◀ 97TH ANNUAL EDITION ▶

WRITER'S MARKET

2018

Robert Lee Brewer, Editor

WD
WRITER'S DIGEST
BOOKS
WritersDigest.com
Cincinnati, Ohio

Writer's Market 2018. Copyright © 2017 F + W Media, Inc. Published by Writer's Digest Books, an imprint of F+W Media, Inc., 10151 Carver Road, Suite 200, Blue Ash, Ohio 45242. Printed and bound in the United States of America. All rights reserved. No part of this book may be reproduced in any form or by any electronic or mechanical means including information storage and retrieval systems without permission in writing from the publisher, except by a reviewer, who may quote brief passages in a review.

Writer's Market website: www.writersmarket.com
Writer's Digest website: www.writersdigest.com

Distributed in Canada by Fraser Direct
100 Armstrong Avenue
Georgetown, Ontario, Canada L7G 5S4
Tel: (905) 877-4411

Distributed in the U.K. and Europe by F&W Media International
Brunel House, Newton Abbot, Devon, TQ12 4PU, England
Tel: (+44) 1626-323200, Fax: (+44) 1626-323319
E-mail: postmaster@davidandcharles.co.uk

Library of Congress Catalog Number 31-20772
ISSN: 0084-2729
ISBN-13: 978-1-44035-263-8
ISBN-13: 978-1-44035-264-5 (Writer's Market Deluxe Edition)
ISBN-10: 1-44035-263-1
ISBN-10: 1-44035-264-X (Writer's Market Deluxe Edition)

Attention Booksellers: This is an annual directory of F + W Media, Inc. Return deadline for this edition is December 31, 2018.

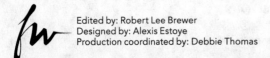

Edited by: Robert Lee Brewer
Designed by: Alexis Estoye
Production coordinated by: Debbie Thomas

CONTENTS

FROM THE EDITOR 1

HOW TO USE *WRITER'S MARKET*...2

FINDING WORK

BEFORE YOUR FIRST SALE 6

QUERY LETTER CLINIC 15

WRITE BETTER QUERIES & SELL MORE ARTICLES,
by Krissy Brady..26

HOW TO FIND SUCCESS IN THE MAGAZINE WORLD,
by Kerrie Flanagan...30

LANDING THE SIX-FIGURE DEAL,
by SJ Hodges..35

WHY, WHEN & HOW TO CO-AUTHOR A BOOK,
by Sue Bradford Edwards... 41

TAPPING INTO A HIDDEN MARKET,
by Joyce Laird...46

EARN A FULL-TIME INCOME FROM BLOGGING,
by Carol Tice...52

FUNDS FOR WRITERS 101,
by C. Hope Clark..58

MANAGING WORK

BUILD A SOLID FOUNDATION,
by Dr. Mike Bechtle 64

CREATE CONTENT TO GROW YOUR AUDIENCE,
by Sage Cohen..70

HOW TO DEVELOP AN EFFECTIVE AUTHOR BRAND,
by Leslie Lee Sanders...76

PROMOTIONS, PR, & PUBLICITY,
by Janice Hussein..81

E-MAIL NEWSLETTERS FOR WRITERS,
by Rebecca Pitts..86

CONTRACTS 101,
by Cindy Ferraino..92

CONTRACTS, COPYRIGHTS, & TAXES,
by David Paul Williams...99

MAKING THE MOST OF THE MONEY YOU EARN,
by Sage Cohen...105

THE ORGANIZED WRITER,
by Jenny Flores...111

HOW MUCH SHOULD I CHARGE?,
by Aaron Belz...116

MARKETS

LITERARY AGENTS 134

BOOK PUBLISHERS 189

CONSUMER MAGAZINES 412

Animal 413
Art & Architecture 416
Associations 417
Astrology, Metaphysical
    & New Age 420
Automotive & Motorcycle 422
Aviation 423
Business & Finance 424
Career, College & Alumni 428
Child Care & Parental Guidance ..429
Consumer Service &
    Business Opportunity................434
Contemporary Culture 434
Disabilities 438
Entertainment 441
Ethnic & Minority 442

Food & Drink 446
Games & Puzzles 449
Gay & Lesbian Interest 450
General Interest 451
Health & Fitness 457
History 460
Hobby & Craft 464
Home & Garden 472
Humor 478
Inflight 479
Juvenile 479
Literary & Little 486
Men's 530
Military 531
Music Consumer 532
Mystery 533

Nature, Conservation
   & Ecology 533
Personal Computers 536
Photography 536
Politics & World Affairs 537
Psychology & Self-Improvement.... 539
Regional 539
Religious 562
Retirement 569

Rural 570
Science 572
Science Fiction, Fantasy
   & Horror 575
Sports 580
Teen & Young Adult 595
Travel, Camping & Trailer 595
Women's 599

TRADE JOURNALS 605

Advertising, Marketing & PR 606
Art, Design & Collectibles 609
Auto & Truck 612
Aviation & Space 615
Beauty & Salon 616
Beverages & Bottling 619
Book & Bookstore 621
Brick, Glass & Ceramics 622
Building Interiors 623
Business Management 624
Church Administration
   & Ministry 628
Clothing 632
Construction & Contracting 632
Education & Counseling 636
Electronics &
   Communication 639
Energy & Utilities 641
Engineering & Technology 642
Entertainment & the Arts 645
Farm 649
Finance 655
Florist, Nurseries &
   Landscapers 657
Government & Public Service 658
Groceries & Food Products 661

Home Furnishings &
   Household Goods 663
Hospitals, Nursing &
   Nursing Homes 663
Hotels, Motels, Clubs, Resorts
   & Restaurants 665
Industrial Operations 667
Information Systems 668
Insurance 669
Jewelry 669
Journalism & Writing 670
Law 675
Lumber 678
Machinery & Metal 678
Maintenance & Safety 681
Management & Supervision 682
Marine & Maritime Industries 683
Medical 683
Music Trade 686
Paper 688
Plumbing, Heating, Air Conditioning
   & Refrigeration 689
Printing 689
Professional Photography 690
Real Estate 691
Resources & Waste Reduction 694

Selling & Merchandising 694
Sport Trade 699
Stone, Quarry & Mining 703
Toy, Novelty & Hobby 704

Transportation 705
Travel Trade 705
Veterinary 706

CONTESTS & AWARDS 708

Playwriting & Scriptwriting...........709
Arts Councils & Fellowships 715
Fiction..719
Nonfiction 739
Writing for Children &
    Young Adults 749

General 761
Journalism.....................................764
Translation.....................................765
Poetry..768
Multiple Writing Areas...................795

RESOURCES

PROFESSIONAL ORGANIZATIONS...818
GLOSSARY...822

INDEXES

BOOK PUBLISHERS SUBJECT INDEX...828
GENERAL INDEX..868

FROM
THE EDITOR

I have a confession to make: Even after more than 17 years of working on *Writer's Market*, I'm still learning. And I'm thankful that I still don't know it all (or think that I do). After all, a constant reshuffling of the deck is often what keeps successful writers successful.

That's why this edition of *Writer's Market* includes articles on industrial writing and co-authoring books, as well as organization skills and how to create an effective e-mail newsletter. Learning new skills and techniques can benefit writers, whether they write ficiton, nonfiction, or poetry (my favorite!).

Of course, the listings are still "where it's at" with *Writer's Market*, and our team went to great lengths (and a lot of time) assembling the most up-to-date information possible to help writers get their queries, proposals, and manuscripts to the right editors, agents, and contests.

Because at the end of the day, my top goal is to provide writers with the best resource to help writers find success with their writing, whether that means getting published, earning more money, or building a career with their writing. Read all the articles, use the listings, and start making success happen for you.

Also, be sure to take advantage of a specially recorded webinar for *Writer's Market* readers. Learn more at www.writersmarket.com/2018-wm-webinar.

Until next we meet, keep writing and marketing what you write.

Robert Lee Brewer
Senior Content Editor
Writer's Market and WritersMarket.com
http://writersdigest.com/editor-blogs/poetic-asides
http://blog.writersmarket.com
http://twitter.com/robertleebrewer

HOW TO USE WRITER'S MARKET

//

Writer's Market is here to help you decide where and how to submit your writing to appropriate markets. Each listing contains information about the editorial focus of the market, how it prefers material to be submitted, payment information, and other helpful tips.

WHAT'S INSIDE?

Since 1921, *Writer's Market* has been giving you the information you need to knowledgeably approach a market. We've continued to develop improvements to help you access that information more efficiently.

NAVIGATIONAL TOOLS. We've designed the pages of *Writer's Market* with you, the writer, in mind. Within the pages you will find **readable market listings** and **accessible charts and graphs**. One such chart can be found in the ever-popular "How Much Should I Charge?" article.

We've taken all of the updated information in this feature and put it into an easy-to-read-and-navigate chart, making it convenient for you to find the rates that accompany the freelance jobs you're seeking.

ICONS. There are a variety of icons that appear before each listing. A complete Key to Icons & Abbreviations appears on the right. Icons let you know whether a book publisher accepts only agented writers (**Ⓐ**), comparative pay rates for a magazine (**$-$$$$**), and more.

CONTACT NAMES, ROYALTY RATES AND ADVANCES. In every section, we identify key contact people with the boldface word **Contact** to help you get your manuscript to the right person.

EDITORS, PAY RATES, ROYALTIES, ADVANCES, AND PERCENTAGE OF MATERIAL WRITTEN BY FREELANCE WRITERS. For Book Publishers, royalty rates and advances are highlighted in boldface, as is other important information on the percentage of first-time writers and unagented writers the company publishes, the number of books published, and the number of manuscripts received each year. In the Consumer Magazines and Trade Journals sections, we identify the amount (percentage) of material accepted from freelance writers, and the pay rates for features, columns and departments, and fillers in boldface to help you quickly identify the information you need to know when considering whether to submit your work.

QUERY FORMATS. We asked editors how they prefer to receive queries and have indicated in the listings whether they prefer them by mail, e-mail, fax or phone. Be sure to check an editor's individual preference before sending your query.

ARTICLES. Writers who want to improve their submission techniques should read the articles in the **Finding Work** section. The **Managing Work** section is geared more toward post-acceptance topics, such as contract negotiation, organization, and self-promotion.

IF THIS BOOK IS NEW TO YOU . . .

Look at the **Contents** pages to familiarize yourself with the arrangement of *Writer's Market*. The three largest sections of the book are the market listings of Book Publishers; Consumer Magazines; and Trade Journals. You will also find other sections of market listings for Literary Agents and Contests & Awards. More opportunities can be found on the WritersMarket.com website.

IMPORTANT LISTING INFORMATION

1. Listings are based on editorial questionnaires and interviews. They are not advertisements; publishers do not pay for their listings. The markets are not endorsed by
   Writer's Market editors. Writer's Digest Books and its employees go to great effort
   to ascertain the validity of information in this book. However, transactions between
   users of the information and individuals and/or companies are strictly between those
   parties.
2. All listings have been verified before publication of this book. If a listing has not
   changed from last year, then the editor said the market's needs have not changed
   and the previous listing continues to accurately reflect its policies.
3. *Writer's Market* reserves the right to exclude any listing.
4. When looking for a specific market, check the index. A market may not be listed for
   one of these reasons:
   - It doesn't solicit freelance material.
   - It doesn't pay for material.
   - It has gone out of business.
   - It has failed to verify or update its listing for this edition.
   - It hasn't answered *Writer's Market* inquiries satisfactorily.

Narrowing your search

After you've identified the market categories that interest you, you can begin researching
specific markets within each section.

Consumer Magazines and Trade Journals are categorized by subject within their respective sections to make it easier for you to identify markets for your work.

There is a subject index available for Book Publishers in the back of the book. It is broken into fiction and nonfiction categories and subcategories.

Contests & Awards are categorized by genre of writing. If you want to find journalism contests, you would search the Journalism category; if you have an unpublished novel,
check the Fiction category.

Interpreting the markets

Once you've identified companies or publications that cover the subjects in which you're interested, you can begin evaluating specific listings to pinpoint the markets most receptive to
your work and most beneficial to you.

In evaluating individual listings, check the location of the company, the types of
material it is interested in seeing, submission requirements, and rights and payment
policies. Depending on your personal concerns, any of these items could be a deciding

factor as you determine which markets you plan to approach. Many listings also include a reporting time.

Whenever possible, obtain submission guidelines before submitting material. You can usually obtain guidelines by sending a SASE to the address in the listing or by checking online. Many of the listings contain instructions on how to obtain sample copies, catalogs or market lists. The more research you do upfront, the better your chances of acceptance, publication and payment.

BEFORE YOUR FIRST SALE

Everything in life has to start somewhere and that somewhere is always at the beginning. Stephen King, Stephenie Meyer, Jeff Kinney, Nora Roberts—they all had to start at the beginning. It would be great to say becoming a writer is as easy as waving a magic wand over your manuscript and "Poof!" you're published, but that's not how it happens. While there's no one true "key" to becoming successful, a long, well-paid writing career *can* happen when you combine four elements:

- Good writing
- Knowledge of writing markets
- Professionalism
- Persistence

Good writing is useless if you don't know which markets will buy your work or how to pitch and sell your writing. If you aren't professional and persistent in your contact with editors, your writing is just that—your writing. But if you are a writer who embraces the above four elements, you have a good chance at becoming a paid, published writer who will reap the benefits of a long and successful career.

As you become more involved with writing, you may read articles or talk to editors and authors with conflicting opinions about the right way to submit your work. The truth is, there are many different routes a writer can follow to get published, but no matter which route you choose, the end is always the same—becoming a published writer.

The following advice on submissions has worked for many writers, but it is by no means the be-all-end-all of proper submission guidelines. It's very easy to get wrapped up in the specifics of submitting (Should I put my last name on every page of my manuscript?) and ignore the more important issues (Will this idea on ice fishing in Alaska be appropriate for a regional magazine in Seattle?). Don't allow yourself to become so blinded by submission procedures that you forget common sense. If you use your common sense and develop professional, courteous relations with editors, you will eventually find your own submission style.

DEVELOP YOUR IDEAS, THEN TARGET THE MARKETS

Writers often think of an interesting story, complete the manuscript, and then begin the search for a suitable publisher or magazine. While this approach is common for fiction, poetry and screenwriting, it reduces your chances of success in many nonfiction writing areas. Instead, choose categories that interest you and study those sections in *Writer's Market*. Select several listings you consider good prospects for your type of writing. Sometimes the individual listings will even help you generate ideas.

Next, make a list of the potential markets for each idea. Make the initial contact with markets using the method stated in the market listings. If you exhaust your list of possibilities, don't give up. Instead, reevaluate the idea or try another angle. Continue developing ideas and approaching markets. Identify and rank potential markets for an idea and continue the process.

As you submit to the various publications listed in *Writer's Market*, it's important to remember that every magazine is published with a particular audience and slant in mind. Probably the number one complaint we receive from editors is the submissions they receive are completely wrong for their magazines or book line. The first mark of professionalism is to know your market well. Gaining that knowledge starts with *Writer's Market*, but you should also do your own detective work. Search out back issues of the magazines you wish to write for, pick up recent issues at your local newsstand, or visit magazines' websites—anything that will help you figure out what subjects specific magazines publish. This research is also helpful in learning what topics have been covered ad nauseum—the topics you should stay away from or approach in a fresh way. Magazines' websites are invaluable as most post the current issue of the magazine, as well as back issues, and most offer writer's guidelines.

The same advice is true for submitting to book publishers. Research publisher websites for their submission guidelines, recently published titles and their backlist. You can use this information to target your book proposal in a way that fits with a publisher's other titles while not directly competing for sales.

Prepare for rejection and the sometimes lengthy wait. When a submission is returned, check your file folder of potential markets for that idea. Cross off the market that rejected the idea. If the editor has given you suggestions or reasons why the manuscript was not accepted, you might want to incorporate these suggestions when revising your manuscript.

After revising your manuscript mail it to the next market on your list.

Take rejection with a grain of salt

Rejection is a way of life in the publishing world. It's inevitable in a business that deals with such an overwhelming number of applicants for such a limited number of positions. Anyone who has published has lived through many rejections, and writers with thin skin are at a distinct disadvantage. A rejection letter is not a personal attack. It simply indicates your submission is not appropriate for that market. Writers who let rejection dissuade them from pursuing their dream or who react to an editor's "No" with indignation or fury do themselves a disservice. Writers who let rejection stop them do not get published. Resign yourself to facing rejection now. You will live through it, and you'll eventually overcome it.

QUERY AND COVER LETTERS

A query letter is a brief, one-page letter used as a tool to hook an editor and get him interested in your idea. When you send a query letter to a magazine, you are trying to get an editor to buy your idea or article. When you query a book publisher, you are attempting to get an editor interested enough in your idea to request your book proposal or your entire manuscript. (Note: Some book editors prefer to receive book proposals on first contact. Check individual listings for which method editors prefer.)

Here are some basic guidelines to help you create a query that's polished and well-organized. For more tips see "Query Letter Clinic" article.

- **LIMIT IT TO ONE PAGE, SINGLE-SPACED**, and address the editor by name (Mr. or Ms. and the surname). *Note*: Do not assume that a person is a Mr. or Ms. unless it is obvious from the name listed. For example, if you are contacting a D.J. Smith, do not assume that D.J. should be preceded by Mr. or Ms. Instead, address the letter to D.J. Smith.
- **GRAB THE EDITOR'S ATTENTION WITH A STRONG OPENING.** Some magazine queries, for example, begin with a paragraph meant to approximate the lead of the intended article.
- **INDICATE HOW YOU INTEND TO DEVELOP THE ARTICLE OR BOOK.** Give the editor some idea of the work's structure and content.
- **LET THE EDITOR KNOW IF YOU HAVE PHOTOS** or illustrations available to accompany your magazine article.
- **MENTION ANY EXPERTISE OR TRAINING THAT QUALIFIES YOU** to write the article or book. If you've been published before, mention it; if not, don't.
- **END WITH A DIRECT REQUEST TO WRITE THE ARTICLE.** Or, if you're pitching a book, ask for the go-ahead to send in a full proposal or the entire manuscript. Give the editor an idea of the expected length and delivery date of your manuscript.

A common question that arises is: If I don't hear from an editor in the reported response time, how do I know when I can safely send the query to another market? Many writers find it helpful to indicate in their queries that if they don't receive a response from the editor (slightly after the listed reporting time), they will assume the editor is not interested. It's best to take this approach, particularly if your topic is timely.

A brief, single-spaced cover letter is helpful when sending a manuscript as it helps personalize the submission. However, if you have previously queried the editor, use the cover letter to politely and briefly remind the editor of that query—when it was sent, what it contained, etc. "Here is the piece on low-fat cooking that I queried you about on December 12. I look forward to hearing from you at your earliest convenience." Do not use the cover letter as a sales pitch.

If you are submitting to a market that accepts unsolicited manuscripts, a cover letter is useful because it personalizes your submission. You can, and should, include information about the manuscript, yourself, your publishing history, and your qualifications.

In addition to tips on writing queries, the "Query Letter Clinic" article offers eight example query letters, some that work and some that don't, as well as comments on why the letters were either successful or failed to garner an assignment or contract.

Querying for fiction

Fiction is sometimes queried, but more often editors prefer receiving material. Many fiction editors won't decide on a submission until they have seen the complete manuscript. When submitting a fiction book idea, most editors prefer to see at least a synopsis and sample chapters (usually the first three). For fiction published in magazines, most editors want to see the complete short story manuscript. If an editor does request a query for fiction, it should include a description of the main theme and story line, including the conflict and resolution. Take a look at individual listings to see what editors prefer to receive.

THE SYNOPSIS

Most fiction books are sold by a complete manuscript, but most editors and agents don't have the time to read a complete manuscript of every wannabe writer. As a result, publishing decision-makers use the synopsis and sample chapters to help the screening process of fiction. The synopsis, on its most basic level, communicates what the book is about.

The length and depth of a synopsis can change from agent to agent or publisher to publisher. Some will want a synopsis that is one to two single-spaced pages; others will want a synopsis that can run up to 25 double-spaced pages. Checking your listings in *Writer's Market*, as well as double-checking with the listing's website, will help guide you in this respect.

The content should cover all the essential points of the novel from beginning to end and in the correct order. The essential points include main characters, main plot points, and, yes, the ending. Of course, your essential points will vary from the editor who wants a one-page synopsis to the editor who wants a 25-page synopsis.

NONFICTION PROPOSALS

Most nonfiction books are sold by a book proposal—a package of materials that details what your book is about, who its intended audience is, and how you intend to write the book. It includes some combination of a cover or query letter, an overview, an outline, author's information sheet, and sample chapters. Editors also want to see information about the audience for your book and about titles that compete with your proposed book.

Submitting nonfiction proposals

A proposal package should include the following items:

- **A COVER OR QUERY LETTER.** This letter should be a short introduction to the material you include in the proposal.
- **AN OVERVIEW.** This is a brief summary of your book. It should detail your book's subject and give an idea of how that subject will be developed.
- **AN OUTLINE.** The outline covers your book chapter by chapter and should include all major points covered in each chapter. Some outlines are done in traditional outline form, but most are written in paragraph form.
- **AN AUTHOR'S INFORMATION SHEET.** This information should acquaint the editor with your writing background and convince her of your qualifications regarding the subject of your book.
- **SAMPLE CHAPTERS.** Many editors like to see sample chapters, especially for a first book. Sample chapters show the editor how you write and develop ideas from your outline.
- **MARKETING INFORMATION.** Facts about how and to whom your book can be successfully marketed are now expected to accompany every book proposal. If you can provide information about the audience for your book and suggest ways the book publisher can reach those people, you will increase your chances of acceptance.
- **COMPETITIVE TITLE ANALYSIS.** Check the *Subject Guide to Books in Print* for other titles on your topic. Write a one- or two-sentence synopsis of each. Point out how your book differs and improves upon existing topics.

For more information on nonfiction book proposals, read Michael Larsen's *How to Write a Book Proposal* (Writer's Digest Books).

A WORD ABOUT AGENTS

An agent represents a writer's work to publishers, negotiates contracts, follows up to see that contracts are fulfilled, and generally handles a writer's business affairs, leaving the writer free to write. Effective agents are valued for their contacts in the publishing industry, their knowledge about who to approach with certain ideas, their ability to guide an author's career, and their business sense.

While most book publishers listed in *Writer's Market* publish books by unagented writers, some of the larger houses are reluctant to consider submissions that have not reached them through a literary agent. Companies with such a policy are noted by an (**A**) icon at the beginning of the listing, as well as in the submission information within the listing.

Writer's Market includes a list of literary agents who are all members of the Association of Authors' Representatives and who are also actively seeking new and established writers.

MANUSCRIPT FORMAT

You can increase your chances of publication by following a few standard guidelines regarding the physical format of your manuscript. It should be your goal to make your manuscript readable. Follow these suggestions as you would any other suggestions: Use what works for you and discard what doesn't.

In general, when submitting a manuscript, you should use white, 8½×11, 20 lb. paper, and you should also choose a legible, professional looking font (i.e., Times New Roman)—no all-italic or artsy fonts. Your entire manuscript should be double-spaced with a 1½-inch margin on all sides of the page. Once you are ready to print your manuscript, you should print either on a laser printer or an ink-jet printer.

ESTIMATING WORD COUNT

All computers provide you with a word count of your manuscript. Your editor will count again after editing the manuscript. Although your computer is counting characters, an editor or production editor is more concerned about the amount of space the text will occupy on a page. Several small headlines or subheads, for instance, will be counted the same by your computer as any other word of text. However, headlines and subheads usually employ a different font size than the body text, so an editor may count them differently to be sure enough space has been estimated for larger type.

For short manuscripts, it's often quickest to count each word on a representative page and multiply by the number of pages. You can get a very rough count by multiplying the

MANUSCRIPT FORMATTING SAMPLE

1 Your Name   50,000 Words **3**
Your Street Address
City State ZIP Code
Day and Evening Phone Numbers
E-mail Address

Website (if applicable)
2

1 Type your real name (even if you use a pseudonym) and contact information **2** Double-space twice **3** Estimated word count **4** Type your title in capital letters, double-space and type "by," double-space again, and type your name (or pseudonym if you're using one) **5** Double-space twice, then indent first paragraph and start text of your manuscript **6** On subsequent pages, type your name, a dash, and the page number in the upper left or right corner

TITLE

by

4 Your Name

5 You can increase your chances of publication by following a few standard guidelines regarding the physical format of your article or manuscript. It should be your goal to make your manuscript readable. Use these suggestions as you would any other suggestions: Use what works for you and discard what doesn't.

In general, when submitting a manuscript, you should use white, 8½×11, 20-lb. bond paper, and you should also choose a legible, professional-looking font (i.e., Times New Roman)—no all-italic or artsy fonts. Your entire manuscript should be double-spaced with a 1½-inch margin on all sides of the page. Once you are ready to print your article or manuscript, you should print either on a laser printer or an ink-jet printer.

Remember, articles should be written after you send a one-page query letter to an editor, and the editor then asks you to write the article. If, however, you are sending an article "on spec" to an editor, you should send both a query letter and the complete article.

Fiction and poetry is a little different from nonfiction articles, in that it is rarely queried. More often than not, poetry and fiction editors want to review the complete manuscript before making a final decision.

number of pages in your manuscript by 250 (the average number of words on a double-spaced typewritten page).

PHOTOGRAPHS AND SLIDES

In some cases, the availability of photographs and slides can be the deciding factor as to whether an editor will accept your submission. This is especially true when querying a publication that relies heavily on photographs, illustrations or artwork to enhance the article (e.g., craft magazines, hobby magazines, etc.). In some instances, the publication may offer additional payment for photographs or illustrations.

Check the individual listings to find out which magazines review photographs and what their submission guidelines are. Most publications prefer you do not send photographs with your submission. However, if photographs or illustrations are available, you should indicate that in your query. As with manuscripts, never send the originals of your photographs or illustrations. Instead, send digital images, which is what most magazine and book publishers prefer to use.

SEND PHOTOCOPIES

If there is one hard-and-fast rule in publishing, it's this: *Never* send the original (or only) copy of your manuscript. Most editors cringe when they find out a writer has sent the only copy of their manuscript. You should always send copies of your manuscript.

Some writers choose to send a self-addressed, stamped postcard with a photocopied submission. In their cover letter they suggest if the editor is not interested in their manuscript, it may be tossed out and a reply sent on the postcard. This method is particularly helpful when sending your submissions to international markets.

MAILING SUBMISSIONS

No matter what size manuscript you're mailing, always include a self-addressed, stamped envelope (SASE) with sufficient return postage. The website for the U.S. Postal Service (www.usps.com) and the website for the Canadian Post (www.canadapost.ca) both have postage calculators if you are unsure how much postage to affix.

A book manuscript should be mailed in a sturdy, well-wrapped box. Enclose a self-addressed mailing label and paper clip your return postage to the label. However, be aware that some book publishers do not return unsolicited manuscripts, so make sure you know the practice of the publisher before sending any unsolicited material.

Types of mail service

There are many different mailing service options available to you whether you are sending a query letter or a complete manuscript. You can work with the U.S. Postal Service, United

Parcel Service, Federal Express, or any number of private mailing companies. The following are the five most common types of mailing services offered by the U.S. Postal Service.

- **FIRST CLASS** is a fairly expensive way to mail a manuscript, but many writers prefer it. First-Class mail generally receives better handling and is delivered more quickly than Standard mail.
- **PRIORITY MAIL** reaches its destination within two or three days.
- **STANDARD MAIL** rates are available for packages, but be sure to pack your materials carefully because they will be handled roughly. To make sure your package will be returned to you if it is undeliverable, print "Return Postage Guaranteed" under your address.
- **CERTIFIED MAIL** must be signed for when it reaches its destination.
- **REGISTERED MAIL** is a high-security method of mailing where the contents are insured. The package is signed in and out of every office it passes through, and a receipt is returned to the sender when the package reaches its destination.

MAILING MANUSCRIPTS

- Fold manuscripts under five pages into thirds, and send in a #10 SASE.
- Mail manuscripts five pages or more unfolded in a 9×12 or 10×13 SASE.
- For return envelope, fold the envelope in half, address it to yourself, and add a stamp, or, if going to Canada or another international destination, International Reply Coupons (available at most post office branches).
- Don't send by Certified Mail—this is a sign of an amateur.

QUERY LETTER CLINIC

Many great writers ask year after year, "Why is it so hard to get published?" In many cases, these writers have spent years developing their craft. They submit to the appropriate markets, yet rejection is always the end result. The culprit? A weak query letter.

The query letter is often the most important piece of the publishing puzzle. In many cases, it determines whether editors or agents will even read your manuscript. A good query makes a good first impression; a bad query earns a swift rejection.

ELEMENTS OF A QUERY

A query letter should sell editors or agents on your idea or convince them to request your finished manuscript. The most effective query letters get into the specifics from the very first line. It's important to remember that the query is a call to action, not a listing of features and benefits.

In addition to selling your idea or manuscript, a query can include information on the availability of photographs or artwork. You can include a working title and projected word count. Depending on the piece, you might also mention whether a sidebar might be appropriate and the type of research you plan to conduct. If appropriate, include a tentative deadline and indicate whether the query is being simultaneously submitted.

Biographical information should be included as well, but don't overdo it unless your background actually helps sell the article or proves that you're the only person who could write your proposed piece.

THINGS TO AVOID IN QUERY

The query is not a place to discuss pay rates. This step comes after an editor has agreed to take on your article or book. Besides making an unprofessional impression, it can also work to your disadvantage in negotiating your fee. If you ask too much, an editor may not even contact you to see if a lower rate works. If you ask for too little, you may start an editorial relationship where you make less than the normal rate.

You should also avoid rookie mistakes, such as mentioning your work is copyrighted or including the copyright symbol on your work. While you want to make it clear that you've researched the market, avoid using flattery as a technique for selling your work. It often has the opposite effect of what you intend. In addition, don't hint that you can rewrite the piece, as this only leads the editor to think there will be a lot of work involved in shaping up your writing.

Also, never admit several other editors or agents have rejected the query. Always treat your new audience as if they are the first place on your list.

HOW TO FORMAT A QUERY

It's OK to break writing rules in a short story or article, but you should follow the rules when it comes to crafting an effective query. Here are guidelines for query writing.

- Use a normal font and typeface, such as Courier and 10- or 12-point type.
- Include your name, address, phone number, e-mail address and website.
- Use one-inch margin on paper queries.
- Address a specific editor or agent. (Note: It's wise to double-check contact names online or by calling.)
- Limit query to one single-spaced page.
- Include self-addressed, stamped envelope or postcard for response with post submissions.

HOW TO FOLLOW UP

Accidents do happen. Queries may not reach your intended reader. Staff changes or interoffice mail snafus may end up with your query letter thrown away. Or the editor may have set your query off to the side for further consideration and forgotten it. Whatever the case may be, there are some basic guidelines you should use for your follow-up communication.

Most importantly, wait until the reported response time, as indicated in *Writer's Market* or their submission guidelines, has elapsed before contacting an editor or agent. Then, you should send a short and polite e-mail describing the original query sent, the date it was sent, and asking if they received it or made a decision regarding its fate.

The importance of remaining polite and businesslike when following up cannot be stressed enough. Making a bad impression on an editor can often have a ripple effect—as that editor may share his or her bad experience with other editors at the magazine or publishing company. Also, don't call.

HOW THE CLINIC WORKS

As mentioned earlier, the query letter is the most important weapon for getting an assignment or a request for your full manuscript. Published writers know how to craft a well-written, hard-hitting query. What follows are eight queries: four are strong; four are not. Detailed comments show what worked and what did not. As you'll see, there is no cut-and-dried "good" query format; every strong query works on its own merit.

GOOD NONFICTION MAGAZINE QUERY

Jimmy Boaz, editor
American Organic Farmer's Digest
8336 Old Dirt Road
Macon GA 00000

Dear Mr. Boaz,

There are 87 varieties of organic crops grown in the United States, but there's only one farm producing 12 of these—Morganic Corporation.

Located in the heart of Arkansas, this company spent the past decade providing great organic crops at a competitive price helping them grow into the ninth leading organic farming operation in the country. Along the way, they developed the most unique organic offering in North America.

As a seasoned writer with access to Richard Banks, the founder and president of Morganic, I propose writing a profile piece on Banks for your Organic Shakers department. After years of reading this riveting column, I believe the time has come to cover Morganic's rise in the organic farming industry. ❸

This piece would run in the normal 800-1,200 word range with photographs available of Banks and Morganic's operation.

I've been published in *Arkansas Farmer's Deluxe, Organic Farming Today* and in several newspapers. ❹

Thank you for your consideration of this article. I hope to hear from you soon.

Sincerely,

Jackie Service
34 Good St.
Little Rock AR 00000
jackie.service9867@email.com

❶ My name is only available on our magazine's website and on the masthead. This writer has done her research. ❷ Here's a story that hasn't been pitched before. I didn't know Morganic was so unique in the market. I want to know more. ❸ The writer has access to her interview subject, and she displays knowledge of the magazine by pointing out the correct section in which her piece would run. ❹ While I probably would've assigned this article based on the idea alone, her past credits do help solidify my decision.

BAD NONFICTION MAGAZINE QUERY

Dear Gentlemen,

I'd like to write the next great article you'll ever publish. My writing credits include amazing pieces I've done for local and community newspapers and for my college English classes. I've been writing for years and years. **2**

Your magazine may not be a big one like *Rolling Stone* or *Sports Illustrated*, but I'm willing to write an interview for you anyway. I know you need material, and I need money. (Don't worry. I won't charge you too much.) **3**

Just give me some people to interview, and I'll do the best job you've ever read. It will be amazing, and I can re-write the piece for you if you don't agree. I'm willing to re-write 20 times if needed. **4**

You better hurry up and assign me an article though, because I've sent out letters to lots of other magazines, and I'm sure to be filled up to capacity very soon. **5**

Later gents,

Carl Bighead
76 Bad Query Lane
Big City NY 00000

1 This is sexist, and it doesn't address any contact specifically. **2** An over-the-top claim by a writer who does not impress me with his publishing background. **3** Insults the magazine and then reassures me he won't charge too much? **4** While I do assign material from time to time, I prefer writers pitch me their own ideas after studying the magazine. **5** I'm sure people aren't going to be knocking down his door anytime soon.

GOOD FICTION MAGAZINE QUERY

Marcus West
88 Piano Drive
Lexington KY 00000

August 8, 2011 **1**

Jeanette Curic, editor
Wonder Stories
45 Noodle Street
Portland OR 00000

Dear Ms. Curic,

Please consider the following 1,200-word story, "Turning to the Melon," a quirky coming-of-age story with a little magical realism thrown in the mix. **2**

After reading *Wonder Stories* for years, I think I've finally written something that would fit with your audience. My previous short story credits include *Stunned Fiction Quarterly* and *Faulty Mindbomb*. **3**

Thank you in advance for considering "Turning to Melon."

Sincerely,

Marcus West
(123) 456-7890
marcusw87452@email.com

Encl: Manuscript and SASE **4**

1 Follows the format we established in our guidelines. Being able to follow directions is more important than many writers realize. **2** Story is in our word count, and the description sounds like the type of story we would consider publishing. It's flattering to know he reads our magazine. While it won't guarantee publication, it does make me a little more hopeful that the story I'm reading will be a good fit. Also, good to know he's been published before. **4** I can figure it out, but it's nice to know what other materials were included in the envelope. This letter is not flashy, but it gives me the basics and puts me in the right frame of mind to read the actual story.

BAD FICTION MAGAZINE QUERY

To: curic@wonderstories808.com ❶
Subject: A Towering Epic Fantasy

Hello there. ❷

I've written a great fantasy epic novel short story of about 25,000 words that may be included in your magazine if you so desire. ❸

More than 20 years, I've spent chained to my desk in a basement writing out the greatest story of our modern time. And it can be yours if you so desire to have it. ❹

Just say the word, and I'll ship it over to you. We can talk money and movie rights after your acceptance. I have big plans for this story, and you can be part of that success. ❺

Yours forever (if you so desire), ❻

Harold
(or Harry for friends)

❶ We do not consider e-mail queries or submissions. ❷ This is a little too informal. ❸ First off, what did he write? An epic novel or short story? Second, 25,000 words is way over our 1,500-word max. ❹ I'm lost for words. ❺ Money and movie rights? We pay moderate rates and definitely don't get involved in movies. ❻ I'm sure the writer was just trying to be nice, but this is a little bizarre and kind of creepy. I do not so desire more contact with "Harry."

GOOD NONFICTION BOOK QUERY

To: corey@bigbookspublishing.com
Subject: Query: Become a Better Parent in 30 Days ①

Dear Mr. Corey,

② As a parent of six and a high school teacher for more than 20 years, I know first hand that being a parent is difficult work. Even harder is being a good parent. My proposed title, ③ *Taking Care of Yourself and Your Kids: A 30-day Program to Become a Better Parent While Still Living Your Life*, would show how to handle real-life situations and still be a good parent.

This book has been years in the making, as it follows the outline I've used successfully in my summer seminars I give on the topic to thousands of parents every year. It really works, because past participants contact me constantly to let me know what a difference my classes have made in their lives. ④

In addition to marketing and selling *Taking Care of Yourself and Your Kids* at my summer seminars, I would also be able to sell it through my website and promote it through my weekly e-newsletter with over 25,000 subscribers. Of course, it would also make a very nice trade title that I think would sell well in bookstores and possibly retail outlets, such as Wal-Mart and Target. ⑤

Please contact me for a copy of my full book proposal today. ⑥

Thank you for your consideration.

Marilyn Parent
8647 Query St.
Norman OK 00000
mparent8647@email.com
www.marilynsbetterparents.com

① Effective subject line. Lets me know exactly what to expect when I open the e-mail. ② Good lead. Six kids and teaches high school. I already trust her as an expert. ③ Nice title that would fit well with others we currently offer. ④ Her platform as a speaker definitely gets my attention. ⑤ 25,000 e-mail subscribers? She must have a very good voice to gather that many readers. ⑥ I was interested after the first paragraph, but every paragraph after made it impossible to not request her proposal.

BAD NONFICTION BOOK QUERY

To: info@bigbookspublishing.com
Subject: a question for you ①

I really liked this book by Mega Book Publishers called *Build Better Trains in Your Own Backyard*. It was a great book that covered all the basics of model train building. My father and I would read from it together and assemble all the pieces, and it was magical like Christmas all through the year. Why wouldn't you want to publish such a book? ②

Well, here it is. I've already copyrighted the material for 2006 and can help you promote it if you want to send me on a worldwide book tour. As you can see from my attached digital photo, I'm not the prettiest person, but I am passionate. ③

There are at least 1,000 model train builders in the United States alone, and there might be even more than that. I haven't done enough research yet, because I don't know if this is an idea that appeals to you. If you give me maybe $500, I could do that research in a day and get back to you on it. ④

Anyway, this idea is a good one that brings back lots of memories for me.

Jacob ⑤

① The subject line is so vague I almost deleted this e-mail as spam without even opening it. ② The reason we don't publish such a book is easy—we don't do hobby titles. ③ I'm not going to open an attachment from an unknown sender via e-mail. Also, copyrighting your work years before pitching is the sign of an amateur. ④ 1,000 possible buyers is a small market, and I'm not going to pay a writer to do research on a proposal. ⑤ Not even a last name? Or contact information? At least I won't feel guilty for not responding.

GOOD FICTION BOOK QUERY

Jeremy Mansfield, editor
Novels R Us Publishing
8787 Big Time Street
New York NY 00000

Dear Mr. Mansfield,

My 62,000-word novel, *The Cat Walk,* is a psychologically complex thriller in the same mold as James Patterson's Alex Cross novels, but with a touch of the supernatural a la Stephenie Meyer. **1**

Rebecca Frank is at the top of the modeling world, posing for magazines in exotic locales all over the world and living life to its fullest. Despite all her success, she feels something is missing in her life. Then she runs into Marcus Hunt, a wealthy bachelor with cold blue eyes and an ambiguous past.

Within 24 hours of meeting Marcus, Rebecca's understanding of the world turns upside down, and she finds herself fighting for her life and the love of a man who may not have the ability to return her the favor.

Filled with demons, serial killers, trolls, maniacal clowns and more, *The Cat Walk* follows Rebecca through a gauntlet of trouble and turmoil, leading up to a final climactic realization that may lead to her own unraveling. **2**

The Cat Walk should fit in well with your other titles, such as *Bone Dead* and *Carry Me Home*, though it is a unique story. Your website mentioned supernatural suspense as a current interest, so I hope this is a good match. **3**

My short fiction has appeared in many mystery magazines, including a prize-winning story in *The Mysterious Oregon Quarterly*. This novel is the first in a series that I'm working on (already half-way through the second). **4**

As stated in your guidelines, I've included the first 30 pages. Thank you for considering *The Cat Walk*.

Sincerely,

Merry Plentiful
54 Willow Road
East Lansing MI 00000
merry865423@email.com

1 Novel is correct length and has the suspense and supernatural elements we're seeking. **2** The quick summary sounds like something we would write on the back cover of our paperbacks. That's a good thing, because it identifies the triggers that draw a response out of our readers. **3** She mentions similar titles we've done and that she's done research on our website. She's not afraid to put in a little extra effort. **4** At the moment, I'm not terribly concerned that this book could become a series, but it is something good to file away in the back of my mind for future use.

BAD FICTION BOOK QUERY

Jeremy Mansfield
Novels R Us Publishing
8787 Big Time Street
New York NY 00000

Dear Editor,

My novel has an amazing twist ending that could make it a worldwide phenomenon overnight while you are sleeping. It has spectacular special effects that will probably lead to a multi-million dollar movie deal that will also spawn action figures, lunch boxes, and several other crazy subsidiary rights. I mean, we're talking big-time money here. **1**

I'm not going to share the twist until I have a signed contract that authorizes me to a big bank account, because I don't want to have my idea stolen and used to promote whatever new initiative "The Man" has in mind for media nowadays. Let it be known that you will be rewarded handsomely for taking a chance on me. **2**

Did you know that George Lucas once took a chance on an actor named Harrison Ford by casting him as Han Solo in Star Wars? Look at how that panned out. Ford went on to become a big actor in the Indiana Jones series, *The Fugitive, Blade Runner*, and more. It's obvious that you taking a risk on me could play out in the same dramatic way. **3**

I realize that you've got to make money, and guess what? I want to make money too. So we're on the same page, you and I. We both want to make money, and we'll stop at nothing to do so.

If you want me to start work on this amazing novel with an incredible twist ending, just send a one-page contract agreeing to pay me a lot of money if we hit it big. No other obligations will apply. If it's a bust, I won't sue you for millions. **4**

Sincerely,

Kenzel Pain
92 Bad Writer Road
Austin TX 00000

1 While I love to hear enthusiasm from a writer about his or her work, this kind of unchecked excitement is worrisome for an editor. **2** I need to know the twist to make a decision on whether to accept the manuscript. Plus, I'm troubled by the paranoia and emphasis on making a lot of money. **3** I'm confused. Does he think he's Harrison Ford? **4** So that's the twist; He hasn't even written the novel yet. There's no way I'm going to offer a contract for a novel that hasn't been written by someone with no experience or idea of how the publishing industry works.

WRITE BETTER QUERIES AND SELL MORE ARTICLES

....

by Krissy Brady

///

The steps to scoring a byline in your favorite publication are straightforward enough: Come up with a mind-blowing article idea for your target market. Write an attention-grabbing query letter. Submit it to the appropriate editor. Rinse. Repeat. But there's one aspect of the pitching process new writers tend to ignore that could spell disaster for them down the line.

Once you've got the nuts-and-bolts of query writing on lockdown, your primary goal as a writer needs to shift from learning how to write quality pitches to learning how to write them more efficiently. As assignments start rolling in (and they will), you'll inevitably have less time to dedicate to pitches—and the last thing you want is your income stream slowing to a trickle.

By making the following tiny changes now, you'll not only avoid the whole assignments vs. pitches tug-of-war as your portfolio grows, but churn out top notch query letters in a fraction of the time. (This is not a drill.)

1. ESTABLISH YOUR EXACT MISSION

Make sure the focus of your primary writing goal is laser sharp. Don't just decide the category of magazine you want to write for: Pinpoint your exact target demographic within that category, the exact magazines that cater to that demographic, and the exact section you want to break into. Focus your attention on the bullseye, not the entire dartboard. It will make the process of breaking in much less overwhelming—and once you've built a solid relationship with the editor of one department, you'll have an automatic referral once you're ready to branch out into others.

2. KEEP TABS ON YOUR MARKETS

Know your markets better than you know yourself. Keep files on each market you'd like to write for, and track everything you learn about them along the way. Include submission guidelines (which you score by signing up for a Mediabistro.com premium membership), the name of the section you want to break into, as well as the name and e-mail address of the editor who runs that department. If they also accept pitches for their website, add their web editor's info to your roster as well.

For unlimited access to your target markets (not to mention years worth of back issues!), sign up for a Texture.com account. Keep track of the articles that are being published in your section: List each headline and sub-headline in your file, along with a brief description of how each article was packaged (feature with sidebars, list post, as told to, etc.). As each new issue launches, update your file. Finally, visit their website on a daily or weekly basis and track what they're publishing online.

Sure, it's a little cyber-stalkerish, but studying your markets on a regular basis takes the guesswork out of what to pitch, who to pitch to, and how to package your ideas, putting you miles ahead of the competition. Over time, your files will become a treasure trove of information that other writers would hand over a kidney for.

3. FIND THE DIAMONDS IN THE ROUGH

While it's important to subscribe to sites like ScienceDaily and EurekAlert! for the latest news on studies and scientific breakthroughs, they're not the best places for new writers to find interesting stories—especially if you don't already have a relationship with the editor you're pitching the story to. More often than not, a staff writer or regular contributor will have written the story before you've so much as decided on a lede.

Instead, visit sites like Google Scholar (scholar.google.com), PubMed (www.ncbi.nlm. nih.gov/pubmed), and ScienceDirect (www.sciencedirect.com). Search for interesting studies that haven't hit the mainstream using keywords that best describe the topics you're most interested in writing about. Best of all, all three sites let you create alerts based on your fave keywords, so you can have the latest studies sent directly to your inbox on a daily or weekly basis. Not sure if a study is worth writing about? Grab a copy of *Basics for Evaluating Medical Research Studies: A Simplified Approach*, by Sheri Ann Strite and Michael E. Stuart, M.D. (Delfini Group, 2013) to help you wade through the medical jargon.

4. LET THE INFORMATION COME TO YOU

Set up an e-mail address specifically for subscribing to scholarly journals, press release websites, and newsletters by the top experts in your field. Each time you read a new article in your niche, look into the studies that were mentioned, where they were published, and subscribe to notifications from those journals. Add the experts that were quoted to your contact list for future reference, and follow them on social media. If applicable, introduce yourself to the PR people who represent these experts and let them know you'd like to be kept in the loop on interesting developments. Use digital doodads like Flipboard (flipboard.com) and Nuzzel (nuzzel.com) to streamline your news hunting experience. Instead of scouring the Internet for new material (which almost always leads to hours of unnecessary Facebook and IMDB creeping), all you'll have to do is check your e-mail and voila—so many ideas, so little time.

5. PITCH LESS

No, but seriously. Focus on the quality of your pitches, not on how fast you can send them out. Once the process of building a solid query is second nature to you, the speed at which you write them will increase naturally. In the meantime, think each of your ideas through from head(line) to toe, and thoughtfully decide which markets you're going to submit them to. I now send one-quarter of the pitches that I used to, but receive (way) more acceptances than rejections—which is the only statistic that matters.

6. BE A PERSONAL PROFESSIONAL

Ditch the business speak and write your pitches like you're writing an e-mail to a friend. Allow the editor to hear your voice as they read your words. I've built an entire writing career using my emotional baggage as bait, and you can too. Define what makes you quirky, and run with it.

7. HONE YOUR PACKAGING SKILLS

Once you've worked with the same editor a few times, you don't have to be as formal with your query letters since they already know you've got the goods. But your pitches still need to pack a punch, and this is where the art of packaging comes in handy. Each time you come up with a new idea, search articles that have been written on the topic in the past and brainstorm ways to package your idea to make it stand out. Consistently putting this habit into practice means the next time a breaking story hits your radar, you'll be able to send your editor an insta-packaged idea that just might lead to an insta-assignment.

8. DON'T LET ANYTHING SLIP THROUGH THE CRACKS

Eventually, you're not only going to have multiple assignments on the go at various stages of completion, but multiple pitches circulating that will need to be followed up on at specific times. Use a program or app like Story Tracker (andrewnicolle.com) to remind yourself of when to touch base with an editor—and when to send your pitch elsewhere.

9. DEVELOP BACKUP ANGLES AND PITCHES

Like you, I was told the odds are slim-to-none that two editors will show interest in the same pitch. And then it happened. Twice. In a row. Naturally, I wasn't prepared, and didn't know whether to do a happy dance or throw up. Save yourself the panic attack by developing 1-2 backup angles for each pitch that can be offered to the second editor if they work for a non-competing market, and a backup pitch that's of equal or higher value if they work for a direct competitor.

10. CREATE YOUR OWN LEARNING EXPERIENCE

Typically, editors only respond to the ideas they're interested in publishing, which means it's on you to determine why your rejected queries were... well, rejected. We've all sent out pitches that were slightly off or "almost" worthy of a sale, and it's important to take stock of what went wrong to refine your process. Compare them to pitches you've nailed in the past, and you'll find the answers are right in front of you: Maybe your intro wasn't catchy enough or your angle was too vague. Maybe your headline was a snore or you sent the pitch from a place of impatience instead of finality. You don't need an editor to write back and confirm your suspicions, because deep down you already know what you need to improve on.

11. PITCH FOR THE RIGHT REASONS

Pitch stories you're drawn to and have a legit interest in covering; don't just pitch an idea because you think it'll sell. If you come across a study that'd make an excellent front-of-book piece for your target market du jour, but you find the subject matter blasé, your query will reflect that. Editors can tell the difference between your heart calling the shots—and your empty wallet.

KRISSY BRADY is so out of shape, it's like she has the innards of an 80-year-old—so naturally, she became a women's health + wellness writer. Since turning her emotional baggage into a writing career, she's been published in magazines like *Cosmopolitan* and *Women's Health*, as well as on websites like Prevention.com and Shape.com. You can follow her shenanigans at writtenbykrissy.com (you know, if you want).

HOW TO FIND SUCCESS IN THE MAGAZINE WORLD

by Kerrie Flanagan

Contrary to popular belief, magazines are still going strong. According to the latest study by the Magazine Publishers of America there are more than 20,000 magazines in print. This is good news if you are looking to write for magazines. But before you jump in, there are a few things you should know that will increase your chances of getting an acceptance letter.

KNOW THE READER

Every magazine has a certain readership; teenage girl, mother of young children, budget traveler and so on. It is imperative you know as much about that reader as you can before submitting a query to the editor, because the more you know about who reads the magazine, the more you can tailor your query, article, or essay to best reach that audience.

Geoff Van Dyke, deputy editor of the Denver magazine *5280* says, "I wish people would truly read the magazine, like cover to cover, and understand our readership and voice and mission before sending queries. Sometimes—more often than not—writers submit queries that make it clear that they don't really understand *5280*, don't understand our readers or our mission, and, thus, the query is a bad fit. If they just spend a little more time on the front end, it would make all the difference."

So how can you find out who is the target audience for a specific magazine? The key is in the advertising. Companies spend thousands of dollars getting their messages out to their consumers. They are only going to invest their money in a magazine directed at their target market. By paying attention to the ads in a publication (and this goes for on-line too) you can learn a lot about the reader. What are the ages of the people in the ads? Are they families? Singles? What types of products are highlighted? Expensive clothes? Organic foods? Luxury cars and world travel or family cars and domestic travel?

Another way to find out the demographics of the reader is to locate the media kit on the magazine's website. This is a document intended to provide information to potential advertisers about their readership, but is a gold mine for freelance writers. The media kit provides information like the average age, income, gender, hobbies, home ownership, education and marital status.

This becomes invaluable when looking at ideas and topics to pitch to a magazine. For instance, in the media kit for *5280* magazine, 71 percent of the readers are married, 93 percent own their own home and 78 percent have lived in Colorado for more than 10 years or are natives of the state. With this little bit of information, pitching an article on where to find the best deals on apartments in Denver, is definitely not a good fit since most of their readers own their own home. An article on the best bars in Denver to meet other singles is also not a good idea for this publication, but one on the most romantic weekend getaways in Colorado to take your spouse is a possibility. It is also clear that, when writing the article, time does not have to be spent explaining to the reader things about Colorado that people who live in the state already know since 78 percent of the readers have been there for more than a decade.

KNOW THE MAGAZINE

Once you understand the reader, then you need to familiarize yourself with the actual magazine. Take the time to explore who are the writers, the length of the articles and the departments.

Tom Hess, editor with *Encompass Magazine*, wishes more writers would take the time to know his magazine, in all its forms, before querying. "Too few writers make the effort, and those who do, get my immediate attention."

One way to do this with print magazines is to literally take apart the magazine. To see who writes for the magazine, find the masthead, the page in the front of the magazine that lists the editors and contributing writers. Tear it out so you have it as a reference. Now, go through the magazine, page by page and make a note by each article with a by-line to find out who wrote the piece. Was it an editor? A contributing editor? If you can't find their names on the masthead, then they are typically freelance writers. A contributing editor is usually not on staff, but writes frequently for the magazine.

Now go through and pay attention to the length of articles and the various departments. How many feature stories are there? Is there a back page essay? Are there short department pieces in the front?

By knowing all of this information, you can better direct your query to the areas of the magazine that are more open to freelance writers and tailor your idea to better fit the type of articles they publish.

KNOW THE STYLE

Each magazine has its own style and tone. It's what makes the difference between *The New Yorker* and *Time*. Some magazines are very literary, others are more informational, so it is important to study the magazines to have a good understanding of their style.

Below are two travel writing examples portraying Ketchikan, Alaska, but with very different styles. As you read over each selection, pay attention to the style by looking at the use of quotes, the point of view (first person, third person…), the descriptions and the overall tone of the article.

EXAMPLE 1

In Ketchikan, there are many great things to see and do. The roots of the three Native Alaskan tribes, the Tlingit, Haida, and Tsimshian run deep on this island where you can find the world's largest collection of totem poles. In a beautiful cove, eight miles north of downtown is Totem Bight State Park where 14 historic totems are found along with a native clanhouse. Totems can also be viewed at the Totem Heritage Center and the Southest Discovery Center. At the Saxman Tribal house and at the Metlakatla Long House, skilled groups bring Native dance to life with regular performances.

EXAMPLE 2

The rest of the world disappeared when I entered this lush, green rainforest. Stillness and peace embraced me while I strolled on the wooden walkway, in awe of the surrounding beauty: moss hung from trees, foliage so dense it provided shelter from the rain and beautiful rivers flowed, in search of the ocean. Ketchikan, Alaska, is in the heart of the Tongass National Forest, and an unlikely place to find the Earth's largest remaining temperate rainforest.

The first article provides information and facts about traveling to Ketchikan to see the totem poles. This article would be a good fit for a magazine like *Family Motor Coaching*. The second article definitely has a different style; one that is more poetic and descriptive and more likely to be found in *National Geographic Traveler*.

Both pieces are good but are unique in their style and tone. By understanding this aspect of a magazine, your query or article can better reflect the voice of the publication and increase your chances of an assignment and well-received article.

KNOW THE GUIDELINES

Most magazines put together submission guidelines, spelling out exactly what they are looking for with articles and how to submit your idea to them.

"I wish writers would understand exactly what kind of material we are looking for," says Russ Lumpkin, managing editor of *Gray's Sporting Journal*, "and that they would adhere strictly to our submission guidelines. We publish fly fishing and hunting stories and accept only digital submissions via e-mail. A poem about watching butterflies submitted through the mail creates work that falls out of my ordinary work flow. And that's aggravating."

The submission guidelines are usually found in the "About Us" or "Contact Us" section on a magazine's website as well as in resources like *Writer's Market*. Read the guidelines carefully and follow them when submitting your query or article.

KNOW HOW TO WRITE AN EFFECTIVE QUERY LETTER

Once you have done all your upfront research and have found a magazine that is a good fit for your idea, it is time to write a good query letter. The letter should be professional and written in a style and tone similar to the article you are pitching.

Robbin Gould, editor of *Family Motor Coaching,* believes a writer needs to submit as comprehensive a query as possible and be fully aware of the magazine's focus, particularly when dealing with a niche publication. "A writer who misuses terms or makes erroneous statements about the subject he or she proposes to cover indicates a lack of knowledge to the editor," says Gould. "Or a query that simply states, 'Would you be interested in an article about XXX?' with minimal explanation wastes everyone's time and suggests the writer is looking for any publication to take the article. If the writer doesn't show much attention to detail up front, the editor probably won't spend much time considering the idea."

There are basic components that should be included in every query letter.

- **SALUTATION (DEAR MR. SMITH).** Find out who the correct editor is to direct your query. You should be able to find this information online. If not make a quick phone call to the publishing company and ask, "Who would I direct a travel query to?" Ask for spelling and the editor's e-mail. Unless you know the editor, use a formal salutation with Mr., Mrs., or Ms. If you are not sure if the editor is a man or woman, put their full name.
- **GOOD HOOK.** You have about 10 seconds to catch the attention of an editor. The opening should be about one to three sentences in length and needs to lure the editor in right away.
- **ARTICLE CONTENT.** This is the bulk of your query and should be about one paragraph. It will focus on the main points of the article and the topics you plan to cover.

- **SPECIFICS.** Here you will include the specifics of the article: word count, department where you think it will fit, possible experts you are going to interview and other information pertinent to the piece.
- **PURPOSE.** In one sentence, share the purpose of your article. Will your article inform, educate, inspire, or entertain?
- **QUALIFICATIONS.** This is not the place to be shy. You need to convince the editor that you are the perfect person to write this article. If you do not have any published clips, then really expand more on your experiences that relate to your article. If you are pitching a parenting article and you have six kids, mention that. It clearly positions you as an expert in the parenting field.
- **SENDING.** Most magazines accept and want queries by e-mail. When sending a query via e-mail, include your information in the body of the message, not in an attachment. Make sure your contact information is at the bottom of the e-mail. Put something noticeable in the subject line. For example: "QUERY: The Benefits of Chocolate and the Creative Process."

By following all the steps in this article you will be ready to set off on a magazine-writing journey equipped with the necessary tools and confidence to get your queries noticed, and, in the end, see your articles in print.

KERRIE FLANAGAN is an author, writing consultant, publisher, and accomplished freelance writer with over 18 years' experience. She is the author of the forthcoming book, *The Writer's Digest Guide to Magazine Article Writing*, as well as seven books published under her label, Hot Chocolate Press. She was the founder and former director of Northern Colorado Writers and now does individual consulting with writers. Feel free to contact her at kerrie.flanagan@gmail.com and www.KerrieFlanagan.com.

LANDING THE SIX-FIGURE DEAL

What Makes Your Proposal Hot

....

by SJ Hodges

It's the question every first-time author wants to ask:

"If I sell my book, will the advance even cover my rent?"

Authors, I am happy to tell you that, yes, the six-figure book deal for a newbie still exists—even if you're not a celebrity with your own television show! As a ghostwriter, I work with numerous authors and personalities to develop both nonfiction and fiction proposals, and I've seen unknown first-timers land life-changing deals even in a down economy. Is platform the ultimate key to their success? You better believe it's a huge consideration for publishers, but here's the good news: Having a killer platform is only one element that transforms a "nice deal" into a "major deal."

You still have to ensure the eight additional elements of your proposal qualify as major attractions. Daniela Rapp, editor at St. Martin's Press explains, "In addition to platform, authors need to have a fantastic, original idea. They have to truly be an expert in their field and they must be able to write." So how do you craft a proposal that conveys your brilliance, your credentials, your talent and puts a couple extra zeroes on your check?

ONE: NARRATIVE OVERVIEW

Before you've even written word one of your manuscript, you are expected to, miraculously, summarize the entirety of your book in such a compelling and visceral way that a publisher or agent will feel as if they are reading *The New York Times* review. Sound impossible? That's because it is.

That's why I'm going to offer two unorthodox suggestions. First, consider writing the first draft of your overview after you've created your table of contents and your chapter outlines. You'll know much more about the content and scope of your material even if you're not 100 percent certain about the voice and tone. That's why you'll take another pass after you complete your sample chapters. Because then you'll be better acquainted with the voice of your book which brings me to unorthodox suggestion number two… treat your overview as literature.

I believe every proposal component needs to be written "in voice" especially because your overview is the first page the editor sees after the title page. By establishing your voice on the page immediately, your proposal becomes less of a sales document and more of a page-turner. Remember, not everyone deciding your fate works in marketing and sales. Editors still have some buying power and they are readers, first and foremost.

TWO: TABLE OF CONTENTS AND CHAPTER OUTLINES

Television writers call this "breaking" a script. This is where you break your book or it breaks you. This is where you discover if what you plan to share with the world actually merits 80,000 words and international distribution.

Regardless of whether you're writing fiction or nonfiction, this element of your proposal must take your buyer on a journey (especially if it's nonfiction) and once more, I'm a big fan of approaching this component with creativity particularly if you're exploring a specific historical time period, plan to write using a regional dialect, rely heavily on "slanguage," and especially if the material is highly technical and dry.

This means you'll need to style your chapter summaries and your chapter titles as a form of dramatic writing. Think about the arc of the chapters, illuminating the escalating conflict, the progression towards a resolution, in a cinematic fashion. Each chapter summary should end with an "emotional bumper," a statement that simultaneously summarizes and entices in the same way a television show punches you in the gut before they cut to a commercial.

Is it risky to commit to a more creative approach? Absolutely. Will it be perfect the first time you write it? No. The fifth time you write it? No. The tenth time? Maybe. But the contents and chapter summary portion of your proposal is where you really get a chance to show off your skills as an architect of plot and structure and how you make an editor's job much, much easier. According to Lara Asher, acquisitions editor at Globe Pequot Press, it is the single most important component of your proposal. "If I can't easily understand what a book is trying to achieve then I can't present it to my colleagues," Asher says. "It won't make it through the acquisitions process."

THREE: YOUR AUTHOR BIO

Your author bio page must prove that you are more than just a pro, that you are recognized by the world at large as "the definitive expert" on your topic, that you have first-hand experience tackling the problems and implementing your solutions, and that you've seen positive results not only in your personal life but in the lives of others. You have to have walked the walk and talked the talk. You come equipped with a built-in audience, mass media attention, and a strong social network. Your bio assures your buyer that you are the right writer exploring the right topic at the right time.

FOUR: YOUR PLATFORM

Platform, platform, platform. Sit through any writing conference, query any agent, lunch with any editor and you'll hear the "P" word over and over again. What you won't hear is hard-and-fast numbers about just how large this platform has to be in order to secure a serious offer. Is there an audience-to-dollar-amount ratio that seems to be in play? Are publishers paying per head?

"I haven't found this to be the case," says Julia Pastore, former editor for Random House. "It's easier to compel someone to 'Like' you on Facebook or follow you on Twitter than it is to compel them to plunk down money to buy your book. Audience engagement is more important than the sheer number of social media followers."

With that said, if you're shooting for six-figures, publishers expect you'll have big numbers and big plans. Your platform will need to include:

Cross-promotional partnerships

These are organizations or individuals that already support you, are already promoting your brand, your products or your persona. If you host a show on HGTV or Nike designed a tennis racket in your honor, they definitely qualify. If, however, you're not rolling like an A-lister just yet, you need to brainstorm any and every possible connection you have to organizations with reach in the 20,000+ range. Maybe your home church is only 200 people but the larger association serves 40,000 and you often write for their newsletter. Think big. Then think bigger.

Specific, verifiable numbers proving the loyalty of your audience

"Publishers want to see that you have direct contact with a loyal audience," says Maura Teitelbaum, an agent at Folio Literary Management. This means having a calendar full of face-to-face speaking engagements, a personal mailing list, extensive database and verifiable traffic to your author website.

But how much traffic does there need to be? How many public appearances? How many e-mails in your Constant Contact newsletter? Publishers are loathe to quote concrete numbers for "Likes" and "Followers" so I'll stick my neck out and do it instead. At a minimum, to land a basic book deal, meaning a low five-figure sum, you'll need to prove that you've got 15,000-20,000 fans willing to follow you into hell and through high water.

For a big six-figure deal, you'll need a solid base of 100,000 rabid fans plus access to hundreds of thousands more. If not millions. Depressed yet? Don't be. Because we live in a time when things as trivial as Angry Oranges or as important as scientific TED talks can go viral and propel a writer out of obscurity in a matter of seconds. It is only your job to become part of the conversation. And once your foot is in the door, you'll be able to gather…

Considerable media exposure

Publishers are risk averse. They want to see that you're a media darling achieving pundit status. Organize and present all your clips, put together a DVD demo reel of your on-air appearances and be able to quote subscriber numbers and demographics about the publications running your articles or features about you.

Advance praise from people who matter

Will blurbs really make a difference in the size of your check? "I would include as many in a proposal as possible," says Teitelbaum. "Especially if those people are willing to write letters of commitment saying they will promote the book via their platform. That shows your efforts will grow exponentially."

FIVE: PROMOTIONAL PLANS

So what is the difference between your platform and your promotional plan? Your promotional plan must demonstrate specifically how you will activate your current platform and the expected sales results of that activation. These are projections starting three to six months before your book release date and continuing for one year after its hardcover publication. They want your guarantee to sell 15,000 books within that first year.

In addition, your promotional plan also issues promises about the commitments you are willing to make in order to promote the book to an even wider market. This is your expansion plan. How will you broaden your reach and who will help you do it? Publishers want to see that your goals are ambitious but doable.

Think about it this way. If you own a nail salon and you apply for a loan to shoot a movie, you're likely to be rejected. But ask for a loan to open your second salon and your odds get much better. In other words, keep your promotional plans in your wheelhouse while still managing to include:

- Television and radio appearances
- Access to print media
- A massive social media campaign
- Direct e-mail solicitations
- E-commerce and back-of-room merchandising
- New joint partnerships
- Your upcoming touring and speaking schedule with expected audience

You'll notice that I did not include hiring a book publicist as a requirement. Gone are the days when an advance-sucking, three-month contract with a book publicist makes any difference. For a six-figure author, publishers expect there is a team in place: a powerful agent, a herd of assistants and a more generalized media publicist already managing the day-to-day affairs of building your brand, growing your audience. Hiring a book publicist at the last minute is useless.

SIX: YOUR MARKET ANALYSIS

It would seem the odds against a first-time author hitting the jackpot are slim but that's where market analysis provides a glimmer of hope. There are actually markets considered more desirable to publishers. "Broader is generally better for us," says Rapp. "Niche generally implies small. Not something we [St. Martin's Press] can afford to do these days. Current affairs books, if they are explosive and timely, can work. Neuroscience is hot. Animal books (not so much animal memoirs) still work. Military books sell."

"The health and diet category will always be huge," says Asher. "But in a category like parenting which is so crowded, we look for an author tackling a niche topic that hasn't yet been covered."

Niche or broad, your market analysis must position your book within a larger context, addressing the needs of the publishing industry, the relevant cultural conversations happening in the zeitgeist, your potential audience and their buying power, and the potential for both domestic and international sales.

SEVEN: YOUR C.T.A.

Choose the books for your Competitive Title Analysis not only for their topical similarities but also because the author has a comparable profile and platform to your own. Says Pastore, "It can be editorially helpful to compare your book to *Unbroken* by Hillenbrand, but unless your previous book was also a bestseller, this comparison won't be helpful to our sales force."

Limit your C.T.A. to five or six solid offerings then get on BookScan and make sure none of the books sold fewer than 10,000 copies. "Higher sales are preferable," says Rapp. "And you should leave it to the publisher to decide if the market can hold one more title or not. We always do our own research anyway, so just because the book is not mentioned in your line-up doesn't mean we won't know about it."

EIGHT: SAMPLE CHAPTERS

Finally, you have to/get to prove you can … write. Oh yeah, that!

This is the fun part, the pages of your proposal where you really get to shine. It is of upmost importance that these chapters, in harmony with your overview and chapter summaries, allow the beauty, wisdom and/or quirkiness of your voice to be heard. Loud and clear.

"Writing absolutely matters and strong sample chapters are crucial." Pastore explains, "An author must be able to turn their brilliant idea into engaging prose on the page."

Approach the presentation of these chapters creatively. Consider including excerpts from several different chapters and not just offering the standard Introduction, Chapter One and Two. Consider the inclusion of photographs to support the narrative, helping your editor put faces to names. Consider using sidebars or box quotes from the narrative throughout your proposal to build anticipation for the actual read.

NINE: YOUR ONE-PAGER

Lastly, you'll need a one-pager, which is a relatively new addition to the book proposal format. Publishers now expect an author to squeeze a 50- or 60-page proposal down to a one-page summary they can hand to their marketing and sales teams. In its brevity, the one-pager must provide your buyer with "a clear vision of what the book is, why it's unique, why you are the best person to write it, and how we can reach the audience," says Pastore. And it must do that in fewer than 1,000 words. There is no room to be anything but impressive.

And if you're shooting for that six-figure deal, impressive is what each component of your book proposal must be. Easy? No. But still possible? Yes.

SJ HODGES is an 11-time published playwright, ghostwriter and editor. Her most recent book, a memoir co-authored with Animal Planet's "Pit Boss" Shorty Rossi was purchased by Random House/Crown, hit #36 on the Amazon bestseller list and went into its 3rd printing less than six weeks after its release date. As a developmental editor, SJ has worked on books published by Vanguard Press, Perseus Book Group and St. Martin's Press. SJ is a tireless advocate for artists offering a free listing for jobs, grants and fellowships at her Facebook page: facebook.com/constantcreator. She can be reached through her website: sjhodges.com.

WHY, WHEN AND HOW TO CO-AUTHOR A BOOK

by Sue Bradford Edwards

Many writers work in isolation. They research and take notes, write and rewrite all on their own. But other writers take the old saying "two heads are better than one" to heart, pairing up to write one or more projects. The reasons they decide to co-author are as varied as the writers themselves.

My co-author launched our partnership. Duchess Harris is an academic and writer of books like *Black Feminist Politics from Kennedy to Obama* (Palgrave MacMillan). She wanted to write about her grandmother's experience as one of NASA's first black computers but she didn't want to write this book for academics. Wanting to inspire young learners, she invited me to co-author an educational book for teens, *Hidden Human Computers* (Abdo). I had already written several books for this audience including *Black Lives Matter* (Abdo) which we worked on together after the publisher brought her into the project as the content expert. I jumped at the opportunity to co-author this story.

Similarly, Corinne Demas had an idea for a science-based picture book. She had expertise as a writer but felt she didn't have the topic knowledge necessary to make the best book possible. "For the science books I needed a co-author who had expertise that I lacked," Demas says. She found that expertise in her daughter, Artemis Roehrig, a research assistant at the University of Massachusetts-Amherst.

Roehrig also benefited from the partnership. "As an unestablished writer, I found working with a well-published author provided a great opportunity for breaking into the publishing world."

Sometimes writers pair off when each develops a similar idea for a manuscript. Sisters Lorraine Campbell and Pam Burks discovered that they both wanted to write a novel based loosely on their lives as two of four sisters. They decided to work together on the manuscript that became *How to Survive Your Sisters* (Across the Pond).

But writers aren't always the ones that come up with the idea for collaboration. Sometimes the initial nudge comes from outside. Liz Scanlon and Audrey Vernick were accountability partners, each making sure the other was writing when their agent suggested they co-author a book. The pair thought that it sounded like fun and were soon passing back and forth the manuscript that became *Bob, Not Bob!* (Disney/Hyperion). After all, deciding to work together is just the start.

Yours vs Mine

For most co-authors, the next step is deciding who does what. With research, writing and communicating with the editor up for grabs, it's important to know who is in charge of each task so that nothing falls through the cracks. Because she knew the topic, Harris led the research while I divvied up the writing, with the math and science for me and the social history for Harris.

Similarly, when they wrote *Does a Fiddler Crab Fiddle?* (Persnickety Press), Roehrig and Demas decided who would do what based on experience. With her science background, Roehrig took responsibility for the research and writing the authors' note. Demas took the lead in developing the book concept and the more creative parts of the text.

Other co-authors take turns writing without a plan. "Our process is so loose," says Scanlon. "One of us—usually the one who gets 'the idea'—gets started. Then we pass a manuscript back and forth via e-mail—adding, subtracting, and revising as we see fit. At some point someone adds a title. Someone re-arranges the first few lines. Someone comes up with the perfect zinger for the end."

This is the same method used by husband and wife team Nicci Gerard and Sean French, who co-author such novels as *Saturday Requiem* (Penguin) and *Sunday Morning Coming Down* (Penguin) as Nicci French. Their novels, from research to writing, are joint endeavors with each taking a turn to write.

Other co-authors divide the writing by each writing the parts of the book that are told from a certain character's point of view (POV). To do this, Campbell and Burks first decide who is writing from which POV. They then know who will write each chapter or other section of the novel based on the POV being used for that part of the story.

Seamless Joins

No matter how the writing is divided, multiple authors mean multiple voices so when two different people write a single book, it's important to make certain it isn't obvious that Author A wrote one part and Author B wrote the other. For some coauthors it is fairly simple to minimize this effect because their voices are so much alike. Campbell and Burks are so similar that, as children, people thought they were twins. They sound alike when they talk and also think much alike. Add to this their common verbal patterns and it isn't surprising that their writing voices are very similar. By the time they make several passes through the manuscript even they aren't entirely sure who drafted which scene.

Some co-authors don't start with similar voices but their joint voice combines each of their strengths. Scanlon uses "pretty metaphors." Vernick writes funny. Says Scanlon, "One of the beauties of writing together is that we get both of those things in each and every story! Any sticky edges get smoothed out by that passing back and forth. Any extremes in her voice or mine get caught."

Vernick agrees. "There is an element of the whole being more than the sum of the parts with our projects," she says. "In addition to including Liz's writing and my writing, there's an element of our writing that magically works its way into the text."

Gerard and French experience something similar. Separately, the two are very different writers, but as they work through a new idea together, a different voice emerges. It isn't the voice of either Gerard or French but the voice of Nicci French.

For their part, Roehrig and Demas make a conscious effort to create a consistent voice. The picture books they write are meant to be read out loud to young readers, so Roehrig and Demas read their stories aloud. By hearing the story the way their audience will, they have the opportunity to make sure the narrative voice is consistent from sentence to sentence and page to page.

FINDING A MATCH

What should you look for in a potential co-author? Here are five things to consider.

- **Do you know and respect this author's work?** Don't just hook up with someone at a conference. Get to know their writing before agreeing to the project. Otherwise you might find you are personally compatible but your styles-of-writing are worlds apart.

- **What does this person write?** Look for someone whose work overlaps your own. If you want to work on novels, don't pick a picture book writer. If your passion is nonfiction, avoid that novelist.

- **Do this person's skills complement your own?** If you are a seat-of-your-pants, how-does-it-sound kind of writer, you might want to pick a co-author who is methodical and linear, but not so much so that you annoy each other.

- **Does this person have a similar work ethic?** If you write, and need feedback, five days a week, don't pick someone who only writes on the weekends. If you are goal oriented, don't saddle yourself with someone who writes only when they feel like it.

> - **Does this person have goals that are similar to your own?** What type of publisher is right for you? If you want a regional publisher, don't pick a co-author who wants one of the big New York houses or is only willing to self-publish.
>
> Answering these questions can help you find a match made in heaven.

Civil Disagreements

Successful co-authors often make writing as part of a team sound simple. In part, this is because they have worked out a way to settle disagreements. After all, with two creative minds, there will eventually be a point where each person wants to do something different with the manuscript.

When that happens, Roehrig and Demas take a break, get something to eat, or go for a walk. Fortunately, as mother and daughter, the two have a track record in working through disagreements. They know they will both have to compromise and they both have the same goal—a top notch manuscript.

When asked how they handle disagreements, Scanlon's initial answer was short. "Sword fights," she said. "Just kidding. Mostly when the other person cuts something we thought we loved, we just trust that the story is better for it! Very occasionally we'll make a case for keeping it. Sometimes we don't even notice an edit's been made because we don't use track changes."

Vernick emphasized just how important that is. "I think that not using track changes is the key to the magic in our process. Writers have such ridiculous, inexplicable attachments to parts of their book and seeing it cut right there, with that cruel line through the words, can evoke a response in a way that having it just disappear does not. I think it's safe to say I usually don't notice what Liz cuts. Also, I have a voodoo doll, and if she doesn't listen at first, I just wait it out." Scanlon and Vernick make it clear that having a sense of humor is an essential part of working closely with another writer.

So is another skill—communication. While Campbell and Burks each copy edit with little or no discussion, big changes, such as taking out a character or sending the story in a new direction, call for a dialogue between the writing partners. Fortunately, they find that the excitement at creating an even better story is contagious and a great way to get a writing partner on board for even a labor-intensive change.

Post Mortem

In spite of the list of co-authored titles these writers have compiled, not every attempt to co-author is a rousing success. Roehrig and Demas encourage writers new to the co-authoring process not to give up if their first attempt isn't a dream come true. Not only does the project have to be something that requires multiple authors to pull off, the paired authors must be carefully chosen to complement each other.

Finding the right writing partner is worth the effort. Says Scanlon, "When you have this much fun working on something, it comes through in the work. There's a kind of embodied joy by the time we finish up, really. When there is success—when we sell a piece—there is a sort of shared giddiness. And when a piece bombs, we are somehow less fragile, less ego-attached. Plus, it already feels like it was time worthwhile, which makes it easier to let it go if we have to."

Vernick agrees. "I've heard many writers talk about how they would write even if there was no chance of publication. I'm not sure I'm of that breed. I want to publish my manuscripts. But as Liz said, when that doesn't come to pass, I still look back on that collaborative writing process as something I'm very happy to have done." Not every manuscript or every author pairing works for collaboration, but when you find one that does it will make you want to try it again.

In addition to writing how-to articles for her fellow writers, **SUE BRADFORD EDWARDS** writes educational nonfiction for young writers from her home in Missouri. Her work includes crafts and activities as well as a variety of books including *Women in Science, Women in Sports, The Zika Virus* and *Hidden Human Computers*. Contact her and learn more at www.suebradford-edwards.com.

TAPPING INTO A HIDDEN MARKET

Industrial Writing

....

by Joyce Laird

//

Industrial writing is a huge market most writers do not consider. It's more profitable than selling short stories to consumer magazines and offers better odds of success than entering "big money fiction contests," which you have to pay to enter. I'm not saying you shouldn't go for the ego boost that publishing a short story or winning a contest brings, but it's not a living. An average industrial feature short is about 500 words and pays $300-750, depending on the magazine. A standard feature article is 1,500-2,500 words and can pay $1,500-3,000.

EXPLORING THE MARKETS

Writing for Industrial Magazines

Industrial publishing houses have at minimun two or three publications under their umbrella, though many have a dozen or more publications. With all magazines keeping in-house staff, most are open to adding freelance writers to lighten the load.

Just to give you an idea of how large this untapped market is, there are about 375 domestic publications who often use freelance writers. Of course these numbers are continually changing. Some publications meld into new publications and all keep adding new online venues. Quite a few industrial publishers also have special projects that they offer to their advertisers. These can be white papers, or even technical brochures. All need to be written.

What makes industrial publications different from consumer is that they exist only by paid advertising, not by subscribed readers. With the exception of a very few special trade publications, all are free to the readers and all keep a very long history of their content online for everyone to read: features, newsletters, webinars and news blogs. These areas all need writers. Some pay very little, but compensate for the low per-piece rate by needing a steady stream of short features on a daily basis. For feature articles, all pay very well.

When given an assignment you only need experts to interview. Some editors will provide a list of "preferred" companies they want included in the feature. Others will expect you to find companies with experts on the topic. You find experts by online searching of the appropriate industry and also using tools such as PR Newswire for Journalists (https://prnmedia.prnewswire.com/).

Proprietary information is what keeps all industrial companies in business.

This type of writing is a kissing-cousin to news journalism, but it is not the same. Fact checking is top priority. For all feature articles it means interviewing a knowledgable source or sources. Each interviewee must have a chance to edit and approve the words you have written from interviews. Proprietary information is what keeps all industrial companies in business. This is even more important when working with medical companies and leading edge scientific research.

Making sure that you have every word signed off and approved before sending the formatted final to your editor will keep everyone happy and cement yourself as a true professional.

Writing for Industrial Manufacturers

There are two types of ghostwriting potentials when working for manufacturing clients. There is pure ghost writing where you interview, write and edit to approved final and give it back to the company to use as they see fit. They may be submitting it as a feature article or using it on their website or in other promotional areas. You are paid to write it. Your job ends there.

The other type of ghostwriting is where you do a synopsis of a topic and pitch it to the magazines that the company prefers. All publications are open to contributed technical features. In this case, you are only paid to write the feature after you get a commitment from an editor with a deadline for the copy and graphics. Then you conduct interviews, write and revise until your client approves the final. After approval you send the full package (formatted copy and grapics) to the publication.

FINDING YOUR MARKET/CONTACTS

All the information you need to make the right contacts is at your fingertips—online. There are no legitimate lists or services that can connect you to everything you need in one tidy spot like you find with consumer magazines or niche fiction, essays or contests. However, every industrial magazine has a website with samples of their publications and the contact information on editors. Online searches such as: Industrial (sub-gender: medical, automotive, aerospace, food processing, machine design, etc.) manufacturing magazines will bring up publication sites for any area you are interested in.

For manufacturers you could search each type individually, but I suggest the best site in the world is the Thomas Register (http://www.thomasnet.com/browse). There are over 170,000 industrial manufacturers are on this site. Add in the medical device manufacturers and it hits roughly 175,000. This is just a very rough count in the USA only because the market is always expanding. Every industrial manufacturer in every niche of the marketplace is listed in the register. You can browse catagories or focus on a specific area of interest, such as medical device manufacturers, electronic assembly systems, solar panel manufacturers, etc. You can review what they do and where they are and follow up on any specific website to learn more.

THREE KINDS OF PITCHES

Seeking freelance assignments from industrial editors

It's most important here to show the editor you know what you're doing and understand what his/her publication needs. If you have samples or a background in industrial writing, use it. If not, explain to the editor why you would be perfect to help him/her with freelance writing.

Pitching a contributed feature to industrial editors

This is the eaiest to pitch, because you already have the information about the feature and should have done an in-depth review of the publication. It's now a matter of presenting why this particular feature would provide excellent new information to the readers. Give all the technical background and who the bylined author and contributing company is. It's free to the publication, so all the editor needs to see is where it fits the best and give you a deadline that you can take back to your client for approval to start the feature.

Seeking freelance writing from industrial manufacturers

In this case, you are presenting yourself as the best writer to help the manufacturer get more exposure in publications. Your writing fee should be lower than buying ad space and offer the company valuable exposure as an industry expert.

WHY YOU NEED A LINK LIST

All industrial features stay online for years. They become a living résumé for you. Keep an updated list of all your published features with associated links. My list consists of the publication, feature title, my byline or ghostwritten for XYZ, and a link. I also save every feature to PDF. Links can change as publications revamp their websites and eventually all fade away so PDF files are a great backup. For example, an editor contacted me last year and wanted to see my writing samples in a particular area. I had written features for his publication long before he became the editor. The links were no longer valid, so I sent him two of the PDF features. I landed the cover feature and made $3,000.

As your list of links builds, it becomes the main tool you use to pitch to editors and to manufacturers. Until then, keep promoting yourself with your education and any background you have that will spark confidence with industrial editors and manufacturers who need freelance writing help.

> The links were no longer valid, so I sent him two of the PDF features. I landed the cover feature and made $3,000.

QUOTES/CONTRACTS

Freelance feature writing for industrial magazines

If they even use them, all editors provide their own contracts. If an editor asks you for a quote, it's always best to ask them what their standard pay rate is. If you quote $1,200 or $1,500 for a standard feature, you may be selling yourself short if their standard rate is $1,800 or $2,500. If the publication only pays a maximum of $750 or $1,000 you might be willing to write a page or two for that rate, or you can turn it down. Never be afraid to ask for a rate range. Editors are used to this question. Then you can base your decision on what the pay is and if the feature is a good addition to your PDF file and link list. Also, it might open up a door to working for that publication on a regular basis. Editors who like you will recommend you, not only to other editors but to their advertisers who are looking for writers for in-house projects.

Ghostwriting for industrial manufacturers

You set your fees. I personally like flat fees for a standard length feature (1,200-2,500 words), and negotiate for short features or larger projects, based on my interest in them. I base my fee at less than the cost of a typical half-page 4-color ad in any industrial publication. This can be from as low as $2,000 up to $8,000, depending on the magazine. A flat rate of $1,600 for instance, makes a very nice comparison when sending industrial manufacturers a query for ghostwriting feature articles for their company. An ad costs a bundle and is just another ad. A feature gives them 3-8 pages or more in color and sets them up as an industry expert. Plus, they can download it, print it, link to it from their website. The uses in marketing are huge.

The legal side

Whether you use it all the time or not, you must have a formal quote/contract template ready. Most publications will never ask for this, but it's good to have just in case. For ghostwriting, a quote/contract is your legal bible. Never start a project without an e-mail approval for your client file.

A formal quote/contract should include:

- Contact information (yours and the company who requested your services)
- Description of the project in detail
- Description of the services you will provide in detail
- Description of what the client must provide in detail
- Breakdown of everything that goes into the total cost of the project
- Time-frame required to complete the project
- Terms of payment*
- Require a signature or e-mail approval of contract before start of project
- Failsafe clause—either party may cancel the contract in writing at any time

*Terms of payment: This may differ depending upon who you are working with. Even with a work quote, all editors have their own payment schedules set by their publisher. I typically just put in net-30 upon receipt of final. I have never been stiffed by a publication in all my 30 years. With electronic deposit, some actually have it in my bank within only days of invoice.

When ghostwriting for industrial manufacturers, I use 50% down upon approval of quote/50% balance payable upon final, approved copy to the client or publication.

You can come up with your own terms, but I highly recommend getting a deposit in advance of starting any project with a manufacturer. Sometimes writing projects can suddenly die due to other issues that may become a priority for the company. If that happens midway, at least you have the deposit up front.

WELCOME TO MY WORLD

The immense size of this market may seem daunting but it offers many opportunities from which to choose. Start slowly and decide where you want to write. There are many publications to choose from and more manufacturers than you could ever contact in your entire lifetime. Start by going after what interests you and let it grow from there. Industrial writing is like a tree that continually springs new branches. New, interesting things always pop up that I never thought of. The secret is to always be open to learning something new. Never attempt to be the expert. Your job is to make the experts sound great.

JOYCE LAIRD has written multiple fiction short stories and essays for *Woman's World* magazine and the *Chicken Soup for the Soul* book series, but she supports her fiction and essay writing by working as a freelance industrial writer. Over the past 30 years, she has written articles and white papers for markets ranging from medical and engineering to renewable energy and electronics manufacturing. To learn more about her, search "industrial features or medical features by Joyce Laird" online and see what comes up. This can very easily soon be you.

EARN A FULL-TIME INCOME FROM BLOGGING

by Carol Tice

//

It sounds like a dream: Instead of sending query letters and relying on editors to give you paying assignments, you start your own blog and turn it into a money-maker. No matter where in the world you want to live, you're able to earn a good living.

For a growing number of writers, it's not a dream. I'm among the writers who now earn more from their own blogs than they do from freelance assignments.

But it's not easy, by any means. The vast majority of blogs never find an audience and their authors never earn a dime. It's hard to stand out—at the end of 2011, pollster Nielsen reported there were over 181 million blogs, up from 36 million in 2006.

In this vast sea of blogs, how can you write one that stands out and becomes the basis for a money-earning business? It begins with setting up the blog to attract a loyal readership. Once you build an audience, there are a limited number of ways you can earn income from your blog audience—I spotlight five of the most popular methods below.

SETTING IT UP TO EARN

Many blogs don't attract readers because they lack basic elements of design and usability that make blogs appealing, says Seattle WordPress trainer Bob Dunn (www.bobwp.com). Dunn's own blog is the platform on which he's built his business.

How do you create an attractive blog?

USE A PROFESSIONAL PLATFORM

Free blog platforms such as Blogger and Moveable Type have limitations that make it hard to look professional (and some free platforms prohibit commerce). If you're serious about blogging, pay for a host and use WordPress—it's now the dominant blogging platform, Technorati reports.

OFFER CONTACT INFORMATION

Many bloggers cultivate an air of mystery, using a pen name and providing no contact info. But readers want to know who you are and be able to e-mail you questions, says Dunn.

HAVE AN "ABOUT" PAGE

With a million scams on the Internet, the About page has become a vital blog component—it's usually the most-visited page after the Home page, Dunn says. This is the place where readers get to know you and learn why you write your blog.

"I can't tell you how many times I go on a blog and there's no About page," says, Dunn. "It should be more than a résumé, too—tell a story."

CLEAN UP THE DESIGN

No matter how wonderful your writing is, if your blog is a clutter of tiny type, dark backgrounds, multiple sidebars, and flashing ads, readers will leave, Dunn says. Begin with a simple, graphical header, title, and tagline that quickly communicate what your blog is about. You have just a few seconds in which to convey what you write about before readers leave, so be clear.

MAKE NAVIGATION SIMPLE

Many bloggers end up with multiple rows of tabs or long drop-down menus. Try to simplify—for every additional click you require, you will lose some readers, Dunn says.

PICK A NICHE TOPIC

While most blogs ramble about whatever the author feels like discussing that day, business-focused blogs stick to a subject or a few related topics, notes Dunn. This allows you to attract and keep readers interested in your subject.

CREATE USEFUL CONTENT

Write with your readers' needs in mind, rather than about your own interests, says Mexico-based Jon Morrow. His year-old blog Boost Blog Traffic (boostblogtraffic.com) earned $500,000 in 2012. If you don't know what readers want, Morrow says, take polls and ask questions to find out.

WRITE STRONG HEADLINES

If you want readers to find your posts online, your headlines need key words and phrases that relate to your topic, to help them rank well in Google searches for your topic. You can do keyword research free using Google's tool (https://adwords.google.com/o/Keyword-Tool). Headlines also need to be lively and interesting to draw readers—Morrow offers a Headline Hacks report on his blog that dissects effective headline styles.

USE BLOG STYLE

Blog posts are different from magazine articles because of how people read—make that skim—online, says Dunn. Good blog-post paragraphs are short, often just one or two sentences. Posts with bold subheads or bulleted or numbered lists are easy to scan and often enjoy higher readership.

MAKE SHARING EASY

To grow your audience, you'll need readers to spread the word, says Dunn. Make that easy with one-click sharing buttons for Twitter, Facebook and other popular social-media platforms. You should be active in these platforms, too, building relationships with influential people who might send you readers.

START GUEST-POSTING

One of the fastest ways to build your blog audience is by guest-posting on popular blogs with lots of traffic. Your guest post will give you a link back to your own blog and allow new readers to find you. This is usually not paid work, but think of it as a marketing cost for your blog-based business. Many top blogs do accept guest posts—look for writer's guidelines on their sites.

"The big secret to making money from blogging is to get serious about marketing," Morrow says.

BUILD AN E-MAIL LIST

The best way to stay in touch with readers is via an e-mail list visitors are encouraged to join, says Dunn. Subscribers who sign up through real simple syndication, or RSS, don't reveal their e-mail address, so it's hard to sell them anything.

START EARNING

Once your blog is set up to entice readers, you're ready to experiment with ways to generate income off your blog. Among the common approaches:

1. Freelance Gigs

Add a "Hire Me" tab to your site to begin attracting freelance blogging gigs from online businesses and publications. That's the approach U.K.-based writer Tom Ewer took when he quit his job and launched his blog Leaving Work Behind (www.leavingworkbehind.com) in 2011.

A brand-new writer at the time, Ewer quickly got a couple of freelance blogging clients by applying to online job ads. More clients approached him after seeing his guest posts on big blogs and finding his blog from there. Ewer was soon blogging for pay about topics including WordPress and government contracting. By late 2012, he was earning $4,000 a month as a paid blogger at $100 a post and up, working part-time hours.

A similar strategy worked for Nigerian blogger Bamidele Onibalusi, who began his online-earning themed blog YoungPrePro (www.youngprepro.com) in 2010, when he was just 16. By 2012, he was making $50,000 a year writing for blog owners who learned of him from his dozens of guest posts on top blogs including DailyBlogTips and ProBlogger.

He's blogged for paying clients in the United States, United Kingdom, Greece, and elsewhere about real estate, accounting, and weight loss, among other topics. Onibalusi says he impresses prospects with long, highly useful posts with strong keywords that attract an ongoing stream of readers.

"Google has sent me most of my business," he says.

2. Books & E-books

Build a major following on your blog, and you can earn good money writing and selling your own books and e-books. That strategy has been successful for Jeff Goins of the writing and social-change blog GoinsWriter (goinswriter.com), who has two Kindle e-books and a traditionally published print book under his belt.

Launched in 2010 and now boasting 25,000 subscribers, GoinsWriter has loyal fans who help drive more than $3,500 a month in sales of his two low-priced e-books, including his co-authored *You Are a Writer (So Start Acting Like One)*, which goes for just $2.99.

Goins first creates excitement around his e-books by blogging about the upcoming release first. Then, as the publication date nears, he gives more than 100 die-hard fans a free PDF of the e-book in exchange for Amazon reviews. When he officially publishes a few days later on Amazon and elsewhere, the glowing reviews help encourage thousands of purchases. The reviews and frequent downloads keep his e-books ranking highly for the writing category, which drives more sales. Links in the e-book also help bring more blog readers.

E-book sales also kicked off the blog-earning career of Pat Flynn, a southern Californian who first had modest blog-monetizing success with an e-book he wrote on how to pass an architectural exam. He started the Smart Passive Income (www.smartpassiveincome.com) blog in 2008 to dissect that success. This second blog went on to greatly surpass the original project, bringing in over $200,000 its first year alone.

3. Affiliate Sales

Flynn earns primarily through affiliate sales, a strategy in which a blogger receives a commission for selling someone else's product or service. It's an approach that works best with a large audience—Smart Passive Income has 57,000 subscribers and gets 100,000 visitors a month.

His audience includes many bloggers who need to set up their websites, so many of his affiliate products are tools or services that enable bloggers. Flynn's top-selling affiliate product in 2012 was website host Bluehost, from which he now typically earns $20,000 or more monthly. He receives a commission every time someone signs up for website hosting through his unique affiliate links.

"I find products that help them get from A to Z," he says. "They're recommended products I've actually used. You want to be sort of an expert in it."

Flynn builds loyalty by creating free blog posts that offer "high value content that would usually require payment." Rather than slapping up ads that might annoy readers, he simply states that site links earn him a commission. Fans are happy to click, and even send him thank-you notes about the products he sells.

Like many top-earning bloggers, Flynn uses videos and podcasts to help promote his blogs. Flynn's Smart Passive Income Podcast has brought many new readers—it's one of the top business-related podcasts on iTunes and has seen more than 2 million downloads.

4. Courses & Coaching

When you've built your reputation through delivering useful blog posts, you can sell your fans more advanced information on your topic. Courses and coaching are the main earners for Boost Blog Traffic's Morrow, who teaches a guest-blogging class and takes just 10 students at a time in his $10,000-a-head, five-month coaching course. The secret sauce in the guest-blogging class includes personal introductions by Morrow to top blog editors.

Build your authority enough, and customers pay just for the opportunity to learn from someone they respect, says Morrow.

"I'm not really selling products," he says. "I'm selling me."

Morrow attributes part of his earning success to hard work to improve the marketing campaigns for his paid programs. He says he's spent hundreds of hours testing and tinkering with marketing e-mails and promotional videos that help sell the courses. Now that he's refined his process, he says he needs to spend only five hours a week on his guest-blogging course. Affiliates do much of the selling of his blogging course for him.

An extension of this teaching niche is public speaking, for which top presenters can earn tens of thousands of dollars per appearance. Morrow recently presented at the New Media Expo (formerly known as BlogWorld), for instance.

5. Membership Community

Once they're publishing, teaching, speaking, and creating audio and video materials on a topic, bloggers can leverage all that content to earn even more through a paid membership community. Inside the community, members can access large amounts of training materials and their favorite expert's advice via chat forums for one low monthly rate, instead of paying for it piecemeal. The community model allows bloggers to earn more as additional members join without having to do much more work, as members mostly access existing content.

Large communities can be major money generators—for instance, A-List Blogger Club (www.alistbloggingbootcamps.com/alist-blogger-club-join), a blog-building training community started by top blogger Leo Babauta of Zen Habits that I used to learn how to build my own blog, had roughly 900 members in 2012 paying $20 apiece per month. The blog Write to Done (writetodone.com) serves as the main platform that introduces writers to the club.

Blogging is not for every writer. It's a lot of work coming up with post ideas and writing several posts a month or even a week. It can be many months until a blog starts to earn money, and there are no guarantees it will ever catch on. But for writers with the drive to stick with it and a willingness to learn about blog marketing, the rewards can be rich.

CAROL TICE writes the Make a Living Writing (www.makealivingwriting.com) blog and runs the writers learning community Freelance Writers Den (freelancewritersden.com). She has written two nonfiction business books and co-authored the Kindle e-book *13 Ways to Get the Writing Done Faster* (www.amazon.com/Ways-Writing-Done-Faster-ebook/dp/B009XM03SK).

FUNDS FOR WRITERS 101

Find Money You Didn't Know Existed

....

by C. Hope Clark

///

When I completed writing my novel over a decade ago, I imagined the next step was simply to find a publisher and watch the book sell. Like most writers, my goal was to earn a living doing what I loved so I could walk away from the day job. No such luck. Between rejection and newfound knowledge that a novel can take years to sell enough for a single house payment, I opened my mind to other writing avenues. I learned that there's no *one* way to find funds to support your writing; instead there are *many*. So many, in fact, that I felt the need to share the volume of knowledge I collected, and I called it FundsforWriters.com.

Funds are money. But obtaining those funds isn't necessarily a linear process, or a one-dimensional path. As a serious writer, you study all options at your fingertips, entertaining financial resources that initially don't make sense as well as the obvious.

GRANTS

Grants come from government agencies, nonprofits, businesses and even generous individuals. They do not have to be repaid, as long as you use the grant as intended. No two are alike. Therefore, you must do your homework to find the right match between your grant need and the grant provider's mission. Grantors like being successful at their mission just as you like excelling at yours. So they screen applicants, ensuring they fit the rules and show promise to follow through.

Don't fear grants. Sure, you're judged by a panel, and rejection is part of the game, but you already know that as a writer. Gigi Rosenberg, author of *The Artist's Guide to*

Grant Writing, states, "If one funder doesn't want to invest in your project, find another who does. And if nobody does, then begin it any way you can. Once you've started, that momentum will help your project find its audience and its financial support."

TYPES OF GRANTS

Grants can send you to retreats, handle emergencies, provide mentors, pay for conferences, or cover travel. They also can be called awards, fellowships, residencies, or scholarships. But like any aspect of your writing journey, define how any tool, even a grant, fits into your plans. Your mission must parallel a grantor's mission.

The cream-of-the-crop grants have no strings attached. Winning recipients are based upon portfolios and an application that defines a work-in-progress. You don't have to be a Pulitzer winner, but you must prove your establishment as a writer.

You find most of these opportunities in state arts commissions. Find them at www.nasaa-arts.org or as a partner listed at the National Endowment for the Arts website, www.nea.gov. Not only does your state's arts commission provide funding, but the players can direct you to other grant opportunities, as well as to artists who've gone before you. Speaking to grant winners gives you a wealth of information and a leg up in designing the best application.

Foundations and nonprofits fund the majority of grants. Most writers' organizations are nonprofits. Both the Mystery Writers of America (www.mysterywriters.org) and Society of Children's Book Writers and Illustrators (www.scbwi.org) offer scholarships and grants.

Many retreats are nonprofits. Journalist and freelancer Alexis Grant (http://alexisgrant.com/) tries to attend a retreat a year. Some ask her to pay, usually on a sliding scale based upon income, and others provide scholarships. Each time, she applies with a clear definition of what she hopes to gain from the two to five-week trips. "It's a great way to get away from the noise of everyday responsibilities, focus on writing well and meet other people who prioritize writing. I always return home with a new perspective." One resource to find writing retreats is the Alliance of Artists Communities (www.artistcommunities.org/).

Laura Lee Perkins won four artist-in-residence slots with the National Park Service (www.nps.gov). The federal agency has 43 locations throughout the United States where writers and artists live for two to four weeks. From Acadia National Park in Maine to Sleeping Bear Dunes National Lakeshore in Michigan, Perkins spoke to tourists about her goals to write a book about Native American music. "Memories of the US National Parks' beauty and profound serenity will continue to enrich my work. Writers find unparalleled inspiration, quietude, housing, interesting staff, and a feeling of being in the root of your artistic desires."

Don't forget writers' conferences. While they may not advertise financial aid, many have funds available in times of need. Always ask as to the availability of a scholarship or work-share program that might enable your attendance.

Grants come in all sizes. FundsforWriters posts emergency grants on its grants page (www.fundsforwriters.com) as well as new grant opportunities such as the Sustainable Arts Foundation (www.sustainableartsfoundation.org) that offers grants to writers and artists with children under the age of 18, or the Awesome Foundation (www.awecomefoundation.org), which gives $1,000 grants to creative projects.

Novelist Joan Dempsey won an Elizabeth George Foundation grant (http://www.elizabethgeorgeonline.com/foundation/index.htm) in early 2012. "I applied to the Foundation for a research grant that included three trips to places relevant to my novel-in-progress, trips I otherwise could not have afforded. Not only does the grant provide travel funds, but it also provides validation that I'm a serious writer worthy of investment, which is great for my psyche and my résumé."

FISCAL SPONSORSHIP

Nonprofits have access to an incredibly large number of grants that individuals do not, and have the ability to offer their tax-exempt status to groups and individuals involved in activities related to their mission. By allowing a nonprofit to serve as your grant overseer, you may acquire funds for your project.

Deborah Marshall is President of the Missouri Writers Guild (www.missouriwritersguild.org) and founder of the Missouri Warrior Writers Project, with ample experience with grants in the arts. "Although grant dollars are available for individual writers, writing the grant proposal becomes difficult without significant publication credits. Partnering with a nonprofit organization, whether it is a writing group, service, community organization, or any 501(c)3, can fill in those gaps to make a grant application competitive. Partnering not only helps a writer's name become known, but it also assists in building that all-important platform."

Two excellent groups that offer fiscal sponsorship for writers are The Fractured Atlas (www.fracturedatlas.org) and Artspire (www.artspire.org), sponsored by the New York Foundation for the Arts and open to all US citizens. Visit The Foundation Center (www.foundationcenter.org) for an excellent tutorial guide to fiscal sponsorship.

CROWD SOURCING

Crowd sourcing is a co-op arrangement where people support artists directly, much like the agricultural co-op movement where individuals fund farming operations in exchange for fresh food. Kickstarter (www.kickstarter.com) has made this funding method successful in the arts.

Basically, the writer proposes his project, and for a financial endorsement as low as $1, donors receive some token in return, like an autographed book, artwork, or bookmark. The higher the donation, the bigger the *wow* factor in the gift. Donors do not receive ownership in the project.

Meagan Adele Lopez (www.ladywholunches.net) presented her debut self-published book *Three Questions* to Kickstarter readers, requesting $4,400 to take her book on tour, create a book trailer, pre-order books, and redesign the cover. Eighty-eight backers pledged a total of $5,202. She was able to hire an editor and a company that designed film trailers. For every $750 she received over her plan, she added a new city to her book tour.

Other up-and-coming crowd sourcing companies include Culture 360 (www.culture360.org) that serves Asia and Europe, and Indiegogo (www.indiegogo.com), as well as Rocket Hub (www.rockethub.com). And nothing stops you from simply asking those you know to support your project. The concept is elementary.

CONTESTS

Contests offer financial opportunity, too. Of course you must win, place or show, but many writers overlook the importance that contests have on a career. These days, contests not only open doors to publishing, name recognition, and money, but listing such achievements in a query letter might make an agent or publisher take a second glance. Noting your wins on a magazine pitch might land a feature assignment. Mentioning your accolades to potential clients could clinch a freelance deal.

I used contests as a barometer when fleshing out my first mystery novel, *A Low-country Bribe* (Bell Bridge Books). After I placed in several contests, earned a total of $750, and reached the semi-finals of the Amazon Breakthrough Novel Award (www.createspace.com/abna), my confidence grew strong enough to pitch agents. My current agent admits that the contest wins drew her in.

Contests can assist in sales of existing books, not only aiding sales but also enticing more deals for future books . . . or the rest of your writing profession.

Whether writing short stories, poetry, novels, or nonfiction, contests abound. As with any call for submission, study the rules. Double checking with entities that screen, like FundsforWriters.com and WinningWriters.com, will help alleviate concerns when selecting where to enter.

FREELANCING

A thick collection of freelancing clips can make an editor sit up and take notice. You've been vetted and accepted by others in the business, and possibly established a following. The more well known the publications, the brighter your aura.

Sooner or later in your career, you'll write an article. In the beginning, articles are a great way to gain your footing. As your career develops, you become more of an expert, and are expected to enlighten and educate about your journey and the knowledge you've acquired. Articles are, arguably, one of the best means to income and branding for writers.

Trade magazines, national periodicals, literary journals, newsletters, newspapers and blogs all offer you a chance to present yourself, earn money, and gain readers for a platform. Do not discount them as income earners.

Linda Formichelli, of Renegade Writer fame (www.therenegadewriter.com) leaped into freelance magazine writing because she simply loved to write, and that love turned her into an expert. "I never loved working to line someone else's pockets." A full-time freelancer since 1997, with credits like *Family Circle*, *Redbook*, and *Writer's Digest*, she also writes articles, books, e-courses, and e-books about her profession as a magazine writer.

JOBS

Part-time, full-time, temporary or permanent, writing jobs hone your skills, pad your resume, and present avenues to movers and shakers you wouldn't necessarily meet on your own. Government and corporate managers hire writers under all sorts of guises like Social Media Specialist and Communications Specialist, as well as the expected Reporter and Copywriter.

Alexis Grant considers her prior jobs as catapults. "Working at a newspaper (*Houston Chronicle*) and a news magazine (*US News & World Report*) for six years provided the foundation for what I'm doing now as a freelancer. Producing stories regularly on tight deadlines will always make you a better writer."

Joan Dempsey chose to return to full-time work and write her novel on the side, removing worries about her livelihood. "My creative writing was suffering trying to freelance. So, I have a day job that supports me now." She still maintains her Facebook presence to continue building her platform for her pending novel.

DIVERSIFICATION

Most importantly, however, is learning how to collect all your funding options and incorporate them into your plan. The successful writer doesn't perform in one arena. Instead, he thrives in more of a three-ring circus.

Grant states it well: "For a long while I thought of myself as only a journalist, but there are so many other ways to use my skills. Today my income comes from three streams: helping small companies with social media and blogging (the biggest source), writing and selling e-guides and courses (my favorite), and taking freelance writing or editing assignments."

Formichelli is proud of being flexible. "When I've had it with magazine writing, I put more energy into my e-courses, and vice versa. Heck, I'm even a certified personal trainer, so if I get really sick of writing I can work out. But a definite side benefit to diversifying is that I'm more protected from the feast-or-famine nature of writing."

Sometimes pursuing the more common sense or lucrative income opportunity can open doors for the dream. When my novel didn't sell, I began writing freelance articles. Then I established FundsforWriters, using all the grant, contest, publisher and market research I did for myself. A decade later, once the site thrived with over 45,000 readers, I used the very research I'd gleaned for my readers to find an agent and sign a publishing contract . . . for the original novel started so long ago.

You can fight to fund one project or study all resources and fund a career. Opportunity is there. Just don't get so wrapped up in one angle that you miss the chance to invest more fully in your future.

C. HOPE CLARK manages FundsForWriters.com and is the author of several books, including *Lowcountry Bribe* and *Palmetto Poison*. Learn more at http://chopeclark.com.

BUILD A SOLID FOUNDATION

For a Long-term Writing Career

by Dr. Mike Bechtle

New writers are anxious to see their name in print. They dream of replacing their day job with a solid writing career, so they do everything they can to get published: attending conferences, joining critique groups, purchasing online courses—and of course, studying *Writer's Market*.

But while focusing on bylines, it's easy to overlook the foundational steps that will ensure a lifetime of writing success. It's like building and decorating a house with no foundation, then wondering why the walls crack over time. The more solid the foundation, the fewer problems you'll have in the process. Once that foundation is in place, it becomes the bedrock for a lifetime of writing success.

It's not a matter of tips and tricks; it's a mindset—a way of looking at your career with a long-term perspective. It won't take time away from your writing; it's simply a different way of thinking. As Stephen Covey said, it's "beginning with the end in mind."

ACT LIKE A PROFESSIONAL

Professionals take full responsibility for their choices, actions and results. They don't blame others or make excuses, because that characterizes an amateur. Agents, editors and publishers don't care why you missed your deadline, and it comes across as whiney when you list the reasons. If your dog dies the day your manuscript is due, your editor might empathize—but he knows you waited until the last minute. An agent recognizes that computer crashes happen to everyone—but she has heard that excuse often, and knows that a professional will religiously backup their work.

Look at writing the same way you'd look at a full-time job in an office. You'll have those days when inspiration flows and the writing is effortless, and you think the muse has moved in to stay. But the next day you can't string three words together in a coherent sentence. The muse is gone and there's a note on the nightstand saying, "I'll call you sometime."

You'll get writer's block; it happens to all of us. But you wouldn't call into a corporate job and say, "I won't be in today. I have worker's block." A professional shows up and does the work.

BUILD HABITS OF PRODUCTIVITY

In an office job, you show up at a certain time, take lunch at a certain time and (hopefully) go home at a certain time. When you're self-employed, that natural structure is missing. So it's easy either to work too much (and lose balance in your life) or work too little (and never succeed in your career). Professionals develop a structure that keeps them productive day after day.

Set writing appointments, and treat them like any other important meeting with a client or boss. You wouldn't skip those meetings, because there would be consequences. When you skip your writing appointments, the consequences aren't immediate—because you think, "I can always do it tomorrow." But when that casual pattern is established, it ensures that you'll never achieve the career success you desire.

> Set writing appointments, and treat them like any other important meeting with a client or boss.

When you sit down to write, the words don't always flow right away. You're not missing inspiration; it just takes time to transition from all the other things you're doing to focus on what you're writing. I've learned to stay seated for at least 20 minutes when I write, even if my mind is totally blank. I might not write anything, but I don't do anything else. Checking my e-mail when my thinking stalls guarantees I won't be able to focus. For the first 15 minutes, I feel like I'm wasting time. But then my mind settles and I manage to write one sentence. That's usually enough to get me into a second sentence, then a third. If I stay in one spot for 20 minutes without any distractions, my mind starts to get into gear.

LEARN TO HANDLE DISTRACTIONS

Goethe said, "Things which matter most must never be at the mercy of things that matter least." In a world filled with distractions, it's hard to stay focused. When the right words don't come, your mind automatically gravitates toward something easier—social media, snacks or solitaire. A thousand good things grab your attention while you're focused on the one great thing.

I get it. My office is never more organized than when I have a writing deadline. I scan documents, print labels for file folders, dust my plants—good things make me feel productive. But they're all distractions that allow me to avoid writing.

Good writing doesn't come from inspiration; it comes from work. That work is rewarding, but it still takes effort. Professionals have learned to triage their priorities, giving their best efforts to the one that has the highest value while prioritizing the others.

When you're driving, you enter your destination in your GPS system. Once that's done, it gives you turn-by-turn directions for the most direct route. Make a wrong turn and it says "make a U-turn" in an attempt to get you back on track. If you don't enter the destination, you have a really nice map that shows you where you are. But you'll be driving in circles.

> Good writing doesn't come from inspiration; it comes from work. That work is rewarding, but it still takes effort.

Professionals have a GPS that keeps them on track. When you enter "complete next chapter" as your goal, every distraction is measured against that destination. It's a commitment that keeps you on track.

THINK LIKE A CEO

Most new writers have worked for other people for years. They get paid to do what the boss says, without giving a lot of thought or input to the direction of the organization. But when you're self-employed, you're the boss. You shape the vision, build the strategy and implement the structures to succeed.

To be successful in your writing career, you need to think like a successful business owner:

- **Watch the bottom line.** Keep accurate records. Don't quit your day job until you've replaced your income; use the security of your current job as an opportunity to build your writing business without the pressure of paying the bills. Don't spend the early money you make writing; invest it in your business.
- **Know who your real customers are.** Agents, editors and publishers are your real customers. Your readers are their customers. As inspiring as your writing is, you have

to put yourselves in an editor's mind and meet their needs. Vicki Crumpton, Executive Editor for Baker Publishing Group says, "Editors increasingly have to think like marketing and sales people. It helps us when authors think like marketing and sales people, too."

- **Sell your writing before worrying about furniture.** When most people start a business, they spend energy and resources decorating an office, designing business cards and building a website. But the successful ones spend their energy making sales. You're a writer, which means your number one job is to write. Don't buy furniture until you've sold a few articles to pay for it.

- **Hire others to complement your strengths.** At the beginning, you'll do everything yourself—design your website, build your platform, go to the post office, choose furniture. But as your business grows, you have to let some of that go. Don't use your writing time to do what others can do better than you. A college student can design a better website than you can, and you can hire her for a few hours for more than she's making as a barista.

- **Invest in your growth.** Whenever you get paid for your writing, set aside 10% for an education fund. Top executives hire the best coaches to build their skills and capacity, and you need to do the same. Save for a writer's conference, platform building sessions and book coaching from an expert. You pay for yoga or golf lessons to improve your health or skill. Why wouldn't you invest in your writing career in the same way?

CAPITALIZE ON YOUR UNIQUENESS

When kids want to get better at a sport, they study their heroes, studying how they move and trying to emulate those same skills. That's OK at the beginning; it's a great way to learn the basics.

But the thing that makes those superstars great is their uniqueness. They don't try to play like anyone else; they build a world-class career on their own unique strengths and abilities, so they can become the absolute best at being themselves.

The more your voice is trained and honed, the more people will pay to hear it.

Nobody in the universe sees the world the way you do. You are the most valuable asset you have as a writer, and imitating someone else cheats your readers. It's called "finding your voice." It means you become the best "you" that you can be, and work constantly to grow and develop that voice. The more your voice is trained and honed, the more people will pay to hear it.

DEVELOP A BIAS FOR ACTION

You're standing at the bottom of a set of steps that reach to the top of a massive stadium. Just the thought of climbing to the top can be paralyzing, because the task is so daunting.

But you can take one step. It doesn't seem like much because there are so many more steps ahead. But even a seasoned athlete can't ignore those single steps. It's the only way up.

> There are no shortcuts to the top. You build a writing career one word at a time.

It's important to have a clear goal, like completing a manuscript. But once it's set, you need to focus on individual steps. Keep the goal in mind, because it keeps us moving in the right direction. Taking single steps helps you overcome inertia and build momentum.

There are no shortcuts to the top. You build a writing career one word at a time.

VACCINATE AGAINST DISCOURAGEMENT

Writing can be a lonely process. You do it in isolation, crafting words while nobody watches. You start critiquing those words, and assume that people won't like them. When you finally press "send," it feels like showing someone your newborn for the first time—and you're afraid they'll think he's ugly. You don't send your work, because you've decided it's no good.

But you're too close to see it accurately. "You'll never know until you try," Crumpton says. "Don't say 'no' to yourself. Let a professional do it." If it's rejected, she says to keep trying. "You may never know until you try again."

Humans function best with community. Think of a time when you've been incapacitated by stress, and nothing seems right in your life. You sit down with a friend and say, "I'm stressed." Your friend says, "Yeah, me too"—and you both feel better.

My editor told me she goes out to lunch every day, just to be around other people. Sometimes she meets with someone, and other times she just enjoys the banter in the restaurant. But having human moments where we connect with others is the best cure for discouragement.

That's why a writing group or a conference can be so valuable. You talk with others about the rejection letters, the nit-picky editors and the low pay rates, and suddenly they're not as overwhelming. Solo careers thrive when they're not completely solo.

Your life is more than what you write. Sharing the journey with others helps us make it through the tough spots in the trail. It gives you the encouragement to keep showing up at the keyboard when you'd rather stay in your pajamas all day and watch reruns.

Building a long-term sustainable writing career is like a river. It starts with a tiny trickle that makes a slight indentation on the ground. As the water continues to flow, it cuts a deepening groove, which becomes a channel, which becomes a raging river, which can eventually carve a canyon.

The choices you make in the early days of your writing determine the path your career will take. It's easier to change that path now than it is to move a raging river later.

Want to be a successful writer for life? Start now—and take the first step toward your dream!

MIKE BECHTLE has had writer's block since 1974. But that hasn't stopped him from publishing a ton of articles for publications like *Writer's Digest* and *Entrepreneur*, and writing five commercially-published books on relationships and communication—including *People Can't Drive You Crazy If You Don't Give Them the Keys* and *I Wish He Had Come With Instructions—A Woman's Guide to a Man's Brain*. As a consultant for FranklinCovey he has taught over 3,000 corporate seminars on productivity, life balance and communication, coaches corporate executives and holds a doctorate from Arizona State. He shares about living an intentional life on his popular blog at www.mikebechtle.com.

CREATE CONTENT TO GROW YOUR AUDIENCE

by Sage Cohen

Writers today have access to a wide range of technology platforms that give us instant access to readers. The key to reaching them effectively and keeping them engaged is consistently delivering great content (meaning information and experiences) that provides real value in the area of our expertise. When we join the conversation and make a meaningful contribution, we can grow our audience, fortify our platform, and sustain our own interest in our work for the long term. Following are some strategies that can help you deliver content that connects—and converts one-time readers into long-term believers.

GIVE YOUR AUDIENCE WHAT YOU PROMISED THEM

We build credibility and connection with our audience/s by having the conversations they have come to us to have. Because many of us have multiple contexts in which we write, live, and serve, we must be intentional about which of our tribes we are speaking to when we share content.

When I am posting in my Radical Divorce blog, for example, I don't share my thoughts about the craft of poetry. And when I'm writing a post on Path of Possibility, my blog for writers, I'm not likely to discuss the challenges and opportunities of coparenting. I have separate Facebook pages for each topic. And I generally hashtag my tweets with #radicaldivorce, #lifepoetic or #productivewriter (my three literary platforms) to make it easier for people to see at a glance if the info I'm sharing is meant for them. On LinkedIn, I share only info related to my marketing communications consulting firm. And when I want to share with my personal network, I tweet without a hashtag, post on my main Facebook page, or upload to a private Vimeo page.

Not sure what kind of content you should be offering, to whom? These questions can help you clarify your approach. If you have multiple platforms, you can run through this list for each one.

- **WHAT IS YOUR TOPIC OR GENRE? AND WHAT IS YOUR UNIQUE ANGLE OR POINT OF VIEW IN THIS AREA?** For example, in my Radical Divorce blog, my topic is doing divorce differently. My unique angle is: I see the breakdown of divorce as a once-in-a-lifetime opportunity for breakthrough—to greater happiness, healing, and wholeness for everyone in the family.
- **WHAT IS YOUR MISSION?** I want to help divorcing parents rewrite their story, reboot their heart, and revise their divorce—so everyone in the family can thrive.
- **WHO IS YOUR AUDIENCE?** I serve divorcing parents with my Radical Divorce blog and digital products. You may not be sure who your readers are (or will be) yet, and that is fine. Start with a clear picture of who you intend your readers to be—and write for them. (I wrote for my friend Sebastian for years, and I believe that helped me eventually attract other readers like her.) As you go, you'll learn more about the people drawn to your work, how it adds value to their lives, and how this influences (or not) the direction you take in your writing.
- **WHO IS YOUR COMMUNITY?** My Radical Divorce community consists of single parents and their support network: coaches, therapists, authors, lawyers, and entrepreneurs. Again, you may not know who your community is yet, and that is fine. As you go deeper into your topic or your genre, you will learn more about your peers and your role models from the content you read, the conversations that your content generates, and the places where your content is shared. Think of content as your trail of crumbs that you scatter to find your way to a new kind of belonging.

With clarity about who your audience is and the value you bring to them comes the opportunity to be in conversation with them, learn with and from them, and relentlessly help and satisfy them.

MAKE IT IRRESISTIBLE

Reader loyalty is established one piece of irresistible content at a time. To discover how you and your readers define irresistible content, consume as much content as you can, from the sources and people you admire in your field. Tune into your favorite podcasts, notice which tweets get you to click on the link to read more, which e-mails you stop everything to read when they arrive in your inbox, which posts on Facebook you share with your community. Through the constellation of content you consume, you can better understand your own passions and preferences—and see what gets you and others to respond.

15 ways to engage

Not sure how to begin, or sustain, a content creation practice? Following are a range of ideas for writing and sharing content that can help grow your audience over time.

1. **REBLOGGING.** This is one of the simplest and most common ways to share content. You can excerpt a provocative quote from a piece of writing you admire, share a link to the full piece, and describe why you think it is valuable.

2. **GUEST-POSTING.** Offer to write a guest post for a blog in your field, or invite a writer you admire to share their work on your blog. This gives both of you greater visibility to each other's audience.

3. **INTERVIEWS.** Interviewing experts in your field or a related field can provide a great service to your audience and bring that expert's audience to you.

4. **CONTESTS, CHALLENGES AND GIVEAWAYS.** Create an exciting opportunity to get something free, try something new, or compete in good company, and people are often inspired to join in—and spread the word.

5. **ENDORSEMENTS.** Share weekly or monthly link lists to the content that you think best serves your audience. This gives them something incredibly useful, while helping the authors of that content increase their traction.

6. **HOW-TO.** Share what you know—from quick tips to step-by-step instructions. This is a great way to become invaluable to readers, and keep them coming back for more.

7. **GENRE-SPECIFIC.** Share insights and make recommendations about the craft of your genre, as well as the related news, products, and services.

8. **SERIALIZATION.** Share small amounts of your writing over time. This is a strategy fiction writers sometimes use to get readers hooked on a story or book.

9. **LITERARY CITIZENSHIP.** Comment on literary news, events, authors, or the publishing industry.

10. **THOUGHT LEADERSHIP.** Whether it's a book, a class or lecture, or a downloadable PDF, give your audience a deep dive into your topic and help them discover something of great importance to their lives or work.

11. **RESPOND TO THE ZEITGEIST.** Reflect on news related to your field of expertise in ways that shed light and share your unique perspective.

12. **PERSONAL VIGNETTES.** Share stories about how you've dealt with or are dealing with a topic in your own life that your readers are also interested in addressing.

13. **INSPIRATION.** Offer quotes, poems, art, wisdom, and insights designed to motivate and inspire.

14. **REVIEWS.** Share a detailed analysis of books, tools, technologies, or other resources that could be valuable to your readers.

15. **PROMPTS.** Offer prompts and provocations to help your audience find new ways forward.

SHARE STRATEGICALLY

What is a writer to do with this range of compelling content? Where and how should you distribute it? First, it's important to understand the ways in which content travels:

- You write/create and share
- Other people or companies or media channels write/create, and you share—adding your own commentary or perspective (I call this "curating" content)
- You write/create and other people share

Next, consider the most common digital channels through which writers today share content. I've described the advantages of each and ways to maximize each share.

CHANNEL	ADVANTAGES
BLOG POSTS	Share content of any length, at the intervals you choose, on your chosen topic. Use any of the 15 content strategies above.
E-MAIL	Arrive in the inbox of people who have opted in to hear from you. Use the content you share to inspire and invite people to join your e-mail list, where you can continue to serve them well.
FACEBOOK	Easily excerpt and share your blog content and others' content. Create specific pages for community engagement related to your platform.
TWITTER	Tweet a compelling excerpt or insight, and link readers directly to the content you are sharing. Use hashtags to make it instantly clear what your content is about and whom it is for.
LINKEDIN	Offer targeted content such as blog posts or reblogging targeted to your colleagues and professional network.
INSTAGRAM	Share the photos and videos that deliver your message.
PINTEREST	Offer visual inspiration that people will want to pin and display.
PERISCOPE	Take them someplace and show them around with live video, if this is meaningful to what you offer.
YOUTUBE	Tell your story in video.
PODCASTS	Are you more of a talker than a writer? Then this could be a powerful channel for you. Share content of any length, at the intervals you choose, on your chosen topic, by audio.

Plus, there are newsletters, billboards, matchbook covers, thank you notes, and endless other channels through which to reach your readers in interesting and compelling ways. I propose that you start with one or two that appeal to you most, then diversify from there over time.

MAKE AN EDITORIAL PLAN, AND STICK TO IT

Creating and sharing fresh content regularly takes discipline, creativity, and stamina. I find it far easier to face the blank page with an editorial calendar in hand that reflects my premeditated goals for reaching my audience. My plan reflects both the content I intend to create and the channels where I intend to share it.

For example, if the main place your tribe gathers is in a Facebook community, you may want your editorial plan to reflect a daily post there. If blogging is your main channel of communication, your plan should reflect how all of your social media revolves around that. If you plan to use Twitter as a channel, you can determine tweet volume and frequency goals. Eventually, when you are generating a great deal of content in multiple channels on a regular basis, you can use social media tools like Buffer or Hootsuite to organize, schedule, and automate the content you share.

Here's an example of how you might plan to generate, share, and promote a weekly blog post.

DAY	CHANNEL	CONTENT TYPE	TOPICS
Mondays	* Blog: Write / publish post * E-mail: Send post by email to blog subscribers * Twitter: Tweet 3X, each featuring unique quotes and linking to blog post with topic hashtag * Facebook: Post an excerpt in FB community page and link to blog post * LinkedIn: Share a different excerpt and link to blog post	* First Mondays: expert interviews * Second Mondays: reblogging * Third Mondays: how-to articles * Fourth Mondays: book reviews	[Here you'd map out every Monday throughout the year with the experts you will interview, the how-to topics you will cover, and the books you will review.]

As you see, you can even weave some of the 15 types of content into your plan, so you have a blueprint for keeping it interesting for readers. In Evernote, I have a notebook for each of my editorial categories for each of my platforms. I use these to log content ideas and save great links. Then, when it's time to write, I usually have a long list of ideas to choose from. This makes it much easier for me to get started—and sustain my momentum.

SERVING YOUR AUDIENCE GROWS YOUR AUDIENCE

Creating and curating content is a practice. I invite you to start small, experiment, and have fun. Over time, you will find the right rhythm for you and your readers. The more you write, read, and share content, the clearer you will be about your platform and what your audience wants and needs from you. As your confidence and expertise grow, a constellation of readers, colleagues, and collaborators will grow with you. Content can be the rich tapestry that weaves you all together in shared purpose, passion, and possibility.

SAGE COHEN is the author of the nonfiction books *Writing the Life Poetic*; *The Productive Writer*; and *Fierce on the Page* (forthcoming) all from Writer's Digest Books and the poetry collection *Like the Heart, the World* from Queen of Wands Press. Her essays, fiction, poems and how-to articles have appeared in a wide range of publications, including: *Rattle*; Hip Mama; The Night, and the Rain, and the River; The Truth of Memoir; Cup of Comfort for Writers, and *Writer's Digest* magazine. Sage holds an MFA from New York University and a BA from Brown University. She offers strategies and support for writers at pathofpossibility.com and for divorcing parents at radicaldivorce.com.

HOW TO DEVELOP AN EFFECTIVE AUTHOR BRAND

....

by Leslie Lee Sanders

///

An author's brand isn't just the specific colors of your website, a catchy tagline, or a recognizable face. Branding is delivering on a promise after setting an expectation. Determining how you want to be perceived and what sets you apart is essential when organizing an author's image, but that is only the tip of the iceberg when it comes to branding. Diving deeper when creating an author brand is a must.

Following is an in-depth look at how to build a successful author brand and become a fierce competitor in the publishing business.

ESTABLISH AN IMAGE

When establishing your image, think beyond color scheme and website layout. Humans are unique for their feeling capabilities, and the way we feel about something usually stays with us longer than any color or image. If applied properly, certain phrases, images, and colors trigger emotions, and this is your main goal when establishing your image. However, you must recognize the emotion you want to convey and how it links people to your brand.

For example, you might want to convey love, calm, excitement, wonder, intrigue, nostalgia, or even hilarity, but deep down the feeling should be universal enough to be relatable.

This is how branding works. A brand effectively engages emotion. Remember the Geico commercial where the massive camel awkwardly strolls through a busy office during the middle of the day asking the workers what day it is? Sure, it is a funny ad, but what is that commercial doing on a deeper level? The commercial is selling a service using a situation most people relate to by making you laugh. Actually, Geico's history of running funny ads have become their brand, from the gecko, the cavemen, Maxwell the Pig, and now the "Hump Day" camel.

Most people relate to the situation of working a demanding nine-to-five and counting the days until the weekend. Most people are probably familiar with a co-worker who, much like the camel, points out the middle of the week in the same tedious way, prompting tired sighs and eye rolls. The commercial triggers something most people "get" and therefore it sticks with them. This is what your brand should do too.

What you do for your readers through your website, blogs, videos, and podcasts is your "service." The books and stories you sell is your "product." How you manage it is your "business." Connect to your audience using emotion to form your reputation and establish your image.

What feelings do you want to trigger?

List the emotions you want others to feel when visiting your website or when reading your books. An easy way to accomplish this is by asking yourself what words you want to associate with your image. Take the third party route, step outside of yourself, and look at what you offer through an objective view. If someone were to describe you and your brand, what words or emotion would you like them to use? Trigger those emotions by using specific words in your content, books, blog posts, and author bio. Use images and colors on your website and book covers to convey your overall message.

What emotion or message do you want to resonate?

Triggering feelings and having them resonate are two different things. The former is what sucks you into the brand. The latter is what you take from it, what you're left with, or what stays with you. What would you like readers to take away from your book after reading it? After visiting your website, what message will they remember you by? Make your mission clear in your work.

What promises do you want to communicate?

By communicating a promise, and most importantly, delivering on that promise, you establish trust that produces satisfied readers, which not only translates into repeat service from avid fans, but generates new readers through word-of-mouth marketing. People will seek you out because you've become the go-to person for your particular service and product. Think Starbucks and coffee. When you've become the go-to person, you have successfully built a brand. Your brand's promise is what your audience comes to expect from your business.

To further expand or maintain your brand requires consistency.

CREATE CONSISTENCY

Being consistent falls under the tier of delivering on your promises. There's a cycle when building a brand; make a promise, deliver, build trust, and repeat. By performing this cycle, you are practicing consistency, which is the reason people come to you instead of your competitor. Take away one of the components and you break the cycle. Break the cycle and your brand might suffer.

You might think to get ahead or to produce sales requires you to beat your competitors, and to be on top means to flaunt what makes you unique. Today, in the writing business, this kind of thinking is retroactive because with so many books and authors flooding the market, being unique is a one in a million chance. The truth is, establishing a brand, building an audience, and keeping your audience satisfied is the trick to success in most businesses. Do this and in return your readers will help you expand your audience by advertising your products and services through recommendations (i.e., word of mouth, social media sharing, and book reviews). This is the tried-and-true formula of every successful brand.

How do you satisfy your audience? Consistency.

Consistency with book releases, series, and the production and design of content

Whatever your service, provide it regularly. Readers expect a new book from you once a year? Meet or exceed that expectation and release a new book every year or sooner. If your newsletter subscribers expect a monthly newsletter and your YouTube videos to highlight important writing techniques for novelist, continue giving them what they come for or give them what they want and more.

Establishing your place within your genre

Sure, you write in a specific genre with no plans of crossing genres anytime soon. Still there are other ways to stay consistent. Do your novels end with happily ever after? Don't try experimenting with the latest story now. You may lose some readers if they're convinced their favorite author or series is becoming something other than what they've grown to love.

Cultivating an overall tone and a distinct voice

Your voice and style, the words you use, and the way you piece them together in your writing is unique to you and your personality. Your audience will grow familiar with your writing mechanics and may even recognize your style in your speaking voice. Keep it consistent. You may have read a book by an author whose writing style reminded you of another author. For example, you may believe the book you are currently hooked on reads like a Stephen King or J.K. Rowling novel. If you're consistent, your style can become recognizable and be a distinctive part of your brand too.

BUILD TRUST

Establishing your image, being consistent, and building trust are some of what it takes to build an effective brand. Let's talk coffee. When mentioning coffee, which establishment do you think of first, Starbucks or McDonalds? Most would say Starbucks. Why? Because Starbucks successfully built their coffeehouse brand.

Starbucks is one of the largest and most successful coffeehouses for many reasons, but one reason is they are consistent with their products, using the same ingredients and measurements to make each coffee the same as the one before. You know exactly how your favorite latte should taste, and they meet that expectation each time. Your brand should build a similar kind of trust with your audience.

Image familiarity, logos, and other insignia

When mentioning branding your business, the next thought might be logos. Your logo is not your brand but the visual symbol of your brand. Your logo is a way to identify your brand in its simplest form, a visual representation of your business.

Here are the best ways to use your logo to maximize your brand's exposure:

- **BOOK SERIES COVER.** A perfect way to use a logo is on the cover of your books in a particular series. It's a recognizable insignia that communicates the promise and trust exchange between you and your readers. When they see that logo on the cover they know each book contains your familiar voice and writing style, and they will know what to expect of the books in that series.
- **STATIONARY, BUSINESS CARDS, BOOKMARKS, LETTERHEAD, ETC.** Office supplies are probably the most obvious place to add your logo. Also make sure your logo appears on business forms like invoices, packing slips, and receipts.
- **ONLINE USE.** Use your logo in place of your profile picture on Twitter and Facebook. Add it to your website header and favicon. Use it in your e-mail signature, in your guest posts, or in your Gravitar (Globally Recognized Avatar) in conjunction with guest posting to get your logo in front of new audiences when commenting on other people's blogs.
- **CUSTOM GOODS.** Add your logo to custom-made apparel, mugs, water bottles, chocolates, pens, totes, etc. Make sure the logo is large enough to be discernable at a distance, and use colors and fonts that can be easily read.

REPUTATION

Overall, your brand, brand identity, logo, content, message, storytelling, and reader experience is your reputation. Your reputation is built from the general feelings, opinions, and beliefs of the majority of people who encounter your brand. And to be just as successful in your niche as Starbucks is to coffee, remember these steps to building your author brand:

1. Establish your image by creating a specific emotion to trigger; message to resonate; and promise to communicate.
2. The following should stay consistent in your brand: identity; voice and style; and production.
3. Build trust by staying consistent; delivering on promises; and creating a visual representation of your business.

LESLIE LEE SANDERS is a published author with over ten years of fiction writing and book publishing experience. She teaches the art and craft of blogging, writing, and publishing on her blog at leslieleesanders.com. Her work has been included in the following Writer's Market books: 2016 Writer's Market, 2016 Novel and Short Story Writer's Market, the 2014 and 2015 editions of Guide to Self-Publishing. She's currently writing the fifth installment of her post-apocalyptic and dystopian book series, Refuge Inc.

PROMOTIONS, PR, AND PUBLICITY:

How to Make Them Work for You

....

by Janice Hussein

///

Book marketing is the process of planning and executing the conception, pricing, promotion, and distribution of a book, and then creating exchanges that satisfy readers. An important part of any marketing strategy in the book business is creating what is called word-of-mouth "buzz." How can you get that word-of-mouth buzz started and moving among your readership or potential readers?

DEVELOP A MARKETING PLAN

First, develop a Marketing Plan, starting at least nine months before a book launch, especially a first book launch. You'll need to establish a website, blog, and set up accounts with social media profiles, such as Twitter and Facebook, and with reader communities like Goodreads.

To develop that Marketing Plan, let's open the marketing toolkit and review the 5 major tools: selling, advertising, and the three P's: promotions, public relations, and publicity. First, briefly, how do these terms differ?

Selling

In publishing, personal selling happens anywhere authors and readers would personally connect—book signings, reader retreats, readers conferences like the Romantic Times Booklover's Convention, and national and regional book festivals, such as Book Expo America (BEA), the fall book festival in Seattle, WA, or Wordstock in Portland, OR.

Advertising

Advertising, a term that seems all-inclusive, refers to activities that are paid for. And the advertiser controls the content—what product to advertise, what to say about it, where to advertise, and when and how it will appear. The TV commercial is the perfect example of this.

Publicity

Publicity is free and usually appears in the form of news coverage. Publicity tools are news releases, news conferences, editorials, or product announcements. Think reviews. No one paid the media outlet or reviewer (usually) to do the interview or to mention the author or book. If it's not paid for, then it's publicity, though there are indirect costs with publicity. And with publicity—unlike advertising—there is little control over what is said.

Promotions

Promotions, like publicity, can be free. Examples are in-store displays, giveaways, and contests. Other examples are coupons, short-term price reductions, samples—the book is offered for free or as a trial size (sample chapters, prequel novellas, or short stories)—and Point-of-Purchase displays, the items we see near cash registers in bookstores.

Public Relations

Public relations, on the other hand, creates an image in the public's mind, one that is attached to the book or author. Examples of authors who do this are Brenda Novak and her campaign against diabetes or David Baldacci's Wish You Well Foundation to combat illiteracy in America.

MAKING PUBLICITY WORK

How can you make publicity work for you? Your publicity tools would be pitch letters, press releases, press kits, media alerts, articles (unless they're paid), interviews, and reviews.

Pitch letters are a single-page letter with a hook and a call to action, targeted to specific journalists at magazines that cover books, such as *The New York Times* and *Publisher's Weekly*, and to radio and television stations.

A press release is a one-page announcement of a newsworthy event. For authors, the first Press Release announces your book launch. Subsequent releases should offer some new or useful information in a way that sells your book—how the book helps readers overcome a problem or satisfies a need—or the book or one of its themes ties into a current event or holiday. Consider your audience when you write these, and target their interests—don't just sell your book. And if your focus is a bookstore buyer, then use a longer-term angle.

The press kit, which should be available in print and online as a PDF or Zip file, is directed at journalists, and usually includes the press release. Maintain an up-to-date press kit. Traditionally, a press kit contains a cover letter, sell sheet, professional author photo and the book cover, blurbs, bio, interviews, reviews, advertisements, a list of past and present events, and excerpts of novels, like booklets and sample chapters. Send these press kits to booksellers, book reviewers, newspapers, television stations, radio stations, libraries, and so on. You have a much better chance of a response from them if the materials are at hand.

Consider writing articles to gain attention for your book(s) and for yourself as a writer, either paid or unpaid (publicity). This can mean big sales for your book. Having written and published a novel, you would be considered a good source of information on the topic of writing. Other ideas are to focus on a theme within the book, to use a large section of the book and make it into an article, or to write something unrelated to your book but which will reach your target market of readers. Remember your audience—the article should address the needs of the magazine's readership. And magazine editors often need filler articles, so offering them a free article saves them money and gives you free publicity. However, request enough space after the article for a very short bio, the book title, and info on how people can order your book.

There are at least two types of reviews: a review by someone else, and an objective ready-made book review—the mock review written by the author—one that a busy editor can just insert into the publication. A book has a better chance of appearing in a publication when accompanied by a press kit and mock review, one that could be used as-is or excerpted. But check submissions guidelines for the publication, as many of them assign articles months ahead of their publication dates. For the mock review, include all the book's details: title, author, ISBN, publisher, price, and where readers could find it, either online or at a bookstore. In the last paragraph, also include a very short bio, with the author's credentials or expertise listed.

Good reviews not only increase your discoverability for readers but they also add a stamp of approval and interest, especially those that are paid, such as *Kirkus Reviews* and *Romantic Times (RT) Review Source*. Lead time for *RT Book Review Magazine* is four months before publication date, and if submitted after publication date, then about four to six weeks for *RT Review Source*. Lead time for *Kirkus* is seven to nine weeks before publication. If you missed the publication date, you can purchase a review through their Indie program, even if you're not self-published. About six to nine months before your launch, familiarize yourself with the blog sites and reviewers that authors of similar books have used for reviews and blog tours, and then approach those blogs and reviewers yourself.

MAKING PROMOTION WORK

How do you make promotions work for you? As previously stated, promotions include giveaways, contests, coupons, short-term price reductions, and samples.

Giveaways and contests have become an important element in any marketing plan, especially for authors who self-publish. These can be done on an author's website and through blog tours, Facebook, and Goodreads. Keep them relatively short in duration, a maximum of three weeks long. Start approaching blog owners several months ahead of your release date, as dates fill up quickly. Also, about a month before your release date—but ending before the launch—run a pre-launch contest, giving away something like a gift card, and then a signed copy of the book when it comes out.

By having a newsletter and developing a list of readers to send it to, you can announce your upcoming releases and book launch, including a short-term price reduction or coupon for those readers. This also helps to develop your relationship with your readers, both by staying in touch and by offering them price reductions. Set up an account with an e-mail marketing service like MailChimp, and start building your list about six to nine months ahead of your launch date, or as soon as you can. On your launch day, send out an e-mail newsletter with a link to buy the book.

Authors often have a year in between book releases, but could offer a free or trial size sample chapter or prequel or short story—related to the current book or to a series or not related. This could promote a new series or a much-awaited conclusion to a series or just keep you in the readers' mind. Some authors offer coupons to their established readership or to those who attend the book launch or book signings.

MAKING PUBLIC RELATIONS WORK

How can you make public relations work for you? Public relations is usually associated with a charity or other worthy cause—literacy, animal rescue, or fund-raising for cures for such diseases as cancer or diabetes.

And authors can become involved with public relations through speaking engagements, a Public Relations tool. Speaking engagements remain one of the bedrocks of any well-constructed PR program, even for authors, positioning the author as an expert or leader. It is excellent for generating extensive media and/or industry exposure.

PUTTING IT ALL TOGETHER

How can the three P's work together? Here's an example of that, using a "fictitious" novel about a rescue dog or the Humane Society. To market the novel, the author starts a contest—using press releases (publicity) to promote the contest and drive participation—asking readers to write letters about adopting a dog, with the most touching and unusual stories winning a prize and attendance at a free luncheon and/or fundraiser with the author. That contest is a promotion. The author could also sell tickets to the fundraiser. Again, press releases and a press kit can promote the event. Then newspapers, television, and radio are pitched to interview you about the contest, your book, and/or the fundraiser. The interviews are publicity. You can also advertise the contest in the local newspaper and in book industry magazines, such as *Writer's Digest*, or *Romantic Times Book Review Magazine*. When you pick the winners and runners-up, hold a dinner for them, while also including the local animal shelter and rescue organizations—the Humane Society, Shelter Pet projects, etc. The dinner is public relations. Invite the media to cover the dinner, and that is publicity.

Marketing pays off when it's done consistently and over time. Building "buzz" usually starts with local media, moves to regional, and then national. Continue your focused marketing efforts up to three months after your launch, seeking reviews, holding contests, and posting regularly to your social media sites. And after the initial campaign is over, stay in contact with readers by blogging and posting to social media. And to anyone who helped to promote your book—reviewers, interviewers, television and radio hosts, the bookstores that carried your book, and the one that hosted your launch party—always send thank-you notes. This helps build relationships for future book releases over the course of your writing career.

JANICE HUSSEIN is a freelance writer, with 5 years of experience. She is also a freelance editor with 12 years of experience and a Master's degree in Writing. She edits short stories and novels, and offers classes and workshops at conferences and elsewhere, to writers at all levels. Hussein is a member of NW Independent Editors Guild, the National Writers Union, RWA, and the Oregon Writers Colony, and I network on Twitter, Facebook, LinkedIn, and Google+. Her articles have been previously published in F+W Media's *2016 Writer's Market*, the *2015 Guide to Self-Publishing*, and *The Novel & Short Story Writer's Market*, for the years 2010, 2011, 2013 (2), and 2014. "The Unsympathetic Protagonist," appeared in the 2010 edition; a tearsheet is available. Her work has also been published with RWR, including "The Espresso Book Machine."

E-MAIL NEWSLETTERS FOR WRITERS

....

by Rebecca Pitts

//

Newsletters are the new blogs. There is simply no better or more direct way to reach your audience in 2018 than to be invited into their inbox. Whether you're just starting out by building a list of loyal readers, or you're an established author who's hoping to convert current fans into subscribers, this article outlines everything you should consider when launching an author's newsletter, from the essential technical questions to big picture strategy.

KNOW YOUR 'WHY' AND 'WHO'

Your list (the e-mail addresses of your subscribers, along with any other information they provide) is a powerful asset and tool that will allow you to:

- communicate directly with readers to share news or exclusive content
- increase your impact by reaching a specific and growing number of people who are interested in your work, invested in your success, and engaged
- sell and market your work directly, if you choose to self-publish
- be more attractive to a publisher, who sees your list as a platform where you can build a relationship with readers and promote your books

Always consider your audience as you develop content for your subscribers. A writer who develops nonfiction craft and DIY books has an audience whose interests likely differ from a travel memoirist living in Istanbul. A homeschooling dad and blogger would likely appeal to parents who are considering this educational arrangement. A writer who is just starting out might not know yet who their people are, and that's ok. You'll likely discover who is opting in to your list (as well as what sort of content you love to share) as you go.

DECIDE WHAT YOU'LL SHARE

Your options for structuring and designing your newsletter are almost endless, but you can't go wrong if you stick to this guiding principle: Your newsletter should feel like a must-have treat that your subscribers truly love to get and read. Here's the good news: You probably have a ton of inspiration in your inbox right now. Spend 30 minutes looking through your inbox at the e-mails you enjoy receiving and reading. What is it about them that keeps you coming back? Are there parts of each e-mail that you find valuable, entertaining, or educational?

> Your newsletter should feel like a must-have treat that your subscribers truly love to get and read.

Here are a few examples of types of formats you might want to consider, along with examples from published authors, journalists, and producers of digital media:

- **The personal letter.** Some of my favorite author newsletters look and feel like a personal letter and are as simple as an essay, delivered in the body of an e-mail. Designer and author Paul Jarvis manages to make each e-mail feel like a letter from a friend, complete with jokes that are actually funny. (https://pjrvs.com/)
- **The interview.** Journalist Nishat Kurwa shares an original interview each week "with dynamic women who rule" in her newsletter Talk Story. (http://tinyletter.com/talkstory)
- **A curated list of links to relevant content around your expertise.** Here's where knowing your audience comes in handy—what are they interested in? Could you save them time by delivering hand-picked content? I open freelance journalist Ann Friedman's e-mail every week for a better sense of what's happening in politics, gender, and the media, delivered via a handful of links to news articles and opinion pieces. (http://www.annfriedman.com/weekly/)
- **A behind-the-scenes peek.** Share a slice of your creative life that isn't available anywhere else—readers will appreciate the insider insight on your thought-process. Author Ryan Holiday does this well in his monthly newsletter, which reads as an annotated bibliography of the books on his nightstand. (https://ryanholiday.net/)

It's worth mentioning that most of the content in these newsletters is exclusive—that is, it's not readily available anywhere else. There's a real reward for a subscriber to join a list—to gain access to information they can't get elsewhere.

If you're consistently delivering value to your audience, promoting your own work will be much easier to do and won't feel like such a struggle. Clearly link to where your readers can buy your books, to specific blog posts on your website, or to event listings you're speaking at. It's a balance: Don't be shy about sharing your wins (like a book deal or a new e-book you're offering) but be sure you're not selling 100% of the time.

CHOOSE AN E-MAIL SERVICE PROVIDER

Choosing the right e-mail service provider will keep you sane and organized. Even if you are just starting out, without a single e-mail address on your list, don't be tempted to cut and paste e-mail addresses into the body of a blank e-mail.

An e-mail service provider:

- manages all of your subscribers in a database
- usually allows for some sort of tagging or organization of those contacts along with additional info like a person's name
- allows you to customize automated emails such as a welcome e-mail
- simplifies design decisions and manages your templates so you're not constantly re-inventing the wheel

TinyLetter, Mailchimp, AWeber, Constant Contact, and ConvertKit are just a few examples of popular e-mail service providers. All of them offer technical support and tutorials for novice users. Several online education platforms, like Skillshare, Lynda.com, and Udemy offer a range of newsletter courses aimed at beginner and advanced students.

....

When in doubt, choose a free e-mail service provider if you're just starting out.

....

When determining the best fit for you and your audience, be sure to consider benefits and costs of each. Many providers offer tiered pricing, with free accounts available to members with lists under a certain number of subscribers. Others, like Tiny Letter, are known for their simplicity of use but lack sophisticated tools like segmentation.

When in doubt, choose a free e-mail service provider if you're just starting out. It's more important that you get started—you can always export your list into a spreadsheet and switch providers once you've gained traction and have outgrown the services offered.

DON'T BE A SPAMMER

It's worth noting upfront that I'm not a lawyer, and you should always consult one for legal advice. Laws around e-mail marketing exist to protect the consumer, and we should all be pleased about this. No one likes getting spam or an unsolicited message. Here are a few things to keep in mind when writing your newsletters and growing your list:

- **You must include a valid mailing address.** Many service providers walk you through this process, and won't let you send an e-mail without your address field populated. If you have privacy concerns, consider getting and using a P.O. box.
- **Don't add people to your list without their consent.** This one couldn't be more plain and simple. Just don't do it. You really don't want people on your list who don't want to be there. Most subscribers will join via an opt-in form (more on this below). If you're speaking at an event, keep a clipboard or notebook open for attendees to join your list. This counts as permission, and later, you can manually add these e-mail addresses to your list.

Does what you're doing feel right?

- **Be thoughtful (and law-abiding) about including your affiliate partnerships.** Affiliate marketing is the promotion of someone else's product or service, with you receiving a commission on the sale. It doesn't cost the customer anything, but it may affect the level of trust a customer has in you (for better or worse). Circle back to your 'why'—if your aim is to communicate with subscribers, share your good news, and grow your list, then you may decide it's not worth promoting someone else's product for the small amount of money you receive. Some affiliate links (like Amazon Associates) aren't even allowed to be shared over e-mail at all. And, finally, if you are sharing affiliate links, you must disclose this information to your subscribers upfront.

Check in with yourself. Does what you're doing feel right? You probably have a good sense of what is and isn't appropriate when growing your list, sharing your ideas, and monetizing your projects.

MAKE IT EASY FOR YOUR READERS TO JOIN YOUR LIST (AND TO TALK TO YOU)

So, you've chosen a provider and have figured out what kind of info you're going to share. It's time to welcome your readers!

- **A newsletter should build on what you're already doing.** Ideally, you have a website as your author platform. It's possible to have a list without a website (I've seen writers with Twitter accounts that link to a 'join' page hosted by an e-mail service provider) but a newsletter list and author website truly go hand-in-hand. Think of the opt-in on your website as a door—you'll want to be clear about what's on the other side, and make the space welcoming and inviting. It doesn't hurt to note that you'll be sharing insider, subscriber-only content as an incentive to your readers.

- **Where should your front door go?** Next, you'll want to determine where you'll place your opt-in on your website. Having a unique URL (in my case, it's rebeccaapitts. com/join) is handy if you're sharing the opt-in elsewhere. In addition, you'll want to include opt-ins on your most heavily trafficked pages as well as your home page.

- **What will you say when a reader walks through your door?** Consider the experience your reader has when they join your list. Be sure to customize the welcome e-mail template within your e-mail service provider—this is a terrific opportunity to write in your own voice, let your sense of humor shine (if that's your thing), and consider adding something of value: either content not shared anywhere else or by linking to the most popular posts on your site.

- **Talk to your readers.** Encourage replies, comments, and questions, just as you would welcome and encourage these on your blog or social media accounts.

GROW YOUR LIST

Numbers are important, sure, but they're not everything. List growth takes time, and is built around consistency and trust.

- **Start with who you already are talking to.** An easy way to gain some momentum is to write a welcome e-mail. Comb through your address book to identify friends, family, and peers that might be interested in hearing from you. Send out an e-mail that explains what you're up to, what you'll be sharing, how often you'll be writing, and ask them to join you if they are interested. Again, don't just add people without their permission.

- **Promote your newsletter.** If you have an existing blog or social media account, use this space to encourage your current followers to join your list. As you develop new content such as a blog post or Instagram post, continue to remind new followers in these spaces that they can keep the conversation going over e-mail by joining your list.

- **Offer a content-upgrade or bonus for subscribers.** A content-upgrade is an offering you make on your blog, social media post, on someone else's website or podcast if you're guest posting, or really in any space where you may meet potential new subscribers. I've even seen them at the beginning of free e-books. The reader, listener, or viewer will hopefully find the offering valuable and subscribe to your list for access. Examples include: a book club study guide, a mini e-book of your list of favorite books of all time, a printable template referenced in a blog post, and access to exclusive audio or video files relating to your expertise.

Your newsletter is a place where you can (and should) be you. Ultimately, your unique voice is what will keep your readers interested beyond any freebie you're offering.

By being upfront about what you'll deliver in your newsletter, how often you'll deliver it, and by following through on your promises, you'll consistently deliver value over time and ultimately build trust. And trust is what will ultimately keep your readers coming back, will fuel your readers' desire to share your news and offerings, and will open the door to real, two-way communication with your subscribers.

Oh yeah, and when it's time to announce a new book, publicize a speaking event, or offer a self-published product to your list, your readers will be right there alongside you, as invested champions of you and your work.

REBECCA PITTS writes and makes stuff for kids and kids at heart. Her work and ideas have been featured in *Country Living, the Etsy Seller Handbook*, the Martha Stewart American Made Market, Craft Industry Alliance, And North, and Dear Handmade Life. She's got a thing for picture books, public libraries, and digging into the archives of female movers & shakers, writers, and artists. Her weekends are usually spent day-tripping in the Hudson Valley, where she lives with her husband, son, and daughter. Learn more at rebeccaapitts.com.

CONTRACTS 101

by Cindy Ferraino

After you do a victory dance about getting the book deal you always dreamed about or your article hitting the top of the content list of a popular magazine, the celebration quickly comes to a halt when you realize you are not at the finish line yet. Your heart begins to beat faster because you know the next possible hurdle is just around the corner—the contract. For many, the idea of reviewing a contract is like being back in first grade. You know you have to listen to the teacher when you could be playing outside. You know you have to read this contract but why because there are terms in there that look like an excerpt from a foreign language syllabus.

Before I changed my status to self-employed writer, I was working as a grants and contracts administrator at a large medical university in Philadelphia. I helped shepherd the M.D. and Ph.D. researchers through the channels of grants and contracts administration. While the researchers provided the technical and scientific pieces that could potentially be the next cure for diabetes, heart disease, or cancer, I was there to make sure they did their magic within the confines of a budget and imposed contractual regulations. The budget process was easy but when it came to contract regulations—oh well, that was a different story. I became familiar with the terms such as indemnifications, property and intellectual rights, and conditions of payments. I was an integral part of reviewing and negotiating a grant or contract that had the best interests for every party involved.

After my son was born, I left the university and my contracts background went on a brief hiatus. Once my son went off to school, I began freelance writing. After a few writing gigs sprinkled with a few too many rejection slips, I landed an assignment for *Dog Fancy* magazine. I was thrilled and eagerly anticipated the arrival of a contract in my inbox. As I opened the document, the hiatus had lifted. I read through the contract and was able to send it back within a few hours.

For many new freelancers or writers who have been around the block, contract administration is not something that they can list as a perk on their resume. Instead of searching through the Yellow Pages for a contract lawyer or trying to call in a special favor to a writer friend, there are some easy ways for a newbie writer or even a seasoned writer to review a contract before putting a smiley face next to the dotted line.

TAKE A DEEP BREATH, THEN READ ON

Remember breaking those seals on test booklets and the voice in the background telling you, "Please read the directions slowly." As you tried to drown out the voice because your stomach was in knots, little did you know that those imparting words of wisdom would come in handy as you perspired profusely over the legal jargon that unfolded before your eyes. The same words go for contracts.

Many writers, including myself, are anxious to get an assignment underway, but the contract carrot continues to loom over our creative minds. "I'm surprised by writers who just skim a contract and then sign it without understanding what it means," says Kelly James-Enger, author of books including *Six Figure Freelancing: The Writer's Guide to Making More* (Random House) and the blog Dollarsanddeadlines.blogspot.com. "Most of the language in magazine contracts isn't that complicated, but it can be confusing when you're new to the business."

When I receive a contract from a new publisher or editor, I make a second copy. My children call it "my sloppy copy." I take out a highlighter and begin to mark up the key points of the contract: beginning and end date, conditions of payment, how my relationship is defined by the publisher, and what the outline of the article should look like.

The beginning and end date of a contract is crucial. After I recently negotiated a contract, the editor changed the due date of the article in an e-mail. I made sure the contract was changed to reflect the new due date. The conditions of the payments are important because it will describe when the writer will be paid and by what method. Most publishers have turned to incremental payment schedules or payments to be made online like PayPal. How the publisher considers your contractor status is important. If you're a freelance contract writer, the contract should reflect that as well as identify you as an independent contractor for IRS tax purposes. Finally, the contract will highlight an outline of what your article or proposal should look like.

As you slowly digest the terms you are about to agree to for your assignment or book project, you gain a better understanding of what an editor or publisher expects from you and when.

CUTTING TO THE LEGAL CHASE

Once you have had a chance to review a contract, you may be scratching your head and saying, "Okay, now what does this all mean to me as a writer?" James-Enger describes

PAYMENT TYPES

There are any number of different arrangements for publishers to pay writers. However, here are three of the most common and what they mean.

- Pays on acceptance. This means a publisher pays (or cuts a check) for the writer upon acceptance of the manuscript. This is usually the best deal a writer can hope to receive.
- Pays on publication. In these cases, a publisher pays (or cuts a check) for the writer by the publication date of the manuscript. For magazines, this could mean several months after the manuscript was accepted and approved. For books, this could mean more than a year.
- Pays after publication. Sometimes contracts will specify exactly how long after publication. Be wary of contracts that leave it open-ended.

three key areas where writers should keep sharp on when it comes to contracts—indemnification, pay and exclusivity provisions.

INDEMNIFICATION is a publisher's way of saying if something goes wrong, we are not responsible. If a claim is brought against another writer's work, a publisher does not want to be responsible for the legal aftermath but you could be the one receiving a notice in the mail. James-Enger warns writers to be on the lookout for indemnification clauses. "In the U.S., anyone can sue anyone over just about anything," she says; "I'm okay with agreeing to indemnification clauses that specify breaches of contract because I know I'm not going to plagiarize, libel or misquote anyone. But I can't promise that the publication will never be sued by anyone whether or not I actually breached the contract."

PAY is where you want the publisher "to show you the money." Writers need to be aware of how publishers will discuss the terms of payment in the contract. James-Enger advises to have "payment on acceptance." This means you will be paid when the editor agrees to accept your manuscript or article. If there is "no payment on acceptance," some publishers will pay when the article is published. "Push for payment whenever you can," she says.

EXCLUSIVITY PROVISIONS are where a particular publisher will not allow the writer to publish an article or manuscript that is "about the same or similar subject" during the time the publisher runs the piece. Because of the nature of the writing business, James-Enger feels writers need to negotiate this part of the contract. "I specialize in health, fitness and nutrition, and I'm always writing about a similar subject," she says.

> ## CONTRACT TIPS
>
> Even seasoned freelancers can find themselves intimidated by contracts. Here are a few things to consider with your contract:
>
> - **KEEP COPY ON RECORD.** If the contract is sent via e-mail, keep a digital copy, but also print up a hard copy and keep it in an easy-to-find file folder.
> - **CHECK FOR RIGHTS.** It's almost never a good idea to sell all rights. But you should also pay attention to whether you're selling any subsidiary or reprint rights. The more rights you release the more payment you should expect (and demand).
> - **WHEN PAYMENT.** Make sure you understand when you are to be paid and have it specified in your contract. You may think that payment will come when the article is accepted or published, but different publishers have different policies. Get it in writing.
> - **HOW MUCH PAYMENT.** The contract should specify exactly how much you are going to be paid. If there is no payment listed on the contract, the publisher could use your work for free.
> - **TURN IN CONTRACT BEFORE ASSIGNMENT.** Don't start working until the contract is signed, and everything is official. As a freelancer, time is as important as money. Don't waste any of your time and effort on any project that is not yet contracted.

WHEN TO HEAD TO THE BARGAINING TABLE

Recently, I became an independent contractor for the American Composites Manufacturing Association (ACMA). When I reviewed the terms of the contract, I was concerned how my independent contractor status was identified. Although I am not an ACMA employee, I wanted to know if I could include my ACMA publications on my resume. Before I signed the contract, I questioned this issue with my editor. My editor told me I may use this opportunity to put on my resume. I signed the contract and finished my assignment.

Writers should be able to talk to an editor or a publisher if there is a question about a term or clause in a contract. "Don't be afraid to talk to the editor about the changes you'd like to make to a contract," James-Enger says; "You don't know what you'll get or if an editor is willing to negotiate it, until you ask."

When writers have to approach an editor for changes to a contract, James-Enger advises writers to act professionally when it comes to the negotiations. "I start out with saying—I am really excited to be working with you on this story and I appreciate the assignment, but I have a couple of issues with the contract that I'd like to talk to you about," she says. "Sure I want a better contract but I also want to maintain a good working relationship with my editor. A scorched-earth policy doesn't benefit any freelancer in the long run."

Negotiating payment terms is a tricky subject for some writers. Writers want to get the most bang for their buck but they don't want to lose a great writing assignment. Do your research first before you decide to ask an editor for more money to complete the assignment. Double check the publisher's website or look to see if the pay scale is equivalent to other publishers in the particular industry. Some publishers have a set publishing fee whereas others may have a little more wiggle room depending on the type of the assignment given. In today's economy, writers are a little more reluctant to ask for a higher rate for an article. If the publisher seems to be open to discussion about the pay scale, just make sure you approach the situation in a professional manner so as to not turn the publisher away from giving you another assignment.

WHO OWNS YOUR WRITING?

Besides payment terms, another area that writers may find themselves on the other end of the negotiation table is with ownership rights. We all want to take credit for the work that we have poured our heart and soul into. Unfortunately, the business of publishing has different ways of saying how a writer can classify their work. Ownership rights vary, but the biggest one that writers have a hard time trying to build up a good case against is "all rights." "All rights" is exactly what it means: *hope you are not in love with what you have just written because you will not be able to use it again.*

In recent months, I have written for two publications that I had given "all rights" to the company. My rationale is that I knew I would never need to use those articles again but I did make sure I was able to include those articles for my byline to show that I have publishing experience.

If you feel that you want to reuse or recycle an article that you had written a few years ago, you might want to consider negotiating an "all rights" clause or maybe going to another publisher. "We don't take all rights so there is no reason for authors to request we change the rights clause," says Angela Hoy, author and owner of WritersWeekly.com and Booklocker.com. "Our contracts were rated 'Outstanding' by Mark Levine (author of *The Fine Print of Self-Publishing*) and has also been called the clearest and fairest in the industry."

James-Enger is also an advocate of negotiating against contracts with an "all rights" clause. "I hate 'all rights' contracts, and try to avoid signing them as they preclude me from ever reselling the piece as a reprint to other markets," she says. "I explain that to editors, and I have been able to get editors to agree to let me retain nonexclusive reprint rights even when they buy all rights—which still lets me market the piece as a reprint." James-Enger also advises that "if the publisher demands all rights, then negotiate if the payment is sub-standard."

So if you are just receiving a contract in the mail for the first time or you are working with a new publisher, you should not be afraid of the legal lingo that blankets the message "we want to work with you." Contracts are meant to protect both the interests of the publishers and writers. Publishers want the commitment from writers that he or she will provide their best work and writers want to be recognized for their best work. But between those contracts lines, the legal lingo can cause writers to feel they need a law degree to review the contract. No, just sit back and relax and enjoy the prose that will take your writing to the next level.

RIGHTS AND WHAT THEY MEAN

A creative work can be used in many different ways. As the author of the work, you hold all rights to the work in question. When you agree to have your work published, you are granting a publisher the right to use your work in any number of ways. Whether that right is to publish the manuscript for the first time in a publication, or to publish it as many times and in as many ways as a publisher wishes, is up to you—it all depends on the agreed-upon terms. As a general rule, the more rights you license away, the less control you have over your work and the money you're paid. You should strive to keep as many rights to your work as you can.

Writers and editors sometimes define rights in a number of different ways. Below you will find a classification of terms as they relate to rights.

- **FIRST SERIAL RIGHTS.** Rights that the writer offers a newspaper or magazine to publish the manuscript for the first time in any periodical. All other rights remain with the writer. Sometimes the qualifier "North American" is added to these rights to specify a geographical limitation to the license. When content is excerpted from a book scheduled to be published, and it appears in a magazine or newspaper prior to book publication, this is also called first serial rights.
- **ONE-TIME RIGHTS.** Nonexclusive rights (rights that can be licensed to more than one market) purchased by a periodical to publish the work once (also known as simultaneous rights). That is, there is nothing to stop the author from selling the work to other publications at the same time.
- **SECOND SERIAL (REPRINT) RIGHTS.** Nonexclusive rights given to a newspaper or magazine to publish a manuscript after it has already appeared in another newspaper or magazine.
- **ALL RIGHTS.** This is exactly what it sounds like. "All rights" means an author is selling every right he has to a work. If you license all rights to your work, you forfeit the right to ever use the work again. If you think you may want to use the article again, you should avoid submitting to such markets or refuse payment and withdraw your material.
- **ELECTRONIC RIGHTS.** Rights that cover a broad range of electronic media, including websites, CD/DVDs, video games, smart phone apps, and more. The contract should

specify if—and which—electronic rights are included. The presumption is unspecified rights remain with the writer.

- **SUBSIDIARY RIGHTS.** Rights, other than book publication rights, that should be covered in a book contract. These may include various serial rights; movie, TV, audio, and other electronic rights; translation rights, etc. The book contract should specify who controls the rights (author or publisher) and what percentage of sales from the licensing of these rights goes to the author.

- **DRAMATIC, TV, AND MOTION PICTURE RIGHTS.** Rights for use of material on the stage, on TV, or in the movies. Often a one-year option to buy such rights is offered (generally for 10 percent of the total price). The party interested in the rights then tries to sell the idea to other people—actors, directors, studios, or TV networks. Some properties are optioned numerous times, but most fail to become full productions. In those cases, the writer can sell the rights again and again.

Sometimes editors don't take the time to specify the rights they are buying. If you sense that an editor is interested in getting stories, but doesn't seem to know what his and the writer's responsibilities are, be wary. In such a case, you'll want to explain what rights you're offering (preferably one-time or first serial rights only) and that you expect additional payment for subsequent use of your work.

The Copyright Law that went into effect January 1, 1978, states writers are primarily selling one-time rights to their work unless they—and the publisher—agree otherwise in writing. Book rights are covered fully by contract between the writer and the book publisher.

CINDY FERRAINO has been blessed with a variety of assignments, including newspaper articles, magazine articles, ghost-written articles, stories for books, and most recently authoring a book on accounting and bookkeeping terminology, *The Complete Dictionary of Accounting & Bookkeeping Terms Explained Simply* (Atlantic Publishing Group).

CONTRACTS, COPYRIGHTS, AND TAXES

by David Paul Williams

You queried an editor or agent and she asked to see your fiction manuscript, book proposal or feature article. The magical day comes with an e-mail attachment that is a pages-long contract. Your strength is your creativity, not your legal knowledge or business acumen. Now what?

Successful writers have split personalities. The creative side crafts great works; the logical side takes care of business. Here are the basics every writer needs to know.

While your contract for agent representation will differ, and magazine article contracts will be much less extensive than book contracts, all publishing contracts should include several important provisions:

- Who is going to write the piece (you!)
- Who is buying the piece (the name of the publisher, not the editor or agent)
- What is the contracted piece (feature article, nonfiction book, essay, novel, memoir, quiz, photo essay, sidebar, round-up, interview, etc.)
- Due date (first draft and post-editing revision dates for book-length works)
- In what format (hard copy, electronic, e-mailed, or Dropbox)
- What rights are being acquired
- What is the offered pay

It would be marvelous if there was a standard industry contract, but alas, like Sasquatch, and Nelly the Loch Ness monster, despite reported sightings no such animal exists. Individual magazines or publishers have different approaches. For magazine and web articles, any missing provisions may be determined by consulting the writer's guidelines, otherwise, immediately contact the editor for clarification. Book contracts can be negotiated to include specifics in order to avoid misunderstandings when it comes to delivering the contracted materials.

A clear understanding of these provisions is important to both parties. Success in writing depends on providing content to the editor on time, and as assigned. Doing so builds a relationship that results in future assignments.

COPYRIGHTS

Copyright protection begins under federal law when the creative work is first reduced to a fixed and tangible medium. That means as soon as you create it, you own the copyright. Registration of the work is not required for the copyright to attach, though registration does provide benefits if the author ever needs to sue for copyright infringement.

> Copyright protection begins under federal law when the creative work is first reduced to a fixed and tangible medium. That means as soon as you create it, you own the copyright.

Registration can be done by paper or electronically. The online method is faster and cheaper (www.copyright.gov/registration). Registration is complete when the Copyright Office receives a properly completed application, payment and a copy of the creative work. It's possible to registered multiple works under one application. Under the current law, the copyright lasts for the life of the author plus 70 years.

RIGHTS SOLD UNDER THE CONTRACT

The writer owns all the rights to their work and grants a license to publish the work to the publisher. There is a natural tension between writer and editor. The writer wants to limit the rights granted and retain as many rights as possible for future use and sale. The editor wants to acquire as many rights as possible, all at once, for the least amount of money. Generally the more rights that are licensed, the more money the writer receives. The process of negotiation is one of compromise. The writer is best served when she has a clear understanding of the rights under consideration.

First Serial Rights. The writer grants a license to a magazine or newspaper to publish the work for the first time in a periodical. Once the work is published, all rights revert to the writer, though the work cannot again be licensed as First Serial. First serial rights are typically limited geographically by adding the qualifier such as "North American." If that qualifier was added, then the writer could license first serial rights elsewhere, like England or India.

One Time Rights. Non-exclusive license for a periodical to run the piece once. One time rights can be licensed multiple times.

Reprint or Second Serial Rights. Grant of a license to a magazine or periodical to publish a piece after it has been previously published.

Electronic Rights. This is an ever-changing area as new and different electronic media and formats are created. The rights may include online magazines, computer software, video games, electronic anthologies, audiobooks, and more. The writer should strive to limit the license to specified media formats.

Subsidiary Rights. The right to produce or publish the original work in different formats, such as a movie based on a book, to translate the book into different languages, or to create toys based on a book. Subsidiary rights may be broken into primary and secondary rights.

All Rights. Just as it sounds, the writer licenses all rights to the publisher. Grant "all rights" with extreme caution.

Work For Hire. Under a "work for hire" contract, the writer is an employee and the employer is treated as the author who owns all rights. The writer does not own the copyright.

Grant 'all rights' with extreme caution.

There are other rights that can be licensed, and the wise writer will research her options before granting those rights.

Now let's talk about legal right of the public to use copyrighted material. The Fair Use Doctrine is a federal law that allows use of copyrighted material without liability for infringement. There are four statutory factors:

- the purpose and character of the use, including whether of a commercial nature or for nonprofit educational use;
- the nature of the copyrighted work;
- the portion used in relation to the copyrighted work as a whole;
- the effect of the use upon the potential market for or value of the copyrighted work.

Application of those factors is what lawyers call 'fact-specific,' meaning that each case is different with few hard and fast rules. Here are a couple: book, song, movie and poem titles cannot be copyrighted, but song lyrics can. A common misconception is that citing the source and giving attribution negates the need to acquire permission or pay the copyright holder for use. It doesn't.

If infringement occurs on the internet, the copyright owner can use the Digital Millennium Copyright Act, a federal law. The Act allows the copyright owner to provide written notice of infringement to the online service provider hosting the infringer. The service provider must take down the copyrighted material. There can be financial consequences as well. There can be substantial penalties for other types of copyright violations. Be mindful and cautious, even if you believe your use of another's copyrighted material is allowed under the Fair Use Doctrine.

Copyright is a form of property known as intangible. You can't see it or touch it or smell it, but it can be inherited. When creating an estate plan, be sure your attorney addresses the money earned by the copyright separately from the decision-making power regarding marketing of copyrighted material.

FEDERAL TAXES

The Internal Revenue Code treats writers in one of two ways: as hobbyist or as a business. It is usually better to be a business, as the Code allows business deductions against income. Under the Code, a business is an activity regularly engaged in with a profit motive. The activity qualifies a business for the IRS if the writer has earned a profit in three of the last five years. If the profit test is not met, the IRS evaluates the intent of the taxpayer by weighing nine relevant factors:

1. does the writer act like a business—a business plan, a separate bank account, business cards, media presence
2. the expertise of the writer—degree or advanced degree, attends writer's conferences and seminars
3. time and effort expended in writing—tracks hours spent researching and writing
4. potential appreciation of business assets—expects gain from business activities
5. track record of profitability in other businesses—previously turned an unprofitable venture into the black
6. history of profit or loss in this activity—were losses during the startup phase or due to events beyond the writer's control, has the writer been profitable in some years
7. relationship of profits and losses—occasional tiny profits following big losses point to hobby
8. does the writer depend on the income—the relationship between writing income and other income sources is relevant
9. elements of personal pleasure or recreation—vacations without corresponding articles/books gets categorized as hobby

No single factor is determinative. If the writer qualifies as a business then the Code allows deduction of the ordinary and necessary expenses of carrying on the business. There are four categories of business expenses with different rules applying to each. Start up expenses can be deducted up to $5,000 the first year of business with the remainder amortized over 15 years. Operating expenses—business travel, research expenses, writer's conferences, supplies—are unlimited in amount (if reasonable and necessary) and deducted in the year incurred. Capital expenses, meaning those assets with a useful life greater than one year, are depreciated over the life of the item. Inventory, the final category, has limited application to writers, except perhaps for indie-published book authors who do advanced print runs rather than print-on-demand.

Writers are exempt from the Uniform Capitalization Rules. This exemption is most applicable to book authors, who may spend years working on a project before they see any money. Writers may deduct expenses in the year incurred, instead of requiring the expense to match the income earned that year. For example, travel and research expenses incurred in the process of writing a book can be deducted when incurred instead of when the book advance is received, which may be years later.

....

Writers are exempt from the Uniform Capitalization Rules. This exemption is most applicable to book authors, who may spend years working on a project before they see any money.

....

The devil is in the details. Unless you are a tax accountant or an avid student of the Internal Revenue Code, Regulations, Rulings and other materials guaranteed to cure insomnia, get professional advice when the amount of money at risk warrants.

BUSINESS ENTITY

To paraphrase the Bard, to incorporate or not to incorporate, that is the question. According to the Small Business Administration, 90% of home businesses are sole proprietorships. These are easily formed and the owners are personally liable for all business debts, just as they would be as individuals.

Partnerships are formed when two or more people enter into business together to earn a profit, as when a formal agreement for co-authoring a book designates the entity a Partnership. Each partner is 100% liable for all business debts, regardless of which partner incurred which debt. Profits are presumed split equally unless the partnership agreement states otherwise.

Corporations are entities distinct from their owners, who enjoy limited personal liability for corporate debts. By default, corporations are "C" corporations unless the entity qualifies as an "S" corporation. The biggest difference is that profits are first taxed to the C corporation, then taxed again if dividends are paid to the shareholders. S corporation profits are passed through to the shareholders who then pay taxes.

Limited liability companies operate much like corporations. The owners typically enjoy the same limited debt liability and same tax benefits as S corporation shareholders.

Corporations and limited liability companies entail more paperwork both in formation and in annual or quarterly reporting. It is important to understand state-specific regulations and to observe legal formalities such as avoiding commingling business money with personal money. To do otherwise risks limited debt liability.

BRANDING

It's been said that 10% of the effort is writing the book, 90% is the author marketing the book. Successful writers are successful marketers and a key to success is developing a brand. An effective brand creates an emotional connection between the writer and the reader, communicates the writer's purpose and intention behind the work, and differentiates the writer from others in the genre or field.

Branding precedes marketing and is part of the writer's platform. It shows up as a cohesive strategy as revealed by the writer's website, social media posts, press releases, query letters, book proposals right down to the look and feel of their business cards.

Make creating your business entity and conducting your business professionally part of your branding strategy. Agents and editors want to work with professionals. Developing a system, a checklist for what doesn't come naturally, gives you the freedom to create.

DAVID PAUL WILLIAMS, attorney, real estate broker, and avid fly fisher turned his education and passion into a writing life. He's the author of *Fly Fishing for Western Smallmouth*, editor-in-chief of *Flyfisher*, department editor for *Flyfishing & Tying Journal*, "In The Field" editor for *Washington-Oregon Game & Fish*, and former Business Topics editor of *ArrowTrade*. A freelance writer for consumer magazines and trade journals since 2004, he also teaches craft and the business of writing workshops at writers conferences and writing groups.

MAKING THE MOST OF THE MONEY YOU EARN

....

by Sage Cohen

///

Writers who manage money well can establish a prosperous writing life that meets their short-term needs and long-term goals. This article will introduce the key financial systems, strategies, attitudes, and practices that will help you cultivate a writing life that makes the most of your resources and sustains you over time.

DIVIDING BUSINESS AND PERSONAL EXPENSES

If you are reporting your writing business to the IRS, it is important that you keep the money that flows from this source entirely separate from your personal finances. Here's what you'll need to accomplish this:

- **BUSINESS CHECKING ACCOUNT:** Only two types of money go into this account: money you have been paid for your writing and/or "capital investments" you make by depositing your own money to invest in the business. And only two types of payments are made from this account: business-related expenses (such as: subscriptions, marketing and advertisement, professional development, fax or phone service, postage, computer software and supplies), and "capital draws" which you make to pay yourself.
- **BUSINESS SAVINGS ACCOUNT OR MONEY MARKET ACCOUNT:** This account is the holding pen where your quarterly tax payments will accumulate and earn interest. Money put aside for your retirement account(s) can also be held here.
- **BUSINESS CREDIT CARD:** It's a good idea to have a credit card for your business as a means of emergency preparedness. Pay off the card responsibly every month and this will help you establish a good business credit record, which can be useful down the line should you need a loan for any reason.

When establishing your business banking and credit, shop around for the best deals, such as highest interest rates, lowest (or no) monthly service fees, and free checking. Mint.com is a good source for researching your options.

EXPENSE TRACKING AND RECONCILING

Once your bank accounts are set up, it's time to start tracking and categorizing what you earn and spend. This will ensure that you can accurately report your income and itemize your deductions when tax time rolls around every quarter. Whether you intend to prepare your taxes yourself or have an accountant help you, immaculate financial records will be the key to speed and success in filing your taxes.

For the most effective and consistent expense tracking, I highly recommend that you use a computer program such as QuickBooks. While it may seem simpler to do accounting by hand, I assure you that it isn't. Even a luddite such as I, who can't comprehend the most basic principles of accounting, can use QuickBooks with great aplomb to plug in the proper categories for income and expenses, easily reconcile bank statements, and with a few clicks prepare all of the requisite reports that make it easy to prepare taxes.

PAYING BILLS ONLINE

While it's certainly not imperative, you might want to check out your bank's online bill pay option if you're not using this already. Once you've set up the payee list, you can make payments in a few seconds every month or set up auto payments for expenses that are recurring. Having a digital history of bills paid can also come in handy with your accounting.

MANAGING TAXES

Self-employed people need to pay quarterly taxes. A quick, online search will reveal a variety of tax calculators and other online tools that can help you estimate what your payments should be. Programs such as TurboTax are popular and useful tools for automating and guiding you step-by-step through tax preparation. An accountant can also be helpful in understanding your unique tax picture, identifying and saving the right amount for taxes each quarter, and even determining SEP IRA contribution amounts (described later in this article). The more complex your finances (or antediluvian your accounting skills), the more likely that you'll benefit from this kind of personalized expertise.

Once you have forecasted your taxes either with the help of a specialized, tax-planning program or an accountant, you can establish a plan toward saving the right amount for quarterly payments. For example, once I figured out what my tax bracket was and the approximate percentage of income that needed to be set aside as taxes, I would immediately transfer a percentage of every deposit to my savings account, where it would sit and grow a little interest until quarterly tax time came around. When I could afford to do so, I would also set aside the appropriate percentage of SEP IRA contribution from each deposit so that I'd be ready at end-of-year to deposit as much as I possibly could for retirement.

THE PRINCIPLE TO COMMIT TO IS THIS: Get that tax-earmarked cash out of your hot little hands (i.e., checking account) as soon as you can, and create whatever deterrents you need to leave the money in savings so you'll have it when you need it.

INTELLIGENT INVESTING FOR YOUR CAREER

Your writing business will require not only the investment of your time but also the investment of money. When deciding what to spend and how, consider your values and your budget in the three, key areas in the chart below: education, marketing and promotion, and keeping the wheels turning.

This is not an absolute formula for spending—just a snapshot of the types of expenses you may be considering and negotiating over time. My general rule would be: start small and modest with the one or two most urgent and/or inexpensive items in each list, and grow slowly over time as your income grows.

The good news is that these legitimate business expenses may all be deducted from your income—making your net income and tax burden less. Please keep in mind that the IRS allows losses as long as you make a profit for at least three of the first five years you are in business. Otherwise, the IRS will consider your writing a non-deductible hobby.

EDUCATION	MARKETING AND PROMOTION	KEEPING THE WHEELS TURNING
Subscriptions to publications in your field	URL registration and hosting for blogs and websites	Technology and application purchase, servicing and back-up
Memberships to organizations in your field	Contact database subscription (such as Constant Contact) for communicating with your audiences	Office supplies and furniture
Books: on topics you want to learn, or in genres you are cultivating	Business cards and stationery	Insurance for you and/or your business

Conferences and seminars	Print promotions (such as direct mail), giveaways and schwag	Travel, gas, parking
Classes and workshops	Online or print ad placement costs	Phone, fax and e-mail

PREPARATION AND PROTECTION FOR THE FUTURE

As a self-employed writer, in many ways your future is in your hands. Following are some of the health and financial investments that I'd recommend you consider as you build and nurture The Enterprise of You. Please understand that these are a layperson's suggestions. I am by no means an accountant, tax advisor, or financial planning guru. I am simply a person who has educated herself on these topics for the sake of her own writing business, made the choices I am recommending, and benefited from them. I'd like you to benefit from them, too.

SEP IRAS

Individual Retirement Accounts (IRAs) are investment accounts designed to help individuals save for retirement. But I do recommend that you educate yourself about the Simplified Employee Pension Individual Retirement Account (SEP IRA) and consider opening one if you don't have one already.

A SEP IRA is a special type of IRA that is particularly beneficial to self-employed people. Whereas a Roth IRA has a contribution cap of $5,000 or $6,000, depending on your age, the contribution limit for self-employed people in 2011 is approximately 20% of adjusted earned income, with a maximum contribution of $49,000. Contributions for a SEP IRA are generally 100% tax deductible and investments grow tax deferred. Let's say your adjusted earned income this year is $50,000. This means you'd be able to contribute $10,000 to your retirement account. I encourage you to do some research online or ask your accountant if a SEP IRA makes sense for you.

CREATING A 9-MONTH SAVINGS BUFFER

When you're living month-to-month, you are extremely vulnerable to fluctuation in the economy, client budget changes, life emergencies and every other wrench that could turn a good working groove into a frightening financial rut. The best way to prepare for the unexpected is to start (or continue) developing a savings buffer. The experts these days are suggesting that we accumulate nine months of living expenses to help us navigate transition in a way that we feel empowered rather than scared and desperate to take the next thing that comes along.

I started creating my savings buffer by opening the highest-interest money market account I could find and setting up a modest, monthly automatic transfer from my checking account. Then, when I paid off my car after five years of monthly payments, I added my car payment amount to the monthly transfer. (I'd been paying that amount for five years, so I was pretty sure I could continue to pay it to myself.) When I paid off one of my credit cards in full, I added that monthly payment to the monthly savings transfer. Within a year, I had a hefty sum going to savings every month before I had time to think about it, all based on expenses I was accustomed to paying, with money that had never been anticipated in the monthly cash flow.

What can you do today—and tomorrow—to put your money to work for your life, and start being as creative with your savings as you are with language?

DISABILITY INSURANCE

If writing is your livelihood, what happens if you become unable to write? I have writing friends who have become incapacitated and unable to work due to injuries to their brains, backs, hands and eyes. Disability insurance is one way to protect against such emergencies and ensure that you have an income in the unlikely event that you're not physically able to earn one yourself.

Depending on your health, age, and budget, monthly disability insurance payments may or may not be within your means or priorities. But you won't know until you learn more about your coverage options. I encourage you to investigate this possibility with several highly rated insurance companies to get the lay of the land for your unique, personal profile and make an informed decision.

HEALTH INSURANCE

Self-employed writers face tough decisions about health insurance. If you're lucky, there's someone in your family with health coverage also available to you. Without the benefit of group health insurance, chances are that self-costs are high and coverage is low. As in disability insurance, age and health status are significant variables in costs and availability.

Ideally, of course, you'll have reasonably-priced health insurance that helps make preventive care and health maintenance more accessible and protects you in case of a major medical emergency. The following are a few possibilities to check out that could reduce costs and improve access to health coverage:

- Join a group that aggregates its members for group coverage, such as a Chamber of Commerce or AARP. Ask an insurance agent in your area if there are any other group coverage options available to you.

- Consider a high-deductible health plan paired with a Health Savings Account (HSA). Because the deductible is so high, these plans are generally thought to be most useful for a major medical emergency. But an HSA paired with such a plan allows you to put aside a chunk of pre-tax change every year that can be spent on medical expenses or remain in the account where it can be invested and grow.

Establishing effective financial systems for your writing business will take some time and energy at the front end. I suggest that you pace yourself by taking an achievable step or two each week until you have a baseline of financial management that works for you. Then, you can start moving toward some of your bigger, longer-term goals. Once it's established, your solid financial foundation will pay you in dividends of greater efficiency, insight, and peace of mind for the rest of your writing career.

SAGE COHEN is the author of *The Productive Writer* and *Writing the Life Poetic,* both from Writer's Digest Books. She's been nominated for a Pushcart Prize, won first prize in the Ghost Road Press Poetry contest and published dozens of poems, essays and articles on the writing life. Sage holds an MFA in creative writing from New York University and a BA from Brown University. Since 1997, she has been a freelance writer serving clients including Intuit, Blue Shield, Adobe, and Kaiser Permanente.

THE ORGANIZED WRITER

From Pitch to Payment and Beyond

....

by Jenny Flores

//

Success is relative for most. But for a writer, success is directly tied to productivity. You will not get paid for what you do not write. Unfortunately, writing is not all that freelance writers are responsible for. By organizing the business aspects of your writing career, you will be more productive creatively and writing for a living will become even more enjoyable.

Much of this advice will be helpful to hobby writers. But for writers who are in the business of writing, the beans I am about to spill are magic beans. When you take yourself seriously enough to organize your writing career, so will everyone else.

A CREATIVE JOB IS STILL A JOB

Ahh, the writer's life. We get to write what we want to write, when we want to write it, and for whom we want to write. Ugh, the writer's life. We must do all the research for what we want to write about, carve out time in our day to write it, and find clients who are willing to pay for what we have written. Our silver lining is also our cloud. With no one telling us what to do and when to do it, it is imperative that we chart our own course. This involves setting long-term writing goals, creating a work space and schedule, setting and meeting milestones on big projects, as well as determining and realizing daily production goals.

If you do not have clear and concrete goals for your writing career, stop what you are doing and decide where you want your business to be 12 months from today. If you need to make a certain amount of money to consider your business a success, be honest with yourself about what that dollar amount is. From there it is a matter of simple math to determine how much you need to produce and what you must charge. If your goal is to break into three new markets, decide which markets you want to crack and dedicate a portion of each day to studying those markets and developing relationships that will help you get your foot in the door.

Once your writing goals are set, take a look at your writing habits. Do you have a work station or are you churning out assignments from the sofa? Do you have a work schedule or are you scribbling notes between laundry and soccer practice? Productivity soars with seriousness. Create an office area that works for you and set inviolable office hours.

Record writing assignments on a calendar, as well as milestones for any large writing projects. Set daily production goals and meet them. Daily production goals include not only writing assignments but networking with writers and editors, sending out e-mails and queries, and updating your website and blog. Everything you do during office hours should advance you toward your long-term writing goals.

PITCH, WRITE, SELL, REPEAT

The more you are able to maximize the value of your work, the more success you will enjoy. Positioning yourself as an expert in a niche market, selling reprints, reslanting your work for new audiences and crossing over into different markets and media outlets are all very good ways to increase your exposure and the value of your writing.

To establish yourself as an expert, you can write for a niche market or you can focus on a niche topic found within that market. For example, homesteading magazines are a niche market whereas "Cultivating Mushrooms" is a niche topic in the homesteading market. The more specific your expertise, the more money you can expect to earn per assignment.

> To establish yourself as an expert, you can write for a niche market or you can focus on a niche topic found within that market.

Create a Manuscript Log in order to examine and track ways in which you can resell your work. If you do this before you start your research, you will be more cognizant of related writing opportunities. For each topic, record the following:

- **IDEA**—This is the overarching topic you will be researching and writing about.
- **MARKET**—This is the market you are targeting first. There are several possibilities within each market. List in order of preference.

- **REPRINT POTENTIAL**—This is where you will record any possible reprint markets. It is always a good idea to retain reprint rights. If you already have a list of markets that are receptive to reprints, you are much more likely to negotiate that clause in your contract.
- **RESLANTS**—List a minimum of three reslants. When you reslant an article you have already written, you are simply altering the article to fit a different audience. You will use the same research but your article will be written to different specs.
- **CROSSOVERS**—List a minimum of three ways this material can cross over into different markets. Full length articles can be trimmed and reformatted into several blog posts. Informational articles can be turned into content for businesses and can also often be tweaked into teaching opportunities such as workshops or instructional videos and podcasts.
- **SERIES**—Is your topic meaty enough to pitch as a series? If you can unpack one info-dense article into three articles, you will be paid three times instead of once for the same amount of research.

IDEA	"CULTIVATING MUSHROOMS"
MARKET	Homesteading magazines: 1. Hobby Farms 2. Mother Earth News 3. Self-Reliant Magazine
REPRINTS	Yes; Capper's Farmer
RESLANTS	1."Medicinal Mushroom Teas" - herbal magazines, holistic living magazines 2."Hearty Mushroom Meals" - women's magazines, vegetarian magazines 3."Can Mushrooms Keep You Young?" - magazine such as AARP
CROSSOVERS	1."Top Five Market Mushrooms" - brochure/newsletter article for farmer's market 2."DIY Mushroom Plugs" - Workshop at local ag office 3."Mushroom Spore Prints" - You Tube instructional video
SERIES	yes

CONTACTS, CLIENTS AND CONTRACTS

Although the actual act of writing is a solitary gig, building a writing business cannot be done in a bubble. You need contacts in order to get clients and contracts. Even though many, if not most, of your contacts will be virtual, it is important to be as professional as you would be if meeting them in person.

Again, organization is the key to the consistency required in creating a working contact list. Start by creating a digital and a physical file of everyone you know. Begin with your family and friends, then editors, publishers, and fellow writers. Once you have listed everyone you know, decide what new contacts you want to make. Follow them on social media, leaving thoughtful and well-written comments two to three times a week. This often leads to being approached with an assignment rather than having to ask for one. If you do query them, mention who you are and which format(s) you follow them on.

As you land clients, create a separate file for each one. Each Client File should include:

- **MARKET**—This is the magazine, business, or blog you are writing for.
- **SUBMISSION GUIDELINES**—Each entity has different submission guidelines. If appearing professional and making your editor glad they hired you is important to you, follow their guidelines to the letter. If you were not sent writer's guidelines with your contract, look for them on their website. You can also Google "submission guidelines + name of market."
- **PERSONAL CONTACT**—This is the contact information (name, title, phone number, e-mail address, social media handles) of the person you will be directly dealing with. Record any of their personal preferences and file all correspondence here.
- **CONTRACT**—This goes without saying but I'm going to say it anyway: Read your contract. Pay special attention to rights, requirements, and payment.
- **RIGHTS**—Your contract should list the rights that are being purchased.
- **REQUIREMENTS**—Contracts will make clear the requirements of the assignment such as word count, photos, sidebars, references, and date due. Early is fine. Late is not.
- **PAYMENT**—Your contract should cover when and how much you are to be paid. If you sign a contract that does not specify pay, you have basically agreed to work for free. Yes, you can fight it in court. Is that how you want to spend time you could be writing?

Read your contract, sign it and send a copy to your editor. Keep a copy for your records. Record the assignment on your work calendar and create a file for this project in your Manuscript Log. Now you are ready to start working on the assignment.

MINDING YOUR MONEY

You are a writer and an entrepreneur. You are in charge of finding and keeping clients, negotiating contracts, researching and writing assignments, and networking on behalf of your business. That is a full plate. I urge you to consider using an accountant to help you navigate the tax requirements for a small business. That being said, there are things you can do to make tax time easier on you and on the aforementioned accountant.

Take a bite out of the taxes you are responsible for by taking advantage of the tax deductions you are allowed. What can you deduct? Almost anything related to your business.

Before you start rifling through your receipts, take a moment to set up a file for your business expenses. This can be anything that you will use, from a cheap notebook to expensive software. Use the IRS Schedule C form to decide on the categories applicable to your situation.

Setting up the system is the easy part. The difficult part is maintaining the discipline it takes to actually file your receipts. It helps to do a mental review of any purchases every evening. Document the purchases that are relevant to your business. Highlight each pertinent line item on the receipt and file.

Depending upon where you are in your career, your accountant may suggest setting up a business banking system. This mainly involves a business checking and savings account, and possibly a business credit card. The savings account is where you will deposit money to be used to pay quarterly taxes, as well as to grow any money you set aside for retirement. The checking account is used for business expenses, including your salary.

Taking some time on the front end to organize your business will alleviate those niggles that tickle your brain to distraction and allow you to focus on what you love—writing.

JENNY FLORES is a contributor to multiple blogs and magazines including *Hobby Farms*, *GRIT*, *Mother Earth Living*, *Bee Culture*, and *GEEZ*. When she is not writing informational and DIY articles, she spends her free time playing with fiction.

HOW MUCH SHOULD I CHARGE?

by Aaron Belz

The first question most aspiring freelance writers ask themselves is, "Where do I find paying gigs?" But once a writer finds that first freelance gig, they often ask, "How much should I charge?"

They ask this question, because often their clients ask them. In the beginning, this can be one of the most stressful parts of the freelancing process: Trying to set rates that don't scare away clients, but that also help put dinner on the table.

Maybe that's why the "How Much Should I Charge?" pay rate chart is one of the most popular and useful pieces of the *Writer's Market*. Freelancers use the rates to justify their worth on the market to potential clients, and clients use the chart as an objective third party authority on what the current market is paying.

Use the following chart to help you get started in figuring out your freelance rates. If you're a beginner, it makes sense to price yourself closer to the lower end of the spectrum, but always use your gut in negotiating rates. The rate on that first assignment often helps set the expectations for future rates.

As you find success in securing work, your rates should naturally increase. If not, consider whether you're building relationships with clients that lead to multiple assignments. Also, take into account whether you're negotiating for higher rates on new assignments with familiar and newer clients.

Remember that smarter freelancers work toward the goal of higher rates, because better rates mean one of two things for writers: Either they're able to earn money, or they're able to earn the same money in less time. For some freelancers, having that extra time is worth more than anything money can buy.

Use the listings in *Writer's Market* to find freelance work for magazines, book publishers, and other traditional publishing markets. But don't restrict your search to the traditional markets if you want to make a serious living as a freelance writer.

As the pay rate chart shows, there are an incredible number of opportunities for writers to make a living doing what they love: writing. Maybe that means writing critiques, editing anthologies, blogging, or something else entirely.

While this pay rate chart covers a wide variety of freelance writing gigs, there are some that are just too unique to get a going rate. If you can't find a specific job listed here, try to find something that is similar to use as a guide for figuring out a rate. There are times when you just have to create the going rate yourself.

Thank you, Aaron Belz, for assembling this pay rate chart and sharing your sources in the sidebar below. I know it will help more than one freelance writer negotiate the freelance rates they deserve.

—*Robert Lee Brewer*

PARTICIPATING ORGANIZATIONS

Here are the organizations surveyed to compile the "How Much Should I Charge?" pay rate chart. You can also find Professional Organizations in the Resources.

- American Medical Writers Association (AMWA), www.amwa.org
- American Society of Journalists & Authors (ASJA), www.asja.org
- American Society of Media Photographers (ASMP), www.asmp.org
- American Society of Picture Professionals (ASPP), www.aspp.com
- American Translators Association (ATA), www.atanet.org
- Association of Independents in Radio (AIR), www.airmedia.org
- Educational Freelancers Association (EFA), www.the-efa.org
- Freelance Success (FLX), www.freelancesucess.com
- Investigative Reporters & Editors (IRE), www.ire.org
- Media Communicators Association International (MCA-I), www.mca-i.org
- National Cartoonists Society (NCS), www.reuben.org/main.asp
- National Writers Union (NWU), www.nwu.org
- National Association of Science Writers (NASW), www.nasw.org
- Society of Professional Journalists (SPJ), www.spj.org
- Women in Film (WIF), www.wif.org
- Writer's Guild of America East (WGAE), www.wgaeast.org
- Writer's Guild of America West (WGA), www.wga.org

AARON BELZ is the author of *The Bird Hoverer* (BlazeVOX), *Lovely, Raspberry* (Persea), and *Glitter Bomb* (Persea). A St. Louis native, he now lives and works in Hillsborough, North Carolina. Visit him online at belz.net or follow him on Twitter @aaronbelz.

	PER HOUR			PER PROJECT			OTHER		
	HIGH	LOW	AVG	HIGH	LOW	AVG	HIGH	LOW	AVG
ADVERTISING & PUBLIC RELATIONS									
Advertising copywriting	$156	$36	$84	$9,000	$160	$2,760	$3/word	30¢/word	$1.57/word
Advertising editing	$125	$20	$65	n/a	n/a	n/a	$1/word	30¢/word	66¢/word
Advertorials	$182	$51	$93	$1,890	$205	$285	$3/word	85¢/word	$1.58/word
Business public relations	$182	$30	$85	n/a	n/a	n/a	$500/day	$200/day	$356/day
Campaign development or product launch	$156	$36	$100	$8,755	$1,550	$4,545	n/a	n/a	n/a
Catalog copywriting	$156	$25	$71	n/a	n/a	n/a	$350/item	$30/item	$116/item
Corporate spokesperson role	$182	$72	$107	n/a	n/a	n/a	$1,200/day	$500/day	$740/day
Direct-mail copywriting	$156	$36	$85	$8,248	$500	$2,839	$4/word	$1/word	$2.17/word
							$400/page	$200/page	$315/page
Event promotions/publicity	$126	$30	$76	n/a	n/a	n/a	n/a	n/a	$500/day
Press kits	$182	$31	$81	n/a	n/a	n/a	$850/60sec	$120/60sec	$458/60sec
Press/news release	$182	$30	$80	$1,500	$125	$700	$2/word	50¢/word	$1.20/word
							$750/page	$150/page	$348/page

	PER HOUR			PER PROJECT			OTHER		
	HIGH	LOW	AVG	HIGH	LOW	AVG	HIGH	LOW	AVG
Radio commercials	$102	$30	$74	n/a	n/a	n/a	$850/60sec	$120/60sec	$456/60sec
Speech writing/editing for individuals or corporations	$168	$36	$92	$10,000	$2,700	$5,036	$355/minute	$105/minute	$208/minute
BOOK PUBLISHING									
Abstracting and abridging	$125	$30	$74	n/a	n/a	n/a	$2/word	$1/word	$1.48/word
Anthology editing	$80	$23	$51	$7,900	$1,200	$4,588	n/a	n/a	n/a
Book chapter	$100	$35	$60	$2,500	$1,200	$1,758	20¢/word	8¢/word	14¢/word
Book production for clients	$100	$40	$67	n/a	n/a	n/a	$17.50/page	$5/page	$10/page
Book proposal consultation	$125	$25	$66	$1,500	$250	$788	n/a	n/a	n/a
Book publicity for clients	n/a	n/a	n/a	$10,000	$500	$2,000	n/a	n/a	n/a
Book query critique	$100	$50	$72	$500	$75	$202	n/a	n/a	n/a
Children's book writing	$75	$35	$50	n/a	n/a	n/a	$5/word $5,000/adv	$1/word $450/adv	$2.75/word $2,286/adv
Content editing (scholarly/textbook)	$125	$20	$51	$15,000	$500	$4,477	$20/page	$3/page	$6.89/page

	PER HOUR			PER PROJECT			OTHER		
	HIGH	LOW	AVG	HIGH	LOW	AVG	HIGH	LOW	AVG
Content editing (trade)	$125	$19	$54	$20,000	$1,000	$6,538	$20/page	$3.75/page	$8/page
Copyediting (trade)	$100	$16	$46	$5,500	$2,000	$2,892	$6/page	$1/page	$4.22/page
Encyclopedia articles	n/a	n/a	n/a	n/a	n/a	n/a	50¢/word $3,000/item	15¢/word $50/item	35¢/word $933/item
Fiction book writing (own)	n/a	n/a	n/a	n/a	n/a	n/a	$40,000/adv	$525/adv	$14,193/adv
Ghostwriting, as told to	$125	$35	$67	$47,000	$5,500	$22,892	$100/page	$50/page	$87/page
Ghostwriting, no credit	$125	$30	$73	n/a	n/a	n/a	$3/word $500/page	50¢/word $50/page	$1.79/word $206/page
Guidebook writing/editing	n/a	n/a	n/a	n/a	n/a	n/a	$14,000/adv	$10,000/adv	$12,000/adv
Indexing	$60	$22	$35	n/a	n/a	n/a	$12/page	$2/page	$4.72/page
Manuscript evaluation and critique	$150	$23	$66	$2,000	$150	$663	n/a	n/a	n/a
Manuscript typing	n/a	n/a	$20	n/a	n/a	n/a	$3/page	95¢/page	$1.67/page
Movie novelizations	n/a	n/a	n/a	$15,000	$5,000	$9,159	n/a	n/a	n/a

	PER HOUR			PER PROJECT			OTHER		
	HIGH	LOW	AVG	HIGH	LOW	AVG	HIGH	LOW	AVG
Nonfiction book writing (collaborative)	$125	$40	$80	n/a	n/a	n/a	$110/page $75,000/adv	$50/page $1,300/adv	$80/page $22,684/adv
Nonfiction book writing (own)	$125	$40	$72	n/a	n/a	n/a	$110/page $50,000/adv	$50/page $1,300/adv	$80/page $14,057/adv
Novel synopsis (general)	$60	$30	$45	$450	$150	$292	$100/page	$10/page	$37/page
Personal history writing/editing (for clients)	$125	$30	$60	$40,000	$750	$15,038	n/a	n/a	n/a
Proofreading	$75	$15	$31	n/a	n/a	n/a	$5/page	$2/page	$3.26/page
Research for writers or book publishers	$150	$15	$52	n/a	n/a	n/a	$600/day	$400/day	$525/day
Rewriting/structural editing	$120	$25	$67	$50,000	$2,500	$13,929	14¢/word	5¢/word	10¢/word
Translation—literary	n/a	n/a	n/a	$95,000	$6,500	$8,000	17¢/target word	4¢/target word	8¢/target word
Translation—nonfiction/technical	n/a	n/a	n/a	n/a	n/a	n/a	30¢/target word	5¢/target word	12¢/target word
BUSINESS									
Annual reports	$185	$60	$102	$15,000	$500	$5,850	$600	$100	$349

	PER HOUR			PER PROJECT			OTHER		
	HIGH	LOW	AVG	HIGH	LOW	AVG	HIGH	LOW	AVG
Brochures, booklets, flyers	$150	$45	$91	$15,000	$300	$4,230	$2.50/word $800/page	35¢/word $50/page	$1.21/word $341/page
Business editing (general)	$155	$40	$80	n/a	n/a	n/a	n/a	n/a	n/a
Business letters	$155	$40	$79	n/a	n/a	n/a	$2/word	$1/word	$1.47/word
Business plan	$155	$40	$87	$15,000	$200	$4,115	n/a	n/a	n/a
Business writing seminars	$155	$70	$112	$8,600	$550	$2,919	n/a	n/a	n/a
Consultation on communications	$155	$50	$80	n/a	n/a	n/a	$1,300/day	$530/day	$830/day
Copyediting for business	$155	$35	$65	n/a	n/a	n/a	$4/page	$2/page	$3/page
Corporate histories	$155	$45	$91	160,000	$5,000	$54,525	$2/word	$1/word	$1.50/word
Corporate periodicals, editing	$155	$45	$74	n/a	n/a	n/a	$2.50/word	75¢/word	$1.42/word
Corporate periodicals, writing	$155	$45	$83	n/a	n/a	$1,880	$3/word	$1/word	$1.71/word
Corporate profiles	$155	$45	$93	n/a	n/a	$3,000	$2/word	$1/word	$1.50/word
Ghostwriting for business execs	$155	$45	$89	$3,000	$500	$1,400	$2.50/word	50¢/word	$2/word

	PER HOUR			PER PROJECT			OTHER		
	HIGH	LOW	AVG	HIGH	LOW	AVG	HIGH	LOW	AVG
Ghostwriting for businesses	$155	$45	$114	$3,000	$500	$1,790	n/a	n/a	n/a
Newsletters, desktop publishing/production	$155	$45	$75	$6,600	$1,000	$3,490	$750/page	$150/page	$429/page
Newsletters, editing	$155	$35	$72	n/a	n/a	$3,615	$230/page	$150/page	$185/page
Newsletters, writing	$155	$35	$82	$6,600	$800	$3,581	$5/word $1,250/page	$1/word $150/page	$2.31/word $514/page
Translation services for business use	$80	$45	$57	n/a	n/a	n/a	$35/ target word $1.41/ target line	7¢/ target word $1/ target line	$2.31/ target word $1.21/ target line
Resume writing	$105	$70	$77	$500	$150	$295	n/a	n/a	n/a
COMPUTER, INTERNET & TECHNICAL									
Blogging—paid	$150	$35	$100	$2,000	$500	$1,250	$500/post	$6/post	$49/post
E-mail copywriting	$135	$30	$85	n/a	n/a	$300	$2/word	30¢/word	91¢/word
Educational webinars	$500	$0	$195	n/a	n/a	n/a	n/a	n/a	n/a
Hardware/Software help screen writing	$95	$60	$81	$6,000	$1,000	$4,000	n/a	n/a	n/a

	PER HOUR			PER PROJECT			OTHER		
	HIGH	LOW	AVG	HIGH	LOW	AVG	HIGH	LOW	AVG
Hardware/Software manual writing	$165	$30	$80	$23,500	$5,000	$11,500	n/a	n/a	n/a
Internet research	$95	$25	$55	n/a	n/a	n/a	n/a	n/a	n/a
Keyword descriptions	n/a	n/a	n/a	n/a	n/a	n/a	$200/page	$130/page	$165/page
Online videos for clients	$95	$60	$76	n/a	n/a	n/a	n/a	n/a	n/a
Social media postings for clients	$95	$25	$62	n/a	n/a	$500	n/a	n/a	$10/word
Technical editing	$150	$30	$65	n/a	n/a	n/a	n/a	n/a	n/a
Technical writing	$160	$30	$80	n/a	n/a	n/a	n/a	n/a	n/a
Web editing	$100	$25	$57	n/a	n/a	n/a	$10/page	$4/page	$5.67/page
Webpage design	$150	$25	$80	$4,000	$200	$1,278	n/a	n/a	n/a
Website or blog promotion	n/a	$30	n/a	$650	$195	$335	n/a	n/a	n/a
Website reviews	n/a	$30	n/a	$900	$50	$300	n/a	n/a	n/a
Website search engine optimization	$89	$30	$76	$50,000	$8,000	$12,000	n/a	n/a	n/a
White papers	$135	$30	$82	$10,000	$2,500	$4,927	n/a	n/a	n/a

	PER HOUR			PER PROJECT			OTHER		
	HIGH	LOW	AVG	HIGH	LOW	AVG	HIGH	LOW	AVG
EDITORIAL/DESIGN PACKAGES									
Desktop publishing	$150	$18	$67	n/a	n/a	n/a	$750/page	$30/page	$202/page
Photo brochures	$125	$60	$87	$15,000	$400	$3,869	$65/picture	$30/picture	$48/picture
Photography	$100	$45	$71	$10,500	$50	$2,100	$2,500/day	$500/day	$1,340/day
Photo research	$75	$45	$49	n/a	n/a	n/a	n/a	n/a	n/a
Picture editing	$100	$45	$64	n/a	n/a	n/a	$65/picture	$30/picture	$53/picture
EDUCATIONAL & LITERARY SERVICES									
Author appearances at national events	n/a	n/a	n/a	n/a	n/a	n/a	$500/hour $30,000/event	$100/hour $500/event	$285/hour $5,000/event
Author appearances at regional events	n/a	n/a	n/a	n/a	n/a	n/a	$1,500/event	$50/event	$615/event
Author appearances at local groups	$63	$40	$47	n/a	n/a	n/a	$400/event	$75/event	$219/event
Authors presenting in schools	$125	$25	$78	n/a	n/a	n/a	$350/class	$50/class	$183/class

	PER HOUR			PER PROJECT			OTHER		
	HIGH	LOW	AVG	HIGH	LOW	AVG	HIGH	LOW	AVG
Educational grant and proposal writing	$100	$35	$67	n/a	n/a	n/a	n/a	n/a	n/a
Manuscript evaluation for theses/dissertations	$100	$15	$53	$1,550	$200	$783	n/a	n/a	n/a
Poetry manuscript critique	$100	$25	$62	n/a	n/a	n/a	n/a	n/a	n/a
Private writing instruction	$60	$50	$57	n/a	n/a	n/a	n/a	n/a	n/a
Readings by poets, fiction writers	n/a	n/a	n/a	n/a	n/a	n/a	$3,000/event	$50/event	$225/event
Short story manuscript critique	$150	$30	$75	$175	$50	$112	n/a	n/a	n/a
Teaching adult writing classes	$125	$30	$82	n/a	n/a	n/a	$800/class $5,000/course	$115/class $500/course	$450/class $2,667/course
Writer's workshop panel or class	$220	$30	$92	n/a	n/a	n/a	$5,000/day	$60/day	$1,186/day
Writing for scholarly journals	$100	$40	$63	$450	$100	$285	n/a	n/a	n/a
FILM, VIDEO, TV, RADIO, STAGE									
Book/novel summaries for film producers	n/a	n/a	n/a	n/a	n/a	n/a	$34/page	$15/page	$23/page $120/book

	PER HOUR			PER PROJECT			OTHER		
	HIGH	LOW	AVG	HIGH	LOW	AVG	HIGH	LOW	AVG
Business film/video scriptwriting	$150	$50	$97	n/a	n/a	$600	$1,000/run min	$50/run min	$334/run min; $500/day
Comedy writing for entertainers	n/a	n/a	n/a	n/a	n/a	n/a	$150/joke; $500/group	$5/joke; $100/group	$50/joke; $283/group
Copyediting audiovisuals	$90	$22	$53	n/a	n/a	n/a	n/a	n/a	n/a
Educational or training film/video scriptwriting	$125	$35	$81	n/a	n/a	n/a	$500/run min	$100/run min	$245/run min
Feature film options	First 18 months, 10% WGA minimum; 10% minimum each 18-month period thereafter.								
TV options	First 180 days, 5% WGA minimum; 10% minimum each 180-day period thereafter.								
Industrial product film/video scriptwriting	$150	$30	$99	n/a	n/a	n/a	$500/run min	$100/run min	$300/run min
Playwriting for the stage	5-10% box office/Broadway, 6-7% box office/off-Broadway, 10% box office/regional theatre.								
Radio editorials	$70	$50	$60	n/a	n/a	n/a	$200/run min; $400/day	$45/run min; $250/day	$124/run min; $325/day
Radio interviews	n/a	n/a	n/a	$1,500	$110	$645	n/a	n/a	n/a

	PER HOUR			PER PROJECT			OTHER		
	HIGH	LOW	AVG	HIGH	LOW	AVG	HIGH	LOW	AVG
Screenwriting (original screenplay-including treatment)	n/a	n/a	n/a	n/a	n/a	n/a	$118,745	$63,526	$92,153
Script synopsis for agent or film	$2,344/30 min, $4,441/60 min, $6,564/90 min								
Script synopsis for business	$75	$45	$62	n/a	n/a	n/a	n/a	n/a	n/a
TV commercials	$99	$60	$81	n/a	n/a	n/a	$2,500/30 sec	$150/30 sec	$1,204/30 sec
TV news story/feature	$1,550/5 min, $3,000/10 min, $4,200/15 min								
TV scripts (non-theatrical)	Prime Time: $33,700/60 min, $47,500/90 min — Not Prime Time: $12,900/30 min, $23,500/60 min, $35,300/90 min								
TV scripts (teleplay/MOW)	$70,000/120 min								
MAGAZINES & TRADE JOURNALS									
Article manuscript critique	$130	$25	$69	n/a	n/a	n/a	n/a	n/a	n/a
Arts query critique	$105	$50	$80	n/a	n/a	n/a	n/a	n/a	n/a
Arts reviewing	$100	$65	$84	$335	$95	$194	$1.25/word	12¢/word	63¢/word
Book reviews	n/a			$900	$12	$348	$1.50/word	20¢/word	73¢/word

	PER HOUR			PER PROJECT			OTHER		
	HIGH	LOW	AVG	HIGH	LOW	AVG	HIGH	LOW	AVG
City magazine calendar	n/a	n/a	n/a	$250	$45	$135	$1/word	35¢/word	75¢/word
Comic book/strip writing	$225 original story, $525 existing story, $50 short script.								
Consultation on magazine editorial	$155	$35	$86	n/a	n/a	n/a	n/a	n/a	$100/page
Consumer magazine column	n/a	n/a	n/a	$2,500	$70	$898	$2.50/word	37¢/word	$1.13/word
Consumer front-of-book	n/a	n/a	n/a	$850	$320	$550	n/a	n/a	n/a
Content editing	$130	$30	$62	$6,500	$2,000	$3,700	15¢/word	6¢/word	11¢/word
Contributing editor	n/a	n/a	n/a	n/a	n/a	n/a	$160,000/ contract	$22,000/ contract	$53,000/ contract
Copyediting magazines	$105	$18	$55	n/a	n/a	n/a	$10/page	$2.90/page	$5.78/page
Fact checking	$130	$15	$46	n/a	n/a	n/a	n/a	n/a	n/a
Gag writing for cartoonists	$35/gag; 25% sale on spec.								
Ghostwriting articles (general)	$225	$30	$107	$3,500	$1,100	$2,200	$10/word	65¢/word	$2.50/word
Magazine research	$125	$20	$53	n/a	n/a	n/a	$500/item	$100/item	$200/item
Proofreading	$80	$20	$40	n/a	n/a	n/a	n/a	n/a	n/a

	PER HOUR			PER PROJECT			OTHER		
	HIGH	LOW	AVG	HIGH	LOW	AVG	HIGH	LOW	AVG
Reprint fees	n/a	n/a	n/a	$1,500	$20	$439	$1.50/word	10¢/word	76¢/word
Rewriting	$130	$25	$74	n/a	n/a	n/a	n/a	n/a	$50/page
Trade journal feature article	$128	$45	$80	$4,950	$150	$1,412	$3/word	20¢/word	$1.20/word
Transcribing interviews	$185	$95	$55	n/a	n/a	n/a	$3/min	$1/min	$2/min
MEDICAL/SCIENCE									
Medical/scientific conference coverage	$125	$50	$85	n/a	n/a	n/a	$800/day	$300/day	$600/day
Medical/scientific editing	$96	$15	$33	n/a	n/a	n/a	$12.50/page	$3/page	$4.40/page
							$600/day	$500/day	$550/day
Medical/scientific writing	$91	$20	$46	$4,000	$500	$2,500	$2/word	25¢/word	$1.12/word
Medical/scientific multimedia presentations	$100	$50	$75	n/a	n/a	n/a	$100/slide	$50/slide	$77/slide
Medical/scientific proofreading	$80	$18	$50	n/a	n/a	$500	$3/page	$2.50/page	$2.75/page
Pharmaceutical writing	$125	$100	$50	n/a	n/a	n/a	n/a	n/a	n/a
NEWSPAPERS									

	PER HOUR			PER PROJECT			OTHER		
	HIGH	LOW	AVG	HIGH	LOW	AVG	HIGH	LOW	AVG
Arts reviewing	$69	$30	$53	$200	$15	$101	60¢/word	6¢/word	36¢/word
Book reviews	$69	$45	$58	$350	$15	$140	60¢/word	25¢/word	44¢/word
Column, local	n/a	n/a	n/a	$600	$25	$206	$1/word	38¢/word	50¢/word
Column, self-syndicated	n/a	n/a	n/a	n/a	n/a	n/a	$35/insertion	$4/insertion	$16/insertion
Copyediting	$35	$15	$27	n/a	n/a	n/a	n/a	n/a	n/a
Editing/manuscript evaluation	$75	$25	$35	n/a	n/a	n/a	n/a	n/a	n/a
Feature writing	$79	$40	$63	$1,040	$85	$478	$1.60/word	10¢/word	59¢/word
Investigative reporting	n/a	n/a	n/a	n/a	n/a	n/a	$10,000/grant	$250/grant	$2,250/grant
Obituary copy	n/a	n/a	n/a	$225	$35	$124	n/a	n/a	n/a
Proofreading	$45	$15	$23	n/a	n/a	n/a	n/a	n/a	n/a
Stringing	n/a	n/a	n/a	$2,400	$40	$525	n/a	n/a	n/a
NONPROFIT									
Grant writing for nonprofits	$150	$12	$75	$3,000	$400	$1,852	n/a	n/a	n/a
Nonprofit annual reports	$100	$28	$60	n/a	n/a	n/a	n/a	n/a	n/a

	PER HOUR			PER PROJECT			OTHER		
	HIGH	LOW	AVG	HIGH	LOW	AVG	HIGH	LOW	AVG
Nonprofit writing	$150	$17	$65	$17,600	$100	$4,706	n/a	n/a	n/a
Nonprofit editing	$125	$16	$50	n/a	n/a	n/a	n/a	n/a	n/a
Nonprofit fundraising literature	$110	$35	$74	$3,500	$200	$1,597	$1,000/day	$300/day	$767/day
Nonprofit presentations	$100	$40	$73	n/a	n/a	n/a	n/a	n/a	n/a
Nonprofit public relations	$100	$30	$60	n/a	n/a	n/a	n/a	n/a	n/a
POLITICS/GOVERNMENT									
Government agency writing/editing	$110	$25	$64	n/a	n/a	n/a	$1.25/word	25¢/word	75¢/word
Government grant writing/editing	$150	$19	$72	n/a	n/a	n/a	n/a	n/a	n/a
Government-sponsored research	$110	$35	$66	n/a	n/a	n/a	n/a	n/a	$600/day
Public relations for political campaigns	$150	$40	$86	n/a	n/a	n/a	n/a	n/a	n/a
Speechwriting for government officials	$200	$40	$96	$4,550	$1,015	$2,755	$200/run min	$110/run min	$155/run min

	PER HOUR			PER PROJECT			OTHER		
	HIGH	LOW	AVG	HIGH	LOW	AVG	HIGH	LOW	AVG
Speechwriting for political campaigns	$155	$65	$101	n/a	n/a	n/a	$200/run min	$100/run min	$162/run min

LITERARY AGENTS

///

The literary agencies listed in this section are open to new clients and are members of the Association of Authors' Representatives (AAR), which means they do not charge for reading, critiquing, or editing. Some agents in this section may charge clients for office expenses such as photocopying, foreign postage, long-distance phone calls, or express mail services. Make sure you have a clear understanding of what these expenses are before signing any agency agreement.

FOR MORE..

The *2018 Guide to Literary Agents* (Writer's Digest Books) offers more than 800 literary agents, as well as information on writers' conferences. It also offers a wealth of information on the author/agent relationship and other related topics.

SUBHEADS

Each listing is broken down into subheads to make locating specific information easier. In the first section, you'll find contact information for each agency. Further information is provided which indicates an agency's size, its willingness to work with a new or previously unpublished writer, and its general areas of interest.

DOMINICK ABEL LITERARY AGENCY, INC.

146 W. 82nd St., #1A, New York NY 10024. (212)877-0710. **E-mail:** agency@dalainc.com. **Website:** dalainc.com. **Contact:** Dominick Abel. Estab. 1975. Member of AAR. Represents 50 clients.

REPRESENTS Fiction, novels. **Considers these nonfiction areas:** business, true crime. **Considers these fiction areas:** action, adventure, crime, detective, mystery, police.

HOW TO CONTACT Query via e-mail. No attachments. "If you wish to submit fiction, describe what you have written and what market you are targeting (you may find it useful to compare your work to that of an established author). Include a synopsis of the novel and the first two or three chapters. If you wish to submit nonfiction, you should, in addition, detail your qualifications for writing this particular book. Identify the audience for your book and explain how your book will be different from and better than already published works aimed at the same market." Accepts simultaneous submissions. Responds in 2-3 weeks.

ADAMS LITERARY

7845 Colony Rd., C4 #215, Charlotte NC 28226. (704)542-1440. **Fax:** (704)542-1450. **E-mail:** info@adamsliterary.com. **Website:** www.adamsliterary.com. **Contact:** Tracey Adams, Josh Adams. Estab. 2004. Member of AAR. Other memberships include SCBWI and WNBA.

MEMBER AGENTS Tracey Adams, Josh Adams, Lorin Oberweger.

REPRESENTS **Considers these fiction areas:** middle grade, picture books, young adult.

➥ Represents "the finest children's book and young adult authors and artists."

HOW TO CONTACT **Submit through online form on website only.** Send e-mail if that is not operating correctly. All submissions and queries should first be made through the online form on website. Will not review—and will promptly recycle—any unsolicited submissions or queries received by mail. Before submitting work for consideration, review complete guidelines online, as the agency sometimes shuts off to new submissions. Accepts simultaneous submissions. Responds in 6 weeks if interested. "While we have an established client list, we do seek new talent—and we accept submissions from both published and aspiring authors and artists."

TERMS Agent receives 15% commission on domestic sales; 20% on foreign sales. Offers written contract.
TIPS "Guidelines are posted (and frequently updated) on our website."

BETSY AMSTER LITERARY ENTERPRISES

6312 SW Capitol Hwy. #503, Portland OR 97239. **E-mail:** b.amster.assistant@gmail.com (for adult titles), b.amster.kidsbooks@gmail.com (for children's and young adult). **Website:** www.amsterlit.com. **Contact:** Betsy Amster (adult), Mary Cummings (children's and young adult). Estab. 1992. Member of AAR. Represents more than 65 clients.

REPRESENTS Nonfiction, novels, juvenile books. **Considers these nonfiction areas:** autobiography, business, cooking, creative nonfiction, cultural interests, decorating, design, foods, gardening, health, history, horticulture, how-to, interior design, investigative, medicine, memoirs, money, multicultural, parenting, popular culture, psychology, self-help, sociology, women's issues. **Considers these fiction areas:** crime, detective, family saga, juvenile, literary, middle grade, multicultural, mystery, picture books, police, suspense, thriller, women's, young adult.

➥ "Actively seeking strong narrative nonfiction, particularly by journalists; outstanding literary fiction (the next Jennifer Haigh or Jess Walter); witty, intelligent commerical women's fiction (the next Elinor Lipman); mysteries and thrillers that open new worlds to us; high-profile self-help and psychology, preferably research-based; and cookbooks and food narratives by West Coast–based chefs and food writers with an original viewpoint and national exposure." Also actively seeking picture books and middle-grade novels. Does not want to receive poetry, romances, western, science fiction, action/adventure, screenplays, fantasy, techno-thrillers, spy capers, apocalyptic scenarios, or political or religious arguments.

HOW TO CONTACT "For fiction or memoirs, please embed the first three pages in the body of your e-mail. For nonfiction, please embed the overview of your proposal." For children's and young adult, see submission requirements online. "For picture books, please embed the entire text in the body of your e-mail. For novels, please embed the first three pages." Accepts simultaneous submissions. Responds in 1 month to queries. Responds in 2 months to mss. Obtains most new clients through recommendations from others, solicitations, and conferences.

TERMS Agent receives 15% commission on domestic sales. Agent receives 20% commission on foreign sales. Offers written contract, binding for 1 year; three-month notice must be given to terminate contract. Charges for photocopying, postage, messengers, galleys/books used in submissions to foreign and film agents and to magazines for first serial rights. (Please note that it is rare to incur much in the way of expenses now that most submissions are made by e-mail.)

APONTE LITERARY AGENCY

E-mail: agents@aponteliterary.com. **Website:** aponteliterary.com. **Contact:** Natalia Aponte. Member of AAR. Signatory of WGA.

MEMBER AGENTS Natalia Aponte (any genre of mainstream fiction and nonfiction, but she is especially seeking women's novels, historical novels, supernatural and paranormal fiction, fantasy novels, political and science thrillers); Victoria Lea (any category, especially interested in women's fiction, science fiction and speculative fiction).

REPRESENTS Novels. **Considers these fiction areas:** fantasy, historical, paranormal, science fiction, supernatural, thriller, women's.

☛ Actively seeking women's novels, historical novels, supernatural and paranormal fiction, fantasy novels, political and science thrillers, science fiction and speculative fiction. In nonfiction, will look at any genre with commercial potential.

HOW TO CONTACT E-query. Accepts simultaneous submissions. Responds in 6 weeks if interested.

THE AXELROD AGENCY

55 Main St., P.O. Box 357, Chatham NY 12037. (518)392-2100. **E-mail:** steve@axelrodagency.com. **Website:** www.axelrodagency.com. **Contact:** Steven Axelrod. Member of AAR. Represents 15-20 clients.

MEMBER AGENTS Steven Axelrod, representation; Lori Antonson, subsidiary rights.

REPRESENTS Novels. **Considers these fiction areas:** crime, mystery, new adult, romance, women's.

☛ Specializes in women's fiction and romance.

HOW TO CONTACT Query via e-mail. Accepts simultaneous submissions. Obtains most new clients through recommendations from others.

TERMS Agent receives 15% commission on domestic sales; 20% commission on foreign sales. No written contract.

BARONE LITERARY AGENCY

385 North St., Batavia OH 45103. (513)732-6740. **Fax:** (513)297-7208. **E-mail:** baroneliteraryagency@roadrunner.com. **Website:** www.baroneliteraryagency.com. **Contact:** Denise Barone. Estab. 2010. Member of AAR and RWA. Signatory of WGA. Represents 10 clients.

REPRESENTS Nonfiction, novels. **Considers these nonfiction areas:** memoirs, theater, young adult. **Considers these fiction areas:** action, adventure, cartoon, comic books, commercial, confession, contemporary issues, crime, detective, erotica, ethnic, experimental, family saga, fantasy, feminist, frontier, gay, glitz, hi-lo, historical, horror, humor, inspirational, juvenile, lesbian, literary, mainstream, metaphysical, military, multicultural, multimedia, mystery, new adult, New Age, occult, paranormal, plays, police, psychic, regional, religious, romance, satire, science fiction, short story collections, spiritual, sports, supernatural, suspense, thriller, translation, urban fantasy, war, westerns, women's, young adult.

☛ Actively seeking adult contemporary romance. Does not want textbooks.

HOW TO CONTACT "We are no longer accepting snail mail submissions; send a query letter via e-mail instead. If I like your query letter, I will ask for the first three chapters and a synopsis as attachments." Accepts simultaneous submissions. "I make every effort to respond within 4 weeks." Obtains new clients by queries/submissions via e-mail only.

TERMS 15% commission on domestic sales, 20% on foreign sales. Offers written contract.

TIPS "The best writing advice I ever got came from a fellow writer, who wrote, 'Learn how to edit yourself,' when signing her book to me."

THE BENT AGENCY

E-mail: info@thebentagency.com. **Website:** www.thebentagency.com. **Contact:** Jenny Bent, Susan Hawk, Molly Ker Hawn, Gemma Cooper, Louise Fury, Brooks Sherman, Beth Phelan, Victoria Lowes, Heather Flaherty. Estab. 2009. Member of AAR.

MEMBER AGENTS Jenny Bent (adult fiction, including women's fiction, romance, and crime/suspense; she particularly likes novels with magical or fantasy elements that fall outside of genre fiction;

young adult and middle-grade fiction; memoir; humor); Susan Hawk (children's books exclusively, from picture books to young adult, including contemporary, mystery, fantasy, science fiction, historical fiction, and humor); Molly Ker Hawn (young adult and middle-grade books, including contemporary, historical, fantasy, science fiction, thrillers, and mystery); Gemma Cooper (all ages of children's and young adult books, including picture books; likes historical, contemporary, thrillers, mystery, humor, and science fiction); Louise Fury (children's fiction: picture books, literary middle-grade, and all young adult; adult fiction: speculative fiction, suspense/thriller, commercial fiction, and all subgenres of romance including erotic; nonfiction: cookbooks and pop culture); Brooks Sherman (speculative and literary adult fiction, select narrative nonfiction; all ages of children's and young adult books, including picture books; likes historical, contemporary, thrillers, humor, fantasy, and horror); Beth Phelan (young adult, thrillers, suspense and mystery, romance and women's fiction, literary and general fiction, cookbooks, lifestyle, and pets/animals); Victoria Lowes (romance and women's fiction, thrillers and mystery, and young adult); Heather Flaherty (young adult and middle-grade fiction: all genres; select adult fiction: upmarket fiction, women's fiction, and female-centric thrillers; select nonfiction: pop culture, humorous, and social media-based projects, as well as teen memoir).

REPRESENTS Nonfiction, novels, short story collections, juvenile books. **Considers these nonfiction areas:** animals, cooking, creative nonfiction, foods, juvenile nonfiction, popular culture, women's issues, young adult. **Considers these fiction areas:** adventure, commercial, crime, erotica, fantasy, feminist, historical, horror, humor, juvenile, literary, mainstream, middle grade, multicultural, mystery, new adult, picture books, romance, short story collections, suspense, thriller, women's, young adult.

HOW TO CONTACT For Jenny Bent, e-mail queries@thebentagency.com; for Susan Hawk, e-mail kidsqueries@thebentagency.com; for Molly Ker Hawn, e-mail hawnqueries@thebentagency.com; for Gemma Cooper, e-mail cooperqueries@thebentagency.com; for Louise Fury, e-mail furyqueries@thebentagency.com; for Brooks Sherman, e-mail shermanqueries@thebentagency.com; for Beth Phelan, e-mail phelanagencies@thebentagency.com; for Victoria Lowes, e-mail lowesqueries@thebentagency.com; for Heather

Flaherty, e-mail flahertyqueries@thebentagency.com. "Tell us briefly who you are, what your book is, and why you're the one to write it. Then include the first 10 pages of your material in the body of your e-mail. We respond to all queries; please resend your query if you haven't had a response within 4 weeks." Accepts simultaneous submissions.

VICKY BIJUR LITERARY AGENCY

27 W. 20th St., Suite 1003, New York NY 10011. **E-mail:** queries@vickybijuragency.com. **Website:** www.vickybijuragency.com. Estab. 1988. Member of AAR.
MEMBER AGENTS Vicky Bijur; Alexandra Franklin.
REPRESENTS Nonfiction, novels. **Considers these nonfiction areas:** memoirs. **Considers these fiction areas:** commercial, literary, mystery, new adult, thriller, women's, young adult, campus novels, coming-of-age.

⌐ "We are not the right agency for screenplays, picture books, poetry, self-help, science fiction, fantasy, horror, or romance."

HOW TO CONTACT "Please send a query letter of no more than 3 paragraphs on what makes your book special and unique, a very brief synopsis, its length and genre, and your biographical information, along with the first 10 pages of your manuscript. Please let us know in your query letter if it is a multiple submission, and kindly keep us informed of other agents' interest and offers of representation. If sending electronically, paste the pages in an e-mail as we don't open attachments from unfamiliar senders. If sending by hard copy, please include an SASE for our response. If you want your material returned, include an SASE large enough to contain pages and enough postage to send back to you." Accepts simultaneous submissions. "We generally respond to all queries within 8 weeks of receipt."

DAVID BLACK LITERARY AGENCY

335 Adams St., Suite 2707, Brooklyn NY 11201. (718)852-5500. **Fax:** (718)852-5539. **Website:** www.davidblackagency.com. **Contact:** David Black, owner. Member of AAR. Represents 150 clients.
MEMBER AGENTS David Black; Jenny Herrera; Gary Morris; Joy E. Tutela (narrative nonfiction, memoir, history, politics, self-help, investment, business, science, women's issues, GLBT issues, parenting, health and fitness, humor, craft, cooking and wine, lifestyle and entertainment, commercial fiction, lit-

erary fiction, MG, YA); Susan Raihofer (commercial fiction and nonfiction, memoir, pop culture, music, inspirational, thrillers, literary fiction); Sarah Smith (memoir, biography, food, music, narrative history, social studies, literary fiction).

REPRESENTS Nonfiction, novels. **Considers these nonfiction areas:** biography, business, cooking, crafts, gay/lesbian, health, history, humor, inspirational, memoirs, music, parenting, popular culture, politics, science, self-help, sociology, sports, women's issues. **Considers these fiction areas:** commercial, literary, middle grade, thriller, young adult.

HOW TO CONTACT "To query an individual agent, please follow the specific query guidelines outlined in the agent's profile on our website. Not all agents are currently accepting unsolicited queries. To query the agency, please send a 1-2 page query letter describing your book, and include information about any previously published works, your audience, and your platform." Do not e-mail your query unless an agent specifically asks for an e-mail. Accepts simultaneous submissions. Responds in 2 months to queries.

BOOK CENTS LITERARY AGENCY, LLC

364 Patteson Dr., #228, Morgantown WV 26505. **E-mail:** cw@bookcentsliteraryagency.com. **Website:** www.bookcentsliteraryagency.com. **Contact:** Christine Witthohn. Estab. 2005. Member of AAR, RWA, MWA, SinC, KOD.

REPRESENTS Novels, juvenile books. **Considers these nonfiction areas:** cooking, gardening, travel, women's issues. **Considers these fiction areas:** commercial, literary, mainstream, multicultural, mystery, new adult, paranormal, romance, suspense, thriller, urban fantasy, women's, young adult.

➣   Actively seeking upmarket fiction, commercial fiction (particularly if it has crossover appeal), women's fiction (emotional and layered), romance (single title or category), mainstream mystery/suspense, thrillers (particularly psychological), and young adult. For detailed list, visit the website. Does not want to receive third party submissions, previously published titles, short stories/novellas, erotica, inspirational, historical, science fiction/fantasy, horror/pulp/slasher thrillers, middle-grade, children's picture books, or poetry. Doesn't want stories with priests/nuns, religion, abuse of children/animals/elderly, rape, or serial killers.

HOW TO CONTACT Submit via form on website. Does not accept mail or e-mail submissions. Accepts simultaneous submissions.

BOOKENDS LITERARY AGENCY

Website: www.bookendsliterary.com. **Contact:** Jessica Faust, Kim Lionetti, Jessica Alvarez, Moe Ferrara, Tracy Marchini, Beth Campbell. Estab. 1999. Member of AAR. RWA, MWA, SCBWI Represents 50+ clients.

MEMBER AGENTS Jessica Faust (women's fiction, mysteries, thrillers, suspense, young adult), Kim Lionetti (romance, women's fiction, young adult), Jessica Alvarez (romance, women's fiction, erotica, romantic suspense), Beth Campbell (fantasy, science fiction, young adult, suspense, romantic suspense, and mystery), Moe Ferrara (middle-grade, young adult, and adult: romance, science fiction, fantasy, horror), Tracy Marchini (picture book, middle-grade, and young adult: fiction and nonfiction).

REPRESENTS Nonfiction, novels, juvenile books. **Considers these nonfiction areas:** art, business, creative nonfiction, ethnic, how-to, inspirational, juvenile nonfiction, money, self-help, women's issues, young adult, picture book, middle grade. **Considers these fiction areas:** adventure, crime, detective, erotica, fantasy, gay, historical, horror, juvenile, lesbian, mainstream, middle grade, multicultural, mystery, paranormal, picture books, police, romance, science fiction, supernatural, suspense, thriller, urban fantasy, women's, young adult.

➣   "BookEnds is currently accepting queries from published and unpublished writers in the areas of romance, mystery, suspense, science fiction and fantasy, horror, women's fiction, picture books, middle-grade, and young adult. In nonfiction we represent titles in the following areas: current affairs, reference, business and career, parenting, pop culture, coloring books, general nonfiction, and nonfiction for children and teens." BookEnds does not represent short fiction, poetry, screenplays, or techno-thrillers.

HOW TO CONTACT Visit website for the most up-to-date guidelines and current preferences. BookEnds agents accept all submissions through their personal Query Manager forms. These forms are accessible on the agency website under Submissions. Accepts simultaneous submissions. "Our response time goals are 6 weeks for queries and 12 weeks on requested partials and fulls."

THE BOOK GROUP

20 W. 20th St., Suite 601, New York NY 10011. (212)803-3360. **E-mail:** submissions@thebookgroup. com. **Website:** www.thebookgroup.com. Estab. 2015. Member of AAR. Signatory of WGA.

MEMBER AGENTS Julie Barer; Faye Bender; Brettne Bloom (fiction: literary and commercial fiction, select young adult; nonfiction, including cookbooks, lifestyle, investigative journalism, history, biography, memoir, and psychology); Elisabeth Weed (upmarket fiction, especially plot-driven novels with a sense of place); Rebecca Stead (innovative forms, diverse voices, and open-hearted fiction for children, young adults, and adults); Dana Murphy (story-driven fiction with a strong sense of place, narrative nonfiction/essays with a pop-culture lean, and YA with an honest voice).

REPRESENTS Considers these nonfiction areas: biography, cooking, history, investigative, memoirs, psychology. **Considers these fiction areas:** commercial, literary, mainstream, women's, young adult.

☛ Please do not send poetry or screenplays.

HOW TO CONTACT Send a query letter and 10 sample pages to submissions@thebookgroup.com, with the first and last name of the agent you are querying in the subject line. All material must be in the body of the e-mail, as the agents do not open attachments. "If we are interested in reading more, we will get in touch with you as soon as possible." Accepts simultaneous submissions.

BRADFORD LITERARY AGENCY

5694 Mission Center Rd., #347, San Diego CA 92108. (619)521-1201. **E-mail:** queries@bradfordlit.com. **Website:** www.bradfordlit.com. **Contact:** Laura Bradford, Natalie Lakosil, Sarah LaPolla, Monica Odom. Estab. 2001. Member of AAR. RWA, SCBWI, ALA Represents 130 clients.

MEMBER AGENTS Laura Bradford (romance [historical, romantic suspense, paranormal, category, contemporary, erotic], mystery, women's fiction, thrillers/suspense, middle grade & YA); Natalie Lakosil (children's literature [from picture book through teen and New Adult], romance [contemporary and historical], cozy mystery/crime, upmarket women's/ general fiction and select children's nonfiction); Sarah LaPolla (YA, middle grade, literary fiction, science fiction, magical realism, dark/psychological mystery, literary horror, and upmarket contemporary fiction);

Monica Odom (nonfiction by authors with demonstrable platforms in the areas of: pop culture, illustrated/graphic design, food and cooking, humor, history and social issues; narrative nonfiction, memoir, literary fiction, upmarket commercial fiction, compelling speculative fiction and magic realism, historical fiction, alternative histories, dark and edgy fiction, literary psychological thrillers, and illustrated/ picture books).

REPRESENTS Nonfiction, fiction, novels, juvenile books. **Considers these nonfiction areas:** biography, cooking, creative nonfiction, cultural interests, foods, history, humor, juvenile nonfiction, memoirs, parenting, popular culture, politics, self-help, women's issues, women's studies, young adult. **Considers these fiction areas:** commercial, crime, ethnic, gay, historical, juvenile, lesbian, literary, mainstream, middle grade, multicultural, mystery, new adult, paranormal, picture books, romance, science fiction, thriller, women's, young adult.

☛ Laura Bradford does not want to receive poetry, screenplays, short stories, westerns, horror, new age, religion, crafts, cookbooks, gift books. Natalie Lakosil does not want to receive inspirational novels, memoir, romantic suspense, adult thrillers, poetry, screenplays. Sarah LaPolla does not want to receive nonfiction, picture books, inspirational/spiritual novels, romance, or erotica. Monica Odom does not want to receive genre romance, erotica, military, poetry, or inspirational/spiritual works.

HOW TO CONTACT Accepts e-mail queries only; For submissions to Laura Bradford or Natalie Lakosil, send to queries@bradfordlit.com. For submissions to Sarah LaPolla, send to sarah@bradfordlit.com. For submissions to Monica Odom, send to Monica@bradfordlit.com. The entire submission must appear in the body of the e-mail and not as an attachment. The subject line should begin as follows: "QUERY: (the title of the ms or any short message that is important should follow)." For fiction: e-mail a query letter along with the first chapter of ms and a synopsis. Include the genre and word count in your query letter. Nonfiction: e-mail full nonfiction proposal including a query letter and a sample chapter. Accepts simultaneous submissions. Responds in 4 weeks to queries; 10 weeks to mss. Obtains most new clients through queries.

TERMS Agent receives 15% commission on domestic sales; 25% commission on foreign sales. Offers written contract. Charges for extra copies of books for foreign submissions.

BRANDT & HOCHMAN LITERARY AGENTS, INC.

1501 Broadway, Suite 2310, New York NY 10036. (212)840-5760. **Fax:** (212)840-5776. **Website:** brandthochman.com. **Contact:** Gail Hochman. Member of AAR. Represents 200 clients.

MEMBER AGENTS Gail Hochman (works of literary fiction, idea-driven nonfiction, literary memoir and children's books); Marianne Merola (fiction, nonfiction and children's books with strong and unique narrative voices); Bill Contardi (voice-driven young adult and middle grade fiction, commercial thrillers, psychological suspense, quirky mysteries, high fantasy, commercial fiction and memoir); Emily Forland (voice-driven literary fiction and nonfiction, memoir, narrative nonfiction, history, biography, food writing, cultural criticism, graphic novels, and young adult fiction); Emma Patterson (fiction from dark, literary novels to upmarket women's and historical fiction; narrative nonfiction that includes memoir, investigative journalism, and popular history; young adult fiction); Jody Kahn (literary and upmarket fiction; narrative nonfiction, particularly books related to sports, food, history, science and pop culture—including cookbooks, and literary memoir and journalism); Henry Thayer (nonfiction on a wide variety of subjects and fiction that inclines toward the literary). The e-mail addresses and specific likes of each of these agents is listed on the agency website.

REPRESENTS Nonfiction, novels. **Considers these nonfiction areas:** biography, cooking, current affairs, foods, health, history, memoirs, music, popular culture, science, sports, narrative nonfiction, journalism. **Considers these fiction areas:** fantasy, historical, literary, middle grade, mystery, suspense, thriller, women's, young adult.

☛ No screenplays or textbooks.

HOW TO CONTACT "We accept queries by e-mail and regular mail; however, we cannot guarantee a response to e-mailed queries. For queries via regular mail, be sure to include a SASE for our reply. Query letters should be no more than 2 pages and should include a convincing overview of the book project and information about the author and his or her writing

credits. Address queries to the specific Brandt & Hochman agent whom you would like to consider your work. Agent e-mail addresses and query preferences may be found at the end of each agent profile on the 'Agents' page of our website." Accepts simultaneous submissions. Obtains most new clients through recommendations from others.

TERMS Agent receives 15% commission on domestic sales; 20% commission on foreign sales.

TIPS "Write a letter which will give the agent a sense of you as a professional writer—your long-term interests as well as a short description of the work at hand."

THE BRATTLE AGENCY

P.O. Box 380537, Cambridge MA 02238. (617)721-5375. **E-mail:** christopher.vyce@thebrattleagency.com; submissions@thebrattleagency.com. **Website:** thebrattleagency.com. **Contact:** Christopher Vyce. Member of AAR. Signatory of WGA.

REPRESENTS Nonfiction, fiction. **Considers these nonfiction areas:** art, cultural interests, history, politics, sports, race studies, American studies. **Considers these fiction areas:** literary, graphic novels.

HOW TO CONTACT Query by e-mail. Include cover letter, brief synopsis, brief CV. Accepts simultaneous submissions. Responds to queries in 72 hours. Responds to approved submissions in 6-8 weeks.

BARBARA BRAUN ASSOCIATES, INC.

7 E. 14th St., #19F, New York NY 10003. **Fax:** (212)604-9023. **E-mail:** bbasubmissions@gmail.com. **Website:** www.barbarabraunagency.com. **Contact:** Barbara Braun. Member of AAR, Authors Guild, PEN Center USA.

REPRESENTS Nonfiction, novels. **Considers these nonfiction areas:** architecture, art, biography, design, film, history, photography, politics, psychology, women's issues, social issues, cultural criticism, fashion, narrative nonfiction. **Considers these fiction areas:** commercial, historical, literary, multicultural, mystery, thriller, women's, young adult, Art-related fiction.

☛ "Our fiction is strong on stories for women, art-related fiction, historical and multicultural stories, and to a lesser extent mysteries and thrillers. We are interested in narrative nonfiction and current affairs books by journalists, as well as YA literature." Does not represent poetry, science fiction, fantasy, horror, or screenplays.

HOW TO CONTACT "We no longer accept submissions by regular mail. Please send all queries via e-mail, marked 'Query' in the subject line. Your query should include: a brief summary of your book, word count, genre, any relevant publishing experience, and the first 5 pages of your manuscript pasted into the body of the e-mail. (No attachments—we will not open these.)" Accepts simultaneous submissions.

TERMS Agent receives 15% commission on domestic sales; 20% commission on foreign sales. No reading fees.

TIPS "Our clients' books are represented throughout Europe, Asia, and Latin America by various subagents. We are also active in selling motion picture rights to the books we represent, and work with various Hollywood agencies."

CURTIS BROWN, LTD.

10 Astor Place, New York NY 10003. (212)473-5400. **Fax:** (212)598-0917. **Website:** www.curtisbrown.com. **Contact:** Ginger Knowlton. Member of AAR. Signatory of WGA.

MEMBER AGENTS Noah Ballard (literary debuts, upmarket thrillers and narrative nonfiction, and he is always on the look-out for honest and provocative new writers); Ginger Clark (science fiction, fantasy, paranormal romance, literary horror, and young adult and middle grade fiction); Kerry D'Agostino (a wide range of literary and commercial fiction, as well as narrative nonfiction and memoir); Katherine Fausset (literary fiction, upmarket commercial fiction, journalism, memoir, popular science, and narrative nonfiction); Holly Frederick; Peter Ginsberg, president; Elizabeth Harding, vice president (represents authors and illustrators of juvenile, middle-grade and young adult fiction); Steve Kasdin (commercial fiction, including mysteries/thrillers, romantic suspense—emphasis on the suspense, and historical fiction; narrative nonfiction, including biography, history and current affairs; and young adult fiction, particularly if it has adult crossover appeal; not interested in SF/fantasy, memoirs, vampires and writers trying to capitalize on trends); Ginger Knowlton, executive vice president (authors and illustrators of children's books in all genres); Timothy Knowlton, CEO; Jonathan Lyons (biographies, history, science, pop culture, sports, general narrative nonfiction, mysteries, thrillers, science fiction and fantasy, and young adult fiction); Laura Blake Peterson, vice president (memoir and biog-

raphy, natural history, literary fiction, mystery, suspense, women's fiction, health and fitness, children's and young adult, faith issues and popular culture); Maureen Walters, senior vice president (working primarily in women's fiction and nonfiction projects on subjects as eclectic as parenting & child care, popular psychology, inspirational/motivational volumes as well as a few medical/nutritional books); Mitchell Waters (literary and commercial fiction and nonfiction, including mystery, history, biography, memoir, young adult, cookbooks, self-help and popular culture); Monika Woods.

REPRESENTS Nonfiction, novels. **Considers these nonfiction areas:** biography, computers, cooking, current affairs, ethnic, health, history, humor, memoirs, popular culture, psychology, science, self-help, spirituality, sports. **Considers these fiction areas:** fantasy, horror, humor, juvenile, literary, mainstream, middle grade, mystery, paranormal, picture books, religious, romance, spiritual, sports, suspense, thriller, women's, young adult.

HOW TO CONTACT Please refer to the "Agents" page on the website for each agent's submission guidelines. Accepts simultaneous submissions. Responds in 3 weeks to queries; 5 weeks to mss. Obtains most new clients through recommendations from others, solicitations, conferences.

TERMS Agent receives 15% commission on domestic sales; 20% on foreign sales. Offers written contract. 75-day notice must be given to terminate contract. Charges for some postage (overseas, etc.).

BROWNE & MILLER LITERARY ASSOCIATES

52 Village Place, Hinsdale IL 60521. (312)922-3063. **E-mail:** mail@browneandmiller.com. **Website:** www.browneandmiller.com. **Contact:** Danielle Egan-Miller, president. Estab. 1971. Member of AAR, RWA, MWA, Authors Guild.

REPRESENTS Nonfiction, novels. **Considers these fiction areas:** commercial, crime, detective, erotica, family saga, historical, inspirational, literary, mainstream, mystery, police, religious, romance, suspense, thriller, women's, Christian/inspirational fiction.

Browne & Miller is most interested in literary and commercial fiction, women's fiction, women's historical fiction, literary-leaning crime fiction, dark suspense/domestic suspense, romance of most subgenres including time travel, Christian/inspirational fiction by established

141

authors, and a wide range of platform-driven nonfiction by nationally-recognized author-experts. Does not want to receive young adult or middle-grade. "We do not represent picture books, horror, science fiction or fantasy, short stories, poetry, original screenplays, articles, or software."

HOW TO CONTACT Query via e-mail only; no attachments. Do not send unsolicited mss. Accepts simultaneous submissions.

ANDREA BROWN LITERARY AGENCY, INC.

E-mail: andrea@andreabrownlit.com; caryn@andreabrownlit.com; lauraqueries@gmail.com; jennifer@andreabrownlit.com; kelly@andreabrownlit.com; jennL@andreabrownlit.com; jamie@andreabrownlit.com; jmatt@andreabrownlit.com; kathleen@andreabrownlit.com; lara@andreabrownlit.com; soloway@andreabrownlit.com. **Website:** www.andreabrownlit.com. Member of AAR.

MEMBER AGENTS Andrea Brown (president); Laura Rennert (executive agent); Caryn Wiseman (senior agent); Jennifer Laughran (senior agent); Jennifer Rofé (senior agent); Kelly Sonnack (agent); Jamie Weiss Chilton (agent); Jennifer Mattson (agent); Kathleen Rushall (agent); Lara Perkins (associate agent, digital manager); Jennifer March Soloway (assistant agent).

REPRESENTS Nonfiction, fiction, juvenile books. **Considers these nonfiction areas:** juvenile nonfiction, young adult, narrative. **Considers these fiction areas:** juvenile, picture books, young adult, middle-grade, all juvenile genres.

☛ Specializes in all kinds of children's books—illustrators and authors. 98% juvenile books. Considers: nonfiction, fiction, picture books, young adult.

HOW TO CONTACT For picture books, submit a query letter and complete ms in the body of the email. For fiction, submit a query letter and the first 10 pages in the body of the email. For nonfiction, submit proposal, first 10 pages in the body of the email. Illustrators: submit a query letter and 2-3 illustration samples (in jpeg format), link to online portfolio, and text of picture book, if applicable. "We only accept queries via e-mail. No attachments, with the exception of jpeg illustrations from illustrators." Visit the agents' bios on our website and choose only *one* agent to whom you will submit your e-query. Send a short e-mail query letter to that agent with "QUERY" in the subject field. Accepts simultaneous submissions. "If we are interested in your work, we will certainly follow up by e-mail or by phone. However, if you haven't heard from us within 6 to 8 weeks, please assume that we are passing on your project." Obtains most new clients through referrals from editors, clients and agents. Check website for guidelines and information.

TERMS Agent receives 15% commission on domestic sales. Agent receives 25% commission on foreign sales. Offers written contract.

SHEREE BYKOFSKY ASSOCIATES, INC.

P.O. Box 706, Brigantine NJ 08203. **E-mail:** shereebee@aol.com. **Website:** www.shereebee.com. **Contact:** Sheree Bykofsky. Estab. 1991. Member of AAR. Author's Guild, Atlantic City Chamber of Commerce, PRC Council Represents 1,000+ clients.

MEMBER AGENTS Sheree Bykofsky, Janet Rosen.

REPRESENTS Nonfiction, novels, scholarly books. **Considers these nonfiction areas:** Americana, animals, anthropology, architecture, art, autobiography, biography, business, child guidance, cooking, crafts, creative nonfiction, cultural interests, current affairs, dance, decorating, diet/nutrition, design, economics, education, environment, ethnic, film, foods, gardening, gay/lesbian, government, health, history, hobbies, how-to, humor, inspirational, language, law, literature, medicine, memoirs, metaphysics, military, money, multicultural, music, New Age, parenting, philosophy, photography, popular culture, politics, psychology, recreation, regional, religious, science, self-help, sex, sociology, software, spirituality, sports, technology, theater, translation, travel, true crime, war, women's issues, creative nonfiction. **Considers these fiction areas:** commercial, contemporary issues, crime, detective, literary, mainstream, mystery, women's.

☛ This agency is seeking nonfiction, both prescriptive and narrative, and some fiction. Prescriptive nonfiction: primarily health and business. Narrative nonfiction: pop culture, biography, history, popular and social science, language, music, cities, medicine, fashion, military, and espionage. Fiction: women's commercial fiction (with a literary quality) and mysteries. Does not want to receive poetry, children's, screenplays, westerns, science fiction, or horror.

HOW TO CONTACT Query via e-mail to submit-bee@aol.com. "We only accept e-queries. We respond only to those queries in which we are interested. No attachments, snail mail, or phone calls, please. We do not open attachments." Fiction: one-page query, one-page synopsis, and first three pages of ms in body of the e-mail. Nonfiction: one-page query in the body of the e-mail. Accepts simultaneous submissions. Responds in 1 month to requested mss. Obtains most new clients through referrals but still reads all submissions closely.

TERMS Agent receives 15% commission on domestic sales. Agent receives 15% commission on foreign sales, plus international co-agent receives another 10%. Offers written contract, binding for 1 year. Charges for international postage.

KIMBERLEY CAMERON & ASSOCIATES

1550 Tiburon Blvd., #704, Tiburon CA 94920. (415)789-9191. **Website:** www.kimberleycameron.com. **Contact:** Kimberley Cameron. Member of AAR. Signatory of WGA.

MEMBER AGENTS Kimberley Cameron; Elizabeth Kracht (temporarily closed to submissions); Amy Cloughley (literary and upmarket fiction, women's, historical, narrative nonfiction, travel or adventure memoir); Mary C. Moore (fantasy, science fiction, upmarket "book club," genre romance, thrillers with female protagonists, and stories from marginalized voices); Lisa Abellera (currently closed to unsolicited submissions); Douglas Lee, douglas@kimberlycameron.com (only accepting submissions via conference and in-person meetings in the Bay Area).

REPRESENTS **Considers these nonfiction areas:** animals, environment, health, memoirs, science, spirituality, travel, true crime, narrative non-fiction. **Considers these fiction areas:** commercial, fantasy, historical, literary, mystery, romance, science fiction, thriller, women's, young adult, LGBTQ.

> "We are looking for a unique and heartfelt voice that conveys a universal truth."

HOW TO CONTACT Prefers queries via site. Only query one agent at a time. For fiction, fill out the correct submissions form for the individual agent and attach the first 50 pages and a synopsis (if requested) as a Word doc or PDF. For nonfiction, fill out the correct submission form of the individual agent and attach a full book proposal and sample chapters (includes the first chapter and no more than 50 pages) as a Word doc or PDF. Accepts simultaneous submissions. Obtains new clients through recommendations from others, solicitations.

CYNTHIA CANNELL LITERARY AGENCY

54 W. 40th St., New York NY 10018. (212)396-9595. **Website:** www.cannellagency.com. **Contact:** Cynthia Cannell. Estab. 1997. Member of AAR.

REPRESENTS Nonfiction, fiction. **Considers these nonfiction areas:** biography, current affairs, memoirs, self-help, spirituality.

> Does not represent screenplays, children's books, illustrated books, cookbooks, romance, category mystery, or science fiction.

HOW TO CONTACT "Please query us with an e-mail or letter. If querying by e-mail, send a brief description of your project with relevant biographical information including publishing credits (if any) to info@cannellagency.com. Do not send attachments. If querying by conventional mail, enclose an SASE." Responds if interested. Accepts simultaneous submissions.

CAPITAL TALENT AGENCY

1330 Connecticut Ave. NW, Suite 271, Washington DC 20036. (202)429-4785. **Fax:** (202)429-4786. **E-mail:** literary.submissions@capitaltalentagency.com. **Website:** capitaltalentagency.com/html/literary.shtml. **Contact:** Cynthia Kane. Estab. 2014. Member of AAR. Signatory of WGA.

MEMBER AGENTS Cynthia Kane; Roger Yoerges; Michelle Muntifering; J. Fred Shiffman.

REPRESENTS Nonfiction, fiction, movie scripts, stage plays.

HOW TO CONTACT "We accept submissions only by e-mail. We do not accept queries via postal mail or fax. For fiction and nonfiction submissions, send a query letter in the body of your e-mail. Please note that while we consider each query seriously, we are unable to respond to all of them. We endeavor to respond within 6 weeks to projects that interest us." Accepts simultaneous submissions.

MARIA CARVAINIS AGENCY, INC.

Rockefeller Center, 1270 Avenue of the Americas, Suite 2915, New York NY 10020. (212)245-6365. **Fax:** (212)245-7196. **E-mail:** mca@mariacarvainisagency.com. **Website:** www.mariacarvainisagency.com. Estab. 1977. Member of AAR. Authors Guild, Women's

Media Group, ABA, MWA, RWA Represents 75 clients.

MEMBER AGENTS Maria Carvainis, president/literary agent; Elizabeth Copps, associate agent.

REPRESENTS Nonfiction, novels. **Considers these nonfiction areas:** biography, business, history, memoirs, popular culture, psychology, science. **Considers these fiction areas:** action, adventure, commercial, contemporary issues, crime, family saga, historical, horror, humor, juvenile, literary, mainstream, middle grade, multicultural, mystery, romance, suspense, thriller, women's, young adult.

☞   The agency does not represent screenplays, children's picture books, science fiction, or poetry.

HOW TO CONTACT If you would like to query the agency, please send a query letter, a synopsis of the work, first 5-10 pages, and note of any writing credentials. Please e-mail queries to mca@mariacarvainisagency.com. All attachments must be either Word documents or PDF files. The agency also accepts queries by mail to Maria Carvainis Agency, Inc., Attention: Query Department. If you want the materials returned to you, please enclose a SASE. Otherwise, please be sure to include your e-mail address. There is no reading fee. Accepts simultaneous submissions. Responds to queries within 1 month. Obtains most new clients through recommendations from others, conferences, query letters.

TERMS Agent receives 15% commission on domestic sales. Agent receives 20% commission on foreign sales. Offers written contract. Charges clients for foreign postage.

CHALBERG & SUSSMAN

115 W. 29th St., Third Floor, New York NY 10001. (917)261-7550. **Website:** www.chalbergsussman.com. Member of AAR. Signatory of WGA.

MEMBER AGENTS Terra Chalberg; Rachel Sussman (narrative journalism, memoir, psychology, history, humor, pop culture, literary fiction); Nicole James (plot-driven fiction, psychological suspense, uplifting female-driven memoir, upmarket self-help, and lifestyle books); Lana Popovic (young adult, middle grade, contemporary realism, speculative fiction, fantasy, horror, sophisticated erotica, romance, select nonfiction, international stories).

REPRESENTS Nonfiction, fiction, novels. **Considers these nonfiction areas:** history, humor, memoirs, popular culture, psychology, self-help, narrative journalism. **Considers these fiction areas:** erotica, fantasy, horror, literary, middle grade, romance, science fiction, suspense, young adult, contemporary realism, speculative fiction.

HOW TO CONTACT To query by e-mail, please contact one of the following: terra@chalbergsussman.com, rachel@chalbergsussman.com, nicole@chalbergsussman.com, lana@chalbergsussman.com. To query by regular mail, please address your letter to one agent and include SASE. Accepts simultaneous submissions.

CK WEBBER ASSOCIATES

E-mail: carlie@ckwebber.com. **Website:** ckwebber.com. **Contact:** Carlisle Webber. Member of AAR. Signatory of WGA.

REPRESENTS Novels, juvenile books. **Considers these fiction areas:** action, adventure, commercial, contemporary issues, crime, detective, family saga, fantasy, feminist, horror, literary, mainstream, middle grade, mystery, new adult, romance, science fiction, suspense, thriller, westerns, women's, young adult.

☞   "We are currently not accepting nonfiction (including memoir), picture books, easy readers, early chapter books, poetry, scripts, novellas, or short story collections."

HOW TO CONTACT Accepts queries via e-mail only. To submit your work for consideration, please send a query letter, synopsis, and the first 30 pages or 3 chapters of your work, whichever is more, to carlie@ckwebber.com and put the word "query" in the subject line of your e-mail. Please include your materials in the body of your e-mail. Blank emails that include an attachment will be deleted unread. Accepts simultaneous submissions.

WM CLARK ASSOCIATES

186 Fifth Ave., Second Floor, New York NY 10010. (212)675-2784. **E-mail:** general@wmclark.com. **Website:** www.wmclark.com. **Contact:** William Clark. Estab. 1997. Member of AAR.

REPRESENTS Nonfiction, novels. **Considers these nonfiction areas:** architecture, art, autobiography, biography, cultural interests, current affairs, dance, design, ethnic, film, history, inspirational, memoirs, music, popular culture, politics, religious, science, sociology, technology, theater, translation, travel. **Considers these fiction areas: contemporary issues, ethnic, historical, literary, mainstream, young adult.

☛ William Clark represents a wide range of titles across all formats to the publishing, motion picture, television, and multimedia fields. Offering individual focus and a global reach, we move quickly and strategically on behalf of domestic and international clients ranging from authors of award-winning, best-selling narrative nonfiction, to authors in translation, chefs, musicians, and artists. The agency undertakes to discover, develop, and market today's most interesting content and the talent that creates it, and forge sophisticated and innovative plans for self-promotion, reliable revenue streams, and an enduring creative career. Agency does not represent screenplays or respond to screenplay pitches. "It is advised that before querying you become familiar with the kinds of books we handle by browsing our Book List, which is available on our website."

HOW TO CONTACT Accepts queries via online query form only. "We will endeavor to respond as soon as possible as to whether or not we'd like to see a proposal or sample chapters from your manuscript." Responds in 1-2 months to queries.

TERMS Agent receives 15% commission on domestic sales; 20% commission on foreign sales. Offers written contract.

TIPS "WCA works on a reciprocal basis with Ed Victor Ltd. (UK) in representing select properties to the US market and vice versa. Translation rights are sold directly in the German, Italian, Spanish, Portuguese, Latin American, French, Dutch, and Scandinavian territories in association with Andrew Nurnberg Associates Ltd. (UK); through offices in China, Bulgaria, Czech Republic, Latvia, Poland, Hungary, and Russia; and through corresponding agents in Japan, Greece, Israel, Turkey, Korea, Taiwan, and Thailand."

FRANCES COLLIN, LITERARY AGENT

P.O. Box 33, Wayne PA 19087-0033. **E-mail:** queries@francescollin.com. **Website:** www.francescollin.com. Estab. 1948. Member of AAR. Represents 50 clients.

MEMBER AGENTS Frances Collin; Sarah Yake.

REPRESENTS Nonfiction, fiction, novels. **Considers these nonfiction areas:** art, autobiography, biography, creative nonfiction, cultural interests, history, literature, memoirs, popular culture, science, sociology, travel, women's issues, women's studies. **Considers these fiction areas:** adventure, commercial, experimental, feminist, historical, juvenile, literary, middle grade, multicultural, science fiction, women's, young adult.

☛ Actively seeking authors who are invested in their unique visions and who want to set trends not chase them. "I'd like to think that my authors are unplagiarizable by virtue of their distinct voices and styles." Does not want previously self-published work. Query with new mss only, please.

HOW TO CONTACT "We ask that writers send a traditional query e-mail describing the project and copy and paste the first 5 pages of the manuscript into the body of the e-mail. We look forward to hearing from you at queries@francescollin.com. Please send queries to that e-mail address. Any queries sent to another e-mail address within the agency will be deleted unread." Accepts simultaneous submissions. Responds in 1-3 weeks for initial queries, longer for full mss.

DON CONGDON ASSOCIATES INC.

110 William St., Suite 2202, New York NY 10038. (212)645-1229. **Fax:** (212)727-2688. **E-mail:** dca@doncongdon.com. **Website:** doncongdon.com. Estab. 1983. Member of AAR.

MEMBER AGENTS Christina Concepcion (crime fiction, narrative nonfiction, political science, journalism, history, books on cities, classical music, biography, science for a popular audience, philosophy, food and wine, iconoclastic books on health and human relationships, essays, and arts criticism); Michael Congdon (commercial and literary fiction, suspense, mystery, thriller, history, military history, biography, memoir, current affairs, and narrative nonfiction [adventure, medicine, science, and nature]); Katie Grimm (literary fiction, historical, women's fiction, short story collections, graphic novels, mysteries, young adult, middle-grade, memoir, science, academic); Katie Kotchman (business [all areas], narrative nonfiction [particularly popular science and social/cultural issues], self-help, success, motivation, psychology, pop culture, women's fiction, realistic young adult, literary fiction, and psychological thrillers); Maura Kye-Casella (narrative nonfiction, cookbooks, women's fiction, young adult, self-help, and parenting); Susan Ramer (literary fiction, upmar-

ket commercial fiction [contemporary and historical], narrative nonfiction, social history, cultural history, smart pop culture [music, film, food, art], women's issues, psychology and mental health, and memoir).
REPRESENTS Nonfiction, novels, short story collections. **Considers these nonfiction areas:** art, biography, business, cooking, creative nonfiction, cultural interests, current affairs, film, foods, history, humor, literature, medicine, memoirs, military, multicultural, music, parenting, philosophy, popular culture, politics, psychology, science, self-help, sociology, sports, women's issues, young adult. **Considers these fiction areas:** crime, hi-lo, historical, literary, middle grade, mystery, short story collections, suspense, thriller, women's, young adult.

☛ Susan Ramer: "Not looking for romance, science fiction, fantasy, espionage, mysteries, politics, health/diet/fitness, self-help, or sports." Katie Kotchman: "Please do not send her screenplays or poetry."

HOW TO CONTACT "For queries via e-mail, you must include the word 'query' and the agent's full name in your subject heading. Please also include your query and sample chapter in the body of the e-mail, as we do not open attachments for security reasons. Please query only one agent within the agency at a time. If you are sending your query via regular mail, please enclose a SASE for our reply. If you would like us to return your materials, please make sure your postage will cover their return." Accepts simultaneous submissions.

CORVISIERO LITERARY AGENCY

275 Madison Ave., at 40th, 14th Floor, New York NY 10016. **E-mail:** query@corvisieroagency.com. **Website:** www.corvisieroagency.com. **Contact:** Marisa A. Corvisiero, senior agent and literary attorney. Member of AAR. Signatory of WGA.
MEMBER AGENTS Marisa A. Corvisiero, senior agent and literary attorney (contemporary romance, thrillers, adventure, paranormal, urban fantasy, science fiction, MG, YA, picture books, Christmas themes, time travel, space science fiction, nonfiction, self-help, science business); Saritza Hernandez, senior agent (all kinds of romance, GLBT, YA, erotica); Doreen Thistle (do not query); Cate Hart (YA, fantasy, magical realism, MG, mystery, fantasy, adventure, historical romance, LGBTQ, erotic, history, biography); Veronica Park (dark or edgy YA/NA, Com-

mercial adult, adult romance and romantic suspense, and funny and/or current/controversial nonfiction); Vanessa Robins (New Adult, human, YA, thrillers, romance, sci-fi, sports-centric plots, memoirs, cultural/ethnic/sexuality, humor, medical narratives); Kelly Peterson (MG, fantasy, paranormal, sci-fi, YA, steampunk, historical, dystopian, sword and sorcery, romance, historical romance, adult, fantasy, romance); Justin Wells; Kaitlyn Johnson.
REPRESENTS Nonfiction, fiction, novels. **Considers these nonfiction areas:** biography, business, history, medicine, memoirs, science, self-help, spirituality. **Considers these fiction areas:** adventure, erotica, fantasy, gay, historical, lesbian, middle grade, mystery, paranormal, picture books, romance, science fiction, suspense, thriller, urban fantasy, young adult, Magical realism, steampunk, dystopian, sword and sorcery.
HOW TO CONTACT Accepts submissions via e-mail only. Include 5 pages of complete and polished ms pasted into the body of an e-mail, and a 1-2 page synopsis. For nonfiction, include a proposal instead of the synopsis. Put "Query for [Agent]" in the e-mail subject line. Accepts simultaneous submissions.

CREATIVE MEDIA AGENCY, INC.

1745 Broadway, 17th Floor, New York NY 10019. (212)812-1494. **E-mail:** paige@cmalit.com. **Website:** www.cmalit.com. **Contact:** Paige Wheeler. Estab. 1997. Member of AAR, WMG, RWA, MWA, Authors Guild. Represents about 30 clients.
REPRESENTS Nonfiction, fiction, novels. **Considers these nonfiction areas:** biography, business, creative nonfiction, diet/nutrition, health, inspirational, memoirs, money, parenting, popular culture, self-help, travel, women's issues, prescriptive nonfiction, narrative nonfiction. **Considers these fiction areas:** commercial, crime, detective, historical, inspirational, mainstream, middle grade, mystery, new adult, romance, suspense, thriller, women's, young adult, general fiction.

☛ Fiction: All commercial and upscale (think book club) fiction, as well as women's fiction, romance (all types), mystery, thrillers, inspirational/Christian and psychological suspense. I enjoy both historical fiction as well as contemporary fiction, so do keep that in mind. I seem to be especially drawn to a story if it has a high concept and a fresh, unique voice. Nonfiction: I'm looking for both narrative nonfiction and prescriptive nonfiction. I'm looking for books where the author has a huge platform and something new to say in a particular area. Some of the areas that I like are lifestyle, relationship, parenting, business/entrepreneurship, food-subsistence-homesteading topics, popular/trendy reference projects and women's issues. I'd like books that would be a good fit on the *Today* show. Does not want to receive children's books, science fiction, fantasy, or academic nonfiction.

HOW TO CONTACT E-query. Write "query" in your e-mail subject line. For fiction, paste in the first 5 pages of the ms after the query. For nonfiction, paste in an extended author bio as well as the marketing section of your book proposal after the query. Accepts simultaneous submissions. Responds in 4-6 weeks.

RICHARD CURTIS ASSOCIATES, INC.

200 E. 72nd St., Suite 28J, New York NY 10021. (212)772-7363. **Fax:** (212)772-7393. **E-mail:** info@ curtisagency.com. **Website:** www.curtisagency.com. Member of AAR, RWA, MWA, ITW, SFWA. Represents 100 clients.
REPRESENTS Nonfiction, novels, juvenile books. **Considers these nonfiction areas:** biography, business, current affairs, dance, gay/lesbian, health, history, how-to, investigative, literature, military, music, politics, psychology, science, sports, theater, true crime, war, women's issues, young adult. **Considers these fiction areas:** commercial, fantasy, romance, science fiction, thriller, young adult.

> ☞ Actively seeking nonfiction (but no memoir), women's fiction (especially contemporary), thrillers, science fiction, middle-grade, and young adult.

HOW TO CONTACT Submit a query letter by mail (with SASE) or e-mail. Do not include sample material unless requested. Accepts simultaneous submissions.
TERMS Agent receives 15% commission on domestic sales. Agent receives 25% commission on foreign sales. Offers written contract. Charges for photocopying, express mail, international freight, book orders.

LAURA DAIL LITERARY AGENCY, INC.

350 Seventh Ave., Suite 2003, New York NY 10001. (212)239-7477. **E-mail:** ldail@ldlainc.com; queries@ ldlainc.com. **Website:** www.ldlainc.com. Member of AAR.

MEMBER AGENTS Laura Dail; Tamar Rydzinski; Elana Roth Parker.
REPRESENTS Nonfiction, fiction, novels, juvenile books. **Considers these nonfiction areas:** biography, cooking, creative nonfiction, current affairs, government, history, investigative, juvenile nonfiction, memoirs, multicultural, popular culture, politics, psychology, sociology, true crime, war, women's studies, young adult. **Considers these fiction areas:** commercial, crime, detective, fantasy, feminist, historical, juvenile, mainstream, middle grade, multicultural, mystery, thriller, women's, young adult.

> ☞ Specializes in women's fiction, literary fiction, young adult fiction, as well as both practical and idea-driven nonfiction. "Tamar is not interested in prescriptive or practical nonfiction, humor, coffee table books or children's books (meaning anything younger than middle grade). She is interested in everything else that is well-written and has great characters, including graphic novels." "Due to the volume of queries and mss received, we apologize for not answering every e-mail and letter. None of us handles children's picture books or chapter books. No New Age. We do not handle screenplays or poetry."

HOW TO CONTACT "If you would like, you may include a synopsis and no more than 10 pages. If you are mailing your query, please be sure to include a self-addressed, stamped envelope; without it, you may not hear back from us. To save money, time and trees, we prefer queries by e-mail to queries@ldlainc.com. We get a lot of spam and are wary of computer viruses, so please use the word 'Query' in the subject line and include your detailed materials in the body of your message, not as an attachment." Accepts simultaneous submissions. Responds in 2-4 weeks.

DANA NEWMAN LITERARY

9720 Wilshire Blvd., 5th Floor, Beverly Hills CA 90212. **E-mail:** dananewmanliterary@gmail.com. **Website:** dananewman.com. **Contact:** Dana Newman. Estab. 2009. Member of AAR, California State Bar. Represents 28 clients.
REPRESENTS Nonfiction, novels, short story collections. **Considers these nonfiction areas:** architecture, art, autobiography, biography, business, child guidance, cooking, creative nonfiction, cultural interests, current affairs, diet/nutrition, design, edu-

cation, ethnic, film, foods, gay/lesbian, government, health, history, how-to, inspirational, investigative, language, law, literature, medicine, memoirs, money, multicultural, music, New Age, parenting, popular culture, politics, psychology, science, self-help, sociology, sports, technology, theater, travel, true crime, women's issues, women's studies. **Considers these fiction areas:** commercial, contemporary issues, family saga, feminist, historical, literary, multicultural, sports, women's.

☛ Ms. Newman has a background as an attorney in contracts, licensing, and intellectual property law. She is experienced in digital content creation and distribution. "We are interested in practical nonfiction (business, health and wellness, psychology, parenting, technology) by authors with smart, unique perspectives and established platforms who are committed to actively marketing and promoting their books. We love compelling, inspiring narrative nonfiction in the areas of memoir, biography, history, pop culture, current affairs/women's interest, sports, and social trends. On the fiction side, we consider a very selective amount of literary fiction and women's upmarket fiction." Does not want religious, children's, poetry, horror, mystery, thriller, romance, or science fiction.

HOW TO CONTACT E-mail queries only. For both nonfiction and fiction, please submit a query letter including a description of your project and a brief biography. "If we are interested in your project, we will contact you and request a full book proposal (nonfiction) or a synopsis and the first 25 pages (fiction)." Accepts simultaneous submissions. "If we have requested your materials after receiving your query, we usually respond within 4 weeks." Obtains new clients through recommendations from others, queries, and submissions.

TERMS Obtains 15% commission on domestic sales; 20% on foreign sales. Offers 1 year written contract. Notice must be given 1 month prior to terminate a contract.

DARHANSOFF & VERRILL LITERARY AGENTS

133 W. 72nd St., Room 304, New York NY 10023. (917)305-1300. **E-mail:** submissions@dvagency.com. **Website:** www.dvagency.com. Member of AAR.

MEMBER AGENTS Liz Darhansoff; Chuck Verrill; Michele Mortimer; Eric Amling.

REPRESENTS Nonfiction, novels. **Considers these nonfiction areas:** creative nonfiction, juvenile nonfiction, memoirs, young adult. **Considers these fiction areas:** literary, middle grade, suspense, young adult.

HOW TO CONTACT Send queries via e-mail. Accepts simultaneous submissions.

LIZA DAWSON ASSOCIATES

350 Seventh Ave., Suite 2003, New York NY 10001. (212)465-9071. **E-mail:** querycaitie@lizadawsonassociates.com. **Website:** www.lizadawsonassociates.com. **Contact:** Caitie Flum. Member of AAR, MWA, Women's Media Group. Represents 50+ clients.

MEMBER AGENTS Liza Dawson, queryliza@lizadawsonassociates.com (plot-driven literary and popular fiction, historical, thrillers, suspense, history, psychology [both popular and clinical], politics, narrative nonfiction, and memoirs); Caitlin Blasdell, querycaitlin@lizadawsonassociates.com (science fiction, fantasy [both adult and young adult], parenting, business, thrillers, and women's fiction; Hannah Bowman, queryhannah@lizadawsonassociates.com (commercial fiction [especially science fiction and fantasy, young adult] and nonfiction in the areas of mathematics, science, and spirituality); Jennifer Johnson-Blalock, queryjennifer@lizadawsonassociates.com (nonfiction, particularly current events, social sciences, women's issues, law, business, history, the arts and pop culture, lifestyle, sports, and food; commercial and upmarket fiction, especially thrillers/mysteries, women's fiction, contemporary romance, young adult, and middle-grade); Caitie Flum, querycaitie@lizadawsonassociates.com (commercial fiction, especially historical, women's fiction, mysteries, crossover fantasy, young adult, and middle-grade; nonfiction in the areas of theater, current affairs, and pop culture).

REPRESENTS Nonfiction, novels. **Considers these nonfiction areas:** agriculture, Americana, animals, anthropology, archeology, architecture, art, autobiography, biography, business, computers, cooking, creative nonfiction, cultural interests, current affairs, environment, ethnic, film, gardening, gay/lesbian, history, humor, investigative, juvenile nonfiction, memoirs, multicultural, parenting, popular culture, politics, psychology, religious, science, sex, sociology, spirituality, theater, travel, true crime, women's issues, women's studies, young adult. **Considers these fiction areas:** action, adventure, commercial, contemporary issues, crime, detective, ethnic, family saga, fantasy, feminist, gay, historical, horror, humor, juvenile, lesbian, mainstream, middle grade, multicultural, mystery, new adult, police, romance, science fiction, supernatural, suspense, thriller, urban fantasy, women's, young adult.

☛ This agency specializes in readable literary fiction, thrillers, mainstream historicals, women's fiction, young adult, middle-grade, academics, historians, journalists, and psychology.

HOW TO CONTACT Query by e-mail only. No phone calls. Each of these agents has their own specific submission requirements, which you can find online at the agency's website. . Obtains most new clients through recommendations from others, conferences, and queries.

TERMS Agent receives 15% commission on domestic sales. Agent receives 20% commission on foreign sales. Offers written contract.

DEFIORE AND COMPANY

47 E. 19th St., 3rd Floor, New York NY 10003. (212) 925-7744. **E-mail:** submissions@defliterary.com. **Website:** www.defliterary.com. Member of AAR. Represents 40 clients.

MEMBER AGENTS Brian DeFiore; Meredith Kaffel; Laurie Abkemeier; Adam Schear; Ashley Collom; Matthew Elblonk; Caryn Karmatz Rudy; Rebecca Strauss; Lisa Gallagher; Nicole Tourtelot; Linda Kaplan; Miriam Altshuler; Reiko Davis; Gabrielle Piraino.

REPRESENTS Novels, short story collections. **Considers these nonfiction areas:** creative nonfiction, how-to, literature, memoirs, multicultural, parenting, psychology, self-help, spirituality, women's issues, young adult. **Considers these fiction areas:** commercial, family saga, historical, literary, middle grade, short story collections, women's, young adult.

☛ Adult literary and commercial fiction and general nonfiction, YA and middle grade fiction. Does not want adult mystery, romance, horror, sci-fi or fantasy, poetry, screenplays, westerns.

HOW TO CONTACT Please send an email to her at querymiriam@defliterary.com. Miriam only accepts email queries. Include the following: A brief description of your book, a brief, relevant bio, the first chapter pasted in the body of your email. Attachments will

not be opened. "I also really want to know what you feel the heart of your book is, in one or two sentences." Accepts simultaneous submissions. Obtains most new clients through recommendations from others.

TERMS Agent receives 15% commission on domestic sales; 20% commission on foreign sales. Charges clients for overseas mailing, photocopies, overnight mail when requested by author.

TIPS See the website for specific submission instructions.

JOELLE DELBOURGO ASSOCIATES, INC.

101 Park St., Montclair NJ 07042. (973)773-0836. **Fax:** (973)783-6802. **E-mail:** joelle@delbourgo.com; submissions@delbourgo.com. **Website:** www.delbourgo. com. Member of AAR. Represents 500+ clients.

MEMBER AGENTS Joelle Delbourgo; Jacqueline Flynn.

REPRESENTS Nonfiction, fiction, novels. **Considers these nonfiction areas:** Americana, animals, anthropology, archeology, autobiography, biography, business, child guidance, cooking, creative nonfiction, current affairs, dance, decorating, diet/nutrition, design, economics, education, environment, film, gardening, gay/lesbian, government, health, history, how-to, humor, inspirational, interior design, investigative, juvenile nonfiction, literature, medicine, memoirs, military, money, multicultural, music, parenting, philosophy, popular culture, politics, psychology, science, self-help, sex, sociology, spirituality, sports, translation, travel, true crime, war, women's issues, women's studies. **Considers these fiction areas:** adventure, commercial, contemporary issues, crime, detective, fantasy, feminist, juvenile, literary, mainstream, middle grade, military, mystery, new adult, New Age, romance, science fiction, thriller, urban fantasy, women's, young adult.

☛ "We are former publishers and editors with deep knowledge and an insider perspective. We have a reputation for individualized attention to clients, strategic management of authors' careers, and creating strong partnerships with publishers for our clients." Do not send scripts, picture books, poetry.

HOW TO CONTACT It's preferable if you submit via e-mail to a specific agent. Query 1 agent only. No attachments. Put the word "Query" in the subject line. "While we do our best to respond to each query, if you have not received a response in 60 days you may consider that a pass. Please do not send us copies of self-published books unless requested. Let us know if you are sending your query to us exclusively or if this is a multiple submission. For nonfiction, let us know if a proposal and sample chapters are available. If not, you should probably wait to send your query when you have a completed proposal. For fiction and memoir, embed the *first* 10 pages of manuscript into the e-mail after your query letter. Please no attachments. If we like your first pages, we may ask to see your synopsis and more manuscript. Please do not cold call us or make a follow-up call unless we call you." Accepts simultaneous submissions.

TERMS Agent receives 15% commission on domestic sales and 20% commission on foreign sales as well as television/film adaptation. Offers written contract. Charges clients for postage and photocopying.

TIPS "Do your homework. Do not cold call. Read and follow submission guidelines before contacting us. Do not call to find out if we received your material. No e-mail queries. Treat agents with respect, as you would any other professional, such as a doctor, lawyer or financial advisor."

SANDRA DIJKSTRA LITERARY AGENCY

1155 Camino del Mar, PMB 515, Del Mar CA 92014. **E-mail:** elise@dijkstraagency.com; queries@dijkstraagency.com. **Website:** www.dijkstraagency.com. Member of AAR, Authors Guild, Organization of American Historians, RWA. Represents 100+ clients.

MEMBER AGENTS President: Sandra Dijkstra (adult only). Acquiring Associate agents: Elise Capron (adult only); Jill Marr (adult only); Thao Le (adult and YA); Roz Foster (adult and YA); Jessica Watterson (subgenres of adult and new adult romance, and women's fiction); Suzy Evans (adult and YA); Jennifer Kim (adult and YA).

REPRESENTS Nonfiction, fiction, novels, short story collections, juvenile books, scholarly books. **Considers these nonfiction areas:** Americana, animals, anthropology, art, biography, business, creative nonfiction, cultural interests, current affairs, design, economics, environment, ethnic, gardening, government, health, history, juvenile nonfiction, literature, memoirs, multicultural, parenting, popular culture, politics, psychology, science, self-help, sports, true crime, women's issues, women's studies, young adult, narrative. **Considers these fiction areas:** commercial, contemporary issues, detective, family saga, fantasy, feminist, historical, horror, juvenile, literary, mainstream, middle grade, multicultural, mystery, new adult, romance, science fiction, short story collections, sports, suspense, thriller, urban fantasy, women's, young adult.

HOW TO CONTACT "Please see guidelines on our website, www.dijkstraagency.com. Please note that we only accept e-mail submissions. Due to the large number of unsolicited submissions we receive, we are only able to respond those submissions in which we are interested." Accepts simultaneous submissions. Responds to queries of interest within 6 weeks.

TERMS Works in conjunction with foreign and film agents. Agent receives 15% commission on domestic sales and 20% commission on foreign sales. Offers written contract. No reading fee.

TIPS "Remember that publishing is a business. Do your research and present your project in as professional a way as possible. Only submit your work when you are confident that it is polished and ready for prime-time. Make yourself a part of the active writing community by getting stories and articles published, networking with other writers, and getting a good sense of where your work fits in the market."

DONADIO & OLSON, INC.

40 West 27th St., 5th Floor, New York NY 10001. (212)691-8077. **Fax:** (212)633-2837. **E-mail:** neil@donadio.com; mail@donadio.com. **Website:** http://donadio.com. **Contact:** Neil Olson. Member of AAR.

MEMBER AGENTS Neil Olson (no queries); Edward Hibbert (no queries); Carrie Howland , carrie@donadio.com (adult literary fiction and narrative nonfiction as well as young adult, middle grade, and picture books).

REPRESENTS Nonfiction, novels. **Considers these nonfiction areas:** creative nonfiction. **Considers these fiction areas:** literary, middle grade, picture books, young adult.

☞   This agency represents mostly fiction, and is very selective.

HOW TO CONTACT "Please send a query letter and the first three chapters/first 25 pages of the manuscript to mail@donadio.com. Please allow a minimum of one month for a reply. Accepts simultaneous submissions.

DUNHAM LITERARY, INC.

110 William St., Suite 2202, New York NY 10038. (212)929-0994. **E-mail:** query@dunhamlit.com. **Web-**

site: www.dunhamlit.com. **Contact:** Jennie Dunham. Estab. 2000. Member of AAR, SCBWI. Represents 50 clients.

MEMBER AGENTS Jennie Dunham, Bridget Smith.

REPRESENTS Nonfiction, fiction, novels, short story collections, juvenile books. **Considers these nonfiction areas:** anthropology, archeology, art, biography, creative nonfiction, cultural interests, environment, health, history, language, literature, medicine, memoirs, multicultural, parenting, popular culture, politics, psychology, science, sociology, technology, women's issues, women's studies, young adult. **Considers these fiction areas:** family saga, fantasy, gay, historical, humor, juvenile, literary, mainstream, middle grade, multicultural, mystery, new adult, picture books, science fiction, short story collections, sports, urban fantasy, women's, young adult.

☛ Westerns, horror, genre romance, poetry.

HOW TO CONTACT E-mail queries preferred, with all materials pasted in the body of the e-mail. Attachments will not be opened. Paper queries are also accepted. Please include a SASE for response and return of materials. If submitting to Bridget Smith, please include the first 5 pages with the query. Accepts simultaneous submissions. Responds in 4 weeks to queries; 2 months to mss. Obtains most new clients through recommendations from others, solicitations.

TERMS Agent receives 15% commission on domestic sales. Agent receives 20% commission on foreign sales.

DUNOW, CARLSON, & LERNER AGENCY

27 W. 20th St., Suite 1107, New York NY 10011. (212)645-7606. **E-mail:** mail@dclagency.com. **Website:** www.dclagency.com. Member of AAR.

MEMBER AGENTS Jennifer Carlson (narrative nonfiction writers and journalists covering current events and ideas and cultural history, as well as literary and upmarket commercial novelists); Henry Dunow (quality fiction–literary, historical, strongly written commercial–and with voice-driven nonfiction across a range of areas–narrative history, biography, memoir, current affairs, cultural trends and criticism, science, sports); Erin Hosier (nonfiction: popular culture, music, sociology and memoir); Betsy Lerner (nonfiction writers in the areas of psychology, history, cultural studies, biography, current events, business; fiction: literary, dark, funny, voice driven); Yishai Seidman (broad range of fiction: literary, postmodern, and thrillers; nonfiction: sports, music, and

pop culture); Amy Hughes (nonfiction in the areas of history, cultural studies, memoir, current events, wellness, health, food, pop culture, and biography; also literary fiction); Eleanor Jackson (literary, commercial, memoir, art, food, science and history); Julia Kenny (fiction—adult, middle grade and YA—and is especially interested in dark, literary thrillers and suspense); Edward Necarsulmer IV (strong new voices in teen & middle grade as well as picture books); Stacia Decker; Arielle Datz (fiction—adult, YA, or middlegrade—literary and commercial, nonfiction—essays, unconventional memoir, pop culture, and sociology).

REPRESENTS Nonfiction, fiction, novels, short story collections. **Considers these nonfiction areas:** art, biography, creative nonfiction, cultural interests, current affairs, foods, health, history, memoirs, music, popular culture, psychology, science, sociology, sports. **Considers these fiction areas:** commercial, literary, mainstream, middle grade, mystery, picture books, thriller, young adult.

HOW TO CONTACT Query via snail mail with SASE, or by e-mail. E-mail preferred, paste 10 sample pages below query letter. No attachments. Will respond only if interested. Accepts simultaneous submissions. Responds in 4-6 weeks if interested.

DYSTEL, GODERICH & BOURRET LLC

1 Union Square W., Suite 904, New York NY 10003. (212)627-9100. **Fax:** (212)627-9313. **Website:** www.dystel.com. Estab. 1994. Member of AAR. Other membership includes SCBWI. Represents 600+ clients.

MEMBER AGENTS Jane Dystel; Miriam Goderich, miriam@dystel.com (literary and commercial fiction as well as some genre fiction, narrative nonfiction, pop culture, psychology, history, science, art, business books, and biography/memoir); Stacey Glick, sglick@dystel.com (adult narrative nonfiction including memoir, parenting, cooking and food, psychology, science, health and wellness, lifestyle, current events, pop culture, YA, middle grade, children's nonfiction, and select adult contemporary fiction); Michael Bourret, mbourret@dystel.com (middle grade and young adult fiction, commercial adult fiction, and all sorts of nonfiction, from practical to narrative; he's especially interested in food and cocktail related books, memoir, popular history, politics, religion (though not spirituality), popular science, and current events); Jim McCarthy, jmccarthy@dystel.com (literary women's fiction, underrepresented voices, mysteries, romance, paranormal fiction, narrative nonfiction, memoir, and paranormal nonfiction); Jessica Papin, jpapin@dystel.com (plot-driven literary and smart commercial fiction, and narrative non-fiction across a range of subjects, including history, medicine, science, economics and women's issues); Lauren Abramo, labramo@dystel.com (humorous middle grade and contemporary YA on the children's side, and upmarket commercial fiction and well-paced literary fiction on the adult side; adult narrative nonfiction, especially pop culture, psychology, pop science, reportage, media, and contemporary culture; in nonfiction, has a strong preference for interdisciplinary approaches, and in all categories she's especially interested in underrepresented voices); John Rudolph, jrudolph@dystel.com (picture book author/illustrators, middle grade, YA, select commercial fiction, and narrative nonfiction—especially in music, sports, history, popular science, "big think", performing arts, health, business, memoir, military history, and humor); Sharon Pelletier, spelletier@dystel.com (smart commercial fiction, from upmarket women's fiction to domestic suspense to literary thrillers, and strong contemporary romance novels; compelling nonfiction projects, especially feminism and religion); Michael Hoogland, mhoogland@dystel.com (thriller, SFF, YA, upmarket women's fiction, and narrative nonfiction); Erin Young, eyoung@dystel.com (YA/MG, literary and intellectual commercial thrillers, memoirs, biographies, sport and science narratives); Amy Bishop, abishop@dystel.com (commercial and literary women's fiction, fiction from diverse authors, historical fiction, YA, personal narratives, and biographies); Kemi Faderin, kfaderin@dystel.com (smart, plot-driven YA, historical fiction/non-fiction, contemporary women's fiction, and literary fiction).

REPRESENTS Considers these nonfiction areas: animals, art, autobiography, biography, business, cooking, cultural interests, current affairs, ethnic, foods, gay/lesbian, health, history, humor, inspirational, investigative, medicine, memoirs, metaphysics, military, New Age, parenting, popular culture, politics, psychology, religious, science, sports, women's issues, women's studies. **Considers these fiction areas:** commercial, ethnic, gay, lesbian, literary, mainstream, middle grade, mystery, paranormal, romance, suspense, thriller, women's, young adult.

☛ "We are actively seeking fiction for all ages, in all genres." No plays, screenplays, or poetry.

HOW TO CONTACT Query via e-mail and put "Query" in the subject line. "Synopses, outlines or sample chapters (say, one chapter or the first 25 pages of your manuscript) should either be included below the cover letter or attached as a separate document. We won't open attachments if they come with a blank e-mail." Accepts simultaneous submissions. Responds in 6 to 8 weeks to queries; within 8 weeks to mss. Obtains most new clients through recommendations from others, solicitations, conferences.

TERMS Agent receives 15% commission on domestic sales; 19% commission on foreign sales. Offers written contract.

TIPS "DGLM prides itself on being a full-service agency. We're involved in every stage of the publishing process, from offering substantial editing on mss and proposals, to coming up with book ideas for authors looking for their next project, negotiating contracts and collecting monies for our clients. We follow a book from its inception through its sale to a publisher, its publication, and beyond. Our commitment to our writers does not, by any means, end when we have collected our commission. This is one of the many things that makes us unique in a very competitive business."

EDEN STREET LITERARY

P.O. Box 30, Billings NY 12510. **E-mail:** info@edenstreetlit.com; submissions@edenstreetlit.com. **Website:** www.edenstreetlit.com. **Contact:** Liza Voges. Member of AAR. Signatory of WGA. Represents over 40 clients.

REPRESENTS Nonfiction, fiction, novels, juvenile books. **Considers these fiction areas:** juvenile, middle grade, picture books, young adult.

HOW TO CONTACT E-mail a picture book ms or dummy; a synopsis and 3 chapters of a MG or YA novel; a proposal and 3 sample chapters for nonfiction. Accepts simultaneous submissions. Responds only to submissions of interest.

EINSTEIN LITERARY MANAGEMENT

27 W. 20th St., No. 1003, New York NY 10011. (212)221-8797. **E-mail:** info@einsteinliterary.com; submissions@einsteinliterary.com. **Website:** http://einsteinliterary.com. **Contact:** Susanna Einstein. Estab. 2015. Member of AAR. Signatory of WGA.

MEMBER AGENTS Susanna Einstein, Susan Graham, Shana Kelly.

REPRESENTS Nonfiction, fiction, novels, short story collections, juvenile books. **Considers these nonfiction areas:** cooking, creative nonfiction, memoirs, blog-to-book projects. **Considers these fiction areas:** comic books, commercial, crime, fantasy, historical, juvenile, literary, middle grade, mystery, picture books, romance, science fiction, suspense, thriller, women's, young adult.

☛ "As an agency we represent a broad range of literary and commercial fiction, including upmarket women's fiction, crime fiction, historical fiction, romance, and books for middle-grade children and young adults, including picture books and graphic novels. We also handle non-fiction including cookbooks, memoir and narrative, and blog-to-book projects. Please see agent bios on the website for specific information about what each of ELM's agents represents." Does not want poetry, textbooks, or screenplays.

HOW TO CONTACT Please submit a query letter and the first 10 double-spaced pages of your manuscript in the body of the e-mail (no attachments). Does not respond to mail queries or telephone queries or queries that are not specifically addressed to this agency. Accepts simultaneous submissions. Responds in 6 weeks if interested.

THE LISA EKUS GROUP, LLC

57 North St., Hatfield MA 01038. (413)247-9325. **Fax:** (413)247-9873. **E-mail:** info@lisaekus.com. **Website:** www.lisaekus.com. **Contact:** Sally Ekus. Member of AAR.

MEMBER AGENTS Lisa Ekus; Sally Ekus.

REPRESENTS Nonfiction. **Considers these nonfiction areas:** cooking, diet/nutrition, foods, health, how-to, humor, women's issues, occasionally health/well-being and women's issues; humor; lifestyle.

☛ "Please note that we do not handle fiction, poetry, or children's books. If we receive a query for titles in these categories, please understand that we do not have the time or resources to respond."

HOW TO CONTACT "For more information about our literary services, visit http://lisaekus.com/services/literary-agency. Submit a query via e-mail or through our contact form on the website. You can also

submit complete hard copy proposal with title page, proposal contents, concept, bio, marketing, TOC, etc. Include SASE for the return of materials." Accepts simultaneous submissions. Responds in 4-6 weeks.

TIPS "Please do not call. No phone queries."

ETHAN ELLENBERG LITERARY AGENCY

155 Suffolk St., No. 2R, New York NY 10002. (212)431-4554. **E-mail:** agent@ethanellenberg.com. **Website:** http://ethanellenberg.com. **Contact:** Ethan Ellenberg. Estab. 1984. Member of AAR, Science Fiction and Fantasy Writer's of American, SCBWI, RWA, and MWA.

MEMBER AGENTS Ethan Ellenberg, president; Evan Gregory, senior agent; Bibi Lewis, associate agent (YA and women's fiction).

REPRESENTS Nonfiction, fiction. **Considers these nonfiction areas:** biography, cooking, current affairs, health, history, memoirs, New Age, popular culture, psychology, science, spirituality, true crime, adventure. **Considers these fiction areas:** commercial, ethnic, fantasy, literary, middle grade, mystery, picture books, romance, science fiction, thriller, women's, young adult, general.

☛ "We specialize in commercial fiction and children's books. In commercial fiction we want to see science fiction, fantasy, romance, mystery, thriller, women's fiction; all genres welcome. In children's books, we want to see everything: picture books, early reader, middle grade and young adult.We do some nonfiction: history, biography, military, popular science, and cutting edge books about any subject. Does not want to receive poetry, short stories, or screenplays.

HOW TO CONTACT Query by e-mail. Paste all of the material in the order listed. Fiction: query letter, synopsis, first 50 pages. Nonfiction: query letter, book proposal. Picture books: query letter, complete ms, 4-5 sample illustrations. Illustrators: query letter, 4-5 sample illustrations, link to online portfolio. Will not respond unless interested. Accepts simultaneous submissions. Responds in 2 weeks.

EMPIRE LITERARY

115 W. 29th St., 3rd Floor, New York NY 10001. (917)213-7082. **E-mail:** abarzvi@empireliterary.com; queries@empireliterary.com. **Website:** www.empire-literary.com. Estab. 2013. Member of AAR. Signatory of WGA.

MEMBER AGENTS Andrea Barzvi; Carrie Howland; Kathleen Schmidt; Penny Moore.

REPRESENTS Nonfiction, novels. **Considers these nonfiction areas:** diet/nutrition, health, memoirs, popular culture. **Considers these fiction areas:** literary, middle grade, women's, young adult.

HOW TO CONTACT Please only query one agent at a time. "If we are interested in reading more we will get in touch with you as soon as possible." Accepts simultaneous submissions.

FELICIA ETH LITERARY REPRESENTATION

555 Bryant St., Suite 350, Palo Alto CA 94301-1700. **E-mail:** feliciaeth.literary@gmail.com. **Website:** eth-literary.com. **Contact:** Felicia Eth. Member of AAR.

REPRESENTS Novels. **Considers these nonfiction areas:** animals, cooking, creative nonfiction, cultural interests, history, investigative, memoirs, parenting, popular culture, psychology, sociology, travel, women's issues. **Considers these fiction areas:** historical, literary, mainstream, suspense.

☛ This agency specializes in high-quality fiction (preferably mainstream/contemporary) and provocative, intelligent, and thoughtful nonfiction on a wide array of commercial subjects. "The agency does not represent genre ficiton, including romance novels, sci fi and fantasy, westerns, anime and graphic novels, mysteries."

HOW TO CONTACT For fiction: Please write a query letter introducing yourself, your book, your writing background. Don't forget to include degrees you may have, publishing credits, awards and endorsements. Please wait for a response before including sample pages. "We only consider material where the manuscript for which you are querying is complete, unless you have previously published." For nonfiction: A query letter is best, introducing idea and what you have written already (proposal, manuscript?). "For writerly nonficiton (narratives, bio, memoir) please let us know if you have a finished manuscript. Also it's important you include information about yourself, your background and expertise, your platform and notoriety, if any. We do not ask for exclusivity in most instances but do ask that you inform us if other agents are considering the same material." Accepts simultaneous submissions.

TERMS Agent receives 15% commission on domestic sales; 20% commission on foreign and film sales.

Charges clients for photocopying and express mail service.

MARY EVANS INC.

242 E. Fifth St., New York NY 10003. (212)979-0880. **Fax:** (212)979-5344. **E-mail:** info@maryevansinc.com. **Website:** maryevansinc.com. Member of AAR.

MEMBER AGENTS Mary Evans (progressive politics, alternative medicine, science and technology, social commentary, American history and culture); Julia Kardon (literary and upmarket fiction, narrative nonfiction, journalism, and history); Tom Mackay (nonfiction that uses sport as a platform to explore other issues and playful literary fiction).

REPRESENTS Nonfiction, novels. **Considers these nonfiction areas:** creative nonfiction, cultural interests, history, medicine, politics, science, technology, social commentary, journalism. **Considers these fiction areas:** literary, upmarket.

☛ No screenplays or stage plays.

HOW TO CONTACT Query by mail or e-mail. If querying by mail, include a SASE. If querying by e-mail, put "Query" in the subject line. For fiction: Include the first few pages, or opening chapter of your novel as a single Word attachment. For nonfiction: Include your book proposal as a single Word attachment. Accepts simultaneous submissions. Responds within 4-8 weeks.

FAIRBANK LITERARY REPRESENTATION

P.O. Box 6, Hudson NY 12534-0006. (617)576-0030. **Fax:** (617)576-0030. **E-mail:** queries@fairbankliterary.com. **Website:** www.fairbankliterary.com. **Contact:** Sorche Fairbank. Member of AAR.

MEMBER AGENTS Sorche Fairbank (narrative nonfiction, commercial and literary fiction, memoir, food and wine); Matthew Frederick, matt@fairbankliterary.com (scout for sports nonfiction, architecture, design).

REPRESENTS Nonfiction, novels, short story collections. **Considers these nonfiction areas:** agriculture, architecture, art, autobiography, biography, cooking, crafts, cultural interests, current affairs, decorating, diet/nutrition, design, environment, ethnic, foods, gay/lesbian, government, hobbies, horticulture, how-to, interior design, investigative, law, memoirs, photography, popular culture, politics, science, sociology, sports, technology, true crime, women's issues, women's studies. **Considers these fiction areas:** action, adventure, feminist, gay, lesbian, literary, mainstream, mystery, sports, suspense, thriller, women's, Southern voices.

☛ "I tend to gravitate toward literary fiction and narrative nonfiction, with a strong interest in women's issues and women's voices, international voices, class and race issues, and projects that simply teach me something new about the greater world and society around us. We have a good reputation for working closely and developmentally with our authors and love what we do." Actively seeking literary fiction, international and culturally diverse voices, narrative nonfiction, topical subjects (politics, current affairs), history, sports, architecture/design and pop culture. Does not want to receive romance, poetry, science fiction, pirates, vampire, young adult, or children's works.

HOW TO CONTACT Query with SASE. Submit author bio. Accepts simultaneous submissions. Obtains most new clients through recommendations from others, solicitations, conferences, ideas generated in-house.

TERMS Agent receives 15% commission on domestic sales; 20% commission on foreign sales. Offers written contract, binding for 12 months; 45-day notice must be given to terminate contract.

TIPS "Be professional from the very first contact. There shouldn't be a single typo or grammatical flub in your query. Have a reason for contacting me about your project other than I was the next name listed on some website. Please do not use form query software! Believe me, we can get a dozen or so a day that look identical—we know when you are using a form. Show me that you know your audience—and your competition. Have the writing and/or proposal at the very, very best it can be before starting the querying process. Don't assume that if someone likes it enough they'll 'fix' it. The biggest mistake new writers make is starting the querying process before they—and the work—are ready. Take your time and do it right."

LEIGH FELDMAN LITERARY

E-mail: assistant@lfliterary.com; query@lfliterary.com. **Website:** lfliterary.com. **Contact:** Leigh Feldman. Estab. 2014. Member of AAR. Signatory of WGA.

REPRESENTS Nonfiction, fiction, novels, short story collections. **Considers these nonfiction areas:** creative nonfiction, memoirs. **Considers these fiction areas:** contemporary issues, family saga, feminist, gay,

historical, lesbian, literary, multicultural, short story collections, women's, young adult.

☛ Does not want mystery, thriller, romance, paranormal, sci-fi.

HOW TO CONTACT E-query. "Please include 'query' in the subject line. Due to large volume of submissions, we regret that we can not respond to all queries individually. Please include the first chapter or the first 10 pages of your manuscript (or proposal) pasted after your query letter. I'd love to know what led you to query me in particular, and please let me know if you are querying other agents as well." Accepts simultaneous submissions.

DIANA FINCH LITERARY AGENCY

116 W. 23rd St., Suite 500, New York NY 10011. (917)544-4470. **E-mail:** diana.finch@verizon.net. **E-mail:** diana.finch@verizon.net or via link at the website (preferred). **Website:** http://dianafinchliteraryagency.blogspot.com ; www.facebook.com/DianaFinchLitAg. **Contact:** Diana Finch. Estab. 2003. Member of AAR. Represents 40 clients.

REPRESENTS Nonfiction, fiction, novels, scholarly books. **Considers these nonfiction areas:** autobiography, biography, business, child guidance, computers, cultural interests, current affairs, dance, diet/nutrition, economics, environment, ethnic, film, government, health, history, how-to, humor, investigative, juvenile nonfiction, law, medicine, memoirs, military, money, music, parenting, photography, popular culture, politics, psychology, satire, science, self-help, sex, sports, technology, theater, translation, true crime, war, women's issues, women's studies, young adult. **Considers these fiction areas:** action, adventure, contemporary issues, crime, detective, ethnic, historical, literary, mainstream, new adult, police, sports, thriller, young adult.

☛ "Does not want romance, mysteries, or children's picture books."

HOW TO CONTACT This agency prefers submissions via its online form. Accepts simultaneous submissions. Obtains most new clients through recommendations from others.

TERMS Agent receives 15% commission on domestic sales. Agent receives 20% commission on foreign sales. Offers written contract. "I charge for overseas postage, galleys, and books purchased, and try to recoup these costs from earnings received for a client, rather than charging outright."

TIPS "Do as much research as you can on agents before you query. Have someone critique your query letter before you send it. It should be only 1 page and describe your book clearly—and why you are writing it—but also demonstrate creativity and a sense of your writing style."

FINEPRINT LITERARY MANAGEMENT

207 W. 106th St., Suite 1D, New York NY 10025. (212)279-1282. **Website:** www.fineprintlit.com. Estab. 2007. Member of AAR.

MEMBER AGENTS Peter Rubie, CEO, peter@fineprintlit.com (nonfiction interests include narrative nonfiction, popular science, spirituality, history, biography, pop culture, business, technology, parenting, health, self help, music, and food; fiction interests include literate thrillers, crime fiction, science fiction and fantasy, military fiction and literary fiction, middle grade and boy-oriented YA fiction); Stephany Evans, stephany@fineprintlit.com (nonfiction: health and wellness, spirituality, lifestyle, food and drink, sustainability, running and fitness, memoir, and narrative nonfiction; fiction interests include mystery/crime, women's fiction, from literary to commercial to romance); Laura Wood, laura@fineprintlit.com (serious nonfiction, especially in the areas of science and nature, along with substantial titles in business, history, religion, and other areas by academics, experienced professionals, and journalists; select genre fiction only (no poetry, literary fiction or memoir) in the categories of science fiction & fantasy and mystery); June Clark, june@fineprintlit.com (nonfiction projects in the areas of entertainment, self-help, parenting, reference/how-to books, food and wine, style/beauty, and prescriptive business titles); Jacqueline Murphy, jacqueline@fineprintlit.com.

REPRESENTS Nonfiction, fiction, novels, short story collections. **Considers these nonfiction areas:** biography, business, cooking, cultural interests, current affairs, diet/nutrition, environment, foods, health, history, how-to, humor, investigative, medicine, memoirs, music, parenting, popular culture, psychology, science, self-help, spirituality, technology, travel, women's issues, fitness, lifestyle. **Considers these fiction areas:** commercial, crime, fantasy, historical, literary, mainstream, middle grade, mystery, romance, science fiction, suspense, thriller, women's, young adult.

HOW TO CONTACT E-query. For fiction, send a query, synopsis, bio, and 30 pages pasted into the e-mail. No attachments. For nonfiction, send a query only; proposal requested later if the agent is interested. Accepts simultaneous submissions. Obtains most new clients through recommendations from others, solicitations.

TERMS Agent receives 15% commission on domestic sales; 20% commission on foreign sales.

FLANNERY LITERARY

1140 Wickfield Ct., Naperville IL 60563. **E-mail:** jennifer@flanneryliterary.com. **Website:** flanneryliterary.com. **Contact:** Jennifer Flannery. Estab. 1992. Represents 40 clients.

REPRESENTS Nonfiction, fiction, novels, juvenile books. **Considers these nonfiction areas:** young adult. **Considers these fiction areas:** juvenile, middle grade, new adult, picture books, young adult.

This agency specializes in children's and young adult fiction and nonfiction. It also accepts picture books. 100% juvenile books.

HOW TO CONTACT Query by e-mail only. "Multiple queries are fine, but please inform us. Please no attachments. If you're sending a query about a novel, please include in the e-mail the first 5-10 pages; if it's a picture book, please include the entire text." Accepts simultaneous submissions. Responds in 2 weeks to queries; 1 month to mss. Obtains new clients through referrals and queries.

TERMS Agent receives 15% commission on domestic sales. Agent receives 20% commission on foreign sales. Offers written contract, binding for life of book in print.

TIPS "Write an engrossing, succinct query describing your work. We are always looking for a fresh new voice."

FLETCHER & COMPANY

78 Fifth Ave., 3rd Floor, New York NY 10011. **E-mail:** info@fletcherandco.com. **Website:** www.fletcherandco.com. **Contact:** Christy Fletcher. Estab. 2003. Member of AAR.

MEMBER AGENTS Christy Fletcher (referrals only); Melissa Chinchillo (select list of her own authors); Rebecca Gradinger (literary fiction, up-market commercial fiction, narrative nonfiction, self-help, memoir, Women's studies, humor, and pop culture); Gráinne Fox (literary fiction and quality commercial authors, award-winning journalists and food writers, American voices, international, literary crime, upmarket fiction, narrative nonfiction); Lisa Grubka (fiction—literary, upmarket women's, and young adult; and nonfiction—narrative, food, science, and more); Sylvie Greenberg (literary fiction, business, sports, science, memoir and history); Donald Lamm (history, biography, investigative journalism, politics, current affairs, and business); Todd Sattersten (business books); Eric Lupfer; Sarah Fuentes; Veronica Goldstein; Mink Choi; Erin McFadden.

REPRESENTS Nonfiction, novels. **Considers these nonfiction areas:** biography, business, creative nonfiction, current affairs, foods, history, humor, investigative, memoirs, popular culture, politics, science, self-help, sports, women's studies. **Considers these fiction areas:** commercial, crime, literary, women's, young adult.

HOW TO CONTACT Send queries to info@fletcherandco.com. Please do not include e-mail attachments with your initial query, as they will be deleted. Address your query to a specific agent. No snail mail queries. Accepts simultaneous submissions.

FOLIO LITERARY MANAGEMENT, LLC

The Film Center Building, 630 Ninth Ave., Suite 1101, New York NY 10036. (212)400-1494. **Fax:** (212)967-0977. **Website:** www.foliolit.com. Member of AAR. Represents 100+ clients.

MEMBER AGENTS Claudia Cross (romance novels, commercial women's fiction, cooking and food writing, serious nonfiction on religious and spiritual topics); Scott Hoffman (literary and commercial fiction, journalistic or academic nonfiction, narrative nonfiction, pop culture books, business, history, politics, spiritual or religious-themed fiction and nonfiction, sci-fi/fantasy literary fiction, heartbreaking memoirs, humorous nonfiction); Jeff Kleinman (book-club fiction (not genre commercial, like mysteries or romances), literary fiction, thrillers and suspense novels, narrative nonfiction, memoir); Dado Derviskadic (nonfiction: cultural history, biography, memoir, pop science, motivational self-help, health/nutrition, pop culture, cookbooks; fiction that's gritty, introspective, or serious); Frank Weimann (biography, business/investing/finance, history, religious, mind/body/spirit, health, lifestyle, cookbooks, sports, African-American, science, memoir, special forces/CIA/FBI/mafia, military, prescriptive nonfiction, humor, celebrity; adult and children's fiction); Michael Harriot (commercial non-fiction (both narrative and prescriptive) and fantasy/science fiction); Erin Harris (book club, historical fiction, literary, narrative nonfiction, psychological suspense, young adult); Katherine Latshaw (blogs-to-books, food/cooking, middle grade, narrative and prescriptive nonfiction); Annie Hwang (literary and upmarket fiction with commercial appeal; select nonfiction: popular science, diet/health/fitness, lifestyle, narrative nonfiction, pop culture, and humor); Erin Niumata (fiction: commercial women's fiction, romance, historical fiction, mysteries, psychological thrillers, suspense, humor; nonfiction: self-help, women's issues, pop culture and humor, pet care/pets, memoirs, and anything blogger); Ruth Pomerance (narrative nonfiction and commercial fiction); Marcy Posner (adult: commercial women's fiction, historical fiction, mystery, biography, history, health, and lifestyle, commercial novels, thrillers, narrative nonfiction; children's: contemporary YA and MG, mystery series for boys, select historical fiction and fantasy); Jeff Silberman (narrative nonfiction, biography, history, politics, current affairs, health, lifestyle, humor, food/cookbook, memoir, pop culture, sports, science, technology; commercial, literary, and book club fiction); Steve Troha; Emily van Beek (YA, MG, picture books), Melissa White (general nonfiction, literary and commercial fiction, MG, YA); John Cusick (middle grade, picture books, YA); Jamie Chambliss.

REPRESENTS Nonfiction, novels. **Considers these nonfiction areas:** animals, art, biography, business, cooking, creative nonfiction, economics, environment, foods, health, history, how-to, humor, inspirational, memoirs, military, parenting, popular culture, politics, psychology, religious, satire, science, self-help, technology, war, women's issues, women's studies. **Considers these fiction areas:** commercial, fantasy, horror, literary, middle grade, mystery, picture books, religious, romance, thriller, women's, young adult.

☛ No poetry, stage plays, or screenplays.

HOW TO CONTACT Query via e-mail only (no attachments). Read agent bios online for specific submission guidelines and e-mail addresses, and to check if someone is closed to queries. "All agents respond to queries as soon as possible, whether interested or not. If you haven't heard back from the individual agent within the time period that they specify on their bio page, it's possible that something has gone wrong, and your query has been lost–in that case, please e-mail a follow-up."

TIPS "Please do not submit simultaneously to more than one agent at Folio. If you're not sure which of us is exactly right for your book, don't worry. We work closely as a team, and if one of our agents gets a query that might be more appropriate for someone else, we'll always pass it along. It's important that you check each agent's bio page for clear directions as to how to submit, as well as when to expect feedback."

JEANNE FREDERICKS LITERARY AGENCY, INC.

221 Benedict Hill Rd., New Canaan CT 06840. (203)972-3011. **Fax:** (203)972-3011. **E-mail:** jeanne.fredericks@gmail.com. **Website:** www.jeannefredericks.com. **Contact:** Jeanne Fredericks. Estab. 1997. Member of AAR. Other memberships include Authors Guild. Represents 75+ clients.

REPRESENTS Nonfiction. **Considers these nonfiction areas:** Americana, animals, autobiography, biography, child guidance, cooking, decorating, diet/nutrition, environment, foods, gardening, health, history, how-to, interior design, medicine, parenting, photography, psychology, self-help, women's issues.

> ☛ This agency specializes in quality adult nonfiction by authorities in their fields. "We do not handle: fiction, true crime, juvenile, textbooks, poetry, essays, screenplays, short stories, science fiction, pop culture, guides to computers and software, politics, horror, pornography, books on overly depressing or violent topics, romance, teacher's manuals, or memoirs."

HOW TO CONTACT Query first by e-mail, then send outline/proposal, 1-2 sample chapters, if requested and after you have consulted the submission guidelines on the agency website. If you do send requested submission materials, include the word "Requested" in the subject line. Accepts simultaneous submissions. Responds in 3-5 weeks to queries; 2-4 months to mss. Obtains most new clients through recommendations from others, solicitations, conferences.

TERMS Agent receives 15% commission on domestic sales. Agent receives 25% commission on foreign sales with co-agent. Offers written contract, binding for 9 months; 2-month notice must be given to terminate contract. Charges client for photocopying of whole proposals and mss, overseas postage, expedited mail

services. Almost all submissions are made electronically so these charges rarely apply.

TIPS "Be sure to research competition for your work and be able to justify why there's a need for your book. I enjoy building an author's career, particularly if he/she is professional, hardworking, and courteous, and actively involved in establishing a marketing platform. Aside from 25 years of agenting experience, I've had 10 years of editorial experience in adult trade book publishing that enables me to help an author polish a proposal so that it's more appealing to prospective editors. My MBA in marketing also distinguishes me from other agents."

GRACE FREEDSON'S PUBLISHING NETWORK

7600 Jericho Turnpike, Suite 300, Woodbury NY 11797. (516)931-7757. **Fax:** (516)931-7759. **E-mail:** gfreedson@gmail.com. **Contact:** Grace Freedson. . Estab. 2000. Member of AAR; Women's Media Group; Author's Guild. Represents 100 clients.

REPRESENTS Nonfiction, scholarly books. **Considers these nonfiction areas:** animals, business, child guidance, computers, cooking, crafts, creative nonfiction, current affairs, diet/nutrition, economics, education, environment, foods, gardening, health, history, hobbies, horticulture, how-to, humor, inspirational, interior design, juvenile nonfiction, language, law, medicine, memoirs, metaphysics, money, multicultural, parenting, philosophy, popular culture, psychology, recreation, regional, satire, science, self-help, sports, technology, true crime, war, women's issues, women's studies.

> ☛ "In addition to representing many qualified authors, I work with publishers as a packager of unique projects—mostly series." Actively seeking true crime and science for the general reader. Does not want to receive fiction.

HOW TO CONTACT Query with SASE. Submit synopsis, SASE. Responds in 2-6 weeks to queries. Obtains most new clients through recommendations from others.

TERMS Agent receives 15% commission on domestic sales. Offers written contract; 30-day notice must be given to terminate contract.

TIPS "At this point, I am only reviewing proposals on nonfiction topics by credentialed authors with platforms."

REBECCA FRIEDMAN LITERARY AGENCY

E-mail: brandie@rfliterary.com. **Website:** www.rfliterary.com. Estab. 2013. Member of AAR. Signatory of WGA.

MEMBER AGENTS Rebecca Friedman (commercial and literary fiction with a focus on literary novels of suspense, women's fiction, contemporary romance, and young adult, as well as journalistic nonfiction and memoir); Susan Finesman, susan@rfliterary.com (fiction, cookbooks, and lifestyle); Abby Schulman, abby@rfliterary.com (YA and nonfiction related to health, wellness, and personal development); Brandie Coonis, brandie@rfliterary.com (writers that defy genre).

REPRESENTS Nonfiction, fiction. **Considers these nonfiction areas:** cooking, health, memoirs, journalistic nonfiction. **Considers these fiction areas:** commercial, fantasy, literary, mystery, new adult, romance, science fiction, suspense, women's, young adult.

HOW TO CONTACT Please submit your query letter and first chapter (no more than 15 pages, double-spaced). If querying Kimberly, paste a full synopsis into the e-mail submission. No attachments. Accepts simultaneous submissions. Tries to respond in 6-8 weeks.

THE FRIEDRICH AGENCY

19 W. 21st St., Suite 201, New York NY 10010. (212)317-8810. **E-mail:** mfriedrich@friedrichagency.com; lcarson@friedrichagency.com; kwolf@friedrichagency.com. **Website:** www.friedrichagency.com. **Contact:** Molly Friedrich; Lucy Carson; Kent D. Wolf. Estab. 2006. Member of AAR. Signatory of WGA. Represents 50+ clients.

MEMBER AGENTS Molly Friedrich, founder and agent (open to queries); Lucy Carson, TV/film rights director and agent (open to queries); Kent D. Wolf, foreign rights director and agent (open to queries).

REPRESENTS Nonfiction, fiction, novels, short story collections. **Considers these nonfiction areas:** creative nonfiction, memoirs. **Considers these fiction areas:** commercial, literary, multicultural, suspense, women's, young adult.

HOW TO CONTACT Query by e-mail only. Please query only 1 agent at this agency. Accepts simultaneous submissions.

FULL CIRCLE LITERARY, LLC

3268 Governor Dr. #323, San Diego CA 92122. **E-mail:** info@fullcircleliterary.com. **Website:** www.fullcircleliterary.com. **Contact:** Stefanie Von Borstel. Estab. 2005. Member of AAR, Society of Children's Books Writers & Illustrators, Authors Guild. Represents 100+ clients.

MEMBER AGENTS Stefanie Von Borstel; Adriana Dominguez; Taylor Martindale Kean (multicultural voices); Lilly Ghahremani.

REPRESENTS **Considers these nonfiction areas:** creative nonfiction, how-to, interior design, multicultural, women's issues, young adult. **Considers these fiction areas:** literary, middle grade, multicultural, picture books, women's, young adult.

☞ Actively seeking nonfiction by authors with a unique voice and strong platform, projects that offer new and diverse viewpoints, and literature with a global or multicultural perspective. "We are particularly interested in books with a Latino or Middle Eastern angle."

HOW TO CONTACT Online submissions only via submissions form online. Please complete the form and submit cover letter, author information and sample writing. For sample writing: fiction please include the first 10 ms pages. For nonfiction, include a proposal with 1 sample chapter. Accepts simultaneous submissions. "Due to the high volume of submissions, please keep in mind we are no longer able to personally respond to every submission. However, we read every submission with care and often share for a second read within the office. If we are interested, we will contact you by email to request additional materials (such as a complete manuscript or additional manuscripts). Please keep us updated if there is a change in the status of your project, such as an offer of representation or book contract."

TERMS Agent receives 15% commission on domestic sales; 25% commission on foreign sales. Offers written contract which outlines responsibilities of the author and the agent.

THE G AGENCY, LLC

P.O. Box 374, Bronx NY 10471. **E-mail:** gagencyquery@gmail.com. **Website:** www.publishersmarketplace.com/members/jeffg/. **Contact:** Jeff Gerecke. Estab. 2012. Member of AAR.

MEMBER AGENTS Jeff Gerecke.

REPRESENTS Nonfiction, fiction. **Considers these nonfiction areas:** biography, business, computers, history, military, money, popular culture, technology.

Considers these fiction areas: historical, mainstream, military, mystery, suspense, thriller, war.

☛ Does not want screenplays, sci-fi/fantasy or romance.

HOW TO CONTACT E-mail submissions required. Please do attach sample chapters or proposal. Enter "QUERY" along with the title in the subject line of e-mails. "I cannot guarantee replies to every submission. If you do not hear from me the first time, you may send me one reminder. I encourage you to make multiple submissions but want to know that is the case if I ask for a manuscript to read." Accepts simultaneous submissions.

TIPS "I am interested in commercial and literary fiction, as well as serious nonfiction and pop culture. My focus as an agent has always been on working with writers to shape their work for its greatest commercial potential. I provide lots of editorial advice in sharpening manuscripts and proposals before submission. I've been a member of the Royalty Committee of the Association of Authors Representatives since its founding and am always keen to challenge publishers for their willfully obscure royalty reporting. Also I have recently taken over the position of Treasurer of the A.A.R. My publishing background includes working at the University of California Press so I am always intrigued by academic subjects which are given a commercial spin to reach an audience outside academia. I've also worked as a foreign scout for publishers like Hodder & Stoughton in England and Wilhelm Heyne in Germany, which gives me a good sense of how American books can be successfully translated overseas."

GELFMAN SCHNEIDER / ICM PARTNERS

850 7th Ave., Suite 903, New York NY 10019. **E-mail:** mail@gelfmanschneider.com. **Website:** www.gelfmanschneider.com. **Contact:** Jane Gelfman, Deborah Schneider. Member of AAR. Represents 300+ clients.

MEMBER AGENTS Deborah Schneider (all categories of literary and commercial fiction and nonfiction); Jane Gelfman; Heather Mitchell (particularly interested in narrative nonfiction, historical fiction and young debut authors with strong voices); Penelope Burns, penelope.gsliterary@gmail.com (literary and commercial fiction and nonfiction, as well as a variety of young adult and middle grade).

REPRESENTS Nonfiction, fiction, juvenile books. **Considers these nonfiction areas:** creative nonfiction, popular culture. **Considers these fiction areas:** commercial, fantasy, historical, literary, mainstream, middle grade, mystery, science fiction, suspense, women's, young adult.

☛ "Among our diverse list of clients are novelists, journalists, playwrights, scientists, activists & humorists writing narrative nonfiction, memoir, political & current affairs, popular science and popular culture nonfiction, as well as literary & commercial fiction, women's fiction, and historical fiction." Does not currently accept screenplays or scripts, poetry, or picture book queries.

HOW TO CONTACT Query. Check Submissions page of website to see which agents are open to queries and further instructions. Accepts simultaneous submissions.

TERMS Agent receives 15% commission on domestic sales; 20% commission on foreign sales; 15% commission on film sales. Offers written contract. Charges clients for photocopying and messengers/couriers.

GHOSH LITERARY

E-mail: submissions@ghoshliterary.com. **Website:** www.ghoshliterary.com. **Contact:** Anna Ghosh. Member of AAR. Signatory of WGA.

REPRESENTS Nonfiction, fiction.

☛ "Anna's literary interests are wide and eclectic and she is known for discovering and developing writers. She is particularly interested in literary narratives and books that illuminate some aspect of human endeavor or the natural world. Anna does not typically represent genre fiction but is drawn to compelling storytelling in most guises."

HOW TO CONTACT E-query. Please send an e-mail briefly introducing yourself and your work. Although no specific format is required, it is helpful to know the following: your qualifications for writing your book, including any publications and recognition for your work; who you expect to buy and read your book; similar books and authors. Accepts simultaneous submissions.

GLASS LITERARY MANAGEMENT

138 W. 25th St., 10th Floor, New York NY 10001. (646)237-4881. **E-mail:** alex@glassliterary.com; rick@glassliterary.com. **Website:** www.glassliterary.com.

Contact: Alex Glass or Rick Pascocello. Estab. 2014. Member of AAR. Signatory of WGA.

MEMBER AGENTS Alex Glass; Rick Pascocello.

REPRESENTS Nonfiction, novels.

☛ Represents general fiction, mystery, suspense/thriller, juvenile fiction, biography, history, mind/body/spirit, health, lifestyle, cookbooks, sports, literary fiction, memoir, narrative nonfiction, pop culture. "We do not represent picture books for children."

HOW TO CONTACT "Please send your query letter in the body of an e-mail and if we are interested, we will respond and ask for the complete manuscript or proposal. No attachments." Accepts simultaneous submissions.

GLOBAL LION INTELLECTUAL PROPERTY MANAGEMENT

P.O. Box 669238, Pompano Beach FL 33066. **E-mail:** queriesgloballionmgt@gmail.com. **Website:** www.globallionmanagement.com. **Contact:** Peter Miller. Estab. 2013. Member of AAR. Signatory of WGA.

☛ "I look for cutting-edge authors of both fiction and nonfiction with global marketing and motion picture/television production potential."

HOW TO CONTACT E-query. Global Lion Intellectual Property Management. Inc. accepts exclusive submissions only. "If your work is under consideration by another agency, please do not submit it to us." Below the query, paste a one page synopsis, a sample of your book (20 pages is fine), a short author bio, and any impressive social media links.

BARRY GOLDBLATT LITERARY LLC

320 7th Ave. #266, Brooklyn NY 11215. **E-mail:** query@bgliterary.com. **Website:** www.bgliterary.com. **Contact:** Barry Goldblatt. Estab. 2000. Member of AAR. Signatory of WGA.

MEMBER AGENTS Barry Goldblatt; Jennifer Udden, query.judden@gmail.com (speculative fiction of all stripes, especially innovative science fiction or fantasy; contemporary/erotic/LGBT/paranormal/historical romance; contemporary or speculative YA; select mysteries, thrillers, and urban fantasies).

REPRESENTS Fiction. **Considers these fiction areas:** fantasy, middle grade, mystery, romance, science fiction, thriller, young adult.

☛ "Please see our website for specific submission guidelines and information on our particular tastes."

HOW TO CONTACT "E-mail queries can be sent to query@bgliterary.com and should include the word 'query' in the subject line. To query Jen Udden specifically, e-mail queries can be sent to query.judden@gmail.com. Please know that we will read and respond to every e-query that we receive, provided it is properly addressed and follows the submission guidelines below. We will not respond to e-queries that are addressed to no one, or to multiple recipients. While we do not require exclusivity, exclusive submissions will receive priority review. If your submission is exclusive to Barry Goldblatt Literary, please indicate so by including the word 'Exclusive' in the subject line of your e-mail. Your e-query should include the following within the body of the e-mail: your query letter, a synopsis of the book, and the first 5 pages of your manuscript. We will not open or respond to any e-mails that have attachments. Our response time is 4 weeks on queries, 6-8 weeks on full manuscripts. If you haven't heard from us within that time, feel free to check in via e-mail." Accepts simultaneous submissions. Obtains clients through referrals, queries, and conferences.

TERMS Agent receives 15% commission on domestic sales; 20% on foreign and dramatic sales. Offers written contract. 60 days notice must be given to terminate contract.

TIPS "We're a hands-on agency, focused on building an author's career, not just making an initial sale. We don't care about trends or what's hot; we just want to sign great writers."

FRANCES GOLDIN LITERARY AGENCY, INC.

214 W. 29th St., Suite 410, New York NY 10001. (212)777-0047. **Fax:** (212)228-1660. **Website:** www.goldinlit.com. Estab. 1977. Member of AAR.

MEMBER AGENTS Frances Goldin, founder/president; Ellen Geiger, vice president/principal (nonfiction: history, biography, progressive politics, photography, science and medicine, women, religion and serious investigative journalism; fiction: literary thriller, and novels in general that provoke and challenge the status quo, as well as historical and multicultural works. Please no New Age, romance, how-to or right-wing politics); Matt McGowan, agent/rights director, mm@goldinlit.com, (literary fiction, essays, history, memoir, journalism, biography, music, popular culture & science, sports [particularly soccer], narrative nonfiction, cultural studies, as well as literary travel, crime, food, suspense and sci-fi); Sam Stoloff, vice president/principal, (literary fiction, memoir, history, accessible sociology and philosophy, cultural studies, serious journalism, narrative and topical nonfiction with a progressive orientation); Ria Julien, agent/counsel; Nina Cochran, literary assistant.

REPRESENTS Nonfiction, novels. **Considers these nonfiction areas:** biography, creative nonfiction, cultural interests, foods, history, investigative, medicine, memoirs, music, philosophy, photography, popular culture, politics, science, sociology, sports, travel, women's issues, crime. **Considers these fiction areas:** historical, literary, mainstream, multicultural, suspense, thriller.

☞ "We are hands on and we work intensively with clients on proposal and manuscript development." "Please note that we do not handle screenplays, romances or most other genre fiction, and hardly any poetry. We do not handle work that is racist, sexist, ageist, homophobic, or pornographic."

HOW TO CONTACT There is an online submission process you can find online. Responds in 4-6 weeks to queries.

IRENE GOODMAN LITERARY AGENCY

27 W. 24th St., Suite 700B, New York NY 10010. **E-mail:** miriam.queries@irenegoodman.com, barbara.queries@irenegoodman.com, rachel.queries@irenegoodman.com, kim.queries@irenegoodman.com, victoria.queries@irenegoodman.com, irene.queries@irenegoodman.com, brita.queries@irenegoodman.com, submissions@irenegoodman.com. **Website:** www.irenegoodman.com. **Contact:** Brita Lundberg. Estab. 1978. Member of AAR. Represents 150 clients.

MEMBER AGENTS Irene Goodman, Miriam Kriss, Barbara Poelle, Rachel Ekstrom, Kim Perel, Brita Lundberg, Victoria Marini.

REPRESENTS Nonfiction, fiction, novels, juvenile books. **Considers these nonfiction areas:** animals, autobiography, cooking, creative nonfiction, cultural interests, current affairs, decorating, diet/nutrition, design, foods, health, history, how-to, humor, interior design, juvenile nonfiction, memoirs, parenting, politics, science, self-help, women's issues, young adult, parenting, social issues, francophilia, anglophilia, Judaica, lifestyles, cooking, memoir. **Considers these fiction areas:** action, crime, detective, family saga, historical, horror, middle grade, mystery, romance, science fiction, suspense, thriller, urban fantasy, women's, young adult.

☞ Commercial and literary fiction and nonfiction. No screenplays, poetry, or inspirational fiction.

HOW TO CONTACT Query. Submit synopsis, first 10 pages pasted into the body of the email. E-mail queries only! See the website submission page. No e-mail attachments. Query 1 agent only. Accepts simultaneous submissions. Responds in 2 months to queries. Consult website for each agent's submission guidelines.

TERMS 15% commission.

TIPS "We are receiving an unprecedented amount of e-mail queries. If you find that the mailbox is full, please try again in two weeks. E-mail queries to our personal addresses will not be answered. E-mails to our personal inboxes will be deleted."

DOUG GRAD LITERARY AGENCY, INC.

68 Jay St., Suite N3, Brooklyn NY 11201. (718)788-6067. **E-mail:** query@dgliterary.com. **Website:** www.dgliterary.com. **Contact:** Doug Grad. Estab. 2008. Member of AAR. Signatory of WGA.

MEMBER AGENTS Doug Grad (narrative nonfiction, military, sports, celebrity memoir, thrillers, mysteries, cozies, historical fiction, music, style, business, home improvement, cookbooks, science and theater).

REPRESENTS Nonfiction, fiction, novels. **Considers these nonfiction areas:** Americana, autobiography, business, cooking, creative nonfiction, current affairs, diet/nutrition, design, film, government, history, humor, military, music, popular culture, politics, science, sports, technology, theater, travel, true crime, war. **Considers these fiction areas:** action, adventure, commercial, crime, detective, historical, horror, literary, mainstream, military, mystery, police, science fiction, suspense, thriller, war, young adult.

☞ Does not want fantasy, young adult, or children's picture books.

HOW TO CONTACT Query by e-mail first. No sample material unless requested; no printed submissions by mail. Accepts simultaneous submissions.

SANFORD J. GREENBURGER ASSOCIATES, INC.

55 Fifth Ave., New York NY 10003. (212)206-5600. **Fax:** (212)463-8718. **Website:** www.greenburger.com. Member of AAR. Represents 500 clients.

MEMBER AGENTS Matt Bialer, LRibar@sjga.com (fantasy, science fiction, thrillers, and mysteries as well as a select group of literary writers, and also loves smart narrative nonfiction including books about current events, popular culture, biography, history, music, race, and sports); Brenda Bowen, queryBB@sjga.com (literary fiction, writers and illustrators of picture books, chapter books, and middle-grade and teen fiction); Faith Hamlin, fhamlin@sjga.com (receives submissions by referral); Heide Lange, queryHL@sjga.com (receives submissions by referral); Daniel Mandel, querydm@sjga.com (literary and commercial fiction, as well as memoirs and non-fiction about business, art, history, politics, sports, and popular culture); Courtney Miller-Callihan, cmiller@sjga.com (YA, middle grade, women's fiction, romance, and historical novels, as well as nonfiction projects on unusual topics, humor, pop culture, and lifestyle books); Nicholas Ellison, nellison@sjga.com; Chelsea Lindman, clindman@sjga.com (playful literary fiction, upmarket crime fiction, and forward thinking or boundary-pushing nonfiction); Rachael Dillon Fried, rfried@sjga.com (both fiction and nonfiction authors, with a keen interest in unique literary voices, women's fiction, narrative nonfiction, memoir, and comedy); Lindsay Ribar, co-agents with Matt Bialer (young adult and middle grade fiction); Bethany Buck querybbuck@sjga.com (middle-grade fiction and chapter books, teen fiction, and a select list of picture book authors and illustrators); Stephanie Delman sdelman@sjga.com (literary/upmarket contemporary fiction, psychological thrillers/suspense, and atmospheric, near-historical fiction); Ed Maxwell emaxwell@sjga.com (expert and narrative nonfiction authors, novelists and graphic novelists, as well as children's book authors and illustrators).

REPRESENTS Nonfiction, fiction, novels, juvenile books. **Considers these nonfiction areas:** art, biography, business, creative nonfiction, current affairs, ethnic, history, humor, memoirs, music, popular culture, politics, sports. **Considers these fiction areas:** commercial, crime, family saga, fantasy, feminist, historical, literary, middle grade, multicultural, mystery, picture books, romance, science fiction, thriller, women's, young adult.

HOW TO CONTACT E-query. "Please look at each agent's profile page for current information about what each agent is looking for and for the correct email address to use for queries to that agent. Please be sure to use the correct query e-mail address for each agent." Agents may not respond to all queries; will respond within 6-8 weeks if interested. Obtains most new clients through recommendations from others.

TERMS Agent receives 15% commission on domestic sales. Agent receives 20% commission on foreign sales. Charges for photocopying and books for foreign and subsidiary rights submissions.

THE GREENHOUSE LITERARY AGENCY

E-mail: submissions@greenhouseliterary.com. **Website:** www.greenhouseliterary.com. **Contact:** Sarah Davies. Estab. 2008. Member of AAR. Other memberships include SCBWI. Represents 50 clients.

MEMBER AGENTS Sarah Davies, vice president (fiction and nonfiction by North American authors, chapter books through to middle grade and young adult); Polly Nolan, agent (fiction by UK, Irish, Commonwealth–including Australia, NZ and India–authors, plus European authors writing in English, author/illustrators (texts under 1,000 words) to young fiction series, through middle grade and young adult).

REPRESENTS Juvenile books. **Considers these nonfiction areas:** juvenile nonfiction, young adult. **Considers these fiction areas:** juvenile, young adult.

➻ "We represent authors writing fiction and nonfiction for children and teens. The agency has offices in both the US and UK, and the agency's commission structure reflects this—taking 15% for sales to both US and UK, thus treating both as 'domestic' market." All genres of children's and YA fiction. Very occasionally, a nonfiction proposal will be considered. Does not want to receive picture books texts (ie, written by writers who aren't also illustrators) or short stories, educational or religious/inspirational work, pre-school/novelty material, screenplays, or writing aimed at adults. Represents novels and some nonfiction.Considers these fiction areas: juvenile, chapter book series, middle grade, young adult. Does not want to receive poetry, picture book texts (unless by author/

illustrators) or work aimed at adults; short stories, educational or religious/inspirational work, pre-school/novelty material, or screenplays.

HOW TO CONTACT Query 1 agent only. Put the target agent's name in the subject line. Paste the first 5 pages of your story (or your complete picture book) after the query. Accepts simultaneous submissions.

TERMS Agent receives 15% commission on domestic sales; 25% commission on foreign sales. Offers written contract. This agency occasionally charges for submission copies to film agents or foreign publishers.

TIPS "Before submitting material, authors should visit the Greenhouse Literary Agency website and carefully read all submission guidelines."

THE JOY HARRIS LITERARY AGENCY, INC.

1501 Broadway, Suite 2310, New York NY 10036. (212)924-6269. **Fax:** (212)540-5776. **E-mail:** contact@joyharrisliterary.com; submissions@joyharrisliterary.com. **Website:** joyharrisliterary.com. **Contact:** Joy Harris. Estab. 1990. Member of AAR. Represents 100+ clients.

MEMBER AGENTS Joy Harris (literary fiction, strongly-written commercial fiction, narrative nonfiction across a broad range of topics, memoir and biography); Adam Reed (literary fiction, science and technology, and pop culture); Elizabeth Trout.

REPRESENTS Nonfiction, fiction. **Considers these nonfiction areas:** art, biography, creative nonfiction, memoirs, popular culture, science, technology. **Considers these fiction areas:** commercial, literary.

> "We are not accepting poetry, screenplays, genre fiction, or self-help submissions at this time."

HOW TO CONTACT Please e-mail all submissions, comprised of a query letter, outline or sample chapter, to submissions@joyharrisliterary.com. Accepts simultaneous submissions. Obtains most new clients through recommendations from clients and editors.

TERMS Agent receives 15% commission on domestic sales; 20% commission on foreign sales. Charges clients for some office expenses.

JOHN HAWKINS & ASSOCIATES, INC.

80 Maiden Ln., Suite 1503, New York NY 10038. (212)807-7040. **E-mail:** jha@jhalit.com. **Website:** www.jhalit.com. **Contact:** Moses Cardona (rights and translations); Annie Kronenberg (permissions); Warren Frazier, literary agent; Anne Hawkins, liter-

ary agent. Member of AAR. The Author Guild Represents 100+ clients.

MEMBER AGENTS Moses Cardona, moses@jhalit.com (commercial fiction, suspense, business, science, and multicultural fiction); Warren Frazier, frazier@jhalit.com (fiction; nonfiction, specifically technology, history, world affairs and foreign policy); Anne Hawkins, ahawkins@jhalit.com (thrillers to literary fiction to serious nonfiction; interested in science, history, public policy, medicine and women's issues).

REPRESENTS Nonfiction, fiction, novels, short story collections, novellas. **Considers these nonfiction areas:** biography, business, history, medicine, politics, science, technology, women's issues. **Considers these fiction areas:** commercial, historical, literary, multicultural, suspense, thriller.

HOW TO CONTACT Query. Include the word "Query" in the subject line. For fiction, include 1-3 chapters of your book as a single Word attachment. For nonfiction, include your proposal as a single attachment. E-mail a particular agent directly if you are targeting one. Accepts simultaneous submissions. Responds in 1 month to queries. Obtains most new clients through recommendations from others.

TERMS Agent receives 15% commission on domestic sales; 20% commission on foreign sales. Charges clients for photocopying.

RICHARD HENSHAW GROUP

145 W. 28th St., 12th Floor, New York NY 10001. (212)414-1172. **E-mail:** submissions@henshaw.com. **Website:** www.richardhenshawgroup.com. **Contact:** Rich Henshaw. Member of AAR.

REPRESENTS Novels. **Considers these fiction areas:** fantasy, historical, horror, literary, mainstream, mystery, police, romance, science fiction, thriller, young adult.

> "We specialize in popular fiction and nonfiction and are affiliated with a variety of writers' organizations. Our clients include *New York Times* bestsellers and recipients of major awards in fiction and nonfiction." "We only consider works between 65,000-150,000 words." "We do not represent children's books, screenplays, short fiction, poetry, textbooks, scholarly works or coffee-table books."

HOW TO CONTACT "Please feel free to submit a query letter in the form of an e-mail of fewer than 250 words to submissions@henshaw.com address." No snail mail queries. Accepts simultaneous submissions. Obtains most new clients through recommendations from others, solicitations, conferences.

TERMS Agent receives 15% commission on domestic sales; 20% commission on foreign sales. No written contract. Charges clients for photocopying and book orders.

TIPS "While we do not have any reason to believe that our submission guidelines will change in the near future, writers can find up-to-date submission policy information on our website. Always include a SASE with correct return postage."

HOLLOWAY LITERARY

P.O. Box 771, Cary NC 27512. **E-mail:** submissions@hollowayliteraryagency.com. **Website:** hollowayliteraryagency.com. **Contact:** Nikki Terpilowski. Estab. 2011. Member of AAR. Signatory of WGA. Represents 26 clients.

MEMBER AGENTS Nikki Terpilowski (romance, women's fiction, Southern fiction, historical fiction, cozy mysteries, military/political thrillers, commercial, upmarket/book club fiction, African-American fiction of all types); Rachel Burkot (young adult contemporary, women's fiction, upmarket/book club fiction, contemporary romance, Southern fiction, literary fiction); Michael Caligaris (literary fiction, autobiographical fiction, short story collections or connected stories as a novel, Americana, crime fiction, mystery/noir, dystopian fiction, civil unrest/political uprising/war novels, memoir, new journalism and/or long-form journalism, essay collections, satirical/humor writing, and environmental writing).

REPRESENTS Nonfiction, fiction, movie scripts, feature film. **Considers these nonfiction areas:** Americana, environment, humor, narrative nonfiction, New Journalism, essays. **Considers these fiction areas:** action, adventure, commercial, contemporary issues, crime, detective, ethnic, family saga, fantasy, glitz, historical, inspirational, literary, mainstream, metaphysical, middle grade, military, multicultural, mystery, new adult, New Age, regional, romance, short story collections, spiritual, suspense, thriller, urban fantasy, war, women's, young adult. **Considers these script areas:** action, adventure, biography, contemporary issues, ethnic, romantic comedy, romantic drama, teen, thriller, TV movie of the week.

HOW TO CONTACT Send query and first 15 pages of ms pasted into the body of e-mail to submissions@hollowayliteraryagency.com. In the subject header write: (Insert Agent's Name)/Title/Genre. Holloway Literary does accept submissions via mail (query letter and first 50 pages). Expect a response time of at least 3 months. Include e-mail address, phone number, social media accounts, and mailing address on your query letter. Accepts simultaneous submissions. Responds in 4-6 weeks. If the agent is interested, he/she'll respond with a request for more material.

HSG AGENCY

37 W. 28th St., 8th Floor, New York NY 10001. **E-mail:** channigan@hsgagency.com; jsalky@hsgagency.com; jgetzler@hsgagency.com; tprasanna@hsgagency.com; leigh@hsgagency.com. **Website:** hsgagency.com. **Contact:** Carrie Hannigan; Jesseca Salky; Josh Getzler;Tanusri Prasanna; Leigh Eisenman. Estab. 2011. Member of AAR. Signatory of WGA.

MEMBER AGENTS Carrie Hannigan; Jesseca Salky (literary and mainstream fiction); Josh Getzler (foreign and historical fiction; both women's fiction, straight-ahead historical fiction, and thrillers and mysteries); Tanusri Prasanna (picture books, children's, MG, YA, select nonfiction); Leigh Eisenman (literary and upmarket fiction, foodie/cookbooks, health and fitness, lifestyle, and select narrative nonfiction).

REPRESENTS Nonfiction, fiction, novels, juvenile books. **Considers these nonfiction areas:** business, cooking, creative nonfiction, current affairs, diet/nutrition, education, environment, foods, health, history, humor, literature, memoirs, multicultural, music, parenting, photography, politics, psychology, science, self-help, sports, women's issues, women's studies, young adult. **Considers these fiction areas:** adventure, commercial, contemporary issues, crime, detective, ethnic, family saga, historical, juvenile, literary, mainstream, middle grade, multicultural, mystery, picture books, thriller, translation, women's, young adult.

HOW TO CONTACT Electronic submissions only. Send query letter, first 5 pages of ms within e-mail to appropriate agent. Avoid submitting to multiple agents within the agency. Picture books: include entire ms. Responds in 4-6 weeks if interested.

HARVEY KLINGER, INC.

300 W. 55th St., Suite 11V, New York NY 10019. (212)581-7068. **E-mail:** queries@harveyklinger.com. **Website:** www.harveyklinger.com. **Contact:** Harvey

Klinger. Estab. 1977. Member of AAR, PEN. Represents 100 clients.

MEMBER AGENTS Harvey Klinger; David Dunton (popular culture, music-related books, literary fiction, young adult, fiction, and memoirs); Andrea Somberg (literary fiction, commercial fiction, romance, sci-fi/fantasy, mysteries/thrillers, young adult, middle grade, quality narrative nonfiction, popular culture, how-to, self-help, humor, interior design, cookbooks, health/fitness); Wendy Levinson (literary and commercial fiction, occasional children's YA or MG, wide variety of nonfiction); Rachel Ridout (children's MG and YA).

REPRESENTS Nonfiction, fiction, novels, juvenile books. **Considers these nonfiction areas:** autobiography, biography, business, child guidance, cooking, crafts, creative nonfiction, cultural interests, current affairs, diet/nutrition, foods, gay/lesbian, health, history, how-to, investigative, literature, medicine, memoirs, money, music, popular culture, psychology, science, self-help, sociology, spirituality, sports, technology, true crime, women's issues, women's studies, young adult. **Considers these fiction areas:** action, adventure, commercial, contemporary issues, crime, detective, erotica, family saga, fantasy, gay, glitz, historical, horror, juvenile, lesbian, literary, mainstream, middle grade, mystery, new adult, police, romance, suspense, thriller, women's, young adult.

➛ This agency specializes in big, mainstream, contemporary fiction and nonfiction. Great debut or established novelists and in nonfiction, authors with great ideas and a national platform already in place to help promote one's book. No Screenplays, poetry, textbooks or anything too technical.

HOW TO CONTACT Use online e-mail submission form on the website, or query with SASE via snail mail. No phone or fax queries. Don't send unsolicited mss or e-mail attachments. Make submission letter to the point and as brief as possible. Accepts simultaneous submissions. Responds in 2-4 weeks to queries, if interested. Obtains most new clients through recommendations from others.

TERMS Agent receives 15% commission on domestic sales; 25% commission on foreign sales. Offers written contract. Charges for photocopying mss and overseas postage for mss.

THE KNIGHT AGENCY

232 W. Washington St., Madison GA 30650. **E-mail:** deidre.knight@knightagency.net; submissions@knightagency.net. **Website:** http://knightagency.net/. **Contact:** Deidre Knight. Estab. 1996. Member of AAR, SCWBI, WFA, SFWA, RWA. Represents 200+ clients.

MEMBER AGENTS Deidre Knight (romance, women's fiction, erotica, commercial fiction, inspirational, m/m fiction, memoir and nonfiction narrative, personal finance, true crime, business, popular culture, self-help, religion, and health); Pamela Harty (romance, women's fiction, young adult, business, motivational, diet and health, memoir, parenting, pop culture, and true crime); Elaine Spencer (romance (single title and category), women's fiction, commercial "book-club" fiction, cozy mysteries, young adult and middle grade material); Lucienne Diver (fantasy, science fiction, romance, suspense and young adult); Nephele Tempest (literary/commercial fiction, women's fiction, fantasy, science fiction, romantic suspense, paranormal romance, contemporary romance, historical fiction, young adult and middle grade fiction); Melissa Jeglinski (romance [contemporary, category, historical, inspirational], young adult, middle grade, women's fiction and mystery); Kristy Hunter (romance, women's fiction, commercial fiction, young adult and middle grade material), Travis Pennington (young adult, middle grade, mysteries, thrillers, commercial fiction, and romance [nothing paranormal/fantasy in any genre for now]).

REPRESENTS Nonfiction, fiction, novels. **Considers these nonfiction areas:** autobiography, business, creative nonfiction, cultural interests, current affairs, diet/nutrition, design, economics, ethnic, film, foods, gay/lesbian, health, history, how-to, inspirational, interior design, investigative, juvenile nonfiction, literature, memoirs, military, money, multicultural, parenting, popular culture, politics, psychology, self-help, sociology, technology, travel, true crime, women's issues, young adult. **Considers these fiction areas:** commercial, crime, erotica, fantasy, gay, historical, juvenile, lesbian, literary, mainstream, middle grade, multicultural, mystery, new adult, paranormal, psychic, romance, science fiction, thriller, urban fantasy, women's, young adult.

➛ Actively seeking Romance in all subgenres, including romantic suspense, paranormal romance, historical romance (a particular love of mine), LGBT, contemporary, and also category romance. Occasionally I represent new adult. I'm also seeking women's fiction with vivid voices, and strong concepts (think me before you). Further seeking YA and MG, and select nonfiction in the categories of personal development, self-help, finance/business, memoir, parenting and health. Does not want to receive screenplays, short stories, poetry, essays, or children's picture books.

HOW TO CONTACT E-queries only. "Your submission should include a one page query letter and the first five pages of your manuscript. All text must be contained in the body of your e-mail. Attachments will not be opened nor included in the consideration of your work. Queries must be addressed to a specific agent. Please do not query multiple agents." Accepts simultaneous submissions. Responds in 1-2 weeks on queries, 6-8 weeks on submissions.

TERMS 15% commission on all domestic sales, 20% on foreign and film.

LINDA KONNER LITERARY AGENCY

10 W. 15th St., Suite 1918, New York NY 10011. **E-mail:** ldkonner@cs.com. **Website:** www.lindakonnerliteraryagency.com. **Contact:** Linda Konner. Estab. 1996. Member of AAR. Other memberships include ASJA. Represents 75 clients.

REPRESENTS Nonfiction. **Considers these nonfiction areas:** business, cooking, diet/nutrition, foods, health, medicine, money, popular culture, psychology, science, self-help, women's issues, biography (celebrity), African American and Latino issues, relationships, popular science.

☛ This agency specializes in health, self-help, and how-to books. Authors/co-authors must be top experts in their field with a substantial media platform. Does not want fiction, children's, YA, illustrated books.

HOW TO CONTACT Query by e-mail (or snail mail with SASE) with synopsis and author bio, including size of social media following, size of website following, appearances in traditional media (print/TV/radio) and frequency/size of speaking engagements. Prefers to read materials exclusively for 2 weeks. Accepts simultaneous submissions. Responds within 2 weeks. Obtains most new clients through recommendations from others, occasional solicitation among established authors/journalists.

TERMS Agent receives 15% commission on domestic sales; 25% commission on foreign sales. Offers written contract. Charges one-time fee for domestic expenses; additional expenses may be incurred for foreign sales.

STUART KRICHEVSKY LITERARY AGENCY, INC.

6 E. 39th St., Suite 500, New York NY 10016. (212)725-5288. **Fax:** (212)725-5275. **Website:** www.skagency.com. Member of AAR.

MEMBER AGENTS Stuart Krichevsky, query@skagency.com (emphasis on narrative nonfiction, literary journalism and literary and commercial fiction); Ross Harris, rhquery@skagency.com (voice-driven humor and memoir, books on popular culture and our society, narrative nonfiction and literary fiction); David Patterson, dpquery@skagency.com (writers of upmarket narrative nonfiction and literary fiction, historians, journalists and thought leaders); Mackenzie Brady Watson, mbwquery@skagency.com (narrative nonfiction, science, history, sociology, investigative journalism, food, business, memoir, and select upmarket and literary YA fiction); Hannah Schwartz, hsquery@skagency; Laura Usselman, luquery@skagency.com.

REPRESENTS Nonfiction, novels. **Considers these nonfiction areas:** business, creative nonfiction, foods, history, humor, investigative, memoirs, popular culture, science, sociology, memoir. **Considers these fiction areas:** commercial, contemporary issues, literary, young adult.

HOW TO CONTACT Please send a query letter and the first few (up to 10) pages of your ms or proposal in the body of an e-mail (not an attachment) to one of the e-mail addresses. No attachments. Responds if interested. Accepts simultaneous submissions. Obtains most new clients through recommendations from others, solicitations.

KT LITERARY, LLC

9249 S. Broadway, #200-543, Highlands Ranch CO 80129. **E-mail:** contact@ktliterary.com; katequery@ktliterary.com, saraquery@ktliterary.com, reneequery@ktliterary.com, hannahquery@ktliterary.com. **Website:** www.ktliterary.com. **Contact:** Kate Schafer Testerman, Sara Megibow, Renee Nyen, Hannah Fergesen, Hilary Harwell. Estab. 2008. Member of AAR. Other agency memberships include SCBWI, YALSA, ALA, SFWA and RWA. Represents 75 clients.

MEMBER AGENTS Kate Testerman (middle grade and young adult); Renee Nyen (middle grade and young adult); Sara Megibow, (middle grade, young adult, romance, erotica, science fiction and fantasy); Hannah Fergesen, (middle grade, young adult and speculative fiction). Always LGBTQ and diversity friendly!

REPRESENTS Fiction. **Considers these fiction areas:** erotica, fantasy, middle grade, romance, science fiction, young adult.

- Kate is looking only at young adult and middle grade fiction and selective nonfiction. Sara seeks authors in middle grade, young adult, and adult romance, erotica, science fiction, and fantasy. Renee is looking for young adult and middle grade fiction only. Hannah is interested in speculative fiction in young adult, middle grade, and adult. "We're thrilled to be actively seeking new clients with great writing, unique stories, and complex characters, for middle grade, young adult, and adult fiction. We are especially interested in diverse voices." Does not want adult mystery, thrillers, or adult literary fiction.

HOW TO CONTACT "To query us, please select one of the agents at kt literary at a time. If we pass, you can feel free to submit to another. Please e-mail your query letter and the first 3 pages of your manuscript in the body of the e-mail to either Kate at katequery@ktliterary.com, Sara at saraquery@ktliterary.com, Renee at reneequery@ktliterary.com, or Hannah at hannahquery@ktliterary.com. The subject line of your e-mail should include the word 'Query' along with the title of your manuscript. Queries should not contain attachments. Attachments will not be read, and queries containing attachments will be deleted unread. We aim to reply to all queries within 2 weeks of receipt. For examples of query letters, please feel free to browse the About My Query archives on the KT Literary website. In addition, if you're an author who is sending a new query, but who previously submitted a novel to us for which we requested chapters but ultimately declined, please do say so in your query letter. If we like your query, we'll ask for the first 5 chapters and a complete synopsis. For our purposes, the synopsis should include the full plot of the book including the conclusion. Don't tease us. Thanks! We are not accepting snail mail queries at this time. If you have an aversion to e-mail, perhaps we're not the best agency for you. We also do not accept pitches on social media." Accepts simultaneous submissions. Responds in 2-4 weeks to queries; 2 months to mss. Obtains most new clients through query slush pile.

TERMS Agent receives 15% commission on domestic sales; 20% commission on foreign sales. Offers written contract; 30-day notice must be given to terminate contract.

THE LESHNE AGENCY

New York NY **E-mail:** info@leshneagency.com. **E-mail:** submissions@leshneagency.com. **Website:** www.leshneagency.com. **Contact:** Lisa Leshne, agent and owner. Estab. 2011. Member of AAR, Women's Media Group.

MEMBER AGENTS Lisa Leshne, agent and owner; Sandy Hodgman, director of foreign rights.

REPRESENTS Nonfiction, fiction, novels. **Considers these nonfiction areas:** business, creative nonfiction, cultural interests, health, how-to, humor, inspirational, memoirs, parenting, politics, science, self-help, sports, women's issues. **Considers these fiction areas:** commercial, middle grade, young adult.

- An avid reader of blogs, newspapers and magazines in addition to books, Lisa is most interested in narrative and prescriptive nonfiction, especially on social justice, sports, health, wellness, business, political and parenting topics. She loves memoirs that transport the reader into another person's head and give a voyeuristic view of someone else's extraordinary experiences. Lisa also enjoys literary and commercial fiction and some young adult and middle-grade books that take the reader on a journey and are just plain fun to read. Wants "authors across all genres. We are interested in narrative, memoir, and prescriptive nonfiction, with a particular interest in sports, wellness, business, political and parenting topics. We will also look at truly terrific commercial fiction and young adult and middle grade books."

HOW TO CONTACT The Leshne Agency is seeking new and existing authors across all genres. "We are especially interested in narrative; memoir; prescriptive nonfiction, with a particular interest in sports, health, wellness, business, political and parenting topics; and truly terrific commercial fiction, young adult and middle-grade books. We are not interested in screenplays; scripts; poetry; and picture books. If your submission is in a genre not specifically listed here, we are still open to considering it, but if your submission is for a genre we've mentioned as not being interested in, please don't bother sending it to us. All submissions should be made through the Authors. me portal by clicking on this link: https://app.authors. me/#submit/the-leshne-agency." Accepts simultaneous submissions.

LEVINE GREENBERG ROSTAN LITERARY AGENCY, INC.

307 Seventh Ave., Suite 2407, New York NY 10001. (212)337-0934. **Fax:** (212)337-0948. **E-mail:** submit@ lgrliterary.com. **Website:** www.lgrliterary.com. Member of AAR. Represents 250 clients.

MEMBER AGENTS Jim Levine (nonfiction, including business, science, narrative nonfiction, social and political issues, psychology, health, spirituality, parenting); Stephanie Rostan (adult and YA fiction; nonfiction, including parenting, health & wellness, sports, memoir); Melissa Rowland; Daniel Greenberg (nonfiction: popular culture, narrative nonfiction, memoir, and humor; literary fiction); Victoria Skurnick; Danielle Svetcov (nonfiction); Lindsay Edgecombe (narrative nonfiction, memoir, lifestyle and health, illustrated books, as well as literary fiction); Monika Verma (nonfiction: humor, pop culture, memoir, narrative nonfiction and style and fashion titles; some young adult fiction (paranormal, historical, contemporary)); Kerry Sparks (young adult and middle grade; select adult fiction and occasional nonfiction); Tim Wojcik (nonfiction, including food narratives, humor, pop culture, popular history and science; literary fiction); Arielle Eckstut (no queries); Sarah Bedingfield (literary and upmarket commercial fiction, Epic family dramas, literary novels with notes of magical realism, darkly gothic stories, psychological suspense).

REPRESENTS Nonfiction, novels. **Considers these nonfiction areas:** business, creative nonfiction, health, history, humor, memoirs, parenting, popular culture, science, spirituality, sports. **Considers these fiction areas:** commercial, literary, mainstream, middle grade, suspense, young adult.

HOW TO CONTACT E-query to submit@lgrliterary.com, or online submission form. "If you would like to direct your query to one of our agents specifically, please feel free to name them in the online form or in the email you send." Cannot respond to submissions by mail. Do not attach more than 50 pages. "Due

to the volume of submissions we receive, we are unable to respond to each individually. If we would like more information about your project, we'll contact you within 3 weeks (though we do get backed up on occasion!)." Accepts simultaneous submissions. Obtains most new clients through recommendations from others.

TERMS Agent receives 15% commission on domestic sales; 20% commission on foreign sales. Offers written contract. Charges clients for out-of-pocket expenses—telephone, fax, postage, photocopying—directly connected to the project.

TIPS "We focus on editorial development, business representation, and publicity and marketing strategy."

LEVY CREATIVE MANAGEMENT

425 E. 58th St., Suite 17F, New York NY 10022. (212)687-6463. **Fax:** (212)661-4839. **E-mail:** info@ levycreative.com. **Website:** www.levycreative.com. **Contact:** Sari S. Schorr. Estab. 1996. Member of AAR. Signatory of WGA.

☛ Currently open to illustrators seeking representation. Open to both new and established illustrators.

HOW TO CONTACT For first contact, send tearsheets, photocopies, SASE. See submission guidelines on website. Portfolio should include professionally presented materials. Accepts simultaneous submissions. Responds only if interested. Finds illustrators through recommendations from others, word of mouth, competitions.

TERMS Offers written contract. Advertising costs are split: 75% paid by illustrators; 25% paid by rep.

STERLING LORD LITERISTIC, INC.

115 Broadway, New York NY 10006. (212)780-6050. **Fax:** (212)780-6095. **E-mail:** info@sll.com. **Website:** www.sll.com. Estab. 1987. Member of AAR. Signatory of WGA.

MEMBER AGENTS Philippa Brophy (represents journalists, nonfiction writers and novelists, and is most interested in current events, memoir, science, politics, biography, and women's issues); Laurie Liss (represents authors of commercial and literary fiction and nonfiction whose perspectives are well developed and unique); Sterling Lord; Peter Matson (abiding interest in storytelling, whether in the service of history, fiction, the sciences); Douglas Stewart (primarily fiction for all ages, from the innovatively literary to the unabashedly commercial); Neeti Madan (memoir, journalism, popular culture, lifestyle, women's issues, multicultural books and virtually any intelligent writing on intriguing topics); Robert Guinsler (literary and commercial fiction (including YA), journalism, narrative nonfiction with an emphasis on pop culture, science and current events, memoirs and biographies); Jim Rutman; Celeste Fine (expert, celebrity, and corporate clients with strong national and international platforms, particularly in the health, science, self-help, food, business, and lifestyle fields); Martha Millard (fiction and nonfiction, including well-written science fiction and young adult); Mary Krienke (literary fiction, memoir, and narrative nonfiction, including psychology, popular science, and cultural commentary); Jenny Stephens (nonfiction: cookbooks, practical lifestyle projects, transportive travel and nature writing, and creative nonfiction; fiction: contemporary literary narratives strongly rooted in place); Alison MacKeen (idea-driven research books: social scientific, scientific, historical, relationships/parenting, learning and education, sexuality, technology, the life-cycle, health, the environment, politics, economics, psychology, geography, and culture; literary fiction, literary nonfiction, memoirs, essays, and travel writing); John Maas (serious nonfiction, specifically business, personal development, science, self-help, health, fitness, and lifestyle); Sarah Passick (commercial nonfiction in the celebrity, food, blogger, lifestyle, health, diet, fitness and fashion categories). **REPRESENTS** Nonfiction, fiction. **Considers these nonfiction areas:** biography, business, cooking, creative nonfiction, current affairs, economics, education, foods, gay/lesbian, history, humor, memoirs, multicultural, parenting, popular culture, politics, psychology, science, technology, travel, women's issues, fitness. **Considers these fiction areas:** commercial, juvenile, literary, middle grade, picture books, science fiction, young adult.

HOW TO CONTACT Query via snail mail. "Please submit a query letter, a synopsis of the work, a brief proposal or the first 3 chapters of the manuscript, a brief bio or resume, and SASE for reply. Original artwork is not accepted. Enclose sufficient postage if you wish to have your materials returned to you. We do not respond to unsolicited e-mail inquiries." Accepts simultaneous submissions.

TERMS Agent receives 15% commission on domestic sales; 20% commission on foreign sales. Offers written contract.

LOWENSTEIN ASSOCIATES INC.

115 E. 23rd St., Floor 4, New York NY 10010. (212)206-1630. **E-mail:** assistant@bookhaven.com. **Website:** www.lowensteinassociates.com. **Contact:** Barbara Lowenstein. Member of AAR.

MEMBER AGENTS Barbara Lowenstein, president (nonfiction interests include narrative nonfiction, health, money, finance, travel, multicultural, popular culture, and memoir; fiction interests include literary fiction and women's fiction); Mary South (literary fiction and nonfiction on subjects such as neuroscience, bioengineering, women's rights, design, and digital humanities, as well as investigative journalism, essays, and memoir).

REPRESENTS Nonfiction, fiction, novels, short story collections. **Considers these nonfiction areas:** autobiography, biography, business, creative nonfiction, cultural interests, health, humor, literature, memoirs, money, multicultural, popular culture, science, technology, travel, women's issues. **Considers these fiction areas:** commercial, literary, middle grade, science fiction, women's, young adult.

Barbara Lowenstein is currently looking for writers who have a platform and are leading experts in their field, including business, women's issues, psychology, health, science and social issues, and is particularly interested in strong new voices in fiction and narrative nonfiction. Does not want westerns, textbooks, children's picture books and books in need of translation.

HOW TO CONTACT "For fiction, please send us a 1-page query letter, along with the first 10 pages pasted in the body of the message by e-mail to assistant@bookhaven.com. If nonfiction, please send a 1-page query letter, a table of contents, and, if available, a proposal pasted into the body of the e-mail. Please put the word 'QUERY' and the title of your project in the subject field of your e-mail and address it to the agent of your choice. Please do not send an attachment as the message will be deleted without being read and no reply will be sent." Accepts simultaneous submissions. Responds in 6 weeks to queries. Obtains most new clients through recommendations from others, solicitations, conferences.

TERMS Agent receives 15% commission on domestic sales; 20% commission on foreign sales. Offers written contract. Charges for large photocopy batches, messenger service, international postage.

TIPS "Know the genre you are working in and read!"

LR CHILDREN'S LITERARY

(312)659-8325. **E-mail:** submissions@lrchildrensliterary.com. **Website:** www.lrchildrensliterary.com. **Contact:** Loretta Caravette. Member of AAR. Signatory of WGA.

REPRESENTS Considers these fiction areas: juvenile, middle grade, picture books, young adult.

☞ "I am very interested in the easy readers and early chapter books. I will take on an author/illustrator combination."

HOW TO CONTACT E-query only. Alert this agent if you are contacting other agencies at the same time. If submitting young adult or middle grade, submit the first 3 chapters and a synopsis. If submitting a picture book, send no more than 2 mss. Illustrations (no more than 5MB) can be sent as .JPG or .PDF formats. Accepts simultaneous submissions. Responds in up to 6 weeks.

TIPS "No phone calls please."

DONALD MAASS LITERARY AGENCY

1000 Dean St., Suite 252, Brooklyn NY 11238. (212)727-8383. **Website:** www.maassagency.com. Estab. 1980. Member of AAR. Other memberships include SFWA, MWA, RWA. Represents more than 100 clients.

MEMBER AGENTS Donald Maass (mainstream, literary, mystery/suspense, science fiction, romance); Jennifer Jackson (science fiction and fantasy for both adult and YA markets, thrillers that mine popular and controversial issues, YA that challenges traditional thinking); Cameron McClure (literary, mystery/suspense, urban, fantasy, narrative nonfiction and projects with multicultural, international, and environmental themes, gay/lesbian); Amy Boggs (fantasy and science fiction, YA/MG, historical fiction about eras that aren't well known); Katie Shea Boutillier (women's fiction/book club, edgy/dark, realistic/contemporary YA, commercial-scale literary fiction, and celebrity memoir); Michael Curry (science fiction and fantasy, near future thrillers); Caitlin McDonald (SF/F [YA/MG/Adult], genre-bending/cross-genre fiction, diversity).

REPRESENTS Nonfiction, fiction, novels, juvenile books. **Considers these nonfiction areas:** creative nonfiction, memoirs, popular culture. **Considers these fiction areas:** contemporary issues, crime, detective, ethnic, fantasy, feminist, gay, historical, horror, juvenile, lesbian, literary, mainstream, middle grade, multicultural, mystery, paranormal, police, regional, romance, science fiction, supernatural, suspense, thriller, urban fantasy, westerns, women's, young adult.

☞ This agency specializes in commercial fiction, especially science fiction, fantasy, thrillers, suspense, women's fiction—for both the adult and YA markets. Does not want poetry, screenplays, picture books.

HOW TO CONTACT Query via e-mail only. All the agents have different submission addresses and instructions. See the website and each agent's online profile for exact submission instructions. Accepts simultaneous submissions.

TERMS Agency receives 15% commission on domestic sales; 20% commission on foreign sales.

TIPS "We are fiction specialists, also noted for our innovative approach to career planning. We are always open to submissions from new writers." Works with subagents in all principle foreign countries and for film and television.

GINA MACCOBY LITERARY AGENCY

P.O. Box 60, Chappaqua NY 10514. (914)238-5630. **E-mail:** query@maccobylit.com. **Website:** www.publishersmarketplace.com/members/ginamaccoby/. **Contact:** Gina Maccoby. Estab. 1986. Member of AAR. AAR Board of Directors; Royalties and Ethics and Contracts subcommittees; Authors Guild, SCBWI.

REPRESENTS Nonfiction, fiction, novels, juvenile books. **Considers these nonfiction areas:** autobiography, biography, cultural interests, current affairs, ethnic, history, juvenile nonfiction, literature, popular culture, women's issues, women's studies, young adult. **Considers these fiction areas:** crime, detective, family saga, juvenile, literary, mainstream, middle grade, multicultural, mystery, new adult, thriller, women's, young adult.

HOW TO CONTACT Query by e-mail only. Accepts simultaneous submissions. Owing to volume of submissions, may not respond to queries unless interested. Obtains most new clients through recommendations.

TERMS Agent receives 15% commission on domestic sales; 20-25% commission on foreign sales, which includes subagents commissions. May recover certain costs, such as purchasing books, shipping books overseas by airmail, legal fees for vetting motion picture contracts, bank fees for electronic funds transfers, overnight delivery services.

CAROL MANN AGENCY

55 Fifth Ave., New York NY 10003. (212)206-5635. **Fax:** (212)675-4809. **E-mail:** submissions@carolmannagency.com. **Website:** www.carolmannagency.com. **Contact:** Isabella Ruggiero. Member of AAR. Represents roughly 200 clients.

MEMBER AGENTS Carol Mann (health/medical, religion, spirituality, self-help, parenting, narrative nonfiction, current affairs); Laura Yorke; Gareth Esersky; Myrsini Stephanides (nonfiction areas of interest: pop culture and music, humor, narrative nonfiction and memoir, cookbooks; fiction areas of interest: offbeat literary fiction, graphic works, and edgy YA fiction); Joanne Wyckoff (nonfiction areas of interest: memoir, narrative nonfiction, personal narrative, psychology, women's issues, education, health and wellness, parenting, serious self-help, natural history; also accepts fiction); Lydia Shamah (edgy, modern fiction and timely nonfiction in the areas of business, self-improvement, relationship and gift books, particularly interested in female voices and experiences); Tom Miller (narrative nonfiction, self-help/psychology, popular culture, body-mind-spirit, wellness, business, and literary fiction).

REPRESENTS Novels. **Considers these nonfiction areas:** anthropology, archeology, architecture, art, autobiography, biography, business, child guidance, cultural interests, current affairs, design, ethnic, government, health, history, law, medicine, money, music, parenting, popular culture, politics, psychology, self-help, sociology, sports, women's issues, women's studies. **Considers these fiction areas:** commercial, literary, young adult, graphic works.

> Does not want to receive genre fiction (romance, mystery, etc.).

HOW TO CONTACT Please see website for submission guidelines. Accepts simultaneous submissions. Responds in 4 weeks to queries.

TERMS Agent receives 15% commission on domestic sales; 20% commission on foreign sales. Offers written contract.

MANSION STREET LITERARY MANAGEMENT

E-mail: querymansionstreet@gmail.com; querymichelle@mansionstreet.com. **Website:** mansionstreet.com. **Contact:** Jean Sagendorph; Michelle Witte. Member of AAR. Signatory of WGA.

MEMBER AGENTS Jean Sagendorph, querymansionstreet@gmail.com (pop culture, gift books, cookbooks, general nonfiction, lifestyle, design, brand extensions), Michelle Witte, querymichelle@mansionstreet.com (young adult, middle grade, early readers, picture books (especially from author-illustrators), juvenile nonfiction).

REPRESENTS Nonfiction, novels. **Considers these nonfiction areas:** cooking, design, popular culture. **Considers these fiction areas:** juvenile, middle grade, young adult.

> Jean is not interested in memoirs or medical/reference. Typically sports and self-help are not a good fit; also does not represent travel books. Michelle is not interested in fiction or nonfiction for adults.

HOW TO CONTACT Send a query letter and no more than the first 10 pages of your ms in the body of an e-mail. Query one specific agent at this agency. No attachments. You must list the genre in the subject line. If the genre is not in the subject line, your query will be deleted. Accepts simultaneous submissions. Responds in up to 6 weeks.

MANUS & ASSOCIATES LITERARY AGENCY, INC.

425 Sherman Ave., Suite 200, Palo Alto CA 94306. (650)470-5151. **Fax:** (650)470-5159. **E-mail:** manuslit@manuslit.com. **Website:** www.manuslit.com. **Contact:** Jillian Manus, Jandy Nelson, Penny Nelson. NYC address: 444 Madison Ave., 39th Floor, New York NY 10022. Member of AAR.

MEMBER AGENTS Jandy Nelson (currently not taking on new clients); Jillian Manus, jillian@manuslit.com (political, memoirs, self-help, history, sports, women's issues, thrillers); Penny Nelson, penny@manuslit.com (memoirs, self-help, sports, nonfiction).

REPRESENTS Nonfiction, novels. **Considers these nonfiction areas:** cooking, history, inspirational, memoirs, politics, psychology, religious, self-help, sports, women's issues. **Considers these fiction areas:** thriller.

> "Our agency is unique in the way that we not only sell the material, but we edit, develop concepts, and participate in the marketing effort. We specialize in large, conceptual fiction and nonfiction, and always value a project that can be sold in the TV/feature film market." Actively seeking high-concept thrillers, commercial

literary fiction, women's fiction, celebrity biographies, memoirs, multicultural fiction, popular health, women's empowerment and mysteries. No horror, romance, science fiction, fantasy, western, young adult, children's, poetry, cookbooks, or magazine articles.

HOW TO CONTACT Snail mail submissions welcome. E-queries also accepted. For nonfiction, send a full proposal via snail mail. For fiction, send a query letter and 30 pages (unbound) if submitting via snail mail. Send only an e-query if submitting fiction via e-mail. If querying by e-mail, submit directly to one of the agents. Accepts simultaneous submissions. Responds in 3 months. Obtains most new clients through recommendations from others, solicitations, conferences.

TERMS Agent receives 15% commission on domestic sales; 20-25% commission on foreign sales. Offers written contract, binding for 2 years; 60-day notice must be given to terminate contract. Charges for photocopying and postage/UPS.

DENISE MARCIL LITERARY AGENCY, LLC

483 Westover Rd., Stamford CT 06902. (203)327-9970. **E-mail:** dmla@denisemarcilagency.com; annemarie@denisemarcilagency.com. **Website:** www.denisemarcilagency.com. **Contact:** Denise Marcil, Anne Marie O'Farrell. Address for Anne Marie O'Farrell: 86 Dennis St., Manhasset, NY 11030. Estab. 1977. Member of AAR, Women's Media Group.

MEMBER AGENTS Denise Marcil (self-help and popular reference books such as wellness, health, women's issues, self-help, and popular reference); Anne Marie O'Farrell (books that convey and promote innovative, practical and cutting edge information and ideas which help people increase their self-awareness and fulfillment and maximize their potential in whatever area they choose; she is dying to represent a great basketball book).

REPRESENTS Nonfiction. **Considers these nonfiction areas:** business, cooking, diet/nutrition, education, health, how-to, New Age, psychology, self-help, spirituality, women's issues. **Considers these fiction areas:** commercial, suspense, thriller, women's.

☛ "In nonfiction we are looking for self-help, personal growth, popular psychology, how-to, business, and popular reference; we want to represent books that help people's lives." Does not want fiction.

HOW TO CONTACT E-query. Accepts simultaneous submissions.

TERMS Agent receives 15% commission on domestic sales. Agent receives 20% commission on foreign sales and film sales. Offers written contract, binding for 2 years.

MARLENA AGENCY

278 Hamilton Ave., Princeton NJ 08540. (609)252-9405. **Fax:** (609)252-9408. **E-mail:** marlena@marlenaagency.com. **Website:** www.marlenaagency.com. Estab. 1990. Member of AAR. Signatory of WGA. Member of Society of Illustrators.

MEMBER AGENTS Staff includes Marlena Torzecka, Anna Pluskota, Tara Barry.

REPRESENTS **Considers these nonfiction areas:** agriculture. **Considers these fiction areas:** action. **Considers these script areas:** action.

☛ Currently open to illustrators seeking representation. Open to both new and established illustrators.

HOW TO CONTACT For first contact, send tearsheets, photocopies, or e-mail low resolution samples only. Submission guidelines available for #10 SASE. Accepts simultaneous submissions. Finds illustrators through queries/solicitations, magazines and graphic design.

TERMS Exclusive representation required. Offers written contract.

TIPS "Be creative and persistent."

THE EVAN MARSHALL AGENCY

1 Pacio Ct., Roseland NJ 07068-1121. (973)287-6216. **Fax:** (973)488-7910. **E-mail:** evan@evanmarshallagency.com. **Website:** www.evanmarshallagency.com. **Contact:** Evan Marshall. Estab. 1987. Member of AAR. Novelists, Inc. Represents 50+ clients.

REPRESENTS Fiction, novels. **Considers these fiction areas:** action, adventure, crime, detective, erotica, ethnic, family saga, fantasy, feminist, frontier, gay, glitz, historical, horror, humor, inspirational, lesbian, literary, mainstream, military, multicultural, multimedia, mystery, new adult, New Age, occult, paranormal, police, psychic, regional, religious, romance, satire, science fiction, spiritual, sports, supernatural, suspense, thriller, translation, urban fantasy, war, westerns, women's, young adult, romance (contemporary, gothic, historical, regency).

☞ "We represent all genres of adult and young adult full-length fiction." Actively seeking high-quality adult and young adult fiction in all genres. Does not want articles, children's books, essays, memoirs, nonfiction, novellas, poetry, screenplays, short stories, stage plays.

HOW TO CONTACT Actively seeking new clients. E-mail query letter, synopsis and first 3 chapters of novel within body of e-mail. Accepts simultaneous submissions. Responds in 1 week to queries. Responds in 1 month to mss. Obtains new clients through queries and through recommendations from editors and current clients.

TERMS Agent receives 15% commission on domestic sales; 20% commission on foreign sales. Offers written contract.

MARGRET MCBRIDE LITERARY AGENCY

P.O. Box 9128, La Jolla CA 92038. (858)454-1550. E-mail: staff@mcbridelit.com. **Website:** www.mcbride-literary.com. Estab. 1981. Member of AAR. Other memberships include Authors Guild.

MEMBER AGENTS Margret McBride; Faye Atchison.

REPRESENTS Nonfiction, fiction, novels. **Considers these nonfiction areas:** autobiography, biography, business, cooking, creative nonfiction, cultural interests, current affairs, diet/nutrition, ethnic, foods, gay/lesbian, health, history, hobbies, how-to, inspirational, investigative, juvenile nonfiction, medicine, memoirs, money, multicultural, music, popular culture, psychology, science, self-help, sex, sociology, theater, travel, true crime, women's issues, young adult. **Considers these fiction areas:** action, adventure, comic books, commercial, confession, contemporary issues, crime, detective, family saga, feminist, historical, horror, juvenile, mainstream, multicultural, multimedia, mystery, new adult, paranormal, police, psychic, regional, supernatural, suspense, thriller, young adult.

☞ This agency specializes in mainstream nonfiction and some commercial fiction. Actively seeking commercial nonfiction, business, health, self-help. Does not want screenplays, romance, poetry, or children's.

HOW TO CONTACT Please check our website, as instructions are subject to change. Only e-mail queries are accepted: staff@mcbridelit.com. In your query letter, provide a brief synopsis of your work, as well as any pertinent information about yourself. We recom-

mend that authors look at book jacket copy of professionally published books to get an idea of the style and content that should be included in a query letter. Essentially, you are marketing yourself and your work to us, so that we can determine whether we feel we can market you and your work to publishers. There are detailed nonfiction proposal guidelines on our website. Please note: The McBride Agency will not respond to queries sent by mail, and will not be responsible for the return of any material submitted by mail. Accepts simultaneous submissions. Responds within 8 weeks to queries; 6-8 weeks to requested mss. "You are welcome to follow up by phone or e-mail after 8 weeks if you have not yet received a response."

TERMS Agent receives 15% commission on domestic sales; 25% commission on translation rights sales (15% to agency, 10% to sub-agent). Charges for overnight delivery and photocopying.

TIPS E-mail queries only. Please don't call to pitch your work by phone.

MCCORMICK LITERARY

37 W. 20th St., New York NY 10011. (212)691-9726. **E-mail:** queries@mccormicklit.com. **Website:** mccormicklit.com. Member of AAR. Signatory of WGA.

MEMBER AGENTS David McCormick; Pilar Queen (narrative nonfiction, practical nonfiction, and commercial women's fiction); Bridget McCarthy (literary and commercial fiction, narrative nonfiction, memoir, and cookbooks); Alia Hanna Habib (literary fiction, narrative nonfiction, memoir and cookbooks); Edward Orloff (literary fiction and narrative nonfiction, especially cultural history, politics, biography, and the arts); Daniel Menaker; Leslie Falk; Emma Borges-Scott.

REPRESENTS Nonfiction, novels. **Considers these nonfiction areas:** biography, cooking, history, memoirs, politics. **Considers these fiction areas:** literary, women's.

HOW TO CONTACT Snail mail queries only. Send an SASE. Accepts simultaneous submissions.

MCINTOSH & OTIS, INC.

353 Lexington Ave., New York NY 10016. (212)687-7400. **Fax:** (212)687-6894. **E-mail:** info@mcintoshandotis.com. **Website:** www.mcintoshandotis.com. **Contact:** Eugene H. Winick, Esq. Estab. 1928. Member of AAR. Signatory of WGA.

MEMBER AGENTS Elizabeth Winick Rubinstein, ewrquery@mcintoshandotis.com (literary fiction, women's fiction, historical fiction, and mystery/suspense, along with narrative nonfiction, spiritual/self-help, history and current affairs); Shira Hoffman, shquery@mcintoshandotis.com (young adult, MG, mainstream commercial fiction, mystery, literary fiction, women's fiction, romance, urban fantasy, fantasy, science fiction, horror and dystopian); Christa Heschke, CHquery@mcintoshandotis.com (picture books, middle grade, young adult and new adult projects); Adam Muhlig, AMquery@mcintoshandotis.com (music–from jazz to classical to punk–popular culture, natural history, travel and adventure, and sports); Eugene Winick.

REPRESENTS Considers these nonfiction areas: creative nonfiction, current affairs, history, popular culture, self-help, spirituality, sports, travel. **Considers these fiction areas:** fantasy, historical, horror, literary, middle grade, mystery, new adult, paranormal, picture books, romance, science fiction, suspense, urban fantasy, women's, young adult.

☛ Actively seeking "books with memorable characters, distinctive voices, and great plots."

HOW TO CONTACT E-mail submissions only. Each agent has their own e-mail address for subs. For fiction: Please send a query letter, synopsis, author bio, and the first 3 consecutive chapters (no more than 30 pages) of your novel. For nonfiction: Please send a query letter, proposal, outline, author bio, and 3 sample chapters (no more than 30 pages) of the ms. For children's & young adult: Please send a query letter, synopsis and the first 3 consecutive chapters (not to exceed 25 pages) of the ms. Accepts simultaneous submissions. Obtains clients through recommendations from others, editors, conferences and queries.

TERMS Agent receives 15% commission on domestic sales; 20% on foreign sales.

MENDEL MEDIA GROUP, LLC

115 W. 30th St., Suite 800, New York NY 10001. (646)239-9896. **Fax:** (212)685-4717. **Website:** www.mendelmedia.com. Member of AAR. Represents 40-60 clients.

REPRESENTS Novels. **Considers these nonfiction areas:** Americana, animals, anthropology, architecture, art, biography, business, child guidance, cooking, current affairs, dance, education, environment, ethnic, foods, gardening, gay/lesbian, government, health, history, how-to, humor, investigative, language, medicine, memoirs, military, money, multicultural, music, par-

enting, philosophy, popular culture, psychology, recreation, regional, religious, science, self-help, sex, sociology, software, spirituality, sports, true crime, war, women's issues, women's studies, Jewish topics; creative nonfiction. **Considers these fiction areas:** action, adventure, contemporary issues, crime, detective, erotica, ethnic, feminist, gay, glitz, historical, humor, inspirational, juvenile, lesbian, literary, mainstream, mystery, picture books, police, religious, romance, satire, sports, thriller, young adult, Jewish fiction.

☛ "I am interested in major works of history, current affairs, biography, business, politics, economics, science, major memoirs, narrative nonfiction, and other sorts of general nonfiction." Actively seeking new, major or definitive work on a subject of broad interest, or a controversial, but authoritative, new book on a subject that affects many people's lives. "I also represent more light-hearted nonfiction projects, such as gift or novelty books, when they suit the market particularly well." Does not want "queries about projects written years ago that were unsuccessfully shopped to a long list of trade publishers by either the author or another agent. I am specifically not interested in reading short, category romances (regency, time travel, paranormal, etc.), horror novels, supernatural stories, poetry, original plays, or film scripts."

HOW TO CONTACT Query with SASE. Do not e-mail or fax queries. For nonfiction, include a complete, fully edited book proposal with sample chapters. For fiction, include a complete synopsis and no more than 20 pages of sample text. Responds in 2 weeks to queries; 4-6 weeks to mss. Obtains most new clients through recommendations from others.

TERMS Agent receives 15% commission on domestic sales; 20% commission on foreign sales.

TIPS "While I am not interested in being flattered by a prospective client, it does matter to me that she knows why she is writing to me in the first place. Is one of my clients a colleague of hers? Has she read a book by one of my clients that led her to believe I might be interested in her work? Authors of descriptive nonfiction should have real credentials and expertise in their subject areas, either as academics, journalists, or policy experts, and authors of prescriptive nonfiction should have legitimate expertise and considerable experience communicating their ideas in seminars and workshops, in a successful business, through the media, etc."

JEAN V. NAGGAR LITERARY AGENCY, INC.

JVNLA, Inc., 216 E. 75th St., Suite 1E, New York NY 10021. (212)794-1082. **Website:** www.jvnla.com. **Contact:** Jennifer Weltz. Estab. 1978. Member of AAR. Other memberships include Women's Media Group, SCBWI, Pace University's Masters in Publishing Board Member. Represents 450 clients.

MEMBER AGENTS Jennifer Weltz (well researched and original historicals, thrillers with a unique voice, wry dark humor, and magical realism; enthralling narrative nonfiction; voice driven young adult, middle grade); Alice Tasman (literary, commercial, YA, middle grade, and nonfiction in the categories of narrative, biography, music or pop culture); Laura Biagi (literary fiction, magical realism, psychological thrillers, young adult novels, middle grade novels, and picture books).

REPRESENTS Nonfiction, fiction, novels, short story collections, novellas, juvenile books, scholarly books, poetry books.

> This agency specializes in mainstream fiction and nonfiction and literary fiction with commercial potential as well as young adult, middle grade, and picture books. Does not want to receive screenplays.

HOW TO CONTACT "Visit our website to send submissions and see what our individual agents are looking for. No snail mail submissions please!" Accepts simultaneous submissions. Depends on the agent. No responses for queries unless the agent is interested.

TERMS Agent receives 15% commission on domestic sales; 20% commission on foreign sales. Offers written contract. Charges for overseas mailing, messenger services, book purchases, photocopying—all deductible from royalties received.

TIPS "We recommend courage, fortitude, and patience: the courage to be true to your own vision, the fortitude to finish a novel and polish it again and again before sending it out, and the patience to accept rejection gracefully and wait for the stars to align themselves appropriately for success."

NELSON LITERARY AGENCY

1732 Wazee St., Suite 207, Denver CO 80202. (303)292-2805. **E-mail:** query@nelsonagency.com; querykristin@nelsonagency.com. **Website:** www.nelsonagency.com.

Contact: Kristin Nelson, President. Estab. 2002. Member of AAR. RWA, SCBWI, SFWA. Represents 37 clients.

REPRESENTS Fiction, novels. **Considers these fiction areas:** commercial, fantasy, historical, horror, literary, mainstream, middle grade, romance, science fiction, suspense, thriller, urban fantasy, women's, young adult.

> NLA specializes in representing commercial fiction and high-caliber literary fiction. "We represent many popular genre categories, including historical romance, steampunk, and all subgenres of YA." Regardless of genre, "we are actively seeking good stories well told." Does not want nonfiction, memoir, stage plays, screenplays, short story collections, poetry, children's picture books, early reader chapter books, or material for the Christian/inspirational market.

HOW TO CONTACT "Please visit our website and carefully read our submission guidelines. We do not accept any queries on Facebook or Twitter. Query by e-mail only. Write the word 'Query' in the e-mail subject line along with the title of your novel. Send no attachments, but please paste the first 10 pages of your novel in the body of the e-mail beneath your query letter." Accepts simultaneous submissions. Makes best efforts to respond to all queries within 10 business day. Response to full mss requested can take up to 3 months.

TERMS Agent charges industry standard commission.

TIPS "If you would like to learn how to write an awesome pitch paragraph for your query letter or would like any info on how publishing contracts work, please visit Kristin's popular industry blog Pub Rants: http://nelsonagency.com/pub-rants/."

NEW LEAF LITERARY & MEDIA, INC.

110 W. 40th St., Suite 2201, New York NY 10018. (646)248-7989. **Fax:** (646)861-4654. **E-mail:** query@newleafliterary.com. **Website:** www.newleafliterary.com. Estab. 2012. Member of AAR.

MEMBER AGENTS Joanna Volpe (women's fiction, thriller, horror, speculative fiction, literary fiction and historical fiction, young adult, middle grade, art-focused picture books); Kathleen Ortiz, Director of Subsidiary Rights and literary agent (new voices in YA and animator/illustrator talent); Suzie Townsend (new adult, young adult, middle grade, romance [all subgenres], fantasy [urban fantasy, science fiction, steampunk, epic fantasy] and crime fiction [mysteries, thrillers]); Pouya Shahbazian, Director of Film and Television (no unsolicited queries); Janet Reid, janet@newleafliterary.com; Jaida Temperly (all fiction: magical realism, historical fiction; literary fiction; stories that are quirky and fantastical; nonfiction: niche, offbeat, a bit strange; middle grade; JL Stermer (nonfiction, smart pop culture, comedy/satire, fashion, health & wellness, self-help, and memoir).

REPRESENTS Nonfiction, fiction, novels, novellas, juvenile books, poetry books. **Considers these nonfiction areas:** cooking, crafts, creative nonfiction, science, technology, women's issues, young adult. **Considers these fiction areas:** crime, fantasy, historical, horror, literary, mainstream, middle grade, mystery, new adult, paranormal, picture books, romance, thriller, women's, young adult.

HOW TO CONTACT Send query via e-mail. Please do not query via phone. The word "Query" must be in the subject line, plus the agent's name, i.e.–Subject: Query, Suzie Townsend. You may include up to 5 double-spaced sample pages within the body of the e-mail. No attachments, unless specifically requested. Include all necessary contact information. You will receive an auto-response confirming receipt of your query. "We only respond if we are interested in seeing your work." Responds only if interested. All queries read within 1 month.

HAROLD OBER ASSOCIATES

425 Madison Ave., New York NY 10017. (212)759-8600. **Fax:** (212)759-9428. **Website:** www.haroldober.com. **Contact:** Appropriate agent. Member of AAR. Represents 250 clients.

MEMBER AGENTS Phyllis Westberg; Craig Tenney (few new clients, mostly Ober backlist and foreign rights).

HOW TO CONTACT Submit concise query letter addressed to a specific agent with the first 5 pages of the ms or proposal and SASE. No fax or e-mail. Does not handle filmscripts or plays. Responds as promptly as possible. Obtains most new clients through recommendations from others.

TERMS Agent receives 15% commission on domestic sales; 20% commission on foreign sales. Charges clients for express mail/package services.

L. PERKINS AGENCY

5800 Arlington Ave., Riverdale NY 10471. (718)543-5344. **E-mail:** submissions@lperkinsagency.com.

Website: lperkinsagency.com. Estab. 1987. Member of AAR. Represents 150 clients.

MEMBER AGENTS Tish Beaty, ePub agent (erotic romance–including paranormal, historical, gay/lesbian/bisexual, and light-BDSM fiction; also, she seeks new adult and YA); Sandy Lu, sandy@lperkinsagency.com (fiction: she is looking for dark literary and commercial fiction, mystery, thriller, psychological horror, paranormal/urban fantasy, historical fiction, YA, historical thrillers or mysteries set in Victorian times; nonfiction: narrative nonfiction, history, biography, pop science, pop psychology, pop culture [music/theatre/film], humor, and food writing); Lori Perkins (not currently taking new clients); Leon Husock (science fiction & fantasy, as well as young adult and middle-grade); Rachel Brooks (picture books, all genres of young adult and new adult fiction, as well as adult romance—especially romantic suspense [NOTE: Rachel is currently closed to unsolicited submissions]); Maximilian Ximinez (fiction: science fiction, fantasy, horror, thrillers; nonfiction: popular science, true crime, arts and trends in developing fields and cultures).

REPRESENTS Nonfiction, fiction, novels, short story collections. **Considers these nonfiction areas:** autobiography, biography, business, creative nonfiction, cultural interests, current affairs, film, foods, gay/lesbian, history, how-to, humor, literature, memoirs, music, popular culture, psychology, science, sex, theater, true crime, women's issues, women's studies, young adult. **Considers these fiction areas:** commercial, crime, detective, erotica, fantasy, feminist, gay, historical, horror, lesbian, literary, middle grade, mystery, new adult, paranormal, picture books, romance, science fiction, short story collections, supernatural, thriller, urban fantasy, women's, young adult.

⚓ "Most of our clients write both fiction and nonfiction. This combination keeps our clients publishing for years. The founder of the agency is also a published author, so we know what it takes to write a good book." Actively seeking erotic romance, romance, young adult, middle grade, science fiction, fantasy, memoir, pop culture, thrillers. Does not want poetry, stand alone short stories or novellas, scripts, plays, westerns, textbooks.

HOW TO CONTACT E-queries only. Include your query, a 1-page synopsis, and the first 5 pages from your novel pasted into the e-mail, or your proposal.

No attachments. Submit to only 1 agent at the agency. No snail mail queries. "If you are submitting to one of our agents, please be sure to check the submission status of the agent by visiting their social media accounts listed [on the agency website]." Accepts simultaneous submissions. Obtains most new clients through recommendations from others, solicitations, conferences.

TERMS Agent receives 15% commission on domestic sales; 20% commission on foreign sales. No written contract. Charges clients for photocopying.

TIPS "Research your field and contact professional writers' organizations to see who is looking for what. Finish your novel before querying agents. Read my book, *An Insider's Guide to Getting an Agent*, to get a sense of how agents operate. Read agent blogs-agentinthemiddle.blogspot.com and ravenousromance. blogspot.com."

PROSPECT AGENCY

551 Valley Rd., PMB 377, Upper Montclair NJ 07043. (718)788-3217. **Fax:** (718)360-9582. **Website:** www. prospectagency.com. Estab. 2005. Member of AAR. Signatory of WGA. Represents 130+ clients.

MEMBER AGENTS Emily Sylvan Kim, esk@ prospectagency.com (romance, women's, commercial, young adult, new adult); Rachel Orr, rko@prospectagency.com (picture books, illustrators, middle grade, young adult); Becca Stumpf, becca@prospectagency. com (young adult and middle grade [all genres, including fantasy/SciFi, literary, mystery, contemporary, historical, horror/suspense], especially MG and YA novels featuring diverse protagonists and life circumstances. Adult SciFi and Fantasy novels with broad appeal, upmarket women's fiction, smart, spicy romance novels); Carrie Pestritto, carrie@prospectagency.com (narrative nonfiction, general nonfiction, biography, and memoir; commercial fiction with a literary twist, women's fiction, romance, upmarket, historical fiction, high-concept YA and upper MG); Linda Camacho, linda@prospectagency.com (middle grade, young adult, and adult fiction across all genres, especially women's fiction/romance, horror, fantasy/sci-fi, graphic novels, contemporary; select literary fiction; fiction featuring diverse/marginalized groups); Kirsten Carleton, kcarleton@prospectagency. com (upmarket speculative, thriller, and literary fiction for adult and YA).

REPRESENTS Nonfiction, fiction, novels, novellas, juvenile books, scholarly books, textbooks. **Considers these nonfiction areas:** biography, memoirs, popular culture, psychology. **Considers these fiction areas:** commercial, contemporary issues, crime, ethnic, family saga, fantasy, feminist, gay, historical, horror, humor, juvenile, lesbian, literary, mainstream, middle grade, multicultural, mystery, new adult, picture books, romance, science fiction, suspense, thriller, urban fantasy, women's, young adult.

➥ "We're looking for strong, unique voices and unforgettable stories and characters."

HOW TO CONTACT All submissions are electronic and must be submitted through the portal at prospectagency.com/submissions. We do not accept any submissions through snail mail. Accepts simultaneous submissions. Obtains new clients through conferences, recommendations, queries, and some scouting.

TERMS Agent receives 15% on domestic sales, 20% on foreign sales sold directly and 25% on sales using a subagent. Offers written contract.

REGAL HOFFMANN & ASSOCIATES LLC

242 W. 38th St., Floor 2, New York NY 10018. (212)684-7900. **Fax:** (212)684-7906. **E-mail:** submissions@rhaliterary.com. **Website:** www.rhaliterary.com. Estab. 2002. Member of AAR. Represents 70 clients.

MEMBER AGENTS Claire Anderson-Wheeler (nonfiction: memoirs and biographies, narrative histories, popular science, popular psychology; adult fiction: primarily character-driven literary fiction, but open to genre fiction, high-concept fiction; all genres of young adult / middle grade fiction); Markus Hoffmann (international and literary fiction, crime, [pop] cultural studies, current affairs, economics, history, music, popular science, and travel literature); Joseph Regal (literary fiction, international thrillers, history, science, photography, music, culture, and whimsy); Stephanie Steiker (serious and narrative nonfiction, literary fiction, graphic novels, history, philosophy, current affairs, cultural studies, biography, music, international writing); Grace Ross (literary fiction, historical fiction, international narratives, narrative nonfiction, popular science, biography, cultural theory, memoir).

REPRESENTS **Considers these nonfiction areas:** biography, creative nonfiction, current affairs, economics, history, memoirs, music, psychology, science, travel. **Considers these fiction areas:** literary, mainstream, middle grade, thriller, young adult.

- "We represent works in a wide range of categories, with an emphasis on literary fiction, outstanding thriller and crime fiction, and serious narrative nonfiction." Actively seeking literary fiction and narrative nonfiction. Does not want romance, science fiction, poetry, or screenplays.

HOW TO CONTACT Query with SASE or via e-mail to submissions@rhaliterary.com. No phone calls. Submissions should consist of a 1-page query letter detailing the book in question, as well as the qualifications of the author. For fiction, submissions may also include the first 10 pages of the novel or one short story from a collection. Responds if interested. Accepts simultaneous submissions. Responds in 4-8 weeks.

TERMS Agent receives 15% commission on domestic sales; 20% commission on foreign sales. "We charge no reading fees."

TIPS "We are deeply committed to every aspect of our clients' careers, and are engaged in everything from the editorial work of developing a great book proposal or line editing a fiction manuscript to negotiating state-of-the-art book deals and working to promote and publicize the book when it's published. We are at the forefront of the effort to increase authors' rights in publishing contracts in a rapidly changing commercial environment. We deal directly with co-agents and publishers in every foreign territory and also work directly and with co-agents for feature film and television rights, with extraordinary success in both arenas. Many of our clients' works have sold in dozens of translation markets, and a high proportion of our books have been sold in Hollywood. We have strong relationships with speaking agents, who can assist in arranging author tours and other corporate and college speaking opportunities when appropriate. We also have a staff publicist and marketer to help promote our clients' and their work."

ANN RITTENBERG LITERARY AGENCY, INC.

15 Maiden Lane, Suite 206, New York NY 10038. (212)684-6936. **E-mail:** info@rittlit.com. **Website:** www.rittlit.com. **Contact:** Ann Rittenberg, president. Member of AAR.

REPRESENTS Nonfiction, novels, juvenile books.

- Does not want to receive screenplays, poetry, or self-help.

HOW TO CONTACT Query via e-mail or postal mail (with SASE). Submit query letter with 3 sample chapters pasted in the body of the e-mail. "If you query by e-mail, we will only respond if interested." Accepts simultaneous submissions. Obtains most new clients through referrals from established writers and editors.

TERMS Agent receives 15% commission on domestic sales. Agent receives 20% commission on foreign sales. Offers written contract. This agency charges clients for photocopying only.

B.J. ROBBINS LITERARY AGENCY

5130 Bellaire Ave., North Hollywood CA 91607-2908. **E-mail:** robbinsliterary@gmail.com. **Website:** www.publishersmarketplace.com/members/bjrobbins. **Contact:** (Ms.) B.J. Robbins. Estab. 1992. Member of AAR.

REPRESENTS Nonfiction, fiction. **Considers these nonfiction areas:** autobiography, biography, cultural interests, current affairs, ethnic, film, health, history, investigative, medicine, memoirs, multicultural, music, popular culture, psychology, science, sociology, sports, theater, travel, true crime, women's issues, women's studies. **Considers these fiction areas:** contemporary issues, crime, detective, ethnic, historical, literary, mainstream, multicultural, mystery, sports, suspense, thriller, women's.

- "We do not represent screenplays, plays, poetry, science fiction, horror, westerns, romance, techno-thrillers, religious tracts, dating books or anything with the word 'unicorn' in the title."

HOW TO CONTACT E-query with no attachments. For fiction, okay to include first 10 pages in body of e-mail. Accepts simultaneous submissions. Only responds to projects if interested. Obtains most new clients through conferences, referrals.

TERMS Agent receives 15% commission on domestic sales; 20% commission on foreign sales. Offers written contract. No fees.

RITA ROSENKRANZ LITERARY AGENCY

440 West End Ave., #15D, New York NY 10024. (212)873-6333. **Website:** www.ritarosenkranzliteraryagency.com. **Contact:** Rita Rosenkranz. Member of AAR. Represents 35 clients.

REPRESENTS Nonfiction. **Considers these nonfiction areas:** Americana, animals, anthropology, architecture, art, autobiography, biography, business, child guidance, computers, cooking, crafts, creative nonfiction, cultural interests, current affairs, dance, decorating, diet/nutrition, design, economics, education, environment, ethnic, film, government, health, history, hobbies, how-to, humor, inspirational, interior design, investigative, language, law, literature, medicine, military, money, music, New Age, parenting, photography, popular culture, politics, psychology, regional, religious, satire, science, self-help, sports, technology, theater, true crime, war, women's issues, women's studies.

☛ "This agency focuses on adult nonfiction, stresses strong editorial development and refinement before submitting to publishers, and brainstorms ideas with authors." Actively seeks authors who are well paired with their subject, either for professional or personal reasons.

HOW TO CONTACT Send query letter only (no proposal) via regular mail or e-mail. Submit proposal package with SASE only on request. No fax queries. Accepts simultaneous submissions. Responds in 2 weeks to queries. Obtains most new clients through directory listings, solicitations, conferences, word of mouth.

TERMS Agent receives 15% commission on domestic sales; 20% commission on foreign sales. Offers written contract, binding for 3 years; 3-month written notice must be given to terminate contract. Charges clients for photocopying. Makes referrals to editing services.

TIPS "Identify the current competition for your project to make sure the project is valid. A strong cover letter is very important."

ANDY ROSS LITERARY AGENCY

767 Santa Ray Ave., Oakland CA 94610. (510)238-8965. **E-mail:** andyrossagency@hotmail.com. **Website:** www.andyrossagency.com. **Contact:** Andy Ross. Estab. 2008. Member of AAR. Represents see website for client list clients.

REPRESENTS Nonfiction, fiction, novels, juvenile books, scholarly books. **Considers these nonfiction areas:** anthropology, autobiography, biography, child guidance, cooking, creative nonfiction, cultural interests, current affairs, economics, education, environment, ethnic, gay/lesbian, government, history, investigative, juvenile nonfiction, language, law, literature, memoirs, military, parenting, philosophy, popular culture, politics, psychology, science, sociology, technology, war, women's issues, women's studies, young adult. **Considers these fiction areas:** commer-

cial, contemporary issues, historical, juvenile, literary, middle grade, picture books, young adult.

☛ "This agency specializes in general nonfiction, politics and current events, history, biography, journalism and contemporary culture as well as literary, commercial, and YA fiction." Does not want to receive poetry.

HOW TO CONTACT Queries should be less than half page. Please put the word "query" in the title header of the e-mail. In the first sentence, state the category of the project. Give a short description of the book and your qualifications for writing. Accepts simultaneous submissions. Responds in 1 week to queries.

TERMS Agent receives 15% commission on domestic sales; 20% commission on foreign sales or other deals made through a sub-agent. Offers written contract.

ROSS YOON AGENCY

1666 Connecticut Ave. NW, Suite 500, Washington DC 20009. (202)328-3282. **E-mail:** submissions@rossyoon.com. **Website:** http://rossyoon.com. **Contact:** Jennifer Manguera. Member of AAR.

MEMBER AGENTS Gail Ross gail@rossyoon.com (represents important commercial nonfiction in a variety of areas; new projects must meet two criteria: it must make her daughters proud and offset their college educations); Howard Yoon howard@rossyoon.com (specializes in narrative nonfiction, memoir, current events, history, science, cookbooks, and popular culture); Anna Sproul-Latimer anna@rossyoon.com (nonfiction of all kinds, particularly working with clients who are driven by curiosity: exploring new worlds, uncovering hidden communities, and creating new connections with enthusiasm so infectious that national audiences have already begun to pay attention).

REPRESENTS Nonfiction.

☛ "We are a Washington, D.C.-based literary agency specializing in serious nonfiction on a variety of topics: everything from memoir and history and biography to popular science, business, and psychology. Our clients include CEOs, Pulitzer Prize-winning journalists, academics, politicos, and radio and television personalities." 'We do not represent fiction, screenplays, poetry, YA, or children's titles."

HOW TO CONTACT E-query submissions@rossyoon.com with a query letter briefly explaining your idea, media platform, and qualifications for writing on this topic; or send a complete book proposal featuring an overview of your idea, author bio, media and marketing strategy, chapter outline, and 1-3 sample chapters. Please send these as attachments in .doc or .docx format. Accepts simultaneous submissions. Attempts to respond in 4-6 weeks to queries, but we cannot guarantee a reply. Obtains most new clients through referrals from current clients.

TERMS Agent receives 15% commission on domestic sales; 20% commission on foreign sales. Reserves the right to bill clients for office expenses.

REGINA RYAN PUBLISHING ENTERPRISES, INC.

251 Central Park W., 7D, New York NY 10024. **E-mail:** https://app.authors.me/submit/regina-ryan-books. **Website:** www.reginaryanbooks.com. **Contact:** Regina Ryan. Estab. 1976. Member of AAR.

REPRESENTS Nonfiction. **Considers these nonfiction areas:** Americana, animals, anthropology, archeology, architecture, autobiography, biography, business, child guidance, cooking, cultural interests, diet/nutrition, environment, foods, gardening, health, history, horticulture, medicine, parenting, popular culture, politics, psychology, recreation, science, self-help, sex, sports, travel, true crime, women's issues, women's studies, adult and juvenile nonfiction: narrative nonfiction; natural history (especially birds and birding); popular science, lifestyle, sustainability, mind-body-spirit;.

☛ "We are always looking for new and exciting books in our areas of interest, including well-written narrative nonfiction, architecture, history, politics, natural history (especially birds), science (especially the brain), the environment, women's issues, parenting, cooking, psychology, health, wellness, diet, lifestyle, sustainability, popular reference, and leisure activities including sports, narrative travel, and gardening. We represent books that have something new and fresh to say, are well-written and that will, if possible, make the world a better place." Actively seeking narrative nonfiction, food related travel projects, brain science.

HOW TO CONTACT All queries must come through the following site https://app.authors.me/submit/regina-ryan-books. Accepts simultaneous submissions. "We try to respond in 4-6 weeks but only if we are interested in pursuing the project. If you don't hear from us in that time frame, it means that we are not interested." Obtains most new clients through internet submissions.

TERMS Agent receives 15% commission on domestic and foreign sales. Offers written contract. Charges clients for all out-of-pocket expenses (e.g., long distance calls, messengers, freight, copying) if it's more than just a nominal amount.

TIPS "It's important to include an analysis of comparable books that have had good sales, as well as an analysis of competitive books, that explains why your proposed book is different. Both are essential."

SADLER CHILDREN'S LITERARY

(815)209-6252. **E-mail:** submissions.sadlerliterary@gmail.com. **Website:** www.sadlerchildrensliterary.com. **Contact:** Jodell Sadler. Member of AAR. Signatory of WGA.

REPRESENTS Nonfiction, fiction, novels, juvenile books. **Considers these nonfiction areas:** creative nonfiction, juvenile nonfiction, young adult. **Considers these fiction areas:** juvenile, middle grade, picture books, young adult.

☛ Actively seeks picture book author-illustrators or illustrators interested in picture book writing, or illustrators of MG illustrated titles or graphic novels. Please place this in the subject line when you query. Does not want fantasy. "It's not for me. I'm open to KidLit categories from board books to YA novels. My particular focus is on picture books from author-illustrators."

HOW TO CONTACT "E-mail submissions only from conferences and events, including participation in webinars and webinar series courses at KidLitCollege. Your subject line should read 'Code provided—(Genre) Title_by_Author' and specifically addressed to me. I prefer a short letter: Hook (why my agency), pitch for you project, and bio (brief background and other categories you work in). All submissions in body of the e-mail, no attachments. Query and complete picture book text; first 10 pages for longer genre category. If you are an illustrator or author-illustrator, I encourage you to contact me, and please send a link to your online portfolio." Accepts simultaneous submissions. "I only obtain clients through writing conferences and SCBWI, Writer's Digest, and KidLitCollege.com webinars and events."

TERMS Standard rate. Provided on contract.

THE SAGALYN AGENCY / ICM PARTNERS

Chevy Chase MD **E-mail:** info@sagalyn.com. **Website:** www.sagalyn.com. Estab. 1980. Member of AAR.
MEMBER AGENTS Raphael Sagalyn.
REPRESENTS Nonfiction. **Considers these nonfiction areas:** biography, business, creative nonfiction, economics, popular culture, science, technology.

> ☛ "Our list includes upmarket nonfiction books in these areas: narrative history, biography, business, economics, popular culture, science, technology."

HOW TO CONTACT Please send e-mail queries only. Accepts simultaneous submissions.

VICTORIA SANDERS & ASSOCIATES

440 Buck Rd., Stone Ridge NY 12484. (212)633-8811. **E-mail:** queriesvsa@gmail.com. **Website:** www.victoriasanders.com. **Contact:** Victoria Sanders. Estab. 1992. Member of AAR. Signatory of WGA. Represents 135 clients.
MEMBER AGENTS Victoria Sanders, Chris Kepner, Bernadette Baker-Baughman.
REPRESENTS Nonfiction, fiction, novels, juvenile books. **Considers these nonfiction areas:** autobiography, biography, cultural interests, current affairs, ethnic, film, gay/lesbian, government, history, humor, law, literature, music, popular culture, politics, psychology, satire, theater, translation, women's issues, women's studies. **Considers these fiction areas:** action, adventure, cartoon, comic books, contemporary issues, crime, detective, ethnic, family saga, feminist, gay, historical, humor, inspirational, juvenile, lesbian, literary, mainstream, middle grade, multicultural, multimedia, mystery, new adult, picture books, thriller, women's, young adult.
HOW TO CONTACT Authors who wish to contact us regarding potential representation should send a query letter with the first 3 chapters (or about 25 pages) pasted into the body of the message to queriesvsa@gmail.com. "We will only accept queries via e-mail. Query letters should describe the project and the author in the body of a single, 1-page e-mail that does not contain any attached files. Important note: Please paste the first 3 chapters of your manuscript (or about 25 pages, and feel free to round up to a chapter break) into the body of your e-mail." Accepts simultaneous submissions. Responds in 1-4 weeks, although occasionally it will take longer. "We will not respond to e-mails with attachments or attached files."

TERMS Agent receives 15% commission on domestic sales; 20% commission on foreign/film sales. Offers written contract.

SUSAN SCHULMAN LITERARY AGENCY LLC

454 W. 44th St., New York NY 10036. (212)713-1633. **E-mail:** susan@schulmanagency.com. **E-mail:** queries@schulmanagency.com. **Website:** www.publishersmarketplace.com/members/schulman/. **Contact:** Susan Schulman. Estab. 1980. Member of AAR. Signatory of WGA. Other memberships include Dramatists Guild, Writers Guild of America, East, New York Women in Film, Women's Media Group, Agents' Roundtable, League of New York Theater Women.
REPRESENTS Nonfiction, fiction, novels, juvenile books, feature film, TV scripts, theatrical stage play. **Considers these nonfiction areas:** anthropology, archeology, architecture, art, biography, business, child guidance, cooking, creative nonfiction, current affairs, economics, ethnic, government, health, history, juvenile nonfiction, law, money, popular culture, politics, psychology, religious, science, spirituality, women's issues, women's studies, young adult. **Considers these fiction areas:** commercial, contemporary issues, juvenile, literary, mainstream, new adult, religious, women's, young adult. **Considers these script areas:** theatrical stage play.

> ☛ "We specialize in books for, by and about women and women's issues including nonfiction self-help books, fiction, and theater projects. We also handle the film, television. and allied rights for several agencies as well as foreign rights for several publishing houses." Actively seeking new nonfiction. Considers plays. Does not want to receive poetry, television scripts or concepts for television.

HOW TO CONTACT "For fiction: query letter with outline and three sample chapters, resume and SASE. For nonfiction: query letter with complete description of subject, at least one chapter, resume and SASE. Queries may be sent via regular mail or email. Please do not submit queries via UPS or Federal Express. Please do not send attachments with e-mail queries Please incorporate the chapters into the body of the email." Accepts simultaneous submissions. Responds in less than 1 week generally to a full query and 6 weeks to a full ms. Obtains most new clients through recommendations from others, solicitations, conferences.

TERMS Agent receives 15% commission on domestic sales; 20% commission on foreign sales. Offers written contract; 30-day notice must be given to terminate contract.

SERENDIPITY LITERARY AGENCY, LLC

305 Gates Ave., Brooklyn NY 11216. **E-mail:** rbrooks@serendipitylit.com; info@serendipitylit.com. **Website:** www.serendipitylit.com; facebook.com/serendipitylit. **Contact:** Regina Brooks. Estab. 2000. Member of AAR. Signatory of WGA. Represents 150 clients.

MEMBER AGENTS Regina Brooks; Dawn Michelle Hardy (nonfiction, including sports, pop culture, blog and trend, music, lifestyle and social science); Folade Bell (literary and commercial women's fiction, YA, literary mysteries & thrillers, historical fiction, African-American issues, gay/lesbian, Christian fiction, humor and books that deeply explore other cultures; nonfiction that reads like fiction, including blog-to-book or pop culture); Nadeen Gayle (romance, memoir, pop culture, inspirational/ religious, women's fiction, parenting, young adult, mystery and political thrillers, and all forms of nonfiction); Rebecca Bugger (narrative nonfiction, investigative journalism, memoir, inspirational self-help, religion/spirituality, international, popular culture, and current affairs; literary and commercial fiction); Christina Morgan (literary fiction, crime fiction, and narrative nonfiction in the categories of pop culture, sports, current events and memoir); Jocquelle Caiby (literary fiction, horror, middle grade fiction, and children's books by authors who have been published in the adult market, athletes, actors, journalists, politicians, and musicians).

REPRESENTS Nonfiction, fiction, novels. **Considers these nonfiction areas:** Americana, anthropology, architecture, art, autobiography, biography, business, cooking, creative nonfiction, cultural interests, current affairs, inspirational, interior design, memoirs, metaphysics, music, parenting, popular culture, religious, self-help, spirituality, sports, travel, true crime, women's issues, women's studies, young adult. **Considers these fiction areas:** commercial, gay, historical, lesbian, literary, middle grade, mystery, romance, thriller, women's, young adult, Christian.

HOW TO CONTACT Check the website, as there are online submission forms for fiction, nonfiction and juvenile. Website will also state if we're temporarily closed to submissions to any areas. Accepts simultaneous submissions. Obtains most new clients through conferences, referrals.

TERMS Agent receives 15% commission on domestic sales; 20% commission on foreign sales. Offers written contract; 2-month notice must be given to terminate contract. Charges clients for office fees, which are taken from any advance.

WENDY SHERMAN ASSOCIATES, INC.

138 W. 25th St., Suite 1018, New York NY 10001. (212)279-9027. **E-mail:** submissions@wsherman.com. **Website:** www.wsherman.com. **Contact:** Wendy Sherman. Estab. 1999. Member of AAR.

MEMBER AGENTS Wendy Sherman (women's fiction that hits that sweet spot between literary and mainstream, Southern voices, historical dramas, suspense with a well-developed protagonist, and writing that illuminates the multicultural experience, anything related to food, dogs, mothers and daughters).

REPRESENTS Nonfiction, fiction, novels. **Considers these nonfiction areas:** creative nonfiction, foods, humor, memoirs, parenting, popular culture, psychology, self-help, narrative nonfiction. **Considers these fiction areas:** Mainstream fiction that hits the sweet spot between literary and commercial.

➤ "We specialize in developing new writers, as well as working with more established writers. My experience as a publisher has proven to be a great asset to my clients."

HOW TO CONTACT Query via e-mail only. "We ask that you include your last name, title, and the name of the agent you are submitting to in the subject line. For fiction, please include a query letter and your first 10 pages copied and pasted in the body of the e-mail. We will not open attachments unless they have been requested. For nonfiction, please include your query letter and author bio. Due to the large number of e-mail submissions that we receive, we only reply to e-mail queries in the affirmative. We respectfully ask that you do not send queries to our individual e-mail addresses." Accepts simultaneous submissions. Obtains most new clients through recommendations from other writers.

TERMS Agent receives standard 15% commission. Offers written contract.

SPENCERHILL ASSOCIATES

8131 Lakewood Main St., Building M, Suite 205, Lakewood Ranch FL 34202. (941)907-3700. **E-mail:** submission@spencerhillassociates.com. **Website:** www.

spencerhillassociates.com. **Contact:** Karen Solem, Nalini Akolekar, Amanda Leuck or Sandy Harding. Member of AAR.

MEMBER AGENTS Karen Solem; Nalini Akolekar; Amanda Leuck; Sandy Harding.

REPRESENTS Fiction, novels. **Considers these fiction areas:** commercial, crime, erotica, family saga, gay, historical, inspirational, literary, mainstream, multicultural, mystery, new adult, paranormal, police, romance, thriller, women's, young adult.

☛ "We handle mostly commercial women's fiction, historical novels, romance (historical, contemporary, paranormal, urban fantasy), thrillers, and mysteries. We also represent Christian fiction only—no nonfiction." No nonfiction, poetry, science fiction, children's picture books, or scripts.

HOW TO CONTACT "We accept electronic submissions and are no longer accepting paper queries. Please send us a query letter in the body of an e-mail, pitch us your project and tell us about yourself: Do you have prior publishing credits? Attach the first three chapters and synopsis preferably in .doc, rtf or txt format to your email. Send all queries to submission@spencerhillassociates.com. We do not have a preference for exclusive submissions, but do appreciate knowing if the submission is simultaneous. We receive thousands of submissions a year and each query receives our attention. Unfortunately, we are unable to respond to each query individually. If we are interested in your work, we will contact you within 12 weeks." Accepts simultaneous submissions.

TERMS Agent receives 15% commission on domestic sales; 20% commission on foreign sales. Offers written contract; 3-month notice must be given to terminate contract.

PHILIP G. SPITZER LITERARY AGENCY, INC

50 Talmage Farm Ln., East Hampton NY 11937. (631)329-3650. **Fax:** (631)329-3651. **E-mail:** lukas.ortiz@spitzeragency.com; spitzer516@aol.com. **E-mail:** kim.lombardini@spitzeragency.com. **Website:** www.spitzeragency.com. **Contact:** Lukas Ortiz. Estab. 1969. Member of AAR.

MEMBER AGENTS Philip G. Spitzer; Lukas Ortiz.

REPRESENTS Novels. **Considers these nonfiction areas:** biography, current affairs, history, politics, sports, travel. **Considers these fiction areas:** juvenile, literary, mainstream, suspense, thriller.

☛ This agency specializes in mystery/suspense, literary fiction, sports, and general nonfiction (no how-to).

HOW TO CONTACT E-mail query containing synopsis of work, brief biography, and a sample chapter (pasted into the e-mail). Be aware that this agency openly says their client list is quite full. Accepts simultaneous submissions. Obtains most new clients through recommendations from others.

TERMS Agent receives 15% commission on domestic sales; 20% commission on foreign sales. Charges clients for photocopying.

STIMOLA LITERARY STUDIO

308 Livingston Ct., Edgewater NJ 07020. **E-mail:** info@stimolaliterarystudio.com. **E-mail:** see submission page on website. **Website:** www.stimolaliterarystudio.com. **Contact:** Rosemary B. Stimola. Estab. 1997. Member of AAR, PEN, Authors Guild, ALA. Represents 50 clients.

MEMBER AGENTS Rosemary B. Stimola; Erica Rand Silverman.

REPRESENTS Juvenile books. **Considers these nonfiction areas:** cooking. **Considers these fiction areas:** young adult.

☛ Actively seeking remarkable middle grade, young adult fiction, and debut picture book author/illustrators. No institutional books.

HOW TO CONTACT Query via e-mail as per submission guidelines on website. Author/illustrators of picture books may attach text and sample art. A PDF dummy is preferred. Accepts simultaneous submissions. Responds in 3 weeks to queries "we wish to pursue further;" 2 months to requested mss. While unsolicited queries are welcome, most clients come through editor, agent, client referrals.

TERMS Agent receives 15% commission on domestic sales; 20% (if subagents are employed) commission on foreign sales. Offers written contract, binding for all children's projects. 60 days notice must be given to terminate contract.

STONESONG

270 W. 39th St. #201, New York NY 10018. (212)929-4600. **E-mail:** editors@stonesong.com. **E-mail:** submissions@stonesong.com. **Website:** stonesong.com. Member of AAR. Signatory of WGA.

MEMBER AGENTS Alison Fargis; Ellen Scordato; Judy Linden; Emmanuelle Morgen; Leila Campoli (business, science, technology, and self improvement); Maria Ribas (cookbooks, self-help, health, diet, home, parenting, and humor, all from authors with demonstrable platforms; she's also interested in narrative nonfiction and select memoir); Melissa Edwards (children's fiction and adult commercial fiction, as well as select pop-culture nonfiction); Alyssa Jennette (children's and adult fiction and picture books, and has dabbled in humor and pop culture nonfiction); Madelyn Burt (adult and children's fiction, as well as select historical nonfiction).

REPRESENTS Nonfiction, fiction, novels, juvenile books. **Considers these nonfiction areas:** architecture, art, biography, business, cooking, crafts, creative nonfiction, cultural interests, current affairs, dance, decorating, diet/nutrition, design, economics, foods, gay/lesbian, health, history, hobbies, how-to, humor, interior design, investigative, literature, memoirs, money, music, New Age, parenting, photography, popular culture, politics, psychology, science, self-help, sociology, spirituality, sports, technology, women's issues, young adult. **Considers these fiction areas:** action, adventure, commercial, confession, contemporary issues, ethnic, experimental, family saga, fantasy, feminist, gay, historical, horror, humor, juvenile, lesbian, literary, mainstream, middle grade, military, multicultural, mystery, new adult, New Age, occult, paranormal, regional, romance, satire, science fiction, supernatural, suspense, thriller, urban fantasy, women's, young adult.

☛ Does not represent plays, screenplays, picture books, or poetry.

HOW TO CONTACT Accepts electronic queries for fiction and nonfiction. Submit query addressed to a specific agent. Include first chapter or first 10 pages of ms. Accepts simultaneous submissions.

ROBIN STRAUS AGENCY, INC.

Wallace Literary Agency, 229 E. 79th St., Suite 5A, New York NY 10075. (212)472-3282. **Fax:** (212)472-3833. **E-mail:** info@robinstrausagency.com. **Website:** www.robinstrausagency.com. **Contact:** Ms. Robin Straus. Estab. 1983. Member of AAR.

REPRESENTS Considers these nonfiction areas: biography, cooking, creative nonfiction, current affairs, environment, foods, health, history, memoirs, multicultural, music, parenting, popular culture, psychology, science, travel, women's issues, mainstream

science. **Considers these fiction areas:** commercial, contemporary issues, literary, mainstream, women's.

☛ Does not represent juvenile, young adult, horror, romance, Westerns, poetry, or screenplays.

HOW TO CONTACT E-query or query via snail mail with SASE. "Send us a query letter with contact information, an autobiographical summary, a brief synopsis or description of your book project, submission history, and information on competition. If you wish, you may also include the opening chapter of your manuscript (pasted). While we do our best to reply to all queries, you can assume that if you haven't heard from us after six weeks, we are not interested." Accepts simultaneous submissions.

TERMS Agent receives 15% commission on domestic sales; 20% commission on foreign sales. Offers written contract.

THE STRINGER LITERARY AGENCY LLC

P.O. Box 770365, Naples FL 34107. **E-mail:** mstringer@stringerlit.com. **Website:** www.stringerlit.com. **Contact:** Marlene Stringer. Estab. 2008. Member of AAR. Signatory of WGA. Represents 50 clients.

REPRESENTS Fiction, novels. **Considers these fiction areas:** commercial, crime, detective, fantasy, historical, horror, mainstream, multicultural, mystery, new adult, paranormal, police, romance, science fiction, suspense, thriller, urban fantasy, women's, young adult. No space opera.

☛ This agency specializes in fiction. "We are an editorial agency, and work with clients to make their manuscripts the best they can be in preparation for submission. We focus on career planning, and help our clients reach their publishing goals. We advise clients on marketing and promotional strategies to help them reach their target readership. Because we are so hands-on, we limit the size of our list; however, we are always looking for exceptional voices and stories that demand we read to the end. You never know where the next great story is coming from." This agency is seeking thrillers, crime fiction (not true crime), mystery, women's fiction, single title and category romance, fantasy (all subgenera), earth-based science fiction (no space opera, aliens, etc.), and YA/teen. Does not want to receive picture books, MG, plays, short stories, or poetry. This is not the agency for inspirational romance or erotica.

No space opera. The agency is not seeking non-fiction as of this time (2016).

HOW TO CONTACT Electronic submissions through website submission form only. Please make sure your ms is as good as it can be before you submit. Agents are not first readers. For specific information on what we like to see in query letters, refer to the information at www.stringerlit.com under the heading "Learn." Accepts simultaneous submissions. "We strive to respond quickly, but current clients' work always comes first." Obtains new clients through referrals, submissions, conferences.

TERMS Standard commission. "We do not charge fees."

EMMA SWEENEY AGENCY, LLC

245 E 80th St., Suite 7E, New York NY 10075. **E-mail:** queries@emmasweeneyagency.com. **Website:** www.emmasweeneyagency.com. Estab. 2006. Member of AAR. Other memberships include Women's Media Group. Represents 80 clients.

MEMBER AGENTS Emma Sweeney, president; Margaret Sutherland Brown (commercial and literary fiction, mysteries and thrillers, narrative nonfiction, lifestyle, and cookbook); Kira Watson (children's literature).

REPRESENTS Nonfiction, fiction, novels, juvenile books. **Considers these nonfiction areas:** biography, cooking, creative nonfiction, cultural interests, decorating, diet/nutrition, design, foods, gardening, history, how-to, interior design, juvenile nonfiction, literature, memoirs, popular culture, psychology, religious, science, sex, sociology, young adult. **Considers these fiction areas:** commercial, contemporary issues, crime, historical, juvenile, literary, mainstream, middle grade, mystery, new adult, suspense, thriller, women's, young adult.

➻ Does not want erotica.

HOW TO CONTACT "We accept only electronic queries, and ask that all queries be sent to queries@emmasweeneyagency.com rather than to any agent directly. Please begin your query with a succinct (and hopefully catchy) description of your plot or proposal. Always include a brief cover letter telling us how you heard about ESA, your previous writing credits, and a few lines about yourself. We cannot open any attachments unless specifically requested, and ask that you paste the first 10 pages of your proposal or novel into the text of your e-mail." Accepts simultaneous submissions.

THOMPSON LITERARY AGENCY

115 W. 29th St., Third Floor, New York NY 10001. (347)281-7685. **E-mail:** submissions@thompsonliterary.com. **Website:** thompsonliterary.com. **Contact:** Meg Thompson, founder. Estab. 2014. Member of AAR. Signatory of WGA.

MEMBER AGENTS Cindy Uh, senior agent; John Thorn, affiliate agent; Sandy Hodgman, director of foreign rights.

REPRESENTS Nonfiction, fiction, novels, juvenile books. **Considers these nonfiction areas:** autobiography, biography, business, cooking, crafts, creative nonfiction, current affairs, diet/nutrition, design, education, foods, health, history, how-to, humor, inspirational, interior design, juvenile nonfiction, memoirs, multicultural, popular culture, politics, science, self-help, sociology, sports, travel, women's issues, women's studies, young adult. **Considers these fiction areas:** commercial, contemporary issues, fantasy, historical, juvenile, literary, middle grade, multicultural, picture books, women's, young adult.

➻ The agency is always on the lookout for both commercial and literary fiction, as well as young adult and children's books. "Nonfiction, however, is our specialty, and our interests include biography, memoir, music, popular science, politics, blog-to-book projects, cookbooks, sports, health and wellness, fashion, art, and popular culture." "Please note that we do not accept submissions for poetry collections or screenplays, and we only consider picture books by established illustrators."

HOW TO CONTACT "For fiction: Please send a query letter, including any salient biographical information or previous publications, and attach the first 25 pages of your manuscript. For nonfiction: Please send a query letter and a full proposal, including biographical information, previous publications, credentials that qualify you to write your book, marketing information, and sample material. You should address your query to whichever agent you think is best suited for your project." Accepts simultaneous submissions. Responds in 6 weeks if interested.

TRIADA US

P.O. Box 561, Sewickley PA 15143. (412)401-3376. **E-mail:** uwe@triadaus.com; brent@triadaus.com; laura@

triadaus.com; mallory@triadaus.com; lauren@triadaus.com. **Website:** www.triadaus.com. **Contact:** Dr. Uwe Stender, President. Estab. 2004. Member of AAR.

MEMBER AGENTS Uwe Stender; Brent Taylor; Laura Crockett; Mallory Brown; Lauren Spieller.

REPRESENTS Nonfiction, fiction, novels, juvenile books. **Considers these nonfiction areas:** biography, business, cooking, crafts, creative nonfiction, cultural interests, current affairs, diet/nutrition, economics, education, environment, ethnic, foods, gardening, health, history, how-to, juvenile nonfiction, literature, memoirs, music, parenting, popular culture, politics, science, self-help, sports, true crime, women's issues, young adult. **Considers these fiction areas:** action, adventure, comic books, commercial, contemporary issues, crime, detective, ethnic, family saga, fantasy, gay, historical, horror, juvenile, lesbian, literary, mainstream, middle grade, multicultural, mystery, new adult, occult, picture books, police, suspense, thriller, urban fantasy, women's, young adult.

⟿ Actively seeking fiction and non-fiction across a broad range of categories of all age levels.

HOW TO CONTACT E-mail queries preferred. Please paste your query letter and the first 10 pages of your ms into the body of a message e-mailed to the agent of your choice. Please note: a rejection from 1 Triada US agent is a rejection from all. Triada US agents personally respond to all queries and requested material and pride themselves on having some of the fastest response times in the industry. Obtains most new clients through submission inbox (query letters and requested mss), client referrals, and conferences.

TERMS Triada US retains 15% commission on domestic sales and 20% commission on foreign and translation sales. Offers written contract; 30-day notice must be given prior to termination.

UNION LITERARY

30 Vandam St., Suite 5A, New York NY 10013. (212)255-2112. **E-mail:** info@unionliterary.com; submissions@unionliterary.com. **Website:** http://unionliterary.com. Member of AAR. Signatory of WGA.

MEMBER AGENTS Trena Keating, tk@unionliterary.com (fiction and nonfiction, specifically a literary novel with an exotic setting, a YA/MG journey or transformation novel, a distinctly modern novel with a female protagonist, a creepy page-turner, a quest memoir that addresses larger issues, nonfiction based on primary research or a unique niche, a great essayist, and a voicy writer who is a great storyteller or makes her laugh); Sally Wofford-Girand, swg@unionliterary.com (history, memoir, women's issues, cultural studies, gripping literary fiction); Jenni Ferrari-Adler, jenni@unionliterary.com (fiction, cookbook/food, young adult and middle grade, narrative nonfiction); Christina Clifford, christina@unionliterary.com (literary fiction, international fiction, narrative nonfiction, specifically historical biography, memoir, business, and science); Shaun Dolan, sd@unionliterary.com (muscular and lyrical literary fiction, narrative nonfiction, memoir, pop culture, and sports narratives).

⟿ "Union Literary is a full-service boutique agency specializing in literary fiction, popular fiction, narrative nonfiction, memoir, social history, business and general big idea books, popular science, cookbooks and food writing." The agency does not represent romance, poetry, science fiction or illustrated books.

HOW TO CONTACT Nonfiction submissions: include a query letter, a proposal and a sample chapter. Fiction submissions: should include a query letter, synopsis, and either sample pages or full ms. "Due to the high volume of submissions we receive, we will only be in contact regarding projects that feel like a match for the respective agent." Accepts simultaneous submissions. Accepts simultaneous submissions. Responds in 1 month.

THE UNTER AGENCY

23 W. 73rd St., Suite 100, New York NY 10023. (212)401-4068. **E-mail:** jennifer@theunteragency.com. **Website:** www.theunteragency.com. **Contact:** Jennifer Unter. Estab. 2008. Member of AAR, Women Media Group.

REPRESENTS Nonfiction, fiction, novels, short story collections, juvenile books. **Considers these nonfiction areas:** animals, art, autobiography, biography, cooking, creative nonfiction, current affairs, diet/nutrition, environment, foods, health, history, how-to, humor, juvenile nonfiction, law, memoirs, popular culture, politics, spirituality, sports, travel, true crime, women's issues, young adult, nature subjects. **Considers these fiction areas:** action, adventure, cartoon, commercial, family saga, inspirational, juvenile, mainstream, middle grade, mystery, paranormal, picture books, thriller, women's, young adult.

⟿ This agency specializes in children's, nonfiction, and quality fiction.

HOW TO CONTACT Send an e-query. There is also an online submission form. If you do not hear back from this agency within 3 months, consider that a no. Accepts simultaneous submissions. Responds in 3 months.

WALES LITERARY AGENCY, INC.

1508 10th Ave. E. #401, Seattle WA 98102. (206)284-7114. **E-mail:** waleslit@waleslit.com. **Website:** www.waleslit.com. **Contact:** Elizabeth Wales; Neal Swain. Estab. 1990. Member of AAR. Other memberships include Authors Guild.

MEMBER AGENTS Elizabeth Wales; Neal Swain.
REPRESENTS Nonfiction, fiction, novels.

☛ This agency specializes in quality mainstream fiction and narrative nonfiction. "We're looking for more narrative nonfiction writing about nature, science, and animals." Does not handle screenplays, children's picture books, genre fiction, or most category nonfiction (such as self-help or how-to books).

HOW TO CONTACT E-query with no attachments. Submission guidelines can be found at the agency website along with a list of current clients and titles. Accepts simultaneous submissions. Responds in 2 weeks to queries, 2 months to mss.

TERMS Agent receives 15% commission on domestic sales; 20% commission on foreign sales.

TIPS "We are especially interested in work that espouses a progressive cultural or political view, projects a new voice, or simply shares an important, compelling story. We also encourage writers living in the Pacific Northwest, West Coast, Alaska, and Pacific Rim countries, and writers from historically underrepresented groups, such as gay and lesbian writers and writers of color, to submit work (but does not discourage writers outside these areas). Most importantly, whether in fiction or nonfiction, the agency is looking for talented storytellers."

WELLS ARMS LITERARY

New York NY **E-mail:** info@wellsarms.com. **Website:** www.wellsarms.com. Estab. 2013. Member of AAR, SCBWI, Society of Illustrators. Represents 25 clients.

REPRESENTS Nonfiction, fiction, novels, juvenile books, children's book illustrators. **Considers these nonfiction areas:** juvenile nonfiction, young adult. **Considers these fiction areas:** juvenile, middle grade, new adult, picture books, young adult.

☛ "We focus on books for young readers of all ages: board books, picture books, readers, chapter books, middle grade, and young adult fiction." Actively seeking middle grade, young adult, magical realism, contemporary, romance, fantasy. "We do not represent to the textbook, magazine, adult romance or fine art markets."

HOW TO CONTACT E-query. Put "query" and your title in your e-mail subject line addressed to info@wellsarms.com. Accepts simultaneous submissions. We try to respond in a month's time. If no response, assume it's a no.

WERNICK & PRATT AGENCY

E-mail: submissions@wernickpratt.com. **Website:** www.wernickpratt.com. **Contact:** Marcia Wernick; Linda Pratt; Emily Mitchell. Member of AAR. Signatory of WGA.

MEMBER AGENTS Marcia Wernick, Linda Pratt, Emily Mitchell.

REPRESENTS Juvenile books. **Considers these fiction areas:** middle grade, young adult.

☛ "Wernick & Pratt Agency specializes in children's books of all genres, from picture books through young adult literature and everything in between. We represent both authors and illustrators. We do not represent authors of adult books." Wants people who both write and illustrate in the picture book genre; humorous young chapter books with strong voice, and which are unique and compelling; middle grade/YA novels, both literary and commercial. No picture book mss of more than 750 words, or mood pieces; work specifically targeted to the educational market; fiction about the American Revolution, Civil War, or World War II unless it is told from a very unique perspective.

HOW TO CONTACT Submit via e-mail only to submissions@wernickpratt.com. "Please indicate to which agent you are submitting." Detailed submission guidelines available on website. "Submissions will only be responded to further if we are interested in them. If you do not hear from us within 6 weeks of your submission, it should be considered declined." Accepts simultaneous submissions. Responds in 6 weeks.

BOOK PUBLISHERS

The markets in this year's Book Publishers section offer opportunities in nearly every area of publishing. Large, commercial houses are here as are their smaller counterparts.

The Book Publishers Subject Index is the best place to start your search. You'll find it in the back of the book, before the General Index. Subject areas for both fiction and nonfiction are broken out for all of the book publisher listings.

When you have compiled a list of publishers interested in books in your subject area, read the detailed listings. Pare down your list by cross-referencing two or three subject areas and eliminating the listings only marginally suited to your book. When you have a good list, send for those publishers' catalogs and manuscript guidelines, or check publishers' websites, which often contain catalog listings, manuscript preparation guidelines, current contact names, and other information helpful to prospective authors. You want to use this information to make sure your book idea is in line with a publisher's list but is not a duplicate of something already published.

You should also visit bookstores and libraries to see if the publisher's books are well represented. When you find a couple of books the house has published that are similar to yours, write or call the company to find out who edited those books. This extra bit of research could be the key to getting your proposal to precisely the right editor.

Publishers prefer different methods of submission on first contact. Most like to see a one-page query, especially for nonfiction. Others will accept a brief proposal package that might include an outline and/or a sample chapter. Some publishers will accept submissions from agents only. Each listing in the Book Publishers section includes specific submission methods, if provided by the publisher. Make sure you read each listing carefully to find out exactly what the publisher wants to receive.

When you write your one-page query, give an overview of your book, mention the intended audience, the competition for your book (check local bookstore shelves), and what sets your book apart from the competition. You should also include any previous publishing experience or special training relevant to the subject of your book. For more on queries, read "Query Letter Clinic."

Personalize your query by addressing the editor individually and mentioning what you know about the company from its catalog or books. Under the heading **Contact**, we list the names of editors who acquire new books for each company, along with the editors' specific areas of expertise. Try your best to send your query to the appropriate editor. Editors move around all the time, so it's in your best interest to look online or call the publishing house to make sure the editor you are addressing your query to is still employed by that publisher.

Author-subsidy publishers' not included

Writer's Market is a reference tool to help you sell your writing, and we encourage you to work with publishers that pay a royalty. Subsidy publishing involves paying money to a publishing house to publish a book. The source of the money could be a government, foundation or university grant, or it could be the author of the book. If one of the publishers listed in this book offers you an author-subsidy arrangement (sometimes called "cooperative publishing," "co-publishing," or "joint venture"); or asks you to pay for part or all of the cost of any aspect of publishing (editing services, manuscript critiques, printing, advertising, etc.); or asks you to guarantee the purchase of any number of the books yourself, we would like you to inform us of that company's practices immediately.

⊘ ABBEVILLE FAMILY

Abbeville Press, 116 W. 23rd St., New York NY 10011. (646)375-2136. **Fax:** (646)375-2359. **E-mail:** abbeville@abbeville.com. **Website:** www.abbeville.com. Estab. 1977. Our list is full for the next several seasons. *Not accepting unsolicited book proposals at this time.* **Publishes 8 titles/year. 10% of books from first-time authors.** Accepts simultaneous submissions.

FICTION Picture books: animal, anthology, concept, contemporary, fantasy, folktales, health, hi-lo, history, humor, multicultural, nature/environment, poetry, science fiction, special needs, sports, suspense. Average word length 300-1,000 words. Please refer to website for submission policy.

⊘ ABBEVILLE PRESS

116 W. 23rd St., New York NY 10011. (646)375-2136. **Fax:** (646)375-2359. **E-mail:** abbeville@abbeville.com. **Website:** www.abbeville.com. Estab. 1977. Mainstay in the art book publishing world. "Our list is full for the next several seasons." **10% of books from first-time authors.** Accepts simultaneous submissions.

NONFICTION Subjects include art. Not accepting unsolicited book proposals at this time.

FICTION Subjects include adventure. Picture books through imprint Abbeville Family. Not accepting unsolicited book proposals at this time.

ABC-CLIO/GREENWOOD

Acquisitions Department, P.O. Box 1911, Santa Barbara CA 93116. (805)968-1911. **E-mail:** acquisition_inquiries@abc-clio.com. **Website:** www.abc-clio.com. Estab. 1955. ABC-CLIO is an award-winning publisher of reference titles, academic and general interest books, electronic resources, and books for librarians and other professionals. **Publishes 600 titles/year. 20% of books from first-time authors. 90% from unagented writers. Pays variable royalty on net price.** Accepts simultaneous submissions. Catalog and guidelines online.

IMPRINTS ABC-CLIO; Greenwood Press; Praeger; Linworth and Libraries Unlimited.

NONFICTION Subjects include business, child guidance, education, government, history, humanities, language, music, psychology, religion, social sciences, sociology, sports. No memoirs, drama. Query with proposal package, including scope, organization, length of project, whether a complete ms is available or when it will be, CV, and SASE. Check guidelines online for each imprint.

TIPS "Looking for reference materials and materials for educated general readers. Many of our authors are college professors who have distinguished credentials and who have published research widely in their fields."

ABDO PUBLISHING CO.

8000 W. 78th St., Suite 310, Edina MN 55439. (800)800-1312. **Fax:** (952)831-1632. **E-mail:** nonfiction@abdopublishing.com. **E-mail:** fiction@abdopublishing.com; illustrations@abdopublishing.com. **Website:** www.abdopublishing.com. Estab. 1985. Publishes hardcover originals. ABDO publishes nonfiction children's books (pre-kindergarten to 8th grade) for school and public libraries—mainly history, sports, biography, geography, science, and social studies. "Please specify each submission as either nonfiction, fiction, or illustration. **Publishes 300 titles/year.** Accepts simultaneous submissions. Guidelines online.

NONFICTION Subjects include animals, history, science, sports, geography, social studies.

ABINGDON PRESS

Imprint of The United Methodist Publishing House, 201 Eighth Ave. S., P.O. Box 801, Nashville TN 37202. (615)749-6000. **Fax:** (615)749-6512. **E-mail:** submissions@umpublishing.org. **Website:** www.abingdonpress.com. Estab. 1789. Publishes hardcover and paperback originals. Abingdon Press, America's oldest theological publisher, provides an ecumenical publishing program dedicated to serving the Christian community—clergy, scholars, church leaders, musicians, and general readers—with quality resources in the areas of Bible study, the practice of ministry, theology, devotion, spirituality, inspiration, prayer, music and worship, reference, Christian education, and church supplies. **Publishes 120 titles/year. 3,000 queries; 250 mss received/year. 85% from unagented writers. Pays 7½% royalty on retail price.** Publishes ms 2 years after acceptance. Responds in 2 months to queries. Book catalog available free. Guidelines online.

NONFICTION Subjects include education, religion, theology. Query with outline and samples only. The author should retain a copy of any unsolicited material submitted.

FICTION Publishes stories of faith, hope, and love that encourage readers to explore life. Agented submissions only for fiction.

⊘ ABRAMS

115 W. 18th St., 6th Floor, New York NY 10011. (212)206-7715. **Fax:** (212)519-1210. **E-mail:** abrams@ abramsbooks.com. **Website:** www.abramsbooks.com. **Contact:** Managing Editor. Estab. 1951. Publishes hardcover and a few paperback originals. **Publishes 250 titles/year.** Accepts simultaneous submissions.

IMPRINTS Stewart, Tabori & Chang; Abrams Appleseed; Abrams Books for Young Readers; Abrams Image; STC Craft; Amulet Books.

🗨 Does not accept unsolicited materials.

NONFICTION Subjects include recreation.

FICTION Subjects include young adult. Publishes hardcover and "a few" paperback originals. Averages 150 total titles/year.

TIPS "We are one of the few publishers who publish almost exclusively illustrated books. We consider ourselves the leading publishers of art books and high-quality artwork in the U.S. Once the author has signed a contract to write a book for our firm the author must finish the manuscript to agreed-upon high standards within the schedule agreed upon in the contract."

⊘ ABRAMS BOOKS FOR YOUNG READERS

115 W. 18th St., New York NY 10011. **Website:** www. abramsyoungreaders.com. Accepts simultaneous submissions.

🗨 Abrams no longer accepts unsolicted mss or queries.

ACADEMY CHICAGO PUBLISHERS

814 N. Franklin St., Chicago IL 60610. (312)337-0747. **Fax:** (312)337-5985. **Website:** www.chicagoreviewpress.com. **Contact:** Yuval Taylor, senior editor. Estab. 1975. Publishes hardcover and some paperback originals and trade paperback reprints. "We publish quality fiction and nonfiction. Our audience is literate and discriminating. No novelized biography, history, or science fiction. No electronic submissions." **Publishes 10 titles/year. Pays 7-10% royalty on wholesale price.** Publishes ms 18 months after acceptance. Accepts simultaneous submissions. Responds in 3 months. Book catalog online. Guidelines online.

NONFICTION Subjects include history, travel. No religion, cookbooks, or self-help. Submit proposal package, outline, bio, 3 sample chapters.

FICTION Subjects include historical, mystery. "We look for quality work, but we do not publish experi-

mental, avant garde, horror, science fiction, thrillers novels." Submit proposal package, synopsis, 3 sample chapters, and short bio.

TIPS "At the moment, we are looking for good nonfiction; we certainly want excellent original fiction, but we are swamped. No fax queries, no disks. No electronic submissions. We are always interested in reprinting good out-of-print books."

⚫⊘ ACE SCIENCE FICTION AND FANTASY

Imprint of the Berkley Publishing Group, Penguin Group (USA), Inc., 375 Hudson St., New York NY 10014. (212)366-2000. **Website:** www. us.penguingroup.com. Estab. 1953. Publishes hardcover, paperback, and trade paperback originals and reprints. Ace publishes science fiction and fantasy exclusively. **Publishes 75 titles/year. Pays royalty. Pays advance.**

🗨 As an imprint of Penguin, Ace is not open to unsolicited submissions.

FICTION Subjects include fantasy, science fiction. No other genre accepted. No short stories. Due to the high volume of manuscripts received, most Penguin Group (USA) Inc. imprints do not normally accept unsolicited mss.

ACTA PUBLICATIONS

4848 N. Clark St., Chicago IL 60640. **Website:** www. actapublications.com. **Contact:** Acquisitions Editor. Estab. 1958. Publishes trade paperback originals. ACTA publishes nonacademic, practical books aimed at the mainline religious market. **Publishes 12 titles/year. 100 queries received/year. 25 mss received/year. 50% of books from first-time authors. 90% from unagented writers. Pays 10-12% royalty on wholesale price.** Publishes book 1 year after acceptance of ms. Responds in 2-3 months to proposals. Book catalog and guidelines online.

🗨 "While some of ACTA's material is specifically Catholic in nature, most of the company's products are aimed at a broadly ecumenical audience."

NONFICTION Subjects include religion, spirituality. True Submit outline, 1 sample chapter. No e-mail submissions. Reviews artwork/photos. Send photocopies.

TIPS "Don't send a submission unless you have examined our catalog, website and several of our books."

ADDICUS BOOKS, INC.

P.O. Box 45327, Omaha NE 68145. (402)330-7493. **Fax:** (402)330-1707. **E-mail:** info@addicusbooks.com. **Website:** www.addicusbooks.com. **Contact:** Acquisitions Editor. Estab. 1994. Addicus Books, Inc. publishes nonfiction books. "Our focus is on consumer health topics and legal topics for consumers, but we will consider other topics. We publish every book in trade paperback and in 3 e-book formats. We partner with a master book distributor that sells books into the trade—bookstores and libraries; we continually seek other sales channels outside the trade. We need at least 1 solid sales channel outside the bookstore market." **Publishes 15 titles/year. 90% of books from first-time authors. 95% from unagented writers. Royalties, paid every 6 months, are based on a percentage of revenue.** Publishes ms 9 months after acceptance. Accepts simultaneous submissions. Responds in 1 month or less to inquiries. Catalog and guidelines online.

NONFICTION Subjects include business, economics, health, law, consumer health, consumer legal topics, economics, investment advice. "We are continuously expanding our line of consumer health and consumer legal titles." Submit inquiry in a brief e-mail. "If we are interested, we may ask for a proposal. See proposal guidelines on our Website. Do not send entire ms unless requested. Please do not mail submissions by certified mail."

TIPS "We focus heavily on the quality of editorial content. We strive for good organization, clarity, and appropriate tone in a manuscript. Our books are concise and reader-friendly."

AHSAHTA PRESS

MFA Program in Creative Writing, Boise State University, 1910 University Dr., MS 1525, Boise ID 83725. (208) 426-3414. **E-mail:** ahsahta@boisestate.edu. **Website:** ahsahtapress.org. **Contact:** Janet Holmes, director. Estab. 1974. Publishes trade paperback originals. A not-for-profit literary publisher, Ahsahta was founded in 1974 at Boise State University to preserve the best works by early poets of the American West. Its name, *ahsahta*, is the Mandan word meaning "Rocky Mountain bighorn sheep," and was first recorded by members of the Lewis and Clark expedition; the founding editors chose the word to honor the press's original mission to publish Western poetry. Peggy Pond Church, H.L. Davis, Hazel Hall, Gwendolen Haste, Haniel Long, and Norman Macleod are among the early Western writers Ahsahta Press restored to print. Soon after its inception, the press began publishing contemporary poetry by Western poets along with its reprint titles. Ahsahta editors discovered and initially published a number of widely popular poets from the West—among them David Baker, Katharine Coles, Wyn Cooper, Gretel Ehrlich, Cynthia Hogue, Leo Romero, and Carolyne Wright. With the inception of the M.F.A. Program in Creative Writing at Boise State University, Ahsahta Press expanded its scope, presenting the work of poets from across the nation whose work is selected through our national competitions or by general submission. These include Julie Carr, Anne Boyer, Kate Greenstreet, Brian Teare, James Meetze, and TC Tolbert. "Ahsahta Press champions and promotes surprising, relevant, and accessible experimental poetry that more commercially minded small presses avoid; in making it widely available, we aim to increase its readership." **Publishes 7-10 titles/year. 1,000 mss received/year. 40% of books from first-time authors. 100% from unagented writers. Pays 8% royalty on retail price for first 1,000 sold; 10% thereafter. Does not usually pay advance.** Publishes ms 2 years after acceptance. Accepts simultaneous submissions. Responds in 3 months to mss. Book catalog online. Guidelines online; submit through submissions manager.

POETRY "We usually hold an open submissions period in May as well as the Sawtooth Poetry Prize competition in January and February, from which we publish 2-3 mss per year. We no longer publish chapbooks." Submit complete ms. The press publishes runners-up as well as winners of the Sawtooth Poetry Prize. Forthcoming, new, and backlist titles available on website. Most backlist titles: $9.95; most current titles: $18.

TIPS "Ahsahta's motto is that poetry is art, so our readers tend to come to us for the unexpected—poetry that makes them think, reflect, question their preconceptions, and even do something they haven't done before."

⊘ ALADDIN

Simon & Schuster, 1230 Avenue of the Americas, 4th Floor, New York NY 10020. (212)698-7000. **Website:** www.simonandschuster.com. **Contact:** Acquisitions Editor. Publishes hardcover/paperback originals and imprints of Simon & Schuster Children's Publishing

Children's Division. Aladdin publishes picture books, beginning readers, chapter books, middle grade and tween fiction and nonfiction, and graphic novels and nonfiction in hardcover and paperback, with an emphasis on commercial, kid-friendly titles. Accepts simultaneous submissions.

FICTION Simon & Schuster does not review, retain or return unsolicited materials or artwork. "We suggest prospective authors and illustrators submit their mss through a professional literary agent."

⊘ ALGONQUIN BOOKS OF CHAPEL HILL

Workman Publishing, P.O. Box 2225, Chapel Hill NC 27515-2225. (919)967-0108. **Website:** www.algonquin. com. **Contact:** Editorial Department. Publishes hardcover originals. Algonquin Books publishes quality literary fiction and literary nonfiction. **Publishes 24 titles/year.** Guidelines online.

IMPRINTS Algonquin Young Readers.

NONFICTION Does not accept unsolicited submissions at this time. "Visit our website for full submission policy to queries."

FICTION Subjects include literary. Does not accept unsolicited submissions at this time.

ALGONQUIN YOUNG READERS

P.O. Box 2225, Chapel Hill NC 27515. **Website:** algonquinyoungreaders.com. Algonquin Young Readers is a new imprint that features books for readers 7-17. "From short illustrated novels for the youngest independent readers to timely and topical crossover young adult fiction, what ties our books together are unforgettable characters, absorbing stories, and superior writing. Accepts simultaneous submissions. Guidelines online.

FICTION Algonquin Young Readers publishes ficiton and a limited number of narrative nonfiction titles for middle grade and young adult readers. "We don't publish poetry, picture books, or genre fiction." Query with 15-20 sample pages and SASE.

ALGORA PUBLISHING

222 Riverside Dr., 16th Floor, New York NY 10025-6809. (212)678-0232. **Fax:** (212)666-3682. **Website:** www.algora.com. Estab. 1992. Publishes hardcover and trade paperback originals and reprints. Algora Publishing is an academic-type press, focusing on works by North and South American, European, Asian, and African authors for the educated general reader. **Publishes 25 titles/year. 1,500 queries; 800 mss received/year. 20% of books from first-time au-**

thors. 85% from unagented writers. Pays $0-1,000 advance. Publishes book 10-18 months after acceptance of ms. Accepts simultaneous submissions. Responds in 1 month to queries/proposals; 3 months to mss. Book catalog and guidelines online.

NONFICTION Subjects include anthropology, archeology, creative nonfiction, dance, education, environment, finance, government, history, language, literature, military, money, music, nature, philosophy, politics, psychology, religion, science, sociology, translation, war, womens issues, womens studies, economics. Algora Publishing welcomes proposals for original mss, but "we do not handle self-help, recovery, or children's books." Submit a query or ms by uploading file to our website.

TIPS "We welcome first-time writers; we help craft an author's raw manuscript into a literary work."

🔁 IAN ALLAN PUBLISHING, LTD.

Terminal House, Shepperton TW17 8AS, United Kingdom. (44)(193)283-4950. **E-mail:** info@ianallan-publishing.co.uk. **Website:** www.ianallanpublishing. com. Publishes hardcover, trade paperback and mass market paperback originals and reprints. **Publishes 120 titles/year. 300 queries; 50 mss received/year. 5% of books from first-time authors. 95% from unagented writers. Payment is subject to contract and type of publication.** Publishes book 6 months after acceptance of ms. Accepts simultaneous submissions. Book catalog available free.

NONFICTION Subjects include history, hobbies, sports, travel. Query with SASE. Reviews artwork/photos.

TIPS "Audience is enthusiasts and historians. We don't publish books with a strong autobiographical bias—e.g., military reminiscences—and no fiction/children's/poetry."

🔁 ALLEN & UNWIN

406 Albert St., East Melbourne VIC 3002, Australia. (61)(3)9665-5000. **E-mail:** fridaypitch@allenandunwin.com. **Website:** www.allenandunwin.com. Allen & Unwin publish over 80 new books for children and young adults each year, many of these from established authors and illustrators. "However, we know how difficult it can be for new writers to get their work in front of publishers, which is why we've decided to extend our innovative and pioneering Friday Pitch service to emerging writers for children and young

adults. Accepts simultaneous submissions. Guidelines online.

ALLWORTH PRESS

An imprint of Skyhorse Publishing, 307 West 36th St., 11th Floor, New York NY 10018. (212)643-6816. **Fax:** (212)643-6819. **E-mail:** allworthsubmissions@ skyhorsepublishing.com. **Website:** www.allworth. com. Estab. 1989. Publishes hardcover and trade paperback originals. Allworth Press publishes business and self-help information for artists, designers, photographers, authors and film and performing artists, as well as books about business, money and the law for the general public. The press also publishes the best of classic and contemporary writing in art and graphic design. Currently emphasizing photography, graphic and industrial design, performing arts, fine arts and crafts, et al. **Publishes 12-18 titles/year. Pays advance.** Responds in 4-6 weeks. Book catalog and ms guidelines free.

NONFICTION Subjects include photography, film, television, graphic design, performing arts, as well as business and legal guides for the public. "We are currently accepting query letters for practical, legal, and technique books targeted to professionals in the arts, including designers, graphic and fine artists, craftspeople, photographers, and those involved in film and the performing arts." Query with 1-2 page synopsis, chapter outline, market analysis, sample chapter, bio, SASE.

TIPS "We are helping creative people in the arts by giving them practical advice about business and success."

ALPINE PUBLICATIONS

38262 Linman Rd., Crawford CO 81415. (970)921-5005. **Fax:** (970)921-5081. **E-mail:** alpinepublishing@aol.com. **Website:** alpinepub.com. **Contact:** B. J. McKinney, Publisher. Estab. 1975. Publishes hardcover and trade paperback originals and reprints. "We specialize in dog and horse books such as training, care, breed books, nutrition, health, and related nonfiction subjects. Alpine Publications is looking for specialized dog training and care manuscripts by experienced trainers, breeders, and other professionals in canine care and performance fields. We do not publish children's books nor first person experiences." **Publishes 1-5 titles/year. 40% of books from first-time authors. 95% from unagented writers. Pays 8-15% royalty on net price. Sometimes offers ad-**

vance. Publishes ms 6-12 months after acceptance. Accepts simultaneous submissions. Responds in 2 weeks. Book catalog online.

NONFICTION Subjects include agriculture, animals. Alpine specializes in books that promote the enjoyment of and responsibility for companion animals with emphasis on dogs and horses. No biographies. Query with a brief synopsis, chapter outline, bio, sample chapter, and market analysis. Reviews artwork with submission. E-mail sample jpg files.

TIPS "Our audience is pet owners, breeders, exhibitors, veterinarians, animal trainers, animal care specialists, and judges. Our books are in-depth and most are heavily illustrated. Look up some of our titles before you submit. See what is unique about our books. Write your proposal to suit our guidelines."

AMACOM BOOKS

American Management Association, 1601 Broadway, New York NY 10019. (212)586-8100. **Fax:** (212)903-8083. **E-mail:** ekadin@amanet.org; spower@amanet. org; tburgard@amanet.org. **Website:** www.amacom-books.org. **Contact:** Ellen Kadin, executive editor (marketing, career, personal development); Stephen Power, senior editor (leadership, management, human resources, training); Tim Burgard, senior editor (sales, customer service, project management, finance, supply chain); all editors (parenting, popular psychology, health & fitness). Book proposals on general business, education, science & technology, popular psychology, parenting, or health & fitness topics may be submitted to any editor. Estab. 1923. Publishes trade hardcover and paperback originals and e-books. AMACOM Books—the publishing arm of the American Management Association (AMA)—is a nonfiction publisher devoted to helping readers lead more satisfying lives by publishing works that enhance their personal and professional growth and success. "Our authors—practitioners, journalists, and world-class educators—are noted experts and leaders in their fields. At AMACOM we can give authors the individual attention of a small publisher as well as the advantage of distributing and selling their books in both print and digital form through multiple channels around the world." **Publishes 40-50 titles/year. Receives 500-1,000 submissions/year. Pays advance.** Depends on the circumstances. Standard schedule is seven months to bound books. Accepts simultaneous submissions. Catalog available. Guidelines online.

NONFICTION Subjects include business, career guidance, child guidance, communications, economics, education, finance, government, health, nutrition, parenting, psychology, real estate, science, womens issues, personal development (business self-help); fitness;. Publishes nonfiction books for consumer and professional markets, including all business topics, parenting, health & fitness, popular psychology, popular science and technology, real estate, and education Submit proposals including brief book description and rationale, TOC, author bio and platform, intended audience, competing books and sample chapters. Proposals returned with SASE only.

TIPS "Platform info in proposal reflects author activities that demonstrate author's visibility, authority, and audience reach."

AMADEUS PRESS

Hal Leonard Publishing Group, 33 Plymouth St., Suite 302, Montclair NJ 07402. (973)337-5034. **Fax:** (973)337-5227. **E-mail:** submissions@halleonardbooks.com. **Website:** www.amadeuspress.com. **Contact:** Carol Flannery, editorial director. Publishes books on classical music and opera. **Publishes 8-10 titles/year. 30% of books from first-time authors. 75% from unagented writers. Pays modest advance.** Publishes ms 18-24 months after acceptance. Accepts simultaneous submissions. Responds in 30-45 days. Guidelines online.

NONFICTION Subjects include education, entertainment, memoirs, music. "Amadeus Press welcomes submissions pertaining to opera and classical music. Send proposal including: a letter describing the purpose and audience for your book, along with your background and qualifications; please indicate which word-processing software you use as we ask that final ms be submitted on disk; an outline or table of contents and an estimate of the length of the completed ms in numbers of words or double-spaced pages; a sample chapter or two, printed out (no electronic file transfers, please); sample illustrations as well as an estimate of the total numbers and types (for example, pen-and-ink artwork for line drawings, black-and-white glossy photographic prints, camera-ready music examples) of illustrations planned for your book; your schedule to complete the book. Generally, we ask authors to submit book proposals early in the writing process as this allows us to give editorial advice during the development phase and cuts down the amount

of revisions needed later. Due to the large volume of submissions, you may not receive a response from us. If you wish to have the materials you submit returned to you, please so indicate and include return postage."

AMBERJACK PUBLISHING

P.O. Box 4668 #89611, New York NY 10163. (888)959-3352. **Website:** www.amberjackpublishing.com. Amberjack Publishing offers authors the freedom to write without burdening them with having to promote the work themselves. They retain all rights. "You will have no rights left to exploit, so you cannot resell, republish or use your story again." Accepts simultaneous submissions.

FICTION Amberjack Publishing is always on the lookout for the next great story. "We are interested in fiction, children's books, graphic novels, science fiction, fantasy, humor, and everything in between." Submit via online query form with book proposal and first 10 pages of ms.

AMERICAN CATHOLIC PRESS

16565 S. State St., South Holland IL 60473. (708)331-5845. **Fax:** (708)331-5484. **E-mail:** acp@acpress.org. **Website:** www.acpress.org. **Contact:** Rev. Michael Gilligan, PhD, editorial director. Estab. 1967. Publishes hardcover originals and hardcover and paperback reprints. **Publishes 4 titles/year. Makes outright purchase of $25-100.** Guidelines online.

NONFICTION Subjects include education, religion, spirituality. "We publish books on the Roman Catholic liturgy—for the most part, books on religious music and educational books and pamphlets. We also publish religious songs for church use, including Psalms, as well as choral and instrumental arrangements. We are interested in new music, meant for use in church services. Books, or even pamphlets, on the Roman Catholic Mass are especially welcome. We have no interest in secular topics and are not interested in religious poetry of any kind."

TIPS "Most of our sales are by direct mail, although we do work through retail outlets."

AMERICAN CHEMICAL SOCIETY

Publications/Books Division, 1155 16th St. NW, Washington DC 20036. (202)452-2120. **Fax:** (202)513-8819. **Website:** pubs.acs.org/books/. Estab. 1876. Publishes hardcover originals. American Chemical Society publishes symposium-based books for chemistry. **Publishes 35 titles/year. Pays royalty.** Accepts simul-

taneous submissions. Responds in 2 months to proposals. Book catalog available free. Guidelines online.
NONFICTION Subjects include science. Emphasis is on meeting-based books. Log in to submission site online.

AMERICAN CORRECTIONAL ASSOCIATION
206 N. Washington St., Suite 200, Alexandria VA 22314. (703)224-0000. **Fax:** (703)224-0179. **Website:** www.aca.org. Estab. 1870. Publishes trade paperback originals. American Correctional Association provides practical information on jails, prisons, boot camps, probation, parole, community corrections, juvenile facilities and rehabilitation programs, substance abuse programs, and other areas of corrections. **Publishes 18 titles/year. 90% of books from first-time authors. 100% from unagented writers.** Publishes ms 1 year after acceptance. Accepts simultaneous submissions. Responds in 4 months to queries. Book catalog available free. Guidelines online.
NONFICTION "We are looking for practical, how-to texts or training materials written for the corrections profession. We are especially interested in books on management, development of first-line supervisors, and security-threat group/management in prisons." No autobiographies or true-life accounts by current or former inmates or correctional officers, theses, or dissertations. No fiction or poetry. Query with SASE. Reviews artwork/photos.
TIPS "Authors are professionals in the field of corrections. Our audience is made up of corrections professionals and criminal justice students. No books by inmates or former inmates. This publisher advises out-of-town freelance editors, indexers, and proofreaders to refrain from requesting work from them."

AMERICAN COUNSELING ASSOCIATION
6101 Stevenson Ave., Suite 600, Alexandria VA 22304. (703)823-9800, x356. **Fax:** (703)823-4786. **E-mail:** cbaker@counseling.org. **Website:** www.counseling.org. **Contact:** Carolyn C. Baker, associate publisher. Estab. 1952. Publishes paperback originals. "The American Counseling Association is dedicated to promoting public confidence and trust in the counseling profession. We publish scholarly texts for graduate level students and mental health professionals. We do not publish books for the general public." **Publishes 8-10 titles/year. 1% of books from first-time authors. 90% from unagented writers. See ACA website for payment information.** Accepts simultaneous sub-

missions. Responds in 1 month to queries. Guidelines available free.
NONFICTION Subjects include career guidance, education, gay, lesbian, multicultural, psychology, religion, social sciences, spirituality, womens issues, womens studies, LGBTQ mental health, school counseling, marriage, family, couples counseling. ACA does not publish self-help books or autobiographies. Query with SASE. Submit proposal package, outline, 2 sample chapters, vitae.
TIPS "Target your market. Your books will not be appropriate for everyone across all disciplines."

AMERICAN FEDERATION OF ASTROLOGERS
6535 S. Rural Rd., Tempe AZ 85283. (480)838-1751. **Fax:** (480)838-8293. **Website:** www.astrologers.com. Estab. 1938. Publishes trade paperback originals and reprints. American Federation of Astrologers publishes astrology books, calendars, charts, and related aids. **Publishes 10-15 titles/year. 10 queries; 20 mss received/year. 50% of books from first-time authors. 100% from unagented writers. Pays 10% royalty.** Publishes book 10 months after acceptance of ms. Accepts simultaneous submissions. Responds in 6 months to mss. Book catalog available free. Guidelines online.
NONFICTION "Our market for beginner books, Sun-sign guides, and similar material is limited and we thus publish very few of these. The ideal word count for a book-length manuscript published by AFA is about 40,000 words, although we will consider manuscripts from 20,000 to 60,000 words." Submit complete ms.
TIPS "AFA welcomes articles for *Today's Astrologer*, our monthly journal for members, on any astrological subject. Most articles are 1,500-3,000 words, but we do accept shorter and longer articles. Follow the guidelines online for book manuscripts. You also can e-mail your article to info@astrologers.com, but any charts or illustrations must be submitted as attachments and not embedded in the body of the e-mail or in an attached document."

AMERICAN QUILTER'S SOCIETY
5801 Kentucky Dam Rd., Paducah KY 42003. (270)898-7903. **Fax:** (270)898-1173. **Website:** www.americanquilter.com. Estab. 1984. Publishes trade paperbacks. American Quilter's Society publishes how-to and pattern books for quilters (beginners

through intermediate skill level). We are not the publisher for non-quilters writing about quilts. We now publish quilt-related craft cozy romance and mystery titles, series only. Humor is good. Graphic depictions and curse words are bad. **Publishes 20-24 titles/year. 100 queries received/year. 60% of books from first-time authors. Pays 5% royalty on retail price for both nonfiction and fiction.** Publishes nonfiction ms 9-18 months after acceptance. Fiction published on a different schedule TBD. Responds in 2 months to proposals. Guidelines online.

○ Accepts simultaneous nonfiction submissions. Does not accept simultaneous fiction submissions.

NONFICTION No queries; proposals only. Note: 1 or 2 completed quilt projects must accompany proposal.

FICTION Submit a synopsis and 2 sample chapters, plus an outline of the next 2 books in the series.

AMERICAN WATER WORKS ASSOCIATION

6666 W. Quincy Ave., Denver CO 80235. (303)347-6260. **Fax:** (303)794-7310. **E-mail:** submissions@awwa.org. **Website:** www.awwa.org. **Contact:** Senior Manager, Acquisitions and Content. Estab. 1881. Publishes hardcover and trade paperback originals. AWWA strives to advance and promote the safety and knowledge of drinking water and related issues to all audiences—from kindergarten through post-doctorate. **Publishes 25 titles/year.** Responds in 4 months to queries. Book catalog and ms guidelines free.

NONFICTION Subjects include science, software, drinking water- and wastewater-related topics, operations, treatment, sustainability. Query with SASE. Submit outline, bio, 3 sample chapters. Reviews artwork/photos. Send photocopies.

TIPS "See website to download submission instructions."

AMG PUBLISHERS

AMG International, Inc., 6815 Shallowford Rd., Chattanooga TN 37421. (423)894-6060. **E-mail:** sales@amgpublishers.com. **Website:** www.amgpublishers.com. **Contact:** Amanda Jenkins, sales manager/author liaison. Estab. 1985. Publishes hardcover and trade paperback originals, electronic originals, and audio Bible and book originals. Publishing division of AMG International began in 1985 with release of the *Hebrew-Greek Key Word Study Bible* in the King James Version. This groundbreaking study Bible is now published in four other Bible translations. In-depth study and examination of original biblical languages provide some of our core Bible study and reference tools. In 1998, AMG launched the successful Following God Bible study series (primarily for women) that examine key characters of the Bible along with life application principles. AMG has also been publishing young adult inspirational fantasy fiction since 2005 but is not currently accepting fiction mss. "Profits from sales of our books and Bibles are funneled back into world missions and childcare efforts of parent organization, AMG Publishers. **Publishes 15-20 titles/year. 2,500 queries; 500 mss received/year. 25% of books from first-time authors. 35% from unagented writers. Pays 10-16% royalty on net sales. Advance negotiable.** Publishes book 12-18 months after acceptance of ms. Accepts simultaneous submissions. Responds in 1 month to queries, 4 months to proposals/mss. Book catalog and guidelines online.

IMPRINTS Living Ink Books; God and Country Press; AMG Bible Studies.

NONFICTION Subjects include Americana, education, history, military, parenting, religion, spirituality, war, womens issues, young adult. Bibles, trade nonfiction books, and workbook Bible studies Does not want self-help, memoir, autobiography, biography, New Age, prosperity gospel. Query with letter first, e-mail preferred.

FICTION Subjects include fantasy, young adult. "We are not presently acquiring fiction of any genre, though we continue to publish a number of titles in the young adult inspirational fantasy category."

TIPS "AMG is open to well-written, niche Bible study, reference, and devotional books that meet immediate needs."

AMHERST MEDIA, INC.

175 Rano Street, Suite 200, Buffalo NY 14207. (716)874-4450. **E-mail:** submissions@amherstmedia.com. **Website:** www.amherstmedia.com. **Contact:** Craig Alesse, publisher. Associate Publisher: Kate Neaverth. Estab. 1974. Publishes trade paperback originals and reprints. Amherst Media publishes illustrated books on all subjects including photographic instruction. **Publishes 50 titles/year. 60% of books from first-time authors. 90% from unagented writers. Pays 15-18% royalty. Pays advance.** Publishes book 1 year after acceptance. Accepts simultaneous

submissions. Responds in 2 weeks to queries. Book catalog online. Guidelines upon request.

NONFICTION Subjects include agriculture, animals, architecture, art, automotive, communications, contemporary culture, crafts, creative nonfiction, environment, gardening, hobbies, horticulture, house and home, marine subjects, medicine, nature, New Age, photography, pop culture, recreation, transportation, womens issues. Looking for author/photographers for illustrated books. 100-200 high quality photographs around a theme. Reviews artwork/photos.

TIPS "Our audience is made up of enthusiasts in all subject areas."

❶❷ AMULET BOOKS

Imprint of Abrams, 115 W. 18th St., 6th Floor, New York NY 10001. **Website:** www.amuletbooks.com. Estab. 2004. *Does not accept unsolicited mss or queries.* **10% of books from first-time authors.** Accepts simultaneous submissions.

FICTION Middle readers: adventure, contemporary, fantasy, history, science fiction, sports. Young adults/teens: adventure, contemporary, fantasy, history, science fiction, sports, suspense.

❸ ANDERSEN PRESS

20 Vauxhall Bridge Rd., London SW1V 2SA, United Kingdom. **E-mail:** anderseneditorial@penguinrandomhouse.co.uk. **Website:** www.andersenpress.co.uk. Andersen Press is a specialist children's publisher. "We publish picture books, for which the required text would be approximately 500 words (maximum 1,000), juvenile fiction for which the text would be approximately 3,000-5,000 words and older fiction up to 75,000 words. We do not publish adult fiction, nonfiction, poetry, or short story anthologies." Accepts simultaneous submissions. Guidelines online.

FICTION Send all submissions by post: Query and full ms for picture books; synopsis and 3 chapters for longer fiction.

ANDREWS MCMEEL UNIVERSAL

1130 Walnut St., Kansas City MO 64106. (816)581-7500. **Website:** www.andrewsmcmeel.com. **Contact:** Book Submissions. Estab. 1973. Publishes hardcover and paperback originals. Andrews McMeel publishes general trade books, humor books, miniature gift books, calendars, and stationery products. **Publishes 300 titles/year. Pays royalty on retail price or net receipts. Pays advance.** Accepts simultaneous submissions. Guidelines online.

NONFICTION Subjects include cooking, games, comics, puzzles. Submit proposal.

❷ ANHINGA PRESS

P.O. Box 3665, Tallahassee FL 32315. **E-mail:** info@anhinga.org. **Website:** www.anhinga.org. **Contact:** Kristine Snodgrass, co-director. Publishes hardcover and trade paperback originals. Publishes only full-length collections of poetry (60-80 pages). No individual poems or chapbooks. **Publishes 5 titles/year. Pays 10% royalty on retail price.** Accepts simultaneous submissions. Responds in 3 months. Guidelines online.

POETRY Not accepting any unsolicited submissions at this time. Enter Robert Dana-Anhinga Prize for Poetry.

ANKERWYCKE

American Bar Association, 321 N. Clark St., Chicago IL 60654. **Website:** www.ababooks.org. Estab. 1878. Publishes hardcover and trade paperback originals. In 1215, the Magna Carta was signed underneath the ancient Ankerwycke Yew tree, starting the process which led to rule by constitutional law—in effect, giving rights and the law to the people. And today, the ABA's Ankerwycke line of books continues to bring the law to the people. With legal fiction, true crime books, popular legal histories, public policy handbooks, and prescriptive guides to current legal and business issues, Ankerwycke is a contemporary and innovative line of books for everyone from a trusted and vested authority. **Publishes 30-40 titles/year. 1,000's of queries received/year. 25% of books from first-time authors. 50% from unagented writers.** Publishes ms 12-18 months after acceptance. Accepts simultaneous submissions. Responds in 1 month to queries and proposals; 3 months to mss. Book catalog and ms guidelines online.

NONFICTION Subjects include business, consumer legal. "Extremely high quality nonfiction with a legal aspect; business books specifically for service professionals; consumer legal on a wide range of topics—we're actively acquiring in all these areas." Query with cover letter; outline or TOC; and CV/bio including other credits. Include e-mail address for response.

FICTION "We're actively acquiring legal fiction with extreme verisimilitude." Query with cover letter; outline or TOC; and CV/bio including other credits. Include e-mail address for response.

⊙⊘ ANNICK PRESS, LTD.

15 Patricia Ave., Toronto ON M2M 1H9, Canada. (416)221-4802. **Fax:** (416)221-8400. **Website:** www.annickpress.com. **Contact:** The Editors. Publishes picture books, juvenile and YA fiction and nonfiction; specializes in trade books. Annick Press maintains a commitment to high quality books that entertain and challenge. Our publications share fantasy and stimulate imagination, while encouraging children to trust their judgment and abilities. *Does not accept unsolicited mss.* **Publishes 25 titles/year. 5,000 queries received/year. 3,000 mss received/year. 20% of books from first-time authors. 80-85% from unagented writers. Pays authors royalty of 5-12% based on retail price. Offers advances (average amount: $3,000). Pays illustrators royalty of 5% minimum.** Publishes a book 2 years after acceptance. Accepts simultaneous submissions. Book catalog and guidelines online.

NONFICTION Works with 20 illustrators/year. Illustrations only: Query with samples.

FICTION Publisher of children's books. Not accepting picture books at this time.

⊙ ANVIL PRESS

P.O. Box 3008 MPO, Vancouver BC V6B 3X5, Canada. (604)876-8710. **Fax:** (604)879-2667. **E-mail:** info@anvilpress.com. **Website:** www.anvilpress.com. Estab. 1988. Publishes trade paperback originals. Anvil Press publishes contemporary adult fiction, poetry, and drama, giving voice to up-and-coming Canadian writers, exploring all literary genres, discovering, nurturing, and promoting new Canadian literary talent. Currently emphasizing urban/suburban themed fiction and poetry; de-emphasizing historical novels. Canadian authors only. No e-mail submissions. **Publishes 8-10 titles/year. 300 queries received/year. 80% of books from first-time authors. 70% from unagented writers. Pays advance. Average advance is $500-2,000, depending on the genre.** Publishes book 8 months after acceptance of ms. Accepts simultaneous submissions. Responds in 2 months to queries; 6 months to mss. Book catalog for 9×12 SAE with 2 first-class stamps. Guidelines online.

NONFICTION Query with 20-30 pages and SASE.

FICTION Subjects include experimental, literary, short story collections. Contemporary, modern literature; no formulaic or genre. Query with 20-30 pages and SASE.

POETRY "Get our catalog, look at our poetry. We do very little poetry-maybe 1-2 titles per year." Query with 8-12 poems and SASE.

TIPS "Audience is informed, educated, aware, with an opinion, culturally active (films, books, the performing arts). No U.S. authors. Research the appropriate publisher for your work."

APA BOOKS

American Psychological Association, 750 First St. NE, Washington DC 20002. (202)336-5500. **Website:** www.apa.org/pubs/books/index.aspx. Publishes hardcover and trade paperback originals. Accepts simultaneous submissions. Book catalog online. Guidelines online.

IMPRINTS Magination Press (children's books).

NONFICTION Subjects include education, multicultural, psychology, science, social sciences, sociology. Submit cv and prospectus with TOC, intended audience, selling points, and outside competition.

TIPS "Our press features scholarly books on empirically supported topics for professionals and students in all areas of psychology."

APPALACHIAN MOUNTAIN CLUB BOOKS

5 Joy St., Boston MA 02138. (617)523-0636. **Fax:** (617)523-0722. **E-mail:** amcbooks@outdoors.org. **Website:** www.outdoors.org. Estab. 1876. Publishes hardcover, trade paperback, and digital originals. AMC Books are written and published by the experts in the Northeast outdoors. "Our mission is to publish authoritative, accurate, and easy-to-use books and maps based on AMC's expertise in outdoor recreation, education, and conservation. We are committed to producing books and maps that appeal to novices and day visitors as well as outdoor enthusiasts in our core activity areas of hiking and paddling. By advancing the interest of the public in outdoor recreation and helping our readers to access back country trails and waterways, and by using our books to educate the public about safety, conservation, and stewardship, we support AMC's mission of promoting the protection, enjoyment, and wise use of the Northeast outdoors. We work with the best professional writers possible and draw upon the experience of our programs staff and chapter leaders from Maine to Washington, DC. **Publishes 8-12 titles/year. 1% of books from first-time authors. 98% from unagented writers. Pays advance.** Publishes ms 1-2 years after accep-

tance. Responds in 4 weeks. Catalog online. Guidelines online.

NONFICTION Subjects include creative nonfiction, environment, nature, recreation, regional, Maps that are based on our direct work with land managers and our on-the-ground collection of data on trails, natural features, and points of interest. Appalachian Mountain Club publishes hiking, paddling, nature, conservation, and mountain-subject guides for America's Northeast. "We also publish narrative titles related to outdoor recreation, mountaineering, and adventure, often with a historical perspective, and always with a deep connection to our region (from Maine to Washington, D.C.). We connect recreation to conservation and education." Please no Appalachian Trail memoirs. Send a query letter and the first three chapters of your ms to the publications department via e-mail. Your query letter should explain the subject of your book and why it would be appropriate for AMC Books to publish. Include information about word count (our guidebooks are typically between 80,000 and 100,000 words) and any special art or graphic treatment that you envision. Tell us how the book would be distinctive by comparing it to similar titles that are already on the market. Also explain the intended audience for your book and why you think your book would generate interest. Present some ideas of how you would help us market the book and reach readers. Conclude with a summary of your relevant experience and credentials, including previously published writing on related topics. Allow us four weeks to respond to your query.

TIPS "Our audience is outdoor recreationists, conservation-minded hikers and canoeists, family outdoor lovers, armchair enthusiasts. Visit our website for proposal submission guidelines and more information. Please no fiction, children's books, or poetry."

ARBORDALE PUBLISHING

612 Johnnie Dodds, Suite A2, Mt. Pleasant SC 29464. (843)971-6722. **Fax:** (843)216-3804. **E-mail:** katie@arbordalepublishing.com. **Website:** www.arbordalepublishing.com. **Contact:** Katie Hall. Estab. 2004. Publishes hardcover, trade paperback, and electronic originals. "The picture books we publish are usually, but not always, fictional stories with nonfiction woven into the story that relate to science or math. All books should subtly convey an educational theme through a warm story that is fun to read and that will grab a child's attention. Each book has a 4-page 'For Creative Minds' section to reinforce the educational component. This section will have a craft and/or game as well as 'fun facts' to be shared by the parent, teacher, or other adult. Authors do not need to supply this information with their submission, but if their ms is accepted, they may be asked to provide additional information for this section. Mss should be less than 1,000 words and meet all of the following 4 criteria: fun to read—mostly fiction with nonfiction facts woven into the story; national or regional in scope; must tie into early elementary school curriculum; must be marketable through a niche market such as a zoo, aquarium, or museum gift shop." **Publishes 12 titles/year. 1,000 mss received/year. 50% of books from first-time authors. 100% from unagented writers. Pays 6-8% royalty on wholesale price. Pays small advance.** Publishes book 18 months after acceptance. May hold onto mss of interest for 1 year until acceptance. Accepts simultaneous submissions. Accepts electronic submissions only. Snail mail submissions are discarded without being opened.

Acknowledges receipt of ms submission within 1 month. Book catalog and guidelines online.

NONFICTION Subjects include animals, creative nonfiction, environment, ethnic, marine subjects, multicultural, science. Prefer fiction, but will consider nonfiction as well All mss should be submitted via e-mail to Katie Hall. Mss should be less than 1,000 words. Reviews artwork/photos. Send 1-2 JPEGS and link to online portfolio

FICTION Subjects include picture books. Picture books: animal, folktales, nature/environment, science- or math-related. No more than 1,000 words. All mss should be submitted via e-mail to Katie Hall. Mss should be less than 1,000 words.

POETRY "We do not accept books of poetry. Will consider mss written in rhyming verse, but prefer prose."

TIPS "Please make sure that you have looked at our website to read our complete submission guidelines and to see if we are looking for a particular subject. Manuscripts must meet all four of our stated criteria. We look for fairly realistic, bright and colorful art- no cartoons. We want the children excited about the books. We envision the books being used at home and in the classroom."

ARCADE PUBLISHING

Skyhorse Publishing, 307 W. 36th St., 11th Floor, New York NY 10018. (212)643-6816. **Fax:** (212)643-6819. **E-mail:** arcadesubmissions@skyhorsepublishing.com. **Website:** www.arcadepub.com. **Contact:** Acquisitions Editor. Estab. 1988. Publishes hardcover originals, trade paperback reprints. Arcade prides itself on publishing top-notch literary nonfiction and fiction, with a significant proportion of foreign writers. **Publishes 35 titles/year. 5% of books from first-time authors. Pays royalty on retail price and 10 author's copies. Pays advance.** Publishes book 18 months after acceptance. Accepts simultaneous submissions. Responds in 2 months if interested. Book catalog and ms guidelines for #10 SASE.

NONFICTION Subjects include history, memoirs, travel, popular science, current events. Submit proposal with brief query, 1-2 page synopsis, chapter outline, market analysis, sample chapter, bio.

FICTION Subjects include literary, short story collections, translation. No romance, historical, science fiction. Submit proposal with brief query, 1-2 page synopsis, chapter outline, market analysis, sample chapter, bio.

ARCADIA PUBLISHING

420 Wando Park Blvd., Mt. Pleasant SC 29464. (843)853-2070. **Fax:** (843)853-0044. **Website:** www.arcadiapublishing.com. Estab. 1993. Publishes trade paperback originals. Arcadia publishes photographic vintage regional histories. "We have more than 3,000 Images of America series in print. We have expanded our California program." **Publishes 600 titles/year. Pays 8% royalty on retail price.** Publishes book 9 months after acceptance. Accepts simultaneous submissions. Book catalog online. Guidelines available free.

NONFICTION Subjects include history. "Arcadia accepts submissions year-round. Our editors seek proposals on local history topics and are able to provide authors with detailed information about our publishing program as well as book proposal submission guidelines. Due to the great demand for titles on local and regional history, we are currently searching for authors to work with us on new photographic history projects. Please contact one of our regional publishing teams if you are interested in submitting a proposal." Specific proposal form to be completed.

TIPS "Writers should know that we only publish history titles. The majority of our books are on a city or region, and contain vintage images with limited text."

ARCHAIA

Imprint of Boom! Studios, 5670 Wilshire Blvd., Suite 450, Los Angeles CA 90036. **Website:** www.archaia.com. Use online submission form. Accepts simultaneous submissions.

FICTION Subjects include adventure, fantasy, horror, mystery, science fiction. Looking for graphic novel submissions that include finished art. "Archaia is a multi-award-winning graphic novel publisher with more than 75 renowned publishing brands, including such domestic and international hits as *Artesia, Mouse Guard*, and a line of Jim Henson graphic novels including *Fraggle Rock* and *The Dark Crystal*. Publishes creator-shared comic books and graphic novels in the adventure, fantasy, horror, pulp noir, and science fiction genres that contain idiosyncratic and atypical writing and art. *Archaia does not generally hire freelancers or arrange for freelance work, so submissions should only be for completed book and series proposals.*"

ARCH STREET PRESS

1122 County Line Rd., Bryn Mawr PA 19010. (877)732-ARCH. **E-mail:** contact@archstreetpress.org. **Website:** www.archstreetpress.org. **Contact:** Robert Rimm, managing editor. Estab. 2010. Publishes hardcover, trade paperback, mass market paperback, and electronic originals. Arch Street Press is an independent nonprofit publisher dedicated to the collaborative work of creative visionaries, social entrepreneurs and leading scholars worldwide. Arch Street Press is part of the Institute for Leadership Education, Advancement and Development, a Pennsylvania-based 501(c)(3) nonprofit with offices in Philadelphia and Bryn Mawr. It has served as a key force for community leadership development since 1995, fostering a degreed citizenry to tangibly improve and sustain the economic, civic and social well-being of communities throughout the United States. Please visit our website, www.archstreetpress.org, for further information, including our Innovate podcast series with international CEOs and leaders, current and upcoming books, wide-ranging blog et al. **Publishes 4 titles/year. 100 queries; 5 mss received/year. 30% of books from first-time authors. 50% from unagented writers. Pays 6-20% royalty on retail price.** Publishes ms 1 year after acceptance. Accepts simultaneous submissions. Responds in 1-2 months. Book catalog and guidelines online.

NONFICTION Subjects include art, business, communications, community, contemporary culture, creative nonfiction, economics, education, environment, finance, foods, government, health, history, humanities, labor, language, law, literary criticism, literature, memoirs, multicultural, music, nature, nutrition, philosophy, social sciences, sociology, spirituality, translation, womens studies, world affairs, leadership. Query with SASE. Submit proposal package including outline and 3 sample chapters. Review artwork. Writers should send photocopies.

FICTION Subjects include literary. Query with SASE. Submit proposal package, including outline and 3 sample chapters.

A-R EDITIONS, INC.

1600 Aspen Commons, Suite 100, Middleton WI 53562. (608)836-9000. **E-mail:** info@areditions.com. **Website:** www.areditions.com. Estab. 1962. A-R Editions publishes modern critical editions of music based on current musicological research. Each edition is devoted to works by a single composer or to a single genre of composition. The contents are chosen for their potential interest to scholars and performers, then prepared for publication according to the standards that govern the making of all reliable, historical editions. **Publishes 30 titles/year. 40 queries; 30 mss received/year. 75% of books from first-time authors. 100% from unagented writers. Pays royalty or honoraria.** Book catalog online. Guidelines online.

NONFICTION Subjects include historical music editions; computer music and digital audio topics. Computer Music and Digital Audio Series titles deal with issues tied to digital and electronic media, and include both textbooks and handbooks in this area.

ARROW PUBLICATIONS, LLC

7716 Bells Mill Rd., Bethesda MD 20817. (301)299-9422. **Fax:** (240)632-8477. **E-mail:** arrow_info@arrowpub.com. **Website:** www.arrowpub.com. **Contact:** Tom King, managing editor. Estab. 1987. No graphic novels until further notice. **Publishes 50 e-book titles/year. Paperback version launched in 2009 with 12 English and 12 Spanish titles/year. 150 queries; 100 mss received/year. 80% of books from first-time authors. 100% from unagented writers. Makes outright purchase of accepted completed scripts.** Publishes book 4-6 months after acceptance

of ms. Accepts simultaneous submissions. Responds in 2 month to queries; 1 month to mss sent upon request. Guidelines online.

NONFICTION Subjects include business, womens issues.

FICTION Subjects include comic books, erotica, ethnic, historical, mainstream, romance. "We are looking for outlines of stories heavy on romance with elements of adventure/intrigue/mystery. We will consider other romance genres such as fantasy, western, inspirational, and historical as long as the romance element is strong." Query with outline first with SASE. Consult submission guidelines online before submitting.

TIPS "Our audience is primarily women 18 and older. Send query with outline only."

ARSENAL PULP PRESS

#202-211 East Georgia St., Vancouver BC V6A 1Z6, Canada. (604)687-4233. **Fax:** (604)687-4283. **E-mail:** info@arsenalpulp.com. **Website:** www.arsenalpulp.com. **Contact:** Editorial Board. Estab. 1980. Publishes trade paperback originals, and trade paperback reprints. "We are interested in literature that traverses uncharted territories, publishing books that challenge and stimulate and ask probing questions about the world around us." **Publishes 14-20 titles/year. 500 queries; 300 mss received/year. 30% of books from first-time authors. 100% from unagented writers.** Publishes ms 1 year after acceptance. Accepts simultaneous submissions. Responds in 2-4 months. Book catalog for 9×12 SAE with IRCs or online. Guidelines online.

NONFICTION Subjects include creative nonfiction, ethnic, history, multicultural, sex, sociology, travel, film, visual art. Rarely publishes non-Canadian authors. No poetry at this time. "We do not publish children's books." Each submission must include: "a synopsis of the work, a chapter by chapter outline for nonfiction, writing credentials, a 50-page excerpt from the ms (*do not send more, it will be a waste of postage; if we like what we see, we'll ask for the rest of the manuscript*), and a marketing analysis. If our editorial board is interested, you will be asked to send the entire ms. We do not accept discs or submissions by fax or e-mail, and we do not discuss concepts over the phone." Reviews artwork/photos.

FICTION Subjects include ethnic, feminist, literary, multicultural, short story collections. No children's books or genre fiction, i.e., westerns, romance, horror, mystery, etc. Submit proposal package, outline, clips, 2-3 sample chapters.

ARTE PUBLICO PRESS

University of Houston, 4902 Gulf Fwy, Bldg 19, Rm 100, Houston TX 77204-2004. **Fax:** (713)743-2847. **E-mail:** submapp@uh.edu. **Website:** artepublicopress. com. Estab. 1979. Publishes hardcover originals, trade paperback originals and reprints. Arte Publico Press is the oldest and largest publisher of Hispanic literature for children and adults in the United States. "We are a showcase for Hispanic literary creativity, arts and culture. Our endeavor is to provide a national forum for U.S.-Hispanic literature." **Publishes 25-30 titles/year. 1,000 queries; 2,000 mss received/year. 50% of books from first-time authors. 80% from unagented writers. Pays 10% royalty on wholesale price. Provides 20 author's copies; 40% discount on subsequent copies. Pays $1,000-3,000 advance.** Publishes book 2 years after acceptance of ms. Accepts simultaneous submissions. Responds in 1 month to queries and proposals; 4 months to mss. Book catalog available free. Guidelines online.

NONFICTION Subjects include ethnic, regional, translation. Hispanic civil rights issues for new series: The Hispanic Civil Rights Series. Submissions made through online submission form.

FICTION Subjects include contemporary, ethnic, literary, mainstream. "Written by U.S.-Hispanics." Submissions made through online submission form.

POETRY Submissions made through online submission form.

TIPS "Include cover letter in which you 'sell' your book—why should we publish the book, who will want to read it, why does it matter, etc. Use our ms submission online form. Format files accepted are: Word, plain/text, rich/text files. Other formats will not be accepted. Manuscript files cannot be larger than 5MB. Once editors review your ms, you will receive an e-mail with the decision. Revision process could take up to 4 months."

ASA, AVIATION SUPPLIES & ACADEMICS

7005 132 Place SE, Newcastle WA 98059. (425)235-1500. **E-mail:** feedback@asa2fly.com. **Website:** www. asa2fly.com. ASA is an industry leader in the development and sales of aviation supplies, publications, and software for pilots, flight instructors, flight engineers and aviation technicians. All ASA products are de-veloped by a team of researchers, authors and editors. Book catalog available free.

NONFICTION Subjects include education. "We are primarily an aviation publisher. Educational books in this area are our specialty; other aviation books will be considered." All subjects must be related to aviation education and training. Query with outline. Send photocopies or MS Word files.

TIPS "Two of our specialty series include ASA's *Focus Series*, and ASA *Aviator's Library*. Books in our *Focus Series* concentrate on single-subject areas of aviation knowledge, curriculum and practice. The *Aviator's Library* is comprised of titles of known and/or classic aviation authors or established instructor/authors in the industry, and other aviation specialty titles."

ASABI PUBLISHING

Asabi Publishing, **E-mail:** submissions@asabipublishing.com. **Website:** www.asabipublishing.com. **Contact:** Tressa Sanders, publisher. Estab. 2004. Publishes hardcover, mass market and trade paperback originals. **Publishes 5 titles/year. Accepts professional queries only. 30% of books from first-time authors. 30% from unagented writers. Pays 40% royalty on wholesale or list price. Pays up to $500 advance.** Publishes ms 2 years after acceptance. Responds in 1 month to queries and proposals, 2-6 months to mss. Book catalog online. Guidelines online.

NONFICTION Subjects include agriculture, alternative lifestyles, environment, ethnic, gay, health, history, house and home, lesbian, medicine, memoirs, nature, psychology, science, sex, travel, true crime, young adult, skilled trades, survival guides. Wants how-to skilled trades, organic agriculture, how-to renewable energy, alternative homebuilding, natural medicine, psychology, sexual instruction, African history, living abroad, non-religious homeschooling, lesbian romance. Anything religious or spiritual, astrology. Submit professional query letter only. "We do not publish poetry or titles containing religious or spiritual content of any kind." Reviews artwork/photos. Writers should send photocopies.

FICTION Subjects include confession, erotica, lesbian, romance. Anything religious or spiritual, astrology, ghosts, aliens. Submit professional query letter.

ASCE PRESS

American Society of Civil Engineers, 1801 Alexander Bell Dr., Reston VA 20191. (703)295-6275. **E-mail:** ascepress@asce.org. **Website:** www.asce.org/bookstore. Estab. 1989. "ASCE Press publishes technical volumes that are useful to practicing civil engineers and civil engineering students, as well as allied professionals. We publish books by individual authors and editors to advance the civil engineering profession. Currently emphasizing geotechnical, structural engineering, sustainable engineering and engineering history. De-emphasizing highly specialized areas with narrow scope." **Publishes 5-10 titles/year. 20% of books from first-time authors. 100% from unagented writers.** Guidelines online.

NONFICTION Subjects include civil engineering. "We are looking for topics that are useful and instructive to the engineering practitioner." Query with proposal, sample chapters, CV, TOC, and target audience.

TIPS "As a traditional publisher of scientific and technical materials, ASCE Press applies rigorous standards to the expertise, scholarship, readability and attractiveness of its books."

ASHLAND POETRY PRESS

401 College Ave., Ashland OH 44805. (419)289-5098. **E-mail:** app@ashland.edu. **Website:** www.ashland-poetrypress.com. **Contact:** Cassandra Brown, managing editor. Estab. 1969. Publishes trade paperback originals. **Publishes 2-3 titles/year. 200-400 mss received/year in Snyder Prize. 50% of books from first-time authors. 100% from unagented writers. Makes outright purchase of $500-1,000.** Publishes book 10 months after acceptance. Accepts simultaneous submissions. Responds in 6 months to mss. Book catalog online. Guidelines online.

NONFICTION Subjects include literature, poetry.

POETRY "We accept unsolicited mss through the Snyder Prize competition each spring, The deadline is April 1." Judges are mindful of dedication to craftsmanship and thematic integrity.

TIPS "We rarely publish a title submitted off the transom outside of our Snyder Prize competition."

ASM PRESS

Book division for the American Society for Microbiology, 1752 N St., NW, Washington DC 20036. (202)737-3600. **Fax:** (202)942-9342. **E-mail:** books@asmusa.org. **Website:** www.asmscience.org. Estab. 1899. Publishes hardcover, trade paperback and electronic originals. **Publishes 30 titles/year. 40% of books from first-time authors. 95% from unagented writers. Pays 5-15% royalty on wholesale price. Pays $1,000-10,000 advance.** Publishes book 6-9 months after acceptance. Accepts simultaneous submissions. Responds in 2 months. Book catalog online. Guidelines online.

NONFICTION Subjects include agriculture, animals, education, history, horticulture, science, microbiology and related sciences. "Must have bona fide academic credentials in which they are writing." Query with SASE or by e-mail. Submit proposal package, outline, prospectus. Reviews artwork/photos. Send photocopies.

TIPS "Credentials are most important."

ASSOCIATION FOR SUPERVISION AND CURRICULUM DEVELOPMENT

ASCD, 1703 N. Beauregard St., Alexandria VA 22311-1714. (703)578-9600. **Fax:** (703)575-5400. **E-mail:** acquisitions@ascd.org. **Website:** www.ascd.org. **Contact:** Genny Ostertag, director, content acquisitions. Estab. 1943. Publishes trade paperback originals. ASCD publishes high-quality professional books for educators. **Publishes 30 titles/year. Receives approximately 200 proposals/year. 30% of books from first-time authors. 95% from unagented writers. Pays negotiable royalty on actual monies received.** Publishes ms 1 year after acceptance. Accepts simultaneous submissions. Responds in 2-3 months to proposals. Book catalog and guidelines online.

NONFICTION Subjects include education. Submit full proposal, 2 sample chapters. Reviews artwork/photos. Send photocopies.

ASTRAGAL PRESS

Finney Company, 5995 149th St. W., Suite 105, Apple Valley MN 55124. (866)543-3045. **E-mail:** info@finneyco.com. **Website:** www.astragalpress.com. Estab. 1983. Publishes trade paperback originals and reprints. Our primary audience includes those interested in antique tool collecting, metalworking, carriage building, early sciences and early trades, and railroading. Accepts simultaneous submissions. Responds in 3 months. Book catalog and ms guidelines free.

NONFICTION Wants books on early tools, trades and technology, and railroads. Query with sample chapters, TOC, book overview, illustration descriptions.

TIPS "We sell to niche markets. We are happy to work with knowledgeable amateur authors in developing titles."

⚠⊘ ATHENEUM BOOKS FOR YOUNG READERS

Simon & Schuster, 1230 Avenue of the Americas, New York NY 10020. **Website:** kids.simonandschuster.com. Estab. 1961. Publishes hardcover originals. Accepts simultaneous submissions. Guidelines for #10 SASE.

NONFICTION Subjects include Americana, animals, history, photography, psychology, recreation, religion, science, sociology, sports, travel. Publishes hardcover originals, picture books for young kids, nonfiction for ages 8-12 and novels for middle-grade and young adults. 100% require freelance illustration. Agented submissions only.

FICTION Subjects include adventure, ethnic, experimental, fantasy, gothic, historical, horror, humor, mystery, science fiction, sports, suspense, western, Animal. All in juvenile versions. "We have few specific needs except for books that are fresh, interesting and well written. Fad topics are dangerous, as are works you haven't polished to the best of your ability. We also don't need safety pamphlets, ABC books, coloring books and board books. In writing picture book texts, avoid the coy and 'cutesy,' such as stories about characters with alliterative names." Agented submissions only. No paperback romance-type fiction.

TIPS "Study our titles."

AVALON TRAVEL PUBLISHING

Avalon Publishing Group, 1700 4th St., Berkeley CA 94710. (510)595-3664. **Fax:** (510)595-4228. **E-mail:** avalon.acquisitions@perseusbooks.com. **Website:** www.avalontravelbooks.com. Estab. 1973. Publishes trade paperback originals. Avalon travel guides feature practicality and spirit, offering a traveler-to-traveler perspective perfect for planning an afternoon hike, around-the-world journey, or anything in between. ATP publishes 7 major series. Each one has a different emphasis and a different geographic coverage. "We have expanded our coverage, with a focus on European and Asian destinations. Our main areas of interest are North America, Central America, South America, the Caribbean, and the Pacific. We are seeking only a few titles in each of our major series. Check online guidelines for our current needs. Follow guidelines closely." **Publishes 100 titles/year. 5,000 queries received/year. 25% of books from first-time authors. 95% from unagented writers. Pays up to $17,000 advance.** Publishes ms an average of 9 months after acceptance. Accepts simultaneous submissions. Responds in 4 months. Guidelines online.

NONFICTION Subjects include regional, travel. "We are not interested in fiction, children's books, and travelogues/travel diaries." Submit cover letter, resume, and up to 5 relevant clips.

AVON ROMANCE

Harper Collins Publishers, 10 E. 53 St., New York NY 10022. **E-mail:** info@avonromance.com. **Website:** www.avonromance.com. Estab. 1941. Publishes paperback and digital originals and reprints. Avon has been publishing award-winning books since 1941. It is recognized for having pioneered the historical romance category and continues to bring the best of commercial literature to the broadest possible audience. **Publishes 400 titles/year.** Accepts simultaneous submissions.

FICTION Subjects include historical, literary, mystery, romance, science fiction, young adult. Submit a query and ms via the online submission form.

BACKBEAT BOOKS

Hal Leonard Publishing Group, 33 Plymouth St., Suite 302, Montclair NJ 07042. (973)337-5034. **E-mail:** bmalavarca@halleonard.com. **Website:** www.backbeatbooks.com. **Contact:** Bernadette Malavarca, senior editor. Publishes hardcover and trade paperback originals; trade paperback reprints. **Publishes 30 titles/year. 30% of books from first-time authors. 60% from unagented writers. Pays modest advance.** Publishes ms 18-24 months after acceptance. Accepts simultaneous submissions. Guidelines online.

NONFICTION Subjects include music, pop culture. Query with TOC, sample chapter, sample illustrations.

THE BACKWATERS PRESS

1124 Pacific St., #8392, Omaha NE 68108. **E-mail:** thebackwaterspress@gmail.com. **Website:** www.thebackwaterspress.org. **Contact:** Michael Catherwood, editor. Editor Emeritus: Greg Kosmicki. Estab. 1998. Publishes poetry in English; no children's poetry. The Backwaters Press is a 501-(C)-3 non-profit literary press that publishes poetry and poetry-related books, including anthologies. The press sponsors an annual book award prize, The Backwaters Prize, which includes a cash prize and publication. **Publishes 2-5 titles/year. 300-400 50% of books from first-time authors. 100% from unagented writers. Pays in copies, publication. Contest winner receives**

$1,000 and copies. Does not pay advance. Publishes ms 6-12 months after acceptance. Accepts simultaneous submissions. Responds to contest: 2-3 months. All others, up to 6 months. Catalog online. Guidelines online.

POETRY Only considers submissions to Backwaters Prize. More details on website. Open to all styles and forms. Complete book mss only.

BAEN BOOKS

P.O. Box 1188, Wake Forest NC 27588. (919)570-1640. **E-mail:** info@baen.com. **Website:** www.baen.com. Estab. 1983. "We publish only science fiction and fantasy. Writers familiar with what we have published in the past will know what sort of material we are most likely to publish in the future: powerful plots with solid scientific and philosophical underpinnings are the sine qua non for consideration for science fiction submissions. As for fantasy, any magical system must be both rigorously coherent and integral to the plot, and overall the work must at least strive for originality." Accepts simultaneous submissions. Responds to mss within 12-18 months.

FICTION "Style: Simple is generally better; in our opinion good style, like good breeding, never calls attention to itself. Length: 100,000-130,000 words Generally we are uncomfortable with manuscripts under 100,000 words, but if your novel is really wonderful send it along regardless of length." "Query letters are not necessary. We prefer to see complete manuscripts accompanied by a synopsis. We prefer not to see simultaneous submissions. Electronic submissions are strongly preferred. *We no longer accept submissions by e-mail.* Send ms by using the submission form at: http://ftp.baen.com/Slush/submit.aspx. No disks unless requested. Attach ms as a Rich Text Format (.rtf) file. Any other format will not be considered."

BAILIWICK PRESS

309 East Mulberry St., Fort Collins CO 80524. (970)672-4878. **Fax:** (970)672-4731. **E-mail:** info@bailiwickpress.com. **E-mail:** aldozelnick@gmail.com. **Website:** www.bailiwickpress.com. "We're a micro-press that produces books and other products that inspire and tell great stories. Our motto is 'books with something to say.' We are now considering submissions, agented and unagented, for children's and young adult fiction. We're looking for smart, funny, and layered writing that kids will clamor for. Authors who already have a following have a leg up. We are only looking for humorous children's fiction. Please do not submit work for adults. Illustrated fiction is desired but not required. (Illustrators are also invited to send samples.) Make us laugh out loud, ooh and aah, and cry, 'Eureka!'" Accepts simultaneous submissions. Responds in 6 months.

FICTION "Please read the Aldo Zelnick series to determine if we might be on the same page, then fill out our submission form. Please do not send submissions via snail mail or phone calls. You must complete the online submission form to be considered. If, after completing and submitting the form, you also need to send us an e-mail attachment (such as sample illustrations or excerpts of graphics), you may e-mail them to aldozelnick@gmail.com."

Ⓐ⊘ BAKER ACADEMIC/BRAZOS PRESS

Division of Baker Publishing Group, 6030 E. Fulton Rd., Ada MI 49301. (616)676-9185. **E-mail:** submissions@bakeracademic.com. **Website:** bakerpublishinggroup.com/bakeracademic. Estab. 1939. "We produce primary and supplementary textbooks, reference works, and scholarly monographs that extend the academic conversation to a range of readers, from students to experts on the cutting edge of research. Our main areas of focus include biblical studies, theology, ethics, cultural studies, and church history. We also publish textbooks on Christian education, mission, and ministry as well as integrative works in a variety of liberal arts disciplines, such as literature, communication, philosophy, and psychology.". Baker Academic serves the academy and the church by publishing works that further the pursuit of knowledge and understanding within the context of Christian faith. "Building on our Reformed and evangelical heritage, we connect authors and readers across the broader academic community by publishing books that reflect historic Christianity and its contemporary expressions. Our authors are scholars who are leaders in their fields, write irenically, and display a healthy respect for other perspectives and traditions. Our goal is to publish books that are notable for their inherent quality and deemed essential reading by students and scholars. Brazos Press publishes books that foster faithful cultural engagement, creatively bringing the riches of our catholic Christian heritage to bear on the complexity and wonder of life. Brazos is animated by a vision of God reaching out to embrace all of humanity with a love as wide and deep as God's creation.

Our books inspire faithful interaction with issues of importance to the church and the world." **Publishes 50 titles/year. Pays advance.** Publishes book 1 year after ms turned in. Accepts simultaneous submissions. Guidelines available.

NONFICTION Subjects include education, psychology, religion, Biblical studies, Christian doctrine, books for pastors and church leaders, contemporary issues.

🅰️ 🚫 BAKER BOOKS

Division of Baker Publishing Group, 6030 E. Fulton Rd., Ada MI 49301. (616)676-9185. **Website:** bakerpublishinggroup.com/bakerbooks. Estab. 1939. Publishes in hardcover and trade paperback originals, and trade paperback reprints. "We will consider unsolicited work only through one of the following avenues. Materials sent through a literary agent will be considered. In addition, our staff attends various writers' conferences at which prospective authors can develop relationships with those in the publishing industry." Accepts simultaneous submissions. Book catalog for 9½×12½ envelope and 3 first-class stamps. Guidelines online.

🔲 "Baker Books publishes popular religious nonfiction reference books and professional books for church leaders. Most of our authors and readers are evangelical Christians, and our books are purchased from Christian bookstores, mail-order retailers, and school bookstores. Does not accept unsolicited queries."

NONFICTION Subjects include Christian doctrines.

TIPS "We are not interested in historical fiction, romances, science fiction, biblical narratives or spiritual warfare novels. Do not call to 'pass by' your idea."

🅰️ BALLANTINE BOOKS

Imprint of Penguin Random House, Inc., 1745 Broadway, 18th Floor, New York NY 10019. (212)782-9000. **Website:** www.penguinrandomhouse.com. Estab. 1952. Publishes hardcover, trade paperback, mass market paperback originals. Ballantine Bantam Dell publishes a wide variety of nonfiction and fiction. Accepts simultaneous submissions. Guidelines online.

NONFICTION Subjects include animals, child guidance, community, creative nonfiction, education, history, memoirs, recreation, religion, sex, spirituality, travel, true crime. Agented submissions only. Reviews artwork/photos. Send photocopies.

FICTION Subjects include confession, ethnic, fantasy, feminist, historical, humor, literary, multicultural, mystery, romance, short story collections, spiritual, suspense, translation, general fiction. Agented submissions only.

🌀 JONATHAN BALL PUBLISHERS

P.O. Box 43265, Woodstock 7915, South Africa. (27)(11)622-2900. **Fax:** (27)(11)601-8183. **E-mail:** tercia.wyngaard@jonathanball.co.za. **Website:** www.jonathanball.co.za. **Contact:** Tercia Wyngaard. Publishes books about South Africa which enlighten and entertain. Accepts simultaneous submissions. Guidelines online.

NONFICTION Subjects include history, sports, travel, politics.

BALL PUBLISHING

P.O. Box 1660, West Chicago IL 60186. (630)231-3675. **Fax:** (630)231-5254. **E-mail:** cbeytes@ballpublishing.com. **Website:** www.ballpublishing.com. **Contact:** Chris Beytes, editor. Publishes hardcover and trade paperback originals. "We publish for the book trade and the horticulture trade. Books on both home gardening/landscaping and commercial production are considered." **Publishes 4-6 titles/year.** Accepts simultaneous submissions. Book catalog for 8 ½×11 envelope and 3 first-class stamps.

NONFICTION Subjects include agriculture, gardening, floriculture. Query with SASE. Submit proposal package, outline, 2 sample chapters. Reviews artwork/photos. Send photocopies.

TIPS "We are expanding our book line to home gardeners, while still publishing for green industry professionals. Gardening books should be well thought out and unique in the market. Actively looking for photo books on specific genera and families of flowers and trees."

🅰️ BALZER & BRAY

HarperCollins Children's Books, 10 E. 53rd St., New York NY 10022. **Website:** www.harpercollinschildrens.com. Estab. 2008. "We publish bold, creative, groundbreaking picture books and novels that appeal directly to kids in a fresh way." **Publishes 10 titles/year. Offers advances. Pays illustrators by the project.** Publishes book 18 months after acceptance. Accepts simultaneous submissions.

NONFICTION Subjects include animals, cooking, dance, environment, history, multicultural, music, nature, science, social sciences, sports. "We will publish very few nonfiction titles, maybe 1-2 per year." Agented submissions only.

FICTION Picture Books, Young Readers: adventure, animal, anthology, concept, contemporary, fantasy, history, humor, multicultural, nature/environment, poetry, science fiction, special needs, sports, suspense. Middle readers, young adults/teens: adventure, animal, anthology, contemporary, fantasy, history, humor, multicultural, nature/environment, poetry, science fiction, special needs, sports, suspense. Agented submissions only.

Ⓐ BANCROFT PRESS

P.O. Box 65360, Baltimore MD 21209-9945. (410)358-0658. **Fax:** (410)764-1967. **E-mail:** bruceb@bancroft-press.com. **Website:** www.bancroftpress.com. **Contact:** Bruce Bortz, editor/publisher (memoirs, health, investment, politics, history, humor, literary novels, mystery/thrillers, chick lit, young adult). Estab. 1992. Publishes hardcover and trade paperback originals as well as e-books and audiobooks. "Bancroft Press is a general trade publisher. Our only mandate is 'books that enlighten.' Our most recent emphasis, with 'The Missing Kennedy' and 'Both Sides of the Line,' has been on memoirs." **Publishes 4-6 titles/year. 50% of books from first-time authors. 80% from unagented writers. Pays 8-15% royalty on retail price. Pays $750-2,500 advances.** Publishes book up to 3 years after acceptance of ms. Accepts simultaneous submissions. Responds in 6-12 months. Guidelines online.

NONFICTION Subjects include business, cinema, creative nonfiction, economics, entertainment, finance, health, history, literature, memoirs, politics, psychology, public affairs, regional, religion, science, spirituality, sports, young adult, popular culture. "We advise writers to visit the website." All quality books on any subject of interest to the publisher. Submit proposal package, outline, 5 sample chapters, competition/market survey.

FICTION Subjects include contemporary, ethnic, feminist, historical, humor, literary, mainstream, military, mystery, regional, religious, science fiction, sports, translation, young adult, thrillers. Submit complete ms.

TIPS "We advise writers to visit our website and to be familiar with our previous work. Patience is the number one attribute contributors must have. It takes us a very long time to get through submitted material, because we are such a small company. Also, we only publish 4-6 books per year, so it may take a long time for your optioned book to be published. We like to be able to market our books to be used in schools and in libraries. We prefer fiction that bucks trends and moves in a new direction. We are especially interested in mysteries and humor (especially humorous mysteries)."

Ⓐ Ⓞ BANTAM BOOKS

Imprint of Penguin Random House, Inc., 1745 Broadway, New York NY 10019. (212)782-9000. **Website:** www.randomhousebooks.com. *Not seeking mss at this time.* Accepts simultaneous submissions.

Ⓞ BARBOUR PUBLISHING, INC.

P.O. Box 719, Urichsville OH 44683. **E-mail:** submissions@barbourbooks.com. **Website:** www.barbourbooks.com. Estab. 1981. "Barbour Books publishes inspirational/devotional material that is nondenominational and evangelical in nature. We're a Christian evangelical publisher." Specializes in short, easy-to-read Christian bargain books. "Faithfulness to the Bible and Jesus Christ are the bedrock values behind every book Barbour's staff produces."

Ⓞ "We no longer accept unsolicited submissions unless they are submitted through professional literary agencies. For more information, we encourage new fiction authors to join a professional writers organization like American Christian Fiction Writers."

Ⓞ BAREFOOT BOOKS

2067 Massachusettes Ave., 5th Floor, Cambridge MA 02140. (617)576-0660. **Fax:** (617)576-0049. **E-mail:** help@barefootbooks.com. **Website:** www.barefootbooks.com. **Contact:** Acquisitions Editor. Publishes hardcover and trade paperback originals. "We are a small, independent publishing company that publishes high-quality picture books for children of all ages and specializes in the work of artists and writers from many cultures. We focus on themes that support independence of spirit, encourage openness to others, and foster a life-long love of learning. Prefers full manuscript." **Publishes 30 titles/year. 2,000 queries received/year. 3,000 mss received/year. 35% of books from first-time authors. 60% from unagented writers. Pays advance.** Accepts simultaneous submissions. Book catalog for 9x12 SAE stamped with $1.80 postage.

FICTION Subjects include juvenile. "Barefoot Books only publishes children's picture books and anthologies of folktales. We do not publish novels." Barefoot Books is not currently accepting ms queries or submissions.

BARRICADE BOOKS, INC.

2037 Lemoine Ave., Suite 362, Fort Lee NJ 07024. (201)944-7600. **Fax:** (201)917-4951. **Website:** www.barricadebooks.com. **Contact:** Carole Stuart, publisher. Estab. 1991. Publishes hardcover and trade paperback originals, trade paperback reprints. "Barricade Books publishes nonfiction, mostly of the controversial type, and books we can promote with authors who can talk about their topics on radio and television and to the press." **Publishes 12 titles/year. 200 queries received/year. 100 mss received/year. 80% of books from first-time authors. 50% from unagented writers. Pays 10-12% royalty on retail price for hardcover. Pays advance.** Publishes book 18 months after acceptance. Accepts simultaneous submissions. Responds in 1 month to queries.

NONFICTION Subjects include ethnic, history, psychology, sociology, true crime. "We look for quality nonfiction mss—preferably with a controversial lean." Query with SASE. Submit outline, 1-2 sample chapters. Material will not be returned or responded to without SASE. "We do not accept proposals on disk or via e-mail." Reviews artwork/photos. Send photocopies.

TIPS "Do your homework. Visit bookshops to find publishers who are doing the kinds of books you want to write. Always submit to a person—not just 'Editor.'"

BARRONS EDUCATIONAL SERIES

250 Wireless Blvd., Hauppauge NY 11788. **Fax:** (631)434-3723. **Website:** www.barronseduc.com. **Contact:** Wayne R. Barr, manuscript acquisitions. Estab. 1945. **Pays authors royalty of 10-12% based on net price or buys ms outright for $2,000 minimum. Pays illustrators by the project based on retail price.** Publishes book 1 year after acceptance. Accepts simultaneous submissions. Due to the large volume of unsolicited submissions received, a complete evaluation of a proposal may take 4-6 weeks. Please do not call about the status of individual submissions. Catalog available for 9x12 SASE. Guidelines available on website.

NONFICTION Picture books: concept, reference. Young readers: biography, how-to, reference, self-help, social issues. Middle readers: hi-lo, how-to, reference, self-help, social issues. Young adults: reference, self-help, social issues, sports. Submit outline/synopsis and sample chapters. "Nonfiction submissions must be accompanied by SASE for response."

FICTION Picture books: animal, concept, multicultural, nature/environment. Young readers: adventure, multicultural, nature/environment, fantasy, suspense/mystery. Middle readers: adventure, fantasy, multicultural, nature/environment, problem novels, suspense/mystery. Young adults: problem novels. "Stories with an educational element are appealing." Query via e-mail with no attached files. Full guidelines are listed on the website.

TIPS Writers: "We publish pre-school storybooks, concept books and middle grade and YA chapter books. No romance novels. Those with an educational element." Illustrators: "We are happy to receive a sample illustration to keep on file for future consideration. Periodic notes reminding us of your work are acceptable." Children's book themes "are becoming much more contemporary and relevant to a child's day-to-day activities, fewer talking animals. We are interested in fiction (ages 7-11 and ages 12-16) dealing with modern problems."

Ⓐ⊘ BASIC BOOKS

Hachette Book Group, 1290 Avenue of the Americas, Suite 1500, New York NY 10104. **Website:** www.basicbooks.com. **Contact:** Editor. Estab. 1952. Publishes hardcover and trade paperback originals and reprints. Accepts simultaneous submissions. Responds in at least 3 months to queries. Book catalog available free. Guidelines online.

NONFICTION Subjects include history, psychology, sociology, politics, current affairs.

BAYLOR UNIVERSITY PRESS

One Bear Place 97363, Waco TX 76798. (254)710-3164. **Fax:** (254)710-3440. **E-mail:** carey_newman@baylor.edu. **Website:** www.baylorpress.com. **Contact:** Dr. Carey C. Newman, director. Estab. 1897. Publishes hardcover and trade paperback originals. "We publish contemporary and historical scholarly works about culture, religion, politics, science, and the arts." **Publishes 30 titles/year. Pays 10% royalty on wholesale price.** Publishes ms 1 year after acceptance. Accepts simultaneous submissions. Responds in 2 months to proposals. Guidelines online.

NONFICTION Submit outline, 1-3 sample chapters via e-mail.

BEACON HILL PRESS OF KANSAS CITY

Nazarene Publishing House, P.O. Box 419527, Kansas City MO 64141. (816)931-1900. **Fax:** (816)412-8306. **E-mail:** crm@nph.com. **Website:** beaconhillbooks. com. Publishes hardcover and paperback originals. "Beacon Hill Press is a Christ-centered publisher that provides authentically Christian resources faithful to God's word and relevant to life." **Publishes 30 titles/ year. Pays royalty.** Publishes ms 2 years after acceptance. Accepts simultaneous submissions. Responds in 3 months to queries.

NONFICTION "Accent on holy living; encouragement in daily Christian life." No fiction, autobiography, poetry, short stories, or children's picture books. Query or submit proposal electronically.

BEACON PRESS

24 Farnsworth St., Boston MA 02210. **E-mail:** editorial@beacon.org. **Website:** www.beacon.org. Estab. 1854. Publishes hardcover originals and paperback reprints. Beacon Press publishes general interest books that promote the following values: the inherent worth and dignity of every person; justice, equity, and compassion in human relations; acceptance of one another; a free and responsible search for truth and meaning; the goal of world community with peace, liberty, and justice for all; respect for the interdependent web of all existence. Currently emphasizing innovative nonfiction writing by people of all colors. De-emphasizing poetry, children's stories, art books, self-help. **Publishes 60 titles/year. 10% of books from first-time authors. Pays royalty. Pays advance.** Accepts simultaneous submissions. Responds in 3 months to queries.

NONFICTION Subjects include child guidance, education, ethnic, philosophy, religion, world affairs. *Strongly prefers agented submissions.* Query by e-mail only. *Strongly prefers referred submissions, on exclusive.*

TIPS "We probably accept only 1 or 2 manuscripts from an unpublished pool of 4,000 submissions/year. No fiction, children's books, or poetry submissions invited. An academic affiliation is helpful."

BEARMANOR MEDIA

P.O. Box 71426, Albany GA 31708. **E-mail:** books@ benohmart.com. **Website:** www.bearmanormedia. com. **Contact:** Ben Ohmart, publisher. Estab. 2000. Publishes trade paperback originals, hardbacks and e-books. "We specialize in entertainment biographies, and books on radio, TV and stage projects, as well as film scripts." **Publishes 70 titles/year. 90% of books from first-time authors. 90% from unagented writers. Negotiable per project. Pays upon acceptance. Occasionally pays advance.** Accepts simultaneous submissions. Responds within a few days. Book catalog online, or free upon request.

IMPRINTS BearManor Bare, MagicImage, BearManor Media.

NONFICTION Subjects include cinema, dance, entertainment, film, memoirs, stage. Only entertainment-related books please. Query with SASE. E-mail queries preferred. Submit proposal package, outline, list of credits on the subject. No.

TIPS "My readers love the past. Radio, old movies, old television. My own tastes include voice actors and scripts, especially of radio and television no longer available. I prefer books on subjects that haven't previously been covered as full books. It doesn't matter to me if you're a first-time author or have a track record. Just know your subject and know how to write a sentence!"

BEAR STAR PRESS

185 Hollow Oak Dr., Cohasset CA 95973. **Website:** www.bearstarpress.com. **Contact:** Beth Spencer, publisher/editor. Estab. 1996. Publishes trade paperback originals. "Bear Star is committed to publishing the best poetry it can attract. Each year it sponsors the Dorothy Brunsman contest, open to poets from Western and Pacific states. From time to time we add to our list other poets from our target area whose work we admire." **Publishes 1-3 titles/year. Pays $1,000, and 25 copies to winner of annual Dorothy Brunsman contest.** Publishes book 9 months after acceptance. Accepts simultaneous submissions. Responds in 2 weeks to queries. Guidelines online.

POETRY Wants well-crafted poems. No restrictions as to form, subject matter, style, or purpose. "Poets should enter our annual book competition. Other books are occasionally solicited by publisher, sometimes from among contestants who didn't win." Online submissions strongly preferred.

TIPS "Send your best work, consider its arrangement. A 'wow' poem early keeps me reading."

BEHRMAN HOUSE INC.

11 Edison Place, Springfield NJ 07081. (973)379-7200. **Fax:** (973)379-7280. **E-mail:** customersupport@behrmanhouse.com. **Website:** www.behrmanhouse.com. **Contact:** Editorial Committee. Estab. 1921. Publishes books on all aspects of Judaism: history, cultural, textbooks, holidays. "Behrman House publishes quality books of Jewish content—history, Bible, philosophy, holidays, ethics—for children and adults." **12% of books from first-time authors. Pays authors royalty of 3-10% based on retail price or buys ms outright for $1,000-5,000. Offers advance. Pays illustrators by the project (range: $500-5,000).** Publishes book 18 months after acceptance. Accepts simultaneous submissions. Responds in 1 month to queries; 2 months to mss. Book catalog free on request. Guidelines online.

NONFICTION All levels: Judaism, Jewish educational textbooks. Average word length: young reader—1,200; middle reader—2,000; young adult—4,000. Submit outline/synopsis and sample chapters.

FREDERIC C. BEIL, PUBLISHER, INC.

609 Whitaker St., Savannah GA 31401. (912)233-2446. **E-mail:** fcb@beil.com. **Website:** www.beil.com. **Contact:** Frederic Beil. Estab. 1982. Publishes original titles in hardcover, softcover, and e-book. Beil publishes books in the fields of biography, history, and fiction. While under way, Beil has published authors of meaningful works and adhered to high standards in bookmaking craftsman. **Publishes 8 titles/year. 950 queries; 8 mss received/year. 60% of books from first-time authors. 100% from unagented writers. Pays 7.5% royalty on retail price. Does not pay advance.** Publishes ms 12-15 months after acceptance. Accepts simultaneous submissions. Responds in 1 week to queries. Catalog online. Upon agreement with author, Beil will provide guidelines to author.

IMPRINTS The Sandstone Press.

NONFICTION Subjects include history, humanities, literature, memoirs, philosophy. Query with SASE.

FICTION Subjects include historical, literary. Query with SASE.

TIPS "Our objectives are to offer carefully selected texts, to adhere to high standards in the choice of materials and in bookmaking craftsmanship; to produce books that exemplify good taste in format and design; and to maintain the lowest cost consistent with quality."

BELLEBOOKS

P.O. Box 300921, Memphis TN 38130. (901)344-9024. **Fax:** (901)344-9068. **E-mail:** bellebooks@bellebooks.com. **Website:** www.bellebooks.com. Estab. 1999. BelleBooks began by publishing Southern fiction. It has become a "second home" for many established authors, who also continue to publish with major publishing houses. **Publishes 30-40 titles/year.** Accepts simultaneous submissions. Guidelines online.

FICTION Subjects include juvenile, young adult. "Yes, we'd love to find the next Harry Potter, but our primary focus for the moment is publishing for the teen market." Query e-mail with brief synopsis and credentials/credits with full ms attached (RTF format preferred).

TIPS "Our list aims for the teen reader and the crossover market. If you're a 'Southern Louise Rennison,' that would catch our attention. Humor is always a plus. We'd love to see books featuring teen boys as protagonists. We're happy to see dark edgy books on serious subjects."

BELLEVUE LITERARY PRESS

New York University School of Medicine, Dept. of Medicine, NYU School of Medicine, 550 First Avenue, OBV 612, New York NY 10016. (212)263-7802. **E-mail:** blpsubmissions@gmail.com. **Website:** blpress.org. **Contact:** Erika Goldman, publisher/editorial director. Estab. 2005. "Publishes literary and authoritative fiction and nonfiction at the nexus of the arts and the sciences, with a special focus on medicine. As our authors explore cultural and historical representations of the human body, illness, and health, they address the impact of scientific and medical practice on the individual and society." Accepts simultaneous submissions.

NONFICTION "If you have a completed ms, a sample of a ms or a proposal that fits our mission as a press feel free to submit it to us by e-mail."

FICTION Subjects include literary. Submit complete ms.

TIPS "We are a project of New York University's School of Medicine and while our standards reflect NYU's excellence in scholarship, humanistic medicine, and science, our authors need not be affiliated with NYU. We are not a university press and do not receive any funding from NYU. Our publishing operations are financed exclusively by foundation grants, private donors, and book sales revenue."

BENBELLA BOOKS

10300 N. Central Expressway, Suite 530, Dallas TX 75231. (214)750-3600. **E-mail:** glenn@benbellabooks. com. **Website:** www.benbellabooks.com. **Contact:** Glenn Yeffeth, publisher. Estab. 2001. Publishes hardcover and trade paperback originals. **Publishes 30-40 titles/year. Pays 6-15% royalty on retail price.** Publishes ms 10 months after acceptance. Accepts simultaneous submissions. Guidelines online.

NONFICTION Subjects include literary criticism, science. Submit proposal package, including: outline, 2 sample chapters (via e-mail).

BENTLEY PUBLISHERS

1734 Massachusetts Ave., Cambridge MA 02138. (617)547-4170. **Fax:** (617)876-9235. **Website:** www. bentleypublishers.com. Estab. 1950. Publishes hardcover and trade paperback originals and reprints. "Bentley Publishers publishes books for automotive enthusiasts. We are interested in books that showcase good research, strong illustrations, and valuable technical information." Automotive subjects only. Query with SASE. Submit sample chapters, bio, synopsis, target market. Reviews artwork/photos. Book catalog and ms guidelines online.

NONFICTION Query with SASE. Submit sample chapters, bio, synopsis, target market. Rreviews artwork/photos.

TIPS "Our audience is composed of serious, intelligent automobile, sports car, and racing enthusiasts, automotive technicians and high-performance tuners."

BERGLI BOOKS

Schwabe Verlag, Steinentorstrasse 11, Basel CH-4010, Switzerland. **E-mail:** info@bergli.ch. **Website:** www. bergli.ch. **Contact:** Richard Harvell, executive editor. Estab. 1991. Bergli Books publishes books in Switzerland that bridge intercultural gaps. "It's mostly English list has included many Swiss-interest bestsellers of the past two decades, including the *Ticking Along* Series, Margaret Oertig's *Beyond Chocolate*, and Sergio Lievano and Nicole Egger's *Hoi* books—the best-selling Swiss German guides of all time. An imprint of Schwabe since 2013, Bergli is unique in Switzerland—connecting English readers to Swiss culture and tradition." **Publishes 3-4 titles/year. Receives 50 queries/year. 50% of books from first-time authors. Pays 7-12% royalties on retail price. Pays $1,000-5,000 advance.** Publishes ms 12 months after acceptance. Accepts simultaneous submissions. Responds in 1 month to queries, proposals, and mss. Catalog available online. Guidelines available for SASE.

NONFICTION Subjects include travel, Swiss culture, Switzerland for expats. "Our chief market is among English speakers in Switzerland." Submit proposal package, outline, and 1 sample chapter. Reviews artwork, submit photocopies.

TIPS "We like illustrated books, show us something that has been done elsewhere but not in Switzerland."

BERKLEY

Penguin Group (USA) Inc., 375 Hudson St., New York NY 10014. **Website:** penguin.com. President: Ivan Held. Estab. 1955. Publishes paperback and mass market originals and reprints. The Berkley Publishing Group publishes a variety of general nonfiction and fiction including the traditional categories of romance, mystery and science fiction. **Publishes 700 titles/year.**

IMPRINTS Ace; Jove; Heat; Sensation; Berkley Prime Crime; Berkley Caliber.

"Due to the high volume of manuscripts received, most Penguin Group (USA) Inc. imprints do not normally accept unsolicited mss. The preferred and standard method for having mss considered for publication by a major publisher is to submit them through an established literary agent."

NONFICTION Subjects include child guidance, creative nonfiction, history, New Age, psychology, true crime, job-seeking communication. No memoirs or personal stories. Prefers agented submissions.

FICTION Subjects include adventure, historical, literary, mystery, romance, spiritual, suspense, western, young adult. No occult fiction. Prefers agented submissions.

BERRETT-KOEHLER PUBLISHERS, INC.

1333 Broadway, Suite #1000, Oakland CA 94612. **E-mail:** bkpub@bkpub.com. **E-mail:** submissions@bk-pub.com. **Website:** www.bkconnection.com. **Contact:** Anna Leinberger, associate editor. Publishes hardcover and trade paperback originals, mass market paperback originals, hardcover and trade paperback reprints. "Berrett-Koehler Publishers' mission is to publish books that support the movement toward a world that works for all. Our titles promote positive change at personal, organizational and societal levels." Please see proposal guidelines online. **Pub-**

lishes 40 titles/year. 1,300 queries received/year. 800 mss received/year. 20-30% of books from first-time authors. 70% from unagented writers. Pays 10-20% royalty. Publishes book 10 months after acceptance. Accepts simultaneous submissions. Responds in 1 month. Book catalog online.

NONFICTION Subjects include community, New Age, spirituality. Submit proposal package, outline, bio, 1-2 sample chapters. Hard-copy proposals only. Do not e-mail, fax, or phone please. Reviews artwork/photos. Send photocopies or originals with SASE.

TIPS "Our audience is business leaders. Use common sense, do your research."

BESS PRESS

3565 Harding Ave., Honolulu HI 96816. (808)734-7159. **Fax:** (808)732-3627. **Website:** www.besspress.com. Estab. 1979. Bess Press is a family-owned independent book publishing company based in Honolulu. For over 30 years, Bess Press has been producing both educational and popular general interest titles about Hawai'i and the Pacific. Accepts simultaneous submissions. Responds in 4 months. Catalog online. Guidelines online.

NONFICTION "We are constantly seeking to work with authors, artists, photographers, and organizations that are developing works concentrating on Hawai'i and the Pacific. Our goal is to regularly provide customers with new, creative, informative, educational, and entertaining publications that are directly connected to or flowing from Hawai'i and other islands in the Pacific region." Not interested in material that is unassociated with Hawai'i or the greater Pacific in theme. Please do not submit works if it does not fall into this regional category. Submit your name, contact information, working title, genre, target audience, short (4-6 sentences) description of your work, identifies target audience(s), explains how your work differs from other books already publishing on the same subject, includes discussion of any additional material with samples. All submissions via e-mail.

TIPS "As a regional publisher, we are looking for material specific to the region (Hawaii and Micronesia), preferably from writers and illustrators living within (or very familiar with) the region.", "As a regional publisher, we are looking for material specific to the region (Hawaii and Micronesia), preferably from writers and illustrators living within (or very familiar with) the region."

BETHANY HOUSE PUBLISHERS

Division of Baker Publishing Group, 6030 E. Fulton Rd., Ada MI 49301. (616)676-9185. **Fax:** (616)676-9573. **Website:** bakerpublishinggroup.com/bethanyhouse. Estab. 1956. Publishes hardcover and trade paperback originals, mass market paperback reprints. Bethany House Publishers specializes in books that communicate Biblical truth and assist people in both spiritual and practical areas of life. Considers unsolicited work only through a professional literary agent or through manuscript submission services, Authonomy or Christian Manuscript Submissions. Guidelines online. *All unsolicited mss returned unopened.* **Publishes 90-100 titles/year. 2% of books from first-time authors. 50% from unagented writers. Pays royalty on net price. Pays advance.** Publishes a book 1 year after acceptance. Accepts simultaneous submissions. Responds in 3 months to queries.

NONFICTION Subjects include child guidance, Biblical disciplines, personal and corporate renewal, emerging generations, devotional, marriage and family, applied theology, inspirational.

FICTION Subjects include historical, young adult, contemporary.

TIPS "Bethany House Publishers' publishing program relates Biblical truth to all areas of life—whether in the framework of a well-told story, of a challenging book for spiritual growth, or of a Bible reference work. We are seeking high-quality fiction and nonfiction that will inspire and challenge our audience."

BETWEEN THE LINES

401 Richmond St. W., Suite 277, Toronto ON M5V 3A8, Canada. (416)535-9914. **Fax:** (416)535-1484. **E-mail:** info@btlbooks.com. **E-mail:** submissions@btlbooks.com. **Website:** www.btlbooks.com. **Contact:** Amanda Crocker, managing editor. Publishes trade paperback originals. "Between the Lines publishes nonfiction books in the following subject areas: politics and public policy issues, social issues, development studies, history, education, the environment, health, gender and sexuality, labour, technology, media, and culture. Please note that we do not publish fiction or poetry. We prefer to receive proposals rather than entire manuscripts for consideration." **Publishes 8 titles/year. 350 queries; 50 mss received/year. 80% of books from first-time authors. 95% from unagented writers. Pays 8% royalty.** Publishes ms 1 year after acceptance. Accepts simultaneous submis-

sions. Responds in 2-4 months. Book catalog online. Guidelines online.

NONFICTION Subjects include education, history, social sciences, sociology, development studies, labor, technology, media, culture. Submit proposal as a PDF by e-mail.

❹❷ BEYOND WORDS PUBLISHING, INC.

20827 NW Cornell Rd., Suite 500, Hillsboro OR 97124. (503)531-8700. **Fax:** (503)531-8773. **E-mail:** info@beyondword.com. **Website:** www.beyondword.com. **Contact:** Submissions Department (for agents only). Estab. 1984. Publishes hardcover and trade paperback originals and paperback reprints. "At this time, we are not accepting any unsolicited queries or proposals, and recommend that all authors work with a literary agent in submitting their work." **Publishes 10-15 titles/year.** Accepts simultaneous submissions.

NONFICTION Subjects include health, young adult. For adult nonfiction, wants whole body health, the evolving human, and transformation. For children and YA, wants health, titles that inspire kids' power to incite change, and titles that allow young readers to explore and/or question traditional wisdom and spiritual practices. Does not want children's picture books, adult fiction, cookbooks, textbooks, reference books, photography books, or illustrated coffee table books. Agent should submit query letter with proposal, including author bio, 5 sample chapters, complete synopsis of book, market analysis, SASE.

FICTION Subjects include juvenile, young adult. Agent should submit query letter with proposal, including author bio, 5 sample chapters, complete synopsis of book, market analysis, SASE.

BILINGUAL REVIEW PRESS

Hispanic Research Center, Arizona State University, P.O. Box 875303, Tempe AZ 85287-5303. (480)965-3867. **Fax:** (480)965-0315. **E-mail:** brp@asu.edu. **Website:** www.asu.edu/brp. **Contact:** Gary Francisco Keller, publisher. Estab. 1973. "We are always on the lookout for Chicano, Puerto Rican, Cuban American, or other U.S. Hispanic themes with strong and serious literary qualities and distinctive and intellectually important topics." Accepts simultaneous submissions. Responds in 3-4 weeks for queries; 3-4 months on requested mss.

NONFICTION Query with SASE. Query should describe book, TOC, sample chapter, and any other in-formation relevant to the rationale, content, audience, etc., for the book.

FICTION Subjects include ethnic, short story collections, translation. Query with SASE. Query should describe book, plot summary, sample chapter, and any other information relevant to the rationale, content, audience, etc., for the book.

POETRY Query with SASE. Query should describe book, TOC, sample poems, and any other information relevant to the rationale, content, audience, etc., for the book.

TIPS "Writers should take the utmost care in assuring that their manuscripts are clean, grammatically impeccable, and have perfect spelling. This is true not only of the English but the Spanish as well. All accent marks need to be in place as well as other diacritical marks. When these are missing it's an immediate first indication that the author does not really know Hispanic culture and is not equipped to write about it. We are interested in publishing creative literature that treats the U.S Hispanic experience in a distinctive, creative, revealing way. The kind of books that we publish we keep in print for a very long time irrespective of sales. We are busy establishing and preserving a U.S. Hispanic canon of creative literature."

BIRCH BOOK PRESS

Birch Brook Impressions, P.O. Box 81, Delhi NY 13753. **Fax:** (607)746-7453. **E-mail:** birchbrook@copper.net. **Website:** www.birchbrookpress.info. **Contact:** Tom Tolnay, editor/publisher; Leigh Eckmair, art & research editor; Joyce Tolnay, account services. Estab. 1982. Occasionally publishes trade paperback originals. Birch Brook Press "is a book printer/typesetter/designer that uses monies from these activities to publish several titles of its own each year with cultural and literary interest." Specializes in literary work, flyfishing, baseball, outdoors, themed short fiction anthologies, and books about books. **Publishes 2 titles/year. 200+ queries; 200+ mss received/year. 95% from unagented writers. Pays modest royalty on acceptance.** Publishes ms 10-18 months after acceptance. Accepts simultaneous submissions. Responds in 3-6 months. Book catalog online.

FICTION "Mostly we do anthologies around a particular theme generated inhouse. We make specific calls for fiction when we are doing an anthology." Currently, BBP is not seeking manuscripts on any subject.

Overstocked. Not currently accepting any submissions.

TIPS "Write well on subjects of interest to BBP, such as outdoors, flyfishing, baseball, music, literary stories, fine poetry, books about books."

BKMK PRESS

University of Missouri - Kansas City, 5101 Rockhill Rd., Kansas City MO 64110-2499. (816)235-1168. **Fax:** (816)235-2611. **E-mail:** bkmk@umkc.edu. **Website:** newletters.org. Estab. 1971. Publishes trade paperback originals. "BkMk Press publishes fine literature. Reading period February-June." **Publishes 4 titles/ year.** Accepts simultaneous submissions. Responds in 4-6 months to queries. Guidelines online.

NONFICTION Creative nonfiction essays. Submit 25-50 sample pages and SASE.

FICTION Subjects include literary, short story collections. Query with SASE.

POETRY Submit 10 sample poems and SASE.

TIPS "We skew toward readers of literature, particularly contemporary writing. Because of our limited number of titles published per year, we discourage apprentice writers or 'scattershot' submissions."

BLACK DOME PRESS CORP.

649 Delaware Ave., Delmar NY 12054. (518)439-6512. **Fax:** (518)439-1309. **Website:** www.blackdomepress.com. Estab. 1990. Publishes cloth and trade paperback originals and reprints. Do not send the entire work. Mail a cover letter, TOC, introduction, sample chapter (or 2), and your CV or brief biography to the Editor. Please do not send computer disks or submit your proposal via e-mail. If your book will include illustrations, please send us copies of sample illustrations. Do not send originals. Accepts simultaneous submissions. Book catalog and guidelines online.

NONFICTION Subjects include history, photography, regional, Native Americans, grand hotels, genealogy, colonial life, French & Indian War (NYS), American Revolution (NYS), quilting, architecture, railroads, hiking and kayaking guidebooks. New York state regional material only. Submit proposal package, outline, bio.

TIPS "Our audience is comprised of New York state residents, tourists, and visitors."

BLACK LAWRENCE PRESS

E-mail: editors@blacklawrencepress.com. **Website:** www.blacklawrencepress.com. **Contact:** Diane Goettel, executive editor. Estab. 2003. Black Lawrence press seeks to publish intriguing books of literature—novels, short story collections, poetry collections, chapbooks, anthologies, and creative nonfiction. Will also publish the occasional translation from German. Publishes 15-20 books/year, mostly poetry and fiction. Mss are selected through open submission and competition. Books are 20-400 pages, offset-printed or high-quality POD, perfect-bound, with 4-color cover. **Accepts submissions during the months of June and November. Pays royalties.** Accepts simultaneous submissions. Responds in 6 months to mss.

FICTION Subjects include literary, short story collections, translation. Submit complete ms.

POETRY Submit complete ms.

BLACK LYON PUBLISHING, LLC

P.O. Box 567, Baker City OR 97814. **E-mail:** info@ blacklyonpublishing.com. **E-mail:** queries@blacklyonpublishing.com. **Website:** www.blacklyonpublishing.com. **Contact:** The Editors. Estab. 2007. Publishes paperback and e-book originals. "Black Lyon Publishing is a small, independent publisher. We are currently closed to all except existing Black Lyon authors through 2017." **Publishes 15-20 titles/year.** Guidelines online.

FICTION Subjects include gothic, historical, romance.

BLACK OCEAN

P.O. Box 52030, Boston MA 02205. **Fax:** (617)849-5678. **E-mail:** carrie@blackocean.org. **Website:** www.blackocean.org. **Contact:** Carrie Olivia Adams, poetry editor. Estab. 2006. **Publishes 6 titles/ year.** Accepts simultaneous submissions. Responds in 6 months to mss.

POETRY Wants poetry that is well-considered, risks itself, and by its beauty and/or bravery disturbs a tiny corner of the universe. Mss are selected through open submission. Books are 60+ pages. Book/chapbook mss may include previously published poems. "We have an open submission period in June of each year; specific guidelines are updated and posted on our website in the months preceding."

BLACK ROSE WRITING

P.O. Box 1540, Castroville TX 78009. **E-mail:** creator@blackrosewriting.com. **Website:** www.blackrosewriting.com. **Contact:** Reagan Rothe. Estab. 2006. Publishes fiction and nonfiction. Black Rose Writing is an independent publishing house that strongly believes in developing a personal relationship with their authors. The Texas-based publishing company doesn't see authors as clients or just another number on a page, but rather as individual people. people who deserve an honest review of their material and to be paid traditional royalties without ever paying any fees to be published. **Publishes 150+ titles/year. 3,500 submissions received/year. 75% of books from first-time authors. 80% from unagented writers. Royalties start at 10%, e-book royalties 15% (25-30% net).** Publishes ms 3-6 months after acceptance. Accepts simultaneous submissions. Responds in 3-6 weeks on queries; 1-2 months on mss. Catalog online. Guidelines online.

IMPRINTS DigiTerra Publishing, Bookend Design.

NONFICTION Subjects include animals, anthropology, archeology, art, business, creative nonfiction, economics, education, ethnic, health, history, medicine, memoirs, military, politics, psychology, science, sociology, sports, transportation, travel, true crime, war. "Our preferred submission method is via Authors.me, please click 'Submit Here' on our website." Reviews artwork.

FICTION Subjects include adventure, fantasy, historical, horror, humor, juvenile, literary, mainstream, military, mystery, occult, picture books, regional, romance, science fiction, sports, suspense, war, western, young adult. "Our preferred submission method is via Authors.me, please click 'Submit Here' on our website."

BLACK VELVET SEDUCTIONS PUBLISHING

E-mail: ric@blackvelvetseductions.com. **E-mail:** submissions@blackvelvetseductions.com. **Website:** www.blackvelvetseductions.com. **Contact:** Richard Savage, CEO. Estab. 2005. Publishes trade paperback and electronic originals and reprints. "We publish across a wide range of romance sub-genres, from soft sweet romance to supernatural romance, domestic discipline to highly erotic romance stories containing D/s and BDSM relationships. We are looking for authors who take something ordinary and make it extraordinary. We want stories with well-developed multi-dimensional characters with back-stories, a high degree of emotional impact, with strong sexual tension between the heroine and hero, and stories that contain strong internal conflict. We prefer stories told in the third person viewpoint, but will consider first person narratives. We put the emphasis on romance, rather than just the erotic. Although we will consider a high level of erotic content, it needs to be in the context of a romance story line. The plots may twist and turn and be full of passion, but please remember that our audience likes a happy ending. Do not be afraid to approach us with a non-traditional character or plot." **Publishes 25 titles/year. 500 queries; 1,000 mss received/year. 75% of books from first-time authors. 100% from unagented writers. Pays 10% royalty for paperbacks; 50% royalty for electronic books.** Publishes ms 6-12 months after acceptance. Accepts simultaneous submissions. Responds as swiftly as possible. Catalog free or online. Guidelines online.

FICTION Subjects include contemporary, erotica, fantasy, gay, historical, lesbian, romance, short story collections, erotic romance, historical romance, multicultural romance, romance, short story collections romantic stories, romantic suspense, western romance. All stories must have a strong romance element. "There are very few sexual taboos in our erotic line. We tend to give our authors the widest latitude. If it is safe, sane, and consensual we will allow our authors latitude to show us the eroticism. However, we will not consider manuscripts with any of the following: bestiality (sex with animals), necrophilia (sex with dead people), pedophillia (sex with children)." Only accepts electronic submissions.

TIPS "We publish romance and erotic romance. We look for books written in very deep point of view. Shallow point of view remains the number one reason we reject manuscripts in which the storyline generally works."

JOHN F. BLAIR, PUBLISHER

1406 Plaza Dr., Winston-Salem NC 27103. (336)768-1374. **Fax:** (336)768-9194. **E-mail:** editorial@blairpub.com. **Website:** www.blairpub.com. **Contact:** Carolyn Sakowski, president. Estab. 1954. No poetry, young adult, children's, science fiction. Fiction must be set in southern U.S. or author must have strong Southern connection. **Publishes 10-15 titles/year. 1,000 proposals received/year. Pays royalties. Pays negotiable advance.** Publishes ms 18 months after acceptance. Accepts simultaneous submissions. Responds in 3-6 months. Catalog online. Guidelines online.

NONFICTION Subjects include cooking, creative nonfiction, history, literature, memoirs, regional, travel. Does not want self-help or business.

FICTION "We specialize in regional books, with an emphasis on nonfiction categories such as history, travel, folklore, and biography. We publish only one or two works of fiction each year. Fiction submitted to us should have some connection with the Southeast. We do not publish children's books, poetry, or category fiction such as romances, science fiction, or spy thrillers. We do not publish collections of short stories, essays, or newspaper columns." Does not want fiction set outside southern U.S. Accepts unsolicited mss. Any fiction submitted should have some connection with the Southeast, either through setting or author's background. Send a cover letter, giving a synopsis of the book. Include the first 2 chapters (at least 50 pages) of the ms. "You may send the entire ms if you wish. If you choose to send only samples, please include the projected word length of your book and estimated completion date in your cover letter. Send a biography of the author, including publishing credits and credentials."

TIPS "We are primarily interested in nonfiction titles. Most of our titles have a tie-in with North Carolina or the southeastern United States, we do not accept short story collections. Please enclose a cover letter and outline with the ms. We prefer to review queries before we are sent complete mss. Queries should include an approximate word count."

BLAZEVOX [BOOKS]

131 Euclid Ave., Kenmore NY 14217. **E-mail:** editor@blazevox.org. **Website:** www.blazevox.org. **Contact:** Geoffrey Gatza, editor/publisher. Estab. 2005. "We are a major publishing presence specializing in innovative fictions and wide-ranging fields of innovative forms of poetry and prose. Our goal is to publish works that are challenging, creative, attractive, and yet affordable to individual readers. Articles of submission depend on many criteria, but overall items submitted must conform to one ethereal trait, your work must not suck. This put plainly, bad art should be punished; we will not promote it. However, all submissions will be reviewed and the author will receive feedback. We are human too." **65% of books from first-time authors. 100% from unagented writers. Pays 10% royalties on fiction and poetry books, based on net receipts. This amount may be split across multiple contributors. "We do not pay advances."** Accepts simultaneous submissions. Guidelines online.

FICTION Subjects include contemporary, experimental, lesbian, literary, poetry, poetry in transla-

tion, short story collections. Submit complete ms via e-mail.

POETRY Submit complete ms via e-mail.

TIPS "We actively contract and support authors who tour, read and perform their work, play an active part of the contemporary literary scene, and seek a readership."

BLIND EYE BOOKS

1141 Grant St., Bellingham WA 98225. **E-mail:** editor@blindeyebooks.com. **Website:** www.blindeyebooks.com. **Contact:** Nicole Kimberling, editor. Estab. 2007. "Blind Eye Books publishes science fiction, fantasy and paranormal romance novels featuring gay or lesbian protagonists. We do not publish short story collections, poetry, erotica, horror or nonfiction. We would hesitate to publish any manuscript that is less than 70,000 or over 150,000 words." Accepts simultaneous submissions. Guidelines online.

FICTION Subjects include fantasy, gay, lesbian, science fiction, paranormal romance. Submit complete ms with cover letter. Accepts queries by snail mail. Send disposable copy of ms and SASE for reply only. Does not return rejected mss. Authors living outside the U.S. can e-mail the editor for submission guidelines.

BLOOMBERG PRESS

Imprint of John Wiley & Sons, Professional Development, 111 River St., Hoboken NJ 07030. **E-mail:** info@wiley.com. **Website:** www.wiley.com. Estab. 1995. Publishes hardcover and trade paperback originals. Bloomberg Press publishes professional books for practitioners in the financial markets. "We publish commercially successful, very high-quality books that stand out clearly from the competition by their brevity, ease of use, sophistication, and abundance of practical tips and strategies; books readers need, will use, and appreciate." **Publishes 18-22 titles/year. 200 queries; 20 mss received/year. 45% from unagented writers. Pays negotiable, competitive royalty. Pays negotiable advance for trade books.** Publishes book 9 months after acceptance. Accepts simultaneous submissions. Responds in 1 month to queries.

NONFICTION Subjects include professional books on finance, investment and financial services, and books for financial advisors. "We are looking for authorities and for experienced service journalists. Do not send us unfocused books containing general information already covered by books in the marketplace. We do not publish business, management, leadership, or career books." Submit outline, sample chapters, SAE with sufficient postage. Submit complete ms.

⊘⊘ BLOOMSBURY CHILDREN'S BOOKS
Imprint of Bloomsbury USA, 1385 Broadway, 5th Floor, New York NY 10018. **Website:** www.bloomsbury.com/us/childrens. No phone calls or e-mails. *Agented submissions only.* **Publishes 60 titles/year. 25% of books from first-time authors. Pays royalty. Pays advance.** Accepts simultaneous submissions. Responds in 6 months. Book catalog online. Guidelines online.

FICTION Subjects include adventure, fantasy, historical, humor, juvenile, multicultural, mystery, picture books, poetry, science fiction, sports, suspense, young adult, animal, anthology, concept, contemporary, folktales, problem novels. *Agented submissions only.*

⊘⊘ BLOOMSBURY CONTINUUM
Imprint of Bloomsbury Group, 1385 Broadway, 5th Floor, New York NY 10018. (212)419-5300. **Website:** www.bloomsbury.com/us/bloomsbury/bloomsbury-continuum. Continuum publishes textbooks, monographs, and reference works in religious studies, the humanities, arts, and social sciences for students, teachers, and professionals worldwide. *Does not accept unsolicited submissions.* Book catalog online.

NONFICTION Subjects include education, history, philosophy, religion, sociology, linguistics.

BLUEBRIDGE
Imprint of United Tribes Media, Inc., (914)301-5901. **E-mail:** janguerth@bluebridgebooks.com. **Website:** www.bluebridgebooks.com. **Contact:** Jan-Erik Guerth, publisher (general nonfiction). Estab. 2004. Publishes hardcover and trade paperbacks. BlueBridge is an independent publisher of international nonfiction based near New York City. BlueBridge book subjects include Culture, History, Biography; Nature and Science; Inspiration and Self-Help. BlueBridge is an imprint of United Tribes Media Inc. **Publishes 4-6 titles/year. Pays variable advance.** Accepts simultaneous submissions.

NONFICTION Subjects include alternative lifestyles, Americana, animals, anthropology, archeology, architecture, art, community, contemporary culture, creative nonfiction, economics, environment, ethnic, gardening, history, humanities, literary criticism, multicultural, nature, philosophy, politics, psychology, public affairs, religion, science, social sciences, sociology, spirituality, travel, womens issues, womens studies, world affairs. BlueBridge only accepts submission queries per e-mail, without any attachments to the e-mail, and only for nonfiction.

TIPS "We target a broad general nonfiction audience."

BLUE LIGHT PRESS
1563 45th Ave., San Francisco CA 94122. **E-mail:** bluelightpress@aol.com. **Website:** www.bluelightpress.com. **Contact:** Diane Frank, chief editor. Estab. 1988. "We like poems that are imagistic, emotionally honest, and push the edge—where the writer pushes through the imagery to a deeper level of insight and understanding. No rhymed poetry." Has published poetry by Stephen Dunn, Kim Addonizio, Jane Hirshfield, Rustin Larson, Mary Kay Rummel, Daniel J. Langton, Loretta Walker, Christopher Seid, and K.B. Ballentine. "Books are elegantly designed and artistic. Our books are professionally printed, with original cover art, and we publish full-length books of poetry and chapbooks." **Publishes 5-8 titles/year. 400 50% of books from first-time authors. 90% from unagented writers. Poetry books retail at 15.95. Authors receive a 30% royalty of profits (not of cover price). Author copies are available at close to a 50% discount, for sale at readings and book events. Does not pay advance.** Publishes ms 2-8 months after acceptance. Accepts simultaneous submissions. Catalog online. Guidelines by e-mail.

NONFICTION Subjects include literature.

FICTION Subjects include poetry, poetry in translation, short story collections, flash fiction, micro fiction. We have published flash fiction and micro fiction.

POETRY Blue Light Press is dedicated to the publication of poetry that is imagistic, inventive, emotionally honest, and pushes the language to a deeper level of insight. "We are a collective of poets based in San Francisco, and our books are artistically designed. We also have an online poetry workshop with a wonderful group of American and international poets—open to new members 3 times/year. Send an e-mail for info — bluelightpress@aol.com." No rhymed poetry. For guidelines, send an e-mail to bluelightpress@aol.com. "Let us know if you want guidelines for a chapbook or full-length ms."

TIPS "To see more than 100 poets we love, get a copy of *River of Earth and Sky: Poems for the Twenty-First Century*. It is full of examples of poems we like to publish."

BLUE MOUNTAIN PRESS

Blue Mountain Arts, Inc., P.O. Box 4219, Boulder CO 80306. (800)525-0642. **E-mail:** bmpbooks@sps.com. **Website:** www.sps.com. **Contact:** Patti Wayant, Director. Estab. 1971. Publishes hardcover originals, trade paperback originals, electronic originals. *"Please note: We are not accepting works of fiction, rhyming poetry, children's books, chapbooks, or memoirs."* **Pays royalty on wholesale price. Royalty advance** Publishes ms 12-16 months after acceptance. Accepts simultaneous submissions. Responds in 2-4 months. E-mail to request submission guidelines.

NONFICTION Subjects include Personal growth, teens/tweens, family, relationships, motivational, and inspirational but not religious. Query with SASE. Submit proposal package including outline and 3-5 sample chapters.

POETRY "We publish poetry appropriate for gift books, self-help books, and personal growth books. We do not publish chapbooks or literary poetry. We do not accept rhyming poetry." Query. Submit 10+ sample poems.

BLUE RIVER PRESS

Cardinal Publishers Group, 2402 N. Shadeland Ave., Suite A, Indianapolis IN 46219. (317)352-8200. **Fax:** (317)352-8202. **E-mail:** dmccormick@cardinalpub.com; tdoherty@cardinalpub.com. **Website:** www.brpressbooks.com; www.cardinalpub.com. **Contact:** Dani McCormick, editor; Tom Doherty, president (adult nonfiction). Estab. 2000. Publishes hardcover, trade paperback, and electronic originals and reprints. Blue River Press released its first book in the spring of 2004. "Today we have more than 100 books and e-books in print on the subjects of sports, health, fitness, games, popular culture, travel and our All About. series for early readers. Our books have been recognized with awards and national and regional review attention. We have had many titles reach Nielsen BookScan category top 50 status in retail sales; illustrating that readers have responded by purchasing Blue River Press titles. Our distributor, Cardinal Publishers Group, has placed our books in chain and independent book retailers, libraries of all sorts, mass-merchant retailers, gift shops, and many specialty retail and wholesale channels. Our authors, editors and designers always keep the reader in mind when creating and developing the content and designing attractive books that are competitively priced. At Blue River Press our mission is to produce and market books that present the reader with good educational and entertaining information at a value." **Publishes 8-12 titles/year. 200 queries received/year. 25% of books from first-time authors. 80% from unagented writers. Pays 10-15% on wholesale price. Outright purchase of $500-5,000. Offers advance up to $5,000.** Publishes ms 6-12 months after acceptance. Accepts simultaneous submissions. Responds to queries in 2 months. Book catalog for #10 SASE or online. Guidelines available by e-mail.

NONFICTION Subjects include Americana, business, career guidance, education, entertainment, environment, games, health, history, recreation, regional, sports, travel. "Most non-religious adult nonfiction subjects are of interest. We like concepts that can develop into series products. Most of our books are paperback or hardcover in the categories of sport, business, health, fitness, lifestyle, yoga, and educational books for teachers and students."

BNA BOOKS

P.O. Box 7814, Edison NJ 08818. (800)960-1220. **Fax:** (723)346-1624. **Website:** www.bnabooks.com. Estab. 1929. Publishes hardcover and softcover originals. BNA Books publishes professional reference books written by lawyers, for lawyers. Accepts simultaneous submissions. Book catalog online. Guidelines online.

NONFICTION No fiction, biographies, bibliographies, cookbooks, religion books, humor, or trade books. Submit detailed TOC or outline, CV, intended market, estimated word length.

TIPS "Our audience is made up of practicing lawyers and law librarians. We look for authoritative and comprehensive treatises that can be supplemented or revised every year or 2 on legal subjects of interest to those audiences."

BOA EDITIONS, LTD.

P.O. Box 30971, Rochester NY 14603. (585)546-3410. **Fax:** (585)546-3913. **E-mail:** contact@boaeditions.org. **Website:** www.boaeditions.org. **Contact:** Ron Martin-Dent, Director of Publicity and Production; Peter Conners, Publisher. Director of Development and Operations: Kelly Hatton. Director of Marketing: Jenna Fisher. Estab. 1976. Publishes hardcover, trade paperback, and digital e-book originals. BOA Editions, Ltd., a not-for-profit publisher of poetry, short fiction, and poetry-in-translation, fosters readership and appreciation of contemporary literature.

By identifying, cultivating, and publishing both new and established poets and selecting authors of unique literary talent, BOA brings high quality literature to the public. **Publishes 10-12 titles/year. 1,000-2,000 queries and mss received/year. 15% of books from first-time authors. 90% from unagented writers. Negotiates royalties. Pays variable advance.** Publishes ms 18 months after acceptance. Accepts simultaneous submissions. Responds in 1 week to queries; 5 months to mss. Book catalog online. Guidelines online.

FICTION Subjects include literary, poetry, poetry in translation, short story collections. BOA publishes literary fiction through its American Reader Series. While aesthetic quality is subjective, our fiction will be by authors more concerned with the artfulness of their writing than the twists and turns of plot. "Our strongest current interest is in short story collections (and short-short story collections). We strongly advise you to read our published fiction collections." *Temporarily closed to novel/collection submissions.*

POETRY Readers who, like Whitman, expect the poet to 'indicate more than the beauty and dignity which always attach to dumb real objects . . They expect him to indicate the path between reality and their souls,' are the audience of BOA's books. BOA Editions, a Pulitzer Prize and National Book Award-winning not-for-profit publishing house, acclaimed for its work, reads poetry mss for the American Poets Continuum Series (new poetry by distinguished poets in mid-to-late career), the Lannan Translations Selection Series (publication of 2 new collections of contemporary international poetry annually, supported by the Lannan Foundation of Santa Fe, NM), the New Poets of America Series (publication of a poet's first book, selected through the A. Poulin, Jr. Poetry Prize), and the America Reader Series (short fiction and prose on poetics). Check BOA's website for reading periods for the American Poets Continuum Series and the Lannan Translation Selection Series. Please adhere to the general submission guidelines for each series. Guidelines online.

BOLD STROKES BOOKS, INC.

P.O. Box 249, Valley Falls NY 12094. (518)677-5127. **Fax:** (518)677-5291. **E-mail:** sandy@boldstrokesbooks. com. **E-mail:** submissions@boldstrokesbooks.com. **Website:** www.boldstrokesbooks.com. **Contact:** Sandy Lowe, senior editor. Estab. 2004. Publishes trade paperback originals and reprints; electronic originals and reprints. **Publishes 120+ titles/year. 300 queries/year; 300 mss/year. 10-20% of books from first-time authors. 95% from unagented writers. Sliding scale based on sales volume and format. Pays advance.** Publishes ms 6-16 months after acceptance. Responds in 1 month to queries; 2 months to proposals; 4 months to mss. Guidelines online.

IMPRINTS BSB Fiction; Victory Editions Lesbian Fiction; Liberty Editions Gay Fiction; Soliloquy Young Adult; Heat Stroke Erotica.

NONFICTION Subjects include gay, lesbian, memoirs, young adult. Submit completed ms with bio, cover letter, and synopsis electronically only. Does not review artwork.

FICTION Subjects include adventure, erotica, fantasy, gay, gothic, historical, horror, lesbian, literary, mainstream, mystery, romance, science fiction, suspense, western, young adult. "Submissions should have a gay, lesbian, transgendered, or bisexual focus and should be positive and life-affirming." We do not publish any non-lgbtqi focused works. Submit completed ms with bio, cover letter, and synopsis—electronically only.

TIPS "We are particularly interested in authors who are interested in craft enhancement, technical development, and exploring and expanding traditional genre definitions and boundaries and are looking for a long-term publishing relationship. LGBTQ-focused works only."

BOOKFISH BOOKS

E-mail: bookfishbooks@gmail.com. **Website:** bookfishbooks.com. **Contact:** Tammy Mckee, acquisitions editor. BookFish Books is looking for novel lengthed young adult, new adult, and middle grade works in all subgenres. Both published and unpublished, agented or unagented authors are welcome to submit. "Sorry, but we do not publish novellas, picture books, early reader/chapter books or adult novels." Responds to every query. Accepts simultaneous submissions. Guidelines online.

FICTION Query via e-mail with a brief synopsis and first 3 chapters of ms.

TIPS "We only accept complete manuscripts. Please do not query us with partial manuscripts or proposals."

BOOKOUTURE

StoryFire Ltd., 23 Sussex Rd., Ickenham UB10 8P, United Kingdom. **Website:** www.bookouture.com.

Contact: Oliver Rhodes, founder and publisher. Estab. 2012. Publishes mass market paperback and electronic originals and reprints. **Publishes 40 titles/year. Receives 200 queries/year; 300 mss/year. Pays 45% royalty on wholesale price.** Publishes ms 4 months after acceptance. Accepts simultaneous submissions. Responds in 1 month. Book catalog online.

FICTION Subjects include contemporary, erotica, ethnic, fantasy, gay, historical, lesbian, mainstream, mystery, romance, science fiction, suspense, western, crime, thriller, new adult. "We are looking for entertaining fiction targeted at modern women. That can be anything from Steampunk to Erotica, Historicals to thrillers. A distinctive author voice is more important than a particular genre or ms length." Submit complete ms.

TIPS "The most important question that we ask of submissions is why would a reader buy the next book? What's distinctive or different about your storytelling that will mean readers will want to come back for more. We look to acquire global English language rights for e-book and Print on Demand."

BOOKS FOR ALL TIMES, INC.

Box 202, Warrenton VA 20188. (540)428-3175. **E-mail:** staff@bfat.com. **Website:** www.bfat.com. **Contact:** Joe David, publisher & editor. Estab. 1981. Accepts simultaneous submissions.

TIPS Interested in "controversial, honest stories which satisfy the reader's curiosity to know. Read Victor Hugo, Fyodor Dostoyevsky and Sinclair Lewis for example."

BOTTOM DOG PRESS, INC.

P.O. Box 425, Huron OH 44839. (419)433-3573. **E-mail:** lsmithdog@smithdocs.net. **Website:** smithdocs. net. **Contact:** Larry Smith, director; Susanna Sharp-Schwacke, associate editor. Estab. 1985. Bottom Dog Press, Inc., "is a nonprofit literary and educational organization dedicated to publishing the best writing and art from the Midwest and Appalachia." **4% of books from first-time authors. 8% from unagented writers. Pays 10 copies and 15% royalty. Does not pay advance.** Publishes ms 4 months after acceptance. Accepts simultaneous submissions.

○ "Query via e-mail first with 2 paragraphs on book and author."

NONFICTION Subjects include alternative lifestyles, contemporary culture, creative nonfiction, humanities, literature, memoirs, New Age, social sciences, spirituality, womens issues, sense of place.

FICTION Subjects include contemporary, ethnic, gay, historical, literary, poetry, short story collections, Appalachian, working-class.

BOYDS MILLS PRESS

Highlights for Children, Inc., 815 Church St., Honesdale PA 18431. (570)253-1164. **Website:** www.boydsmillspress.com. Estab. 1990. Boyds Mills Press publishes picture books, nonfiction, activity books, and paperback reprints. Their titles have been named notable books by the International Reading Association, the American Library Association, and the National Council of Teachers of English. They've earned numerous awards, including the National Jewish Book Award, the Christopher Medal, the NCTE Orbis Pictus Honor, and the Golden Kite Honor. Boyds Mills Press welcomes unsolicited submissions from published and unpublished writers and artists. Submit a ms with a cover letter of relevant information, including experience with writing and publishing. Label the package "Manuscript Submission" and include an SASE. For art samples, label the package "Art Sample Submission." All submissions will be evaluated for all imprints. Responds to mss within 3 months. Catalog online. Guidelines online.

POETRY Send a book-length collection of poems. Do not send an initial query. Keep in mind that the strongest collections demonstrate a facility with multiple poetic forms.

GEORGE BRAZILLER, INC.

277 Broadway, Suite 708, New York NY 10007. **Website:** www.georgebraziller.com. Publishes hardcover and trade paperback originals and reprints. Accepts simultaneous submissions.

FICTION Subjects include ethnic, gay, lesbian, literary. "We rarely do fiction but when we have published novels, they have mostly been literary novels." Submit 4-6 sample chapter(s), SASE. Agented fiction 20%. Responds in 3 months to proposals.

NICHOLAS BREALEY PUBLISHING

53 State St., 9th Floor, Boston MA 02109. (617)523-3801. **Fax:** (617)523-3708. **Website:** www.nicholasbrealey.com. **Contact:** Aquisitions Editor. Estab. 1992. "Nicholas Brealey Publishing has a reputation for publishing high-quality and thought-provoking business books with international appeal. Over time our list has grown to focus also on careers, professional and

personal development, travel narratives and crossing cultures. We welcome fresh ideas and new insights in all of these subject areas." Submit via e-mail and follow the guidelines on the website. Accepts simultaneous submissions.

BREWERS PUBLICATIONS

Imprint of Brewers Association, 1327 Spruce St., Boulder CO 80302. **E-mail:** kristi@brewersassociation. org. **Website:** www.brewerspublications.com. **Contact:** Kristi Switzer, publisher. Estab. 1986. Publishes trade paperback originals. "BP is the largest publisher of contemporary and relevant brewing literature for today's craft brewers and homebrewers." **Publishes 2 titles/year. 50% of books from first-time authors. 100% from unagented writers. Pays advance.** Publishes book 9 months after acceptance. Accepts simultaneous submissions. Responds in 3 months to relevant queries. "Only those submissions relevant to our needs will receive a response to queries.". Guidelines online.

NONFICTION Subjects include professional brewing, homebrewing, technical brewing. "We seek to do this in a positive atmosphere, create lasting relationships and shared pride in our contributions to the brewing and beer community. The books we select to carry out this mission include titles relevant to homebrewing, professional brewing, starting a brewery, books on particular styles of beer, industry trends, ingredients, processes and the occasional broader interest title on cooking or the history/impact of beer in our society." Query first with proposal and sample chapter.

☯ BRICK BOOKS

Box 20081, 431 Boler Rd., London ON N6K 4G6, Canada. (519)657-8579. **E-mail:** brick.books@sympatico. ca. **Website:** www.brickbooks.ca. **Contact:** Kitty Lewis, General Manager. Estab. 1975. Publishes trade paperback originals. Brick Books has a reading period of January 1-April 30. Mss received outside that period will be returned. No multiple submissions. Pays 10% royalty in book copies only. "We publish only poetry." **Publishes 7 titles/year. 100 mss received/year. 30% of books from first-time authors. 100% from unagented writers.** Publishes ms 2 years after acceptance. Responds in 3-4 months to queries. Book catalog free or online. Guidelines online.

POETRY Submit only poetry.

TIPS "Writers without previous publications in literary journals or magazines are rarely considered by Brick Books for publication."

BRICK ROAD POETRY PRESS, INC.

513 Broadway, Columbus GA 31901. (706)221-4370. **Fax:** (706)649-3094. **E-mail:** kbadowski@brickroad-poetrypress.com. **Website:** www.brickroadpoetry-press.com. **Contact:** Ron Self and Keith Badowski, co-editors/founders. Estab. 2009. Publishes poetry only: books (single author collections). The mission of Brick Road Poetry Press is to publish and promote poetry that entertains, amuses, edifies, and surprises a wide audience of appreciative readers. "We concentrate on publishing what we enjoy. Our preference is for poetry geared toward dramatizing the human experience in language rich with sensory image and metaphor, recognizing that poetry can be, at one and the same time, both familiar as the perspiration of daily labor and as outrageous as a carnival sideshow. We prefer poetry that offers a coherent human voice, a sense of humor, attentiveness to words and language, narratives with surprise twists, persona poems, and/or philosophical or spiritual themes explored through the concrete scenes and images." Does not want intentional obscurity or riddling, highfalutin vocabulary, greeting card verse, and/or abstractions. **Publishes 3-6 titles/year. 500 submissions received/year. 80% of books from first-time authors. 100% from unagented writers. Pays royalties and 15 author copies. Initial print run of 150, print-on-demand thereafter. Does not pay advance.** Publishes ms 1 year after acceptance. Accepts simultaneous submissions. Responds in 3-9 months. Guidelines available.

POETRY Publishes poetry only: books (single author collections) "We prefer poetry that offers a coherent human voice, a sense of humor, attentiveness to words and language, narratives with surprise twists, persona poems, and/or philosophical or spiritual themes explored through the concrete scenes and images." Publishes 3-6 poetry books/year Mss accepted through open submission December-January and competition August-November. "We accept .doc, .rtf, or .pdf file formats. We prefer electronic submissions but will reluctantly consider hard copy submissions by mail if USPS Flat Rate Mailing Envelope is used and with the stipulation that, should the author's work be chosen for publication, an electronic version (.doc or .rtf) must be prepared in a timely manner and at the poet's expense." Please include cover letter with poetry publication/recognition highlights and something intriguing about your life story or ongoing pursuits. "We would like to develop a connection with the poet as well as the poetry." Please include the collection title in the cover letter. "We want to publish poets who are engaged in the literary community, including regular submission of work to various publications and participation in poetry readings, workshops, and writers' groups. That said, we would never rule out an emerging poet who demonstrates ability and motivation to move in that direction." Does not want intentional obscurity or riddling, highfalutin vocabulary, greeting card verse, and/or abstractions. Publishes poetry only: books (single author collections) "We accept .doc, .rtf, or .pdf file formats. We prefer electronic submissions but will reluctantly consider hard copy submissions by mail if USPS Flat Rate Mailing Envelope is used and with the stipulation that, should the author's work be chosen for publication, an electronic version (.doc or .rtf) must be prepared in a timely manner and at the poet's expense." Please include cover letter with poetry publication/recognition highlights and something intriguing about your life story or ongoing pursuits. "We would like to develop a connection with the poet as well as the poetry." Please include the collection title in the cover letter. "We want to publish poets who are engaged in the literary community, including regular submission of work to various publications and participation in poetry readings, workshops, and writers' groups. That said, we would never rule out an emerging poet who demonstrates ability and motivation to move in that direction."

TIPS "The best way to discover all that poetry can be and to expand the limits of your own poetry is to read expansively. We recommend the following poets: Kim Addonizio, Ken Babstock, Coleman Barks, Billy Collins, Morri Creech, Cynthia Cruz, Alice Friman, John Glenday, Beth A. Gylys, Jane Hirshfield, Jane Kenyon, Ted Kooser, Stanley Kunitz, Thomas Lux, Barry Marks, Michael Meyerhofer, Linda Pastan, Mark Strand, and Natasha D. Trethewey. Support your fellow poets and poetry in general by buying and reading lots of poetry books!"

⦿ BROADVIEW PRESS, INC.

P.O. Box 1243, Peterborough ON K9J 7H5, Canada. (705)743-8990. **Fax:** (705)743-8353. **E-mail:** mather@ broadviewpress.com; slatta@broadviewpress.com; dema@broadviewpress.com; brett@broadviewpress. com. **Website:** www.broadviewpress.com. **Contact:** Marjorie Mather, publisher/editor (English studies); Stephen Latta, editor (philosophy); Leslie Dema, acquisitions editor (Broadview Editions in philosophy); Brett McLenithan, acquisitions editor. Estab. 1985. "We publish in a broad variety of subject areas in the arts and social sciences. We are open to a broad range of political and philosophical viewpoints, from liberal and conservative to libertarian and Marxist, and including a wide range of feminist viewpoints." **Publishes over 40 titles/year. 500 queries; 200 mss received/year. 10% of books from first-time authors. 99% from unagented writers. Pays royalty.** Publishes ms 12 months after acceptance. Accepts simultaneous submissions. Responds in 1 month to queries; 2 months to proposals; 4 months to mss. Book catalog available free. Guidelines online.

NONFICTION Subjects include philosophy, religion, politics. "Our focus is very much on English studies and Philosophy, but within those 2 core subject areas we are open to a broad range of academic approaches and political viewpoints. We welcome feminist perspectives, and we have a particular interest in addressing environmental issues. Our publishing program is internationally-oriented, and we publish for a broad range of geographical markets-but as a Canadian company we also publish a broad range of titles with a Canadian emphasis." Query with SASE. Submit proposal package. Reviews artwork/photos. Send photocopies.

TIPS "Our titles often appeal to a broad readership; we have many books that are as much of interest to the general reader as they are to academics and students."

Ⓐⵔ BROADWAY BOOKS

Penguin Random House, 1745 Broadway, New York NY 10019. (212)782-9000. **Fax:** (212)782-9411. **Website:** crownpublishing.com/imprint/broadway-books. Estab. 1995. Publishes hardcover and trade paperback books. "Broadway publishes high quality general interest nonfiction and fiction for adults." **Receives thousands of mss/year. Pays royalty on retail price. Pays advance.** Accepts simultaneous submissions.

IMPRINTS Broadway Books; Broadway Business; Doubleday; Doubleday Image; Doubleday Religious Publishing; Main Street Books; Nan A. Talese.

NONFICTION Subjects include child guidance, contemporary culture, history, memoirs, multicultural, New Age, psychology, sex, spirituality, sports, travel, current affairs, motivational/inspirational, popular culture, consumer reference. *Agented submissions only.*

FICTION *Agented submissions only.*

BRONZE MAN BOOKS

Millikin University, 1184 W. Main, Decatur IL 62522. (217)424-6264. **E-mail:** rbrooks@millikin.edu. **Website:** www.bronzemanbooks.com. **Contact:** Dr. Randy Brooks, editorial board; Edwin Walker, editorial board. Estab. 2006. Publishes hardcover, trade paperback, literary chapbooks and mass market paperback originals. A student-owned and operated press located on Millikin University's campus in Decatur, Ill., Bronze Man Books is dedicated to integrating quality design and meaningful content. The company exposes undergraduate students to the process of publishing by combining the theory of writing, publishing, editing and designing with the practice of running a book publishing company. This emphasis on performance learning is a hallmark of Millikin's brand of education. **Publishes 3-4 titles/year. 80% of books from first-time authors. 100% from unagented writers. Outright purchase based on wholesale value of 10% of a press run.** Publishes book 6-12 months after acceptance. Accepts simultaneous submissions. Responds in 1-3 months.

NONFICTION Subjects include architecture, art, child guidance, literature, parenting. Query with SASE. E-mail inquiries are welcome.

FICTION Subjects include picture books, poetry. Subjects include art, graphic design, exhibits, general. Submit completed ms.

POETRY Submit completed ms.

TIPS "The art books are intended for serious collectors and scholars of contemporary art, especially of artists from the Midwestern US. These books are published in conjunction with art exhibitions at Millikin University or the Decatur Area Arts Council. The children's books have our broadest audience, and the literary chapbooks are intended for readers of contemporary fiction, drama, and poetry."

☼ THE BRUCEDALE PRESS

P.O. Box 2259, Port Elgin ON N0H 2C0, Canada. (519)832-6025. **E-mail:** info@brucedalepress.ca. **Website:** brucedalepress.ca. Estab. 1994. Publishes hardcover and trade paperback originals. The Brucedale Press publishes books and other materials of regional interest and merit, as well as literary, historical, and/or pictorial works. **Publishes 3 titles/year. 50 queries; 30 mss received/year. 75% of books from first-time authors. 100% from unagented writers. Pays royalty.** Publishes book 1 year after acceptance. Accepts simultaneous submissions. Book catalog online. "Unless responding to an invitation to submit, query first by Canada Post with outline and sample chapter to book-length manuscripts. Send full manuscripts for work intended for children." Guidelines online.

🗨 *Accepts works by Canadian authors only. Book submissions reviewed November to January. Submissions to* The Leaf Journal *accepted in September and March only. Manuscripts must be in English and thoroughly proofread before being sent. Use Canadian spellings and style.*

NONFICTION Subjects include history, memoirs, photography. Reviews artwork/photos from Canadians only.

FICTION Subjects include fantasy, feminist, historical, humor, juvenile, literary, mystery, plays, poetry, romance, short story collections, young adult.

TIPS "Our focus is very regional. In reading submissions, I look for quality writing with a strong connection to the Queen's Bush area of Ontario. All authors should visit our website, get a catalog, and read our books before submitting."

BUCKNELL UNIVERSITY PRESS

Bucknell University, 1 Dent Dr., Lewisburg PA 17837. (570)577-3674. **E-mail:** universitypress@bucknell.edu. **Website:** www.bucknell.edu/universitypress. **Contact:** Greg Clingham, director. Estab. 1968. Publishes hardcover, paperback, and e-books on various platforms. "In all fields, our criteria are scholarly excellence, critical originality, and interdisciplinary and theoretical expertise and sensitivity." **Publishes 35-40 titles/year.** Book catalog available free. Guidelines online.

NONFICTION Subjects include environment, ethnic, history, law, literary criticism, multicultural, philosophy, psychology, sociology, Luso-Hispanic studies, Latin American studies, 18-century studies, ecocriticism, African studies, Irish literature, cultural studies, historiography, legal theory. Series: Transits: Literature, Thought & Culture 1650-1850; Bucknell

Series in Latin American Literature and Theory; Eighteenth-Century Scotland; New Studies in the Age of Goethe; Contemporary Irish Writers; Griot Project Book Series; Apercus: Histories Texts Cultures. Submit full proposal and CV by Word attachment.

BULL PUBLISHING CO.

P.O. Box 1377, Boulder CO 80306. (800)676-2855. **Fax:** (303)545-6354. **Website:** www.bullpub.com. **Contact:** James Bull, publisher. Estab. 1974. Publishes hardcover and trade paperback originals. "Bull Publishing publishes health and nutrition books for the public with an emphasis on self-care, nutrition, women's health, weight control and psychology." **Publishes 6-8 titles/year. Pays 10-16% royalty on wholesale price (net to publisher).** Publishes ms 6 months after acceptance. Accepts simultaneous submissions. Book catalog available free.

NONFICTION Subjects include education. Subjects include self-care, nutrition, fitness, child health and nutrition, health education, mental health. "We look for books that fit our area of strength: responsible books on health that fill a substantial public need, and that we can market primarily through professionals." Submit outline, sample chapters. Reviews artwork/photos.

BURFORD BOOKS

101 E. State St., #301, Ithaca NY 14850. (607)319-4373. **E-mail:** info@burfordbooks.com. **Website:** www.burfordbooks.com. **Contact:** Burford Books Editorial Department. Estab. 1997. Publishes hardcover originals, trade paperback originals and reprints. Burford Books publishes books on all aspects of the outdoors, from backpacking to sports, practical and literary, as well as books on food & wine, military history, and the Finger Lakes region of New York State. **Publishes 12 titles/year. 300 queries; 200 mss received/year. 30% of books from first-time authors. 60% from unagented writers. Pays royalty on wholesale price.** Publishes book 18 months after acceptance. Accepts simultaneous submissions. Responds in 1 week to queries; 1 month to proposals; 2 months to mss. Book catalog and ms guidelines online.

NONFICTION Subjects include Americana, animals, cooking, foods, gardening, history, hobbies, military, recreation, sports, travel, war, fitness. "Burford Books welcomes proposals on new projects, especially in the subject areas in which we specialize: sports, the outdoors, golf, nature, gardening, food and wine, travel, and military history. We are not currently considering fiction or children's books. In general it's sufficient to send a brief proposal letter that outlines your idea, which should be e-mailed to info@burfordbooks.com with the word 'query' in the subject line." Reviews artwork/photos. Send digital images.

BUSTER BOOKS

16 Lion Yard, Tremadoc Rd., London WA SW4 7NQ, United Kingdom. (020)7720-8643. **Fax:** (022)7720-8953. **E-mail:** enquiries@mombooks.com. **Website:** www.busterbooks.co.uk. **Contact:** Buster Submissions. "We are dedicated to providing irresistible and fun books for children of all ages. We typically publish black & white nonfiction for children aged 8-12 novelty titles-including doodle books." Accepts simultaneous submissions.

NONFICTION Prefers synopsis and sample text over complete ms.

TIPS "We do not accept picturebook or poetry submissions. Please do not send original artwork as we cannot guarantee its safety." Visit website before submitting.

C&T PUBLISHING

1651 Challenge Dr., Concord CA 94520-5206. (925)677-0377. **Fax:** (925)677-0373. **E-mail:** roxanec@ctpub.com. **E-mail:** support@ctpub.com. **Website:** www.ctpub.com. **Contact:** Roxane Cerda. Estab. 1983. Publishes hardcover and trade paperback originals. "C&T publishes well-written, beautifully designed books on quilting and fiber crafts, embroidery, doll-making, knitting and paper crafts." **Publishes 60 titles/year. 50% of books from first-time authors. 90% from unagented writers.** Accepts simultaneous submissions. Responds in 3 months to queries. Book catalog free; guidelines online.

IMPRINTS Stash Books, Kansas City Star Quilts, Fun Stitch Studio.

NONFICTION Subjects include art, crafts, hobbies, quilting books, occasional quilt picture books, quilt-related crafts, wearable art, needlework, fiber and surface embellishments, other books relating to fabric crafting and paper crafting. Extensive proposal guidelines are available on the company's website.

TIPS "In our industry, we find that how-to books have the longest selling life. Quiltmakers, sewing enthusiasts, needle artists, fiber artists and paper crafters are our audience. We like to see new concepts or techniques. Include some great samples, and you'll get our attention quickly. Dynamic design is hard to resist, and if that's your forte, show us what you've done."

CALKINS CREEK

Boyds Mills Press, 815 Church St., Honesdale PA 18431. **Website:** www.boydsmillspress.com. Estab. 2004. "We aim to publish books that are a well-written blend of creative writing and extensive research, which emphasize important events, people, and places in U.S. history." **Pays authors royalty or work purchased outright.** Accepts simultaneous submissions. Guidelines online.

NONFICTION Subjects include history. Submit outline/synopsis and 3 sample chapters.

FICTION Subjects include historical. Submit outline/synopsis and 3 sample chapters.

TIPS "Read through our recently published titles and review our catalog. When selecting titles to publish, our emphasis will be on important events, people, and places in U.S. history. Writers are encouraged to submit a detailed bibliography, including secondary and primary sources, and expert reviews with their submissions."

⊘ CALYX BOOKS

P.O. Box B, Corvallis OR 97339-0539. (541)753-9384. **Fax:** (541)753-0515. **E-mail:** info@calyxpress.org. **E-mail:** editor@calyxpress.org. **Website:** www.calyxpress.org. **Contact:** The Editor. A. Bublitz Estab. 1986. Accepts simultaneous submissions.

○   "Due to the high volume of book manuscripts received, CALYX Books is currently closed for manuscript submissions until further notice except for the Sarah Lantz Poetry Book Prize."

FICTION Closed to submissions until further notice.

ⒶⒹ CANDLEWICK PRESS

99 Dover St., Somerville MA 02144. (617) 661-3330. **Fax:** (617) 661-0565. **E-mail:** bigbear@candlewick. com. **Website:** www.candlewick.com. Estab. 1991. Publishes hardcover and trade paperback originals, and reprints. "Candlewick Press publishes high-quality, illustrated children's books for ages infant through young adult. We are a truly child-centered publisher." **Publishes 200 titles/year. 5% of books from first-time authors. Pays authors royalty of 2½-10% based on retail price. Offers advance.** Accepts simultaneous submissions.

IMPRINTS Big Picture Press, Candlewick Entertainment, Candlewick Studio, Nosy Crow, Templar Books.

○   *Candlewick Press is not accepting queries or unsolicited mss at this time.*

NONFICTION Picture books: concept, biography, geography, nature/environment. Young readers: biography, geography, nature/environment.

FICTION Subjects include juvenile, picture books, young adult. Picture books: animal, concept, contemporary, fantasy, history, humor, multicultural, nature/environment, poetry. Middle readers, young adults: contemporary, fantasy, history, humor, multicultural, poetry, science fiction, sports, suspense/mystery. "We currently do not accept unsolicited editorial queries or submissions. If you are an author or illustrator and would like us to consider your work, please read our submissions policy (online) to learn more."

TIPS *"We no longer accept unsolicited mss. See our website for further information about us."*

CANTERBURY HOUSE PUBLISHING, LTD.

4535 Ottawa Trail, Sarasota FL 34233. (941)312-6912. **Website:** www.canterburyhousepublishing.com. **Contact:** Sandra Horton, editor. Estab. 2009. Publishes hardcover, trade paperback, and electronic originals. "Our audience is made up of readers looking for wholesome fiction with good southern stories, with elements of mystery, romance, and inspiration and/or are looking for true stories of achievement and triumph over challenging circumstances. We are very strict on our submission guidelines due to our small staff, and our target market of Southern regional settings." **Publishes 3-6 titles/year. 35% of books from first-time authors. 100% from unagented writers. Pays 10-15% royalty on wholesale price.** Publishes ms 9-12 months after acceptance. Accepts simultaneous submissions. Responds in 1 month to queries; 3 months to mss. Book catalog online. Guidelines online.

NONFICTION Subjects include memoirs, regional. Query with SASE and through website e-mail upon request. Reviews artwork. Send photocopies.

FICTION Subjects include contemporary, historical, literary, mainstream, mystery, regional, romance, suspense. Query with SASE and through website.

TIPS "Because of our limited staff, we prefer authors who have good writing credentials and submit edited manuscripts. We also look at authors who are business and marketing savvy and willing to help promote their books."

 CAPALL BANN PUBLISHING

Auton Farm, Milverton, Somerset TA4 1NE, United Kingdom. (44)(182)340-1528. **E-mail:** enquiries@ capallbann.co.uk. **Website:** www.capallbann.co.uk. **Contact:** Julia Day (MBS, healing, animals and religion). Publishes trade and mass market paperback originals and trade paperback and mass market paperback reprints. "Our mission is to publish books of real value to enhance and improve readers' lives." **Publishes 46 titles/year. 800 queries; 450 mss received/year. 50% of books from first-time authors. 100% from unagented writers. Pays 10% royalty on net sales.** Publishes ms 4-8 months after acceptance. Accepts simultaneous submissions. Responds in 2-6 weeks to queries; 2 months to proposals and mss. Book catalog free. Guidelines online.

NONFICTION Subjects include animals, astrology, crafts, creative nonfiction, gardening, New Age, philosophy, psychic, religion, spirituality, witchcraft, paganism, druidry, ritual magic. Submit outline. Reviews artwork/photos. Send photocopies.

CAPSTONE PRESS

Capstone Young Readers, 1710 Roe Crest Dr., North Mankato MN 56003. **E-mail:** author.sub@capstonepub.com; il.sub@capstonepub.com. **Website:** www.capstonepub.com. Estab. 1991. The Capstone Press imprint publishes nonfiction with accessible text on topics kids love to capture interest and build confidence and skill in beginning, struggling, and reluctant readers, grades pre-K-9. Responds only if submissions fit needs. Mss and writing samples will not be returned. "If you receive no reply within 6 months, you should assume the editors are not interested.". Catalog available upon request. Guidelines online.

CAPSTONE PROFESSIONAL

Maupin House, Capstone, 1710 Roe Crest Dr., North Mankato MN 56003. (312)324-5200. **Fax:** (312)324-5201. **E-mail:** author.sub@capstonepub.com. **Website:** www.capstonepd.com. Marketing Director: David Willette. Marketing Specialist: Mary McCarthy. Associate Marketing Manager: Patty Corcoran. Estab. 2013. Capstone Professional publishes professional learning resources for K-12 educators under the imprint of Maupin House. **Publishes 6-8 titles/year. Receives 25 submissions/year. 60% of books from first-time authors. 100% from unagented writers. Pays**

royalty. Not usually. Publishes 6 months after acceptance. Accepts simultaneous submissions. Responds in less than 1 month. Catalog and guidelines online.

IMPRINTS Maupin House.

NONFICTION Subjects include education. Professional development offerings by Capstone Professional range from webinars and workshops to conference speakers and author visits. Submissions for products that speak to the needs of educators today are always accepted. "We continue to look for professional development resources that support grades K–8 classroom teachers in areas, such as these: Literacy, Language Arts, Content-Area Literacy, Research-Based Practices, Assessment, Inquiry, Technology, Differentiation, Standards-Based Instruction, School Safety, Classroom Management, and School Community." Reviews artwork/photos as part of the ms package. Writers should send photocopies, digital.

THE CAREER PRESS, INC.

12 Parish Dr., Wayne NJ 07470. **Website:** www.careerpress.com. Estab. 1985. Publishes hardcover and paperback originals. Career Press publishes books for adult readers seeking practical information to improve themselves in careers, business, HR, sales, entrepreneurship, and other related topics, as well as titles on supervision, management and CEOs. New Page Books publishes in the areas of New Age, new science, paranormal, the unexplained, alternative history, spirituality. Accepts simultaneous submissions. Guidelines online.

NONFICTION Subjects include recreation, nutrition. Look through our catalog; become familiar with our publications. "We like to select authors who are specialists on their topic." Submit outline, bio, TOC, 2-3 sample chapters, marketing plan, SASE. Or, send complete ms (preferred).

CARNEGIE MELLON UNIVERSITY PRESS

5032 Forbes Ave., Pittsburgh PA 15289. (412)268-2861. **Fax:** (412)268-8706. **E-mail:** carnegiemellonuniversitypress@gmail.com. **Website:** www.cmu.edu/universitypress/. **Contact:** Poetry Editor or Nonfiction Editor. Estab. 1972. Publishes hardcover and trade paperback originals. **Publishes 6 titles/year.** Accepts simultaneous submissions. Book catalog and guidelines online.

NONFICTION Subjects include education, history, literary criticism, memoirs, science, sociology, translation. Query with SASE.

FICTION Subjects include literary, poetry, poetry in translation, short story collections, drama, epistolary novel.

POETRY Holds annual reading period. "This reading period is only for poets who have not previously been published by CMP." Submit complete ms. **Requires reading fee of $15.**

CAROLINA WREN PRESS

120 Morris St., Durham NC 27701. (919)560-2738. **E-mail:** carolinawrenpress@earthlink.net. **Website:** www.carolinawrenpress.org. **Contact:** Robin Miura, Editor & Director. Estab. 1976. "We publish poetry, fiction, and memoirs by or about people of color, women, gay/lesbian issues, and work by writers from, living in, or writing about the U.S. South." Accepts simultaneous submissions, but "let us know if work has been accepted elsewhere." **We pay our authors an honorarium.** Publishes ms 2 year after acceptance. Accepts simultaneous submissions. Responds in 3 months to queries; 6 months to mss. Guidelines online.

NONFICTION Subjects include ethnic, gay, lesbian, literature, multicultural, womens issues.

FICTION Subjects include ethnic, experimental, feminist, literary, poetry, short story collections. "We are no longer publishing children's literature of any topic." Books: 6×9 paper; typeset; various bindings; illustrations. Distributes titles through John F. Blair, Amazon.com, Barnes & Noble, Baker & Taylor, and on their website. "We very rarely accept any unsolicited manuscripts, but we accept submissions for the Doris Bakwin Award for Writing by a Woman in Jan-June of even-numbered years and submissions for the Lee Smith Novel Prize in Jan-June of odd-numbered years." "We will accept e-mailed queries—a letter in the body of the e-mail describing your project—but please do not send large attachments." All other submissions are accepted via Submittable as part of our annual contests.

POETRY Publishes 2 poetry books/year, "usually through the Carolina Wren Press Poetry Series Contest. Otherwise we primarily publish women, minorities, and authors from, living in, or writing about the U.S. South." Not accepting unsolicited submissions except through Poetry Series Contest. Accepts e-mail queries, but send only letter and description of work, no large files. Carolina Wren Press Poetry Contest for a First or Second Book takes submissions, electronically, from January to June of odd-numbered years. **TIPS** "Best way to get read is to submit to a contest."

⊘ CAROLRHODA BOOKS, INC.

1251 Washington Ave. N., Minneapolis MN 55401. **Website:** www.lernerbooks.com. Editorial Director: Alix Reid. Estab. 1959. "We will continue to seek targeted solicitations at specific reading levels and in specific subject areas. The company will list these targeted solicitations on our website and in national newsletters, such as the SCBWI Bulletin." Interested in "boundary-pushing" teen fiction. *Lerner Publishing Group no longer accepts submissions to any of their imprints except for Kar-Ben Publishing.* Accepts simultaneous submissions.

⊘ CARSON-DELLOSA PUBLISHING CO., INC.

P.O. Box 35665, Greensboro NC 27425. (336)632-0084. **E-mail:** freelancesamples@carsondellosa.com. **Website:** www.carsondellosa.com. Does not accept unsolicited product ideas or book proposals at this time. **Publishes 80-90 titles/year. 15-20% of books from first-time authors. 95% from unagented writers. Makes outright purchase.** Book catalog online. Guidelines available free.

NONFICTION Subjects include education. "We publish supplementary educational materials, such as teacher resource books, workbooks, and activity books." No textbooks or trade children's books, please.

🅐⊘ CARTWHEEL BOOKS

Imprint of Scholastic Trade Division, 557 Broadway, New York NY 10012. (212)343-6100. **Website:** www.scholastic.com. Estab. 1991. Publishes novelty books, easy readers, board books, hardcover and trade paperback originals. Cartwheel Books publishes innovative books for children, up to age 8. "We are looking for 'novelties' that are books first, play objects second. Even without its gimmick, a Cartwheel Book should stand alone as a valid piece of children's literature." Accepts simultaneous submissions. Guidelines available free.

NONFICTION Subjects include animals, history, recreation, science, sports. Cartwheel Books publishes for the very young, therefore nonfiction should be written in a manner that is accessible to preschoolers through 2nd grade. Often writers choose topics that are too narrow or "special" and do not appeal to the mass market. Also, the text and vocabulary are frequently too difficult for our young audience. *Accepts mss from agents only.* Reviews artwork/photos. Send Please do not send original artwork.

FICTION Subjects include humor, juvenile, mystery, picture books. Again, the subject should have mass market appeal for very young children. Humor can be helpful, but not necessary. Mistakes writers make are a reading level that is too difficult, a topic of no interest or too narrow, or mss that are too long. *Accepts mss from agents only.*

CATHOLIC UNIVERSITY OF AMERICA PRESS

620 Michigan Ave. NE, Washington DC 20064. (202)319-5052. **E-mail:** cua-press@cua.edu. **Website:** cuapress.org. Estab. 1939. The Catholic University of America Press publishes in the fields of history (ecclesiastical and secular), literature and languages, philosophy, political theory, social studies, and theology. "We have interdisciplinary emphasis on patristics, and medieval studies. We publish works of original scholarship intended for academic libraries, scholars and other professionals and works that offer a synthesis of knowledge of the subject of interest to a general audience or suitable for use in college and university classrooms." **Publishes 30-35 titles/year. 50% of books from first-time authors. 100% from unagented writers. Pays variable royalty on net receipts.** Publishes book 18 months after acceptance. Accepts simultaneous submissions. Responds in 5 days to queries. Book catalog on request. Guidelines online.

NONFICTION Subjects include history, philosophy, religion, Church-state relations. No unrevised doctoral dissertations. Length: 40,000-120,000 words. Query with outline, sample chapter, CV, and list of previous publications.

TIPS "Scholarly monographs and works suitable for adoption as supplementary reading material in courses have the best chance."

CATO INSTITUTE

1000 Massachusetts Ave. NW, Washington DC 20001. (202)842-0200. **Website:** www.cato.org. **Contact:** Submissions Editor. Estab. 1977. Publishes hardcover originals, trade paperback originals and reprints. Cato Institute publishes books on public policy issues from a free-market or libertarian perspective. **Publishes 12 titles/year. 25% of books from first-time authors. 90% from unagented writers. Makes outright purchase of $1,000-10,000. Pays advance.** Pub-

lishes ms 9 months after acceptance. Accepts simultaneous submissions. Responds in 3 months to queries. Book catalog online.

NONFICTION Subjects include education, sociology, public policy. Query with SASE.

CAVE HOLLOW PRESS

P.O. Drawer J, Warrensburg MO 64093. **E-mail:** gbcrump@cavehollowpress.com. **Website:** www.cavehollowpress.com. **Contact:** G.B. Crump, editor. Estab. 2001. Publishes trade paperback originals. **Publishes 1 titles/year. 85 queries; 6 mss received/year. 80% of books from first-time authors. 100% from unagented writers. Pays 7-12% royalty on wholesale price. Pays negotiable amount in advance.** Publishes ms 1 year after acceptance. Accepts simultaneous submissions. Responds in 1-2 months to queries and proposals; 3-6 months to mss. Catalog online. Guidelines available free.

FICTION Subjects include contemporary, literary, mainstream, mystery. "We publish fiction by Midwestern authors and/or with Midwestern themes and/or settings. Our website is updated frequently to reflect the current type of fiction Cave Hollow Press is seeking." Query with SASE.

TIPS "Our audience varies based on the type of book we are publishing. We specialize in Missouri and Midwest regional fiction. We are interested in talented writers from Missouri and the surrounding Midwest. Check our submission guidelines on the website for what type of fiction we are interested in currently."

CEDAR FORT, INC.

2373 W. 700 S, Springville UT 84663. (801)489-4084. **Website:** www.cedarfort.com. Estab. 1986. Publishes hardcover, trade paperback originals and reprints, mass market paperback and electronic reprints. "Each year we publish well over 100 books, and many of those are by first-time authors. At the same time, we love to see books from established authors. As one of the largest book publishers in Utah, we have the capability and enthusiasm to make your book a success, whether you are a new author or a returning one. We want to publish uplifting and edifying books that help people think about what is important in life, books people enjoy reading to relax and feel better about themselves, and books to help improve lives. Although we do put out several children's books each year, we are extremely selective. Our children's books must have strong religious or moral values, and must contain outstanding writing and an excellent storyline." **Publishes 150 titles/year. Receives 200 queries/year; 600 mss/year. 60% of books from first-time authors. 95% from unagented writers. Pays 10-12% royalty on wholesale price. Pays $2,000-50,000 advance.** Publishes book 10-14 months after acceptance. Accepts simultaneous submissions. Responds in 1 month on queries; 2 months on proposals; 4 months on mss. Catalog and guidelines online.

IMPRINTS Council Press, Sweetwater Books, Bonneville Books, Front Table Books, Hobble Creek Press, CFI, Plain Sight Publishing, Horizon Publishers, Pioneer Plus.

NONFICTION Subjects include agriculture, Americana, animals, anthropology, archeology, business, child guidance, communications, cooking, crafts, creative nonfiction, economics, education, foods, gardening, health, history, hobbies, horticulture, house and home, military, nature, recreation, regional, religion, social sciences, spirituality, war, womens issues, young adult. Query with SASE; submit proposal package, including outline, 2 sample chapters; or submit completed ms. Reviews artwork as part of the ms package. Send photocopies.

FICTION Subjects include adventure, contemporary, fantasy, historical, humor, juvenile, literary, mainstream, military, multicultural, mystery, regional, religious, romance, science fiction, spiritual, sports, suspense, war, western, young adult. Submit completed ms.

TIPS "Our audience is rural, conservative, mainstream. The first page of your ms is very important because we start reading every submission, but good writing and plot keep us reading."

CENTERSTREAM PUBLISHING LLC

P.O. Box 17878, Anaheim Hills CA 92817. (714)779-9390. **Fax:** (714)779-9390. **E-mail:** centerstrm@aol.com. **Website:** www.centerstream-usa.com. **Contact:** Ron Middlebrook. Estab. 1980. Publishes music hardcover and mass market paperback originals, trade paperback and mass market paperback reprints. Centerstream publishes music history and instructional books, all instruments plus DVDs. **Publishes 12 titles/year. 15 queries; 15 mss received/year. 80% of books from first-time authors. 100% from unagented writers. Pays 10-15% royalty on wholesale price. Pays $300-3,000 advance.** Publishes ms 8 months after acceptance. Accepts simultaneous sub-

missions. Responds in 3 months to queries. Book catalog and ms guidelines for #10 SASE.

NONFICTION Query with SASE.

CHALICE PRESS

CBP Books, Christian Board of Publication, 483 E. Lockwood Ave., Suite 100, St. Louis MO 63119. (314)231-8500. **E-mail:** submissions@chalicepress.com. **Website:** www.chalicepress.com. **Contact:** Brad Lyons, president and publisher. Estab. 1911. Publishes hardcover and trade paperback originals. The mission of CBP/Chalice Press is to publish resources inviting all people into deeper relationship with God, equipping them as disciples of Jesus Christ, and sending them into ministries as the Holy Spirit calls them. CBP is a 501(c)3 not-for-profit organization. **Publishes 20 titles/year. 300 queries; 50 mss received/year. 10% of books from first-time authors. 95% from unagented writers. Pays negotiable advance.** Publishes ms 1 year after acceptance. Accepts simultaneous submissions. Responds in 2 months to queries; 3 months to proposals and mss. Book catalog online. Guidelines online.

IMPRINTS Chalice Press, TCP Books, CBP, Inside-Out Church Camp Curriculum.

NONFICTION Subjects include community, multicultural, public affairs, religion, social sciences, spirituality, womens issues, Christian spirituality, social justice. Submit query as directed on www.chalicepress.com.

TIPS "We publish for lay Christian readers, church ministers, and educators."

⚫ S. CHAND & COMPANY LTD.

7361 Ram Nagar, Qutab Rd., New Delhi 110055, India. (91)(11)2367-2080. **Fax:** (91)(11)2367-7446. **Website:** www.schandpublishing.com. Accepts simultaneous submissions. Guidelines online.

NONFICTION Subjects include history, botany, chemistry, engineering, technical, English, mathematics, physics, political science, zoology. Query through website.

CHANGELING PRESS LLC

315 N. Centre St., Martinsburg WV 25404. **E-mail:** submissions.changelingpress@gmail.com. **Website:** www.changelingpress.com. **Contact:** Margaret Riley, publisher. Estab. 2004. Publishes e-books. Erotic romance, novellas only (10,000-30,000 words). "We're currently looking for contemporary and futuristic short fiction, single title, series, and serials in the fol-

lowing genres and themes: sci-fi/futuristic, dark and urban fantasy, paranormal, BDSM, action adventure, guilty pleasures (adult contemporary kink), new adult, menage, bisexual and more, gay, interracial, BBW, cougar (M/F), silver fox (M/M), men and women in uniform, vampires, werewolves, elves, dragons and magical creatures, other shape shifters, magic, dark desires (demons and horror), and hentai (tentacle monsters)." **Publishes 165 titles/year. 400+ 5% of books from first-time authors. 100% from unagented writers. Pays 35% gross royalties on site, 50% gross off site monthly. Does not pay advance.** Publishes ms 60-90 days after acceptance. Responds in 1 week to queries. Catalog online. Guidelines online.

IMPRINTS Razor's Edge Press.

FICTION Subjects include adventure, erotica, ethnic, fantasy, gay, horror, humor, literary, military, multicultural, romance, science fiction, short story collections, suspense, young adult. Please read and follow our submissions guidelines available at http://changelingpress.com/submissions.php. All submissions which do not follow the submissions guidelines will be rejected unread. No lesbian fiction submissions without prior approval, please. Absolutely no lesbian fiction written by men. E-mail submissions only. Please read and follow our submissions guidelines available at http://changelingpress.com/submissions.php. All submissions which do not follow the submissions guidelines will be rejected unread.

CHARLESBRIDGE PUBLISHING

85 Main St., Watertown MA 02472. (617)926-0329. **Fax:** (617)926-5720. **E-mail:** tradeeditorial@charlesbridge.com. **E-mail:** yasubs@charlesbridge.com. **Website:** www.charlesbridge.com. Estab. 1980. Publishes hardcover and trade paperback nonfiction and fiction, children's books for the trade and library markets. "Charlesbridge publishes high-quality books for children, with a goal of creating lifelong readers and lifelong learners. Our books encourage reading and discovery in the classroom, library, and home. We believe that books for children should offer accurate information, promote a positive worldview, and embrace a child's innate sense of wonder and fun. To this end, we continually strive to seek new voices, new visions, and new directions in children's literature. As of September 2015, we are now accepting young adult novels for consideration." **Publishes 45 titles/year. 2,000 submissions/year. 10-20% of books from first-time authors. 50% from unagented writers. Pays royalty. Pays advance.** Publishes ms 2-4 years after acceptance. Accepts simultaneous submissions. Responds in 3 months. Guidelines online.

IMPRINTS Charlesbridge Teen: Charlesbridge Teen features storytelling that presents new ideas and an evolving world. Our carefully curated stories give voice to unforgettable characters with unique perspectives. We publish books that inspire teens to cheer or sigh, laugh or reflect, reread or share with a friend, and ultimately, pick up another book. Our mission—to make reading irresistible!

NONFICTION Subjects include animals, creative nonfiction, history, multicultural, science, social science. Strong interest in nature, environment, social studies, and other topics for trade and library markets. Please submit only 1 or 2 chapters at a time. For nonfiction books longer than 30 ms pages, send a detailed proposal, a chapter outline, and 1-3 chapters of text.

FICTION Subjects include young adult. Strong stories with enduring themes. Charlesbridge publishes both picture books and transitional bridge books (books ranging from early readers to middle-grade chapter books). Our fiction titles include lively, plot-driven stories with strong, engaging characters. No alphabet books, board books, coloring books, activity books, or books with audiotapes or CD-ROMs. Please submit only 1 ms at a time. For picture books and shorter bridge books, please send a complete ms. For fiction books longer than 30 ms pages, please send a detailed plot synopsis, a chapter outline, and 3 chapters of text. If sending a young adult novel, mark the front of the envelope with "YA novel enclosed." Please note, for YA, e-mail submissions are preferred to the following address; yasubs@charlesbridge.com. Only responds if interested. Full guidelines on site.

TIPS "To become acquainted with our publishing program, we encourage you to review our books and visit our website where you will find our catalog."

THE CHARLES PRESS, PUBLISHERS

230 North 21st St., Ste. 312, Philadelphia PA 19103. (215)561-2786. **Fax:** (215)600-1248. **E-mail:** mail@charlespresspub.com. **E-mail:** submissions@charlespresspub.com. **Website:** www.charlespresspub.com. **Contact:** Lauren Meltzer, publisher. Estab. 1982. Publishes hardcover and trade paperback originals. Currently emphasizing mental and physical health (especially holistic, complementary and alternative

healthcare), psychology, animals/pets/veterinary medicine, how-to (especially relating to healthcare and wellness), aging/eldercare/geriatrics and medical reference books. **Publishes 7-9 titles/year. 300 Does not usually pay advance for scholarly books, but possibly for other types.** Publishes ms 10 months after acceptance. Accepts simultaneous submissions. Responds in 1-2 months. Book catalog online. Guidelines online.

NONFICTION Subjects include animals, beauty, child guidance, cooking, counseling, education, ethnic, foods, health, history, humanities, medicine, nutrition, parenting, philosophy, psychology, religion, science, sex, social sciences, sociology, spirituality, true crime, Medical nursing healthcare aging/eldercare wellness nutrition food nutrition cookbooks animals veterinary parenting. No autobiographies, children's books, or poetry. Query first, then submit proposal package that includes a description of the book, a few representative sample chapters, intended audience, competing titles, author's qualifications/ background. No faxed submissions. Reviews artwork/ photos. Send photocopies or transparencies.

CHELSEA GREEN PUBLISHING CO.

85 N. Main St., Suite 120, White River Junction VT 05001. (802)295-6300. **Fax:** (802)295-6444. **E-mail:** web@chelseagreen.com. **E-mail:** submissions@chelseagreen.com. **Website:** www.chelseagreen.com. Estab. 1984. Publishes hardcover and trade paperback originals and reprints. "Since 1984, Chelsea Green has been the publishing leader for books on the politics and practice of sustainable living." **Publishes 18-25 titles/year. 600-800 queries; 200-300 mss received/year. 30% of books from first-time authors. 80% from unagented writers. Pays royalty on publisher's net. Pays $2,500-10,000 advance.** Publishes book 18 months after acceptance. Accepts simultaneous submissions. Responds in 2 weeks to queries; 1 month to proposals/mss. Book catalog online. Guidelines online.

NONFICTION Subjects include agriculture, alternative lifestyles, business, community, cooking, creative nonfiction, economics, environment, foods, gardening, government, health, horticulture, medicine, nature, nutrition, politics, science, simple living, renewable energy, and other sustainability topics. Academic, self-help, spiritual. Prefers electronic queries and proposals via e-mail (as a single attachment). If sending via snail mail, submissions will only be returned with SASE. Please review our guidelines on our website carefully before submitting. Reviews artwork/photos.

TIPS "Our readers and our authors are passionate about finding sustainable and viable solutions to contemporary challenges in the fields of energy, food production, economics, and building. It would be helpful for prospective authors to have a look at several of our current books, as well as our website."

CHEMICAL PUBLISHING CO., INC.

P.O. Box 676, Revere MA 02151. **Website:** www.chemical-publishing.com. **Contact:** Heather Carr, editor. Estab. 1934. Publishes hardcover originals. Chemical Publishing Co., Inc., publishes professional chemistry-technical titles aimed at people employed in the chemical industry, libraries and graduate courses. "We invite the submission of manuscripts whether they are technical, scientific or serious popular expositions. All submitted manuscripts and planned works will receive prompt attention. The staff will consider finished and proposed manuscripts by authors whose works have not been previously published as sympathetically as those by experienced authors. Please do not hesitate to consult us about such manuscripts or about your ideas for writing them." **Publishes 10-15 titles/year. 20 queries received/year. 50% of books from first-time authors. 100% from unagented writers. Pays 10% royalty on retail price or makes negotiable outright purchase. Pays negotiable advance.** Publishes ms 8 months after acceptance. Responds in 3 weeks to queries; 5 weeks to proposals; 1 months to mss. Book catalog available free. Guidelines online.

NONFICTION Subjects include science, analytical methods, chemical technology, cosmetics, dictionaries, engineering, environmental science, food technology, formularies, industrial technology, medical, metallurgy, textiles. Submit outline, a few pages of 3 sample chapters, SASE. Download CPC submission form online and include with submission. Reviews, artwork and photos should also be part of the ms package.

TIPS "Audience is professionals in various fields of chemistry, corporate and public libraries, college libraries. We request a fax letter with an introduction of the author and the kind of book written. Afterwards, we will reply. If the title is of interest, then we will request samples of the manuscript."

CHICAGO REVIEW PRESS

814 N. Franklin St., Chicago IL 60610. (312)337-0747. **Fax:** (312)337-5110. **E-mail:** csherry@chicagoreviewpress.com; jpohlen@chicagoreviewpress.com; lreardon@chicagoreviewpress.com; ytaylor@chicagoreviewpress.com. **Website:** www.chicagoreviewpress.com. **Contact:** Cynthia Sherry, publisher; Yuval Taylor, senior editor; Jerome Pohlen, senior editor; Lisa Reardon, senior editor. Estab. 1973. "Chicago Review Press publishes high-quality, nonfiction, educational activity books that extend the learning process through hands-on projects and accurate and interesting text. We look for activity books that are as much fun as they are constructive and informative." **Pays authors royalty of 7.5-12.5% based on retail price. Offers advances of $3,000-6,000. Pays illustrators and photographers by the project (range varies considerably).** Publishes a book 1-2 years after acceptance. Accepts simultaneous submissions. Responds in 2 months. Book catalog available for $3. Ms guidelines available for $3.

IMPRINTS Academy Chicago; Ball Publishing; Chicago Review Press; Lawrence Hill Books; Zephyr Press.

NONFICTION Young readers, middle readers and young adults: activity books, arts/crafts, multicultural, history, nature/environment, science. "We're interested in hands-on, educational books; anything else probably will be rejected." Average length: young readers and young adults—144-160 pages. Enclose cover letter and a brief synopsis of book in 1-2 paragraphs, table of contents and first 3 sample chapters; prefers not to receive e-mail queries. For children's activity books include a few sample activities with a list of the others. Full guidelines available on site.

FICTION Guidelines now available on website.

TIPS "We're looking for original activity books for small children and the adults caring for them—new themes and enticing projects to occupy kids' imaginations and promote their sense of personal creativity. We like activity books that are as much fun as they are constructive. Please write for guidelines so you'll know what we're looking for."

⊘ CHILDREN'S BRAINS ARE YUMMY (CBAY) BOOKS

P.O. Box 670296, Dallas TX 75367. **E-mail:** submissions@cbaybooks.com. **Website:** www.cbaybooks.com. **Contact:** Madeline Smoot, publisher. Estab.

2008. "CBAY Books currently focuses on quality fantasy and science fiction books for the middle grade and teen markets. We are not currently accepting unsolicited submissions. We do not publish picture books." **Publishes 3-6 titles/year. 30% of books from first-time authors. 80% from unagented writers. Pays authors royalty 10%-15% based on wholesale price. Offers advances against royalties. Average amount $500. Pays advance.** Publishes ms 24 months after acceptance. Accepts simultaneous submissions. Responds in 2 months. "We are distributed by IPG. Our books can be found in their catalog at www.ipgbooks.com.". Brochure and guidelines online.

FICTION Subjects include adventure, fantasy, juvenile, mystery, science fiction, short story collections, suspense, young adult, folktales.

⊘⊘ CHILD'S PLAY (INTERNATIONAL) LTD.

Child's Play, Ashworth Rd. Bridgemead, Swindon, Wiltshire SN5 7YD, United Kingdom. 01793 616286. **E-mail:** neil@childs-play.com; office@childs-play.com. **Website:** www.childs-play.com. **Contact:** Sue Baker, Neil Burden, manuscript acquisitions. Art Director: Annie Kubler. Estab. 1972. Specializes in nonfiction, fiction, educational material, multicultural material. Produces 30 picture books/year; 10 young readers/year. "A child's early years are more important than any other. This is when children learn most about the world around them and the language they need to survive and grow. Child's Play aims to create exactly the right material for this all-important time." **Publishes 40 titles/year.** Publishes book 2 years after acceptance. Accepts simultaneous submissions.

○ "Due to a backlog of submissions, Child's Play is currently no longer able to accept anymore manuscripts."

NONFICTION Picture books: activity books, animal, concept, multicultural, music/dance, nature/environment, science. Young readers: activity books, animal, concept, multicultural, music/dance, nature/environment, science. Average word length: picture books—2,000; young readers—3,000.

FICTION Picture books: adventure, animal, concept, contemporary, folktales, multicultural, nature/environment. Young readers: adventure, animal, anthology, concept, contemporary, folktales, humor, multicultural, nature/environment, poetry. Average word length: picture books—1,500; young readers—2,000.

TIPS "Look at our website to see the kind of work we do before sending. Do not send cartoons. We do not publish novels. We do publish lots of books with pictures of babies/toddlers."

CHRISTIAN FOCUS PUBLICATIONS

Geanies House, Fearn, Tain Ross-shire Scotland IV20 1TW, United Kingdom. (44)1862-871-011. **Fax:** (44)1862-871-699. **E-mail:** submissions@christian-focus.com. **Website:** www.christianfocus.com. **Contact:** Director of Publishing. Estab. 1975. Specializes in Christian material, nonfiction, fiction, educational material. **Publishes 22-32 titles/year. 2% of books from first-time authors.** Publishes book 1 year after acceptance. Accepts simultaneous submissions. Responds to queries in 2 weeks; mss in 3-6 months.

NONFICTION All levels: activity books, biography, history, religion, science. Average word length: picture books—5,000; young readers—5,000; middle readers—5,000-10,000; young adult/teens—10,000-20,000. Query or submit outline/synopsis and 3 sample chapters. Include Author Information Form from site with submission. Will consider electronic submissions and previously published work.

FICTION Picture books, young readers, adventure, history, religion. Middle readers: adventure, problem novels, religion. Young adult/teens: adventure, history, problem novels, religion. Average word length: young readers—5,000; middle readers—max 10,000; young adult/teen—max 20,000.

TIPS "Be aware of the international market as regards writing style/topics as well as illustration styles. Our company sells rights to European as well as Asian countries. Fiction sales are not as good as they were. Christian fiction for youngsters is not a product that is performing well in comparison to nonfiction such as Christian biography/Bible stories/church history, etc."

CHRONICLE BOOKS

680 Second St., San Francisco CA 94107. **E-mail:** submissions@chroniclebooks.com. **Website:** www.chroniclebooks.com. "We publish an exciting range of books, stationery, kits, calendars, and novelty formats. Our list includes children's books and interactive formats; young adult books; cookbooks; fine art, design, and photography; pop culture; craft, fashion, beauty, and home decor; relationships, mind-body-spirit; innovative formats such as interactive journals,

kits, decks, and stationery; and much, much more." **Publishes 90 titles/year. Generally pays authors in royalties based on retail price, "though we do occasionally work on a flat fee basis." Advance varies. Illustrators paid royalty based on retail price or flat fee.** Publishes a book 1-3 years after acceptance. Accepts simultaneous submissions. Responds to queries in 1 month. Book catalog for 9x12 SAE and 8 first-class stamps. Ms guidelines for #10 SASE.

NONFICTION Subjects include art, beauty, cooking, crafts, house and home, New Age, pop culture. "We're always looking for the new and unusual. We do accept unsolicited manuscripts and we review all proposals. However, given the volume of proposals we receive, we are not able to personally respond to unsolicited proposals unless we are interested in pursuing the project." Submit via mail or e-mail (prefers e-mail for adult submissions; only by mail for children's submissions). Submit proposal (guidelines online) and allow 3 months for editors to review and for children's submissions, allow 6 months. If submitting by mail, do not include SASE since our staff will not return materials.

FICTION Only interested in fiction for children and young adults. No adult fiction. Submit complete ms (picture books); submit outline/synopsis and 3 sample chapters (for older readers). Will not respond to submissions unless interested. Will not consider submissions by fax, e-mail or disk. Do not include SASE; do not send original materials. No submissions will be returned.

POETRY Submit via mail only. Children's submissions only. Submit proposal (guidelines online) and allow up to 3 months for editors to review. If submitting by mail, do not include SASE since our staff will not return materials.

CHRONICLE BOOKS FOR CHILDREN

680 Second St., San Francisco CA 94107. (415)537-4200. **Fax:** (415)537-4460. **Website:** www.chronicle-kids.com. Publishes hardcover and trade paperback originals. "Chronicle Books for Children publishes an eclectic mixture of traditional and innovative children's books. Our aim is to publish books that inspire young readers to learn and grow creatively while helping them discover the joy of reading. We're looking for quirky, bold artwork and subject matter." **Publishes 100-110 titles/year. 30,000 queries received/year. 6% of books from first-time authors. 25% from un-**

agented writers. **Pays variable advance.** Publishes a book 18-24 months after acceptance. Accepts simultaneous submissions. Responds in 2-4 weeks to queries; 6 months to mss. Book catalog for 9x12 envelope and 3 first-class stamps. Guidelines online.

NONFICTION Subjects include animals, multicultural, science. Query with synopsis. Reviews artwork/photos.

FICTION Subjects include multicultural, young adult, picture books. Does not accept proposals by fax, via e-mail, or on disk. When submitting artwork, either as a part of a project or as samples for review, do not send original art.

TIPS "We are interested in projects that have a unique bent to them—be it in subject matter, writing style, or illustrative technique. As a small list, we are looking for books that will lend our list a distinctive flavor. Primarily we are interested in fiction and nonfiction picture books for children ages up to 8 years, and nonfiction books for children ages up to 12 years. We publish board, pop-up, and other novelty formats as well as picture books. We are also interested in early chapter books, middle grade fiction, and young adult projects."

CHURCH PUBLISHING INC.

19 E. 34th St., New York NY 10016. (800)223-6602. **Fax:** (212)779-3392. **E-mail:** nabryan@cpg.org. **Website:** www.churchpublishing.org. **Contact:** Nancy Bryan, VP editorial. Estab. 1884. "With a religious publishing heritage dating back to 1918 and headquartered today in New York City, CPI is an official publisher of worship materials and resources for The Episcopal Church, plus a multi-faceted publisher and supplier to the broader ecumenical marketplace. In the nearly 100 years since its first publication, Church Publishing has emerged as a principal provider of liturgical and musical resources for The Episcopal Church, along with works on church leadership, pastoral care and Christian formation. With its growing portfolio of professional books and resources, Church Publishing was recognized in 1997 as the official publisher for the General Convention of the Episcopal Church in the United States. Simultaneously through the years, Church Publishing has consciously broadened its program, reach, and service to the church by publishing books for and about the worldwide Anglican Communion." Accepts simultaneous submissions.

IMPRINTS Church Publishing, Morehouse Publishing, Seabury Books.

TIPS "Prefer using freelancers who are located in central Pennsylvania and are available for meetings when necessary."

CITY LIGHTS BOOKS

261 Columbus Ave., San Francisco CA 94133. (415)362-8193. **Fax:** (415)362-4921. **Website:** www.citylights.com. Estab. 1953. Accepts simultaneous submissions.

CLARION BOOKS

Houghton Mifflin Co., 215 Park Ave. S., New York NY 10003. **Website:** www.hmhco.com. Estab. 1965. Publishes hardcover originals for children. "Clarion Books publishes picture books, nonfiction, and fiction for infants through grade 12. Avoid telling your stories in verse unless you are a professional poet. *We are no longer responding to your unsolicited submission unless we are interested in publishing it. Please do not include a SASE. Submissions will be recycled, and you will not hear from us regarding the status of your submission unless we are interested. We regret that we cannot respond personally to each submission, but we do consider each and every submission we receive.*" **Publishes 50 titles/year. Pays 5-10% royalty on retail price. Pays minimum of $4,000 advance.** Publishes a book 2 years after acceptance. Accepts simultaneous submissions. Responds in 2 months to queries. Guidelines online.

NONFICTION Subjects include Americana, history, photography, holiday. No unsolicited mss. Query with SASE. Submit proposal package, sample chapters, SASE. Reviews artwork/photos. Send photocopies.

FICTION Subjects include adventure, historical, humor, mystery, suspense, strong character studies, contemporary. "Clarion is highly selective in the areas of historical fiction, fantasy, and science fiction. A novel must be superlatively written in order to find a place on the list. Mss that arrive without an SASE of adequate size will *not* be responded to or returned. Accepts fiction translations." Submit complete ms. No queries, please. Send to only *one* Clarion editor.

TIPS "Looks for freshness, enthusiasm—in short, life."

CLARITY PRESS, INC.

2625 Piedmont Rd. NE, Suite 56, Atlanta GA 30324. (404)647-6501. **Fax:** (877)613-7868. **E-mail:** claritypress@usa.net. **Website:** www.claritypress.com. **Contact:** Diana G. Collier, editorial director (contemporary social justice issues). Estab. 1984. Publishes hardcover and trade paperback originals and e-books. **Publishes 8 titles/year. 20% of books from first-time authors. 100% from unagented writers.** Accepts simultaneous submissions. Responds to queries only if interested. Guidelines available.

IMPRINTS Clear Day Books.

NONFICTION Subjects include contemporary culture, economics, environment, ethnic, government, history, labor, law, military, multicultural, politics, public affairs, world affairs, human rights/socioeconomic and minority issues, globalization, social justice. Publishes books on contemporary global issues in U.S., Middle East and Africa, on US public and foreign policy. No fiction. Query by e-mail only with synopsis, TOC, résumé, publishing history.

TIPS "Check our titles on the website."

Ⓐ CLARKSON POTTER

Penguin Random House, 1745 Broadway, New York NY 10019. (212)782-9000. **Website:** www.clarksonpotter.com. Estab. 1959. Publishes hardcover and trade paperback originals. Accepts agented submissions only. Clarkson Potter specializes in publishing cooking books, decorating and other around-the-house how-to subjects.

NONFICTION Subjects include child guidance, memoirs, photography, psychology, translation. Agented submissions only.

CLEIS PRESS

101 Hudson St., 37th Floor, Suite 3705, Jersey City NJ 07302. **Fax:** (510)845-8001. **Website:** www.cleispress.com. Estab. 1980. Publishes books that inform, enlighten, and entertain. Areas of interest include gift, inspiration, health, family and childcare, self-help, women's issues, reference, cooking. "We do our best to bring readers quality books that celebrate life, inspire the mind, revive the spirit, and enhance lives all around. Our authors are practical visionaries; people who offer deep wisdom in a hopeful and helpful manner.". Cleis Press publishes provocative, intelligent books in the areas of sexuality, gay and lesbian studies, erotica, fiction, gender studies, and human rights. **Publishes 45 titles/year. 10% of books from first-time authors. 40% from unagented writers.** Publishes ms 2 years after acceptance. Accepts simultaneous submissions. Responds in 2 month to queries.

NONFICTION Subjects include sexual politics. "Cleis Press is interested in books on topics of sexual-

ity, human rights and women's and gay and lesbian literature. Please consult our website first to be certain that your book fits our list." Query or submit outline and sample chapters.

FICTION Subjects include feminist, literary. "We are looking for high quality fiction and nonfiction." Submit complete ms. Include brief bio, list of publishing credits. Send SASE for return of ms or send a disposable ms and SASE for reply only.

TIPS "Be familiar with publishers' catalogs; be absolutely aware of your audience; research potential markets; present fresh new ways of looking at your topic; avoid 'PR' language and include publishing history in query letter."

CLEVELAND STATE UNIVERSITY POETRY CENTER

2121 Euclid Ave., RT 1841, Cleveland OH 44115. (216)687-3986. **Fax:** (216)687-6943. **E-mail:** poetrycenter@csuohio.edu. **Website:** www.csupoetrycenter.com. **Contact:** Dan Dorman, managing editor. Estab. 1962. The Cleveland State University Poetry Center was established in 1962 at the former Fenn College of Engineering to promote poetry through readings and community outreach. In 1971, it expanded its mission to become a national non-profit independent press under the auspices of the Cleveland State University Department of English, and has since published nearly 200 rangy, joyful, profound, astonishing, complicated, surprising, and aesthetically diverse collections of contemporary poetry and prose by established and emerging authors. The Cleveland State University Poetry Center publishes between three and five collections of contemporary poetry and prose a year, with a national distribution and reach. The Poetry Center currently acquires manuscripts through three annual contests (one dedicated to publishing and promoting first books of poetry, one to supporting an established poet's career, and one to publishing collections of literary essays). **Publishes 3-5 titles/year. 500-1,200 submissions received/year. 50% of books from first-time authors. 100% from unagented writers. Pays $1,000 for competition winners.** Publishes ms 1-2 years after acceptance. Accepts simultaneous submissions. Responds in less than a year. Catalog online. Guidelines online.

POETRY Most mss are accepted through the competitions. All mss sent for competitions are considered for publication. Outside of competitions, mss are accepted by solicitation only.

COACHES CHOICE

P.O. Box 1828, Monterey CA 93942. (888)229-5745. **E-mail:** info@coacheschoice.com. **Website:** www.coacheschoice.com. Publishes trade paperback originals and reprints. "We publish books for anyone who coaches a sport or has an interest in coaching a sport—all levels of competition." Detailed descriptions, step-by-step instructions, and easy-to-follow diagrams set our books apart. Accepts simultaneous submissions. Book catalog available free.

NONFICTION Subjects include sports, sports specific training. Submit proposal package, outline, resume, 2 sample chapters. Reviews artwork/photos. Send photocopies and diagrams.

○ COACH HOUSE BOOKS

80 bpNichol Ln., Toronto ON M5S 3J4, Canada. (416)979-2217. **Fax:** (416)977-1158. **E-mail:** mail@chbooks.com. **E-mail:** editor@chbooks.com. **Website:** www.chbooks.com. **Contact:** Alana Wilcox, editorial director. Publishes trade paperback originals by Canadian authors. Independent Canadian publisher of innovative poetry, literary fiction, nonfiction and drama. **Publishes 18 titles/year. 80% of books from first-time authors. Pays 10% royalty on retail price.** Publishes ms 1 year after acceptance. Responds in 6-8 months to queries. Guidelines online.

NONFICTION Query.

FICTION Subjects include experimental, literary, poetry. We much prefer to receive electronic submissions. Please put your cover letter and CV into one Word or PDF file along with the manuscript and email it to editor@chbooks.com. We'd appreciate it if you would name your file following this convention: Last Name, First Name - MS Title. For fiction and poetry submissions, please send your complete manuscript, along with an introductory letter that describes your work and compares it to at least two current Coach House titles, explaining how your book would fit our list, and a literary CV listing your previous publications and relevant experience.

POETRY We much prefer to receive electronic submissions. Please put your cover letter and CV into one Word or PDF file along with the manuscript and email it to editor@chbooks.com. We'd appreciate it if you would name your file following this convention: Last Name, First Name - MS Title. For fiction and poetry submissions, please send your complete manuscript, along with an introductory letter that describes your work and compares it to at least two current Coach House titles, explaining how your book would fit our list, and a literary CV listing your previous publications and relevant experience.

TIPS "We are not a general publisher, and publish only Canadian poetry, fiction, select nonfiction and drama. We are interested primarily in innovative or experimental writing."

COFFEE HOUSE PRESS

79 13th Ave. NE, Suite 110, Minneapolis MN 55413. (612)338-0125. **Fax:** (612)338-4004. **Website:** www.coffeehousepress.org. Estab. 1984. Publishes hardcover and trade paperback originals. This successful nonprofit small press has received numerous grants from various organizations including the NEA, the McKnight Foundation and Target. Books published by Coffee House Press have won numerous honors and awards. Example: *The Book of Medicines*, by Linda Hogan won the Colorado Book Award for Poetry and the Lannan Foundation Literary Fellowship. **Publishes 16-18 titles/year.** Accepts simultaneous submissions. Responds in 4-6 weeks to queries; up to 6 months to mss. Book catalog and ms guidelines online.

NONFICTION Subjects include creative nonfiction, memoirs, book-length essays, collections of essays. Query with outline and sample pages during annual reading periods (March 1-31 and September 1-30).

FICTION Seeks literary novels, short story collections and poetry. Query first with outline and samples (20-30 pages) during annual reading periods (March 1-31 and September 1-30).

POETRY Coffee House Press will not accept unsolicited poetry submissions. Please check our web page periodically for future updates to this policy.

TIPS "Look for our books at stores and libraries to get a feel for what we like to publish. No phone calls, e-mails, or faxes."

THE COLLEGE BOARD

College Entrance Examination Board, 250 Vesey St., New York NY 10281. (212)713-8000. **Website:** www.collegeboard.com. Publishes trade paperback originals. The College Board publishes guidance information for college-bound students. **Publishes 2 titles/year. 25% of books from first-time authors. 50% from unagented writers. Pays royalty on retail price. Pays advance.** Publishes ms 9 months after acceptance. Accepts simultaneous submissions. Responds in 2 months to queries. Book catalog available free.

NONFICTION Subjects include education, college guidance. "We want books to help students make a successful transition from high school to college." Query with SASE. Submit outline, sample chapters, SASE.

COLLEGE PRESS PUBLISHING CO.

P.O. Box 1132, 2111 N. Main St., Suite C, Joplin MO 64801. (800)289-3300. **Fax:** (417)623-1929. **E-mail:** collpressbooks@gmail.com. **Website:** www.college-press.com. **Contact:** Acquisitions Editor. Estab. 1959. Publishes hardcover and trade paperback originals and reprints. College Press is a traditional Christian publishing house. Seeks proposals for Bible studies, topical studies (biblically based), apologetic studies. Accepts simultaneous submissions. Responds in 3 months to proposals; 2 months to mss. Guidelines online.

NONFICTION Seeks Bible studies, topical studies, apologetic studies. No poetry, games/puzzles, books on prophecy from a premillennial or dispensational viewpoint, or any book without a Christian message. Query with SASE.

TIPS "Our core market is Christian Churches/Churches of Christ and conservative evangelical Christians. Have your material critically reviewed prior to sending it. Make sure that it is non-Calvinistic and that it leans more amillennial (if it is apocalyptic writing)."

🌑 COLOURPOINT BOOKS

Jubilee Business Park, 21 Jubilee Rd., Newtownards, Northern Ireland BT23 4YH, United Kingdom. (44)(289)182-0505. **Fax:** (44)(289)182-1900. **E-mail:** info@colourpoint.co.uk. **Website:** www.colourpoint.co.uk. Estab. 1993. **Publishes 25 titles/year. Pays royalty.** Accepts simultaneous submissions. Responds in 2-3 months. Guidelines online.

NONFICTION Subjects include education. "Our specialisms are educational textbooks and transport subjects—mainly trains and buses. When e-mailing queries, please put 'submission query' in the subject line." Does not want fiction, poetry or plays. Query with SASE. Submit outline, outline/proposal, resume, publishing history, bio, 2 sample pages, SASE.

TIPS "Before approaching any publisher with a proposal, be sure that you are sending it to the right company. Publishing houses have their own personalities and specialisms and much time can be saved—including yours—by not submitting to a totally unsuitable publisher."

CONARI PRESS

Red Wheel/Weiser, LLC., 665 Third Street Suite 400, San Fransisco CA 94107. **E-mail:** submissions@rwwbooks.com: info@rwwbooks.com. **Website:** www.redwheelweiser.com. Estab. 1987. "Conari Press, an imprint of Red Wheel/Weiser, publishes books on topics ranging from spirituality, personal growth, and relationships to women's issues, parenting, and social issues. Our mission is to publish quality books that will make a difference in people's lives—how we feel about ourselves and how we relate to one another. We value integrity, compassion, and receptivity, both in the books we publish and in the way we do business." Accepts simultaneous submissions.

NONFICTION Subjects include foods, health, parenting, spirituality, womens issues, womens studies. "Inspire, literally to breathe life into. That's what Conari Press books aim to do—inspire all walks of life, mind, body, and spirit; inspire creativity, laughter, gratitude, good food, good health, and all good things in life." Guidelines online.

TIPS "Review our website to make sure your work is appropriate."

CONCORDIA PUBLISHING HOUSE

3558 S. Jefferson Ave., St. Louis MO 63118. (314)268-1187. **Fax:** (314)268-1329. **E-mail:** editorial.concordia@cph.org. **Website:** www.cph.org. Estab. 1869. Publishes hardcover and trade paperback originals. Concordia Publishing House is the publishing arm of The Lutheran Church—Missouri Synod. "We develop, produce, and distribute (1) resources that support pastoral and congregational ministry, and (2) scholary and professional books in exegetical, historical, dogmatic, and practical theology." Accepts simultaneous submissions.

🅐🌑⊘ CONSTABLE & ROBINSON, LTD.

50 Victoria Embankment, London EC4Y 0DZ, United Kingdom. **E-mail:** info@littlebrown.co.uk. **Website:** https://www.littlebrown.co.uk/ConstableRobinson/about-constable-publisher.page. Publishes hardcover and trade paperback originals. **Publishes 60 titles/year. 3,000 queries/year; 1,000 mss/year. Pays royalty. Pays advance.** Publishes book 1 year after acceptance. Accepts simultaneous submissions. Responds in 1-3 months. Book catalog available free.

NONFICTION Subjects include health, history, medicine, military, photography, politics, psychology, science, travel, war. Query with SASE. Submit synopsis. Reviews artwork/photos. Send photocopies. **FICTION** Subjects include historical, mystery. Publishes "crime fiction (mysteries) and historical crime fiction." Length 80,000 words minimum; 130,000 words maximum. *Agented submissions only.*

COPPER CANYON PRESS

P.O. Box 271, Port Townsend WA 98368. (360)385-4925. **Fax:** (360)385-4985. **E-mail:** poetry@copper-canyonpress.org. **Website:** www.coppercanyonpress.org. **Contact:** Joseph Bednarik and George Knotek, co-publishers. Managing Editor: Tonaya Craft. Estab. 1972. Copper Canyon Press is a nonprofit publisher that believes poetry is vital to language and living. Since 1972, the press has published poetry exclusively and has established an international reputation for its commitment to authors, editorial acumen, and dedication to the poetry audience. Accepts simultaneous submissions. Catalog online. Guidelines online.

POETRY Has open submission periods throughout the year; see website for details. Charges $35 fee for each submission, which entitles poets to select 2 Copper Canyon Press titles from a list. Submit complete ms via Submittable.

TIPS "Please familiarize yourself with our mission, catalog, and submissions FAQ before submitting a manuscript."

CORNELL UNIVERSITY PRESS

Sage House, 512 E. State St., Ithaca NY 14850. (607)277-2338. **Fax:** (607)277-2374. **Website:** www.cornellpress.cornell.edu. **Contact:** Mahinder Kingra, editor-in-chief; Roger Haydon, executive editor; Emily Andrew, senior editor; James Lance, senior editor; Michael J. McGandy, senior editor. Estab. 1869. Publishes hardcover and paperback originals. "Cornell Press is an academic publisher of nonfiction with particular strengths in anthropology, Asian studies, biological sciences, classics, history, labor and business, literary criticism, politics and international relations, women's studies, Slavic studies, philosophy, urban studies, health care work, regional titles, and security studies. Currently emphasizing sound scholarship that appeals beyond the academic community." **Publishes 150 titles/year. Pays royalty. Pays $0-5,000 advance.** Publishes ms 1 year after acceptance.

Accepts simultaneous submissions. Book catalog and guidelines online.

NONFICTION Subjects include agriculture, ethnic, history, philosophy, regional, sociology, translation, classics, life sciences. Submit résumé, cover letter, and prospectus.

CORWIN PRESS, INC.

2455 Teller Rd., Thousand Oaks CA 91320. (800)818-7243. **Fax:** (805)499-2692. **E-mail:** ariel.bartlett@corwin.com; erin.null@corwin.com; jessica.allan@corwin.com. **Website:** www.corwinpress.com. **Contact:** Ariel Bartlett, acquisitions editor; Erin Null, acquisitions editor; Jessica Allan, senior acquisitions editor. Estab. 1990. Publishes paperback originals. **Publishes 150 titles/year.** Publishes ms 7 months after acceptance. Accepts simultaneous submissions. Responds in 1-2 months to queries. Guidelines online.

🔾 "Corwin Press, Inc., publishes leading-edge, user-friendly publications for education professionals."

NONFICTION Subjects include education. Seeking fresh insights, conclusions, and recommendations for action. Prefers theory or research-based books that provide real-world examples and practical, hands-on strategies to help busy educators be successful. Professional-level publications for administrators, teachers, school specialists, policymakers, researchers and others involved with Pre K-12 education. No textbooks that simply summarize existing knowledge or mass-market books. Query with SASE.

☯ COTEAU BOOKS

Thunder Creek Publishing Co-operative Ltd., 2517 Victoria Ave., Regina SK S4P 0T2, Canada. (306)777-0170. **Fax:** (306)522-5152. **E-mail:** coteau@coteaubooks.com. **Website:** www.coteaubooks.com. **Contact:** Geoffrey Ursell, publisher. Estab. 1975. Publishes trade paperback originals and reprints. "Our mission is to publish the finest in Canadian fiction, nonfiction, poetry, drama, and children's literature, with an emphasis on Saskatchewan and prairie writers. De-emphasizing science fiction, picture books." Publishes chapter books for young readers aged 9-12 and novels for older kids ages 13-15 and for ages 15 and up. **Publishes 12 titles/year. 200 queries; 40 mss received/year. 25% of books from first-time authors. 90% from unagented writers. Pays 10% royalty on retail price.** Publishes book 1 year after acceptance.

Responds in 3 months. Book catalog available free. Guidelines online.

NONFICTION Subjects include creative nonfiction, ethnic, history, memoirs, regional, sports, travel. *Canadian authors only*. Submit hard copy query, bio, 3-4 sample chapters, SASE.

FICTION Subjects include ethnic, fantasy, feminist, historical, humor, juvenile, literary, multicultural, multimedia, mystery, plays, poetry, regional, short story collections, spiritual, sports, novels/short fiction, adult/middle years. No science fiction. No children's picture books. Query.

POETRY Submit 20-25 sample poems.

TIPS "Look at past publications to get an idea of our editorial program. We do not publish romance, horror, or picture books but are interested in juvenile and teen fiction from Canadian authors. Submissions, even queries, must be made in hard copy only. We do not accept simultaneous/multiple submissions. Check our website for new submission timing guidelines."

COVENANT COMMUNICATIONS, INC.

Deseret Book Company, P.O. Box 416, American Fork UT 84003. (801)756-1041. **Fax:** (801)756-1049. **E-mail:** submissionsdesk@covenant-lds.com. **Website:** www.covenant-lds.com. **Contact:** Kathryn Gordon, managing editor. Estab. 1958. "Currently emphasizing inspirational, doctrinal, historical, biography, and fiction." **Publishes 80-100 titles/year. Receives 1,200 mss/year. 30% of books from first-time authors. 99% from unagented writers. Pays 6-15% royalty on retail price.** Publishes book 6-12 months after acceptance. Responds in 1 month on queries; 4-6 months on mss. Guidelines online.

NONFICTION Subjects include history, religion, spirituality. "We target an audience of members of The Church of Jesus Christ of Latter-day Saints, LDS, or Mormon. All mss must be acceptable to that audience." We do not accept anything dealing with the occult or alternative lifestyles. Submit complete ms. Reviews artwork. Send photocopies.

FICTION Subjects include adventure, historical, mystery, regional, religious, romance, spiritual, suspense. "Manuscripts do not necessarily have to include LDS/Mormon characters or themes, but cannot contain profanity, sexual content, gratuitous violence, witchcraft, vampires, and other such material." We do not accept nor publish young adult, middle grade, science fiction, fantasy, occult, steampunk, or gay/lesbian/bisexual/transgender themes. Submit complete ms.

TIPS "We are actively looking for new, fresh Regency romance authors."

CQ PRESS

2455 Teller Rd., Thousand Oaks CA 91320. (805)410-7582. **Website:** www.cqpress.com. Estab. 1945. Publishes hardcover and online paperback titles. CQ Press seeks to educate the public by publishing authoritative works on American and international politics, policy, and people. Accepts simultaneous submissions. Book catalog available free.

NONFICTION Subjects include history. "We are interested in American government, public administration, comparative government, and international relations." Submit proposal package, including prospectus, TOC, 1-2 sample chapters.

TIPS "Our books present important information on American government and politics, and related issues, with careful attention to accuracy, thoroughness, and readability."

⊘ CRABTREE PUBLISHING COMPANY

350 Fifth Ave., 59th Floor, New York NY 10118. (212)496-5040; (800)387-7650. **Fax:** (800)355-7166. **Website:** www.crabtreebooks.com. Estab. 1978. Crabtree Publishing Company is dedicated to producing high-quality books and educational products for K-8+. Each resource blends accuracy, immediacy, and eye-catching illustration with the goal of inspiring nothing less than a life-long interest in reading and learning in children. The company began building its reputation in 1978 as a quality children's nonfiction book publisher with acclaimed author Bobbie Kalman's first series about the early pioneers. The Early Settler Life Series became a mainstay in schools as well as historic sites and museums across North America. Accepts simultaneous submissions.

> "Crabtree does not accept unsolicited manuscripts. Crabtree Publishing has an editorial team in-house that creates curriculum-specific book series."

TIPS "Since our books are for younger readers, lively photos of children and animals are always excellent." Portfolio should be diverse and encompass several subjects rather than just 1 or 2; depth of coverage of subject should be intense so that any publishing company could, conceivably, use all or many of a photographer's photos in a book on a particular subject."

CRAFTSMAN BOOK CO.

6058 Corte Del Cedro, Carlsbad CA 92011. (760)438-7828 or (800)829-8123. **Fax:** (760)438-0398. **E-mail:** jacobs@costbook.com. **Website:** www.craftsman-book.com. **Contact:** Laurence D. Jacobs, editorial manager. Estab. 1957. Publishes paperback originals. Publishes how-to manuals for professional builders. Currently emphasizing construction software for cost estimating, insurance replacement costs, contract and lien writing software and construction forms. **Publishes 10 titles/year. 4 85% of books from first-time authors. 98% from unagented writers. Pays 7-12% royalty on wholesale price and 12-1/2% on retail price. Does not pay advance.** Publishes ms 2 years after acceptance. Accepts simultaneous submissions. Responds in 2 months to queries. Book catalog and ms guidelines free.

NONFICTION Subjects include business, software. All titles are related to construction for professional builders. Reviews artwork/photos.

TIPS "The book submission should be loaded with step-by-step instructions, illustrations, charts, reference data, forms, samples, cost estimates, rules of thumb, and examples that solve actual problems in the builder's office and in the field. It must cover the subject completely, become the owner's primary reference on the subject, have a high utility-to-cost ratio, and help the owner make a better living in his chosen field."

CRAIGMORE CREATIONS

PMB 114, 4110 SE Hawthorne Blvd., Portland OR 97124. (503)477-9562. **E-mail:** info@craigmorecreations.com. **Website:** www.craigmorecreations.com. Estab. 2009. Accepts simultaneous submissions.

NONFICTION Subjects include animals, anthropology, archeology, creative nonfiction, environment, multicultural, nature, regional, science, young adult, Earth sciences, natural history. "We publish books that make time travel seem possible: nonfiction that explores pre-history and Earth sciences for children." Submit proposal package. See website for detailed submission guidelines. Send photocopies.

FICTION Subjects include juvenile, picture books, young adult. Submit proposal package. See website for detailed submission guidelines.

CREATIVE COMPANY

P.O. Box 227, Mankato MN 56002. (800)445-6209. **Fax:** (507)388-2746. **E-mail:** info@thecreativecom-pany.us. **Website:** www.thecreativecompany.us. Estab. 1932. "We are currently not accepting fiction submissions." **Publishes 140 titles/year.** Publishes a book 2 years after acceptance. Accepts simultaneous submissions. Responds in 3-6 months. Guidelines available for SAE.

IMPRINTS Creative Editions (picture books); Creative Education (nonfiction).

NONFICTION Picture books, young readers, young adults: animal, arts/crafts, biography, careers, geography, health, history, hobbies, multicultural, music/dance, nature/environment, religion, science, social issues, special needs, sports. Average word length: young readers—500; young adults—6,000. Submit outline/synopsis and 2 sample chapters, along with division of titles within the series.

TIPS "We are accepting nonfiction, series submissions only. Fiction submissions will not be reviewed or returned. Nonfiction submissions should be presented in series (4, 6, or 8) rather than single."

CRESCENT MOON PUBLISHING

P.O. Box 1312, Maidstone Kent ME14 5XU, United Kingdom. (44)(162)272-9593. **E-mail:** cresmopub@yahoo.co.uk. **Website:** www.crmoon.com. **Contact:** Jeremy Robinson, director (arts, media, cinema, literature); Cassidy Hughes (visual arts). Estab. 1988. Publishes hardcover and trade paperback originals. "Our mission is to publish the best in contemporary work, in poetry, fiction, and critical studies, and selections from the great writers. Currently emphasizing nonfiction (media, film, music, painting). De-emphasizing children's books." **Publishes 25 titles/year. 300 queries; 400 mss received/year. 1% of books from first-time authors. 1% from unagented writers. Pays royalty. Pays negotiable advance.** Publishes ms 18 months after acceptance. Accepts simultaneous submissions. Responds in 2 months to queries; 4 months to proposals and mss. Book catalog and ms guidelines free.

IMPRINTS Joe's Press; Pagan America Magazine; Passion Magazine.

NONFICTION Subjects include Americana, anthropology, cinema, contemporary culture, film, gardening, literary criticism, literature, philosophy, pop culture, religion, social sciences, spirituality, travel, womens issues, womens studies, cinema, the media, cultural studies. Query with SASE. Submit outline, 2 sample chapters, bio. Reviews artwork/photos. Send photocopies.

FICTION Subjects include erotica, experimental, feminist, literary, short story collections, translation. "We do not publish much fiction at present but will consider high quality new work." Query with SASE. Submit outline, clips, 2 sample chapters, bio.

POETRY "We prefer a small selection of the poet's very best work at first. We prefer free verse or non-rhyming poetry. Do not send too much material." Query and submit 6 sample poems.

TIPS "Our audience is interested in new contemporary writing."

CRESTON BOOKS

P.O. Box 9369, Berkeley CA 94709. **E-mail:** submissions@crestonbooks.co. **Website:** crestonbooks. co. Estab. 2013. Creston Books is author-illustrator driven, with talented, award-winning creators given more editorial freedom and control than in a typical New York house. **50% of books from first-time authors. 50% from unagented writers. Pays advance.** Accepts simultaneous submissions. Catalog online. Guidelines online.

FICTION Subjects include juvenile, multicultural, picture books, young adult. Please paste text of picture books or first chapters of novels in the body of e-mail. Words of Advice for submitting authors listed on the site.

CROSS-CULTURAL COMMUNICATIONS

Cross-Cultural Literary Editions, CROSS-CULTURAL COMMUNICATIONS, 239 Wynsum Ave., Merrick NY 11566-4725. (516)869-5635. **Fax:** (516)379-1901. **E-mail:** info@cross-culturalcommunications. com; cccpoetry@aol.com. **Website:** www.cross-culturalcommunications.com. **Contact:** Stanley H. Barkan; Bebe Barkan. Estab. 1971. Publishes hardcover and trade paperback originals. **Publishes 10 titles/ year. 200 queries; 50 mss received/year. 10-25% of books from first-time authors. 100% from unagented writers.** Publishes book 1 year after acceptance. Responds in 1 month to proposals; 2 months to mss. Book catalog (sample flyers) for #10 SASE.

NONFICTION Subjects include language, literature, memoirs, multicultural. "Query first; we basically do not want the focus on nonfiction." Query with SASE. Reviews artwork/photos. Send photocopies.

FICTION Subjects include historical, multicultural, poetry, poetry in translation, translation, bilingual poetry. Query with SASE.

POETRY For bilingual poetry submit 3-6 short poems in original language with English translation, a brief (3-5 lines) bio of the author and translator(s).

TIPS "Best chance: poetry from a translation."

THE CROSSROAD PUBLISHING COMPANY

83 Chestnut Ridge Rd., Chestnut Ridge NY 10977. **Fax:** (845)517-0181. **E-mail:** submissions@crossroadpublishing.com. **Website:** www.crossroadpublishing.com. Estab. 1980. Publishes hardcover and trade paperback originals and reprints. **Publishes 45 titles/year. 1,000 queries received/year. 200 mss received/year. 10% of books from first-time authors. 75% from unagented writers. Pays 6-14% royalty on wholesale price.** Publishes ms 14 months after acceptance. Accepts simultaneous submissions. Responds in 6 weeks to queries and proposals; 12 weeks to mss. Book catalog available free. Guidelines online.

IMPRINTS Crossroad (trade); Herder (classroom/academic).

NONFICTION Subjects include creative nonfiction, ethnic, religion, spirituality, leadership, Catholicism. "We want hopeful, well-written books on religion and spirituality." Query with SASE.

TIPS "Refer to our website and catalog for a sense of the range and kinds of books we offer. Follow our application guidelines as posted on our website."

CROSSWAY

A publishing ministry of Good News Publishing, 1300 Crescent St., Wheaton IL 60174. (630)682-4300. **Fax:** (630)682-4785. **E-mail:** info@crossway.org. **E-mail:** submissions@crossway.org. **Website:** www.crossway.org. **Contact:** Jill Carter, editorial administrator. Estab. 1938. "'Making a difference in people's lives for Christ' as its maxim, Crossway Books lists titles written from an evangelical Christian perspective." Member ECPA. Distributes titles through Christian bookstores and catalogs. Promotes titles through magazine ads, catalogs. *Does not accept unsolicited mss.* **Publishes 85 titles/year. Pays negotiable royalty.** Publishes ms 18 months after acceptance. Accepts simultaneous submissions.

NONFICTION "Send us an e-mail query and, if your idea fits within our acquisitions guidelines, we'll invite a proposal."

ⓐ CROWN BUSINESS

Penguin Random House, 1745 Broadway, New York NY 10019. (212)572-2275. **Website:** crownpublishing.com. Estab. 1995. Publishes hardcover and trade paperback originals. *Agented submissions only.* Accepts simultaneous submissions. Book catalog online.

ⓐⓞ CROWN PUBLISHING GROUP

Penguin Random House, 1745 Broadway, New York NY 10019. (212)782-9000. **Website:** crownpublishing.com. Estab. 1933. Publishes popular fiction and nonfiction hardcover originals. Accepts simultaneous submissions. *Agented submissions only.* See website for more details.

IMPRINTS Amphoto Books; Back Stage Books; Billboard Books; Broadway Books; Clarkson Potter; Crown; Crown Archetype; Crown Business; Crown Forum; Harmony Books; Image Books; Potter Craft; Potter Style; Ten Speed Press; Three Rivers Press; Waterbrook Multnomah; Watson-Guptill.

CRYSTAL SPIRIT PUBLISHING, INC.

P.O. Box 12506, Durham NC 27709. **E-mail:** crystalspiritinc@gmail.com. **E-mail:** submissions@crystalspiritinc.com. **Website:** www.crystalspiritinc.com. **Contact:** Vanessa S. O'Neal, Senior Managing Editor. Estab. 2004. Publishes hardcover, trade paperback, mass market paperback, and electronic originals. "Our readers are lovers of high-quality books that are sold as direct sales, in bookstores, gift shops and placed in libraries and schools. They support independent authors and they expect works that will provide them with entertainment, inspiration, romance, and education. Our audience loves to read and will embrace niche authors that love to write." **Publishes 3-5 titles/year. Receives 1,100 mss/year. 80% of books from first-time authors. 100% from unagented writers. Pays 20-45% royalty on retail price.** Publishes ms 3-6 months after acceptance. Accepts simultaneous submissions. Responds in 30-45 days. Book catalog and ms guidelines online. Guidelines for submissions are stated on the website.

NONFICTION Subjects include alternative lifestyles, business, career guidance, child guidance, community, contemporary culture, cooking, counseling, creative nonfiction, economics, entertainment, ethnic, fashion, film, finance, foods, gay, health, house and home, humanities, language, law, lesbian, literary criticism, literature, medicine, memoirs, money, multicultural, music, New Age, nutrition, parenting, philosophy, pop culture, public affairs, real estate, recreation, religion, sex, social sciences, sociology, spirituality, sports, travel, womens issues, womens studies, world affairs, young adult, inspirational, Christian romance. Full completed mss can be submitted via the website. Mss submitted by mail must include the cover letter and information as stated in the submission guidelines on the website.

FICTION Subjects include confession, contemporary, erotica, ethnic, feminist, gay, humor, juvenile, literary, mainstream, multicultural, religious, romance, short story collections, spiritual, young adult, inspirational, Christian romance. Full completed mss can be submitted via the website. Mss submitted by mail must include the cover letter and information as stated in the submission guidelines on the website.

TIPS "Submissions are accepted for publication throughout the year. Works should be positive and non-threatening. Typed pages only. Non-typed entries will not be reviewed or returned. Ensure that all contact information is correct, abide by the submission guidelines and do not send follow-up e-mails or calls."

CSLI PUBLICATIONS

Condura Hall, Stanford University, 210 Panama St., Stanford CA 94305. (650)723-1839. **Fax:** (650)725-2166. **E-mail:** pubs@csli.stanford.edu. **Website:** csli-publications.stanford.edu. Publishes hardcover and scholarly paperback originals. CSLI Publications, part of the Center for the Study of Language and Information, specializes in books in the study of language, information, logic, and computation. Book catalog available free. Guidelines online.

NONFICTION Subjects include science, logic, cognitive science. "We do not accept unsolicited mss."

CURIOSITY QUILLS

Whampa, LLC, P.O. Box 2160, Reston VA 20195. (800)998-2509. **Fax:** (800)998-2509. **E-mail:** editor@curiosityquills.com. **E-mail:** acquisitions@curiosityquills.com. **Website:** curiosityquills.com. **Contact:** Alisa Gus. Additional Contacts: Eugene Teplitsky, Nikki Tetreault. Estab. 2011. Firm publishes sci-fi, speculative fiction, steampunk, paranormal and urban fantasy, and corresponding romance titles under its new Rebel Romance imprint. Curiosity Quills is a publisher of hard-hitting dark sci-fi, speculative fiction, and paranormal works aimed at adults, young adults, and new adults. **Publishes 75 titles/year.**

1,000 submissions/year. 60% of books from first-time authors. 65% from unagented writers. Pays variable royalty. Does not pay advance. Publishes ms 9-12 months after acceptance. Accepts simultaneous submissions. Responds in 1-6 weeks. Catalog available. Guidelines online.

IMPRINTS Curiosity Quills Press, Rebel Romance.

NONFICTION Writer's guides, on a strictly limited basis.

FICTION Subjects include adventure, contemporary, erotica, fantasy, gay, gothic, hi-lo, historical, horror, humor, juvenile, lesbian, literary, mainstream, multicultural, multimedia, mystery, romance, science fiction, suspense, young adult, steampunk, dieselpunk, space opera. Looking for "thought-provoking, mind-twisting rollercoasters—challenge our mind, turn our world upside down, and make us question. Those are the makings of a true literary marauder." Submit ms using online submission form or e-mail to acquisitions@curiosityquills.com.

CURIOUS FOX

Brunel Rd., Houndmills, Basingstoke Hants RG21 6XS, United Kingdom. **E-mail:** submissions@curious-fox.com. **Website:** www.curious-fox.com. "Do you love telling good stories? If so, we'd like to hear from you. Curious Fox is on the lookout for UK-based authors, whether new talent or established authors with exciting ideas. We take submissions for books aimed at ages 3-young adult. If you have story ideas that are bold, fun, and imaginative, then please do get in touch!" Accepts simultaneous submissions. Guidelines online.

FICTION "Send your submission via e-mail to submissions@curious-fox.com. Include the following in the body of the email, not as attachments: Sample chapters, Résumé, List of previous publishing credits, if applicable. We will respond only if your writing samples fit our needs."

CYCLE PUBLICATIONS, INC.

Van der Plas Publications, 1282 Seventh Ave., San Francisco CA 94112. (415)665-8214. **Fax:** (415)753-8572. **Website:** www.cyclepublishing.com. Estab. 1985. "Van der Plas Publications/Cycle Publishing was started in 1997 with 4 books. Since then, we have introduced about 4 new books each year, and in addition to our 'mainstay' of cycling books, we now also have books on manufactured housing, golf, baseball, and strength training. Our offices are located in San Francisco, where we do editorial work, as well as administration, publicity, and design. Our books are warehoused in Kimball, Michigan, which is close to the companies that print most of our books and is conveniently located to supply our book trade distributors and the major book wholesalers." Accepts simultaneous submissions.

CYCLOTOUR GUIDE BOOKS

160 Harvard St., Rochester NY 14607-3174. **E-mail:** cyclotour@cyclotour.com. **Website:** www.cyclotour.com. Estab. 1994. Publishes trade paperback originals. **Publishes 1 titles/year. Receives 25 queries/year and 2 mss/year. 25% of books from first-time authors. 100% from unagented writers. Does not pay advance.** Publishes ms 2 years after acceptance. Accepts simultaneous submissions. Responds in 1 month. Book catalog and ms guidelines online.

NONFICTION Subjects include transportation, travel, bicycle tour guides. Query with SASE. Reviews artwork/photos as part of ms package. Send photocopies.

TIPS Bicyclists. Folks with a dream of bicycle touring. "Check your grammar and spelling. Write logically."

DA CAPO PRESS

Perseus Books Group, 44 Farnsworth St., 3rd Floor, Boston MA 02210. (617)252-5200. **Website:** www.dacapopress.com. Estab. 1975. Publishes hardcover originals and trade paperback originals and reprints. **Publishes 115 titles/year. 500 queries; 300 mss received/year. 25% of books from first-time authors. 1% from unagented writers. Pays 7-15% royalty. Pays $1,000-225,000 advance.** Publishes book 1 year after acceptance. Accepts simultaneous submissions. Book catalog and guidelines online.

NONFICTION Subjects include contemporary culture, creative nonfiction, history, memoirs, social sciences, sports, translation, travel, world affairs. No unsolicited mss or proposals. Agented submissions only.

DARBY CREEK PUBLISHING

Lerner Publishing Group, 1251 Washington Ave. N., Minneapolis MN 55401. (612)332-3344. **Fax:** (612)332-7615. **Website:** www.lernerbooks.com. "Darby Creek publishes series fiction titles for emerging, striving and reluctant readers ages 7 to 18 (grades 2-12). From beginning chapter books to intermediate fiction and page-turning YA titles, Darby Creek books engage readers with strong characters and formats they'll want to pursue." Darby Creek does not publish picture books. Publishes children's chapter books, middle readers, young adult. Mostly series. **Publishes 25 titles/year. Offers advance-against-royalty contracts.** Accepts simultaneous submissions.

◯   "We are currently not accepting any submissions. If that changes, we will provide all children's writing publications with our new info."

NONFICTION Middle readers: biography, history, science, sports. Recently published *Albino Animals*, by Kelly Milner Halls, illustrated by Rick Spears; *Miracle: The True Story of the Wreck of the Sea Venture*, by Gail Karwoski.

FICTION Middle readers, young adult. Recently published: *The Surviving Southside* series, by various authors; *The Agent Amelia* series, by Michael Broad; *The Mallory McDonald* series, by Laurie B. Friedman; and *The Alien Agent* series, by Pam Service.

DARK HORSE COMICS, INC.

10956 SE Main St., Milwaukie OR 97222. (503)652-8815. **Fax:** (503)654-9440. **E-mail:** dhcomics@darkhorse.com. **E-mail:** dhsubsproposals@darkhouse.com. **Website:** www.darkhorse.com. "In addition to publishing comics from top talent like Frank Miller, Mike Mignola, Stan Sakai and internationally-renowned humorist Sergio Aragonés, Dark Horse is recognized as the world's leading publisher of licensed comics." Accepts simultaneous submissions.

FICTION Subjects include comic books. Comic books, graphic novels. Published *Astro Boy Volume 10 TPB*, by Osamu Tezuka and Reid Fleming; *Flaming Carrot Crossover #1* by Bob Burden and David Boswell. Submit synopsis to dhcomics@darkhorse.com. See website (www.darkhorse.com) for detailed submission guidelines and submission agreement, which must be signed. Include a full script for any short story or single-issue submission, or the first eight pages of the first issue of any series. Submissions can no longer be mailed back to the sender.

TIPS "If you're looking for constructive criticism, show your work to industry professionals at conventions."

● DARTON, LONGMAN AND TODD

1 Spencer Ct., 140-142 Wandsworth High St., London SW18 4JJ, United Kingdom. (44)(208)875-0155. **Fax:** (44)(208)875-0133. **E-mail:** editorial@darton-longman-todd.co.uk. **Website:** www.dltbooks.com. **Contact:** Editorial Department. Estab. 1959. Darton, Longman and Todd is an internationally-respected publisher of brave, ground-breaking, independent books and e-books on matters of heart, mind, and soul that meet the needs and interests of ordinary people. **Publishes 30 titles/year. Pays royalty.** Accepts simultaneous submissions. Guidelines online.

NONFICTION Subjects include counseling, politics, religion, spirituality, womens issues, womens studies. Simultaenous submissions accepted, but inform publisher if submitting elsewhere. Does not want poetry, scholarly monographs or children's books. Query by e-mail only.

TIPS "Our books are read by people inside and outside the Christian churches, by believers, seekers and sceptics, and by thoughtful non-specialists as well as students and academics. The books are widely sold throughout the religious and the general trade."

DAW BOOKS, INC.

Penguin Random House, 375 Hudson St., New York NY 10014. (212)366-2096. **Fax:** (212)366-2090. **E-mail:** daw@penguinrandomhouse.com. **Website:** www.dawbooks.com. **Contact:** Peter Stampfel, submissions editor. Estab. 1971. Publishes hardcover and paperback originals and reprints. DAW Books publishes science fiction and fantasy. **Publishes 50-60 titles/year. Pays in royalties with an advance negotiable on a book-by-book basis.** Responds in 3 months. Guidelines online.

FICTION Subjects include fantasy, science fiction. "Currently seeking modern urban fantasy and paranormals. We like character-driven books with appealing protagonists, engaging plots, and well-constructed worlds. We accept both agented and unagented manuscripts." Submit entire ms, cover letter, SASE. "Do not submit your only copy of anything. The average length of the novels we publish varies but is almost never less than 80,000 words."

DAWN PUBLICATIONS

12402 Bitney Springs Rd., Nevada City CA 95959. (530)274-7775. **Fax:** (530)274-7778. **Website:** www.dawnpub.com. **Contact:** Carol Malnor, associate editor. Estab. 1979. Publishes hardcover and trade paperback originals. "Dawn Publications is dedicated to inspiring in children a sense of appreciation for all life on earth. Dawn looks for nature awareness and appreciation titles that promote a relationship with the natural world and specific habitats, usually through inspiring treatment and nonfiction." Dawn accepts mss submissions by e-mail; follow instructions posted on website. Submissions by mail OK. **Publishes 6 titles/year. 2,500 queries or mss received/year. 15% of books from first-time authors. 90% from unagented writers. Pays advance.** Publishes book 1-2 years after acceptance. Accepts simultaneous submissions. Automated confirmation of submission sent upon receipt. Followup in 2 months if interested. Book catalog and guidelines online.

NONFICTION Subjects include animals, creative nonfiction, marine subjects, nature.

TIPS "Publishes mostly creative nonfiction with lightness and inspiration." Looking for "picture books expressing nature awareness with inspirational quality leading to enhanced self-awareness." Does not publish anthropomorphic works; no animal dialogue.

KATHY DAWSON BOOKS

Penguin Random House, 375 Hudson St., New York NY 10014. (212)366-2000. **Website:** kathydawsonbooks.tumblr.com. **Contact:** Kathy Dawson, vice-president and publisher. Estab. 2014. Mission statement: Publish stellar novels with unforgettable characters for children and teens that expand their vision of the world, sneakily explore the meaning of life, celebrate the written word, and last for generations. The imprint strives to publish tomorrow's award contenders: quality books with strong hooks in a variety of genres with universal themes and compelling voices—books that break the mold and the heart. Responds only if interested. Guidelines online.

FICTION Accepts fiction queries via snail mail only. Include cover sheet with one-sentence elevator pitch, main themes, author version of catalog copy for book, first 10 pages of ms (double-spaced, Times Roman, 12 point type), and publishing history. No SASE needed. Responds only if interested.

🅐⊘ DELACORTE PRESS

an imprint of Random House Children's Books, a division of Penguin Random House LLC, New York, 1745 Broadway, New York NY 10019. (212)782-9000. **Website:** randomhousekids.com; randomhouseteens.com. Publishes middle grade and young adult fiction in hard cover, trade paperback, mass market and digest formats. Accepts simultaneous submissions.

○ All query letters and manuscript submissions must be submitted through an agent or at the request of an editor.

🅐⊘ DEL REY BOOKS

Penguin Random House, 1745 Broadway, 18th Floor, New York NY 10019. (212)782-9000. **Website:** www.penguinrandomhouse.com. Estab. 1977. Publishes hardcover, trade paperback, and mass market originals and mass market paperback reprints. Del Rey publishes top level fantasy, alternate history, and science fiction. **Pays royalty on retail price. Pays competitive advance.**

IMPRINTS Del Rey/Manga, Del Rey/Lucas Books.

FICTION Subjects include fantasy, science fiction, alternate history. *Agented submissions only.*

TIPS "Del Rey is a reader's house. Pay particular attention to plotting, strong characters, and dramatic, satisfactory conclusions. It must be/feel believable. That's what the readers like. In terms of mass market, we basically created the field of fantasy bestsellers. Not that it didn't exist before, but we put the mass into mass market."

DIAL BOOKS FOR YOUNG READERS

Imprint of Penguin Group (USA), 345 Hudson St., New York NY 10014. (212)366-2000. **Website:** www.penguin.com/children. Estab. 1961. Publishes hardcover originals. "Dial Books for Young Readers publishes quality picture books for ages 18 months-6 years; lively, believable novels for middle readers and young adults; and occasional nonfiction for middle readers and young adults." **Publishes 50 titles/year. 5,000 queries received/year. 20% of books from first-time authors. Pays royalty. Pays varies advance.** Responds in 4-6 months to queries. Book catalog and guidelines online.

NONFICTION Only responds if interested. "We accept entire picture book manuscripts and a maximum of 10 pages for longer works (novels, easy-to-reads). When submitting a portion of a longer work, please provide an accompanying cover letter that briefly describes your manuscript's plot, genre (i.e. easy-to-read, middle grade or YA novel), the intended age group, and your publishing credits, if any."

FICTION Subjects include adventure, fantasy, juvenile, picture books, young adult. Especially looking for lively and well-written novels for middle grade and young adult children involving a convincing plot and believable characters. The subject matter or theme should not already be overworked in previously published books. The approach must not be demeaning to any minority group, nor should the

247

roles of female characters (or others) be stereotyped, though we don't think books should be didactic, or in any way message-y. No topics inappropriate for the juvenile, young adult, and middle grade audiences. No plays. Accepts unsolicited queries and up to 10 pages for longer works and unsolicited mss for picture books. Will only respond if interested.

TIPS "Our readers are anywhere from preschool age to teenage. Picture books must have strong plots, lots of action, unusual premises, or universal themes treated with freshness and originality. Humor works well in these books. A very well-thought-out and intelligently presented book has the best chance of being taken on. Genre isn't as much of a factor as presentation."

ⒶⒹ DIAL PRESS

1745 Broadway, New York NY 10019. **Website:** www.randomhouse.com/bantamdell/. Estab. 1924. Accepts simultaneous submissions.

FICTION Subjects include literary. *Agented submissions only.*

DIGITAL MANGA PUBLISHING

1487 West 178th St., Suite 300, Gardenia CA 90248. **Website:** www.dmpbooks.com. "Submissions must be original and not infringe on copyrighted works by other creators. Please note that we are a manga publisher; we do not distribute Western style comics or literary novels. Completed works must contain a minimum of 90 pages of content. Submissions may be in black and white or full color. We accept submissions for all genres of manga which comply to US law and we only accept submissions from persons aged 18 and over. Please do not send your original copies as we cannot return them to you. If your work is published online elsewhere, please feel free to include a link for us to further view your portfolio." Accepts simultaneous submissions.

DIVERTIR

P.O. Box 232, North Salem NH 03073. **E-mail;** info@divertirpublishing.com. **E-mail:** query@divertirpublishing.com. **Website:** www.divertirpublishing.com. **Contact:** Kenneth Tupper, Publisher. Estab. 2009. Publishes trade paperback and electronic originals. Divertir Publishing is an independent publisher located in Salem, NH. "Our goal is to provide interesting and entertaining books to our readers, as well as to offer new and exciting voices in the writing community the opportunity to publish their work. We seek to combine an understanding of traditional publishing with a unique understanding of the modern market to best serve both our authors and readers." **Publishes 6-12 titles/year. 1,000 submissions received/year. 70% of books from first-time authors. 100% from unagented writers. Pays 10-15% royalty on wholesale price (for novels and nonfiction). Does not pay advance.** Publishes ms 9-12 months after acceptance. Accepts simultaneous submissions. Responds in 1-3 months on queries; 3-4 months on proposals and mss. Catalog online. Guidelines online.

NONFICTION Subjects include contemporary culture, government, history, hobbies, politics, public affairs, world affairs, young adult. "We are particularly interested in the following: political/social commentary, current events, history, and humor/satire. We currently do not publish memoirs." Reviews artwork/photos as part of the ms package. Submit electronically.

FICTION Subjects include adventure, contemporary, fantasy, gothic, horror, humor, mainstream, mystery, romance, science fiction, suspense, young adult. "We are particularly interested in the following: science fiction, fantasy, historical, alternate history, contemporary mythology, mystery and suspense, paranormal, and urban fantasy." Does not consider erotica or mss with excessive violence. Electronically submit proposal package, including synopsis and query letter with author's bio.

TIPS "Please see our Author Info page (online) for more information."

ⒶⒼⒹ DK PUBLISHING

Penguin Random House, 80 Strand, London WC2R 0RL, United Kingdom. **Website:** www.dk.com. "DK publishes photographically illustrated nonfiction for children of all ages." *DK Publishing does not accept unagented mss or proposals.* Accepts simultaneous submissions.

ⒶⒸ DOUBLEDAY CANADA

1 Toronto St., Suite 300, Toronto ON M5C 2V6, Canada. **Website:** www.randomhouse.ca. Accepts simultaneous submissions.

DOVER PUBLICATIONS, INC.

31 E. Second St., Mineola NY 11501. (516)294-7000. **Fax:** (516)873-1401. **Website:** www.doverpublications.com. Estab. 1941. Publishes trade paperback originals and reprints. **Publishes 660 titles/year. Makes out-**

right purchase. Accepts simultaneous submissions. Book catalog online.

NONFICTION Subjects include agriculture, Americana, animals, history, hobbies, philosophy, photography, religion, science, sports, translation, travel. Publishes mostly reprints. Accepts original paper doll collections, game books, coloring books (juvenile). Query with SASE. Reviews artwork/photos.

DOWN THE SHORE PUBLISHING

P.O. Box 100, West Creek NJ 08092. **Fax:** (609)812-5098. **E-mail:** info@down-the-shore.com. **Website:** www.down-the-shore.com. **Contact:** Acquisitions Editor. Publishes hardcover and trade paperback originals and reprints. "Bear in mind that our market is regional-New Jersey, the Jersey Shore, the mid-Atlantic, and seashore and coastal subjects." **Publishes 4-10 titles/year. Pays royalty on wholesale or retail price, or makes outright purchase.** Accepts simultaneous submissions. Responds in 3 months to queries. Book catalog online. Guidelines online.

NONFICTION Subjects include Americana, history, regional. Query with SASE. Submit proposal package, 1-2 sample chapters, synopsis. Reviews artwork/photos. Send photocopies.

FICTION Subjects include regional. Query with SASE. Submit proposal package, clips, 1-2 sample chapters.

POETRY "We do not publish poetry, unless it is to be included as part of an anthology."

TIPS "Carefully consider whether your proposal is a good fit for our established market."

○ DRAGON MOON PRESS

3521 43A Ave., Red Deer AB T4N 3E9, Canada. **Website:** www.dragonmoonpress.com. Estab. 1994. "Dragon Moon Press is dedicated to new and exciting voices in science fiction and fantasy." Publishes trade paperback and electronic originals. Books: 60 lb. offset paper; short run printing and offset printing. Average print order: 250-3,000. **Published several debut authors within the last year.** Plans 5 first novels this year. Averages 4-6 total titles, 4-5 fiction titles/year. Distributed through Baker & Taylor. Promoted locally through authors and online at leading retail bookstores like Amazon, Barnes & Noble, Chapters, etc. Accepts simultaneous submissions.

FICTION "At present, we are only accepting solicited manuscripts via referral from our authors and partners. All manuscripts already under review will still be considered by our readers, and we will notify you of our decision." For solicited submissions: Market: "We prefer manuscripts targeted to the adult market or the upper border of YA. No middle grade or children's literature, please. Fantasy, science fiction (soft/sociological). No horror or children's fiction, short stories or poetry."

TIPS "First, be patient. Read our guidelines. Not following our submission guidelines can be grounds for automatic rejection. Second, be patient, we are small and sometimes very slow as a result, especially during book launch season. Third, we view publishing as a family affair. Be ready to participate in the process and show some enthusiasm and understanding in what we do. Remember also, this is a business and not about egos, so keep yours on a leash! Show us a great story with well-developed characters and plot lines, show us that you are interested in participating in marketing and developing as an author, and show us your desire to create a great book and you may just find yourself published by Dragon Moon Press."

DREAM OF THINGS

P.O. Box 872, Downers Grove IL 60515. **Website:** dreamofthings.com. Estab. 2009. Publishes trade paperback originals and reprints, electronic originals and reprints. Publishes memoirs, essay collections, and creative nonfiction. **Publishes 3-4 titles/year. 90% of books from first-time authors. 90% from unagented writers. Pays 10% royalties on retail price. No advance.** Accept to publish time is 6 months. Accepts simultaneous submissions. Catalog online. Guidelines online.

NONFICTION Subjects include creative nonfiction, memoirs, essay collections. Submit via online form. For memoirs, submit 1 sample chapter. For essay collections, submit 2-3 essays. Does not review artwork.

DUFOUR EDITIONS

P.O. Box 7, 124 Byers Rd., Chester Springs PA 19425. (610)458-5005. **Fax:** (610)458-7103. **Website:** www.dufoureditions.com. Estab. 1948. Publishes hardcover originals, trade paperback originals and reprints. "We publish literary fiction by good writers which is well received and achieves modest sales. De-emphsazing poetry and nonfiction." **Publishes 3-4 titles/year. 200 queries; 15 mss received/year. 20-30% of books from first-time authors. 80% from unagented writers. Pays $100-500 advance.** Publishes ms 18 months after acceptance. Accepts simultaneous submissions. Responds in 3-6 months. Book catalog available free.

NONFICTION Subjects include history, translation. Query with SASE. Reviews artwork/photos. Send photocopies.

FICTION Subjects include literary, short story collections, translation. "We like books that are slightly offbeat, different and well-written." Query with SASE.

POETRY Query.

THE DUNDURN GROUP

3 Church St., Suite 500, Toronto ON M5E 1M2, Canada. **Website:** www.dundurn.com. Estab. 1972. Dundurn prefers work by Canadian authors. First-time authors are welcome. Publishes hardcover and trade paperback originals and reprints. Accepts simultaneous submissions.

FICTION Subjects include literary, mystery, young adult. Query with SASE or submit 3 sample chapter(s), synopsis. Accepts queries by mail. Include estimated word count. Responds in 3-4 months to queries. Accepts simultaneous submissions. No electronic submissions.

DUNDURN PRESS, LTD.

3 Church St., Suite 500, Toronto ON M5E 1M2, Canada. (416)214-5544. **E-mail:** info@dundurn.com. **E-mail:** submissions@dundurn.com. **Website:** www. dundurn.com. **Contact:** Acquisitions Editor. Estab. 1972. Publishes hardcover, trade paperback, and e-book originals and reprints. Dundurn publishes books by Canadian authors. **600 queries received/ year. 25% of books from first-time authors. 50% from unagented writers.** Publishes ms 1-2 year after acceptance. Accepts simultaneous submissions. Responds in 6 months to queries. Guidelines online.

NONFICTION Subjects include history, regional, art history, theater, serious and popular nonfiction. Submit cover letter, synopsis, CV, TOC, writing sample, e-mail contact. Do not submit original materials. Submissions will not be returned.

FICTION Subjects include literary, mystery, young adult. No romance, science fiction, or experimental."Important note: Dundurn is not currently accepting fiction submissions, including mysteries or YA, nor is it accepting children's non-fiction submissions."

DUNEDIN ACADEMIC PRESS LTD

Hudson House, 8 Albany St., Edinburgh EH1 3QB, United Kingdom. (44)(131)473-2397. **E-mail:** mail@ dunedinacademicpress.co.uk. **Website:** www.dunedinacademicpress.co.uk. **Contact:** Anthony Kinahan, director. Estab. 2001. Dunedin Academic Press Ltd is a lively small independent academic publishing house. **Publishes 15-20 titles/year. 10% of books from first-time authors. 100% from unagented writers. Pays royalty.** Book catalog and proposal guidelines online.

"Read and respond to the proposal guidelines on our website before submitting. Do not send mss unless requested to do so. Do not send hard copy proposals. Approach first by e-mail, outlining proposal and identifying the market."

NONFICTION Subjects include earth science, health and social care, child protection. Reviews artwork/photos.

TIPS "Dunedin's list contains authors and subjects from across the international the academic world. DAP's horizons are far broader than our immediate Scottish environment. One of the strengths of Dunedin is that we are able to offer our authors that individual support that comes from dealing with a small independent publisher committed to growth through careful treatment of its authors. Most of our publishing is commissioned from the academic authors who write in the narrow subject areas in which the company publishes"

THOMAS DUNNE BOOKS

Imprint of St. Martin's Press, 175 Fifth Ave., New York NY 10010. (212)674-5151. **E-mail:** thomasdunnebooks@stmartins.com. **Website:** www.thomasdunnebooks.com. Estab. 1986. Publishes hardcover and trade paperback originals, and reprints. "Thomas Dunne Books publishes popular trade fiction and nonfiction. With an output of approximately 175 titles each year, his group covers a range of genres including commercial and literary fiction, thrillers, biography, politics, sports, popular science, and more. The list is intentionally eclectic and includes a wide range of fiction and nonfiction, from first books to international bestsellers." Accepts simultaneous submissions. Book catalog and ms guidelines free.

NONFICTION Subjects include history, sports, political commentary. *Accepts agented submissions only.*

FICTION Subjects include mystery, suspense, thrillers, women's. *Accepts agented submissions only.*

DUQUESNE UNIVERSITY PRESS

600 Forbes Ave., Pittsburgh PA 15282. (412)396-6610. **Fax:** (412)396-5984. **E-mail:** dupress@duq.edu. **Website:** www.dupress.duq.edu. Estab. 1927. Publishes hardcover and trade paperback originals. "Duquesne publishes scholarly monographs in the fields of literary studies (medieval and Renaissance), continental philosophy, ethics, religious studies, philosophy of communication, and humanistic psychology. Interdisciplinary works are also of interest. Duquesne University Press does not publish fiction, poetry, children's books, technical or 'hard' science works, or unrevised theses or dissertations." **Publishes 8-12 titles/year. 400 queries; 65 mss received/year. 30% of books from first-time authors. 95% from unagented writers. Pays royalty on net price. Pays (some) advance.** Publishes ms 1 year after acceptance. Accepts simultaneous submissions. Responds in 1-3 months. Book catalog available. Guidelines online.

NONFICTION Subjects include communications, humanities, literary criticism, philosophy, psychology, religion, social sciences. "We look for quality of scholarship." For scholarly books, query or submit outline, 1 sample chapter, and SASE.

⊕⊘ 🖉 DUTTON ADULT TRADE

Penguin Random House, 375 Hudson St., New York NY 10014. (212)366-2000. **Website:** penguin.com. Estab. 1852. Publishes hardcover originals. "Dutton currently publishes 45 hardcovers a year, roughly half fiction and half nonfiction." **Pays royalty. Pays negotiable advance.** Book catalog online.

NONFICTION Agented submissions only. *No unsolicited mss.*

FICTION Subjects include adventure, historical, literary, mystery, short story collections, suspense. Agented submissions only. *No unsolicited mss.*

TIPS "Write the complete ms and submit it to an agent or agents. They will know exactly which editor will be interested in a project."

DUTTON CHILDREN'S BOOKS

Penguin Random House, 375 Hudson St., New York NY 10014. **Website:** www.penguin.com. Estab. 1852. Publishes hardcover originals as well as novelty formats. Dutton Children's Books publishes high-quality fiction and nonfiction for readers ranging from preschoolers to young adults on a variety of subjects. Currently emphasizing middle grade and young adult novels that offer a fresh perspective. De-emphasizing photographic nonfiction and picture books that teach a lesson. **Publishes 100 titles/year. 15% of books from first-time authors. Pays royalty on retail price. Pays advance.** Accepts simultaneous submissions.

🗨 "Cultivating the creative talents of authors and illustrators and publishing books with purpose and heart continue to be the mission and joy at Dutton."

NONFICTION Subjects include animals, history, science. Query. Only responds if interested.

FICTION Subjects include juvenile, young adult. Dutton Children's Books has a diverse, general interest list that includes picture books; easy-to-read books; and fiction for all ages, from first chapter books to young adult readers. Query. Responds only if interested.

DYNAMITE ENTERTAINMENT

113 Gaither Dr., Suite 205, Mt. Laurel NJ 8054. **E-mail:** submissions@dynamite.com. **Website:** www.dynamiteentertainment.com. Accepts simultaneous submissions.

FICTION Query first. Does not accept unsolicited submissions. Include brief bio, list of publishing credits.

DZANC BOOKS

Dzanc Books, Inc., 2702 Lillian, Ann Arbor MI 48104. **Website:** www.dzancbooks.org. Accepts simultaneous submissions.

FICTION Subjects include literary. "We're an independent non-profit publishing literary fiction. We also set up writer-in-residence programs and help literary journals develop their subscription bases." Publishes paperback originals. Query with outline/synopsis and 35 sample pages. Accepts queries by e-mail. Include brief bio. Agented fiction: 3%. Accepts unsolicited mss. Considers simultaneous submissions, submissions on CD or disk. Rarely critiques/comments on rejected mss. Responds to mss in 5 months.

TIPS "Every word counts—it's amazing how many submissions have poor first sentences or paragraphs and that first impression is hard to shake when it's a bad one."

EASTLAND PRESS

P.O. Box 99749, Seattle WA 98139. (800)453-3278. **Fax:** (760)598-6463. **E-mail:** info@eastlandpress.com. **Website:** www.eastlandpress.com. **Contact:** John O'Connor, managing editor. Estab. 1981. Publishes hardcover and trade paperback originals. "Eastland Press is interested in textbooks for practitioners of alternative medical therapies, primarily Chinese and physical therapies, and related bodywork." **Publishes 3-4 titles/year. 25 queries received/year. 30% of books from first-time authors. 90% from unagented writers. Pays 12-15% royalty on receipts.** Publishes ms 1-2 years after acceptance. Accepts simultaneous submissions. Responds in 1 month to queries. Catalog online.

NONFICTION Subjects include medicine. "We prefer that a ms be completed or close to completion before we will consider publication. Proposals are rarely considered, unless submitted by a published author or teaching institution." Submit TOC and 2-3 sample chapters. Reviews artwork/photos

THE ECCO PRESS

195 Broadway, New York NY 10007. (212)207-7000. **Fax:** (212)702-2460. **Website:** www.harpercollins.com. Estab. 1970. Publishes hardcover and trade paperback originals and reprints. **Publishes 60 titles/year. Pays royalty. Pays negotiable advance.** Publishes ms 1 year after acceptance. Accepts simultaneous submissions.

FICTION Literary, short story collections. "We can publish possibly 1 or 2 original novels a year." *Does not accept unsolicited mss.*

TIPS "We are always interested in first novels and feel it's important that they be brought to the attention of the reading public."

EDGE SCIENCE FICTION AND FANTASY PUBLISHING

Hades Publications, Box 1714, Calgary AB T2P 2L7, Canada. (403)254-0160. **Website:** www.edgewebsite.com. **Contact:** Editorial Manager. Estab. 1996. Publishes hardcover, trade paperback and e-book originals. EDGE publishes thought-provoking full length novels and anthologies of Science Fiction, Fantasy and Horror. Featuring works by established authors and emerging new voices, EDGE is pleased to provide quality literary entertainment in both print and pixels. **Publishes 20+ titles/year. 300-400 20% of books from first-time authors. 90% from unagented writers. Pays 10% royalty on net price. Negotiable advance.** Publishes ms 18-20 months after acceptance. Responds in 4-5 months to mss. Catalog online. Guidelines online.

IMPRINTS EDGE, EDGE-Lite, Absolute XPress.

FICTION Subjects include fantasy, horror, science fiction, young adult. "We are looking for all types of fantasy, science fiction, and horror - except juvenile, erotica, and religious fiction. Short stories and poetry are only required for announced anthologies." Length: 75,000-100,000/words. Does not want juvenile, erotica, and religious fiction. Submit first 3 chapters and synopsis. Check website for guidelines. Include estimated word count.

ÉDITIONS DU NOROÎT

4609 D'Iberville, Bureau 202, Montreal QC H2H 2L9, Canada. (514)727-0005. **Fax:** (514)723-6660. **E-mail:** lenoroit@lenoroit.com. **Website:** www.lenoroit.com. Publishes trade paperback originals and reprints. "Editions du Noiroît publishes poetry and essays on poetry." **Publishes 20 titles/year. 500 queries; 500 mss received/year. Pays 10% royalty on retail price.** Publishes ms 1 year after acceptance. Accepts simultaneous submissions. Responds in 4 months to mss.

POETRY Submit 40 sample poems.

EDUPRESS, INC.

Teacher Created Resources, 12621 Western Ave., Garden Grove CA 92841. (800)662-4321. **Fax:** (800)525-1254. **Website:** www.edupress.com. **Contact:** Editor-in-Chief. Estab. 1979. Edupress, Inc., publishes supplemental curriculum resources for PK-6th grade. Currently emphasizing Common Core reading and math games and materials. **Work purchased outright from authors.** Publishes ms 1-2 years after acceptance. Accepts simultaneous submissions. Responds in 2-4 months. Catalog online.

"Our mission is to create products that make kids want to go to school."

NONFICTION Submit complete ms via mail or e-mail with "Manuscript Submission" as the subject line.

TIPS "We are looking for unique, research-based, quality supplemental materials for Pre-K through 6th grade. We publish mainly reading and math materials in many different formats, including games. Our materials are intended for classroom and home schooling use. We do not publish picture books."

WILLIAM B. EERDMANS PUBLISHING CO.

2140 Oak Industrial Dr. NE, Grand Rapids MI 49505. (616)459-4591. **Fax:** (616)459-6540. **E-mail:** info@eerdmans.com. **E-mail:** submissions@eerdmans.com. **Website:** www.eerdmans.com. Estab. 1911. Publishes hardcover and paperback originals and reprints. "The majority of our adult publications are religious and most of these are academic or semi-academic in character (as opposed to inspirational or celebrity books), though we also publish general trade books on the Christian life. Our nonreligious titles, most of them in regional history or on social issues, aim, similarly, at an educated audience." Accepts simultaneous submissions. Responds in 4 weeks. Book catalog and ms guidelines free.

NONFICTION Subjects include history, philosophy, psychology, regional, religion, sociology, translation, Biblical studies. "We prefer that writers take the time to notice if we have published anything at all in the same category as their manuscript before sending it to us." Query with TOC, 2-3 sample chapters, and SASE for return of ms. Reviews artwork/photos.

FICTION Subjects include religious. Query with SASE.

ELM BOOKS

1175 Hwy. 130, Laramie WY 82070. (610)529-0460. **E-mail:** leila.monaghan@gmail.com. **Website:** www.elm-books.com. **Contact:** Leila Monaghan, publisher. "We are eager to publish stories by new writers that have real stories to tell. We are looking for short stories (5,000-10,000 words) with real characters and true-to-life stories. Whether your story is fictionalized autobiography, or other stories of real-life mayhem and debauchery, we are interested in reading them!" **Pays royalties.** Accepts simultaneous submissions.

FICTION "We are looking for short stories (1,000-5,000 words) about kids of color that will grab readers' attentions—mysteries, adventures, humor, suspense, set in the present, near past or near future that reflect the realities and hopes of life in diverse communities." Also looking for middle grade novels (20,000-50,000 words). Send complete ms for short stories; synopsis and 3 sample chapters for novels.

EMIS, INC.

P.O. Box 270666, Fort Collins CO 80527. (800)225-0694. **Fax:** (970)672-8606. **Website:** www.emispub.com. Publishes trade paperback originals. "Medical text designed for physicians; fit in the lab coat pocket as a quick reference. Currently emphasizing women's health." **Publishes 2 titles/year. Pays 12% royalty on retail price.** Accepts simultaneous submissions. Responds in 3 months to queries. Book catalog available free. Guidelines available free.

NONFICTION Subjects include psychology, women's health/medicine. Submit 3 sample chapters with SASE.

⊘ ENCANTE PRESS, LLC

1572 Blue Lupine Ln., Victor MT 59875. (406)642-3333. **Fax:** (406)642-6373. **E-mail:** books@encante-press.com. **Website:** www.encantepress.com. **Contact:** Marty Essen, president. Estab. 2007. Nonfiction publisher interested in nature, wildlife, animals, environment, travel, sciences, and politics. Encarte Press has a temporary hold on new submissions. "We are working on too many projects to consider anything new at this time." **Publishes 3-6 titles/year. 75% of books from first-time authors. 75% from unagented writers. Pays 10-20% royalty on net. "We offer a small advance, depending on the author and the book."** Publishes book 1 year after acceptance. Guidelines via e-mail.

NONFICTION Subjects include animals, environment, government, nature, politics, science, travel, wildlife.

ⒶⓄ ENCOUNTER BOOKS

900 Broadway, Suite 601, New York NY 10003. (212)871-6310. **Fax:** (212)871-6311. **Website:** www.encounterbooks.com. **Contact:** Acquisitions. Publisher/President: Roger Kimball. Publishes hardcover, trade paperback, and e-book originals and trade paperback reprints. Encounter Books publishes serious nonfiction—books that can alter our society, challenge our morality, stimulate our imaginations—in the areas of history, politics, religion, biography, education, public policy, current affairs, and social sciences. Encounter Books is an activity of Encounter for Culture and Education, a tax-exempt, non profit corporation dedicated to strengthening the marketplace of ideas and engaging in educational activities to help preserve democratic culture. Accepts simultaneous submissions. Book catalog online. Guidelines online.

NONFICTION Subjects include child guidance, education, ethnic, history, memoirs, multicultural, philosophy, psychology, religion, science, sociology, gender studies. Only considers agented submissions.

ENETE ENTERPRISES

1321 Upland Dr. #6536, Houston TX 77043. **E-mail:** eneteenterprises@gmail.com. **Website:** www.eneteenterprises.com. **Contact:** Shannon Enete, editor. Estab. 2011. Publishes trade paperback originals, mass market paperback originals, electronic originals. **Publishes 6 titles/year. 290 queries received/ year. 95% of books from first-time authors. 100% from unagented writers. Pays royalties of 10-20%.** Publishes book 3-6 months after acceptance. Accepts simultaneous submissions. Responds to queries/proposals in 1 month; mss in 1-3 months. Guidelines online.

NONFICTION Subjects include education, health, memoirs, travel, travel guides, travel memoirs, life abroad, retired living abroad. Submit query, proposal, or ms with marketing plan by e-mail.

TIPS "Send me your best work. Do not rush a draft. If you don't follow the submission guidelines your work will not be reviewed. A marketing plan is required."

ENSLOW PUBLISHERS, INC.

101 W. 23rd St., Suite 240, New York NY 10011. (973)771-9400. **Fax:** (877)980-4454. **E-mail:** customerservice@enslow.com. **Website:** www.enslow.com. Estab. 1977. Publishes hardcover originals. 10% require freelance illustration. Enslow publishes nonfiction and fiction series books for young adults and school-age children. **Publishes 250 titles/year. Pays royalty on net price with advance or flat fee. Pays advance.** Publishes ms 1 year after acceptance. Accepts simultaneous submissions. Responds in 1 month to queries. Guidelines via e-mail.

NONFICTION Subjects include history, recreation, science, sociology, sports. "Interested in new ideas for series of books for young people." No fiction, fictionalized history, or dialogue.

TIPS "We love to receive resumes from experienced writers with good research skills who can think like young people."

ENTANGLED TEEN

Website: www.entangledteen.com. "Entangled Teen and Entangled digiTeen, our young adult imprints publish the swoonworthy young adult romances readers crave. Whether they're dark and angsty or fun and sassy, contemporary, fantastical, or futuristic. We are seeking fresh voices with interesting twists on popular genres." **Pays royalty.** Accepts simultaneous submissions.

IMPRINTS Teen Crush; Teen Crave.

FICTION "We are seeking novels in the subgenres of romantic fiction for contemporary, upper young adult with crossover appeal." E-mail using site. "All submissions must have strong romantic elements. YA novels should be 50K to 100K in length. Revised backlist titles will be considered on a case by case basis." Agented and unagented considered.

ENTREPRENEUR PRESS

Entrepreneur Media Inc., 18061 Fitch, Irvine CA 92614. (949)261-2325. **Fax:** (949)622-7106. **E-mail:** press@entrepreneur.com. **Website:** www.entrepreneurbookstore.com. **Contact:** Vanessa Campos, marketing manager. Acquisitions Director: Jen Dorsey. "We specialize in quality paperbacks and e-books that focus on the entrepreneur in us all. Addressing the diverse challenges at all stages of business, each Entrepreneur Press book aims to provide actionable solutions to help entrepreneurs excel in all ventures they take on." **Publishes 20+ titles/year. Pays competitive net royalty.** Accepts simultaneous submissions. Catalog online. Guidelines online.

NONFICTION Subjects include business, career guidance, business start-up, small business management, business planning, marketing, finance, careers, personal finance, accounting, motivation, leadership, legal advise, management. When submitting work to us, please send as much of the proposed book as possible. Proposal should include: cover letter, preface, marketing plan, analysis of competition and comparative titles, author bio, TOC, 2 sample chapters. Go to website for more details. Reviews artwork/photos. Send transparencies and all other applicable information.

TIPS "We are currently seeking proposals covering sales, small business, startup, online businesses, marketing, etc."

EPICENTER PRESS, INC.

Aftershocks Media, 6524 NE 181st St. #2, Kenmore WA 98028. (425)485-6822. **Fax:** (425)481-8253. **E-mail:** info@epicenterpress.com. **Website:** www.epicenterpress.com. **Contact:** Lael Morgan, acquisitions editor. Estab. 1987. Publishes hardcover and trade paperback originals. "We are a regional press founded in Alaska whose interests include but are not limited to the arts, history, environment, and diverse cultures and lifestyles of the North Pacific and high latitudes. Our affiliated company, Aftershocks Media, provides a range of services to self-publisher industry distributors." **Publishes 4-8 titles/year. 200 queries; 100 mss received/year. 75% of books from first-time authors. 90% from unagented writers.** Publishes book 1-2 years after acceptance. Accepts simultaneous submissions. Responds in 6 months to queries. Book catalog and guidelines online.

NONFICTION Subjects include animals, ethnic, history, recreation, regional. "Our focus is Alaska and the Pacific Northwest. We do not encourage nonfiction titles from outside this region." Submit outline and 3 sample chapters. Reviews artwork/photos. Send photocopies.

⬤ EYEWEAR PUBLISHING

United Kingdom. **E-mail:** info@eyewearpublishing.com. **Website:** store.eyewearpublishing.com. **Contact:** Dr. Todd Swift, director/editor. Senior Editor: Kelly Davio. Estab. 2012. Firm publishes fiction, nonfiction, and poetry. Eyewear Publishing is an independent press, passionate about producing beautifully designed, fascinating books that remain affordable. "Based in London and New York, we celebrate the best writing in English from the UK and abroad." **Publishes 30 titles/year. Royalties vary from 10% to 20% Pays variable advance.** Accepts simultaneous submissions. Response time varies. Guidelines online.

IMPRINTS Maida Vale Publishing.

NONFICTION Subjects include Americana, art, community, contemporary culture, creative nonfiction, ethnic, gay, government, history, humanities, lesbian, literary criticism, literature, memoirs, multicultural, politics, pop culture, public affairs, regional, religion, social sciences, translation, womens issues, womens studies, world affairs.

FICTION Subjects include contemporary, ethnic, feminist, lesbian, literary, poetry, poetry in translation, regional, translation.

FACTS ON FILE, INC.

Infobase Learning, 132 W. 31st St., 16th Floor, New York NY 10001. (800)322-8755. **Fax:** (800)678-3633. **E-mail:** llikoff@infobaselearning.com; custserv@infobaselearning.com. **Website:** www.infobaselearning.com. **Contact:** Laurie Likoff. Estab. 1941. Publishes hardcover originals and reprints and e-books as well as reference databases. Facts On File produces high-quality reference materials in print and digital format on a broad range of subjects for the school and public library market and the general nonfiction trade. **Publishes 150-200 titles/year. 10% of books from first-time authors. 45% from unagented writers. Pays 10% royalty on retail price. Pays $3-5,000 advance.** Responds in 6 months to 1 year. Accepts simultane-ous submissions. Responds in 2 months to queries. Reference catalog available free. Guidelines online.

IMPRINTS Bloom's Literature; Ferguson's; Chelsea House; World Almanac.

NONFICTION Subjects include career guidance, contemporary culture, education, environment, government, history, literary criticism, multicultural, nutrition, politics, religion, sports, womens studies, young adult, careers, entertainment, natural history, popular culture. "We publish serious, informational books and e-books for a targeted audience. All our books must have strong library interest, but we also distribute books effectively to the trade. Our library books fit the junior and senior high school curriculum." No computer books, technical books, cookbooks, biographies (except YA), pop psychology, humor, fiction or poetry. Query or submit outline and sample chapter with SASE. No submissions returned without SASE.

TIPS "Our audience is school and public libraries for our more reference-oriented books and libraries, schools and bookstores for our less reference-oriented informational titles."

FAIRLEIGH DICKINSON UNIVERSITY PRESS

285 Madison Ave., M-GH2-01, Madison NJ 07940. (973)443-8564. **Fax:** (973)443-8364. **E-mail:** fdupress@fdu.edu. **Website:** www.fdupress.org. **Contact:** Harry Keyishian, Director. Estab. 1967. Publishes in hardcover originals and all electronic formats. Publishes a selection of volumes in paperback. Fairleigh Dickinson publishes scholarly books for the academic market, in the humanities and social sciences through a co-publishing partnership with Rowman & Littlefield, Lanham, MD. **Publishes 35-45 titles/year. 33% of books from first-time authors. 95% from unagented writers.** Publishes ms 6-7 months after acceptance. Responds in 2 weeks to queries.

⬤ "Contracts are arranged through The Rowman & Littlefield Publishing Group, which also handles editing and production. Publication decisions are made by our Editorial and Advisory Board. FDU Press is open to quality scholarly submissions in all humanities/social science field. We also have developed several book series: American History and Culture; Communication Studies; Italian Studies; Law, Culture and the Humanities; Mormon Studies; Shakespeare and the Stage; Studies in Willa Cather.

Activate your FREE subscription to WritersMarket.com to find even more agent listings!

255

NONFICTION Subjects include architecture, art, cinema, communications, contemporary culture, dance, economics, ethnic, film, gay, government, history, law, lesbian, literary criticism, multicultural, music, philosophy, psychology, regional, religion, sociology, womens issues, womens studies, world affairs, local, world literature, Italian Studies (series), Communication Studies (series), Willa Cather (series), American history and culture, Civil War, Jewish studies. "The Press discourages submissions of unrevised dissertations. We will consider scholarly editions of literary works in all fields, in English, or translation. We welcome inquiries about essay collections if the the material is previously unpublished, he essays have a unifying and consistent theme, and the editors provide a substantial scholarly introduction." No non-scholarly books. "We do not publish textbooks, or original fiction, poetry or plays." Query with outline, detailed abstract, and sample chapters (if possible), and CV. Does not review artwork.

FAMILIUS

1254 Commerce Way, Sanger CA 93657. (559)876-2170. **Fax:** (559)876-2180. **E-mail:** bookideas@familius.com. **Website:** familius.com. **Contact:** Acquisitions. Design & Digital: David Miles. Managing Editor: Brooke Jorden. Marketing & Publicity: Erika Riggs. Estab. 2011. Publishes hardcover, trade paperback, and electronic originals and reprints. Familius is all about strengthening families. Collective, the authors and staff have experienced a wide slice of the family-life spectrum. Some come from broken homes. Some are married and in the throes of managing a bursting household. Some are preparing to start families of their own. Together, they publish books and articles that help families be happy. **Publishes 40 titles/year. 200 queries; 100 mss received/year. 30% of books from first-time authors. 70% from unagented writers. Authors are paid 10-30% royalty on wholesale price.** Publishes book 12 months after acceptance. Accepts simultaneous submissions. Responds in 1 month to queries and proposals; 2 months to mss. Catalog online and print. Guidelines online.
NONFICTION Subjects include Americana, beauty, child guidance, cooking, counseling, crafts, finance, foods, games, gardening, health, hobbies, medicine, memoirs, military, nutrition, parenting. All mss must align with Familius mission statement to help families succeed. Submit a proposal package, including

an outline, 1 sample chapter, competition evaluation, and your author platform. Reviews JPEGS if sent as part of the submission package.
FICTION Subjects include juvenile, picture books. All picture books must align with Familius values statement listed on the website footer. Submit a proposal package, including a synopsis, 3 sample chapters, and your author platform.

FAMILYLIFE PUBLISHING

FamilyLife, a division of Campus Crusade for Christ, P.O. Box 7111, Little Rock AR 72223. (800)358-6329. **Website:** www.familylife.com. Publishes hardcover and trade paperback originals. FamilyLife is dedicated to effectively developing godly families. We publish connecting resources—books, videos, audio resources, and interactive multi-piece packs—that help husbands and wives communicate better, and parents and children build stronger relationships. **Publishes 3-12 titles/year. 250 queries received/year. 50 mss received/year. 1% of books from first-time authors. 90% from unagented writers. Pays 2-18% royalty on wholesale price. Makes outright purchase of 250.** Publishes ms 2 years after acceptance. Accepts simultaneous submissions. Responds in 3 months to queries; 6 months to proposals and mss. Book catalog online.
NONFICTION Subjects include child guidance, education, religion, sex, spirituality. FamilyLife Publishing exists to create resources to connect your family. "We publish very few books. Become familiar with what we offer. Our resources are unique in the marketplace. Discover what makes us unique, match your work to our style, and then submit." Query with SASE. Submit proposal package, outline, 2 sample chapters. Reviews artwork/photos.

FANTAGRAPHICS BOOKS, INC.

7563 Lake City Way NE, Seattle WA 98115. (206)524-1967. **Fax:** (206)524-2104. **Website:** www.fantagraphics.com. **Contact:** Submissions Editor. Estab. 1976. Publishes original trade paperbacks. Publishes comics for thinking readers. Does not want mainstream genres of superhero, vigilante, horror, fantasy, or science fiction. Accepts simultaneous submissions. Responds in 2-3 months to queries. Book catalog online. Guidelines online.
FICTION Subjects include comic books. "Fantagraphics is an independent company with a modus operandi different from larger, factory-like corporate

comics publishers. If your talents are limited to a specific area of expertise (i.e. inking, writing, etc.), then you will need to develop your own team before submitting a project to us. We want to see an idea that is fully fleshed-out in your mind, at least, if not on paper. Submit a minimum of 5 fully-inked pages of art, a synopsis, SASE, and a brief note stating approximately how many issues you have in mind."

TIPS "Take note of the originality and diversity of the themes and approaches to drawing in such Fantagraphics titles as *Love & Rockets* (stories of life in Latin America and Chicano L.A.), *Palestine* (journalistic autobiography in the Middle East), *Eightball* (surrealism mixed with kitsch culture in stories alternately humorous and painfully personal), and *Naughty Bits* (feminist humor and short stories which both attack and commiserate). Try to develop your own, equally individual voice; originality, aesthetic maturity, and graphic storytelling skill are the signs by which Fantagraphics judges whether or not your submission is ripe for publication."

FARCOUNTRY PRESS

P.O. Box 5630, Helena MT 59604. (800)821-3874. **Fax:** (406)443-5480. **E-mail:** will@farcountrypress.com. **Website:** www.farcountrypress.com. **Contact:** Will Harmon, Sr. Editor. Estab. 1980. Award-winning publisher Farcountry Press specializes in softcover and hardcover color photography books showcasing the nation's cities, states, national parks, and wildlife. Farcountry also publishes several children's series, as well as guidebooks, cookbooks, and regional history titles nationwide. **Publishes The staff produces about 30 books annually; the backlist has grown to more than 400 titles. titles/year.** Accepts simultaneous submissions. Guidelines online.

NONFICTION Subjects include agriculture, Americana, animals, community, cooking, environment, foods, history, memoirs, nature, photography, regional, travel.

FARRAR, STRAUS & GIROUX

18 W. 18th St., New York NY 10011. (646)307-5151. **Website:** us.macmillan.com/fsg. **Contact:** Editorial Department. Estab. 1946. Publishes hardcover originals and trade paperback reprints. "We publish original and well-written material for all ages." **Publishes 75 titles/year. 6,000 queries and mss received/year. 5% of books from first-time authors. 50% from un-agented writers. Pays 2-6% royalty on retail price** for paperbacks, 3-10% for hardcovers. **Pays $3,000-25,000 advance.** Publishes ms 18 months after acceptance. Accepts simultaneous submissions. Responds in 2-3 months. Catalog available by request. Guidelines online.

NONFICTION All levels. Send cover letter describing submission with first 50 pages.

FICTION Subjects include juvenile, picture books, young adult. Do not query picture books; just send ms. Do not fax or e-mail queries or mss. Send cover letter describing submission with first 50 pages.

POETRY Send cover letter describing submission with 3-4 poems. By mail only.

FARRAR, STRAUS & GIROUX FOR YOUNG READERS

Macmillan Children's Publishing Group, 175 Fifth Ave., New York NY 10010. (212)741-6900. **Fax:** (212)633-2427. **E-mail:** childrens.editorial@fsgbooks.com. **Website:** www.fsgkidsbooks.com. Estab. 1946. Accepts simultaneous submissions. Book catalog available by request. Ms guidelines online.

NONFICTION All levels: all categories. "We publish only literary nonfiction." Submit cover letter, first 50 pages by mail only.

FICTION All levels: all categories. "Original and well-written material for all ages." Submit cover letter, first 50 pages by mail only.

POETRY Submit cover letter, 3-4 poems by mail only.

TIPS "Study our catalog before submitting. We will see illustrators' portfolios by appointment. Don't ask for criticism and/or advice—due to the volume of submissions we receive, it's just not possible. Never send originals. Always enclose SASE."

🌀 FAT FOX BOOKS

The Den, P.O. Box 579, Tonbridge TN9 9NG, United Kingdom. (44)(0)1580-857249. **E-mail:** hello@fatfoxbooks.com. **Website:** fatfoxbooks.com. "Can you write engaging, funny, original and brilliant stories? We are looking for fresh new talent as well as exciting new ideas from established writers and illustrators. We publish books for children from 3-14, and if we think the story is brilliant and fits our list, then as one of the few publishers who accepts unsolicited material, we will take it seriously. We will consider books of all genres." Accepts simultaneous submissions. Guidelines online. Currently closed to submissions.

FICTION For picture books, send complete ms; for longer works, send first 3 chapters and estimate of final word count.

FATHER'S PRESS

590 N.W. 1921 St. Rd., Kingsville MO 64063. (816) 550-1138. **E-mail:** mike@fatherspress.com. **Website:** www.fatherspress.com. **Contact:** Mike Smitley, owner (fiction, nonfiction). Estab. 2006. Publishes hardcover, trade paperback, and mass market paperback originals and reprints. **Publishes 6-10 titles/year. Pays 10-15% royalty on wholesale price.** Publishes ms 6 months after acceptance. Responds in 1-3 months. Guidelines online.

NONFICTION Subjects include animals, creative nonfiction, history, religion. Query with SASE. Unsolicited mss returned unopened. Call or e-mail first. Reviews artwork/photos. Send photocopies.

FICTION Subjects include adventure, historical, juvenile, literary, mystery, regional, religious, suspense, western, young adult. Query with SASE. Unsolicited mss returned unopened. Call or e-mail first.

F+W, A CONTENT + ECOMMERCE COMPANY (BOOK DIVISION)

10151 Carver Rd., Suite 200, Blue Ash OH 45242. (513)531-2690. **Website:** www.fwcommunity.com. Estab. 1913. Publishes trade paperback originals and reprints. F+W connects passionate, like-minded groups of people to share an ongoing exchange of information, ideas, and inspiration. "We are committed to providing the very best experience for our consumers across our niche categories–craft, art, writing, design, outdoors, and lifestyle. We offer exclusive programs and products, best-in-industry customer service, curated kit flash sales, rewards and VIP programs, personalized 1-to-1 marketing, and more." **Publishes 400+ titles/year.** Accepts simultaneous submissions. Guidelines online.

IMPRINTS HOW Books (graphic design, illustrated, humor, pop culture); IMPACT Books (fantasy art, manga, creative comics and popular culture); Interweave (knitting, beading, crochet, jewelry, sewing); Krause Books (antiques and collectibles, automotive, coins and paper money, comics, crafts, games, firearms, militaria, outdoors and hunting, records and CDs, sports, toys); North Light Books (crafts, decorative painting, fine art); Popular Woodworking Books (shop skills, woodworking); Tyrus Books (mystery and literary fiction); Warman's (antiques and collectibles, field guides); Writer's Digest Books (writing and reference).

- ◖ Please see individual listings for specific submission information about the company's imprints.

❶❷⊘ FEIWEL AND FRIENDS

Macmillan Children's Publishing Group, 175 Fifth Ave., New York NY 10010. (646)307-5151. **Website:** us.macmillan.com. Feiwel and Friends is a publisher of innovative children's fiction and nonfiction literature, including hardcover, paperback series, and individual titles. The list is eclectic and combines quality and commercial appeal for readers ages 0-16. The imprint is dedicated to "book by book" publishing, bringing the work of distinctive and oustanding authors, illustrators, and ideas to the marketplace. This market does not accept unsolicited mss due to the volume of submissions; they also do not accept unsolicited queries for interior art. The best way to submit a ms is through an agent. Catalog online.

FENCE BOOKS

Science Library 320, Univ. of Albany, 1400 Washington Ave., Albany NY 12222. (518)591-8162. **E-mail:** jessp.fence@gmail.com. **Website:** www.fenceportal.org. **Contact:** Submissions Manager. Publishes hardcover originals. "Fence Books publishes poetry, fiction, and critical texts and anthologies, and prioritizes sustained support for its authors, many of whom come to us through our book contests and then go on to publish second, third, fourth books." Accepts simultaneous submissions. Guidelines online.

FICTION Subjects include literary, poetry. Submit via contests and occasional open reading periods.

POETRY Submit via contests and occasional open reading periods.

FERGUSON PUBLISHING CO.

Infobase Publishing, 132 W. 31st St., 17th Floor, New York NY 10001. (800)322-8755. **E-mail:** editorial@factsonfile.com. **Website:** www.infobasepublishing.com. Estab. 1940. Publishes hardcover and trade paperback originals. "We are primarily a career education publisher that publishes for schools and libraries. We need writers who have expertise in a particular career or career field (for possible full-length books on a specific career or field)." **Publishes 50 titles/year. Pays by project.** Accepts simultaneous submissions. Responds in 6 months to queries. Guidelines online.

NONFICTION "We publish work specifically for the elementary/junior high/high school/college library reference market. Works are generally encyclopedic in nature. Our current focus is career encyclopedias and young adult career sets and series. We consider manuscripts that cross over into the trade market." No mass market, poetry, scholarly, or juvenile books, please. Query or submit an outline and 1 sample chapter.

TIPS "We like writers who know the market—former or current librarians or teachers or guidance counselors."

✪ FERNWOOD PUBLISHING, LTD.

32 Ocenavista Ln., Black Point NS B0J 1B0, Canada. (902)857-1388. **Fax:** (902) 857-1328. **E-mail:** info@fernpub.ca. **E-mail:** editorial@fernpub.ca. **Website:** www.fernwoodpublishing.ca. **Contact:** Errol Sharpe, publisher. Estab. 1993. Publishes trade paperback originals. "Fernwood's objective is to publish critical works which challenge existing scholarship. We are a political and academic publisher. We publish critical books in the social sciences and humanities and for the trade market." **Publishes 35-40 titles/year. 120 queries received/year. 50 mss received/year. 40% of books from first-time authors. 100% from unagented writers. Pays 7-10% royalty on wholesale price. Pays advance.** Publishes ms 12-18 months after acceptance. Accepts simultaneous submissions. Responds in 6 weeks to proposals. Guidelines online.

IMPRINTS Roseway Publishing.

NONFICTION Subjects include agriculture, anthropology, communications, community, contemporary culture, creative nonfiction, economics, education, environment, ethnic, gay, government, health, history, humanities, labor, law, lesbian, multicultural, philosophy, politics, regional, sex, social sciences, sociology, translation, womens issues, womens studies, world affairs, young adult, contemporary culture, world affairs. "Our main focus is in the social sciences and humanities, emphasizing Indigenous resistance and resurgence, politics, capitalism, political economy, women, gender, sexuality, crime and law, international development and social work-for use in college and university courses." Submit proposal package, outline, sample chapters. Reviews artwork/photos. Send photocopies.

FICTION Subjects include ethnic, feminist, gay, historical, lesbian, literary, multicultural, regional, young adult, environment. Roseway Publishing is our social justice literary imprint. Roseway publishes fiction, young adult fiction, children's fiction and autobiography that deals with social justice issues. Guidelines online.

● DAVID FICKLING BOOKS

31 Beamont St., Oxford OX1 2NP, United Kingdom. (018)65-339000. **Fax:** (018)65-339009. **Website:** www.davidficklingbooks.co.uk. **Contact:** Simon Mason, managing director. David Fickling Books is a story house." For nearly twelve years DFB has been run as an imprint—first as part of Scholastic, then of Random House. Now we've set up as an independent business." **Publishes 12-20 titles/year.** Accepts simultaneous submissions. Responds to mss in 3 months, if interested. Guidelines online. Closed to submissions. Check website for when they open to submissions and for details on the Inkpot competition.

FICTION Considers all categories. Submit cover letter and 3 sample chapters as PDF attachment saved in format "Author Name_Full Title."

TIPS "We adore stories for all ages, in both text and pictures. Quality is our watch word."

FILBERT PUBLISHING

Box 326, Kandiyohi MN 56251-0326. **E-mail:** filbertpublishing@filbertpublishing.com. **Website:** filbertpublishing.com. **Contact:** Maurice Erickson, acquisitions. Estab. 2001. Publishes trade paperback and electronic originals and reprints. "We really like to publish books that creative entrepreneurs can use to help them make a living following their dream. This includes books on marketing, books that encourage living a full life, freelancing, self-help, we'll consider a fairly wide range of subjects under this umbrella. The people who purchase our titles (and visit our website) tend to be in their fifties, female, well-educated; many are freelancers who want to make a living writing. Any well-written manuscript that would appeal to that audience is nearly a slam dunk to get added to our catalog." **Publishes 6-12 titles/year. 85% of books from first-time authors. 99% from unagented writers. Paperback authors receive 10% royalty on retail price. E-books receive 50% net.** Publishes book 6-9 months after acceptance. Accepts simultaneous submissions. Responds in 1-2 months. Catalog online. Guidelines online.

NONFICTION Subjects include business, communications, creative nonfiction, spirituality, reference books for freelancers and creative entrepreneurs with an emphasis on marketing. "Our projects tend to be evergreen. If you've got a great project that's as relevant today as it will be 10 years from now, something that you're passionate about, query." Submit a query via SASE with a proposal package, including an outline and 2 sample chapters. "You can also query via e-mail. However, sometimes legit queries get lost because we get a ton of e-mail. If you haven't received a reply within a couple weeks, don't hesitate to resend." Will review artwork. Writers should send photocopies or query about sending electronically.

FICTION Subjects include contemporary, mainstream, romance, suspense. "We're thrilled when we find a story that sweeps us off our feet. Fiction queries have been very sparse the last couple of years, and we're keen on expanding our current romance line in the coming year." Query via SASE with a proposal package, including a synopsis, 5 sample chapters, information regarding your web platform, and a brief mention of your current marketing plan. If you'd like to submit a query via e-mail, that's fine. However, we get a lot of e-mail and if you don't receive a reply within a couple weeks, don't hesitate to resend.

TIPS "Get to know us. Subscribe to Writing Etc./The Creative Entrepreneur to capture our preferred tone. Dig through our website, you'll get many ideas of what we're looking for. We love nurturing new writing careers and most of our authors have stuck with us since our humble beginning. All new authors begin their journey with us with e-book publication. If that goes well, we move on to print. We love words. We enjoy marketing. We really love the publishing business. If you share those passions, feel free to query."

FILTER PRESS, LLC

P.O. Box 95, Palmer Lake CO 80133. (888)570-2663. **Fax:** (719)481-2420. **E-mail:** info@filterpressbooks. com. **Website:** www.filterpressbooks.com. **Contact:** Doris Baker, president. Estab. 1957. Publishes trade paperback originals and reprints. "Filter Press specializes in nonfiction of the West." **Publishes 4-6 titles/year. Pays 10-12% royalty on wholesale price.** Publishes ms 18 months after acceptance. Accepts simultaneous submissions.

NONFICTION Subjects include Americana, ethnic, history, regional, crafts and crafts people of the Southwest. Query with outline and SASE. Reviews artwork/photos.

FINDHORN PRESS

Delft Cottage, Dyke, Forres Scotland IV36 2TF, United Kingdom. (44)(1309)690-582. **Fax:** (44)(131)777-2711. **E-mail:** info@findhornpress.com. **E-mail:** submissions@findhornpress.com. **Website:** www.findhornpress.com. **Contact:** Thierry Bogliolo, publisher. Estab. 1971. Publishes trade paperback originals, CDs and e-books. **Publishes 20 titles/year. 1,000 queries received/year. 50% of books from first-time authors. 80% from unagented writers. Pays 10-15% royalty on wholesale price.** Publishes ms 12-18 months after acceptance. Accepts simultaneous submissions. Responds in 3-4 months to proposals. Book catalog and ms guidelines online.

IMPRINTS Earthdancer, Camino Guides.

No fiction or poetry.

NONFICTION Subjects include alternative lifestyles, animals, community, health, nature, New Age, psychology, spirituality, alternative health. No autobiographies.

FINNEY COMPANY, INC.

5995 149th St. W., Suite 105, Apple Valley MN 55124. **E-mail:** info@finneyco.com. **Website:** www.finneyco. com. **Contact:** Acquisitions. Publishes trade paperback originals. **Publishes 2 titles/year. Pays 10% royalty on wholesale price. Does not pay advance.** Publishes ms 1 year after acceptance. Accepts simultaneous submissions. Responds in 2-3 months to queries.

NONFICTION Subjects include education, career exploration/development. Finney publishes career development educational materials. Query with SASE. Reviews artwork/photos.

FIRST SECOND

Macmillan Children's Publishing Group, 175 5th Ave., New York NY 10010. **E-mail:** mail@firstsecondbooks. com. **Website:** www.firstsecondbooks.com. First Second is a publisher of graphic novels and an imprint of Macmillan Children's Publishing Group. First Second does not accept unsolicited submissions. Responds in about 6 weeks. Catalog online.

FITZHENRY & WHITESIDE LTD.

195 Allstate Pkwy., Markham ON L3R 4T8, Canada. (905)477-9700. **Fax:** (905)477-2834. **E-mail:** godwit@ fitzhenry.ca. **Website:** www.fitzhenry.ca/. Emphasis on Canadian authors and illustrators, subject or perspective. "Until further notice, we will not be accepting unsolicited submissions." **Publishes 15 titles/**

year. 10% of books from first-time authors. Pays authors 8-10% royalty with escalations. Offers "respectable" advances for picture books, split 50/50 between author and illustrator. Pays illustrators by project and royalty. Pays photographers per photo. Publishes book 1-2 years after acceptance. **TIPS** "We respond to quality."

FLASHLIGHT PRESS

527 Empire Blvd., Brooklyn NY 11225. (718)288-8300. **Fax:** (718)972-6307. **E-mail:** submissions@flashlight-press.com. **Website:** www.flashlightpress.com. **Contact:** Shari Dash Greenspan, editor. Estab. 2004. Publishes hardcover original children's picture books for 4-8 year olds. **Publishes 2-3 titles/year. 2,000 queries received/year. 50% of books from first-time authors. 50% from unagented writers. Pays 8-10% royalty on net. Pays advance.** Publishes ms up to 3 years after acceptance. Accepts simultaneous submissions. "Only accepts e-mail queries according to submission guidelines.". Book catalog online. Guidelines online.
NONFICTION See art submission guidelines online.
FICTION Subjects include juvenile, picture books. Average word length: 1,000 words. Picture books: contemporary, humor, multicultural. "Query by e-mail only, after carefully reading our submission guidelines online. Do not send anything by snail mail."

🦉 FLYING EYE BOOKS

62 Great Eastern St., London EC2A 3QR, United Kingdom. (44)(0)207-033-4430. **E-mail:** picturbksubs@nobrow.net. **Website:** www.flyingeyebooks.com. Estab. 2013. Flying Eye Books is the children's imprint of award-winning visual publishing house Nobrow. FEB seeks to retain the same attention to detail and excellence in illustrated content as its parent publisher, but with a focus on the craft of children's storytelling and nonfiction. Accepts simultaneous submissions. Guidelines online.

🦉 FLYLEAF PRESS

Ancestor Network Ltd, 4 Spencer Villas, Glenageary, County Dublin Ireland. (353)(1)285-4658. **E-mail:** books@flyleaf.ie. **Website:** www.flyleaf.ie. **Contact:** James Ryan, managing editor (family history). Sales: Brian Smith. Estab. 1987. Publishes Irish-interest family history and genealogy titles. Flyleaf Press is the publishing arm of Ancestor Network Ltd. (http://ancestornetwork.ie) which provides research services to personal and professional clients. Flyleaf Press was founded in 1987 and is Ireland's major specialist publisher of family history and genealogy titles. Flyleaf specialize in high-quality 'how-to' guides for research in various counties of Ireland. To date guides for 12 counties have been published. They also publish reference works on Church Records, Census records and wills. **Publishes 3 titles/year. 15 queries; 10 mss received/year. 60% of books from first-time authors. 100% from unagented writers. Pays 7-10% royalty on wholesale price. Does not pay advance.** Publishes book 6 months after acceptance. Responds in 1 month to mss. Book catalog online.
NONFICTION Subjects include history, hobbies, family history. Submit proposal package, outline, 1 sample chapter.
TIPS "Audience is family history hobbyists, history students, local historians."

FOCAL PRESS

Imprint of Elsevier (USA), Inc., 711 3rd Ave., 8th Floor, New York NY 10017. **Website:** routledge.com/focalpress. Estab. US, 1981; UK, 1938. Publishes hardcover and paperback originals and reprints. "Focal Press provides excellent books for students, advanced amateurs, and working professionals involved in all areas of media technology. Topics of interest include photography (digital and traditional techniques), film/video, audio, broadcasting, and cinematography, through to journalism, radio, television, video, and writing. Currently emphasizing graphics, gaming, animation, and multimedia." **Publishes 80-120 UK-US titles/year; entire firm publishes over 1,000 titles/year. 25% of books from first-time authors. 90% from unagented writers.** Publishes ms 6 months after acceptance. Accepts simultaneous submissions. Responds in 2 months to queries. Guidelines online.
NONFICTION Subjects include photography, film, cinematography, broadcasting, theater and performing arts, audio, sound and media technology. Does not publish collections of photographs or books composed primarily of photographs. To submit a proposal for consideration by Elsevier, complete the proposal form online. "Once we have had a chance to review your proposal in line with our publishing plan and budget, we will contact you to discuss the next steps." Reviews artwork/photos.

FODOR'S TRAVEL PUBLICATIONS, INC.

Imprint of Random House, Inc., 1745 Broadway, 15th Floor, New York NY 10019. **E-mail:** editors@fodors.com. **Website:** www.fodors.com. Estab. 1936. Publishes trade paperback originals. Fodor's publishes travel books on many regions and countries. "Remember that most Fodor's writers live in the areas they cover. Note that we do not accept unsolicited mss." **Most titles are collective works, with contributions as works for hire. Most contributions are updates of previously published volumes.** Accepts simultaneous submissions. Responds in 2 months to queries. Book catalog available free.

NONFICTION Subjects include travel. "We are interested in unique approaches to favorite destinations. Writers seldom review our catalog or our list and often query about books on topics that we're already covering. Beyond that, it's important to review competition and to say what the proposed book will add. Do not send originals without first querying as to our interest in the project. We're not interested in travel literature or in proposals for general travel guidebooks." Submit writing clips and résumé via mail or e-mail. In cover letter, explain qualifications and areas of expertise.

TIPS "In preparing your query or proposal, remember that it's the only argument Fodor's will hear about why your book will be a good one, and why you think it will sell; and it's also best evidence of your ability to create the book you propose. Craft your proposal well and carefully so that it puts your best foot forward."

FOLDED WORD

79 Tracy Way, Meredith NH 03253. **Website:** www.foldedword.com. **Contact:** Barbara Flaherty, acquisitions editor. Editor-in-Chief: JS Graustein. Poetry Editor: Rose Auslander. Fiction Editor: Casey Tingle. Estab. 2008. Folded Word is a literary micro-press that explores the world, one voice at a time. "Our list includes globally-distributed work by authors from four continents. We give individualized attention to the editing and design of each title." **Publishes 12 titles/year. 30% of books from first-time authors. 99% from unagented writers. Pays royalty. Advance only in rare cases with solicited books.** Publishes ms 2 years after acceptance. Accepts simultaneous submissions. Responds in 60 days for queries. If a full ms is requested, it may take 6 months for a final decision. Catalog online. Guidelines online.

NONFICTION Subjects include creative nonfiction, literature, nature, travel. "We are seeking creative nonfiction of 5,000-10,000 words that is well-researched, concise, and poetic. We are looking for a re-spite from the predictable and formulaic. We are also looking for manuscripts that are ecologically and culturally aware. We enjoy humor, word-play, and strong images. Please, surprise us." "We are especially seeking 5,000-10,000 word travel and literary essays that can be published as stand-alone chapbooks."

FICTION Subjects include contemporary, historical, humor, literary, poetry, poetry in translation, regional, short story collections. "We are seeking non-formulaic narratives that have a strong sense of place and/or time, especially the exploration of unfamiliar place/time. We are looking for manuscripts that are an escape from the everyday, be it a cleansing laugh, a cathartic cry, a virtual holiday, or even a respite from predictable plots. We are also looking for manuscripts that are ecologically aware. We enjoy quirky characters, voices that take a chance, humor, and word-play. Please, surprise us." "We are only seeking 5,000-10,000 word manuscripts that can be published as stand-alone chapbooks and chapbook-length collections of flash fiction. We no longer publish novels."

POETRY "We enjoy narrative poetry that has a strong sense of place and/or time, especially the exploration of unfamiliar place/time. We enjoy mind-bending images and creative spacing on the page. We are also looking for poetry that is ecologically and culturally aware. We enjoy humor, word-play, and voices that take a chance. Please, surprise us." "We are especially seeking regional poetry (any region), haiku (and other Japanese-form poetry), and bilingual chapbooks of poetry in translation."

TIPS "Please be sure you have read some of our recent titles prior to submitting."

FORDHAM UNIVERSITY PRESS

2546 Belmont Ave., University Box L, Bronx NY 10458. (718)817-4795. **Fax:** (718)817-4785. **Website:** www.fordhampress.com. **Contact:** Tom Lay, acquisitions editor. Editorial Director: Richard W. Morrison. Publishes hardcover and trade paperback originals and reprints. "We are a publisher in humanities, accepting scholarly monographs, collections, occasional reprints and general interest titles for consideration. No fiction." Accepts simultaneous submissions. Book catalog and ms guidelines free.

NONFICTION Subjects include education, history, philosophy, regional, religion, science, sociology, translation, business, Jewish studies, media, music. Submit query letter, CV, SASE.

TIPS "We have an academic and general audience."

FOREIGN POLICY ASSOCIATION

470 Park Ave. S., New York NY 10016. (212)481-8100. **Fax:** (212)481-9275. **Website:** www.fpa.org. Publishes 2 periodicals, an annual eight episode PBS Television series with DVD and an occasional hardcover and trade paperback original. The Foreign Policy Association, a nonpartisan, not-for-profit educational organization founded in 1918, is a catalyst for developing awareness, understanding of and informed opinion on US foreign policy and global issues. Through its balanced, nonpartisan publications, FPA seeks to encourage individuals in schools, communities and the workplace to participate in the foreign policy process. Accepts simultaneous submissions. Book catalog available free.

IMPRINTS Headline Series (quarterly); Great Decisions (annual).

NONFICTION Subjects include history, foreign policy.

TIPS "Audience is students and people with an interest, but not necessarily any expertise, in foreign policy and international relations."

✪ FORMAC PUBLISHING CO. LTD.

5502 Atlantic St., Halifax NS B3H 1G4, Canada. (902)421-7022. **Fax:** (902)425-0166. **Website:** www.formac.ca. **Contact:** Acquisitions Editor. Estab. 1977. Publishes hardcover and trade paperback originals. **Publishes 15-20 titles/year. 200 queries received/year. 150 mss received/year. 20% of books from first-time authors. 75% from unagented writers. Pays 5-10% royalty on wholesale price.** Publishes book 1 year after acceptance of ms. Accepts simultaneous submissions. Responds in 2 months to queries and to proposals; 4 months to mss. Book catalog available free. Guidelines online.

NONFICTION Subjects include animals, creative nonfiction, history, multicultural, regional, travel, marine subjects, transportation. Submit proposal package, outline, 2 sample chapters, CV or résumé of author(s).

TIPS "For our illustrated books, our audience includes adults interestsed in regional topics. For our travel titles, the audience is Canadians and visitors looking for cultural and outdoor experiences. Check out our website to see if you think your books fits anywhere in our list before submitting it. We are primarily interested in the work of Canadian authors."

FORTRESS PRESS

P.O. Box 1209, Minneapolis MN 55440. (612)330-3300. **Website:** www.fortresspress.com. Publishes hardcover and trade paperback originals. "Fortress Press publishes academic books in Biblical studies, theology, Christian ethics, church history, and professional books in pastoral care and counseling." **Pays royalty on retail price.** Accepts simultaneous submissions. Book catalog free. Guidelines online.

NONFICTION Subjects include religion, church history, African-American studies. Use online form. Please study guidelines before submitting.

FORWARD MOVEMENT

412 Sycamore St., Cincinnati OH 45202. (513)721-6659; (800)543-1813. **Fax:** (513)721-0729. **E-mail:** editorial@forwardmovement.org. **Website:** www.forwardmovement.org. Estab. 1934. "Forward Movement was established to help reinvigorate the life of the church. Many titles focus on the life of prayer, where our relationship with God is centered, death, marriage, baptism, recovery, joy, the Episcopal Church and more. Currently emphasizing prayer/spirituality." **Publishes 30 titles/year.** Accepts simultaneous submissions. Responds in 1 month. Book catalog free. Guidelines online.

NONFICTION Subjects include religion. "We are an agency of the Episcopal Church. There is a special need for tracts of under 8 pages. (A page usually runs about 200 words.) On rare occasions, we publish a full-length book." Query with SASE or by e-mail with complete ms attached.

FICTION Subjects include juvenile.

TIPS "Audience is primarily Episcopalians and other Christians."

WALTER FOSTER PUBLISHING, INC.

6 Orchard, Suite 100, Lake Forest CA 92630. (949)380-7510. **Fax:** (949)380-7575. **E-mail:** walterfoster@quarto.com. **Website:** www.walterfoster.com. **Contact:** Submissions. Estab. 1922. Publishes trade paperback originals. "Walter Foster publishes instructional how-to/craft instruction as well as licensed products." Accepts simultaneous submissions. Guidelines online.

NONFICTION Art, craft, activity books. Submit proposal package.

FOUR WAY BOOKS

Box 535, Village Station, New York NY 10014. **E-mail:** editors@fourwaybooks.com. **Website:** www.fourwaybooks.com. Estab. 1993. "Four Way Books is a not-for-profit literary press dedicated to publishing poetry and short fiction by emerging and established writers. Each year, Four Way Books publishes the winners of its national poetry competitions, as well as collections accepted through general submission, panel selection, and solicitation by the editors." Accepts simultaneous submissions.

FICTION Open reading period: June 1-30. Book-length story collections and novellas. Submission guidelines will be posted online at end of May. Does not want novels or translations.

POETRY Four Way Books publishes poetry and short fiction. Considers full-length poetry mss only. Books are about 70 pages, offset-printed digitally, perfect-bound, with paperback binding, art/graphics on covers. Does not want individual poems or poetry intended for children/young readers. See website for complete submission guidelines and open reading period in June. Book mss may include previously published poems. Responds to submissions in 4 months. Payment varies. Order sample books from Four Way Books online or through bookstores.

FOX CHAPEL PUBLISHING

1970 Broad St., East Petersburg PA 17520. (800)457-9112. **Fax:** (717)560-4702. **Website:** www.foxchapelpublishing.com. Publishes hardcover and trade paperback originals and trade paperback reprints. Fox Chapel publishes craft, lifestyle, and woodworking titles for professionals and hobbyists. **Publishes 90-150 titles/year. 30% of books from first-time authors. 100% from unagented writers. Pays royalty or makes outright purchase. Pays variable advance.** Accepts simultaneous submissions. Submission guidelines online.

NONFICTION Subjects include cooking, crafts, creative nonfiction.

TIPS "We're looking for knowledgeable artists, craftspeople and woodworkers, all experts in their fields, to write books of lasting value."

FRANCES LINCOLN BOOKS

74-77 White Lion St., London N1 9PF, United Kingdom. (44)(20)7284-4009. **Website:** www.franceslincoln.com. Estab. 1977. **Publishes 100 titles/year. 6% of books from first-time authors.** Publishes book 18 months after acceptance. Accepts simultaneous submissions. Responds in 6 weeks to mss.

NONFICTION Subjects include animals, career guidance, cooking, environment, history, multicul-

tural, nature, religion, social issues, special needs. Query by e-mail.

FRANCES LINCOLN CHILDREN'S BOOKS

Frances Lincoln, 74-77 White Lion St., London N1 9PF, United Kingdom. (44)(20)7284-4009. **Website:** www.franceslincoln.com. Estab. 1977. "Our company was founded by Frances Lincoln in 1977. We published our first books two years later, and we have been creating illustrated books of the highest quality ever since, with special emphasis on gardening, walking and the outdoors, art, architecture, design and landscape. In 1983, we started to publish illustrated books for children. Since then we have won many awards and prizes with both fiction and nonfiction children's books." **Publishes 100 titles/year. 6% of books from first-time authors.** Publishes book 18 months after acceptance. Accepts simultaneous submissions. Responds in 6 weeks to mss.

NONFICTION Subjects include animals, career guidance, cooking, environment, history, multicultural, nature, religion, young adult, social issues, special needs. Average word length: picture books—1,000; middle readers—29,768. Query by e-mail.

FICTION Subjects include adventure, fantasy, historical, humor, juvenile, multicultural, picture books, sports, young adult, antholology, folktales, nature. Average word length: picture books—1,000; young readers— 9,788; middle readers— 20,653; young adults— 35,407. Query by e-mail.

FRANCISCAN MEDIA PRESS

28 W. Liberty St., Cincinnati OH 45202-6498. (513)241-5615. **Fax:** (513)241-0399. **E-mail:** info@franciscanmedia.org. **Website:** www.americancatholic.org. Estab. 1970. Publishes trade paperback originals. "St. Anthony Messenger Press/Franciscan Communications seeks to communicate the word that is Jesus Christ in the styles of Saints Francis and Anthony. Through print and electronic media marketed in North America and worldwide, we endeavor to evangelize, inspire, and inform those who search for God and seek a richer Catholic, Christian, human life. Our efforts help support the life, ministry, and charities of the Franciscan Friars of St. John the Baptist Province, who sponsor our work. Currently emphasizing prayer/spirituality." **Publishes 20-25 titles/year. 300 queries received/year. 50 mss received/year. 5% of**

books from first-time authors. **99% from unagented writers. Pays $1,000 average advance.** Publishes ms 18 months after acceptance. Accepts simultaneous submissions. Responds in 2 months. Guidelines online.

IMPRINTS Servant Books.

NONFICTION Query with SASE. Submit outline. Reviews artwork/photos.

ⒶⓈⓄ FRANKLIN WATTS

Hachette Children's Books, Carmelite House, 50 Victoria Embankment, London EC4Y 0DZ, United Kingdom. (44)(20)7873-6000. **Fax:** (44)(20)7873-6024. **Website:** www.franklinwatts.co.uk. Estab. 1942. Franklin Watts is well known for its high quality and attractive information books, which support the National Curriculum and stimulate children's enquiring minds. *Generally does not accept unsolicited mss.* Accepts simultaneous submissions.

FREE SPIRIT PUBLISHING, INC.

6325 Sandburg Rd., Suite 100, Minneapolis MN 55427-3674. (612)338-2068. **Fax:** (612)337-5050. **E-mail:** acquisitions@freespirit.com. **Website:** www. freespirit.com. Estab. 1983. Publishes trade paperback originals and reprints. "Free Spirit is the leading publisher of learning tools that support young people's social-emotional health and educational needs. We help children and teens think for themselves, overcome challenges, and make a difference in the world." Free Spirit does not accept general fiction, poetry or storybook submissions. **Publishes 25-30 titles/year.** Accepts simultaneous submissions. Responds to proposals in 2-6 months. Book catalog and guidelines online.

NONFICTION Subjects include child guidance, counseling, education, educator resources; early childhood education. "Many of our authors are educators, mental health professionals, and youth workers involved in helping kids and teens." No general fiction or picture storybooks, poetry, single biographies or autobiographies, books with mythical or animal characters, or books with religious or New Age content. "We are not looking for academic or religious materials, or books that analyze problems with the nation's school systems." Query with cover letter stating qualifications, intent, and intended audience and market analysis (comprehensive list of similar titles and detailed explanation of how your book stands out from the field), along with your promotional plan, outline, 2 sample chapters (note: for early childhood

submissions, the entire text is required for evaluation), resume, SASE. Do not send original copies of work.

FICTION "Please review catalog and author guidelines (both available online) for details before submitting proposal. If you'd like material returned, enclose a SASE with sufficient postage."

TIPS "Our books are issue-oriented, jargon-free, and solution-focused. Our audience is children, teens, teachers, parents and youth counselors. We are especially concerned with kids' social and emotional well-being and look for books with ready-to-use strategies for coping with today's issues at home or in school—written in everyday language. We are not looking for academic or religious materials, or books that analyze problems with the nation's school systems. Instead, we want books that offer practical, positive advice so kids can help themselves, and parents and teachers can help kids succeed."

FULCRUM PUBLISHING

4690 Table Mountain Dr., Suite 100, Golden CO 80403. **E-mail:** acquisitions@fulcrumbooks.com. **Website:** www.fulcrum-books.com. **Contact:** T. Baker, acquisitions editor. Estab. 1984. **Pays authors royalty based on wholesale price. Offers advances.** Accepts simultaneous submissions. Catalog for SASE. Guidelines online.

NONFICTION Subjects include Americana, anthropology, history, literature, nature, politics, recreation, regional, science, travel, true crime, young adult. Looking for nonfiction-based graphic novels and comics, U.S. history and culture, Native American history or culture studies, conservation-oriented materials. "We do not accept memoir or fiction manuscripts." "Your submission must include: a proposal of your work, including a brief synopsis, 2-3 sample chapters, brief biography of yourself, description of your audience, your assessment of the market for the book, list of competing titles, and what you can do to help market your book. We are a green company and therefore only accept e-mailed submissions. Paper queries submitted via US Mail or any other means (including fax, FedEx/UPS, and even door-to-door delivery) will not be reviewed or returned. Please help us support the preservation of the environment by e-mailing your query to acquisitions@fulcrumbooks. com."

TIPS "Research our line first. We look for books that appeal to the school market and trade."

FUTURECYCLE PRESS

Lexington KY **Website:** www.futurecycle.org. **Contact:** Diane Kistner, director/editor-in-chief. Estab. 2007. Publishes English-language poetry books, chapbooks, and anthologies in print-on-demand and digital editions. Awards the FutureCycle Poetry Book Prize and honorarium for the best full-length book the press publishes each year. **Pays in deeply discounted author copies (no purchase required).** Accepts simultaneous submissions. Responds in 3 months. Guidelines, sample contract, and detailed *Guide for Authors* online.

POETRY Wants "poetry from imaginative, highly skilled poets, whether well known or emerging. We abhor the myopic, self-absorbed, and sloppy, but otherwise are eclectic in our tastes." Does not want concrete or visual poetry. Publishes 15+ poetry books/year and 5+ chapbooks/year. Ms. selected through open submission. Books average 62-110 pages; chapbooks 30-42 pages; anthologies 100+ pages. Submit complete ms. No need to query.

FUTURE HORIZONS

721 W. Abram St., Arlington TX 76013. (817)277-0727. **Fax:** (817)277-2270. **Website:** www.fhautism.com. **Contact:** Jennifer Gilpin-Yacio, editorial director. Publishes hardcover originals, trade paperback originals and reprints. **Publishes 10 titles/year. 250 queries received/year. 125 mss received/year. 75% of books from first-time authors. 95% from unagented writers. Pays 10% royalty. Makes outright purchase.** Publishes book 2 months after acceptance of ms. Accepts simultaneous submissions. Responds in 1 month to queries; 2 months to proposals. Book catalog available free. Guidelines online.

NONFICTION Subjects include education, autism. Submit proposal package, outline by mail (no e-mail). Reviews artwork/photos. Send photocopies.

TIPS "Audience is parents, teachers."

GENEALOGICAL PUBLISHING CO., INC

Genealogical.com, 3600 Clipper Mill Rd., Suite 260, Baltimore MD 21211. (410)837-8271. **Fax:** (410)752-8492. **E-mail:** info@genealogical.com. **E-mail:** jgaronzi@genealogical.com. **Website:** www.genealogical.com. **Contact:** Joe Garonzik, marketing director. Production Manager: Eileen Perkins. Estab. 1959. Publishes hardcover and trade paperback originals and reprints. **Publishes 50 titles/year. Receives 100 queries/year; 20 mss/year. 10% of books from first-**

time authors. 99% from unagented writers. Pays 10% royalty on selling price. Does not pay advance. Publishes book 6 months after acceptance. Accepts simultaneous submissions. Responds in 1 month. Catalog free on request.

IMPRINTS Clearfield Company.

NONFICTION Subjects include Americana, ethnic, history, hobbies. Submit outline, 1 sample chapter. Reviews artwork/photos as part of the mss package.

TIPS "Our audience is genealogy hobbyists."

GERTRUDE PRESS

P.O. Box 28281, Portland OR 97228. (503)515-8252. **E-mail:** editorgertrudepress@gmail.com. **Website:** www.gertrudepress.org. Estab. 2005. "Gertrude Press is a nonprofit organization developing and showcasing the creative talents of lesbian, gay, bisexual, trans, queer-identified and allied individuals. We publish limited-edition fiction and poetry chapbooks plus the biannual literary journal, *Gertrude*." Reads chapbook mss only through contests. Accepts simultaneous submissions.

FICTION Subjects include ethnic, experimental, feminist, gay, humor, lesbian, literary, mainstream, multicultural, short story collections.

TIPS Sponsors poetry and fiction chapbook contest. Prize is $175 and 50 contributor's copies. Submission guidelines and fee information on website. "Read the journal and sample published work. We are not impressed by pages of publications; your work should speak for itself."

GIBBS SMITH

P.O. Box 667, Layton UT 84041. (801)544-9800. **Fax:** (801)544-8853. **E-mail:** debbie.uribe@gibbs-smith.com. **Website:** www.gibbs-smith.com. Estab. 1969. **Publishes 3 titles/year. 50% of books from first-time authors. 50% from unagented writers. Pays authors royalty of 2% based on retail price or work purchased outright ($500 minimum). Offers advances (average amount: $2,000).** Publishes ms 1-2 years after acceptance. Accepts simultaneous submissions. Responds in 2 months. Book catalog available for 9×12 SAE and $2.30 postage. Ms guidelines available by e-mail.

NONFICTION Middle readers: activity, arts/crafts, cooking, how-to, nature/environment, science. Average word length: picture books—under 1,000 words; activity books—under 15,000 words. Submit an outline and writing samples for activity books; query for other types of books.

TIPS "We target ages 5-11. We do not publish young adult novels or chapter books."

GIVAL PRESS

Gival Press, LLC, P.O. Box 3812, Arlington VA 22203. (703)351-0079. **E-mail:** givalpress@yahoo.com. **Website:** www.givalpress.com. **Contact:** Robert L. Giron, editor-in-chief (area of interest: literary). Estab. 1998. Publishes trade paperback, electronic originals, and reprints. "We publish literary works: fiction, nonfiction (essays, academic), and poetry in English, Spanish, and French." **Publishes 2-3 titles/year. 200 queries; 60 mss received/year. 50% of books from first-time authors. 70% from unagented writers. Pays royalty. Per the contest prize, amount per the content. Outside of contests, yes.** Publishes ms usually 1 to 2 years after acceptance, per contract. Accepts simultaneous submissions. Responds in 3-5 months. Book catalog online. Guidelines online.

NONFICTION Subjects include creative nonfiction, education, gay, lesbian, literature, memoirs, multicultural, translation, womens issues, womens studies, scholarly. Submit between May 15-August 15. Always query first via e-mail; provide plan/ms content, bio, and supportive material. Best to submit via our portal at: www.givalpress.submittable.com. Reviews artwork/photos; query first.

FICTION Subjects include contemporary, feminist, gay, historical, lesbian, literary, multicultural, poetry, poetry in translation, translation. Always query first via e-mail; provide description, author's bio, and supportive material.

POETRY Query via e-mail; provide description, bio, etc.; submit 5-6 sample poems via e-mail.

TIPS "Our audience is those who read literary works with depth to the work. Visit our website—there is much to be read/learned from the numerous pages."

GLENBRIDGE PUBLISHING, LTD.

19923 E. Long Ave., Centennial CO 80016. (800)986-4135. **Fax:** (720)230-1209. **E-mail:** glenbridge10@gmail.com. **Website:** www.glenbridgepublishing.com. Estab. 1986. Publishes hardcover originals and reprints, trade paperback originals. "Glenbridge has an eclectic approach to publishing. We look for titles that have long-term capabilities." **Publishes 6-8 titles/year. Pays 10% royalty.** Publishes ms 1 year after acceptance. Accepts simultaneous submissions. Re-

sponds in 2 months to queries. Book catalog online. Guidelines for #10 SASE.

NONFICTION Subjects include Americana, history, philosophy, sociology. Send e-mail on website. Query with outline/synopsis, sample chapters.

THE GLENCANNON PRESS

P.O. Box 1428, El Cerrito CA 94530. (510)528-4216. **E-mail:** merships@yahoo.com. **Website:** www.glencannon.com. **Contact:** Bill Harris (maritime, maritime children's). Estab. 1993. Publishes hardcover and paperback originals and hardcover reprints. "We publish quality books about ships and the sea." Average print order: 500. Member PMA, BAIPA. Distributes titles through Baker & Taylor. Promotes titles through direct mail, magazine advertising and word of mouth. Accepts unsolicited mss. Often comments on rejected mss. **Publishes 4-5 titles/year. 25% of books from first-time authors. 100% from unagented writers. Pays 10-20% royalty.** Publishes ms 6-24 months after acceptance. Accepts simultaneous submissions. Responds in 1 month to queries; 2 months to mss.

IMPRINTS Smyth: perfect binding; illustrations.

NONFICTION Subjects include history, marine subjects, transportation, travel, war.

FICTION Subjects include adventure, historical, mainstream, military, multicultural, mystery, war, western, young adult. Submit complete ms. Include brief bio, list of publishing credits. Send SASE for return of ms or send a disposable ms and SASE for reply only.

TIPS "Write a good story in a compelling style."

Ⓐⵁ DAVID R. GODINE, PUBLISHER

15 Court Square, Suite 320, Boston MA 02108. (617)451-9600. **Fax:** (617)350-0250. **E-mail:** info@godine.com. **Website:** www.godine.com. Estab. 1970. "We publish books that matter for people who care." This publisher is no longer considering unsolicited mss of any type. Only interested in agented material. Accepts simultaneous submissions.

IMPRINTS Black Sparrow Books, Verba Mundi, Nonpareil.

NONFICTION Subjects include Americana, art, creative nonfiction, gardening, history, language, law, literary criticism, literature, photography, young adult, typography.

FICTION Subjects include literary, multicultural, poetry, poetry in translation, translation, young adult.

▲∅ GOLDEN BOOKS FOR YOUNG READERS GROUP

1745 Broadway, New York NY 10019. **Website:** www. penguinrandomhouse.com. Estab. 1935. "Random House Books aims to create books that nurture the hearts and minds of children, providing and promoting quality books and a rich variety of media that entertain and educate readers from 6 months to 12 years." *Random House-Golden Books does not accept unsolicited mss, only agented material.* They reserve the right not to return unsolicited material. **2% of books from first-time authors. Pays authors in royalties; sometimes buys mss outright.** Accepts simultaneous submissions. Book catalog free on request.

GOLDEN WEST BOOKS

P.O. Box 80250, San Marino CA 91118. (626)458-8148. **Fax:** (626)458-8148. **Website:** www.goldenwestbooks. com. Publishes hardcover originals. "Golden West Books specializes in railroad history. We are always interested in new material. Please use the form online to contact us; we will follow up with you as soon as possible." **Publishes 3-4 titles/year. 8-10 queries; 5 mss received/year. 75% of books from first-time authors. 100% from unagented writers. Pays 8-10% royalty on wholesale price.** Publishes ms 3 months after acceptance. Responds in 3 months to queries. Book catalog and ms guidelines free.

NONFICTION Subjects include Americana, history. Use online form. Reviews artwork/photos.

∅ GOOSEBOTTOM BOOKS

543 Trinidad Ln., Foster City CA 94404. **Fax:** (888)407-5286. **E-mail:** submissions@goosebottombooks.com. **Website:** goosebottombooks.com. **Contact:** Shirin Bridges. Estab. 2010. Middle grade nonfiction and fiction. Goosebottom Books is a small press dedicated to "fun non-fiction" founded by Shirin Yim Bridges, author of *Ruby's Wish*. *The Thinking Girl's Treasury of Dastardly Dames* was named by *Booklist* as one of the Top 10 Nonfiction Series for Youth of 2012. *Horrible Hauntings* made the IRA Children's Choices list with a mention that it "motivated even the most reluctant reader." And *Call Me Ixchel, Goddess of the Moon* was named one of the Top 10 Middle Grade Novels 2013 by Foreword Reviews. **Publishes less than 6 titles/year. 1,000 submissions received/ year. 50% of books from first-time authors. 100% from unagented writers. Goosebottom Books: Pays advance plus royalties; Gosling Press: Pays royal-** **ties only.** Publishes ms 18 months after acceptance. Responds in 1 month. Catalog online. Goosebottom Books is not accepting submissions at this time. Goosebottom Books never accepts hard copy submissions. "We like trees.".

IMPRINTS Goosebottom Books, Gosling Press.

NONFICTION Subjects include creative nonfiction, history, multicultural, social sciences, womens studies, young adult.

FICTION Subjects include adventure, ethnic, fantasy, feminist, gay, historical, horror, humor, juvenile, literary, mainstream, multicultural, mystery, picture books, science fiction, suspense, young adult. Gosling Press is a new partnership publishing imprint for children's middle grade fiction. Any fiction for adults.

✪ GOOSE LANE EDITIONS

500 Beaverbrook Ct., Suite 330, Fredericton NB E3B 5X4, Canada. (506)450-4251. **Fax:** (506)459-4991. **E-mail:** info@gooselane.com. **Website:** www.gooselane. com. Estab. 1954. Publishes hardcover and paperback originals and occasional reprints. "Goose Lane publishes literary fiction and nonfiction from well-read and highly skilled Canadian authors." **Publishes 16-20 titles/year. 20% of books from first-time authors. 60% from unagented writers. Pays 8-10% royalty on retail price. Pays $500-3,000, negotiable advance.** Responds in 6 months to queries.

NONFICTION Subjects include history, regional. Query with SASE.

FICTION Subjects include literary, short story collections, contemporary. Our needs in fiction never change: Substantial, character-centered literary fiction. No children's, YA, mainstream, mass market, genre, mystery, thriller, confessional or science fiction. Query with SAE with Canadian stamps or IRCs. No U.S. stamps.

POETRY Considers mss by Canadian poets only. Submit cover letter, list of publications, synopsis, entire ms, SASE.

TIPS "Writers should send us outlines and samples of books that show a very well-read author with highly developed literary skills. Our books are almost all by Canadians living in Canada; we seldom consider submissions from outside Canada. We consider submissions from outside Canada only when the author is Canadian and the book is of extraordinary interest to Canadian readers. We do not publish books for children or for the young adult market."

GRAYWOLF PRESS

250 Third Ave. N., Suite 600, Minneapolis MN 55401. (651)641-0077. **Fax:** (651)641-0036. **Website:** www. graywolfpress.org. Estab. 1974. Publishes trade cloth and paperback originals. "Graywolf Press is an independent, nonprofit publisher dedicated to the creation and promotion of thoughtful and imaginative contemporary literature essential to a vital and diverse culture." **Publishes 30 titles/year. Pays royalty on retail price. Pays $1,000-25,000 advance.** Publishes 18 months after acceptance. Accepts simultaneous submissions. Responds in 3 months to queries. Book catalog free. Guidelines online.

NONFICTION Subjects include contemporary culture, culture. Agented submissions only.

FICTION Subjects include short story collections, literary novels. "Familiarize yourself with our list first." No genre books (romance, western, science fiction, suspense). Agented submissions only.

POETRY "We are interested in linguistically challenging work." Agented submissions only.

GREAT POTENTIAL PRESS

1650 N. Kolb Rd., #200, Tucson AZ 85715. (520)777-6161. **Fax:** (520)777-6217. **Website:** www.greatpotentialpress.com. President: James T. Webb, Ph.D. Estab. 1986. Publishes trade paperback originals. Specializes in nonfiction books that address academic, social and emotional issues of gifted and talented children and adults. **Publishes 6-10 titles/year. 75 queries; 20-30 mss received/year. 50% of books from first-time authors. 100% from unagented writers. Pays 10% royalty on retail price.** Publishes book 1 year after acceptance. Accepts simultaneous submissions. Responds in 2 months to queries; 3 months to proposals; 4 months to mss. Book catalog free or on website. Guidelines online.

NONFICTION Subjects include child guidance, education, multicultural, psychology, translation, travel, gifted/talented children and adults, misdiagnosis of gifted, parenting gifted, teaching gifted, meeting the social and emotional needs of gifted and talented, and strategies for working with gifted children and adults. Use online submission form.

TIPS "Mss should be clear, cogent, and well-written and should pertain to gifted, talented, and creative persons and/or issues."

GREENHAVEN PRESS

27500 Drake Rd., Farmington Hills MI 48331. (800)877-4523. **Website:** www.gale.com/greenhaven. Estab. 1970. Publishes 220 young adult academic reference titles/year. 50% of books by first-time authors. Greenhaven continues to print quality nonfiction anthologies for libraries and classrooms. "Our well-known Opposing Viewpoints series is highly respected by students and librarians in need of material on controversial social issues." Greenhaven accepts no unsolicited mss. Send query, resume, and list of published works by e-mail. Work purchased outright from authors; write-for-hire, flat fee. Accepts simultaneous submissions.

NONFICTION Young adults (high school): controversial issues, social issues, history, literature, science, environment, health.

GREENWILLOW BOOKS

HarperCollins Publishers, 10 E. 53rd St., New York NY 10022. (212)207-7000. **Website:** www.greenwillowblog.com. Estab. 1974. Publishes hardcover originals, paperbacks, e-books, and reprints. *Does not accept unsolicited mss.* "Unsolicited mail will not be opened and will not be returned." **Publishes 40-50 titles/year. Pays 10% royalty on wholesale price for first-time authors. Offers variable advance.** Publishes ms 2 years after acceptance. Accepts simultaneous submissions.

FICTION Subjects include fantasy, humor, literary, mystery, picture books. *Agented submissions only.*

GREY GECKO PRESS

565 S. Mason Rd., Suite 154, Katy TX 77450. Phone/**Fax:** (866)535-6078. **E-mail:** info@greygeckopress. com. **E-mail:** submissions@greygeckopress.com. **Website:** www.greygeckopress.com. **Contact:** Submissions Coordinator. Estab. 2011. Publishes hardcover, trade paperback, audiobook, and electronic originals. Grey Gecko focuses on new and emerging authors and great books that might not otherwise get a chance to see the light of day. "We publish all our titles in hardcover, trade paperback, and e-book formats (both Kindle and ePub), as well as audiobook and foreign-language editions. Our books are available worldwide, for readers of all types, kinds, and interests." Not currently open for submissions; check website for updates. **Publishes 5 titles/year. 200+ queries; 30-40 mss received/year. 79% of books from first-time authors. 100% from unagented writ-**

ers. **Pays 50-75% royalties on net revenue. Does not pay advance.** Publishes ms 18-36 months after acceptance. Accepts simultaneous submissions. Responds in 6-12 months. Catalog online. Guidelines online.

NONFICTION Subjects include architecture, art, contemporary culture, cooking, creative nonfiction, environment, foods, history, marine subjects, military, nature, photography, travel, war. All nonfiction submissions are evaluated on a case-by-case basis. "We focus mainly on fiction, but we'll take a look at nonfiction works when submissions are open." Use online submission page. Reviews artwork. Send photocopies or link to photo website.

FICTION Subjects include adventure, contemporary, ethnic, experimental, fantasy, feminist, gay, historical, horror, humor, juvenile, lesbian, literary, mainstream, military, multicultural, mystery, occult, regional, romance, science fiction, short story collections, sports, suspense, war, western, young adult. "We do not publish extreme horror, erotica, or religious fiction. New and interesting stories by unpublished authors will always get our attention. Innovation is a core value of our company." Does not want extreme horror (e.g. *Saw* or *Hostel*), religious, or erotica. When open, use online submission page.

TIPS "Be willing to be a part of the Grey Gecko family. Publishing with us is a partnership, not indentured servitude. Authors are expected and encouraged to be proactive and contribute to their book's success."

⚠⊘ GROSSET & DUNLAP PUBLISHERS

Penguin Random House, 345 Hudson St., New York NY 10014. **Website:** www.penguin.com. Estab. 1898. Publishes hardcover (few) and mass market paperback originals. Grosset & Dunlap publishes children's books that show children that reading is fun, with books that speak to their interests, and that are affordable so that children can build a home library of their own. Focus on licensed properties, series and readers. "Grosset & Dunlap publishes high-interest, affordable books for children ages 0-10 years. We focus on original series, licensed properties, readers and novelty books." **Publishes 140 titles/year. Pays royalty. Pays advance.**

NONFICTION Subjects include science. *Agented submissions only.*

FICTION Subjects include juvenile. *Agented submissions only.*

☺ GROUNDWOOD BOOKS

128 Sterling Rd., Lower Level, Attention: Submissions, Toronto ON M6R 2B7, Canada. (416)363-4343. **Fax:** (416)363-1017. **E-mail:** submissions@groundwood-books.com. **Website:** groundwoodbooks.com. "We are always looking for new authors of novel-length fiction for children of all ages. Our mandate is to publish high-quality, character-driven literary fiction. We do not generally publish stories with an obvious moral or message, or genre fiction such as thrillers or fantasy." Publishes 19 picture books/year; 2 young readers/year; 3 middle readers/year; 3 young adult titles/year, approximately 2 nonfiction titles/year. **Offers advances.** Accepts simultaneous submissions. Responds to mss in 6-8 months. Visit website for guidelines.

FICTION Submit a cover letter, synopsis and sample chapters via e-mail. "Due to the large number of submissions we receive, Groundwood regrets that we cannot accept unsolicited manuscripts for picture books."

GROUP PUBLISHING, INC.

1515 Cascade Ave., Loveland CO 80539. **E-mail:** info@group.com. **Website:** www.group.com. Estab. 1974. Publishes trade paperback originals. "Our mission is to equip churches to help children, youth, and adults grow in their relationship with Jesus." **Publishes 65 titles/year. 500 queries; 500 mss received/year. 40% of books from first-time authors. 95% from unagented writers. Pays up to 10% royalty on wholesale price or makes outright purchase or work for hire. Pays up to $1,000 advance.** Publishes ms 18 months after acceptance. Accepts simultaneous submissions. Responds in 1 month to queries; 6 months to proposals and mss. Book catalog for 9x12 envelope and 2 first-class stamps.

NONFICTION Subjects include education, religion. "We're an interdenominational publisher of resource materials for people who work with adults, youth or children in a Christian church setting. We also publish materials for use directly by youth or children (such as devotional books, workbooks or Bibles stories). Everything we do is based on concepts of active and interactive learning as described in *Why Nobody Learns Much of Anything at Church: And How to Fix It*, by Thom and Joani Schultz. We need new, practical, hands-on, innovative, out-of-the-box ideas—things that no one's doing. yet." Query with SASE. Submit proposal package, outline, 3 sample chapters, cover letter, introduction to book, and sample activities if appropriate.

TIPS "Our audience consists of pastors, Christian education directors, youth leaders, and Sunday school teachers."

⚫⊘ GROVE/ATLANTIC, INC.

154 W. 14th St., 12th Floor, New York NY 10011. **E-mail:** info@groveatlantic.com. **Website:** www.grove-atlantic.com. Estab. 1917. Publishes hardcover and trade paperback originals, and reprints. "Due to limited resources of time and staffing, Grove/Atlantic cannot accept manuscripts that do not come through a literary agent. In today's publishing world, agents are more important than ever, helping writers shape their work and navigate the main publishing houses to find the most appropriate outlet for a project." **Publishes 100 titles/year. 1,000+ queries; 1,000+ mss received/year. 10% of books from first-time authors. Pays 7 ½-12 ½% royalty. Makes outright purchase of $5-500,000.** Book published 9 months after acceptance of ms. Accepts simultaneous submissions. Responds in 1 month to queries; 2 months to proposals; 4 months to mss. Book catalog available online.

IMPRINTS Black Cat, Atlantic Monthly Press, Grove Press.

NONFICTION Subjects include creative nonfiction, education, memoirs, philosophy, psychology, science, social sciences, sports, translation. Agented submissions only.

FICTION Subjects include erotica, horror, literary, science fiction, short story collections, suspense, western. Agented submissions only.

POETRY Agented submissions only.

GRYPHON HOUSE, INC.

P.O. Box 10, 6848 Leon's Way, Lewisville NC 27023. (800)638-0928. **E-mail:** info@ghbooks.com. **Website:** www.gryphonhouse.com. Estab. 1981. Publishes trade paperback originals. "At Gryphon House, our goal is to publish books that help teachers and parents enrich the lives of children from birth through age 8. We strive to make our books useful for teachers at all levels of experience, as well as for parents, caregivers, and anyone interested in working with children." Query. Submit outline/synopsis and 2 sample chapters. Responds to queries/mss in 6 months. Publishes a book 18 months after acceptance. Will consider simultaneous submissions, e-mail submissions. Book catalog and ms guidelines available via website

or with SASE. **Publishes 12-15 titles/year. Pays royalty on wholesale price.** Responds in 3-6 months to queries. Guidelines available online.

NONFICTION Subjects include child guidance, education. Currently emphasizing social-emotional intelligence and classroom management; de-emphasizing literacy after-school activities. "We prefer to receive a letter of inquiry and/or a proposal, rather than the entire manuscript. Please include: the proposed title, the purpose of the book, table of contents, introductory material, 20-40 sample pages of the actual book. In addition, please describe the book, including the intended audience, why teachers will want to buy it, how it is different from other similar books already published, and what qualifications you possess that make you the appropriate person to write the book. If you have a writing sample that demonstrates that you write clear, compelling prose, please include it with your letter."

TIPS "We are looking for books of creative, participatory learning experiences that have a common conceptual theme to tie them together. The books should be on subjects that parents or teachers want to do on a daily basis."

⊙⊘ GUERNICA EDITIONS

1569 Heritage Way, Oakville ON L6M 2Z7, Canada. (905)599-5304. **Fax:** (416)981-7606. **E-mail:** michaelmirolla@guernicaeditions.com. **Website:** www.guernicaeditions.com. **Contact:** Michael Mirolla, editor/publisher (poetry, nonfiction, short stories, novels). Anna Geisler (publicist): annageisler@guernicaeditions.com Estab. 1978. Publishes trade paperback originals and reprints. Guernica Editions is a literary press that produces works of poetry, fiction and nonfiction often by writers who are ignored by the mainstream. "We also feature a new imprint (Miro-Land) which accepts memoirs, how-to books, graphic novels, genre fiction with the possibility of children's and cook books" **Publishes 25-30 titles/year. Several hundred mss received/year. 20% of books from first-time authors. 99% from unagented writers. Pays 8-10% royalty on retail price, or makes outright purchase of $200-5,000. Pays $450-750 advance.** Publishes 24-36 months after acceptance. Accepts simultaneous submissions. Responds in 1 month to queries; 6 months to proposals; 1 year to mss. Book catalog online. Queries and submissions accepted via e-mail between January 1 and April 30.

NONFICTION Subjects include contemporary culture, creative nonfiction, ethnic, gay, history, lesbian, literary criticism, literature, memoirs, multicultural, philosophy, politics, pop culture, psychology, regional, social sciences, translation, womens issues, womens studies. Query by e-mail only. Reviews artwork/photos. Send photocopies.

FICTION Subjects include comic books, contemporary, ethnic, experimental, feminist, gay, historical, lesbian, literary, multicultural, mystery, plays, poetry, poetry in translation, science fiction, short story collections, translation. "We wish to open up into the fiction world and focus less on poetry. We specialize in European, especially Italian, translations." E-mail queries only.

POETRY Feminist, gay/lesbian, literary, multicultural, poetry in translation. We wish to have writers in translation. Any writer who has translated Italian poetry is welcomed. Full books only. No single poems by different authors, unless modern, and used as an anthology. Query.

GULF PUBLISHING COMPANY

P.O. Box 2608, Houston TX 77252. (713)529-4301. **Fax:** (713)520-4433. **Website:** www.gulfpub.com. Estab. 1916. Publishes hardcover originals and reprints; electronic originals and reprints. "Gulf Publishing Company is the leading publisher to the oil and gas industry. Our specialized publications reach over 100,000 people involved in energy industries worldwide. Our magazines and catalogs help readers keep current with information important to their field and allow advertisers to reach their customers in all segments of petroleum operations. More than half our editorial staff have engineering degrees. The others are thoroughly trained and experienced business journalists and editors." **Publishes 12-15 titles/year. 3-5 queries and mss received in a year. 30% of books from first-time authors. 80% from unagented writers. Royalties on retail price. Pays $1,000-$1,500 advance.** Publishes ms 8-9 months after acceptance. Accepts simultaneous submissions. Responds in 2 months to queries; 1 month to proposals and mss. Catalog free on request. Guidelines available by e-mail.

NONFICTION Subjects include Engineering. "We don't publish a lot in the year, therefore we are able to focus more on marketing and sales—we are hoping to grow in the future." Submit outline, 1-2 sample chap-

ters, completed ms. Reviews artwork. Send high res file formats with high dpi in b&w.

TIPS "Our audience would be engineers, engineering students, academia, professors, well managers, construction engineers. We recommend getting contributors to help with the writing process—this provides a more comprehensive overview for technical and scientific books. Work harder on artwork. It's expensive and time-consuming for a publisher to redraw a lot of the figures."

❹ GUN DIGEST BOOKS

F+W Media, 700 E. State St., Iola WI 54990. (888)457-2873. **E-mail:** gundigestonline@fwmedia.com. **Website:** www.gundigest.com. Estab. 1944. Hardcover, trade paperback, mass market paperback, and electronic originals (all). **Publishes 25 titles/year. 75 submissions received/year. 30% of books from first-time authors. 80% from unagented writers. 10-20% royalty on wholesale price. Pays advance between $2,800-5,000.** Publishes book 7 months after acceptance. Accepts simultaneous submissions. Responds immediately to queries; 2 months to proposals/ms. Catalog online. Guidelines available.

IMPRINTS Gun Digest Books, Krause Publications.

NONFICTION Subjects include Firearms, hunting-related titles only. "Must have mainstream appeal and not be too narrowly focused." Submit proposal package, including outline, 2 sample chapters, and author bio; submit completed ms. Review artwork/photos (required); high-res digital only (.jpg, .tif).

TIPS "Our audience is shooters, collectors, hunters, outdoors enthusiasts. We prefer not to work through agents."

HACHAI PUBLISHING

527 Empire Blvd., Brooklyn NY 11225. (718)633-0100. **Fax:** (718)633-0103. **E-mail:** info@hachai.com; dlr@hachai.com. **Website:** www.hachai.com. **Contact:** Devorah Leah Rosenfeld, editor. Estab. 1988. Publishes hardcover originals. Hachai is dedicated to producing high quality Jewish children's literature, ages 2-10. Story should promote universal values such as sharing, kindness, etc. **Publishes 5 titles/year. 75% of books from first-time authors. Work purchased outright from authors for $800-1,000.** Accepts simultaneous submissions. Responds in 2 months to mss. Guidelines online.

🔾 "All books have spiritual/religious themes, specifically traditional Jewish content. We're seeking books about morals and values; the Jewish experience in current and Biblical times; and Jewish observance, Sabbath and holidays."

NONFICTION Subjects include ethnic, religion. Submit complete ms. Reviews artwork/photos. Send photocopies.

FICTION Subjects include juvenile. Picture books and young readers: contemporary, historical fiction, religion. Middle readers: adventure, contemporary, problem novels, religion. Does not want to see fantasy, animal stories, romance, problem novels depicting drug use or violence. Submit complete ms.

TIPS "We are looking for books that convey the traditional Jewish experience in modern times or long ago; traditional Jewish observance such as Sabbath and holidays and mitzvos such as mezuzah, blessings etc.; positive character traits (middos) such as honesty, charity, respect, sharing, etc. We are also interested in historical fiction for young readers (7-10) written with a traditional Jewish perspective and highlighting the relevance of Torah in making important choices. Please, no animal stories, romance, violence, preachy sermonizing. Write a story that incorporates a moral, not a preachy morality tale. Originality is the key. We feel Hachai publications will appeal to a wider readership as parents become more interested in positive values for their children."

HADLEY RILLE BOOKS

P.O. Box 25466, Overland Park KS 66225. **E-mail:** contact@hadleyrillebooks.com. **E-mail:** subs@hadleyrillebooks.com. **Website:** https://hadleyrillebks. wordpress.com. **Contact:** Eric T. Reynolds, editor/publisher. Estab. 2005. Currently closed to submissions. Check website for future reading periods. Accepts simultaneous submissions.

FICTION Subjects include fantasy, science fiction, short story collections.

TIPS "We aim to produce books that are aligned with current interest in the genres. Anthology markets are somewhat rare in SF these days, we feel there aren't enough good anthologies being published each year and part of our goal is to present the best that we can. We like stories that fit well within the guidelines of the particular anthology for which we are soliciting manuscripts. Aside from that, we want stories with strong characters (not necessarily characters with strong personalities, flawed characters are welcome). We want a sense of wonder and awe. We want to feel the world around the character and so scene description is important (however, this doesn't always require a lot of text, just set the scene well so we don't wonder where the character is). We strongly recommend workshopping the story or having it critiqued in some way by readers familiar with the genre. We prefer clichés be kept to a bare minimum in the prose and avoid re-working old story lines."

HAMPTON ROADS PUBLISHING CO., INC.

65 Parker St, Suite 7, Newburyport MA 01950. **E-mail:** submissions@rwwbooks.com. **Website:** www. redwheelweiser.com. Estab. 1989. Publishes and distributes hardcover and trade paperback originals on subjects including metaphysics, health, complementary medicine, and other related topics. "Our reason for being is to impact, uplift, and contribute to positive change in the world. We publish books that will enrich and empower the evolving consciousness of mankind. Though we are not necessarily limited in scope, we are most interested in manuscripts on the following subjects: Body/Mind/Spirit, Health and Healing, Self-Help. Please be advised that at the moment we are not accepting fiction or novelized material that does not pertain to body/mind/spirit, channeled writing." **Publishes 35-40 titles/year. 1,000 queries; 1,500 mss received/year. 50% of books from first-time authors. 70% from unagented writers. Pays royalty. Pays $1,000-50,000 advance.** Publishes ms 1 year after acceptance. Accepts simultaneous submissions. Responds in 2-4 months to queries; 1 month to proposals; 6-12 months to mss. Guidelines online.

NONFICTION Subjects include New Age, spirituality. Submit by e-mail.

HANCOCK HOUSE PUBLISHERS

Unit 104, 4550 Birch Bay-Lynden Rd., Blaine WA 98230. (800)938-1114. **Fax:** (604)538-2262. **E-mail:** submissions@hancockhouse.com. **Website:** www. hancockhouse.com. Estab. 1971. Publishes hardcover, trade paperback, and e-book originals and reprints. "Hancock House Publishers is the largest North American publisher of wildlife and Native Indian titles. We also cover Pacific Northwest, fishing, history, Canadiana, biographies. We are seeking agriculture, natural history, and popular science titles with a regional (Pacific Northwest), national, or international focus. Currently emphasizing nonfiction wildlife, cryptozoology, guide books, native history, biography, fishing." **Publishes 12-20 titles/year. 50% of books from**

first-time authors. 90% from unagented writers. Pays 10% royalty. Publishes book 1 year after acceptance. Accepts simultaneous submissions. Responds to proposals in 3-6 months. Book catalog available free. Guidelines online.

NONFICTION Subjects include agriculture, animals, ethnic, history, horticulture, regional. Centered around Pacific Northwest, local history, nature guide books, international ornithology, and Native Americans. Query via e-mail, including outline with word count, a short author bio, table of contents, 3 sample chapters. Accepts double-spaced word .docs or PDFs. Reviews artwork/photos. Send photocopies.

HANSER PUBLICATIONS

6915 Valley Ave., Cincinnati OH 45244. (800)950-8977. **Fax:** (513)527-8801. **E-mail:** info@hanserpublications.com. **Website:** www.hanserpublications.com. **Contact:** Development Editor. Estab. 1993. Publishes hardcover and paperback originals, and digital educational and training programs. "Hanser Publications publishes books and electronic media for the manufacturing (both metalworking and plastics) industries. Publications range from basic training materials to advanced reference books." **Publishes 10-15 titles/year. 100 queries received/year. 10-20 mss received/year. 50% of books from first-time authors. 100% from unagented writers.** Publishes ms 10 months after acceptance. Accepts simultaneous submissions. Responds in 2 weeks to queries; 1 month to proposals/mss. Book catalog available free. Guidelines available online.

○ "Hanser Publications is currently seeking technical experts with strong writing skills to author training and reference books and related products focused on various aspects of the manufacturing industry. Our goal is to provide manufacturing professionals with insightful, easy-to-reference information, and to educate and prepare students for technical careers through accessible, concise training manuals. Do your publishing ideas match this goal? If so, we'd like to hear from you. Submit your detailed product proposals, resume of credentials, and a brief writing sample to: Development Editor, Prospective Authors."

NONFICTION "We publish how-to texts, references, technical books, and computer-based learning materials for the manufacturing industries. Titles include

award-winning management books, encyclopedic references, and leading references." Submit outline, sample chapters, resume, preface, and comparison to competing or similar titles.

TIPS "E-mail submissions speed up response time."

○ HARLEQUIN BLAZE

225 Duncan Mill Rd., Don Mills ON M3B 3K9, Canada. (416)445-5860. **Website:** www.harlequin.com. **Contact:** Kathleen Scheibling, senior editor. Publishes paperback originals. "Harlequin Blaze is a red-hot series. It is a vehicle to build and promote new authors who have a strong sexual edge to their stories. It is also the place to be for seasoned authors who want to create a sexy, sizzling, longer contemporary story." Accepts simultaneous submissions. Guidelines online.

FICTION Subjects include romance. "Sensuous, highly romantic, innovative plots that are sexy in premise and execution. The tone of the books can run from fun and flirtatious to dark and sensual. Submissions should have a very contemporary feel—what it's like to be young and single today. We are looking for heroes and heroines in their early 20s and up. There should be a a strong emphasis on the physical relationship between the couples. Fully described love scenes along with a high level of fantasy and playfulness." Length: 55,000-60,000 words.

TIPS "Are you a *Cosmo* girl at heart? A fan of *Sex and the City*? Or maybe you have a sexually adventurous spirit. If so, then Blaze is the series for you!"

HARLEQUIN DESIRE

233 Broadway, Suite 1001, New York NY 10279. (212)553-4200. **Website:** www.harlequin.com. **Contact:** Stacy Boyd, senior editor. Publishes paperback originals and reprints. Always powerful, passionate, and provocative. "Desire novels are sensual reads and a love scene or scenes are still needed. But there is no set number of pages that needs to be fulfilled. Rather, the level of sensuality must be appropriate to the storyline. Above all, every Silhouette Desire novel must fulfill the promise of a powerful, passionate and provocative read." **Pays royalty. Offers advance.** Accepts simultaneous submissions. Guidelines online.

FICTION Subjects include romance. Looking for novels in which "the conflict is an emotional one, springing naturally from the unique characters you've chosen. The focus is on the developing relationship, set in a believable plot. Sensuality is key, but lovemaking is never taken lightly. Secondary characters and subplots need to blend with the core story. Innovative new directions in storytelling and fresh approaches to classic romantic plots are welcome." Manuscripts must be 50,000-55,000 words.

⊘ HARLEQUIN INTRIGUE

225 Duncan Mill Rd., Don Mills ON M3B 3K9, Canada. **Website:** www.harlequin.com. **Contact:** Denise Zaza, senior editor. Wants crime stories tailored to the series romance market packed with a variety of thrilling suspense and whodunit mystery. Word count: 55,000-60,000. Accepts simultaneous submissions. Guidelines online.

FICTION Subjects include mystery, romance, suspense. Submit online.

⊘ HARLEQUIN SUPERROMANCE

225 Duncan Mill Rd., Don Mills ON M3B 3K9, Canada. **Website:** www.harlequin.com. **Contact:** Victoria Curran, senior editor. Publishes paperback originals. "The Harlequin Superromance line focuses on believable characters triumphing over true-to-life drama and conflict. At the heart of these contemporary stories should be a compelling romance that brings the reader along with the hero and heroine on their journey of overcoming the obstacles in their way and falling in love. Because of the longer length relevant subplots and secondary characters are welcome but not required. This series publishes a variety of story types—family sagas, romantic suspense, Westerns, to name a few—and tones from light to dramatic, emotional to suspenseful. Settings also vary from vibrant urban neighborhoods to charming small towns. The unifying element of Harlequin Superromance stories is the realistic treatment of character and plot. The characters should seem familiar to readers—similar to people they know in their own lives—and the circumstances within the realm of possibility. The stories should be layered and complex in that the conflicts should not be easily resolved. The best way to get an idea of we're looking for is to read what we're currently publishing. The aim of Superromance novels is to produce a contemporary, involving read with a mainstream tone in its situations and characters, using romance as the major theme. To achieve this, emphasis should be placed on individual writing styles and unique and topical ideas." **Pays royalties. Pays advance.** Accepts simultaneous submissions. Guidelines online.

FICTION Subjects include romance. "The criteria for Superromance books are flexible. Aside from length (80,000 words), the determining factor for publication will always be quality. Authors should strive to break free of stereotypes, clichés and worn-out plot devices to create strong, believable stories with depth and emotional intensity. Superromance novels are intended to appeal to a wide range of romance readers." Submit online.

TIPS "A general familiarity with current Superromance books is advisable to keep abreast of ever-changing trends and overall scope, but we don't want imitations. We look for sincere, heartfelt writing based on true-to-life experiences the reader can identify with. We are interested in innovation."

HARMONY INK PRESS

Dreamspinner Press, 5032 Capital Circle SW, Suite 2 PMB 279, Tallahassee FL 32305. (850)632-4648. **Fax:** (888)308-3739. **E-mail:** submissions@harmonyinkpress.com. **Website:** harmonyinkpress.com. **Contact:** Anne Regan. Estab. 2010. Teen and new adult fiction featuring at least 1 strong LGBTQ+ main character who shows significant personal growth through the course of the story. **Publishes 26 titles/year. Pays royalty. Pays $500-1,000 advance.** Accepts simultaneous submissions.

FICTION "We are looking for stories in all subgenres, featuring primary characters across the whole LGBTQ+ spectrum between the ages of 14 and 21 that explore all the facets of young adult, teen, and new adult life. Sexual content should be appropriate for the characters and the story." Submit complete ms.

⊘⊘ HARPERBUSINESS

Imprint of HarperCollins General Books Group, 195 Broadway, New York NY 10007. (212)207-7000. **Website:** www.harpercollins.com. Estab. 1991. Publishes hardcover, trade paperback originals and reprints. HarperBusiness publishes the inside story on ideas that will shape business practices with cutting-edge information and visionary concepts. **Pays royalty on retail price. Pays advance.** Accepts simultaneous submissions.

○ "The gold standard of business book publishing for 50 years, Harper Business brings you innovative, authoritative, and creative works from world-class thinkers. Building upon this rich legacy of paradigm-shifting books, Harper Business authors continue to help readers see the future and to lead and live successfully."

NONFICTION Subjects include marketing subjects. "We don't publish how-to, textbooks or things for academic market; no reference (tax or mortgage guides), our reference department does that. Proposals need to be top notch. We tend not to publish people who have no business standing. Must have business credentials." Agented submissions only.

⊛⊘ HARPERCOLLINS

195 Broadway, New York NY 10007. (212)207-7000. **Website:** www.harpercollins.com. Publishes hardcover and paperback originals and paperback reprints. HarperCollins, one of the largest English language publishers in the world, is a broad-based publisher with strengths in academic, business and professional, children's, educational, general interest, and religious and spiritual books, as well as multimedia titles. **Pays royalty. Pays negotiable advance.** Accepts simultaneous submissions.

NONFICTION Agented submissions only. Unsolicited mss returned unopened.

FICTION Subjects include adventure, fantasy, gothic, historical, literary, mystery, science fiction, suspense, western. "We look for a strong story line and exceptional literary talent." Agented submissions only. *All unsolicited mss returned.*

TIPS "We do not accept any unsolicited material."

◐⊘ HARPERCOLLINS CANADA, LTD.

2 Bloor St. E., 20th Floor, Toronto ON M4W 1A8, Canada. (416)975-9334. **Fax:** (416)975-5223. **Website:** www.harpercollins.ca. Estab. 1989. *HarperCollins Canada is not accepting unsolicited material at this time.* Accepts simultaneous submissions.

◓ HARPERCOLLINS CHILDREN'S BOOKS/ HARPERCOLLINS PUBLISHERS

195 Broadway, New York NY 10007. (212)207-7000. **Website:** www.harpercollins.com. Publishes hardcover and paperback originals and paperback reprints. HarperCollins, one of the largest English language publishers in the world, is a broad-based publisher with strengths in academic, business and professional, children's, educational, general interest, and religious and spiritual books, as well as multimedia titles. **Publishes 500 titles/year. Negotiates payment upon acceptance.** Accepts simultaneous submissions.

Responds in 1 month, will contact only if interested. Does not accept any unsolicited texts. Catalog online.

IMPRINTS HarperCollins Australia/New Zealand: Angus & Robertson, Fourth Estate, HarperBusiness, HarperCollins, HarperPerenniel, HarperReligious, HarperSports, Voyager; **HarperCollins Canada**: HarperFlamingoCanada, PerennialCanada; **HarperCollins Children's Books Group:** Amistad, Julie Andrews Collection, Avon, Joanna Cotler Books, Eos, Laura Geringer Books, Greenwillow Books, HarperAudio, HarperCollins Children's Books, HarperFestival, HarperTempest, HarperTrophy, Rayo, Katherine Tegen Books; **HarperCollins General Books Group:** Access, Amistad, Avon, Caedmon, Ecco, Eos, Fourth Estate, HarperAudio, HarperBusiness, HarperCollins, HarperEntertainment, HarperLargePrint, HarperResource, HarperSanFrancisco, HarperTorch, Harper Design International, Perennial, PerfectBound, Quill, Rayo, ReganBooks, William Morrow, William Morrow Cookbooks; **HarperCollins UK:** Collins Bartholomew, Collins, HarperCollins Crime & Thrillers, Collins Freedom to Teach, HarperCollins Children's Books, Thorsons/Element, Voyager Books; **Zondervan:** Inspirio, Vida, Zonderkidz, Zondervan.

NONFICTION *No unsolicited mss or queries.* Agented submissions only. Unsolicited mss returned unopened.

FICTION Subjects include picture books, young adult, chapter books, middle grade, early readers. "We look for a strong story line and exceptional literary talent." Agented submissions only. *All unsolicited mss returned.*

TIPS "We do not accept any unsolicited material."

◓ HARPER PERENNIAL

10 E. 53rd St., New York NY 10022. **E-mail:** harperperennial@harpercollins.com. **Website:** harperperennial.tumblr.com. Harper Perennial is one of the paperback imprints of HarperCollins. "We publish paperback originals and reprints of authors like Ann Patchett, Justin Taylor, Barbara Kingsolver, and Blake Butler. Accepts simultaneous submissions.

⊛⊘ HARPER VOYAGER

Imprint of HarperCollins General Books Group, 195 Broadway, New York NY 10007. (212)207-7000. **Website:** www.harpercollins.com. Estab. 1998. Publishes hardcover originals, trade and mass market paperback originals, and reprints. Eos publishes quality science fiction/fantasy with broad appeal. **Pays royalty** on retail price. **Pays variable advance.** Accepts simultaneous submissions. Guidelines online.

FICTION Subjects include fantasy, science fiction. No horror or juvenile. Agented submissions only. *All unsolicited mss returned.*

HARTMAN PUBLISHING, INC.

1313 Iron Ave. SW, Albuquerque NM 87102. **E-mail:** info@hartmanonline.com. **Website:** www.hartmanonline.com. **Contact:** Managing Editor. Publishes trade paperback originals. "We publish educational books for employees of nursing homes, home health agencies, hospitals, and providers of eldercare." **Publishes 5-10 titles/year. 50 queries received/year. 25 mss received/year. 50% of books from first-time authors. 100% from unagented writers. Pays 6-12% royalty on wholesale or retail price, or makes outright purchase of $200-600.** Publishes book 4-12 months after acceptance of ms. Accepts simultaneous submissions. Responds in 2 months to proposals; 3 months to mss. Book catalog available free. Guidelines online.

IMPRINTS Care Spring.

NONFICTION "Writers should request our books-wanted list, as well as view samples of our published material." Submit via online form.

THE HARVARD COMMON PRESS

100 Cummings Center, Suite 406-L, Beverly MA 01915. (978)282-9590. **Fax:** (978)282-7765. **E-mail:** info@harvardcommonpress.com. **E-mail:** editorial@harvardcommonpress.com. **Website:** https://www.quartoknows.com/Harvard-Common-Press. **Contact:** Submissions. Estab. 1976. Publishes hardcover and trade paperback originals and reprints. "We want strong, practical books that help people gain control over a particular area of their lives. Currently emphasizing cooking, child care/parenting, health. De-emphasizing general instructional books, travel." **Publishes 16 titles/year. 20% of books from first-time authors. 40% from unagented writers. Pays royalty. Pays average $2,500-10,000 advance.** Publishes ms 1 year after acceptance. Accepts simultaneous submissions. Responds in 2 months to queries. Guidelines online.

NONFICTION Subjects include child guidance. "A large percentage of our list is made up of books about cooking, child care, and parenting; in these areas we are looking for authors who are knowledgeable, if not experts, and who can offer a different approach to the subject. We are open to good nonfiction proposals that show evidence of strong organization and writing, and clearly demonstrate a need in the marketplace. First-time authors are welcome." Submit outline. Potential authors may also submit a query letter or e-mail of no more than 300 words, rather than a full proposal; if interested, will ask to see a proposal. Queries and questions may be sent via e-mail. "We will not consider e-mail attachments containing proposals. No phone calls, please."

TIPS "We are demanding about the quality of proposals; in addition to strong writing skills and thorough knowledge of the subject matter, we require a detailed analysis of the competition."

🅐🚫 HARVEST HOUSE PUBLISHERS

990 Owen Loop, Eugene OR 97402. (541)343-0123. **Fax:** (541)302-0731. **Website:** www.harvesthouse-publishers.com. Estab. 1974. Publishes hardcover, trade paperback, and mass market paperback originals and reprints. **Publishes 160 titles/year. 1,500 queries; 1,000 mss received/year. 1% of books from first-time authors. Pays royalty.** Accepts simultaneous submissions.

NONFICTION Subjects include child guidance, religion, Bible studies. *No unsolicited mss.*

FICTION *No unsolicited mss, proposals, or artwork.* Agented submissions only.

TIPS "For first time/nonpublished authors we suggest building their literary résumé by submitting to magazines, or perhaps accruing book contributions."

🅐 HAY HOUSE, INC.

P.O. Box 5100, Carlsbad CA 92018. (760)431-7695. **Fax:** (760)431-6948. **E-mail:** editorial@hayhouse.com. **Website:** www.hayhouse.com. Estab. 1985. Publishes hardcover, trade paperback and e-book/POD originals. "We publish books, audios, and videos that help heal the planet." **Publishes 50 titles/year. Pays standard royalty.** Accepts simultaneous submissions. Guidelines online.

IMPRINTS Hay House Lifestyles; Hay House Insights; Hay House Visions; SmileyBooks.

NONFICTION Subjects include alternative lifestyles, astrology, cooking, education, foods, health, New Age, nutrition, philosophy, psychic, psychology, sociology, spirituality, womens issues, mind/body/spirit. "Hay House is interested in a variety of subjects as long as they have a positive self-help slant to them. No poetry, children's books, or negative concepts that are not conducive to helping/healing ourselves or our planet." Accepts e-mail submissions from agents.

TIPS "Our audience is concerned with our planet, the healing properties of love, and general self-help principles. If I were a writer trying to market a book today, I would research the market thoroughly to make sure there weren't already too many books on the subject I was interested in writing about. Then I would make sure I had a unique slant on my idea. Simultaneous submissions from agents must include SASEs."

HEALTH COMMUNICATIONS, INC.

3201 SW 15th St., Deerfield Beach FL 33442. (954)360-0909, ext. 232. **Fax:** (954)360-0034. **E-mail:** editorial@hcibooks.com. **Website:** www.hcibooks.com. **Contact:** Editorial Committee. Estab. 1976. Publishes hardcover and trade paperback nonfiction only. "While HCI is a best known for recovery publishing, today recovery is only one part of a publishing program that includes titles in self-help and psychology, health and wellness, spirituality, inspiration, women's and men's issues, relationships, family, teens and children, memoirs, mind/body/spirit integration, and gift books." **Publishes 60 titles/year.** Accepts simultaneous submissions. Responds in 3-6 months. Guidelines online.

NONFICTION Subjects include child guidance, health, parenting, psychology, young adult, self-help.

TIPS "Due to the volume of submissions, Health Communications cannot guarantee response times or personalize responses to individual proposals. Under no circumstances do we accept phone calls or e-mails pitching submissions."

HEALTH PROFESSIONS PRESS

P.O. Box 10624, Baltimore MD 21285-0624. (410)337-9585. **Fax:** (410)337-8539. **E-mail:** mmagnus@healthpropress.com. **Website:** www.healthpropress.com. **Contact:** Acquisitions Department. Publishes hardcover and trade paperback originals. "We are a specialty publisher. Our primary audiences are professionals, students, and educated consumers interested in topics related to aging, eldercare, and healthcare management." **Publishes 8-10 titles/year. 70 queries; 12 mss received/year. 50% of books from first-time authors. 100% from unagented writers. Pays 8-15% royalty on wholesale price.** Publishes ms 8-10 months after acceptance. Accepts simultaneous submissions. Responds in 1 month to queries; 3 months

to proposals; 4 months to mss. Book catalog free or online. Guidelines online.

NONFICTION Subjects include health, psychology. Query with SASE. Submit proposal package, outline, resume, 1-2 sample chapters, cover letter.

WILLIAM S. HEIN & CO., INC.

2350 N. Forest Rd., Getzville NY 14068. (716)882-2600. **Fax:** (716)883-8100. **E-mail:** mail@wshein.com. **Website:** www.wshein.com. Estab. 1961. "William S. Hein & Co. publishes reference books for law librarians, legal researchers, and those interested in legal writing. Currently emphasizing legal research, legal writing, and legal education." **Publishes 18 titles/year. 30 queries received/year. 15 mss received/year. 30% of books from first-time authors. 99% from unagented writers. Pays 10-20% royalty on net price for print; higher royalties if published as an e-book.** Publishes book 9 months after acceptance. Accepts simultaneous submissions. Responds in 6 weeks to queries. Book catalog online. Guidelines by e-mail.

NONFICTION Subjects include education, law, world affairs, legislative histories.

HELLGATE PRESS

L&R Publishing, LLC, P.O. Box 3531, Ashland OR 97520. (541)973-5154. **E-mail:** sales@hellgatepress.com. **Website:** www.hellgatepress.com. **Contact:** Harley B. Patrick. Estab. 1996. "Hellgate Press specializes in military history, veteran memoirs, other military topics, travel adventure, and historical/adventure fiction." **Publishes 15-25 titles/year. 85% of books from first-time authors. 95% from unagented writers. Pays royalty.** Publishes ms 6-9 months after acceptance. Accepts simultaneous submissions. Responds in 2 months to queries.

NONFICTION Subjects include history, memoirs, military, war, womens issues, world affairs, young adult. Query/proposal by e-mail only. No phone queries, please. *Do not send mss.*

FICTION Subjects include historical, military, war, young adult.

HENDRICK-LONG PUBLISHING CO., INC.

10635 Tower Oaks, Suite D, Houston TX 77070. (832)912-READ. **Fax:** (832)912-7353. **E-mail:** hendrick-long@att.net. **Website:** hendricklongpublishing.com. Estab. 1969. Publishes hardcover and trade paperback originals and hardcover reprints. "Hendrick-Long publishes historical fiction and nonfiction about Texas and the Southwest for children and young adults." **Publishes 4 titles/year. 90% from unagented writers. Pays royalty on selling price. Pays advance.** Publishes ms 18 months after acceptance. Responds in 3 months to queries. Book catalog available. Guidelines online.

NONFICTION Subjects include history, regional. Subject must be Texas related; other subjects cannot be considered. "We are particularly interested in material from educators that can be used in the classroom as workbooks, math, science, history with a Texas theme or twist." Query, or submit outline and 2 sample chapters. Reviews artwork/photos. Send photocopies.

FICTION Subjects include juvenile, young adult. Query with SASE. Submit outline, clips, 2 sample chapters.

⊘ HENDRICKSON PUBLISHERS, INC.

P.O. Box 3473, Peabody MA 01961. **Fax:** (978)573-8276. **E-mail:** editorial@hendrickson.com. **Website:** www.hendrickson.com. Estab. 1981. Publishes trade reprints, bibles, and scholarly material in the areas of New Testament; Hebrew Bible; religion and culture; patristics; Judaism; and practical, historical, and Biblical theology. "Hendrickson is an academic publisher of Biblical scholarship and trade books that encourage spiritual growth. Currently emphasizing Biblical language and reference, pastoral resources, and Biblical studies." **Publishes 35 titles/year. 800 queries received/year. 10% of books from first-time authors. 90% from unagented writers.** Publishes ms 1 year after acceptance. Guidelines online.

NONFICTION Subjects include contemporary culture, creative nonfiction, education, entertainment, film, history, humanities, language, literature, religion, social sciences, spirituality. "We cannot accept unsolicited mss or book proposals except through one of the 2 following avenues: Materials sent to our editorial staff through a professional literary agent will be considered; Our staff would be happy to discuss book ideas at the various conferences we attend throughout the year (most notably, the AAR/SBL annual meeting)."

HERITAGE BOOKS, INC.

5810 Ruatan St., Berwyn Heights MD 20740. (800)876-6103. **E-mail:** info@heritagebooks.com. **E-mail:** submissions@heritagebooks.com. **Website:** www.heritagebooks.com. Estab. 1978. Publishes hardcover and paperback originals and reprints.

"Our goal is to celebrate life by exploring all aspects of American life: settlement, development, wars, and other significant events, including family histories, memoirs, etc. Currently emphasizing early American life, early wars and conflicts, ethnic studies." **Publishes 200 titles/year. 25% of books from first-time authors. 100% from unagented writers. Pays 10% royalty on list price. Does not pay advance.** Accepts simultaneous submissions. Responds in 3 months to queries. Book catalog and ms guidelines free.

NONFICTION Subjects include Americana, ethnic, history, memoirs, military, regional. Military memoirs. Query with SASE. Submit outline via e-mail. Reviews artwork/photos.

TIPS "The quality of the book is of prime importance; next is its relevance to our fields of interest."

♻ HERITAGE HOUSE PUBLISHING CO., LTD.

103-1075 Pendergast St., Victoria BC V8V 0A1, Canada. (250)360-0829. **E-mail:** heritage@heritagehouse.ca. **Website:** www.heritagehouse.ca. **Contact:** Lara Kordic, senior editor. Publishes mostly trade paperback and some hardcovers. "Heritage House publishes books that celebrate the historical and cultural heritage of Canada, particularly Western Canada and the Pacific Northwest. We also publish some children's titles, titles of national interest and a series of books aimed at young and casual readers, called *Amazing Stories*. We accept simultaneous submissions, but indicate on your query that it is a simultaneous submission." **Publishes 25-30 titles/year. 200 queries; 100 mss received/year. 50% of books from first-time authors. 90% from unagented writers. Pays 12-15% royalty on net proceeds. Advances are rarely paid.** Publishes book within 1-2 years of acceptance. Accepts simultaneous submissions. Responds in 6 months to queries. Catalog and guidelines online.

NONFICTION Subjects include animals, anthropology, art, business, community, contemporary culture, creative nonfiction, environment, ethnic, history, humanities, marine subjects, multicultural, politics, pop culture, public affairs, regional, war, womens issues, adventure, contemporary Canadian culture. Query by e-mail. Include synopsis, outline, 2-3 sample chapters with indication of illustrative material available, and marketing strategy.

TIPS "Our books appeal to residents of and visitors to the northwest quadrant of the continent. We're looking for good stories and good storytellers. We focus on work by Canadian authors."

HEYDAY BOOKS

c/o Acquisitions Editor, Box 9145, Berkeley CA 94709. **Fax:** (510)549-1889. **E-mail:** heyday@heydaybooks. com. **Website:** www.heydaybooks.com. **Contact:** Gayle Wattawa, acquisitions and editorial director. Estab. 1974. Publishes hardcover originals, trade paperback originals and reprints. "Heyday Books publishes nonfiction books and literary anthologies with a strong California focus. We publish books about Native Americans, natural history, history, literature, and recreation, with a strong California focus." **Publishes 12-15 titles/year. 50% of books from first-time authors. 90% from unagented writers. Pays 8% royalty on net price.** Publishes book 18 months after acceptance. Responds in 3 months. Book catalog online. Guidelines online.

NONFICTION Subjects include Americana, ethnic, history, recreation, regional, travel. Books about California only. Query with outline and synopsis. "Query or proposal by traditional post. Include a cover letter introducing yourself and your qualifications, a brief description of your project, a table of contents and list of illustrations, notes on the market you are trying to reach and why your book will appeal to them, a sample chapter, and a SASE if you would like us to return these materials to you." Reviews artwork/photos.

FICTION Publishes picture books, beginning readers, and young adult literature. Submit complete ms for picture books; proposal with sample chapters for longer works. include a chapter by chapter summary. Mark attention: Children's Submission. Reviews manuscript/illustration packages; but may consider art and text separately. Tries to respond to query within 12 weeks.

HIGH PLAINS PRESS

P.O. Box 123, 403 Cassa Rd., Glendo WY 82213. (307)735-4370. **Fax:** (307)735-4590. **E-mail:** editor@ highplainspress.com. **Website:** www.highplainspress. com. **Contact:** Nancy Curtis, publisher. Estab. 1984. Publishes hardcover and trade paperback originals. High Plains Press is a regional book publishing company specializing in books about the American West, with special interest in things relating to Wyoming. **Publishes 3 titles/year. 50 queries; 75 mss received/ year. 75% of books from first-time authors. 100% from unagented writers. Pays 10% royalty on whole-**

sale price. **Pays $200-2,000 advance.** Publishes book 2 years after acceptance of ms. Accepts simultaneous submissions. Responds in 1 month to queries and proposals; 6 months on mss. Book catalog and guidelines online.

NONFICTION Subjects include agriculture, Americana, environment, history, horticulture, memoirs, nature, regional, womens studies. "We consider only books with strong connection to the West." Query with SASE. Reviews artwork/photos. Send photocopies.

POETRY "We publish 1 poetry volume a year. Sometimes we skip a year. Require connection to West. Consider poetry in August." Submit 5 sample poems.

TIPS "Our audience comprises general readers interested in history and culture of the Rockies."

ⒶⓍ HILL AND WANG

Farrar Straus & Giroux, Inc., 18 W. 18th St., New York NY 10011. (212)741-6900. **Fax:** (212)633-9385. **Website:** www.fsgbooks.com. Estab. 1956. Publishes hardcover and trade paperbacks. "Hill and Wang publishes serious nonfiction books, primarily in history, science, mathematics and the social sciences. We are not considering new fiction, drama, or poetry." **Publishes 12 titles/year. 1,500 queries received/year. 50% of books from first-time authors. 50% from unagented writers.** Publishes ms 1 year after acceptance. Accepts simultaneous submissions. Book catalog available free.

NONFICTION Subjects include history. *Agented submissions only.*

LAWRENCE HILL BOOKS

Chicago Review Press, 814 N. Franklin St., 2nd Floor, Chicago IL 60610. (312)337-0747. **Fax:** (312)337-5110. **Website:** www.chicagoreviewpress.com. **Contact:** Yuval Taylor, senior editor. Publishes hardcover originals and trade paperback originals and reprints. **Publishes 3-10 titles/year. 20 queries; 10 mss received/ year. 40% of books from first-time authors. 50% from unagented writers. Pays 7-12% royalty on retail price. Pays $3,000-10,000 advance.** Publishes ms 1 year after acceptance. Accepts simultaneous submissions. Responds in 1 month to queries; 2 months to proposals and mss. Book catalog available free.

NONFICTION Subjects include ethnic, history, multicultural. Submit proposal package, outline, 2 sample chapters.

HIPPOCRENE BOOKS, INC.

171 Madison Ave., Suite 1605, New York NY 10016. 212-685-4371. **E-mail:** info@hippocrenebooks.com. **Website:** www.hippocrenebooks.com. Estab. 1971. *Mastering Arabic 1 and 2, Beginner's Russian with Interactive Online Workbook, Farsi Concise Dictionary, Tagalog Standard Dictionary, The Ghana Cookbook, Muy Bueno, Latin Twist, Healthy South Indian Cooking.* "Over the last forty years, Hippocrene Books has become one of America's foremost publishers of foreign language reference books and ethnic cookbooks. As a small publishing house in a marketplace dominated by conglomerates, Hippocrene has succeeded by continually reinventing its list while maintaining a strong international and ethnic orientation." Accepts simultaneous submissions. Please include summary, author background/resume including ability to promote book, sample chapter, table of contents, and audience. Do not send entire manuscript (hard copy or document file).

Hippocrene Books offers guides to over 120 languages and cookbooks in 80 inernational cuisines. We're seeking new languages not a part of our catalog, or additional titles in top-selling languages. Our cookbooks highlight a specific region or country, and stay clear of trends or fads.

FICTION No fiction is accepted.

POETRY Not seeking new poetry submissions.

HIPPOPOTAMUS PRESS

22 Whitewell Rd., Frome Somerset BA11 4EL, United Kingdom. (44)(173)466-6653. **E-mail:** rjhippopress@aol.com. **Contact:** R. John, editor; M. Pargitter (poetry); Anna Martin (translation). Estab. 1974. Publishes hardcover and trade paperback originals. "Hippopotamus Press publishes first, full collections of verse by those well represented in the mainstream poetry magazines of the English-speaking world." **Publishes 3 - 4 titles/year. 90% of books from first-time authors. 90% from unagented writers. Pays 7½-10% royalty on retail price. Pays advance.** Publishes book 10 months after acceptance. Accepts simultaneous submissions. Responds in 1 month to queries. Book catalog available free.

NONFICTION Subjects include literature. Query with SASE. Submit complete ms.

FICTION Subjects include poetry, poetry in translation.

POETRY "Read one of our authors—poets often make the mistake of submitting poetry without knowing the type of verse we publish." Query and submit complete ms.

TIPS "We publish books for a literate audience. We have a strong link to the Modernist tradition. Read what we publish."

HISTORY PUBLISHING COMPANY, LLC

P.O. Box 700, Palisades NY 10964. (845)359-1765. **Fax:** (845)231-6167. **E-mail:** djb@historypublishingco.com. **Website:** www.historypublishingco.com. **Contact:** Don Bracken, editorial director. Estab. 2001. Publishes hardcover and trade paperback originals and electronic books. "History Publishing is looking for interesting stories told in a creative nonfiction manner. Stories should be suitable for presentation on a television or motion picture screen. History Publishing Company will also consider select novels with an American history story line." **Publishes 20 titles/ year. Receives 45 submissions/year. 50% of books from first-time authors. 50% from unagented writers. Pays 7-10% royalty on wholesale list price. More if story is placed for optical presentation. Does not pay advances to unpublished authors.** Publishes ms 1 year after acceptance. Responds in 4 months to full mss. Guidelines online.

IMPRINTS Chronology Books; Today's Books.

NONFICTION Subjects include Americana, business, contemporary culture, creative nonfiction, environment, finance, government, history, memoirs, military, politics, social sciences, sociology, true crime, war, world affairs. Query with SASE. Submit proposal package, outline, 3 sample chapters or submit complete ms. Reviews artwork/photos. Send photocopies.

FICTION Subjects include adventure, historical, war.

TIPS "We focus on an audience interested in the events that shaped the world we live in and the events of today that continue to shape that world. Focus on interesting and serious events that will appeal to the contemporary reader who likes easy-to-read history that flows from one page to the next."

HOBAR PUBLICATIONS

A division of Finney Co., 5995 149th St. W., Suite 105, Apple Valley MN 55124. (952)469-6699. **Fax:** (952)469-1968. **E-mail:** feedback@finney-hobar.com; info@finneyco.com. **Website:** www.finney-hobar.com. **Contact:** Alan E. Krysan, president. Publishes trade paperback originals. "Hobar publishes career and technical educational materials." **Publishes 4-6 titles/year. 30 queries; 10 mss received/year. 35% of books from first-time authors. 100% from unagented writers. Pays 10% royalty on wholesale price. Does not pay advance.** Publishes ms 1 year after acceptance. Accepts simultaneous submissions. Responds in 10-12 weeks to queries.

NONFICTION Subjects include agriculture, animals, education, gardening, science, building trades. Query with SASE. Reviews artwork/photos.

HOHM PRESS

P.O. Box 4410, Chino Valley AZ 86323. (800)381-2700. **Fax:** (928)717-1779. **Website:** www.hohmpress.com. **Contact:** Acquisitions Editor. Estab. 1975. Publishes hardcover and trade paperback originals. "*Hohm Press* publishes a range of titles in the areas of transpersonal psychology and spirituality, herbistry, alternative health methods, and nutrition. Not interested in personal health survival stories." **Publishes 6-8 titles/year. 50% of books from first-time authors. Pays 10% royalty on net sales.** Publishes ms 18 months after acceptance. Accepts simultaneous submissions. Responds in 3 months to queries.

NONFICTION Subjects include philosophy, religion, yoga. "We look for writers who have an established record in their field of expertise. The best buy of recent years came from 2 women who fully substantiated how they could market their book. We believed they could do it. We were right." No children's books please. Query with SASE. No e-mail inquiries, please.

POETRY "We are not accepting poetry at this time except for translations of recognized religious/spiritual classics."

HOLIDAY HOUSE, INC.

425 Madison Ave., New York NY 10017. (212)688-0085. **Fax:** (212)421-6134. **E-mail:** info@holidayhouse.com. **Website:** holidayhouse.com. Estab. 1935. Publishes hardcover originals and paperback reprints. "Holiday House publishes children's and young adult books for the school and library markets. We have a commitment to publishing first-time authors and illustrators. We specialize in quality hardcovers from picture books to young adult, both fiction and nonfiction, primarily for the school and library market." **Publishes 50 titles/year. 5% of books from first-time authors. 50% from unagented writers. Pays royalty on list price, range varies.** Publishes 1-2 years after acceptance. Responds in 4 months. Guidelines for #10 SASE.

NONFICTION Subjects include Americana, history, science, Judaica. Please send the entire ms, whether submitting a picture book or novel. "All submissions should be directed to the Editorial Department, Holiday House. We do not accept certified or registered mail. There is no need to include a SASE. We do not consider submissions by e-mail or fax. Please note that you do not have to supply illustrations. However, if you have illustrations you would like to include with your submission, you may send detailed sketches or photocopies of the original art. Do not send original art." Reviews artwork/photos. Send photocopies-no originals.

FICTION Subjects include adventure, historical, humor, literary, Judaica and holiday, animal stories for young readers. Children's books only. Query with SASE. No phone calls, please.

TIPS "We need manuscripts with strong stories and writing."

⚠ ⊘ HENRY HOLT

175 Fifth Ave., New York NY 10011. (646)307-5095. **Fax:** (212)633-0748. **Website:** www.henryholt.com. *Agented submissions only.* Accepts simultaneous submissions.

HOLY CROSS ORTHODOX PRESS

Hellenic College, Inc., 50 Goddard Ave., Brookline MA 02445. (617)850-1321. **Fax:** (617)850-1457. **E-mail:** press@hchc.edu. **Website:** www.hchc.edu/community/administrative_offices/holy.cross.orthodox.press/. **Contact:** Mrs. Sarah Parro, production manager. Managing Director: Kevin Kovalycsik (kkovalycsik@hchc.edu). Estab. 1974. Publishes trade paperback originals. "Holy Cross publishes titles that are rooted in the tradition of the Eastern Orthodox Church." **Publishes 8 titles/year. 10-15 queries; 10-15 mss received/year. 85% of books from first-time authors. 100% from unagented writers. Pays 10% royalty on net revenue from retail sales.** Publishes ms 2 years after acceptance. Accepts simultaneous submissions. Responds in 6 months to mss. Guidelines online.

NONFICTION Subjects include ethnic, religion. Holy Cross Orthodox Press publishes scholarly and popular literature in the areas of Orthodox Christian theology and Greek letters. Submissions are often far too technical usually with very limited audiences.

Submit outline. Submit complete ms. Reviews artwork/photos. Digital formats preferred.

HOPEWELL PUBLICATIONS

P.O. Box 11, Titusville NJ 08560. **Website:** www.hopepubs.com. **Contact:** E. Martin, publisher. Estab. 2002. Format publishes in hardcover, trade paperback, and electronic originals; trade paperback and electronic reprints. "Hopewell Publications specializes in classic reprints—books with proven sales records that have gone out of print—and the occasional new title of interest. Our catalog spans from 1 to 60 years of publication history. We print fiction and nonfiction, and we accept agented and unagented materials. Submissions are accepted online only." **Publishes 20-30 titles/year. Receives 2,000 queries/year; 500 mss/year. 25% of books from first-time authors. 75% from unagented writers. Pays royalty on retail price.** Publishes ms 6-12 months after acceptance. Accepts simultaneous submissions. Responds in 3 months to queries; 6 months to proposals; 9 months to mss. Catalog online. Guidelines online.

IMPRINTS Egress Books, Legacy Classics.

NONFICTION Subjects include All nonfiction subjects acceptable. Query online using online guidelines.

FICTION Subjects include adventure, contemporary, experimental, fantasy, gay, historical, humor, juvenile, literary, mainstream, mystery, plays, short story collections, spiritual, suspense, young adult, All fiction subjects acceptable. Query online using our online guidelines.

HOUGHTON MIFFLIN HARCOURT BOOKS FOR CHILDREN

Imprint of Houghton Mifflin Trade & Reference Division, 222 Berkeley St., Boston MA 02116. (617)351-5000. **Fax:** (617)351-1111. **Website:** www.houghtonmifflinbooks.com. Publishes hardcover originals and trade paperback originals and reprints. Houghton Mifflin Harcourt gives shape to ideas that educate, inform, and above all, delight. *Does not respond to or return mss unless interested.* **Publishes 100 titles/year. 5,000 queries received/year. 14,000 mss received/year. 10% of books from first-time authors. 60% from unagented writers. Pays 5-10% royalty on retail price. Pays variable advance.** Publishes ms 2 years after acceptance. Accepts simultaneous submissions. Responds in 4-6 months to queries. Guidelines online.

NONFICTION Subjects include animals, ethnic, history, science, sports. Interested in innovative books and subjects about which the author is passionate. Query with SASE. Submit sample chapters, synopsis. Reviews artwork/photos. Send photocopies.

FICTION Subjects include adventure, ethnic, historical, humor, juvenile, literary, mystery, picture books, suspense, young adult, board books. Submit complete ms.

ⒶⓄ HOUGHTON MIFFLIN HARCOURT CO.

222 Berkeley St., Boston MA 02116. (617)351-5000. **Website:** www.hmhco.com. Estab. 1832. Publishes hardcover originals and trade paperback originals and reprints. "Houghton Mifflin Harcourt gives shape to ideas that educate, inform and delight. In a new era of publishing, our legacy of quality thrives as we combine imagination with technology, bringing you new ways to know." Accepts simultaneous submissions.

NONFICTION "We are not a mass market publisher. Our main focus is serious nonfiction. We do practical self-help but not pop psychology self-help." *Agented submissions only. Unsolicited mss returned unopened.*

ⒸⓄ HOUSE OF ANANSI PRESS

128 Sterling Rd., Lower Level, Toronto ON M6R 2B7, Canada. (416)363-4343. **Fax:** (416)363-1017. **Website:** www.anansi.ca. Estab. 1967. House of Anansi publishes literary fiction and poetry by Canadian and international writers. **Pays 8-10% royalties. Pays $750 advance and 10 author's copies.** Responds to queries within 1 year; to mss (if invited) within 4 months. Accepts simultaneous submissions.

NONFICTION Avoids dry, jargon-filled academic prose and has a literary twist that will interest general readers and experts alike. Query with SASE.

FICTION Publishes literary fiction that has a unique flair, memorable characters, and a strong narrative voice. Query with SASE.

POETRY "We seek to balance the list between well-known and emerging writers, with an interest in writing by Canadians of all backgrounds. We publish Canadian poetry only, and poets must have a substantial publication record—if not in books, then definitely in journals and magazines of repute." Does not want "children's poetry or poetry by previously unpublished poets." Canadian poets should query first with 10 sample poems (typed double-spaced) and a cover letter with brief bio and publication credits. Considers simultaneous submissions. Poems are circulated to an editorial board. Often comments on rejected poems.

HOW BOOKS

F+W, a Content + eCommerce Company, 10151 Carver Rd., Suite 200, Blue Ash OH 45242. (513)531-2690. **Website:** www.howdesign.com. Estab. 1985. Publishes hardcover and trade paperback originals. **Publishes 15 titles/year. 50 queries; 5 mss received/year. 50% of books from first-time authors. 50% from unagented writers. Pays 10% royalty on wholesale price. Pays $2,000-6,000 advance.** Publishes ms 18-24 months after acceptance. Accepts simultaneous submissions. Responds in 1 month to queries and proposals; 3 months to mss. Book catalog available online. Guidelines available online.

NONFICTION Subjects include , graphic design, web design, creativity, pop culture. "We look for material that reflects the cutting edge of trends, graphic design, and culture. Nearly all HOW Books are intensely visual, and authors must be able to create or supply art/illustration for their books." Query via e-mail. Submit proposal package, outline, 1 sample chapter, sample art or sample design. Reviews artwork/photos. Send as PDF's.

TIPS "Audience comprised of graphic designers. Your art, design, or concept."

HUMAN KINETICS PUBLISHERS, INC.

P.O. Box 5076, Champaign IL 61825-5076. (800)747-4457. **Fax:** (217)351-1549. **E-mail:** acquisitions@hkusa.com. **Website:** www.humankinetics.com. Estab. 1974. Publishes hardcover, ebooks, and paperback text and reference books, trade paperback originals, course software and audiovisual. "*Human Kinetics* publishes books which provide expert knowledge in sport and fitness training and techniques, physical education, sports sciences and sports medicine for coaches, athletes and fitness enthusiasts and professionals in the physical action field." **Publishes 160 titles/year. Pays 10-15% royalty on net income.** Publishes ms up to 18 months after acceptance. Accepts simultaneous submissions. Responds in 2 months to queries. Book catalog available free. Guidelines online.

NONFICTION Subjects include education, psychology, recreation, sports. "Here is a current listing of our divisions: Amer. Sport Education; Aquatics Edu.; Professional Edu.; HPERD Div., Journal Div.; STM Div., Trade Div." Submit outline, sample chapters. Reviews artwork/photos.

IBEX PUBLISHERS

P.O. Box 30087, Bethesda MD 20824. (301)718-8188. **Fax:** (301)907-8707. **E-mail:** info@ibexpub.com. **Website:** www.ibexpublishers.com. Estab. 1979. Publishes hardcover and trade paperback originals and reprints. "Ibex publishes books about Iran and the Middle East and about Persian culture and literature." **Publishes 10-12 titles/year. Payment varies.** Accepts simultaneous submissions. Book catalog available free.

IMPRINTS Iranbooks Press.

NONFICTION Subjects include history, humanities, language, literary criticism, literature, spirituality, translation. Query with SASE, or submit proposal package, including outline and 2 sample chapters.

POETRY "Translations of Persian poets will be considered."

ICONOGRAFIX/ENTHUSIAST BOOKS

2017 O'Neil Rd., Hudson WI 54016. (715)381-9755. **Website:** www.enthusiastbooks.com. Estab. 1992. Publishes trade paperback originals. "Iconografix publishes special, historical-interest photographic books for transportation equipment enthusiasts. Currently emphasizing emergency vehicles, buses, trucks, railroads, automobiles, auto racing, construction equipment, snowmobiles." **Publishes 6-10 titles/year. 50 queries received/year. 20 mss received/year. 50% of books from first-time authors. 100% from unagented writers. Pays 8-12% royalty on wholesale price. Pays $1,000-3,000 advance.** Publishes book 1 year after acceptance. Accepts simultaneous submissions. Responds in 1 month to queries; 3 months to proposals and mss. Book catalog and ms guidelines free.

NONFICTION Subjects include Americana, history, hobbies, transportation (older photos of specific vehicles). Interested in photo archives. Query with SASE, or submit proposal package, including outline. Reviews artwork/photos. Send photocopies.

IDW PUBLISHING

2765 Truxtun Rd., San Diego CA 92106. **E-mail:** letters@idwpublishing.com. **Website:** www.idwpublishing.com. Estab. 1999. Publishes hardcover, mass market and trade paperback originals. IDW Publishing currently publishes a wide range of comic books and graphic novels including titles based on GI Joe, Star Trek, Terminator: Salvation, and Transformers. Creator-driven titles include Fallen Angel by Peter David and JK Woodward, Locke & Key by Joe Hill and Gabriel Rodriguez, and a variety of titles by writer Steve Niles including Wake the Dead, Epilogue, and Dead, She Said. Accepts simultaneous submissions.

IDYLL ARBOR, INC.

39129 264th Ave. SE, Enumclaw WA 98022. (360)825-7797. **Fax:** (360)825-5670. **E-mail:** editors@idyllarbor.com. **Website:** www.idyllarbor.com. **Contact:** Tom Blaschko. Estab. 1984. Publishes hardcover and trade paperback originals, and trade paperback reprints. "Idyll Arbor publishes practical information on the current state and art of healthcare practice. Currently emphasizing therapies (recreational, horticultural), and activity directors in long-term care facilities. Issues Press looks at problems in society from video games to returning veterans and their problems reintegrating into the civilian world. Pine Winds Press publishes books about strange phenomena such as Bigfoot and the life force." **Publishes 6 titles/year. 40% of books from first-time authors. 100% from unagented writers. Pays 8-15% royalty on wholesale price or retail price.** Publishes book 1 year after acceptance. Accepts simultaneous submissions. Responds in 1 month; 2 months to proposals; 6 months to mss. Book catalog and ms guidelines free.

IMPRINTS Issues Press; Pine Winds Press.

NONFICTION Subjects include health, medicine, New Age, psychic, psychology, recreation, science, spirituality, horticulture (used in long-term care activities or health care therapy). "Idyll Arbor is currently developing a line of books under the imprint Issues Press, which treats emotional issues in a clear-headed manner. We look for mss from authors with recent clinical experience. Good grounding in theory is required, but practical experience is more important." Query preferred with outline and 1 sample chapter. Reviews artwork/photos. Send photocopies.

TIPS "The books must be useful for the health practitioner who meets face to face with patients or the books must be useful for teaching undergraduate and graduate level classes. Pine Winds Press books should be compatible with the model of the soul found on weallhavesouls.com."

ILIUM PRESS

2407 S. Sonora Dr., Spokane WA 99037. (509)701-8866. **E-mail:** iliumpress@outlook.com. **Contact:** John Lemon, owner/editor. Estab. 2010. Publishes trade paperback originals and reprints, electronic originals and reprints. "Ilium Press is a small, 1-person press that I created to cultivate and promote the relevance of epic poetry in today's world. My focus is book-length narrative poems in blank (non-rhyming) metered verse, such as iambic parameter or sprung verse. I am very selective about my projects, but I provide extensive editorial care to those projects I take on." **Publishes 1-3 titles/year. 25% of books from first-time authors. Pays 20-50% royalties on receipts. Does not pay advance.** Publishes ms up to 1 year after acceptance. Accepts simultaneous submissions. Responds in 6 months.

POETRY Ilium Press specializes in original, book-length narrative epic poems written in blank (non-rhyming) metered verse (such as iambic pentameter or sprung verse) in contemporary language. "I'm looking for original work that shows how epic poetry is still relevant in today's world. Please query via e-mail if you have questions." Submit via e-mail (preferred) or via mail with first 20 pages. Don't forget to include your contact information!

ILR PRESS

Cornell University Press, Sage House, 512 E. State St., Ithaca NY 14850. (607)277-2338. **Fax:** (607)277-2374. **E-mail:** fgb2@cornell.edu. **Website:** www.ilr.cornell.edu/ilrpress. **Contact:** Frances Benson, editorial director. Estab. 1945. Publishes hardcover and trade paperback originals and reprints. "We are interested in manuscripts with innovative perspectives on current workplace issues that concern both academics and the general public." **Publishes 10-15 titles/year. Pays royalty.** Responds in 2 months to queries. Book catalog available free. Guidelines online.

NONFICTION Subjects include history, sociology. All titles relate to labor relations and/or workplace issues including relevant work in the fields of history, sociology, political science, economics, human resources, and organizational behavior. Special series: culture and politics of health care work. Query with SASE. Submit outline, sample chapters, CV.

TIPS "Manuscripts must be well documented to pass our editorial evaluation, which includes review by academics in related fields."

IMAGE COMICS

2701 NW Vaughn St., Suite 780, Portland OR 97210. **E-mail:** submissions@imagecomics.com. **Website:** www.imagecomics.com. Estab. 1992. Publishes creator-owned comic books, graphic novels. See this company's website for detailed guidelines. Does not accept writing samples without art. Accepts simultaneous submissions.

FICTION Query with 1-page synopsis and 5 pages or more of samples. "We do not accept writing (that is plots, scripts, whatever) samples! If you're an established pro, we might be able to find somebody willing to work with you but it would be nearly impossible for us to read through every script that might find its way our direction. Do not send your script or your plot unaccompanied by art—it will be discarded, unread."

TIPS "We are not looking for any specific genre or type of comic book. We are looking for comics that are well written and well drawn, by people who are dedicated and can meet deadlines."

IMBRIFEX BOOKS

Flattop Productions, Inc., 8275 S. Eastern Ave., Suite 200, Las Vegas NV 89123. (702)309-0130. **E-mail:** acquisitions@imbrifex.com. **Website:** https://imbrifex.com. **Contact:** Mark Sedenquist. Estab. 2016. Based in Las Vegas, Nevada, Imbrifex Books publishes both fiction and nonfiction, with a particular interest in books for road trip aficionados and books that have a connection with Las Vegas and the desert Southwest. Titles are distributed world-wide through Legato Publishers Group, IPS and Audible.com. **Publishes 6-8 titles/year. 70% of books from first-time authors. 60% from unagented writers. Pays advance.** Accepts simultaneous submissions. Responds in 2 months. Guidelines online.

NONFICTION Subjects include community, marine subjects, multicultural, travel, true crime, womens issues, young adult.

FICTION Subjects include adventure, experimental, feminist, gay, humor, lesbian, literary, mainstream, multicultural, mystery, poetry, short story collections, suspense.

IMMEDIUM

P.O. Box 31846, San Francisco CA 94131. (415)452-8546. **Fax:** (360)937-6272. **Website:** www.immedium.com. **Contact:** Submissions Editor. Estab. 2005. Publishes hardcover and trade paperback originals. "Immedium focuses on publishing eye-catching children's picture books, Asian-American topics, and contemporary arts, popular culture, and multicultural issues." **Publishes 4 titles/year. 50 queries received/year. 25 mss received/year. 50% of books from first-time authors. 90% from unagented writers. Pays 5% royalty on wholesale price. Pays on**

publication. Publishes book 2 years after acceptance. Accepts simultaneous submissions. Responds in 1-3 months. Catalog online. Guidelines online.

NONFICTION Subjects include multicultural. Submit complete ms. Reviews artwork/photos. Send photocopies.

FICTION Subjects include comic books, picture books. Submit complete ms.

TIPS "Our audience is children and parents. Please visit our site."

IMPACT BOOKS

F+W Media, Inc., 10151 Carver Rd., Suite 200, Blue Ash OH 45242. **E-mail:** mona.clough@fwmedia.com. **Website:** www.northlightshop.com; www.impactbooks.com. **Contact:** Mona Clough, content director (art instruction for fantasy, comics, manga, anime, popular culture, science fiction, cartooning and body art). Estab. 2004. Publishes trade paperback originals. IMPACT Books publishes titles that emphasize illustrated how-to-draw-manga, science- fiction, fantasy and comics art instruction. Currently emphasizing manga and anime art, science fiction, traditional American comics styles, including humor, and pop art. Looking for good science fiction art instruction. This market is for experienced artists who are willing to work with an IMPACT editor to produce a step-by-step how-to book about how to create the art and the artist's creative process. **Publishes 9 titles/year. 50 queries; 10-12 mss received/year. 70% of books from first-time authors. 80% from unagented writers. Pays advance.** Publishes ms 11 months after acceptance. Accepts simultaneous submissions. Responds in 4 months. Visit website for booklist. Guidelines available online.

NONFICTION Subjects include art, contemporary culture, creative nonfiction, hobbies. Submit via email only. Submit proposal package, outline, 1 sample chapter, at least 20 examples of sample art. Reviews artwork/photos. Send digital art.

TIPS "Audience comprised primarily of 12- to 18-year-old beginners along the lines of comic buyers, in general—mostly teenagers—but also appealing to a broader audience of young adults 19-30 who need basic techniques. Art must appeal to teenagers and be submitted in a form that will reproduce well. Authors need to know how to teach beginners step-by-step. A sample step-by-step demonstration is important."

IMPACT PUBLISHERS, INC.

5674 Shattuck Ave., Oakland CA 94609. **E-mail:** proposals@newharbinger.com. **Website:** www.newharbinger.com/imprint/impact-publishers. **Contact:** Acquisitions Department. Estab. 1970. "Our purpose is to make the best human services expertise available to the widest possible audience. We publish only popular psychology and self-help materials written in everyday language by professionals with advanced degrees and significant experience in the human services." **Publishes 3-5 titles/year. 20% of books from first-time authors. Pays authors royalty of 10-12%. Offers advances.** Accepts simultaneous submissions. Responds in 3 months. Book catalog for #10 SASE with 2 first-class stamps. Guidelines for SASE.

IMPRINTS Little Imp Books, Rebuilding Books, The Practical Therapist Series.

NONFICTION Young readers, middle readers, young adults: self-help. Query or submit complete ms, cover letter, résumé.

TIPS "Please do not submit fiction, poetry or narratives."

INCENTIVE PUBLICATIONS, INC.

233 N. Michigan Ave., Suite 2000, Chicago IL 60601. **E-mail:** incentive@worldbook.com. **Website:** www.incentivepublications.com. Estab. 1970. Publishes paperback originals. "Incentive publishes developmentally appropriate teacher/school administrator/parent resource materials and supplementary instructional materials for children in grades K-12. Actively seeking proposals for student workbooks, all grades/all subjects, and professional development resources for pre K-12 classroom teachers and school administrators." **Publishes 10-15 titles/year. 25% of books from first-time authors. 100, but agent proposals welcome% from unagented writers. Pays royalty, or makes outright purchase.** an average of 1 year Accepts simultaneous submissions. Responds in 1 month to queries.

NONFICTION Subjects include education. Instructional, teacher/administrator professional development books in pre-K through 12th grade. Query with synopsis and detailed outline.

INDIANA HISTORICAL SOCIETY PRESS

450 W. Ohio St., Indianapolis IN 46202. (317)233-6073. **Fax:** (317)233-0857. **E-mail:** ihspress@indianahistory.org. **Website:** www.indianahistory.org. **Contact:** Submissions Editor. Estab. 1830. Publishes hardcover and paperback originals. **Publishes 10 titles/year.** Accepts simultaneous submissions. Responds in 1 month to queries.

NONFICTION Subjects include agriculture, ethnic, history, sports, family history, children's books. All topics must relate to Indiana. "We seek book-length manuscripts that are solidly researched and engagingly written on topics related to Indiana: biography, history, literature, music, politics, transportation, sports, agriculture, architecture, and children's books." Query with SASE.

INFORMATION TODAY, INC.

143 Old Marlton Pike, Medford NJ 08055. (609)654-6266. **Fax:** (609)654-4309. **E-mail:** rcolding@infotoday.com. **Website:** www.infotoday.com. **Contact:** Rob Colding, Book Marketing Manager. Publishes hardcover and trade paperback originals. "We look for highly-focused coverage of cutting-edge technology topics. Written by established experts and targeted to a tech-savvy readership. Virtually all our titles focus on how information is accessed, used, shared, and transformed into knowledge that can benefit people, business, and society. Currently emphasizing Web 2.0, internet/online technologies, including their social significance: biography, how-to, technical, reference, scholarly. De-emphasizing fiction." **Publishes 15-20 titles/year. 200 queries; 30 mss received/year. 30% of books from first-time authors. 90% from unagented writers. Pays 10-15% royalty on wholesale price. Pays $500-2,500 advance.** Publishes book 9 months after acceptance. Accepts simultaneous submissions. Responds in 1 month to queries; 2 months to proposals; 3 months to mss. Book catalog free or on website. Proposal guidelines free or via e-mail as attachment.

IMPRINTS ITI (academic, scholarly, library science); CyberAge Books (high-end consumer and business technology books-emphasis on Internet/WWW topics including online research).

NONFICTION Subjects include business, computers, education, science, Internet and cyberculture. Query with SASE. Reviews artwork/photos. Send photocopies.

TIPS "Our readers include scholars, academics, educators, indexers, librarians, information professionals (ITI imprint), as well as high-end consumer and business users of Internet/WWW/online technologies, and people interested in the marriage of technology with issues of social significance (i.e., Web 2.0 relevance)."

INSOMNIAC PRESS

520 Princess Ave., London ON N6B 2B8, Canada. (416)504-6270. **Website:** www.insomniacpress.com. Estab. 1992. Publishes trade paperback originals and reprints, mass market paperback originals, and electronic originals and reprints. **Publishes 20 titles/year. 250 queries received/year. 1,000 mss received/year. 50% of books from first-time authors. 80% from unagented writers. Pays 10-15% royalty on retail price. Pays $500-1,000 advance.** Publishes ms 6 months after acceptance. Accepts simultaneous submissions. Guidelines online.

NONFICTION Subjects include multicultural, religion, true crime. Very interested in areas such as true crime and well-written and well-researched nonfiction on topics of wide interest. Query via e-mail, submit proposal package including outline, 2 sample chapters, or submit complete ms. Reviews artwork/photos. Send photocopies.

FICTION Subjects include comic books, ethnic, experimental, humor, literary, mystery, poetry, suspense. "We publish a mix of commercial (mysteries) and literary fiction." Query via e-mail, submit proposal.

POETRY "Our poetry publishing is limited to 2-4 books per year and we are often booked up a year or two in advance." Submit complete ms.

TIPS "We envision a mixed readership that appreciates up-and-coming literary fiction and poetry as well as solidly researched and provocative nonfiction. Peruse our website and familiarize yourself with what we've published in the past."

INTERLINK PUBLISHING GROUP, INC.

46 Crosby St., Northampton MA 01060. (413)582-7054. **E-mail:** info@interlinkbooks.com. **E-mail:** submissions@interlinkbooks.com. **Website:** www.interlinkbooks.com. Estab. 1987. Publishes hardcover and trade paperback originals. Interlink is an independent publisher of general trade adult fiction and nonfiction with an emphasis on books that have a wide appeal while also meeting high intellectual and literary standards. "Our list is devoted to works of literature, history, contemporary politics, travel, art, and cuisine from around the world, often from areas underrepresented in Western media." **Publishes 50 titles/year. 30% of books from first-time authors. 50% from unagented writers. Pays 6-8% royalty on retail price.**

Pays small advance. Publishes ms 18 months after acceptance. Accepts simultaneous submissions. Responds in 3-6 months to queries. Book catalog and guidelines online.

IMPRINTS Olive Branch Press; Crocodile Books; Interlink Books.

NONFICTION Subjects include contemporary culture, creative nonfiction, ethnic, foods, history, humanities, literary criticism, literature, multicultural, politics, regional, translation, war, womens issues, world affairs. Submit outline and sample chapters via e-mail.

FICTION Subjects include ethnic, feminist, literary, multicultural, translation, international. "We are looking for translated works relating to the Middle East, Africa or Latin America. The only fiction we publish falls into our 'Interlink World Fiction' series. Most of these books, as you can see in our catalog, are translated fiction from around the world. The series aims to bring fiction from other countries to a North American audience. In short, unless you were born outside the United States, your novel will not fit into the series." No science fiction, romance, plays, erotica, fantasy, horror. Query by e-mail. Submit outline, sample chapters.

TIPS "Any submissions that fit well in our publishing program will receive careful attention. A visit to our website, your local bookstore, or library to look at some of our books before you send in your submission is recommended."

INTERNATIONAL FOUNDATION OF EMPLOYEE BENEFIT PLANS

18700 W. Bluemound Rd., Brookfield WI 53045. (262)786-6700. **Fax:** (262)786-8780. **Website:** www.ifebp.org. Estab. 1954. Publishes trade paperback originals. IFEBP publishes general and technical monographs on all aspects of employee benefits—pension plans, health insurance, etc. **Publishes 6 titles/year. 15% of books from first-time authors. 80% from unagented writers. Pays 5-15% royalty on wholesale and retail price.** Publishes ms 1 year after acceptance. Accepts simultaneous submissions. Responds in 3 months to queries. Book catalog online. Guidelines online.

NONFICTION Subjects limited to health care, pensions, retirement planning and employee benefits and compensation. Query with outline.

TIPS "Be aware of interests of employers and the marketplace in benefits topics, for example, pension plan changes, healthcare cost containment."

INTERNATIONAL MARINE

The McGraw-Hill Companies, 90 Mechanic St., Camden ME 04843. (207)236-4838. **Fax:** (207)236-6314. **E-mail:** christopher.brown@mheducation.com. **Website:** www.internationalmarine.com. **Contact:** Acquisitions Editor. Estab. 1969. Publishes hardcover and paperback originals. International Marine publishes the best books about boats. **Publishes 50 titles/year. 500-700 mss received/year. 30% of books from first-time authors. 60% from unagented writers. Pays standard royalties based on net price. Pays advance.** Publishes ms 1 year after acceptance. Accepts simultaneous submissions. Responds in 2 months to queries. Guidelines online.

IMPRINTS Ragged Mountain Press (sports and outdoor books that take you off the beaten path).

NONFICTION All books are illustrated. Material in all stages welcome. Publishes a wide range of subjects include: sea stories, seamanship, boat maintenance, etc. Query first with outline and 2-3 sample chapters. Reviews artwork/photos.

TIPS "Writers should be aware of the need for clarity, accuracy and interest. Many progress too far in the actual writing."

INTERNATIONAL PRESS

P.O. Box 502, Somerville MA 02143. (617)623-3855. **Fax:** (617)623-3101. **E-mail:** ipb-mgmt@intlpress.com. **Website:** www.intlpress.com. **Contact:** Brian Bianchini. Estab. 1992. Publishes hardcover originals and reprints. International Press of Boston, Inc. is an academic publishing company that welcomes book publication inquiries from prospective authors on all topics in Mathematics and Physics. International Press also publishes high-level mathematics and mathematical physics book titles and textbooks. **Publishes 12 titles/year. 200 queries received/year. 500 mss received/year. 10% of books from first-time authors. 100% from unagented writers. Pays 3-10% royalty.** Publishes ms 6 months after acceptance. Responds in 5 months to queries and proposals; 1 year to mss. Book catalog available free. Guidelines online.

NONFICTION Subjects include science. All our books will be in research mathematics. Authors need to provide ready to print latex files. Submit complete ms. Reviews artwork/photos. Send EPS files.

TIPS "Audience is PhD mathematicians, researchers and students."

INTERNATIONAL SOCIETY FOR TECHNOLOGY IN EDUCATION (ISTE)

1530 Wilson Blvd., Suite 730, Arlington VA 22209. (703)348-4784. **E-mail:** iste@iste.org. **Website:** www.iste.org. Publishes trade paperback originals. "Currently emphasizing books on educational technology standards, curriculum integration, professional development, and assessment. De-emphasizing software how-to books." **Publishes 10 titles/year. 100 queries received/year. 40 mss received/year. 75% of books from first-time authors. 95% from unagented writers. Pays 10% royalty on retail price.** Publishes ms 6-9 months after acceptance. Accepts simultaneous submissions. Responds in 2 weeks to queries; 1 month to proposals and mss. Book catalog and guidelines online.

NONFICTION Submit proposal package, outline, sample chapters, TOC, vita. Reviews artwork/photos. Send photocopies.

TIPS "Our audience is K-12 teachers, teacher educators, technology coordinators, and school and district administrators."

INTERNATIONAL WEALTH SUCCESS INC.

IWS Inc., P.O. Box 186, Merrick NY 11570. (516)766-5850. **Fax:** (516)766-5919. **E-mail:** admin@iwsmoney.com. **Website:** www.iwsmoney.com. **Contact:** Tyler G. Hicks, president. Estab. 1966. International Wealth Success Inc. (IWS) is a full-service newsletter, book and self-study course publisher of print and digital media on small business and income real estate. The company's mission is to help beginning and experienced business people choose, start, finance, and succeed in their own small businesses. Topics include real estate investment, import-export, mail order, home-based business, marketing, fundraising, and financing. **Publishes 10 titles/year. Pays 10% royalty on wholesale or retail price.** Publishes ms 4 months after acceptance. Accepts simultaneous submissions. Responds within 1 month to queries. Catalog online.

NONFICTION Subjects include business, career guidance, finance, real estate, private money, financial institutions, homebased business, marketing, export-import, grants and fundraising. Techniques, methods, sources for building wealth. Personal, how-to-do-it with case histories and examples. Publications are aimed at aspiring wealth builders and are sympathetic to their problems and challenges. Publications present a wide range of business opportunities while providing practical, hands-on, step-by-step instructions aimed at helping readers achieve their personal goals in as short a time as possible while adhering to ethical and professional business standards. Length: 60,000-70,000 words. Does not want anything that doesn't pertain to small business, entrepreneurism, business opportunities, or real estate. Query. Reviews artwork/photos.

INTERVARSITY PRESS

P.O. Box 1400, Downers Grove IL 60515. **E-mail:** email@ivpress.com. **Website:** www.ivpress.com/submissions. Estab. 1947. Publishes hardcover originals, trade paperback and mass market paperback originals. "InterVarsity Press publishes a full line of books from an evangelical Christian perspective targeted to an open-minded audience. We serve those in the university, the church, and the world, by publishing books from an evangelical Christian perspective." **Publishes 115 titles/year. 1,000 queries; 900 mss received/year. 13% of books from first-time authors. 80% from unagented writers. Pays 14-16% royalty on retail price. Outright purchase is $75-1,500. Pays negotiable advance.** Publishes book 18 months after acceptance. Accepts simultaneous submissions. "We are unable to provide updates on the review process or personalized responses to unsolicited proposals. We regret that submissions will not be returned." Book catalog online. Guidelines online.

IMPRINTS IVP Academic; IVP Connect; IVP Books.

NONFICTION Subjects include business, child guidance, contemporary culture, economics, ethnic, history, multicultural, philosophy, psychology, religion, science, social sciences, sociology, spirituality. "InterVarsity Press publishes a full line of books from an evangelical Christian perspective targeted to an open-minded audience. We serve those in the university, the church, and the world, by publishing books from an evangelical Christian perspective. We review The Writer's Edge at writersedgeservice.com." Does not review artwork.

TIPS "The best way to submit to us is to go to a conference where one of our editors is attending. Networking is key. We are seeking writers who have good ideas and a presence/platform where they have been testing out their ideas (a church, university, on a prominent blog). We need authors who will bring resources to the table for helping to publicize and sell their books (speaking at seminars and conferences, writing for national magazines or newspapers, etc.)."

INTERWEAVE PRESS

F+W Media, Inc., 4868 Innovation Dr, Ft. Collins CO 80525. (970)669-7672. **Fax:** (970)667-8317. **E-mail:** kerry.bogert@fwcommunity.com. **Website:** www.interweave.com. **Contact:** Kerry Bogert, editorial director. Estab. 1975. Publishes hardcover and trade paperback originals. Interweave Press publishes instructive titles relating to the fiber arts and beadwork topics. **Publishes 40-45 titles/year. 60% of books from first-time authors. 90% from unagented writers.** Publishes ms 6-18 months after acceptance. Accepts simultaneous submissions. Responds in 2 months to queries. Book catalog and guidelines online.

NONFICTION Subjects include crafts, hobbies. Subjects limited to fiber arts (spinning, knitting, dyeing, weaving) and jewelry making (beadwork, stringing, wireworking, metalsmithing). Submit outline, sample chapters. Accepts simultaneous submissions if informed of non-exclusivity. Reviews artwork/photos.

TIPS "We are looking for very clear, informally written, technically correct manuscripts, generally of a how-to nature, in our specific fiber and beadwork fields only. Our audience includes a variety of creative self-starters who appreciate inspiration and clear instruction. They are often well educated and skillful in many areas."

INVERTED-A

P.O. Box 267, Licking MO 65542. **E-mail:** Katzaya@gmail.com. **Website:** http://inverteda.com/. **Contact:** Aya Katz, chief editor (poetry, novels, political); Nets Katz, science editor (scientific, academic). Estab. 1985. Publishes paperback originals. Books: POD. Distributes through Amazon, Bowker, Barnes Noble. **Pays 10 author's copies.** Publishes ms 1 year after acceptance. Accepts simultaneous submissions. Responds in 1 month to queries; 3 months to mss. Guidelines for SASE.

NONFICTION Subjects include Americana, literature, politics, stage, translation, Libertarian.

FICTION Subjects include historical, picture books, translation, war, young adult, Utopian, political. Does not accept unsolicited mss. Query with SASE. Reading period open from January 2 to March 15. Accepts queries by e-mail. Include estimated word count.

TIPS "Read our books. Read the *Inverted-A Horn*. We are different. We do not follow industry trends."

IRISH ACADEMIC PRESS

Tuckmill House, 10 George's St., Newbridge Co. Kildare Ireland. (353)(45)432497. **E-mail:** info@iap.ie. **E-mail:** conor.graham@iap.ie. **Website:** www.iap.ie. **Contact:** Conor Graham. Estab. 1974. Publishes nonfiction. **Publishes 10 titles/year. Pays royalty.** Accepts simultaneous submissions. Responds in 8 weeks. Guidelines online.

IMPRINTS Merrion Press.

NONFICTION Subjects include art, history, humanities, literary criticism, military, politics, social sciences, womens studies, genealogy, Irish history. Does not want fiction or poetry.

IRON GATE PUBLISHING

P.O. Box 999, Niwot CO 80544. **E-mail:** editor@irongate.com. **Website:** www.irongate.com. **Contact:** Dina C. Carson, publisher (how-to, genealogy, local history). Publishes hardcover and trade paperback originals. "Our readers are people who are looking for solid, how-to advice on self-publishing a family or local history, or who are conducting genealogical or local history research in Colorado." **Publishes 20-30 titles/year. 100 queries; 20 mss received/year. 30% of books from first-time authors. 10% from unagented writers. Pays royalty on a case-by-case basis.** Publishes book 6 months after acceptance. Accepts simultaneous submissions. Responds in 2 months to proposals. Book catalog and writer's guidelines free or online.

NONFICTION Subjects include history, genealogy, local history. Query with SASE, or submit proposal package, including outline, 2 sample chapters, and marketing summary. Reviews artwork/photos. Send photocopies.

TIPS "Please look at the other books we publish and tell us in your query letter why your book would fit into our line of books."

ITALICA PRESS

595 Main St., Suite 605, New York NY 10044. (917)371-0563. **E-mail:** inquiries@italicapress.com. **Website:** www.italicapress.com. Estab. 1985. Publishes hardcover and trade paperback originals. "Italica Press publishes English translations of modern Italian fiction and medieval and Renaissance nonfiction." **Publishes 6 titles/year. 600 queries; 60 mss received/year. 5% of books from first-time authors.**

100% from unagented writers. Pays 7-15% royalty on wholesale price; author's copies. Publishes ms 1 year after acceptance. Accepts simultaneous submissions. Responds in 1 month to queries; 4 months to mss. Book catalog and guidelines online.

NONFICTION Subjects include translation. "We publish English translations of medieval and Renaissance source materials and English translations of modern Italian fiction." Query via e-mail. Reviews artwork/photos.

FICTION "First-time translators published. We would like to see translations of Italian writers who are well-known in Italy who are not yet translated for an American audience." Query via e-mail.

POETRY Poetry titles are always translations and generally dual language. Query with 10 sample translations of medieval and Renaissance Italian poets. Include cover letter, bio, and list of publications.

TIPS "We are interested in considering a wide variety of medieval and Renaissance topics (not historical fiction), and for modern works we are only interested in translations from Italian fiction by well-known Italian authors. *Only* fiction that has been previously published in Italian. A *brief* e-mail saves a lot of time. 90% of proposals we receive are completely off base— but we are very interested in things that are right on target."

JAIN PUBLISHING CO.

P.O. Box 3523, Fremont CA 94539. (510)659-8272. **Fax:** (510)659-0501. **E-mail:** mail@jainpub.com. **Website:** www.jainpub.com. **Contact:** Mukesh Jain, editor-in-chief. Estab. 1989. Publishes hardcover and paperback originals and reprints. Jain Publishing Co. is a humanities and social sciences publisher that publishes academic and scholarly references, as well as books for the general reader in both print and electronic formats. A substantial part of its publishing program pertains to books dealing with Asia, commonly categorized as "Asian Studies." **Publishes 6-8 titles/year. 300 queries received/year. 100% from unagented writers. Pays 5-10% royalty on net sales.** Publishes ms 1-2 years after acceptance. Accepts simultaneous submissions. Responds in 3 months to mss. Book catalog and ms guidelines online.

NONFICTION Subjects include cinema, environment, film, humanities, multicultural, philosophy, psychology, religion, social sciences, spirituality,

Asian studies. Submit proposal package, publishing history. Reviews artwork/photos. Send photocopies.

ALICE JAMES BOOKS

114 Prescott St., Farmington ME 04938. (207)778-7071. **Fax:** (207)778-7766. **Website:** www.alicejames-books.org. Estab. 1973. Publishes trade paperback originals. "Alice James Books is a nonprofit cooperative poetry press. The founders' objectives were to give women access to publishing and to involve authors in the publishing process. The cooperative selects mss for publication through both regional and national competitions." **Publishes 6 titles/year. Approximately 1,000 mss received/year. 50% of books from first-time authors. 100% from unagented writers. Pays through competition awards.** Publishes ms 1 year after acceptance. Accepts simultaneous submissions. Responds promptly to queries; 4 months to mss. Book catalog online. Guidelines online.

POETRY "Alice James Books is a nonprofit cooperative poetry press. The founders' objectives were to give women access to publishing and to involve authors in the publishing process. The cooperative selects mss for publication through both regional and national competitions." Does not want children's poetry or light verse.

TIPS "Send SASE for contest guidelines or check website. Do not send work without consulting current guidelines."

JEWISH LIGHTS PUBLISHING

LongHill Partners, Inc., Sunset Farm Offices, Rt. 4, P.O. Box 237, Woodstock VT 05091. (802)457-4000. **Fax:** (802)457-4004. **E-mail:** submissions@turner-publishing.com. **Website:** www.jewishlights.com. Estab. 1990. Publishes hardcover and trade paperback originals, trade paperback reprints. "Jewish Lights publishes books for people of all faiths and all backgrounds who yearn for books that attract, engage, educate and spiritually inspire. Our authors are at the forefront of spiritual thought and deal with the quest for the self and for meaning in life by drawing on the Jewish wisdom tradition. Our books cover topics including history, spirituality, life cycle, children, self-help, recovery, theology and philosophy. We do not publish autobiography, biography, fiction, haggadot, poetry or cookbooks. At this point we plan to do only two books for children annually, and one will be for younger children (ages 4-10)." **Publishes 30 titles/year. 50% of books from first-time authors.**

75% from unagented writers. Pays authors royalty of 10% of revenue received; 15% royalty for subsequent printings. Publishes ms 1 year after acceptance. Accepts simultaneous submissions. Responds in 6 months to queries. Book catalog and guidelines online.

NONFICTION Subjects include history, philosophy, religion, spirituality. Picture book, young readers, middle readers: activity books, spirituality. "We do *not* publish haggadot, biography, poetry, memoirs, or cookbooks." Query. Reviews artwork/photos. Send photocopies.

FICTION Picture books, young readers, middle readers: spirituality. "We are not interested in anything other than spirituality." Query with outline/synopsis and 2 sample chapters; submit complete ms for picture books.

TIPS "We publish books for all faiths and backgrounds that also reflect the Jewish wisdom tradition. Explain in your cover letter why you're submitting your project to us in particular. Make sure you know what we publish."

THE JOHNS HOPKINS UNIVERSITY PRESS

2715 N. Charles St., Baltimore MD 21218. (410)516-6900. **Fax:** (410)516-6968. **Website:** www.press.jhu.edu. Estab. 1878. Publishes hardcover originals and reprints, and trade paperback reprints. **Publishes 140 titles/year. Pays royalty.** Publishes ms 1 year after acceptance. Accepts simultaneous submissions.

NONFICTION Subjects include history, humanities, literary criticism, regional, religion, science. Submit proposal package, outline, 1 sample chapter, CV. Reviews artwork/photos. Send photocopies.

POETRY "One of the largest American university presses, Johns Hopkins publishes primarily scholarly books and journals. We do, however, publish short fiction and poetry in the series Johns Hopkins: Poetry and Fiction, edited by John Irwin."

JOHNSON BOOKS

Imprint of Big Earth Publishing, 3005 Center Green Dr., Suite 225, Boulder CO 80301. (303)443-9766. **Fax:** (303)443-9687. **E-mail:** books@bigearthpublishing.com. **Website:** bigearthpublishing.com/johnson-books. Estab. 1979. Publishes hardcover and paperback originals and reprints. Johnson Books specializes in books on the American West, primarily outdoor, useful titles that will have strong national appeal. **Publishes 20-25 titles/year. 30% of books** from first-time authors. **90% from unagented writers. Royalties vary.** Publishes ms 1 year after acceptance. Accepts simultaneous submissions. Responds in 4 months to queries. Book catalog for 9 x 12 SAE with 5 first-class stamps. Guidelines available.

NONFICTION Subjects include history, recreation, regional, science, travel, general nonfiction. "We are primarily interested in books for the informed popular market, though we will consider vividly written scholarly works. Looks for good writing, thorough research, professional presentation, and appropriate style. Marketing suggestions from writers are helpful." Submit outline/synopsis, 3 sample chapters and a author bio.

JOSSEY-BASS

John Wiley & Sons, Inc., One Montgomery St., Suite 1000, San Francisco CA 94104. **Website:** www.wiley. com. Jossey-Bass is an imprint of Wiley, specializing in books and periodicals for thoughtful professionals and researchers in the areas of business and management, leadership, human resource development, education, health, psychology, religion, and the public and nonprofit sectors. **Publishes 250 titles/year. Pays variable royalties. Pays occasional advance.** Publishes ms 1 year after acceptance. Accepts simultaneous submissions. Responds in 2-3 months to queries. Guidelines online.

NONFICTION Subjects include education, psychology, religion. Jossey-Bass publishes first-time and unagented authors. Publishes books on topics of interest to a wide range of readers: business and management, conflict resolution, mediation and negotiation, K-12 education, higher and adult education, healthcare management, psychology/behavioral healthcare, nonprofit and public management, religion, human resources and training. Also publishes 25 periodicals. See guidelines online.

JOURNEYFORTH

Imprint of BJU Press, 1700 Wade Hampton Blvd., Greenville SC 29614. (864)770-1317. **E-mail:** journeyforth@bjupress.com. **Website:** www.journeyforth. com. **Contact:** Nancy Lohr. Estab. 1974. Publishes paperback originals. JourneyForth Books publishes fiction and nonfiction that reflects a worldview based solidly on the Bible and that encourages Christians to live out their faith. JourneyForth is an imprint of BJU Press. **Publishes 8-10 titles/year. 400+ 30% of books from first-time authors. 80% from unagent-**

ed writers. **Pays royalty. yes** Publishes book 12-18 months after acceptance. Accepts simultaneous submissions. Responds in 1 month to queries; 3 months to mss. Book catalog available free or online. Guidelines online.

NONFICTION Subjects include animals, contemporary culture, history, music, nature, religion, spirituality, young adult, Bible studies, Christian living, Christian apologetics. Christian living, Bible studies, church and ministry, church history. "We produce books for the adult Christian market that are from a conservative Christian worldview."

FICTION Subjects include adventure, hi-lo, historical, juvenile, mystery, sports, western, young adult. "Our fiction is all based on a Christian worldview." Does not want short stories, poetry, picture books, or fiction for the adult market. Submit proposal with synopsis, market analysis of competing works, and first 5 chapters.

TIPS "Study the publisher's guidelines. We are looking for engaging text and a biblical worldview. Will read hard copy submissions, but prefer e-mail queries/proposals/submissions."

JUDAICA PRESS

123 Ditmas Ave., Brooklyn NY 11218. (718)972-6200. **Fax:** (718)972-6204. **E-mail:** submissions@judaica-press.com. **Website:** www.judaicapress.com. Estab. 1963. Publishes hardcover and trade paperback originals and reprints. "We cater to the Orthodox Jewish market." **Publishes 12 titles/year.** Accepts simultaneous submissions. Responds in 3 months to queries. Book catalog in print and online.

NONFICTION Subjects include religion, prayer, holidays, life cycle. Looking for Orthodox Judaica in all genres. Submit ms with SASE.

JUDSON PRESS

P.O. Box 851, Valley Forge PA 19482. (610)768-2127. **Fax:** (610)768-2441. **E-mail:** acquisitions@judson-press.com. **Website:** www.judsonpress.com. **Contact:** Acquisitions Editor. Estab. 1824. Publishes hardcover and paperback originals. "Our audience is comprised primarily of pastors, leaders, and Christians who seek a more fulfilling personal spiritual life and want to serve God in their churches, communities, and relationships. We have a large African American and multicultural readership. Currently emphasizing Baptist identity and small group resources. Not accepting biography, memoir, children's books, poetry." **Pub-**

lishes 10-12 titles/year. 500 queries received/year. 50% of books from first-time authors. 85% from unagented writers. Pays royalty or makes outright purchase. Publishes ms 12-18 months after acceptance. Accepts simultaneous submissions. Responds in 3-6 months to queries. Catalog online. Guidelines online.

NONFICTION Subjects include community, multicultural, parenting, religion, spirituality, womens issues. Adult religious nonfiction of 30,000-80,000 words. Does not want biography, autobiography, memoir. Query by e-mail or mail. Submit annotated outline, sample chapters, CV, competing titles, marketing plan.

TIPS "Writers have the best chance selling us practical books assisting clergy or laypersons in their ministry and personal lives. Our audience consists of Protestant church leaders and members. Be informed about the market's needs and related titles. Be clear about your audience, and be practical in your focus. Books on multicultural issues are very welcome. Also seeking books that respond to real (felt) needs of pastors and churches."

JUST US BOOKS, INC.

P.O. Box 5306, East Orange NJ 07019. (973)672-7701. **Fax:** (973)677-7570. **Website:** justusbooks.com. Estab. 1988. "Just Us Books is the nation's premier independent publisher of Black-interest books for young people. Our books focus primarily on the culture, history, and contemporary experiences of African Americans." Accepts simultaneous submissions. Guidelines online.

IMPRINTS Marimba Books.

NONFICTION Query with synopsis and 3-5 sample pages.

FICTION Subjects include juvenile. Just Us Books is currently accepting queries for chapter books and middle reader titles only. "We are not considering any other works at this time."

TIPS "We are looking for realistic, contemporary characters; stories and interesting plots that introduce both conflict and resolution. We will consider various themes and story-lines, but before an author submits a query we urge them to become familiar with our books."

KAEDEN BOOKS

P.O. Box 16190, Rocky River OH 44116. **Website:** www.kaeden.com. Estab. 1986. Publishes paperback originals. "Children's book publisher for education K-3 market: reading stories, fiction/nonfiction,

chapter books, science, and social studies materials." Publishes 12-20 titles/year. 1,000 mss received/year. 30% of books from first-time authors. 95% from unagented writers. Work purchased outright from authors. Pays royalties to previous authors. Publishes ms 6-9 months after acceptance. Accepts simultaneous submissions. Responds only if interested. Book catalog and guidelines online.

NONFICTION Subjects include animals, creative nonfiction, science, social sciences. Mss should have interesting topics and information presented in language comprehensible to young students. Content should be supported with details and accurate facts. Submit complete ms. "Can be as minimal as 25 words for the earliest reader or as much as 2,000 words for the fluent reader. Beginning chapter books are welcome. Our readers are in kindergarten to third grade, so vocabulary and sentence structure must be appropriate for young readers. Make sure that all language used in the story is of an appropriate level for the students to read independently. Sentences should be complete and grammatically correct." Reviews artwork/photos. Send photocopies.

FICTION Subjects include adventure, fantasy, historical, humor, mystery, short story collections, sports, suspense. "We are looking for stories with humor, surprise endings, and interesting characters that will appeal to children in kindergarten through third grade." No sentence fragments. Please do not submit: queries, ms summaries, or résumés, mss that stereotype or demean individuals or groups, mss that present violence as acceptable behavior. Submit complete ms. "Can be as minimal as 25 words for the earliest reader or as much as 2,000 words for the fluent reader. Beginning chapter books are welcome. Our readers are in kindergarten to third grade, so vocabulary and sentence structure must be appropriate for young readers. Make sure that all language used in the story is of an appropriate level for the students to read independently. Sentences should be complete and grammatically correct."

TIPS "Our audience ranges from kindergarten-third grade school children. We are an educational publisher. We are particularly interested in humorous stories with surprise endings and beginning chapter books."

KALMBACH PUBLISHING CO.

21027 Crossroads Circle, P.O. Box 1612, Waukesha WI 53186. (262)796-8776. **Fax:** (262)798-6468. **Website:**

www.kalmbach.com. Estab. 1934. Publishes paperback originals and reprints. **Publishes 40-50 titles/year. 50% of books from first-time authors. 99% from unagented writers. Pays 7% royalty on net receipts. Pays $1,500 advance.** Publishes ms 18 months after acceptance. Accepts simultaneous submissions. Responds in 2 months to queries.

NONFICTION "Focus on beading, wirework, and one-of-a-kind artisan creations for jewelry-making and crafts and in the railfan, model railroading, plastic modeling and toy train collecting/operating hobbies. Kalmbach publishes reference materials and how-to publications for hobbyists, jewelry-makers, and crafters." Query with 2-3 page detailed outline, sample chapter with photos, drawings, and how-to text. Reviews artwork/photos.

TIPS "Our how-to books are highly visual in their presentation. Any author who wants to publish with us must be able to furnish good photographs and rough drawings before we'll consider his or her book."

Ⓐ KANE/MILLER BOOK PUBLISHERS

4901 Morena Blvd., Suite 213, San Diego CA 92117. (858)456-0540. **Fax:** (858)456-9641. **E-mail:** submissions@kanemiller.com. **Website:** www.kanemiller.com. **Contact:** Editorial Department. Estab. 1985. "Kane/Miller Book Publishers is a division of EDC Publishing, specializing in award-winning children's books from around the world. Our books bring the children of the world closer to each other, sharing stories and ideas, while exploring cultural differences and similarities. Although we continue to look for books from other countries, we are now actively seeking works that convey cultures and communities within the US. We are committed to expanding our picture book list and are interested in great stories with engaging characters, especially those with particularly American subjects. When writing about the experiences of a particular community, we will express a preference for stories written from a firsthand experience." Submission guidelines on site. Accepts simultaneous submissions. If interested, responds in 90 days to queries.

NONFICTION Subjects include Americana, history, sports, young adult.

FICTION Subjects include adventure, fantasy, historical, juvenile, multicultural, mystery, picture books. Picture Books: concept, contemporary, health, humor, multicultural. Young Readers: contemporary, multicultural, suspense. Middle Readers: contemporary, humor, multicultural, suspense. "At this time, we are not considering holiday stories (in any age range) or self-published works."

TIPS "We like to think that a child reading a Kane/Miller book will see parallels between his own life and what might be the unfamiliar setting and characters of the story. And that by seeing how a character who is somehow or in some way dissimilar—an outsider—finds a way to fit comfortably into a culture or community or situation while maintaining a healthy sense of self and self-dignity, she might be empowered to do the same."

KAR-BEN PUBLISHING

Lerner Publishing Group, 1251 Washington Ave. N., Minneapolis MN 55401. **E-mail:** editorial@karben.com. **Website:** www.karben.com. Estab. 1974. Publishes hardcover, trade paperback and e-books. Kar-Ben publishes exclusively children's books on Jewish themes. **Publishes 20 titles/year. 800 mss received/year. 20% of books from first-time authors. 70% from unagented writers. Pays 5% royalty on NET sale. Pays $500-2,500 advance.** Most mss published within 2 years. Accepts simultaneous submissions. Responds in 12 weeks. Book catalog online; free upon request. Guidelines online.

NONFICTION Subjects include religion. "In addition to traditional Jewish-themed stories about Jewish holidays, history, folktales and other subjects, we especially seek stories that reflect the rich diversity of the contemporary Jewish community." Picture books, young readers; Jewish history, Israel, Holocaust, folktales, religion, social issues, special needs; must be of Jewish interest. No textbooks, games, or educational materials. Submit completed ms. Reviews artwork separately. Works with 10-12 illustrators/year. Prefers four-color art in any medium that is scannable. Reviews illustration packages from artists. Submit sample of art or online portfolio (no originals).

FICTION "We seek picture book mss 800-1,000 words on Jewish-themed topics for children." Picture books: Adventure, concept, folktales, history, humor, multicultural, religion, special needs; must be on a Jewish theme. Average word length: picture books–1,000. Submit full ms. Picture books only.

TIPS "Authors: Do a literature search to make sure similar title doesn't already exist. Illustrators: Look at our online catalog for a sense of what we like—bright colors and lively composition."

KAYA PRESS

c/o USC ASE, 3620 S. Vermont Ave. KAP 462, Los Angeles CA 90089. (213) 740-2285. **E-mail:** info@kaya.com. **E-mail:** acquisitions@kaya.com. **Website:** www.kaya.com. Estab. 1994. Publishes hardcover originals and trade paperback originals and reprints. Kaya is an independent literary press dedicated to the publication of innovative literature from the Asian Pacific diaspora. Accepts simultaneous submissions. Responds in 6 months to mss. Book catalog available free. Guidelines online.

NONFICTION Subjects include multicultural. Submit proposal package, outline, sample chapters, previous publications, SASE. Reviews artwork/photos. Send photocopies.

FICTION Submit 2-4 sample chapters, clips, SASE.

POETRY Submit complete ms.

TIPS "Audience is people interested in a high standard of literature and who are interested in breaking down easy approaches to multicultural literature."

KELSEY STREET PRESS

Poetry by Women, 2824 Kelsey St., Berkeley CA 94705. **Website:** www.kelseyst.com. Estab. 1974. Hardcover and trade paperback originals and electronic originals. "A Berkeley, California press publishing collaborations between women poets and artists. Many of the press's collaborations focus on a central theme or conceit, like the sprawl and spectacle of New York in *Arcade* by Erica Hunt and Alison Saar." Accepts simultaneous submissions.

FICTION Subjects include experimental, horror, multicultural, mystery, poetry, prose, women of color.

POETRY Query.

KENSINGTON PUBLISHING CORP.

119 W. 40th St., New York NY 10018. (212)407-1500. **Fax:** (212)935-0699. **E-mail:** jscognamiglio@kensingtonbooks.com. **Website:** www.kensingtonbooks.com. **Contact:** John Scognamiglio, editorial director, fiction (historical romance, Regency romance, women's contemporary fiction, gay and lesbian fiction and nonfiction, mysteries, suspense, mainstream fiction); Michaela Hamilton, editor-in-chief, Citadel Press (thrillers, mysteries, mainstream fiction, true crime, current events); Selena James, executive editor, Dafina Books (African American fiction and nonfiction, inspirational, young adult, romance); Peter Senf-

tleben, assistant editor (mainstream fiction, women's contemporary fiction, gay and lesbian fiction, mysteries, suspense, thrillers, romantic suspense, paranormal romance). Estab. 1975. Publishes hardcover and trade paperback originals, mass market paperback originals and reprints. "Kensington focuses on profitable niches and uses aggressive marketing techniques to support its books." **Publishes over 500 titles/year. 5,000 queries received/year. 2,000 mss received/year. 10% of books from first-time authors. Pays 6-15% royalty on retail price. Makes outright purchase. Pays $2,000 and up advance.** Publishes ms 9-12 months after acceptance. Accepts simultaneous submissions. Responds in 1 month to queries and proposals; 4 months to mss. Book catalog and guidelines online.

NONFICTION Subjects include Americana, animals, child guidance, contemporary culture, history, hobbies, memoirs, multicultural, philosophy, psychology, recreation, regional, sex, sports, travel, true crime, pop culture. Query.

FICTION Subjects include ethnic, historical, horror, mainstream, multicultural, mystery, occult, romance, suspense, western, thrillers, women's. No science fiction/fantasy, experimental fiction, business texts or children's titles. Query.

TIPS "Agented submissions only, except for submissions to romance lines. For those lines, query with SASE or submit proposal package including 3 sample chapters, synopsis."

KENT STATE UNIVERSITY PRESS

P.O. Box 5190, 1118 University Library, Kent OH 44242. **Fax:** (330)672-3104. **E-mail:** ksupress@kent.edu. **Website:** www.kentstateuniversitypress.com. **Contact:** Will Underwood, acquiring editor. Estab. 1965. Publishes hardcover and paperback originals and some reprints. "Kent State publishes primarily scholarly works and titles of regional interest. Currently emphasizing US history, US literary criticism." **Publishes 30-35 titles/year. Non-author subsidy publishes 20% of books. Standard minimum book contract on net sales.** Accepts simultaneous submissions. Responds in 4 months to queries. Book catalog available free.

NONFICTION Subjects include history, literary criticism, regional, true crime, literary criticism, material culture, textile/fashion studies, US foreign relations. "Especially interested in scholarly works in history (US and world) and US literary studies of high quality, any titles of regional interest for Ohio, scholarly biographies and general nonfiction. Send a letter of inquiry before submitting mss. Decisions based on in-house readings and 2 by outside scholars in the field of study." Please, no faxes, phone calls, or e-mail submissions.

☺ KIDS CAN PRESS

25 Dockside Dr., Toronto ON M5A 0B5, Canada. (416)479-7000. **Fax:** (416)960-5437. **Website:** www. kidscanpress.com. **Contact:** Corus Quay, acquisitions. Estab. 1973. Publishes book 18-24 months after acceptance. Accepts simultaneous submissions. Responds in 6 months only if interested.

☺ *Kids Can Press is currently accepting unsolicited mss from Canadian adult authors only.*

NONFICTION Picture books: activity books, animal, arts/crafts, biography, careers, concept, health, history, hobbies, how-to, multicultural, nature/environment, science, social issues, special needs, sports. Young readers: activity books, animal, arts/crafts, biography, careers, concept, history, hobbies, how-to, multicultural. Middle readers: cooking, music/dance. Average word length: picture books 500-1,250; young readers 750-2,000; middle readers 5,000-15,000.

FICTION Picture books, young readers: concepts. "We do not accept young adult fiction or fantasy novels for any age." Adventure, animal, contemporary, folktales, history, humor, multicultural, nature/environment, special needs, sports, suspense/mystery. Average word length: picture books 1,000-2,000; young readers 750-1,500; middle readers 10,000-15,000; young adults over 15,000. Submit outline/synopsis and 2-3 sample chapters. For picture books submit complete ms.

KIRKBRIDE BIBLE CO., INC.

1102 Deloss St., Indianapolis IN 46203. (800)428-4385. **Fax:** (317)633-1444. **E-mail:** info@kirkbride.com. **Website:** www.kirkbride.com. **Contact:** Paula Haggard, David Gage, Bill Cross. Estab. 1915. Publishes Thompson Chain-Reference Bible hardcover originals and quality leather bindings styles and translations of the Bible. Types of books include reference and religious. Specializes in reference and study material. Accepts simultaneous submissions.

DENIS KITCHEN PUBLISHING CO., LLC

P.O. Box 2250, Amherst MA 01004. (413)259-1627. **Fax:** (413)259-1812. **E-mail:** help@deniskitchen. com. **Website:** www.deniskitchen.com. **Contact:** Denis Kitchen, publisher. Publishes hardcover and trade paperback originals and reprints. **Publishes 4 titles/year. 15% of books from first-time authors. 50% from unagented writers. Pays 6-10% royalty on retail price. Occasionally makes deals based on percentage of wholesale if idea and/or bulk of work is done in-house. Pays $1-5,000 advance.** Publishes ms 9-12 months after acceptance. Responds in 4-6 weeks.

☺ This publisher strongly discourages e-mail submissions.

NONFICTION Query with SASE. Submit proposal package, outline, illustrative matter. Submit complete ms. Reviews artwork/photos. Send photocopies and transparencies.

FICTION Subjects include adventure, erotica, historical, horror, humor, literary, mystery, occult, science fiction. "We do not want pure fiction. We seek cartoonists or writer/illustrator teams who can tell compelling stories with a combination of words and pictures." No pure fiction (meaning text only). Query with SASE. Submit sample illustrations/comic pages. Submit complete ms.

TIPS "Our audience is readers who embrace the graphic novel revolution, who appreciate historical comic strips and books, and those who follow popular and alternative culture. We like to discover new talent. The artist who has a day job but a great idea is encouraged to contact us. The pop culture historian who has a new take on an important figure is likewise encouraged. We have few preconceived notions about manuscripts or ideas, though we are decidedly selective. Historically, we have published many first-time authors and artists, some of whom developed into award-winning creators with substantial followings. Artists or illustrators who do not have confidence in their writing should send us self-promotional postcards (our favorite way of spotting new talent)."

KNOPF

Imprint of Random House, 1745 Broadway, New York NY 10019. **Fax:** (212)940-7390. **Website:** knopfdoubleday.com/imprint/knopf. Estab. 1915. Publishes hardcover and paperback originals. **Publishes 200 titles/year. Royalties vary. Offers advance.** Publishes ms 1 year after acceptance. Accepts simultaneous submissions. Responds in 2-6 months to queries.

NONFICTION Usually only accepts mss submitted by agents. However, writers may submit sample 25-50 pages with SASE.

FICTION Publishes book-length fiction of literary merit by known or unknown writers. Length: 40,000-150,000 words. Usually only accepts mss submitted by agents. However, writers may submit sample 25-50 pages with SASE.

KNOX ROBINSON PUBLISHING

Knox Robinson Holdings, LLC, 3104 Briarcliff RD NE #98414, Atlanta GA 30345. (404)478-8696. **E-mail:** info@knoxrobinsonpublishing.com. **Website:** www.knoxrobinsonpublishing.com. Estab. 2010. Publishes fiction and nonfiction. Knox Robinson Publishing began as an international, independent, specialist publisher of historical fiction, historical romance and fantasy. Now open to well-written literature in all genres. **Publishes 20 titles/year. Pays royalty.** Accepts simultaneous submissions. Responds within 6 months to submissions of first 3 chapters. "We do not accept proposals.". Catalog available. Guidelines online.

IMPRINTS Under The Maple Tree Books (Children's Literature), Mithras Books (Young Adult Literature).

NONFICTION Subjects include history, humanities, religion, general nonfiction. "Our goal is to publish history books, monographs and historical fiction that satisfies history buffs and encourages general readers to learn more." Submit first 3 chapters and author questionnaire found on website. Reviews artwork/photos. Send photocopies. Does not accept printed submissions; electronic only.

FICTION Subjects include adventure, contemporary, fantasy, historical, horror, literary, mainstream, romance, science fiction. "We are seeking historical fiction featuring obscure historical figures." Submit first 3 chapters and author questionnaire found on website.

KRAUSE PUBLICATIONS

A Division of F+W Media, Inc., 700 E. State St., Iola WI 54990. (715)445-2214. **Fax:** (715)445-4087. **E-mail:** paul.kennedy@fwcommunity.com. **Website:** www.krausebooks.com. **Contact:** Paul Kennedy (antiques and collectibles, rocks, gems and minerals, music, sports, militaria, numismatics); Chris Berens (outdoors); Brian Earnest (automotive). Publishes hardcover and trade paperback originals. "We are the world's largest hobby and collectibles publisher."

Publishes 30 titles/year. 100 queries received/year. 25% of books from first-time authors. 95% from unagented writers. Pays advance. Photo budget. Publishes ms 18 months after acceptance. Responds in 1 month to proposals; 1 month to mss.

NONFICTION Submit proposal package, including outline, TOC, a sample chapter, and letter explaining your project's unique contributions. Reviews artwork/photos. Accepts only digital photography. Send sample photos.

TIPS Audience consists of serious hobbyists. "Your work should provide a unique contribution to the special interest."

⊘ KREGEL PUBLICATIONS

2450 Oak Industrial Dr. NE, Grand Rapids MI 49505. (616)451-4775. **Fax:** (616)451-9330. **E-mail:** kregelbooks@kregel.com. **Website:** www.kregelpublications.com. Estab. 1949. Publishes hardcover and trade paperback originals and reprints. "Our mission as an evangelical Christian publisher is to provide—with integrity and excellence—trusted, Biblically based resources that challenge and encourage individuals in their Christian lives. Works in theology and Biblical studies should reflect the historic, orthodox Protestant tradition." **Publishes 90 titles/year. 20% of books from first-time authors. 10% from unagented writers. Pays royalty on wholesale price. Pays negotiable advance.** Publishes ms 12-16 months after acceptance. Accepts simultaneous submissions. Responds in 2-3 months. Guidelines online.

IMPRINTS Kregel Publications, Kregel Academic, Kregel Childrens, Kregel Classics.

NONFICTION Subjects include history, religion. "We serve evangelical Christian readers and those in career Christian service." Finds works through The Writer's Edge and Christian Manuscript Submissions ms screening services.

FICTION Subjects include religious, young adult. Fiction should be geared toward the evangelical Christian market. Wants books with fast-paced, contemporary storylines presenting a strong Christian message in an engaging, entertaining style. Finds works through The Writer's Edge and Christian Manuscript Submissions ms screening services.

TIPS "Our audience consists of conservative, evangelical Christians, including pastors and ministry students."

KRIEGER PUBLISHING CO.

1725 Krieger Ln., Malabar FL 32950. (321)724-9542. **Fax:** (321)951-3671. **E-mail:** info@krieger-publishing. com. **Website:** www.krieger-publishing.com. **Contact:** Sharan B. Merriam and Ronald M. Cervero, series editor (adult education); David E. Kyvig, series director (local history); James B. Gardner, series editor (public history). Also publishes in the fields of natural sciences, history and space sciences. Estab. 1969. Publishes hardcover and paperback originals and reprints. "We are a short-run niche publisher providing accurate and well-documented scientific and technical titles for text and reference use, college level and higher." **Publishes 30 titles/year. 30% of books from first-time authors. 100% from unagented writers. Pays royalty on net price.** Publishes ms 9-18 months after acceptance. Accepts simultaneous submissions. Responds in 3 months to queries. Book catalog online.

IMPRINTS Anvil Series; Orbit Series; Public History; Professional Practices in Adult Education and Lifelong Learning Series.

NONFICTION Subjects include agriculture, animals, education, history, horticulture, science, herpetology. Query with SASE. Reviews artwork/photos.

LANGMARC PUBLISHING

P.O. Box 90488, Austin TX 78709-0488. (512)394-0989. **Fax:** (512)394-0829. **E-mail:** langmarc@book-sails.com. **Website:** www.langmarc.com. Publishes trade paperback originals. **Publishes 3 titles/year. 150 queries; 80 mss received/year. 60% of books from first-time authors. 80% from unagented writers. Pays 14% royalty on sales price.** Publishes ms 8-14 months after acceptance. Accepts simultaneous submissions. Responds in 3 months to queries. Book catalog online. Guidelines online.

NONFICTION Subjects include creative nonfiction. Query with SASE.

LANTANA PUBLISHING

London United Kingdom. **E-mail:** info@lantana-publishing.com. **E-mail:** submissions@lantanapublishing.com. **Website:** www.lantanapublishing.com. Estab. 2014. "Lantana Publishing is an independent and award-winning publishing company committed to addressing the widespread lack of cultural diversity in children's publishing in the UK. As a publishing house with a strong social mission to increase the availability and visibility of diverse children's writing, we provide opportunities for authors and illustrators of minority backgrounds to create children's books that are resonant of their own experiences, places and cultures." **Pays royalty. Pays advance.** Accepts simultaneous submissions. Responds in 6 weeks. Guidelines online.

"We are currently focusing on picture books for 4 to 8 year olds."

FICTION Subjects include adventure, ethnic, experimental, fantasy, multicultural, picture books. "We love writing that is new, unusual or quirky, and that interweaves mythic, historical or spiritual elements into fun, contemporary stories full of colour and excitement. We particularly like stories with modern-day settings and strong role models, positive relationships between communities and their environment, and evocative storylines that can provide a glimpse into the belief systems, traditions or world views of other cultures." No nonfiction. "If you are a picture book author, please send us the complete text of your ms. Illustrations are not necessary. If we like your story, we will commission an illustrator to work with you. A picture book ms should not normally exceed 1,000 words. If your story does exceed this word limit please include a justification for its length in your covering letter."

LAPWING PUBLICATIONS

1 Ballysillan Dr., Belfast BT14 8HQ, Northern Ireland. (44)2890-500-796. **Fax:** (44)2890-295-800. **E-mail:** lapwing.poetry@ntlworld.com. **Website:** www.lapwingpoetry.com. **Contact:** Dennis Greig, editor. Estab. 1989. **Pays 20 author's copies, no royalties.** Accepts simultaneous submissions. Responds to queries in 1 month; mss in 2 months.

Lapwing will produce work only if and when resources to do so are available.

POETRY Lapwing publishes "emerging Irish poets and poets domiciled in Ireland, plus the new work of a suitable size by established Irish writers. Non-Irish poets are also published. Poets based in continental Europe have become a major feature. Emphasis on first collections preferrably not larger than 80 pages. "Submit 6 poems in the first instance; depending on these, an invitation to submit more may follow." Considers simultaneous submissions. Accepts e-mail submissions in body of message or in DOC format. Cover letter is required. "All submissions receive a first reading. If these poems have minor errors or faults, the writer is advised. Those which appeal at first reading are retained, and a conditional offer is sent." Often comments on rejected poems. "After initial publication, irrespective of the quantity, the work will be permanently available using 'print-on-demand' production; such publications may not always be printed exactly as the original, although the content will remain the same."

TIPS "We are unable to accept new work from beyond mainland Europe and the British Isles due to delivery costs."

LEAPFROG PRESS

Box 505, Fredonia NY 14063. (508)274-2710. **E-mail:** leapfrog@leapfrogpress.com. **Website:** www.leapfrogpress.com. **Contact:** Rebecca Schwab, acquisitions editor; Layla Al-Bedawi, publicity. Estab. 1996. **Publishes 4-6 titles/year. 2,000-3,000 submissions received/year. 50% of books from first-time authors. 90% from unagented writers. Pays 10% royalty on net receipts. Average advance: negotiable.** Publishes ms approximately 1 year after acceptance. Accepts simultaneous submissions. Response time varies. Guidelines online.

FICTION Subjects include adventure, ethnic, experimental, feminist, gay, historical, juvenile, lesbian, literary, mainstream, multicultural, poetry, science fiction, short story collections, young adult. "We search for beautifully written literary titles and market them aggressively to national trade and library accounts. We also sell film, translation, foreign, and book club rights." Publishes paperback originals. Books: acid-free paper; sewn binding. Average print order: 3,000. First novel print order: 2,000 (average). Member, Publishers Marketing Association, PEN. Distributes titles through Consortium Book Sales and Distribution, St. Paul, MN. Promotes titles through all national review media, bookstore readings, author tours, website, radio shows, chain store promotions, advertisements, book fairs. "Genres often blur; look for good writing. We are most interested in works that are quirky, that fall outside of any known genre,and of course well written and finely crafted. We are most interested in literary fiction." Query by e-mail only. Send letter and first 5-10 ms pages within e-mail message. No attachments. Responds in 2-3 weeks to queries by e-mail; 6 months to mss. May consider simultaneous submissions.

TIPS "We like anything that is superbly written and genuinely original. We like the idiosyncratic and the peculiar. We rarely publish nonfiction. Send only your best work, and send only completed work that is ready. That means the completed ms has already been through extensive editing and is ready to be judged. We consider submissions from both previously published and unpublished writers. We are uninterested in an impressive author bio if the work is poor; if the work is excellent, the author bio is equally unimportant."

LEE & LOW BOOKS

95 Madison Ave., #1205, New York NY 10016. (212)779-4400. **E-mail:** general@leeandlow.com. **Website:** www.leeandlow.com. Estab. 1991. Publishes hardcover originals and trade paperback reprints. "Our goals are to meet a growing need for books that address children of color, and to present literature that all children can identify with. We only consider multicultural children's books. Sponsors a yearly New Voices Award for first-time picture book authors of color. Contest rules online at website or for SASE." **Publishes 12-14 titles/year. Receives 100 queries/year; 1,200 mss/year. 20% of books from first-time authors. 50% from unagented writers. Pays net royalty. Pays authors advances against royalty. Pays illustrators advance against royalty. Photographers paid advance against royalty.** Publishes book 2 years after acceptance. Responds in 6 months to mss if interested. Book catalog available online. Guidelines available online or by written request with SASE.

NONFICTION Picture books: concept. Picture books, middle readers: biography, history, multicultural, science and sports. Average word length: picture books-1,500-3,000. Submit complete ms. Reviews artwork/photos only if writer is also a professional illustrator or photographer. Send photocopies and nonreturnable art samples only.

FICTION Picture books, young readers: anthology, contemporary, history, multicultural, poetry. Picture book, middle reader: contemporary, history, multicultural, nature/environment, poetry, sports. Average word length: picture books—1,000-1,500 words. "We do not publish folklore or animal stories." Submit complete ms.

POETRY Submit complete ms.

TIPS "Check our website to see the kinds of books we publish. Do not send mss that don't fit our mission."

LEHIGH UNIVERSITY PRESS

B040 Christmas-Saucon Hall, 14 E. Packer Ave., Bethlehem PA 18015. (610)758-3933. **Fax:** (610)758-6331. **E-mail:** inlup@lehigh.edu. **Website:** https://lupress.cas2.lehigh.edu. **Contact:** Kate Crassons. Estab. 1985. Publishes nonfiction hardcover originals. Currently emphasizing works on 18th-century studies, history of technology, literary criticism, and topics involving Asian Studies. **Publishes 10 titles/year. 90-100 queries; 50-60 mss received/year. 70% of books from first-time authors. 100% from unagented writers. Pays royalty.** Publishes ms 18 months after acceptance. Responds in 3 months to queries. Book catalog available free. Guidelines online.

NONFICTION Subjects include Americana, history, science. Lehigh University Press is a conduit for nonfiction works of scholarly interest to the academic community. Submit proposal package with cover letter, several sample chapters, current CV and SASE.

HAL LEONARD BOOKS

Hal Leonard Publishing Group, 33 Plymouth St., Suite 302, Montclair NJ 07042. (973)337-5034. **Website:** www.halleonardbooks.com. **Contact:** John Cerullo, publisher. **Publishes 30 titles/year.** Accepts simultaneous submissions.

NONFICTION Subjects include music. Query with SASE.

⊘ LES FIGUES PRESS

P.O. Box 7736, Los Angeles CA 90007. **E-mail:** info@lesfigues.com. **Website:** www.lesfigues.com. **Contact:** Teresa Carmody, director. Estab. 2005. Les Figues Press is an independent, nonprofit publisher of poetry, prose, visual art, conceptual writing, and translation. With amission is to create aesthetic conversations between readers, writers, and artists, Les Figues Press favors projects which push the boundaries of genre, form, and general acceptability. "We are currently closed to all submissions." Accepts simultaneous submissions.

LETHE PRESS

118 Heritage Ave., Maple Shade NJ 8052. (609)410-7391. **Website:** www.lethepressbooks.com. Estab. 2001. "Welcomes submissions from authors of any sexual or gender identity." Accepts simultaneous submissions. Guidelines online.

NONFICTION Query via e-mail.

FICTION Subjects include gay, lesbian, occult, science fiction. "Named after the Greek river of memory and forgetfulness (and pronounced Lee-Thee), Lethe Press is a small press devoted to ideas that are often neglected or forgotten by mainstream, profit-oriented publishers." Distributes/promotes titles. Lethe Books are distributed by Ingram Publications and Bookazine, and are available at all major bookstores, as well as the major online retailers. Query via e-mail.

POETRY "Lethe Press is a small press seeking gay and lesbian themed poetry collections." Lethe Books are distributed by Ingram Publications and Bookazine, and are available at all major bookstores, as well as the major online retailers. Query with 7-10 poems, list of publications.

ARTHUR A. LEVINE BOOKS

Scholastic, Inc., 557 Broadway, New York NY 10012. (212)343-4436. **Fax:** (212)343-6143. **Website:** www.arthuralevinebooks.com. Estab. 1996. Publishes hardcover, paperback, and e-book editions. Publishes a book 18 months after acceptance. Accepts simultaneous submissions. Responds in 1 month to queries; 5 months to mss. Picture Books: Query letter and full text of pb. Novels: Send Query letter, first 2 chapters and synopsis. Other: Query letter, 10-page sample and synopsis/proposal.

NONFICTION Please follow submission guidelines. Works with 8 illustrators/year. Will review ms/illustration packages from artists. Query first. Illustrations only: Send postcard sample with tearsheets. Samples not returned.

FICTION Subjects include juvenile, picture books, young adult. "Arthur A. Levine is looking for distinctive literature, for children and young adults, for whatever's extraordinary." Averages 18-20 total titles/year. Query.

◎ LEXISNEXIS CANADA, INC.

111 Gordon Baker Rd., Suite 900, Toronto ON M2H 3R1, Canada. (905)479-2665. **Fax:** (905)479-2826. **Website:** www.lexisnexis.ca. **Contact:** Product Development Director. LexisNexis Canada, Inc., publishes professional reference material for the legal, business, and accounting markets under the Butterworths imprint and operates the Quicklaw and LexisNexis online services. **Publishes 100 titles/year. 50% of books from first-time authors. 100% from unagented writers. Pays 5-15% royalty on wholesale price.** Publishes ms 4 months after acceptance. Accepts simultaneous submissions. Responds in 1 month to queries. Book catalog available free. Guidelines online.

TIPS "Audience is legal community, business, medical, accounting professions."

◉ LIFE CYCLE BOOKS

20 - 1085 Bellamy Rd N, Toronto ON M1H 3C7, Canada. **Website:** www.lifecyclebooks.com. **Contact:** Paul Broughton, general manager. Estab. 1973. Publishes trade paperback originals and reprints, and mass market reprints. **Publishes 6 titles/year. 50+ queries received/year. 50% of books from first-time authors. 100% from unagented writers. Pays 8-10% royalty on wholesale price. Pays $250+ advance.** Publishes book 1 year after acceptance. Responds within 1-2 months. Catalog online.

NONFICTION Subjects include pro-life issues. "We specialize in pro-life issues. Please look at our website before submitting your manuscript." Query with SASE. Submit complete ms.

LIGUORI PUBLICATIONS

One Liguori Dr., Liguori MO 63057. (636)464-2500. **Fax:** (636)464-8449. **Website:** www.liguori.org. Estab. 1947. Publishes paperback originals and reprints under the Ligouri and Libros Ligouri imprints. Liguori Publications, faithful to the charism of St. Alphonsus, is an apostolate within the mission of the Denver Province. Its mission, a collaborative effort of Redemptorists and laity, is to spread the gospel of Jesus Christ primarily through the print and electronic media. It shares in the Redemptorist priority of giving special attention to the poor and the most abandoned. Currently emphasizing practical spirituality, prayers and devotions, how-to spirituality. **Publishes 20-25 titles/year. Pays royalty. Makes outright purchase. Pays varied advance.** Publishes ms 2 years after acceptance. Responds in 2-3 months. Guidelines online.

NONFICTION Subjects include religion, spirituality. Mostly adult audience; limited children/juvenile. Mss with Catholic sensibility. Query with SASE. Submit outline, 1 sample chapter.

TIPS "As a rule, Liguori Publications does not accept unsolicited fiction, poetry, art books, biography, autobiography, private revelations."

LILLENAS PUBLISHING CO.

Imprint of Lillenas Drama Resources, P.O. Box 419527, Kansas City MO 64141. (800)877-0700. **Fax:** (816)412-8390. **E-mail:** drama@lillenas.com. **Website:** www.lillenasdrama.com. Publishes mass market paperback and electronic originals. "We purchase only original, previously unpublished materials. Also, we require that all scripts be performed at least once before it is submitted for consideration. We do not accept scripts that are sent via fax or e-mail. Direct all manuscripts to the Drama Resources Editor." **Publishes 50+ titles/year. Pays royalty on net price. Makes outright purchase.** Responds in 4-6 months to material. Guidelines online.

NONFICTION No musicals. Query with SASE. Submit complete ms.

FICTION "Looking for sketch and monologue collections for all ages – adults, children and youth. For these collections, we request 12 - 15 scripts to be submitted at one time. Unique treatments of spiritual themes, relevant issues and biblical messages are of interest. Contemporary full-length and one-act plays that have conflict, characterization, and a spiritual context that is neither a sermon nor an apologetic for youth and adults. We also need wholesome so-called secular full-length scripts for dinner theatres and schools." No musicals.

TIPS "We never receive too many manuscripts."

LINDEN PUBLISHING, INC.

2006 S. Mary, Fresno CA 93721. (559)233-6633. **Fax:** (559)233-6933. **E-mail:** richard@lindenpub.com. **Website:** www.lindenpub.com and www.quilldriverbooks.com. **Contact:** Richard Sorsky, president; Kent Sorsky, vice president. Estab. 1976. Publishes hardcover and trade paperback originals; hardcover and trade paperback reprints. **Publishes 10-12 titles/year. 30+ queries; 5-15 mss received/year. 40% of books from first-time authors. 50% from unagented writers. Pays 7½ -12% royalty on wholesale price. Pays $500-6,000 advance.** Publishes ms 18 months after acceptance. Responds in 1 month. Book catalog online. Guidelines available via e-mail.

IMPRINTS Quill Driver Books, Craven Street Books. Pace Press.

NONFICTION Subjects include crafts, health, history, hobbies, regional, true crime, Regional California history. Submit proposal package, outline, 3 sample chapters, bio. Reviews artwork/photos. Send electronic files, if available.

FICTION Subjects include adventure, fantasy, gothic, historical, horror, mystery, occult, science fiction, suspense.

LISTEN & LIVE AUDIO

1700 Manhattan Ave., Union City NJ 07087. (201)558-9000. **Website:** www.listenandlive.com. **Contact:** Alfred C. Martino, president. Independent audiobook publisher. "We also license audiobooks for the download market. We specialize in the following genres: fiction, mystery, nonfiction, self-help, business, children's, and teen." **Publishes 10+ titles/year.** Accepts simultaneous submissions. Catalog online.

⊘⊘ LITTLE, BROWN AND CO. ADULT TRADE BOOKS

1290 Avenue of the Americas, New York NY 10104. **Website:** www.littlebrown.com. Estab. 1837. Publishes hardcover originals and paperback originals and reprints. "The general editorial philosophy for all divisions continues to be broad and flexible, with high quality and the promise of commercial success as always the first considerations." **Publishes 100 titles/year. Pays royalty. Offer advance.** Accepts simultaneous submissions. Guidelines online.

NONFICTION *Agented submissions only.*

FICTION Subjects include contemporary, literary, mainstream. *Agented submissions only.*

⊘⊘ LITTLE, BROWN BOOKS FOR YOUNG READERS

Hachette Book Group USA, 1290 Avenue of the Americas, New York NY 10104. (212)364-1100. **Fax:** (212)364-0925. **Website:** littlebrown.com. Estab. 1837. "Little, Brown and Co. Children's Publishing publishes all formats including board books, picture books, middle grade fiction, and nonfiction YA titles. We are looking for strong writing and presentation, but no predetermined topics." *Only interested in solicited agented material.* **Publishes 100-150 titles/year. Pays authors royalties based on retail price. Pays illustrators and photographers by the project or royalty based on retail price. Sends galleys to authors; dummies to illustrators. Pays negotiable advance.** Publishes ms 2 years after acceptance. Accepts simultaneous submissions. Responds in 1-2 months.

NONFICTION Subjects include animals, ethnic, history, hobbies, recreation, science, sports. "Writers should avoid looking for the 'issue' they think publishers want to see, choosing instead topics they know best and are most enthusiastic about/inspired by." *Agented submissions only.*

FICTION Subjects include adventure, fantasy, feminist, historical, humor, mystery, science fiction, suspense, chick lit, multicultural. Average word length: picture books—1,000; young readers—6,000; middle readers—15,000- 50,000; young adults—50,000 and up. *Agented submissions only.*

TIPS "In order to break into the field, authors and illustrators should research their competition and try to come up with something outstandingly different."

LITTLE PICKLE PRESS

3701 Sacramento St., #494, San Francisco CA 94118. (415)340-3344. **Fax:** (415)366-1520. **E-mail:** info@march4thinc.com. **Website:** www.littlepicklepress.com. Little Pickle Press is a 21st Century publisher dedicated to helping parents and educators cultivate conscious, responsible little people by stimulating explorations of the meaningful topics of their generation through a variety of media, technologies, and techniques. Submit through submission link on site. Includes YA imprint Relish Media. Accepts simultaneous submissions. Uses Author.me for submissions for Little Pickle and YA imprint Relish Media. Guidelines available on site.

TIPS "We have lots of manuscripts to consider, so it will take up to 8 weeks before we get back to you."

⊘⊘ LITTLE SIMON

Imprint of Simon & Schuster, 1230 Avenue of the Americas, New York NY 10020. (212)698-1295. **Fax:** (212)698-2794. **Website:** www.simonandschuster.com/kids. Publishes novelty and branded books only. "Our goal is to provide fresh material in an innovative format for preschool to age 8. Our books are often, if not exclusively, format driven." **Offers advance and royalties.** Accepts simultaneous submissions.

NONFICTION "We publish very few nonfiction titles." No picture books. *Currently not accepting unsolicited mss.*

FICTION Novelty books include many things that do not fit in the traditional hardcover or paperback format, such as pop-up, board book, scratch and sniff, glow in the dark, lift the flap, etc. Children's/juvenile. No picture books. Large part of the list is holiday-themed. *Currently not accepting unsolicited mss.*

⊘⊘ LITTLE TIGER PRESS

1 The Coda Centre, 189 Munster Rd., London SW6 6AW, United Kingdom. (44)(20)7385-6333. **Website:** www.littletigerpress.com. Little Tiger Press is a dynamic and busy independent publisher. Also includes imprints: Caterpillar Books and Stripes Publishing.

FICTION Picture books: animal, concept, contemporary, humor. Average word length: picture books—750 words or less. "We are no longer accepting unsolicited manuscripts. We will however, continue to accept illustration submissions and samples."

LIVINGSTON PRESS

University of West Alabama, 100 N. Washington St., Station 22, University of West Alabama, Livingston AL 35470. **Fax:** (205)652-3717. **E-mail:** jwt@uwa.edu. **Website:** www.livingstonpress.uwa.edu. **Contact:** Joe Taylor, director. Estab. 1974. Publishes hardcover and trade paperback originals, plus Kindle. "Livingston Press, as do all literary presses, looks for authorial excellence in style. Currently emphasizing novels." Reading in June only. Check back for details. **Publishes 7-10 titles/year. 50% of books from first-time authors. 100% from unagented writers. Pays 80 contributor's copies, after sales of 1,000, standard royalty.** Publishes ms 18 months after acceptance. Accepts simultaneous submissions. Responds in 4 months to queries; 6-12 months to mss. Book catalog online. Guidelines online.

IMPRINTS Swallow's Tale Press.

FICTION Subjects include experimental, literary, offbeat or Southern. "We are interested in form and, of course, style." No genre fiction, please.

TIPS "Our readers are interested in literature, often quirky literature that emphasizes form and style. Please visit our website for current needs."

LLEWELLYN PUBLICATIONS

Imprint of Llewellyn Worldwide, Ltd., 2143 Wooddale Dr., Woodbury MN 55125. (651)291-1970. **Fax:** (651)291-1908. **E-mail:** submissions@llewellyn.com. **Website:** www.llewellyn.com. Estab. 1901. Publishes trade and mass market paperback originals. "Llewellyn publishes New Age fiction and nonfiction exploring new worlds of mind and spirit. Currently emphasizing astrology, alternative health and healing, tarot. De-emphasizing fiction, channeling." **Publishes 100+ titles/year. 30% of books from first-time authors. 50% from unagented writers. Pays 10% royalty on wholesale or retail price.** Accepts simultaneous submissions. Responds in 3 months to queries. Book catalog online.

NONFICTION Subjects include New Age, psychology. Submit outline, sample chapters. Reviews artwork/photos.

LONELY PLANET PUBLICATIONS

124 Linden St., Oakland CA 94607. (510)250-6400. **Fax:** (510)893-8572. **Website:** www.lonelyplanet. com. Estab. 1973. Publishes trade paperback originals.

"Lonely Planet publishes travel guides, atlases, travel literature, phrasebooks, condensed pocket guides, diving and snorkeling guides." **Work-for-hire: on contract, 1/3 on submission, 1/3 on approval. Pays advance.** Accepts simultaneous submissions. Responds in 3 months to queries. Book catalog online. Guidelines online.

NONFICTION Subjects include travel. "We only work with contract writers on book ideas that we originate. We do not accept original proposals. Request our writer's guidelines. Send resume and clips of travel writing." Query with SASE.

LOOSE ID

P.O. Box 806, San Francisco CA 94104. **E-mail:** submissions@loose-id.com. **Website:** www.loose-id.com. **Contact:** Treva Harte, editor-in-chief. Estab. 2004. "*Loose Id* is love unleashed. We're taking romance to the edge." Publishes e-books and some print books. Distributes/promotes titles. "The company promotes itself through web and print advertising wherever readers of erotic romance may be found, creating a recognizable brand identity as the place to let your id run free and the people who unleash your fantasies. It is currently pursuing licensing agreements for foreign translations, and has a print program of 2 to 5 titles per month." **Pays e-book royalties of 40%.** Publishes ms within 1 year after acceptance. Accepts simultaneous submissions. Responds to queries in 1 month. Guidelines online.

○   "Loose Id is actively acquiring stories from both aspiring and established authors."

FICTION Subjects include erotica, romance. Wants nontraditional erotic romance stories, including gay, lesbian, heroes and heroines, multi-culturalism, cross-genre, fantasy, and science fiction, straight contemporary or historical romances. Query with outline/synopsis and 3 sample chapters. Accepts queries by e-mail. Include estimated word count, list of publishing credits, and why your submission is love unleashed. "Before submitting a query or proposal, please read the guidelines on our website. Please don't hesitate to contact us by e-mail for any information you don't see there."

LOYOLA PRESS

3441 N. Ashland Ave., Chicago IL 60657. (773)281-1818. **Fax:** (773)281-0152. **E-mail:** durepos@loyolapress.com. **Website:** www.loyolapress.org. **Contact:** Joseph Durepos, acquisitions editor. Estab. 1912.

Publishes hardcover and trade paperback. **Publishes 20-30 titles/year. 500 queries received/year. Pays standard royalties. Offers reasonable advance.** Accepts simultaneous submissions. Book catalog online. Guidelines online.

NONFICTION Subjects include memoirs, religion, spirituality, inspirational, prayer, Catholic life, parish and adult faith formation resources with a special focus on Ignatian spirituality and Jesuit history. E-mail query, or snail mail query with SASE.

TIPS "Check our submission guidelines."

LRP PUBLICATIONS, INC.

360 Hiatt Dr., Palm Beach Gardens FL 33418. **Website:** www.lrp.com. Estab. 1977. Publishes hardcover and trade paperback originals. "LRP publishes two industry-leading magazines, *Human Resource Executive*® and *Risk & Insurance*®, as well as hundreds of newsletters, books, videos and case reporters in the fields of: human resources, federal employment, workers' compensation, public employment law, disability, bankruptcy, education administration and law." **Pays royalty.** Book catalog free. Guidelines free.

NONFICTION Subjects include education. Submit proposal package, outline.

LSU PRESS

338 Johnston Hall, Baton Rouge LA 70803. (225)578-6294. **Website:** lsupress.org. Estab. 1935. LSU Press has established itself as one of the nation's outstanding scholarly presses and garners national and international accolades, including 4 Pulitzer Prizes. Accepts simultaneous submissions. Responds in 4-6 months. Catalog online. Guidelines online.

POETRY Poetry proposals should include a cover letter, 4-5 sample pages from the ms, and a current resume.

⊘ LUNA BISONTE PRODS

137 Leland Ave., Columbus OH 43214-7505. **E-mail:** bennettjohnm@gmail.com. **Website:** www.johnmbennett.net. **Contact:** John M. Bennett, editor/publisher. Estab. 1967. **Publishes 5 titles/year. Pays copy or copies of book; further copies at cost. Does not pay advance.** Not considering unsolicited submissions at this time.

NONFICTION Subjects include language, literature, poetry, visual poetry.

POETRY "Interested in avant-garde and highly experimental work only." Has published poetry by Jim Leftwich, Sheila E. Murphy, Al Ackerman, Richard

Kostelanetz, Carla Bertola, Olchar Lindsann, and many others. Query first, with a few sample poems and cover letter with brief bio and publication credits. "Keep it brief. Chapbook publishing usually depends on grants or other subsidies, and is usually by solicitation. **Will also consider subsidy arrangements on negotiable terms.**" A sampling of various Luna Bisonte Prods products is available for $20.

⊘ THE LYONS PRESS

The Globe Pequot Press, Inc., Box 480, 246 Goose Ln., Guilford CT 6437. (203)458-4500. **Fax:** (203)458-4668. **Website:** www.lyonspress.com. Estab. 1984 (Lyons & Burford), 1997 (The Lyons Press). Publishes hardcover and trade paperback originals and reprints. The Lyons Press publishes practical and literary books, chiefly centered on outdoor subjects—natural history, all sports, gardening, horses, fishing, hunting, survival, self-reliant living, plus cooking, memoir, bio, nonfiction. "At this time, we are not accepting unsolicited mss or proposals." Check back for updates. **Pays $3,000-25,000 advance.** Book catalog online. Guidelines online.

NONFICTION Subjects include agriculture, Americana, animals, history, recreation, sports, adventure, fitness, the sea, woodworking.

♲ MAGENTA FOUNDATION

151 Winchester St., Toronto ON M4X 1B5, Canada. **E-mail:** info@magentafoundation.org. **Website:** www.magentafoundation.org. **Contact:** Submissions. Estab. 2004. "Established in 2004, The Magenta Foundation is Canada's pioneering non-profit, charitable arts publishing house. Magenta was created to organize promotional opportunities for artists, in an international context, through circulated exhibitions and publications. Projects mounted by Magenta are supported by credible international media coverage and critical reviews in all mainstream-media formats (radio, television and print). Magenta works with respected individuals and international organizations to help increase recognition for artists while uniting the global photography community." Accepts simultaneous submissions.

MAGE PUBLISHERS, INC.

1780 Crossroads Dr., Odenton MD 21113. (202)342-1642. **Fax:** (202)342-9269. **E-mail:** as@mage.com. **Website:** www.mage.com. Estab. 1985. Publishes hardcover originals and reprints, trade paperback originals. Mage publishes books relating to Persian/

Iranian culture. **Pays royalty.** Accepts simultaneous submissions. Responds in 1 month to queries. Book catalog available free. Guidelines online.

NONFICTION Subjects include ethnic, history, sociology, translation. Submit outline, bio, SASE. Query via mail or e-mail. Reviews artwork/photos. Send photocopies.

FICTION Subjects include ethnic, feminist, historical, literary, short story collections. Must relate to Persian/Iranian culture. Submit outline, SASE. Query via mail or e-mail.

POETRY Must relate to Persian/Iranian culture. Query.

TIPS "Audience is the Iranian-American community in America and Americans interested in Persian culture."

MAGINATION PRESS

750 First St. NE, Washington DC 20002. (202)336-5618. **Fax:** (202)336-5624. **E-mail:** magination@apa.org. **Website:** www.apa.org. Estab. 1988. Magination Press is an imprint of the American Psychological Association. "We publish books dealing with the psycho/therapeutic resolution of children's problems and psychological issues with a strong self-help component." Submit complete ms. Full guidelines available on site. Materials returned only with SASE. **Publishes 12 titles/year. 75% of books from first-time authors.** Publishes a book 18-24 months after acceptance. Accepts simultaneous submissions. Responds to queries in 1-2 months; mss in 2-6 months.

NONFICTION All levels: psychological and social issues, self-help, health, multicultural, special needs.

FICTION All levels: psychological and social issues, self-help, health, parenting concerns and, special needs. Picture books, middle school readers.

MANDALA PUBLISHING

Mandala Publishing and Earth Aware Editions, 800 A St., San Rafael CA 94901. **E-mail:** info@mandalapublishing.com. **Website:** www.mandalaeartheditions.com. Estab. 1989. Publishes hardcover, trade paperback, and electronic originals. "In the traditions of the East, wisdom, truth, and beauty go hand in- hand. This is reflected in the great arts, music, yoga, and philosophy of India. Mandala Publishing strives to bring to its readers authentic and accessible renderings of thousands of years of wisdom and philosophy from this unique culture-timeless treasures that are our inspirations and guides. At Mandala, we believe that the arts, health, ecology, and spirituality of the great Vedic traditions are as relevant today as they were in sacred India thousands of years ago. As a distinguished publisher in the world of Vedic literature, lifestyle, and interests today, Mandala strives to provide accessible and meaningful works for the modern reader." **Publishes 12 titles/year. 200 queries received/year. 100 mss received/year. 40% of books from first-time authors. 100% from unagented writers. Pays 3-15% royalty on retail price.** Publishes ms 8 months after acceptance. Accepts simultaneous submissions. Responds in 6 months. Book catalog online.

NONFICTION Subjects include education, philosophy, photography, religion, spirituality. Query with SASE. Reviews artwork/photos. Send photocopies and thumbnails.

FICTION Subjects include juvenile, religious, spiritual. Query with SASE.

⚙ MANOR HOUSE PUBLISHING, INC.

452 Cottingham Crescent, Ancaster ON L9G 3V6, Canada. (905)648-2193. **E-mail:** mbdavie@manor-house.biz. **Website:** www.manor-house.biz. **Contact:** Mike Davie, president (novels and nonfiction). Estab. 1998. Publishes hardcover, trade paperback, and mass market paperback originals (and reprints if they meet specific criteria - best to inquire with publisher). Manor House is currently looking for new fully edited, ready-to-run titles to complete our spring-fall 2017 release lineup. This is a rare opportunity for authors, including self-published, to have existing or ready titles picked up by Manor House and made available to retailers throughout the world, while our network of rights agents provide more potential revenue streams via foreign language rights sales. We are currently looking for titles that are ready or nearly ready for publishing to be released this fall. Such titles should be written by Canadian citizens residing in Canada and should be profitable or with strong market sales potential to allow full cost recovery and profit for publisher and author. Of primary interest are business and self-help titles along with other nonfiction, including new age. **Publishes 5-6 titles/year. 30 queries; 20 mss received/year. 90% of books from first-time authors. 90% from unagented writers. Pays 10% royalty on retail price.** Publishes book 6 mos to 1 year after acceptance. Queries and mss to be sent by e-mail only. "We will respond in 30 days if interested-if not, there is no response. Do not

follow up unless asked to do so.". Book catalog online. Guidelines available.

NONFICTION Subjects include history, sex, social sciences, sociology, spirituality. We are currently looking for titles that are ready or nearly ready for publishing to be released in 2017 onward. Such titles should be written by Canadian citizens residing in Canada and should be profitable or with strong market sales potential to allow full cost recovery and profit for publisher and author. Of primary interest are Business and self-help titles along with other nonfiction, including new age. We are also open to publishing non-Canadian authors (nonfiction works only) - provided non-Canadian authors can further provide us with a very good indication of demand for their book (Eg: actual or expected advance book orders from speaker venues, corporations, agencies or authors on a non-returnable basis) so we are assured the title will likely be a profitable venture for both author and publisher. Query via e-mail. Submit proposal package, outline, bio, 3 sample chapters. Submit complete ms. Reviews artwork/photos. Send photocopies.

FICTION Subjects include adventure, experimental, gothic, historical, horror, humor, juvenile, literary, mystery, occult, poetry, regional, romance, short story collections, young adult. Stories should mainly be by Canadian authors residing in Canada, have Canadian settings and characters should be Canadian, but content should have universal appeal to wide audience. In some cases, we will consider publishing non-Canadian fiction authors - provided they demonstrate publishing their book will be profitable for author and publisher. Query via e-mail. Submit proposal package, clips, bio, 3 sample chapters. Submit complete ms.

POETRY Poetry should engage, provoke, involve the reader (and be written by Canadian authors residing in Canada).

TIPS "Our audience includes everyone-the general public/mass audience. Self-edit your work first, make sure it is well written and well edited with strong Canadian content and/or content of universal appeal (preferably with a Canadian connection of some kind)."

Ⓐ MARINER BOOKS

222 Berkeley St., Boston MA 2116. (617)351-5000. **Website:** www.hmco.com. Estab. 1997. Accepts simultaneous submissions.

POETRY Has published poetry by Thomas Lux, Linda Gregerson, and Keith Leonard. Agented submissions only.

MARTIN SISTERS PUBLISHING COMPANY

P.O. Box 1154, Barbourville KY 40906-1499. **Website:** www.martinsisterspublishing.com. Estab. 2011. Firm/imprint publishes trade and mass market paperback originals; electronic originals. **Publishes 12 titles/year. 75% of books from first-time authors. 100% from unagented writers. Pays 7.5% royalty/max on print net; 35% royalty/max on e-book net. No advance offered.** Publishes ms 9 months after acceptance. Accepts simultaneous submissions. Responds in 1 month on queries, 2 months on proposals, 3-6 months on mss. Catalog and guidelines online.

NONFICTION Subjects include Americana, child guidance, contemporary culture, cooking, creative nonfiction, education, gardening, history, house and home, humanities, labor, language, law, literature, memoirs, money, nutrition, parenting, psychology, regional, sociology, spirituality, womens issues, womens studies, western. Does not review artwork.

FICTION Subjects include adventure, confession, fantasy, historical, humor, juvenile, literary, mainstream, military, mystery, poetry in translation, regional, religious, romance, science fiction, short story collections, spiritual, sports, suspense, war, western, young adult. "Please place query letter, marketing plan and the first 5-10 pages of your manuscript (if you are submitting fiction) directly into your e-mail." Guidelines available on site.

MARVEL COMICS

135 W. 50th St., 7th Floor, New York NY 10020. **Website:** www.marvel.com. Publishes hardcover originals and reprints, trade paperback reprints, mass market comic book originals, electronic reprints. **Pays on a per page work for hire basis or creator-owned which is then contracted. Pays negotiable advance.** Responds in 3-5 weeks to queries. Guidelines online.

FICTION Subjects include adventure, comic books, fantasy, horror, humor, science fiction, young adult. Our shared universe needs new heroes and villains; books for younger readers and teens needed. Submit inquiry letter, idea submission form (download from website), SASE.

MASTER BOOKS

P.O. Box 726, Green Forest AR 72638. **E-mail:** submissions@newleafpress.net. **Website:** www.masterbooks.

com. **Contact:** Craig Froman, acquisitions editor. Estab. 1975. Publishes 3 middle readers/year; 2 young adult nonfiction titles/year; 10 homeschool curriculum titles; 20 adult trade books/year. **500 5% of books from first-time authors. 99% from unagented writers. Pays authors royalty of 3-15% based on wholesale price.** Publishes book 1 year after acceptance. Accepts simultaneous submissions. We are no longer able to respond to every query. If you have not heard from us within 90 days, it means we are unable to partner with you on that particular project. Book catalog available upon request. Guidelines online.

NONFICTION Subjects include archeology, religion, science, womens issues, world affairs. Picture books: activity books, animal, nature/environment, creation. Young readers, middle readers, young adults: activity books, animal, biography Christian, nature/environment, science, creation. Submission guidelines on website.

TIPS "All of our children's books are creation-based, including topics from the Book of Genesis. We look also for home school educational material as we are expanding our home school curriculum resources."

MAVEN HOUSE PRESS

4 Snead Ct., Palmyra VA 22963. (610)883-7988. **Fax:** (888)894-3403. **E-mail:** jim@mavenhousepress.com. **Website:** www.mavenhousepress.com. **Contact:** Jim Pennypacker, publisher. Estab. 2012. Publishes hardcover, trade paperback, and electronic originals. Maven House Press publishes business books for executives and managers to help them lead their organizations to greatness. **Publishes 4 titles/year. 50% of books from first-time authors. 50% from unagented writers. Pays 10-50% royalty based on wholesale price. Does not pay advance.** Publishes ms 12 months after acceptance. Accepts simultaneous submissions. Responds in 1 month.

NONFICTION Subjects include business, career guidance, communications, economics, finance, business/management/personal success. Submit proposal package including: outline, 1-2 sample chapters. See submission form online.

MAVERICK DUCK PRESS

E-mail: maverickduckpress@yahoo.com. **Website:** www.maverickduckpress.com. **Contact:** Kendall A. Bell, editor. Assistant Editors: Kayla Marie Middlebrook and Brielle Kelton. Estab. 2005. Maverick Duck Press is a "publisher of chapbooks from undiscovered talent. We are looking for fresh and powerful work that shows a sense of innovation or a new take on passion or emotion. Previous publication in print or online journals could increase your chances of us accepting your manuscript." Does not want "unedited work." **Pays 20 author's copies.**

POETRY Send ms in Microsoft Word format with a cover letter with brief bio and publication credits. Chapbook mss may include previously published poems. "Previous publication is always a plus, as we may be more familiar with your work. Chapbook mss should have 16-24 poems, but no more than 24 poems."

MAVERICK MUSICALS AND PLAYS

17, Tarnkun St., Alexandra Headlands QLD 4572, Australia. Phone/**Fax:** (61)(7)5448 4093. **E-mail:** tahlia@maverickmusicals.com. **Website:** www.maverickmusicals.com. **Contact:** Tahlia Wilkins. Estab. 1978. Accepts simultaneous submissions. Guidelines online.

FICTION "Looking for two-act musicals and one-and two-act plays. See website for more details."

MCBOOKS PRESS

ID Booth Building, 520 N. Meadow St., Ithaca NY 14850. (607)272-2114. **E-mail:** mcbooks@mcbooks.com. **E-mail:** alex@mcbooks.com. **Website:** www.mcbooks.com. **Contact:** Alexander G. Skutt, publisher. Art Director & Associate Publisher: Panda Musgrove. Estab. 1979. Publishes trade paperback and hardcover originals and reprints. McBooks Press has been publishing books independently for over 30 years in Ithaca, New York. McBooks' extensive list of publications features works of historical fiction—including naval and military fiction in series. We continue to seek excellent historical naval adventures that are suitable for publication in series. In the past, we have also published nonfiction, including books on boxing, food and health, and the Finger Lakes Region of New York State. **Publishes 5 titles/year. 15% of books from first-time authors. 30% from unagented writers. Pays a percentage of cover price for physical books plus a percentage of net income for e-books. Pays advance.** Publishes ms over 1 year after acceptance. Accepts simultaneous submissions. Responds in 2 months. Guidelines online.

"Currently not accepting submissions or queries for fiction or nonfiction." The only exceptions that we would look at are: 1) well-written nautical historical fiction that could grow into a series 2) great books about the Finger Lakes or adjacent regions of Upstate New York.

NONFICTION Subjects include history, marine subjects.

FICTION Subjects include adventure, military, war. Publishes Julian Stockwin, John Biggins, Colin Sargent, and Douglas W. Jacobson. Distributes titles through Independent Publishers Group.

TIPS "We are currently only publishing authors with whom we have a pre-existing relationship. If this policy changes, we will announce the change on our website."

⟳ MCCLELLAND & STEWART, LTD.

The Canadian Publishers, 320 Front St. W., Suite 1400, Toronto ON M5V 3B6, Canada. (416)364-4449. **Fax:** (416)598-7764. **Website:** www.mcclelland.com. Publishes hardcover, trade paperback, and mass market paperback originals and reprints. **Publishes 80 titles/year. 1,500 queries received/year. 10% of books from first-time authors. 30% from unagented writers. Pays 10-15% royalty on retail price (hardcover rates). Pays advance.** Publishes ms 1 year after acceptance. Accepts simultaneous submissions. Responds in 3 months to proposals.

NONFICTION Subjects include history, philosophy, photography, psychology, recreation, religion, science, sociology, sports, translation, travel, Canadiana. "We publish books primarily by Canadian authors." Submit outline. *All unsolicited mss returned unopened.*

FICTION "We publish work by established authors, as well as the work of new and developing authors." Query. *All unsolicited mss* returned unopened.

POETRY Only Canadian poets should apply. We publish only 4 titles each year. Query. *No unsolicited mss.*

THE MCDONALD & WOODWARD PUBLISHING CO.

695 Tall Oaks Dr., Newark OH 43055. (740)641-2691. **Fax:** (740)641-2692. **E-mail:** mwpubco@mwpubco.com. **Website:** www.mwpubco.com. **Contact:** Jerry N. McDonald, publisher. Estab. 1986. Publishes hardcover and trade paperback originals. McDonald & Woodward publishes books in natural history, cultural history, and natural resources. Currently emphasizing travel, natural and cultural history, and natural resource conservation. **Publishes 5 titles/year. 25 queries received/year. 20 mss received/year. Pays 10% royalty.** Accepts simultaneous submissions.

Responds in less than 1 month. Book catalog online. Guidelines free on request; by e-mail.

NONFICTION Subjects include animals, architecture, environment, history, nature, science, travel, natural history. Query with SASE. Reviews artwork/photos. Photos are not required.

FICTION Subjects include historical. Query with SASE.

TIPS "Our books are meant for the curious and educated elements of the general population."

⊘ MARGARET K. MCELDERRY BOOKS

Imprint of Simon & Schuster Children's Publishing Division, 1230 Sixth Ave., New York NY 10020. (212)698-7200. **Website:** imprints.simonandschuster.biz/margaret-k-mcelderry-books. VP/Publisher: Justin Chanda. Estab. 1971. "Margaret K. McElderry Books publishes hardcover and paperback trade books for children from pre-school age through young adult. This list includes picture books, middle grade and teen fiction, poetry, and fantasy. The style and subject matter of the books we publish is almost unlimited. We do not publish textbooks, coloring and activity books, greeting cards, magazines, pamphlets, or religious publications." **Publishes 30 titles/year. 15% of books from first-time authors. 50% from unagented writers. Pays authors royalty based on retail price. Pays illustrator royalty of by the project. Pays photographers by the project. Original artwork returned at job's completion. Offers $5,000-8,000 advance for new authors.** Accepts simultaneous submissions. Guidelines for #10 SASE.

NONFICTION Subjects include history, adventure. *No unsolicited mss. Agented submissions only.*

FICTION Subjects include adventure, fantasy, historical, mystery, picture books, young adult. *No unsolicited mss. Agented submissions only.*

TIPS "Read! The children's book field is competitive. See what's been done and what's out there before submitting. We look for high quality: an originality of ideas, clarity and felicity of expression, a well organized plot, and strong character-driven stories. We're looking for strong, original fiction, especially mysteries and middle grade humor. We are always interested in picture books for the youngest age reader. Study our titles."

MCFARLAND & CO., INC., PUBLISHERS

Box 611, Jefferson NC 28640. (336)246-4460. **Fax:** (336)246-5018. **E-mail:** info@mcfarlandpub.com.

Website: www.mcfarlandpub.com. **Contact:** Editorial Department. Estab. 1979. Publishes hardcover and quality paperback originals. "McFarland publishes serious nonfiction in a variety of fields, including general reference, performing arts, popular culture, sports (particularly baseball); women's studies, librarianship, literature, Civil War, history and international studies. Currently emphasizing medieval history, automotive history. De-emphasizing memoirs." **Publishes 350 titles/year. 50% of books from first-time authors. 95% from unagented writers.** Publishes book 10 months after acceptance. Accepts simultaneous submissions. Responds in 1 month to queries. Guidelines online.

NONFICTION Subjects include history, recreation, sociology, African-American studies (very strong). Reference books are particularly wanted—fresh material (i.e., not in head-to-head competition with an established title). "We prefer manuscripts of 250 or more double-spaced pages or at least 75,000 words." No fiction, New Age, exposes, poetry, children's books, devotional/inspirational works, Bible studies, or personal essays. Query with SASE. Submit outline, sample chapters. Reviews artwork/photos.

TIPS "We want well-organized knowledge of an area in which there is not information coverage at present, plus reliability so we don't feel we have to check absolutely everything. Our market is worldwide and libraries are an important part."

MCGRAW-HILL PROFESSIONAL BUSINESS

Imprint of The McGraw-Hill Companies, 2 Penn Plaza, New York NY 10121. (212)438-1000. **Website:** www.mcgraw-hill.com. McGraw Hill Professional is a publishing leader in business/investing, management, careers, self-help, consumer health, language reference, test preparation, sports/recreation, and general interest titles. Publisher not responsible for returning mss or proposals. Accepts simultaneous submissions. Guidelines online.

NONFICTION Subjects include child guidance, education, sports, management, consumer reference, English and foreign language reference. Current, up-to-date, original ideas are needed. Good self-promotion is key. Submit proposal package, outline, concept of book, competition and market info, CV.

MC PRESS

3695 W. Quail Heights Ct., Boise ID 83703. (208)629-7275. **Fax:** (208)639-1231. **E-mail:** duptmor@mcpressonline.com. **Website:** www.mc-store.com. **Contact:** David Uptmor, publisher. Editor: Anne Grubb. Estab. 2001. Publishes trade paperback originals. **Publishes 12 titles/year. 50 queries received/year. 15 mss received/year. 50% of books from first-time authors. 100% from unagented writers. Pays 10-16% royalty on wholesale price.** Publishes book 5 months after acceptance. Accepts simultaneous submissions. Responds in 1 month. Book catalog and ms guidelines free.

IMPRINTS MC Press, IBM Press.

NONFICTION "We specialize in computer titles targeted at IBM technologies." Submit proposal package, outline, 2 sample chapters, abstract. Reviews artwork/photos. Send photocopies.

MCSWEENEY'S POETRY SERIES

San Francisco CA **E-mail:** poetry@mcsweeneys.net. **Website:** mcsweeneys.net. McSweeney's regularly publishes poetry collections, as part of the McSweeney's Poetry Series. Accepts simultaneous submissions. Catalog online. Guidelines online.

POETRY The McSweeney's Poetry Series publishes new collections of poetry. "We are open to all styles. Book-length mss should be sent as PDF to poetry@mcsweeneys.net. In the cover letter, include your name, phone number, and e-mail address.

TIPS "We're a very small operation, and we may not be able to get back to you about the manuscript. We will do our very best."

MEDALLION PRESS

4222 Meridian Pkwy., Aurora IL 60504. (630)513-8316. **E-mail:** emily@medallionpress.com. **Website:** medallionpress.com. **Contact:** Emily Steele, editorial director. Estab. 2003. Publishes trade paperback, hardcover, e-book originals. "We are an independent, innovative publisher looking for compelling, memorable stories told in distinctive voices." **Offers advance.** Publishes ms 1-2 years after acceptance. Accepts simultaneous submissions. Responds in 2-3 months to mss. Guidelines online. Currently closed to submissions.

NONFICTION Subjects include art, health, celebrity, design, fitness. *Agented only.* Please query.

FICTION Subjects include fantasy, historical, horror, literary, mainstream, mystery, romance, science fiction, suspense, young adult, thriller, YA-YA (YA written by young adults). Word count: 40,000-90,000 for YA; 60,000-120,000 for all others. No short stories, anthologies, erotica, middle grade, children's fiction.

Submit first 3 consecutive chapters and a synopsis through our online submission form. Please check if submissions are currently open before submitting. **TIPS** "Please visit our website for the most current guidelines prior to submitting anything to us. Please check if submissions are currently open before submitting."

MEDICAL GROUP MANAGEMENT ASSOCIATION

104 Inverness Terrace E., Englewood CO 80112. (303)799-1111. **E-mail:** support@mgma.com. **Website:** www.mgma.org. Estab. 1926. Publishes professional and scholarly hardcover, paperback, and electronic originals, and trade paperback reprints. **Publishes 6 titles/year. 18 queries received/year. 6 mss received/year. 30% of books from first-time authors. 100% from unagented writers. Pays 8-17% royalty on net sales (twice a year). Pays $2,000-5,000 advance.** Publishes ms 6 months after acceptance. Accepts simultaneous submissions. Responds in less than 3 weeks to queries. Book catalog online. Guidelines online.

NONFICTION Subjects include education, health. Submit proposal package, outline, 3 sample chapters. Submit complete ms. Reviews artwork/photos. Send photocopies.

TIPS "Audience includes medical practice managers and executives. Our books are geared at the business side of medicine."

MEDICAL PHYSICS PUBLISHING

4555 Helgesen Dr., Madison WI 53718. (608)224-4508. **Fax:** (608)224-5016. **E-mail:** todd@medicalphysics.org. **Website:** www.medicalphysics.org. **Contact:** Todd Hanson, editor. Estab. 1985. Publishes hardcover and paperback originals and reprints. "We are a nonprofit publisher of affordable books in medical physics and related fields." **Publishes 5-6 titles/year. 10-20 queries received/year. 10% of books from first-time authors. 100% from unagented writers. Pays 10% royalty on net price. Does not pay advance.** Publishes most mss 1 year after acceptance. Accepts simultaneous submissions. Responds in 3 months to mss. Book catalog available via website or upon request.

NONFICTION Subjects include medicine, science, Symposium proceedings in the fields of medical physics and radiology. Submit complete ms. Reviews artwork/photos. Send disposable copies.

MELANGE BOOKS, LLC

White Bear Lake MN 55110-5538. **E-mail:** melange-books@melange-books.com. **E-mail:** submissions@melange-books.com. **Website:** www.melange-books.com. **Contact:** Nancy Schumacher, publisher and acquiring editor for Melange and Satin Romance; Caroline Andrus, acquiring editor for Fire and Ice for Young Adult. Estab. 2011. Publishes trade paperback originals and electronic originals. Melange is a royalty-paying company publishing e-books and print books. **Publishes 75 titles/year. Receives 1,000 queries/year; 700 mss/year. 65% of books from first-time authors. 75% from unagented writers. Authors receive a minimum of 20% royalty on print sales, 40% on electronic book sales. Does not offer an advance.** Publishes book 12-15 months after acceptance. Accepts simultaneous submissions. Responds in 1 month on queries; 2 months on proposals; 4-6 months on mss. Send SASE for book catalog. Guidelines online.

IMPRINTS Fire and Ice (young and new adult); Satin Romance.

FICTION Subjects include adventure, contemporary, erotica, fantasy, gay, gothic, historical, lesbian, mainstream, multicultural, mystery, romance, science fiction, suspense, western, young adult. Submit a clean mss by following guidelines on website. Query electronically by clicking on "submissions" on website. Include a synopsis and 4 chapters.

MELBOURNE UNIVERSITY PUBLISHING, LTD.

Subsidiary of University of Melbourne, Level 1, 11-15 Argyle Pl. S., Carlton VIC 3053, Australia. (61)(3)934-20300. **Fax:** (61)(3)9342-0399. **E-mail:** mup-contact@unimelb.edu.au. **E-mail:** mup-submissions@unimelb.edu.au. **Website:** www.mup.com.au. **Contact:** The Executive Assistant. Estab. 1922. **Publishes 80 titles/year.** Accepts simultaneous submissions. Responds to queries in 4 months if interested. Guidelines online.

IMPRINTS Melbourne University Press; The Miegunyah Press (strong Australian content); Victory Books.

NONFICTION Subjects include philosophy, science, social sciences, Aboriginal studies, cultural studies, gender studies, natural history. Submit using MUP Book Proposal Form available online.

MENASHA RIDGE PRESS

AdventureKEEN, 2204 First Ave. S., Suite 102, Birmingham AL 35233. (205)322-0439. **E-mail:** tim@adventurewithkeen.com. **Website:** www.menasharidge. com. **Contact:** Tim Jackson, acquisitions editor. Publishes hardcover and trade paperback originals. Menasha Ridge Press publishes distinctive books in the areas of outdoor sports, recreation, and travel. We are primarily looking for outdoors guidebooks. "Our authors are among the best in their fields." **Publishes 20 titles/year. 30% of books from first-time authors. 90% from unagented writers. Pays varying royalty. Pays varying advance.** Publishes ms 1 year after acceptance. Accepts simultaneous submissions. Responds in 2 months to queries.

NONFICTION Subjects include nature, recreation, sports, travel, outdoors. Most concepts are generated in-house, but a few come from outside submissions. Submit proposal package, resume, clips. Reviews artwork/photos.

MERRIAM PRESS

489 South St., Hoosick Falls NY 12090. **E-mail:** ray@ merriam-press.com. **Website:** www.merriam-press. com. **Contact:** Ray Merriam, owner. Estab. 1988. Publishes hardcover and softcover trade paperback original works and reprints. Titles are also made available in e-book editions. Merriam Press specializes in military history, particularly World War II history. We are also branching out into other genres, including fiction, historical fiction, poetry, children. Provide brief synopsis of ms. Never send any files in body of e-mail or as an attachment. Publisher will ask for full ms for review. **Publishes 50+ titles/year. 70-90% of books from first-time authors. 100% from unagented writers. Pays 10% royalty for printed editions and 50% royalty for eBook editions. Royalty payment is based on the amount paid to the publisher, not the retail or list prices. Does not pay advance.** Publishes ms 6 months or less after acceptance. Responds quickly (e-mail preferred) to queries. Book catalog available in print and PDF editions. Author guidelines and additional information are available on publisher's website.

○ Publisher requires unformatted mss. Mss must be thoroughly edited and error-free.

NONFICTION Subjects include Americana, creative nonfiction, history, memoirs, military, war. Especially but not limited to military history. Query with SASE or by e-mail first. Do not send ms (in whole or in part) unless requested to do so. When

asked to submit ms, include all artwork, photos and other materials.

FICTION Subjects include historical, military, poetry, war. Especially but not limited to military history. Query with SASE or by e-mail first. Do not send ms (in whole or in part) unless requested to do so.

POETRY Especially but not limited to military topics. Query with SASE or by e-mail first. Do not send ms (in whole or in part) unless requested to do so.

TIPS "Our military history books are geared for military historians, collectors, model kit builders, wargamers, veterans, general enthusiasts. We now publish some historical fiction and poetry and will consider well-written books on a variety of non-military topics."

MESSIANIC JEWISH PUBLISHERS

6120 Day Long Ln., Clarksville MD 21029. (410)531-6644. **E-mail:** editor@messianicjewish.net. **Website:** www.messianicjewish.net. Publishes hardcover and trade paperback originals and reprints. **Publishes 6-12 titles/year. Pays 7-15% royalty on wholesale price.** Accepts simultaneous submissions. Guidelines via e-mail.

NONFICTION Subjects include religion. Text must demonstrate keen awareness of Jewish culture and thought, and Biblical literacy. Jewish themes only. Query with SASE. Unsolicited mss are not returned.

FICTION Subjects include religious. "We publish very little fiction. Jewish or Biblical themes are a must. Text must demonstrate keen awareness of Jewish culture and thought." Query with SASE. Unsolicited mss are not return.

METAL POWDER INDUSTRIES FEDERATION

105 College Rd. E., Princeton NJ 08540. (609)452-7700. **Fax:** (609)987-8523. **Website:** www.mpif.org. Estab. 1946. Publishes hardcover originals. "Metal Powder Industries publishes monographs, textbooks, handbooks, design guides, conference proceedings, standards, and general titles in the field of powder metallurgy or particulate materials." **Publishes 10 titles/year. Pays 3-12% royalty on wholesale or retail price. Pays $3,000-5,000 advance.** Accepts simultaneous submissions. Responds in 1 month to queries.

NONFICTION Work must relate to powder metallurgy or particulate materials.

❥ METHUEN PUBLISHING LTD

Editorial Department, 35 Hospital Fields Rd., York YO10 4DZ, United Kingdom. **E-mail:** editorial@metheun.co.uk. **Website:** www.methuen.co.uk. Estab. 1889. **Pays royalty.** Accepts simultaneous submissions. Guidelines online.

○ No unsolicited mss; synopses and ideas welcome. Prefers to be approached via agents or a letter of inquiry. No first novels, cookery books or personal memoirs.

NONFICTION Subjects include contemporary culture, history, psychology, sports. No cookbooks or memoirs. Query with SASE. Submit outline, resume, publishing history, clips, bio, SASE.

FICTION No first novels. Query with SASE. Submit proposal package, outline, outline/proposal, resume, publishing history, clips, bio, SASE.

TIPS "We recommend that all prospective authors attempt to find an agent before submitting to publishers and we do not encourage unagented submissions."

⊘ MIAMI UNIVERSITY PRESS

356 Bachelor Hall, Miami University, Oxford OH 45056. **E-mail:** mupress@miamioh.edu. **Website:** www.miamioh.edu/mupress. **Contact:** Keith Tuma, editor; Amy Toland, managing editor. Estab. 1992. Publishes 1-2 books of poetry and/or poetry in translation per year and 1 novella, in paperback editions. Accepts simultaneous submissions.

NONFICTION Subjects include literature.

FICTION Subjects include contemporary, experimental, feminist, gay, literary, multicultural, poetry, poetry in translation, translation.

POETRY Miami University Press is unable to respond to unsolicited mss and queries.

MICHIGAN STATE UNIVERSITY PRESS

1405 S. Harrison Rd., Suite 25, East Lansing MI 48823. (517)355-9543. **Fax:** (517)432-2611. **E-mail:** msupress@msu.edu. **Website:** msupress.org. **Contact:** Alex Schwartz and Julie Loehr, acquisitions. Estab. 1947. Publishes hardcover and softcover originals. Michigan State University Press has notably represented both scholarly publishing and the mission of Michigan State University with the publication of numerous award-winning books and scholarly journals. In addition, they publish nonfiction that addresses, in a more contemporary way, social concerns, such as diversity and civil rights. They also publish literary fiction and poetry. **Pays variable royalty.** Book catalog and ms guidelines online.

NONFICTION Distributes books for: University of Calgary Press, University of Alberta Press, and University of Manitoba Press. Submit proposal/outline and sample chapter. Hard copy is preferred but email proposals are also accepted. Initial submissions to MSU Press should be in the form of a short letter of inquiry and a sample chapter(s), as well as our preliminary Marketing Questionnaire, which can be downloaded from their website. We do not accept: Festschrifts, conference papers, or unrevised dissertations. Reviews artwork/photos.

FICTION Subjects include literary. Publishes literary fiction. Submit proposal.

POETRY Publishes poetry collections. Submit proposal with sample poems.

MICROSOFT PRESS

E-mail: 4bkideas@microsoft.com. **Website:** www.microsoft.com/learning/en/us/microsoft-press-books.aspx. **Publishes 80 titles/year. 25% of books from first-time authors. 90% from unagented writers.** Accepts simultaneous submissions. Book proposal guidelines online.

NONFICTION Subjects include software. A book proposal should consist of the following information: TOC, a resume with author biography, a writing sample, and a questionnaire. "We place a great deal of emphasis on your proposal. A proposal provides us with a basis for evaluating the idea of the book and how fully your book fulfills its purpose."

MILKWEED EDITIONS

1011 Washington Ave. S., Suite 300, Minneapolis MN 55415. (612)332-3192. **Fax:** (612)215-2550. **Website:** www.milkweed.org. Estab. 1979. Publishes hardcover, trade paperback, and electronic originals; trade paperback and electronic reprints. "Milkweed Editions publishes with the intention of making a humane impact on society, in the belief that literature is a transformative art uniquely able to convey the essential experiences of the human heart and spirit. To that end, Milkweed Editions publishes distinctive voices of literary merit in handsomely designed, visually dynamic books, exploring the ethical, cultural, and esthetic issues that free societies need continually to address." **Publishes 15-20 titles/year. 25% of books from first-time authors. 75% from unagented writers. Pays authors variable royalty based on** retail price. **Offers advance against royalties. Pays varied advance from $500-10,000.** Publishes book in 18 months. Accepts simultaneous submissions. Responds in 6 months. Book catalog online. Only accepts submissions during open submission periods. See website for guidelines.

NONFICTION Subjects include agriculture, animals, art, contemporary culture, creative nonfiction, environment, gardening, gay, government, history, humanities, language, literature, multicultural, nature, politics, translation, world affairs. Does not review artwork.

FICTION Subjects include experimental, short story collections, translation, young adult. Novels for adults and for readers 8-13. High literary quality. For adult readers: literary fiction, nonfiction, poetry, essays. Middle readers: adventure, contemporary, fantasy, multicultural, nature/environment, suspense/mystery. Average length: middle readers—90-200 pages. No romance, mysteries, science fiction. "Please submit a query letter with three opening chapters (of a novel) or three representative stories (of a collection). Publishes YR."

POETRY Milkweed Editions is "looking for poetry manuscripts of high quality that embody humane values and contribute to cultural understanding." Not limited in subject matter. Open to writers with previously published books of poetry or a minimum of 6 poems published in nationally distributed commercial or literary journals. Considers translations and bilingual mss. Query with SASE; submit completed ms.

TIPS "We are looking for excellent writing with the intent of making a humane impact on society. Please read submission guidelines before submitting and acquaint yourself with our books in terms of style and quality before submitting. Many factors influence our selection process, so don't get discouraged. Nonfiction is focused on literary writing about the natural world, including living well in urban environments."

MILKWEED FOR YOUNG READERS

Milkweed Editions, Open Book Building, 1011 Washington Ave. S., Suite 300, Minneapolis MN 55415. (612)332-3192. **Fax:** (612)215-2550. **Website:** www. milkweed.org. Estab. 1984. Publishes hardcover and trade paperback originals. "We are looking first of all for high quality literary writing. We publish books with the intention of making a humane impact on society." **Publishes 3-4 titles/year. 25% of books from first-time authors. 50% from unagented writers. Pays 7% royalty on retail price. Pays variable advance.** Publishes ms 1 year after acceptance. Accepts simultaneous submissions. Responds in 6 months to queries. Book catalog for $1.50. Guidelines online.

FICTION Subjects include adventure, fantasy, historical, humor, animal, environmental. "Milkweed Editions now accepts manuscripts online through our Submission Manager. If you're a first-time submitter, you'll need to fill in a simple form and then follow the instructions for selecting and uploading your manuscript. Please make sure that your manuscript follows the submission guidelines."

⊘ THE MILLBROOK PRESS

Lerner Publishing Group, 1251 Washington Ave N, Minneapolis MN 55401. **E-mail:** info@lernerbooks. com. **Website:** www.lernerbooks.com. **Contact:** Carol Hinz, editorial director. "Millbrook Press publishes informative picture books, illustrated nonfiction titles, and inspiring photo-driven titles for grades K–5. Our authors approach curricular topics with a fresh point of view. Our fact-filled books engage readers with fun yet accessible writing, high-quality photographs, and a wide variety of illustration styles. We cover subjects ranging from the parts of speech and other language arts skills; to history, science, and math; to art, sports, crafts, and other interests. Millbrook Press is the home of the best-selling Words Are CATegorical® series and Bob Raczka's Art Adventures. We do not accept unsolicited manuscripts from authors. Occasionally, we may put out a call for submissions, which will be announced on our website." Accepts simultaneous submissions.

MINNESOTA HISTORICAL SOCIETY PRESS

Minnesota Historical Society, 345 Kellogg Blvd. W., St. Paul MN 55102. (651)259-3200. **Fax:** (651)297-1345. **E-mail:** ann.regan@mnhs.org. **Website:** www. mnhspress.org. **Contact:** Ann Regan, editor-in-chief. Estab. 1852. Publishes hardcover, trade paperback and electronic originals; trade paperback and electronic reprints. The Minnesota Historical Society Press is a leading publisher of the history and culture of Minnesota and the Upper Midwest. The Minnesota Historical Society Press seeks proposals for book manuscripts relating to the history and culture of Minnesota and the Upper Midwest. We are especially interested in excellent works of history and in well-researched and well-written manuscripts that use the best tools of narrative journalism to tell history for general audiences. Successful manuscripts will address themes or issues that are important to understanding life in this region and will reveal a strong sense of place. Preferred topics include Native American studies, Scandinavian studies, nature and environment, women's history, popular culture, food, adventure and travel, true crime, war and conflict, and the histories of Minnesota's diverse peoples. **Publishes 20 titles/year. 300 queries; 150 mss received/year. 60% of books from first-time authors. 95% from unagented writers. Royalties are negotiated; 5-10% on wholesale price. Pays $1,000 and up.** Publishes ms 16 months after acceptance. Accepts simultaneous submissions. Responds in 1-4 months. Book catalog online. Guidelines online.

NONFICTION Subjects include Americana, community, contemporary culture, cooking, creative nonfiction, ethnic, history, memoirs, multicultural, music, photography, politics, pop culture, regional, Native American studies. Books must have a connection to the Midwest. Regional works only. Submit proposal package, outline, 1 sample chapter and other materials listed in our online website in author guidelines: CV, brief description, intended audience, readership, length of ms, schedule. Reviews artwork/photos. Send photocopies.

MISSOURI HISTORICAL SOCIETY PRESS

The Missouri Historical Society, P.O. Box 11940, St. Louis MO 63112. (314)746-4558 or (314)746-4556. **Fax:** (314)746-4548. **E-mail:** jtebbe@mohistory.org. **Website:** www.mohistory.org. Publishes hardcover and trade paperback originals and reprints. **Publishes 2-4 titles/year. 30 queries; 20 mss received/year. 10% of books from first-time authors. 80% from unagented writers. Pays 5-10% royalty.** Accepts simultaneous submissions. Responds in 1-2 months.

NONFICTION Subjects include history, multicultural, regional, sports, popular culture, photography, children's nonfiction. Query with SASE and request author-proposal form.

TIPS "We're looking for new perspectives, even if the topics are familiar. You'll get our attention with nontraditional voices and views."

MITCHELL LANE PUBLISHERS, INC.

P.O. Box 196, Hockessin DE 33009. (302) 234-9426. **Fax:** (866) 834-4164. **E-mail:** barbaramitchell@mitchelllane.com; customerservice@mitchelllane.com. **Website:** www.mitchelllane.com. **Contact:** Barbara Mitchell. Estab. 1993. Publishes hardcover and library bound originals. **Publishes 80 titles/year. 100 queries received/year. 5 mss received/year. 0% of books from first-time authors. 90% from unagented writers. Work purchased outright from authors (range: $350-2,000). Pays illustrators by the project (range: $40-400).** Publishes ms 1 year after acceptance. Responds only if interested to queries. Book catalog available free.

NONFICTION Subjects include ethnic, multicultural. Young readers, middle readers, young adults: biography, nonfiction, and curriculum-related subjects. Average word length: 4,000-50,000 words. Recently published: *My Guide to US Citizenship*, *Rivers of the World* and *Vote America*. Query with SASE. *All unsolicited mss discarded.*

TIPS "We hire writers on a 'work-for-hire' basis to complete book projects we assign. Send résumé and writing samples that do not need to be returned."

MONDIAL

203 W. 107th St., Suite 6C, New York NY 10025. 212-864-7095. **Fax:** (208)361-2863. **E-mail:** contact@mondialbooks.com. **Website:** www.mondialbooks.com; www.librejo.com. **Contact:** Andrew Moore, editor. Estab. 1996. Publishes hard cover, trade paperback originals and reprints. Mondial publishes fiction and non-fiction in English, Esperanto, and Hebrew: novels, short stories, poetry, textbooks, dictionaries, books about history, linguistics, and psychology, among others. Since 2007, it has been publishing a literary magazine in Esperanto. **Publishes 20 titles/year. 2,000 queries; 500 mss received/year. 20% of books from first-time authors. 100% from unagented writers. Pays 10% royalty on wholesale price. Does not pay advance.** Publishes ms 4 months after acceptance. Accepts simultaneous submissions. Responds to queries in 3 months, only if interested. Guidelines online.

NONFICTION Subjects include ethnic, history, literary criticism, memoirs, multicultural, philosophy, psychology, sex, sociology, translation. Submit proposal package, outline, 1 sample chapters. Send only electronically by e-mail.

FICTION Subjects include adventure, erotica, ethnic, historical, literary, multicultural, mystery, poetry, romance, short story collections, translation. Query through online submission form.

MONSOON BOOKS

No.1 Duke of Windsor Suite, Burrough Court, Burrough on the Hill Leicestershire LE14 2QS, United Kingdom. **E-mail:** sales@monsoonbooks.co.uk. **Website:** www.monsoonbooks.co.uk. **Contact:** Philip Tatham, Publisher. Estab. 2002. Monsoon Books is a UK-based trade publisher of English-language fiction and narrative nonfiction relating to Asia. All titles have an Asian, usually a SE Asian, angle. Accepts simultaneous submissions. Guidelines online.

NONFICTION Subjects include contemporary culture, history, humanities, literature, memoirs, military, sex, true crime, war, world affairs.

FICTION Subjects include adventure, confession, contemporary, erotica, gay, historical, horror, lesbian, literary, mainstream, military, multicultural, mystery, romance, short story collections, suspense, translation, war. Query with outline/synopsis and submit complete ms with cover letter. Accepts queries by snail mail, fax, and e-mail (submissions@monsoonbooks.com.sg. Please include estimated word count, brief bio, list of publishing credits, and list of three comparative titles. Send hard copy submissions to: Monsoon Books Pte Ltd, 71 Ayer Rajah Crescent #01-01, Mediapolis Phase, Singapore 139951. We are not able to return hard copy manuscripts. We do not encourage hand deliveries. Agented fiction 20%. Responds in 8 weeks to your submissions. If you do not hear from us by then, e-mail us. Accepts simultaneous submissions, submissions on CD or disk. Rarely comments on rejected manuscripts. Monsoon Books regularly works with literary agents from the UK and Australia (such as David Higham Associates in London and Cameron's Management in Sydney) and we are particularly keen to hear from agents with manuscripts set in Southeast or North Asia as well as mss written by authors from this region.

TIPS "Monsoon welcomes unsolicited manuscripts from agented and unagented authors writing books set in Asia, particularly Southeast Asia."

MONTANA HISTORICAL SOCIETY PRESS

225 N. Roberts St., Helene MT 59620. (406)444-2694. **E-mail:** mholz@mt.gov. **Website:** https://mhs.mt.gov/pubs/press. **Contact:** Molly Holz, editor. Estab. 1956. Publishes hardcover originalsand trade paperback originals and reprints. **Publishes 4 titles/year. 24 queries received/year. 16 mss received/year. 50% of books from first-time authors. 100% from unagented writers. Pays 5-10% royalty on wholesale price.** Publishes ms 1 year after acceptance. Responds in 1 month to queries; 2 months to proposals; 4 months to mss. Book catalog online. Guidelines online.

NONFICTION Subjects include history, regional, travel. "We publish history and environmental studies books focusing on the northern plains and Rocky Mountains." Query with SASE.

TIPS "Audience includes history buffs; people with an interest in Yellowstone National Park."

MOODY PUBLISHERS

Moody Bible Institute, 820 N. LaSalle Blvd., Chicago IL 60610. (800)678-8812. **Fax:** (312)329-4157. **Website:** www.moodypublishers.org. **Contact:** Acquisitions Coordinator. Estab. 1894. Publishes hardcover, trade, and mass market paperback originals. "The mission of Moody Publishers is to educate and edify the Christian and to evangelize the non-Christian by ethically publishing conservative, evangelical Christian literature and other media for all ages around the world, and to help provide resources for Moody Bible Institute in its training of future Christian leaders." **Publishes 60 titles/year. 1,500 queries received/year. 2,000 mss received/year. 1% of books from first-time authors. 80% from unagented writers. Royalty varies.** Publishes book 1 year after acceptance. Responds in 2-3 months to queries. Book catalog for 9×12 envelope and 4 first-class stamps. Guidelines online.

NONFICTION Subjects include child guidance, religion, spirituality. "We are no longer reviewing queries or unsolicited manuscripts unless they come to us through an agent,are from an author who has published with us, an associate from a Moody Bible Institute ministry or a personal contact at a writer's conference. Unsolicited proposals will be returned only if proper postage is included. We are not able to acknowledge the receipt of your unsolicited proposal." Does not accept unsolicited nonfiction submissions.

FICTION Subjects include fantasy, historical, mystery, religious, science fiction, young adult. *Agented submissions only.*

TIPS "In our fiction list, we're looking for Christian storytellers rather than teachers trying to present a message. Your motivation should be to delight the reader. Using your skills to create beautiful works is glorifying to God."

MOTORBOOKS

Quarto Publishing Group, 400 First Ave. N., Suite 400, Minneapolis MN 55401. (612)344-8100. **Fax:** (612)344-8691. **E-mail:** zack.miller@quarto.com. **Website:** www.motorbooks.com. **Contact:** Zack Miller. Estab. 1973. Publishes hardcover and paperback originals. "Motorbooks is one of the world's leading transportation publishers, covering subjects from classic motorcycles to heavy equipment to today's latest automotive technology. We satisfy our customers' high expectations by hiring top writers and photographers and presenting their work in handsomely designed books that work hard in the shop and look good on the coffee table." **Publishes 200 titles/year. 300 queries; 50 mss received/year. 95% from unagented writers. Pays $5,000 average advance.** Publishes ms 1 year after acceptance. Accepts simultaneous submissions. Responds in 6-8 months to proposals. Book catalog available free. Guidelines online.
NONFICTION Subjects include Americana, history, hobbies, photography, translation. State qualifications for doing book. Transportation-related subjects. Query with SASE. Reviews artwork/photos. Send photocopies.

MOUNTAINEERS BOOKS

1001 SW Klickitat Way, Suite 201, Seattle WA 98134. (206)223-6303. **Fax:** (206)223-6306. **E-mail:** submissions@mountaineersbooks.org. **Website:** www.mountaineersbooks.org. Estab. 1961. Publishes hardcover and trade paperback originals and reprints. "Mountaineers Books specializes in expert, authoritative books dealing with mountaineering, hiking, backpacking, skiing, snowshoeing, etc. These can be either how-to-do-it or where-to-do-it (guidebooks). Currently emphasizing regional conservation and natural history." **Publishes 40 titles/year. 25% of books from first-time authors. 98% from unagented writers. Pays advance.** Publishes ms 1 year after acceptance. Responds in 3 months to queries. Guidelines online.
NONFICTION Subjects include recreation, regional, sports, translation, travel, natural history, conservation. Accepts nonfiction translations. Looks for expert knowledge, good organization. Also interested in nonfiction adventure narratives. Does not want to

see anything dealing with hunting, fishing, or motorized travel. Submit outline, 2 sample chapters, bio.
TIPS "The type of book the writer has the best chance of selling to our firm is an authoritative guidebook (*in our field*) to a specific area not otherwise covered; or a how-to that is better than existing competition (again, *in our field*)."

MOUNTAIN PRESS PUBLISHING CO.

P.O. Box 2399, Missoula MT 59806. (406)728-1900 or (800)234-5308. **Fax:** (406)728-1635. **E-mail:** info@mtnpress.com. **Website:** www.mountain-press.com. **Contact:** Jennifer Carey, editor. Estab. 1948. Publishes hardcover and trade paperback originals. "We are expanding our Roadside Geology, Geology Underfoot, and Roadside History series (done on a state-by-state basis). We are interested in well-written regional field guides—plants and flowers—and readable history and natural history." **Publishes 15 titles/year. 50% of books from first-time authors. 90% from unagented writers. Pays 7-12% royalty on wholesale price.** Publishes ms 2 years after acceptance. Accepts simultaneous submissions. Responds in 3 months to queries. Book catalog online.

○ Expanding children's/juvenile nonfiction titles.
NONFICTION Subjects include animals, history, regional, science. No personal histories or journals, poetry or fiction. Query with SASE. Submit outline, sample chapters. Reviews artwork/photos.
TIPS "Find out what kind of books a publisher is interested in and tailor your writing to them; research markets and target your audience. Research other books on the same subjects. Make yours different. Don't present your manuscript to a publisher—sell it. Give the information needed to make a decision on a title. Please learn what we publish before sending your proposal. We are a 'niche' publisher."

⊘ MOVING PARTS PRESS

10699 Empire Grade, Santa Cruz CA 95060. (831)427-2271. **E-mail:** frice@movingpartspress.com. **Website:** www.movingpartspress.com. **Contact:** Felicia Rice, poetry editor. Estab. 1977. Moving Part Press publishes handsome, innovative books, broadsides, and prints that "explore the relationship of word and image, typography and the visual arts, the fine arts and popular culture." Accepts simultaneous submissions.
POETRY *Does not accept unsolicited mss.*

MSI PRESS

1760-F Airline Hwy, #203, Hollister CA 95023. **Fax:** (831)886-2486. **E-mail:** editor@msipress.com. **Website:** www.msipress.com. **Contact:** Betty Leaver, managing editor (self-help, spirituality, religion, memoir, mind/body/spirit, some humor, popular psychology, foreign tales, parenting). Estab. 2003. Publishes trade paperback originals and corresponding e-books. "We are a small, 'boutique' press that specializes in award-winning quality publications, refined through strong personal interactions and productive working relationships between our editors and our authors. A small advance may be offered to previously published authors with a strong book, strong platform, and solid sales numbers. We will accept first-time authors with credibility in their fields and a strong platform, but we do not offer advances to first-time authors. We may refer authors with a good book but little credibility or lacking a strong platform to San Juan Books, our co-publishing venture." **Publishes 15-20 titles/year. 100-200 10% of books from first-time authors. 100% from unagented writers. Pays 10% royalty on retail price. By exception, pays small advance to previously published authors with good sales history.** Publishes ms 8-12 months after acceptance. Responds in 2 weeks to queries sent by e-mail and to proposals submitted via the template on our website. If response not received in 2 weeks, okay to query. Catalog online. Guidelines online.

IMPRINTS MSI Press, LLC; San Juan Books.

NONFICTION Subjects include creative nonfiction, education, health, humanities, memoirs, parenting, philosophy, psychology, religion, spirituality, travel, womens issues, Ask; we are open to new ideas. "We continue to expand our spirituality, psychology, and self-help lines and are interested in adding to our collection of books in Spanish. We do not do or publish translations." Does not want erotica. Submit proposal package, including: outline, 1 sample chapter, professional resume, platform. Prefers electronic submissions. Note that we are open to foreign writers (non-native speakers of English), but please have an English editor proofread the submission prior to sending;if the query letter or proposal is written in poor English, we will not take a chance on a manuscript. Reviews artwork/photos; send computer disk, or, preferably, e-file.

TIPS "Learn the mechanics of writing. Too many submissions are full of grammar and punctuation errors and poorly worded with trite expressions. Read to write; observe and analyze how the great authors of all time use language to good avail. Capture our attention with active verbs, not bland description. Before writing your book, determine its audience, write to that audience, and go about developing your credibility with that audience—and then tell us what you have done and are doing in your proposal."

MUSSIO VENTURES PUBLISHING LTD.

106 - 1500 Hartley Ave., Coquitlam BC V3K 7A1, Canada. **Website:** www.backroadmapbooks.com. Estab. 1993. "We are in the business of producing, publishing, distributing and marketing Outdoor Recreation guidebooks and maps. We are also actively looking to advance our digital side of the business including making our products Google Earth, cell phone or iPhone and GPS compatible." **Publishes 5 titles/year. 5 queries received/year. 2 mss received/year. 25% of books from first-time authors. Makes outright purchase of $2,000-4,800. Pays $1,000 advance.** Publishes ms 12 months after acceptance. Accepts simultaneous submissions. Responds in 1 month. Book catalog available free.

NONFICTION Subjects include maps and guides. Submit proposal package, outline/proposal, 1 sample chapter. Reviews artwork/photos. Send photocopies and digital files.

TIPS "Audience includes outdoor recreation enthusiasts and travellers. Provide a proposal including an outline and samples."

NATIONAL GEOGRAPHIC CHILDREN'S BOOKS

1145 17th St. NW, Washington DC 20090-8199. (800)647-5463. **Website:** kids.nationalgeographic.com. National Geographic CHildren's Books provides quality nonfiction for children and young adults by award-winning authors. *This market does not currently accept unsolicited mss.*

NATUREGRAPH PUBLISHERS, INC.

P.O. Box 1047, 3543 Indian Creek Rd., Happy Camp CA 96039. (530)493-5353. **Fax:** (530)493-5240. **E-mail:** nature@sisqtel.net. **Website:** www.naturegraph.com. **Contact:** Barbara Brown, owner. Estab. 1946. Publishes trade paperback originals. **Publishes 2 titles/year. 100 queries; 6 mss received/year. 80% of books from first-time authors. 90% from unagented writers. Pays royalties. Does not pay advance.** Publishes ms 2 years after acceptance. Accepts simultaneous submissions. Responds in 1 month to queries; 2 months to mss. Book catalog for #10 SASE.

NONFICTION Subjects include ethnic, multicultural, New Age, science, crafts.

TIPS "Please-always send a stamped reply envelope. Publishers get hundreds of manuscripts yearly."

NAVAL INSTITUTE PRESS

US Naval Institute, 291 Wood Rd., Annapolis MD 21402. (410)268-6110. **Fax:** (410)295-1084. **Website:** www.usni.org. Estab. 1873. "The Naval Institute Press publishes trade and scholarly nonfiction. We are interested in national and international security, naval, military, military jointness, intelligence, and special warfare, both current and historical." **Publishes 80-90 titles/year. 50% of books from first-time authors. 90% from unagented writers.** Accepts simultaneous submissions. Guidelines online.

NONFICTION Submit proposal package with outline, author bio, TOC, description/synopsis, sample chapter(s), page/word count, number of illustrations, ms completion date, intended market; or submit complete ms. Send SASE with sufficient postage for return of ms. Send by postal mail only. No e-mail submissions, please.

⊘ NAVPRESS

3820 N. 30th St., Colorado Springs CO 80904. **Website:** www.navpress.com. Estab. 1975. Publishes hardcover, trade paperback, direct and mass market paperback originals and reprints; electronic books and Bible studies. **Pays royalty. Pays low or no advances.** Accepts simultaneous submissions. Book catalog available free.

NONFICTION Subjects include child guidance.

NBM PUBLISHING

160 Broadway, Suite 700, East Bldg., New York NY 10038. **E-mail:** nbmgn@nbmpub.com. **Website:** nbmpub.com. **Contact:** Terry Nantier, editor. Estab. 1976. Publishes graphic novels for an audience of YA/adults. Types of books include fiction, mystery, biographies and social parodies. **Publishes 16 titles/year. 5% of books from first-time authors. 90% from unagented writers. Advance negotiable.** Publishes ms 1 year after acceptance. Accepts simultaneous submissions. Responds to e-mail 1-2 days; mail 1 week. Catalog online.

NONFICTION Subjects include biographies.

FICTION Subjects include comic books, contemporary, erotica, humor, literary, translation, young adult.

⊘ THOMAS NELSON, INC.

HarperCollins Christian Publishing, Box 141000, Nashville TN 37214. (615)889-9000. **Website:** www.thomasnelson.com. Publishes hardcover and paperback orginals. Thomas Nelson publishes Christian lifestyle nonfiction and fiction, and general nonfiction. **Publishes 100-150 titles/year. Rates negotiated for each project. Pays advance.** Publishes ms 1-2 years after acceptance. Accepts simultaneous submissions.

NONFICTION Subjects include gardening, religion, spirituality, adult inspirational, motivational, devotional, Christian living, prayer and evangelism, Bible study, personal development, political, biography/autobiography. *Does not accept unsolicited mss.* No phone queries.

FICTION Publishes authors of commercial fiction who write for adults from a Christian perspective. *Does not accept unsolicited mss.* No phone queries.

⊘ TOMMY NELSON

Imprint of Thomas Nelson, Inc., P.O. Box 141000, Nashville TN 37214-1000. (615)889-9000. **Fax:** (615)902-2219. **Website:** www.tommynelson.com. Publishes hardcover and trade paperback originals. "Tommy Nelson publishes children's Christian nonfiction and fiction for boys and girls up to age 14. We honor God and serve people through books, videos, software and Bibles for children that improve the lives of our customers." **Publishes 50-75 titles/year.** Guidelines online.

NONFICTION Subjects include religion. *Does not accept unsolicited mss.*

FICTION Subjects include adventure, juvenile, mystery, picture books, religious. No stereotypical characters. *Does not accept unsolicited mss.*

TIPS "Know the Christian Booksellers Association market. Check out the Christian bookstores to see what sells and what is needed."

NEW DIRECTIONS

80 Eighth Ave., New York NY 10011. **Fax:** (212)255-0231. **E-mail:** editorial@ndbooks.com. **Website:** www.ndbooks.com. **Contact:** Editorial Assistant. Estab. 1936. Hardcover and trade paperback originals. "Currently, New Directions focuses primarily on fiction in translation, avant garde American fiction, and experimental poetry by American and foreign authors. If your work does not fall into one of those categories, you would probably do best to sub-

mit your work elsewhere." **Publishes 30 titles/year.** Responds in 3-4 months to queries. Book catalog and guidelines online.

FICTION Subjects include ethnic, experimental, historical, humor, literary, poetry, poetry in translation, regional, short story collections, suspense, translation. No juvenile or young adult, occult or paranormal, genre fiction (formula romances, sci-fi or westerns), arts & crafts, and inspirational poetry. Brief query only.

POETRY Query.

TIPS "Our books serve the academic community."

NEWEST PUBLISHERS LTD.

201, 8540-109 St., Edmonton AB T6G 1E6, Canada. (780)432-9427. **Fax:** (780)433-3179. **E-mail:** info@newestpress.com. **E-mail:** submissions@newest-press.com. **Website:** www.newestpress.com. Estab. 1977. Publishes trade paperback originals. NeWest publishes Western Canadian fiction, nonfiction, poetry, and drama. **Publishes 13-16 titles/year. 40% of books from first-time authors. 85% from unagented writers. Pays 10% royalty.** Publishes ms 2-3 years after acceptance. Accepts simultaneous submissions. Responds in 6-8 months to queries. Book catalog for 9×12 SASE. Guidelines online.

NONFICTION Subjects include ethnic, history, Canadian. Query.

FICTION Subjects include literary. Submit complete ms.

NEW FORUMS PRESS

New Forums, 1018 S. Lewis St., Stillwater OK 74074. (405)372-6158. **Fax:** (405)377-2237. **E-mail:** contact@newforums.com. **E-mail:** submissions@newforums.com. **Website:** www.newforums.com. **Contact:** Doug Dollar, president (interests: higher education, Oklahoma-Regional, US military). Estab. 1981. Hardcover and trade paperback originals. "New Forums Press is an independent publisher offering works devoted to various aspects of professional development in higher education, home and office aides, US military, and various titles of a regional interest. We welcome suggestions for thematic series of books and thematic issues of our academic journals—addressing a single issue, problem, or theory." **60% of books from first-time authors. 100% from unagented writers. 10% of Gross Sales paid as royalty. Does not pay advance.** Publishes ms 4 months after acceptance. Accepts

simultaneous submissions. Responds in 1-2 weeks. Guidelines online.

NONFICTION Subjects include business, education, history, literature, military, regional, sociology, war. "We are actively seeking new authors—send for review copies and author guidelines, and visit our website." Mss should be submitted as a Microsoft Word document, or a similar standard word processor document (saved in RTF rich text), as an attachment to an e-mail sent to submissions@newforums.com. Otherwise, submit your ms on 8 ½ x 11 inch white bond paper (one original). The name and complete address, telephone, fax number, and e-mail address of each author should appear on a separate cover page, so it can be removed for the blind review process.

NEW HARBINGER PUBLICATIONS

5674 Shattuck Ave., Oakland CA 94609. (510)652-0215. **Fax:** (510)652-5472. **E-mail:** proposals@newharbinger.com. **Website:** www.newharbinger.com. Estab. 1973. "We look for psychology and health self-help books that teach readers how to master essential life skills. Mental health professionals who want simple, clear explanations or important psychological techniques and health issues also read our books. Thus, our books must be simple ane easy to understand but also complete and authoritative. Most of our authors are therapists or other helping professionals." **Publishes 55 titles/year. 1,000 queries received/year. 300 mss received/year. 60% of books from first-time authors. 75% from unagented writers.** Publishes ms 1 year after acceptance. Accepts simultaneous submissions. Responds in 2 weeks to queries; 1 month to proposals; 2 months to mss. Book catalog free. Guidelines online.

NONFICTION Subjects include psychology, psycho spirituality, anger management, anxiety, coping, mindfulness skills. Authors need to be qualified psychotherapists or health practitioners to publish with us. Submit proposal package, outline, 2 sample chapters, TOC, competing titles, and a compelling, supported reason why the book is unique.

TIPS "Audience includes psychotherapists and lay readers wanting step-by-step strategies to solve specific problems. Our definition of a self-help psychology or health book is one that teaches essential life skills. The primary goal is to train the reader so that, after reading the book, he or she can deal more effectively with health and/or psychological challenges."

⊘ NEW HOPE PUBLISHERS

Woman's Missionary Union, P.O. Box 12065, Birmingham AL 35202-2065. (205)991-4950. **Fax:** (205)991-4015. **E-mail:** new_hope@wmu.org. **Website:** www.newhopepublishers.com. **Contact:** Acquisitions Editor. "Our vision is to challenge believers to understand and be radically involved in the missions of God. This market does not accept unsolicited mss. We encourage you to post your proposal at ChristianManuscriptSubmissions.com." **Publishes 20-28 titles/year. 25% of books from first-time authors.** Publishes ms 2 years after acceptance. Accepts simultaneous submissions.

NONFICTION Subjects include child guidance, education, multicultural, religion, church leadership. "We publish books dealing with all facets of Christian life for women and families, including health, discipleship, missions, ministry, Bible studies, spiritual development, parenting, and marriage. We currently do not accept adult fiction or children's picture books. We are particularly interested in niche categories and books on lifestyle development and change." "We do not accept or review any unsolicited queries, proposals, or manuscripts."

NEW HORIZON PRESS

P.O. Box 669, Far Hills NJ 07931. (908)604-6311. **Fax:** (908)604-6330. **Website:** www.newhorizonpressbooks.com. **Contact:** Acquisitions Editor. Estab. 1983. Publishes hardcover and trade paperback originals. "New Horizon publishes adult nonfiction featuring true stories of uncommon heroes, true crime, social issues, and self help." **Publishes 12 titles/year. 90% of books from first-time authors. 50% from unagented writers. Pays standard royalty on net receipts. Pays advance.** Publishes book within 2 years of acceptance. Accepts simultaneous submissions. Book catalog available free. Guidelines online.

IMPRINTS Small Horizons.

NONFICTION Subjects include child guidance, creative nonfiction, psychology, true crime. Submit proposal package, outline, résumé, bio, 3 sample chapters, photo, marketing information.

TIPS "We are a small publisher, thus it is important that the author/publisher have a good working relationship. The author must be willing to promote his book."

NEW ISSUES POETRY & PROSE

Western Michigan University, 1903 W. Michigan Ave., Kalamazoo MI 49008-5463. (269)387-8185. **E-mail:** new-issues@wmich.edu. **Website:** wmich.edu/newissues. **Contact:** Managing Editor. Estab. 1996. **50% of books from first-time authors. 95% from unagented writers.** Publishes 18 months after acceptance. Accepts simultaneous submissions. Guidelines online.

FICTION Subjects include poetry. Only considers submissions to book contests.

POETRY New Issues Poetry & Prose offers two contests annually. The Green Rose Prize is awarded to an author who has previously published at least one full-length book of poems. The New Issues Poetry Prize, an award for a first book of poems, is chosen by a guest judge. Past judges have included Philip Levine, C.K. Williams, C.D. Wright, and Campbell McGrath. New Issues does not read mss outside our contests. Graduate students in the Ph.D. and M.F.A. programs of Western Michigan Univ. often volunteer their time reading mss. Finalists are chosen by the editors. New Issues often publishes up to 2 additional mss selected from the finalists.

⊛ NEW LIBRI PRESS

4907 Meridian Ave. N., Seattle WA 98103. **E-mail:** query@newlibri.com. **Website:** www.newlibri.com. **Contact:** Michael Muller, editor; Stanislav Fritz, editor. Estab. 2011. Publishes trade paperback, electronic original, electronic reprints. "We only accept e-mail submissions, not USPS." **Publishes 5 titles/year. Receives over 100 submissions/year. 90% of books from first-time authors. 100% from unagented writers. Pays 20-35% royalty on wholesale price. No advance.** Publishes ms 9-12 months after acceptance. Accepts simultaneous submissions. Responds in 3 months to mss. Catalog online. Guidelines online. Electronic submissions only.

NONFICTION Subjects include agriculture, automotive, business, child guidance, computers, cooking, creative nonfiction, economics, electronics, environment, gardening, hobbies, house and home, nature, parenting, recreation, science, sex, software, translation, travel. "Writers should know we embrace e-books. This means that some formats and types of books work well and others don't." Religious. Prefers e-mail. Submit proposal package, including outline, 2 sample chapters, and summary of market from author's perspective. Prefers complete ms.

FICTION Subjects include adventure, experimental, fantasy, historical, horror, literary, mainstream, military, mystery, science fiction, translation, war, western, young adult. "Open to most ideas right now; this will change as we mature as a press. As a new press, we are more open than most and time will probably shape the direction. That said, trite as it is, we want good writing that is fun to read. While we currently are not looking for some sub-genres, if it is well written and a bit off the beaten path, submit to us. We are e-book focused. **We may not create a paper version if the e-book does not sell**, which means some fiction may be less likely to currently sell (e.g. picture books are problematic). Submit query, synopsis, and full manuscript (so we don't have to ask for it later if we like it. We will read about 50 pages to start).

TIPS "Our audience is someone who is comfortable reading an e-book,or someone who is tired of the recycled authors of mainstream publishing, but still wants a good, relatively fast, reading experience. The industry is changing, while we accept for the traditional model, we are searching for writers who are interested in sharing the risk and controlling their own destiny. We embrace writers with no agent."

NEW RIVERS PRESS

1104 Seventh Ave. S., Moorhead MN 56563. **Website:** www.newriverspress.com. **Contact:** Nayt Rundquist, managing editor. Estab. 1968. New Rivers Press publishes collections of poetry, novels, nonfiction, translations of contemporary literature, and collections of short fiction and nonfiction. "We continue to publish books regularly by new and emerging writers, but we also welcome the opportunity to read work of every character and to publish the best literature available nationwide. Each fall through the Many Voices Project competition, we choose 2 books: 1 poetry and 1 prose." Accepts simultaneous submissions.

FICTION Sponsors American Fiction Prize to find best unpublished short stories by American writers.

POETRY The Many Voices Project awards $1,000, a standard book contract, publication of a book-length ms by New Rivers Press, and national distribution. All previously published poems must be acknowledged. "We will consider simultaneous submissions if noted as such. If your manuscript is accepted elsewhere during the judging, you must notify New Rivers Press immediately. If you do not give such notification and your manuscript is selected, your entry gives New

Rivers Press permission to go ahead with publication." Guidelines online.

NEWSAGE PRESS

P.O. Box 607, Troutdale OR 97060. (503)695-2211. **E-mail:** info@newsagepress.com. **Website:** www.newsagepress.com. Estab. 1985. Publishes trade paperback originals. "We focus on nonfiction books. No 'how-to' books or cynical, despairing books. Photo-essay books in large format are no longer published by Newsage Press. No novels or other forms of fiction." Accepts simultaneous submissions. Guidelines online.

NONFICTION Subjects include animals, multicultural, death/dying. Submit 2 sample chapters, proposal (no more than 1 page), SASE.

⊙ NEW SOCIETY PUBLISHERS

P.O. Box 189, Gabriola Island BC V0R 1X0, Canada. (250)247-9737. **Fax:** (250)247-7471. **E-mail:** editor@newsociety.com. **Website:** www.newsociety.com. Publishes trade paperback originals and reprints and electronic originals. **Publishes 25 titles/year. 400 queries; 300 mss received/year. 50% of books from first-time authors. 80% from unagented writers. Pays 10-12% royalty on wholesale price. Pays $0-5,000 advance.** Publishes ms about 9 months after acceptance. Accepts simultaneous submissions. Responds in 1-2 months. Book catalog and guidelines online.

NONFICTION Subjects include agriculture, alternative lifestyles, animals, beauty, business, child guidance, communications, community, contemporary culture, cooking, economics, education, environment, fashion, finance, foods, gardening, health, horticulture, house and home, humanities, labor, money, nature, nutrition, parenting, philosophy, politics, regional, science, social sciences, spirituality, sustainability, open building, peak oil, renewable energy, post carbon prep, sustainable living, gardening & cooking, green building, natural building, ecological design & planning, environment & economy. Query with SASE. Submit proposal package, outline, 2 sample chapters. Reviews artwork/photos. Send photocopies.

TIPS "Audience is activists, academics. Don't get an agent!"

NEW WORLD LIBRARY

14 Pamaron Way, Novato CA 94949. (415)884-2100. **Fax:** (415)884-2199. **E-mail:** submit@newworldlibrary.com. **Website:** www.newworldlibrary.com. **Contact:** Joel Prins, submissions editor. Estab. 1977.

Publishes nonfiction hardcover and trade paperback originals and reprints and ebooks. "NWL is dedicated to publishing books that inspire and challenge us to improve the quality of our lives and our world." Prefers e-mail submissions. No longer accepting children's mss. **Publishes 30-35 titles/year. 10% of books from first-time authors. 25% from unagented writers. Pays advance.** Publishes ms 12 months after acceptance. Accepts simultaneous submissions. Responds in 3 months to queries if interested. Reviews all queries. Book catalog free. Guidelines online.

NONFICTION Subjects include alternative lifestyles, animals, business, career guidance, child guidance, contemporary culture, counseling, environment, nature, New Age, parenting, psychic, religion, spirituality, womens issues. Submit outline, overview, bio, 2-3 sample chapters via email. Does not review artwork.

NEW YORK UNIVERSITY PRESS

838 Broadway, 3rd Floor, New York NY 10003. (212)998-2575. **Fax:** (212)995-3833. **E-mail:** nyupressinfo@nyu.edu. **Website:** www.nyupress.org. **Contact:** Ellen Chodosh, director. Estab. 1916. Hardcover and trade paperback originals. "New York University Press embraces ideological diversity. We often publish books on the same issue from different poles to generate dialogue, engender and resist pat categorizations." **Publishes 100 titles/year. 800-1,000 queries received/year. 30% of books from first-time authors. 90% from unagented writers.** Publishes ms 9-11 months after acceptance. Accepts simultaneous submissions. Responds in 1-4 months (peer reviewed) to proposals. Guidelines online.

NONFICTION Subjects include ethnic, psychology, regional, religion, sociology, American history, anthropology. New York University Press is a publisher primarily of academic books and is a department of the New York University Division of Libraries. NYU Press publishes in the humanities and social sciences, with emphasis on sociology, law, cultural and American studies, religion, American history, anthropology, politics, criminology, media and film, and psychology. The Press also publishes books on New York regional history, politics, and culture. Query with SASE. Submit proposal package, outline, 1 sample chapter. Reviews artwork/photos. Send photocopies.

NIGHTBOAT BOOKS

P.O. Box 10, Callicoon NY 12723. **Fax:** (603)448-9429. **Website:** nightboat.org. Estab. 2003. Nightboat Books, a nonprofit organization, seeks to develop audiences for writers whose work resists convention and transcends boundaries, by publishing books rich with poignancy, intelligence and risk. Accepts simultaneous submissions. Catalog online. Guidelines online.

POETRY Considers poetry submitted to its poetry prize. More information online.

TIPS "The name Nightboat signifies travel, passage, and possibility—of mind and body, and of language. The night boat maneuvers in darkness at the mercy of changing currents and weather, always immersed in forces beyond itself."

NIGHTSCAPE PRESS

P.O. Box 1948, Smyrna TN 37167. **E-mail:** info@nightscapepress.com. **E-mail:** submissions@nightscapepress.com. **Website:** www.nightscapepress.com. Estab. 2012. Nightscape Press is seeking quality book-length words of at least 50,000 words (40,000 for young adult). **Pays monthly royalties. Offers advance.** Accepts simultaneous submissions. Guidelines online. Currently closed to submissions. Will announce on site when they re-open to submissions.

FICTION Subjects include experimental, fantasy, horror, science fiction, short story collections, suspense, young adult. "We are not interested in erotica or graphic novels." Query.

⊘ NINETY-SIX PRESS

Special Collections, James B. Duke Library, 3300 Poinsett Hwy., Greenville SC 29613. (864)294-2194. **Website:** library.furman.edu/specialcollections/96Press/index.htm. Estab. 1991. For a sample, send $10.

TIPS "Between 1991 and 2015, the Ninety-Six Press published only poetry by South Carolina authors. The Press is not considering new publishing projects at this time. Check our website for up-to-date information."

NOLO

950 Parker St., Berkeley CA 94710. (510)549-1976. **Fax:** (510)859-0025. **Website:** www.nolo.com. **Contact:** Editorial Department. Estab. 1971. Publishes trade paperback originals. "We publish practical, do-it-yourself books, software and various electronic products on financial and legal issues that affect individuals, small business, and nonprofit organizations. We specialize in helping people handle their own legal tasks; i.e., write a will, file a small claims lawsuit, start a small business or nonprofit, or apply for a patent." **Publishes 75 new editions and 15 new**

titles/year. 20% of books from first-time authors. **Pays advance.** Accepts simultaneous submissions. Responds in 3 weeks to queries. Responds in 5 weeks to proposals. Guidelines online.

NONFICTION Subjects include legal guides in various topics including employment, small business, intellectual property, parenting and education, finance and investment, landlord/tenant, real estate, and estate planning. Query with SASE. Submit outline, 1 sample chapter.

NOMAD PRESS

2456 Christain St., White River Junction VT 05001. (802)649-1995. **E-mail:** info@nomadpress.net. **Website:** www.nomadpress.net. **Contact:** Acquisitions Editor. Estab. 2001. "We produce nonfiction children's activity books that bring a particular science or cultural topic into sharp focus. Nomad Press does not accept unsolicited manuscripts. If authors are interested in contributing to our children's series, please send a writing resume that includes relevant experience/expertise and publishing credits." **Pays authors royalty based on retail price or work purchased outright. Offers advance against royalties.** Publishes book 1 year after acceptance. Accepts simultaneous submissions. Responds to queries in 3-4 weeks. Catalog online.

○ Nomad Press does not accept picture books, fiction, or cookbooks.

NONFICTION Middle readers: activity books, history, science. Average word length: middle readers—30,000.

TIPS "We publish a very specific kind of nonfiction children's activity book. Please keep this in mind when querying or submitting."

NORTH ATLANTIC BOOKS

2526 Martin Luther King Jr. Way, Berkeley CA 94704. **E-mail:** submissions@northatlanticbooks.com. **Website:** www.northatlanticbooks.com. **Contact:** Acquisitions Board. Estab. 1974. Publishes hardcover, trade paperback, and electronic originals; trade paperback and electronic reprints. **Publishes 60 titles/year. Receives 200 mss/year. 50% of books from first-time authors. 75% from unagented writers. Pays royalty percentage on wholesale price.** Publishes ms 14 months after acceptance. Accepts simultaneous submissions. Responds in 3-6 months. Book catalog free on request (if available). Guidelines online.

IMPRINTS Evolver Editions, Blue Snake Books.

NONFICTION Subjects include agriculture, anthropology, archeology, architecture, art, astrology, business, child guidance, community, contemporary culture, cooking, economics, electronics, environment, finance, foods, gardening, gay, health, horticulture, lesbian, medicine, memoirs, money, multicultural, nature, New Age, nutrition, philosophy, politics, psychic, psychology, public affairs, religion, science, social sciences, sociology, spirituality, sports, travel, womens issues, womens studies, world affairs. Submit proposal package including an outline, 3-4 sample chapters, and "a 75-word statement about the book, your qualifications as an author, marketing plan/audience, for the book, and comparable titles." Reviews artwork with ms package.

FICTION Subjects include adventure, literary, multicultural, mystery, regional, science fiction, spiritual. "We only publish fiction on rare occasions." Submit proposal package including an outline, 3-4 sample chapters, and "a 75-word statement about the book, your qualifications as an author, marketing plan/audience, for the book, and comparable titles."

POETRY Submit 15-20 sample poems.

NORTH CAROLINA OFFICE OF ARCHIVES AND HISTORY

109 E. Jones St., Mail Service Center 4601, Raleigh NC 27601. (919)733-7442. **Fax:** (919)733-1439. **Website:** www.ncdcr.gov/about/history/historical-publications. Publishes hardcover and trade paperback originals. "We publish *only* titles that relate to North Carolina. The North Carolina Office of Archives and History also publishes the *North Carolina Historical Review,* a quarterly scholarly journal of history." **Publishes 1 titles/year. 10 queries received/year. 5 mss received/year. 5% of books from first-time authors. 100% from unagented writers. Makes one-time payment upon delivery of completed ms.** Publishes ms 2 years after acceptance. Accepts simultaneous submissions. Responds in 1 week to queries and to proposals; 2 months to mss. Guidelines for $3.

NONFICTION Subjects include history, regional. Query with SASE. Reviews artwork/photos. Send photocopies.

NORTH LIGHT BOOKS

F+W, a Content + eCommerce Company, 10151 Carver Rd., Suite 200, Blue Ash OH 45242. **E-mail:** mona. clough@fwmedia.com. **Website:** www.fwmedia.com; www.artistsnetwork.com; www.createmixedmedia.

com. Publishes hardcover and trade paperback how-to books. "North Light Books publishes art books, including watercolor, drawing, mixed media, acrylic that emphasize illustrated how-to art instruction. Currently emphasizing drawing including traditional, activity books and creativity and inspiration." **Publishes 50 titles/year. 50% of books from first-time authors. 80% from unagented writers. Pays 8% royalty on net receipts and $3,000 advance. Pays advance.** Publishes ms 10-24 months after acceptance. Accepts simultaneous submissions. Responds in 3 months to queries. Book catalog online. Does not return submissions.

❍ This market is mainly for experienced fine artists and workshop instructors who are willing to work with an North Light editor to produce a step-by-step how-to book that teaches readers how to accomplish art techniques.

NONFICTION Subjects include art, watercolor, oil painting, acrylic painting realistic drawing, creativity, decorative painting, paper arts, collage and other craft instruction books. Interested in books on acrylic painting, basic drawing and sketching, journaling, pen and ink, colored pencil, decorative painting, art and how-to. Do not submit coffee table art books without how-to art instruction. Query via e-mail only. Submit outline with JPEG low-resolution images. Submissions via snail mail will not be returned.

NORTHSOUTH BOOKS

600 Third Ave., 2nd Floor, New York NY 10016. (917)210-5868. **E-mail:** hlennon@northsouth.com. **E-mail:** submissionsnsb@gmail.com. **Website:** www.northsouth.com. Accepts simultaneous submissions. Guidelines online.

FICTION Looking for fresh, original fiction with universal themes that could appeal to children ages 3-8. "We typically do not acquire rhyming texts, since our books must also be translated into German." Submit picture book mss (1,000 words or less) via e-mail.

RECENT TITLE(S) *Surf's Up*, by Kwame Alexander and Daniel Miyares; *Lindbergh: Tale of a Flying Mouse*, by Torben Kuhlmann.

NORTIA PRESS

Santa Ana CA **E-mail:** acquisitions@nortiapress.com. **Website:** www.nortiapress.com. Estab. 2009. Publishes trade paperback and electronic originals. **Publishes 6 titles/year. 0% of books from first-time authors. 80% from unagented writers. Pays negotiable royal-**ties on wholesale price. Publishes ms 7 months after acceptance. Accepts simultaneous submissions. Responds in 1 month.

NONFICTION Subjects include ethnic, government, humanities, military, public affairs, religion, social sciences, sociology, war, womens issues.

FICTION Subjects include ethnic, historical, literary, military, war. "We focus mainly on nonfiction as well as literary and historical fiction, but are open to other genres. No vampire stories, science fiction, or erotica, please." Submit a brief e-mail query. Please include a short bio, approximate word count of book, and expected date of completion (fiction titles should be completed before sending a query, and should contain a sample chapter in the body of the e-mail). All unsolicited snail mail or attachments will be discarded without review.

TIPS "We specialize in working with experienced authors who seek a more collaborative and fulfilling relationship with their publisher. As such, we are less likely to accept pitches form first-time authors, no matter how good the idea. As with any pitch, please make your e-mail very brief and to the point, so the reader is not forced to skim it. Always include some biographic information. Your life is interesting."

W.W. NORTON & COMPANY, INC.

500 Fifth Ave., New York NY 10110. (212)354-5500. **Fax:** (212)869-0856. **Website:** www.wwnorton.com. Estab. 1923. "W. W. Norton & Company, the oldest and largest publishing house owned wholly by its employees, strives to carry out the imperative of its founder to 'publish books not for a single season, but for the years' in fiction, nonfiction, poetry, college textbooks, cookbooks, art books and professional books. Due to the workload of our editorial staff and the large volume of materials we receive, *Norton is no longer able to accept unsolicited submissions*. If you are seeking publication, we suggest working with a literary agent who will represent you to the house." Accepts simultaneous submissions.

NO STARCH PRESS, INC.

245 8th St., San Francisco CA 94103. (415)863-9900. **Fax:** (415)863-9950. **E-mail:** editors@nostarch.com. **Website:** www.nostarch.com. **Contact:** William Pollock, publisher. Estab. 1994. Publishes trade paperback originals. "No Starch Press publishes the finest in geek entertainment—unique books on technology, with a focus on open source, security, hacking,

programming, alternative operating systems, LEGO, science, and math. Our titles have personality, our authors are passionate, and our books tackle topics that people care about." **Publishes 25-30 titles/year. 300 queries; 50 mss received/year. 80% of books from first-time authors. 90% from unagented writers. Pays 10-15% royalty on wholesale price. Pays advance.** Publishes ms 4 months after acceptance. Accepts simultaneous submissions. Responds in 1-2 weeks. Book catalog online. Guidelines online.

NONFICTION Subjects include computers, electronics, science, software, technology, computing, mathematics, science, STEM, LEGO. Submit outline, bio, 1 sample chapter, market rationale. Reviews artwork/photos. Send digitally please.

TIPS "Books must be relevant to tech-savvy, geeky readers."

NOSY CROW PUBLISHING

The Crow's Nest, 10a Lant St., London SE1 1QR, United Kingdom. (44)(0)207-089-7575. **Fax:** (44)(0)207-089-7576. **E-mail:** hello@nosycrow.com. **E-mail:** submissions@nosycrow.com. **Website:** nosycrow.com. "We publish books for children 0-14. We're looking for 'parent-friendly' books, and we don't publish books with explicit sex, drug use or serious violence, so no edgy YA or edgy cross-over. And whatever New Adult is, we don't do it. We also publish apps for children from 2-7, and may publish apps for older children if the idea feels right." Accepts simultaneous submissions. Guidelines online.

NONFICTION Prefers submissions by e-mail, but post works if absolutely necessary.

FICTION "As a rule, we don't like books with 'issues' that are in any way overly didactic." Prefers submissions by e-mail, but post works if absolutely necessary.

TIPS "Please don't be too disappointed if we reject your work! We're a small company and can only publish a few new books and apps each year, so do try other publishers and agents: publishing is necessarily a hugely subjective business. We wish you luck!"

NOVA PRESS

P.O. Box 692023, West Hollywood CA 90069. (310)275-3513. **Fax:** (310)281-5629. **E-mail:** novapress@aol.com. **Website:** www.novapress.net. **Contact:** Jeff Kolby, president. Estab. 1993. Publishes trade paperback originals. "Nova Press publishes only test prep books for college entrance exams (SAT, GRE, GMAT, LSAT, etc.), and closely related reference

books, such as college guides and vocabulary books." **Publishes 6 titles/year.** Publishes book 2 months after acceptance. Accepts simultaneous submissions. Book catalog available free.

NONFICTION Subjects include education, software.

NURSESBOOKS.ORG

American Nurses Association, 8515 Georgia Ave., Suite 400, Silver Spring MD 20901. (800)274-4ANA. **Fax:** (301)628-5003. **E-mail:** anp@ana.org. **Website:** www.nursesbooks.org. Publishes professional paperback originals and reprints. "Nursebooks.org publishes books designed to help professional nurses in their work and careers. Through the publishing program, Nursebooks.org provides nurses in all practice settings with publications that address cutting edge issues and form a basis for debate and exploration of this century's most critical health care trends." **Publishes 10 titles/year. 50 queries received/year. 8-10 mss received/year. 75% of books from first-time authors. 100% from unagented writers.** Publishes ms 4 months after acceptance. Responds in 3 months. Book catalog online. Guidelines available free.

NONFICTION Subjects include advanced practice, computers, continuing education, ethics, health care policy, nursing administration, psychiatric and mental health, quality, nursing history, workplace issues, key clinical topics, such as geriatrics, pain management, public health, spirituality and home health. Submit outline, 1 sample chapter, CV, list of 3 reviewers and paragraph on audience and how to reach them. Reviews artwork/photos. Send photocopies.

OAK KNOLL PRESS

310 Delaware St., New Castle DE 19720. (302)328-7232. **Fax:** (302)328-7274. **E-mail:** publishing@oakknoll.com. **Website:** www.oakknoll.com. **Contact:** Robert D. Fleck III, president. Estab. 1976. Publishes hardcover and trade paperback originals and reprints. "Oak Knoll specializes in books about books and manuals on the book arts: preserving the art and lore of the printed word." **Publishes 40 titles/year. 250 queries; 100 mss received/year. 50% of books from first-time authors. 100% from unagented writers.** Publishes ms 1 year after acceptance. Accepts simultaneous submissions. Guidelines online.

NONFICTION Reviews artwork/photos. Send photocopies.

OBERLIN COLLEGE PRESS

50 N. Professor St., Oberlin OH 44074. (440)775-8408. **Fax:** (440)775-8124. **E-mail:** oc.press@oberlin.edu. **Website:** www.oberlin.edu/ocpress. **Contact:** Marco Wilkinson, managing editor. Estab. 1969. Publishes hardcover and trade paperback originals. **Publishes 2-3 titles/year. Pays 7½-10% royalty.** Accepts simultaneous submissions. Responds promptly to queries; 2 months to mss.

POETRY *FIELD Magazine*—submit 2-6 poems through website "submissions" tab; FIELD Translation Series—query with SASE and sample poems; FIELD Poetry Series—*no unsolicited mss.* Enter mss in FIELD Poetry Prize ($1,000 and a standard royalty contract) held annually in May. Submit complete ms.

TIPS "Queries for the FIELD Translation Series: send sample poems and letter describing project. Winner of the annual FIELD poetry prize determines publication. Do not send unsolicited manuscripts."

OCEANVIEW PUBLISHING

595 Bay Isles Rd., Suite 120-G, Longboat Key FL 34228. **E-mail:** mail@oceanviewpub.com. **E-mail:** submissions@oceanviewpub.com. **Website:** www. oceanviewpub.com. Estab. 2006. Publishes hardcover and electronic originals. "Independent publisher of nonfiction and fiction, with primary interest in original mystery, thriller and suspense titles. Accepts new and established writers." Accepts simultaneous submissions. Responds in 3 months on mss. Catalog and guidelines online.

FICTION Subjects include mystery, suspense, thriller. Accepting adult mss with a primary interest in the mystery, thriller and suspense genres—from new and established writers. No children's or YA literature, poetry, cookbooks, technical manuals or short stories. Within body of e-mail only, include author's name and brief bio (Indicate if this is an agent submission), ms title and word count, author's mailing address, phone number and e-mail address. Attached to the e-mail should be the following: A synopsis of 750 words or fewer. The first 30 pages of the ms. Please note that we accept only Word documents as attachments to the submission e-mail. Do not send query letters or proposals.

OHIO STATE UNIVERSITY PRESS

1070 Carmack Rd., 180 Pressey Hall, Columbus OH 43210-1002. (614)292-6930. **Fax:** (614)292-2065. **E-mail:** eugene@osupress.org. **E-mail:** lindsay@osu-press.org. **Website:** www.ohiostatepress.org. **Contact:** Eugene O'Connor, acquisitions editor (medieval studies and classics); Lindsay Martin, acquisitions editor (literary studies). Estab. 1957. The Ohio State University Press publishes scholarly nonfiction, and offers short fiction and short poetry prizes. Currently emphasizing history, literary studies, political science, women's health, classics, Victoria studies. **Publishes 30 titles/year. Pays royalty. Pays advance.** Accepts simultaneous submissions. Responds in 3 months to queries. Guidelines online.

NONFICTION Subjects include education, history, literary criticism, multicultural, regional, sociology, criminology, literary criticism, women's health. Query.

POETRY Offers poetry competition through *The Journal.*

OHIO UNIVERSITY PRESS

31 S. Court St., Suite 143, Athens OH 45701. (740)593-1159. **Fax:** (740)593-4536. **E-mail:** berchowi@ohio.edu. **Website:** www.ohioswallow.com. **Contact:** Gillian Berchowitz, director. Estab. 1964. Publishes hardcover and trade paperback originals and reprints. "Ohio University Press publishes and disseminates the fruits of research and creative endeavor, specifically in the areas of literary studies, regional works, philosophy, contemporary history, and African studies. Its charge to produce books of value in service to the academic community and for the enrichment of the broader culture is in keeping with the university's mission of teaching, research and service to its constituents." **Publishes 45-50 titles/year. 500 queries received/year. 50 mss received/year. 20% of books from first-time authors. 95% from unagented writers.** Publishes ms 1 year after acceptance. Accepts simultaneous submissions. Responds in 1-3 months. Book catalog available free. Guidelines online.

NONFICTION Subjects include Americana, anthropology, government, history, language, literature, military, nature, politics, regional, sociology, African studies. "We prefer queries or detailed proposals, rather than manuscripts, pertaining to scholarly projects that might have a general interest." Proposals should explain the thesis and details of the subject matter, not just sell a title. Query with SASE. Reviews artwork/photos. Send photocopies.

TIPS "Rather than trying to hook the editor on your work, let the material be compelling enough and well-presented enough to do it for you."

OMNIDAWN PUBLISHING

2200 Adeline St., Suite 150, Oakland CA 94607. **Website:** www.omnidawn.com. Estab. 1999. Publishes ms 6-12 months after acceptance. Accepts simultaneous submissions. Guidelines online.

TIPS "Check our website for latest information."

ONEWORLD

Oneworld Publications, 10 Bloomsbury St., London WC1B 3SR, United Kingdom. **E-mail:** submissions@oneworld-publications.com. **Website:** www.oneworld-publications.com. Estab. 1986. Publishes hardcover and trade paperback originals and mass market paperback. "We publish general trade nonfiction, which must be accessible but authoritative, mainly by academics or experts for a general readership and where appropriate a cross-over student market. Currently emphasizing current affairs, popular science, history, psychology, politics and business; de-emphasizing self-help. We also publish literary fiction by international authors, both debut and established, throughout the English language world as well as selling translation rights. Our focus is on well-written literary and high-end commercial fiction from a variety of cultures and periods, many exploring interesting themes and issues. In addition we publish fiction in translation, crime fiction and YA fiction." **Publishes 100 titles/year. 20% of books from first-time authors. 20% from unagented writers.** Publishes ms 12-15 months after acceptance. Book catalog online. Guidelines online.

IMPRINTS Point Blank, Rock the Boat.

NONFICTION Submit through online proposal form.

FICTION Submit through online proposal forms.

ONSTAGE PUBLISHING

190 Lime Quarry Rd., Suite 106-J, Madison AL 35758-8962. (256)542-3213. **Fax:** (256)542-3213. **E-mail:** submissions@onstagepublishing.com. **Website:** www.onstagepublishing.com. **Contact:** Dianne Hamilton, senior editor. Estab. 1999. "At this time, we only produce fiction books for ages 8-18. We have added an e-book only side of the house for mysteries for grades 6-12. See our website for more information. We will not do anthologies of any kind. Query first for nonfiction projects as nonfiction projects must spark our inter-

est. We no longer are accepting written submissions. We want e-mail queries and submissions. For submissions: Put the first 3 chapters in the body of the e-mail. Do not use attachments! We will delete any submission with an attachment without acknowledgment." Suggested ms lengths: Chapter books: 3,000-9,000 words, Middle Grade novels: 10,000-40,000 words, Young adult novels: 40,000-60,000 words. **Publishes 1-5 titles/year. 500 + 80% of books from first-time authors. Pays authors/illustrators/photographers advance plus royalties.** Accepts simultaneous submissions. Responds in 1-3 months. Guidelines online.

FICTION Subjects include adventure, historical, mystery, young adult. Middle readers: adventure, contemporary, fantasy, history, nature/environment, science fiction, suspense/mystery. Young adults: adventure, contemporary, fantasy, history, humor, science fiction, suspense/mystery. Average word length: chapter books—4,000-6,000 words; middle readers—5,000 words and up; young adults—25,000 and up. Recently published *Mission: Shanghai* by Jamie Dodson (an adventure for boys ages 12+); *Birmingham, 1933: Alice* (a chapter book for grades 3-5). "We do not produce picture books."

TIPS "Study our titles and get a sense of the kind of books we publish, so that you know whether your project is likely to be right for us."

☺ ON THE MARK PRESS

15 Dairy Ave., Napanee ON K7R 1M4, Canada. (800)463-6367. **Fax:** (800)290-3631. **E-mail:** lisa@onthemarkpress.com. **Website:** www.onthemarkpress.com. Estab. 1986. Publishes books for the Canadian curriculum. **15% of books from first-time authors.** Accepts simultaneous submissions.

☺ OOLICHAN BOOKS

P.O. Box 2278, Lantzville BC V0B 1M0, Canada. (250)423-6113. **E-mail:** info@oolichan.com. **Website:** www.oolichan.com. Publisher: Randal Macnair. Estab. 1974. Publishes hardcover and trade paperback originals and reprints. **Publishes 8 titles/year. 2,000 mss received/year. 30% of books from first-time authors. Pays royalty on retail price.** Publishes ms 6-12 months after acceptance. Accepts simultaneous submissions. Responds in 1-3 months. Book catalog online. Guidelines online.

☺ Only publishes Canadian authors.

NONFICTION Subjects include history. "We try to publish creative nonfiction titles each year which are of regional, national, and international interest." Submit proposal package, publishing history, bio, cover letter, 3 sample chapters, SASE.

FICTION Subjects include literary. "We try to publish at least 2 literary fiction titles each year. We receive many more deserving submissions than we are able to publish, so we publish only outstanding work. We try to balance our list between emerging and established writers, and have published many first-time writers who have gone on to win or be shortlisted for major literary awards, both nationally and internationally." Submit proposal package, publishing history, clips, bio, cover letter, 3 sample chapters, SASE.

POETRY "We are one of the few small literary presses in Canada that still publishes poetry. We try to include 2-3 poetry titles each year. We attempt to balance our list between emerging and established poets. Our poetry titles have won or been shortlisted for major national awards, including the Governor General's Award, the BC Book Prizes, and the Alberta Awards." Submit 10 sample poems.

TIPS "Our audience is adult readers who love good books and good literature. Our audience is regional and national, as well as international. Follow our submission guidelines. Check out some of our titles at your local library or bookstore to get an idea of what we publish. Don't send us the only copy of your manuscript. Let us know if your submission is simultaneous, and inform us if it is accepted elsewhere. Above all, keep writing!"

OPEN COURT PUBLISHING CO.

70 E. Lake St., Suite 800, Chicago IL 60601. **E-mail:** opencourt@cricketmedia.com. **Website:** www.opencourtbooks.com. **Contact:** Acquisitions Editor. Estab. 1887. Publishes hardcover and trade paperback originals. "Regrettably, now, and for the forseeable future, Open Court can consider no new unsolicited manuscripts for publication, with the exception of works suitable for our Popular Culture and Philosophy series." **Publishes 20 titles/year. Pays 5-15% royalty on wholesale price.** Publishes ms 2 years after acceptance. Book catalog online. Guidelines online.

NONFICTION Subjects include philosophy, Asian thought, religious studies and popular culture. Query with SASE. Submit proposal package, outline, 1 sample chapter, TOC, author's cover letter, intended audience.

TIPS "Audience consists of philosophers and intelligent general readers. Only accepting submissions to Popular Culture and Philosophy series."

⚙ ORCA BOOK PUBLISHERS

1016 Balmoral Rd., Victoria BC V8T 1A8, Canada. (800)210-5277. **Fax:** (877)408-1551. **E-mail:** orca@orcabook.com. **Website:** www.orcabook.com. **Contact:** Amy Collins, editor (picture books); Sarah Harvey, editor (young readers); Andrew Wooldridge, editor (juvenile and teen fiction); Bob Tyrrell, publisher (YA, teen); Ruth Linka, associate editor (rapid reads). Estab. 1984. Publishes hardcover and trade paperback originals, and mass market paperback originals and reprints. Only publishes Canadian authors. **Publishes 30-50 titles/year. 2,500 queries; 1,000 mss received/year. 20% of books from first-time authors. 75% from unagented writers. Pays 10% royalty.** Publishes book 12-18 months after acceptance. Responds in 1 month to queries; 2 months to proposals and mss. Book catalog for 8½x11 SASE. Guidelines online.

NONFICTION Subjects include gay, lesbian, marine subjects, multicultural, sports, young adult, picture books. Only publishes Canadian authors. Query with a SASE.

FICTION Subjects include adventure, gay, hi-lo, juvenile, lesbian, literary, multicultural, mystery, picture books, sports, young adult. Picture books: animals, contemporary, history, nature/environment. Middle readers: contemporary, history, fantasy, nature/environment, problem novels, graphic novels. Young adults: adventure, contemporary, hi-lo (Orca Soundings), history, multicultural, nature/environment, problem novels, suspense/mystery, graphic novels. Average word length: picture books—500-1,500; middle readers—20,000-35,000; young adult—25,000-45,000; Orca Soundings—13,000-15,000; Orca Currents—13,000-15,000. No romance, science fiction. Query with SASE. Submit proposal package, outline, clips, 2-5 sample chapters, SASE.

TIPS "Our audience is students in grades K-12. Know our books, and know the market."

🅐⊘ ORCHARD BOOKS (US)

557 Broadway, New York NY 10012. **Website:** www.scholastic.com. *Orchard is not accepting unsolicited mss.* **Publishes 20 titles/year. 10% of books from first-time authors. Most commonly offers an ad-**

vance against list royalties. Accepts simultaneous submissions.

FICTION Picture books, early readers, and novelty: animal, contemporary, history, humor, multicultural, poetry.

OREGON STATE UNIVERSITY PRESS

121 The Valley Library, Corvallis OR 97331. (541)737-3873. **Fax:** (541)737-3170. **E-mail:** mary.braun@oregonstate.edu. **Website:** osupress.oregonstate.edu. **Contact:** Mary Elizabeth Braun, acquisitions editor. Estab. 1962. Publishes hardcover, paperback, and e-book originals. **Publishes 20-25 titles/year. 40% of books from first-time authors.** Publishes book 1 year after acceptance. Responds in 3 months to queries. Book catalog for 6x9 SAE with 2 first-class stamps. Guidelines online.

NONFICTION Subjects include regional, science. Publishes scholarly books in history, biography, geography, literature, natural resource management, with strong emphasis on Pacific or Northwestern topics and Native American and indigenous studies. Submit outline, sample chapters.

O'REILLY MEDIA

1005 Gravenstein Highway N., Sebastopol CA 95472. (707)827-7000. **Fax:** (707)829-0104. **E-mail:** workwithus@oreilly.com. **Website:** www.oreilly.com. **Contact:** Acquisitions Editor. "We're always looking for new authors and new book ideas. Our ideal author has real technical competence and a passion for explaining things clearly." Accepts simultaneous submissions. Guidelines online.

NONFICTION "At the same time as you might say that our books are written 'by and for smart people,' they also have a down to earth quality. We like straight talk that goes right to the heart of what people need to know." Submit proposal package, outline, publishing history, bio.

TIPS "It helps if you know that we tend to publish 'high end' books rather than books for dummies, and generally don't want yet another book on a topic that's already well covered."

OUR SUNDAY VISITOR, INC.

200 Noll Plaza, Huntington IN 46750. **E-mail:** jlindsey@osv.com. **Website:** www.osv.com. Publishes paperback and hardbound originals. "We are a Catholic publishing company seeking to educate and deepen our readers in their faith. Currently emphasizing devotional, inspirational, Catholic identity, apologetics,

and catechetics." **Publishes 40-50 titles/year. Pays authors royalty of 10-12% net. Pays illustrators by the project (range: $25-1,500).** Publishes ms 1-2 years after acceptance. Accepts simultaneous submissions. Responds in 2 months. Book catalog for 9×12 envelope and first-class stamps; ms guidelines available online.

Our Sunday Visitor, Inc. is publishing only those children's books that are specifically Catholic. See website for submission guidelines.

NONFICTION Prefers to see well-developed proposals as first submission with annotated outline and definition of intended market; Catholic viewpoints on family, prayer, and devotional books, and Catholic heritage books. Picture books, middle readers, young readers, young adults. Query, submit complete ms, or submit outline/synopsis and 2-3 sample chapters. Reviews artwork/photos.

TIPS "Stay in accordance with our guidelines."

RICHARD C. OWEN PUBLISHERS, INC.

P.O. Box 585, Katonah NY 10536. (914)232-3903; (800)262-0787. **E-mail:** richardowen@rcowen.com. **Website:** www.rcowen.com. **Contact:** Richard Owen, publisher. Estab. 1982. "We publish child-focused books, with inherent instructional value, about characters and situations with which 5, 6, and 7-year-old children can identify—books that can be read for meaning, entertainment, enjoyment and information. We include multicultural stories that present minorities in a positive and natural way. Our stories show the diversity in America." Not interested in lesson plans, or books of activities for literature studies or other content areas. Submit complete ms and cover letter. **Pays authors royalty of 5% based on net price or outright purchase (range: $25-500). Offers no advances. Pays illustrators by the project (range: $100-2,000) or per photo (range: $50-150).** Publishes book 2-3 years after acceptance. Accepts simultaneous submissions. Responds to mss in 1 year. Book catalog available with SASE. Ms guidelines with SASE or online.

"Due to high volume and long production time, we are currently limiting to nonfiction submissions only."

NONFICTION Subjects include history, recreation, science, sports, music, diverse culture, nature. "Our books are for kindergarten, first- and second-grade children to read on their own. The stories are very brief—up to 2,000 words—yet well structured and crafted with memorable characters, language, and plots. Picture books, young readers: animals, careers, history, how-to, music/dance, geography, multicultural, nature/environment, science, sports. Multicultural needs include: Good stories respectful of all heritages, races, cultural—African-American, Hispanic, American Indian, Asian, European, Middle Eastern." Wants lively stories. No "encyclopedic" type of information stories. Average word length: under 500 words.

PETER OWEN PUBLISHERS

81 Bridge Rd., London N8 9NP, United Kingdom. (44)(208)350-1775. **Fax:** (44)(208)340-9488. **E-mail:** info@peterowen.com. **Website:** www.peterowen.com. Publishes hardcover originals and trade paperback originals and reprints. "We are far more interested in proposals for nonfiction than fiction at the moment. No poetry or short stories." **Publishes 20-30 titles/year. 3,000 queries received/year. 800 mss received/year. 70% from unagented writers. Pays 7½-10% royalty. Pays negotiable advance.** Publishes ms 1 year after acceptance. Responds in 2 months to queries; 3 months to proposals and mss. Book catalog for SASE, SAE with IRC or on website.

NONFICTION Subjects include history, literature, memoirs, translation, travel, art, drama, literary, biography. Query with synopsis, sample chapters.

FICTION "No first novels. Authors should be aware that we publish very little new fiction these days." Query with synopsis, sample chapters.

OXFORD UNIVERSITY PRESS

198 Madison Ave., New York NY 10016. (212)726-6000. **E-mail:** custserv.us@oup.com. **Website:** www.oup.com/us. World's largest university press with the widest global audience. Accepts simultaneous submissions. Guidelines online.

NONFICTION Query with outline, proposal, sample chapters.

OXFORD UNIVERSITY PRESS: SOUTHERN AFRICA

P.O. Box 12119, NI City Cape Town 7463, South Africa. (27)(21)596-2300. **Fax:** (27)(21)596-1234. **E-mail:** oxford.za@oup.com. **Website:** www.oxford.co.za. Academic publisher known for its educational books for southern African schools. Also publishes general and reference titles. **Publishes 150 titles/year.** Accepts simultaneous submissions. Book catalog online. Guidelines online.

NONFICTION Submit cover letter, synopsis, first few chapters, and submission form (available online) via mail.

FICTION Submit cover letter, synopsis.

OZARK MOUNTAIN PUBLISHING, INC.

Cannon Holdings, LLC, P.O. Box 754, Huntsville AR 72740. (479)738-2348. **Fax:** (479)738-2448. **E-mail:** brandy@ozarkmt.com. **Website:** www.ozarkmt.com. **Contact:** Nancy Vernon, general manager. Estab. 1992. Publishes trade paperback originals. "We publish new age/metaphysical, spiritual nonfiction books." **Publishes 8-10 titles/year. 50-75 queries; 150-200 mss received/year. 50% of books from first-time authors. 95% from unagented writers. Pays 10-15% royalty on retail or wholesale price. Pays $250-500 advance.** Publishes ms within 18 months after acceptance. Accepts simultaneous submissions. Responds in 6 months to queries; 7 months to mss. Book catalog online. Guidelines online. Postcard included for notification of receipt. No phone call please.

NONFICTION Subjects include astrology, New Age, philosophy, psychic, spirituality, metaphysical. No phone calls please. Query with SASE. Submit TOC and 4-5 sample chapters. Guidelines online. No phone calls please.

TIPS "We envision our audience to be open minded, spiritually expanding. Please do not call to check on submissions. Do not submit electronically. Send hard copy only."

P & R PUBLISHING CO.

P.O. Box 817, Phillipsburg NJ 08865. **Fax:** (908)859-2390. **E-mail:** editorial@prpbooks.com. **Website:** www.prpbooks.com. Estab. 1930. Publishes hardcover originals and trade paperback originals and reprints. **Publishes 40 titles/year. Up to 300 queries; 100 mss received/year. 5% of books from first-time authors. 95% from unagented writers. Pays 10-16% royalty on wholesale price.** Accepts simultaneous submissions. Responds in 3 months to proposals. Guidelines online.

NONFICTION Subjects include history, religion, spirituality, translation. Only accepts electronic submission with completion of online Author Guidelines. Hard copy mss will not be returned.

TIPS "Our audience is evangelical Christians and seekers. All of our publications are consistent with Biblical teaching, as summarized in the Westminster Standards."

PACIFIC PRESS PUBLISHING ASSOCIATION

Trade Book Division, 1350 N. Kings Rd., Nampa ID 83687. (208)465-2500. **Fax:** (208)465-2531. **Website:** www.pacificpress.com. Estab. 1874. Publishes hardcover and trade paperback originals and reprints. "We publish books that fit Seventh-day Adventist beliefs only. All titles are Christian and religious. For guidance, see www.adventist.org/beliefs/index.html. Our books fit into the categories of this retail site: www.adventistbookcenter.com." **Publishes 35 titles/year. 35% of books from first-time authors. 100% from unagented writers. Pays 8-16% royalty on wholesale price.** Publishes book 2 years after acceptance. Responds in 3 months to queries. Guidelines online.

NONFICTION Subjects include child guidance, philosophy, religion, spirituality, family living, Christian lifestyle, Bible study, Christian doctrine, prophecy. Query with SASE or e-mail, or submit 3 sample chapters, cover letter with overview of book. Electronic submissions accepted. Reviews artwork/photos.

FICTION Subjects include religious. "Pacific Press rarely publishes fiction, but we're interested in developing a line of Seventh-day Adventist fiction in the future. Only proposals accepted; no full manuscripts."

TIPS "Our primary audience is members of the Seventh-day Adventist denomination. Almost all are written by Seventh-day Adventists. Books that do well for us relate the Biblical message to practical human concerns and focus more on the experiential rather than theoretical aspects of Christianity. We are assigning more titles, using less unsolicited material—although we still publish manuscripts from freelance submissions and proposals."

PAGESPRING PUBLISHING

P.O. Box 2113, Columbus OH 43221. **E-mail:** sales@pagespringpublishing.com. **E-mail:** submissions@pagespringpublishing.com. **Website:** www.pagespringpublishing.com. **Contact:** Lucky Marble Books Editor or Cup of Tea Books Editor. Estab. 2012. Publishes trade paperback and electronic originals. PageSpring Publishing publishes women's fiction under the Cup of Tea Books imprint and YA/middle grade titles under the Lucky Marble Books imprint. Visit the PageSpring Publishing website for submission details. **Publishes 4-7 titles/year. 50% of books from first-time authors. 90% from unagented writers. Pays royalty on wholesale price.** Publishes ms 9-12 months after acceptance. Accepts simultaneous submissions. Endeavors to respond to queries within 3 months. Catalog online. Guidelines online.

IMPRINTS Cup of Tea Books, Lucky Marble Books.

FICTION Subjects include adventure, contemporary, gothic, historical, humor, juvenile, mainstream, mystery, regional, romance, suspense, young adult. Cup of Tea Books publishes women's fiction. Lucky Marble Books specializes in middle grade and young adult fiction. Send submissions for both Cup of Tea Books and Lucky Marble Books to submissions@pagespringpublishing.com. Send a query, synopsis, and the first 30 pages of the manuscript in the body of the email. please. NO attachments.

TIPS Cup of Tea Books would love to see more cozy mysteries and humor. Lucky Marble Books is looking for humor and engaging contemporary stories for middle grade and young adult readers.

PAGESPRING PUBLISHING

PageSpring Publishing, P.O. Box 21133, Columbus OH 43221. **E-mail:** submissions@pagespringpublishing.com. **Website:** www.pagespringpublishing.com. Estab. 2012. Publishes trade paperback and electronic originals. PageSpring Publishing is a small independent publisher with two imprints: Cup of Tea Books and Lucky Marble Books. Cup of Tea Books publishes women's fiction, with particular emphasis on mystery and humor. Lucky Marble Books publishes young adult and middle grade fiction. "We are looking for engaging characters and well-crafted plots that keep our readers turning the page. We accept e-mail queries only; see our website for details." **Publishes 4-5 titles/year. 75% of books from first-time authors. 100% from unagented writers. Pays royalty.** Publishes ms 12 months after acceptance. Accepts simultaneous submissions. Responds in 3 months. Guidelines online.

IMPRINTS Cup of Tea Books and Lucky Marble Books.

FICTION Subjects include adventure, contemporary, fantasy, feminist, hi-lo, historical, humor, juvenile, literary, mainstream, multicultural, mystery, regional, romance, science fiction, sports, suspense, young adult. Cup of Tea Books publishes women's fiction. Lucky Marble Books publishes middle grade and young adult novels. No children's picture books. Submit proposal package via e-mail only. Include synopsis and 30 sample pages.

TIPS "Cup of Tea Books is particularly interested in cozy mystery novels. Lucky Marble Books is looking for funny, age-appropriate tales for middle grade and young adult readers."

⊙ PAJAMA PRESS

181 Carlaw Ave., Suite 207, Toronto ON M4M 2S1, Canada. 4164662222. **E-mail:** annfeatherstone@ pajamapress.ca. **Website:** pajamapress.ca. **Contact:** Ann Featherstone, senior editor. Publisher: Gail Winskill (gailwinskill@pajamapress.ca). Estab. 2011. "We publish picture books—both for the very young and for school-aged readers, as well as novels for middle grade readers and contemporary or historical fiction for young adults aged 12+. Our nonfiction titles typically contain a strong narrative element. Pajama Press is also looking for mss from authors of diverse backgrounds. Stories about immigrants are of special interest." **Publishes 15-20 titles/year. 1,000 20% of books from first-time authors. 80% from unagented writers. Pays advance.** Publishes ms 1-3 years after acceptance. Responds in 6 weeks. Guidelines online.

NONFICTION Subjects include animals, contemporary culture, cooking, creative nonfiction, environment, gay, history, literature, nature, science, social sciences, sports, war, young adult. "Our nonfiction titles typically contain a strong narrative element; for example, juvenile biographies and narratives about wildlife rescue." Does not want how-to books, activity books, books for adults, psychology books, educational resources Pajama Press considers digital queries accompanied by picture books texts or the first 3 chapters of novel length projects. Your query should include an overview of your submission and some information about your writing background. Pajama Press prefers not to look at simultaneous submissions. Please notify us if you are submitting your project to another publisher. Please e-mail your queries and submissions to annfeatherstone@pajamapress.ca. In the interest of saving trees, Pajama Press does not accept physical mss. Any mss mailed to our office will be recycled unopened.

FICTION Subjects include contemporary, gay, juvenile, literary, multicultural, mystery, picture books, poetry, sports, young adult, All children's fiction. vampire novels; romance (except as part of a literary novel); fiction with overt political or religious messages

PALADIN PRESS

5540 Central Ave., Suite 200, Boulder CO 80301. (303)443-7250. **Fax:** (303)442-8741. **E-mail:** editorial@paladin-press.com. **Website:** www.paladin-press. com. Estab. 1970. Publishes hardcover originals and paperback originals and reprints, videos. "Paladin Press publishes the action library of nonfiction in military science, police science, weapons, combat, personal freedom, self-defense, survival." **Publishes 50 titles/year. 50% of books from first-time authors. 95% from unagented writers. "We pay royalties in full and on time." Pays advance.** Publishes ms 1 year after acceptance. Accepts simultaneous submissions. Responds in 2 months to proposals. Book catalog available free.

IMPRINTS Sycamore Island Books; Flying Machines Press; Outer Limits Press; Romance Book Classics.

NONFICTION If applicable, send sample photographs and line drawings with complete outline and sample chapters. Paladin Press primarily publishes original manuscripts on military science, weaponry, self-defense, personal privacy, financial freedom, espionage, police science, action careers, guerrilla warfare, and fieldcraft. To submit a book proposal to Paladin Press, send an outline or chapter description along with 1-2 sample chapters (or the entire ms) to the address below. If applicable, samples of illustrations or photographs are also useful. Do not send a computer disk at this point, and be sure keep a copy of everything you send us. We are not accepting mss as electronic submissions at this time. Please allow 2-6 weeks for a reply. If you would like your sample material returned, a SASE with proper postage is required. Editorial Department, Paladin Press Gunbarrel Tech Center, 5540 Central Ave., Boulder, CO 80301, or e-mail us at: editorial@paladin-press.com. Query with SASE. Submitting a proposal for a video project is not much different than a book proposal. See guidelines online and send to: All materials related to video proposals should be addressed directly to: David Dubrow, Video Production Manager.

TIPS "We need lucid, instructive material aimed at our market and accompanied by sharp, relevant illustrations and photos. As we are primarily a publisher of `how-to' books, a manuscript that has step-by-step instructions, written in a clear and concise manner (but not strictly outline form) is desirable. No fiction, first-person accounts, children's, religious, or joke books.

We are also interested in serious, professional videos and video ideas (contact Michael Rigg)."

PALETTES & QUILLS

1935 Penfield Rd., Penfield NY 14526. (585)383-0812. **E-mail:** palettesnquills@gmail.com. **Website:** http://palettesandquills.simplesite.com/. **Contact:** Donna M. Marbach, publisher/owner. Estab. 2002. Publishes chapbooks, broadsides, e-newsletter. Palettes & Quills is devoted to the celebration and expansion of the literary and visual arts, offering both commissioned and consulting services. It works to support beginning and emerging writers and artists to expand their knowledge, improve their skills, and connect to other resources in the community. Further, Palettes & Quills seeks to increase the public's awareness and appreciation of these arts through education, advocacy, hands-on program assistance, and functioning as a small literary press. "We publish a chapbook every other year in a contest judged by a well-known poet. We also publish a monthly e-newsletter, and chapbooks/anthologies/ and broadsides on an irregular schedule. Reprints accepted only for our e-newsletter." **Contest winner gets $200 and 50 books. Others are paid copies.** Publishes ms 12 months after acceptance. Accepts simultaneous submissions. Response time varies. "We try to respond as quick as we can.". Guidelines online.

NONFICTION Subjects include art, crafts, creative nonfiction, entertainment, literary criticism, literature, music, photography. Does not want political and religious diatribes. Our preference is for book reviews, how to for literature and the arts, interviews with artists/authors/essay of interest for writing style or art and literature interest. Artwork can be photos, copies of paintings, collages, photos of sculptures. Photos can be on any subject but should be of interest to literary and visual artists. Reviews art work and photos for covers.

FICTION "We prefer short-shorts and stories. We might consider a novella, but we are too small for long epic novels. Encourage short essays, short stories, reviews for our monthy newsletter."

POETRY Palettes & Quills "is at this point is only considering chapbooks that are poetry, creative nonfiction, or fiction, a poetry press only, and produces only a handful of publications each year, specializing in anthologies, individual chapbooks, and broadsides." Wants "work that should appeal to a wide audience." Does not want "poems that are sold blocks of text, long-lined and without stanza breaks. Wildly elaborate free-verse would be difficult and in all likelihood fight with art background, amateurish rhyming poem, overly sentimental poems, poems that use excessive profanity, or which denigrate other people, or political and religious diatribes." Query first with 3-5 poems and a cover letter with brief bio and publication credits for individual unsolicited chapbooks. May include previously published poems. Chapbook poets would get 20 copies of a run; broadside poets and artists get 5-10 copies and occasionally paid $10 for reproduction rights. Anthology poets get 1 copy of the anthology. All poets and artists get a discount on purchases that include their work.

TIPS "We are very small and the best bet with us with our monthly e-newsletter Pencil Marks."

PALGRAVE MACMILLAN

St. Martin's Press, 175 Fifth Ave., New York NY 10010. (212)982-3900. **Fax:** (212)777-6359. **E-mail:** proposals@palgrave.com. **Website:** www.palgrave.com. Publishes hardcover and trade paperback originals. "Palgrave wishes to expand on our already successful academic, trade, and reference programs so that we will remain at the forefront of publishing in the global information economy of the 21st century. We publish high-quality academic works and a distinguished range of reference titles, and we expect to see many of our works available in electronic form. We do not accept fiction or poetry." Accepts simultaneous submissions. Book catalog and ms guidelines online.

Palgrave Macmillan is a cross-market publisher specializing in cutting edge academic and trade non-fiction titles. Our list consists of top authors ranging from academics making original contributions in their disciplines to trade authors, including journalists and experts, writing news-making books for a broad, educated readership.

NONFICTION Subjects include creative nonfiction, education, ethnic, history, multicultural, philosophy, regional, religion, sociology, spirituality, translation, humanities. We are looking for good solid scholarship. Query with proposal package including outline, 3-4 sample chapters, prospectus, cv and SASE. Reviews artwork/photos.

⚫⊘ PANTHEON BOOKS

Penguin Random House, 1745 Broadway, New York NY 10019. **Website:** www.pantheonbooks.com. Estab. 1942. Publishes hardcover and trade paperback originals and trade paperback reprints. Accepts simultaneous submissions.

💬 Pantheon Books publishes both Western and non-Western authors of literary fiction and important nonfiction. "We only accept mss submitted by an agent."

NONFICTION *Does not accept unsolicited mss. Agented submissions only.*

FICTION *Does not accept unsolicited mss. Agented submissions only.*

PANTS ON FIRE PRESS

2062 Harbor Cove Way, Winter Garden FL 34787. (863)546-0760. **E-mail:** submission@pantsonfirepress.com. **Website:** www.pantsonfirepress.com. **Contact:** Becca Goldman, senior editor; Emily Gerety, editor. Estab. 2012. Publishes hardcover originals and reprints, trade paperback originals and reprints, and electronic originals and reprints. Pants On Fire Press is an award-winning book publisher of picture, middle-grade, young adult, and adult books. **Publishes 10-15 titles/year. Receives 36,300 queries and mss per year. 60% of books from first-time authors. 80% from unagented writers. Pays 10-50% royalties on wholesale price.** Publishes ms approximately 7 months after acceptance. Accepts simultaneous submissions. Responds in 3 months. Catalog online. Guidelines online.

FICTION Subjects include adventure, fantasy, historical, horror, humor, juvenile, mainstream, military, mystery, picture books, religious, romance, science fiction, spiritual, sports, suspense, war, young adult. Publishes big story ideas with high concepts, new worlds, and meaty characters for children, teens, and discerning adults. Always on the lookout for action, adventure, animals, comedic, dramatic, dystopian, fantasy, historical, paranormal, romance, sci-fi, supernatural, and suspense stories. Submit a proposal package including a synopsis, 3 sample chapters, and a query letter via e-mail.

PAPERCUTZ

160 Broadway, Suite 700E, New York NY 10038. (646)559-4681. **Fax:** (212)643-1545. **Website:** www.papercutz.com. Estab. 2004. Publishes major licenses and author created comics. Publisher of graphic novels for kids and teens. **Publishes 60 titles/year. 5% of books from first-time authors. 90% from unagented writers. Pays advance.** Publishes ms 1 year after acceptance. Accepts simultaneous submissions. Responds in 2-4 weeks.

IMPRINTS SuperGenius, Charmz.

NONFICTION Subjects include literature, pop culture, translation, young adult.

FICTION Subjects include comic books, fantasy, historical, horror, humor, juvenile, literary, mainstream, translation, young adult. "Independent publisher of graphic novels based on popular existing properties aimed at the teen and tween market."

TIPS "Be familiar with our titles—that's the best way to know what we're interested in publishing. If you are somehow attached to a successful tween or teen property and would like to adapt it into a graphic novel, we may be interested. We also take submissions for new series preferably that have already a following online."

PARACLETE PRESS

P.O. Box 1568, Orleans MA 02653. (508)255-4685. **Fax:** (508)255-5705. **E-mail:** phil@paracletepress.com. **Website:** www.paracletepress.com. **Contact:** Phil Fox Rose. Estab. 1981. Publishes hardcover and trade paperback originals. Publisher of books on prayer, Christian living, spirituality, fiction, devotionals, new editions of classics. Also publishes audio and video. **Publishes 40 titles/year. 250 mss received/year.** Publishes ms up to 2 years after acceptance.

💬 Does not accept unsolicited submissions of poetry, memoirs, or children's books.

NONFICTION Subjects include art, religion, spirituality. E-mail. Submit proposal, with intro plus 2-3 sample chapters, TOC, chapter summaries.

PARADISE CAY PUBLICATIONS

P.O. Box 29, Arcata CA 95518-0029. (800)736-4509. **Fax:** (707)822-9163. **Website:** www.paracay.com. Publishes hardcover and trade paperback originals and reprints. "Paradise Cay Publications, Inc. is a small independent publisher specializing in nautical books, videos, and art prints. Our primary interest is in manuscripts that deal with the instructional and technical aspects of ocean sailing. We also publish and will consider fiction if it has a strong nautical theme." **Publishes 5 titles/year. 360-480 queries received/year. 240-360 mss received/year. 10% of books from first-time authors. 100% from unagented writers.**

Pays 10-15% royalty on wholesale price. Makes outright purchase of $1,000-10,000. Does not normally pay advances to first-time or little-known authors. Publishes book 4 months after acceptance. Accepts simultaneous submissions. Responds in 1 month to queries/proposals; 2 months to mss. Book catalog and ms guidelines free on request or online.

IMPRINTS Pardey Books.

NONFICTION Subjects include recreation, sports, travel. Must have strong nautical theme. Include a cover letter containing a story synopsis and a short bio, including any plans to promote their work. The cover letter should describe the book's subject matter, approach, distinguishing characteristics, intended audience, author's qualifications, and why the author thinks this book is appropriate for Paradise Cay. Call first. Reviews artwork/photos. Send photocopies.

FICTION Subjects include adventure. All fiction must have a nautical theme. Query with SASE. Submit proposal package, clips, 2-3 sample chapters.

TIPS "Audience is recreational sailors. Call Matt Morehouse (publisher)."

PARAGON HOUSE PUBLISHERS

3600 Labore Rd., Suite 1, St. Paul MN 55110. (651)644-3087. **Fax:** (651)644-0997. **E-mail:** paragon@paragonhouse.com. **Website:** www.paragonhouse.com. **Contact:** Gordon Anderson, acquisitions editor. Estab. 1962. Publishes hardcover and trade paperback originals and trade paperback reprints and e-books. "We publish general-interest titles and textbooks that provide the readers greater understanding of society and the world. Currently emphasizing religion, philosophy, economics, and society." **Publishes 5-10 titles/year. 1,500 queries; 150 mss received/year. 7% of books from first-time authors. 90% from unagented writers. Does not generally pay advance. Royalties paid as-earned.** Publishes ms 1 year after acceptance. Accepts simultaneous submissions. Guidelines online.

IMPRINTS Omega Books.

NONFICTION Subjects include anthropology, economics, environment, government, history, military, New Age, parenting, philosophy, politics, psychology, religion, social sciences, spirituality, integral studies. Submit proposal package, outline, 2 sample chapters, market breakdown, SASE.

PARALLAX PRESS

P.O. Box 7355, Berkeley CA 94707. (510)525-0101, ext. 113. **Fax:** (510)525-7129. **Website:** www.parallax.org.

Contact: Acquisitions Editor. Estab. 1985. Publishes hardcover and trade paperback originals. "We focus primarily on engaged Buddhism." **Publishes 5-8 titles/year.** Responds in 6-8 weeks to queries. Guidelines online.

NONFICTION Subjects include multicultural, religion, spirituality. Query with SASE. Submit 1 sample chapter, 1-page proposal. Reviews artwork/photos. Send photocopies.

PASSKEY PUBLICATIONS

5438 Vegas Dr., PMB 1670, Las Vegas NV 89108. (702)418-3326. **Fax:** (702)418-3326. **E-mail:** support@passkeylearningsystems.com. **Website:** www.passkeypublications.com. Estab. 2007. Publishes trade paperback originals. **Publishes 15 titles/year. Receives 375 queries/year; 120 mss/year. 15% of books from first-time authors. 90% from unagented writers. Pay varies on retail price.** Publishes ms 1 year after acceptance. Accepts simultaneous submissions. Responds in 1 month. Catalog and guidelines online.

IMPRINTS Passkey Publications, PassKey EA Review.

NONFICTION Subjects include business, economics, finance, money, real estate, accounting, taxation, study guides for professional examinations. "Books on taxation and accounting are generally updated every year to reflect tax law changes, and the turnaround on a ms must be less than 3 months for accounting and tax subject matter. Books generally remain in publication only 11 months and are generally published every year for updates." Submit complete ms. Nonfiction mss only. Reviews artwork/photos as part of ms package. Send electronic files on disk, via e-mail, or jump drive.

TIPS "Accepting business, accounting, tax, finance and other related subjects only."

⊘ PAUL DRY BOOKS

1700 Sansom St., Suite 700, Philadelphia PA 19103. (215)231-9939. **Fax:** (215)231-9942. **E-mail:** editor@pauldrybooks.com. **E-mail:** pdry@pauldrybooks.com. **Website:** pauldrybooks.com. Hardcover and trade paperback originals, trade paperback reprints. "We publish fiction, both novels and short stories, and nonfiction, biography, memoirs, history, and essays, covering subjects from Homer to Chekhov, bird watching to jazz music, New York City to shogunate Japan." Accepts simultaneous submissions. Book catalog online.

NONFICTION Subjects include agriculture, architecture, contemporary culture, education, history, language, literary criticism, literature, memoirs, multicultural, philosophy, religion, science, translation, travel, young adult, popular mathematics. "We do not accept unsolicited manuscripts."

FICTION Subjects include literary, short story collections, translation, young adult, novels. "We do not accept unsolicited manuscripts."

TIPS "Our aim is to publish lively books 'to awaken, delight, and educate'—to spark conversation. We publish fiction and nonfiction, and essays covering subjects from Homer to Chekhov, bird watching to jazz music, New York City to shogunate Japan."

PAULINE BOOKS & MEDIA

50 St. Paul's Ave., Boston MA 02130. (617)522-8911. **Fax:** (617)541-9805. **E-mail:** design@paulinemedia.com; editorial@paulinemedia.com. **Website:** www.pauline.org. Estab. 1932. Publishes trade paperback originals and reprints. "Submissions are evaluated on adherence to Gospel values, harmony with the Catholic faith tradition, relevance of topic, and quality of writing." For board books and picture books, the entire manuscript should be submitted. For easy-to-read, young readers, and middle reader books and teen books, please send a cover letter accompanied by a synopsis and two sample chapters. "Electronic submissions are encouraged. We make every effort to respond to unsolicited submissions within 2 months." **Publishes 40 titles/year. 5% from unagented writers. Varies by project, but generally are royalties with advance. Flat fees sometimes considered for smaller works.** Publishes a book approximately 11-18 months after acceptance. Responds in 2 months. Book catalog online. Guidelines online.

NONFICTION Subjects include child guidance, religion, spirituality, young adult. Picture books, young readers, middle readers, teen: religion and fiction. Average word length: picture books—500-1,000; young readers—8,000-10,000; middle readers—15,000-25,000; teen—30,000-50,000. Recently published children's titles: *Bible Stores for Little Ones* by Genny Monchapm; *I Forgive You: Love We Can Hear, Ask For and Give* by Nicole Lataif; *Shepherds To the Rescue* (first place Catholic Book Award Winner) by Maria Grace Dateno; *FSP; Jorge from Argentina; Prayers for Young Catholics*. Teen Titles: *Teens Share the Mission* by Teens; *Martyred: The Story of Saint Lorenzo Ruiz; Ten Commandmenst for Kissing Gloria Jean* by Britt Leigh; *A.K.A. Genius* (2nd Place Catholic Book Award Winner) by Marilee Haynes; *Tackling Tough Topics* with Faith and Fiction by Diana Jenkins. No memoir/autobiography, poetry, or strictly nonreligious works currently considered. Submit proposal package, including outline, 1-2 sample chapters, cover letter, synopsis, intended audience and proposed length.

FICTION Subjects include adventure, comic books, contemporary, juvenile, picture books, religious, romance, spiritual, young adult. Children's and teen fiction only. "We are now accepting submissions for easy-to-read and middle reader chapter, and teen well documented historical fiction. We would also consider well-written fantasy, fairy tales, myths, science fiction, mysteries, or romance if approached from a Catholic perspective and consistent with church teaching. Please see our Writer's Guidelines." "Submit proposal package, including synopsis, 2 sample chapters, and cover letter; complete ms."

TIPS "Manuscripts may or may not be explicitly catechetical, but we seek those that reflect a positive worldview, good moral values, awareness and appreciation of diversity, and respect for all people. All material must be relevant to the lives of readers and must conform to Catholic teaching and practice."

PAULIST PRESS

997 Macarthur Blvd., Mahwah NJ 07430. (201)825-7300. **Fax:** (201)825-8345. **E-mail:** submissions@paulistpress.com. **Website:** www.paulistpress.com. Estab. 1865. Paulist Press publishes ecumenical theology, Roman Catholic studies, and books on scripture, liturgy, spirituality, church history, and philosophy, as well as works on faith and culture. "Our publishing is oriented toward adult-level nonfiction. We do not publish memoirs, poetry, or works of fiction, and we have scaled back on children's books. Offer of a subsidy is no guarantee of acceptance—we are not a vanity press." **Receives 250 submissions/year. 10% of books from first-time authors. 95% from unagented writers. Royalties and advances are negotiable. Pays negotiable advance.** Publishes a book 12-18 months after receipt of final, edited ms. Responds in 3 months to queries and proposals; 3-4 months on mss. Book catalog available online. Guidelines available on website and by e-mail.

NONFICTION Subjects include religion. Accepts submissions via e-mail. Hard copy submissions returned only if accompanied by self-addressed envelope with adequate postage.

PAYCOCK PRESS

3819 N. 13th St., Arlington VA 22201. (703)525-9296. **E-mail:** rchrdpeabody9@gmail.com. **E-mail:** gargoyle@gargoylemagazine.com. **Website:** www.gargoylemagazine.com. **Contact:** Richard Peabody. Estab. 1976. "Too academic for the underground, too outlaw for the academic world. We tend to be edgy and look for ultra-literary work." Publishes paperback originals. Books: POD printing. Average print order: 500. Averages 1 total title/year. Member CLMP. Distributes through Amazon and website. Publishes ms 1 year after acceptance. Accepts simultaneous submissions. Responds to queries in 1 month; mss in 4 months.

FICTION Subjects include experimental, literary, poetry, short story collections. Accepts unsolicited mss. Accepts queries by e-mail. Include brief bio. Send SASE for return of ms or send a disposable ms and SASE for reply only.

POETRY Considers experimental, edgy poetry collections. Accepts unsolicited mss. Accepts queries by e-mail. Include brief bio. Send SASE for return of ms or send a disposable ms and SASE for reply only.

TIPS "Check out our website. Two of our favorite writers are Paul Bowles and Jeanette Winterson."

PEACHTREE CHILDREN'S BOOKS

Peachtree Publishers, Ltd., 1700 Chattahoochee Ave., Atlanta GA 30318. (404)876-8761. **Fax:** (404)875-2578. **E-mail:** hello@peachtree-online.com. **Website:** www. peachtree-online.com. **Contact:** Helen Harriss, submissions editor. Publishes hardcover and trade paperback originals. "We publish a broad range of subjects and perspectives, with emphasis on innovative plots and strong writing." **Publishes 30 titles/year. 25% of books from first-time authors. 25% from unagented writers. Pays royalty on retail price.** Publishes ms 1 year after acceptance. Accepts simultaneous submissions. Responds in 6 months and mss. Book catalog for 6 first-class stamps. Guidelines online.

NONFICTION Subjects include animals, child guidance, creative nonfiction, education, ethnic, gardening, history, literary criticism, multicultural, recreation, regional, science, social sciences, sports, travel. No e-mail or fax queries of mss. Submit complete ms

with SASE, or summary and 3 sample chapters with SASE.

FICTION Subjects include juvenile, picture books, young adult. Looking for very well-written middle grade and young adult novels. No adult fiction. No collections of poetry or short stories; no romance or science fiction. Submit complete ms with SASE.

PEACHTREE PUBLISHERS, LTD.

1700 Chattahoochee Ave., Atlanta GA 30318. (404)876-8761. **Fax:** (404)875-2578. **E-mail:** hello@peachtree-online.com. **Website:** www.peachtree-online.com. Estab. 1977. **Publishes 30-35 titles/year.** Publishes book 1-2 years after acceptance. Accepts simultaneous submissions. Responds in 6-7 months.

NONFICTION Picture books: animal, history, nature/environment. Young readers, middle readers, young adults: animal, biography, nature/environment. Does not want to see religion. Submit complete ms or 3 sample chapters by postal mail only.

FICTION Picture books, young readers: adventure, animal, concept, history, nature/environment. Middle readers: adventure, animal, history, nature/environment, sports. Young adults: fiction, mystery, adventure. Does not want to see science fiction, romance. Submit complete ms or 3 sample chapters by postal mail only.

⊙⊘ PEDLAR PRESS

113 Bond St., St. John's NL A16 1T6, Canada. (709)738-6702. **E-mail:** feralgrl@interlog.com. **Website:** www.pedlarpress.com. **Contact:** Beth Follett, owner/editor. Estab. 1996. **Publishes 7 titles/year. 27% of books from first-time authors. 100% from unagented writers. Pays 10% royalty on retail price. Average advance: $200-400.** Publishes ms 18 months after acceptance. Accepts simultaneous submissions. Catalog online.

NONFICTION Subjects include art, creative nonfiction, gay, literary criticism, literature.

FICTION Subjects include experimental, feminist, gay, lesbian, literary, poetry, short story collections. Experimental, feminist, gay/lesbian, literary, short story collections. Canadian writers only. Query with SASE, sample chapter(s), synopsis.

TIPS "I select manuscripts according to my taste, which fluctuates. Be familiar with some if not most of Pedlar's recent titles."

PELICAN PUBLISHING COMPANY

1000 Burmaster St., Gretna LA 70053. (504)368-1175. **Fax:** (504)368-1195. **E-mail:** editorial@pelicanpub.com. **Website:** www.pelicanpub.com. Estab. 1926. Publishes hardcover, trade paperback and mass market paperback originals and reprints. "We believe ideas have consequences. One of the consequences is that they lead to a best-selling book. We publish books to improve and uplift the reader. Currently emphasizing business and history titles." Publishes 20 young readers/year; 1 middle reader/year. "Our children's books (illustrated and otherwise) include history, biography, holiday, and regional. Pelican's mission is to publish books of quality and permanence that enrich the lives of those who read them." **Pays authors in royalties; buys ms outright "rarely." Illustrators paid by "various arrangements." Advance considered.** Publishes a book 9-18 months after acceptance. Responds in 1 month to queries; 3 months to mss. Requires exclusive submission. Book catalog and ms guidelines online.

NONFICTION Subjects include Americana, ethnic, history, multicultural, regional, religion, sports, motivational (with business slant). "We look for authors who can promote successfully. We require that a query be made first. This greatly expedites the review process and can save the writer additional postage expenses." Young readers: biography, history, holiday, multicultural. Middle readers: Louisiana history, holiday, regional. No multiple queries or submissions. Reviews artwork/photos.

FICTION Subjects include historical, juvenile. We publish no adult fiction. Young readers: history, holiday, science, multicultural and regional. Middle readers: Louisiana History. Multicultural needs include stories about African-Americans, Irish-Americans, Jews, Asian-Americans, and Hispanics. Does not want animal stories, general Christmas stories, "day at school" or "accept yourself" stories. Maximum word length: young readers—1,100; middle readers—40,000. No young adult, romance, science fiction, fantasy, gothic, mystery, erotica, confession, horror, sex, or violence. Also no psychological novels. Submit outline, clips, 2 sample chapters, SASE. Full guidelines on website.

POETRY Considers poetry for "hardcover children's books only (1,100 words maximum), preferably with a regional focus. However, our needs for this are very limited; we publish 20 juvenile titles per year, and most of these are prose, not poetry." Books are 32 pages, magazine-sized, include illustrations.

TIPS "We do extremely well with cookbooks, popular histories, and business. We will continue to build in these areas. The writer must have a clear sense of the market and knowledge of the competition. A query letter should describe the project briefly, give the author's writing and professional credentials, and promotional ideas."

Ⓐ♺ PENGUIN CANADA, LTD.

The Penguin Group, 320 Front St. W., Suite 1400, Toronto ON M5V 3B6, Canada. (416)364-4449. **Fax:** (416)598-7764. **Website:** www.penguinrandomhouse.ca. Estab. 1974. **Pays advance.**

NONFICTION Any Canadian subject by any Canadian authors. Agented submissions only.

ⒶⓄ PENGUIN GROUP USA

375 Hudson St., New York NY 10014. (212)366-2000. **Website:** www.penguin.com. General interest publisher of both fiction and nonfiction. *No unsolicited mss.* Submit work through a literary agent. DAW Books is the lone exception. Guidelines online.

ⒶⓄ PENGUIN RANDOM HOUSE, LLC

Division of Bertelsmann Book Group, 1745 Broadway, New York NY 10019. (212)782-9000. **Website:** www.penguinrandomhouse.com. Estab. 1925. Penguin Random House LLC is the world's largest English-language general trade book publisher. *Agented submissions only. No unsolicited mss.* Accepts simultaneous submissions.

IMPRINTS Crown Publishing Group; Knopf Doubleday Publishing Group; Random House Publishing Group; Random House Children's Books; RH Digital Publishing Group; RH International.

THE PERMANENT PRESS

Second Chance Press, Attn: Judith Shepard, 4170 Noyac Rd., Sag Harbor NY 11963. (631)725-1101. **E-mail:** judith@thepermanentpress.com; shepard@thepermanentpress.com. **Website:** www.thepermanentpress.com. **Contact:** Judith and Martin Shepard, acquisitions/co-publishers. Estab. 1978. Publishes hardcover originals. Mid-size, independent publisher of literary fiction. "We keep titles in print and are active in selling subsidiary rights." Average print order: 1,000-2,500. Averages 16 total titles. Accepts unsolicited mss. Pays 10-15% royalty on wholesale price. Offers $1,000 advance. *Will not accept simultaneous* *submissions*. **20% of books from first-time authors. 45% from unagented writers. Pays 10-15% royalty on wholesale price. Offers $1,000 advance.** Publishes ms within 18 months after acceptance. Responds in weeks or months. Catalog available.

NONFICTION Subjects include literature, memoirs, sex, true crime.

FICTION Subjects include adventure, contemporary, erotica, experimental, historical, literary, mainstream, mystery, science fiction, suspense, translation. Promotes titles through reviews. Literary, mainstream/contemporary, mystery. Especially looking for high-line literary fiction, "artful, original and arresting." Accepts any fiction category as long as it is a "well-written, original full-length novel."

TIPS "We are looking for good books—be they 10th novels or first ones, it makes little difference. The fiction is more important than the track record. Send us the first 25 pages; it's impossible to judge something that begins on page 302. Also, no outlines—let the writing present itself."

PERSEA BOOKS

277 Broadway, Suite 708, New York NY 10007. (212)260-9256. **Fax:** (212)267-3165. **E-mail:** info@perseabooks.com. **Website:** www.perseabooks.com. Estab. 1975. The aim of Persea is to publish works that endure by meeting high standards of literary merit and relevance. "We have often taken on important books other publishers have overlooked, or have made significant discoveries and rediscoveries, whether of a single work or writer's entire oeuvre. Our books cover a wide range of themes, styles, and genres. We have published poetry, fiction, essays, memoir, biography, titles of Jewish and Middle Eastern interest, women's studies, American Indian folklore, and revived classics, as well as a notable selection of works in translation." Accepts simultaneous submissions. Responds in 8 weeks to proposals; 10 weeks to mss. Guidelines online.

NONFICTION Subjects include contemporary culture, literary criticism, literature, memoirs, translation, travel, young adult.

FICTION Subjects include contemporary, literary, short story collections, translation, young adult. Queries should include a cover letter, author background and publication history, a detailed synopsis of the proposed work, and a sample chapter. Please indicate if the work is simultaneously submitted.

POETRY "We have a longstanding commitment to publishing extraordinary contemporary poetry and maintain an active poetry program. At this time, due to our commitment to the poets we already publish, we are limited in our ability to add new collections." Send an e-mail to poetry@perseabooks.com describing current project and publication history, attaching a pdf or Word document with up to 12 sample pages of poetry. "If the timing is right and we are interested in seeing more work, we will contact you."

⊘ PERUGIA PRESS

P.O. Box 60364, Florence MA 01062. **Website:** www.perugiapress.com. **Contact:** Rebecca Olander, director. Estab. 1997. The best new women poets for 20 years. "Contact us through our website." Accepts simultaneous submissions.

PETER PAUPER PRESS, INC.

202 Mamaroneck Ave., 4th Floor, White Plains NY 10601. **Website:** www.peterpauper.com. Estab. 1928. Publishes hardcover originals. "PPP publishes small and medium format, illustrated gift books for occasions and in celebration of specific relationships such as mom, sister, friend, teacher, grandmother, granddaughter. PPP has expanded into the following areas: books for teens and tweens, activity books for children, organizers, books on popular topics of nonfiction for adults and licensed books by best-selling authors." **Publishes 40-50 titles/year. 100 queries received/year. 150 mss received/year. 5% from unagented writers. Makes outright purchase only. Pays advance.** Publishes ms 1 year after acceptance. Responds in 2 months to queries.

NONFICTION "We do not publish fiction or poetry. We publish brief, original quotes, aphorisms, and wise sayings. Please do not send us other people's quotes." Submit cover letter and hard copy ms.

TIPS "Our readers are primarily female, age 10 and over, who are likely to buy a 'gift' book or gift book set in a stationery, gift, book, or boutique store or national book chain. Writers should become familiar with our previously published work. We publish only small- and medium-format, illustrated, hardcover gift books and sets of between 1,000-4,000 words. We have much less interest in work aimed at men."

PETERSON'S

121 S. 13 St., Lincoln NE 68508. **E-mail:** support@petersons.com. **Website:** www.petersons.com. Estab. 1966. Publishes trade and reference books. Peterson's

publishes guides to graduate and professional programs, colleges and universities, financial aid, distance learning, private schools, summer programs, international study, executive education, job hunting and career opportunities, educational and career test prep, as well as online products and services offering educational and career guidance and information for adult learners and workplace solutions for education professionals. **Pays royalty. Pays advance.** Book catalog available free.

NONFICTION Subjects include education, careers. Looks for appropriateness of contents to our markets, author's credentials, and writing style suitable for audience.

PFEIFFER

John Wiley & Sons, Inc., 989 Market St., San Francisco CA 94103. **Website:** www.wiley.com. Pfeiffer is an imprint of Wiley. **Publishes 250 titles/year. Pays variable royalties. Pays occasional advance.** Publishes ms 1 year after acceptance. Accepts simultaneous submissions. Responds in 2-3 months to queries. Guidelines online.

NONFICTION Subjects include education, psychology, religion. See proposal guidelines online.

PFLAUM PUBLISHING GROUP

3055 Kettering Blvd., Suite 100, Dayton OH 45439. (800)543-4383. **Website:** www.pflaum.com. "Pflaum Publishing Group, a division of Peter Li, Inc., serves the specialized market of religious education, primarily Roman Catholic. We provide high quality, theologically sound, practical, and affordable resources that assist religious educators of and ministers to children from preschool through senior high school." **Publishes 20 titles/year. Payment by outright purchase.** Accepts simultaneous submissions. Book catalog and ms guidelines free.

NONFICTION Query with SASE.

PHAIDON PRESS

65 Bleecker St., 8th Floor, New York NY 10012. (212)652-5400. **Fax:** (212)652-5410. **E-mail:** submissions@phaidon.com. **Website:** www.phaidon.com. Estab. 1923. Publishes hardcover and trade paperback originals and reprints. Phaidon Press is the world's leading publisher of books on the visual arts, with offices in London, Paris, Berlin, Barcelona, Milan, New York and Tokyo. Their books are recognized worldwide for the highest quality of content, design, and production. They cover everything from art, architecture, photography, design, performing arts, decorative arts, contemporary culture, fashion, film, travel, cookery and children's books. **Publishes 100 titles/year. 500 mss received/year. 40% of books from first-time authors. 90% from unagented writers. Pays royalty on wholesale price, if appropriate. Offers advance, if appropriate.** Publishes ms 1 year after acceptance. Accepts simultaneous submissions. Responds in 3 months to proposals. Book catalog available free. Guidelines online.

NONFICTION Subjects include photography, design. Submit proposal package and outline, or submit complete ms. Submissions by e-mail or fax will not be accepted. Reviews artwork/photos. Send photocopies.

TIPS "Please do not contact us to obtain an update on the status of your submission until we have had your submission for at least three months, as we will not provide updates before this period of time has elapsed. Phaidon does not assume any responsibility for any unsolicited submissions, or any materials included with a submission."

ⓐⓩ PHILOMEL BOOKS

Imprint of Penguin Group (USA), Inc., 375 Hudson St., New York NY 10014. (212)414-3610. **Website:** www.penguin.com. **Contact:** Michael Green, president/publisher. Estab. 1980. Publishes hardcover originals. "We look for beautifully written, engaging manuscripts for children and young adults." **Publishes 8-10 titles/year. 5% of books from first-time authors. 20% from unagented writers. Pays authors in royalties. Average advance payment "varies." Illustrators paid by advance and in royalties. Pays negotiable advance.** Accepts simultaneous submissions.

NONFICTION Picture books. *Agented submissions only.*

FICTION Subjects include adventure, ethnic, fantasy, historical, juvenile, literary, picture books, regional, short story collections, translation, western, young adult. *No unsolicited mss.*

PHILOSOPHY DOCUMENTATION CENTER

P.O. Box 7147, Charlottesville VA 22906-7147. (434)220-3300. **Fax:** (434)220-3301. **E-mail:** leaman@pdcnet.org. **Website:** www.pdcnet.org. **Contact:** Dr. George Leaman, director. Estab. 1966. The Philosophy Documentation Center specializes in the publication of reference materials, scholarly journals, book series, and conference proceedings. It has a unique commitment to support teaching, research, and professional activities in philosophy and related fields. **Publishes 20 titles/year. 20 queries; 4-6 mss received/year. 20% of books from first-time authors. Pays 2-10% royalty. Pays advance (special cases only).** Publishes ms 1 year after acceptance. Responds in 1 week to queries.

NONFICTION Subjects include philosophy, software. "We want to increase the range of philosophical titles that are available online, and we support online publication of philosophical work in multiple languages." Query with SASE. Submit outline.

PIANO PRESS

P.O. Box 85, Del Mar CA 92014. (619)884-1401. **Fax:** (858)755-1104. **E-mail:** pianopress@pianopress.com. **Website:** www.pianopress.com. **Contact:** Elizabeth C. Axford, editor. Estab. 1984. "We publish music-related books, either fiction or nonfiction, music-related coloring books, songbooks, sheet music, CDs, and music-related poetry." **Pays authors, illustrators, and photographers royalties based on the retail price.** Publishes book 1 year after acceptance. Accepts simultaneous submissions. Responds if interested. Book catalog online.

NONFICTION Subjects include music. Picture books, young readers, middle readers, young adults: multicultural, music/dance. Average word length: picture books—1,500-2,000.

FICTION Subjects include multicultural, multimedia, picture books. Picture books, young readers, middle readers, young adults: folktales, multicultural, poetry, music. Average word length: picture books—1,500-2,000.

TIPS "We are looking for music-related material only for the juvenile market. Please do not send non-music-related materials. Query by e-mail first before submitting anything."

🅰🐾⊘ PIATKUS BOOKS

Little, Brown Book Group, Carmelite House, 50 Victoria Embankment, London EC4Y 0DZ, United Kingdom. (020)3122-7000. **Fax:** (020)3122-7000. **E-mail:** info@littlebrown.co.uk. **Website:** piatkus.co.uk. Estab. 1979. Publishes hardcover originals, paperback originals, and paperback reprints. **10% from unagented writers.** Publishes ms 1 year after acceptance. Accepts simultaneous submissions. Guidelines online.

NONFICTION *Agented submissions only.*

FICTION Romance fiction, women's fiction, book-club fiction. *Agented submissions only.*

🅰⊘ PICADOR USA

MacMillan, 175 Fifth Ave., New York NY 10010. (212)674-5151. **Website:** us.macmillan.com/picador. Estab. 1994. Picador publishes high-quality literary fiction and nonfiction. "We are open to a broad range of subjects, well written by authoritative authors." Publishes hardcover and trade paperback originals and reprints. Does not accept unsolicited mss. *Agented submissions only.* **Publishes 70-80 titles/year. Pays 7-15% on royalty. Advance varies.** Publishes ms 18 months after acceptance. Accepts simultaneous submissions.

PICCADILLY BOOKS, LTD.

P.O. Box 25203, Colorado Springs CO 80936. (719)550-9887. **Fax:** (719)550-8810. **E-mail:** info@piccadillybooks.com. **Website:** www.piccadillybooks.com. Estab. 1985. Publishes hardcover originals and trade paperback originals and reprints. "Picadilly publishes nonfiction, diet, nutrition, and health-related books with a focus on alternative and natural medicine." **Publishes 5-8 titles/year. 70% of books from first-time authors. 95% from unagented writers. Pays 6-10% royalty on retail price.** Publishes ms 1 year after acceptance. Accepts simultaneous submissions. Responds only if interested, unless accompanied by a SASE to queries. Responds to all e-mail queries.

NONFICTION Subjects include health, medicine, nutrition, health, nutrition, diet, and physical fitness. "Do your research. Let us know why there is a need for your book, how it differs from other books on the market, and how you will promote the book. No phone calls. We prefer to see the entire ms, but will accept a minimum of 3 sample chapters on your first inquiry. A cover letter is also required; please provide a brief overview of the book, information about similar books already in print and explain why yours is different or better. Tell us the prime market for your book and what you can do to help market it. Also, provide us with background information on yourself and explain what qualifies you to write this book."

TIPS "We publish nonfiction, general interest, self-help books currently emphasizing alternative health."

⊘ THE PILGRIM PRESS

700 Prospect Ave. E., Cleveland OH 44115-1100. (216)736-3755. **Fax:** (216)736-2207. **Website:** www.thepilgrimpress.com. Publishes hardcover and trade paperback originals. No longer accepting unsolicited

ms proposals. **Publishes 25 titles/year. 60% of books from first-time authors. 80% from unagented writers. Pays standard royalties. Pays advance.** Publishes ms an average of 18 months after acceptance. Responds in 3 months to queries. Book catalog and ms guidelines online.

NONFICTION Subjects include religion, ethics, social issues with a strong commitment to justice—addressing such topics as public policy, sexuality and gender, human rights and minority liberation—primarily in a Christian context, but not exclusively.

PIÑATA BOOKS

Imprint of Arte Publico Press, University of Houston, 4902 Gulf Fwy., Bldg. 19, Room 100, Houston TX 77204-2004. (713)743-2845. **Fax:** (713)743-3080. **E-mail:** submapp@uh.edu. **Website:** www.artepublicopress.com. Estab. 1994. Publishes hardcover and trade paperback originals. "Piñata Books is dedicated to the publication of children's and young adult literature focusing on U.S. Hispanic culture by U.S. Hispanic authors. Arte Publico's mission is the publication, promotion and dissemination of Latino literature for a variety of national and regional audiences, from early childhood to adult, through the complete gamut of delivery systems, including personal performance as well as print and electronic media." **Publishes 10-15 titles/year. 80% of books from first-time authors. Pays 10% royalty on wholesale price. Pays $1,000-3,000 advance.** Publishes book 2 years after acceptance. Accepts simultaneous submissions. Responds in 2-3 months to queries; 4-6 months to mss. Book catalog and guidelines online.

NONFICTION Subjects include ethnic. Piñata Books specializes in publication of children's and young adult literature that authentically portrays themes, characters and customs unique to U.S. Hispanic culture. Submissions made through online submission form.

FICTION Subjects include adventure, juvenile, picture books, young adult. Submissions made through online submission form.

POETRY Appropriate to Hispanic theme. Submissions made through online submission form.

TIPS "Include cover letter with submission explaining why your manuscript is unique and important, why we should publish it, who will buy it, etc."

PINEAPPLE PRESS, INC.

P.O. Box 3889, Sarasota FL 34230. (941)706-2507. **Fax:** (800)746-3275. **Website:** www.pineapplepress.com. **Contact:** June Cussen, executive editor. Estab. 1982. Publishes hardcover and trade paperback originals. "We are seeking quality nonfiction on diverse topics for the library and book trade markets. Our mission is to publish good books about Florida." **Publishes 21 titles/year. 1,000 queries; 500 mss received/year. 50% of books from first-time authors. 95% from unagented writers. Pays authors royalty of 10-15%.** Publishes a book 1 year after acceptance. Accepts simultaneous submissions. Responds in 2 months. Book catalog for 9×12 SAE with $1.32 postage. Guidelines online.

NONFICTION Subjects include regional, Florida. Picture books: animal, history, nature/environmental, science. Young readers, middle readers, young adults: animal, biography, geography, history, nature/environment, science. Query or submit outline/synopsis and intro and 3 sample chapters. Reviews artwork/photos. Send photocopies.

FICTION Subjects include regional. Picture books, young readers, middle readers, young adults: animal, folktales, history, nature/environment. Query or submit outline/synopsis and 3 sample chapters.

TIPS "Quality first novels will be published, though we usually only do one or two novels per year and they must be set in Florida. We regard the author/editor relationship as a trusting relationship with communication open both ways. Learn all you can about the publishing process and about how to promote your book once it is published. A query on a novel without a brief sample seems useless."

⊘ PLAN B PRESS

2714 Jefferson Dr., Alexandria VA 22303. (215)732-2663. **E-mail:** planbpress@gmail.com. **Website:** www.planbpress.com. **Contact:** Steven Allen May, president. Estab. 1999. Plan B Press is a "small publishing company with an international feel. Our intention is to have Plan B Press be part of the conversation about the direction and depth of literary movements and genres. Plan B Press's new direction is to seek out authors rarely-to-never published, sharing new voices that might not otherwise be heard. Plan B Press is determined to merge text with image, writing with art." Publishes poetry and short fiction. Wants "experimental poetry, concrete/visual work." **Pays author's**

copies. Accepts simultaneous submissions. Responds to queries in 1 month; mss in 3 months.

NONFICTION Subjects include literature.

FICTION Subjects include poetry.

POETRY Wants to see: experimental, concrete, visual poetry. Does not want "sonnets, political or religious poems, work in the style of Ogden Nash."

PLAYLAB PRESS

P.O. Box 3701, South Brisbane BC 4101, Australia. E-mail: info@playlab.org.au. **Website:** www.playlab.org.au. Estab. 1978. **Publishes 1 titles/year.** Accepts simultaneous submissions. Responds in 3 months to mss. Guidelines online.

NONFICTION Subjects include literary criticism.

FICTION Subjects include plays. Submit 2 copies of ms, cover letter.

TIPS "Playlab Press is committed to the publication of quality writing for and about theatre and performance, which is of significance to Australia's cultural life. It values socially just and diverse publication outcomes and aims to promote these outcomes in local, national, and international contexts."

PLEXUS PUBLISHING, INC.

143 Old Marlton Pike, Medford NJ 08055. (609)654-6500. **Fax:** (609)654-4309. **E-mail:** rcolding@plexuspublishing.com. **Website:** www.plexuspublishing.com. **Contact:** Rob Colding, Book Marketing Manager. Estab. 1977. Publishes hardcover and paperback originals. Plexus publishes regional-interest (southern New Jersey and the greater Philadelphia area) fiction and nonfiction including mysteries, field guides, nature, travel and history. **Pays $500-1,000 advance.** Accepts simultaneous submissions. Responds in 3 months to proposals. Book catalog and book proposal guidelines for 10x13 SASE.

NONFICTION Subjects include Americana, environment, history, memoirs, true crime. Query with SASE.

FICTION Subjects include adventure, contemporary, historical, mystery, suspense. Mysteries and literary novels with a strong regional (southern New Jersey) angle. Query with SASE.

POCKET BOOKS

Simon & Schuster, 1230 Avenue of the Americas, New York NY 10020. (212)698-7000. **Website:** www.simonandschuster.com. Estab. 1939. Publishes paperback originals and reprints, mass market and trade paperbacks. Pocket Books publishes commercial fiction and genre fiction (WWE, Downtown Press, Star Trek). Book catalog available free. Guidelines online.

NONFICTION *Agented submissions only.*

FICTION Subjects include mystery, romance, suspense, western. *Agented submissions only.*

POCOL PRESS

Box 411, Clifton VA 20124. (703)830-5862. **Website:** www.pocolpress.com. **Contact:** J. Thomas Hetrick, editor. Estab. 1999. Publishes trade paperback originals. "Pocol Press is dedicated to producing high-quality print books and e-books from first-time, non-agented authors. However, all submissions are welcome. We're dedicated to good storytellers and to the written word, specializing in short fiction and baseball. Several of our books have been used as literary texts at universities and in book group discussions around the nation. Pocol Press does not publish children's books, romance novels, or graphic novels. Our authors are comprised of veteran writers and emerging talents." **Publishes 6 titles/year. 90 queries; 20 mss received/year. 90% of books from first-time authors. 100% from unagented writers. Pays 10-12% royalty on wholesale price.** Publishes book less than 1 year after acceptance. Responds in 1 month to queries; 2 months to mss. Book catalog and guidelines online.

NONFICTION Subjects include computers, history, literature, medicine, military, sports, war, womens studies.

FICTION Subjects include adventure, historical, horror, literary, mainstream, military, mystery, religious, short story collections, spiritual, sports, suspense, western, baseball fiction. "We specialize in thematic short fiction collections by a single author, westerns, war stories, and baseball fiction. Expert storytellers welcome." Does not accept or return unsolicited mss. Query with SASE or submit 1 sample chapter.

TIPS "Our audience is aged 18 and over. Pocol Press is unique; we publish good writing and great storytelling. Write the best stories you can. Read them to you friends/peers. Note their reaction. Publishes some of the finest fiction by a small press."

THE POISONED PENCIL

Poisoned Pen Press, 6962 E. 1st Ave., Suite 103, Scottsdale AZ 85251. (480)945-3375. **Fax:** (480)949-1707. **E-mail:** info@thepoisonedpencil.com. **E-mail:** ellen@thepoisonedpencil.com. **Website:** www.thepoisonedpencil.com. **Contact:** Ellen Larson, editor. Robert Rosenwald, publisher Estab. 2012. Publishes trade paperback and electronic originals. **Publishes 4-6 titles/year. 150 submissions received/year. Pays 9-15% for trade paperback; 25-35% for e-books. Pays advance of $1,000.** Publishes ms 15 months after acceptance. Responds in 6 weeks to mss. Guidelines online.

◑ *Accepts young adult mysteries only.*

FICTION Subjects include mystery, young adult. "We publish only young adult mystery novels, 45,000 to 90,000 words in length. For our purposes, a young adult book is a book with a protagonist between the ages of 13 and 18. We are looking for both traditional and cross-genre young adult mysteries. We encourage off-beat approaches and narrative choices that reflect the complexity and ambiguity of today's world. Submissions from teens are very welcome. Avoid serial killers, excessive gore, and vampires (and other heavy supernatural themes). We only consider authors who live in the US or Canada, due to practicalities of marketing promotion. Avoid coincidence in plotting. Avoid having your sleuth leap to conclusions rather than discover and deduce. Pay attention to the resonance between character and plot; between plot and theme; between theme and character. We are looking for clean style, fluid storytelling, and solid structure. Unrealistic dialogue is a real turn-off." Submit proposal package including synopsis, complete ms, and cover letter.

TIPS "Our audience is made up of young adults and adults who love YA mysteries."

POISONED PEN PRESS

6962 E. 1st Ave., Suite 103, Scottsdale AZ 85251. E-mail: submissions@poisonedpenpress.com. **Website:** www.poisonedpenpress.com. **Contact:** Diane DiBiase, Assistant Publisher. Estab. 1997. Publishes hardcover and trade paperback originals, and hardcover and trade paperback reprints. "Our publishing goal is to offer well-written mystery novels of crime and/or detection where the puzzle and its resolution are the main forces that move the story forward." **Publishes 60 titles/year. 1,000 queries; 300 mss received/year. 35% of books from first-time authors. 65% from unagented writers. Pays 9-15% royalty on retail price.** Publishes book 10-12 months after acceptance. Responds in 2-3 months to queries and proposals; 6 months to mss. Book catalog and guidelines online.

◑ *Not currently accepting submissions. Check website.*

FICTION Subjects include mystery. Mss should generally be longer than 65,000 words and shorter than 100,000 words. Member Publishers Marketing Associations, Arizona Book Publishers Associations, Publishers Association of West. Distributes through Ingram, Baker & Taylor, Brodart. Does not want novels centered on serial killers, spousal or child abuse, drugs, or extremist groups, although we do not entirely rule such works out. Accepts unsolicited mss. Electronic queries only. "Submit clips, first 3 pages. We must receive both the synopsis and ms pages electronically as separate attachments to an e-mail message."

TIPS "Audience is adult readers of mystery fiction."

POLIS BOOKS

E-mail: info@polisbooks.com. **E-mail:** submissions@polisbooks.com. **Website:** www.polisbooks.com. Estab. 2013. "Polis Books is an independent publishing company actively seeking new and established authors for our growing list. We are actively acquiring titles in mystery, thriller, suspense, procedural, traditional crime, science fiction, fantasy, horror, supernatural, urban fantasy, romance, erotica, commercial women's fiction, commercial literary fiction, young adult and middle grade books." **Publishes 40 titles/year. 500+ 33% of books from first-time authors. 10% from unagented writers. Offers advance against royalties.** For e-book originals, ms published 6-9 months after acceptance. For front list print titles, 9-15 months. Accepts simultaneous submissions. Only responds to submissions if interested. Guidelines online.

FICTION Query with 3 sample chapters and bio via e-mail.

POPULAR WOODWORKING BOOKS

Imprint of F+W Media, Inc., 10151 Carver Rd., Suite 200, Blue Ash OH 45242. (513) 531-2690. **E-mail:** scott.francis@fwcommunity.com. **Website:** www.popular-woodworking.com. **Contact:** Scott Francis, content editor. Publishes trade paperback and hardcover originals and reprints. "Popular Woodworking Books is one of the largest publishers of woodworking books in the world. From perfecting a furniture design to putting on the final coat of finish, our books provide step-by-step instructions and trusted advice from the pros that make them valuable tools for both beginning and advanced woodworkers. Currently emphasizing woodworking jigs and fixtures, woodworking techniques, furniture and cabinet projects, smaller finely crafted boxes, all styles of furniture. We are also looking for DIY-style maker projects for clever furniture projects or home decor created using wood and woodworking techiniques; techniques creating space-saving, modular furniture." **Publishes 8-10 titles/year. 20 queries; 10 mss received/year. 20% of books from first-time authors. 95% from unagented writers.** Accepts simultaneous submissions. Responds in 1 month to queries.

NONFICTION "We publish heavily illustrated how-to woodworking books that show, rather than tell, our readers how to accomplish their woodworking goals." Query with SASE, or electronic query. Proposal package should include an outline and digital photos.

TIPS "Our books are for beginning to advanced woodworking enthusiasts."

PPI (PROFESSIONAL PUBLICATIONS, INC.)

1250 Fifth Ave., Belmont CA 94002. (650)593-9119. **Fax:** (650)592-4519. **E-mail:** info@ppi2pass.com. **E-mail:** acquisitions@ppi2pass.com. **Website:** www.ppi2pass.com. Estab. 1975. Publishes hardcover, paperback, and electronic products, CD-ROMs and DVDs. "PPI publishes professional, reference, and licensing preparation materials. PPI wants submissions from both professionals practicing in the field and from experienced instructors. Currently emphasizing engineering, interior design, architecture, landscape architecture and LEED exam review." **Publishes 10 titles/year. 5% of books from first-time authors. 100% from unagented writers.** Publishes ms 4-18 months after acceptance. Accepts simultaneous submissions. Responds in 1 month to queries. Book catalog and ms guidelines free.

NONFICTION Subjects include architecture, science, landscape architecture, engineering mathematics, engineering, surveying, interior design, green-building, sustainable development, and other professional licensure subjects. Especially needs review and reference books for all professional licensing examinations. Please submit ms and proposal outlining market potential, etc. Proposal template available upon request. Reviews artwork/photos.

TIPS "We specialize in books for those people who want to become licensed and/or accredited professionals: engineers, architects, surveyors, interior designers, LEED APs, etc. Demonstrating your understanding of the market, competition, appropriate de-livery methods, and marketing ideas will help sell us on your proposal."

PRESA PRESS

P.O. Box 792, Rockford MI 49341. **E-mail:** presapress@aol.com. **Website:** www.presapress.com. **Contact:** Roseanne Ritzema, editor. Estab. 2003. Presa Press publishes perfect-bound paperbacks of poetry. Wants "imagistic poetry where form is an extension of content, surreal, experimental, and personal poetry." Does not want "overtly political or didactic material." **Pays 5+ author/quotes copies.** Time between acceptance and publication is 8-12 weeks. Accepts simultaneous submissions. Responds to queries in 2-4 weeks; to mss in 8-12 weeks.

NONFICTION Subjects include literary criticism, literature.

FICTION Subjects include poetry.

POETRY Acquires first North American serial rights and the right to reprint in anthologies. Rights include e-book publishing rights. Rights revert to poets upon publication. Accepts postal submissions only. Cover letter is preferred. Reads submissions year round. Poems are circulated to an editorial board. Send materials for review consideration to Roseanne Ritzema. Query first, with a few sample poems and a cover letter with brief bio and publication credits. Book/chapbook mss may include previously published poems.

PRESS 53

560 N. Trade St., Suite 103, Winston-Salem NC 27101. (336)770-5353. **E-mail:** editor@press53.com. **Website:** www.press53.com. **Contact:** Kevin Morgan Watson, publisher. Estab. 2005. Poetry and short fiction collections only. "Press 53 was founded in October 2005 and quickly began earning a reputation as a quality publishing house of short fiction and poetry collections." **Publishes 14-15 titles/year. Finds mss through contest, referrals, and scouting journals, magazines, and contests. 60% of books from first-time authors. 90% from unagented writers. Pays 10% royalty on gross sales. Pays advance only for contest winners.** Publishes ms 1 year after acceptance. Catalog online. Guidelines online.

FICTION Subjects include literary, short story collections. "We publish roughly 3-4 short fiction collections each year by writers who are active and earning recognition through publication and awards, plus the winner of our Press 53 Award for Short Fiction." Collections should be between 100 and 250 pages (give or take) with 70% or more of those stories previously published in journals, magazines, anthologies, etc. Does not want novels. Finds mss through contest, referrals, and scouting magazines, journals, and contests.

POETRY "We love working with poets who have been widely published and are active in the poetry community. We publish roughly 6-8 full-length poetry collections of around 70 pages or more each year, plus the winner of our Press 53 Award for Poetry." Prefers that at least 30-40% of the poems in the collection be previously published in magazines, journals, anthologies, etc. Does not want experimental, overtly political or religious. Finds mss through contest, referrals, and scouting magazines, journals, and contests.

TIPS "We are looking for writers who are actively involved in the writing community, writers who are submitting their work to journals, magazines and contests, and who are getting published, building readership, and earning a reputation for their work."

⟳ PRESSES DE L'UNIVERSITÉ DE MONTREAL

C.P. 6128, succ. Centre-ville, Montreal QC H3C 3J7, Canada. (514)343-6933. **Fax:** (514)343-2232. **E-mail:** sb@editionspum.ca. **Website:** www.pum.umontreal. ca. **Contact:** Patrick Poirier, rights and sales. Publishes hardcover and trade paperback originals. **Publishes 40 titles/year.** Publishes ms 6 months after acceptance. Accepts simultaneous submissions. Responds in 1 month. Book catalog and ms guidelines free.

NONFICTION Subjects include anthropology, art, contemporary culture, education, history, philosophy, politics, psychology, sociology, translation, world affairs. Submit outline, 2 sample chapters.

PRESS HERE

22230 NE 28th Place, Sammamish WA 98074-6408. **Website:** www.gracecuts.com/press-here. **Contact:** Michael Dylan Welch, editor/publisher. Estab. 1989. Press Here publishes award-winning books of haiku, tanka, and related poetry by the leading poets of these genres, as well as essays, criticism, and interviews about these genres. "We publish work only by those poets who are already frequently published in the leading haiku and tanka journals." Publishes 1-2 poetry books/year, plus occasional books of essays or interviews. Mss are selected nearly always by invitation. **Pays a negotiated percentage of author's cop-**

ies (out of a press run of 200-1,000). Accepts simultaneous submissions. Responds to queries in up to 1 month; to mss in up to 2 months. Catalog available for #10 SASE.

◷ Press Here publications have won the 1st-place Merit Book Award and other awards from the Haiku Society of America.

POETRY Does not want any poetry other than haiku, tanka, and related genres. Has published poetry by Lee Gurga, paul m., Paul O. Williams, Adele Kenny, Pat Shelley, Cor van den Heuvel, and William J. Higginson. Query first, with a few sample poems and a cover letter with brief bio and publication credits. Book mss may include previously published poems ("previous publication strongly preferred"). "All proposals must be by well-established haiku or tanka poets, and must be for haiku or tanka poetry, or criticism/discussion of these genres. If the editor does not already know your work well from leading haiku and tanka publications, then he is not likely to be interested in your manuscript."

PRESTWICK HOUSE, INC.

P.O. Box 658, Clayton DE 19938. **E-mail:** info@prestwickhouse.com. **Website:** www.prestwickhouse.com. Estab. 1980. Accepts simultaneous submissions.

NONFICTION Submit proposal package, outline, resume, 1 sample chapter, TOC.

TIPS "We market our books primarily for middle and high school English teachers. Submissions should address a direct need of grades 7-12 language arts teachers. Current and former English teachers are encouraged to submit materials developed and used by them successfully in the classroom."

⊘⊘ PRICE STERN SLOAN, INC.

Penguin Group, 375 Hudson St., New York NY 10014. (212)366-2000. **Website:** www.penguin.com. Estab. 1963. "Price Stern Sloan publishes quirky mass market novelty series for childrens as well as licensed movie tie-in books." Price Stern Sloan only responds to submissions it's interested in publishing. Accepts simultaneous submissions. Book catalog online.

FICTION Publishes picture books and novelty/board books. *Agented submissions only.*

TIPS "Price Stern Sloan publishes unique, fun titles."

PRINCETON ARCHITECTURAL PRESS

37 E. 7th St., New York NY 10003. (212)995-9620. **Fax:** (212)995-9454. **E-mail:** submissions@papress.com.

Website: www.papress.com. Publishes hardcover and trade paperback originals. **Publishes 50 titles/year. 300 queries; 150 mss received/year. 65% of books from first-time authors. 95% from unagented writers. Pays royalty on wholesale price.** Publishes ms 1 year after acceptance. Accepts simultaneous submissions. Responds in 2 months. Book catalog online. Guidelines online.

NONFICTION Submit proposal package, outline, 1 sample chapter, TOC, sample of art, and survey of competitive titles. Reviews artwork/photos. Do not send originals.

TIPS "Princeton Architecture Press publishes fine books on architecture, design, photography, landscape, and visual culture. Our books are acclaimed for their strong and unique editorial vision, unrivaled design sensibility, and high production values at affordable prices."

PRINCETON BOOK CO.

614 Route 130, Hightstown NJ 08520. (609)426-0602. **Fax:** (609)426-1344. **Website:** www.dancehorizons. com. **Contact:** Charles Woodford, president. Publishes hardcover and trade paperback originals and reprints. **Publishes 5-6 titles/year. 50 queries received/ year. 100 mss received/year. 80% of books from first-time authors. 100% from unagented writers. Pays negotiable royalty on net receipts.** Publishes ms 9-12 months after acceptance. Accepts simultaneous submissions. Responds in 1 week. Book catalog and guidelines online.

IMPRINTS Dance Horizons, Elysian Editions.

NONFICTION "We publish all sorts of dance-related books including those on fitness and health." Does not accept memoir. Submit proposal package, outline, 3 sample chapters. Reviews artwork/photos. Send photocopies.

PRINCETON UNIVERSITY PRESS

41 William St., Princeton NJ 08540. (609)258-4900. **Fax:** (609)258-6305. **Website:** press.princeton.edu. **Contact:** Susan Stewart, editor. "The Lockert Library of Poetry in Translation embraces a wide geographic and temporal range, from Scandinavia to Latin America to the subcontinent of India, from the Tang Dynasty to Europe of the modern day. It especially emphasizes poets who are established in their native lands and who are being introduced to an English-speaking audience. Manuscripts are judged with several criteria in mind: the ability of the translation to stand on its own as poetry in English; fidelity to the tone and spirit of the original, rather than literal accuracy; and the importance of the translated poet to the literature of his or her time and country." Accepts simultaneous submissions. Responds in 3-4 months. Guidelines online.

NONFICTION Query with SASE.

POETRY Submit hard copy of proposal with sample poems or full ms. Cover letter is required. Reads submissions year round. Mss will not be returned. Comments on finalists only.

PRINTING INDUSTRIES OF AMERICA

301 Brush Creek Rd., Warrendale PA 15086. (412)741-6860. **Fax:** (412)741-2311. **E-mail:** printing@printing. org. **Website:** www.printing.org. Estab. 1921. Publishes trade paperback originals and reference texts. "Printing Industries of America, along with its affiliates, delivers products and services that enhance the growth and profitability of its members and the industry through advocacy, education, research, and technical information." Printing Industries of America's mission is to serve the graphic communications community as the major resource for technical information and services through research and education. **Publishes 8-10 titles/year. 20 mss; 30 queries received/year. 50% of books from first-time authors. 100% from unagented writers. Pays 15% royalty on wholesale price.** Publishes ms 18 months after acceptance. Accepts simultaneous submissions. Responds in 1 month to queries.

NONFICTION Subjects include business, communications, economics, education, printing and graphic arts reference, technical, textbook. Currently emphasizing technical textbooks as well as career guides for graphic communications and turnkey training curricula. Query with SASE, or submit outline, sample chapters, and SASE. Reviews artwork. Send photocopies.

PROMETHEUS BOOKS

59 John Glenn Dr., Amherst NY 14228. (800)421-0351. **Fax:** (716)564-2711. **Website:** www.prometheusbooks. com. Estab. 1969. Publishes hardcover originals, trade paperback originals and reprints. "Prometheus Books is a leading independent publisher in philosophy, social science, popular science, and critical thinking. We publish authoritative and thoughtful books by distinguished authors in many categories. Currently emphasizing popular science, health, psychology, so-

cial science, current events, business and economics, atheism and critiques of religion." **Publishes 90-100 titles/year. 30% of books from first-time authors. 40% from unagented writers.** Accepts simultaneous submissions. Responds in 2 months to queries; 3 months to proposals; 4 months to mss. Book catalog and guidelines online.

NONFICTION Subjects include education, history, New Age, philosophy, psychology, religion, contemporary issues. Ask for a catalog, go to the library or our website, look at our books and others like them to get an idea of what our focus is. Submit proposal package including outline, synopsis, potential market, tentative ms length, résumé, and a well-developed query letter with SASE, two or three of author's best chapters. Reviews artwork/photos. Send photocopies.

TIPS "Audience is highly literate with multiple degrees; an audience that is intellectually mature and knows what it wants. They are aware, and we try to provide them with new information on topics of interest to them in mainstream and related areas."

PRUFROCK PRESS, INC.

P.O. Box 8813, Waco TX 76714. (800)988-2208. **Fax:** (800)240-0333. **Website:** www.prufrock.com. "Prufrock Press offers award-winning products focused on gifted education, gifted children, advanced learning, and special needs learners, including trade nonfiction (not narrative nonfiction, however) for adults and children/teens. For more than 20 years, Prufrock has supported gifted children and their education and development. The company publishes more than 300 products that enhance the lives of gifted children and the teachers and parents who support them." Accepts simultaneous submissions, but must be notified about it. **50 queries; 40 mss received/year. 20% of books from first-time authors. 100% from unagented writers.** Publishes ms 1-2 year after acceptance. Accepts simultaneous submissions. Book catalog available. Guidelines online.

NONFICTION Subjects include education. "We are always looking for truly original, creative materials for teachers." Query with SASE. Submit outline, 1-3 sample chapters.

FICTION Prufrock Press "offers award-winning products focused on gifted education, gifted children, advanced learning, and special needs learners. For more than 20 years, Prufrock has supported gifted children and their education and development.

The company publishes more than 300 products that enhance the lives of gifted children and the teachers and parents who support them." No picture books. "Prufrock Press does not consider unsolicited manuscripts."

🅐🚫 PUFFIN BOOKS

Imprint of Penguin Group (USA), Inc., 375 Hudson St., New York NY 10014. (212)366-2000. **Website:** www.penguin.com. Publishes trade paperback originals and reprints. "Puffin Books publishes high-end trade paperbacks and paperback reprints for preschool children, beginning and middle readers, and young adults." **Publishes 175-200 titles/year.** Publishes book 1 year after acceptance.

NONFICTION Subjects include education, history, womens issues, womens studies. "Women in history books interest us." *No unsolicited mss. Agented submissions only.*

FICTION Subjects include fantasy, picture books, science fiction, young adult, middle grade, easy-to-read grades 1-3, graphic novels, classics. *No unsolicited mss. Agented submissions only.*

TIPS "Our audience ranges from little children 'first books' to young adult (ages 14-16). An original idea has the best luck."

PURDUE UNIVERSITY PRESS

504 West State St., West Lafayette IN 47907-2058. (765)494-2038. **E-mail:** pupress@purdue.edu. **E-mail:** lpennywa@purdue.edu. **Website:** www.thepress.purdue.edu. **Contact:** Leah Pennywark, acquisitions assistant. Estab. 1960. Purdue University Press is administratively a unit of Purdue University Libraries and its Director reports to the Dean of Libraries. There are 3 full-time staff and 2 part-time staff, as well as student assistants. Dedicated to the dissemination of scholarly and professional information, the Press provides quality resources in several key subject areas including business, technology, health, veterinary sciences, and other selected disciplines in the humanities and sciences. As well as publishing 30 books a year, and 5 subscription-based journals, the Press is committed to broadening access to scholarly information using digital technology. As part of this initiative, the Press distributes a number of Open Access electronic-only journals. An editorial board of 9 Purdue faculty members is responsible for the imprint of the Press and meets twice a semester to consider mss and proposals, and guide the editorial program. A manage-

ment advisory board advises the Director on strategy, and meets twice a year. Purdue University Press is a member of the Association of American University Presses.

G.P. PUTNAM'S SONS, PENGUIN YOUNG READERS GROUP

345 Hudson St., 14th Floor, New York NY 10014. (212)366-2000. **Website:** www.penguin.com. **Contact:** Dave Kopka, Junior Designer. Accepts simultaneous submissions.

ⒶⓍ G.P. PUTNAM'S SONS HARDCOVER

Imprint of Penguin Group (USA), Inc., 375 Hudson, New York NY 10014. (212)366-2000. **Fax:** (212)366-2664. **Website:** www.penguin.com. Publishes hardcover originals. **Pays variable royalties on retail price. Pays varies advance.** Accepts simultaneous submissions. Request book catalog through mail order department.

NONFICTION Subjects include animals, child guidance, contemporary culture, religion, science, sports, travel, celebrity-related topics. *Agented submissions only. No unsolicited mss.*

FICTION Subjects include adventure, literary, suspense, women's. *Agented submissions only.*

QUE

Pearson Education, 800 E. 96th St., Indianapolis IN 46240. (317)581-3500. **E-mail:** greg.wiegand@pearson.com. **Website:** www.quepublishing.com. **Contact:** Greg Wiegand, associate publisher. Estab. 1981. Publishes hardcover, trade paperback and mass market paperback originals and reprints. **Publishes 100 titles/year. 80% from unagented writers. Pays variable royalty on wholesale price or makes work-for-hire arrangements. Pays varying advance.** Accepts simultaneous submissions. Book catalog and guidelines online.

NONFICTION Subjects include technology, certification. Submit proposal package, resume, TOC, writing sample, competing titles.

QUILL DRIVER BOOKS

2006 S. Mary St., Fresno CA 93721. (559)233-6633. **E-mail:** info@lindenpub.com. **E-mail:** kent@lindenpub.com. **Website:** www.quilldriverbooks.com. **Contact:** Kent Sorsky. Publishes hardcover and trade paperback originals and reprints. Quill Driver Books publishes a mix of nonfiction titles, with an emphasis on how-to books. "Our books, we hope, make a worth-

while contribution to the human community, and we have a little fun along the way." **Publishes 10-12 titles/year. 50% of books from first-time authors. 75% from unagented writers. Pays 4-10% royalty on retail price. Pays $500-5,000 advance.** Publishes ms 12 months after acceptance. Accepts simultaneous submissions. Responds in 1 month to queries and proposals; 3 months to mss. Book catalog and ms guidelines for #10 SASE.

NONFICTION Subjects include regional, writing, aging. Query with SASE. Submit proposal package. Reviews artwork/photos. Send photocopies.

Ⓧ QUITE SPECIFIC MEDIA GROUP, LTD.

7373 Pyramid Place, Hollywood CA 90046. **E-mail:** info@quitespecificmedia.com; info@silmanjamespress.com. **Website:** www.quitespecificmedia.com. Estab. 1967. Publishes hardcover originals, trade paperback originals and reprints. "Quite Specific Media Group is an umbrella company of 5 imprints specializing in costume and fashion, theater and design." **Publishes 12 titles/year. 75 queries; 30 mss received/year. 75% of books from first-time authors. 85% from unagented writers. Pays royalty on wholesale price. Pays varies advance.** Publishes ms 18 months after acceptance. Accepts simultaneous submissions. Responds to queries. Book catalog online.

NONFICTION Subjects include fashion, history, literary criticism, translation. Query by e-mail please. Reviews artwork/photos.

RAGGED SKY PRESS

270 Griggs Dr., Princeton NJ 08540. **E-mail:** raggedskyanthology@gmail.com. **Website:** www.raggedsky.com. **Contact:** Ellen Foos, publisher; Vasiliki Katsarou, managing editor; Arlene Weiner, editor. Produces poetry anthologies and single-author poetry collections along with occasional inspired prose. Ragged Sky is a small, highly selective cooperative press. "We work with our authors closely." Individual poetry collections currently by invitation only. Learn more online. **Publishes 5 titles/year. 25 50% of books from first-time authors. 100% from unagented writers.** Publishes ms 1 year after acceptance. Accepts simultaneous submissions. Responds in 3 weeks.

NONFICTION Subjects include literature, poetry.

FICTION Subjects include literary.

Ⓐ⊘ RANDOM HOUSE CHILDREN'S BOOKS

1745 Broadway, New York NY 10019. (212)782-9000. **Website:** www.penguinrandomhouse.com. Estab. 1925. "Producing books for preschool children through young adult readers, in all formats from board to activity books to picture books and novels, Random House Children's Books brings together world-famous franchise characters, multimillion-copy series and top-flight, award-winning authors, and illustrators." Submit mss through a literary agent. Accepts simultaneous submissions.

IMPRINTS Kids@Random; Golden Books; Princeton Review; Sylvan Learning.

FICTION "Random House publishes a select list of first chapter books and novels, with an emphasis on fantasy and historical fiction." Chapter books, middle-grade readers, young adult. *Does not accept unsolicited mss.*

TIPS "We look for original, unique stories. Do something that hasn't been done before."

ⒶⒺ⊘ RANDOM HOUSE CHILDREN'S PUBLISHERS UK

20 Vauxhall Bridge Rd., London SW1V 2SA, United Kingdom. **Website:** www.randomhousechildrens.co.uk. *Only interested in agented material.* **Publishes 250 titles/year. Pays authors royalty. Offers advances.** Accepts simultaneous submissions.

IMPRINTS Bantam, Doubleday, Corgi, Johnathan Cape, Hutchinson, Bodley Head, Red Fox, Tamarind Books.

FICTION Picture books: adventure, animal, anthology, contemporary, fantasy, folktales, humor, multicultural, nature/environment, poetry, suspense/mystery. Young readers: adventure, animal, anthology, contemporary, fantasy, folktales, humor, multicultural, nature/environment, poetry, sports, suspense/mystery. Middle readers: adventure, animal, anthology, contemporary, fantasy, folktales, humor, multicultural, nature/environment, problem novels, romance, sports, suspense/mystery. Young adults: adventure, contemporary, fantasy, humor, multicultural, nature/environment, problem novels, romance, science fiction, suspense/mystery. Average word length: picture books—800; young readers—1,500-6,000; middle readers—10,000-15,000; young adults—20,000-45,000.

TIPS "Although Random House is a big publisher, each imprint only publishes a small number of books each year. Our lists for the next few years are already full. Any book we take on from a previously unpublished author has to be truly exceptional. Manuscripts should be sent to us via literary agents."

Ⓐ⊘ RANDOM HOUSE PUBLISHING GROUP

Division of Random House, Inc., 1745 Broadway, New York NY 10019. (212)782-9000. **Website:** www.penguinrandomhouse.com. Estab. 1925. Publishes hardcover and paperback trade books. Random House is the world's largest English-language general trade book publisher. It includes an array of prestigious imprints that publish some of the foremost writers of our time. **Publishes 120 titles/year.** Accepts simultaneous submissions.

IMPRINTS Ballantine Books; Bantam; Delacorte; Dell; Del Rey; Modern Library; One World; Presidio Press; Random House Trade Group; Random House Trade Paperbacks; Spectra; Spiegel & Grau; Triumph Books; Villard.

NONFICTION *Agented submissions only.*

FICTION *Agented submissions only.*

⊘ RATTAPALLAX PRESS

217 Thompson St., Suite 353, New York NY 10012. **Website:** www.rattapallax.com. **Contact:** Ram Devineni, founder/president; Flavia Rocha, editor-in-chief. Estab. 1998. Rattapallax Press publishes "contemporary poets and writers with unique, powerful voices." Publishes 5 paperbacks and 3 chapbooks/year. Books are usually 64 pages, digest-sized, offset-printed, perfect-bound, with 12-pt. CS1 covers. Accepts simultaneous submissions.

POETRY Query first, with a few sample poems and cover letter with brief bio and publication credits. Include SASE. Requires authors to first be published in *Rattapallax.* Responds to queries in 1 month; to mss in 2 months. Pays royalties of 10-25%. Order sample books from website.

RAZORBILL

Penguin Young Readers Group, 345 Hudson St., New York NY 10014. (212)414-3427. **E-mail:** asanchez@penguinrandomhouse.com; bschrank@penguinrandomhouse.com; jharriton@penguinrandomhouse.com. **Website:** www.razorbillbooks.com. **Contact:** Jessica Almon, executive editor; Casey McIntyre, associate publisher; Deborah Kaplan, vice president and executive art director, Marissa Grossman; assistant editor, Tiffany Liao; associate editor. Estab. 2003. "This division of Penguin Young Readers is looking for the best and the most original of commercial contemporary fiction titles for middle grade and YA readers. A select quantity of nonfiction titles will also be considered." **Publishes 30 titles/year. Offers advance against royalties.** Publishes book 1-2 after acceptance. Accepts simultaneous submissions. Responds in 1-3 months.

NONFICTION Middle readers and young adults/teens: concept. Submit cover letter with up to 30 sample pages.

FICTION Middle Readers: adventure, contemporary, graphic novels, fantasy, humor, problem novels. Young adults/teens: adventure, contemporary, fantasy, graphic novels, humor, multicultural, suspense, paranormal, science fiction, dystopian, literary, romance. Average word length: middle readers—40,000; young adult—60,000. Submit cover letter with up to 30 sample pages.

TIPS "New writers will have the best chance of acceptance and publication with original, contemporary material that boasts a distinctive voice and well-articulated world. Check out website to get a better idea of what we're looking for."

REBELIGHT PUBLISHING, INC.

23-845 Dakota St., Suite 314, Winnipeg Manitoba R2M 5M3, Canada. **Website:** www.rebelight.com. **Contact:** Editor. Estab. 2014. Publishes paperback and electronic originals. Rebelight Publishing is interested in "crack the spine, blow your mind" manuscripts for middle grade, young adult and new adult novels. *Only considers submissions from Canadian writers.* **Publishes 6-10 titles/year. Receive about 500 submissions/year. 25-50% of books from first-time authors. 100% from unagented writers. Pays 12-22% royalties on retail price. Does not offer an advance.** Publishes ms 12-18 months after acceptance. Accepts simultaneous submissions. Responds in 3 months to queries and mss. Submissions accepted via email only. Catalog online or PDF available via e-mail request. Guidelines online.

FICTION Subjects include adventure, contemporary, fantasy, historical, horror, humor, juvenile, mainstream, multicultural, mystery, romance, science fiction, sports, suspense, young adult. All genres are considered, provided they are for a middle grade,

young adult, or new adult audience. "Become familiar with our books. Study our website. Stick within the guidelines. Our tag line is 'crack the spine, blow your mind'—we are looking for well-written, powerful, fresh, fast-paced fiction. Keep us turning the pages. Give us something we just have to spread the word about." Submit proposal package, including a synopsis and 3 sample chapters. Read guidelines carefully.

TIPS "Review your manuscript for passive voice prior to submitting! (And that means get rid of it.)"

RED DEER PRESS

195 Allstate Pkwy., Markham ON L3R 4TB, Canada. (905)477-9700. **Fax:** (905)477-9179. **E-mail:** rdp@reddeerpress.com. **Website:** www.reddeerpress.com. **Contact:** Richard Dionne, publisher. Estab. 1975. **Pays 8-10% royalty.** Publishes ms 18 months after acceptance. Book catalog for 9 x 12 SASE.

Red Deer Press is an award-winning publisher of children's and young adult literary titles.

FICTION Publishes young adult, adult science fiction, fantasy, and paperback originals "focusing on books by, about, or of interest to Canadians." Books: offset paper; offset printing; hardcover/perfect-bound. Average print order: 5,000. First novel print order: 2,500. Distributes titles in Canada and the US, the UK, Australia and New Zealand. Young adult (juvenile and early reader), contemporary. No romance or horror.

TIPS "We're very interested in young adult and children's fiction from Canadian writers with a proven track record (either published books or widely published in established magazines or journals) and for manuscripts with regional themes and/or a distinctive voice. We publish Canadian authors exclusively."

RED HEN PRESS

P.O. Box 40820, Pasadena CA 91114. (626)356-4760. **Fax:** (626)356-9974. **Website:** www.redhen.org. **Contact:** Mark E. Cull, publisher/executive director. Managing Editor: Kate Gale. Estab. 1993. Publishes trade paperback originals. "At this time, the best opportunity to be published by Red Hen is by entering one of our contests. Please find more information in our award submission guidelines." **Publishes 22 titles/year. 2,000 queries; 500 mss received/year. 10% of books from first-time authors. 90% from unagented writers.** Publishes ms 1 year after acceptance. Accepts simultaneous submissions. Responds in 1-2 months. Book catalog available free. Guidelines online.

NONFICTION Subjects include ethnic, memoirs, political/social interest. Query with synopsis and either 20-30 sample pages or complete ms using online submission manager.

FICTION Subjects include ethnic, experimental, feminist, historical, literary, poetry, poetry in translation, short story collections. Query with synopsis and either 20-30 sample pages or complete ms using online submission manager.

POETRY Submit to Benjamin Saltman Poetry Award.

TIPS "Audience reads poetry, literary fiction, intelligent nonfiction. If you have an agent, we may be too small since we don't pay advances. Write well. Send queries first. Be willing to help promote your own book."

REDLEAF LANE

Redleaf Press, 10 Yorkton Ct., St. Paul MN 55117. (800)423-8309. **E-mail:** info@redleafpress.org. **E-mail:** acquisitions@redleafpress.org. **Website:** www.redleafpress.org. **Contact:** David Heath, director. Redleaf Lane publishes engaging, high-quality picture books for children. "Our books are unique because they take place in group-care settings and reflect developmentally appropriate practices and research-based standards." Accepts simultaneous submissions. Guidelines online.

NONFICTION Subjects include child guidance, education.

⊘ RED MOON PRESS

P.O. Box 2461, Winchester VA 22604. (540)722-2156. **E-mail:** jim.kacian@redmoonpress.com. **Website:** www.redmoonpress.com. **Contact:** Jim Kacian, editor/publisher. Estab. 1993. English-language haiku, contemporary haiku in other languages in English translation, haiku anthologies, books of haiku theory and criticism, books on related genres (tanka, haibun, haiga, renga, renku, etc.). Red Moon Press "is the largest and most prestigious publisher of English-language haiku and related work in the world." Publishes 10-15 volumes/year, usually 2-3 anthologies, 6-8 individual collections of English-language haiku, and 1-3 books of essays, translations, or criticism of haiku. Under other imprints, the press also publishes chapbooks of various sizes and formats. **Publishes 10-15 titles/year. 100+ 75% of books from first-time authors. 100% from unagented writers. Every book is a separate consideration.** Publishes ms 1 month after

acceptance. Accepts simultaneous submissions. Catalog online. Guidelines available.

NONFICTION Subjects include alternative lifestyles, art, contemporary culture, education, environment, ethnic, history, hobbies, humanities, language, literary criticism, literature, memoirs, multicultural, music, nature, New Age, philosophy, photography, pop culture, psychology, recreation, spirituality, translation, travel.

POETRY Query first with book concept (not just "I've written a few haiku . ."); if interested we'll ask for samples. "Each contract separately negotiated."

RED ROCK PRESS

205 W. 57th St., Suite 8B, New York NY 10024. **Fax:** (212)362-6216. **Website:** www.redrockpress.com. **Contact:** Ilene Barth. Estab. 1998. Publishes hardcover and trade paperback originals. **Publishes 6-8 titles/year. Pays royalty on wholesale price. The amount of the advance offered depends on the project.** Responds in 3-4 months to queries.

NONFICTION Subjects include creative nonfiction. All of our books are pegged to gift-giving holidays.

RED SAGE PUBLISHING, INC.

P.O. Box 4844, Seminole FL 33775. (727)391-3847. **E-mail:** submissions@eredsage.com. **Website:** www.eredsage.com. **Contact:** Alexandria Kendall. Estab. 1995. Publishes books of romance fiction, written for the adventurous woman. **Publishes 12 titles/year. 50% of books from first-time authors. Pays author royalty.** Guidelines online and all submissions via e-mail.

FICTION Subjects include adventure, contemporary, erotica, fantasy, gay, historical, horror, military, multicultural, mystery, occult, regional, romance, science fiction, suspense, war, western, Whatever your imagination can come up with. :). Read guidelines.

◐ RED TUQUE BOOKS, INC.

477 Martin St., Unit #6, Penticton BC V2A 5L2, Canada. (778)476-5750. **Fax:** (778)476-5651. **E-mail:** dave@redtuquebooks.ca. **E-mail:** Not accepting email submissions. Queries only. **Website:** www.redtuquebooks.ca. **Contact:** David Korinetz, executive editor. Estab. 2009. Red Tuque Books is primarily a book distributor, that also publishes catalogues and anthologies. Interested in Canadian authors only, except for the Annual Canadian Tales Anthology, which will accept stories written about Canada or Canadians by non-Canadians. Publication in the anthology is only

through submissions via the Canadian Tales writing contest. See website for details. **125 50% of books from first-time authors. 100% from unagented writers. Pays fixed award amount for anthology ($25 to $500). Does not pay advance.** Publishes ms 1-2 years after acceptance. Accepts simultaneous submissions. Responds in 3-6 weeks. Contest submissions only.

FICTION Subjects include short story collections. Novels Submit a query letter, 1-page synopsis, and first 5 pages only. Include total word count. Accepts ms only by mail. SASE or e-mail address for reply.

TIPS "Well-plotted, character-driven stories, preferably with happy endings, will have the best chance of being accepted. Keep in mind that authors who like to begin sentences with 'and, or, and but' are less likely to be considered. Don't send anything gruesome or overly explicit; tell us a good story, but think PG."

RED WHEEL/WEISER

65 Parker St., Suite 7, Newburyport MA 01950. (978)465-0504. **Fax:** (978)465-0504. **E-mail:** submissions@rwwbooks.com. **Website:** www.redwheelweiser.com. **Contact:** Pat Bryce, acquisitions editor. Estab. 1956. Publishes hardcover and trade paperback originals and reprints. **Publishes 60-75 titles/year. 2,000 queries; 2,000 mss received/year. 20% of books from first-time authors. 50% from unagented writers. Pays royalty.** Publishes ms 1 year after accceptance. Accepts simultaneous submissions. Responds in 3-6 months. Book catalog available free. Guidelines online.

NONFICTION Subjects include New Age, spirituality, parenting. Guidelines online.

ROBERT D. REED PUBLISHERS

P.O. Box 1992, Bandon OR 97411. (541)347-9882. **Fax:** (541)347-9883. **E-mail:** cleone@rdrpublishers.com; bob@rdrpublishers.com. **Website:** www.rdrpublishers.com. **Contact:** Cleone L. Reed. Estab. 1991. Publishes hardcover and trade paperback originals and e-books. **Publishes 5-10 titles/year. 75% of books from first-time authors. 90% from unagented writers. Pays 12-17% royalty on wholesale price.** Publishes ms 5 months after acceptance. Accepts simultaneous submissions. Responds in 1 month. Catalog and guidelines online.

NONFICTION Subjects include alternative lifestyles, business, career guidance, child guidance, communications, community, contemporary culture, counseling, education, entertainment, environment, ethnic,

gay, health, history, humanities, language, lesbian, literature, memoirs, military, money, multicultural, nature, New Age, nutrition, parenting, philosophy, psychology, social sciences, sociology, spirituality, travel, true crime, womens issues, womens studies, world affairs. "We want titles that have a large audience with at least 10-year sales potential, and author's workshop, speaking and seminar participation. We like titles that are part of author's career." Submit proposal package with outline. Reviews artwork.

TIPS "We publish books to make this a better world. Nonfiction only."

REFERENCE SERVICE PRESS

1945 Golden Way, Mountain View CA 94040. **Website:** www.rspfunding.com. Estab. 1977. Publishes hardcover originals. "Reference Service Press focuses on the development and publication of financial aid resources in any format (print, electronic, e-book, etc.). We are interested in financial aid publications aimed at specific groups (e.g., minorities, women, veterans, the disabled, undergraduates majoring in specific subject areas, specific types of financial aid, etc.)." **Publishes 10-20 titles/year. 100% from unagented writers. Pays 10% royalty. Pays advance.** Publishes book 6 months after acceptance. Responds in 2 months to queries. Book catalog for #10 SASE.

NONFICTION Subjects include history, disabled. Submit outline, sample chapters.

TIPS "Our audience consists of librarians, counselors, researchers, students, re-entry women, scholars, and other fundseekers."

⚠️⊘ REVELL

Division of Baker Publishing Group, 6030 E. Fulton Rd., Ada MI 49301. (616)676-9185. **Fax:** (616)676-9573. **Website:** www.bakerbooks.com. Estab. 1870. Publishes hardcover, trade paperback and mass market paperback originals. "Revell publishes to the heart (rather than to the head). For 125 years, Revell has been publishing evangelical books for the personal enrichment and spiritual growth of general Christian readers." Accepts simultaneous submissions. Book catalog and ms guidelines online.

⊘ *No longer accepts unsolicited mss.*

NONFICTION Subjects include child guidance, religion, Christian living, marriage.

FICTION Subjects include historical, religious, suspense, contemporary.

RING OF FIRE PUBLISHING LLC

6523 California Ave. SW #409, Seattle WA 98136. E-mail: contact@ringoffirebooks.com. **Website:** www.ringoffirebooks.com. Estab. 2011. Publishes trade paperback and electronic originals. "We are currently closed to submissions." Check website for updates. **Publishes 6-12 titles/year. 75% of books from first-time authors. 100% from unagented writers. Pays royalties.** Publishes ms 6 months after acceptance. Accepts simultaneous submissions. Book catalog and ms guidelines online.

FICTION Subjects include adventure, contemporary, experimental, fantasy, gothic, horror, juvenile, literary, mainstream, mystery, occult, romance, science fiction, short story collections, suspense, western, young adult.

RIO NUEVO PUBLISHERS

Imprint of Treasure Chest Books, P.O. Box 5250, Tucson AZ 85703. **Fax:** (520)624-5888. **E-mail:** info@rionuevo.com. **Website:** www.rionuevo.com. Estab. 1975. Publishes hardcover and trade paperback originals and reprints. **Publishes 12-20 titles/year. 30 queries received/year. 10 mss received/year. 30% of books from first-time authors. 100% from unagented writers. Pays $1,000-4,000 advance.** Publishes book 1 year after acceptance. Accepts simultaneous submissions. Responds in 6 months. Book catalog online. Guidelines online.

NONFICTION Subjects include animals, gardening, history, regional, religion, spirituality, travel. "We cover the Southwest but prefer titles that are not too narrow in their focus. We want our books to be of broad enough interest that people from other places will also want to read them." Query with SASE or via e-mail. Submit proposal package, outline, 2 sample chapters. Reviews artwork/photos. Send photocopies.

TIPS "We have a general audience of intelligent people interested in the Southwest-nature, history, culture. Many of our books are sold in gift shops throughout the region. Look at our books and website for inspiration and to see what we do."

RIPPLE GROVE PRESS

P.O. Box 86740, Portland OR 97286. **E-mail:** submit@ripplegrovepress.com. **Website:** www.ripplegrovepress.com. **Contact:** Amanda Broder, Rob Broder. Estab. 2013. Publishes hardcover originals. Ripple Grove Press is a family-owned children's picture book publishing company. "We started Ripple Grove Press because we have a passion for well-told and beautifully illustrated stories for children. Our mission is to surround ourselves with great writers and talented illustrators to make the most beautiful books possible. We hope our books that find their way to the cozy spot in your home." **Publishes 3-6 titles/year. 3,000 Authors and illustrators receive royalties on net receipts Pays negotiable advance.** Average length of time between acceptance of a book-length ms and publication is 12-18 months. Accepts simultaneous submissions. Given the volume of submissions we receive we are no longer able to individually respond to each. Please allow 5 months for us to review your submission. If we are interested in your story, you can expect to hear from us within that time. If you do not hear from us after that time, we are not interested in publishing your story. It's not you, it's us! We receive thousands of submissions and only publish a few books each year. Don't give up!. Catalog online. Guidelines online.

NONFICTION We do review artwork. Illustrators should send samples or links to their website and online portfolio.

FICTION Subjects include adventure, contemporary, fantasy, humor, juvenile, literary, mainstream, multicultural, picture books. We are looking for something unique, that has not been done before; an interesting story that captures a moment with a timeless feel. We are looking for picture driven stories for children ages 2-6. Please do not send early readers, middle grade, or YA mss. No religious or holiday themed stories. Please do not submit your story with page breaks or illustration notes. Do not submit a story with doodles or personal photographs. Do not send your "idea" for a story, send your story in manuscript form. Submit completed mss. Accepts submissions by mail and e-mail. E-mail preferred. Please submit a cover letter including a summary of your story, the age range of the story, a brief biography of yourself, and contact information.

TIPS Please read children's picture books. We create books that children and adults want to read over and over again. Our books showcase art as well as stories and tie them together in a unique and creative way.

RIVER CITY PUBLISHING

1719 Mulberry St., Montgomery AL 36106. **E-mail:** fnorris@rivercitypublishing.com. **Website:** www.rivercitypublishing.com. **Contact:** Fran Norris, editor.

Estab. 1989. Publishes hardcover and trade paperback originals. Midsize independent publisher. River City publishes literary fiction, regional, short story collections. No poetry, memoir, or children's books. We also consider narrative histories, sociological accounts, and travel; however, only biographies and memoirs from noted persons will be considered. **Publishes 6 titles/year.** Accepts simultaneous submissions. Responds within 9 months.

NONFICTION "We do not publish self-help, how-to, business, medicine, religion, education, or psychology." Accepts unsolicited submissions and submissions from unagented authors, as well as those from established and agented writers. Submit 5 consecutive sample chapters or entire ms for review. "Please include a short biography that highlights any previous writing and publishing experience, sales opportunities the author could provide, ideas for marketing the book, and why you think the work would be appropriate for River City." Send appropriate-sized SASE or IRC, "otherwise, the material will be recycled." Also accepts queries by e-mail.

FICTION Subjects include literary, regional, short story collections. No poetry, memoir, or children's books. Send appropriate-sized SASE or IRC, "otherwise, the material will be recycled." Also accepts queries by e-mail. "Please include your electronic query letter as inline text and not an as attachment; we do not open unsolicited attachments of any kind." No multiple submissions. Rarely comments on rejected mss.

TIPS "Only send your best work after you have received outside opinions. From approximately 1,000 submissions each year, we publish no more than 8 books and few of those come from unsolicited material. Competition is fierce, so follow the guidelines exactly. First-time novelists are also encouraged to send work."

Ⓐⵁ RIVERHEAD BOOKS

Penguin Putnam, 375 Hudson St., New York NY 10014. **Website:** www.penguin.com. Accepts simultaneous submissions.

FICTION Subjects include contemporary, literary, mainstream. *Submit through agent only. No unsolicited mss.*

Ⓐⵁ ROARING BROOK PRESS

Macmillan Children's Publishing Group, 175 Fifth Ave., New York NY 10010. (646)307-5151. **Website:**

us.macmillan.com. Estab. 2000. Roaring Brook Press is an imprint of MacMillan, a group of companies that includes Henry Holt and Farrar, Straus & Giroux. *Roaring Brook is not accepting unsolicited mss.* **Pays authors royalty based on retail price.** Accepts simultaneous submissions.

NONFICTION Picture books, young readers, middle readers, young adults: adventure, animal, contemporary, fantasy, history, humor, multicultural, nature/environment, poetry, religion, science fiction, sports, suspense/mystery. *Not accepting unsolicited mss or queries.*

FICTION Picture books, young readers, middle readers, young adults: adventure, animal, contemporary, fantasy, history, humor, multicultural, nature/environment, poetry, religion, science fiction, sports, suspense/mystery. *Not accepting unsolicited mss or queries.*

TIPS "You should find a reputable agent and have him/her submit your work."

ⵁ ROCKY MOUNTAIN BOOKS

103 - 1075 Pendergast St., Victoria BC V8V 0A1, Canada. (250)360-0829. **E-mail:** don@rmbooks.com. **Website:** www.rmbooks.com. **Contact:** Don Gorman, publisher. Publishes trade paperback and hardcover books. "RMB is a dynamic book publisher located in western Canada. We specialize in quality nonfiction on the outdoors, travel, environment, social and cultural issues." **Rarely offers advance.** Accepts simultaneous submissions. Responds in 2-6 months to queries. Book catalog and ms guidelines online.

NONFICTION "Our main area of publishing is outdoor recreation guides to Western and Northern Canada."

Ⓐⵁ RODALE BOOKS

400 S. Tenth St., Emmaus PA 18098. (610)967-5171. **Fax:** (610)967-8961. **Website:** www.rodaleinc.com. Estab. 1932. "Rodale Books publishes adult trade titles in categories such health & fitness, cooking, spirituality, and pet care." Accepts simultaneous submissions.

ⵁ RONSDALE PRESS

3350 W. 21st Ave., Vancouver BC V6S 1G7, Canada. (604)738-4688. **Fax:** (604)731-4548. **E-mail:** ronsdale@shaw.ca. **Website:** ronsdalepress.com. **Contact:** Ronald B. Hatch (fiction, poetry, nonfiction, social commentary); Veronica Hatch (YA novels and short stories). Estab. 1988. Publishes trade paperback originals. "Ronsdale Press is a Canadian literary publishing house that publishes 12 books each year, four of which are young adult titles. Of particular interest are books involving children exploring and discovering new aspects of Canadian history." **Publishes 12 titles/year. 40 queries; 800 mss received/year. 40% of books from first-time authors. 95% from unagented writers. Pays 10% royalty on retail price.** Publishes book 1 year after acceptance. Accepts simultaneous submissions. Responds to queries in 2 weeks; mss in 2 months. Book catalog for #10 SASE. Guidelines online.

NONFICTION Subjects include history, literary criticism, literature, regional. Middle readers, young adults: animal, biography, history, multicultural, social issues. Average word length: young readers—90; middle readers—90. "We publish a number of books for children and young adults in the age 10 to 15 range. We are especially interested in YA historical novels. We regret that we can no longer publish picture books." Submit complete ms.

FICTION Subjects include literary, short story collections, novels. Young adults: Canadian novels. Average word length: middle readers and young adults—50,000. Submit complete ms.

POETRY Poets should have published some poems in magazines/journals and should be well-read in contemporary masters. Submit complete ms.

TIPS "Ronsdale Press is a literary publishing house, based in Vancouver, and dedicated to publishing books from across Canada, books that give Canadians new insights into themselves and their country. We aim to publish the best Canadian writers."

ROSE ALLEY PRESS

4203 Brooklyn Ave. NE, #103A, Seattle WA 98105-5911, USA. (206)633-2725. **E-mail:** rosealleypress@juno.com. **Website:** www.rosealleypress.com. **Contact:** David D. Horowitz. Estab. 1995. "Rose Alley Press primarily publishes books featuring rhymed metrical poetry and an annually updated booklet about writing and publication. We do not read or consider unsolicited manuscripts." Accepts simultaneous submissions.

NONFICTION Subjects include literature, philosophy.

ROSEN PUBLISHING

29 E. 21st St., New York NY 10010. (800)237-9932. **Fax:** (888)436-4643. **Website:** www.rosenpublishing.

com. Estab. 1950. Rosen Publishing is an independent educational publishing house, established to serve the needs of students in grades Pre-K-12 with high interest, curriculum-correlated materials. Rosen publishes more than 700 new books each year and has a backlist of more than 7,000.

ROTOVISION

Fourth Floor, Ovest House, 58 West St., Brighton BN1 2RA, United Kingdom. (44)(127)371-6000. **Website:** https://www.quartoknows.com/RotoVision. **Contact:** Isheeta Mustafi. Publishes hardcover and trade paperback originals, and trade paperback reprints. Accepts simultaneous submissions. Book catalog available free. Guidelines available free.

"RotoVision books showcase the works of top writers and designers reflecting excellence and innovation in the visual arts. If you wish to submit a book proposal, in the first instance please familiarise yourself with our publishing portfolio to ensure your proposal fits into our focus area."

NONFICTION Subjects include art, creative nonfiction. "Our books are aimed at keen amateurs and professionals who want to improve their skills." Submit an e-mail with "Book Proposal" in the subject line. Reviews artwork/photos. Send transparencies and PDFs.

TIPS "Our audience includes professionals, keen amateurs, and students of visual arts including graphic design, general design, advertising, and photography. Make your approach international in scope. Content not to be less than 35% US."

ROWMAN & LITTLEFIELD PUBLISHING GROUP

4501 Forbes Blvd., Suite 200, Lanham MD 20706. (301)459-3366. **Fax:** (301)429-5748. **Website:** www.rowmanlittlefield.com. **Contact:** Linda Ganster. Estab. 1949. Textbooks, nonfiction general interest titles, professional development works, and references in hardcover and paperback. "We are an independent press devoted to publishing social science and humanities titles that engage, inform and educate: innovative, thought-provoking texts for college courses; research-based titles for professionals eager to remain abreast of developments within their domains; and general interest books intended to convey important trends to an educated readership. Our approach emphasizes thought leadership balanced with a deep understanding of the areas in which we publish. We offer a forum for responsible voices representing the diversity of opinion on college campuses, and take special pride in our commitment to covering critical societal issues." **Pays advance.** Book catalog online. Guidelines online.

NONFICTION Subjects include alternative lifestyles, Americana, anthropology, archeology, architecture, art, career guidance, child guidance, cinema, communications, community, contemporary culture, counseling, education, environment, ethnic, fashion, film, foods, gay, government, health, history, humanities, lesbian, literary criticism, military, multicultural, music, nutrition, parenting, philosophy, politics, pop culture, psychology, public affairs, religion, sex, sociology, sports, stage, war, womens issues, world affairs, young adult. "Rowman & Littlefield is seeking proposals in the serious nonfiction areas of history, politics, current events, religion, sociology, philosophy, communication and education. All proposal inquiries can be e-mailed or mailed to the respective acquisitions editor listed on the contacts page on our website."

RUKA PRESS

P.O. Box 1409, Washington DC 20013. **E-mail:** contact@rukapress.com. **E-mail:** submissions@rukapress.com. **Website:** www.rukapress.com. **Contact:** Daniel Kohan, owner. Estab. 2010. Publishes in trade paperback originals, electronic. "We publish nonfiction books with a strong environmental component for a general audience. We are looking for books that explain things, that make an argument, that demystify. We are interested in economics, science, nature, climate change, and sustainability. We like building charts and graphs, tables and timelines. Our politics are progressive, but our books need not be political." **Publishes 1-3 titles/year. 40% of books from first-time authors. 80% from unagented writers. Pays advance. Royalties are 10-25% on wholesale price.** Publishes book an average of 9-12 months after acceptance of ms. Accepts simultaneous submissions. Responds in 1 month. Book catalog online. Guidelines online.

NONFICTION Subjects include environment, nature, science. Submit proposal package, including outline, resume, bio, or CV, and 1 sample chapter.

TIPS "We appeal to an audience of intelligent, educated readers with broad interests. Be sure to tell us why your proposal is unique, and why you are especially qualified to write this book. We are looking for originality and expertise."

RUTGERS UNIVERSITY PRESS

106 Somerset St., 3rd Floor, New Brunswick NJ 08901. (732)445-7762. **Fax:** (732)445-7039. **E-mail:** lmitch@rutgers.edu. **Website:** rutgerspress.rutgers.edu. **Contact:** Leslie Mitchner, editor-in-chief/associate director (humanities); Peter Micklaus, editor (social sciences); Kel McGowan, editor (science, health and medicine); Elisabeth Maselli, editor (Jewish studies), Lisa Banning (Asian American Studies, human rights, new media), Kimberly Guinta, editor (higher education, anthropology, women's studies). Estab. 1936. Publishes hardcover and trade paperback originals and reprints. "Our press aims to reach audiences beyond the academic community with accessible scholarly and regional books." **Publishes 100 titles/year. 1,500 queries; 300 mss received/year. 30% of books from first-time authors. 70% from unagented writers. Pays 7 1/2-15% royalty. Pays $1,000-10,000 advance.** Publishes ms 1 year after acceptance. Accepts simultaneous submissions. Responds in 1 month to proposals. Book catalog online. Guidelines online.

NONFICTION Subjects include ethnic, history, multicultural, regional, religion, sociology, African-American studies. Books for use in undergraduate courses. Submit outline, 2-3 sample chapters. Reviews artwork/photos. Send photocopies.

TIPS "Both academic and general audiences. Many of our books have potential for undergraduate course use. We are more trade-oriented than most university presses. We are looking for intelligent, well-written, and accessible books. Avoid overly narrow topics."

SADDLEBACK EDUCATIONAL PUBLISHING

3120-A Pullman St., Costa Mesa CA 92626. (888)735-2225. **E-mail:** contact@sdlback.com. **Website:** www.sdlback.com. Saddleback is always looking for fresh, new talent. "Please note that we primarily publish books for kids ages 12-18." Accepts simultaneous submissions.

FICTION "We look for diversity for our characters and content." Mail typed submission along with a query letter describing the work simply and where it fits in with other titles.

SAE INTERNATIONAL

400 Commonwealth Dr., Warrendale PA 15096-0001. (724)776-4841. **Website:** www.sae.org/writeabook. Estab. 1905. Publishes hardcover and trade paperback

originals, e-books. Automotive means anything self-propelled. "We are a professional society serving engineers, scientists, and researchers in the automobile, aerospace, and off-highway industries." **Publishes approximately 10 titles/year. 50 queries received/year. 20 mss received/year. 70% of books from first-time authors. 100% from unagented writers. Pays royalty. Pays possible advance.** Publishes ms 9-10 months after acceptance. Accepts simultaneous submissions. Responds in 4 months to queries. Book catalog free. Guidelines online.

NONFICTION Query with proposal.

TIPS "Audience is automotive and aerospace engineers and managers, automotive safety and biomechanics professionals, students, educators, enthusiasts, and historians."

SAFER SOCIETY PRESS

P.O. Box 340, Brandon VT 05733. (802)247-3132. **Fax:** (802)247-4233. **E-mail:** maryfalcon@safersociety.org. **Website:** www.safersociety.org. **Contact:** Mary Falcon, editorial director. Estab. 1985. Publishes trade paperback originals. "Our mission is the prevention and treatment of sexual abuse." **Publishes 3-4 titles/year. 15-20 queries received/year. 15-20 mss received/year. 90% of books from first-time authors. 100% from unagented writers. Pays 10% royalty on retail price.** Publishes ms 1 year after acceptance. Accepts simultaneous submissions. Book catalog available free. Guidelines online.

NONFICTION Subjects include psychology. "We are a small, nonprofit, niche press. We want well-researched books dealing with any aspect of sexual abuse: treatment, prevention, understanding; works on subject in Spanish." Memoirs generally not accepted. Query with SASE, submit proposal package, or complete ms Reviews artwork/photos. Send photocopies.

TIPS "Audience is persons working in mental health/persons needing self-help books. Pays small fees or low royalties."

SAGUARO BOOKS, LLC

16201 E. Keymar Dr., Fountain Hills AZ 85268. **Fax:** (480)284-4855. **E-mail:** mjnickum@saguarobooks.com. **Website:** www.saguarobooks.com. **Contact:** Mary Nickum, CEO. Estab. 2012. Publishes trade paperback and electronic originals. Saguaro Books, LLC is a publishing company specializing in middle grade and young adult ficiton by first-time authors.

Publishes 4-6 titles/year. Receives 60-80 queries/year, 8-10 mss/year. 100% of books from first-time authors. 100% from unagented writers. Pays 20% royalties after taxes and publication costs. Does not offer advance. Publishes ms 18-24 months after acceptance. Responds within 3 months only if we're interested. Catalog online. Guidelines by e-mail.

FICTION Subjects include adventure, fantasy, historical, juvenile, military, multicultural, mystery, occult, science fiction, sports, suspense, war, western, young adult. Ms should be well-written; signed letter by a professional editor is required. Does not want agented work. Query via e-mail before submitting work. Any material sent before requested will be ignored.

TIPS "Visit our website before sending us a query. Pay special attention to the For Authors Only page."

ⓐⓞ ST. MARTIN'S PRESS, LLC

Holtzbrinck Publishers, 175 Fifth Ave., New York NY 10010. (212)674-5151. **Fax:** (212)420-9314. **Website:** www.stmartins.com. Estab. 1952. Publishes hardcover, trade paperback and mass market originals. General interest publisher of both fiction and nonfiction. **Publishes 1,500 titles/year. Pays royalty. Pays advance.** Accepts simultaneous submissions.

NONFICTION Subjects include sports, general nonfiction. *Agented submissions only. No unsolicited mss.*

FICTION Subjects include contemporary, fantasy, historical, horror, literary, mystery, science fiction, suspense, western, general fiction. *Agented submissions only. No unsolicited mss.*

SAINT MARY'S PRESS

702 Terrace Heights, Winona MN 55987. (800)533-8095. **Fax:** (800)344-9225. **E-mail:** submissions@smp.org. **Website:** www.smp.org. Accepts simultaneous submissions. Ms guidelines online or by e-mail.

NONFICTION Subjects include religion. Titles for Catholic youth and their parents, teachers, and youth ministers. High school Catholic religious education textbooks and primary source readings. Query with SASE. Submit proposal package, outline, 1 sample chapter, SASE. Brief author biography.

TIPS "Request product catalog and/or do research online of Saint Mary Press book lists before submitting proposal."

ST PAULS

Society of St. Paul, 2187 Victory Blvd., Staten Island NY 10314. (718)761-0047. **Fax:** (718)761-0057. **E-mail:** edmund_lane@juno.com. **Website:** www.stpauls.us.

Contact: Edmund C. Lane, SSP, acquisitions editor. Estab. 1957. Publishes trade paperback and mass market paperback originals and reprints. **Publishes 22 titles/year. 250 queries; 150 mss received/year. 10% of books from first-time authors. 100% from unagented writers. Pays 5-10% royalty.** Publishes ms 10 months after acceptance. Responds in 1 month to queries and proposals; 2 months to mss. Book catalog and ms guidelines free.

NONFICTION Subjects include philosophy, religion, spirituality. Alba House is the North American publishing division of the Society of St. Paul, an International Roman Catholic Missionary Religious Congregation dedicated to spreading the Gospel message via the media of communications. Does not want fiction, children's books, poetry, personal testimonies, or autobiographies. Submit complete ms. Reviews artwork/photos. Send photocopies.

TIPS "Our audience is educated Roman Catholic readers interested in matters related to the Church, spirituality, Biblical and theological topics, moral concerns, lives of the saints, etc."

SAKURA PUBLISHING & TECHNOLOGIES

805 Lindaraxa Park North, Alhambra CA 91801. (330)360-5131. **E-mail:** skpublishing124@gmail.com. **Website:** www.sakura-publishing.com. **Contact:** Derek Vasconi, submissions coordinator. Estab. 2007. Publishes trade paperback, mass market paperback and electronic originals and reprints. Currently accepts only the following genres: Asian fiction, Japanese fiction (in English), Nonfiction, and horror. Please do not send queries for any other genres. Visit our website for query guidelines. Mss that don't follow guidelines will not be considered. Sakura Publishing is a traditional, independent book publishing company that seeks to publish Asian-themed books, particularly Asian-Horror, or anything dealing with Japan, Japanese culture, and Japanese horror. **Publishes 1-3 titles/year. 90% of books from first-time authors. 80% from unagented writers. Royalty payments on paperback, e-book, wholesale, and merchandise Does not pay advance.** Publishes ms 6 months after acceptance. Accepts simultaneous submissions. Responds in 1 week. Book catalog available for #10 SASE. Guidelines online.

NONFICTION Subjects include contemporary culture, creative nonfiction, entertainment, ethnic, film, games, history, hobbies, humanities, literature, memoirs, military, music, philosophy, pop culture, psychology, regional, religion, sex, travel, true crime, world affairs. Looking for memoirs by Asians, or any nonfiction that deals with Asia, especially Japan, or American experiences while living in Japan. No memoirs other than what we have listed above, cookbooks, humor, textbooks, technical, and definitely no books about suffering from diseases and overcoming them. Follow guidelines online.

FICTION Subjects include contemporary, erotica, ethnic, historical, horror, multicultural, occult, Asian, horror, occult. Only looking for Asian horror, with preference given to Japanese horror, as well as Japanese fiction, Japanese erotica, Asian erotica. Will consider other types of Asian-centered fiction, but top preference will be on fiction centered in or dealing with Japan or Japanese people living in America. Follow guidelines online.

POETRY Follow guidelines online.

TIPS "Please make sure you visit our submissions page at our website and follow all instructions exactly as written. Also, Sakura Publishing has a preference for fiction/nonfiction books specializing in Asian culture."

SALEM PRESS, INC.

P.O. Box 56, 4919 Rt. 22, Amenia NY 12501. **E-mail:** lmars@greyhouse.com. **Website:** www.salempress.com. **Contact:** Laura Mars, editorial director. **Publishes 20-22 titles/year. 15 queries received/year. Work-for-hire pays 5-15¢/word.** Accepts simultaneous submissions. Responds in 3 months to queries; 1 month to proposals. Book catalog online.

NONFICTION Subjects include ethnic, history, philosophy, psychology, science, sociology. "We accept vitas for writers interested in supplying articles/entries for encyclopedia-type entries in library reference books. Will also accept multi-volume book ideas from people interested in being a general editor." Query with SASE.

SALINA BOOKSHELF

1120 W. University Ave., Suite 102, Flagstaff AZ 86001. (877)527-0070. **Fax:** (928)526-0386. **Website:** www.salinabookshelf.com. Publishes trade paperback originals and reprints. **Publishes 4-5 titles/year. 50% of books from first-time authors. 100% from unagented writers. Pays varying royalty. Pays advance.** Publishes ms 1 year after acceptance. Accepts simultaneous submissions. Responds in 3 months to queries.

NONFICTION Subjects include education, ethnic, science. "We publish children's bilingual readers." Nonfiction should be appropriate to science and social studies curriculum grades 3-8. Query with SASE.

FICTION Subjects include juvenile. Submissions should be in English or Navajo. "All our books relate to the Navajo language and culture." Query with SASE.

POETRY "We accept poetry in English/Southwest language for children." Submit 3 sample poems.

◗ SALMON POETRY

Knockeven, Cliffs of Moher, County Clare Ireland. 353(0)852318909. **E-mail:** info@salmonpoetry.com. **E-mail:** jessie@salmonpoetry.com. **Website:** www.salmonpoetry.com. **Contact:** Jessie Lendennie, editor. Estab. 1981. Publishes contemporary poetry and literary nonfiction. **Publishes 30 titles/year. 300+ 5% of books from first-time authors. 100% from unagented writers. Pays advance.** Publishes ms 2 years after acceptance. Responds in 3 months. Guidelines available.

NONFICTION Subjects include literature, marine subjects.

POETRY "Salmon Press is one of the most important publishers in the Irish literary world; specializing in the promotion of new poets, particularly women. Established in 1981 as an alternative voice in Irish literature, Salmon is known for its international list and over the years has developed a cross-cultural literary dialog, broadening Irish Literature and urging new perspectives on established traditions." E-mail query with short biographical note and 5-10 sample poems.

TIPS "Read as much poetry as you can, and always research the publisher before submitting!"

SALVO PRESS

An imprint of Start Publishing, 101 Hudson St., 37th Floor, Suite 3705, Jersey City NJ 07302. **E-mail:** info@salvopress.com. **Website:** www.salvopress.com. Estab. 1998. Salvo Press proudly publishes mysteries, thrillers, and literary books in e-book and audiobook formats. **Publishes 6-12 titles/year. 75% from unagented writers. Pays 10% royalty.** Publishes ms 9-12 months after acceptance. Responds in 5 minutes to 1 month to queries; 2 months to mss. Book catalog and ms guidelines online.

FICTION Subjects include adventure, literary, mystery, science fiction, suspense, thriller/espionage. "We are a small press specializing in mystery, suspense, espionage and thriller fiction. Our press publishes in trade paperback and most e-book formats." Query by e-mail.

SANTA MONICA PRESS

P.O. Box 850, Solana Beach CA 92075. (858)793-1890; (800)784-9553. **E-mail:** books@santamonicapress.com. **E-mail:** acquisitions@santamonicapress.com. **Website:** www.santamonicapress.com. Estab. 1994. Publishes hardcover and trade paperback originals. Santa Monica Press has been publishing an eclectic line of books since 1994. "Our critically acclaimed titles are sold in chain, independent, online, and university bookstores around the world, as well as in some of the most popular retail outlets in North America. Our authors are recognized experts who are sought after by the media and receive newspaper, magazine, radio, and television coverage both nationally and internationally. At Santa Monica Press, we're not afraid to cast a wide editorial net. Our list of lively and modern non-fiction titles includes books in such categories as popular culture, film history, photography, humor, biography, travel, and reference." **Publishes 12 titles/year. 25% of books from first-time authors. 75% from unagented writers. Pays 6-10% royalty on net price. Pays $500-10,000+ advance.** Publishes book 1 year after acceptance. Accepts simultaneous submissions. Responds in 1-2 months to proposals. Guidelines available.

NONFICTION Subjects include Americana, art, cinema, contemporary culture, creative nonfiction, education, entertainment, film, history, humanities, language, literature, memoirs, music, parenting, photography, pop culture, regional, social sciences, sports, stage, travel. Submit proposal package, including outline, 2-3 sample chapters, biography, marketing and publicity plans, analysis of competitive titles, SASE with appropriate postage. Reviews artwork/photos. Send photocopies.

TIPS "Visit our website before submitting to view our author guidelines and to get a clear idea of the types of books we publish. Carefully analyze your book's competition and tell us what makes your book different—and what makes it better. Also let us know what promotional and marketing opportunities you, as the author, bring to the project."

SARABANDE BOOKS, INC.

822 E. Market St., Louisville KY 40206. (502)458-4028. **Fax:** (502)458-4065. **E-mail:** info@sarabande-

books.org. **Website:** www.sarabandebooks.org. **Contact:** Sarah Gorham, Editor-in-Chief. Estab. 1994. Publishes trade paperback originals. "Sarabande Books was founded to publish poetry, short fiction, and creative nonfiction. We look for works of lasting literary value. Please see our titles to get an idea of our taste. Accepts submissions through contests and open submissions." **Publishes 10 titles/year. 1,500 queries; 3,000 mss received/year. 35% of books from first-time authors. 75% from unagented writers. Pays royalty. 10% on actual income received. Also pays in author's copies. Pays $500-1,000 advance.** Publishes ms 18 months after acceptance. Accepts simultaneous submissions. Book catalog available free. Contest guidelines for #10 SASE or on website.

○ Charges $15 handling fee with alternative option of purchase of book from website (e-mail confirmation of sale must be included with submission).

FICTION Subjects include literary, short story collections, novellas, short novels (300 pages maximum, 150 pages minimum). "We consider novels and nonfiction in a wide variety of genres. We do not consider genre fiction such as science fiction, fantasy, or horror. Our target length is 70,000-90,000 words." Queries can be sent via e-mail, fax, or regular post.

POETRY Poetry of superior artistic quality; otherwise no restraints or specifications. Sarabande Books publishes books of poetry of 48 pages minimum. Wants "poetry that offers originality of voice and subject matter, uniqueness of vision, and a language that startles because of the careful attention paid to it—language that goes beyond the merely competent or functional." Mss selected through literary contests, invitation, and recommendation by a well-established writer.

TIPS "Sarabande publishes for a general literary audience. Know your market. Read-and buy-books of literature. Sponsors contests for poetry and fiction. Make sure you're not writing in a vacuum, that you've read and are conscious of contemporary literature. Have someone read your manuscript, checking it for ordering, coherence. Better a lean, consistently strong manuscript than one that is long and uneven. We like a story to have good narrative, and we like to be engaged by language."

SAS PUBLISHING

100 SAS Campus Dr., Cary NC 27513. (919)677-8000. **Fax:** (919)677-4444. **E-mail:** saspress@sas.com. **Website:** support.sas.com/saspress. Estab. 1976. Publishes hardcover and trade paperback originals. "SAS publishes books for SAS and JMP software users, both new and experienced." **Publishes 40 titles/year. 50% of books from first-time authors. 100% from unagented writers. Payment negotiable. Pays negotiable advance.** Responds in 2 weeks to queries. Book catalog and ms guidelines online.

NONFICTION Subjects include software, statistics. SAS Publishing jointly Wiley and SAS Business Series titles. "Through SAS, we also publish books by SAS users on a variety of topics relating to SAS software. SAS titles enhance users' abilities to use SAS effectively. We're interested in publishing manuscripts that describe or illustrate using any of SAS products, including JMP software. Books must be aimed at SAS or JMP users, either new or experienced." Mss must reflect current or upcoming software releases, and the author's writing should indicate an understanding of SAS and the technical aspects covered in the ms. Query with SASE. Submit outline, sample chapters. Reviews artwork/photos.

SASQUATCH BOOKS

1904 Third Ave., Suite 710, Seattle WA 98101. (206)467-4300. **Fax:** (206)467-4301. **E-mail:** custserv@sasquatchbooks.com. **Website:** www.sasquatchbooks.com. Estab. 1986. Publishes regional hardcover and trade paperback originals. "Sasquatch Books publishes books for and from the Pacific Northwest, Alaska, and California is the nation's premier regional press. Sasquatch Books' publishing program is a veritable celebration of regionally written words. Undeterred by political or geographical borders, Sasquatch defines its region as the magnificent area that stretches from the Brooks Range to the Gulf of California and from the Rocky Mountains to the Pacific Ocean. Our top-selling Best Places® travel guides serve the most popular destinations and locations of the West. We also publish widely in the areas of food and wine, gardening, nature, photography, children's books, and regional history, all facets of the literature of place. With more than 200 books brimming with insider information on the West, we offer an energetic eye on the lifestyle, landscape, and worldview of our region. Considers queries and proposals from authors and agents for new projects that fit into our West Coast regional publishing program. We can evaluate query letters, proposals, and complete mss." **Publishes 30 titles/year. 20% of books from first-time authors. 75% from unagented writers. Pays royalty on cover price. Pays wide range advance.** Publishes book 6-9 months after acceptance. Accepts simultaneous submissions. Responds to queries in 3 months. Guidelines online.

NONFICTION Subjects include animals, gardening, history, recreation, regional, sports, travel, outdoors. "We are seeking quality nonfiction works about the Pacific Northwest and West Coast regions (including Alaska to California). The literature of place includes how-to and where-to as well as history and narrative nonfiction." Picture books: activity books, animal, concept, nature/environment. "We publish a variety of nonfiction books, as well as children's books under our Little Bigfoot imprint." Query first, then submit outline and sample chapters with SASE. Send submissions to The Editors. E-mailed submissions and queries are not recommended. Please include return postage if you want your materials back.

FICTION Young readers: adventure, animal, concept, contemporary, humor, nature/environment.

TIPS "We sell books through a range of channels in addition to the book trade. Our primary audience consists of active, literate residents of the West Coast."

SATURNALIA BOOKS

105 Woodside Rd., Ardmore PA 19003. (267)278-9541. **E-mail:** info@saturnaliabooks.com. **Website:** www.saturnaliabooks.org. **Contact:** Henry Israeli, publisher. Estab. 2002. Publishes trade paperback originals and digital versions for e-readers. "We do not accept unsolicited submissions. We hold a contest, the Saturnalia Books Poetry Prize, annually in which 1 anonymously submitted title is chosen by a poet with a national reputation for publication. Submissions are accepted during the month of March. The submission fee is $30, and the prize is $2,000 and 20 copies of the book. See website for details." **Publishes 5 titles/year. Receives 600 mss/year. 33% of books from first-time authors. 100% from unagented writers. Pays authors 4-6% royalty on retail price. Pays $400-2,000 advance.** Accepts simultaneous submissions. Responds in 4 months on mss. Catalog online. No unsolicited submissions. Contest guidelines online.

POETRY "Saturnalia Books has no bias against any school of poetry, but we do tend to publish writers who take chances and push against convention in some way, whether it's in form, language, content, or musicality." Submit complete ms to contest only.

TIPS "Our audience tend to be young avid readers of contemporary poetry. Read a few sample books first."

SCARECROW PRESS, INC.

Imprint of Rowman & Littlefield Publishing Group, 4501 Forbes Blvd., Suite 200, Lanham MD 20706. (301)459-3366. **Fax:** (301)429-5748. **Website:** www.scarecrowpress.com. Estab. 1955. Publishes hardcover originals. Scarecrow Press publishes several series: Historical Dictionaries (includes countries, religions, international organizations, and area studies); Studies and Documentaries on the History of Popular Entertainment (forthcoming); Society, Culture and Libraries. Emphasis is on any title likely to appeal to libraries. Currently emphasizing jazz, Africana, and educational issues of contemporary interest. **Publishes 165 titles/year. 70% of books from first-time authors. 99% from unagented writers. Pays 8% royalty on net of first 1,000 copies; 10% of net price thereafter.** Publishes ms 18 months after acceptance. Responds in 2 months to queries. Catalog and ms guidelines online.

NONFICTION Subjects include religion, sports, annotated bibliographies, handbooks and biographical dictionaries in the areas of women's studies and ethnic studies, parapsychology, fine arts and handicrafts, genealogy, sports history, music, movies, stage, library and information science. Query with SASE.

SCHIFFER PUBLISHING, LTD.

4880 Lower Valley Rd., Atglen PA 19310. (610)593-1777. **Fax:** (610)593-2002. **E-mail:** info@schifferbooks.com. **Website:** www.schifferbooks.com. Estab. 1975. **Publishes 10-20 titles/year. Pays royalty on wholesale price.** Accepts simultaneous submissions. Responds in 2 weeks to queries. Book catalog available free. Guidelines online.

NONFICTION Art-quality illustrated regional histories. Looking for informed, entertaining writing and lots of subject areas to provide points of entry into the text for non-history buffs who buy a beautiful book because they are from, or love, an area. Full color possible in the case of historic postcards. Fax or e-mail outline, photos, and book proposal.

TIPS "We want to publish books for towns or cities with relevant population or active tourism to support book sales. A list of potential town vendors is a helpful start toward selling us on your book idea."

SCHOCKEN BOOKS

Imprint of Knopf Publishing Group, Division of Random House, Inc., 1745 Broadway, New York NY 10019. (212)572-9000. **Fax:** (212)572-6030. **Website:** www. schocken.com. Estab. 1945. Publishes hardcover and trade paperback originals and reprints. "Schocken publishes quality Judaica in all areas-fiction, history, biography, current affairs, spirituality and religious practices, popular culture, and cultural studies." *Does not accept unsolicited mss. Agented submissions only.* **Publishes 9-12 titles/year. Pays varied advance.** Accepts simultaneous submissions.

SCHOLASTIC PRESS

Imprint of Scholastic, Inc., 557 Broadway, New York NY 10012. (212)343-6100. **Fax:** (212)343-4713. **Website:** www.scholastic.com. Publishes hardcover originals. Scholastic Press publishes fresh, literary picture book fiction and nonfiction; fresh, literary nonseries or nongenre-oriented middle grade and young adult fiction. Currently emphasizing subtly handled treatments of key relationships in children's lives; unusual approaches to commonly dry subjects, such as biography, math, history, or science. De-emphasizing fairy tales (or retellings), board books, genre, or series fiction (mystery, fantasy, etc.). **Publishes 60 titles/year. 2,500 queries received/year. 1% of books from first-time authors. Pays royalty on retail price. Pays variable advance.** Publishes book 2 years after acceptance. Responds in 3 months to queries; 6-8 months to mss. **NONFICTION** Agented submissions and previously published authors only.
FICTION Subjects include juvenile, picture books, novels. Looking for strong picture books, young chapter books, appealing middle grade novels (ages 8-11) and interesting and well-written young adult novels. Wants fresh, exciting picture books and novels—inspiring, new talent. *Agented submissions only.*
TIPS "Read *currently* published children's books. Revise, rewrite, rework and find your own voice, style and subject. We are looking for authors with a strong and unique voice who can tell a great story and have the ability to evoke genuine emotion. Children's publishers are becoming more selective, looking for irresistible talent and fairly broad appeal, yet still very willing to take risks, just to keep the game interesting."

SCHWARTZ & WADE BOOKS

Random House Children's Books, 1745 Broadway, New York NY 10019. **Website:** www.randomhousekids.com. Estab. 2006. Schwartz & Wade Books is an imprint of Random House Children's Books, co-directed by Anne Schwartz and Lee Wade, who take a unique approach to the creative process and believe that the best books for children grow from a seamless collaboration between editorial and design.

This market does not accept unsolicited submissions, proposals, mss, or submission queries. Recommends that authors work with an established literary agent.

SCRIBE PUBLICATIONS

18-20 Edward St., Brunswick VIC 3056, Australia. (61)(3)9388-8780. **E-mail:** info@scribepub.com.au. **E-mail:** submissions@scribepub.com.au. **Website:** www. scribepublications.com.au. **Contact:** Anna Thwaites. Estab. 1976. Scribe has been operating as a wholly independent trade-publishing house for almost 40 years. What started off in 1976 as a desire on publisher Henry Rosenbloom's part to publish 'serious non-fiction' as a one-man band has turned into a multi-award-winning company with 20 staff members in two locations — Melbourne, Australia and London, England — and a scout in New York. Scribe publishes over 65 nonfiction and fiction titles annually in Australia and about 40 in the United Kingdom. "We currently have acquiring editors working in both our Melbourne and London offices. We spend each day sifting through submissions and manuscripts from around the world, and commissioning and editing local titles, in an uncompromising pursuit of the best books we can find, help create, and deliver to readers. We love what we do, and we hope you will, too." **Publishes 70 titles/year. 10-20% from unagented writers.** Guidelines online.
IMPRINTS Scribble.
NONFICTION Subjects include environment, history, memoirs, psychology, current affairs, social history. "Please refer first to our website before contacting us or submitting anything, because we explain there who we will accept proposals from."
FICTION Subjects include contemporary, historical, humor, literary, military, mystery, picture books, poetry, short story collections, suspense, translation, war, young adult. Submit synopsis, sample chapters, CV.

TIPS "We are only able to consider unsolicited submissions if you have a demonstrated background of writing and publishing for general readers."

◐ ⊘ SCRIBNER

Imprint of Simon & Schuster Adult Publishing Group, 1230 Avenue of the Americas, 12th Floor, New York NY 10020. (212)698-7000. **Website:** www.simonsays. com. Publishes hardcover originals. **Publishes 70-75 titles/year. Thousands queries received/year. 20% of books from first-time authors. Pays 7-15% royalty. Pays variable advance.** Publishes ms 9 months after acceptance. Accepts simultaneous submissions. Responds in 3 months to queries.

NONFICTION Subjects include education, ethnic, history, philosophy, psychology, religion, science, criticism. *Agented submissions only.*

FICTION Subjects include literary, mystery, suspense. *Agented submissions only.*

SEAL PRESS

Perseus Books Group, 1700 4th St., Berkeley CA 94710. (510)595-3664. **E-mail:** seal.press@perseusbooks.com. **E-mail:** emma.rose@perseusbooks.com. **Website:** www.sealpress.com. Estab. 1976. Publishes hardcover and trade paperback originals. "Seal Press is an imprint of the Perseus Book Group, a feminist book publisher interested in original, lively, radical, empowering and culturally diverse nonfiction by women addressing contemporary issues with the goal of informing women's lives. Currently emphasizing women outdoor adventurists, young feminists, political issues, health and fitness, parenting, personal finance, sex and relationships, and LGBT and gender topics. *Not accepting fiction at this time.*" **Publishes 30 titles/year. 1,000 queries received/year. 750 mss received/year. 25% of books from first-time authors. 50% from unagented writers. Pays 7-10% royalty on retail price. Pays variable royalty on retail price. Pays wide ranging advance.** Publishes ms 1 year after acceptance. Accepts simultaneous submissions. Responds in 2 months to queries. Book catalog and ms guidelines for SASE or online.

NONFICTION Subjects include alternative lifestyles, Americana, child guidance, contemporary culture, creative nonfiction, ethnic, gay, health, lesbian, memoirs, multicultural, parenting, politics, pop culture, sex, travel, womens issues, womens studies, popular culture, politics, domestic violence, sexual abuse. Query with SASE. Reviews artwork/photos. Send photocopies. No original art or photos accepted.

TIPS "Seeking empowering and progressive nonfiction that can impact a woman's life across categories."

SEARCH INSTITUTE PRESS

Search Institute, 615 First Ave. NE, Suite 125, Minneapolis MN 55413. (612)376-8955. **Fax:** (612)692-5553. **E-mail:** si@search-institute.org. **Website:** www. search-institute.org. Estab. 1958. Publishes trade paperback originals. **Publishes 12-15 titles/year. Pays royalty.** Publishes book 1 year after acceptance. Accepts simultaneous submissions. Responds in 6 months. Catalog and guidelines online.

NONFICTION Subjects include career guidance, child guidance, community, counseling, education, entertainment, games, parenting, public affairs, social sciences, youth leadership, prevention, activities. Does not want children's picture books, poetry, New Age and religious-themes, memoirs, biographies, and autobiographies. Query with SASE. Does not review artwork/photos.

TIPS "Our audience is educators, youth program leaders, mentors, parents."

SEAWORTHY PUBLICATIONS, INC.

2023 N. Atlantic Ave., #226, Cocoa Beach FL 32931. (321)610-3634. **E-mail:** queries@seaworthy.com. **Website:** www.seaworthy.com. **Contact:** Joseph F. Janson, publisher. Estab. 1992. Publishes trade paperback originals, hardcover originals, and reprints. "Seaworthy Publications is a nautical book publisher that primarily publishes books of interest to recreational boaters and bluewater cruisers, including cruising guides, how-to books about boating. Currently emphasizing cruising guides." **Publishes 8 titles/year. 50 queries; 10 mss received/year. 60% of books from first-time authors. 100% from unagented writers. Pays 10% starting royalty based on wholesale price with increases up to 15% based on sales. Pays $1,000 advance.** Publishes ms 6 months after acceptance. Responds in 1 month to queries. Book catalog and guidelines online.

IMPRINTS Tablet Publications.

NONFICTION Subjects include environment, marine subjects, regional, sports, travel, sailing, boating, regional, boating guide books, boating how-to, Bahamas, Caribbean, travel. Regional guide books, first-person adventure, reference, how-to, technical— all dealing with boating. Query with SASE. Submit 3 sample chapters, TOC. Prefers electronic query via e-mail. Reviews artwork/photos. Send photocopies, color prints, or jpeg files.

TIPS "Our audience consists of sailors, boaters, and those interested in the sea, sailing, or long-distance cruising."

☼ SECOND STORY PRESS

20 Maud St., Suite 401, Toronto ON M5V 2M5, Canada. (416)537-7850. **Fax:** (416)537-0588. **E-mail:** info@secondstorypress.ca. **Website:** www.secondstorypress.ca. "Please keep in mind that as a feminist press, we are looking for non-sexist, non-racist and non-violent stories, as well as historical fiction, chapter books, novels and biography." Accepts simultaneous submissions.

NONFICTION Subjects include community, contemporary culture, creative nonfiction, environment, gay, health, history, labor, lesbian, literature, memoirs, multicultural, politics, sociology, womens issues, womens studies, young adult. Picture books: biography. Accepts appropriate material from residents of Canada only. "Send a synopsis and up to 3 sample chapters. If you are submitting a picture book you can send the entire manuscript. Illustrations are not necessary." No electronic submissions or queries. Guidelines on site.

FICTION Considers non-sexist, non-racist, and non-violent stories, as well as historical fiction, chapter books, picture books.

SEEDLING CONTINENTAL PRESS

520 E. Bainbridge St., Elizabethtown PA 17022. (800)233-0759. **Website:** www.continentalpress.com. "Continental publishes educational materials for grades K-12, specializing in reading, mathematics, and test preparation materials. We are not currently accepting submissions for Seedling leveled readers or instructional materials." **Work purchased outright from authors.** Publishes book 1-2 years after acceptance. Accepts simultaneous submissions. Responds to mss in 6 months.

NONFICTION Young readers: animal, arts/crafts, biography, careers, concept, multicultural, nature/environment, science. Does not accept texts longer than 12 pages or over 300 words. Average word length: young readers—100.

FICTION Young readers: adventure, animal, folktales, humor, multicultural, nature/environment. Does not accept texts longer than 12 pages or over

300 words. Average word length: young readers—100. Submit complete ms.

TIPS "See our website. Follow writers' guidelines carefully and test your story with children and educators."

☼ SELF-COUNSEL PRESS

1481 Charlotte Rd., North Vancouver BC V7J 1H1, Canada. (360)676-4530. **E-mail:** editor@self-counsel.com. **Website:** www.self-counsel.com. **Contact:** Linda L. Richards. Estab. 1971. Publishes trade paperback originals. Self-Counsel Press publishes a range of quality self-help books written in practical, nontechnical style by recognized experts in the fields of business, financial, or legal guidance for people who want to help themselves. **Publishes 20 titles/year. 1,500 queries received/year. 50% of books from first-time authors. 95% from unagented writers. Pays rare advance.** Publishes ms 8 months after acceptance. Accepts simultaneous submissions. Responds in 2 months to queries. Book catalog online. Guidelines online.

NONFICTION Subjects include legal and business issues for lay people. Submit proposal package, outline, resume, 2 sample chapters.

⊘ SENTIENT PUBLICATIONS

P.O. Box 7204, Boulder CO 80306. **Website:** www.sentientpublications.com. Estab. 2001. Publishes hardcover and trade paperback originals; trade paperback reprints. "We are not currently accepting submissions." **Publishes 4 titles/year. 200 queries; 100 mss received/year. 70% of books from first-time authors. 50% from unagented writers. Pays royalty on wholesale price. Sometimes pays advance.** Publishes ms 10 months after acceptance. Responds in 1 month to queries; 2 months to proposals and mss. Book catalog online.

NONFICTION Subjects include child guidance, contemporary culture, creative nonfiction, education, environment, gardening, history, philosophy, photography, psychology, science, social sciences, sociology, spirituality, travel. Does not review artwork/photos.

SEVEN STORIES PRESS

140 Watts St., New York NY 10013. (212)226-8760. **Fax:** (212)226-1411. **E-mail:** info@sevenstories.com. **Website:** www.sevenstories.com. **Contact:** Acquisitions. Estab. 1995. Publishes hardcover and trade paperback originals. Founded in 1995 in New York City, and named for the seven authors who committed to a

home with a fiercely independent spirit, Seven Stories Press publishes works of the imagination and political titles by voices of conscience. While most widely known for its books on politics, human rights, and social and economic justice, Seven Stories continues to champion literature, with a list encompassing both innovative debut novels and National Book Award–winning poetry collections, as well as prose and poetry translations from the French, Spanish, German, Swedish, Italian, Greek, Polish, Korean, Vietnamese, Russian, and Arabic. **Publishes 40-50 titles/year. 15% of books from first-time authors. 50% from unagented writers. Pays 7-15% royalty on retail price. Pays advance.** Publishes ms 1-3 years after acceptance. Accepts simultaneous submissions. Responds in 1 month. Book catalog and ms guidelines free.

NONFICTION Responds only if interested. Submit cover letter with 2 sample chapters.

FICTION Subjects include literary. Submit cover letter with 2 sample chapters.

SEVERN HOUSE PUBLISHERS

Salatin House, 19 Cedar Rd., Sutton, Surrey SM2 5DA, United Kingdom. (44)(208)770-3930. **Fax:** (44)(208)770-3850. **Website:** www.severnhouse.com. Publishes hardcover and trade paperback originals and reprints. Severn House is currently emphasizing suspense, romance, mystery. Large print imprint from existing authors. **Publishes 150 titles/year. 400-500 queries received/year. 50 mss received/year. Pays 7-15% royalty on retail price. Pays $750-5,000 advance.** Accepts simultaneous submissions. Responds in 3 months to proposals. Book catalog available free.

FICTION Subjects include adventure, fantasy, historical, horror, mystery, romance, short story collections, suspense. *Agented submissions only.*

SHAMBHALA PUBLICATIONS, INC.

4720 Walnut St., Boulder CO 80304. **E-mail:** submissions@shambhala.com. **Website:** www.shambhala.com. Estab. 1969. Publishes hardcover and trade paperback originals and reprints. **Publishes 90-100 titles/year. 500 queries; 1,200 mss/proposals received/year. 30% of books from first-time authors. 70% from unagented writers. Pays 8% royalty on retail price.** Publishes ms 1 year after acceptance. Accepts simultaneous submissions. Responds in 4 months. Book catalog free. Guidelines online.

IMPRINTS Roost Books; Snow Lion.

NONFICTION Subjects include cooking, crafts, parenting, Buddhism, martial arts, yoga, natural health, Eastern philosophy, creativity, green living, nature writing. To send a book proposal, include a synopsis of the book, see the submissions guidelines online. "We strongly prefer electronic submissions and do not take phone calls regarding book ideas or proposals."

SHEARSMAN BOOKS, LTD

50 Westons Hills Dr., Emersons Green, Bristol BS16 7DF, United Kingdom. **E-mail:** editor@shearsman.com. **Website:** www.shearsman.com. **Contact:** Tony Frazer, editor. Estab. 1981. Publishes trade paperback originals. **Publishes 45-60 titles/year. Receives 2,000 submissions/year. 10% of books from first-time authors. 95% from unagented writers. Pays 10% royalty on retail price after 150 copies have sold; authors also receive 10 free copies of their books. Does not pay advance.** Publishes ms 9-18 months after acceptance. Accepts simultaneous submissions. Responds in 3 months to mss. Book catalog online. Print copies available on request. Guidelines online.

NONFICTION Subjects include literature, memoirs, translation, essays. All nonfiction has to do with poetry in some way. "We don't publish nonfiction unless it's related to poetry."

POETRY "Shearsman only publishes poetry, poetry collections, and poetry in translation (from any language but with an emphasis on work in Spanish & in German). Some critical work on poetry and also memoirs and essays by poets. Mainly poetry by British, Irish, North American, and Australian poets." No poetry by or for children. No devotional or religious verse.

TIPS "Book ms submission: most of the ms must have already appeared in the UK or USA magazines of some repute, and it has to fill 70-72 pages of half letter or A5 pages. You must have sufficient return postage, or permit email responses. Submissions can also be made by email. It is unlikely that a poet with no track record will be accepted for publication as there is no obvious audience for the work. Try to develop some exposure to UK and US magazines and try to assemble a MS only later."

SHIPWRECKT BOOKS PUBLISHING COMPANY LLC

309 W. Stevens Ave., Rushford MN 55971. **E-mail:** editor@shipwrecktbooks.com. **E-mail:** contact@ship-

wrecktbooks.com. **Website:** www.shipwrecktbooks. com. **Contact:** Tom Driscoll, managing editor. Publishes trade paperback originals, mass market paperback originals, and electronic originals. **Publishes 6 titles/year. Receives 700 submissions/year. 60% of books from first-time authors. 80% from unagented writers. Authors receive a maximum of 35% royalties.** Average length of time between acceptance of a book-length ms and publication is 6 months. Accepts simultaneous submissions. Responds to queries within 6 months. Catalog and guidelines online.

IMPRINTS Rocket Science Press (literary); Up On Big Rock Poetry Series; Lost Lake Folk Art (memoir, biography, essays, fiction and nonfiction).

NONFICTION Subjects include agriculture, alternative lifestyles, Americana, animals, anthropology, architecture, creative nonfiction, environment, ethnic, foods, gardening, gay, government, health, history, hobbies, horticulture, house and home, lesbian, medicine, memoirs, military, multicultural, nature, nutrition, politics, recreation, regional, spirituality, sports, war, womens issues, world affairs, young adult. Does not want religious. E-mail query first. All unsolicited mss returned unopened. Does not review artwork.

FICTION Subjects include adventure, comic books, contemporary, erotica, ethnic, experimental, fantasy, historical, humor, literary, mainstream, military, multicultural, mystery, poetry, poetry in translation, regional, science fiction, short story collections, sports, suspense, war, young adult. E-mail query first. All unsolicited mss returned unopened.

POETRY Poetry bar is very high. No religious or holiday verse. Submit 3 sample poems by e-mail.

TIPS "Quality writing. Query first. Development and full editorial services available."

SIBLING RIVALRY PRESS

P.O. Box 26147, Little Rock AR 72221. **E-mail:** info@ siblingrivalrypress.com. **Website:** siblingrivalrypress. com. **Contact:** Bryan Borland, publisher; Seth Pennington, editor. Estab. 2010. While we champion our LGBTIQ authors and artists, and while we've been very fortunate in our successes in LGBTIQ publishing, we are an inclusive publishing house and welcome all authors, artists, and readers regardless of sexual orientation or identity. We publish work we love. Merit trumps category. SRP is the only press to ever win Lambda Literary Awards in both gay poetry and lesbian poetry. All SRP titles are housed permanently in the Library of Congress Rare Book and Special Collections Vault. **50% of books from first-time authors. 95% from unagented writers. 30% royalties for print Does not pay advance.** Accepts simultaneous submissions. Catalog online. Guidelines online.

POETRY Opening reading period: March 1-June 1. Submit complete ms.

SILMAN-JAMES PRESS

3624 Shannon Rd., Los Angeles CA 90027. (323)661-9922. **Fax:** (323)661-9933. **Website:** www.silman-jamespress.com. Publishes trade paperback originals and reprints. **Pays variable royalty on retail price.** Accepts simultaneous submissions. Book catalog available free.

NONFICTION Pertaining to film, theatre, music, performing arts. Submit proposal package, outline, 1+ sample chapters. Will accept phone queries. Reviews artwork/photos. Send photocopies.

TIPS "Our audience ranges from people with a general interest in film (fans, etc.) to students of film and performing arts to industry professionals. We will accept 'query' phone calls."

SILVER DOLPHIN BOOKS

(858)457-2500. **E-mail:** infosilverdolphin@reader-link.com. **Website:** www.silverdolphinbooks.com. Silver Dolphin Books publishes activity, novelty, and educational nonfiction books for preschoolers to 12-year-olds. Highly interactive formats such as the Field Guides and Uncover series both educate and entertain older children. "We will consider submissions only from authors with previously published works." Accepts simultaneous submissions.

FICTION Submit cover letter with full proposal and SASE.

SILVERFISH REVIEW PRESS

P.O. Box 3541, Eugene OR 97403. (541)344-5060. **E-mail:** sfrpress@earthlink.net. **Website:** www.silverfishreviewpress.com. Estab. 1978. Publishes trade paperback originals. "Sponsors the Gerald Cable Book Award. This prize is awarded annually to a book length manuscript of original poetry by an author who has not yet published a full-length collection. There are no restrictions on the kind of poetry or subject matter; translations are not acceptable. Winners will receive $1,000, publication, and 25 copies of the book. Entries must be postmarked by October 15. Entries may be submitted by e-mail. See website for instructions." **Publishes 2-3 titles/year. 50%**

of books from first-time authors. **100% from unagented writers.** Accepts simultaneous submissions. Guidelines online.

TIPS "Read recent Silverfish titles."

SILVER LAKE PUBLISHING

P.O. Box 173, Aberdeen WA 98520. (360)532-5758. **Fax:** (360)532-5728. **E-mail:** publisher@silverlakepub.com. **Website:** www.silverlakepub.com. Estab. 1998. Publishes hardcover and trade paperback originals and reprints. **Pays royalty.** Accepts simultaneous submissions. Responds in 6-8 weeks to proposals. Book catalog available free. Guidelines available free.

NONFICTION No fiction or poetry. Submit outline, resume, 2 sample chapters, cover letter, synopsis. Submit via mail only.

◑◿ SIMON & SCHUSTER

1230 Avenue of the Americas, New York NY 10020. (212)698-7000. **Website:** www.simonandschuster.com. *Accepts agented submissions only.* Accepts simultaneous submissions.

IMPRINTS Aladdin; Atheneum Books for Young Readers; Atria; Beach Lane Books; Folger Shakespeare Library; Free Press; Gallery Books; Howard Books; Little Simon; Margaret K. McElderry Books; Pocket; Scribner; Simon & Schuster; Simon & Schuster Books for Young Readers; Simon Pulse; Simon Spotlight; Threshold; Touchstone; Paula Wiseman Books.

◑◿ SIMON & SCHUSTER BOOKS FOR YOUNG READERS

Imprint of Simon & Schuster Children's Publishing, 1230 Avenue of the Americas, New York NY 10020. (212)698-7000. **Fax:** (212)698-2796. **Website:** www.simonsayskids.com. Publishes hardcover originals. "Simon and Schuster Books For Young Readers is the Flagship imprint of the S&S Children's Division. We are committed to publishing a wide range of contemporary, commercial, award-winning fiction and nonfiction that spans every age of children's publishing. BFYR is constantly looking to the future, supporting our foundation authors and franchises, but always with an eye for breaking new ground with every publication. We publish high-quality fiction and nonfiction for a variety of age groups and a variety of markets. Above all, we strive to publish books that we are passionate about." *No unsolicited mss.* All unsolicited mss returned unopened. **Publishes 75 titles/year. Pays variable royalty on retail price.** Publishes ms 2-4 years after acceptance. Accepts simultaneous submissions. Guidelines online.

NONFICTION Subjects include history, biography. Picture books: concept. All levels: narrative, current events, biography, history. "We're looking for picture books or middle grade nonfiction that have a retail potential. No photo essays." *Agented submissions only.*

FICTION Subjects include fantasy, historical, humor, juvenile, mystery, picture books, science fiction, young adult. *Agented submissions only.*

TIPS "We're looking for picture books centered on a strong, fully-developed protagonist who grows or changes during the course of the story; YA novels that are challenging and psychologically complex; also imaginative and humorous middle-grade fiction. And we want nonfiction that is as engaging as fiction. Our imprint's slogan is 'Reading You'll Remember.' We aim to publish books that are fresh, accessible and family-oriented; we want them to have an impact on the reader."

◔ SIMPLY READ BOOKS

501-5525 W. Blvd., Vancouver BC V6M 3W6, Canada. **E-mail:** go@simplyreadbooks.com. **Website:** www.simplyreadbooks.com. Simply Read Books is current seeking mss in picture books, early readers, early chapter books, middle grade fiction, and graphic novels. Accepts simultaneous submissions.

FICTION Query or submit complete ms.

SKINNER HOUSE BOOKS

The Unitarian Universalist Association, 24 Farnsworth St., Boston MA 02210. (617)742-2100, ext. 603. **Fax:** (617)948-6466. **E-mail:** bookproposals@uua.org. **Website:** www.uua.org/publications/skinnerhouse. **Contact:** Betsy Martin. Estab. 1975. Publishes trade paperback originals and reprints. "We publish titles in Unitarian Universalist faith, liberal religion, history, biography, worship, and issues of social justice. Most of our children's titles are intended for religious education or worship use. They reflect Unitarian Universalist values. We also publish inspirational titles of poetic prose and meditations. Writers should know that Unitarian Universalism is a liberal religious denomination committed to progressive ideals. Currently emphasizing social justice concerns." **Publishes 10-20 titles/year. 30% of books from first-time authors. 100% from unagented writers.** Publishes book 1 year after acceptance. Accepts simultaneous submissions.

Responds to queries in 1 month. Book catalog for 6×9 SAE with 3 first-class stamps. Guidelines online.

NONFICTION Subjects include religion, inspirational, church leadership. All levels: activity books, multicultural, music/dance, nature/environment, religion. Query or submit proposal with cover letter, TOC, 2 sample chapters. Reviews artwork/photos. Send photocopies.

FICTION Only publishes fiction for children's titles for religious instruction. Query.

TIPS "From outside our denomination, we are interested in manuscripts that will be of help or interest to liberal churches, Sunday School classes, parents, ministers, and volunteers. Inspirational/spiritual and children's titles must reflect liberal Unitarian Universalist values."

Ⓐⵔ LIZZIE SKURNICK BOOKS

Ig Publishing, (718)797-0676. **Website:** lizzieskurnickbooks.com. Estab. 2013. Lizzie Skurnick Books, an imprint of Ig Publishing, is devoted to reissuing the very best in young adult literature, from the classics of the 1930s and 1940s to the social novels of the 1970s and 1980s. Ig does not accept unsolicited mss, either by e-mail or regular mail. If you have a ms that you would like Ig to take a look at, send a query through online contact form. If interested, they will contact. All unsolicited mss will be discarded. Accepts simultaneous submissions.

SKY PONY PRESS

307 W. 36th St., 11th Floor, New York NY 10018. (212)643-6816. **Fax:** (212)643-6819. **Website:** skyponypress.com. Estab. 2011. Sky Pony Press is the children's book imprint of Skyhorse Publishing. "Following in the footsteps of our parent company, our goal is to provide books for readers with a wide variety of interests." Accepts simultaneous submissions. Guidelines online.

NONFICTION "Our parent company publishes many excellent books in the fields of ecology, independent living, farm living, wilderness living, recycling, and other green topics, and this will be a theme in our children's books. We are also searching for books that have strong educational themes and that help inform children of the world in which they live." Submit proposal via e-mail.

FICTION "We will consider picture books, early readers, midgrade novels, novelties, and informational books for all ages." Submit ms or proposal.

SLEEPING BEAR PRESS

2395 South Huron Parkway #200, Ann Arbor MI 48104. (800)487-2323. **Fax:** (734)794-0004. **E-mail:** submissions@sleepingbearpress.com. **Website:** www.sleepingbearpress.com. **Contact:** Manuscript Submissions. Estab. 1998. Accepts simultaneous submissions. Book catalog available via e-mail.

FICTION Picture books: adventure, animal, concept, folktales, history, multicultural, nature/environment, religion, sports. Young readers: adventure, animal, concept, folktales, history, humor, multicultural, nature/environment, religion, sports. Average word length: picture books—1,800. Accepts unsolicited queries 3 times per year. See website for details. Query with sample of work (up to 15 pages) and SASE. Please address packages to Manuscript Submissions.

SMALL BEER PRESS

150 Pleasant St., #306, Easthampton MA 01027. (413)203-1636. **Fax:** (413)203-1636. **E-mail:** info@smallbeerpress.com. **Website:** www.smallbeerpress.com. Estab. 2000. Small Beer Press also publishes the zine *Lady Churchill's Rosebud Wristlet.* "SBP's books have recently received the Tiptree and Crawford Awards." **Publishes 6-10 titles/year. Advance and standard royalties.**

FICTION Subjects include experimental, literary, short story collections, speculative. Does not accept unsolicited novel or short story collection mss. Send queries with first 10-20 pages and SASE.

TIPS "Please be familiar with our books first to avoid wasting your time and ours, thank you. E-mail queries will be deleted. Really."

SMITH AND KRAUS PUBLISHERS, INC.

177 Lyme Rd., Hanover NH 03755. (603)643-6431. **E-mail:** editor@smithandkraus.com. **E-mail:** carolb@smithandkraus.com. **Website:** smithandkraus.com. Estab. 1990. Publishes hardcover and trade paperback originals. **Publishes 35-40 titles/year. 10% of books from first-time authors. 10-20% from unagented writers. Pays 7% royalty on retail price. Pays $500-2,000 advance.** Publishes ms 1 year after acceptance. Responds in 1 month to queries; 2 months to proposals; 4 months to mss. Book catalog available free.

NONFICTION Subjects include drama. Does not return submissions. Query with SASE.

FICTION Does not return submissions. Query with SASE.

GIBBS SMITH, PUBLISHER

P.O. Box 667, Layton UT 84041. (801)544-9800. **Fax:** (801)546-8853. **Website:** www.gibbs-smith.com. Estab. 1969. Publishes hardcover and trade paperback originals. "We publish books that enrich and inspire humankind. Currently emphasizing interior decorating and design, home reference. De-emphasizing novels and short stories." **Publishes 80 titles/year. 3,000-4,000 queries received/year. 50% of books from first-time authors. 75% from unagented writers. Pays 8-14% royalty on gross receipts. Offers advance based on first year saleability projections.** Publishes ms 1-2 years after acceptance. Accepts simultaneous submissions. Responds in 1 month to queries; 10 weeks to proposals and mss. Guidelines online.

NONFICTION Subjects include regional, interior design, cooking, business, western, outdoor/sports/recreation. Query by e-mail only.

SOFT SKULL PRESS INC.

Counterpoint, 2650 Ninth St., Suite 318, Berkeley CA 94710. (510)704-0230. **Fax:** (510)704-0268. **E-mail:** info@counterpointpress.com. **Website:** www.softskull.com. Publishes hardcover and trade paperback originals. "Here at Soft Skull we love books that are new, fun, smart, revelatory, quirky, groundbreaking, cage-rattling and/or otherwise unusual." **Publishes 40 titles/year. Pays 7-10% royalty. Average advance: $100-15,000.** Publishes ms 6 months after acceptance. Accepts simultaneous submissions. Responds in 2 months to proposals; 3 months to mss. Book catalog and guidelines online.

NONFICTION Subjects include contemporary culture, creative nonfiction, entertainment, literature, pop culture. Send a cover letter describing your project and a full proposal along with 2 sample chapters.

FICTION Subjects include comic books, confession, contemporary, erotica, experimental, gay, lesbian, literary, mainstream, multicultural, short story collections. Does not consider poetry. Soft Skull Press no longer accepts digital submissions. Send a cover letter describing your project in detail and a completed ms. For graphic novels, send a minimum of five fully inked pages of art, along with a synopsis of your storyline. "Please do not send original material, as it will not be returned."

TIPS "See our website for updated submission guidelines."

SOHO PRESS, INC.

853 Broadway, New York NY 10003. (212)260-1900. **E-mail:** soho@sohopress.com. **Website:** www.sohopress.com. **Contact:** Bronwen Hruska, publisher; Mark Doten, senior editor. Estab. 1986. Publishes hardcover and trade paperback originals; trade paperback reprints. Soho Press publishes primarily fiction, as well as some narrative literary nonfiction and mysteries set abroad. No electronic submissions, only queries by e-mail. **Publishes 60-70 titles/year. 15-25% of books from first-time authors. 10% from unagented writers. Pays 10-15% royalty on retail price (varies under certain circumstances).** Publishes ms 18 months after acceptance. Accepts simultaneous submissions. Responds in 3 months. Guidelines online.

NONFICTION Subjects include creative nonfiction, ethnic, memoirs. "Independent publisher known for sophisticated fiction, mysteries set abroad, women's interest (no genre) novels and multicultural novels." Publishes hardcover and trade paperback originals and reprint editions. Books: perfect binding; halftone illustrations. First novel print order varies. We do not buy books on proposal. We always need to see a complete ms before we buy a book, though we prefer an initial submission of 3 sample chapters. We do not publish books with color art or photographs or a lot of graphical material." No self-help, how-to, or cookbooks. Submit 3 sample chapters and a cover letter with a synopsis and author bio; SASE. Send photocopies.

FICTION Subjects include ethnic, historical, humor, literary, mystery, In mysteries, we only publish series with foreign or exotic settings, usually procedurals. Adventure, ethnic, feminist, historical, literary, mainstream/contemporary, mystery (police procedural), suspense, multicultural. Submit 3 sample chapters and cover letter with synopsis, author bio, SASE. *No e-mailed submissions.*

TIPS "Soho Press publishes discerning authors for discriminating readers, finding the strongest possible writers and publishing them. Before submitting, look at our website for an idea of the types of books we publish, and read our submission guidelines."

SOURCEBOOKS, INC.

1935 Brookdale Rd., Suite 139, Naperville IL 60563. (630)961-3900. **Fax:** (630)961-2168. **E-mail:** editorialsubmissions@sourcebooks.com. **Website:** www.sourcebooks.com. Estab. 1987. Publishes hardcover and trade paperback originals. "Sourcebooks publishes many forms of fiction and nonfiction titles, including books on parenting, self-help/psychology, business, and health. Focus is on practical, useful information and skills. It also continues to publish in the reference, New Age, history, current affairs, and humor categories. Currently emphasizing gift, women's interest, history, reference, historical fiction, romance genre, and children's." **Publishes 300 titles/ year. 30% of books from first-time authors. 25% from unagented writers. Pays royalty on wholesale or list price. Pays advance.** Publishes ms 1 year after acceptance. Accepts simultaneous submissions. Responds in 3 months to queries. Book catalog online. Guidelines online.

NONFICTION Subjects include child guidance, history, psychology, science, sports, contemporary culture. Books for small business owners, entrepreneurs, and students. A key to submitting books to us is to explain how your book helps the reader, why it is different from the books already out there (please do your homework), and the author's credentials for writing this book. Books likely to succeed with us are self-help, parenting and childcare, psychology, women's issues, how-to, history, reference, biography, humor, gift books, or books with strong artwork. "We seek unique books on traditional subjects and authors who are smart and aggressive." Query with SASE, 2-3 sample chapters (not the first). *No complete mss.* Reviews artwork/photos.

TIPS "Our market is a decidedly trade-oriented bookstore audience. We also have very strong penetration into the gift-store market. Books which cross over between these 2 very different markets do extremely well with us. Our list is a solid mix of unique and general audience titles and series-oriented projects. We are looking for products that break new ground either in their own areas or within the framework of our series of imprints."

SOURCEBOOKS CASABLANCA

Sourcebooks, Inc., 232 Madison Ave., Suite 1100, New York NY 10016. **E-mail:** romance@sourcebooks. com. **Website:** www.sourcebooks.com. **Contact:** Deb Werksman (deb.werksman@sourcebooks.com). "Our romance imprint, Sourcebooks Casablanca, publishes single title romance in all subgenres." Accepts simultaneous submissions. Responds in 2-3 months. Guidelines online.

FICTION "Our editorial criteria call for: a heroine the reader can relate to, a hero she can fall in love with, a world gets created that the reader can escape into, there's a hook that we can sell within 2-3 sentences, and the author is out to build a career with us."

TIPS "We are actively acquiring single-title and single-title series romance fiction (90,000-100,000 words) for our Casablanca imprint. We are looking for strong writers who are excited about marketing their books and building their community of readers, and whose books have something fresh to offer in the genre of romance."

SOURCEBOOKS FIRE

1935 Brookdale Rd., Suite 139, Naperville IL 60563. (630)961-3900. **Fax:** (630)961-2168. **E-mail:** submissions@sourcebooks.com. **Website:** www.sourcebooks. com. "We're actively acquiring knockout books for our YA imprint. We are particularly looking for strong writers who are excited about promoting and building their community of readers, and whose books have something fresh to offer the ever-growing young adult audience. We are not accepting any unsolicited or unagented manuscripts at this time. Unfortunately, our staff can no longer handle the large volume of manuscripts that we receive on a daily basis. We will continue to consider agented manuscripts." See website for details. Accepts simultaneous submissions.

FICTION Query with the full ms attached in Word doc.

SOURCEBOOKS LANDMARK

Sourcebooks, Inc., Sourcebooks, Inc., 232 Madison Ave., Suite 1100, New York NY 10016. **E-mail:** editorialsubmissions@sourcebooks.com. **Website:** www. sourcebooks.com. "Our fiction imprint, Sourcebooks Landmark, publishes a variety of commercial fiction, including specialties in historical fiction and Austenalia. We are interested first and foremost in books that have a story to tell." Accepts simultaneous submissions. Responds in 2-3 months.

FICTION "We are actively acquiring contemporary, book club, and historical fiction for our Landmark imprint. We are looking for strong writers who are excited about marketing their books and building their community of readers." Submit synopsis and full ms preferred. Receipt of e-mail submissions acknowledged within 3 weeks of e-mail.

SOUTHERN ILLINOIS UNIVERSITY PRESS

1915 University Press Dr., SIUC Mail Code 6806, Carbondale IL 62901. (618)453-6613. **Fax:** (618)453-1221. **E-mail:** kageff@siu.edu. **Website:** www.siupress.com. **Contact:** Karl Kageff, editor-in-chief. Estab. 1956. Publishes hardcover and trade paperback originals and reprints. Scholarly press specializes in theater studies, rhetoric and composition studies, American history, Civil War, regional and nonfiction trade, poetry. No fiction. Currently emphasizing theater and American history, especially Civil War. **Publishes 36-40 titles/year. 300 queries; 80 mss received/year. 40% of books from first-time authors. 99% from unagented writers. Pays 5-10% royalty on wholesale price. Rarely offers advance.** Publishes ms 1 year after acceptance. Responds in 2 months to queries. Book catalog and ms guidelines free.

NONFICTION Subjects include archeology, history, language, military, regional, stage, transportation, war, womens studies.

POETRY Crab Orchard Series in Poetry. Guidelines online.

SPENCER HILL PRESS

27 W. 20th St., Suite 1102, New York NY 10011. **Website:** www.spencerhillpress.com. Spencer Hill Press is an independent publishing house specializing in sci-fi, urban fantasy, and paranormal romance for young adult readers. "Our books have that 'I couldn't put it down!' quality." Accepts simultaneous submissions. Guidelines online.

FICTION "We are interested in young adult, new adult, and middle grade sci-fi, psych-fi, paranormal, or urban fantasy, particularly those with a strong and interesting voice." Check website for open submission periods.

SPINNER BOOKS

University Games, 2030 Harrison St., San Francisco CA 94110. (415)503-1600. **Fax:** (415)503-0085. **E-mail:** info@ugames.com. **Website:** www.ugames.com. Estab. 1985. "Spinners Books publishes books of puzzles, games and trivia." Publishes book 6 months after acceptance. Accepts simultaneous submissions. Responds to queries in 3 months; mss in 2 months only if interested.

NONFICTION Picture books: games and puzzles. Query.

SPLASHING COW BOOKS

P.O. Box 867, Manchester VT 05254. **Website:** www.splashingcowbooks.com. **Contact:** Gordon McClellan, publisher. Estab. 2014. Publishes mass market paperback and hardcover books. We do not publish digital books. Splashing Cow Books publishes books under three imprints: Splashing Cow (children), Blue Boot (women) and Yellow Dot (family). **Publishes 10 titles/year. 100% of books from first-time authors. 100% from unagented writers. Pays royalties on retail price. Does not offer an advance.** Accepts simultaneous submissions. We try to reply as soon as possible, but may take up to 3 months. Catalog online. Guidelines online.

IMPRINTS Blue Boot Books imprint publishes books for women. Yellow Dot publishes general interest topics.

NONFICTION Open to any topic that would be of interest to children, women or families.

FICTION Subjects include adventure, comic books, contemporary, ethnic, fantasy, historical, humor, juvenile, literary, mainstream, multicultural, mystery, picture books, romance, science fiction, short story collections, spiritual, sports, suspense, western, young adult. Interested in a wide range of subject matter for children, women and families. Please check our website for submission guidelines.

SQUARE ONE PUBLISHERS, INC.

115 Herricks Rd., Garden City Park NY 11040. (516)535-2010. **Fax:** (516)535-2014. **Website:** www.squareonepublishers.com. **Contact:** Acquisitions Editor. Publishes trade paperback originals. **Publishes 20 titles/year. 500 queries; 100 mss received/year. 95% of books from first-time authors. 95% from unagented writers. Pays 10-15% royalty on wholesale price. Pays variable advance.** Publishes ms 10 months after acceptance. Accepts simultaneous submissions. Responds in 1 month. Book catalog and ms guidelines online.

NONFICTION Subjects include child guidance, cooking, health, hobbies, nutrition, psychology, religion, spirituality, sports, travel, writers' guides, cooking/foods, gaming/gambling. Query with SASE. Submit proposal package, outline, bio, introduction, synopsis, SASE. Reviews artwork/photos. Send photocopies.

TIPS "We focus on making our books accessible, accurate, and interesting. They are written for people who are looking for the best place to start, and who don't appreciate the terms 'dummy,' 'idiot,' or 'fool,' on the cover of their books. We look for smartly written, informative books that have a strong point of view, and that are authored by people who know their subjects well."

STANDARD PUBLISHING

Standex International Corp., 4050 Lee Vance View, Colorado Springs CO 80918. (800)323-7543. **Fax:** (800)323-0726. **Website:** www.standardpub.com. Estab. 1866. Publishes resources that meet church and family needs in the area of children's ministry. Guidelines online.

STANFORD UNIVERSITY PRESS

500 Broadway St., Redwood City CA 94063. (650)723-9434. **Fax:** (650)725-3457. **Website:** www.sup.org. Estab. 1925. "Stanford University Press publishes scholarly books in the humanities and social sciences, along with professional books in business, economics and management science; also high-level textbooks and some books for a more general audience." *Submit to specific editor.* **Pays variable royalty (sometimes none). Pays occasional advance.** Guidelines online.

NONFICTION Subjects include ethnic, history, humanities, literary criticism, philosophy, psychology, religion, science, social sciences, sociology, political science, law, education, history and culture of China, Japan and Latin America, European history, linguistics, geology, medieval and classical studies. Query with prospectus and an outline. Reviews artwork/photos.

TIPS "The writer's best chance is a work of original scholarship with an argument of some importance."

STAR BRIGHT BOOKS

13 Landsdowne St., Cambridge MA 02139. (617)354-1300. **Fax:** (617)354-1399. **E-mail:** info@starbright-books.com. **Website:** www.starbrightbooks.com. Star Bright Books does accept unsolicited mss and art submissions. "We welcome submissions for picture books and longer works, both fiction and nonfiction." Also beginner readers and chapter books. Query first. **Publishes 18 titles/year. 75% of books from first-time authors. 99% from unagented writers. Pays advance.** Publishes ms 1-2 years after acceptance. Accepts simultaneous submissions. Responds in several months. Catalog available.

NONFICTION Almost anything of interest to children. Very keen on Biographies and any thing of interest to children.

ST. AUGUSTINE'S PRESS

17917 Killington Way, South Bend IN 46614-9773. (574)291-3500. **Fax:** (574)291-3700. **E-mail:** bruce@staugustine.net. **Website:** www.staugustine.net. **Contact:** Bruce Fingerhut, president. Estab. 1996. Publishes hardcover originals and trade paperback originals and reprints. "Our market is scholarly in the humanities. We publish in philosophy, religion, cultural history, and history of ideas only." **Publishes 30+ titles/year. 350 queries; 300 mss received/year. 2% of books from first-time authors. 95% from unagented writers. Pays 6-15% royalty. Pays $500-5,000 advance.** Publishes book 8-18 months after acceptance. Accepts simultaneous submissions. Responds in 2-6 months to queries; 3-8 months to proposals; 4-8 months to mss. Book catalog available free.

IMPRINTS Carthage Reprints.

NONFICTION Subjects include humanities, philosophy, religion. Query with SASE. Reviews artwork/photos. Send photocopies.

TIPS "Scholarly and college student audience."

STC CRAFT

Imprint of Abrams, 115 W. 18th St., 6th Floor, New York NY 10011. **Website:** abramscraft.com. Publishes a vibrant collection of exciting and visually stunning craft books specializing in knitting, sewing, quilting, felting, and other popular craft genres. Accepts simultaneous submissions. Guidelines online.

NONFICTION Subjects include crafts. Please submit via e-mail.

STEEL TOE BOOKS

Department of English, Western Kentucky University, 1906 College Heights Blvd. #11086, Bowling Green KY 42101. (270)745-5769. **E-mail:** tom.hunley@wku.edu. **Website:** www.steeltoebooks.com. **Contact:** Dr. Tom C. Hunley, director. Estab. 2003. Steel Toe Books publishes "full-length, single-author poetry collections. Our books are professionally designed and printed. We look for workmanship (economical use of language, high-energy verbs, precise literal descriptions, original figurative language, poems carefully arranged as a book); a unique style and/or a distinctive voice; clarity; emotional impact; humor (word plays, hyperbole, comic timing); performability (a Steel Toe poet is at home on the stage as well as on the page)." Does not want "dry verse, purposely obscure language, poetry by people who are so wary of being called 'sentimental' they steer away from any recognizable human emotions, poetry that takes itself so seriously that it's unintentionally funny." Has published poetry by Allison Joseph, Susan Browne, James Doyle, Martha Silano, Mary Biddinger, John Guzlowski, Jeannine Hall Gailey, and others. Publishes 1-3 poetry books/year. Mss are normally selected through open submission. Accepts simultaneous submissions.

POETRY "Check the website for news about our next open reading period." Book mss may include previously published poems. Responds to mss in 3 months. Pays $500 advance on 10% royalties and 10 author's copies. Order sample books by sending $12 to Steel Toe Books. *Must purchase a ms in order to submit.* See website for submission guidelines.

STENHOUSE PUBLISHERS

P.O. Box 11020, Portland ME 04104. **E-mail:** editors@stenhouse.com. **Website:** www.stenhouse.com. **Contact:** Philippa Stratton, editorial director. Estab. 1993. Publishes paperback originals. Stenhouse publishes exclusively professional books for teachers, K-12. **Publishes 15 titles/year. 300 queries received/year. 30% of books from first-time authors. 99% from unagented writers. Pays royalty on wholesale price.** Accepts simultaneous submissions. Responds in 2 weeks to queries; 1 month to mss. Book catalog free or online. Guidelines online.

NONFICTION Subjects include education, specializing in literary with offerings in elementary and middle level math and science. All of our books are a combination of theory and practice. No children's books or student texts. Query by e-mail (preferred) or SASE. Reviews artwork/photos. Send photocopies.

STERLING PUBLISHING CO., INC.

1166 Avenue of the Americas, 17th Floor, New York NY 10036. (212)532-7160. **Website:** www.sterlingpublishing.com. Publishes hardcover and paperback originals and reprints. "Sterling publishes highly illustrated, accessible, hands-on, practical books for adults and children. Our mission is to publish high-quality books that educate, entertain, and enrich the lives of our readers." **15% of books from first-time authors. Pays royalty or work purchased outright. Offers advances (average amount: $2,000).** Accepts simultaneous submissions. Catalog online. Guidelines online.

NONFICTION Subjects include animals, ethnic, gardening, hobbies, New Age, recreation, science, sports, fiber arts, games and puzzles, children's humor, children's science, nature and activities, pets, wine, home decorating, dolls and puppets, ghosts, UFOs, woodworking, crafts, medieval, Celtic subjects, alternative health and healing, new consciousness. Proposals on subjects such as crafting, decorating, outdoor living, and photography should be sent directly to Lark Books at their Asheville, North Carolina offices. Complete guidelines can be found on the Lark site: www.larkbooks.com/submissions. Publishes nonfiction only. Submit outline, publishing history, 1 sample chapter (typed and double-spaced), SASE. "Explain your idea. Send sample illustrations where applicable. For children's books, please submit full mss. We do not accept electronic (e-mail) submissions. Be sure to include information about yourself with particular regard to your skills and qualifications in the subject area of your submission. It is helpful for us to know your publishing history—whether or not you've written other books and, if so, the name of the publisher and whether those books are currently in print." Reviews artwork/photocopies.

FICTION Publishes fiction for children. Submit to attention of "Children's Book Editor."

TIPS "We are primarily a nonfiction activities-based publisher. We have a picture book list, but we do not publish chapter books or novels. Our list is not trend-driven. We focus on titles that will backlist well. "

STIPES PUBLISHING LLC

P.O. Box 526, Champaign IL 61824. (217)356-8391. **Fax:** (217)356-5753. **E-mail:** stipes01@sbcglobal.net. **Website:** www.stipes.com. Estab. 1925. Publishes hardcover and paperback originals. "Stipes Publishing is oriented towards the education market and educational books with some emphasis in the trade market." **Publishes 15-30 titles/year. 50% of books from first-time authors. 95% from unagented writers. Pays 15% maximum royalty on retail price.** Publishes ms 4 months after acceptance. Responds in 2 months to queries. Guidelines online.

NONFICTION Subjects include agriculture, recreation, science. "All of our books in the trade area are books that also have a college text market. No books unrelated to educational fields taught at the college level." Submit outline, 1 sample chapter.

STONE ARCH BOOKS

1710 Roe Crest Rd., North Mankato MN 56003. **Website:** www.stonearchbooks.com. **Work purchased outright from authors.** Accepts simultaneous submissions. Catalog online.

FICTION Imprint of Capstone Publishers. Young readers, middle readers, young adults: adventure, contemporary, fantasy, humor, light humor, mystery, science fiction, sports, suspense. Average word length: young readers—1,000-3,000; middle readers and early young adults—5,000-10,000. Submit outline/synopsis and 3 sample chapters. Electronic submissions preferred. Full guidelines available on website.

TIPS "A high-interest topic or activity is one that a young person would spend their free time on without adult direction or suggestion."

STONE BRIDGE PRESS

P.O. Box 8208, Berkeley CA 94707. **E-mail:** sbp@stonebridge.com. **Website:** www.stonebridge.com. **Contact:** Peter Goodman, publisher. Estab. 1989. "Independent press focusing on books about Asia, primarily Japan and China, in English (business, language, culture, literature, animation)." Publishes hardcover and trade paperback originals. Books: 60-70 lb. offset paper; web and sheet paper; perfect bound; some illustrations. Distributes titles through Consortium. Promotes titles through Internet announcements, special-interest magazines and niche tie-ins to associations. **Publishes 6 titles/year. 90% from unagented writers. Pays royalty on wholesale price.** Publishes ms 2 years after acceptance. Accepts simultaneous submissions. Responds to queries in 4 months; mss in 8 months. Catalog online.

NONFICTION Subjects include business, cinema, crafts, creative nonfiction, ethnic, film, house and home, language, literature, memoirs, nature, philosophy, pop culture, sex, spirituality, travel, womens issues. Query with e-mail first.

FICTION Subjects include comic books, contemporary, erotica, literary, translation. Experimental, gay/lesbian, literary, Asia-themed. "Primarily looking at material relating to Asia, especially Japan and China. " Does not accept unsolicited mss. Accepts queries by e -mail.

TIPS "Query first before submitting. Research us first and avoid sending mss not in our subject area. Generic and bulk submissions will be ignored. No po-etry. Looking also for graphic novels, not manga or serializations."

STONESLIDE BOOKS

Stoneslide Media LLC, P.O. Box 8331, New Haven CT 06530. **Website:** www.stoneslidecorrective.com. Estab. 2012. Publishes trade paperback and electronic originals. "We like novels with strong character development and narrative thrust, brought out with writing that's clear and expressive." **Publishes 3-5 titles/year. Receives 300 queries/year; 150 mss/year. 100% of books from first-time authors. 100% from unagented writers. Pays 20-80% royalty.** Publishes book 8 months after acceptance. Responds in 1-2 months. Book catalog and guidelines online.

FICTION Subjects include adventure, contemporary, experimental, fantasy, gothic, historical, humor, literary, mainstream, mystery, science fiction, short story collections, suspense. "We will look at any genre. The important factor for us is that the story use plot, characters, emotions, and other elements of storytelling to think and move the mind forward." Submit proposal package via online submission form including: synopsis and 3 sample chapters.

TIPS "Read the Stoneslide Corrective to see if your work fits with our approach."

STOREY PUBLISHING

210 MASS MoCA Way, North Adams MA 01247. (800)793-9396. **Fax:** (413)346-2199. **E-mail:** feedback@storey.com. **Website:** www.storey.com. Estab. 1983. Publishes hardcover and trade paperback originals and reprints. "The mission of Storey Publishing is to serve our customers by publishing practical information that encourages personal independence in harmony with the environment. We seek to do this in a positive atmosphere that promotes editorial quality, team spirit, and profitability. The books we select to carry out this mission include titles on gardening, small-scale farming, building, cooking, home brewing, crafts, part-time business, home improvement, woodworking, animals, nature, natural living, personal care, and country living. We are always pleased to review new proposals, which we try to process expeditiously. We offer both work-for-hire and standard royalty contracts." **Publishes 40 titles/year. 600 queries received/year. 150 mss received/year. 25% of books from first-time authors. 60% from unagented writers. We offer both work-for-hire and standard royalty contracts. Pays advance.** Publishes book 2

years after acceptance. Accepts simultaneous submissions. Responds in 1-3 months. Book catalog available free. Guidelines online.

NONFICTION Subjects include animals, gardening, home, mind/body/spirit, birds, beer and wine, crafts, building, cooking. Submit a proposal. Reviews artwork/photos.

STRATEGIC MEDIA BOOKS

782 Wofford St., Rock Hill SC 29730. (803)366-5440. **E-mail:** contact@strategicmediabooks.com. **Website:** strategicmediabooks.com. Estab. 2010. Publishes hardcover, trade paperback, and electronic originals. "Strategic Media Books, LLC is an independent U.S. publisher that aims to bring extraordinary true-life stories to the widest possible audience. Founded in 2010, Strategic Media Books intends to be one of the most energetic and hard-hitting nonfiction publishers in the business. While we currently specialize in true crime, we plan to expand and publish great books in any nonfiction genre." **Publishes 16-20 titles/year. 100 queries received/year. 30-35 mss received/year. 20% of books from first-time authors. 85% from unagented writers. Authors receive 15-20% royalty on retail price.** Publishes book 9 months after acceptance. Accepts simultaneous submissions. Responds in 1-2 months. Catalog online. Guidelines via e-mail.

NONFICTION Subjects include Americana, contemporary culture, environment, ethnic, government, history, memoirs, military, multicultural, nature, politics, regional, war, world affairs, true crime. Planning to increase the number of books for the 2014 and 2015 seasons. Query with SASE. Will review artwork. Writers should send photocopies.

FICTION Subjects include mystery, suspense. "We are very selective in our publication of fiction. If writers want to submit, make sure mss fits the mystery or suspense genres." Query with SASE.

STRAWBERRIES PRESS

750 Pinehurst Dr., Rio Vista CA 94571. (707)398-6430. **E-mail:** books@strawberriespress.com. **Website:** www.strawberriespress.com. **Contact:** Susan Zhang, Executive Editor. Estab. 2015. Publishes interactive picture books in the 8-1/2" x 11" softcover format. Strawberries books are beautifully illustrated and designed to be high-quality publications that children will love and treasure. For example, our interactive picture book for train enthusiasts entitled Choo-Choo Charlie Presents Steam Locomotives provides a fun story by Charlie the Locomotive while teaching kids about steam engines and how they work, the definition of a train, the history of steam locomotives, and how to determine a locomotive's wheel configuration number. Children even get to watch a singing cartoon video of Choo-Choo Charlie the Engineer and how he uses candy to make his train run. A fun test is included at the end of each book. Just send Strawberries the completed test and your child will receive a beautifully printed Reading Certificate that he or she can proudly frame and display for all his or her friends to see. Reading traditional picture books, watching videos, visiting websites that contain associated subjects, taking fun tests, and earning Reading Certificates represent the interactive parts of the Strawberries reading and learning concept. **Publishes 6 titles/ year. Receives 12-20 queries/year; 12 mss/year. 50% of books from first-time authors. 100% from unagented writers. Pays for outright purchase between $250-500.** Publishes mss in 3-4 months upon acceptance. Responds in 1 month. Catalog available online. Guidelines available by e-mail.

NONFICTION Subjects include anthropology, archeology, architecture, art, creative nonfiction, education, environment, ethnic, hobbies, marine subjects, nature, photography, science, sports, transportation, young adult. Interested in topics that explore exciting subjects that stimulate young minds in both the fiction and nonfiction genres. For examples of subject matter and format requirements, see online catalog of picture book titles. "We only publish wholesome learning resources and educationally constructive subject matter that retains, promotes, and enhances the innocence of children. Political, immoral, antisocial, propagandist, and other age-inappropriate themes are strictly prohibited at Strawberries Press. We do not use our publications as social engineering and brainwashing tools." Submit completed ms. Writers should sent artwork/photographs with manuscript, if available. All art/photo submissions are provided as unsolicited; Strawberries Press is not responsible for the loss or damage of art/photos; therefore, do not send irreplaceable original work. Send copies only.

TIPS "Although there are no restrictions on the number of sentences on a single page, all picture books are limited to 40 pages. For text, illustrating, and formatting examples, view our sample online picture book."

STYLUS PUBLISHING, LLC

22883 Quicksilver Dr., Sterling VA 20166. **E-mail:** sylusinfo@styluspub.com. **Website:** styluspub.com. Estab. 1996. Publishes hardcover and trade paperback originals. "We publish in higher education (diversity, professional development, distance education, teaching, administration)." **Publishes 10-15 titles/year. 50 queries received/year. 6 mss received/year. 50% of books from first-time authors. 100% from unagented writers. Pays 5-10% royalty on wholesale price. Pays advance.** Publishes ms 6 months after acceptance. Responds in 1 month to queries. Book catalog available free. Guidelines online.

NONFICTION Query or submit outline, 1 sample chapter with SASE. Reviews artwork/photos. Send photocopies.

SUBITO PRESS

University of Colorado at Boulder, Dept. of English, 226 UCB, Boulder CO 80309-0226. **E-mail:** subitopressucb@gmail.com. **Website:** www.subitopress.org. Publishes trade paperback originals. Subito Press is a non-profit publisher of literary works. Each year Subito publishes one work of fiction and one work of poetry through its contest. Accepts simultaneous submissions. Guidelines online.

FICTION Subjects include experimental, literary, translation. Submit complete ms to contest.

POETRY Submit complete ms to contest.

TIPS "We publish 2 books of innovative writing a year through our poetry and fiction contests. All entries are also considered for publication with the press."

SUN BOOKS / SUN PUBLISHING

P.O. Box 5588, Santa Fe NM 87502. (505)471-5177. **E-mail:** info@sunbooks.com. **Website:** www.sunbooks.com. Estab. 1973. Publishes trade paperback originals and reprints. Not accepting new mss at this time. **Publishes 10-15 titles/year. 5% of books from first-time authors. 90% from unagented writers. Pays 5% royalty on retail price. Occasionally makes outright purchase.** Publishes ms 16-18 months after acceptance. Accepts simultaneous submissions. "Will respond within 2 months, via e-mail, to queries if interested.". Book catalog online. Queries via e-mail only, please.

NONFICTION Subjects include agriculture, alternative lifestyles, Americana, astrology, career guidance, environment, history, New Age, regional, self-help, leadership, motivational, recovery, inspirational.

SUNBURY PRESS, INC.

105 S. Market St., Mechanicsburg PA 17055. **E-mail:** info@sunburypress.com. **E-mail:** proposals@sunburypress.com. **Website:** www.sunburypress.com. Estab. 2004. Publishes trade paperback and hardcover originals and reprints; electronic originals and reprints. Sunbury Press, Inc., headquartered in Mechanicsburg, PA is a publisher of trade paperback, hard cover and digital books featuring established and emerging authors in many fiction and non-fiction categories. Sunbury's books are printed in the USA and sold through leading booksellers worldwide. "Please use our online submission form." **Publishes 60 titles/year. Receives 1,000 queries/year; 500 mss/year. 40% of books from first-time authors. 95% from unagented writers. Pays 10% royalty on wholesale price.** Publishes ms 6 months after acceptance. Accepts simultaneous submissions. Responds in 3 months. Catalog and guidelines online.

NONFICTION Subjects include agriculture, Americana, animals, anthropology, archeology, architecture, art, astrology, business, career guidance, child guidance, communications, computers, contemporary culture, counseling, crafts, creative nonfiction, economics, education, electronics, entertainment, ethnic, film, finance, government, health, history, hobbies, house and home, humanities, labor, language, law, literature, medicine, memoirs, military, money, multicultural, music, nature, New Age, parenting, philosophy, politics, pop culture, psychic, psychology, public affairs, real estate, recreation, regional, religion, science, sex, sociology, spirituality, sports, transportation, travel, true crime, war, womens issues, world affairs, young adult. "We are currently seeking war memoirs of all kinds and local / regional histories and biographies." Reviews artwork.

FICTION Subjects include adventure, confession, contemporary, ethnic, experimental, fantasy, gothic, historical, horror, humor, juvenile, literary, mainstream, military, multicultural, mystery, occult, regional, religious, romance, science fiction, short story collections, spiritual, sports, suspense, war, western, young adult. "We are especially seeking climate change / dystopian fiction and books of regional interest."

POETRY Submit complete ms.

TIPS "Our books appeal to very diverse audiences. We are building our list in many categories, focusing on many demographics. We are not like traditional publishers—we are digitally adept and very creative. Don't be surprised if we move quicker than you are accustomed to!"

SUNRISE RIVER PRESS

838 Lake St. S., Forest Lake MN 55025. (800)895-4585. **Fax:** (651)277-1203. **E-mail:** info@sunriseriverpress. com. **E-mail:** submissions@sunriseriverpress.com. **Website:** www.sunriseriverpress.com. Estab. 1992. "E-mail is preferred method of contact." **Publishes 30 titles/year. Pays advance.** Accepts simultaneous submissions. Guidelines online.

Sunrise River Press is part of a 3-company publishing house that also includes CarTech Books and Specialty Press. "Sunrise River Press is currently seeking book proposals from health/medical writers or experts who are interested in authoring consumer-geared trade paperbacks on healthcare, fitness, and nutrition topics."

NONFICTION Subjects include genetics, immune system maintenance, fitness; also some professional healthcare titles. Check website for submission guidelines. No phone calls, please; no originals.

SUNSTONE PRESS

Box 2321, Santa Fe NM 87504. (800)243-5644. **Website:** www.sunstonepress.com. **Contact:** Submissions Editor. Sunstone's original focus was on nonfiction subjects that preserved and highlighted the richness of the American Southwest but it has expanded its view over the years to include mainstream themes and categories—both nonfiction and fiction—that have a more general appeal. Accepts simultaneous submissions. Guidelines online.
NONFICTION Query with 1 sample chapter.
FICTION Query with 1 sample chapter.

SUPERCOLLEGE

3286 Oak Ct., Belmont CA 94002. (650)618-2221. **Website:** www.supercollege.com. Estab. 1998. Publishes trade paperback originals. "We only publish books on admission, financial aid, scholarships, test preparation, student life, and career preparation for college and graduate students." **Publishes 8-10 titles/ year. 50% of books from first-time authors. 70% from unagented writers. Pays royalty on wholesale price or makes outright purchase.** Publishes ms 7-9 months after acceptance. Accepts simultaneous submissions. Book catalog and writers guidelines online.

NONFICTION Subjects include education. Submit complete ms. Reviews artwork/photos. Send photocopies.
TIPS "We want titles that are student and parent friendly, and that are different from other titles in this category. We also seek authors who want to work with a small but dynamic and ambitious publishing company."

SWAN SCYTHE PRESS

1468 Mallard Way, Sunnyvale CA 94087. **E-mail:** robert.pesich@gmail.com. **Website:** www.swanscythepress.com. **Contact:** Robert Pesich, editor. Estab. 1999. Accepts simultaneous submissions.
POETRY "Swan Scythe Press, a publishing group located in Northern California, is committed to discovering and publishing the best new poets in America today. Its authors have won many national and local grants, awards and fellowships, and have distinguished themselves as artists and educators throughout the U.S. and in foreign countries. Founding Editor and Publisher Sandra McPherson, a widely-known and honored poet, along with the present Editor, James DenBoer, have now turned over the editorial functions of the press to Robert Pesich." Query first before submitting a ms via e-mail or through website.

SWEDENBORG FOUNDATION

320 N. Church St., West Chester PA 19380. (610)430-3222. **Fax:** (610)430-7982. **E-mail:** info@swedenborg.com. **Website:** www.swedenborg.com. Estab. 1849. Publishes trade paperback originals and reprints. The Swedenborg Foundation publishes books by and about Emanuel Swedenborg (1688-1772), his ideas, how his ideas have influenced others, and related topics. Appropriate topics include Swedenborgian concepts, such as: near-death experience, angels, Biblical interpretation, mysteries of good and evil, etc. A work must actively engage the thought of Emanuel Swedenborg and show an understanding of his philosophy in order to be accepted for publication. **Publishes 5 titles/year.** Responds in 1 month to queries; 3 months to proposals and mss. Book catalog available free. Guidelines online.
NONFICTION Subjects include philosophy, religion, spirituality. Submit proposal package, outline, sample chapters, synopsis via e-mail. Reviews artwork/photos. Send photocopies.

🍬 SWEET CHERRY PUBLISHING

Unit 36, Vulcan Business Complex, Vulcan Rd., Leicester Leicestershire LE5 3EF, United Kingdom. **E-mail:** info@sweetcherrypublishing.com. **E-mail:** submissions@sweetcherrypublishing.com. **Website:** www.sweetcherrypublishing.com. Estab. 2011. Sweet Cherry Publishing is an independent publishing company based in Leicester. Our aim is to provide children with compelling worlds and engaging characters that they will want to revisit time and time again. **Offers one-time fee for work that is accepted.** Accepts simultaneous submissions. Guidelines online.

NONFICTION Freelance illustrators are welcome to submit via our website.

FICTION Subjects include adventure, contemporary, ethnic, fantasy, gothic, horror, humor, juvenile, mainstream, multicultural, picture books, science fiction, young adult. No erotica. Submit a cover letter and a synopsis with 3 sample chapters via post or e-mail. Please note that we strongly prefer e-mail submissions.

TIPS "We strongly prefer e-mail submissions over postal submissions. If your work is accepted, Sweet Cherry may consider commissioning you for future series."

SYRACUSE UNIVERSITY PRESS

621 Skytop Rd., Suite 110, Syracuse NY 13244. (315)443-5534. **Fax:** (315)443-5545. **E-mail:** seguiod@syr.edu; dmmanion@syr.edu. **Website:** syracuseuniversitypress.syr.edu. **Contact:** Suzanne Guiod, editor-in-chief; Deborah Manion, acquisitions editor. Estab. 1943. "Currently emphasizing Middle East studies, Jewish studies, Irish studies, peace studies, disability studies, television and popular culture, sports and entertainment, Native American studies, gender and ethnic studies, New York State." **Publishes 50 titles/year. 25% of books from first-time authors. 95% from unagented writers.** Publishes book 15 months after acceptance. Book catalog online. Guidelines online.

NONFICTION Subjects include anthropology, history, humanities, literature, politics, pop culture, regional, religion, sociology, sports, translation, womens studies. "Special opportunity in our nonfiction program for books on New York state, sports history, Jewish studies, Irish studies, the Middle East, religion and politics, television and popular culture, disability studies, peace studies, Native American studies. Provide precise descriptions of subjects, along with background description of project. The author must make a case for the importance of his or her subject." Submit query via e-mail with the book proposal form found on our website and a copy of your CV. Reviews artwork/photos.

TIPS "We're seeking well-written and thoroughly researched books that will make a significant contribution to the subject areas listed above and will be favorably received in the marketplace."

🌍 TAFELBERG PUBLISHERS

Imprint of NB Publishers, P.O. Box 879, Cape Town 8000, South Africa. (27)(21)406-3033. **Fax:** (27)(21)406-3812. **E-mail:** engela.reinke@nb.co.za. **Website:** www.tafelberg.com. **Contact:** Engela Reinke. General publisher best known for Afrikaans fiction, authoritative political works, children's/youth literature, and a variety of illustrated and nonillustrated nonfiction. **Publishes 10 titles/year. Pays authors royalty of 15-18% based on wholesale price.** Publishes book 1 year after acceptance. Accepts simultaneous submissions. Responds to queries in 2 weeks; mss in 6 months.

NONFICTION Subjects include memoirs, politics. Submit outline, information on intended market, bio, and 1-2 sample chapters.

FICTION Subjects include juvenile, romance. Picture books, young readers: animal, anthology, contemporary, fantasy, folktales, hi-lo, humor, multicultural, nature/environment, scient fiction, special needs. Middle readers, young adults: animal (middle reader only), contemporary, fantasy, hi-lo, humor, multicultural, nature/environment, problem novels, science fiction, special needs, sports, suspense/mystery. Average word length: picture books—1,500-7,500; young readers—25,000; middle readers—15,000; young adults—40,000. Submit complete ms.

TIPS "Writers: Story needs to have a South African or African style. Illustrators: I'd like to look, but the chances of getting commissioned are slim. The market is small and difficult. Do not expect huge advances. Editorial staff attended or plans to attend the following conferences: IBBY, Frankfurt, SCBWI Bologna."

🅰️🌗 NAN A. TALESE

Imprint of Doubleday, Random House, 1745 Broadway, New York NY 10019. (212)782-8918. **Fax:** (212)782-8448. **Website:** www.nanatalese.com. Publishes hardcover originals. Nan A. Talese publishes nonfiction with a powerful guiding narrative and relevance to larger cultural interests, and literary fiction of the highest quality. **Publishes 15 titles/year. 400 queries received/year. 400 mss received/year. Pays variable royalty on retail price. Pays varying advance.** Accepts simultaneous submissions.

NONFICTION Subjects include contemporary culture, history, philosophy, sociology. *Agented submissions only.*

FICTION Subjects include literary. Well-written narratives with a compelling story line, good characterization and use of language. We like stories with an edge. *Agented submissions only.*

TIPS "Audience is highly literate people interested in story, information and insight. We want well-written material submitted by agents only. See our website."

TANTOR MEDIA

Recorded Books, 6 Business Park Rd., Old Saybrook CT 06475. (860)395-1155. **Fax:** (860)395-1154. **E-mail:** rightsemail@tantor.com. **Website:** www.tantor.com. **Contact:** Ron Formica, director of acquisitions. Estab. 2001. Publishes audiobooks only. Tantor Media, a division of Recorded Books, is a leading audiobook publisher, producing more than 100 new titles every month. We do not publish print or e-books. **Publishes 1,500 titles/year.** Accepts simultaneous submissions. Responds in 2 months. Catalog online. Not accepting print or e-book queries. We only publish audiobooks.

NONFICTION Subjects include agriculture, alternative lifestyles, Americana, animals, anthropology, astrology, business, child guidance, communications, contemporary culture, cooking, creative nonfiction, economics, education, entertainment, foods, games, gay, government, health, history, horticulture, law, lesbian, literary criticism, marine subjects, memoirs, military, money, multicultural, music, New Age, philosophy, psychology, religion, science, sex, social sciences, sociology, spirituality, sports, womens issues, womens studies, world affairs, young adult. Not accepted print submissions.

FICTION Subjects include adventure, contemporary, erotica, experimental, fantasy, feminist, gay, gothic, historical, horror, humor, juvenile, lesbian, literary, mainstream, military, multicultural, multimedia, mystery, occult, religious, romance, science fiction, short story collections, spiritual, sports, suspense, western, young adult.

TEACHERS COLLEGE PRESS

1234 Amsterdam Ave., New York NY 10027. (212)678-3929. **Fax:** (212)678-4149. **E-mail:** tcp.cs@aidcvt.com. **Website:** www.teacherscollegepress.com. Estab. 1904. Publishes hardcover and paperback originals and reprints. "Teachers College Press publishes a wide range of educational titles for all levels of students: early childhood to higher education. Publishing books that respond to, examine, and confront issues pertaining to education, teacher training, and school reform." **Publishes 60 titles/year. Pays industry standard royalty. Pays advance.** Publishes ms 1 year after acceptance. Responds in 2 months to queries. Book catalog available free. Guidelines online.

NONFICTION Subjects include education, history, philosophy, sociology. This university press concentrates on books in the field of education in the broadest sense, from early childhood to higher education: good classroom practices, teacher training, special education, innovative trends and issues, administration and supervision, film, continuing and adult education, all areas of the curriculum, computers, guidance and counseling, and the politics, economics, philosophy, sociology, and history of education. We have recently added women's studies to our list. The Press also issues classroom materials for students at all levels, with a strong emphasis on reading and writing and social studies. Submit outline, sample chapters.

TEBOT BACH

P.O. Box 7887, Huntington Beach CA 92615. (714)968-0905. **Fax:** (714)968-0905. **E-mail:** info@tebotbach.org. **Website:** www.tebotbach.org. **Contact:** Mifanwy Kaiser, editor/publisher. Estab. 1999. Publishes mss 6 months-1 year after acceptance. Accepts simultaneous submissions. Responds in 3 months.

POETRY Offers 2 contests per year. The Patricia Bibby First Book Contest and The Clockwise Chapbook contest. Go online for more information. Query first via e-mail, with a few sample poems and cover letter with brief bio.

Ⓐ⊘ KATHERINE TEGEN BOOKS

HarperCollins, 10 E. 53rd St., New York NY 10022. **Website:** www.harpercollins.com. Estab. 2003. Katherine Tegen Books publishes high-quality, commercial literature for children of all ages, including teens. Talented authors and illustrators who offer powerful narratives that are thought-provoking, well-written, and entertaining are the core of the Katherine Tegen

Books imprint. *Katherine Tegen Books accepts agented work only.*

TEMPLE UNIVERSITY PRESS

1852 N. 10th St., Philadelphia PA 19122. (215)926-2140. **Fax:** (215)926-2141. **Website:** www.temple.edu/tempress/. Estab. 1969. "Temple University Press has been publishing path-breaking books on Asian-Americans, law, gender issues, film, women's studies and other interesting areas for nearly 40 years." **Publishes 60 titles/year. Pays advance.** Publishes ms 10 months after acceptance. Responds in 2 months to queries. Book catalog available free. Guidelines online.

NONFICTION Subjects include ethnic, history, photography, regional, sociology, labor studies, urban studies, Latin American/Latino, Asian American, African American studies, public policy, women's studies. No memoirs, fiction or poetry. Query with SASE. Reviews artwork/photos.

❷⊘ TEN SPEED PRESS

Penguin Random House, The Crown Publishing Group, Attn: Acquisitions, 2625 Alcatraz Ave. #505, Berkeley CA 94705. (510)559-1600. **Fax:** (510)524-1052. **Website:** crownpublishing.com/imprint/ten-speed-press. Estab. 1971. Publishes trade paperback originals and reprints. "Ten Speed Press publishes authoritative books for an audience interested in innovative ideas. Currently emphasizing cookbooks, career, business, alternative education, and offbeat general nonfiction gift books." **Publishes 120 titles/year. 40% of books from first-time authors. 40% from unagented writers. Pays $2,500 average advance.** Publishes ms 1 year after acceptance. Accepts simultaneous submissions. Responds in 3 months to queries; 6-8 weeks to proposals. Book catalog for 9×12 envelope and 6 first-class stamps. Guidelines online.

NONFICTION Subjects include business, career guidance, cooking, crafts, relationships, how-to, humor, and pop culture. *Agented submissions only.*

TIPS "We like books from people who really know their subject, rather than people who think they've spotted a trend to capitalize on. We like books that will sell for a long time, rather than 9-day wonders. Our audience consists of a well-educated, slightly weird group of people who like food, the outdoors, and take a light, but serious, approach to business and careers. Study the backlist of each publisher you're submitting to and tailor your proposal to what you perceive as their needs. Nothing gets a publisher's attention like someone who knows what he or she is talking about, and nothing falls flat like someone who obviously has no idea who he or she is submitting to."

TEXAS TECH UNIVERSITY PRESS

1120 Main St., Second Floor, Box 41037, Lubbock TX 79415. (806)742-2982. **Fax:** (806)742-2979. **E-mail:** ttup@ttu.edu. **Website:** www.ttupress.org. Estab. 1971. Texas Tech University Press, the book publishing office of the university since 1971 and an AAUP member since 1986, publishes nonfiction titles in the areas of natural history and the natural sciences; 18th century and Joseph Conrad studies; studies of modern Southeast Asia, particularly the Vietnam War; costume and textile history; Latin American literature and culture; and all aspects of the Great Plains and the American West, especially history, biography, memoir, sports history, and travel. In addition, the Press publishes several scholarly journals, acclaimed series for young readers, an annual invited poetry collection, and literary fiction of Texas and the West. Accepts simultaneous submissions. Guidelines online.

NONFICTION Subjects include environment, ethnic, history, law, literary criticism, literature, regional, sports. Submit proposal that includes introduction, 2 sample chapters, cover letter, working title, anticipated ms length, description of audience, comparison of book to others published on the subject, brief bio or CV.

FICTION Subjects include ethnic, multicultural, religious, western. Fiction rooted in the American West and Southwest, Jewish literature, Latin American and Latino fiction (in translation or English).

POETRY "TTUP publishes an annual invited first-book poetry manuscript (please note that we cannot entertain unsolicited poetry submissions)."

⊘ TEXAS WESTERN PRESS

The University of Texas at El Paso, 500 W. University Ave., El Paso TX 79968. (915)747-5688. **Fax:** (915)747-5345. **E-mail:** ctavarez@utep.edu. **Website:** twp.utep.edu. **Contact:** Carmen P. Tavarez. Estab. 1952. Publishes hardcover and paperback originals. "Texas Western Press publishes books on the history and cultures of the American Southwest, particularly historical and biographical works about West Texas, New Mexico, northern Mexico, and the U.S. borderlands." **Publishes 1 titles/year. Pays standard 10% royalty. Pays advance.** Responds in 2 months to queries. Book catalog available free. Guidelines online.

IMPRINTS Southwestern Studies.

NONFICTION Subjects include education, history, regional, science, social sciences. "Historic and cultural accounts of the Southwest (West Texas, New Mexico, northern Mexico). Also art, photographic books, Native American and limited regional fiction reprints." *Not currently seeking mss.*

TIPS "We try to treat our authors professionally, produce handsome, long-lived books and aim for quality, rather than quantity of titles carrying our imprint."

THISTLEDOWN PRESS LTD.

410 2nd Ave., Saskatoon SK S7K 2C3, Canada. (306)244-1722. **Fax:** (306)244-1762. **E-mail:** editorial@thistledownpress.com. **Website:** www.thistledownpress.com. **Contact:** Allan Forrie, publisher. Estab. 1975. "Thistledown originates books by Canadian authors only, although we have co-published titles by authors outside Canada. We do not publish children's picture books." **150 -250 40% of books from first-time authors. 40% from unagented writers. Pays authors royalty of 10-12% based on net dollar sales. Pays illustrators and photographers by the project (range: $250-750). Rarely pays advance.** Publishes book 1 year after acceptance. Responds to queries in 6 months. Book catalog on website. Guidelines online.

NONFICTION Subjects include environment, literature, young adult.

FICTION Subjects include literary, short story collections. Young adults: adventure, anthology, contemporary, fantasy, humor, poetry, romance, science fiction, suspense/mystery, short stories. Average word length: young adults—40,000. Submit outline/synopsis and sample chapters. *Does not accept mss.* Do not query by e-mail. "Please note: we are not accepting middle years (ages 8-12) nor children's manuscripts at this time." See Submission Guidelines on Website.

POETRY "We do not publish cowboy poetry, inspirational poetry, or poetry for children."

TIPS "Send cover letter including publishing history and SASE."

THOMSON REUTERS

One Corporate Plaza, 2075 Kennedy Rd., Toronto ON M1T 3V4, Canada. (416)298-5024. **Fax:** (416)298-5094. **Website:** www.carswell.com. Publishes hardcover originals. "Thomson Carswell is Canada's national resource of information and legal interpretations for law, accounting, tax and business professionals." **Publishes 150-200 titles/year. 30-50% of books from first-time authors. Pays 5-15% royalty on wholesale price.** Publishes ms 6 months after acceptance. Accepts simultaneous submissions. Responds in 3 months to queries. Book catalog and ms guidelines free.

NONFICTION Canadian information of a regulatory nature is our mandate. Submit proposal package, outline, resume.

TIPS "Audience is Canada and persons interested in Canadian information; professionals in law, tax, accounting fields; business people interested in regulatory material."

THUNDERSTONE BOOKS

6575 Horse Dr., Las Vegas NV 89131. **E-mail:** info@thunderstonebooks.com. **Website:** www.thunderstonebooks.com. **Contact:** Rachel Noorda, editorial director. Estab. 2014. Publishes hardcover, trade paperback, mass market paperback, and electronic originals. "At ThunderStone Books, we aim to publish children's books that have an educational aspect. We are not looking for curriculum for learning certain subjects, but rather stories that encourage learning for children, whether that be learning about a new language/culture or learning more about science and math in a fun, fictional format. We want to help children to gain a love for other languages and subjects so that they are curious about the world around them. We are currently accepting fiction and nonfiction submissions. Picture books without accompanying illustration will not be accepted." **Publishes 2-5 titles/year. Receives 30 queries and mss/year. 100% of books from first-time authors. 100% from unagented writers. Pays 5-15% royalties on retail price. Pays $300-1,000 advance.** Publishes ms 6 months after acceptance. Accepts simultaneous submissions. Responds in 3 months. Catalog available for SASE. Guidelines available.

NONFICTION Subjects include creative nonfiction, education, language, literature, multicultural, regional, science, translation. Looking for engaging educational materials, not a set curriculum, but books that teach as well as have some fun. Open to a variety of educational subjects, but specialty and main interest lies in language exposure/learning, science, math, and history. Reviews photocopies of artwork.

FICTION Subjects include multicultural, picture books, regional. Interested in multicultural stories with an emphasis on authentic culture and language (these may include mythology). "If you think your book is right for us, send a query letter with a word attachment of the first 50 pages to info@thunderstonebooks.com. If it is a picture book or chapter book for young readers that is shorter than 50 pages send the entire manuscript."

TIA CHUCHA PRESS

13197 Gladstone Ave., Unit A, Sylmar CA 91342. (818)939-3433. **Fax:** (818)367-5600. **E-mail:** info@tiachucha.com. **Website:** www.tiachucha.com. Interim Executive Director: Trini Rodriguez. Estab. 1989. Publishes hardcover and trade paperback originals. Tia Chucha's Centro Cultural is a nonprofit learning and cultural arts center. "We support and promote the continued growth, development and holistic learning of our community through the many powerful means of the arts. Tia Centra provides a positive space for people to activate what we all share as humans: the capacity to create, to imagine and to express ourselves in an effort to improve the quality of life for our community." **Publishes 2-4 titles/year. 25-30 queries received/year. 150 mss received/year. Pays 10% royalty on wholesale price.** Publishes ms 1 year after acceptance. Responds in 9 months to mss. Guidelines online.

POETRY No restrictions as to style or content. "We only publish poetry at this time. We do cross-cultural and performance-oriented poetry. It has to work on the page, however." Query and submit complete ms.

TIPS "We will cultivate the practice. Audience is those interested."

◑⊘ TIGHTROPE BOOKS

#207-2 College St., Toronto ON M5G 1K3, Canada. (416)928-6666. **E-mail:** tightropeasst@gmail.com. **Website:** www.tightropebooks.com. Estab. 2005. Publishes trade paperback originals. **Publishes 12 titles/year. 60% of books from first-time authors. 90% from unagented writers. Pays 5-15% royalty on retail price. Pays advance of $200-300.** Publishes book 1-2 years after acceptance. Accepts simultaneous submissions. Responds if interested. Catalog and guidelines online.

◑ Accepting submissions for literary fiction, nonfiction and poetry from Canadian citizens and permanent Canadian residents only.

NONFICTION Subjects include alternative lifestyles, art, contemporary culture, creative nonfiction, ethnic, gay, language, lesbian, literary criticism, literature, memoirs, multicultural, womens issues, womens studies. No genres

FICTION Subjects include contemporary, ethnic, experimental, feminist, gay, lesbian, literary, multicultural, poetry, poetry in translation, short story collections, young adult.

TIPS "Audience is urban, literary, educated, unconventional."

TILBURY HOUSE PUBLISHERS

WordSplice Studio, Inc., 12 Starr St., Thomaston ME 04861. (800)582-1899. **Fax:** (207)582-8772. **E-mail:** info@tilburyhouse.com. **Website:** www.tilburyhouse.com. Estab. 1990. **Publishes 10 titles/year. Pays royalty based on wholesale price.** Publishes ms 1 year after acceptance. Accepts simultaneous submissions. Responds to mss in 3 months. Guidelines and catalog online.

NONFICTION Regional adult biography/history/maritime/nature, and children's picture books that deal with issues, such as bullying, multiculturalism, etc., science/nature. Submit complete ms for picture books or outline/synopsis for longer works. Now uses online submission form. Reviews artwork/photos. Send photocopies.

FICTION Picture books: multicultural, nature/environment. Special needs include books that teach children about tolerance and honoring diversity. Send art/photography samples and/or complete ms to Audrey Maynard, children's book editor.

TIPS "We are always interested in stories that will encourage children to understand the natural world and the environment, as well as stories with social justice themes. We really like stories that engage children to become problem solvers as well as those that promote respect, tolerance and compassion. We do not publish books with personified animal characters; historical fiction; YA or middle grade fiction or chapter books; fantasy."

ⒶTIN HOUSE BOOKS

2617 NW Thurman St., Portland OR 97210. (503)473-8663. **Fax:** (503)473-8957. **E-mail:** masie@tinhouse.com. **Website:** www.tinhouse.com. **Contact:** Masie Cochran, editor; Tony Perez, editor. Publishes hardcover originals, paperback originals, paperback reprints. "We are a small independent publisher dedicated to nurturing new, promising talent as well as showcasing the work of established writers." Distributes/promotes titles through W. W. Norton. **Publish-**

es 10-12 titles/year. Publishes ms 1 year after acceptance. Accepts simultaneous submissions. Responds to queries in 2-3 weeks; mss in 2-3 months. Guidelines online.

NONFICTION *Agented mss only.* "We no longer read unsolicited submissions by authors with no representation. We will continue to accept submissions from agents."

FICTION *Agented mss only.* "We no longer read unsolicited submissions by authors with no representation. We will continue to accept submissions from agents."

TITAN PRESS

PMB 17897, Encino CA 91416. **E-mail:** titan91416@yahoo.com. **Website:** https://www.facebook.com/RVClef. **Contact:** Romana V. Clef, editor. Estab. 1981. Publishes hardcover and paperback originals. Little literary publisher. **Publishes 12 titles/year. Receives 100-200 submissions/year. 50% from unagented writers. Pays 20-40% royalty.** Publishes ms 1 year after acceptance. Accepts simultaneous submissions. Responds to queries in 3 months.

NONFICTION Subjects include creative nonfiction, entertainment, literary criticism.

FICTION Subjects include contemporary, literary, mainstream, short story collections. Does not accept unsolicited mss. Query with SASE. Include brief bio, list of publishing credits.

POETRY Literary, not MFA banality.

TIPS "Look, act, sound, and *be* professional."

TOP COW PRODUCTIONS, INC.

3812 Dunn Dr., Culver City CA 90232. **Website:** www.topcow.com. Accepts simultaneous submissions. Guidelines online.

FICTION *No unsolicited submissions.* Prefers submissions from artists. See website for details and advice on how to break into the market.

TOR BOOKS

Tom Doherty Associates, 175 Fifth Ave., New York NY 10010. **Website:** www.tor-forge.com. Tor Books is the "world's largest publisher of science fiction and fantasy, with strong category publishing in historical fiction, mystery, western/Americana, thriller, YA." **Publishes 10-20 titles/year. Pays author royalty. Pays illustrators by the project.** Accepts simultaneous submissions. Book catalog available. Guidelines online.

FICTION Subjects include adventure, fantasy, historical, humor, mystery, picture books, science fiction, suspense, young adult. Submit first 3 chapters, 3-10 page synopsis, dated cover letter, SASE.

TORREY HOUSE PRESS

2806 Melony Dr., Salt Lake City UT 84124. **E-mail:** kirsten@torreyhouse.com. **Website:** torreyhouse.org. **Contact:** Kirsten Allen. Estab. 2010. Publishes hardcover, trade paperback, and electronic originals. Torrey House Press is an independent nonprofit publisher promoting environmental conservation through literature. **Publishes 6 titles/year. Receives 500 queries/year; 200 mss/year. 50% of books from first-time authors. 80% from unagented writers. Pays 5-15% royalty on retail price.** Publishes ms 12-18 months after acceptance. Accepts simultaneous submissions. Responds in 3 months. Catalog online. Guidelines online.

NONFICTION Subjects include creative nonfiction, environment, nature. Query; submit proposal package, including: outline, ms, bio. Does not review artwork.

FICTION Subjects include historical, literary. "Torrey House Press publishes literary fiction and creative nonfiction about the world environment and the American West." Submit proposal package including: synopsis, complete ms, bio.

POETRY Query; submit complete ms.

TIPS "Include writing experience (none okay)."

⊙ TOUCHWOOD EDITIONS

The Heritage Group, 103-1075 Pendergast St., Victoria BC V8V 0A1, Canada. (250)360-0829. **Fax:** (250)386-0829. **E-mail:** edit@touchwoodeditions.com. **Website:** www.touchwoodeditions.com. **Contact:** Renée Layberry, Editor. Publishes trade paperback, originals and reprints. **Publishes 20-25 titles/year. 40% of books from first-time authors. 70% from unagented writers. Pays 15% royalty on net price.** Publishes ms 12-24 months after acceptance. Accepts simultaneous submissions. Responds in 6 months to queries. Book catalog and guidelines online.

NONFICTION Subjects include cooking, creative nonfiction, history, memoirs, recreation, regional, regional travel or guidebooks with a focus on food, wine, art or similar topics, regional history or biography, biography (well-known and western Canadian figures only), cultural studies, aboriginal history and writing, for adult and young readers, historical fiction, relating to western Canada. Submit TOC, outline, word count,

2-3 sample chapters, synopsis. Reviews artwork/photos. Send photocopies.

FICTION Subjects include historical, mainstream, mystery, regional. Submit bio/CV, marketing plan, TOC, outline, word count.

TIPS "Our area of interest is western Canada. We would like more creative nonfiction and fiction from First Nations authors, and welcome authors who write about notable individuals in Canada's history. Please note we do not publish poetry."

TOWER PUBLISHING

588 Saco Rd., Standish ME 04084. (207)642-5400. **Fax:** (207)642-5463. **E-mail:** info@towerpub.com. **E-mail:** michaell@towerpub.com. **Website:** www.towerpub.com. **Contact:** Michael Lyons, president. Estab. 1772. Publishes hardcover originals and reprints, trade paperback originals. Tower Publishing specializes in legal publications. **Publishes 22 titles/year. 60 queries; 30 mss received/year. 10% of books from first-time authors. 90% from unagented writers.** Publishes ms 6 months after acceptance. Accepts simultaneous submissions. Responds in 1 month to queries; 2 months to proposals and mss. Book catalog and ms guidelines online.

NONFICTION Subjects include law. Looking for legal books of a national stature. Query with SASE. Submit outline.

◎ TRADEWIND BOOKS

202-1807 Maritime Mews, Granville Island, Vancouver BC V6H 3W7, Canada. (604)662-4405. **Website:** www.tradewindbooks.com. Publishes hardcover and trade paperback originals. "Tradewind Books publishes juvenile picture books and young adult novels. Requires that submissions include evidence that author has read at least 3 titles published by Tradewind Books." **Publishes 5 titles/year. 15% of books from first-time authors. 50% from unagented writers. Pays 7% royalty on retail price. Pays variable advance.** Publishes book 3 years after acceptance. Accepts simultaneous submissions. Responds to mss in 2 months. Book catalog and ms guidelines online.

FICTION Subjects include juvenile, multicultural, picture books. Average word length: 900 words. Send complete ms for picture books. *YA novels by Canadian authors only. Chapter books by US authors considered.* For chapter books/Middle Grade Fiction, submit the first three chapters, a chapter outline and plot summary.

POETRY Please send a book-length collection only.

TRAFALGAR SQUARE BOOKS

388 Howe Hill Rd., P.O. Box 257, North Pomfret VT 05053. (802)457-1911. **Website:** www.horseandriderbooks.com. **Contact:** Rebecca Didier. Estab. 1985. Publishes hardcover and trade paperback originals. "We publish high-quality instructional books for horsemen and horsewomen, always with the horse's welfare in mind." **Publishes 12 titles/year. 50% of books from first-time authors. 80% from unagented writers. Pays royalty. Pays advance.** Publishes ms 18 months after acceptance. Responds in 1 month to queries; 2 months to proposals; 2-3 months to mss. Catalog free on request and by e-mail.

NONFICTION Subjects include animals. "We rarely consider books for complete novices." Query with SASE. Submit proposal package including outline, 1-3 sample chapters, letter of introduction including qualifications for writing on the subject and why the proposed book is an essential addition to existing publications. Reviews artwork/photos as part of the ms package. We prefer color laser thumbnail sheets or duplicate prints (do not send original photos or art!).

TIPS "Our audience is comprised of horse lovers and riders interested in pursuing their passion and/or sport while doing what is best for horses."

TRAVELERS' TALES

Solas House, Inc., 2320 Bowdoin St., Palo Alto CA 94306. (650)462-2110. **Fax:** (650)462-6305. **Website:** www.travelerstales.com. Estab. 1993. Publishes inspirational travel books, mostly anthologies and travel advice books. "Due to the volume of submissions, we do not respond unless the material submitted meets our immediate editorial needs. All stories are read and filed for future use contingent upon meeting editorial guidelines." **Publishes 4-6 titles/year. Receives hundreds of submissions/year. 30% of books from first-time authors. 80% from unagented writers. Pays $100 honorarium for anthology pieces. Does not pay advance.** Accepts simultaneous submissions. "We contact you if we'd like to publish your work.". Guidelines online.

NONFICTION Subjects include creative nonfiction, literature, memoirs, spirituality, travel, womens issues, world affairs. Subjects include all aspects of travel.

TIPS "We publish personal nonfiction stories and anecdotes—funny, illuminating, adventurous, frightening, or grim. Stories should reflect that unique alchemy that occurs when you enter unfamiliar territory and begin to see the world differently as a result. Stories that have already been published, including book excerpts, are welcome as long as the authors retain the copyright or can obtain permission from the copyright holder to reprint the material."

TRIANGLE SQUARE

Seven Stories Press, 140 Watts St., New York NY 10013. (212)226-8760. **Fax:** (212)226-1411. **E-mail:** info@sevenstories.com. **Website:** https://www.sevenstories.com/imprints/triangle-square. Triangle Square is a children's and young adult imprint of Seven Story Press. Accepts simultaneous submissions.
FICTION Send a cover letter with 2 sample chapters and SASE. Send c/o Acquisitions.

THE TRINITY FOUNDATION

P.O. Box 68, Unicoi TN 37692. (423)743-0199. **Fax:** (423)743-2005. **E-mail:** tjtrinityfound@aol.com. **Website:** www.trinityfoundation.org. **Contact:** Thomas W. Juodaitis, editor. Publishes hardcover and paperback originals and reprints. **Publishes 2-3 titles/year.** Publishes ms 9 months after acceptance. Accepts simultaneous submissions. Responds in 1 month to queries and proposals; 3 months to mss. Book catalog online.
NONFICTION Subjects include economics, education, philosophy, religion. Only books that conform to the philosophy and theology of the Westminster Confession of Faith. Textbooks subjects include business/economics, education, government/politics, history, philosophy, religion, science. Query with SASE.

TRISTAN PUBLISHING

2355 Louisiana Ave. N, Golden Valley MN 55427. (763)545-1383. **Fax:** (763)545-1387. **E-mail:** info@tristanpublishing.com; manuscripts@tristanpublishing.com. **Website:** www.tristanpublishing.com. **Contact:** Brett Waldman, publisher. Estab. 2002. Publishes hardcover originals. **Publishes 6-10 titles/year. 1,000 queries and mss/year. 15% of books from first-time authors. 100% from unagented writers. Pays royalty on wholesale or retail price; outright purchase.** Publishes book 2 years after acceptance. Accepts simultaneous submissions. Responds in 3 months. Catalog and guidelines online.
NONFICTION Subjects include inspirational. "Our mission is to create books with a message that inspire and uplift in typically 1,000 words or less." Query

with SASE; submit completed mss. Reviews artwork/photos; send photocopies.
FICTION Subjects include inspirational, gift books. Query with SASE; submit completed mss.
TIPS "Our audience is adults and children."

TRIUMPH BOOKS

814 N. Franklin St., Chicago IL 60610. (312)337-0747. **Fax:** (312)280-5470. **Website:** www.triumphbooks. com. Estab. 1990. Publishes hardcover originals and trade paperback originals and reprints. Accepts simultaneous submissions. Book catalog available free.
NONFICTION Subjects include recreation, sports, health, sports business/motivation. Query with SASE. Reviews artwork/photos. Send photocopies.

TRUMAN STATE UNIVERSITY PRESS

100 E. Normal Ave., Kirksville MO 63501. (660)785-7336. **Fax:** (660)785-4480. **E-mail:** tsup@truman. edu. **E-mail:** bsm@truman.edu. **Website:** tsup.truman.edu. **Contact:** Barbara Smith-Mandell, editor-in-chief. Estab. 1986. Truman State University Press (TSUP) publishes peer-reviewed research in the humanities for the scholarly community and the broader public, and publishes creative literary works. Accepts simultaneous submissions. Guidelines online.
NONFICTION Subjects include creative nonfiction, history, contemporary nonfiction, early modern studies, American Midwest, poetry. Submit book ms proposals in American Midwest/American history and in creative nonfiction to Barbara Smith-Mandell at bsm@truman.edu; early modern studies to Michael. Wolfe@qc.cuny.edu.
POETRY Not accepting unsolicited poetry mss. Submit to annual T.S. Eliot Prize for Poetry.

TU BOOKS

Lee & Low Books, 95 Madison Ave., Suite #1205, New York NY 10016. **Website:** www.leeandlow.com/imprints/3. **Contact:** Stacy Whitman, Publisher. Estab. 2010. Young adult and middle grade novels and graphic novels: science fiction, fantasy, contemporary realism, mystery, historical fiction, and more, with particular interest in books with strong literary hooks. The Tu imprint spans many genres: science fiction, fantasy, mystery, contemporary, and more. We don't believe in labels or limits, just great stories. Join us at the crossroads where fantasy and real life collide. You'll be glad you did. **Publishes 3-6 titles/year. 25% of books from first-time authors. Advance against**

royalties. Pays advance. Accepts simultaneous submissions. Responds only if interested.

○ For new writers of color, please be aware of the New Visions Award writing contest, which runs every year from June-October. Previously unpublished writers of color and Native American writers may submit their middle grade and young adult novels. See submission guidelines for the contest at https://www.lee-andlow.com/writers-illustrators/new-visions-award.

NONFICTION Not seeking nonfiction. Graphic novel manuscripts for author/illustrators as well as portfolios of illustrators for cover art/spot art in illustrated novels. Submission guidelines at https://www.leeandlow.com/writers-illustrators/illustrator-guide-lines-tu-books.

FICTION Subjects include adventure, comic books, contemporary, ethnic, fantasy, hi-lo, historical, horror, juvenile, literary, multicultural, mystery, romance, science fiction, sports, suspense, translation, war, young adult, Middle grade. At Tu Books, an imprint of Lee & Low Books, our focus is on well-told, exciting, adventurous fantasy, science fiction, and mystery novels and graphic novels starring people of color. We also selectively publish realism that explores the contemporary and historical experiences of people of color. We look for fantasy set in worlds inspired by non-Western folklore or culture, contemporary mysteries and fantasy set all over the world starring people of color, and science fiction that centers the possibilities for people of color in the future. We welcome intersectional narratives that feature LGBTQIA and disabled POC as heroes in their own stories. We are looking specifically for stories for both middle grade (ages 8-12) and young adult (ages 12-18) readers. Occasionally a manuscript might fall between those two categories; if your manuscript does, let us know. We are not looking for picture books, chapter books, or short stories at this time. Please do not send submissions in these categories. Unsolicited mss should be submitted online.

TUMBLEHOME LEARNING

P.O. Box 71386, Boston MA 02117. **E-mail:** info@tumblehomelearning.com. **E-mail:** submissions@tumblehomelearning.com. **Website:** www.tumblehome-learning.com. **Contact:** Pendred Noyce, editor. Estab. 2011. Publishes hardcover, trade paperback, and electronic originals. Tumblehome Learning helps kids imagine themselves as young scientists or engineers and encourages them to experience science through adventure and discovery. "We do this with exciting mystery and adventure tales as well as experiments carefully designed to engage students from ages 8 and up." **Publishes 8-10 titles/year. Receives 20 queries and 20 mss/year. 50% of books from first-time authors. 100% from unagented writers. Pays authors 8-12% royalties on retail price. Pays $500 advance.** Publishes ms 8 months after acceptance. Accepts simultaneous submissions. Responds in 1 month to queries and proposals, and 2 months to mss. Catalog available online. Guidelines available on request for SASE.

NONFICTION Subjects include science. Rarely publishes nonfiction. Book would need to be sold to trade, not just the school market.

FICTION Subjects include adventure, juvenile. "All our fiction has science at its heart. This can include using science to solve a mystery (see *The Walking Fish* by Rachelle Burk or *Something Stinks!* by Gail Hedrick), realistic science fiction, books in our Galactic Academy of Science series, science-based adventure tales, and the occasional picture book with a science theme, such as appreciation of the stars and constellations in *Elizabeth's Constellation Quilt* by Olivia Fu. A graphic novel about science would also be welcome." Submit completed ms electronically.

TIPS "Please don't submit to us if your book is not about science. We don't accept generic books about animals or books with glaring scientific errors in the first chapter. That said, the book should be fun to read and the science content can be subtle. We work closely with authors, including first-time authors, to edit and improve their books. As a small publisher, the greatest benefit we can offer is this friendly and respectful partnership with authors."

◎ TURNSTONE PRESS

Artspace Building, 206-100 Arthur St., Winnipeg MB R3B 1H3, Canada. (204)947-1555. **Fax:** (204)942-1555. **Website:** www.turnstonepress.com. **Contact:** Submissions Assistant. Estab. 1976. "Turnstone Press is a literary publisher, not a general publisher, and therefore we are only interested in literary fiction, literary nonfiction—including literary criticism—and poetry. We do publish literary mysteries, thrillers, and noir under our Ravenstone imprint. We publish only Canadian authors or landed immigrants, we strive to publish a significant number of new writers, to publish in a variety of genres, and to have 50% of each year's list be Manitoba writers and/or books with Manitoba content." Publishes ms 2 years after acceptance. Accepts simultaneous submissions. Responds in 4-7 months. Guidelines online.

NONFICTION "Samples must be 40 to 60 pages, typed/printed in a minimum 12 point serif typeface such as Times, Book Antiqua, or Garamond."

FICTION "Samples must be 40 to 60 pages, typed/printed in a minimum 12 point serif typeface such as Times, Book Antiqua, or Garamond."

POETRY Poetry mss should be a minimum 70 pages. Submit complete ms. Include cover letter.

TIPS "As a Canadian literary press, we have a mandate to publish Canadian writers only. Do some homework before submitting works to make sure your subject matter/genre/writing style falls within the publishers area of interest."

TWILIGHT TIMES BOOKS

P.O. Box 3340, Kingsport TN 37664. **E-mail:** publisher@twilighttimesbooks.com. **Website:** www.twilighttimesbooks.com. **Contact:** Andy M. Scott, managing editor. Estab. 1999. "We publish compelling literary fiction by authors with a distinctive voice." Published 5 debut authors within the last year. Averages 120 total titles; 15 fiction titles/year. Member: AAP, PAS, SPAN, SLF. **85% from unagented writers. Pays 8-15% royalty.** Accepts simultaneous submissions. Responds in 4 weeks to queries; 2 months to mss. Guidelines online.

NONFICTION Subjects include creative nonfiction, literary criticism, memoirs, military, nature, New Age, womens studies, young adult.

FICTION Subjects include fantasy, historical, humor, juvenile, literary, mainstream, military, mystery, regional, science fiction, suspense, war, young adult. Accepts unsolicited mss. Do not send complete mss. Queries via e-mail only. Include estimated word count, brief bio, list of publishing credits, marketing plan.

TIPS "The only requirement for consideration at Twilight Times Books is that your novel must be entertaining and professionally written."

TWO DOLLAR RADIO

Website: www.twodollarradio.com. **Contact:** Eric Obenauf, editorial director. Estab. 2005. Two Dollar Radio is a boutique family-run press, publishing bold works of literary merit, each book, individually and collectively, providing a sonic progression that "we believe to be too loud to ignore." Targets readers who admire ambition and creativity. Range of print runs: 2,000-7,500 copies. **Publishes 5-6 (plus a biannual journal of nonfiction essays, *Frequencies*) titles/year. Advance: $500-1,000.**

FICTION Submit entire, completed ms with a brief cover letter, via Submittable. No previously published work. No proposals. No excerpts. There is a $2 reading fee per submission. Accepts submissions every other month (January, March, May, July, September, November).

TIPS "We want writers who show an authority over language and the world that is being created, from the very first sentence on."

TWO SYLVIAS PRESS

P.O. Box 1524, Kingston WA 98346. **E-mail:** twosylviaspress@gmail.com. **Website:** twosylviaspress.com. **Contact:** Kelli Russell Agodon and Annette Spaulding-Convy. Estab. 2010. Two Sylvias Press is an independent press located in the Seattle area. "We publish poetry, memoir, essays, books on the craft of writing, and creativity tools, such as The Poet Tarot and The Daily Poet. The press draws its inspiration from the poetic literary talent of Sylvia Plath and the editorial business sense of Sylvia Beach." Two Sylvias Press values inclusiveness, diversity, respect, creativity, and freedom of expression. "We welcome all readers and writers." Accepts simultaneous submissions. Catalog online.

NONFICTION Subjects include Books on Creativity & Writing Craft. Two Sylvias Press focuses on books of creativity and writing craft/writing prompt books, but also publishes memoir/essay.

POETRY Chapbook & Full Length Poetry Book Prizes. Occasional calls for submissions for specific poetry anthologies. Subscribe to the Two Sylvias Press newsletter (www.tinyletter.com/twosylviaspress) for updates on submission periods.

TIPS "Created with the belief that great writing is good for the world, Two Sylvias Press mixes modern technology, classic style, and literary intellect with an eco-friendly heart."

TYNDALE HOUSE PUBLISHERS, INC.

351 Executive Dr., Carol Stream IL 60188. (800)323-9400. **Fax:** (800)684-0247. **Website:** www.tyndale.

com. Estab. 1962. Publishes hardcover and trade paperback originals and mass paperback reprints. "Tyndale House publishes practical, user-friendly Christian books for the home and family." **Publishes 15 titles/year. Pays negotiable royalty. Pays negotiable advance.** Accepts simultaneous submissions. Guidelines online.

NONFICTION Subjects include child guidance, religion, devotional/inspirational. *Agented submissions only. No unsolicited mss.*

FICTION Subjects include juvenile, romance, Christian (children's, general, inspirational, mystery/suspense, thriller, romance). "Christian truths must be woven into the story organically. No short story collections. Youth books: character building stories with Christian perspective. Especially interested in ages 10-14. We primarily publish Christian historical romances, with occasional contemporary, suspense, or standalones." *Agented submissions only. No unsolicited mss.*

TIPS "All accepted manuscripts will appeal to Evangelical Christian children and parents."

UMI (URBAN MINISTRIES, INC.)

P.O. Box 436987, Chicago IL 60643. **Website:** www.urbanministries.com. Estab. 1970. Publishes trade paperback originals and reprints. **Publishes 2-3 titles/year.**

NONFICTION Subjects include education, religion, spirituality, Christian living, Christian doctrine, theology. "The books we publish are generally those we have a specific need for (i.e., Vacation Bible School curriculum topics); to complement an existing resource or product line; or those with a potential to develop into a curriculum." Query with SASE. Submit proposal package, outline, 2-3 sample chapters, letter why UMI should publish the book and why the book will sell.

UNBRIDLED BOOKS

8201 E. Highway WW, Columbia MO 65201. **E-mail:** michalsong@unbridledbooks.com. **Website:** unbridledbooks.com. **Contact:** Greg Michalson. Estab. 2004. "Unbridled Books is a premier publisher of works of rich literary quality that appeal to a broad audience." Accepts simultaneous submissions.

FICTION Please query first by e-mail. "Due to the heavy volume of submissions, we regret that at this time we are not able to consider uninvited mss."

TIPS "We try to read each ms that arrives, so please be patient."

⊘ UNITY HOUSE

1901 N.W. Blue Pkwy., Unity Village MO 64065. (816)524-3550. **Fax:** (816)347-5518. **E-mail:** unity@unityonline.org. **Website:** www.unityonline.org. Estab. 1889. Publishes hardcover, trade paperback, and electronic originals. Unity House publishes metaphysical Christian books based on Unity principles, as well as inspirational books on metaphysics and practical spirituality. All manuscripts must reflect a spiritual foundation and express the Unity philosophy, practical Christianity, universal principles, and/or metaphysics. **Publishes 5-7 titles/year. 50 queries received/year. 5% of books from first-time authors. 95% from unagented writers. Pays 10-15% royalty on retail price. Pays advance.** Publishes ms 13 months after acceptance. Responds in 6-8 months. Catalog and guidelines online.

NONFICTION Subjects include religion. "Writers should be familiar with principles of metaphysical Christianity but not feel bound by them. We are interested in works in the related fields of holistic health, spiritual psychology, and the philosophy of other world religions." *Not accepting mss for new books at this time.* Reviews artwork/photos. Writers should send photocopies.

FICTION Subjects include spiritual, inspirational, metaphysical, visionary fiction. "We are a bridge between traditional Christianity and New Age spirituality. Unity is based on metaphysical Christian principles, spiritual values and the healing power of prayer as a resource for daily living." *Not accepting mss for new books at this time.*

TIPS "We target an audience of spiritual seekers."

THE UNIVERSITY OF AKRON PRESS

120 E. Mill St., Suite 415, Akron OH 44308. **E-mail:** uapress@uakron.edu. **Website:** www.uakron.edu/uapress. **Contact:** Dr. Jon Miller, director and acquisitions. Estab. 1988. Publishes hardcover and paperback originals. "The University of Akron Press is the publishing arm of The University of Akron and is dedicated to the dissemination of scholarly, professional, and regional books and other content." **Publishes 10-12 titles/year. 100 queries; 50-75 mss received/year. 40% of books from first-time authors. 80% from unagented writers. Pays 7-15% royalty.** Publishes book 9-12 months after acceptance. Accepts simultaneous

submissions. Responds in 4 weeks to queries/proposals; 3-4 months to solicited mss. Query prior to submitting. Guidelines online.

NONFICTION Subjects include Americana, anthropology, archeology, creative nonfiction, environment, foods, history, humanities, labor, law, literary criticism, literature, memoirs, multicultural, politics, pop culture, psychology, regional. "For our readers in and of Northeast Ohio, we are always looking for new books on our history and culture. We've published books on our people and neighborhoods, our institutions, our sports teams, our parks, and through our cookbooks, on our food. For readers all over the world, we publish peer-reviewed books and collections on the history and culture of Akron and Ohio. In our Bliss Institute series, we publish scholarship on applied politics. With the Drs. Nicholas and Dorothy Cummings Center for the History of Psychology, we publish books and textbooks on the history of psychology." Query by e-mail. Mss cannot be returned unless SASE is included.

POETRY "Follow the guidelines and submit mss only for the contest: www.uakron.edu/uapress/poetry.html. The Akron Series in Poetry brings forth at least 2 new books of poetry every year, mainly through our prestigious and long-running Akron Poetry Prize. We also publish scholarship on poetics."

THE UNIVERSITY OF ALABAMA PRESS

200 Hackberry Lane, 2nd Floor, Tuscaloosa AL 35487. (205)348-5180 or (205)348-1571. **Fax:** (205)348-9201. **E-mail:** waterman@uapress.ua.edu. **Website:** www.uapress.ua.edu. **Contact:** Daniel Waterman, editor-in-chief. Publishes nonfiction hardcover and paperbound originals. **Publishes 70-75 titles/year. 70% of books from first-time authors. 95% from unagented writers. Pays advance in very limited number of circumstances.** Accepts simultaneous submissions. Responds in 2-3 weeks to queries. Book catalog available free.

NONFICTION Subjects include history, literary criticism, politics, religion. Considers upon merit almost any subject of scholarly interest, but specializes in communications, military history, public administration, literary criticism and biography, history, Judaic studies, and American archaeology. Accepts nonfiction translations. Query with SASE.

TIPS "Please direct inquiry to appropriate acquisitions editor. University of Alabama Press responds to an author within 2-3 weeks upon receiving the ms or proposal. If they think it is unsuitable for Alabama's program, they tell the author as soon as possible. If the ms warrants it, they begin the peer-review process, which may take 2-4 months to complete. During that process, they keep the author fully informed."

UNIVERSITY OF ALASKA PRESS

P.O. Box 756240, Fairbanks AK 99775-6240. (907)474-5831 or (888)252-6657. **Fax:** (907)474-5502. **Website:** www.uaf.edu/uapress. Estab. 1967. Publishes hardcover originals, trade paperback originals and reprints. "The mission of the University of Alaska Press is to encourage, publish, and disseminate works of scholarship that will enhance the store of knowledge about Alaska and the North Pacific Rim, with a special emphasis on the circumpolar regions." **Publishes 10 titles/year.** Publishes ms within 2 years of acceptance. Accepts simultaneous submissions. Responds in 2 months to queries. Book catalog available free. Guidelines online.

NONFICTION Subjects include Americana, animals, education, ethnic, history, regional, science, translation. Northern or circumpolar only. Query with SASE and proposal. Reviews artwork/photos.

FICTION Subjects include literary. Alaska literary series with Peggy Shumaker as series editor. Publishes 1-3 works of fiction/year. Submit proposal.

TIPS "Writers have the best chance with scholarly nonfiction relating to Alaska, the circumpolar regions and North Pacific Rim. Our audience is made up of scholars, historians, students, libraries, universities, individuals, and the general Alaskan public."

♻⊘ THE UNIVERSITY OF ALBERTA PRESS

Ring House 2, Edmonton AB T6G 2E1, Canada. (780)492-3662. **Fax:** (780)492-0719. **E-mail:** pmidgley@ualberta.ca. **Website:** www.uap.ualberta.ca. **Contact:** Peter Midgley. Estab. 1969. Publishes originals and reprints. "We do not accept unsolicited novels, short story collections, or poetry. Please see our website for details." **Publishes 18-25 titles/year. Royalties are negotiated.** Publishes ms within 2 years after acceptance. Responds in 3 months to queries. Guidelines online.

NONFICTION Subjects include history, regional, natural history, social policy. Submit cover letter, word count, CV, 1 sample chapter, TOC.

UNIVERSITY OF ARIZONA PRESS

Main Library Building, 5th Floor, 1510 E. University Blvd., Tucson AZ 85721. (520)621-1441. **Fax:** (520)621-8899. **E-mail:** kbuckles@uapress.arizona.edu. **Website:** www.uapress.arizona.edu. **Contact:** Kristen Buckles, acquiring editor. Estab. 1959. Publishes hardcover and paperback originals and reprints. "University of Arizona is a publisher of scholarly books and books of the Southwest." **Royalty terms vary; usual starting point for scholarly monography is after sale of first 1,000 copies. Pays advance.** Responds in 3 months to queries. Book catalog online. Guidelines online.

NONFICTION Subjects include Americana, ethnic, regional, environmental studies, western, and environmental history. Scholarly books about anthropology, Arizona, American West, archeology, Native American studies, Latino studies, environmental science, global change, Latin America, Native Americans, natural history, space sciences, and women's studies. Submit sample chapters, resume, TOC, ms length, audience, comparable books. Reviews artwork/photos.

TIPS "Perhaps the most common mistake a writer might make is to offer a book manuscript or proposal to a house whose list he or she has not studied carefully. Editors rejoice in receiving material that is clearly targeted to the house's list ('I have approached your firm because my books complement your past publications in') and presented in a straightforward, businesslike manner."

THE UNIVERSITY OF ARKANSAS PRESS

McIlroy House, 105 N. McIlroy Ave., Fayetteville AR 72701. (479)575-3246. **Fax:** (479)575-6044. **E-mail:** mbieker@uark.edu. **Website:** uapress.com. **Contact:** Mike Bieker, director. Estab. 1980. Publishes hardcover and trade paperback originals and reprints. "The University of Arkansas Press publishes series on Ozark studies, the Civil War in the West, poetry and poetics, food studies, and sport and society." **Publishes 22 titles/year. 30% of books from first-time authors. 95% from unagented writers.** Publishes book 1 year after acceptance. Accepts simultaneous submissions. Responds in 3 months to proposals. Book catalog and ms guidelines online.

NONFICTION Subjects include architecture, foods, history, humanities, literary criticism, regional, Arkansas. Accepted mss must be submitted electronically. Query with SASE. Submit outline, sample chapters, resume.

FICTION Subjects include historical, regional.

POETRY University of Arkansas Press publishes 4 poetry books per year through the Miller Williams Poetry Prize.

☯ UNIVERSITY OF CALGARY PRESS

2500 University Dr. NW, Calgary AB T2N 1N4, Canada. (403)220-7578. **Fax:** (403)282-0085. **E-mail:** brian.scrivener@ucalgary.ca. **Website:** press.ucalgary.ca. **Contact:** Brian Scrivener, Director. Estab. 1984. Publishes scholarly and trade paperback originals and reprints. **Publishes 10 titles/year. 40% of books from first-time authors. 90% from unagented writers.** Publishes ms 20 months after acceptance. Book catalog available for free. Guidelines online.

NONFICTION Subjects include architecture, art, cinema, communications, environment, film, history, humanities, literary criticism, literature, memoirs, military, politics, public affairs, regional, social sciences, womens studies, Canadian studies, postmodern studies, native studies, history, international relations, arctic studies, Africa, Latin American and Caribbean studies, and heritage of the Canadian and American heartland.

UNIVERSITY OF CALIFORNIA PRESS

155 Grand Ave., Suite 400, Oakland CA 94612. **Website:** www.ucpress.edu. **Contact:** Kate Marshall, acquisitions editor. Estab. 1893. Publishes hardcover and paperback originals and reprints. "University of California Press publishes mostly nonfiction written by scholars." **Pays advance.** Accepts simultaneous submissions. Response time varies, depending on the subject. Enclose return postage to queries. Guidelines online.

NONFICTION Subjects include history, translation, art, literature, natural sciences, some high-level popularizations. No length preference. Submit proposal package.

FICTION Publishes fiction only in translation.

⊘ THE UNIVERSITY OF CHICAGO PRESS

1427 East 60th St., Chicago IL 60637. (773)702-7700. **Fax:** (773)702-9756. **Website:** www.press.uchicago.edu. **Contact:** Randolph Petilos, Poetry and Medieval Studies Editor. Estab. 1891. "The University of Chicago Press has been publishing scholarly books and journals since 1891. Annually, we publish an average of 4 books in our Phoenix Poets series and 2 books of poetry in translation. Occasionally, we may publish a book of poetry outside Phoenix Poets, or as a paperback reprint from another publisher." Has recently published work by Peter Balakian, Charles Bernstein, Maggie Dietz, Reginald Gibbons, Nate Klug, Gail Mazur, Robert Pack, Vanesha Pravin, Alan Shapiro, and Connie Voisine. Accepts simultaneous submissions.

UNIVERSITY OF GEORGIA PRESS

Main Library, Third Floor, 320 S. Jackson St., Athens GA 30602. (706)369-6130. **Fax:** (706)369-6131. **Website:** www.ugapress.org. **Contact:** Mick Gusinde-Duffy, executive editor; Walter Biggins, executive editor; Pat Allen, acquisitions editor; Beth Snead, assistant acquisitions editor. Estab. 1938. Publishes hardcover originals, trade paperback originals, and reprints. University of Georgia Press is a midsized press that publishes fiction only through the Flannery O'Connor Award for Short Fiction competition. **Publishes 85 titles/year. Pays 7-10% royalty on net receipts. Pays rare, varying advance.** Publishes book 1 year after acceptance. Responds in 2 months to queries. Book catalog and guidelines online.

NONFICTION Subjects include history, regional, environmental studies, literary nonfiction. Query with SASE. Submit bio, 1 sample chapter. Reviews artwork/photos. Send if essential to book.

FICTION Short story collections published in Flannery O'Connor Award Competition.

TIPS "Please visit our website to view our book catalogs and for all manuscript submission guidelines."

UNIVERSITY OF ILLINOIS PRESS

1325 S. Oak St., Champaign IL 61820-6903. (217)333-0950. **Fax:** (217)244-8082. **E-mail:** uipress@uillinois. edu. **Website:** www.press.uillinois.edu. **Contact:** Laurie Matheson, director; Daniel Nasset, acquisitions editor; Dawn Durante, acquisitions editor; James Engelhardt, acquisitions editor. Estab. 1918. Publishes hardcover and trade paperback originals and reprints. University of Illinois Press publishes scholarly books and serious nonfiction with a wide range of study interests. Currently emphasizing American history, especially immigration, labor, African-American, and military; American religion, music, women's studies, and film. **Publishes 150 titles/year. 35% of books from first-time authors. 95% from unagented writers. Pays $1,000-1,500 (rarely) advance.** Publishes ms 1 year after acceptance. Accepts simultaneous sub-

missions. Responds in 1 month to queries. Guidelines online.

NONFICTION Subjects include Americana, animals, communications, ethnic, history, philosophy, regional, sociology, sports, translation, film/cinema/stage. "Always looking for solid, scholarly books in American history, especially social history; books on American popular music, and books in the broad area of American studies." Query with SASE. Submit outline.

TIPS "As a university press, we are required to submit all mss to rigorous scholarly review. Mss need to be clearly original, well written, and based on solid and thorough research. We cannot encourage memoirs or autobiographies."

UNIVERSITY OF IOWA PRESS

100 Kuhl House, 119 W. Park Rd., Iowa City IA 52242. (319)335-2000. **Fax:** (319)335-2055. **E-mail:** james-mccoy@uiowa.edu. **Website:** www.uiowapress.org. **Contact:** James McCoy, director. Estab. 1969. Publishes hardcover and paperback originals. The University of Iowa Press publishes both trade and academic work in a variety of fields. **Publishes 35 titles/year. 30% of books from first-time authors. 95% from unagented writers.** Accepts simultaneous submissions. Book catalog available free. Guidelines online.

NONFICTION Subjects include agriculture, contemporary culture, creative nonfiction, environment, history, humanities, literary criticism, multicultural, nature, pop culture, regional, travel, true crime, womens studies. "Looks for evidence of original research, reliable sources, clarity of organization, complete development of theme with documentation, supportive footnotes and/or bibliography, and a substantive contribution to knowledge in the field treated. Use *Chicago Manual of Style*." Query with SASE. Submit outline. Reviews artwork/photos.

FICTION Currently publishes the Iowa Short Fiction Award selections. "We do not accept any fiction submissions outside of the Iowa Short Fiction Award. See www.uiowapress.org for contest details."

POETRY Currently publishes winners of the Iowa Poetry Prize Competition and Kuhl House Poets (by invitation only). Competition guidelines available on website.

UNIVERSITY OF MAINE PRESS

5729 Fogler Library, Orono ME 04469. (207)581-1652. **Fax:** (207)581-1653. **E-mail:** michael.alpert@umit.

maine.edu. **Website:** www.umaine.edu/umpress. **Contact:** Michael Alpert, editorial director. Publishes hardcover and trade paperback originals and reprints. **Publishes 4 titles/year. 50 queries received/year. 25 mss received/year. 50% of books from first-time authors. 90% from unagented writers.** Publishes ms 1 year after acceptance. Accepts simultaneous submissions.

NONFICTION Subjects include history, regional, science. "We are an academic book publisher, interested in scholarly works on regional history, regional life sciences, Franco-American studies. Authors should be able to articulate their ideas on the potential market for their work." Query with SASE.

UNIVERSITY OF MICHIGAN PRESS

839 Greene St., Ann Arbor MI 48106. (734)764-4388. **Fax:** (734)615-1540. **Website:** www.press.umich.edu. **Contact:** Mary Francis, editorial director. "In partnership with our authors and series editors, we publish in a wide range of humanities and social sciences disciplines." Accepts simultaneous submissions. Guidelines online.

NONFICTION Submit proposal.

FICTION Subjects include literary, regional. In addition to the annual Michigan Literary Fiction Awards, this publishes literary fiction linked to the Great Lakes region. Submit cover letter and first 30 pages.

UNIVERSITY OF NEVADA PRESS

Mail Stop 0166, Reno NV 89557. (775)784-6573. **Fax:** (775)784-6200. **Website:** www.unpress.nevada.edu. **Contact:** Justin Race, director. Estab. 1961. Publishes hardcover and paperback originals and reprints. "University Press specializing in regional titles, fiction and memoir, and books in the fields of environmental studies, Basque studies, mining studies, nature, and the American West." **Publishes 25 titles/year.** Publishes ms 18 months after acceptance. Responds in 3-5 weeks. Guidelines online.

NONFICTION Subjects include agriculture, animals, archeology, architecture, creative nonfiction, environment, history, memoirs, nature, regional, western literature, gambling and gaming, Basque studies. No juvenile books. Submit electronically, instructions on website. Reviews artwork/photos. Send electronically.

FICTION Fiction should have some connection to the American West, whether in setting or theme. We do not publish historical fiction.

UNIVERSITY OF NEW MEXICO PRESS

1717 Roma Ave. NE, Albuquerque NM 87106. (505)277-3495 or (800)249-7737. **Fax:** (505)277-3343. **Website:** www.unmpress.com. **Contact:** John W. Byram, Director. Estab. 1929. Publishes hardcover originals and trade paperback originals and reprints. "The Press is well known as a publisher in the fields of anthropology, archeology, Latin American studies, art and photography, architecture and the history and culture of the American West, fiction, some poetry, Chicano/a studies and works by and about American Indians. We focus on American West, Southwest and Latin American regions." **Publishes 75 titles/year. 1,500 submissions received/year. 20% of books from first-time authors. 80% from unagented writers. Pays variable royalty. May pay advance.** Publishes ms 10 months after acceptance. Responds in 6 weeks. Book catalog available free. Guidelines online.

NONFICTION Subjects include Americana, anthropology, archeology, architecture, art, cooking, environment, ethnic, foods, gardening, history, humanities, literary criticism, literature, memoirs, military, multicultural, music, nature, photography, politics, pop culture, public affairs, regional, religion, science, social sciences, sports, translation, travel, true crime, womens issues, womens studies, world affairs, contemporary culture, cinema/stage, true crime, general nonfiction. No how-to, humor, juvenile, self-help, software, technical or textbooks. Query with SASE. Reviews artwork/photos. Send photocopies.

FICTION Subjects include ethnic, literary, multicultural, regional, translation.

THE UNIVERSITY OF NORTH CAROLINA PRESS

116 S. Boundary St., Chapel Hill NC 27514. (919)966-3561. **Fax:** (919)966-3829. **E-mail:** mark_simpson-vos@unc.edu. **Website:** www.uncpress.unc.edu. **Contact:** Mark Simpson-Vos, editorial director. Publishes hardcover originals, trade paperback originals and reprints. "UNC Press publishes nonfiction books for academic and general audiences. We have a special interest in trade and scholarly titles about our region. We do not, however, publish original fiction, drama, or poetry, memoirs of living persons, or festshriften." **Publishes 90 titles/year. 500 queries received/year. 200 mss received/year. 50% of books from first-time authors. 90% from unagented writers. Pays variable royalty on wholesale price. Offers variable advance.**

Publishes ms 1 year after acceptance. Accepts simultaneous submissions. Responds in 3-4 weeks. Book catalog and guidelines online.

NONFICTION Subjects include Americana, gardening, history, multicultural, philosophy, photography, regional, religion, translation, African-American studies, American studies, cultural studies, Latin-American studies, American-Indian studies, media studies, gender studies, social medicine, Appalachian studies. Submit proposal package, outline, CV, cover letter, abstract, and TOC. Reviews artwork/photos. Send photocopies.

UNIVERSITY OF NORTH TEXAS PRESS

1155 Union Circle, #311336, Denton TX 76203. (940)565-2142. **Fax:** (940)565-4590. **E-mail:** karen. devinney@unt.edu. **Website:** untpress.unt.edu. **Contact:** Ronald Chrisman, director; Karen De Vinney, assistant director. Estab. 1987. Publishes hardcover and trade paperback originals and reprints. "We are dedicated to producing the highest quality scholarly, academic, and general interest books. We are committed to serving all peoples by publishing stories of their cultures and experiences that have been overlooked. Currently emphasizing military history, Texas history, music, Mexican-American studies." **Publishes 14-16 titles/year. 500 queries received/year. 50% of books from first-time authors. 95% from unagented writers.** Publishes ms 1-2 years after acceptance. Responds in 1 month to queries. Book catalog for 8 ½×11 SASE. Guidelines online.

NONFICTION Subjects include Americana, art, cooking, creative nonfiction, ethnic, government, history, humanities, military, multicultural, music, nature, photography, politics, regional, social sciences, war, womens issues, womens studies. Query by e-mail. Reviews artwork/photos. Send photocopies.

FICTION Subjects include short story collections. "The only fiction we publish is the winner of the Katherine Anne Porter Prize in Short Fiction, an annual, national competition with a $1,000 prize, and publication of the winning ms each Fall."

POETRY "The only poetry we publish is the winner of the Vassar Miller Prize in Poetry, an annual, national competition with a $1,000 prize and publication of the winning ms each Spring." Query.

TIPS "We publish series called War and the Southwest; Texas Folklore Society Publications; the Western Life Series; Practical Guide Series; Al-Filo: Mexican-American studies; North Texas Crime and Criminal Justice; Katherine Anne Porter Prize in Short Fiction; and the North Texas Lives of Musicians Series."

UNIVERSITY OF OKLAHOMA PRESS

2800 Venture Dr., Norman OK 73069. (405)325-5609. **E-mail:** adam.kane@ou.edu. **Website:** www.oupress. com. **Contact:** Adam C. Kane, editor-in-chief. Estab. 1928. Publishes hardcover and paperback originals and reprints. University of Oklahoma Press publishes books for both scholarly and nonspecialist readers. **Publishes 90 titles/year. Pays standard royalty.** Responds promptly to queries. Book catalog online.

IMPRINTS Plains Reprints.

NONFICTION Subjects include political science (Congressional, area and security studies), history (regional, military, natural), language/literature (American Indian, US West), American Indian studies, classical studies. Query with SASE or by e-mail. Submit outline, resume, 1-2 sample chapters. Use *Chicago Manual of Style* for ms guidelines. Reviews artwork/photos.

◯ UNIVERSITY OF OTTAWA PRESS

542 King Edward Ave., Ottawa ON K1N 6N5, Canada. (613)562-5246. **Fax:** (613)562-5247. **E-mail:** puo-uop@ uottawa.ca. **Website:** www.press.uottawa.ca. **Contact:** Lara Mainville, director; Dominike Thomas, acquisitions editor. Estab. 1936. "UOP publishes books and journals, in French and English, and in any and all editions and formats, that touch upon the human condition: anthropology, sociology, political science, psychology, criminology, media studies, economics, education, language and culture, law, history, literature, translation studies, philosophy, public administration, health sciences, and religious studies." Accepts simultaneous submissions. Book catalog and ms guidelines online.

NONFICTION Submit outline, proposal form (please see website), CV, 1-2 sample chapters (for monographs only), ms (for collected works only), TOC, 2-5 page proposal/summary, contributor names, short bios, and citizenships (for collected works only).

TIPS "Please note that the University of Ottawa Press does not accept: bilingual works (texts must be either entirely in English or entirely in French), undergraduate or masters theses, or doctoral theses that have not been substantially revised."

UNIVERSITY OF PENNSYLVANIA PRESS

3905 Spruce St., Philadelphia PA 19104. (215)898-6261. **Fax:** (215)898-0404. **E-mail:** agree@upenn.edu. **Website:** www.pennpress.org. **Contact:** Peter Agree, editor-in-chief. Estab. 1890. Publishes hardcover and paperback originals, and reprints. "Manuscript submissions are welcome in fields appropriate for Penn Press's editorial program. The Press's acquiring editors, and their fields of responsibility, are listed in the Contact Us section of our Web site. Although we have no formal policies regarding manuscript proposals and submissions, what we need minimally, in order to gauge our degree of interest, is a brief statement describing the manuscript, a copy of the contents page, and a reasonably current vita. Initial inquiries are best sent by letter, in paper form, to the appropriate acquiring editor." **Publishes 100+ titles/year. 20-30% of books from first-time authors. 95% from unagented writers. Royalty determined on book-by-book basis. Pays advance.** Publishes ms 10 months after acceptance. Responds in 3 months to queries. Book catalog online. Guidelines online.

NONFICTION Subjects include Americana, history, literary criticism, sociology, anthropology, literary criticism, cultural studies, ancient studies, medieval studies, urban studies, human rights. Follow the *Chicago Manual of Style*. "Serious books that serve the scholar and the professional, student and general reader." Query with SASE. Submit outline, resume.

UNIVERSITY OF PITTSBURGH PRESS

7500 Thomas Blvd., Pittsburgh PA 15260. (412)383-2456. **Fax:** (412)383-2466. **E-mail:** info@upress.pitt.edu. **Website:** www.upress.pitt.edu. **Contact:** Sandy Crooms, editorial director. Estab. 1936. The University of Pittsburgh Press is a scholarly publisher with distinguished books in several academic areas and in poetry and short fiction, as well as books about Pittsburgh and western Pennsylvania for general readers, scholars, and students. "Our mission is to extend the reach and reputation of the university through the publication of scholarly, artistic, and educational books that advance learning and knowledge and through the publication of regional books that contribute to an understanding of and are of special benefit to western Pennsylvania and the Upper Ohio Valley region. Accepts simultaneous submissions. Book catalog online. Guidelines online.

POETRY Publishes at least 4 books by poets who have previously published full-length collections of poetry. Submit complete ms in September and October only.

TIPS "We pride ourselves on the eclectic nature of our list. We are not tied to any particular style or school of writing, but we do demand that any book we publish be of exceptional merit."

UNIVERSITY OF SOUTH CAROLINA PRESS

1600 Hampton St., 5th Floor, Columbia SC 29208. (803)777-5243. **Fax:** (803)777-0160. **E-mail:** batesvc@mailbox.sc.edu. **Website:** www.sc.edu/uscpress. **Contact:** Jonathan Haupt, director. Estab. 1944. Publishes hardcover originals, trade paperback originals and reprints. "We focus on scholarly monographs and regional trade books of lasting merit." **Publishes 50 titles/year. 500 queries received/year. 150 mss received/year. 30% of books from first-time authors. 95% from unagented writers.** Publishes ms 1 year after acceptance. Accepts simultaneous submissions. Responds in 3 months to mss. Book catalog available free. Guidelines online.

NONFICTION Subjects include history, regional, religion, rhetoric, communication. Query with SASE, or submit proposal package and outline, and 1 sample chapter and resume with SASE Reviews artwork/photos. Send photocopies.

POETRY Palmetto Poetry Series, a South Carolina-based original poetry series edited by Nikky Finney. Director: Jonathan Haupt, director (jhaupt@mailbox.sc.edu).

UNIVERSITY OF TAMPA PRESS

The University of Tampa, 401 W. Kennedy Blvd., Tampa FL 33606. (813)253-6266. **E-mail:** utpress@ut.edu. **Website:** www.ut.edu/tampapress. **Contact:** Richard Mathews, editor. Estab. 1952. Publishes hardcover originals and reprints; trade paperback originals and reprints. "We are a small university press publishing a limited number of titles each year, primarily in the areas of local and regional history, poetry, and printing history. We do not accept e-mail submissions." **Publishes 4-6 titles/year. Does not pay advance.** Publishes ms 6 months-2 years after acceptance. Responds in 3-4 months to queries. Book catalog online.

NONFICTION Subjects include Florida history. Does not consider unsolicited mss.

FICTION Subjects include literary, poetry.

POETRY "We consider original poetry collections through the annual Tampa Review Prize for Poetry competition, with a deadline of December 31 each year." Submit to the Tampa Review Prize for Poetry.

THE UNIVERSITY OF TENNESSEE PRESS

The University of Tennessee, 110 Conference Center, 600 Henley St., Knoxville TN 37996. (865)974-3321. **Fax:** (865)974-3724. **E-mail:** twells@utk.edu. **Website:** www.utpress.org. **Contact:** Thomas Wells, acquisitions editor. Estab. 1940. "Our mission is to stimulate scientific and scholarly research in all fields; to channel such studies, either in scholarly or popular form, to a larger number of people; and to extend the regional leadership of the University of Tennessee by stimulating research projects within the South and by nonuniversity authors." **Publishes 35 titles/year. 35% of books from first-time authors. 99% from unagented writers. Pays negotiable royalty on net receipts. Rarely offers advance.** Publishes ms 18 months after acceptance. Accepts simultaneous submissions. Guidelines online.

NONFICTION Subjects include Americana, archeology, architecture, history, literary criticism, military, music, regional, religion, war, African-American studies, Appalachian studies, folklore/folklife, material culture. Prefers scholarly treatment and a readable style. Authors usually have advanced degrees. Submissions in other fields, fiction or poetry, textbooks, and plays and translations are not invited Submit cover letter, outline, bio or CV, and sample chapters. Reviews artwork/photos.

FICTION The press no longer publishes works of fiction.

UNIVERSITY OF TEXAS PRESS

3001 Lake Austin Blvd., 2.200, Stop E4800, Austin TX 78703. **Fax:** (512)232-7178. **Website:** www.utexaspress.com. Estab. 1952. "In addition to publishing the results of advanced research for scholars worldwide, UT Press has a special obligation to the people of its state to publish authoritative books on Texas. We do not publish fiction or poetry, except as invited by a series editor, and some Latin American and Middle Eastern literature in translation." **Publishes 90 titles/year. 50% of books from first-time authors. 99% from unagented writers. Pays occasional advance.** Publishes ms 18-24 months after acceptance. Responds in 3 months to queries. Guidelines online.

NONFICTION Subjects include ethnic, history, literary criticism, regional, science, translation, natural history, American, Latin American, Native American, Latino, and Middle Eastern studies; classics and the ancient world, film, contemporary regional architecture, geography, ornithology, biology. Also uses specialty titles related to Texas and the Southwest, national trade titles and regional trade titles. Submit cover letter, TOC, CV, sample chapter.

UNIVERSITY OF WASHINGTON PRESS

P.O. Box 359570, Seattle WA 98195. (206)543-4050. **Fax:** (206)543-3932. **E-mail:** uwapress@uw.edu. **E-mail:** lmclaugh@uw.edu. **Website:** www.washington.edu/uwpress/. **Contact:** Laurin McLaughlin, editor-in-chief. Publishes in hardcover originals. **Publishes 70 titles/year.** Accepts simultaneous submissions. Book catalog guidelines online.

NONFICTION Subjects include ethnic, history, multicultural, photography, regional, social sciences. Go to our Book Search page for complete subject listing. We publish academic and general books, especially in anthropology, Asian studies, art, environmental studies, Middle Eastern Studies & regional interests. International Studies with focus on Asia; Jewish Studies; Art & Culture of the Northwest coast; Indians & Alaskan Eskimos; The Asian-American Experience; Southeast Asian Studies; Korean and Slavic Studies; Studies in Modernity & National Identity; Scandinavian Studies. Query with SASE. Submit proposal package, outline, sample chapters.

UNIVERSITY OF WISCONSIN PRESS

1930 Monroe St., 3rd Floor, Madison WI 53711. **E-mail:** kadushin@wisc.edu; gcwalker@wisc.edu. **Website:** uwpress.wisc.edu. **Contact:** Raphael Kadushin, executive editor; Gwen Walker, editorial director. Estab. 1937. **Publishes 50 titles/year. Pays royalty.** Publishes 10-14 months after acceptance of final ms. Accepts simultaneous submissions. Responds in 1-3 weeks to queries; 3-6 weeks to proposals. Rarely comments on rejected work. See submission guidelines on our website.

NONFICTION Subjects include cinema, contemporary culture, creative nonfiction, entertainment, environment, film, foods, gay, government, history, labor, lesbian, memoirs, politics, public affairs, travel, African Studies, classical studies, human rights, Irish studies, Jewish studies, Latin American studies, Latino/a memoirs, modern Western European history, Slavic studies, Southeast Asian studies. Does not accept unsolicited mss. See website for submission guidelines.

FICTION Subjects include gay, hi-lo, lesbian, mystery, regional, short story collections. Query with SASE or submit outline, 1-2 sample chapter(s), synopsis.

POETRY The University of Wisconsin Press Awards the Brittingham Prize in Poetry and Felix Pollack Prize in Poetry. More details online.

TIPS "Make sure the query letter and sample text are well-written, and read guidelines carefully to make sure we accept the genre you are submitting."

UNIVERSITY PRESS OF KANSAS

2502 Westbrooke Circle, Lawrence KS 66045. (785)864-4154. **Fax:** (785) 864-4586. **E-mail:** upress@ku.edu. **Website:** www.kansaspress.ku.edu. **Contact:** Conrad Roberts, interim director & business manager; Joyce Harrison, editor-in-chief; Kim Hogeland, acquisitions editor. Estab. 1946. Publishes hardcover originals, trade paperback originals and reprints. "The University Press of Kansas publishes scholarly books that advance knowledge and regional books that contribute to the understanding of Kansas, the Great Plains, and the Midwest." **Publishes 55 titles/year. 600 queries received/year. 20% of books from first-time authors. 98% from unagented writers. Pays selective advance.** Publishes book 10 months after acceptance. Responds in 1 month to proposals. Book catalog and ms guidelines free.

NONFICTION Subjects include Americana, archeology, environment, government, military, nature, politics, regional, war, American History, Native Studies, American Cultural Studies. "We are looking for books on topics of wide interest based on solid scholarship and written for both specialists and informed general readers. Do not send unsolicited, complete manuscripts." Submit outline, sample chapters, cover letter, CV, prospectus. Reviews artwork/photos. Send photocopies.

UNIVERSITY PRESS OF KENTUCKY

663 S. Limestone St., Lexington KY 40508. (859)257-8434. **Fax:** (859)323-1873. **E-mail:** adwatk0@email.uky.edu. **Website:** www.kentuckypress.com. **Contact:** Anne Dean Dotson, senior acquisitions editor. Estab. 1943. Publishes hardcover and paperback originals and reprints. "We are a scholarly publisher, publishing chiefly for an academic and professional audience, as well as books about Kentucky, the upper South, Ap-

palachia, and the Ohio Valley." **Publishes 60 titles/year. Royalty varies.** Publishes ms 1 year after accceptance. Accepts simultaneous submissions. Responds in 2 months to queries. Book catalog available free. Guidelines online.

NONFICTION Subjects include history, regional, political science. No textbooks, genealogical material, lightweight popular treatments, how-to books, or books unrelated to our major areas of interest. The Press does not consider original works of fiction or poetry. Query with SASE.

UNIVERSITY PRESS OF MISSISSIPPI

3825 Ridgewood Rd., Jackson MS 39211. (601)432-6205. **Fax:** (601)432-6217. **E-mail:** press@mississippi.edu. **Website:** www.upress.state.ms.us. **Contact:** Craig W. Gill, Director. Estab. 1970. Publishes hardcover and paperback originals and reprints and e-books. "University Press of Mississippi publishes scholarly and trade titles, as well as special series, including: American Made Music; Conversations with Comics Artists; Conversations with Filmmakers; Faulkner and Yoknapatawpha; Great Comic Artists; Literary Conversations; Hollywood Legends; Caribbean Studies, Willie Morris Books in Memoir and Biography." **Publishes 70 titles/year. 80% of books from first-time authors. 90% from unagented writers. Pays competitive royalties and terms. Pays advance.** Publishes ms 1 year after acceptance. Responds in 3 months to queries.

NONFICTION Subjects include Americana, art, ethnic, history, literary criticism, regional, sports, womens studies, African American studies, comics studies, film studies, folklife, popular culture with scholarly emphasis, literary studies. "We prefer a proposal that describes the significance of the work and a chapter outline." Submit outline, sample chapters, CV.

ⒶⓈⓄ USBORNE PUBLISHING

83-85 Saffron Hill, London EC1N 8RT, United Kingdom. (44)207430-2800. **Fax:** (44)207430-1562. **E-mail:** mail@usborne.co.uk. **Website:** www.usborne.com. "Usborne Publishing is a multiple-award-winning, worldwide children's publishing company publishing almost every type of children's book for every age from baby to young adult." **Pays authors royalty.** Accepts simultaneous submissions.

FICTION Young readers, middle readers: adventure, contemporary, fantasy, history, humor, multicultural, nature/environment, science fiction, suspense/mystery, strong concept-based or character-led series. Average word length: young readers—5,000-10,000; middle readers—25,000-50,000; young adult—50,000-100,000. *Agented submissions only.*

TIPS "Do not send any original work and, sorry, but we cannot guarantee a reply."

UTAH STATE UNIVERSITY PRESS

3078 Old Main Hill, Logan UT 84322. **Website:** www.usu.edu/usupress. Estab. 1972. Publishes hardcover and trade paperback originals and reprints. Utah State University Press publishes scholarly works in the academic areas noted below. Currently interested in book-length scholarly mss dealing with folklore studies, composition studies, Native American studies, and history. **Publishes 18 titles/year. 8% of books from first-time authors.** Publishes ms 18 months after acceptance. Responds in 1 month to queries. Book catalog available free. Guidelines online.

NONFICTION Subjects include history, regional, folklore, the West, Native-American studies, studies in composition and rhetoric. Query via online submission form. Reviews artwork/photos. Send photocopies.

TIPS "Utah State University Press also sponsors the annual May Swenson Poetry Award."

VANDERBILT UNIVERSITY PRESS

PMB 351813, 2301 Vanderbilt Place, Nashville TN 37235. (615)322-3585. **Fax:** (615)343-8823. **E-mail:** vupress@vanderbilt.edu. **E-mail:** beth.itkin@vanderbilt.edu. **Website:** www.vanderbiltuniversitypress.com. Publishes hardcover originals and trade paperback originals and reprints. "Vanderbilt University Press publishes books on healthcare, social sciences, education, and regional studies, for both academic and general audiences that are intellectually significant, socially relevant, and of practical importance." **Publishes 20-25 titles/year. 500 queries received/year. 25% of books from first-time authors. 90% from unagented writers. Pays rare advance.** Publishes ms 10 months after acceptance. Accepts simultaneous submissions. Responds in 2 weeks to proposals. Book catalog online. Guidelines online.

NONFICTION Subjects include Americana, education, ethnic, history, multicultural, philosophy. Submit cover letter, TOC, CV, 1-2 sample chapters.

TIPS "Our audience consists of scholars and educated, general readers."

VAN SCHAIK PUBLISHERS

1059 Francis Baard St., Hatfield 0028, South Africa. **E-mail:** vanschaik@vanschaiknet.com. **Website:** www.vanschaiknet.com. **Contact:** Julia Read. Accepts simultaneous submissions. Guidelines online.

NONFICTION Subjects include education, social sciences, nursing/medicine, language, accounting, public administration. Submit proposal package, outline, sample text.

VÉHICULE PRESS

P.O.B. 42094 BP Roy, Montreal QC H2W 2T3, Canada. (514)844-6073. **Fax:** (514)844-7543. **E-mail:** sd@vehiculepress.com. **E-mail:** admin@vehiculepress.com. **Website:** www.vehiculepress.com. **Contact:** Simon Dardick, nonfiction; Carmine Starnino, poetry; Dimitri Nasrallah, fiction. Estab. 1973. Publishes trade paperback originals by Canadian authors mostly. "Montreal's Véhicule Press has published the best of Canadian and Quebec literature-fiction, poetry, essays, translations, and social history." **Publishes 15 titles/year. 20% of books from first-time authors. 95% from unagented writers. Pays 10-15% royalty on retail price. Pays $200-500 advance.** Publishes ms 1 year after acceptance. Accepts simultaneous submissions. Responds in 4 months to queries. Book catalog for 9 x 12 SAE with IRCs.

IMPRINTS Signal Editions (poetry); Esplanade Editions (fiction).

NONFICTION Subjects include history, memoirs, regional, sociology. Especially looking for Canadian social history. Query with SASE. Reviews artwork/photos.

FICTION Subjects include feminist, literary, regional, translation, literary novels. No romance or formula writing. Query with SASE.

POETRY Vehicule Press is a "literary press with a poetry series, Signal Editions, publishing the work of Canadian poets only." Publishes flat-spined paperbacks. Publishes Canadian poetry that is "first-rate, original, content-conscious."

TIPS "Quality in almost any style is acceptable. We believe in the editing process."

VELÁZQUEZ PRESS

Division of Academic Learning Press, 9682 Telstar Ave., Suite 110, El Monte CA 91731. (626)448-3448. **Website:** www.velazquezpress.com. Publishes hardcover and trade paperback originals and reprints. **Publishes 5-10 titles/year. Pays 10% royalty on re-**

BOOK PUBLISHERS

tail price. Publishes ms 6 months after acceptance. Accepts simultaneous submissions. Responds in 2 months. Book catalog and guidelines via e-mail.

IMPRINTS WBusiness Books; ZHealth.

NONFICTION Subjects include education. "We are interested in publishing bilingual educational materials." Submit proposal package, outline, 2 sample chapters, cover letter. Submit complete ms. Reviews artwork/photos. Send photocopies.

VENTURE PUBLISHING, INC.

1807 N. Federal Dr., Urbana IL 61801. (217)359-5940. **Website:** www.sagamorepub.com. Estab. 1978. Publishes hardcover and paperback originals and reprints. "Venture Publishing produces quality educational publications, also workbooks for professionals, educators, and students in the fields of recreation, parks, leisure studies, therapeutic recreation and long term care." **Pays royalty on wholesale price. Pays advance.** Book catalog and ms guidelines online.

NONFICTION Subjects include recreation, sociology, long-term care nursing homes, therapeutic recreation. Textbooks and books for recreation activity leaders high priority. Submit 1 sample chapter, book proposal, competing titles.

VERSO

20 Jay St., 10th Floor, Brooklyn NY 11201. (718)246-8160. **Fax:** (718)246-8165. **E-mail:** verso@verso-books.com. **E-mail:** submissions@versobooks.com. **Website:** www.versobooks.com. **Contact:** Editorial Department. Estab. 1970. Publishes hardcover and trade paperback originals. "Our books cover economics, politics, cinema studies, and history (among other topics), but all come from a critical, Leftist viewpoint, on the border between trade and academic." **Publishes 100 titles/year. Pays royalty. Pays advance.** Accepts simultaneous submissions. Book catalog available free. Guidelines online.

NONFICTION Subjects include history, philosophy, sociology. Submit proposal package.

⊘ VERTIGO

DC Universe, Vertigo-DC Comics, 1700 Broadway, New York NY 10019. **Website:** www.vertigocomics.com. At this time, DC Entertainment does not accept unsolicited artwork or writing submissions. Accepts simultaneous submissions.

🅐⊘ VIKING

Imprint of Penguin Group (USA), Inc., 375 Hudson St., New York NY 10014. (212)366-2000. **Website:** www.penguin.com. Estab. 1925. Publishes hardcover and originals. Viking publishes a mix of academic and popular fiction and nonfiction. **Publishes 100 titles/year. Pays 10-15% royalty on retail price.** Publishes ms 18 months after acceptance. Accepts simultaneous submissions.

NONFICTION Subjects include child guidance, history, philosophy. *Agented submissions only.*

FICTION Subjects include literary, mystery, suspense. *Agented submissions only.*

🅐⊘ VIKING CHILDREN'S BOOKS

375 Hudson St., New York NY 10014. **Website:** www.penguin.com. Publishes hardcover originals. "Viking Children's Books is known for humorous, quirky picture books, in addition to more traditional fiction. We publish the highest quality fiction, nonfiction, and picture books for pre-schoolers through young adults." *Does not accept unsolicited submissions.* **Publishes 70 titles/year. Pays 2-10% royalty on retail price or flat fee. Pays negotiable advance.** Publishes book 1-2 years after acceptance. Accepts simultaneous submissions. Responds in 6 months.

NONFICTION All levels: biography, concept, history, multicultural, music/dance, nature/environment, science, and sports. *Agented submissions only.*

FICTION All levels: adventure, animal, contemporary, fantasy, history, humor, multicultural, nature/environment, poetry, problem novels, romance, science fiction, sports, suspense/mystery. *Accepts agented mss only.*

TIPS "No 'cartoony' or mass-market submissions for picture books."

🅐⊘ VILLARD BOOKS

Penguin Random House, 1745 Broadway, New York NY 10019. (212)572-2600. **Website:** www.penguinrandomhouse.com. Estab. 1983. "Villard Books is the publisher of savvy and sometimes quirky, best-selling hardcovers and trade paperbacks." **Pays negotiable royalty. Pays negotiable advance.**

NONFICTION *Agented submissions only.*

FICTION Commercial fiction. *Agented submissions only.*

Ⓐ⊘ VINTAGE ANCHOR PUBLISHING

Penguin Random House, 1745 Broadway, New York NY 10019. **Website:** www.penguinrandomhouse.com. **Pays 4-8% royalty on retail price. Average advance: $2,500 and up.** Publishes ms 1 year after acceptance. Accepts simultaneous submissions.

FICTION Subjects include contemporary, literary, mainstream, short story collections. *Agented submissions only.*

VIVISPHERE PUBLISHING

675 Dutchess Turnpike, Poughkeepsie NY 12603. (845)463-1100, ext. 314. **Fax:** (845)463-0018. **E-mail:** cs@vivisphere.com. **Website:** www.vivisphere.com. **Contact:** Submissions. Estab. 1995. Publishes trade paperback originals and reprints and e-books. Vivisphere Publishing is now considering new submissions from any genre as follows: game of bridge (cards), nonfiction, history, military, new age, fiction, feminist/gay/lesbian, horror, contemporary, self-help, science fiction and cookbooks. **Pays royalty.** Publishes ms 6 months-2 years after acceptance. Accepts simultaneous submissions. Responds in 6-24 months. Book catalog and ms guidelines online.

▢ "Cookbooks should have a particular slant or appeal to a certain niche. Also publish out-of-print books."

NONFICTION Subjects include game of bridge. Query with SASE. Please submit a proposal package (printed paper copy) including: outline and 1st chapter along with your contact information. If submitting, please use above guidelines and e-mail cs@vivisphere.com.

FICTION Query with SASE.

⊘ VIZ MEDIA LLC

P.O. Box 77010, San Francisco CA 94107. (415)546-7073. **Website:** www.viz.com. "VIZ Media, LLC is one of the most comprehensive and innovative companies in the field of manga (graphic novel) publishing, animation and entertainment licensing of Japanese content. Owned by three of Japan's largest creators and licensors of manga and animation, Shueisha Inc., Shogakukan Inc., and Shogakukan-Shueisha Productions, Co., Ltd., VIZ Media is a leader in the publishing and distribution of Japanese manga for English speaking audiences in North America, the United Kingdom, Ireland, and South Africa and is a global ex-Asia licensor of Japanese manga and animation.

The company offers an integrated product line including magazines such as *Shonen Jump* and *Shojo Beat*, graphic novels, and DVDs, and develops, markets, licenses, and distributes animated entertainment for audiences and consumers of all ages." Accepts simultaneous submissions.

FICTION "At the present, all of the manga that appears in our magazines come directly from manga that has been serialized and published in Japan."

VOYAGEUR PRESS

401 Second Ave. N., Suite 310, Minneapolis MN 55401. (800)458-0454. **Fax:** (612)344-8691. **Website:** https://www.quartoknows.com/Voyageur-Press. Publisher: Jeff Serena. Estab. 1972. Publishes hardcover and trade paperback originals. "Voyageur Press (and its sports imprint MVP Books) is internationally known as a leading publisher of quality music, sports, country living, crafts, natural history, and regional books. No children's or poetry books." **Publishes 80 titles/year. 1,200 queries received/year. 500 mss received/year. 10% of books from first-time authors. 90% from unagented writers. Pays royalty. Pays advance.** Publishes ms 1 year after acceptance. Accepts simultaneous submissions. Responds in 3 months to queries.

NONFICTION Subjects include Americana, cooking, environment, history, hobbies, music, nature, regional, sports, collectibles, country living, knitting and quilting, outdoor recreation. Query with SASE. Submit outline. Send sample digital images or transparencies (duplicates and tearsheets only).

TIPS "We publish books for an audience interested in regional, natural, and cultural history on a wide variety of subjects. We seek authors strongly committed to helping us promote and sell their books. Please present as focused an idea as possible in a brief submission (1-page cover letter; 2-page outline or proposal). Note your credentials for writing the book. Tell all you know about the market niche and marketing possibilities for proposed book. We use more book designers than artists or illustrators, since most of our books are illustrated with photographs."

⊘ WAKE FOREST UNIVERSITY PRESS

P.O. Box 7333, Winston-Salem NC 27109. (336)758-5448. **Fax:** (336)758-5636. **E-mail:** wfupress@wfu.edu. **Website:** wfupress.wfu.edu. **Contact:** Jefferson Holdridge, director/poetry editor; Dillon Johnston, advisory editor. Estab. 1976. "We publish only poetry from Ireland. I am able to consider only poetry written by native Irish poets. I must return, unread, poetry from American poets." Query with 4-5 samples and cover letter. Sometimes sends prepublication galleys. Buys North American or U.S. rights. **Publishes 4-6 titles/year. Pays on 8% list royalty contract, plus 6-8 author's copies. Negotiable advance.** Responds to queries in 1-2 weeks; to submissions (*if invited*) in 2-3 months.

WALCH PUBLISHING

40 Walch Dr., Portland ME 04103. (207)772-3105. **Fax:** (207)774-7167. **Website:** www.walch.com. Estab. 1927. "We focus on English/language arts, math, social studies and science teaching resources for middle school through adult assessment titles." **Publishes 100 titles/year. 10% of books from first-time authors. 95% from unagented writers. Pays 5-8% royalty on flat rate.** Publishes ms 6 months after acceptance. Accepts simultaneous submissions. Responds in 2 months to queries.

NONFICTION Subjects include education, history, science, technology. "Most titles are assigned by us, though we occasionally accept an author's unsolicited submission. We have a great need for author/artist teams and for authors who can write at third- to seventh-grade levels." Looks for sense of organization, writing ability, knowledge of subject, skill of communicating with intended audience. Formats include teacher resources, reproducibles. "We do *not* want textbooks or anthologies. All authors should have educational writing experience." Query first.

WASHINGTON STATE UNIVERSITY PRESS

P.O. Box 645910, Pullman WA 99164-5910. (800)354-7360. **E-mail:** wsupress@wsu.edu. **E-mail:** robert.clark@wsu.edu. **Website:** wsupress.wsu.edu. **Contact:** Robert A. Clark, editor-in-chief. Beth DeWeese (beth.deweese@wsu.edu) Estab. 1928. Publishes hardcover originals, trade paperback originals, and reprints. WSU Press publishes scholarly nonfiction books on the history, pre-history, culture, and politics of the West, particularly the Pacific Northwest. **Publishes 8-10 titles/year. 40% of books from first-time authors. 95% from unagented writers. Pays 5% royalty graduated according to sales.** Publishes ms 18 months after acceptance. Accepts simultaneous submissions. Responds in 1 month to queries. Guidelines online.

NONFICTION Subjects include essays. "We welcome engaging and thought-provoking mss that focus on the greater Pacific Northwest (primarily Washington, Oregon, Idaho, British Columbia, western Montana, and southeastern Alaska). Currently we are not accepting how-to books, literary criticism, memoirs, novels, or poetry." Submit outline, sample chapters. Reviews artwork/photos.

TIPS "We have developed our marketing in the direction of regional and local history, and use this as the base upon which to expand our publishing program. For history, the secret is to write strong narratives on significant topics or events. Stories should be told in imaginative, clever ways and be substantiated factually. Have visuals (photos, maps, etc.) available to help the reader envision what has happened. Explain stories in ways that tie them to wider-ranging regional, national—or even international—events. Weave them into the large pattern of history."

WASHINGTON WRITERS' PUBLISHING HOUSE

P.O. Box 15271, Washington DC 20003. **Website:** www.washingtonwriters.org. Estab. 1975. **Offers $1,000 and 50 copies of published book plus additional copies for publicity use.** Accepts simultaneous submissions. Guidelines online.

FICTION Washington Writers' Publishing House considers book-length mss for publication by fiction writers living within 75 driving miles of the U.S. Capitol, Baltimore area included, through competition only. Mss may include previously published stories and excerpts. "Author should indicate where they heard about WWPH." Submit an electronic copy by e-mail (use PDF, .doc, or rich text format) or 2 hard copies by snail mail of a short story collection or novel (no more than 350 pages, double or 1-1/2 spaced; author's name should not appear on any ms pages). Include separate page of publication acknowledgments plus 2 cover sheets: one with ms title, poet's name, address, telephone number, and e-mail address, the other with ms title only. Include SASE for results only; mss will not be returned (will be recycled).

POETRY Washington Writers' Publishing House considers book-length mss for publication by poets living within 75 driving miles of the U.S. Capitol (Baltimore area included) through competition only. Publishes 1-2 poetry books/year. "No specific criteria, except literary excellence."

⚫⊘ WATERBROOK MULTNOMAH PUBLISHING GROUP

10807 New Allegiance Dr., Suite 500, Colorado Springs CO 80921. (719)590-4999. **Fax:** (719)590-8977. **Website:** www.waterbrookmultnomah.com. Estab. 1996. Publishes hardcover and trade paperback originals. **Publishes 70 titles/year. 2,000 queries received/year. 15% of books from first-time authors. Pays royalty.** Publishes book 1 year after acceptance. Accepts simultaneous submissions. Responds in 2-3 months. Book catalog online.

NONFICTION Subjects include child guidance, religion, spirituality, marriage, Christian living. "We publish books on unique topics with a Christian perspective." *Agented submissions only.*

FICTION Subjects include adventure, historical, literary, mystery, religious, romance, science fiction, spiritual, suspense. *Agented submissions only.*

WAVE BOOKS

1938 Fairview Ave. E., Suite 201, Seattle WA 98102. (206)676-5337. **E-mail:** info@wavepoetry.com. **Website:** www.wavepoetry.com. Estab. 2005. Publishes hardcover and trade paperback originals. "Wave Books is an independent poetry press based in Seattle, Washington, dedicated to publishing the best in contemporary American poetry, poetry in translation, and writing by poets. The Press was founded in 2005, merging with established publisher Verse Press. By publishing strong innovative work in finely crafted trade editions and handmade ephemera, we hope to continue to challenge the values and practices of readers and add to the collective sense of what's possible in contemporary poetry." Accepts simultaneous submissions. Catalog online.

POETRY "Please no unsolicited mss or queries. We will post calls for submissions on our website."

WAVELAND PRESS, INC.

4180 Illinois Rt. 83, Suite 101, Long Grove IL 60047. (847)634-0081. **Fax:** (847)634-9501. **E-mail:** info@waveland.com. **Website:** www.waveland.com. Estab. 1975. Waveland Press, Inc. is a publisher of college textbooks and supplements. "We are committed to providing reasonably priced teaching materials for the classroom and actively seek to add new titles to our growing lists in a variety of academic disciplines. If you are currently working on a project you feel serves a need and would have promise as an adopted text in the college market, we would like to hear from you." Accepts simultaneous submissions.

THE WAYWISER PRESS

P.O. Box 6205, Baltimore MD 21206. **E-mail:** info@waywiser-press.com. **Website:** waywiser-press.com. **Contact:** Philip Hoy. Estab. 2001. The Waywiser Press is a small independent company, with its main office in the UK, and a subsidiary in the USA. It publishes literary works of all kinds, but has a special interest in contemporary poetry in English. **Publishes 4-5 titles/year. Royalties paid.** Ms published 6-9 months after acceptance. Accepts simultaneous submissions. Responds in 3-6 months. Guidelines online.

NONFICTION Subjects include literary criticism, literature, memoirs.

POETRY Poets who've published one or no collections should submit to the Anthony Hecht Poetry Prize, open for submissions between August 1st and December 1st annually. Submit complete ms by post (if prospective author has already published 2 or more collections).

TIPS "We are keen to promote the work of new as well as established authors, and would like to rescue still others from undeserved neglect."

WESLEYAN PUBLISHING HOUSE

P.O. Box 50434, Indianapolis IN 46250. (800)493-7539. **E-mail:** submissions@wesleyan.org. **Website:** www.wesleyan.org/wg. **Contact:** Katie Long, Communications Coordinator. Estab. 1843. Publishes hardcover and trade paperback originals. **100 submissions received/year. Pays royalty on wholesale price. Pays advance occasionally.** Publishes book 11 months after acceptance. Responds within 2 months to proposals. Catalog online. Guidelines online.

NONFICTION Subjects include religion, Christianity. Does not want biographies, memoirs, children's products, plays, poems, art work. Not accepting unsolicited proposals. Does not review artwork.

TIPS "Our books help evangelical Christians learn about the faith or grow in their relationship with God."

⊘ WESLEYAN UNIVERSITY PRESS

215 Long Ln., Middletown CT 06459. (860)685-7711. **Fax:** (860)685-7712. **E-mail:** stamminen@wesleyan.edu. **Website:** www.wesleyan.edu/wespress. **Contact:** Suzanna Tamminen, director and editor-in-chief. Estab. 1959. Publishes hardcover originals and paperbacks. "Wesleyan University Press is a scholarly press with a focus on poetry, music, dance and cultural

studies." Wesleyan University Press is one of the major publishers of poetry in the nation. Poetry publications from Wesleyan tend to get widely (and respectfully) reviewed. **"We are accepting manuscripts by invitation only until further notice." Pays royalties, plus 10 author's copies.** Accepts simultaneous submissions. Responds to queries in 2 months; to mss in 4 months. Book catalog available free. Guidelines online.

NONFICTION Subjects include film/TV & media studies, science fiction studies, dance and poetry. *Does not accept unsolicited mss.*

POETRY *Does not accept unsolicited mss.*

WESTERN PSYCHOLOGICAL SERVICES

625 Alaska Ave., Torrance CA 90503. (424)201-8800 or (800)648-8857. **Fax:** (424)201-6950. **Website:** www.wpspublish.com. Estab. 1948. Publishes psychological and educational assessments and some trade paperback originals. "Western Psychological Services publishes psychological and educational assessments that practitioners trust. Our products allow helping professionals to accurately screen, diagnose, and treat people in need. WPS publishes practical books and games used by therapists, counselors, social workers, and others in the helping professionals who work with children and adults." **Publishes 2 titles/year. 60 queries received/year. 30 mss received/year. 90% of books from first-time authors. 95% from unagented writers. Pays 5-10% royalty on wholesale price.** Publishes ms 1 year after acceptance. Accepts simultaneous submissions. Responds in 2 months to queries. Book catalog available free. Guidelines online.

NONFICTION Subjects include child guidance. "We publish children's books dealing with feelings, anger, social skills, autism, family problems." Submit complete ms. Reviews artwork/photos. Send photocopies.

WESTMINSTER JOHN KNOX PRESS

Division of Presbyterian Publishing Corp., 100 Witherspoon St., Louisville KY 40202. **Fax:** (502)569-5113. **E-mail:** jkelley@wjkbooks.com. **Website:** www.wjkbooks.com. **Contact:** Jessica Miller Kelley, acquisitions editor. Publishes hardcover and paperback originals and reprints. "All WJK books have a religious/spiritual angle, but are written for various markets—scholarly, professional, and the general reader. Westminster John Knox is affiliated with the Presbyterian Church USA. No phone queries. We do not publish fiction, poetry, memoir, children's books, or disser-

tations. We will not return or respond to submissions without an accompanying SASE with sufficient postage." **Publishes 70 titles/year. 2,500 queries received/year. 750 mss received/year. 10% of books from first-time authors. Pays royalty on net price.** Responds in 3 months. Proposal guidelines online.

NONFICTION Subjects include religion, spirituality. Submit proposal package according to the WJK book proposal guidelines found online.

WHITAKER HOUSE

1030 Hunt Valley Circle, New Kensington PA 15068. **E-mail:** publisher@whitakerhouse.com. **Website:** www.whitakerhouse.com. **Contact:** Editorial Department. Estab. 1970. Publishes hardcover, trade paperback, and mass market originals. **Publishes 70 titles/year. 600 queries; 200 mss received/year. 15% of books from first-time authors. 60% from unagented writers. Pays 5-15% royalty on wholesale price.** Publishes ms 9 months after acceptance. Accepts simultaneous submissions. Responds in 3 months. Book catalog online. Guidelines online.

NONFICTION Subjects include religion. Accepts submissions on topics with a Christian perspective. Query with SASE. Does not review artwork/photos.

FICTION Subjects include religious. All fiction must have a Christian perspective. Query with SASE.

TIPS "Audience includes those seeking uplifting and inspirational fiction and nonfiction."

✪ WHITECAP BOOKS, LTD.

210 - 314 W. Cordova St., Vancouver BC V6B 1 E8, Canada. (604)681-6181. **Fax:** (905)477-9179. **Website:** www.whitecap.ca. Publishes hardcover and trade paperback originals. "Whitecap Books is a general trade publisher with a focus on food and wine titles. Although we are interested in reviewing unsolicited ms submissions, please note that we only accept submissions that meet the needs of our current publishing program. Please see some of most recent releases to get an idea of the kinds of titles we are interested in." **Publishes 30 titles/year. 500 queries received/year; 1,000 mss received/year. 20% of books from first-time authors. 90% from unagented writers. Pays royalty. Pays negotiated advance.** Publishes book 1 year after acceptance. Accepts simultaneous submissions. Responds in 2-3 months to proposals. Catalog and guidelines online.

NONFICTION Subjects include animals, gardening, history, recreation, regional, travel. Young children's and middle reader's nonfiction focusing mainly on nature, wildlife and animals. "Writers should take the time to research our list and read the submission guidelines on our website. This is especially important for children's writers and cookbook authors. We will only consider submissions that fall into these categories: cookbooks, wine and spirits, regional travel, home and garden, Canadian history, North American natural history, juvenile series-based fiction. At this time, we are not accepting the following categories: self-help or inspirational books, political, social commentary, or issue books, general how-to books, biographies or memoirs, business and finance, art and architecture, religion and spirituality." Submit cover letter, synopsis, SASE via ground mail. See guidelines online. Reviews artwork/photos. Send photocopies.

FICTION No children's picture books or adult fiction. See guidelines.

TIPS "We want well-written, well-researched material that presents a fresh approach to a particular topic."

WHITE MANE KIDS

73 W. Burd St., Shippensburg PA 17257. (717)532-2237. **Fax:** (717)532-6110. **E-mail:** marketing@whitemane. com. **Website:** www.whitemane.com. **Contact:** Harold Collier, acquisitions editor. Estab. 1987. **Pays authors royalty of 7-10%. Pays illustrators and photographers by the project.** Publishes book 18 months after acceptance. Accepts simultaneous submissions. Responds to queries in 1 month, mss in 6-9 months. Book catalog and writer's guidelines available for SASE.

IMPRINTS White Mane Books, Burd Street Press, White Mane Kids, Ragged Edge Press.

NONFICTION Middle readers, young adults: history. Average word length: middle readers—30,000. Does not publish picture books. Submit outline/synopsis and 2-3 sample chapters. Book proposal form on website.

FICTION Middle readers, young adults: history (primarily American Civil War). Average word length: middle readers—30,000. Does not publish picture books. Query.

TIPS "Make your work historically accurate. We are interested in historically accurate fiction for middle and young adult readers. We do *not* publish picture books. Our primary focus is the American Civil War and some America Revolution topics."

⊘ WHITE PINE PRESS

P.O. Box 236, Buffalo NY 14201. (716)627-4665. **Fax:** (716)627-4665. **E-mail:** wpine@whitepine.org. **Website:** www.whitepine.org. **Contact:** Dennis Maloney, editor. Estab. 1973. Publishes trade paperback originals. **Publishes 8-10 titles/year. Receives 500 queries/year. 1% of books from first-time authors. 100% from unagented writers. Pays contributor's copies.** Publishes ms 18 months after acceptance. Accepts simultaneous submissions. Responds in 1 month to queries and proposals; 4 months to mss. Catalog online. Guidelines online.

NONFICTION Subjects include language, literature, multicultural, translation, poetry. *"We are currently not considering nonfiction mss."*

POETRY "Only considering submissions for our annual poetry contest."

ALBERT WHITMAN & COMPANY

250 S. Northwest Hwy., Suite 320, Park Ridge IL 60068. (800)255-7675. **Fax:** (847)581-0039. **E-mail:** submissions@albertwhitman.com. **Website:** www.albertwhitman.com. Estab. 1919. Publishes in original hardcover, paperback, boardbooks. Albert Whitman & Company publishes books for the trade, library, and school library market. Interested in reviewing the following types of projects: Picture book manuscripts for ages 2-8; novels and chapter books for ages 8-12; young adult novels; nonfiction for ages 3-12 and YA; art samples showing pictures of children. Best known for the classic series The Boxcar Children® Mysteries. "We are no longer reading unsolicited queries and manuscripts sent through the US mail. We now require these submissions to be sent by e-mail. You must visit our website for our guidelines, which include instructions for formatting your e-mail. E-mails that do not follow this format may not be read. We read every submission within 4 months of receipt, but we can no longer respond to every one. If you do not receive a response from us after four months, we have declined to publish your submission." **Publishes 60 titles/year. 10% of books from first-time authors. 50% from unagented writers.** Accepts simultaneous submissions. Guidelines online.

NONFICTION Picture books up to 1,000 words. Submit cover letter, brief description.

FICTION Picture books (up to 1,000 words); middle grade (up to 35,000 words); young adult (up to 70,000 words). For picture books, submit cover letter and brief description. For middle grade and young adult, send query, synopsis, and first 3 chapters.

WILDERNESS PRESS

2204 First Ave. S., Suite 102, Birmingham AL 35233. (800)443-7227. **Fax:** (205)326-1012. **Website:** www. wildernesspress.com. Estab. 1967. Publishes paperback originals. "Wilderness Press has a long tradition of publishing the highest quality, most accurate hiking and other outdoor activity guidebooks." **Publishes 12 titles/year.** Publishes ms 8-12 months after acceptance. Accepts simultaneous submissions. Responds in 2 months to queries. Book catalog and ms guidelines online.

NONFICTION Subjects include recreation, trail guides for hikers and backpackers. "We publish books about the outdoors and some general travel guides. Many are trail guides for hikers and backpackers, but we also publish climbing, kayaking, and other outdoor activity guides, how-to books about the outdoors and urban walking books. The manuscript must be accurate. The author must research an area in person. If writing a trail guide, you must walk all the trails in the area your book is about. Outlook must be strongly conservationist. Style must be appropriate for a highly literate audience." Download proposal guidelines from website.

THE WILD ROSE PRESS

P.O. Box 708, Adams Basin NY 14410-0708. (585)752-8770. **E-mail:** queryus@thewildrosepress.com. **Website:** www.thewildrosepress.com. **Contact:** Rhonda Penders, Editor in Chief. Estab. 2006. Publishes paperback originals, reprints, and e-books in a POD format. **Publishes approx. 60 fiction titles/year. Pays royalty of 7% minimum; 40% maximum. Sends prepublication galleys to author.** Publishes ms 1 year after acceptance. Responds to queries in 4 weeks; mss in 12 weeks. Guidelines online.

FICTION Subjects include fantasy, gothic, historical, romance, short story collections, suspense, young adult, futuristic/time travel, regency, romantic suspense, erotic, and paranormal romances. Plans several anthologies "in several lines of the company in the next year, including Cactus Rose, Yellow Rose, American Rose, Black Rose, and Scarlet Rose.". *Does not accept unsolicited mss.* Send query letter with outline and synopsis of up to 5 pages. Accepts all queries by e-mail. Include estimated word count, brief bio, and

list of publishing credits. Agented fiction less than 1%. Always comments on rejected mss.

TIPS "Polish your manuscript, make it as error free as possible, and follow our submission guidelines."

JOHN WILEY & SONS, INC.

111 River St., Hoboken NJ 07030. (201)748-6000. **Fax:** (201)748-6088. **Website:** www.wiley.com. Estab. 1807. Publishes hardcover originals, trade paperback originals and reprints. **Pays competitive rates.** Accepts simultaneous submissions. Book catalog online. Guidelines online.

NONFICTION Subjects include business, communications, computers, economics, education, finance, health, psychology, science. Wiley is a global publisher of print and electronic products—including scientific, scholarly, professional, consumer, and educational content. "Please visit our website to review our submissions guidelines for Books and Journals authors."

Ⓐⵔ WILLIAM MORROW

HarperCollins, 195 Broadway, New York NY 10007. (212)207-7000. **Fax:** (212)207-7145. **Website:** www. harpercollins.com. Estab. 1926. "William Morrow publishes a wide range of titles that receive much recognition and prestige—a most selective house." **Pays standard royalty on retail price. Pays varying advance.** Accepts simultaneous submissions. Book catalog available free.

NONFICTION Subjects include history. Length 50,000-100,000 words. *No unsolicited mss or proposals. Agented submissions only.*

FICTION Publishes adult fiction. Morrow accepts only the highest quality submissions in adult fiction. *No unsolicited mss or proposals. Agented submissions only.*

WILLOW CREEK PRESS

P.O. Box 147, Minocqua WI 54548. (715)358-7010. **Fax:** (715)358-2807. **Website:** www.willowcreekpress. com. **Contact:** Sara Olson, Designer. Estab. 1986. Publishes hardcover and trade paperback originals and reprints. "We specialize in nature, outdoor, and sporting topics, including gardening, wildlife, and animal books. Pets, cookbooks, and a few humor books and essays round out our titles. Currently emphasizing pets (mainly dogs and cats), wildlife, outdoor sports (hunting, fishing). De-emphasizing essays, fiction." **Publishes 25 titles/year. 400 queries; 150 mss received/year. 15% of books from first-time authors.**

50% from unagented writers. **Pays 6-15% royalty on wholesale price. Pays $2,000-5,000 advance.** Publishes ms 18 months after acceptance. Accepts simultaneous submissions. Responds in 2 months to queries. Guidelines online.

NONFICTION Subjects include animals, gardening, recreation, sports, travel, wildlife, pets. Submit cover letter, chapter outline, 1-2 sample chapters, brief bio, SASE. Reviews artwork/photos.

WINDWARD PUBLISHING

Finney Company, 5995 149th St. W., Suite 105, Apple Valley MN 55124. **E-mail:** info@finneyco.com. **Website:** www.finneyco.com. **Contact:** Alan E. Krysan, President. Estab. 1973. Publishes trade paperback originals. Windward publishes illustrated natural history, recreation books, and children's books. "Covers topics of natural history and science, outdoor recreation, and children's literature. Its principal markets are book, retail, and specialty stores. While primarily a nonfiction publisher, we will occasionally accept fiction books with educational value." **Publishes 6-10 titles/year. 120 queries; 50 mss received/year. 50% of books from first-time authors. 100% from unagented writers. Pays 10% royalty on wholesale price. No advance.** Publishes book 1 year after acceptance. Accepts simultaneous submissions. Responds in 8-10 weeks to queries.

NONFICTION Subjects include agriculture, animals, gardening, recreation, science, sports, natural history. Young readers, middle readers, young adults: activity books, animal, careers, nature/environment, science. Young adults: textbooks. Query with SASE. Does not accept e-mail or fax submissions. Reviews artwork/photos.

WISCONSIN HISTORICAL SOCIETY PRESS

816 State St., Madison WI 53706. (608)264-6465. **Fax:** (608)264-6486. **Website:** www.wisconsinhistory.org/whspress/. Estab. 1855. Publishes hardcover and trade paperback originals; trade paperback reprints. **Publishes 12-14 titles/year. 60-75 queries received/year. 20% of books from first-time authors. 90% from unagented writers. Pays royalty on wholesale price.** Publishes ms 2 years after acceptance. Accepts simultaneous submissions. Book catalog available free. Guidelines online.

NONFICTION Subjects include history. Submit book proposal, form from website. Reviews artwork/photos. Send photocopies.

TIPS "Our audience reads about Wisconsin. Carefully review the book."

WISDOM PUBLICATIONS

199 Elm St., Somerville MA 02144. (617)776-7416, ext. 28. **Fax:** (617)776-7841. **E-mail:** editors@wisdompubs.org. **Website:** www.wisdompubs.org. **Contact:** David Kittelstrom, senior editor. Estab. 1976. Publishes hardcover originals and trade paperback originals and reprints. "Wisdom Publications is dedicated to making available authentic Buddhist works for the benefit of all. We publish translations, commentaries, and teachings of past and contemporary Buddhist masters and original works by leading Buddhist scholars. Currently emphasizing popular applied Buddhism, scholarly titles." **Publishes 30-35 titles/year. 300 queries received/year. 50% of books from first-time authors. 95% from unagented writers. Pays 8% royalty on wholesale price. Sometimes pays advance.** Publishes ms within 2 years of acceptance. Book catalog and ms guidelines online.

NONFICTION Subjects include philosophy, psychology, religion, spirituality, Buddhism, Tibet, Mindfulness. Submissions should be made electronically.

TIPS "Wisdom Publications is the leading publisher of contemporary and classic Buddhist books and practical works on mindfulness. Please see our catalog or our website before you send anything to us to get a sense of what we publish."

🅐⊘ PAULA WISEMAN BOOKS

1230 Sixth Ave., New York NY 10020. (212)698-7000. **Fax:** (212)698-2796. **Website:** kids.simonandschuster.com. Estab. 2003. Paula Wiseman Books is an imprint of Simon & Schuster Children's Publishing that launched in 2003. It has since gone on to publish over 70 award-winning and bestselling books, including picture books, novelty books, and novels. The imprint focuses on stories and art that are childlike, timeless, innovative, and centered in emotion. "We strive to publish books that entertain while expanding the experience of the children who read them, as well as stories that will endure, including those based in other cultures. We are committed to publishing new talent in both picture books and novels. We are actively seeking submissions from new and published authors and artists through agents and from SCBWI conferences." **Publishes 30 titles/year. 15% of books from first-time authors.** Accepts simultaneous submissions.

NONFICTION Picture books: animal, biography, concept, history, nature/environment. Young readers: animal, biography, history, multicultural, nature/environment, sports. Average word length: picture books—500; others standard length. Does not accept unsolicited or unagented mss. By mail preferably.

FICTION Considers all categories. Average word length: picture books—500; others standard length.

WOODBINE HOUSE

6510 Bells Mill Rd., Bethesda MD 20817. (301)897-3570. **Fax:** (301)897-5838. **E-mail:** info@woodbinehouse.com. **Website:** www.woodbinehouse.com. **Contact:** Acquisitions Editor. Estab. 1985. Publishes trade paperback originals. Woodbine House publishes books for or about individuals with disabilities to help those individuals and their families live fulfilling and satisfying lives in their homes, schools, and communities. **Publishes 10 titles/year. 15% of books from first-time authors. 90% from unagented writers. Pays 10-12% royalty.** Publishes ms 18 months after acceptance. Accepts simultaneous submissions. Responds in 3 months to queries. Guidelines online.

NONFICTION Publishes books for and about children with disabilities. No personal accounts or general parenting guides. Submit outline, and at least 3 sample chapters. Reviews artwork/photos.

FICTION Subjects include picture books. Receptive to stories re: developmental and intellectual disabilities, e.g., autism and cerebral palsy. Submit complete ms with SASE.

TIPS "Do not send us a proposal on the basis of this description. Examine our catalog or website and a couple of our books to make sure you are on the right track. Put some thought into how your book could be marketed (aside from in bookstores). Keep cover letters concise and to the point; if it's a subject that interests us, we'll ask to see more."

Ⓐ WORDSONG

815 Church St., Honesdale PA 18431. **Fax:** (570)253-0179. **Website:** www.wordsongpoetry.com. Estab. 1990. "We publish fresh voices in contemporary poetry." **Pays authors royalty or work purchased outright.** Accepts simultaneous submissions. Responds to mss in 3 months.

POETRY *Agented submissions only.*

TIPS "Collections of original poetry, not anthologies, are our biggest need at this time. Keep in mind that the strongest collections demonstrate a facility with multiple poetic forms and offer fresh images and insights. Check to see what's already on the market and on our website before submitting."

WORKMAN PUBLISHING CO.

225 Varick St., New York NY 10014. **E-mail:** info@workman.com. **Website:** www.workman.com. Estab. 1967. Publishes hardcover and trade paperback originals, as well as calendars. "We are a trade paperback house specializing in a wide range of popular nonfiction. We publish no adult fiction and very little children's fiction. We also publish a full range of full-color wall and Page-A-Day calendars." **Publishes 40 titles/year. thousands of queries received/year. Open to first-time authors. Pays variable royalty on retail price. Pays variable advance.** Publishes ms approximately 1 year after acceptance. Accepts simultaneous submissions. Responds in 5 months to queries. Guidelines online.

NONFICTION Subjects include child guidance, gardening, sports, travel. Query.

TIPS "We prefer electronic submissions."

WORLD BOOK, INC.

180 N. LaSalle St., Suite 900, Chicago IL 60601. (312)729-5800. **Fax:** (312)729-5600. **E-mail:** service@worldbook.com. **Website:** www.worldbook.com. World Book, Inc. (publisher of The World Book Encyclopedia), publishes reference sources and nonfiction series for children and young adults in the areas of science, mathematics, English-language skills, basic academic and social skills, social studies, history, and health and fitness. "We publish print and nonprint material appropriate for children ages 3-14. WB does not publish fiction, poetry, or wordless picture books." **Payment negotiated on project-by-project basis.** Publishes book 18 months after acceptance. Accepts simultaneous submissions. Responds to queries in 2 months.

NONFICTION Young readers: animal, arts/crafts, careers, concept, geography, health, reference. Middle readers: animal, arts/crafts, careers, geography, health, history, hobbies, how-to, nature/environment, reference, science. Young adult: arts/crafts, careers, geography, health, history, hobbies, how-to, nature/environment, reference, science. Query.

WORLD WEAVER PRESS

Albuquerque NM 87111. **E-mail:** submissions@worldweaverpress.com. **Website:** www.worldweaverpress.com. **Contact:** WWP Editors. Estab. 2012. World Weaver

Press publishes digital and print editions of speculative fiction at various lengths for adult, young adult, and new adult audiences. "We believe in great storytelling." **Publishes 10-12 titles/year. 85% from unagented writers. Average royalty rate of 39% net on all editions. No advance.** Publishes ms 6-24 months after acceptance. Accepts simultaneous submissions. Responds to query letters within 3 weeks. Responses to mss requests take longer. Catalog online. Guidelines on website.

NONFICTION Subjects include pop culture, folklore and fairy tale studies.

FICTION Subjects include adventure, erotica, fantasy, feminist, gay, lesbian, multicultural, romance, science fiction, young adult. "We believe that publishing speculative fiction isn't just printing words on the page — it's the act of weaving brand new worlds. Seeking speculative fiction in many varieties: protagonists who have strength, not fainting spells; intriguing worlds with well-developed settings; characters that are to die for (we'd rather find ourselves in love than just in lust)." Full list of interests on website. Does not want giant bugs, ghosts, post-apocalyptic and/or dystopia, angels, zombies, magical realism, surrealism, middle grade (MG) or younger. Queries accepted only during February unless otherwise stated on website. Full guidelines will be updates approximately one month before submissions open.

TIPS "Use your letter to pitch us the story, not talk about its themes or inception."

WORTHY KIDS/IDEALS BOOKS

6100 Tower Circle, Suite 210, Franklin TN 37067. **Website:** www.idealsbooks.com. Estab. 1944. Accepts simultaneous submissions.

NONFICTION Worthy Kids/Ideals publishes for ages birth to 8, no longer than 800 words. Submit complete ms.

FICTION Subjects include juvenile. Picture books: animal, concept, history, religion. Board books: animal, history, nature/environment, religion. Worthy Kids/Ideals publishes for ages birth to 8, no longer than 800 words. Submit complete ms.

WRITE BLOODY PUBLISHING

Austin TX **Website:** writebloody.com. **Contact:** Derrick Brown, president. We publish and promote great books of poetry every year. We are a small press with a snappy look, dedicated to quality literature that is proud to be printed in the USA. We are not a printer. We are a sweet publishing house located on the outskirts of Austin, Texas. Accepts simultaneous submissions. Catalog online. Guidelines online.

POETRY Reading period August 1-31. Check online for details.

TIPS "You must tour if you are part of our family. At least 20 shows a year. Just like a band."

WRITER'S DIGEST BOOKS

Imprint of F+W, a Content + eCommerce Company, 10151 Carver Rd., Suite #200, Cincinnati OH 45242. **E-mail:** writersdigest@fwmedia.com. **Website:** www.writersdigest.com. **Contact:** Cris Freese. Estab. 1920. Publishes hardcover originals and trade paperbacks. "Writer's Digest Books is the premiere source for instructional books on writing and publishing for an audience of aspirational writers. Typical mss are 80,000 words. E-mail queries strongly preferred; no phone calls please." **Publishes 18-20 titles/year. 300 queries; 50 mss received/year. 30% from unagented writers. Pays average $3,000 advance.** Publishes book 1 year after acceptance. Accepts simultaneous submissions. Responds in 3 months to queries. "Our catalog of titles is available to view online at www.WritersDigestShop.com.".

Writer's Digest Books accepts query letters and complete proposals via e-mail at writersdigest@fwcommunity.com.

NONFICTION "Our instruction books stress results and how to achieve them. Should be well-researched, yet lively and readable. We do not want to see books telling readers how to crack specific nonfiction markets: *Writing for the Computer Market* or *Writing for Trade Publications*, for instance. We are most in need of fiction-technique books written by published authors. Be prepared to explain how the proposed book differs from existing books on the subject." No fiction or poetry. Query with SASE. Submit outline, sample chapters, SASE.

TIPS "Most queries we receive are either too broad (how to write fiction) or too niche (how to write erotic horror), and don't reflect a knowledge of our large backlist of 150 titles. We rarely publish new books on journalism, freelancing, magazine article writing or marketing/promotion. We are actively seeking fiction and nonfiction writing technique books with fresh perspectives, interactive and visual writing instruction books, similar to *The Pocket Muse* by Monica Wood, and general reference works that appeal to an audience beyond writers."

YALE UNIVERSITY PRESS

P.O. Box 209040, New Haven CT 06520. (203)432-0960. **Fax:** (203)432-0948. **E-mail:** Contact specific editor (see website). **Website:** yalebooks.com. Estab. 1908. Publishes hardcover and trade paperback originals. "Yale University Press publishes scholarly and general interest books." Accepts simultaneous submissions. Book catalog and ms guidelines online.

NONFICTION Subjects include Americana, education, history, philosophy, psychology, religion, science, sociology. "Our nonfiction has to be at a very high level. Most of our books are written by professors or journalists, with a high level of expertise. *Submit proposals only. We'll ask if we want to see more. No unsolicited mss. We won't return them.*" Submit sample chapters, cover letter, prospectus, CV, TOC, SASE. Reviews artwork/photos. Send photocopies.

POETRY Submit to Yale Series of Younger Poets Competition. Guidelines online.

TIPS "Audience is scholars, students and general readers."

YELLOW SHOE FICTION SERIES

LSU Press, P.O. Box 25053, Baton Rouge LA 70894. **Website:** www.lsu.edu/lsupress. **Contact:** Michael Griffith, editor. Estab. 2004. **Publishes 2 titles/year. Pays royalty. Offers advance.** Accepts simultaneous submissions.

> "Looking first and foremost for literary excellence, especially good manuscripts that have fallen through the cracks at the big commercial presses. I'll cast a wide net."

FICTION Does not accept unsolicited mss. Accepts queries by mail, Attn: James W. Long.

YMAA PUBLICATION CENTER

P.O. Box 480, Wolfeboro NH 03894. (603)569-7988. **Fax:** (603)569-1889. **Website:** ymaa.com. Estab. 1982. Publishes trade paperback originals and reprints. Publishes 6-8 DVD titles/year. YMAA publishes books on Chinese Chi Kung (Qigong), Taijiquan, (Tai Chi) and Asian martial arts. We are expanding our focus to include books on healing, wellness, meditation and subjects related to Asian culture and Asian medicine. **Publishes 6-8 titles/year. 50 queries; 20 mss received/year. 25% of books from first-time authors. 100% from unagented writers.** Publishes ms 18 months after acceptance. Accepts simultaneous submissions. Responds in 3 months to proposals. Book catalog online. Guidelines available free.

NONFICTION Subjects include ethnic, history, philosophy, spirituality, sports, Asian martial arts, Chinese Qigong. "We no longer publish or solicit books for children. We also produce instructional DVDs and videos to accompany our books on traditional Chinese martial arts, meditation, massage, and Chi Kung. We are most interested in Asian martial arts, Chinese medicine, and Chinese Qigong. We publish Eastern thought, health, meditation, massage, and East/West synthesis." Submit proposal package, outline, bio, 1 sample chapter, SASE. Reviews artwork/photos. Send Send photocopies and 1-2 originals to determine quality of photo/line art.

TIPS "If you are submitting health-related material, please refer to an Asian tradition. Learn about author publicity options as your participation is mandatory."

YOGI IMPRESSIONS BOOKS PVT. LTD.

1711, Centre 1, World Trade Centre, Cuffe Parade Mumbai 400 005, India. **E-mail:** yogi@yogiimpressions.com. **Website:** www.yogiimpressions.com. Estab. 2000. "Yogi Impressions are Self-help, Personal Growth and Spiritual book publishers based in Mumbai, India. Established at the turn of the millennium, at Mumbai, Yogi Impressions publishes books which seek to revive interest in spirituality, enhance the quality of life and, thereby, create the legacy of a better world for future generations." Accepts simultaneous submissions. Guidelines online.

NONFICTION Subjects include child guidance, multicultural, religion, spirituality, alternative health, enlightened business, self-improvement/personal growth. Submit outline/proposal, bio, 2-3 sample chapters, market assessment, SASE.

ZEBRA BOOKS

Kensington, 119 W. 40th St., New York NY 10018. (212)407-1500. **E-mail:** esogah@kensingtonbooks.com. **Website:** www.kensingtonbooks.com. **Contact:** Esi Sogah, senior editor. Publishes hardcover originals, trade paperback and mass market paperback originals and reprints. Zebra Books is dedicated to women's fiction, which includes, but is not limited to romance. Publishes ms 12-18 months after acceptance. Accepts simultaneous submissions. Book catalog online.

FICTION Query.

ZEST BOOKS

2443 Fillmore St., Suite 340, San Francisco CA 94115. (415)777-8654. **Fax:** (415)777-8653. **E-mail:** info@zestbooks.net. **Website:** zestbooks.net. **Contact:** Dan

Harmon, publishing director. Zest Books is a leader in young adult nonfiction, publishing books on entertainment, history, science, health, fashion, and lifestyle advice since 2006. Zest Books is distributed by Houghton Mifflin Harcourt. Accepts simultaneous submissions. Guidelines online.

NONFICTION Submit proposal.

TIPS "If you're interested in becoming a member of our author pool, send a cover letter stating why you are interested in young adult nonfiction, plus your specific areas of interest and specialties, your resume, 3-5 writing samples."

ZUMAYA PUBLICATIONS, LLC

3209 S. Interstate 35, Austin TX 78741. (512)537-3145. **Fax:** (512)276-6745. **E-mail:** business@zumayapublishing.com. **E-mail:** acquisitions@zumayapublications.com. **Website:** www.zumayapublications.com. **Contact:** Rie Sheridan Rose, acquisitions editor. Estab. 1999. Publishes trade paperback and electronic originals and reprints. Zumaya Publications is a digitally-based micro-press publishing mainly in on-demand trade paperback and e-book formats. "We currently offer approximately 190 fiction titles in the mystery, SF/F, historical, romance, LGBTQ, horror, and occult genres in adult, young adult, and middle reader categories. In 2016, we plan to officially launch our graphic and illustrated novel imprint, Zumaya Fabled Ink. We publish approximately 10-15 new titles annually, at least five of which are from new authors. We do not publish erotica or graphic erotic romance at this time. We accept only electronic queries; all others will be discarded unread. A working knowledge of computers and relevant software is a necessity, as our production process is completely digital." **Publishes 10-15 titles/year. 1,000 queries; 50 mss requested/year. 5% of books from first-time authors. 98% from unagented writers. Pay 20% of net on paperbacks, net defined as cover price less printing and other associated costs; 50% of net on all e-books. Does not pay advance.** Publishes book 2 years after acceptance. Responds in 3 months to queries and proposals; 6 months to mss. Guidelines online.

IMPRINTS Zumaya Arcane (New Age, inspirational fiction & nonfiction), Zumaya Boundless (GLBTQ); Zumaya Embraces (romance/women's fiction); Zumaya Enigma (mystery/suspense/thriller); Zumaya Thresholds (YA/middle grade); Zumaya Otherworlds (SF/F/H), Zumaya Yesterdays (memoirs, historical fiction, fiction, western fiction); Zumaya Fabled Ink (graphic and illustrated novels).

NONFICTION Subjects include creative nonfiction, memoirs, New Age, psychic, spirituality, true crime, true ghost stories. "The easiest way to figure out what we're looking for is to look at what we've already done. Our main nonfiction interests are in collections of true ghost stories, ones that have been investigated or thoroughly documented, memoirs that address specific regions and eras from a 'normal person' viewpoint and books on the craft of writing. That doesn't mean we won't consider something else." Electronic query only. Reviews artwork/photos. Send digital format.

FICTION Subjects include adventure, contemporary, ethnic, fantasy, feminist, gay, gothic, historical, horror, humor, juvenile, lesbian, literary, military, multicultural, mystery, occult, romance, science fiction, short story collections, spiritual, suspense, war, western, young adult. "We are open to all genres, particularly GLBT and YA/middle grade, historical and western, New Age/inspirational (no overtly Christian materials, please), non-category romance, thrillers. We encourage people to review what we've already published so as to avoid sending us more of the same, at least, insofar as the plot is concerned. While we're always looking for good mysteries, especially cozies, mysteries with historical settings, and police procedurals, we want original concepts rather than slightly altered versions of what we've already published. We do not publish erotica or graphically erotic romance at this time." Does not want erotica, graphically erotic romance, experimental, literary (unless it fits into one of our established imprints). A copy of our rules of submission is posted on our website and can be downloaded. They are rules rather than guidelines and should be read carefully before submitting. It will save everyone time and frustration.

TIPS "We're catering to readers who may have loved last year's best seller but not enough to want to read 10 more just like it. Have something different. If it does not fit standard pigeonholes, that's a plus. On the other hand, it has to have an audience. And if you're not prepared to work with us on promotion and marketing, particularly via social media, it would be better to look elsewhere."

CONSUMER MAGAZINES

Selling your writing to consumer magazines is as much an exercise of your marketing skills as it is of your writing abilities. Editors of consumer magazines are looking for good writing which communicates pertinent information to their readers.

Marketing skills will help you successfully discern a magazine's editorial slant, and write queries and articles that prove your knowledge of the magazine's readership. You can gather clues about a magazine's readership—and establish your credibility with the editor—in a number of ways: Read the listing in *Writer's Market*; study a magazine's writer's guidelines; check a magazine's website; and read current issues of the magazine.

Writers who can correctly and consistently discern a publication's audience and deliver stories that speak to that target readership will win out every time over writers who submit haphazardly.

In nonfiction, editors continue to look for short feature articles covering specialized topics. Editors want crisp writing and expertise. If you are not an expert in the area about which you are writing, make yourself one through research. Always query before sending your manuscript.

Fiction editors prefer to receive complete manuscripts. Writers must keep in mind that fiction is competitive, and editors receive far more material than they can publish. For this reason, they often do not respond to submissions unless they are interested in using the story.

Most magazines listed here have indicated pay rates; some give very specific payment-per-word rates, while others state a range. Any agreement you come to with a magazine, whether verbal or written, should specify the payment you are to receive and when you are to receive it.

ANIMAL

AKC GAZETTE

American Kennel Club, 260 Madison Ave., New York NY 10016. (212)696-8200. **Website:** www.akc.org/pubs/gazette. **85% freelance written.** Monthly magazine. "Geared to interests of fanciers of purebred dogs as opposed to commercial interests or pet owners. We require solid expertise from our contributors—we are *not* a pet magazine." Estab. 1889. Circ. 60,000. Byline given. Pays on publication. Offers 10% kill fee. Publishes ms an average of 6 months after acceptance. Submit seasonal material 6 months in advance. Accepts queries by mail. Accepts simultaneous submissions. Responds in 2 months to queries. Guidelines for #10 SASE.

NONFICTION Needs general interest, how-to, humor, interview, photo feature, travel, dog art, training and canine performance sports. No poetry, tributes to individual dogs, or fiction. **Buys 30-40 mss/year.** Length: 1,000-3,000 words. **Pays $300-500.**

PHOTOS Photo contest guidelines for #10 SASE. State availability. Captions, identification of subjects, model releases required. Reviews color transparencies, prints. Pays $50-200/photo. Buys one-time rights.

FICTION Annual short fiction contest only. Guidelines for #10 SASE. Send entries to AKC Publications Fiction Contest.

TIPS "Contributors should be involved in the dog fancy or be an expert in the area they write about (veterinary, showing, field trialing, obedience training, dogs in legislation, dog art or history or literature). All submissions are welcome but author must be a credible expert or be able to interview and quote the experts. Veterinary articles must be written by or with veterinarians. Humorous features or personal experiences relative to purebred dogs should have broader applications. For features, know the subject thoroughly and be conversant with jargon peculiar to the sport of dogs."

THE AMERICAN QUARTER HORSE JOURNAL

AQHA, 1600 Quarter Horse Dr., Amarillo TX 79104. (806)376-4811. **Website:** www.aqha.com. Editor-in-Chief: Becky Newell. **30% freelance written. Prefers to work with published/established writers.** Monthly official publication of the american quarter horse association. covering American Quarter Horses/ horse activities/western lifestyle. "Covers the American Wuarter Horse breed and more than 30 disciplines in which Quarter Horses compete. Business stories, lifestyles stories, how-to stories and others related to the breed and horse activities." Estab. 1948. Circ. 60,000. Byline given. Pays on acceptance. Offers 60% kill fee. Publishes ms an average of 3 months after acceptance. Editorial lead time 3 months. Submit seasonal material 3 months in advance. Accepts queries by mail, e-mail. Accepts simultaneous submissions. Responds in 1 week to queries. Responds in 1 month to mss. Sample copy free. Guidelines free.

NONFICTION Needs book excerpts, essays, general interest, historical, how-to, humor, inspirational, interview, "Must be about established horses or people who have made a contribution to the business, new prod, opinion, personal exp, photo, technical, equine updates, new surgery procedures, etc." Special issues: Annual stallion issue dedicated to the breeding of horses. **Buys 10 mss/year.** Query with published clips. Length: 700-3,000 words. **Pays $250-1,500 for assigned articles. Pays $250-1,500 for unsolicited articles.**

PHOTOS State availability. Captions, identification of subjects required. Reviews GIF/JPEG files. Buys all rights.

COLUMNS/DEPARTMENTS Quarter's Worth (Industry news); Horse Health (health items), 750 words. **Buys 6 mss/yr. mss/year.** Query with published clips. **Pays $100-$400.**

TIPS "Writers must have a knowledge of the horse business."

🟢🟢 APPALOOSA JOURNAL

2720 W. Pullman Rd., Moscow ID 83843. (208)882-5578. **Fax:** (208)882-8150. **E-mail:** editor@appaloosajournal.com; designer2@appaloosajournal.com. **Website:** www.appaloosajournal.com. **Contact:** Dana Russell, editor; John Langston, art director. **40% freelance written.** Monthly magazine covering Appaloosa horses. "*Appaloosa Journal* is the authoritative, association-based source for information about the Appaloosa Horse Club, the Appaloosa breed and the Appaloosa industry. Our mission is to cultivate a broader membership base and instill enthusiasm for the breed by recognizing the needs and achievements of the Appaloosa, ApHC members, enthusiasts and our readers. The Appaloosa Horse Club is a not-for-profit organization. Serious inquiries within specified budget only." Estab. 1946. Circ. 25,000. Byline given. Pays on publication. Publishes ms an average of 3 months after acceptance. Accepts simultaneous submissions. Responds in 1 month to queries. Responds in 2 months to mss. Sample copy free. Guidelines available online.

○ *Appaloosa Journal* no longer accepts material for columns.

NONFICTION Needs historical, interview. **Buys 15-20 mss/year.** Send complete ms. *Appaloosa Journal* is not responsible for unsolicited materials. All freelance correspondence should be directed to editor Dana Russell via e-mail, with the subject line "'Freelance.' Article-length reports of timely and newsworthy events, such as shows, races, and overseas competition, are welcome but must be pre-approved by the editor. Mss exceeding the preferred word length will be evaluated according to relevance and content matter. Lengthy stories, opinion pieces, or poorly written pieces will be rejected. Mss may be sent on a CD or via e-mail in Microsoft Word or text-only format. If sent via CD, an accompanying hard copy should be printed, double spaced, following the guidelines." Length: 1,500-1,800 words (features); 600-800 words (article-length). **Pays $200-400.**

PHOTOS In photographer's samples, wants to see "high-quality color photos of world-class, characteristic (coat patterned) Appaloosa horses in appealing, picturesque outdoor environments." Send photos. Captions, identification of subjects required. Payment varies. Pays $200 for color cover; $25 minimum for color inside. Pays on publication. Credit line given. Buys first rights.

TIPS "Articles by writers with horse knowledge, news sense, and photography skills are in great demand. If it's a strong article about an Appaloosa, the writer has a pretty good chance of publication. A good understanding of the breed and the industry, breeders, and owners is helpful. Make sure there's some substance and a unique twist."

○ HORSE CANADA

Horse Publications Group, Box 670, Aurora ON L4G 4J9 Canada. (905)727-0107. **Fax:** (905)841-1530. **E-mail:** hceditor@horse-canada.com. **Website:** www. horse-canada.com. **Contact:** Amy Harris, managing editor. **80% freelance written.** National magazine for horse lovers of all ages. Readers are committed horse owners with many different breeds involved in a variety of disciplines—from beginner riders to industry

professionals. Circ. 20,000. No kill fee. Editorial lead time 2 months. Accepts queries by e-mail. Accepts simultaneous submissions. Guidelines available online.

NONFICTION Query. Length: 750-1,500 words. **Payment varies.**

PHOTOS State availability of or send photos.

COLUMNS/DEPARTMENTS **Payment varies.**

⊖ ⊖ HORSE ILLUSTRATED

I-5 Publishing, 470 Conway Ct., Suite b-6, Lexington KY 40511. (800)546-7730. **E-mail:** horseillustrated@ luminamedia.com. **Website:** www.horseillustrated. com. **Contact:** Elizabeth Moyer, editor. **90% freelance written. Prefers to work with published/established writers, but will work with new/unpublished writers.** Monthly magazine covering all aspects of horse ownership. "Our readers are adults, mostly women, between the ages of 18 and 40; stories should be geared to that age group and reflect responsible horse care." Estab. 1976. Circ. 160,660. Byline given. Pays on publication. Publishes ms an average of 8 months after acceptance. Submit seasonal material 6 months in advance. Accepts queries by mail. Accepts simultaneous submissions. Responds in 3 months to queries. Guidelines available at www.horsechannel.com/horse-magazines/horse-illustrated/submission-guidelines.aspx.

NONFICTION Needs general interest, how-to, inspirational, photo feature. "No little girl horse stories, cowboy and Indian stories, or anything not *directly* relating to horses." **Buys 20 mss/year.** Query or send complete ms. Length: 1,000-2,000 words. **Pays $200-475.**

PHOTOS Send high-res digital images on a CD with thumbnails.

TIPS "Freelancers can break in at this publication with feature articles on Western and English training methods; veterinary and general care how-to articles; and horse sports articles. We rarely use personal experience articles. Submit photos with training and how-to articles whenever possible. We have a very good record of developing new freelancers into regular contributors/columnists. We are always looking for fresh talent, but certainly enjoy working with established writers who know the ropes as well. We are accepting less unsolicited freelance work—much is now assigned and contracted."

JUST LABS

Willow Creek Press, 2779 Aero Park Dr., Traverse City MI 49686. (231)946-3712; (800)-447-7367. **E-**

mail: jake@villagepress.com; jillian.lacross@villagepress.com. **E-mail:** jillian.lacross@villagepress.com. **Website:** www.justlabsmagazine.com. **Contact:** Jason Smith, editor; Jill LaCross, managing and web editor. **50% freelance written.** Bimonthly magazine covering all aspects of the Labrador Retriever. "*Just Labs* is targeted toward the family Labrador Retriever, and all of our articles help people learn about, live with, train, take care of, and enjoy their dogs. We do not look for articles that pull at the heart strings, but rather we look for articles that teach, inform, and entertain." Estab. 2001. Circ. 15,000. Byline given. Pays on publication. Offers 40% kill fee. Publishes ms an average of 6 months after acceptance. Editorial lead time 6 months. Submit seasonal material 6-8 months in advance. Accepts queries by mail, e-mail. Accepts simultaneous submissions. Responds in 4-6 weeks to queries; in 2 months to mss. Guidelines by e-mail.

NONFICTION Needs essays, how-to, humor, inspirational, interview, photo feature, technical, travel. "We don't want tributes to dogs that have passed on. This is a privilege we reserve for our subscribers." **Buys 30 mss/year.** Query. Length: 1,200-1,800 words. **Pays $250-400.**

PHOTOS Send photos. Captions required. Reviews contact sheets, transparencies, prints, GIF/JPEG files. Offers no additional payment for photos accepted with ms. Buys one-time rights.

TIPS "Be professional, courteous, and understanding of our time. Please be aware that we have been around for several years and have probably published an article on almost every 'dog topic' out there. Those queries providing fresh, unique, and interesting angles on common topics will catch our eye."

USDF CONNECTiON

United States Dressage Federation, 4051 Iron Works Pkwy., Lexington KY 40511. **E-mail:** connection@usdf.org. **E-mail:** editorial@usdf.org. **Website:** www.usdf.org. **Contact:** Jennifer Bryant. **40% freelance written.** Magazine published 10 times/year covering dressage (an equestrian sport). All material must relate to the sport of dressage in the U.S. Estab. 2000. Circ. 35,000. Byline given. Pays on acceptance. Offers 50% kill fee. Publishes ms an average of 6 months after acceptance. Editorial lead time: 3 months. Submit seasonal material 6 months in advance. Accepts queries by e-mail. Responds in 1 month to queries; in 1-2 months to mss. Sample copy: $5. Guidelines available online.

NONFICTION Needs book excerpts, essays, how-to, interview, opinion, personal experience. Does not want general-interest equine material or stories that lack a U.S. dressage angle. **Buys 20 mss/year.** Query. Length: 500-2,000 words. **Pays $100-400 for assigned articles. Pays $100-300 for unsolicited articles. Byline only for "The Tail End," a one-page personal or op/ed column pertaining to USDF members' dressage experiences.**

PHOTOS State availability. Captions, identification of subjects required. Reviews JPEG files. Negotiates payment individually. Buys one-time rights.

COLUMNS/DEPARTMENTS Amateur Hour (profiles of and service pieces of interest to USDF's adult amateur members), 1,200-1,500 words; Under 21 (profiles of and service pieces of interest to USDF's young members), 1,200-1,500 words; Horse-Health Connection (dressage-related horse health), 1,200-1,800 words. **Buys 12 mss/year.** Query with published clips. **Pays $150-300.**

TIPS "Know the organization and the sport. Most successful contributors are active in the horse industry and bring valuable perspectives and insights to their stories and images."

YOUNG RIDER

2030 Main Street, Irvine CA 92614. (949) 855-8822. **Fax:** (949) 855-3045. **E-mail:** yreditor@i5publishing.com. **Website:** www.youngrider.com. "*Young Rider* magazine teaches young people, in an easy-to-read and entertaining way, how to look after their horses properly, and how to improve their riding skills safely." Byline given. Accepts simultaneous submissions. Guidelines available online.

NONFICTION young adults: animal, careers, famous equestrians, health (horse), horse celebrities, riding. Special issues: Wants "'horsey-interest type stories. Stories or events that will interest kids ALL over the country that the editor is not able to personally attend. We need 4-5 good color photos with stories like this; the pictures must be color and tack sharp." Query with published clips. Length: 800-1,000 words. **Pays $200/story.**

FICTION young adults: adventure, animal, horses. "We would prefer funny stories, with a bit of conflict, which will appeal to the 13-year-old age group. They should be written in the third person, and about kids." Query. Length: 800-1,000 words. **Pays $150.**

TIPS "Fiction must be in third person. Read magazine before sending in a query. No 'true story from when I was a youngster.' No moralistic stories. Fiction must be up-to-date and humorous, teen-oriented. No practical or how-to articles—all done in-house."

ART & ARCHITECTURE

$$ THE ARTIST'S MAGAZINE

F+W Media, 10151 Carver Rd., Suite 200, Blue Ash OH 45242. (513)531-2690, ext. 11731. **Fax:** (513)891-7153. **Website:** www.artistsmagazine.com. **Contact:** Maureen Bloomfield, editor in chief; Brian Roeth, senior art director. **80% freelance written.** Magazine published 10 times/year covering primarily two-dimensional art for working artists. Maureen Bloomfield says, "Ours is a highly visual approach to teaching serious amateur and professional artists techniques that will help them improve their skills and market their work. The style should be crisp and immediately engaging, written in a voice that speaks directly to artists. We do not accept unsolicited mss. Artists should send digital images of their work; writers should send clips of previously published work, along with a query letter." Circ. 100,000. Bionote given for features and columns. Pays on receiving ms. Offers 8% kill fee. Publishes ms an average of 6 months-1 year after acceptance. Responds in 6 months to queries. Sample copy: $6.99. Guidelines available online.

 Sponsors 3 annual contests. Look online for information on contests.

NONFICTION Needs book excerpts, essays, historical, how-to, interview, new product, profile. No unillustrated articles. **Buys 60 mss/year.** Length: 500-1,200 words. **Pays $300-500 and up.**

PHOTOS Images of artwork must be in the form of high-quality, high-resolution digital files. Full captions must accompany these. Buys all rights.

TIPS "Look at several current issues and read the author's guidelines carefully. Remember that our readers are professional artists. Pitch an article; send clips. Do not send a finished article."

$$ ARTLINK

Artlink Australia, P.O. Box 182, Fullarton SA 5063 Australia. (61)(8)8271-6228. **E-mail:** info@artlink. com.au. **Website:** www.artlink.com.au. **Contact:**

Eve Sullivan, executive editor. Quarterly magazine covering contemporary art in Australia. Estab. 1981. Accepts simultaneous submissions. Guidelines available online.

NONFICTION Needs general interest. Special issues: "*Artlink* welcomes proposals for writing and information on associated projects and exhibition programs that relate to forthcoming themed issues." See website for upcoming themes. Write or e-mail the editor with your CV and 2-3 examples of previously published writing. **Pays $300/1,000 words.**

TIPS "Because *Artlink* is a themed magazine which tries to make art relevant across society, we often need to find contributors who have expert knowledge of subjects outside of the art area who can put the work of artists in a broader context."

$$$$ AZURE (ARCHITECTURE, DESIGN, INTERIORS, CURIOSITY)

213 Sterling Rd., Suite 206, Toronto ON M6R 2B2 Canada. 416-203-9674. **E-mail:** editorial@azureonline.com; azure@azureonline.com. **Website:** www.azuremagazine.com. **Contact:** David Dick-Agnew, senior editor. **75% freelance written.** Magazine covering design and architecture. "*AZURE* is an award-winning magazine with a focus on contemporary architecture and design. In 8 visually stunning issues per year, *AZURE* explores inventive projects, emerging trends, and design issues that relate to our changing society. In recent years, *AZURE* has evolved into a media brand offering digital editions, weekly e-newsletters featuring the latest design news, an interactive website updated daily, and an international awards program celebrating excellence in design." Estab. 1985. Byline given. Pays on publication. Offers variable kill fee. Publishes ms an average of 1 month after acceptance. Editorial lead time up to 45 days. Accepts queries by e-mail. Accepts simultaneous submissions. Responds in 6 weeks to queries.

NONFICTION Needs new product, profile, technical, travel. Special issues: January/February: Houses; March/April: Iconic Buildings; June: Office Spaces; July/August: AZ Awards Annual; October: Trends; December: Interiors and Higher Ed. Does not want "anything other than architecture, design, urbanism and landscape, and tangentially related topics." **Buys 25-30 mss/year.** Length: 300-1,500 words. **Pays $1/word (Canadian).**

COLUMNS/DEPARTMENTS Groundbreaker (profiles of new, large architectural projects) 350 words; book and documentary reviews, 300 words; Field Trip (profiles of hospitality/travel spaces with design angle), 800 words; Trailer (idiosyncratic design stories) 300 words. **Buys 30 mss/year.** Query. **Pays $1/ word (Canadian).**

TIPS "Try to understand what the magazine is about. Writers must be well versed in the field of architecture and design. It's very unusual to get something from someone I haven't worked quite closely with and gotten a sense of who the writer is. The best way to introduce yourself is by sending clips or writing samples and describing what your background is in the field."

☾☻❸ ESPACE

Le Centre de Diffusion 3D, 423-5445 Avenue De Gaspé, Montreal QC H2J 3B2 Canada. (514)907-6147. **E-mail:** info@espaceartactuel.com. **Website:** www. espaceartactuel.com. **Contact:** Serge Fisette, editor. **95% freelance written.** Quarterly magazine covering sculpture events. Estab. 1987. Circ. 1,400. Byline given. Pays on publication. No kill fee. Publishes ms an average of 3 months after acceptance. Editorial lead time 5 months. Submit seasonal material 3 months in advance. Accepts queries by e-mail. Accepts simultaneous submissions. Sample copy free. Guidelines online.

NONFICTION Needs interview, reviews, sculpture events. **Buys 60 mss/year.** Send complete ms. Length: up to 1,000 words for reviews; 1,500-2,000 words for interviews, events. **Pays $65/page.**

PHOTOS Send photos. Reviews transparencies, prints. Offers no additional payment for photos accepted with ms.

FORM: PIONEERING DESIGN

Balcony Media, Inc., 812 E. Fremont, Suite 205, South Pasadena CA 91030. (626)460-8339. **E-mail:** edit@ formmag.net. **Website:** www.formmag.net. **80% freelance written.** Bimonthly magazine covering architecture, interiors, landscape, and other design disciplines. *Form: Pioneering Design* is interested in architecture, interiors, product, graphics, and landscape design as well as news about the arts. We encourage designers to keep us informed on projects, techniques, and products that are innovative, new, or nationally newsworthy. We are especially interested in new and renovated projects that illustrate a high degree of design integrity and unique answers to typical problems in the urban cultural and physical environment. Es-

tab. 1999. Circ. 20,000. Byline given. Pays on publication. No kill fee. Publishes ms an average of 3 months after acceptance. Editorial lead time 4 months. Submit seasonal material 4 months in advance. Accepts queries by mail, e-mail, fax. Accepts simultaneous submissions. Responds in 1 month.

NONFICTION Needs book excerpts, essays, historical, interview, new product. **Buys 20 mss/year.** Length: 500-2,000 words. **Payment negotiable.**

PHOTOS State availability. Captions, identification of subjects, model releases required. Offers no additional payment for photos accepted with ms. Buys one time rights.

ASSOCIATIONS

AMERICAN EDUCATOR

American Federation of Teachers, 555 New Jersey Ave. NW, Washington DC 20001. **E-mail:** ae@aft. org. **Website:** www.aft.org/ae. **Contact:** Amy Hightower, editor. **5% freelance written.** Quarterly magazine covering education, condition of children, and labor issues. *American Educator*, the quaterly magazine of the American Federation of Teachers, reaches over 900,000 public school teachers, higher education faculty, and education researchers and policymakers. The magazine concentrates on significant ideas and practices in education, civics, and the condition of children in America and around the world. Estab. 1977. Circ. 900,000. Byline given. Pays on publication. Offers 50% kill fee. Publishes ms an average of 2-6 months after acceptance. Editorial lead time 1 year. Submit seasonal material 6 months in advance. Accepts queries by mail, e-mail. Accepts simultaneous submissions. Responds in 2 months to queries. Responds in 6 months to mss. Sample copy and guidelines online.

○ "We prefer queries to mss. When sending a ms, please keep at least 1 copy of your article on file, as we cannot be responsible for unsolicited mss. Be sure to include your contact information in the event we need to reach you. Payment varies according to length and topic. The minimum payment for an article is $300."

NONFICTION Needs book excerpts, essays, historical, interview, discussions of educational research. No pieces that are not supportive of the public schools. **Buys 8 mss/year.** Query with published clips. Length:

1,000-7,000 words. **Pays $750-3,000 for assigned articles. Pays $300-1,000 for unsolicited articles.**
PHOTOS State availability. Captions, identification of subjects, model releases required. Reviews contact sheets, negatives, transparencies, 8x10 prints, GIF/JPEG files. Negotiates payment individually. Buys one-time rights.

LION

Lions Clubs International, 300 W. 22nd St., Oak Brook IL 60523-8842. (630)468-6909. **Fax:** (630)571-1685. **E-mail:** magazine@lionsclubs.org. **Website:** www.lionsclubs.org. **Contact:** Jay Copp, senior editor. **35% freelance written. Works with a small number of new/unpublished writers each year.** Monthly magazine covering service club organization for Lions Club members and their families. Estab. 1918. Circ. 350,000. Byline given. Pays on acceptance. No kill fee. Publishes ms an average of 5 months after acceptance. Accepts queries by mail, e-mail, fax, phone. Accepts simultaneous submissions. Responds in 1 month to queries. Sample copy and writer's guidelines free.

○ *LION* magazine welcomes freelance article submissions with accompanying photos that depict the service goals and projects of Lions clubs on the local, national, and international level. Lions Clubs International is the world's largest service club organization. Lions are recognized globally for their commitment to projects that benefit the blind, visually impaired, and people in need.

NONFICTION Needs photo feature. No travel, biography, or personal experiences. **Buys 40 mss/year.** "Article length should not exceed 2,000 words, and is subject to editing. No gags, fillers, quizzes or poems are accepted. Photos must be color prints or sent digitally. *LION* magazine pays upon acceptance of material. Advance queries save your time and ours. Address all submissions to Jay Copp, senior editor, by mail or e-mail text and .tif or .jpg (300 dpi) photos." Length: 500-2,000 words. **Pays $100-$1,500.**
PHOTOS Purchased with accompanying ms. Photos should be at least 5x7 glossies; color prints or slides are preferred. "We also accept digital photos by e-mail. Be sure photos are clear and as candid as possible." Captions required. Total purchase price for ms includes payment for photos accepted with ms.
TIPS "Send detailed description of proposed article. Query first and request writer's guidelines and sample

copy. Incomplete details on how the Lions involved actually carried out a project and poor quality photos are the most frequent mistakes made by writers in completing an article assignment for us. No gags, fillers, quizzes, or poems are accepted. We are geared increasingly to an international audience. Writers who travel internationally could query for possible assignments, although only locally related expenses could be paid."

NEW MOBILITY

United Spinal Association, 120-34 Queens Blvd., #320, Kew Gardens NY 11415. (718)803-3782. **E-mail:** tgilmer@unitedspinal.org; jbyzek@unitedspinal.org. **Website:** www.spinalcord.org/. **Contact:** Tim Gilmer, editor; Josie Byzek, managing editor. **50% freelance written.** Bimonthly magazine covering living with spinal cord injury/disorder (SCI/D). The bimonthly membership magazine for the National Spinal Cord Injury Association, a program of United Spinal Association. Members include people with spinal cord injury or disorder, as well as caregivers, parents, and some spinal cord injury/disorder professionals. All articles should reflect this common interest of the audience. Assume that your audience is better educated in the subject of spinal cord injury than average, but be careful not to be too technical. Each issue has a theme (available from editor) that unites features in addition to a series of departments focused on building community and providing solutions for the SCI/D community. Articles that feature members, chapters or the organization are preferred, but any article that deals with issue pertinent to SCI/D community will be considered. Estab. 2011. Circ. 35,000. Byline given. Pays on publication. No kill fee. Publishes ms an average of 1-2 months after acceptance. Accepts queries by e-mail. Accepts simultaneous submissions. Sample copy and guidelines available on website.
NONFICTION Needs essays, general interest, how-to, humor, interview, new product, personal experience, photo feature, travel, medical research. Does not want "articles that treat disabilities as an affliction or cause for pity, or that show the writer does not get that people with disabilities are people like anyone else. We aren't interested in 'courageous' or 'inspiring' tales of 'overcoming disability.'" **Buys 36 mss/year.** Query. Length: 800-1,600 words. **Pays 15¢/word for new writers.**

PHOTOS Send photos. Identification of subjects required. Reviews high-quality GIF/JPEG files. Offers no additional payment for photos accepted with ms.

COLUMNS/DEPARTMENTS Travel (report on access of a single travel destination based on conversations with disabled travelers), Access (hands-on look at how to improve access for a specific type of area), Ask Anything (tap members and experts to answer community question relating to life w/SCI/D), Advocacy (investigation of ongoing advocacy issue related to SCI/D). **Buys 40 mss/year.** Length: 800 words. Query with published clips. **Pays 15¢/word for new writers.**

TIPS "It helps (though is not necessary) if you have a disability, or if you are comfortable with people with disabilities; they are the subjects of most of our articles as well as the bulk of our readership. Our readers are looking for tips on how to live well with mobility impairment. They're concerned with access to jobs, travel, recreation, education, etc. They like to read about how others deal with like situations and hear about resources or ideas that will help them in their daily lives. They are sophisticated about spinal cord injuries and don't need to be 'inspired' by the typical stories about people with disabilities that appear in the human interest section of most newspapers."

SCOUTING

Boy Scouts of America, 1325 W. Walnut Hill Lane, P.O. Box 152079, Irving TX 75015-2079. **Website:** www.scoutingmagazine.org. **80% freelance written.** Magazine published 6 times/year covering Scouting activities for adult leaders of the Boy Scouts, Cub Scouts, and Venturing. Estab. 1913. Circ. 1 million. Byline given. Pays on acceptance for major features and some shorter features. Publishes ms an average of 18 months after acceptance. Editorial lead time 1 year. Submit seasonal material 1 year in advance. Accepts queries by mail. Accepts simultaneous submissions. Responds in 3 weeks to queries; in 2 months to mss. Sample copy: $2.50 and 9x12 SAE with 4 first-class stamps, or online.

NONFICTION Needs inspirational, interview. **Buys 20-30 mss/year.** Query with SASE. Length: short features, 500-700 words; some longer features, up to 1,200 words, usually the result of a definite assignment to a professional writer. **Pays $650-800 for major articles, $300-500 for shorter features. Rates depend on professional quality of article.**

REPRINTS Send photocopy of article and information about when and where the article previously appeared. First-person accounts of meaningful Scouting experiences (previously published in local newspapers, etc.) are a popular subject.

PHOTOS State availability. Identification of subjects required. Reviews transparencies, prints. Buys one-time rights.

COLUMNS/DEPARTMENTS Way It Was (Scouting history), 600-750 words; Family Talk (family, raising kids, etc.), 600-750 words. **Buys 8-12 mss/year.** Query. **Pays $300-500.**

FILLERS Limited to personal accounts of humorous or inspirational Scouting experiences. Needs anecdotes, short humor. **Buys 15-25 mss/year.** Length: 50-150 words. **Pays $25 on publication.**

TIPS "*Scouting* magazine articles are mainly about successful program activities conducted by or for Cub Scout packs, Boy Scout troops, and Venturing crews. We also include features on winning leadership techniques and styles, profiles of outstanding individual leaders, and inspirational accounts (usually first person) of *Scouting*'s impact on an individual, either as a youth or while serving as a volunteer adult leader. Because most volunteer Scout leaders are also parents of children of Scout age, *Scouting* is also considered a family magazine. We publish material we feel will help parents in strengthening their families (because they often deal with communicating and interacting with young people, many of these features are useful to a reader in both roles as parent and Scout leader)."

TOASTMASTER

Toastmasters International, P.O. Box 9052, Mission Viejo CA 92690. 949-858-8255. **E-mail:** submissions@toastmasters.org. **Website:** www.toastmasters.org. **Contact:** submissions@toastmasters.org. **50% freelance written.** Monthly magazine covers public speaking, leadership, communication and club-related topics. The monthly Toastmaster magazine is distributed to members of Toastmasters International, a nonprofit organization and world leader in communication and leadership development. The publications team prizes article originality, depth of research, timeliness, and excellence of expression. Unsolicited article queries and photos are accepted via email. All accepted articles are subject to editing for length and/or clarity. Articles and photos may be published in print and digital versions. Estab. 1924. Circ. 345,000 members in more than 15,800 clubs in 142 countries. Byline given. Pays upon acceptance. No kill fee. Submit seasonal material 3-4 months in advance. Accepts queries by e-mail, online submission form. Accepts simultaneous submissions. Guidelines available at www.toastmasters.org/Submissions. Please refer to the submissions guidelines on the Toastmasters website first, and then submit your query via email to submissions@toastmasters.org. Tip: We highly recommend that you review several issues of the Toastmaster magazine before submitting a query.

○ Freelancer reports that editors only pay when articles are assigned. Be sure to query first and turn in articles only after contract is negotiated.

NONFICTION Needs how-to, humor, interview, profile, communications, leadership, language use. Articles with political or religious slants or sexist or nationalist language will not be accepted. **Buys 50 mss/year.** Need: Leadership and communication "How To …" articles, expert advice and tips for public speakers, impromptu speaking, humorous speeches, persuasive speeches, storytelling, and cross-cultural communication. Profiles of prominent international speakers and leaders relative to an international audience. Length: 650-1,800 words. **Compensation for accepted articles (word count: 650–1,800) is $200–$650, and is based on readability, thoroughness of the research performed, compliance with submissions guidelines, and the article's value to the publications team and to members of Toastmasters.**

TIPS "Our readers are knowledgeable and experienced public speakers, and therefore only authentic, well-researched, and well-crafted stories will be accepted. Articles of the most value to our readers are "How To's" on subjects within the broad fields of communication and leadership, which can be applied by our members for self-improvement and increased club-experience value. The most popular stories have style, depth, emotional impact, and take-away value for readers. Feature articles must tell a compelling story that has an unusual hook, or a unique angle, that is of interest to our international readers. Articles must be complete with anecdotes and/or examples. Profiles of prominent speakers and leaders are welcome only if they are of interest to our international audience. All submissions must be in English."

VFW MAGAZINE

Veterans of Foreign Wars of the United States, 406 W. 34th St., Kansas City MO 64111. (816)756-3390. **Fax:** (816)968-1169. **E-mail:** kwilliams@vfw.org; magazine@vfw.org. **Website:** www.vfwmagazine. org. **Contact:** Kari Williams, editorial associate. **40% freelance written.** Monthly magazine on veterans' affairs, military history, patriotism, defense, and current events. *VFW Magazine* goes to its members worldwide, all having served honorably in the armed forces overseas from World War II through the Iraq and Afghanistan Wars. Estab. 1904. Circ. 1.3 million. Byline given. Pays on acceptance. Offers 50% kill fee. Publishes ms 3-6 months after acceptance. Editorial lead time is 6 months. Submit seasonal material 6 months in advance. Accepts queries by mail, e-mail, fax. Accepts simultaneous submissions. Responds in 2 months to queries. Sample copy for 9x12 SAE with 5 first-class stamps. Guidelines available online.

○ Unsolicited manuscripts and photographs must be accompanied by return postage, and no responsibility is assumed for safe handling. Poetry submissions not accepted.

NONFICTION Needs general interest, historical, inspirational. **Buys 25-30 mss/year.** Query with two-sentence outline, résumé, and published clips. Do not send unsolicited mss. Length: 1,000 words. **Pays up to $500-1,000 maximum for assigned articles; $500-750 maximum for unsolicited articles.**

PHOTOS Send photos. Reviews contact sheets, negatives, hi-res, TIF/JPEG files, 5x7, or 8x10 prints. Buys first North American rights.

TIPS "Absolute accuracy and quotes from relevant individuals are a must. Bibliographies useful if subject required extensive research and/or is open to dispute. Consult *The Associated Press Stylebook* for correct grammar and punctuation. Please enclose a brief and your military experience (if applicable) in the field in which you are writing. No phone queries."

ASTROLOGY, METAPHYSICAL & NEW AGE

FATE MAGAZINE

Fate Magazine, Inc., P.O. Box 460, Lakeville MN 55044. (952)431-2050. **E-mail:** fate@fatemag.com. **Website:** www.fatemag.com. **Contact:** Phyllis Galde, editor in chief. **75% freelance written.** Covers the paranormal, ghosts, UFOs, strange science. "Reports a wide variety of strange and unknown phenomena. We are open to receiving any well-written, well-documented article. Our readers especially like reports of current investigations, experiments, theories, and experiences." Estab. 1948. Circ. 15,000. Byline given. Pays after publication. Publishes ms 3-6 months after acceptance. Editorial lead time 3-6 months. Accepts queries by mail, e-mail. Accepts simultaneous submissions. Responds in 1-3 months to queries. Sample copy available for free online, by e-mail. Guidelines available online.

○ "*Fate* prefers first-person accounts and investigations of the topics we cover. We do not publish fiction or opinion pieces or book-length mss."

NONFICTION Needs general interest, historical, how-to, personal experience, photo feature, technical. "We do not publish poetry, fiction, editorial/opinion pieces, or book-length mss." **Buys 100 mss/year.** Submit complete ms by e-mail or on CD accompanied by hard copy. Length: 1,500-3,000 words. **Pays $50.** Pays with merchandise or ad space if requested.

PHOTOS Buys slides, prints, or digital photos/illustrations with ms. Send photos with submission. Reviews hi-res (300 dpi) GIF/JPEG files, 4x6 prints.

COLUMNS/DEPARTMENTS True Mystic Experiences (short reader-submitted stories of strange experiences); My Proof of Survival (short reader-submitted stories of proof of life after death), up to 500 words. Submit complete ms by e-mail or on CD accompanied by hard copy. **Pays $10.**

FILLERS Fillers are especially welcomed and must be fully authenticated. Needs Needs anecdotes and facts. Length: 150-500 words. **Pays $10.**

TIPS "*Fate* is looking for exciting, first-hand accounts of UFO and paranormal experiences and investigations."

WITCHES AND PAGANS

BBI Media, Inc., P.O. Box 687, Forest Grove OR 97116. (503)430-8817. **E-mail:** editor2@bbimedia.com. **Website:** www.witchesandpagans.com. **Contact:** Anne Newkirk Niven. **100%.** Thrice-yearly magazine covering modern Paganism, Witchcraft, Heathen, and Polytheism movements. "Devoted exclusively to promoting and covering contemporary Pagan culture, *W&P* features exclusive interviews with the teachers, writers, and activists who create and lead our traditions, visits to the sacred places and people who inspire us, and in-depth discussions of our ever-evolving practices. You'll also find practical daily magic, ideas for solitary ritual and devotion, God/dess-friendly craft-projects, Pagan poetry and short fiction, reviews, and much more in every 88-page issue. *W&P* is available in either traditional paper copy sent by postal mail or as a digital PDF e-zine download that is compatible with most computers and readers." Estab. 2002. Circ. 10,000. Byline given. No cash payment, but 4 contributor's copies and one-year subscription given for published submissions. 3 months to 2 years Editorial lead time is 3-4 months. Submit seasonal material 6 months in advance. Accepts queries by mail, e-mail, fax, phone. Accepts simultaneous submissions. Responds in 1-2 weeks to queries; 1 month to mss. Sample copy: $6. Guidelines available online.

NONFICTION Needs essays, how-to, inspirational, interview, personal experience, photo feature, religious, reviews, travel. Special issues: Features (articles, essays, fiction, interviews, and rituals) should range between 1,000-5,000 words. "We most often publish items between 1,500-3000 words; we prefer in-depth coverage to tidbits in most cases, and the upper ranges are usually reserved for lead pieces assigned to specific writers." **Buys 15-35 mss/year.** Send complete ms. "Submit all written material in electronic format. Our first choice is Open Office writer file attachments e-mailed directly to editor2@bbimedia.com. This e-mail address is being protected from spambots. You need JavaScript enabled to view it; other acceptable file attachment formats include text files and commonly used word processing programs; you may also paste the text of your ms directly into an e-mail message. Use a plain, legible font or typeface large enough to read easily. Sidebars can be 500-1,300 words or so. Reviews have specific lengths and formats; e-mail editor2@bbimedia.com." Length: 1,000-4,000 words.

FICTION Needs erotica, horror, suspense, Contemporary fiction featuring protagonists from our area of interest. No "Harry Potter" style fantasy magic please. Does not want faction (fictionalized retellings of real events). Avoid gratuitous sex, violence, sentimentality, and pagan moralizing. Don't beat our readers with the Rede or the Threefold Law. **Buys 3-4 mss/year.** Send complete ms. Length: 1,000-5,000 words.

POETRY Needs avant-garde, free verse, haiku, light verse, traditional. Submit maximum 3-5 poems.

TIPS "Read the magazine, do your research, write the piece, send it in. That's really the only way to get started as a writer; everything else is window dressing."

AUTOMOTIVE & MOTORCYCLE

AMERICAN MOTORCYCLIST

American Motorcyclist Association, 13515 Yarmouth Dr., Pickerington OH 43147. (614)856-1900. **E-mail:** submissions@ama-cycle.org. **Website:** www.americanmotorcyclist.com. **Contact:** Grant Parsons, director of communications; James Holter, managing editor. **25% freelance written.** Monthly magazine for enthusiastic motorcyclists investing considerable time and money in the sport, emphasizing the motorcyclist, not the vehicle. Monthly magazine of the American Motorcyclist Association. Emphasizes people involved in, and events dealing with, all aspects of motorcycling. Readers are "enthusiastic motorcyclists, investing considerable time in road riding or all aspects of the sport." Estab. 1947. Circ. 200,000. Byline given. Pays on publication. No kill fee. Editorial lead time 3 months. Submit seasonal material 4 months in advance. Accepts queries by mail, e-mail. Accepts simultaneous submissions. Responds in 5 weeks to queries. Responds in 6 weeks to mss. Sample copy for $1.50. Guidelines free.

NONFICTION Needs interview, personal experience, travel. **Buys 8 mss/year.** Send complete ms. Length: 1,000-2,500 words. **Pays minimum $8/published column inch.**

PHOTOS Buys 10-20 photos/issue. Subjects include: travel, technical, sports, humorous, photo essay/feature and celebrity/personality. Photo captions preferred. Send photos. Captions, identification of subjects required. Reviews transparencies, prints. Pays $50/photo minimum. Pays $50-150/photo; $250 minimum for cover. Also buys photos in photo/text packages according to same rate; pays $8/column inch minimum for story. Pays on publication. Buys one-time rights, First North American serial rights.

TIPS "Our major category of freelance stories concerns motorcycling trips to interesting North American destinations. Prefers stories of a timeless nature."

$$$$ AUTOWEEK

Crain Communications, Inc., 1155 Gratiot Ave., Detroit MI 48207. (313)446-6000. **Fax:** (313)446-1027. **E-mail:** awletter@autoweek.com. **Website:** www.autoweek.com. Editor: Wes Raynal. **5% freelance written, most by regular contributors.** *AutoWeek* is a biweekly magazine for auto enthusiasts. Estab. 1958. Circ. 300,000. Byline given. Pays on publication. Publishes ms an average of 1 month after acceptance. Accepts queries by e-mail. Accepts simultaneous submissions.

NONFICTION Needs historical, interview. **Buys 5 mss/year.** Query. Length: 100-400 words. **Pays $1/word.**

CAR AND DRIVER

Hearst Communications, Inc., 1585 Eisenhower Place, Ann Arbor MI 48108. **E-mail:** editors@caranddriver.com. **Website:** www.caranddriver.com. **Contact:** Eddie Alterman, editor in chief; Mike Fazioli, managing editor. Monthly magazine for auto enthusiasts; readers are college-educated, professional, median 24-35 years of age. Estab. 1956. Circ. 1,212,555. Byline given. Pays on acceptance. Offers 25% kill fee. Accepts queries by mail, e-mail. Accepts simultaneous submissions. Responds in 2 months to queries.

NONFICTION Query with published clips before submitting.

PHOTOS Color slides and b&w photos sometimes purchased with accompanying ms.

TIPS "It is best to start off with an interesting query and to stay away from nuts-and-bolts ideas, because that will be handled in-house or by an acknowledged expert. Our goal is to be absolutely without flaw in our presentation of automotive facts, but we strive to be every bit as entertaining as we are informative. We do not print this sort of story: 'My Dad's Wacky, Lovable Beetle.'"

MOTOR TREND

TEN: The Enthusiast Network, 831 S. Douglas St., El Segundo CA 90245. **Website:** www.motortrend.com. **5-10% freelance written. Only works with published/established writers.** Monthly magazine for automotive enthusiasts and general interest consumers. Estab. 1949. Circ. 1,250,000. No kill fee. Publishes ms an average of 3 months after acceptance. Accepts queries by mail. Accepts simultaneous submissions. Responds in 1 month to queries.

NONFICTION Query before submitting.

PHOTOS Buys photos of prototype cars and assorted automotive matter.

AVIATION

AFRICAN PILOT

Wavelengths 10 (Pty) Ltd., 6 Barbeque Heights, 9 Dytchley Rd., Barbeque Downs, Midrand 1684 South Africa. +27(0)11-466-8524/6. **Fax:** +27(0)86-767-4333. **E-mail:** editor@africanpilot.co.za. **Website:** www.africanpilot.co.za. **Contact:** Athol Franz, editor. **50% freelance written.** "*African Pilot* is southern Africa's premier monthly aviation magazine. It publishes a high-quality magazine that is well known and respected within the aviation community of southern Africa. The magazine offers a number of benefits to readers and advertisers, including a weekly e-mail, Aviation News, annual service guide, aviation training supplement, executive wall calendar, and an extensive website. The monthly aviation magazine is also available online as an exact replica of the paper edition but where all major advertising pages are hyperlinked to the advertisers' websites. The magazine offers clean layouts with outstanding photography and reflects editorial professionalism as well as a responsible approach to journalism. The magazine offers a complete and tailored promotional solution for all aviation businesses operating in the African region." Estab. 2001. Circ. 7,000+ online; 6,600+ print. Byline given. No kill fee. Editorial lead time 2-3 months. Accepts queries by e-mail. Accepts simultaneous submissions. Responds only if interested; send nonreturnable samples. Sample copies available upon request. Writer's guidelines online or via e-mail.

NONFICTION Needs general interest, historical, interview, new product, personal experience, photo feature, technical. No articles on aircraft accidents. **Buys up to 60 mss/year.** Send complete ms. Length: 1,200-2,800 words.

PHOTOS Send photos. Captions required. Negotiates payment individually. Buys one-time rights.

TIPS "The website is updated monthly, and all articles are fully published online."

AIR & SPACE

Smithsonian Institution, P.O. Box 37012, MRC 513, Washington DC 20013. (202)633-6070. **Fax:** (202)633-6085. **E-mail:** editors@si.edu. **Website:** www.airspacemag.com. **80% freelance written.** Bimonthly magazine covering aviation and aerospace for a nontechnical audience. "*Air & Space* is a general interest magazine about flight. Its goal is to show readers, both the knowledgeable and the novice, facets of the enterprise of flight that they are unlikely to encounter elsewhere. The emphasis is on the human rather than the technological, on the ideas behind events, rather than a simple recounting of details." Estab. 1985. Circ. 225,000. Byline given. Pays on acceptance. Offers kill fee. Accepts queries by mail, e-mail, online submission form. Accepts simultaneous submissions. Responds in 3 months to queries. Sample copy: $7. Guidelines available online.

NONFICTION Needs book excerpts, essays, general interest, historical, humor, photo feature, technical. **Buys 50 mss/year.** Query with published clips. Length: 1,500-3,000 words. **Pay varies.**

PHOTOS Refuses unsolicited material. State availability. Reviews 35 mm transparencies, digital files.

COLUMNS/DEPARTMENTS Above & Beyond (first-person narrative of an adventure in air or space), 1,500 words; Flights & Fancy (whimsical, brief reflection), 800-1,000 words; Soundings (short, current news items reporting oddball or amusing events, efforts, or situations), 300-1,000 words; Reviews & Previews (a description and critique of a recent or soon-to-be-released book, video, movie, aerospace-related recreational product, or software), 200-450 words. **Buys 25 mss/year.** Query with published clips. **Pay varies.**

TIPS "We continue to be interested in stories about space exploration. Also, writing should be clear, accurate, and engaging. It should be free of technical and insider jargon, and generous with explanation and background. The first step every aspiring contributor should take is to study recent issues of the magazine."

AVIATION HISTORY

HistoryNet, LLC, 1919 Gallows Rd., Ste. 400, Vienna VA 22182. **E-mail:** aviationhistory@historynet.com. **Website:** www.historynet.com/aviation-history. **Contact:** Carl von Wodtke, editor. **95% freelance written.** Bimonthly magazine covering military and civilian aviation from first flight to the space age. "*Aviation History* aims to make aeronautical history not only factually accurate and complete but also enjoyable to a varied subscriber and newsstand audience." Estab. 1990. Circ. 40,000. Byline given. Pays on publication. No kill fee. Publishes ms an average of 2 years after acceptance. Editorial lead time 6 months. Submit seasonal material 1 year in advance. Accepts queries by mail, e-mail. Accepts simultaneous submissions.

Responds in 2 months to queries; 3 months to mss. Sample copy: $6. Guidelines with #10 SASE, or online. **NONFICTION** Needs historical, interview, personal experience. **Buys 24 mss/year.** Query. Length: up to 3,000 words, with a 500-word sidebar where appropriate, author bio, and book suggestions for further reading. **Pays minimum of $300.**

COLUMNS/DEPARTMENTS Aviators; Restored; Extremes, all up to 1,100 words. **Pays minimum of $150. Book reviews, 250-500 words, pays minimum of $75.**

TIPS "Choose stories with strong narrative and art possibilities. Write an entertaining, informative, and unusual story that grabs the reader's attention and holds it. All stories must be true. We do not publish fiction or poetry."

💲💲 FLIGHT JOURNAL

Air Age Media, 88 Danbury Rd., Wilton CT 06897. (203)431-9000. **E-mail:** flight@airage.com. **Website:** www.flightjournal.com. Bimonthly magazine covering aviation-oriented material, for the most part with a historical overtone, but also with some modern history in the making reporting. "*Flight Journal* is like no other aviation magazine in the world, covering the world of flight from its simple beginnings to its high-tech, no-holds-barred future. We put readers in the cockpit and let them live the thrill and adventure of the aviation experience, narrated by those who know the technology and made the history. Each issue brings the stories of flight—past, present and future—to life." No kill fee. Accepts queries by mail, e-mail. Accepts simultaneous submissions.

NONFICTION Needs historical, humor, interview, new product, personal experience, photo feature, technical. "We do not want any general aviation articles as in 'My Flight to Baja in my 172,' nor detailed recitations of the technical capabilities of an aircraft. Avoid historically accurate but bland chronologies of events." Send a single page outline of your idea. Provide 1 or more samples of prior articles, if practical. Length: 2,500-3,000 words. Lengthier pieces should be discussed in advance with the editors. **Pays $600.**

PHOTOS See submission guidelines. Reviews 5x7 prints. Negotiates payment individually.

TIPS "Use an unusual slant that makes your story idea unique; unusual pictures for an exciting presentation; fantastic but true accounts; lots of human interest. The designers, builders, pilots, and mechanics

are what aviation is all about. We like an upbeat style, with humor, where it fits. Use sidebars to divide content of technically dense subjects. If you have a good personal story but aren't a professional-quality writer, we'll help with the writing."

FLYING ADVENTURES

Aviation Publishing Corporation, El Monte Airport (EMT), P.O. Box 93613, Pasadena CA 91109-3613. (626)618-4000. **E-mail:** editor@flyingadventures.com. **Website:** www.flyingadventures.com. **Contact:** Lyn Freeman, Editor in Chief

Li Wu, Editor & Research Chief. **20% freelance written.** Bimonthly magazine covering lifestyle travel for owners and passengers of private aircraft. Articles cover upscale travelers. Estab. 1994. Circ. 135,000. Byline given for features. Pays on acceptance. No kill fee. Editorial lead time 2-8 weeks. Accepts queries by e-mail. Accepts simultaneous submissions. Responds immediately.

NONFICTION "Nothing nonrelevant or not our style. See magazine." Query with published clips. Length: 500-1,500 words. **Pays $150-300 for assigned and unsolicited articles.**

PHOTOS State availability. Captions, identification of subjects, model releases required. Reviews GIF/JPEG files. Negotiates payment individually. Buys all rights.

COLUMNS/DEPARTMENTS Publication has numerous departments; see magazine. **Buys 100+ mss/year.** Query with published clips. **Pays up to $150.**

TIPS "Send clip that fits our content and style. Must fit our style!"

BUSINESS & FINANCE

💲💲 ALASKA BUSINESS MONTHLY

Alaska Business Publishing Company, Inc., 501 W. Northern Lights Blvd., Ste. 100, Anchorage AK 99503-2577. (907)276-4373; (800)770-4373. **Fax:** (907)279-2900. **E-mail:** editor@akbizmag.com. **Website:** www.akbizmag.com. **Contact:** Susan Harrington, managing editor. **80% freelance written.** *Alaska Business Monthly,* produced in Alaska for Alaskans and other U.S. and international audiences interested in the business affairs of the 49th state, aims to provide a thorough and objective analysis of issues and trends of interest to the Alaska business community. Estab. 1985. Circ. 13,000-15,000. Byline given. Pays in month of publication. Offers $50 kill fee. Publishes ms an average of 2 months after acceptance. Assignments are due 2 months before date published. Editorial lead time 3-6 months. Deadlines are 2 months prior to month published. Ideas generally need to be submitted 4-6 months in advance for approval and assignment. Accepts queries by e-mail, online submission form. Responds immediately to queries. Past issues available on website: www.akbizmag.com/digital-archives. Send to editor@akbizmag.com as inline text of an e-mail.

◒ Story queries and pitches should be focused on special sections and topics listed on the editorial calendar, which is on the editorial page of the website: www.akbizmag.com/editorial. "We are an Alaska-centric publication and typically feature Alaskan writers."

NONFICTION Needs interview, new product, opinion, profile, technical, travel, Engineering, Architecture, Construction, Travel, Conventions & Meetings, Oil & Gas, Transportation, Pacific Northwest, Telecom & Technology, International Trade, Environmental Services, Energy & Power, Alaska Native Corporations, Mining, Healthcare, Resource Development, Employee Relations, Small Business Tips, Entrepreneur Advice. Special issues: "A different industry is featured each month in a special section. Read our magazine and editorial calendar for an idea of the material we assign." No fiction, poetry, or anything not pertinent to Alaska business. Rarely uses any unsolicited or unassigned articles. **Buys 200 mss/year.** Send query and 3 clips of previously published articles. Do not send complete mss. Does not republish blog posts. Length: 500-2,500 words. **Pays $100-500 for assigned articles.** Does not pay expenses.

REPRINTS Rarely publishes reprints from other publications. Reprint payment varies.

PHOTOS Contact: Susan Harrington, managing editor. State availability. Captions, identification of subjects, model releases required. Reviews high-res JPEG files. Pays $25-50/photo. Buys all rights.

TIPS "Always query the pro-Alaska business angle. Read our magazine for ideas on style and content. Send a well-written query on a subject of importance to Alaska businesses that is on the editorial calendar. We seek informative, entertaining articles on everything from entrepreneurs to heavy industry. We cover all sectors of *Alaska Business* and industry. Read the

magazine and study the website before submitting anything."

◒ ALBERTA VENTURE

Venture Publishing Inc., 10339–124 St., #300, Edmonton AB T5N 3W1 Canada. (780)990-0839. **E-mail:** admin@albertaventure.com. **Website:** www.albertaventure.com. **70% freelance written.** Monthly magazine covering business in Alberta. "Our readers are mostly business owners and managers in Alberta who read the magazine to keep up with trends and run their businesses better." Estab. 1997. Circ. 35,000. Byline given. Pays on publication. Offers 30% kill fee. Publishes ms an average of 2 months after acceptance. Editorial lead time 3 months. Submit seasonal material 3 months in advance. Accepts queries by e-mail. Accepts simultaneous submissions. Responds in 2 weeks to queries. Sample copy available online. Guidelines by e-mail.

NONFICTION Does not want company or product profiles. **Buys 75 mss/year.** Query. Length: 1,000-3,000 words. **Pays $300-2,000 (Canadian).**

PHOTOS Contact: Contact Kim Larson, art director.. State availability. Identification of subjects required. Reviews GIF/JPEG files. Negotiates payment individually. Buys one-time rights.

◒$$ ATLANTIC BUSINESS MAGAZINE

Communications Ten, Ltd., P.O. Box 2356, Station C, St. John's NL A1C 6E7 Canada. (709)726-9300. **Fax:** (709)726-3013. **E-mail:** dchafe@atlanticbusinessmagazine.com. **Website:** www.atlanticbusinessmagazine.net. **Contact:** Dawn Chafe, executive editor. **80% freelance written.** Bimonthly magazine covering business in Atlantic Canada. "We discuss positive business developments, emphasizing that the 4 Atlantic provinces are a great place to do business." Estab. 1989. Circ. 30,000. Byline given. Pays within 30 days of publication. No kill fee. Publishes ms an average of 2 months after acceptance. Editorial lead time 6 months. Accepts queries by e-mail. Accepts simultaneous submissions. Sample copy free. Guidelines online.

NONFICTION Needs general interest, interview, new product. "We don't want religious, technical, or scholarly material. We are not an academic magazine. We are interested only in stories concerning business topics specific to the 4 Canadian provinces of Nova Scotia, New Brunswick, Prince Edward Island, and Newfoundland and Labrador." **Buys 36 mss/year.** Query with published clips. Length: 1,000-

1,200 words for features; 3,500-4,000 for cover stories. **Pays 40¢/word.**

PHOTOS Send photos. Captions, identification of subjects required. Reviews contact sheets, transparencies, prints. Negotiates payment individually. Buys one-time rights.

COLUMNS/DEPARTMENTS Query with published clips.

TIPS "Writers should submit their areas of interest as well as samples of their work and, if possible, suggested story ideas."

BLOOMBERG BUSINESSWEEK

Bloomberg LP, 731 Lexington Ave., New York NY 10022. **E-mail:** letters@bloomberg.net. **Website:** www.businessweek.com. Weekly business magazine that provides information and interpretation about what is happening in the business world. Estab. 1929. Accepts simultaneous submissions.

◐ Query before submitting. Difficult market to break into.

BUSINESS NH MAGAZINE

Millyard Communications, 55 S. Commercial St., Manchester NH 03101. (603)626-6354. **Fax:** (603)626-6359. **E-mail:** edit@businessnhmagazine.com. **Website:** www.millyardcommunications.com. **Contact:** Matt Mowry, editor. **25% freelance written.** Monthly magazine covering business, politics, and people of New Hampshire. "Our audience consists of the owners and top managers of New Hampshire businesses." Estab. 1983. Circ. 14,800. Byline given. Pays on publication. Publishes an average of 2 months after acceptance. three months Accepts queries by e-mail, phone.

NONFICTION Needs how-to, interview, profile. No unsolicited articles; interested in New Hampshire writers only and NH, business-centric topics. **Buys 24 mss/year.** Query with published clips and résumé. Length: 800-2,500 words. **Payment varies.**

PHOTOS only color photos are used. Model/property release preferred. Photo captions required; include names, locations, contact phone number. Payment varies. Pays on publication. Buys one-time rights.

TIPS "We always want clips and résumés with queries. Freelance stories are almost always assigned. Stories must be local to New Hampshire."

💲💲 ELLIOTT WAVE INTERNATIONAL PUBLICATIONS

Elliott Wave International, P.O. Box 1618, Gainesville GA 30503. (770)536-0309. **E-mail:** customercare@elliottwave.com. **Website:** www.elliottwave.com. **10% freelance written.** Our publications are weekly to monthly in print and online formats covering investment markets. An understanding of technical market analysis is indispensable, knowledge of Elliott wave analysis even better. Clear, conversational prose is mandatory. Estab. 1979. Circ. 80,000. Byline sometimes given. Pays on publication. Publishes ms an average of 1 month after acceptance. Editorial lead time 1 month. Accepts queries by e-mail. Accepts simultaneous submissions.

NONFICTION Needs essays, how-to, technical. **Buys 12 mss/year.** Query with published clips. Length: 500-800 words. **Pays $100-200.**

COLUMNS/DEPARTMENTS Pop culture and the stock market, 500-800 words. **Buys 12 mss/year.** Query with published clips. **Pays $100-200.**

FORBES

Forbes, Inc., 499 Washington Blvd., Jersey City NJ 07310. **Website:** www.forbes.com. Biweekly magazine. Edited for top business management professionals and for those aspiring to positions of corporate leadership. Circ. 1,000,000. No kill fee. Editorial lead time 2 months. Accepts simultaneous submissions.

◐ Query before submitting.

FORTUNE

Time, Inc., 225 Liberty St., New York NY 10281. (212)522-1212. **Fax:** (212)522-0810. **E-mail:** letters@fortune.com. **Website:** www.fortune.com. Biweekly magazine covering business and finance. Edited primarily for high-demographic business people. Specializes in big stories about companies, business personalities, technology, managing, Wall Street, media, marketing, personal finance, politics, and policy. Circ. 1,066,000. No kill fee. Editorial lead time 6 weeks. Accepts simultaneous submissions.

◐ Query before submitting.

💲💲 THE LANE REPORT

Lane Communications Group, 201 E. Main St., 14th Floor, Lexington KY 40507. (859)244-3500. **E-mail:** markgreen@lanereport.com. **Website:** www.lanereport.com. **Contact:** Mark Green, managing editor. **60% freelance written.** Monthly magazine covering statewide business. *The Lane Report* is an intelligent, enterprising magazine that informs readers and drives a statewide dialogue by highlighting important business stories in Kentucky. Estab. 1985. Circ. 15,000. Byline given. Pays on publication. No kill fee. Editorial lead time 6 weeks. Submit seasonal material 3 months in advance. Accepts queries by mail, e-mail. Accepts simultaneous submissions. Responds in 1 month to queries. Sample copy and writer's guidelines free.

NONFICTION Needs essays, interview, new product, photo feature. **Buys 30-40 mss/year.** Query with published clips. Do not send unsolicited mss. Looking for major trends shaping the state, noteworthy business and practices, and stories with sweeping implications across industry sectors and state regions. Length: 750-3,000 words. **Pays $150-375.**

PHOTOS State availability. Identification of subjects required. Reviews contact sheets, negatives, transparencies, prints, digital images. Negotiates payment individually. Buys one-time rights.

COLUMNS/DEPARTMENTS Fast Lane Briefs (recent news and trends and how they might shape the future), 100-400 words; Opinion (opinion on a business or economic issue about which you, the writer, feel passionate and qualified to write), 750 words; Entrepreneurs (profile of a particularly interesting or quirky member of the business community), 750-1,400 words. Query.

TIPS "As Kentucky's only statewide business and economics publication, we look for stories that incorporate perspectives from the Commonwealth's various regions and prominent industries—tying it into the national picture when appropriate. We also look for insightful profiles and interviews of Kentucky's entrepreneurs and business leaders."

MONEY

Time, Inc., 1271 Avenue of the Americas, 17th Floor, New York NY 10020. (212)522-1212. **E-mail:** editor@money.timeinc.com. **Website:** time.com/money. Monthly magazine covering finance. *Money* magazine offers sophisticated coverage in all aspects of personal finance for individuals, business executives, and personal investors. Estab. 1972. Circ. 1,967,420. No kill fee. Accepts simultaneous submissions.

Query before submitting.

NATIONAL BLACK MBA MAGAZINE

400 West Peachtree Street NW, Suite 203, Atlanta GA 30308. (312)236-2622. **Fax:** (312)236-0390. **E-mail:** elaine@naylor.com. **Website:** www.nbmbaa.org. **80% freelance written.** Online magazine covering business career strategy, economic development, and financial management. Estab. 1997. Circ. 45,000. Byline given. Pays after publication. Offers 10-20% or $500 kill fee. Publishes ms an average of 1 month after acceptance. Editorial lead time 2-3 months. Submit seasonal material 3-4 months in advance. Accepts queries by mail, e-mail, fax.

PHOTOS State availability of or send photos. Identification of subjects required. Reviews ZIP disk. Offers no additional payment for photos accepted with ms. Buys one-time rights.

COLUMNS/DEPARTMENTS Management Strategies (leadership development), 1,200-1,700 words; Features (business management, entreprenuerial finance); Finance; Technology. Send complete ms. **Pays $500-1,000.**

THE NETWORK JOURNAL

The Network Journal Communication, 39 Broadway, Suite 2430, New York NY 10006. (212)962-3791. **Fax:** (212)962-3537. **E-mail:** tnjeditors@tnj.com. **Website:** www.tnj.com. **25% freelance written.** Monthly magazine covering business and career articles. *The Network Journal* caters to black professionals and small-business owners, providing quality coverage on business, financial, technology, and career news germane to the black community. Estab. 1993. Circ. 25,000. Byline given. Pays on publication. Editorial lead time 2 months. Submit seasonal material 3 months in advance. Accepts queries by mail, e-mail, fax, phone. Accepts simultaneous submissions. Sample copy for $1 or online. Writer's guidelines for SASE.

NONFICTION Needs how-to, interview. Send complete ms. Length: 1,200-1,500 words. **Pays $150-200.**

PHOTOS Send photos. Identification of subjects required. Offers $25/photo. Buys one time rights.

COLUMNS/DEPARTMENTS Book reviews, 700-800 words; career management and small business development, 800 words. **Pays $100.**

TIPS We are looking for vigorous writing and reporting for our cover stories and feature articles. Pieces should have gripping leads, quotes that actually say something and that come from several sources. Unless it is a column, please do not submit a 1-source story. Always remember that your article must contain a nutgraph—that's usually the third paragraph telling the reader what the story is about and why you are telling it now. Editorializing should be kept to a minimum. If you're writing a column, make sure your opinions are well-supported.

PACIFIC COAST BUSINESS TIMES

14 E. Carrillo St., Suite A, Santa Barbara CA 93101. (805)560-6950. **E-mail:** hdubroff@pacbiztimes.com. **E-mail:** Grabinowitz@pacbiztimes.com. **Website:** www.pacbiztimes.com. **Contact:** Glenn Rabinowitz, Managing Editor. **10% freelance written.** Weekly tabloid covering financial news specific to Santa Barbara, Ventura, San Luis Obispo counties in California. Estab. 2000. Circ. 5,000. Byline given. No kill fee. Editorial lead time 1 month. Accepts queries by e-mail, phone. Accepts simultaneous submissions. Sample copy free. Guidelines free.

NONFICTION Needs book excerpts, interview, opinion, personal finance. Does not want first person, promo, or fluff pieces. **Buys 20 mss/year.** Query. Length: 500-800 words. **Pays $75-175.**

CAREER, COLLEGE & ALUMNI

AFRICAN-AMERICAN CAREER WORLD

Equal Opportunity Publications, Inc., 445 Broad Hollow Rd., Suite 425, Melville NY 11747. (631)421-9421. **E-mail:** bloehr@eop.com. **Website:** www.eop.com. **Contact:** Barbara Capella Loehr, editor. **60% freelance written.** Semiannual magazine focused on African-American students and professionals in all disciplines. Estab. 1969. Byline given. Pays on publication. No kill fee. Publishes ms an average of 3 months after acceptance. Editorial lead time 3 months. Accepts queries by mail, e-mail. Accepts simultaneous submissions. Sample copy free. Guidelines free.

NONFICTION Needs how-to, interview, personal experience. "We do not want articles that are too general." Query. Length: 1,500-2,500 words. **Pays $350 for assigned articles.**

TIPS "Gear articles to our audience."

⊕⑤ HISPANIC CAREER WORLD

Equal Opportunity Publications, Inc., 445 Broad Hollow Rd., Suite 425, Melville NY 11747. (631)421-9421,

ext. 12. **Fax:** (631)421-1352. **E-mail:** bloehr@eop.com. **Website:** www.eop.com. **Contact:** Barbara Capella Loehr, editor. **60% freelance written.** Semiannual magazine aimed at Hispanic students and professionals in all disciplines. Estab. 1969. Byline given. Pays on publication. No kill fee. Publishes ms an average of 3 months after acceptance. Editorial lead time 3 months. Accepts queries by mail, e-mail, fax, phone. Accepts simultaneous submissions. Responds in 2 weeks to queries; 2 months to mss. Sample copy free. Guidelines free.

NONFICTION Needs how-to, interview, personal experience. Query. Length: 1,500-2,500 words. **Pays $350 for assigned articles.**

TIPS "Gear articles to our audience."

⑤ NEXTSTEPU MAGAZINE

NextStepSTEM Magazine, Next Step Universe, 1460 Broadway, New York NY 10036. **E-mail:** info@nextstepu.com. **Website:** www.nextstepu.com. **Contact:** Amelia Mezrahi. **75% freelance written.** Covers college planning, careers, college searches, paying for college, test prep, STEM. *NextStepU Magazine*, published 2 times/school year, is an objective publication that prepares students for life after high school. Articles cover college, careers, life, and financial aid. It is in a digital format as well as limited print distribution. *NextStepSTEM* focuses on STEM college and careers. Distributed to more than 20,500 high schools and student organizations. Estab. 1995. No kill fee. Editorial lead time 3 months. Submit seasonal material 3 months in advance. Accepts queries by e-mail. Sample copy available online. Guidelines online at www.nextstepu.com/pdf-handouts/writerguidelines.pdf.

NONFICTION Needs book excerpts, essays, general interest, how-to, interview, personal experience, travel. Articles "should be focused on (1) helping counselors do their jobs better and (2) helping college-bound students with college planning, careers, and scholarship help." Past articles have included what college admissions want, college essays, how to find scholarships, FAFSA, and extracurricular activities. Length: 800-1,500 words.

COLUMNS/DEPARTMENTS **Contact:** Laura Jeanne Hammond. College Planning (college types, making a decision, admissions); Financial Aid (scholarships, financial aid options); SAT/ACT (preparing for the SAT/ACT, study tips), 400-1,000 words; Career Profiles (profile at least 3 professionals in different aspects of a specific industry), 800-1,000 words; Military (careers in the military, different branches, how to join), 400-600 words.

NOTRE DAME MAGAZINE

University of Notre Dame, 500 Grace Hall, Notre Dame IN 46556-5612. (574)631-5335. **Fax:** (574)631-6767. **E-mail:** ndmag@nd.edu. **Website:** magazine. nd.edu. **Contact:** Kerry Temple, editor; Kerry Prugh, art director. **50% freelance written.** "We are a university magazine with a scope as broad as that found at a university, but we place our discussion in a moral, ethical, and spiritual context reflecting our Catholic heritage." Estab. 1972. Circ. 150,000. Byline given. Pays on acceptance. No kill fee. Publishes ms an average of 1 year after acceptance. Accepts queries by mail, e-mail. Accepts simultaneous submissions. Responds in 2 months to queries. Sample copy available online and by request. Guidelines available online.

NONFICTION Needs essays, general interest, personal experience, profile. **Buys 35 mss/year.** Query with published clips. Length: 600-3,000 words. **Pays $250-3,000.**

PHOTOS State availability. Identification of subjects, model releases required. Buys one-time, first and electronic rights.

COLUMNS/DEPARTMENTS CrossCurrents (essays, deal with a wide array of issues—some topical, some personal, some serious, some light). Query with or without published clips or send complete ms.

TIPS "The editors are always looking for new writers and fresh ideas. However, the caliber of the magazine and frequency of its publication dictate that the writing meet very high standards. The editors value articles strong in storytelling quality, journalistic technique, and substance. They do not encourage promotional or nostalgia pieces, stories on sports, or essays that are sentimentally religious."

WORKFORCE DIVERSITY FOR ENGINEERING & IT PROFESSIONALS

Equal Opportunity Publications, Inc., 445 Broad Hollow Rd., Suite 425, Melville NY 11747. (631)421-9421. **Fax:** (631)421-1352. **E-mail:** info@eop.com; bloehr@eop.com. **Website:** www.eop.com. **Contact:** Barbara Capella Loehr, editor. **60% freelance written.** Quarterly magazine addressing workplace issues affecting technical professional women, members of minority groups, and people with disabilities. Estab. 1969. Byline given. Pays on publication. No kill fee. Publishes

ms an average of 3 months after acceptance. Editorial lead time 3 months. Accepts queries by mail, e-mail, fax, phone. Accepts simultaneous submissions. Responds in 2 weeks to queries. Responds in 2 months to mss. Sample copy free. Guidelines free.

NONFICTION Needs how-to, interview, personal experience. We do not want articles that are too general. Query. Length: 1,500-2,500 words. **Pays $350 for assigned articles.**

TIPS "Gear articles to our audience."

CHILD CARE & PARENTAL GUIDANCE

AMERICAN BABY

Meredith Corp., 125 Park Ave., 6th Floor, New York NY 10017. **Website:** www.americanbaby.com. **Contact:** Dana Points, editor-in-chief. **70% freelance written.** Monthly magazine covering health, medical, and child care concerns for expectant and new parents, particularly those having their first child or those whose child is between the ages of birth and 2 years old. Mothers are the primary readers, but fathers' issues are equally important. Prefers to work with published/established writers; works with a small number of new/unpublished writers each year. Estab. 1938. Circ. 2,000,000. Byline given. Pays on acceptance. Offers 25% kill fee. Publishes ms an average of 6 months after acceptance. Editorial lead time 5 months. Submit seasonal material 6 months in advance. Accepts queries by mail. Accepts simultaneous submissions.

NONFICTION Needs book excerpts, essays, general interest, how-to, humor, new product. No "hearts and flowers" or fantasy pieces. **Buys 60 mss/year.** Length: 1,000-2,000 words. **Pays $800-1,000 for features, depending on article length and whether the author has previously written for** American Baby. **First-person experiences pay $500.**

REPRINTS Send photocopy and information about when and where the material previously appeared. Pays 50% of original price.

PHOTOS State availability. Identification of subjects, model releases required. Reviews transparencies, prints. Buys one-time rights.

COLUMNS/DEPARTMENTS Personal essays (700-1,000 words) and shorter items for Crib Notes (news and features) and Medical Updates (50-350 words) are also accepted. **Pays $200-1,000.**

TIPS "Get to know our style by thoroughly reading a recent issue of the magazine. Don't send something we recently published. Our readers want to feel connected to other parents, both to share experiences and to learn from one another. They want reassurance that the problems they are facing are solvable and not uncommon. They want to keep up with the latest issues affecting their new family, particularly health and medical news, but they don't have a lot of spare time to read. We forgo the theoretical approach to offer quick-to-read, hands-on information that can be put to use immediately. A simple, straightforward, clear approach is mandatory."

💲 ATLANTA PARENT

2346 Perimeter Park Dr., Atlanta GA 30341. (770)454-7599. **E-mail:** editor@atlantaparent.com; atlantaparent@atlantaparent.com. **Website:** www.atlantaparent.com. **Contact:** Editor. **50% freelance written.** Monthly magazine for parents in the Atlanta metro area with children from birth to 18 years old. "*Atlanta Parent* magazine has been a valuable resource for Atlanta families since 1983. It is the only magazine in the Atlanta area providing pertinent, local, and award-winning family-oriented articles and information. Atlanta parents rely on us for features that are timely, informative, and reader-friendly on important issues such as childcare, family life, education, adolescence, motherhood, health, and teens. Fun, easy, and inexpensive family activities and crafts as well as the humorous side of parenting are also important to our readers." Estab. 1983. Byline given. Pays on publication. Publishes ms an average of 3 months after acceptance. Submit seasonal material 6 months in advance. Accepts queries by mail, e-mail. Accepts simultaneous submissions. Responds in 4 months to queries. Sample copy: $3.

NONFICTION Needs general interest, how-to, humor, interview, travel. No religious or philosophical discussions. **Buys 60 mss/year.** Send complete ms by mail or e-mail. Length: 800-1,200 words. **Pays $5-50.**

REPRINTS Send tearsheet or photocopy with rights for sale noted and information about when and where the material previously appeared. Pays $30-50.

PHOTOS State availability of or send photos. Reviews 3x5 photos. Offers $10/photo. Buys one-time rights.

TIPS "Articles should be geared to problems or situations of families and parents. Should include down-to-earth tips and be clearly written. No philosophical discussions. We're also looking for well-written humor."

💲💲 BIRMINGHAM PARENT

Evans Publishing LLC, 3590-B Hwy 31S. #289, Pelham AL 35124. (205)987-7700. **Fax:** (205)987-7600. **E-mail:** carol@biringhamparent.com. **Website:** www.birminghamparent.com. **Contact:** Carol Evans, publisher/editor. **75% freelance written.** Monthly magazine covering family issues, parenting, education, babies to teens, health care, anything involving parents raising children. "We are a free, local parenting publication in central Alabama. All of our stories carry some type of local slant. Parenting magazines abound: we are the source for the local market." Estab. 2004. Circ. 30,000. Byline given. Pays within 30 days of publication. Offers 20% kill fee. Publishes ms an average of 3-4 months after acceptance. Editorial lead time 3-4 months. Submit seasonal material 4 months in advance. Accepts queries by e-mail. Accepts simultaneous submissions. Responds in 2-3 weeks to queries. Responds in 2-3 months to mss. Sample copy for $3. Guidelines available online.

NONFICTION Needs book excerpts, general interest, how-to, interview, parenting. Does not want first person pieces. "Our pieces educate and inform; we don't take stories without sources." **Buys 24 mss/year.** Send complete ms. Length: 350-2,500 words. **Pays $50-350 for assigned articles. Pays $35-200 for unsolicited articles.**

PHOTOS State availability. Captions, identification of subjects, model releases required. Reviews GIF/JPEG files. Negotiates payment individually; offers no additional payment for photos accepted with ms. Buys one-time rights.

COLUMNS/DEPARTMENTS Parenting Solo (single parenting), 650 words; Baby & Me (dealing with newborns or pregnancy), 650 words; Teens (raising teenagers), 650-1,500 words. **Buys 36 mss/year.** Query with published clips or send complete ms. **Pays $35-200.**

TIPS "Present your story so that you can add local slant to it, or suggest to us how to do so. Please no first person opinion pieces—no '10 great gifts for teachers,' for example, without sources. We expect some sources for our informative stories."

CHESAPEAKE FAMILY LIFE

Jefferson Communications, 121 Cathedral Street, Third Floor, Annapolis MD 21401. (410) 263-1641. **Fax:** (410) 280-0255. **E-mail:** editor@chesapeakefamily.com; calendar@jecoannapolis.com. **Website:** www.chesapeakefamily.com. **Contact:** Betsy Stein, editor. **80% freelance written.** Monthly magazine, website and e-mail newsletters covering parenting and other topics of interest to parents in Maryland. *Chesapeake Family LIFE* publishes a free, regional parenting publication, annual publications and e-mail newsletters serving readers in the Anne Arundel, Calvert, Prince George's and Queen Anne's counties of Maryland. Our goal is to identify tips, resources, and products that will make our readers' lives easier. "We answer the questions they don't have time to ask, doing the research for them so they have the information they need to make better decisions for their families' health, education, and well-being." Articles must have local angle and resources. Estab. 1990. Circ. 34,000. Byline given. Publishes ms an average of 2 months after acceptance. Editorial lead time 3-6 months. Submit seasonal material 4 months in advance. Accepts queries by mail, e-mail, fax. Accepts simultaneous submissions. Guidelines available online.

NONFICTION Needs how-to, interview, profile, travel. No general personal essays (however, personal anecdotes leading into a story with general applicability is fine). **Buys 25 mss/year.** Send complete ms. Length: 800-1,200 words. **Pays $75-150.**

PHOTOS State availability. Model releases required. Reviews prints, GIF/JPEG files. Offers no additional payment for photos accepted with ms, unless original, assigned photo is selected for the cover.

COLUMNS/DEPARTMENTS Buys 25 mss/year. Pays $35-50.

TIPS "A writer's best chance is to know the issues specific to our local readers. Know how to research the issues well, answer the questions our readers need to know, and give them information they can act on—and present it in a friendly, conversational tone."

CHICAGO PARENT

141 S. Oak Park Ave., Oak Park IL 60302. (708)386-5555. **E-mail:** tamara@chicagoparent.com; chiparent@chicagoparent.com. **Website:** www.chicagoparent.com. **Contact:** Tamara O'Shaughnessy, editor. **80% freelance written.** Monthly parenting magazine covering the six-county Chicago metropolitan area. *Chicago Parent* has a distinctly local approach. Offers information, inspiration, perspective, and empathy to Chicago-area parents. Lively editorial mix has a "we're all in this together" spirit, and articles are thoroughly researched and well written. Estab. 1988. Circ. 100,000. Byline given. Pays on publication. Offers 10-50% kill fee. Publishes ms an average of 2 months after acceptance. Editorial lead time 4 months. Submit seasonal material 4 months in advance. Accepts queries by e-mail. Responds in 6 weeks to queries. Sample copy for $4.95 and 11×17 SAE with $1.65 postage direct to circulation. Guidelines available on website.

NONFICTION Needs essays, expose, general interest, how-to, humor, interview, personal experience, profile, travel. No pot-boiler parenting pieces or nonlocal writers (from outside the six-county Chicago metropolitan area and Northwest Indiana). **Buys 40-50 mss/year.** Query with links to published clips. Length: 200-2,500 words. **Pays $50-450 for assigned articles.**

FAMILYFUN

Parents Magazine Group, **Website:** www.parents.com/familyfun-magazine. Family magazine published 10 times/year. Written for parents with children ages 3-12, focusing on family cooking, vacations, parties, holidays, crafts, and learning. Estab. 1991. Circ. 2.1 million. Accepts queries by mail, e-mail. Accepts simultaneous submissions. Guidelines available upon request.

NONFICTION Interested in stories that will appeal to a wide variety of parents. Query before submitting. Queries should describe the content, structure, and tone of a proposed article. Include published clips with query. Works only with experienced writers.

⑤ HUDSON VALLEY PARENT

The Professional Image, 174 South St., Newburgh NY 12550. (845)562-3606. **E-mail:** editor@excitingread.com. **Website:** www.hvparent.com. **Contact:** Sara Dunn. **95% freelance written.** Monthly magazine covering local parents and families. Estab. 1994. Circ. 80,000. Byline given. Pays on publication. No kill fee. Publishes ms an average of 3 months after acceptance. Editorial lead time 4 months. Submit seasonal material 4 months in advance. Accepts queries by e-mail. Accepts simultaneous submissions. Responds in 2-4 weeks to mss. Sample copy free. Guidelines available online.

NONFICTION Needs expose, general interest, humor, interview, personal experience. **Buys 20 mss/year.** Query. Length: 700-1,200 words. **Pays $80-120 for assigned articles. Pays $25-35 for unsolicited articles.**

REPRINTS Pays $25-35 for reprints.

⑤ MEDIA FOR LIVING, VALLEY LIVING MAGAZINE

Shalom Foundation, 1251 Virginia Ave., Harrisonburg VA 22802. (540)433-5351. **E-mail:** info@valleyliving.org. **E-mail:** melodie@valleyliving.org. **Website:** www.valleyliving.org. Lindsey Shantz. **80% freelance written.** Quarterly tabloid covering family living. Articles focus on giving general encouragement for families of all ages and stages. Estab. 1990. Circ. 11,000. Byline given. Pays on publication. No kill fee. Publishes ms an average of 6-12 months after acceptance. Editorial lead time 4-6 months. Submit seasonal material 6 months in advance. Accepts queries by mail, e-mail, online submission form. Accepts simultaneous submissions. Responds in 2 months to queries; 2-4 months to mss. Sample copy for SAE with 9x12 envelope and 4 first-class stamps.

○ "Our bias is to use articles *showing* rather than telling readers how to raise families (stories rather than how-to). We aim for articles that are well written, understandable, challenging (not the same old thing you've read elsewhere); they should stimulate readers to dig a little deeper, but not too deep with academic or technical language; that are interesting and fit our theological perspective (Christian) but are not preachy or overly patriotic. No favorable mentions of smoking, drinking, cursing, etc."

NONFICTION Needs general interest, how-to, humor, inspirational, personal experience. "We do not use devotional materials intended for Christian audiences. We seldom use pet stories and receive way too many grief/death/dealing-with-serious-illness stories. We publish in March, June, September, and December, so holidays that occur in other months are not usually the subject of articles." **Buys 48-52 mss/year.** Query. Length: 500-1,200 words. **Pays $35-60.**

PHOTOS Contact: Lindsey Shantz. State availability. Captions, identification of subjects, model releases required. Reviews 4x6 prints, GIF/JPEG files. Offers $15-25/photo. Buys one-time rights.

TIPS "We prefer 'good news' stories that are uplifting and noncontroversial in nature. We want articles that tell stories of people solving problems and dealing with personal issues rather than essays or 'preaching.' If you submit electronically, it is very helpful if you put the specific title of the submission in the subject line, and please include your e-mail address in the body of the e-mail or on your ms. Also, always include your address and phone number."

⑤ METROKIDS

Kidstuff Publications, Inc., 1412-1414 Pine St., Philadelphia PA 19102. (215)291-5560, ext. 102. **Fax:** (215)291-5565. **E-mail:** editor@metrokids.com. **Website:** www.metrokids.com. **Contact:** Sara Murphy, managing editor. **25% freelance written.** Monthly magazine providing information for parents and kids in Philadelphia and surrounding counties, South Jersey, and Delaware. "*MetroKids*, a free monthly magazine, is a resource for parents living in the greater Delaware Valley. The Pennsylvania, South Jersey, and Delaware editions of *MetroKids* are available in supermarkets, libraries, daycares, and hundreds of other locations. The magazine and website feature the area's most extensive calendar of day-by-day family events; child-focused camp, day care, and party directories; local family fun suggestions; and articles that offer parenting advice and insights. Other *MetroKids* publications include *The Ultimate Family Guide*, a guide to area attractions, service providers, and community resources; SpecialKids, a resource guide for families of children with special needs; and Educator's Edition, a directory of field trips, assemblies, and school enrichment programs." Estab. 1990. Circ. 90,000. Byline given. Pays on publication. Submit seasonal material 4 months in advance. Accepts queries by e-mail. Accepts simultaneous submissions. Guidelines available by e-mail.

○ Responds only if interested.

NONFICTION Needs general interest, how-to, new product. Special issues: See editorial calendar online for current needs. **Buys 40 mss/year.** Query with published clips. Length: 575-1,500 words. **Pays $50.**

REPRINTS E-mail summary or complete article and information about when and where the material previously appeared. Pays $35, or $50 if localized after discussion.

COLUMNS/DEPARTMENTS Tech Talk, Mom Matters, Health, Money, Your Home, Parenting, Toddlers, Tweens/Teens, Education, Food & Nutrition, Play, Toddlers, Camp, Classes, Features, all 650-850 words. **Buys 25 mss/year.** Query. **Pays $25-50.**

TIPS "We prefer e-mail queries or submissions. Because they're so numerous, we don't reply unless interested. We are interested in feature articles (on specified topics) or material for our regular departments (with a regional/seasonal base). Articles should cite expert sources, preferably from the Philadelphia/South Jersey/Delaware area, and the most up-to-date theories and facts. We are looking for a journalistic style of writing. We are also interested in finding local writers for assignments."

PARENTS

Meredith Corp., 805 Third Ave., New York NY 10022. (212)499-2000. **Website:** www.parents.com. **Contact:** See masthead for specific department editors. Monthly magazine that focuses on the daily needs and concerns of mothers with young children. Provides high-quality content that informs, entertains, and joins parents in celebrating the joys of parenthood. Features information about child health, safety, behavior, discipline, and education. There are also stories on women's health, nutrition, pregnancy, marriage, and beauty. Estab. 1926. Circ. 2.2 million. Pays on acceptance. Offers 25% kill fee. Submit seasonal material 6-8 months in advance. Accepts queries by mail. Accepts simultaneous submissions. Responds in 4-6 weeks to queries. Guidelines available online.

NONFICTION Query before submitting. "Include one-page letter detailing the topic you'd like to address as well as your strategy for writing the story. Demonstrate that you are adept at doing research by mentioning the kinds of sources you intend to use. Keep in mind that all of our articles include expert advice and real-parent examples as well as study data." Include SASE.

TIPS "We're a national publication, so we're mainly interested in stories that will appeal to a wide variety of parents. We're always looking for compelling human-interest stories, so you may want to check your local newspaper for ideas. Keep in mind that we can't pursue stories that have appeared in competing national publications."

☯💲💲💲💲💲 TODAY'S PARENT

Rogers Media, Inc., 1 Mt. Pleasant Rd., 8th Floor, Toronto Ontario M4Y 2Y5 Canada. (416)764-2883. **Fax:** (416)764-2894. **E-mail:** editors@todaysparent.com.

Website: www.todaysparent.com. **Contact:** Alicia Kowalewski, art director. Monthly magazine for parents with children up to the age of 12. Circ. 2 million. No kill fee. Editorial lead time 5 months. Accepts simultaneous submissions.

NONFICTION Length: 1,800-2,500 words. **Pays $1,500-2,200.**

COLUMNS/DEPARTMENTS What's New (games/apps/movies/toys); Health (parents and children); Behaviour; Relationships; Steps and Stages; How Does He/She Do It; Bright Idea; Food/In the Kitchen.

TIPS "Because we promote ourselves as a Canadian magazine, we try to use only Canadian writers and focus on Canadian content."

WORKING MOTHER

Bonnier Corporation, 2 Park Ave., 10th Floor, New York NY 10016. (212)779-5000. **Website:** www.workingmother.com. **90% freelance written. Prefers to work with published/established writers; works with a small number of new/unpublished writers each year.** Magazine published 8 times/year for women who balance a career, home, and family. Estab. 1981. Circ. 760,000. Byline given. Offers kill fee. Publishes ms an average of 4 months after acceptance. Submit seasonal material 6 months in advance. Accepts queries by e-mail. Accepts simultaneous submissions. Sample copy available. Guidelines available online.

NONFICTION Needs humor, service, child development, material pertinent to the working mother's predicament. **Buys 9-10 mss/year.** Query with published clips. Feature queries should specifically relate to the working mom, whether geared to her work, family, personal well-being, or a mixture of these. Length: 1,000-2,000 words.

COLUMNS/DEPARTMENTS Most of columns are staff written, but some are assigned out occasionally. E-mail queries, including links or files of clips of previously published work. Include all contact info. If pitching about a specific working mom, include recent photographs/JPGs (at least 300 dpi) if possible. Unsolicited mss will not be returned. Does not respond to every proposal, only if interested. If interested, will respond in 90 days. Columns topics (sorted by editor): All Best Companies initiatives: krista.karothers@workingmother.com and/or jennifer.owens@workingmother.com; non-initiative features, celebrities, executive moms ("From the Corner

Office"), parenting, travel, food, money and finance, personal essays ("IMHO"); all online articles: barbara. turvett@workingmother.com; celebrities, workplace issues, entrepreneur moms, mom health and fitness, pregnancy, books, products: marisa.lascala@workingmother.com.

CONSUMER SERVICE & BUSINESS OPPORTUNITY

⊕⊕ HOME BUSINESS MAGAZINE

20664 Jutland Place, Lakeville MN 55044. **E-mail:** editor@homebusinessmag.com. **Website:** www.homebusinessmag.com. **Contact:** Sherilyn Colleen. **75% freelance written.** Covers every angle of the home-based business market including: cutting edge editorial by well-known authorities on sales and marketing, business operations, the home office, franchising, business opportunities, network marketing, mail order, and other subjects to help readers choose, manage, and prosper in a home-based business; display advertising, classified ads and a directory of home-based businesses; technology, the Internet, computers, and the future of home-based business; home-office editorial including management advice, office set-up, and product descriptions; business opportunities, franchising and work-from-home success stories. Estab. 1993. Circ. 105,000. No kill fee. Publishes ms an average of 6 months after acceptance. Editorial lead time 6 months. Submit seasonal material 6 months in advance. Accepts queries by e-mail. Accepts simultaneous submissions. Sample copy for sae with 9x12 envelope and 8 first-class stamps. Guidelines for #10 SASE.

NONFICTION Needs book excerpts, general interest, how-to, inspirational, interview, new product, personal experience, photo feature. No non-home business related topics. **Buys 40 mss/year.** Send complete ms. "Send complete information by e-mail. We encourage writers to submit feature articles (2-3 pages) and departmental articles (1 page). Please submit polished, well-written, organized material. It helps to provide subheadings within the article. Boxes, lists, and bullets are encouraged because they make your article easier to read, use, and reference by the reader. A primary problem in the past is that articles do not stick to the subject of the title. Please pay attention to the focus of your article and to your title. Please

don't call to get the status of your submission. We will call if we're interested in publishing the submission." Length: 200-1,000 words. **Pays 20¢/published word for work-for-hire assignments; 50-word byline for unsolicited articles.**

PHOTOS Identification of subjects required. Offers no additional payment for photos accepted with ms.

COLUMNS/DEPARTMENTS Marketing & Sales; Money Corner; Home Office; Management; Technology; Working Smarter; Franchising; Network Marketing, all 650 words. Send complete ms.

KIPLINGER'S PERSONAL FINANCE

1100 13th St. NW, Washington DC 20005. (202)887-6400; (646) 695-7046. **E-mail:** jbodnar@kiplinger. com; alex@rosengrouppr.com. **Website:** www.kiplinger.com. **Contact:** Janet Bodnar, editor; Stacie Harrison, art director; Alex Kutler, account executive. **10% freelance written. Prefers to work with published/established writers.** Monthly magazine for general, adult audience interested in personal finance and consumer information. "*Kiplinger's* is a highly trustworthy source of information on saving and investing, taxes, credit, home ownership, paying for college, retirement planning, automobile buying, and many other personal finance topics." Estab. 1947. Circ. 800,000. Pays on acceptance. No kill fee. Publishes ms an average of 2 months after acceptance. Accepts simultaneous submissions. Responds in 1 month to queries.

NONFICTION Query with published clips.

TIPS "We are looking for a heavy emphasis on personal finance topics. Currently most work is provided by in-house writers."

CONTEMPORARY CULTURE

A&U

Art & Understanding, Inc., 25 Monroe St., Suite 205, Albany NY 12210-2729. (518)426-9010. **Fax:** (518)436-5354. **E-mail:** chaelneedle@mac.com. **E-mail:** aumaglit@gmail.com. **Website:** www.aumag.org. Brent Calderwood, literary editor. **Contact:** Chael Needle, managing editor. **50% freelance written.** Monthly national nonprofit print magazine covering cultural, political, and medical responses to HIV/AIDS, including poetry, fiction and drama. Estab. 1991. Circ. 180,000. Byline given. Pays 1-3 months after publication. Publishes ms an average of 1-3 months after acceptance. Editorial lead time 6 months. Accepts queries by mail, e-mail. Accepts simultaneous submissions. Responds in 1 month to queries; in 2 months to mss. Sample copy: $5. Guidelines available online.

NONFICTION Needs book excerpts, essays, general interest, humor, interview, opinion, personal experience, photo feature, profile. **Buys 6 mss/year.** Query with published clips. Length: 800-1,200 words. **Pays $150-300 for assigned articles.**

COLUMNS/DEPARTMENTS The Culture of AIDS (reviews of books, music, film), 300 words; Viewpoint (personal opinion), 750 words. **Buys 8 mss/year.** Send complete ms. **Pays $50-150.**

FICTION Literary electronic submissions, as Word attachments, may be mailed to Brent Calderwood, literary editor, at aumaglit@gmail.com. Pay rate schedule available upon request. Send complete ms. Length: up to 1,500 words. **Pays $50.**

POETRY Accepts any length/style (shorter works preferred). **Pays $25.**

TIPS "We're looking for more articles on youth and HIV/AIDS; more international coverage; celebrity interviews; more coverage of how the pandemic is affecting historically underrepresented communities. We are also looking for literary submissions that address the past and present AIDS epidemic in fresh ways. Each year, we sponsor the Christopher Hewitt Award, given to the best poem, short story, creative nonfiction piece, and drama submitted."

◑ ADBUSTERS

Adbusters Media Foundation, 1243 W. Seventh Ave., Vancouver BC V6H 1B7 Canada. (604)736-9401. **E-mail:** editor@adbusters.org. **Website:** www.adbusters.org. **50% freelance written.** Bimonthly magazine on consumerism. "Based in Vancouver, British Columbia, Canada, *Adbusters* is a not-for-profit, reader-supported magazine concerned with the erosion of our physical and cultural environments by commercial forces. Since 1989, the magazine has been featured in hundreds of alternative and mainstream newspapers, magazines, television, and radio shows. Known worldwide for sparking Occupy Wall Street, *Adbusters* is also responsible for social media campaigns such as Buy Nothing Day and Digital Detox Week. Included in the magazine are incisive philosophical articles and activist commentary, coupled with impact design that seeks to unbound the traditional magazine format. Issues relevant to our contemporary moment, such as media concentration, climate change, and genetically modified foods, are regularly featured. We seek out a world where economy and ecology exist in harmony. By challenging people to become participants as opposed to spectators, *Adbusters* takes aim at corporate disinformation, global injustice, and the industries and governments who actively pollute and destroy our physical and mental commons." Estab. 1989. Circ. 90,000. Byline given. Pays 1 month after publication. Accepts queries by mail, e-mail, fax. Accepts simultaneous submissions. Guidelines available online.

NONFICTION Needs essays, expose, interview, opinion. **Buys variable mss/year.** Query. Length: 250-3,000 words. **Pays $100/page for unsolicited articles; 50¢/word for solicited articles.**

FICTION Inquire about themes.

POETRY Inquire about themes.

BOSTON REVIEW

P.O. Box 425786, Cambridge MA 02142. (617)324-1360. **E-mail:** review@bostonreview.net. **Website:** www.bostonreview.net. **Contact:** Deborah Chasman and Joshua Cohen, editors. **90% freelance written.** Online and print magazine of cultural and political analysis, reviews, fiction, and poetry. The editors are committed to a society that fosters human diversity and a democracy in which we seek common grounds of principle amidst our many differences. In the hope of advancing these ideals, *Boston Review* acts as a forum that seeks to enrich the language of public debate. Estab. 1975. Byline given. Time between acceptance and publication is 4 months for nonfiction, 1 year for fiction and poetry. Accepts queries by e-mail, online submission form. Accepts simultaneous submissions. Responds in 4 months to queries. Sample copy for $10 plus shipping; purchase online at bostonreview.net/store. Guidelines online.

◗ *Boston Review* is a recipient of the Pushcart Prize in Poetry.

NONFICTION Needs book excerpts, essays, expose, general interest, historical, interview, reviews, Philosophy, Political Studies. **Buys 200 mss/year.** Submit query letters and unsolicited nonfiction up to 5,000 words via the online submissions system.

FICTION Currently closed to general fiction submissions but assembling a special issue of fiction on global dystopias, edited by Junot Díaz. See submission page for details. Needs ethnic, experimental, fantasy, horror, science fiction, short stories, Afrofuturist, dystopian, speculative. **Buys 20 mss/year.** Send complete ms. Length: up to 5,000 words, but can be much shorter. **Pays $100-300 and contributor's copies.**

POETRY "We are open to both traditional and experimental forms. What we value most is originality and a strong sense of voice." Send materials for review consideration. Buys 50 poems/year. Submit maximum 6 poems. **Payment varies.**

TIPS "The best way to get a sense of the kind of material *Boston Review* is looking for is to read the magazine. It is all available online for free."

COMMON GROUND

Common Ground Publishing, 3152 W 8th Ave., Vancouver BC V6K 2C3 Canada. (604)733-2215. **Fax:** (604)733-4415. **E-mail:** editor@commonground.ca. **Website:** www.commonground.ca. **90% freelance written.** Monthly tabloid covering health, environment, spirit, creativity, and wellness. "We serve the cultural creative community." Estab. 1982. Circ. 70,000. Byline given. Pays on publication. No kill fee. Publishes ms an average of 1 month after acceptance. Editorial lead time 2 months. Submit seasonal material 3 months in advance. Accepts queries by e-mail. Accepts simultaneous submissions. Responds in 6 weeks to queries. Responds in 3 months to mss. Sample copy for $5. Guidelines available online.

"We prefer to receive a completed article for consideration. The maximum word count is 2,000 words. The minimum word count is 600 words. Also include a brief biography as well as an explanation of why the author is qualified to write on this subject. Please do not send any attachments with your query. Please read past issues of Common Ground to understand the nature and style of the editorial content. The offices of Common Ground have past issues available to you for $5 each. Generally we accept articles on health, wellness, the environment, transformational travel and personal growth. We prefer articles by Canadian authors, and we very rarely accept fiction and poetry. For current needs, please refer to the Editorial Calendar."

NONFICTION Needs book excerpts, how-to, inspirational, interview, opinion, personal experience, travel, call to action. Send complete ms. Length: 500-2,500 words. **Pays 10¢/word (Canadian).**

PHOTOS State availability. Captions, True required. Buys one-time rights.

FAST COMPANY

7 World Trade Center, New York NY 10007-2195. (212) 389-5300. **Fax:** (212) 389-5496. **E-mail:** pr@fastcompany.com. **Website:** www.fastcompany.com. **Contact:** Lori Hoffman, managing editor. Magazine published 10 times/year that inspires readers and users to think beyond traditional boundaries, lead conversations, and create the future of business. *Fast Company* is the world's leading progressive business media brand, with a unique editorial focus on innovation in technology, ethonomics (ethical economics), leadership, and design. Estab. 1996. Circ. 750,000. Accepts queries by e-mail. Accepts simultaneous submissions. No formal guidelines. Familiarize yourself with the magazine.

Difficult market to break into.

NONFICTION Rarely accepts unsolicited freelancer contributions. If you have a person, company, product, or any other story idea you'd like to see in *Fast Company*, query with a pitch. If interested, *Fast Company* will contact you.

FLAUNT

1422 N. Highland Ave., Los Angeles CA 90028. (323)836-1000. **E-mail:** info@flauntmagazine.com. **Website:** www.flaunt.com. **Contact:** Luis Barajas, editor in chief. **40% freelance written.** Monthly magazine covering culture, arts, entertainment, music, fashion, and film. "*Flaunt* features the bold work of emerging photographers, writers, artists, and musicians. The quality of the content is mirrored in the sophisticated, interactive format of the magazine, using advanced printing techniques, fold-out articles, beautiful papers, and inserts to create a visually stimulating, surprisingly readable, and intelligent book that pushes the magazine into the realm of art-object. *Flaunt* has, since 1998, made it a point to break new ground, earning itself a reputation as an engine of the avant-garde and an outlet for the culture of the cutting edge. *Flaunt* takes pride in reinventing itself each month, while consistently representing a hybrid of all that is interesting in entertainment, fashion, music, design, film, art, and literature." Estab. 1998. Circ. 100,000. Byline given. No kill fee. Publishes ms an average of 3 months after acceptance. Editorial lead time 3 months. Submit seasonal material 3 months in advance. Accepts queries by mail, e-mail. Accepts simultaneous submissions. Responds in 2 weeks to queries; in 1 month to mss.

NONFICTION Needs book excerpts, essays, general interest, historical, humor, interview, new product, opinion, personal experience, photo feature, travel. Special issues: Special issues: September and March (fashion issues); February (men's issue); May (music issue). **Buys 20 mss/year.** Query with published clips. Length: 500-5,000 words. **Pays up to $500.**

PHOTOS State availability. Identification of subjects, model releases required. Reviews contact sheets, transparencies, prints, GIF/JPEG files. Buys one-time rights.

GOOD MAGAZINE

601 West 26th Street, Suite 235, New York NY 10001. (323)556-6780. **E-mail:** submissions@goodinc.com. **Website:** www.goodmagazine.com. *GOOD* is the integrated media platform for people who want to live well and do good. Has themed issues. Estab. 2006. Accepts simultaneous submissions.

🟢🟢🟢🟢 MOTHER JONES

Foundation for National Progress, 222 Sutter St., Suite 600, San Francisco CA 94108. (415)321-1700. **E-mail:** query@motherjones.com. **Website:** www.mother-jones.com. **Contact:** Mark Murrmann, photo editor; Ivylise Simones, creative director; Monika Bauerlein and Clara Jeffery, editors. **80% freelance written.** Bi-monthly magazine covering politics, investigative reporting, social issues, and pop culture. *"Mother Jones* is a 'progressive' magazine—but the core of its editorial well is reporting (i.e., fact-based). No slant required. Estab. 1976. Circ. 240,000. Byline given. Pays on publication. Offers 33% kill fee. Publishes ms an average of 4 months after acceptance. Editorial lead time 4 months. Submit seasonal material 6 months in advance. Accepts simultaneous submissions. Responds in 2 months to queries. Sample copy for $6 and 9x12 SASE. Guidelines available online.

> *"Mother Jones* magazine and *MotherJones. com* will consider solidly reported, hard-hitting, groundbreaking news stories. We're also open to thought-provoking, timely opinion and analysis pieces on important current issues. We're interested in just about anything that will raise our readers' eyebrows, but we focus especially on these areas: national poli-

tics, environmental issues, corporate wrongdoing, human rights, and political influence in all spheres.

NONFICTION Needs interview, photo feature, current issues, policy, investigative reporting. **Buys 70-100 mss/year.** Query with published clips. "Please also include your rèsumè and two or three of your most relevant clips. If the clips are online, please provide the complete URLs. Web pieces are generally less than 1,500 words. Because we have staff reporters it is extremely rare that we will pay for a piece whose timeliness or other qualities work for the Web only. Magazine pieces can range up to 5,000 words. There is at least a two-month lead time. No phone calls please." Length: 2,000-5,000 words. **Pays $1/word.**

PHOTOS Contact: Mark Murrmann.

COLUMNS/DEPARTMENTS Outfront (short, newsy and/or outrageous and/or humorous items), 200-800 words; Profiles of Hellraisers, 500 words. **Pays $1/word.**

TIPS "We're looking for hard-hitting, investigative reports exposing government cover-ups, corporate malfeasance, scientific myopia, institutional fraud or hypocrisy; thoughtful, provocative articles which challenge the conventional wisdom (on the right or the left) concerning issues of national importance; and timely, people-oriented stories on issues such as the environment, labor, the media, healthcare, consumer protection, and cultural trends. Send a great, short query and establish your credibility as a reporter. Explain what you plan to cover and how you will proceed with the reporting. The query should convey your approach, tone and style, and should answer the following: What are your specific qualifications to write on this topic? What 'ins' do you have with your sources? Can you provide full documentation so that your story can be fact-checked?"

🟢 THE OLDIE MAGAZINE

Oldie Publications Ltd, 65 Newman St., London England W1T 3EG United Kingdom. (44)(207)436-8801. **Fax:** (44)(207)436-8804. **E-mail:** jeremylewis@the-oldie.co.uk. **Website:** www.theoldie.co.uk. **Contact:** Jeremy Lewis, features editor. No kill fee. Accepts queries by mail. Accepts simultaneous submissions. Responds in 1 month to mss. Sample copy by e-mail. Guidelines available online.

NONFICTION Send complete ms. Length: 600-1,300 words.

PHOTOS Send photocopies of photographs, cartoons, and illustrations.

COLUMNS/DEPARTMENTS Modern Life (puzzling aspects of today's world); Anorak (owning up to an obsession); The Old Un's Diary (oldun@theoldie.co.uk).

TIPS "Please do not submit anything to us unless you have read at least two or three copies of *The Oldie* and have a good feel for the magazine. *The Oldie* is one of the very few magazines in the country who believe in dedicating time and effort from our limited resources to reading all unsolicited pieces, so please do your bit–pay attention to these guidelines and make sure you're familiar with the magazine."

PEOPLE STYLEWATCH

Time Inc., 1271 Avenue of the Americas, 27th Floor, New York NY 10020. (212)522-1388. **Fax:** (212)467-3127. **E-mail:** editor@people.com. **Website:** www.peoplestylewatch.com. **Contact:** Ariel Foxman, editor. Monthly magazine focusing on celebrity style, fashion, and beauty. *People StyleWatch* is an extension of *People Magazine's* StyleWatch column. Estab. 2002. Accepts simultaneous submissions.

 Query before submitting.

UTNE READER

1503 SW 42nd St, Topeka KS 66609. (785)274-4300; (800) 678-5779. **E-mail:** editor@utne.com. **Website:** www.utne.com. **Contact:** Carolyn Lang, art director. Estab. 1984. Circ. 250,000. Accepts queries by mail, e-mail. Accepts simultaneous submissions. Guidelines available online.

REPRINTS Send tearsheet or photocopy with rights for sale noted and information about when and where the material previously appeared.

TIPS "State the theme(s) clearly, let the narrative flow, and build the story around strong characters and a vivid sense of place. Give us rounded episodes, logically arranged. We do not publish fiction or poetry."

VANITY FAIR

Conde Nast Publications, Inc., One World Trade Center, New York NY 10007. **E-mail:** letters@vf.com. **Website:** www.vanityfair.com. Monthly magazine. *Vanity Fair* is edited for readers with an interest in contemporary society. No kill fee. Accepts simultaneous submissions.

 Does not buy freelance material, use freelance writers, or respond to queries.

DISABILITIES

⚙ ABILITIES

Canadian Abilities Foundation, 225 Duncan Mill Road, Suite 803, Toronto ON M3B 3H9 Canada. (416)421-7944. **Fax:** (416)421-8418. **E-mail:** abilities@bcsgroup.com. **Website:** www.abilities.ca. **Contact:** Caroline Tapp-McDougall, managing editor. **50% freelance written.** Quarterly magazine covering disability issues. "*Abilities* is Canada's foremost cross-disability lifestyle magazine. The mission of the magazine is to provide **information** about lifestyle topics, including travel, health, careers, education, relationships, parenting, new products, social policy and much more; **inspiration** to participate in organizations, events, and activities and pursue opportunities in sports, education, careers, and more; and **opportunity** to learn about a wealth of Canadian resources that facilitate self empowerment of people with disabilities." Estab. 1987. Circ. 20,000. Byline given. Pays on publication. Offers 50% kill fee. Publishes ms an average of 3 months after acceptance. Editorial lead time 3 months. Submit seasonal material 4 months in advance. Accepts queries by mail, e-mail. Responds in 3 months to queries. Sample copy free. Writer's guidelines for #10 SASE, online, or by e-mail.

NONFICTION Needs general interest, how-to, humor, inspirational, interview, new product, personal experience, photo feature, travel. Does not want articles that 'preach to the converted'—this means info that people with disabilities likely already know, such as what it's like to have a disability. **Buys 30-40 mss/year.** Query or send complete ms. Length: 500-2,000 words. **Pays $50-325 (Canadian) for assigned articles.**

REPRINTS Sometimes accepts previously published submissions (if stated as such).

PHOTOS State availability.

COLUMNS/DEPARTMENTS The Lighter Side (humor), 700 words; Profile, 1,200 words.

TIPS "We strongly prefer e-mail queries. When developing story ideas, keep in mind that our readers are in Canada."

💲💲💲💲 ARTHRITIS TODAY

Arthritis Foundation, 1355 Peachtree St. NE, 6th Floor, Atlanta GA 30309. **Website:** www.arthritis-today.org. **50% freelance written.** Bimonthly magazine covering living with arthritis and the latest in research/treatment. *Arthritis Today* is a consumer health magazine and is written for the more than 70 million Americans who have arthritis and for the millions of others whose lives are touched by an arthritis-related disease. The editorial content is designed to help the person with arthritis live a more productive, independent, and pain-free life. The articles are upbeat and provide practical advice, information, and inspiration. Estab. 1987. Circ. 650,000. Byline given. Pays on acceptance. Offers kill fee. Offers kill fee. Editorial lead time 6 months. Submit seasonal material 6 months in advance. Accepts queries by mail, online submission form. Accepts simultaneous submissions. Responds in 2 months to queries. Sample copy for 9x11 SAE with 4 first-class stamps.

NONFICTION Needs general interest, how-to, inspirational, new product, opinion, personal experience, photo feature, technical, travel. **Buys 12 unsolicited mss/year.** Query with published clips. Length: 150-2,500 words. **Pays $100-2,500.**

PHOTOS Send photos. Identification of subjects required. Reviews prints. Negotiates payment individually. Buys one-time rights.

COLUMNS/DEPARTMENTS Nutrition, 100-600 words; Fitness, 100-600 words; Balance (emotional coping), 100-600 words; MedWatch, 100-800 words; Solutions, 100-600 words; Life Makeover, 400-600 words.

FILLERS Needs facts, gags, short humor. **Buys 2 mss/year.** Length: 40-100 words. **Pays $80-150.**

TIPS "Our readers are already well informed. We need ideas and writers that give in-depth, fresh, interesting information that truly adds to their understanding of their condition and their quality of life. Quality writers are more important than good ideas. The staff generates many of our ideas but needs experienced, talented writers who are good reporters to execute them. Please provide published clips. In addition to articles specifically about living with arthritis, we look for articles to appeal to an older audience on subjects such as hobbies, general health, lifestyle, etc."

CAREERS & THE DISABLED

Equal Opportunity Publications, 445 Broad Hollow Rd., Suite 425, Melville NY 11747. (631)421-9421, ext. 12. **E-mail:** bloehr@eop.com. **Website:** www.eop.com. **Contact:** Barbara Capella Loehr, editor. **60% freelance written.** Magazine published 6 times/year, with Fall, Winter, Spring, Summer, Expo and Veterans' editions, offering role-model profiles and career guidance articles geared toward disabled college students and professionals, and promoting personal and professional growth. Estab. 1968: EOP; 1986: CAREERS & the disABLED magazine. Circ. 10,000. Byline given. Pays on publication. Publishes ms an average of 6 months after acceptance. Editorial lead time 6 months. Submit seasonal material 6 months in advance. Accepts queries by mail, e-mail, phone. Accepts simultaneous submissions. Responds in 3 weeks to queries. Sample copy for 9x12 SAE with 5 first-class stamps. Guidelines free.

NONFICTION Needs essays, general interest, how-to, interview, new product, opinion, personal experience. **Buys 30 mss/year.** Query. Length: 1,000-2,500 words. **Pays 10¢/word.**

PHOTOS Captions, identification of subjects, model releases required. Reviews transparencies, prints. Buys one-time rights.

TIPS "Be as targeted as possible. Role-model profiles and specific career guidance strategies that offer advice to disabled college students are most needed."

⊗⊗ DIABETES HEALTH

P.O. Box 1199, Woodacre CA 94973. **E-mail:** editor@diabeteshealth.com. **Website:** www.diabeteshealth.com. **Contact:** Nadia Al-Samarrie, editor in chief. **60% freelance written.** Monthly tabloid covering diabetes care. *Diabetes Health* covers the latest in diabetes care, medications, and patient advocacy. Personal accounts are welcome as well as medical-oriented articles by MDs, RNs, and CDEs (certified diabetes educators). Estab. 1991. Circ. 150,000. Byline given. Pays on publication. No kill fee. Publishes ms an average of 2 months after acceptance. Editorial lead time 2 months. Submit seasonal material 2 months in advance. Accepts queries by e-mail. Accepts simultaneous submissions. Sample copy available online. Guidelines free.

Accepts solicited submissions from contributing writers for feature-length stories.

NONFICTION Needs book excerpts, essays, how-to, humor, inspirational, interview, memoir, new product, nostalgic, opinion, personal experience, photo feature, reviews, technical, travel. *Diabetes Health* does not accept mss that promote a product, philosophy, or personal view. **Buys 25 mss/year.** Send complete ms. Length: 400-1,500 words. **Pays 10¢/word.**

POETRY Needs Personal poetry from people living with diabetes.

TIPS "Be actively involved in the diabetes community, or have diabetes. Writers need not have diabetes to write an article, but it must be diabetes-related."

DIABETES SELF-MANAGEMENT

Madavor Media, LLC, 25 Braintree Hill Office Park, Suite 404, Braintree MA 02184. **E-mail:** dsmwebeditor@madavor.com. **Website:** www.diabetesselfmanagement.com. **20% freelance written.** Bimonthly magazine. "We publish how-to health care articles for motivated, intelligent readers who have diabetes and who are actively involved in their own health care management. All articles must have immediate application to their daily living." Estab. 1983. Byline given. Pays on publication. Offers 20% kill fee. Submit seasonal material 6 months in advance. Accepts queries by e-mail. Accepts simultaneous submissions. Responds in 6 weeks to queries. Guidelines online.

NONFICTION Needs how-to, technical, travel. No personal experiences, personality profiles, exposés, or research breakthroughs. **Buys 10-12 mss/year.** Query with published clips. Length: 2,000-3,000 words. **Pay varies.**

TIPS "The rule of thumb for any article we publish is that it must be clear, concise, useful, and instructive, and it must have immediate application to the lives of our readers. If your query is accepted, expect heavy editorial supervision."

DIALOGUE

Blindskills, Inc., P.O. Box 5181, Salem OR 97304. **E-mail:** magazine@blindskills.com. **Website:** www.blindskills.com. **60% freelance written.** Quarterly journal covering visually impaired people. Estab. 1962. Circ. 1,100. Byline given. Pays on publication. Publishes ms an average of 6 months after acceptance. Editorial lead time 3 months. Accepts queries by e-mail. Accepts simultaneous submissions. Sample copy: 1 free copy on request. Available in large print, Braille, digital audio Cartridge, and e-mail. Guidelines available online.

NONFICTION Needs essays, general interest, historical, how-to, humor, interview, new product, opinion, personal experience, profile. No controversial, explicit sex, religious, or political topics. **Buys 50-60 mss/year.** Send complete ms. Length: 200-1,200 words. **Pays $15-35 for assigned articles. Pays $15-25 for unsolicited articles.**

COLUMNS/DEPARTMENTS All material should be relative to blind and visually impaired readers. Living with Low Vision, 1,000 words; Hear's How (dealing with sight loss), 1,000 words; Technology Answer Book, 1,000 words. **Buys 80 mss/year.** Send complete ms. **Pays $25-50.**

KALEIDOSCOPE

United Disability Services, 701 S. Main St., Akron OH 44311-1019. (330)762-9755. **Fax:** (330)762-0912. **E-mail:** kaleidoscope@udsakron.org. **Website:** www.kaleidoscopeonline.org. **Contact:** Gail Willmott, editor in chief. **90% freelance written. Eager to work with new/unpublished writers.** Semiannual free online magazine. Kaleidoscope magazine creatively focuses on the experiences of disability through literature and the fine arts. As a pioneering literary resource for the field of disability studies, this award-winning publication expresses the diversity of the disability experience from a variety of perspectives including: individuals, families, friends, caregivers, educators, and healthcare professionals, among others." Estab. 1979. Byline given. Pays on publication. No kill fee. 1-3 years 3 months prior to publication Accepts queries by mail, e-mail, fax, phone, online submission form. Accepts simultaneous submissions. Responds in 6-9 months. Guidelines available online. Submissions and queries electronically via website and e-mail.

○ Kaleidoscope has received awards from the Great Lakes Awards Competition and Ohio Public Images; received the Ohioana Award of Editorial Excellence.

NONFICTION Needs essays, interview, personal experience, reviews, articles relating to both literary and visual arts. For book reviews: "Reviews that are substantive, timely, powerful works about publications in the field of disability and/or the arts. The writer's opinion of the work being reviewed should be clear. The review should be a literary work in its own right." **Buys 40-50 mss/year.** Submit complete ms by website or e-mail. Include cover letter. Length: up to 5,000 words. **Pays $25.**

REPRINTS Send double-spaced, typed ms with complete author's/artist's contact information, rights for sale noted, and information about when and where the material previously appeared. Reprints permitted with credit given to original publication. All rights revert to author upon publication

PHOTOS Send digital images.

FICTION Wants short stories with a well-crafted plot and engaging characters. Needs historical, humorous, mainstream, short stories, slice-of-life vignettes. No fiction that is stereotypical, patronizing, sentimental, erotic, or maudlin. No romance, religious or dogmatic fiction; no children's literature. Submit complete ms by website or e-mail. Include cover letter. Length: up to 5,000 words. **Pays $25.**

POETRY Wants poems that have strong imagery, evocative language. Submit up to 5 poems by website or e-mail. Include cover letter. Do not get caught up in rhyme scheme. Reviews any style. **$10 per poem.**

TIPS "The material chosen for Kaleidoscope challenges and overcomes stereotypical, patronizing, and sentimental attitudes about disability. We accept the work of writers with and without disabilities; however the work of a writer without a disability must focus on some aspect of disability. The criteria for good writing apply: effective technique, thought-provoking subject matter, and, in general, a mature grasp of the art of storytelling. Writers should avoid using offensive language and always put the person before the disability."

ENTERTAINMENT

DANCE INTERNATIONAL

Scotiabank Dance Centre, Level 6 - 677 Davie St., Vancouver BC V6B 2G6 Canada. (604)681-1525. **Fax:** (604)681-7732. **E-mail:** editor@danceinternational.org; info@danceinternational.org. **Website:** www.danceinternational.org. **100% freelance written.** Quarterly magazine covering dance arts. Articles and reviews on current activities in world dance, with occasional historical features. Estab. 1977. Circ. 3,000. Byline given. Pays on publication. Offers 50% kill fee. Publishes ms an average of 3 months after acceptance. Editorial lead time 3 months. Long lead times necessary for quarterly publication. Accepts queries by mail, e-mail. Responds promptly to queries. Sample copy: $7.50 plus p&p, or on Kobo.

NONFICTION Needs book excerpts, essays, historical, interview, memoir, personal experience, profile, reviews, technical. **Buys 100 mss/year.** Query with a brief proposal and short bio. Length: 1,200-2,200 words.

PHOTOS Offers no additional payment for photos accepted with ms.

COLUMNS/DEPARTMENTS Mediawatch (recent books, DVDs, media reviewed), 700-800 words; Regional Reports (quarterly roundups from cities worldwide), 800 words. **Buys 100 mss/year.** Query. **Pays $80.**

TIPS Send résumé and samples of recent writing.

ENTERTAINMENT WEEKLY

Time, Inc., 135 West 50th Street, New York NY 10020. (212)522-5600. **Fax:** (212)522-0074. **Website:** www.ew.com. **Contact:** Matt Bean, editor. Weekly magazine. *Entertainment Weekly* is an all-access pass to Hollywood's most creative minds and fascinating stars. Written for readers who want the latest reviews, previews, and updates of the entertainment world. Circ. 1,600,000. No kill fee. Editorial lead time 4 weeks. Accepts simultaneous submissions.

Query before submitting.

GLOBE

American Media, Inc., 1000 American Media Way, Boca Raton FL 33464. **Website:** www.globemagazine.com. Weekly tabloid covering celebrities. *Globe* is edited for an audience interested in a wide range of human-interest stories, with particular emphasis on celebrities. Does not buy freelance material or use freelance writers. Circ. 631,705. No kill fee. Accepts simultaneous submissions.

IN TOUCH WEEKLY

270 Sylvan Ave., Englewood Cliffs NJ 07632. (201)569-6699. **E-mail:** contactus@intouchweekly.com. **Website:** www.intouchweekly.com. **10% freelance written.** Weekly magazine covering celebrity news and entertainment. Estab. 2002. Circ. 1,300,000. No byline given. Pays on publication. Editorial lead time 1 week. Accepts queries by mail, e-mail. Accepts simultaneous submissions.

NONFICTION Needs interview, gossip. **Buys 1,300 mss/year.** Query. Send a tip about a celebrity by e-mail. Length: 100-1,000 words. **Pays $50.**

METRO MAGAZINE (AUSTRALIA)

Australian Teachers of Media (ATOM), P.O. Box 2040, St. Kilda West VIC 3182 Australia. (61)(3)9525-5302. **Fax:** (61)(3)9537-2325. **E-mail:** metro@atom.org.au. **Website:** www.metromagazine.com.au. **Contact:** Adolfo Aranjuez. Quarterly magazine specializing in longform articles, analytical reviews, and critical essays on film, TV, and media from Australia, New Zealand, and the Asia-Pacific region. Estab. 1968. Pays on publication. Accepts queries by e-mail. Accepts simultaneous submissions. Guidelines available online.

NONFICTION Needs essays, general interest, interview, reviews, technical. Send complete ms via e-mail. Length: 1,000-3,000 words. **Pay rates available online.**

PHOTOS Send photos. Reviews TIFF/JPEG files.

🟢 🟢 MOVIEMAKER MAGAZINE

MovieMaker Media LLC, 2525 Michigan Ave., Building I, Santa Monica CA 90404. (310)828-8388. **E-mail:** tim@moviemaker.com. **Website:** www.moviemaker.com. **Contact:** Timothy Rhys, editor in chief. **75% freelance written.** Bimonthly magazine covering film, independent cinema, and Hollywood. "*MovieMaker's* editorial is a progressive mix of in-depth interviews and criticism, combined with practical techniques and advice on financing, distribution, and production strategies. Behind-the-scenes discussions with Hollywood's top moviemakers, as well as independents from around the globe, are routinely found in *MovieMaker's* pages. E-mail is the preferred submission method, but we will accept queries via mail as well. Please, no telephone pitches. We want to read the idea with clips." Estab. 1993. Circ. 55,000. Byline given. Pays 30 days after newsstand publication. Offers variable kill fee. Publishes ms an average of 2 months after acceptance. Editorial lead time 3 months. Submit seasonal material 4 months in advance. Accepts queries by mail, e-mail. Accepts simultaneous submissions. Responds in 2-4 weeks to queries; in 4-6 weeks to mss. Sample copy available online. Guidelines by email.

NONFICTION Needs expose, general interest, historical, how-to, interview, new product, technical. **Buys 20 mss/year.** Query with published clips. Length: 800-3,000 words. **Pays $75-500 for assigned articles.**

PHOTOS State availability. Identification of subjects required. Payment varies for photos accepted with ms. Rights purchased negotiable.

COLUMNS/DEPARTMENTS Documentary; Home Cinema (home video/DVD reviews); How They Did It (first-person filmmaking experiences); Festival Beat (film festival reviews); World Cinema (current state of cinema from a particular country). Query with published clips **Pays $75-300.**

TIPS "The best way to begin working with *MovieMaker* is to send a list of 'pitches' along with your résumé and clips. As we receive a number of résumés each week, we want to get an early sense of not just your style of writing but the kinds of subjects that interest you most as they relate to film. We also want to know that you understand the magazine and our audience. The fastest way to have your story rejected (besides a typo in the pitch) is to clearly have never read a copy of the magazine. Please allow 1 month before following up on a query or résumé. All queries must be submitted in writing. No phone calls, please."

TV GUIDE

11 W. 42nd St., 16th Floor, New York NY 10036. (212)852-7500. **Fax:** (212)852-7470. **Website:** www.tvguide.com. **Contact:** Mickey O'Connor, editor-in-chief. Weekly magazine. Focuses on all aspects of network, cable, and pay television programming and how it affects and reflects audiences. Estab. 1953. Circ. 9 million. No kill fee. Accepts simultaneous submissions.

⚲ Query before submitting.

US WEEKLY

Wenner Media LLC, 1290 Avenue of the Americas, New York NY 10104. **Fax:** (212)651-7890. **E-mail:** letters@usmagazine.com. **Website:** www.usmagazine.com. Weekly celebrity and entertainment magazine. Estab. 1977. Circ. 2 million. Accepts simultaneous submissions.

⚲ Query to gauge interest before submitting unsolicited mss.

ETHNIC & MINORITY

🟢 🟢 AMBASSADOR MAGAZINE

National Italian American Foundation, 1860 19th St. NW, Washington DC 20009. (202)939-3108. **E-mail:** don@niaf.org. **Website:** www.niaf.org. **Contact:** Don Oldenburg, director of publications and editor. **65% freelance written.** "We publish original nonfiction articles on the Italian American experience, culture, and traditions. We also publish profiles of Italian Americans (famous and not famous but doing something exceptional) and travel features, especially in Italy, but also relevant U.S. travel pieces." Estab. 1989. Circ. 28,000. Byline given. Pays on publication. $50 kill fee for assigned stories. Time between acceptance and publication varies. Editorial lead time 4 months. Accepts queries by e-mail. Responds within 2 months to e-mailed queries. Sample copy free. Writer's guidelines available by e-mail.

○ *Ambassador* is a glossy, high-quality consumer magazine for Italian Americans, Italians, and Italophiles.

NONFICTION Needs general interest, interview, personal experience, photo feature, profile, reviews, travel. Query via e-mail before submitting ms. When submitting ms, send as a Word e-mail attachment. Phone and mailed queries and mss are discouraged. Length: 800-1,500 words. **Pays $300 for full feature or profile; $350 for full feature or profile with photos taken by writer.**

PHOTOS Photos must be high resolution (300 dpi) and relevant to an assigned story. Offers additional $50 total for original photos taken to support a story. Otherwise, pay is negotiable. Buys one-time rights.

TIPS "Good photos, clear prose, and professional storytelling ability are all prerequisites."

○ **CELTIC LIFE INTERNATIONAL**

Clansman Publishing, Ltd., P.O. Box 8805, Station A, Halifax NS B3K 5M4 Canada. (902)835-2358. **Fax:** (902)835-0080. **E-mail:** info@celticlife.ca. **Website:** www.celticlife.com. **Contact:** Patrick Smart, editor. **50% freelance written.** Bi-monthly publication for those with a passion for Celtic culture. *Celtic Life International* is a global community for a living, breathing Celtic culture. Home to an extensive collection of feature stories, interviews, history, heritage, news, views, reviews, recipes, events, trivia, humor, and tidbits from across all Seven Celtic Nations and beyond. The flagship publication, *Celtic Life International Magazine*, is published 4 times/year in both print and digital formats, and is distributed around the world. The online home, CelticLife.ca, is an informative and interactive community that engages Celts from all walks of life. Estab. 1987. Circ. 201,340. Byline given. Pays after publication. No kill fee. Editorial lead time 2 months. Submit seasonal material 3 months in advance. Responds in 1 week to queries; in 1 month to mss.

NONFICTION Needs essays, general interest, historical, interview, opinion, personal experience, profile, travel, Gaelic language, Celtic music reviews, profiles of Celtic musicians, Celtic history, traditions, and folklore. Also buys short fiction. No fiction, poetry, historical stories already well publicized. **Buys 100 mss/year.** Query or send complete ms. Length: 700-2,500 words. **All writers receive a complimentary subscription.**

PHOTOS State availability. Captions, identification of subjects, model releases required. Reviews 35mm transparencies, 5x7 prints, JPEG files (300 dpi). "We pay for photographs."

COLUMNS/DEPARTMENTS Query.

GERMAN LIFE

Zeitgeist Publishing, Inc., 1068 National Hwy., LaVale MD 21502. **E-mail:** editor@germanlife.com. **Website:** www.germanlife.com. **Contact:** Mark Slider. **80% freelance written.** Bimonthly magazine covering German-speaking Europe (Germany, Austria, Switzerland). "*German Life* is for all interested in the diversity of German-speaking culture—past and present—and in the various ways that the US (and North America in general) has been shaped by its German immigrants. The magazine is dedicated to solid reporting on travel, cultural, historical, social, genealogical, culinary and political topics." Estab. 1994. Circ. 40,000. Byline given. Pays on publication. Editorial lead time 4 months. Submit seasonal material 6-12 months in advance. Accepts queries by mail, e-mail. Responds in 2 months to queries; in 3 months to mss. Sample copy for $4.95 and SASE with 4 first-class stamps. Guidelines available online at www.germanlife.com.

NONFICTION Needs general interest, historical, interview, photo feature, reviews, travel. Special issues: February/March: Food, wine, beer; April/May: travel in Germany and other parts of German-speaking Europe; June/July: German-American travel destinations; August/September: Education; October/November: Oktoberfest;. December/January:Holiday Issue. **Buys 50 mss/year.** Query with published clips. Length: up to 1,200 words. **Pays $100-500.**

PHOTOS State availability. Identification of subjects required. High res digital images. Offers no additional payment for photos accepted with ms. Buys one-time rights.

COLUMNS/DEPARTMENTS German-Americana (regards specific German-American communities, organizations, and/or events past or present), 1,200 words; Profile (portrays prominent Germans, Americans, or German-Americans), 1,000 words; At Home (cuisine, etc. relating to German-speaking Europe), 800 words; Library (reviews of books, videos, CDs, etc.), 300 words. **Buys 30 mss/year.** Query with published clips. **Pays $100-130.**

FILLERS Needs facts, newsbreaks. Length: 100-300 words. **Pays $80.**

TIPS "The best queries include several informative proposals. Writers should avoid overemphasizing autobiographical experiences or stories. Please avoid 'superficial' travel articles. *GL* has been in publication for 20+ years and readers are savvy travelers, so we look for articles with substance."

HADASSAH MAGAZINE

Hadassah, WZOA, 40 Wall St., Eighth Floor, New York NY 10005. **Fax:** (212)451-6257. **E-mail:** magazine@hadassah.org. **Website:** www.hadassahmagazine.org. **Contact:** Elizabeth Barnea. **90% freelance written.** Bimonthly magazine. Bimonthly publication of the Hadassah Women's Zionist Organization of America. Emphasizes Jewish life, Israel. Readers are 85% females who travel and are interested in Jewish affairs, average age 59. Circ. 255,000. Byline given. Pays on acceptance. Accepts simultaneous submissions. Responds in 4 months to mss. Sample copy and writer's guidelines with 9x12 SASE.

NONFICTION Needs historical. **Buys 10 unsolicited mss/year.** Query. Length: 1,500-2,000 words.

PHOTOS "We buy photos only to illustrate articles. Always interested in striking cover photos." Offers $50 for first photo, $35 for each additional photo.

COLUMNS/DEPARTMENTS "We have a family column and a travel column, but a query for topic or destination should be submitted first to make sure the area is of interest and the story follows our format."

FICTION Wants short stories with strong plots and positive Jewish values. Receives 20-25 unsolicited mss/month. Publishes some new writers/year. Needs ethnic. No personal memoirs, "schmaltzy" or shelter magazine fiction. Length: 1,500-2,000 words. **Pays $500 minimum.**

TIPS "Stories on a Jewish theme should be neither self-hating nor schmaltzy."

INTERNATIONAL EXAMINER

409 Maynard Ave. S., #203, Seattle WA 98104. (206)624-3925. **Fax:** (206)624-3046. **E-mail:** editor@iexaminer.org. **Website:** www.iexaminer.org. **Contact:** Travis Quezon, editor in chief. **75% freelance written.** Biweekly journal of Asian American news, politics, and arts. "*International Examiner* is about

Asian American issues and things of interest to Asian Americans. We do not want stuff about Asian things (stories on your trip to China, Japanese Tea Ceremony, etc. will be rejected). Yes, we are in English." Estab. 1974. Circ. 12,000. Pays on publication. No kill fee. Publishes ms an average of 1 month after acceptance. Editorial lead time 1 month. Submit seasonal material 2 months in advance. Accepts queries by mail, e-mail, fax. Accepts simultaneous submissions. Guidelines for #10 SASE.

NONFICTION Needs essays, general interest, historical, humor, interview, opinion, personal experience, photo feature. **Buys 100 mss/year.** Query with published clips. Length: 750-5,000 words, depending on subject. **Pays $25-100.**

REPRINTS Accepts previously published submissions (as long as published in same area). Send typed ms with rights for sale noted and information about when and where the material previously appeared. Payment negotiable.

PHOTOS State availability. Captions, identification of subjects required. Reviews contact sheets. Negotiates payment individually. Buys one-time rights.

FICTION Asian American authored fiction by or about Asian Americans only. **Buys 1-2 mss/year.** Query.

TIPS "Write decent, suitable material on a subject of interest to the Asian American community. All submissions are reviewed; all good ones are contacted. It helps to call and run an idea by the editor before or after sending submissions."

ITALIAN AMERICA

219 E St. NE, Washington DC 20002. (202)547-2900. **Fax:** (202)546-8168. **E-mail:** ddesanctis@osia.org; mfisher@osia.org. **Website:** www.osia.org. **Contact:** Dona De Sanctis, editor; Miles Ryan Fisher, Editor-in-Chief. **20% freelance written.** Quarterly magazine. "*Italian America* provides timely information about OSIA, while reporting on individuals, institutions, issues, and events of current or historical significance in the Italian-American community." Estab. 1996. Circ. 65,000. Byline given. Pays on publication. Offers 50% kill fee. Publishes ms an average of 3 months after acceptance. Editorial lead time 3 months. Accepts queries by mail, e-mail, fax. Accepts simultaneous submissions. Sample copy free. Guidelines available online.

NONFICTION Needs historical, interview, opinion, current events. **Buys 8 mss/year.** Query with published clips. Length: 750-1,000 words. **Pays $50-250.**

TIPS "We pay particular attention to the quality of graphics that accompany the stories. We are interested in little known facts about historical/cultural Italian America."

🅢 KHABAR

3635 Savannah Place Dr., Suite 400, Duluth GA 30096. (770)451-3067, ext. 4. **E-mail:** editor@khabar.com. **Website:** www.khabar.com. **50% freelance written.** "*Khabar* is a monthly magazine for the Indian community, free in Georgia, Alabama, Tennessee, and South Carolina. Besides Indian-Americans, *Khabar* also reaches other South Asian immigrants in Georgia—those from countries such as Pakistan, Bangladesh, Nepal, and Sri Lanka who share common needs for good and services. 'Khabar' means 'news' or 'to know' in many Indian languages, but we are a features magazine rather than a news publication." Estab. 1992. Circ. 27,000. Pays on publication. Offers 25% kill fee. Publishes ms an average of 2 months after acceptance. Editorial lead time 2 months. Submit seasonal material 2 months in advance. Accepts queries by e-mail. Accepts simultaneous submissions. Sample copy free. Guidelines by e-mail.

NONFICTION Needs essays, interview, opinion, personal experience, travel. **Buys 5 mss/year.** Send complete ms. Length: 750-4,000 words. **Pays $100-300 for assigned articles. Pays $75 for unsolicited articles.**

PHOTOS State availability of or send photos. Captions, identification of subjects required. Negotiates payment individually.

COLUMNS/DEPARTMENTS Book Review, 1,200 words; Music Review, 800 words; Spotlight (profiles), 1,200-3,000 words. **Buys 5 mss/year.** Query with or without published clips or send complete ms. **Pays $75 minimum.**

FICTION Needs ethnic. **Buys 5 mss/year.** Query or send complete ms. **Pays $50-100.**

TIPS "Ask for our 'editorial guidelines' document by e-mail."

LILITH MAGAZINE: INDEPENDENT, JEWISH & FRANKLY FEMINIST

119 West 57th St., Suite 1210, New York NY 10019. (212)757-0818. **Fax:** (212)757-5705. **E-mail:** info@lilith.org. **Website:** www.lilith.org. **Contact:** Susan Weidman Schneider, editor in chief; Naomi Danis, managing editor. *Lilith Magazine: Independent, Jewish & Frankly Feminist*, published quarterly, welcomes submissions of high-quality, lively writing: reportage, opinion pieces, memoirs, fiction, and poetry on subjects of interest to Jewish women. Estab. 1976. Accepts queries by mail, e-mail, online submission form. Responds in 3 months. Sample copy: $7. Guidelines online.

Lilith Magazine is 48 pages, magazine-sized, with glossy color cover. Press run is about 10,000 (about 6,000 subscribers). Subscription: $26/year. For all submissions: Make sure name and contact information appear on each page of mss. Include a short bio (1-2 sentences), written in third person. Accepts submissions year round.

NONFICTION Send complete ms via online submissions form or mail. Length: up to 2,500 words for features, up to 500 words for news briefs.

FICTION Send complete ms via online submissions form or mail. Length: up to 3,000 words.

POETRY Has published poetry by Irena Klepfisz, Lyn Lifshin, Marcia Falk, Adrienne Rich, and Muriel Rukeyser. Send up to 3 poems at a time via online submissions form or mail; no e-mail submissions. Copy should be neatly typed and proofread for typos and spelling errors. Buys 4 poems/year.

TIPS "Read a copy of the publication before you submit your work. Please be patient."

🅢🅢🅢 MOMENT

4115 Wisconsin Ave. NW, Suite LL10, Washington DC 20016. (202)363-6422. **Fax:** (202)362-2514. **E-mail:** editor@momentmag.com. **Website:** www.momentmag.com. **Contact:** Sarah Breger, deputy editor. **90% freelance written.** Bimonthly magazine on Judaism. *Moment* is committed to portraying intellectual, political, cultural, and religious debates within the community, and to educating readers about Judaism's rich history and contemporary movements, ranging from left to right, fundamentalist to secular. Estab. 1975. Circ. 65,000. Byline given. Pays on publication. Publishes ms an average of 6 months after acceptance. Editorial lead time 3 months. Submit seasonal material 6 months in advance. Accepts queries by mail, e-mail. Accepts simultaneous submissions. Responds in 1 month to queries; in 3 months to mss. Sample copy for $4.50 and SAE. Guidelines available online.

CONSUMER MAGAZINES

NONFICTION Buys 25-30 mss/year. Query with published clips. Length: 2,500-7,000 words. **Pays $200-1,200.**

PHOTOS State availability. Identification of subjects required. Negotiates payment individually. Buys one-time rights.

COLUMNS/DEPARTMENTS 5765 (snappy pieces about quirky events in Jewish communities, news and ideas to improve Jewish living), 250 words maximum; Olam (first-person pieces, humor, and colorful reportage), 600-1,500 words; book eviews (fiction and nonfiction) are accepted but generally assigned, 400-800 words. **Buys 30 mss/year.** Query with published clips. **Pays $50-250.**

TIPS "Successful features offer readers an in-depth journalistic treatment of an issue, phenomenon, institution, or individual. The more the writer can follow the principle of 'show, don't tell,' the better. The majority of the submissions we receive are about The Holocaust and Israel. A writer has a better chance of having an idea accepted if it is not on these subjects."

⊗⊗ NATIVE PEOPLES MAGAZINE

5333 N. Seventh St., Suite C-224, Phoenix AZ 85014. (602)265-4855. **Fax:** (602)265-3113. **E-mail:** sphillips@nativepeoples.com. **Website:** www.nativepeoples.com. **Contact:** Stephen Phillips, Publisher. Bimonthly magazine covering Native Americans. High-quality reproduction with full color throughout. The primary purpose of this magazine is to offer a sensitive portrayal of the arts and lifeways of native peoples of the Americas. Estab. 1987. Circ. 40,000. Byline given. Pays on publication. Accepts queries by mail, e-mail, fax. Accepts simultaneous submissions. Responds in 2 months to queries. Guidelines by request.

NONFICTION Needs personal experience. **Buys 35 mss/year.** Length: 1,000-2,500 words. **Pays 25¢/word.**

PHOTOS State availability. Identification of subjects required. Reviews transparencies, prefers high-res digital images and 35mm slides. Inquire for details. Offers $45-150/page rates, $250/cover photos. Buys one-time rights and nonexclusive web and reprint rights.

TIPS "We are focused upon authenticity and a positive portrayal of present-day Native American life and cultural practices. Our stories portray role models of Native people, young and old, with a sense of pride in their heritage and culture. Therefore, it is important that the Native American point of view be incorporated in each story."

UPSCALE MAGAZINE

Bronner Brothers, 2141 Powers Ferry Rd. SE, Marietta GA 30067. (770)988-0015. **E-mail:** social@upscalemagazine.com. **Website:** www.upscalemagazine.com. Monthly magazine covering topics for upscale African-American/black interests. *Upscale* offers to take the reader to the 'next level' of life's experience. Written for the black reader and consumer, *Upscale* provides information in the realms of business, news, lifestyle, fashion and beauty, and arts and entertainment. "*Upscale* is the ultimate lifestyle magazine addressing the needs of stylish, informed and progressive African-Americans." Estab. 1989. Circ. 250,000. Byline given. Pays on publication. Offers 25% kill fee. Publishes ms an average of 4 months after acceptance. Editorial lead time 3-4 months. Accepts queries by mail. Accepts simultaneous submissions. Responds in 1 month to queries. Sample copy available online. Guidelines available online.

PHOTOS State availability. Captions, identification of subjects, model releases required. Negotiates payment individually.

COLUMNS/DEPARTMENTS News & Business (factual, current); Lifestyle (travel, home, wellness, etc.); Beauty & Fashion (tips, trends, upscale fashion, hair); and Arts & Entertainment (artwork, black celebrities, entertainment). **Buys 6-10 mss/year.** Query with published clips. **Payment different for each department.**

TIPS Make queries informative and exciting. Include entertaining clips. Be familiar with issues affecting black readers. Be able to write about them with ease and intelligence.

FOOD & DRINK

AMERICAN WINE SOCIETY JOURNAL

American Wine Society, P.O. Box 889, Scranton PA 18501. (888)297-9070. **Website:** www.americanwinesociety.org. **100% freelance written.** The nonprofit American Wine Society is the largest consumer-based wine education organization in the U.S. The *Journal* reflects the varied interests of AWS members, which may include wine novices, experts, grape growers, amateur and professional winemakers, chefs, wine appreciators, wine educators, restauranteurs, and anyone wanting to learn more about wine and gastronomy. Estab. 1967. Circ. 5,000. Byline given. Pays on publication. No kill fee. Publishes 3 months after acceptance. Editorial lead time 3 months. Accepts queries by mail, e-mail. Accepts simultaneous submissions. Responds in 2 weeks to queries, 3 months to mss. Sample copy available on website. Writer's guidelines available by e-mail at rink@americanwinesociety.org.

NONFICTION Needs general interest, historical, how-to, nostalgic, technical, travel. Submit query with published clips.

PHOTOS Freelancers should send photos with submission. Requires captions and identification of subjects. Reviews GIF/JPEG files. Offers no additional payment for photos accepted with ms. Buys one-time rights.

COLUMNS/DEPARTMENTS Columns include wine reviews, book reviews, food and wine articles. Writer should send query with published clips.

TIPS "Request a sample copy, which we can provide in PDF format. The readership is diverse, and you may see a travel piece next to a technical piece on malolactic fermentation. Use proper grammar and spelling. Please proofread copy before sending. We're always looking for engaging pieces related to winemaking, grape growing, food and wine, wine and travel, book reviews, recipes, and new developments in the field."

BON APPETIT

Conde Nast Publications, Inc., One World Trade Center, New York NY 10007. (212)286-3535. **E-mail:** askba@bonappetit.com. **Website:** www.bonappetit. com. **50% freelance written.** Monthly magazine covering fine food, restaurants, and home entertaining. *Bon Appetit* celebrates the world of great food and the pleasure of sharing it with others. Every issue invites readers into a hands-on experience, engaging them in all aspects of the epicurean lifestyle-cooking, dining, travel, entertaining, shopping and design. Estab. 1956. Circ. 1,529,385. Byline given. Pays on acceptance. Submit seasonal material 1 year in advance. Accepts queries by mail. Accepts simultaneous submissions. Guidelines for #10 SASE.

NONFICTION Needs travel, food feature, personal essays. No cartoons, quizzes, poetry, historic food features, or obscure food subjects. **Buys 50 mss/year.** Query with resume and published clips. No phone calls or e-mails. Length: 150-2,000 words.

PHOTOS Never send photos.

TIPS "Writers must have a good knowledge of *Bon Appetit* and the related topics of food, travel, and entertaining (as shown in accompanying clips). A light, lively style is a plus."

COOKING LIGHT

Southern Progress Corporation (Time Inc.), 4100 Old Montgomery Highway, Birmingham AL 35201. (205)445-6000. **Fax:** (205)445-6600. **Website:** www. cookinglight.com. Monthly American food and lifestyle magazine. Each magazine issue includes approximately 100 original recipes, plus editorial content covering food trends, fitness tips, and other culinary and health-related news. Estab. 1987. Circ. 1.8 million. Accepts simultaneous submissions.

Query before submitting. Difficult market to break into.

❸❸❸ DRAFT

300 W. Clarendon Ave., Suite 155, Phoenix AZ 85013. **E-mail:** editorial@draftmag.com. **Website:** www. draftmag.com. **Contact:** Sally Benford. **60% freelance written.** Bimonthly magazine covering beer and lifestyle (including food, travel, sports, and leisure). "*DRAFT* is a national magazine devoted to beer, breweries, and the lifestyle and culture that surrounds it. Read by nearly 300,000, aged 21-45, *DRAFT* offers formal beer reviews, plus coverage of food, travel, sports, and leisure. Writers need not have formal beer knowledge (though that's a plus!), but they should be experienced journalists who can appreciate beer and beer culture." Estab. 2006. Circ. 275,000. Byline given. Pays on publication. Offers 20% kill fee. Publishes ms an average of 2 months after acceptance. Editorial lead time 4 months. Submit seasonal material 6 months in advance. Accepts queries by e-mail. Accepts simultaneous submissions. Responds in 1 month to queries. Sample copy: $3 (magazine can also be found on most newsstands for $4.99). Guidelines available at draft-mag.com/submissions.

NONFICTION Does not want unsolicited mss, beer reviews, brewery profiles. **Buys 80 mss/year.** Query with published clips. Length: 250-2,500 words. **Pays**

50-90¢ for assigned articles. Expenses limit agreed upon in advance.

PHOTOS Reviews GIF/JPEG files. Offers no additional payment for photos accepted with ms. Acquires either one-time rights or no rights.

TIPS "Please see 'What to pitch' and 'what not to pitch' in writer's guidelines."

EVERY DAY WITH RACHAEL RAY

Meredith Corporation, **E-mail:** comments@rachaelraymag.com. **Website:** www.rachaelraymag.com. Magazine published 10 times/year, providing recipes, shopping tricks to save time and money, and new ideas for fun things to do with friends and family. Estab. 2005. Circ. 1.2 million. Accepts simultaneous submissions.

○ Currently closed to submissions.

FOOD & WINE

Time Inc., Affluent Media Group, 1120 Avenue of the Americas, 9th Floor, New York NY 10036. (212)522-1387. **Fax:** (212)764-2177. **Website:** www.foodandwine.com. **Contact:** Morgan Goldberg. Monthly magazine for the reader who enjoys the finer things in life. Editorial focuses on upscale dining, covering resturants, entertaining at home, and travel destinations. Circ. 964,000. No kill fee. Editorial lead time 6 months. Accepts simultaneous submissions.

○ Query before submitting to ensure magazine is currently accepting mss.

FOOD NETWORK MAGAZINE

Hearst Corporation, 75 Ninth Ave., New York NY 10011. **Website:** www.foodnetwork.com. Food Network Magazine is a food entertainment magazine published 10 times/year based on the popular television network. The only magazine in the epicurean category to offer unprecedented access to many of America's favorite TV chefs and personalities. Circ. 1.4 million. Accepts simultaneous submissions.

○ Query before submitting. Difficult market to break into.

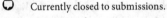 GOURMET TRAVELLER WINE

GT Wine Magazine Pty Limited, Level 6, 10-14 Waterloo Street, Surry Hills 2010, PO Box 323, Darlinghurst NSW 1300 Australia. (61)(2)91990601. **E-mail:** jsarris@gourmettravellerwine.com. **Website:** www.gourmettravellerwine.com. Julian Rifkin. **Contact:** Judy Sarris, editor. Bimonthly magazine for the world

of wine, celebrating both local and overseas industries. *Gourmet Traveller Wine* is for wine lovers: It's for those who love to travel, to eat out, and to entertain at home, and for those who want to know more about the wine in their glass. Estab. 1996. Circ. 22,088. Accepts queries by e-mail. Accepts simultaneous submissions.

NONFICTION Needs general interest, how-to, interview, new product, profile, reviews, travel. Query.

KASHRUS MAGAZINE

The Kashrus Institute, P.O. Box 204, Brooklyn NY 11204. (718)336-8544. **Fax:** (718)336-8550. **E-mail:** editorial@kashrusmagazine.com. **Website:** www.kashrusmagazine.com. **Contact:** Rabbi Yosef Wikler, editor. *Kashrus Magazine* is the kosher consumer's most established, authoritative, and independent source of news about kosher foods. Estab. 1981. Circ. 10,000. Byline given. Pays on publication. Offers 50% kill fee. Publishes ms an average of 2 months after acceptance. Submit seasonal material 2 months in advance. Accepts queries by mail, phone. Accepts simultaneous submissions. Responds in 2 weeks. Sample copy by e-mail.

NONFICTION Needs personal experience, photo feature, religious, technical. Special issues: International Kosher Travel (October); Passover Shopping Guide (March); Domestic Kosher Travel Guide (June). **Buys 8-12 mss/year.** Query with published clips. Length: 1,000-1,500 words. **Pays $100-250 for assigned articles. Pays up to $100 for unsolicited articles.**

REPRINTS Send tearsheet or photocopy and information about when and where the material previously appeared. Pays 25-50% of amount paid for an original article.

PHOTOS No guidelines; send samples or call. State availability. Offers no additional payment for photos accepted with ms. Buys one-time rights.

COLUMNS/DEPARTMENTS Health/Diet/Nutrition, 1,000-1,500 words; Book Review (cookbooks, food technology, kosher food), 250-500 words; People in the News (interviews with kosher personalities), 1,000-1,500 words; Regional Kosher Supervision (report on kosher supervision in a city or community), 1,000-1,500 words; Food Technology (new technology or current technology with accompanying pictures), 1,000-1,500 words; Kosher Travel (international, national—must include Kosher information and Jewish communities), 1,000-1,500 words; Regional Kosher Cooking, 1,000-1,500 words. **Buys 8-12 mss/year.** Query with published clips. **Pays $50-250.**

TASTE OF HOME

Reader's Digest Association, Inc., 1610 N. Second St., Ste. 102, Milwaukee WI 53207. (414)423-0100. **Fax:** (414)423-8463. **E-mail:** feedback@tasteofhome.com. **Website:** www.tasteofhome.com. Bimonthly magazine. *Taste of Home* is dedicated to home cooks, from beginners to the very experienced. Editorial includes recipes and serving suggestions, interviews and ideas from the publication's readers and field editors based around the country, and reviews of new cooking tools and gadgets. Circ. 2.5 million. No kill fee. Accepts queries by mail, e-mail. Accepts simultaneous submissions.

○ Query before submitting.

NONFICTION Submit recipes through website. Submit stories, tips, and other nonrecipe content by e-mail or mail.

WINE ENTHUSIAST MAGAZINE

Wine Enthusiast Media, 200 Summit Lake Drive, Valhalla NY 10595. **E-mail:** editor@wineenthusiast. net. **E-mail:** jczerwin@wineenthusiast.net; jfink@ wineenthusiast.net; lbortolot@wineenthusiast.net. **Website:** www.winemag.com. **Contact:** Joe Czerwinski, managing editor; Jameson Fink, digital senior editor; Lana Bortolot, senior editor. **25% freelance written.** Monthly magazine covering the lifestyle of wine. Demystifying wine without dumbing it down, and tapping into current trends of spirits, travel, entertaining and art through a savvy wine lovers' lens, Wine Enthusiast is the modern tome of popular wine culture—a magazine that provokes and drives global dialogue in one of the world's most vibrant and fast-paced lifestyle categories, educating and entertaining legions of smart and sophisticated consumers. Estab. 1988. Circ. 180,000. Byline given. Pays on acceptance. Offers 25% kill fee. Editorial lead time 4 months. Submit seasonal material 5 months in advance. Accepts queries by e-mail. Responds in 2 weeks to queries. Responds in 2 months to mss.

NONFICTION Needs essays, humor, interview, new product, nostalgic, personal experience, travel. **Buys 5 mss/year.** Submit a proposal (1 or 2 paragraphs) with clips and a resume. Submit short, web items to Jameson Fink; submit feature proposals to Joe Czerwinski.

Submit short, front-of-book items to Lana Bortolot. **$1/word**

PHOTOS Send photos. Reviews GIF/JPEG files. Offers $135-400/photo.

GAMES & PUZZLES

⊘ GAME INFORMER

GameStop, 724 N. First St., Fourth Floor, Minneapolis MN 55401. (612)486-6154. **Fax:** (612)486-6101. **Website:** www.gameinformer.com. **Contact:** Andy McNamara, editor in chief; Matt Bertz, managing editor. Monthly video game magazine featuring articles, news, strategy, and reviews of video games and associated consoles. Estab. 1991. Circ. 7.6 million. Accepts simultaneous submissions.

○ *Game Informer* is closed to freelance submissions.

GAMES WORLD OF PUZZLES

Kappa Publishing Group, Inc., 6198 Butler Pike, Suite 200, Blue Bell PA 19422. (215)643-6385. **Fax:** (215)628-3571. **E-mail:** games@kappapublishing.com. **Website:** www.gamesmagazine-online.com. **Contact:** Jennifer Orehowsky, senior editor. **50% freelance written.** *Games World of Puzzles*, published 10 times/year, features visual and verbal puzzles, quizzes, game reviews, contests, and feature articles. Estab. 1977. Circ. 75,000. Byline given. Pays on publication. Offers 25% kill fee. Publishes ms an average of 4 months after acceptance. Editorial lead time 3 months. Submit seasonal material 6 months in advance. Accepts queries by mail, e-mail. Accepts simultaneous submissions. Responds in 6-8 weeks to queries and mss. Sample copy: $5. Guidelines available online.

NONFICTION Needs humor, photo feature, game- and puzzle-related events or people, wordplay. Query or submit complete ms by e-mail. Length: 2,000-2,500 words. **Pays $500-1,000.**

PHOTOS State availability. Captions, identification of subjects, model releases required. Reviews contact sheets, negatives, transparencies, prints. Negotiates payment individually. Buys one-time rights.

COLUMNS/DEPARTMENTS Puzzles, tests, quizzes. **Buys 50 mss/year.** Query or send complete ms. **Payment varies.**

TIPS "We look for fresh, lively ideas, carefully worked out for solvability. Visual appeal, a sense of humor, and the incorporation of pictures/objects from popular culture and everyday life are big pluses. Novelty is essential."

GAY & LESBIAN INTEREST

THE ADVOCATE

Here Media, Inc., 10990 Wilshire Blvd., Penthouse, Los Angeles CA 90024. (310)806-4288. **Fax:** (310)806-4268. **E-mail:** newsroom@advocate.com. **Website:** www.advocate.com. **Contact:** Matthew Breen, editor in chief; Meg Thomann, managing editor. Biweekly magazine covering national news events with a gay and lesbian perspective on the issues. Estab. 1967. Circ. 120,000. Byline given. Pays on publication. Accepts simultaneous submissions. Responds in 1 month to queries. Sample copy: $3.95. Guidelines on website.

NONFICTION Needs expose. Query. Length: 800 words. **Pays $550.**

COLUMNS/DEPARTMENTS Arts & Media (news and profiles of well-known gay or lesbians in entertainment); 750 words. Query. **Pays $100-500.**

TIPS "*The Advocate* is a unique newsmagazine. While we report on gay and lesbian issues and are published by one of the country's oldest and most established gay-owned companies, we also play by the rules of mainstream-not-gay-community journalism."

CURVE MAGAZINE

P.O Box 467, New York NY 10034. **E-mail:** editor@curvemag.com; merryn@curvemag.com. **E-mail:** merryn@curvemag.com. **Website:** www.curvemag.com. **Contact:** Merryn Johns, editor in chief. **60% freelance written.** Magazine published 6 times/year covering lesbian entertainment, culture, and general interest categories. "We want dynamic and provocative articles that deal with issues, ideas, or cultural moments that are of interest or relevance to gay women." Estab. 1990. Circ. 250,000. Byline given. Pays on publication. Offers 25% kill fee. Up to 3 months between acceptance and publication. Editorial lead time 6 months. Submit seasonal material 6 months in advance. Accepts queries by mail, e-mail, fax. Accepts simultaneous submissions. Sample copy for $4.95 with $2 postage. Guidelines available online.

Ⓞ   Does not publish fiction or poetry.

NONFICTION Needs general interest, interview, new product, photo feature, profile, reviews, travel, celebrity interview/profile. Special issues: See website

for calendar. No fiction or poetry. **Buys 100 mss/year.** Query. Length: 200-2,000 words. **Pays 15¢/word.**

PHOTOS Send hi-res photos with submission. Captions, identification of subjects, model releases required. Offers $25-100/photo; negotiates payment individually. Buys one time rights.

TIPS "Feature articles generally fit into 1 of the following categories: Celebrity profiles (lesbian, bisexual, or straight women who are icons for the lesbian community or actively involved in coalition-building with the lesbian community); community segment profiles—i.e., lesbian firefighters, drag kings, sports teams (multiple interviews with a variety of women in different parts of the country representing a diversity of backgrounds); noncelebrity profiles (activities of unknown or low-profile lesbian and bisexual activists/political leaders, athletes, filmmakers, dancers, writers, musicians, etc.); controversial issues (spark a dialogue about issues that divide us as a community, and the ways in which lesbians of different backgrounds fail to understand and support one another). We are not interested in inflammatory articles that incite or enrage readers without offering a channel for action, but we do look for challenging, thought-provoking work. The easiest way to get published in *Curve* is with a front-of-the-book piece for our Curvatures section, topical/fun/newsy pop culture articles that are 100-350 words."

THE GAY & LESBIAN REVIEW

Gay & Lesbian Review, Inc., P.O. Box 16477, Hollywood CA 91615. (844)752-7829. **E-mail:** glreview@hubservice.com. **E-mail:** richard.schneider@glreview.org. **Website:** www.glreview.org. Stephen Hemrick, *Director of Advertising* stephen.hemrick@glreview.org. **Contact:** Richard Schneider, Jr., editor. **100% freelance written.** "*The Gay & Lesbian Review* is a bimonthly magazine targeting an educated readership of gay, lesbian, bisexual, and transgendered (GLBT) men and women. Under the tagline 'a bimonthly journal of history, culture, and politics,' the *G&LR* publishes essays in a wide range of disciplines as well as reviews of books, movies, and plays." Estab. 1994. Circ. 12,000. A bimonthly magazine of history, culture, and politics. Pays on publication. No kill fee. Editorial lead time 2 months. Accepts simultaneous submissions. Sample copy free. Guidelines available online at http://www.glreview.org/writers-guidelines-for-submission/.

NONFICTION Needs book excerpts, essays, historical, humor, interview, memoir, opinion, photo feature, reviews, travel, book reviews. Special issues: See website: http://www.glreview.org/writers-guidelines-for-submission/. Query or send complete ms by e-mail. Length: 2,000-4,000 words for features; 600-1,200 words for book reviews. **Pays $50-100.**

COLUMNS/DEPARTMENTS Guest Opinion (op-ed pieces by GLBT writers and activists), 500-1,000 words; Artist's Profile (focuses on the creative output of a visual artist, musician, or writer), 1,000-1,500 words; Art Memo (reflections on a work or artist of the past who made a difference for gay culture), 1,000-1,500 words; International Spectrum (the state of GLBT rights or culture in city or region outside the U.S.), 1,000-1,500 words. Query or submit complete ms by e-mail.

POETRY Needs avant-garde, free verse, traditional. Submit poems by postal mail (no e-mail submissions) with SASE for reply. Submit maximum 3 poems. Length: "While there is no hard-and-fast limit on length, poems of over 50 lines become hard to accommodate."

TIPS "We prefer that a proposal be e-mailed before a completed draft is sent."

GERTRUDE

P.O. Box 28281, Portland OR 97228. **E-mail:** editorgertrudepress@gmail.com. **Website:** www.gertrudepress.org. **Contact:** Tammy. *Gertrude*, the annual literary arts journal of Gertrude Press, is a "publication featuring the voices and visions of the gay, lesbian, bisexual, transgender, and supportive community." Estab. 1999. Accepts simultaneous submissions. Responds in 9-12 months to mss. Sample copy: $8. Subscription: $18 for 1 year, $32 for 2 years.

NONFICTION creative nonfiction. Submit 1-2 pieces via online submissions manager. Include word count for each piece in your cover letter. For interviews, query the editor. Length: up to 3,000 words.

FICTION Has published work by Carol Guess, Demrie Alonzo, Henry Alley, and Scott Pomfret. ethnic/multicultural, feminist, gay, humor/satire, lesbian, literary, mainstream. Submit 1-2 pieces via online submissions manager, double-spaced. Include word count for each piece in cover letter. Length: up to 3,000 words.

POETRY Has published poetry by Judith Barrington, Deanna Kern Ludwin, Casey Charles, Michael Montlack, Megan Kruse, and Noah Tysick. Submit up to 6 poems via online submissions manager. Length: open, but "poems less than 60 lines are preferable."

TIPS "We look for strong characterization and imagery, and new, unique ways of writing about universal experiences. Follow the construction of your work until the ending. Many stories start out with zest, then flipper and die. Show us, don't tell us."

GENERAL INTEREST

THE ALMANAC FOR FARMERS & CITY FOLK

Greentree Publishing, Inc., Box 319, 840 S. Rancho Dr., Suite 4, Las Vegas NV 89106. (702)387-6777. **Fax:** (702)385-1370. **Website:** www.thealmanac.com. **30-40% freelance written.** Annual almanac of "down-home, folksy material pertaining to farming, gardening, homemaking, animals, etc." Estab. 1983. Circ. 300,000. Byline given. Pays on publication. No kill fee. Publishes ms an average of 6 months after acceptance. Accepts queries by mail. Accepts simultaneous submissions. Sample copy: $4.99.

NONFICTION Needs essays, general interest, historical, how-to, humor. "No fiction or controversial topics. Please, no first-person pieces!" **Buys 30-40 mss/year.** No queries, please. Editorial decisions made from mss only. Send complete ms by mail. Length: 350-1,400 words. **Pays $45/page.**

FILLERS Needs anecdotes, facts, short humor, gardening hints. Length: up to 125 words. **Pays $15 for short fillers or page rate for longer fillers.**

TIPS "Material should appeal to a wide range of people and should be on the 'folksy' side, preferably with a thread of humor woven in. No first-person pieces (using 'I' or 'my')."

THE AMERICAN LEGION MAGAZINE

700 N. Pennsylvania St., P.O. Box 1055, Indianapolis IN 46206-1055. (317)630-1253; (317) 630-1298. **Fax:** (317)630-1280. **E-mail:** magazine@legion.org; mgrills@legion.org; hsoria@legion.org. **Website:** www.legion.org. **Contact:** Matt Grills, cartoon editor; Holly Soria, art director. **70% freelance written. Prefers to work with published/established writers, but works with a small number of new/unpublished writers each year.** Monthly magazine. Working through 15,000 community-level posts, the honorably discharged wartime veterans of The Ameri-

can Legion dedicate themselves to God, country, and traditional American values. They believe in a strong defense; adequate and compassionate care for veterans and their families; community service; and the wholesome development of our nation's youth. Publishes articles that reflect these values. Informs readers and their families of significant trends and issues affecting the nation, the world and their way of life. Major features focus on the American flag, national security, foreign affairs, business trends, social issues, health, education, ethics, and the arts. Also publishes selected general feature articles, articles of special interest to veterans, and question-and-answer interviews with prominent national and world figures. Estab. 1919. Circ. 2,550,000. Byline given. Pays on acceptance. No kill fee. Publishes ms an average of 6 months after acceptance. Accepts queries by mail, e-mail, fax. Accepts simultaneous submissions. Responds in 2 months to queries. Sample copy for $3.50 and 9x12 SAE with 6 first-class stamps. Guidelines for #10 SASE.

NONFICTION Needs general interest, interview. No regional topics or promotion of partisan political agendas. No personal experiences or war stories. **Buys 50-60 mss/year.** Query with SASE should explain the subject or issue, article's angle and organization, writer's qualifications, and experts to be interviewed. Length: 300-2,000 words. **Pays 40¢/word and up.**

PHOTOS On assignment.

TIPS "Queries by new writers should include clips/background/expertise; no longer than 1 1/2 pages. Submit suitable material showing you have read several issues. *The American Legion Magazine* considers itself 'the magazine for a strong America.' Reflect this theme (which includes economy, educational system, moral fiber, social issues, infrastructure, technology and national defense/security). We are a general interest, national magazine, not a strictly military magazine. We are widely read by members of the Washington establishment and other policy makers."

THE AMERICAN SCHOLAR

Phi Beta Kappa, 1606 New Hampshire Ave. NW, Washington DC 20009. (202)265-3808. **Fax:** (202)265-0083. **E-mail:** scholar@pbk.org. **E-mail:** theamericanscholar.submittable.org/submit. **Website:** www.theamericanscholar.org. **Contact:** Robert Wilson, editor. **100% freelance written.** Quarterly magazine dedicated to current events, politics, history, science, culture and the arts. "Our intent is to have articles written by scholars and experts but written in non-technical language for an intelligent audience. Material covers a wide range in the arts, sciences, current affairs, history, and literature." Estab. 1932. Circ. 30,000. Byline given. Pays on publication. Offers 50% kill fee. Publishes ms an average of 1 year after acceptance. Editorial lead time 6 months. Submit seasonal material 6 months in advance. Accepts queries by online submission form. Accepts simultaneous submissions. Responds in 2 weeks to queries; 2 months to mss. Guidelines online.

NONFICTION Needs essays, general interest, historical, humor, memoir, reviews, travel. **Buys 40 mss/year.** Query. Length: 3,000-5,000 words. **Pays $500 maximum.**

POETRY Contact: Sandra Costich. "We're not considering any unsolicited poetry."

THE ATLANTIC MONTHLY

The Watergate, 600 New Hampshire Ave., NW, Washington DC 20037. (202)266-6000. **Fax:** (202)266-6001. **E-mail:** submissions@theatlantic.com; pitches@theatlantic.com. **Website:** www.theatlantic.com. **Contact:** Scott Stossel, magazine editor; Ann Hulbert, literary editor. Covers poetry, fiction, and articles of the highest quality. General magazine for an educated readership with broad cultural and public-affairs interests. "*The Atlantic* considers unsolicited mss, either fiction or nonfiction. A general familiarity with what we have published in the past is the best guide to our needs and preferences." Estab. 1857. Circ. 500,000. Byline given. Pays on acceptance. No kill fee. Accepts queries by mail, e-mail. Responds in 4-6 weeks to mss. Guidelines online.

NONFICTION Needs book excerpts, essays, general interest, humor, travel. Query with or without published clips to pitches@theatlantic.com, or send complete ms to "Editorial Department" at address above. All unsolicited mss must be accompanied by SASE. "A general familiarity with what we have published in the past is the best guide to our needs and preferences." Length: 1,000-6,000 words **Payment varies.** Sometimes pays expenses.

FICTION "Seeks fiction that is clear, tightly written with strong sense of 'story' and well-defined characters." No longer publishes fiction in the regular magazine. Instead, it will appear in a special newsstand-only fiction issue. Receives 1,000 unsolicited mss/month.

Accepts 7-8 mss/year. **Publishes 3-4 new writers/year.** literary, contemporary. Submit via e-mail with Word document attachment to submissions@theatlantic. com. Mss submitted via postal mail must be typewritten and double-spaced. Preferred length: 2,000-6,000 words. **Payment varies.**

POETRY *The Atlantic Monthly* publishes some of the most distinguished poetry in American literature. "We read with interest and attention every poem submitted to the magazine and, quite simply, we publish those that seem to us to be the best." Has published poetry by Maxine Kumin, Stanley Plumly, Linda Gregerson, Philip Levine, Ellen Bryant Voigt, and W.S. Merwin. Receives about 60,000 poems/year. Submit 2-6 poems by e-mail or mail. Buys 30-35 poems/year.

TIPS "Writers should be aware that this is not a market for beginner's work (nonfiction and fiction), nor is it truly for intermediate work. Study this magazine before sending only your best, most professional work. When making first contact, cover letters are sometimes helpful, particularly if they cite prior publications or involvement in writing programs. Common mistakes: melodrama, inconclusiveness, lack of development, unpersuasive characters and/or dialogue."

THE CHRISTIAN SCIENCE MONITOR

210 Massachussetts Ave., Boston MA 02115 USA. **E-mail:** homeforum@csmonitor.com. **Website:** www. csmonitor.com. **Contact:** Editor, The Home Forum. **95% freelance written.** *The Christian Science Monitor*, a Web-first publication that also publishes a weekly print magazine, regularly features personal nonfiction essays and, occasionally, poetry in its Home Forum section. "We're looking for upbeat essays of 600-800 words and short (20 lines maximum) poems that explore and celebrate daily life." Estab. 1908. Pays on publication. Offers 50% kill fee. Publishes ms 1-8 months after acceptance. Editorial lead time 6-8 weeks. Accepts queries by e-mail, online submission form. Responds in 3 weeks to mss; only responds to accepted mss. Sample copy available online. Guidelines available online or by e-mail.

NONFICTION Needs essays, humor, personal experience. **Buys 2,000+ mss/year.** 600-800 **Pays $75-150.**

POETRY Accepts submissions via online form. Does not want "work that presents people in helpless or hopeless states; poetry about death, aging, or illness; or dark, violent, sensual poems. No poems that are overtly religious or falsely sweet." Submit maximum

5 poems. Length: up to 20 lines/poem. **Pays $25/haiku; $50/poem.**

EBONY

Ebony Media Corporation, 200 Michigan Ave., Chicago IL 60605. **E-mail:** digitalpitches@ebony.com. **Website:** www.ebony.com. **Contact:** Teryn Payne, editorial assistant. Monthly magazine covering topics ranging from education and history to entertainment, art, government, health, travel, sports, and social events. "*Ebony* is the top source for an authoritative perspective on the Black-American community. *Ebony* features the best thinkers, trendsetters, hottest celebrities, and next-generation leaders of Black America. It ignites conversation, promotes empowerment, and celebrates aspiration." Circ. 11,000,000. No kill fee. Editorial lead time 3 months. Accepts queries by e-mail. Accepts simultaneous submissions.

 Query before submitting.

NONFICTION Needs interview, profile. Query.

FAMILY CIRCLE

Meredith Corp., Articles Department, 805 Third Ave., 24th Floor, New York NY 10022. **Website:** www.familycircle.com. Lisa Kelsey, art director. **80% freelance written.** A national general interest women's magazine that focuses on all subjects relating to the family. Estab. 1932. Circ. 4 million. Byline given. Offers 20% kill fee. Editorial lead time 4 months. Submit seasonal material 4 months in advance. Accepts queries by mail. Accepts simultaneous submissions. Responds in 2 months to queries; in 2 months to mss. Guidelines available online.

NONFICTION Needs essays, opinion, personal experience, women's interest subjects such as family and personal relationships, children, physical and mental health, nutrition, and self-improvement. No fiction or poetry. **Buys 200 mss/year.** Submit detailed outline, 2 clips, cover letter describing your publishing history, SASE or IRCs. Length: 1,000-2,500 words. **Pays $1/word.**

TIPS "Query letters should be concise and to the point. Also, writers should keep close tabs on *Family Circle* and other women's magazines to avoid submitting recently run subject matter."

NATIONAL GEOGRAPHIC

P.O. Box 98199, Washington DC 20090-8199. (202)857-7000. **Fax:** (202)828-5460. **Website:** www. nationalgeographic.com. **Contact:** Susan Goldberg, editor in chief; David Brindley, managing editor. **60% freelance written. Prefers to work with published/ established writers.** Monthly magazine for members of the National Geographic Society. *National Geographic* magazine is the global leader in empowering people to navigate the world, providing authoritative, unbiased content that addresses today's complex issues, while uncovering the wonders of our time. Each issue captivates millions of curious readers with world-class, award-winning photography and reporting that inspire them to make informed decisions and effect positive change. As part of the world's largest nonprofit scientific, education, and entertainment organizations, *National Geographic* has unmatched reach to a national audience that influences opinions on the Beltway, in the board room, in Silicon Valley, and beyond. Estab. 1888. Circ. 3.1 million. Accepts queries by mail. Accepts simultaneous submissions. Guidelines available online.

NONFICTION Query (500 words with clips of published articles). Do not send mss. Length: 2,000-8,000 words.

PHOTOS Query in care of the Photographic Division.

TIPS "State the theme(s) clearly, let the narrative flow, and build the story around strong characters and a vivid sense of place. Give us rounded episodes, logically arranged."

THE NEW YORKER

1 World Trade Center, New York NY 10007. **E-mail:** themail@newyorker.com. **E-mail:** poetry@newyorker.com. **Website:** www.newyorker.com. **Contact:** David Remnick, editor in chief. A quality weekly magazine of distinct news stories, articles, essays, and poems for a literate audience. Estab. 1925. Circ. 938,600. Pays on acceptance. No kill fee. Accepts queries by mail, e-mail. Responds in 3 months to mss. Subscription: $59.99/year (47 issues), $29.99 for 6 months (23 issues).

○ *The New Yorker* receives approximately 4,000 submissions per month.

NONFICTION Submissions should be sent as PDF attachments. Do not paste them into the message field. Due to volume, cannot consider unsolicited "Talk of the Town" stories or other nonfiction.

FICTION Contact: fiction@newyorker.com. Publishes 1 ms/issue. Send complete ms by e-mail (as

PDF attachment) or mail (address to Fiction Editor). **Payment varies.**

POETRY Submit up to 6 poems at a time by e-mail (as PDF attachment) or mail (address to Poetry Department). **Pays top rates.**

TIPS "Be lively, original, not overly literary. Write what you want to write, not what you think the editor would like."

⑤⑤⑤⑤ PEOPLE

Time, Inc., 1271 Avenue of the Americas, 28th Floor, New York NY 10020. (212)522-1212. **Fax:** (212)522-1359. **E-mail:** editor@people.com. **Website:** www.people.com. Weekly magazine. Designed as a forum for personality journalism through the use of short articles on contemporary news events and people. Circ. 3.4 million. No kill fee. Editorial lead time 3 months. Accepts simultaneous submissions.

○ Query before submitting.

⑤⑤ READER'S DIGEST

The Reader's Digest Association, Inc., Box 100, Pleasantville NY 10572. **E-mail:** letters@rd.com. **E-mail:** articleproposals@rd.com. **Website:** www.rd.com. *Reader's Digest* is an American general interest family magazine, published monthly. "We create content that is real, optimistic, authentic, inspiring, and actionable. *Reader's Digest* is a read of lasting value and importance—an oasis from snark, celebrity hype, and pessimism." Estab. 1922. Circ. 3 million. Accepts queries by e-mail. Accepts simultaneous submissions. Guidelines available online.

○ Query before submitting.

NONFICTION Accepts one-page queries that clearly detail the article idea, with special emphasis on the arc of the story, interview access to the main characters, access to documents, etc. Looks for dramatic narratives, articles about everyday heroes, crime dramas, adventure stories. Include a separate page for writing credentials.

COLUMNS/DEPARTMENTS Life; @Work; Off Base, **pays $300.** Laugh; Quotes, **pays $100.** Address your submission to the appropriate humor category.

TIPS "Full-length, original articles are usually assigned to regular contributors to the magazine. We do not accept or return unpublished mss. We do, however, accept one-page queries that clearly detail the article idea—with special emphasis on the arc of the story, your interview access to the main characters, your access to special documents, etc. We look for dramatic narratives, articles about everyday heroes, crime dramas, and adventure stories. Do include a separate page of your writing credits. We are not interested in poetry, fiction, or opinion pieces. Please submit article proposals on the website."

REUNIONS MAGAZINE

P.O. Box 11727, Milwaukee WI 53211-0727. (414)263-4567. **Fax:** (414)263-6331. **E-mail:** editor@reunions-mag.com. **Website:** www.reunionsmag.com. **Contact:** Edith Wagner, editor. **85% freelance written.** Occasional print magazine covering all aspects of reunion planning, Our only focus is reunion planning; our only audience is reunion planners: the people who make reunion purchasing decisions. "*Reunions Magazine* is primarily for people actively planning family, class, military, and other reunions. We want easy, practical ideas about organizing, planning, researching/searching, attending, or promoting reunions." Estab. 1990. Circ. 15,000. Byline given. Pays on publication. Publishes ms an average of 1 year after acceptance. Editorial lead time 6 months. Submit seasonal material 1 year in advance. Accepts queries by mail, e-mail. Accepts simultaneous submissions. Responds in about 1 year. Sample copy, sent $3; writer's guidelines send #10 SASE or see both online. Prefer email. See guidelines.

○ Our only focus is reunion planning; our only audience is reunion planners: the people who make reunion purchasing decisions.

NONFICTION Needs how-to, humor, new product, personal experience, photo feature, travel. **Buys 40 mss/year.** Query with published clips. Length: 500-2,500 (prefers work on the short side). **"Rarely able to pay, but when we can pays $25-50."**

REPRINTS Send tearsheet, photocopy or typed ms with rights for sale noted and information about when and where the material previously appeared. Usually pays $10, if at all.

PHOTOS Always looking for vertical cover photos screaming *Reunion!* Prefers print or e-mail pictures. State availability. Captions, identification of subjects required. Reviews contact sheets, negatives, 35mm transparencies, prints, TIFF/JPEG files (300 dpi or higher) as e-mail attachments. Send to reunionsmag@gmail.com. Offers no additional payment for photos accepted with ms.

FILLERS Must be reunion-related. Needs anecdotes, facts, short humor. **Buys 20-40 fillers/year mss/year.** Length: 50-250 words. **Pays $5.**

TIPS "All copy must be reunion-related with strong, real reunion examples and experiences. Write a lively account of an interesting or unusual reunion, either upcoming or soon after while it's hot. Tell readers why the reunion is special, what went into planning it, and how attendees reacted. Our 'Masterplan' section, about family reunion planning, is a great place for a freelancer to start by telling her/his own reunion story. Send us how-tos or tips about any of the many aspects of reunion organizing or activities. Open your minds to different types of reunions—they're all around!"

SMITHSONIAN MAGAZINE

Capital Gallery, Suite 6001, MRC 513, P.O. Box 37012, Washington DC 20013. (202)275-2000. **E-mail:** smithsonianmagazine@si.edu. **Website:** www.smithsonianmag.com. **Contact:** Molly Roberts, photo editor; Jeff Campagna, art services coordinator. **90% freelance written.** Monthly magazine for associate members of the Smithsonian Institution; 85% with college education. *Smithsonian Magazine's* mission is to inspire fascination with all the world has to offer by featuring unexpected and entertaining editorial that explores different lifestyles, cultures and peoples, the arts, the wonders of nature and technology, and much more. The highly educated, innovative readers of *Smithsonian* share a unique desire to celebrate life, seeking out the timely as well as timeless, the artistic as well as the academic, and the thought-provoking as well as the humorous. Circ. 2.3 million. Pays on acceptance. Offers 33% kill fee. Publishes ms an average of 6 months after acceptance. Editorial lead time 2 months. Submit seasonal material 3 months in advance. Accepts simultaneous submissions. Sample copy for $5. Guidelines available online.

NONFICTION Buys 120-130 feature (up to 5,000 words) and 12 short (500-650 words) mss/year. Use online submission form. *Smithsonian* magazine accepts unsolicited proposals from established freelance writers for features and some departments. Submit a proposal of 250 to 300 words as a preliminary query. Background information and writing credentials are helpful. The proposal text box on the Web submission form holds 10,000 characters (approximately 2,000 words), ample room for a cover letter and proposal. All unsolicited proposals are sent on speculation.

Supporting material or clips of previously published work can be provided with links. Article length ranges from a 700-word humor column to a 4,000-word full-length feature. Considers focused subjects that fall within the general range of Smithsonian Institution interests, such as: cultural history, physical science, art and natural history. **Pays various rates per feature, $1,500 per short piece.**

PHOTOS Purchased with or without ms and on assignment. Illustrations are not the responsibility of authors, but if you do have photographs or illustration materials, please include a selection of them with your submission. In general, 35mm color transparencies or black-and-white prints are perfectly acceptable. Photographs published in the magazine are usually obtained through assignment, stock agencies, or specialized sources. No photo library is maintained and photographs should be submitted only to accompany a specific article proposal. Send photos. Captions required. Pays $400/full color page.

COLUMNS/DEPARTMENTS Length: 1,000-2,000 words. Last Page humor, 550-700 words. **Buys 12-15 mss/year.** Use online submission form. **Pays $1,000-1,500.**

TIPS "Send proposals through online submission form only. No e-mail or mail queries, please."

TIME

1271 Avenue of the Americas, New York NY 10020. **E-mail:** letters@time.com. **Website:** www.time.com. **Contact:** Nancy Gibbs, editor. Weekly magazine. *TIME* covers the full range of information that is important to people today—breaking news, national and world affairs, business news, societal and lifestyle issues, culture, and entertainment news and reviews. Estab. 1923. Circ. 4 million. No kill fee. Accepts simultaneous submissions.

　Query before submitting.

⑤⑤⑤ YES! MAGAZINE

284 Madrona Way NE, Suite 116, Bainbridge Island WA 98110. **E-mail:** editors@yesmagazine.org. **E-mail:** submissions@yesmagazine.org. **Website:** www.yesmagazine.org. **70% freelance written.** Quarterly magazine covering sustainability, social justice, grassroots activism, contemporary culture; nature, conservation, ecology, politics, and world affairs. "*YES! Magazine* documents how people are creating a more just, sustainable and compassionate world. Each issue includes articles focused on a theme—about solutions to a significant challenge facing our world—and a number of timely, non-theme articles. Our non-theme section provides ongoing coverage of issues like health, climate change, globalization, media reform, faith, democracy, economy and labor, social and racial justice and peace building. To inquire about upcoming themes, send an e-mail to submissions@yesmagazine.org; please be sure to type 'themes' as the subject line." Estab. 1997. Circ. 55,000. Byline given. Pays on publication. Rarely offers kill fee. Publishes ms an average of 1-6 months after acceptance. Editorial lead time 3-6 months. Submit seasonal material 2-6 months in advance. Accepts queries by e-mail. Accepts simultaneous submissions. Responds in 3 months. Sample copy and writer's guidelines online.

NONFICTION Needs book excerpts, opinion. "We don't want stories that are negative or too politically partisan." **Buys 30 mss/year mss/year.** Query with published clips. Length: 100-2,500 words. **Pays $50-1,250 for assigned articles. Pays $50-600 for unsolicited articles.**

REPRINTS Send photocopy or typed ms with rights for sale noted and information about when and where the material previously appeared.

PHOTOS Buys one time rights.

COLUMNS/DEPARTMENTS Signs of Life (positive news briefs), 100-250 words; Commentary (opinion from thinkers and experts), 500 words; Book and film reviews, 500-800 words. **Pays $20-300.**

TIPS "We practice positive, solution-oriented journalism. We're interested in articles that: 'Change the story' about what is possible; tell specific success stories of individuals, communities, movements, nations, or regions that are addressing society's challenges and problems; offer visions of a better world. Our material exemplifies our tagline: 'Powerful Ideas, Practical Actions.' We're less interested in articles that only describe or update a problem (unless there are dramatically new developments, reframings, or insights); primarily reinforce a sense of being a victim (and therefore powerless); are written in styles or about topics relevant or accessible only to narrow groups; lack grounding in research or reporting (except for occasional essays). Our readers are well-educated, well-informed, and politically and socially engaged. We seek to present complex topics in a way that is accessible to laypeople and is jargon-free. Our magazine content is available online at yesmagazine.org. We urge you to familiarize yourself with the content, tone, and angle of our material before you submit."

HEALTH & FITNESS

AMERICAN FITNESS

1750 E. Northrop Blvd., Suite 200, Chandler AZ 85286. (800)446-2322, ext. 200. **E-mail:** americanfitness@afaa.com. **Website:** www.afaa.com. **Contact:** Meg Jordan, editor. **75% freelance written.** Bimonthly magazine covering exercise and fitness, health, and nutrition. "We need timely, in-depth, informative articles on health, fitness, aerobic exercise, sports nutrition, age-specific fitness, and outdoor activity. Absolutely no first-person accounts. Need well-researched articles for professional readers." Estab. 1983. Circ. 42,900. Byline given. Pays 30 days after publication. No kill fee. Publishes ms an average of 6 months after acceptance. Submit seasonal material 4 months in advance. Accepts queries by mail, fax. Accepts simultaneous submissions. Responds in 2 months to queries. Sample copy for $4.50 and SASE with 6 first-class stamps.

NONFICTION Needs historical, inspirational, interview, new product, personal experience, photo feature, travel. No articles on unsound nutritional practices, popular trends, or unsafe exercise gimmicks. **Buys 18-25 mss/year.** Send complete ms. Length: 800-1,200 words. **Pays $200 for features, $80 for news.**

PHOTOS Sports, action, fitness, aquatic aerobics competitions, and exercise class. We are especially interested in photos of high-adrenalin sports like rock climbing and mountain biking. No answer. Captions, identification of subjects, model releases required. Reviews transparencies, prints. Pays $35 for transparencies. Usually buys all rights; other rights purchased depend on use of photo.

COLUMNS/DEPARTMENTS Research (latest exercise and fitness findings); Alternative paths (non-mainstream approaches to health, wellness, and fitness); Strength (latest breakthroughs in weight training); Clubscene (profiles and highlights of fitness club industry); Adventure (treks, trails, and global challenges); Food (low-fat/nonfat, high-flavor dishes); Homescene (home-workout alternatives); Clip 'n' Post (concise exercise research to post in health clubs, offices or on refrigerators). Length: 800-1,000 words. Query with published clips or send complete ms. **Pays $100-200.**

TIPS "Make sure to quote scientific literature or good research studies and several experts with good credentials to validate exercise trend, technique, or issue. Cover a unique aerobics or fitness angle, provide accurate and interesting findings, and write in a lively, intelligent manner. Please, no first-person accounts of 'how I lost weight or discovered running.' *AF* is a good place for first-time authors or regularly published authors who want to sell spin-offs or reprints."

HEALTH

Time, Inc., Southern Progress Corp., 1271 Avenue of The Americas, New York NY 10020. **E-mail:** christine.mattheis@health.com; theresa_tamkins@health.com. **Website:** www.health.com. **Contact:** Kathleen Mulpeter, senior editor; Theresa Tamkins, editor in chief. Magazine published 10 times/year covering health, fitness, and nutrition. Readers are predominantly college-educated women in their 30s, 40s, and 50s. Edited to focus not on illness but on wellness news, events, ideas, and people. Estab. 1987. Circ. 1,360,000. Byline given. Pays on acceptance. Offers 33% kill fee. Accepts queries by mail, e-mail. Accepts simultaneous submissions. Responds in 2 months to queries. Sample copy: $5. Guidelines for #10 SASE or via e-mail.

🞇 Query before submitting.

NONFICTION No unsolicited mss. **Buys 25 mss/year.** Query with published clips and SASE. Length: up to 1,200 words.

COLUMNS/DEPARTMENTS Body, Mind, Fitness, Beauty, Food.

TIPS "We look for well-articulated ideas with a narrow focus and broad appeal. A query that starts with an unusual local event and hooks it legitimately to some national trend or concern is bound to get our attention. Use quotes, examples, and statistics to show why the topic is important and why the approach is workable. We need to see clear evidence of credible research findings pointing to meaningful options for our readers. Stories should offer practical advice and give clear explanations."

🞇🞇🞇 IMPACT MAGAZINE

IMPACT Productions, 2007 Second St. SW, Calgary AB T2S 1S4 Canada. (403)228-0605. **E-mail:** editor@impactmagazine.ca. **E-mail:** info@impactmagazine.ca. **Website:** www.impactmagazine.ca. **Contact:** Chris Welner, editor. **10% freelance written.** Bimonthly magazine covering fitness and sport performance. A leader in the industry, *IMPACT Magazine* is committed to publishing content provided by the best experts in their fields for those who aspire to higher levels of health, fitness, and sport performance. Estab. 1991. Circ. 90,000. Byline given. Pays 30 days after publication. Offers 25% kill fee. Publishes ms an average of 4-6 months after acceptance. Editorial lead time 6 months. Submit seasonal material 6 months in advance. Accepts queries by e-mail. Accepts simultaneous submissions. Responds in 4 weeks to queries. Sample copy and guidelines available online.

○ "Query first, outlining the parameters of the article, the length, sources, etc., before submitting a completed ms. We do not accept editorial articles that profile and promote a specific business or service. *IMPACT Magazine* is a bimonthly publication; submission deadlines are16 weeks prior to the publishing date. E-mail the article in a MS Word or text format (Mac or PC format). *IMPACT Magazine* compensates writers whose qualifications and work meet our specific guidelines (available from the editor). We are happy to accept photos or illustrations and will give photos credit where due. Digital images must be a minimum of 300 dpi."

NONFICTION Needs general interest, how-to, interview, new product, opinion, technical. **Buys 4 mss/year.** Query before submitting. Length: 600-1,800 words. **Pays 25¢/word maximum for assigned articles. Pays 25¢/word maximum for unsolicited articles.**

PHOTOS State availability. Identification of subjects, model releases required. Reviews contact sheets, GIF/JPEG files (300 dpi or greater). Negotiates payment individually. Acquires first-time print and all electronic rights.

PREVENTION

Rodale, Inc., 33 E. Minor St., Emmaus PA 18098-0099. **E-mail:** editor@prevention.com. **Website:** www.prevention.com. Monthly magazine covering health and fitness. Written to motivate, inspire and enable male and female readers ages 35 and over to take charge of their health, to become healthier and happier, and to improve the lives of family and friends. Estab. 1950. Circ. 3,150,000. No kill fee. Accepts simultaneous submissions.

○ Query before submitting.

⑤⑤⑤⑤ SHAPE

American Media, 4 New York Plaza, 4th Floor, New York NY 10004. (212)545-4800. **Website:** www.shape. com. **70% freelance written. Prefers to work with published/established writers.** Monthly magazine covering health, fitness, nutrition, and beauty for women ages 18-34. *Shape* reaches women who are committed to healthful, active lifestyles. Readers participate in a variety of fitness-related activities in the gym, at home, and outdoors. They are also proactive about their health and are nutrition conscious. Estab. 1981. Circ. 2.5 million. Pays on acceptance. Offers 33% kill fee. Submit seasonal material 8 months in advance. Accepts queries by mail. Accepts simultaneous submissions. Responds in 2 months to queries. Sample copy for SAE with 9x12 envelope and 4 first-class stamps.

○ Query before submitting.

NONFICTION Needs book excerpts, expose, how-to. Rarely publishes celebrity question-and-answer stories, celebrity profiles, or menopausal/hormone replacement therapy stories. Query with published clips. Length: 2,500 words for features; 1,000 words for shorter pieces. **Pays $1.50/word (on average).**

TIPS "Review a recent issue of the magazine. Not responsible for unsolicited material. We reserve the right to edit any article."

VIBRANT LIFE

Pacific Press Publishing Association, P.O. Box 5353, Nampa ID 83653-5353. (208)465-2579. **Fax:** (208)465-2531. **E-mail:** vibrantlife@pacificpress.com. **Website:** www.vibrantlife.com. **Contact:** Heather Quintana, Editor. **80% freelance written. Enjoys working with published/established writers; works with a small number of new/unpublished writers each year.** Bimonthly magazine covering health articles (especially from a prevention angle and with a Christian slant). "Whether you are fit and vigorous or have just received a frightening diagnosis, *Vibrant Life* has health information that will help you move closer to the life you were designed to live. It is perfect for sharing with people who may have never heard of this Christian approach to whole-person health. It's a wonderful way to introduce people to God's plan for us to have harmony of mind, body, and spirit. You can give a subscription to neighbors, friends, or coworkers; order a stack to place in a local grocery store, business, or doctor's office; or use it as a part of local church health initiatives, such as blood drives or cooking classes." Estab. 1885. Circ. 30,000. Byline given. Pays on acceptance. Submit seasonal material 9 months in advance. Accepts queries by mail, e-mail, fax. Accepts simultaneous submissions. Sample copy for $1. Guidelines available online.

NONFICTION Needs interview. **Buys 50-60 feature articles/year and 40 short mss/year.** Send complete ms. Length: 1,500-1,800 words for features; 650-750 words for short pieces. **Pays $100-300 for articles.**

REPRINTS Send tearsheet and information about when and where the material previously appeared. Pays 50% of amount paid for an original article.

PHOTOS Not interested in b&w photos. Send photos.

TIPS "We encourage writers to include practical information, true stories, and encouraging tips in each article. We have an easy-to-read style that includes sidebars and quick-read boxes."

WEBMD THE MAGAZINE

WebMD, 39 Hudson St., 3rd Floor, New York NY 10014. (212)624-3700. **Website:** www.webmd.com/magazine. **80% freelance written.** Bimonthly magazine covering health, lifestyle health, and well-being, some medical. Published by WebMD Health, *WebMD the Magazine* is the print sibling of the website WebMD.com. It aims to broaden the company-wide mandate: "Better information, better health." It is a health magazine, with a difference. It is specifically designed and written for people who are about to have what may be the most important conversation of the year with their physician or other medical professional. The magazine's content is therefore developed to be most useful at this critical point of care, to improve and enhance the dialogue between patient and doctor. Readers are adults (65% women, 35% men) in their 30s, 40s, and 50s (median age is 41) who care about their health, take an active role in their own and their family's wellness, and want the best information possible to make informed healthcare decisions. Estab. 2005. Circ. 1 million. Byline given. Pays on acceptance. Offers 30% kill fee. Publishes ms an average of 3 months after acceptance. Editorial lead time 3-4 months. Submit seasonal material 3-4 months in advance. Accepts queries by e-mail. Accepts simultaneous submissions. Sample copy available online.

Query before submitting.

TIPS "We only want experienced magazine writers, in the topic areas of consumer health. Writers with experience writing for national women's health magazines preferred. Relevant clips required. Fresh, witty, smart, well-written style, with solid background in health. This is not a publication for writers breaking into the field."

WEIGHT WATCHERS

14 W. 23rd St. #2, New York NY 10010. (212)929-7054. **Website:** www.weightwatchers.com/magazine. The official magazine of Weight Watchers International, an international company that offers various products and services to assist weight loss and service. Estab. 1963. Accepts simultaneous submissions.

Query before submitting.

YOGA JOURNAL

Active Interest Media, Healthy Living Group, 475 Sansome St., Suite 850, San Francisco CA 94111. (415)591-0555. **Fax:** (415)591-0733. **E-mail:** queries@yjmag.com. **Website:** www.yogajournal.com. **Contact:** Kaitlin Quistgaard, editor in chief. **75% freelance written.** Magazine published 9 times a year covering the practice and philosophy of yoga. Estab. 1975. Circ. 300,000. Byline given. Pays within 90 days of acceptance. Offers kill fee. Offers kill fee on assigned articles. Publishes ms an average of 10 months after acceptance. Submit seasonal material 7 months in advance. Accepts queries by e-mail. Accepts simultaneous submissions. Responds in 6 weeks to queries if interested. Sample copy: $4.99. Guidelines on website.

NONFICTION Needs book excerpts, how-to, interview, opinion, photo feature, travel. Does not want unsolicited poetry or cartoons. "Please avoid New Age jargon and in-house buzz words as much as possible." **Buys 50-60 mss/year.** Query with SASE. Length: 3,000-5,000 words. **Pays $800-2,000.**

REPRINTS Send tearsheet or photocopy with rights for sale noted and information about when and where the material previously appeared.

COLUMNS/DEPARTMENTS Om: Covers myriad aspects of the yoga lifestyle (150-400 words). This department includes Yoga Diary, a 250-word story about a pivotal moment in your yoga practice. Eating Wisely: A popular, 1,400-word department about relationship to food. Most stories focus on vegetarian and whole-foods cooking, nutritional healing, and contemplative pieces about the relationship between yoga and food. Yoga Scene: Featured on the back page of the magazine, this photo depicts some expression of your yoga practice. Please tell us where the photo is from, what was going on during the moment the photo was taken, and any other information that will help put the photo into context. E-mail a well-written query.

TIPS "Please read several issues of *Yoga Journal* before submitting a query. Pitch your article idea to the appropriate department with the projected word count, and what sources you'd use. In your query letter, please indicate your writing credentials. If we are interested in your idea, we will require writing samples. Please note that we do not accept unsolicited mss for any departments except Yoga Diary, a first person, 250-word story that tells about a pivotal moment in the writer's yoga experience (diary@yjmag.com). Please read our writer's guidelines before submission. Do not e-mail or fax unsolicited mss."

HISTORY

AMERICAN HERITAGE

90 Fifth Ave., New York NY 10011. (212)367-3100. **E-mail:** editor@americanheritage.com. **Website:** www.americanheritage.com. **70% freelance written.** Magazine published 6 times/year. *American Heritage* writes from a historical point of view on politics, business, art, current and international affairs, and our changing lifestyles. The articles are written with the intent to enrich the reader's appreciation of the sometimes nostalgic, sometimes funny, always stirring panorama of the American experience. Circ. 350,000. Byline given. Pays on acceptance. Publishes ms an average of 6-12 months after acceptance. Submit seasonal material 1 year in advance. Accepts simultaneous submissions. Responds in 2 months to queries. Guidelines for #10 sase.

NONFICTION Buys 10-15 unsolicited mss/year. Query. Length: 1,500-6,000 words. **Payment varies**

TIPS We have over the years published quite a few 'firsts' from young writers whose historical knowledge, research methods, and writing skills met our standards. The scope and ambition of a new writer tell us a lot about his or her future usefulness to us. A major article gives us a better idea of the writer's value. Everything depends on the quality of the material. We don't really care whether the author is 20 and unknown, or 80 and famous, or vice versa. No phone calls, please.

AMERICAN HISTORY

Historynet.com, 1919 Gallows Rd., #400, Vienna VA 22182. **E-mail:** americanhistory@historynet.com. **E-mail:** mdolan@historynet.com. **Website:** www.historynet.com/magazines/american_history. **Contact:** Michael Dolan. **75% freelance written.** Bimonthly magazine of cultural, social, military, and political history published for a general audience. "Presents American history for general-interest readers in an authoritative, informative, thought-provoking, and entertaining style. Lively narratives take readers on an adventure with history, complemented by rare photographs, paintings, illustrations, and maps." Estab. 1966. Circ. 95,000. Byline given. Pays on acceptance. 20% kill fee. Accepts queries by e-mail. Accepts simultaneous submissions. Responds in 10 weeks to queries. Sample copy: $6. Guidelines by e-mail.

NONFICTION "*American History* commissions assignments based on one-page pitches by prospective authors explaining topic, significance, key character(s), setting, and narrative arc. We do not encourage speculative submissions." *Unsolicited mss not considered.* Inappropriate materials include book reviews, travelogues, personal/family narratives not of national significance, articles about collectibles/antiques, living artists, local/individual historic buildings/landmarks, and articles of a current editorial nature. **Buys 30 mss/year.** Query by e-mail with published clips. Length: 2,000-4,000 words. **Payment varies.**

PHOTOS Welcomes suggestions for illustrations.

TIPS "The best guide to writing for our magazines is our magazines. Before querying, pick up a few recent copies and study them to see how we do what we do and gain a sense of the topics and writing styles we seek."

AMERICAN LEGACY

28 W. 23rd St., 10th Floor, New York NY 10010-5254. (212)367-3100. **Fax:** (212)367-3151. **E-mail:** apeterson@americanlegacymag.com. **Website:** www.americanlegacymag.com. Quarterly magazine spotlighting the historical and cultural achievements of African American men and women throughout history. No kill fee. Editorial lead time 6 months. Accepts simultaneous submissions.

🜨 Query before submitting.

AMERICA'S CIVIL WAR

Weider History Group, 1600 Tysons Blvd., Suite 1140, Tysons VA 22102. **E-mail:** acw@historynet.com. **E-mail:** submissions@historynet.com. **Website:** www.historynet.com/americas-civil-war. **Contact:** editor. **60% freelance written.** Bimonthly magazine covering popular history and straight historical narrative for both the general reader and the American Civil War buff featuring firsthand accounts, remarkable photos, expert commentary, and maps in making the whole story of the most pivotal era in American history accessible and showing why it still matters in the 21st century. Estab. 1988. Circ. 78,000. Byline given. Pays on publication. No kill fee. Accepts queries by e-mail. Accepts simultaneous submissions. Guidelines online.

NONFICTION Buys 18 mss/year. "Query. Submit a page outlining the subject and your approach to it, and why you believe this would be an important article for the magazine. Briefly summarize your prior writing experience in a cover note." Length: 3,500 words; 250-word sidebar. **Pays $300 and up.**

PHOTOS Send photos with submission or cite sources. Captions, identification of subjects required.

TIPS "All stories must be true. We do not publish fiction or poetry. Write an entertaining, well-researched, informative and unusual story that grabs the reader's attention and holds it. Submit queries or mss by e-mail. All submissions are on speculation."

❺ THE ARTILLERYMAN

Jack W. Melton Jr. LLC, 520 Folly Road, Suite P-379, Charleston SC 29412. (706)940-2673. **E-mail:** mail@artillerymanmagazine.com. **Website:** www.artillerymanmagazine.com. **Contact:** Jack Melton, Publisher. **60% freelance written.** Quarterly magazine covering antique artillery, fortifications, and crew-served weapons 1750-1900 for competition shooters, collectors, and living history reenactors using artillery. Estab. 1979. Circ. 1,200. Byline given. Pays on publication. Publishes ms an average of 6 months after acceptance. Accepts queries by mail, e-mail, fax. Accepts simultaneous submissions. Responds in 3 weeks to queries. Sample copy online.

NONFICTION Needs historical, how-to, interview, photo feature, technical, travel. **Buys 12 mss/year.** Send complete ms. Length: 300 words minimum. **Pays $40-60.**

PHOTOS Send photos. Captions, identification of subjects required.

TIPS "We regularly use freelance contributions for Places-to-Visit and Unit Profiles departments and welcome pieces on unusual cannon or cannon with a known and unique history. Writers should ask themselves if they could knowledgeably talk artillery with an expert."

❺ BRITISH HERITAGE TRAVEL

Kliger Heritage Group, 81 Winter St., Exeter NH 03833. (603)580-5022. **E-mail:** editor@britishheritage.com. **Website:** www.britishheritage.com. **Contact:** Dana Huntley, Editor. Bimonthly magazine covering British travel, history and culture. The American magazine of British travel, history and culture, especially written for those who love England, Scotland, and Wales. A must-read for Anglophiles, *British Heritage Travel* shows them what they can see and do, how to get there, and where to stay, with information that even veteran travelers may overlook. Circ. 50,485. Byline given. Pays on acceptance. Editorial lead time 6 months. Accepts queries by e-mail.

NONFICTION Buys 50 mss/year. Query by e-mail. Length: 1,000-1,600 words.

TIPS "The first rule still stands: Know thy market."

GATEWAY

Missouri History Museum, P.O. Box 11940, St. Louis MO 63112. (314)746-4558. **Fax:** (314)746-4548. **E-mail:** lmitchell@mohistory.org. **Website:** www.mohistory.org. **Contact:** Lauren Mitchell. **75% freelance written.** Annual magazine covering Missouri history and culture. "*Gateway* is a popular cultural history magazine that is primarily a member benefit of the Missouri History Museum. Thus, we have a general audience with an interest in the history and culture of Missouri and St. Louis in particular." Estab. 1980. Circ. 9,000. Byline given. Publishes ms an average of 6 months-1 year after acceptance. Editorial lead time 6 months. Accepts queries by mail, e-mail. Accepts simultaneous submissions. Responds in 1 month to queries; in 2 months to mss. Sample copy: $10. Guidelines available online.

NONFICTION Needs book excerpts, essays, historical, interview, photo feature, scholarly essays, Missouri biographies, viewpoints on events, first-hand historical accounts, regional architectural history, literary history. No genealogies. **Buys 4-6 mss/year.** Query with writing samples or complete ms. Length: 2,000-5,000 words.

PHOTOS State availability with submission.

TIPS "You'll get our attention with queries reflecting new perspectives on historical and cultural topics."

✪❸❺ HISTORY MAGAZINE

Moorshead Magazines, 82 Church St. S., Suite 101, Ajax ON L1S 6B3 Canada. **E-mail:** edward@moorshead.com. **E-mail:** edward@moorshead.com. **Website:** www.history-magazine.com. **Contact:** Edward Zapletal, publisher/editor. **99% freelance written.** Bimonthly magazine covering social history. A general interest history magazine, focusing on social history up to about 1960. Estab. 1999. Byline given. Pays on publication. See author notes. Publishes ms an average of 6 months after acceptance. Editorial lead time 6 months. Submit seasonal material 6 months in advance. Accepts queries by e-mail. Accepts simultaneous submissions. Responds in 1 to 2 months to queries. Sample PDF copy available on request. Guidelines available online.

○ "Please see our author notes at history-magazine.com/anotes.html for details."

NONFICTION Needs book excerpts, historical. Does not want first-person narratives or revisionist history. **Buys 50 mss/year.** Query. Do not submit complete ms. "PLEASE NOTE: Submissions must be accompanied by the author's name, telephone number, postal address, and e-mail address. If not present in the ms, we will delay publication until we receive the necessary contact information." Length: 500-2,500 words. **Pays 8¢/word; $7/image submitted and used in the final layout.**

PHOTOS State availability. Captions required. Reviews JPEG files. See author guidelines. Prefers public domain images only. Buys one-time rights.

TIPS "A love of history helps a lot, as does a willingness to work with us to present interesting articles on the past to our readers."

LIGHTHOUSE DIGEST

Lighthouse Digest, P.O. Box 250, East Machias ME 04630. (207)259-2121. **E-mail:** Editor@LighthouseDigest.com. **Website:** www.lighthousedigest.com. **Contact:** Tim Harrison, editor. **12% freelance written.** Monthly magazine covering historical, fiction and news events about lighthouses and similar maritime stories. Full color lighthouse news and history magazine. Estab. 1989. Circ. 20,000. Byline given. Pays on publication. No kill fee. Publishes ms an average of 4 months after acceptance. Editorial lead time 3 months. Submit seasonal material 3 months in advance. Accepts queries by e-mail. Accepts simultaneous submissions. Responds in 6 weeks to queries. Sample copy free.

NONFICTION Needs expose, general interest, historical, humor, inspirational, personal experience, photo feature, reviews, technical, travel. No historical data taken from books. **Buys 30 mss/year.** Send complete ms. Length: 2,500 words maximum.

PHOTOS Photos can be sent via e-mail but they must be high resolution images, one attachment per e-mail. Captions, identification of subjects required. Reviews prints. Offers no additional payment for photos accepted with ms. Buys all rights.

FICTION Needs adventure, historical, humorous, mystery, romance, suspense. **Buys 2 mss/year.** Send complete ms. 2,500 words maximum.

TIPS "Read our publication and visit the website."

MHQ: THE QUARTERLY JOURNAL OF MILITARY HISTORY

HistoryNet, LLC, 1919 Gallows Road, Suite 400, Vienna VA 22182-4038. **E-mail:** mhq@historynet.com. **Website:** www.historynet.com/magazines/mhq. **Contact:** Dr. Michael W. Robbins, editor. **80% freelance written.** Quarterly journal covering military history. *MHQ* offers readers in-depth articles on the history of warfare from ancient times into the 21st century. Authoritative features and departments cover military strategies, philosophies, campaigns, battles, personalities, weaponry, espionage, and perspectives, all written in a lively and readable style. Articles are accompanied by classic works of art, photographs, and maps. Readers include serious students of military tactics, strategy, leaders, and campaigns, as well as general world history enthusiasts. Many readers are currently in the military or retired officers. Estab. 1988. Circ. 22,000. Byline given. Pays on publication. No kill fee. Editorial lead time 1 year. Submit seasonal material 1 year in advance. Accepts queries by mail, e-mail. Sample copy: $6. Guidelines available online.

NONFICTION Needs historical, personal experience, photo feature. No fiction or stories pertaining to collectibles or reenactments. **Buys 36 mss/year.** Query by mail or e-mail with published clips. Length: 750-5,000 words.

PHOTOS Send photos/art with submission. Identification of subjects required. Reviews transparencies, prints. Negotiates payment individually. Buys all rights.

COLUMNS/DEPARTMENTS Artists on War (description of artwork of a military nature); Experience of War (first-person accounts of military incidents); Strategic View (discussion of military theory, strategy); Arms & Men (description of military hardware or unit), all up to 2,500 words. **Buys 16 mss/year.** Send complete ms.

TIPS "Less common topic areas—medieval, Asian, or South American military history, for example—are more likely to attract our attention. The likelihood that articles can be effectively illustrated often determines the ultimate fate of mss. Many otherwise excellent articles have been rejected due to a lack of suitable art or photographs. While the information we publish is scholarly and substantive, we prefer writing that is anecdotal, and, above all, engaging rather than didactic."

MILITARY HISTORY

HistoryNet, 1919 Gallows Rd., Suite 400, Vienna VA 22182-4038. (703)771-9400. **Fax:** (703)779-8345. **E-mail:** militaryhistory@historynet.com. **Website:** www.historynet.com/magazines/military_history. **Contact:** Stephen Harding, editor. **70% freelance written.** Magazine published 6 times/year covering world military history of all ages. "We strive to give the general reader accurate, highly readable, often narrative popular history, richly accompanied by period art." Byline given. Pays on publication. No kill fee. Submit seasonal material 1 year in advance. Accepts queries by mail, e-mail. Accepts simultaneous submissions. Sample: $6. Guidelines for #10 SASE or by e-mail.

NONFICTION Needs historical, interview. **Buys 20-30 mss/year.** Query by mail or e-mail with published clips. Length: 2,000-3,000 words with a 200- to 500-word sidebar.

COLUMNS/DEPARTMENTS Interview; What We Learned (lessons from history); Valor (those who have earned medals/awards); Hallowed Ground (battlegrounds of significance); and Reviews (books, video, games, all relating to military history). Length: 700-1,300 words.

TIPS "We seek professional submissions that are thoroughly researched and fact-checked and adhere to the *Associated Press Stylebook*."

TRAINS

Kalmbach Publishing Co., P.O. Box 1612, Waukesha WI 53187-1612. (262)796-8776. **Fax:** (262)796-1142. **E-mail:** editor@trainsmag.com; photoeditor@trainsmag.com. **Website:** www.trn.trains.com. **Contact:** Jim Wrinn, editor; Tom Danneman, art director. Monthly magazine covering railroading. "Appeals to consumers interested in learning about the function and history of the railroad industry." Estab. 1940. Circ. 92,419. No kill fee. Editorial lead time 2 months. Accepts simultaneous submissions.

🔾   Query before submitting.

NONFICTION *Trains* buys news stories and feature articles covering railroading's past and present, including first-person recollections. Before submitting a feature-length article, send a written query via e-mail. Send a brief paragraph explaining the story, its theme, and highlights. Queries should include a possible headline. **Payment: 10¢/word.**

VIETNAM

HistoryNet LLC, Editor, Vietnam Magazine, 1919 Gallows Road, Suite 400, Vienna VA 22182-4038. **E-mail:** vietnam@historynet.com. **Website:** www.historynet.com/vietnam. **Contact:** Chuck Springston, editor. **90% freelance written.** Bimonthly magazine providing in-depth and authoritative accounts of the many complexities that made the war in Vietnam unique, including the people, battles, strategies, perspectives, analysis, and weaponry. Estab. 1988. Circ. 46,000. Byline given. Pays on publication. No kill fee. Accepts queries by e-mail. Accepts simultaneous submissions. Sample copy: $9.95. Send manuscripts in Microsoft Word or plain text documents as email attachments.

NONFICTION **Buys 24 mss/year.** Length: up to 3,000 words, including sidebars.

PHOTOS Send photos with submission or state availability. Identification of subjects required.

COLUMNS/DEPARTMENTS Query.

WILD WEST

World History Group, Wild West Story Idea, 1919 Gallows Road, Suite 400, Vienna VA 22182-4038. **E-mail:** wildwest@historynet.com. **Website:** www.historynet.com. **Contact:** Gregory J. Lalire, editor. **95% freelance written.** Bimonthly magazine covering the history of the American frontier, from its eastern beginnings to its western terminus. *Wild West* covers the popular (narrative) history of the American West—events, trends, personalities, anything of general interest. Estab. 1988. Circ. 83,500. Byline given. Pays on publication. No kill fee. Publishes ms an average of 2 years after acceptance. Editorial lead time 10 months. Submit seasonal material 1 year in advance. Accepts queries by mail, e-mail. Accepts simultaneous submissions. Responds in 3 months to queries; in 6 months to mss. Single issue: $9.95. Writer's guidelines for #10 SASE or online.

NONFICTION Needs historical. No excerpts, travel, etc. Articles can be adapted from book. No fiction or poetry. Nothing current. **Buys 36 mss/year.** Query. Length: 3,500 words with a 500-word sidebar. **Pays $300.**

PHOTOS State availability. Captions, identification of subjects required. Reviews negatives, transparencies. Offers no additional payment for photos accepted with ms. Buys one-time rights.

COLUMNS/DEPARTMENTS Gunfighters & Lawmen, 2,000 words; Westerners, 2,000 words; Warriors & Chiefs, 2,000 words; Western Lore, 2,000 words; Guns of the West, 1,500 words; Artists West, 1,500 words; Books Reviews, 250 words. **Buys 36 mss/year.** Query. **Pays $150 for departments; book reviews paid by the word, minimum $40.**

TIPS "Always query the editor with your story idea. Successful queries include a description of sources of information and suggestions for color and b&w photography or artwork. The best way to break into our magazine is to write an entertaining, informative, and unusual story that grabs the reader's attention and holds it. We favor carefully researched, third-person articles that give the reader a sense of experiencing historical events."

HOBBY & CRAFT

AMERICAN CRAFT

American Craft Council, 1224 Marshall St. NE, Suite 200, Minneapolis MN 55413. (612)206-3115. **E-mail:** mmoses@craftcouncil.org. **E-mail:** query@craftcouncil.org. **Website:** www.americancraftmag.org. **Contact:** Monica Moses, editor in chief. **75% freelance written.** Bimonthly magazine covering art, craft, design. "American Craft Council is a national nonprofit aimed at supporting artists and craft enthusiasts. We want to inspire people to live a creative life. *American Craft* magazine celebrates the age-old human impulse to make things by hand." Estab. 1941. Circ. 40,000. Byline given. Pays on acceptance. Offers 25% kill fee. Publishes ms an average of 2 months after acceptance. Editorial lead time 4-6 months. Submit seasonal material 4-6 months in advance. Accepts queries by mail, e-mail. Accepts simultaneous submissions. Responds in 1 month to queries; in 2 months to mss. See writer's guidelines online.

NONFICTION Needs essays, interview, profile, travel, craft artist profiles, art travel pieces, interviews with creative luminaries, essays on creativity. Query with images. Include medium (glass, clay, fiber, metal, wood, paper, etc.) and department in subject line. Length: 500-2,000 words. **Pays $1/word, according to assigned length.**

COLUMNS/DEPARTMENTS On Our Radar (profiles of emerging artists doing remarkable work); Product Placement (stylish, inventive, practical, and generally affordable goods in production and the people who design them); Shop Talk (Q&As with owners of galleries); Material Matters (an artist using unusual materials to make fine craft); Personal Paths (an artist doing very individual—even idiosyncratic—work from a personal motivation); Spirit of Craft (art forms that might not typically be considered fine craft but may entail the sort of devotion generally associated with craft); Craft in Action (artists or organizations using craft to make the world better); Crafted Lives (photo-driven Q&A with a person or people living in a particularly creative space); Ideas (Q&A with a thinker or practitioner whose views represent a challenge to the status quo); Wide World of Craft (foreign or U.S. travel destination for craft lovers). **Buys 10-12 mss/year.** Query with published clips.

TIPS "Keep pitches short and sweet, a paragraph or 2 at most. Please include visuals with any pitches."

AMERICAN DIGGER

The Publication for Diggers and Collectors, Greybird Publishers, P.O. Box 126, Acworth GA 30101. (770)362-8671. **E-mail:** publisher@americandigger.com. **Website:** americandigger.com. **Contact:** Butch Holcombe, publisher. **95% freelance written.** Covers hobby of metal detecting and collecting historical artifacts. *American Digger* is published bimonthly for the pleasure and education of relic hunters, metal detectorists, digging enthusiasts, and collectors of historical artifacts. Care is taken to create a publication that is accurate, informative, exciting, enjoyable, and comprehensive, with an emphasis on spreading information about metal detecting and collecting historical artifacts. Estab. 2005. Circ. 15,000. Byline given. Pays on publication. Publishes ms an average of 6-12 months after acceptance. Accepts queries by mail, e-mail. Sample copies available online. Guidlines available by e-mail.

NONFICTION Needs how-to, interview, memoir, personal experience, profile, technical. Please do not send any fiction or poetry. **Buys 25-40 mss/year.** Query first on any topic. Any stories should be related to the hobby, whether technical (equipment), personal stories, or how-tos. Word length: 1,200-1,500 words. **Pays 3 contributor copies of the issue and a business card ad.**

PHOTOS Contact: Butch Holcombe, publisher. Freelancers should send photos with submission. Captions, model releases, and identification of subjects are required with photos. Reviews prints (4x6) and GIF/JPEG files (300dpi). Offers no additional payment for photos accepted with ms. Purchases one-time rights.

TIPS "Know your subject matter and the hobby you're writing about. View the sample copies on our website. Always query before submission!"

ANTIQUE TRADER

F+W, a Content + eCommerce Company, 700 E. State St., Iola WI 54990. (715)445-2214. **Fax:** (715)445-4087. **E-mail:** karen.knapstein@fwcommunity.com. **Website:** www.antiquetrader.com. **Contact:** Karen Knapstein, print editor. **60% freelance written.** Published 26 times per year. "We publish quote-heavy stories of timely interest in the antiques field. We cover antiques shows, auctions, and news events." Estab. 1957. Circ. 50,000. Byline given. Pays on publication. No kill fee. Publishes ms an average of 1-3 months after acceptance. Editorial lead time 2 months. Accepts queries by mail, e-mail, fax. Accepts simultaneous submissions. Responds in 1 week to queries; 2 months to mss. Sample copy for cover price, plus postage. Guidelines online.

NONFICTION Needs book excerpts, general interest, interview, personal experience, show and auction coverage. Does not want the same, dry textbook, historical stories on antiques that appear elsewhere. Our readers want personality and timeliness. **Buys 1,000+ mss/year.** Send complete ms. Length: 750-1,200 words. **Pays $50-150, plus contributor copy.**

PHOTOS State availability. Identification of subjects required. Reviews transparencies, prints, GIF/JPEG files. Offers no additional payment for photos accepted with ms. Buys one-time rights.

COLUMNS/DEPARTMENTS Dealer Profile (interviews with interesting antiques dealers), 750-1,200 words; Collector Profile (interviews with interesting collectors), 750-1,000 words. **Buys 30-60 mss/year.** Query with or without published clips or send complete ms.

AUTOGRAPH MAGAZINE

P.O. Box 25559, Santa Ana CA 92799. (951)734-9636. **Fax:** (951)371-7139. **E-mail:** steve.cyrkin@autograph-magazine.com. **Website:** autographmagazine.com. **Contact:** Steve Cyrkin, publisher. **80% freelance written.** Monthly magazine covering the autograph collecting hobby. The focus of *Autograph* is on documents, photographs, or any collectible item that has been signed by a famous person, whether a current celebrity or historical figure. Articles stress how and where to locate celebrities and autograph material, authenticity of signatures and what they are worth. Byline given. Offers negotiable kill fee. Editorial lead time 2 months. Submit seasonal material 3 months in advance. Accepts queries by mail, e-mail. Accepts simultaneous submissions. Responds in 2 weeks to queries.

NONFICTION Needs historical, how-to, interview, personal experience. **Buys 25-35 mss/year.** Query. Length: 1,600-2,000 words. **Pays 5¢/word.**

PHOTOS State availability. Captions, identification of subjects required. Reviews transparencies, prints. Offers $3/photo. Buys one-time rights.

COLUMNS/DEPARTMENTS *Autograph Collector* buys 8-10 columns per month written by regular contributors. **Buys 90-100 mss/year.** Query. **Pays $50 or as determined on a per case basis.**

FILLERS Needs anecdotes, facts. **Buys 20-25 mss/year.** Length: 200-300 words. **$15.**

TIPS "Ideally writers should be autograph collectors themselves and know their topics thoroughly. Articles must be well-researched and clearly written. Writers should remember that *Autograph Collector* is a celebrity-driven magazine and name recognition of the subject is important."

BEADWORK

Interweave Press, 4868 Innovation Drive, Ft. Collins CO 80525. **E-mail:** beadworksubmissions@interweave.com. **Website:** www.beadingdaily.com. "*Beadwork* is a bimonthly magazine devoted to everything about beads and beadwork. Our pages are filled with projects for all levels of beaders, with a focus on the learning needs of those who seek to master beadweaving stitches. We pride ourselves on our easy-to-follow instructions and technical illustrations as well as our informative and entertaining features." Pays on publication. Accepts simultaneous submissions. Guidelines available on website.

NONFICTION step-by-step beading projects, features on beading and bead artists. Query by e-mail or mail. If submitting a project idea, include high-resolution photo of project and contact info. If querying for a feature, submit proposal and contact info.

☘ CANADIAN WOODWORKING AND HOME IMPROVEMENT

Sawdust Media, Inc., 51 Maple Ave. N., RR #3, Burford ON N0E 1A0 Canada. (519)449-2444. **Fax:** (519)449-2445. **E-mail:** pfulcher@canadianwoodworking.com. **E-mail:** rbrown@canadianwoodworking.com. **Website:** www.canadianwoodworking.com. **20% freelance written.** Bi-monthly magazine covering woodworking and home improvement; only accepts work from Canadian writers. Estab. 1999. Byline given. Pays on publication. Offers 50% kill fee. Accepts queries by e-mail. Accepts simultaneous submissions. Sample copy available online. Guidelines available by e-mail.

NONFICTION Needs how-to, humor, inspirational, new product, personal experience, photo feature, technical. Does not want profile on a woodworker. Query. Length: 500-4,000 words. **Pays $250-600 for assigned articles. Pays $250-400 for unsolicited articles.**

PHOTOS State availability. Negotiates payment individually. Buys all rights.

CLASSIC TOY TRAINS

Kalmbach Publishing Co., P.O. Box 1612, 21027 Crossroads Circle, Waukesha WI 53187. (262)796-8776, ext. 524. **Fax:** (262)796-1142. **E-mail:** editor@classictoytrains.com. **Website:** www.classictoytrains.com. **Contact:** Carl Swanson, editor. **80% freelance written.** Magazine published 9 times/year covering collectible toy trains (O, S, Standard) like Lionel and American Flyer, etc. For the collector and operator of toy trains, *CTT* offers full-color photos of layouts and collections of toy trains, restoration tips, operating information, new product reviews and information, and insights into the history of toy trains. Estab. 1987. Circ. 40,000. Byline given. Pays on acceptance. Publishes ms an average of 1 year after acceptance.

Editorial lead time 3 months. Submit seasonal material 6 months in advance. Accepts queries by mail, e-mail. Accepts simultaneous submissions. Responds in 3 weeks to queries; in 1 month to mss. Sample copy for $6.95, plus postage. Guidelines available online.

NONFICTION Needs general interest, historical, how-to, interview, personal experience, photo feature, technical. **Buys 90 mss/year.** Query. Length: 500-3,000 words. **Pays $75-500.**

PHOTOS Send photos. Captions required. Reviews hi-res digital photos. Offers no additional payment for photos accepted with ms or $15-75/photo. Buys all rights.

TIPS "It's important to have a thorough understanding of the toy train hobby; most of our freelancers are hobbyists themselves. One-half to two-thirds of *CTT*'s editorial space is devoted to photographs; superior photography is critical."

F+W MEDIA (MAGAZINE DIVISION)

10151 Carver Rd., Suite 200, Cincinnati OH 45242. (513)531-2690. **Website:** www.fwcommunity.com. **Contact:** Dave Pulvermacher, marketing research. Each month, millions of enthusiasts turn to the magazines from F+W for inspiration, instruction, and encouragement. "Readers are as varied as our categories, but all are assured of getting the best possible coverage of their favorite hobby." Publishes magazines in the following categories: antiques and collectibles (*Antique Trader*); astronomy (*Sky & Telescope*); automotive (*Military Vehicles, Old Cars Report Price Guide, Old Cars Weekly*); beading (*Beadwork*); coins and paper money (*Bank Note Reporter, Coins Magazine, Numismatic News, World Coin News*); construction (*Frame Building News, Metal Roofing Magazine, Rural Builder*); crocheting (*Interweave Crochet, Love of Crochet*); fine art (*Acrylic Artist, Collector's Guide, Drawing, Pastel Journal, Southwest Art, The Artist's Magazine, Watercolor Artist*); firearms and knives (*Blade, Gun Digest The Magazine*); genealogy (*Family Tree Magazine*); graphic design (*HOW Magazine, PRINT*); horticulture (*Horticulture*); jewelry (*Jewelry Stringing, Lapidary Journal Jewelry Artist, Step by Step Wire Jewelry*); knitting (*Interweave Knits, Knitscene, Love of Knitting*) militaria (*Military Trader*); mixed media (*Cloth Paper Scissors*); outdoors and hunting (*Deer & Deer Hunting, Trapper & Predator Caller*); quilting (*Fons & Porter's Easy Quilts, Fons & Porter's Love of Quilting, McCall's Quick Quilts, McCall's*

Quilting, *Quilting Arts Magazine, Quiltmaker*); records and CDs (*Goldmine*); sewing (*Creative Machine Embroidery, Piecework, Sew News*); spinning (*Spin Off*); sports (*Sports Collectors Digest*); woodworking (*Popular Woodworking Magazine*); weaving (*Handwoven*); writing (*Writer's Digest*). Accepts simultaneous submissions.

○ Please see individual listings in the Consumer Magazines and Trade Journals sections for specific submission information about each magazine.

❸❸❸ FAMILY TREE MAGAZINE

F+W, a Content and eCommerce Company, 10151 Carver Rd., Suite 200, Blue Ash OH 45242. (513)531-2690. **Fax:** (513)891-7153. **Website:** www.familytreemagazine.com. **75% freelance written.** Magazine covering family history, heritage, and genealogy research. "*Family Tree Magazine* is a special-interest consumer magazine that helps readers discover, preserve, and celebrate their family's history. We cover genealogy, ethnic heritage, genealogy websites and software, photography and photo preservation, and other ways that families connect with their past." Estab. 1999. Circ. 75,000. Byline given. Pays on acceptance. Offers 25% kill fee. Publishes ms an average of 6 months after acceptance. Editorial lead time 8 months. Submit seasonal material 8 months in advance. Accepts queries by mail, e-mail. Responds in 6-8 weeks to queries. Sample copy: $8 from website. Guidelines online.

○ Please note that Family Tree Magazine does not cover general family or parenting topics.

NONFICTION Needs book excerpts, historical, how-to, new product, technical. Does not publish personal experience stories (except brief stories in the Tree Talk column, which does not pay) or histories of specific families. Does not cover general family or parenting topics. **Buys 40 mss/year.** Query with a specific story idea and published clips. Length: 250-4,500 words. **Pays up to $800.**

PHOTOS State availability. Captions required. Reviews color transparencies. Negotiates payment individually. Buys all rights.

TIPS "Always query with a specific story idea. Look at sample issues before querying to get a feel for appropriate topics and angles. We see too many broad, general stories on genealogy or records and personal accounts of 'How I found great-aunt Sally' without how-to value."

○ FIBRE FOCUS

The Ontario Handweavers & Spinners, 1188 Walker Lake Dr., RR4, Huntsville ON P1H 2J6 Canada. **E-mail:** ffeditor@ohs.on.ca. **Website:** www.ohs.on.ca. **Contact:** Flannery Surette, editor. **75% freelance written.** Quarterly magazine covering handweaving, spinning, basketry, beading, and other fiber arts. "Our readers are weavers and spinners who also do dyeing, knitting, basketry, feltmaking, papermaking, sheep raising, and craft supply. All articles deal with some aspect of these crafts." Estab. 1957. Circ. 700. Byline given. Pays within 30 days after publication. Publishes ms 2-5 months after acceptance. Editorial lead time 3 months. Submit seasonal material 6 months in advance. Accepts simultaneous submissions. Responds in 1 month to queries. Sample copy: $8 (Canadian). Guidelines available online.

○ "Articles must reflect a true understanding of weaving, spinning, or fiber art you are writing about. Good-quality photographs and/or graphics are an essential part of any story. Travel articles focusing on fiber arts discovered in other countries are also considered."

NONFICTION Needs historical, how-to, interview, new product, opinion, personal experience, photo feature, profile, reviews, technical, travel. **Buys 40-60 mss/year.** Contact the *Fibre Focus* editor before undertaking a project or an article. Mss may be submitted c/o Flannery Surette by e-mail for anything you have to contribute for upcoming issues. Feature article deadlines: December 31, March 31, June 30, and September 15. Length: varies, but generally 600-1,800 words. **Pays $30 (Canadian)/published page.**

REPRINTS Pays $20 (Canadian) per published page.

PHOTOS Send photos. Captions, identification of subjects required. Payment is included as part of the article. Buys one-time rights.

TIPS "Visit the OHS website for current information."

FINE WOODWORKING

The Taunton Press, Inc., 63 South Main St., P.O. Box 5506, Newtown CT 06470-5506. (203)426-8171. **Fax:** (203)426-3434. **E-mail:** fw@taunton.com. **Website:** www.finewoodworking.com. **Contact:** Tom McKenna, senior editor. Bimonthly magazine on woodworking in the small shop. Estab. 1975. Circ. 270,000. Byline given. Pays on acceptance. Offers variable kill

CONSUMER MAGAZINES

fee. Submit seasonal material 6 months in advance. Accepts simultaneous submissions. Responds in 1 month to queries. Guidelines online at www.fine-woodworking.com/pages/fw_authorguideline.asp.

NONFICTION Needs how-to. **Buys 120 mss/year.** Send article outline, helpful drawings or photos, and proposal letter. **Pays $150/magazine page.**

COLUMNS/DEPARTMENTS Fundamentals (basic how-to and concepts for beginning woodworkers); Master Class (advanced techniques); Finish Line (finishing techniques); Question & Answer (woodworking Q&A); Methods of Work (shop tips); Tools & Materials (short reviews of new tools). **Buys 400 mss/year. Pays $50-150/published page.**

TIPS "Look for authors guidelines and follow them. Stories about woodworking reported by non-woodworkers are *not* used. Our magazine is essentially reader-written by woodworkers."

🅢 FINESCALE MODELER

Kalmbach Publishing Co., 21027 Crossroads Circle, P.O. Box 1612, Waukesha WI 53187-1612. (414)796-8776. **Website:** www.finescale.com. **80% freelance written. Eager to work with new/unpublished writers.** Magazine published 10 times/year devoted to how-to-do-it modeling information for scale model builders who build non-operating aircraft, tanks, boats, automobiles, figures, dioramas, and science fiction and fantasy models. Circ. 60,000. Byline given. Pays on acceptance. No kill fee. Publishes ms an average of 14 months after acceptance. Accepts simultaneous submissions. Responds in 6 weeks to queries. Responds in 3 months to mss. Sample copy with 9x12 SASE and 3 first-class stamps. Guidelines available on website.

NONFICTION Needs how-to, technical. Query or send complete ms via www.contribute.kalmbach.com. Length: 750-3,000 words. **Pays $60/published page minimum.**

PHOTOS "Send original high-res digital images, slides, or prints with submission. You can submit digital images at www.contribute.kalmbach.com." Captions, identification of subjects required. Reviews transparencies, color prints. Pays $7.50 minimum for transparencies and $5 minimum for color prints. Buys one-time rights.

COLUMNS/DEPARTMENTS *FSM* Showcase (photos plus description of model); *FSM* Tips and Techniques (model building hints and tips). **Buys 25-50 mss/year.** Send complete ms. **Pays $25-50.**

TIPS "A freelancer can best break in first through hints and tips, then through feature articles. Most people who write for *FSM* are modelers first, writers second. This is a specialty magazine for a special, quite expert audience. Essentially, 99% of our writers will come from that audience."

HANDWOVEN

F+W Media, 4868 Innovation Dr., Fort Collins CO 80525. **E-mail:** osterhaug@att.net; cgarton@interweave.com. **E-mail:** handwoven@interweave.com. **Website:** www.interweave.com/weaving. **Contact:** Anita Osterhaug, editor; Christina Garton, associate editor; Kathy Mallo, managing editor. "The main goal of *Handwoven* articles is to inspire our readers to weave. Articles and projects should be accessible to weavers of all skill levels, even when the material is technical. The best way to prepare an article for *Handwoven* is to study the format and style of articles in recent issues." Estab. 1979. Pays on publication. Editorial lead time is 6-12 months. Accepts queries by mail, e-mail. Responds in 6 weeks to queries. Guidelines available on website.

NONFICTION Needs essays, historical, how-to, humor, personal experience, profile, reviews, travel. Special issues: Query or submit full ms by e-mail or mail. Include written intro, relevant photos or other visuals (include photo credits), 25-word author bio, and photo.

COLUMNS/DEPARTMENTS What's Happening, Spotlight, Endnotes. **Buys 10 mss/year.** Submit materials to Christina Garton, associate editor.

INTERWEAVE CROCHET

F+W Media, 4868 Innovation Dr., Fort Collins CO 80525. **E-mail:** crochet@interweave.com. **Website:** www.interweave.com/crochet. **Contact:** Lisa Shroyer. "*Interweave Crochet* is a quarterly publication for all those who love to crochet. In each issue we present beautifully finished projects, accompanied by clear step-by-step instructions, as well as stories and articles of interest to crocheters. The projects range from quick but intriguing projects that can be accomplished in a weekend to complex patterns that may take months to complete. Engaging and informative feature articles come from around the country and around the world. Fashion sensibility and striking examples of craft technique are important to us." Pays on publication. Accepts queries by mail. Guidelines available online.

NONFICTION Needs how-to, profile. Special issues: "We are interested in articles on a broad range of topics, including technical pieces, profiles of inspiring crochet designers, and features about regions of the world where crochet has played or continues to play an important role." See website for current calls for submission. Query by mail. Include submission form (available online). "Please send a detailed proposal— complete outline, written description—to give us a clear idea of what to expect in the finished piece."

INTERWEAVE KNITS

Interweave Press, 4868 Innovation Dr., Ft. Collins CO 80537. **E-mail:** custserv@fwmedia.com. **Website:** www.interweave.com/knitting. *Interweave Knits* is a quarterly publication of Interweave Press for all those who love to knit. In each issue we present beautifully finished projects, accompanied by clear step-by-step instruction, and stories and articles of interest to knitters. The projects range from quick but intriguing items that can be accomplished in a weekend, to complex patterns that may take months to complete. Feature articles (personally arresting but information rich) come from around the country and around the world. Fashion sensibility and striking examples of craft technique are important to us. *Interweave Knits* is published quarterly. Pays on publication. Editorial lead time is 6-12 months. Responds in 6 weeks to queries. Guidelines available on website.

NONFICTION Special issues: "We are interested in articles of all lengths on a broad range of topics, including technical pieces; profiles of inspiring knitwear designers and others in textile industries; and features about regions of the world where knitting has played or continues to play an important role. We take knitting seriously and want articles that do the same. The best way to understand what we're looking for is to read a recent issue of the magazine carefully. For all article queries, send a detailed proposal: For shorter submissions, a brief description will do; for feature articles, send an outline and a sample paragraph or two. If the proposal is accepted, and once we've made any adjustments to the concept and agreed on the details, you will begin work on the article." Query by mail. Include submission form (available online). Do not address queries to Eunny Jang. "Beyond the Basics" (useful, accurate, high-quality technical information;

2,000-2,200 words); "Ravelings" (the personal side of knitting; 700-750 words, send whole articles)

COLUMNS/DEPARTMENTS "Knitted Artifact" (examines a knitted artifact, exploring the societal and cultural importance of the craft; 250-300 words); "Where it Comes From (educates readers about fiber and yarn; 250-300 words); "Yarn Review" (1,200-1,400 words); Profiles (showcasing a designer; 1,500-1,800 words).

TIPS "Remember that your submission is a representation of who you are and how you work—if you send us a thoughtful, neat, and well-organized submission, we are likely to be intrigued."

🟢🟢 KITPLANES

P.O. Box 1295, Dayton NV 89403. **E-mail:** editorial@ kitplanes.com. **Website:** www.kitplanes.com. **Contact:** Paul Dye, editor in chief; Mark Schrimmer, managing editor. **50% freelance written. Eager to work with new/unpublished writers.** Monthly magazine covering self-construction of private aircraft for pilots and builders. Estab. 1984. Circ. 72,000. Byline given. Pays on publication. Publishes ms an average of 3 months after acceptance. Submit seasonal material 6 months in advance. Accepts queries by mail, e-mail. Accepts simultaneous submissions. Responds in 1 month to queries; in 6 weeks to mss. Sample copy: $6. Guidelines available online.

NONFICTION Needs general interest, how-to, interview, new product, personal experience, photo feature, technical. No general-interest aviation articles, or "My First Solo" type of articles. **Buys 80 mss/year.** Query. Interested in articles on all phases of aircraft construction, from basic design to flight trials to construction technique in wood, metal, and composite. Length: varies, but feature articles average about 2,000 words. **Pays $250-1,000, including story photos.**

PHOTOS State availability of or send photos. Captions, identification of subjects required. Pays $300 for cover photos. Buys one-time rights.

TIPS "*Kitplanes* contains very specific information— a writer must be extremely knowledgeable in the field. Major features are entrusted only to known writers. We cannot emphasize enough that articles must be directed at the individual aircraft builder. We need more 'how-to' photo features in all areas of homebuilt aircraft."

LAPIDARY JOURNAL JEWELRY ARTIST

F+W, a Content + eCommerce Company, 4868 Innovation Dr., Fort Collins CO 80525. (800)272-2193. **Website:** www.interweave.com/jewelry. **70% freelance written.** Monthly magazine covering gem, bead, and jewelry arts. Our audience is hobbyists who usually have some knowledge of and proficiency in the subject before they start reading. Our style is conversational and informative. There are how-to projects and profiles of artists and materials. Estab. 1947. Circ. 53,000. Byline given. Pays on acceptance. No kill fee. Publishes ms an average of 4 months after acceptance. Editorial lead time 3 months. Accepts queries by mail, e-mail. Accepts simultaneous submissions. Sample copy available online.

NONFICTION Needs how-to, interview, new product, personal experience, technical, travel. **Buys 100 mss/year.** Query. 1,500-2,500 words preferred; 1,000-3,500 words acceptable; longer works occasionally published serially.

REPRINTS Send photocopy.

TIPS "Some knowledge of jewelry, gemstones, and/or minerals is a definite asset. Step-by-Step is a section within *Lapidary Journal* that offers illustrated, step-by-step instruction in gem-cutting, jewelry-making, and beading. Please request a copy of the Step-by-Step guidelines for greater detail."

LOST TREASURE, INC.

P.O. Box 451589, Grove OK 74345. (866)469-6224. **Fax:** (918)786-2192. **E-mail:** managingeditor@losttreasure.com. **Website:** www.losttreasure.com. **Contact:** Carla Nielsen, Managing Editor. **75% freelance written.** Monthly and annual magazines covering lost treasure. Estab. 1966. Circ. 55,000. Byline given. Pays on publication. Approximately 2 months. Accepts queries by e-mail. Accepts simultaneous submissions. Responds within two weeks to queries via e-mail and website. For a sample copy send #10 SASE. Submission guidelines can be requested by e-mailing managingeditor@losttreasure.com.

NONFICTION Needs historical, how-to, personal experience, technical, All must be related to treasure hunting. **Buys 225 mss/year.** Query on Treasure Cache/Treasure Facts only. "Will buy articles, photographs, and cartoons that meet our editorial approval." Enclose SASE with all editorial submissions. Length: 1,000-2,000 words. **Pays 4¢/word.**

PHOTOS "Color or b&w prints, copied maps, art with source credit with mss will help sell your story. We are always looking for cover photos with or without accompanying ms. Pays $100/published cover photo. Must be vertical." High quality JPEG..Captions required. Pays $5/published photo.

TIPS "Queries welcome but not required. If you write about famous treasures and lost mines, be sure we haven't used your selected topic recently—the story must have a new slant or new information. Source documentation required. How-tos should cover some aspect of treasure hunting, and how-to steps should be clearly defined."

💲💲 MILITARY VEHICLES

F+W Media, Inc., 700 E. State St., Iola WI 54990-0001. (715)445-4612. **Fax:** (715)445-4087. **E-mail:** john.adams-graf@fwmedia.com. **Website:** www.militarytrader.com. **Contact:** John Adams-Graf, editor. **50% freelance written.** Bimonthly magazine covering historic military vehicles. Dedicated to serving people who collect, restore, and drive historic military vehicles. Estab. 1987. Circ. 18,500. Byline given. Pays on publication. No kill fee. Publishes ms an average of 1 month after acceptance. Accepts queries by mail, e-mail. Accepts simultaneous submissions. Responds in 1 week to queries. Responds in 1 month to mss. Sample copy for $5.

NONFICTION Needs historical, how-to, technical. **Buys 20 mss/year.** Send complete ms. Length: 1,300-2,600 words. **Pays $0-200.**

PHOTOS True required. Buys all rights.

COLUMNS/DEPARTMENTS Pays $0-75.

TIPS "Be knowledgeable about military vehicles. This magazine is for a very specialized audience. General automotive journalists will probably not be able to write for this group. The bulk of our content addresses U.S.-manufactured and used vehicles. Plenty of good photos will make it easier to be published in our publication. Write for the collector/restorer: Assume that they already know the basics of historical context. Articles that show how to restore or repair military vehicles are given the highest priority."

💲 NATIONAL COMMUNICATIONS MAGAZINE

SCAN Services Co., P.O. Box 1, Aledo IL 61231-0001. (309)228-8000. **Fax:** (888)287-SCAN. **E-mail:** editor@natcommag.com. **Website:** www.natcommag.com. **Contact:** Chuck Gysi, editor and publisher. **50%**

freelance written. Covers scanner radios and listening (VHF/UHF), citizens band (CB) radio, and other hobby two-way radio services such as GMRS, FRS, and MURS. *National Communications Magazine* was created for the hobby radio user. Estab. 1988. Circ. 5,000. Byline given. Pays *immediately* on publication. No kill fee. Publishes ms an average of 2 months after acceptance. Editorial lead time 2 months. Submit seasonal material 4 months in advance. Accepts queries by e-mail. Responds in 1 day-1 week. Current-issue sample copy: $6. Free recent PDF sample download at www.nat-com.org/sample.pdf.

NONFICTION Needs how-to, interview, new product, personal experience, photo feature, technical. Does not want articles off-topic of the publication's audience (radio hobbyists). "If you aren't writing about police scanners, CB radios, or two-way radios and don't know our audience, we're not interested in your article. It's essential to know your subject matter." **Buys 18 mss/year.** Query by e-mail only. "Inquire before writing with an outline of your proposed article. We're also interested in working with new authors, but we like to work with them in shaping articles before they are started. Photos and graphics are needed for all articles and must be provided by the author." Length: 2,500-3,000 words. **Pays $75 or more.** No expenses paid.

PHOTOS Attach photos and/or graphics with all submissions. Captions, identification of subjects required. Photos must be author generated, or permission must be obtained for publication. Photos should be copyright-free. Reviews GIF/JPEG/TIF files. Offers no additional payment for photos accepted with ms. Buys all rights.

POETRY Does not accept any poetry whatsoever.

TIPS "If you don't know our subject matter well, which is the use and enjoyment of police scanners, citizens band radio, and two-way radios in the GMRS/FRS/MURS radio services, please do not waste our time and your time. We'll know instantly if you are a radio hobbyist or not. Make sure all submissions include artwork. Great artwork in a vertical format may be featured on our cover and help turn your article into a cover feature. The editor is a long-time journalist willing to work with new writers who are radio communications hobbyists."

POPULAR MECHANICS

Hearst Corp., 300 W. 57th St., New York NY 10019-5899. (212)649-2000. **E-mail:** popularmechanics@hearst.com; pmwebmaster@hearst.com. **Website:** www.popularmechanics.com. **Contact:** Ryan D'Agostino, editor-in-chief. **Up to 50% freelance written.** Monthly magazine on technology, science, automotive, home, outdoors. A men's service magazine that addresses the diverse interests of today's male, providing him with information to improve the way he lives. Covers stories from do-it-yourself projects to technological advances in aerospace, military, automotive, and so on. Estab. 1902. Circ. 1,200,000. Byline given. Pays on acceptance. Offers 25% kill fee. Publishes ms an average of 6 months after acceptance. Submit seasonal material 6 months in advance. Accepts simultaneous submissions. Guidelines available on website.

NONFICTION Query before submitting a ms. Send ms to the appropriate departmental editor. In any article query, be specific as to what makes the development new, better, different, interesting, or less expensive. All articles must be submitted in a word processing app. Editorial interests include automotive, home journal, science/technology/aerospace, boating/outdoors, electronics/photography/telecommunications, and general interest articles. **Pays $300-1,000 for features.**

POPULAR WOODWORKING MAGAZINE

F+W, A Content + Ecommerce Company, 8469 Blue Ash Rd., Suite 100, Cincinnati OH 45236. **E-mail:** rodney.wilson@fwmedia.com. **E-mail:** rodney.wilson@fwmedia.com. **Website:** www.popularwoodworking.com. **Contact:** Rodney Wilson, Managing Editor. **75% freelance written.** Magazine published 7 times/year. "*Popular Woodworking Magazine* invites woodworkers of all skill levels into a community of professionals who share their hard-won shop experience through in-depth projects and technique articles, which help readers hone their existing skills and develop new ones for both hand and power tools. Related stories increase the readers' understanding and enjoyment of their craft. Any project submitted must be aesthetically pleasing, of sound construction, and offer a challenge to readers. On the average, we use 5 freelance features per issue. Our primary needs are 'how-to' articles on woodworking. Our secondary need is for articles that will inspire discussion concerning woodworking. Tone of articles should be conversational and informal but knowledgeable, as if the writer is speaking directly to the reader. Our readers are the woodworking hobbyist and small woodshop owner. Writers should have an extensive knowledge of woodworking and excellent woodworking techniques and skills." Estab. 1981. Circ. 150,000. Byline given. Pays on acceptance. No kill fee. Publishes ms an average of 10 months after acceptance. Submit seasonal material 6 months in advance. Accepts queries by mail, e-mail. Responds in 2 months to queries. Sample copy: $6.99 plus 9x12 SAE with 6 first-class stamps, or online. Guidelines available online at http://www.popularwoodworking.com/submission-guidelines.

○   For build articles, professional-quality Sketch-Up models are strongly encouraged. Must be able to submit publishable, high-resolution digital images.

NONFICTION Needs how-to, profile, technical. No tool reviews. **Buys 35 mss/year.** Query first; see guidelines and sample query on website. Length: 1,200-2,500 words. **Pay starts at $275/published page.**

REPRINTS For previously published material, send photocopy with rights for sale noted and information about when and where the material previously appeared. Pays 25% of amount paid for an original article.

PHOTOS Photographic quality affects acceptance. Need professional quality, high-resolution digital images. Send photos. Captions, identification of subjects required. Pays $75/page.

COLUMNS/DEPARTMENTS Tricks of the Trade (helpful techniques) 250 words; End Grain (thoughts on woodworking as a profession or hobby, can be humorous or serious) 500-550 words. **Buys 20 mss/year.** Query. **Pays $350 for End Grain and $50-$100 for Tricks of the Trade.**

TIPS "Write an 'End Grain' column for us and then follow up with photos of your projects. Submissions should include materials list, SketchUp model or hand illustration (SU preferred), and discussion of the step-by-step process. We select attractive, practical projects with quality construction for which the authors can supply quality digital photography."

WESTERN & EASTERN TREASURES

People's Publishing Co., Inc., P.O. Box 647, Pacific Grove CA 93950-0647 USA. **E-mail:** editor@wetreasures.com. **Website:** www.wetreasures.com. **100%**

freelance written. Monthly magazine on the newsstand, in print and in digital format through subscription, covering hobby/sport of metal detecting/treasure hunting. "*Western & Eastern Treasures* provides concise yet comprehensive coverage of every aspect of the sport/hobby of metal detecting and treasure hunting with a strong emphasis on current, accurate information; innovative, field-proven advice and instruction; and entertaining, effective presentation." Estab. 1966. Circ. 50,000. Byline given. Pays on publication. No kill fee. Publishes ms an average of 3+ months after acceptance. Editorial lead time 4 months. Submit seasonal material 3-4 months in advance. Responds in 2 months to mss. Sample copy for SAE with 9x12 envelope and 5 first-class stamps. Request our current Freelancer's Guidelines by sending an email to: editor@wetreasures.com.

NONFICTION Needs how-to, personal experience. Special issues: *Silver & Gold Annual* (editorial deadline February each year)—looking for articles 1,500+ words, plus photos on the subject of locating silver and/or gold using a metal detector. No fiction, poetry, or puzzles. **Buys 150+ mss/year.** Send complete ms by e-mail or mail (include SASE). Be sure you have read a current copy of our Freelancer's Guidelines before submitting any articles/photos. Simply request a copy via e-mail to: editor@wetreasures.com Thank you. Length: 1,000-2,000 words. **Pays 5¢/word.**

PHOTOS Our Freelancer's Guidelines also include specifics on how to submit photos. Send photos. Captions, identification of subjects required. Reviews digital scans (minimum 300 dpi) and original prints in certain cases. Offers $5/photo used in article and $100 for main cover photo paid on publication. Buys all rights.

HOME & GARDEN

THE AMERICAN GARDENER

American Horticultural Society, 7931 E. Boulevard Dr., Alexandria VA 22308-1300. (703)768-5700. **E-mail:** editor@ahsgardening.org. **Website:** www.ahsgardening.org. **Contact:** David Ellis, Editor. **60% freelance written.** Bimonthly, 64-page, four-color magazine covering gardening and horticulture. "This is the official publication of the American Horticultural Society (AHS), a national, nonprofit, membership organization for gardeners, founded in 1922. The AHS mission is 'to open the eyes of all Americans to the vital connection between people and plants, and to inspire all Americans to become responsible caretakers of the earth, to celebrate America's diversity through the art and science of horticulture, and to lead this effort by sharing the society's unique national resources with all Americans.' All articles are also published in the digital edition." Estab. 1922. Circ. 20,000. Byline given. Pays on publication. Offers 25% kill fee. Publishes ms an average of 6 months after acceptance. Editorial lead time 6 months. Submit seasonal material at least 1 year in advance. Accepts queries by mail, e-mail. Responds in 3 to 4 months to queries. Sample copy: $8. Writer's guidelines by e-mail and online.

○ "*The American Gardener* goes out bimonthly to about 20,000 members of the American Horticultural Society. *The American Gardener* is primarily freelance written, and its content differs considerably from that of other gardening publications. Articles are intended to bring this knowledgeable group new information, ranging from the latest scientific findings that affect plants, to the history of gardening and gardens in America. We introduce readers to unusual plants, personalities, and issues that will enrich what we assume is already a passionate commitment to gardening."

NONFICTION Needs general interest, how-to, photo feature, profile, reviews, travel. No personal essays about your garden. **Buys 20 mss/year.** Query with published clips. Length: 1,500-2,000 words. **Pays $300-600, depending on complexity and author's experience.**

REPRINTS Rarely purchases second rights. Send PDF file of article with information about when and where the material previously appeared. Payment varies.

PHOTOS E-mail or check website for guidelines before submitting. It is very important to include some kind of plant list for your stock so we can determine if you specialize in the types of plants we cover. The list does not have to be comprehensive, but it should give some idea of the breadth of your photo archive. If, for instance, your list contains mostly tulips, pansies, roses, and other popular plants like these, your stock will not be a good match for our articles. Also, if your list does not include the botanical names for all plants, we will not be able to use the photos. Identification of subjects required. Photo captions required; include

complete botanical names of plants including genus, species, and botanical variety or cultivar. Pays $350 maximum for color cover; $80-130 for color inside. Pays on publication. Credit line given. Buys one-time North American and nonexclusive rights. Buys one-time print rights, plus limited rights to run article on members-only website.

COLUMNS/DEPARTMENTS Natural Connections (explains a natural phenomenon—plant and pollinator relationships, plant and fungus relationships, parasites—that may be observed in nature or in the garden), 750-1,000 words; Homegrown Harvest (articles on edible plants delivered in a personal, reassuring voice. Each issue focuses on a single crop, such as carrots, blueberries, or parsley), 800-900 words; Plant in the Spotlight (profiles of a single plant species or cultivar, including a personal perspective on why it's a favored plant), 600 words. **Buys 5 mss/year.** Query with published clips. **Pays $100-250.**

TIPS "The majority of our readers are advanced, passionate amateur gardeners; about 20% are horticultural professionals. Most prefer not to use synthetic chemical pesticides."

ATLANTA HOME IMPROVEMENT

Network Communications, Inc. (NCI), 80 W. Wieuca Rd., Atlanta GA 30342. (404)303-9333. **Fax:** (404)303-0030. **E-mail:** jhallock@nci.com. **Website:** www.atlantahomeimprovement.com. **30% freelance written.** Monthly magazine covering home improvement in Atlanta, Georgia. Estab. 2001. Circ. 75,000. Byline given. Pays on acceptance. No kill fee. Publishes ms an average of 2 months after acceptance. Editorial lead time 3 months. Submit seasonal material 4-5 months in advance. Accepts queries by mail, e-mail. Accepts simultaneous submissions. Responds in 2 weeks to queries. Sample copy and guidelines free.

○ "Our audience is very local; magazine caters to Atlanta homeowners, so must have an Atlanta slant and include Atlanta home/garden businesses."

PHOTOS State availability of or send photos. Identification of subjects required. Reviews GIF/JPEG files. Buys one-time rights.

$$ ATLANTA HOMES AND LIFESTYLES

Esteem Media, 1117 Perimeter Center W., Suite N118, Atlanta GA 30338. (404)252-6670. **E-mail:** editor@atlantahomesmag.com. **Website:** www.atlantahomesmag.com. **Contact:** Elizabeth Ralls, editor in chief;

Elizabeth Anderson, art director. **65% freelance written.** Magazine published 12 times/year. *Atlanta Homes and Lifestyles* is designed for the action-oriented, well-educated reader who enjoys his or her shelter, its design and construction, its environment, and living and entertaining in it. Estab. 1983. Circ. 30,000. Byline given. Pays on publication. Publishes ms an average of 6 months after acceptance. Accepts queries by mail, fax. Accepts simultaneous submissions. Responds in 3 months to queries. Sample copy online.

NONFICTION Needs interview, new product. "We do not want articles outside the respective market area, not written for magazine format, or that are excessively controversial, investigative, or that cannot be appropriately illustrated with attractive photography." **Buys 35 mss/year.** Query with published clips. Length: 500-1,200 words. **Pays $100-500.** Sometimes pays expenses of writer on assignment.

PHOTOS Most photography is assigned. State availability. Captions, identification of subjects, model releases required. Reviews transparencies. Pays $40-50/photo. Buys one-time rights.

COLUMNS/DEPARTMENTS Pays $50-200.

TIPS "Query with specific new story ideas rather than previously published material."

🟢🟢🟢 BETTER HOMES AND GARDENS

1716 Locust St., Des Moines IA 50309. **Website:** www.bhg.com. **Contact:** Nancy Hopkins, deputy editor, Food and Entertaining; Oma Blaise Ford, senior deputy editor, Home Design; Elvin McDonald, deputy editor, Garden and Outdoor Living; Terry Michael, associate editor, Travel; Laura O'Neil, senior building and environmental editor; Christian Millman, health editor; Stephen George, deputy editor, Features; Brenda Lesch, creative director. **10-15% freelance written.** Magazine providing home service information for people who have a serious interest in their homes. *Better Homes and Gardens* is the vibrant, down-to-earth guide for the woman who is passionate about her home and garden and the life she creates there. Estab. 1922. Circ. 7,605,000. Pays on acceptance. Accepts queries by mail. Accepts simultaneous submissions.

NONFICTION Needs travel, education, gardening, health, cars, home, entertainment. Does not deal with political subjects or with areas not connected with the home, community, and family. No poetry or fiction. **Pay rates vary.**

TIPS "Most stories published by this magazine go through a lengthy process of development involving both editor and writer. Some editors will consider only query letters, not unsolicited manuscripts. Direct queries to the department that best suits your storyline."

BIRDS & BLOOMS

Reiman Media Group, 1610 N. 2nd St., Suite 102, Milwaukee WI 53212. (414)423-0100. **E-mail:** editors@birdsandblooms.com. **Website:** www.birdsandblooms.com. **15% freelance written.** Bimonthly magazine focusing on "the beauty in your own backyard." *Birds & Blooms* is a sharing magazine that lets backyard enthusiasts chat with each other by exchanging personal experiences. This makes *Birds & Blooms* more like a conversation than a magazine, as readers share tips and tricks on producing beautiful blooms and attracting feathered friends to their backyards. Estab. 1995. Circ. 1,900,000. Byline given. Pays on publication. No kill fee. Publishes ms an average of 7 months after acceptance. Editorial lead time 2 months. Submit seasonal material 4 months in advance. Accepts queries by mail. Accepts simultaneous submissions. Responds in 2 months to queries and mss. Sample copy: $2, plus 9x12 SAE and $1.95 postage. Guidelines online.

NONFICTION Needs essays, how-to, humor, inspirational, personal experience. No bird rescue or captive bird pieces. **Buys 12-20 mss/year.** Query or send complete ms, along with full name, daytime phone number, e-mail address, and mailing address. If submitting for a particular column, note that as well. Each reader contributor whose story, photo, or short item is published receives a *Birds & Blooms* tote bag. See guidelines online. Length: up to 1,000 words. **Pays $100-400.**

PHOTOS Send photos. Identification of subjects required. Reviews transparencies, prints. Buys one-time rights.

COLUMNS/DEPARTMENTS Bird Tales (birding experiences); Front Porch (gardening and birding tips and tricks, reader-created gardening, birding DIYs, etc.); From Your Backyard (more casual writing). **Buys 12-20 mss/year.** Send complete ms. **Pays $50-75.**

FILLERS Needs anecdotes, facts, gags. **Buys 25 mss/year.** Length: 10-250 words. **Pays $10-75.**

TIPS "Focus on conversational writing, like you're chatting with a neighbor over your fence. Mss full of tips and ideas that people can use in backyards across the country have the best chance of being used. Photos that illustrate these points also increase chances of being used."

COUNTRY LIVING

The Hearst Corp., 300 W. 57th St., 22nd Floor, New York NY 10019. (212)649-3501. **E-mail:** countryliving@hearst.com. **Website:** www.countryliving.com. **Contact:** Rachel Hardage Barrett, editor-in-chief; Amy Lower Mitchell, managing editor. Monthly magazine covering home design and interior decorating with an emphasis on country style. A lifestyle magazine for readers who appreciate the warmth and traditions associated with American home and family life. Each monthly issue embraces American country decorating and includes features on furniture, antiques, gardening, home building, real estate, cooking, entertaining and travel. Estab. 1978. Circ. 1,600,000. No kill fee. Accepts simultaneous submissions.

NONFICTION Buys 20-30 mss/year. Query to see if market is currently accepting submissions. Then, send complete ms and SASE. **Payment varies.**

COLUMNS/DEPARTMENTS Query first.

TIPS "Know the magazine, know the market, and know how to write a good story that will interest *our* readers."

EARLY AMERICAN LIFE

Firelands Media Group LLC, 16759 W Park Circle Dr, Chagrin Falls OH 44023 USA. 440-543-8566. **E-mail:** queries@firelandsmedia.com. **Website:** www.EarlyAmericanLife.com. **Contact:** Jeanmarie Andrews, executive editor. **60% freelance written.** Our readers are interested in our founding heritage including antiques, traditional crafts, architecture, restoration, collecting, and re-enacting. We are particularly interested in using antiques and crafts in decorating, restoring old homes and building replicas of period examples, judging and making handcrafts of the period (including how-to's), and experiencing period lifestyles, be it though military re-enacting, playing old games and sports, or cooking on a hearth. Early American Life is a bimonthly magazine for people who are interested in experiencing the warmth and beauty of the 1600-1840 period, using period style in their homes and lives today, re-enacting past events and how people lived, and visiting historic sites and museums. Estab. 1970. Circ. 90,000. Byline given. Pays on acceptance. 25% kill fee. Publishes ms an average of 1 year after acceptance. For upcoming events, submit material at least four months before the event. We are geared to the seasons, so we prepare a year ahead. Accepts queries by mail, e-mail. Responds within one week to queries. Sample copy for 9x12 SAE with $2.50 postage. Guidelines available online at: www.EarlyAmericanLife.com/editorial/guidelines.php.

Style book available online at: www.EarlyAmericanLife.com/editorial/stylebook.php.

NONFICTION Contact: Jeanmarie Andrews, executive editor. Needs book excerpts, historical, how-to, photo feature, travel, architecture and decorating, antiques, heritage studio crafts, historic destinations. Special issues: Christmas. No material outside our period (1600-1840). **Buys 40 mss/year.** Query. Length: 750-2,500 words. **Pays $250-700; additional payment for photos.**

PHOTOS 300 dpi at size to appear; Model releases required.

TIPS "Our readers are eager for ideas on how to bring early America into their lives. Conceive a new approach to satisfy their related interests in arts, crafts, travel to historic sites, and especially in houses decorated in the Early American style. Write to entertain and inform at the same time. We are visually oriented, so writers are asked to supply images or suggest sources for illustrations."

THE FAMILY HANDYMAN

Reader's Digest Association, 2915 Commers Dr., #700, Eagan MN 55121. **E-mail:** editors@thefamilyhandyman.com. **Website:** www.familyhandyman.com. *The Family Handyman* is an American home-improvement magazine. Estab. 1951. Circ. 1.1 million. Byline given. Pays on acceptance. Accepts queries by online submission form. Accepts simultaneous submissions.

NONFICTION Submit to *Family Handyman* via online submission form. Accepts mss for home projects that writers want to share. **Pays $100/ms.**

COLUMNS/DEPARTMENTS Accepts mss for Handy Hint, Great Goof, and Shop Tips. Accepts submissions online. **Pays $100/ms.**

⑤⑤⑤⑤ GOOD HOUSEKEEPING

Hearst Corporation, Article Submissions, 300 W. 57th St., 28th Floor, New York NY 10019. **Website:** www.goodhousekeeping.com. Monthly magazine covering women's interests. *Good Housekeeping* is edited for the new traditionalist. Articles which focus on food, fitness, beauty, and childcare draw upon the resources of the Good Housekeeping Institute. Editorial includes human interest stories, articles that focus on social issues, money management, health news, and travel. Circ. 4.3 million. Byline given. Pays on acceptance. Offers 25% kill fee. Submit seasonal material 6 months in advance. Accepts queries by mail. Accepts simultaneous submissions. Responds in 2-3 months to queries and mss. Call for a sample copy. Guidelines online.

NONFICTION Needs personal experience, travel. **Buys 4-6 mss/year.** Query by mail with published clips. Include SASE. Length: 500 words.

PHOTOS Photos purchased mostly on assignment. State availability. Model releases required. Pays $100-350 for b&w; $200-400 for color photos.

COLUMNS/DEPARTMENTS Blessings (about a person or event that proved to be a blessing), 500 words. Query by mail with published clips. Include SASE. **Pays $1/word.**

TIPS "Always send an SASE and clips. We prefer to see a query first. Do not send material on subjects already covered in house by the Good Housekeeping Institute—these include food, beauty, needlework, and crafts."

HGTV MAGAZINE

Hearst Corporation, 320 W. 57th St., 5th Floor, New York NY 10019. **E-mail:** hgtvmagazine@hearst.com. **Website:** hgtvmagonline.com. *HGTV Magazine* is a fresh home lifestyle magazine that gives readers inspiring, real-life solutions for all the things that homeowners deal with every day in an upbeat and engaging way. The magazine offers value of insider advice from trusted experts, as well as the enjoyment of taking a look inside real people's homes. Accepts queries by mail, e-mail. Accepts simultaneous submissions.

◒ Query before submitting. Difficult market to break into.

NONFICTION Query.

⑤⑤⑤⑤ HORTICULTURE

F+W, a Content + eCommerce Company, 10151 Carver Rd., Suite #200, Blue Ash OH 45242. (513)531-2690. **Fax:** (513)891-7153. **E-mail:** edit@hortmag.com. **Website:** www.hortmag.com. Bimonthly magazine. *Horticulture*, the country's oldest gardening magazine, is designed for active home gardeners. Our goal is to offer a blend of text, photographs and illustrations that will both instruct and inspire readers. Circ. 160,000.

Byline given. Offers kill fee. Submit seasonal material 10 months in advance. Accepts queries by mail, e-mail, fax. Accepts simultaneous submissions. Responds in 3 months to queries. Guidelines for SASE or by e-mail.

NONFICTION **Buys 70 mss/year.** Query with published clips, subject background material and SASE. Length: 800-1,000 words. **Pays $500.**

COLUMNS/DEPARTMENTS Length: 200-600 words. Query with published clips, subject background material and SASE. Include disk where possible. **Pays $250.**

TIPS "We believe every article must offer ideas or illustrate principles that our readers might apply on their own gardens. Our readers want to become better, more creative gardeners."

HOUSE BEAUTIFUL

The Hearst Corp., 300 W. 57th St., 27th Floor, New York NY 10019. **E-mail:** readerservices@housebeautiful.com. **Website:** www.housebeautiful.com. **Contact:** Jeffrey Bauman, executive managing editor. Monthly magazine covering home decoration and design. Targeted toward affluent, educated readers ages 30-40. Covers home design and decoration, gardening and entertaining, interior design, architecture, and travel. Circ. 865,352. No kill fee. Editorial lead time 3 months. Accepts simultaneous submissions.

◒ Query before submitting.

LOG HOME LIVING

Home Buyer Publications, Inc., 5720 Flatiron Parkway, Boulder CO 80301. (703)222-9411; (800)826-3893. **Fax:** (703)222-3209. **E-mail:** editor@timberhomeliving.com. **Website:** www.loghome.com. **90% freelance written.** Monthly magazine for enthusiasts who are dreaming of, planning for, or actively building a log home. Estab. 1989. Circ. 132,000. Byline given. Pays on acceptance. Offers $100 kill fee. Publishes ms an average of 6 months after acceptance. Editorial lead time 6 months. Submit seasonal material 6 months in advance. Accepts queries by mail, e-mail. Accepts simultaneous submissions. Responds in 6 weeks to queries. Sample copy for $4. Guidelines available online.

◒ Also publishes *Timber Home Living, Log Home Design Ideas* and *Building Systems.*

NONFICTION Needs personal experience, technical, travel. **Buys 60 mss/year.** Query with SASE. Length: 1,000-2,000 words. **Payment depends on length, nature of the work, and writer's expertise.**

CONSUMER MAGAZINES

REPRINTS Send tearsheet, photocopy or typed ms and information about when and where the material previously appeared.

PHOTOS State availability. Reviews contact sheets, 4x5 transparencies, 4x6 prints. Negotiates payment individually. Buys one-time rights.

TIPS "*Log Home Living* is devoted almost exclusively to modern manufactured and handcrafted kit log homes. Our interest in historical or nostalgic stories of very old log cabins, reconstructed log homes, or one-of-a-kind owner-built homes is secondary and should be queried first."

MIDWEST HOME

Greenspring Media, 706 S. Second Ave. S., Suite 1000, Minneapolis MN 55402. (612)371-5800. **Fax:** (612)371-5801. **E-mail:** clee@greenspring.com. **Website:** midwesthomemag.com. **Contact:** Chris Lee, editor. **50% freelance written.** "*Midwest Home* is an upscale shelter magazine showcasing innovative architecture, interesting interior design, and beautiful gardens of Minnesota. Estab. 1997. Circ. 50,000. Byline given. Pays on acceptance. Offers 20% kill fee. Accepts queries by e-mail. Accepts simultaneous submissions. Guidelines available online.

NONFICTION Needs book excerpts, how-to, interview, new product, photo feature, profile. Query with résumé and published clips. Length: 300-1,000 words. **Payment negotiable.**

TIPS "We are always looking for great new interior design, architecture, and gardens—in Minnesota and eastern Wisconsin.

💲💲 MOUNTAIN LIVING

Wiesner Media Network Communications, Inc., 1780 S. Bellaire St., Suite 505, Denver CO 80222. (303)248-2060. **Fax:** (303)248-2066. **E-mail:** greatideas@mountainliving.com; hscott@mountainliving.com; cdeorio@mountainliving.com. **Website:** www.mountainliving.com. **Contact:** Holly Scott, publisher; Christine DeOrio, editor-in-chief. **50% freelance written.** Magazine published 7 times/year covering architecture, interior design, and lifestyle issues for people who live in, visit, or hope to live in the mountains. Estab. 1994. Circ. 40,000. Byline given. Pays on acceptance. Offers 15% kill fee. Publishes ms an average of 4 months after acceptance. Editorial lead time 6 months. Submit seasonal material 8-12 months in advance. Responds in 6-8 weeks to queries. Responds in 2 months to mss. Sample copy for $7. Guidelines by e-mail.

NONFICTION Needs photo feature, travel, home features. **Buys 30 mss/year.** Query with published clips. Length: 200-600 words. **Pays $250-600.**

PHOTOS Provide photos (digital files only, saved as JPEG or TIFF and at least 300 dpi). State availability. All features photography is assigned to photographers who specialize in architectural and interior photography. Negotiates payment individually. Buys one-time rights, plus rights to run photo on website.

COLUMNS/DEPARTMENTS ML Recommends; Short Travel Tips; New Product Information; Art; Insider's Guide; Entertaining. Length: 150-400 words.

TIPS "*Mountain Living* is an image-driven magazine and selects its featured homes for their exceptional architecture and interior design. The editorial staff will not consider queries that are not accompanied by professional or scouting photos. Story angles are determined by the editorial staff and assigned to freelance writers. To be considered for freelance assignments, please send your résumé and 4 published clips. Before you query, please read the magazine to get a sense of who we are and what we do."

MARTHA STEWART LIVING

Omnimedia, 601 W. 26th St., New York NY 10001. (212)827-8000. **Fax:** (212)827-8204. **Website:** www.marthastewart.com. Monthly magazine for gardening, entertaining, renovating, cooking, collecting, and creating. Magazine, featuring Martha Stewart, that focuses on the domestic arts. Estab. 1990. Circ. 2.1 million. Accepts simultaneous submissions.

💬 Query before submitting. Difficult market to break into.

TEXAS GARDENER

Suntex Communications, Inc., P.O. Box 9005, Waco TX 76714. (254)848-9393. **Fax:** (254)848-9779. **E-mail:** info@texasgardener.com. **Website:** www.texasgardener.com. **Contact:** Chris Corby. **80% freelance written. Works with a small number of new/unpublished writers each year.** Bimonthly magazine covering vegetable and fruit production, ornamentals, and home landscape information for home gardeners in Texas. Estab. 1981. Circ. 20,000. Byline given. Pays on publication. No kill fee. Publisher pays at time of publication. Submit seasonal material 6 months in advance. Accepts queries by mail, e-mail, fax. Accepts simultaneous submissions. Responds in 2 months to queries. Sample copy for $6.00 (includes postage). Writers' guidelines available online at website.

NONFICTION Needs how-to, humor, interview, photo feature. **Buys 50-60 mss/year.** Query with published clips. Length: 800-2,400 words. **Pays $50-200.**

PHOTOS "We prefer superb color and b&w photos; 90% of photos used are color. Send low resolution jpgs files for review to info@texasgardener.com. High resolution jpg files are required for publication if photos are accepted." Send photos. Identification of subjects, model releases required. Digital images in either jpeg or tif format. Send low resolution images for review. High resolution images are required if photos are accepted. Pays negotiable rates.

COLUMNS/DEPARTMENTS Between Neighbors. See sample issue for style and content. **Buys 6 mss/ year. Pays $50.**

TIPS "First, be a Texan. Then come up with a good idea of interest to home gardeners in this state. Be specific. Stick to feature topics like 'How Alley Gardening Became a Texas Tradition.' Leave topics like 'How to Control Fire Blight' to the experts. High quality photos could make the difference. We would like to add several writers to our group of regular contributors and would make assignments on a regular basis. Fillers are easy to come up with in-house. We want good writers who can produce accurate and interesting copy. Frequent mistakes made by writers in completing an article assignment for us are that articles are not slanted toward Texas gardening, show inaccurate or too little gardening information, or lack good writing style."

THIS OLD HOUSE

Time Inc., 262 Harbor Drive, Stamford CT 06902. (475)209-8665. **Fax:** (212)522-9435. **E-mail:** toh_letters@thisoldhouse.com; scott@thisoldhouse.com. **Website:** www.thisoldhouse.com. **Contact:** Scott Omelianuk, editor. **40% freelance written.** Magazine published 10 times/year covering home design, renovation, and maintenance. "*This Old House* is the ultimate resource for readers whose homes are their passions. The magazine's mission is threefold: to inform with lively service journalism and reporting on innovative new products and materials, to inspire with beautiful examples of fine craftsmanship and elegant architectural design, and to instruct with clear step-by-step projects that will enhance a home or help a homeowner maintain one. The voice of the magazine is not that of a rarefied design maven or a linear Mr. Fix It but rather that of an eyes-wide-open, in-the-trenches homeowner who's eager for advice, tools, and techniques that'll help him realize his dream of a home." Estab. 1995. Circ. 960,000. Byline given. Pays on acceptance. Publishes ms an average of 3-6 months after acceptance. Editorial lead time 3-12 months. Submit seasonal material 1 year in advance. Accepts queries by mail, e-mail. Accepts simultaneous submissions.

NONFICTION Needs essays, how-to, new product. **Buys 70 mss/year.** Query with published clips. Length: 250-2,500 words. **Pays $1/word.**

COLUMNS/DEPARTMENTS Around the House (news, new products), 250 words. **Pays $1/word.**

TRADITIONAL HOME

Meredith Corp., 1716 Locust St., Des Moines IA 50309-3023. **E-mail:** traditionalhome@meredith.com. **Website:** www.traditionalhome.com. Magazine published 8 times/year. Features articles on building, renovating, and decorating homes in the traditional style. From home, garden, and green living to fashion, beauty, entertaining, and travel, *Traditional Home* is a celebration of quality, craftsmanship, authenticity, and family. Estab. 1989. Circ. 950,000. No kill fee. Editorial lead time 6 months. Accepts simultaneous submissions.

Query before submitting.

NONFICTION Query.

HUMOR

FUNNY TIMES

Funny Times, Inc., P.O. Box 18530, Cleveland Heights OH 44118. (216)371-8600. **Fax:** (216)371-8696. **E-mail:** info@funnytimes.com. **Website:** www.funnytimes.com. **Contact:** Ray Lesser and Susan Wolpert, editors. **50% freelance written.** Monthly tabloid for humor. "*Funny Times* is a monthly review of America's funniest cartoonists and writers. We are the *Reader's Digest* of modern American humor with a progressive/peace-oriented/environmental/politically activist slant." Estab. 1985. Circ. 65,000. Byline given. Pays on publication. Publishes ms an average of 3 months after acceptance. Editorial lead time 2 months. Accepts simultaneous submissions. Responds in 3 months to mss. Sample copy for $3 or 9x12 SAE with 3 first-class stamps ($1.61 postage). Guidelines available online.

NONFICTION Needs essays, humor, interview, opinion, personal experience. **Buys 60 mss/year.** Send complete ms. Length: 500-700 words. **Pays $60 minimum.**

COLUMNS/DEPARTMENTS Query with published clips.

FICTION Wants anything funny. Needs humorous. **Buys 6 mss/year.** Query with published clips. Length: 500-700 words. **Pays $50-150.**

TIPS "Send us a small packet (1-3 items) of only your very funniest stuff. If this makes us laugh, we'll be glad to ask for more. We particularly welcome previously published material that has been well received elsewhere."

INFLIGHT

💲💲 HORIZON EDITION MAGAZINE

Paradigm Communications Group, 2701 First Ave., Suite 250, Seattle WA 98121. (206)441-5871. **Fax:** (206)448-6939. **E-mail:** info@paradigmcg.com. **Website:** www.alaskaairlinesmagazine.com/horizonedition. **Contact:** Michele Andrus Dill, editor. **90% freelance written.** Monthly inflight magazine covering travel, business, and leisure in the Pacific Northwest. "*Horizon Edition Magazine* is the monthly in-flight magazine for Horizon Air, reaching more than 574,000 travelers in Washington, Oregon, Idaho, Montana, California, Nevada, Western Canada and Baja, Mexico, each month." Estab. 1990. Byline given. Pays on publication. Offers 33% kill fee. Publishes ms an average of 1 year after acceptance. Editorial lead time 6 months. Submit seasonal material 6 months in advance. Accepts queries by mail, fax. Accepts simultaneous submissions. Sample copy for 9x12 SASE. Guidelines available online.

NONFICTION Needs essays, general interest, historical, how-to, humor, interview, personal experience, photo feature, travel, business. Special issues: Meeting planners' guide, golf, gift guide. No material unrelated to the Pacific Northwest. **Buys approximately 36 mss/year.** Query with published clips. Length: 2,000-2,500 words. **Pays $250 minimum.**

PHOTOS State availability. Captions, identification of subjects, model releases required. Reviews transparencies, prints. Negotiates payment individually. Buys one-time rights.

COLUMNS/DEPARTMENTS Region (Northwest news/profiles), 200-500 words. **Buys 15 mss/year.** Query with published clips. **Pays $100 minimum.**

JUVENILE

💲 AQUILA

Studio 2 Willowfield Studios, 67a Willowfield Rd., Eastbourne BN22 8AP England. (44)(132)343-1313. **E-mail:** editor@aquila.co.uk. **Website:** www.aquila.co.uk. "*Aquila* is an educational magazine for readers ages 8-13 including factual articles (no pop/celebrity material), arts/crafts, and puzzles." Entire publication aimed at juvenile market. Estab. 1993. Circ. 40,000. Pays on publication. Accepts queries by mail, e-mail. Accepts simultaneous submissions. Sample copy: £5. Guidelines online.

NONFICTION Young Readers: animal, arts/crafts, concept, cooking, games/puzzles, health, history, how-to, interview/profile, math, nature/environment, science, sports. Middle Readers: animal, arts/crafts, concept, cooking, games/puzzles, health, history, interview/profile, math, nature/environment, science, sports. Query. Length: 600-800 words. **Pays £90.**

FICTION Young Readers: animal, contemporary, fantasy, folktales, health, history, humorous, multicultural, nature/environment, problem solving, religious, science fiction, sports, suspense/mystery. Middle Readers: animal, contemporary, fantasy, folktales, health, history, humorous, multicultural, nature/environment, problem solving, religious, romance, science fiction, sports, suspense/mystery. Length: 1,000-1,150 words. **Pays £90.**

TIPS "We only accept a high level of educational material for children ages 8-13 with a good standard of literacy and ability."

BOYS' LIFE

Boy Scouts of America, P.O. Box 152079, 1325 W. Walnut Hill Ln., Irving TX 75015. **Website:** www.boyslife.org. **Contact:** Paula Murphey, senior editor; Clay Swartz, associate editor. **75% freelance written. Prefers to work with published/established writers; works with small number of new/unpublished writers each year.** *Boys' Life* is a monthly 4-color general interest magazine for boys 7-18, most of whom are Cub Scouts, Boy Scouts, or Venturers. Estab. 1911. Circ. 1.1 million. Byline given. Pays on acceptance. Publishes ms approximately 1 year after acceptance.

Accepts queries by mail. Accepts simultaneous submissions. Responds to queries/mss in 2 months. Sample copy: $3.95 plus 9x12 SASE. Guidelines online.

NONFICTION scouting activities and general interests. **Buys 60 mss/year.** Query senior editor with SASE. No phone or e-mail queries. Length: 500-1,500 words. **Pay ranges from $400-1,500.**

PHOTOS Photo guidelines free with SASE. Pays $500 base editorial day rate against placement fees, plus expenses. **Pays on acceptance.** Buys one-time rights.

COLUMNS/DEPARTMENTS Science; Nature; Earth; Health; Sports; Space and Aviation; Cars; Computers; Entertainment; Pets; History; Music, all 600 words. Query associate editor. **Pays $100-400.**

TIPS "We strongly recommend reading at least 12 issues of the magazine before submitting queries. We are a good market for any writer willing to do the necessary homework. Write for a boy you know who is 12. Our readers demand punchy writing in relatively short, straightforward sentences. The editors demand well-reported articles that demonstrate high standards of journalism. We follow the *Associated Press* manual of style and usage. Learn and read our publications before submitting anything."

⑤ CADET QUEST MAGAZINE

Calvinist Cadet Corps, 1333 Alger St. SE, Grand Rapids MI 49507. (616)241-5616. **Fax:** (616)241-5558. **E-mail:** submissions@calvinistcadets.org. **Website:** www.calvinistcadets.org. **Contact:** Steve Bootsma, editor. Magazine published 7 times/year. *Cadet Quest Magazine* shows boys 9-14 how God is at work in their lives and in the world around them. Estab. 1958. Circ. 6,000. Byline given. Pays on acceptance. No kill fee. Publishes ms 4-11 months after acceptance. Accepts simultaneous submissions. Responds in 2 months to mss. Sample copy for 9x12 SASE and $1.45 postage. Guidelines online.

NONFICTION informational. Special issues: New themes list available online in January or for SASE. "Articles about Christian athletes, coaching tips, and developing Christian character through sports are appreciated. Photos of these sports or athletes are also welcomed. Be original in presenting these topics to boys. Articles about camping, nature, and survival should be practical—the 'how-to' approach is best. 'God in nature' articles, if done without being preachy, are appreciated." Send complete ms via postal mail or e-mail (in body of e-mail; no attachments). Length: up to 1,500 words. **Pays 5¢/word and 1 contributor's copy.**

REPRINTS For reprints, send typed ms with rights for sale noted or e-mail (in body of e-mail; no attachments). Payment varies.

PHOTOS Pays $5 each for photos purchased with ms.

COLUMNS/DEPARTMENTS Project/Hobby articles (simple projects boys 9-14 can do on their own, made with easily accessible materials; must provide clear, accurate instructions); Cartoons and Puzzles (wholesome and boy-oriented logic puzzles, crosswords, and hidden pictures).

TIPS "The best time to submit stories/articles is early in the year (January-April). Also remember readers are boys ages 9-14. Stories must reflect or add to the theme of the issue and be from a Christian perspective."

DIG INTO HISTORY

Cricket Media, Inc., 70 E. Lake Street, #800m, Chicago IL 60601. **E-mail:** dig@cricketmedia.com. **E-mail:** dig@cricketmedia.com. **Website:** www.cricketmedia.com. **Contact:** Rosalie F. Baker. *Dig into History* is a magazine on world history and archaeology for kids ages 10-14. Publishes engaging, accurate, educational stories about historical events and people. Its Let's Go Digging section includes articles on archaeological discoveries, as well as the people who discovered them and those who help to preserve them. Estab. 1999. Yes Pays after publication. Three to six months Accepts queries by mail, e-mail. Accepts simultaneous submissions. Sample copy available online. Guidelines available online.

○ Kids who love DIG are seriously curious and want to immerse themselves in the world of the past. They love the thrill of being transported to ancient times and want to know more about what people did then and why they did it. They are particularly fascinated by traces of long-ago peoples and cultures that have been digging in the dirt and in historical records—and how these traces offer insights into how people live and act today.

NONFICTION Special issues: Wants feature articles (in-depth nonfiction, plays, and biographies); supplemental nonfiction (subjects directly and indirectly related to the theme; editors want little-known information but encourage writers not to overlook the obvious); activities (crafts, recipes, woodworking, or any other interesting projects that can be done either by children alone or with adult supervision; sketches and description of how activity relates to theme should accompany queries). Query by e-mail with brief cover letter, one-page outline, bibliography. Length: 750-1000 words for feature articles; 250-500 words for supplemental nonfiction; up to 700 words for activities.

FICTION authentic historical and biographical fiction, adventure, and retold legends relating to the theme. Query by e-mail with brief cover letter, one-page outline, bibliography. Length: 750-1,000 words.

FILLERS Needs Puzzles and Games: crossword and other word puzzles using the vocabulary of the edition's theme; mazes and picture puzzles that relate to the theme. Please, no word finds. Query by e-mail with brief cover letter, one-page outline, bibliography.

TIPS "We are looking for writers who can communicate world history and archaeological concepts in a conversational, interesting, informative, and accurate style for kids. Always welcome if authors can suggest where photography can be located to support their articles."

◑◑ FACES

Cricket Media, Inc., **E-mail:** faces@cricketmedia.com. **Website:** www.cricketmedia.com. **90-100% freelance written.** "Published 9 times/year, *Faces* covers world culture for ages 9-14. It stands apart from other children's magazines by offering a solid look at 1 subject and stressing strong editorial content, color photographs throughout, and original illustrations. *Faces* offers an equal balance of feature articles and activities, as well as folktales and legends." Estab. 1984. Circ. 15,000. Byline given. Pays on publication. Offers 50% kill fee. Accepts simultaneous submissions. Sample copy available online. Guidelines available online.

NONFICTION Needs historical, interview, personal experience, photo feature, feature articles (in-depth nonfiction highlighting an aspect of the featured culture, interviews, and personal accounts), 700-800 words; supplemental nonfiction (subjects directly and indirectly related to the theme), 300-600 words. Special issues: See website for upcoming themes. **Buys 45-50 mss/year.** Query by e-mail with cover letter, one-page outline, bibliography. **Pays 20-25¢/word.**

FICTION Fiction accepted: retold legends, folktales, stories, and original plays from around the world, etc., relating to the theme. Needs ethnic. Query with cover letter, one-page outline, bibliography. **Pays 20-25¢/word.**

FILLERS Needs Puzzles and Games (word puzzles using the vocabulary of the edition's theme, mazes and picture puzzles that relate to the theme); Activities (crafts, games, recipes, projects, etc., which children can do either alone or with adult supervision; should be accompanied by sketches and description of how activity relates to theme), up to 700 words. No crossword puzzles. **Pays on an individual basis.**

TIPS "Writers are encouraged to study past issues of the magazine to become familiar with our style and content. Writers with anthropological and/or travel experience are particularly encouraged; *Faces* is about world cultures. All feature articles, recipes, and activities are freelance contributions."

THE FRIEND MAGAZINE

The Church of Jesus Christ of Latter-day Saints, 50 E. North Temple St., Salt Lake City UT 84150. (801)240-2210. **Fax:** (801)240-2270. **E-mail:** friend@ldschurch. org. **Website:** www.lds.org/friend. **Contact:** Paul B. Pieper, editor; Mark W. Robison, art director. Monthly magazine for 3-12 year olds. "The *Friend* is published by The Church of Jesus Christ of Latter-day Saints for boys and girls up to 3-12 years of age." Estab. 1971. Available online.

NONFICTION Needs historical, humor, inspirational.

FICTION Wants illustrated stories and "For Little Friends" stories. See guidelines online.

POETRY Pays $30 for poems.

FUN FOR KIDZ

P.O. Box 227, Bluffton OH 45817. 419-358-4610. **Website:** funforkidz.com. **Contact:** Marilyn Edwards, articles editor. "*Fun For Kidz* is an activity magazine that maintains the same wholesome values as the other publications. Each issue is also created around a theme. There is nothing in the magazine to make it out dated. *Fun For Kidz* offers creative activities for children with extra time on their hands." Estab. 2002. Byline given. Pays on acceptance. Accepts queries by mail. Accepts simultaneous submissions. Sample copy: $6 in U.S., $9 in Canada, and $12.25 internationally. Guidelines online.

NONFICTION picture-oriented material, young readers, middle readers: animal, arts/crafts, cooking, games/puzzles, history, hobbies, how-to, humorous, problem-solving, sports, carpentry projects. Submit complete ms with SASE, contact info, and notation of which upcoming theme your content should be considered for. Length: 300-750 words. **Pays minimum 5¢/word for articles; variable rate for games and projects, etc.**

TIPS "Our point of view is that every child deserves the right to be a child for a number of years before he or she becomes a young adult. As a result, *Fun for Kidz* looks for activities that deal with timeless topics, such as pets, nature, hobbies, science, games, sports, careers, simple cooking, and anything else likely to interest a child."

GIRLS' LIFE

3 S. Frederick St., Suite 806, Baltimore MD 21202. (410)426-9600. **Fax:** (866)793-1531. **E-mail:** writeforgl@girlslife.com. **Website:** www.girlslife.com. **Contact:** Karen Bokram, founding editor and publisher; Kelsey Haywood, senior editor; Chun Kim, art director. Bimonthly magazine covering girls ages 9-15. Estab. 1994. Circ. 2.16 million. Byline given. Pays on publication. Publishes an average of 3 months after acceptance. Editorial lead time 4 months. Submit seasonal material 5 months in advance. Accepts queries by mail, e-mail. Accepts simultaneous submissions. Responds in 1 month to queries. Sample copy for $5 or online. Guidelines available online.

NONFICTION Needs book excerpts, essays, general interest, how-to, humor, inspirational, interview, new product, travel. Special issues: Special issues: Back to School (August/September); Fall, Halloween (October/November); Holidays, Winter (December/January); Valentine's Day, Crushes (February/March); Spring, Mother's Day (April/May); and Summer, Father's Day (June/July). **Buys 40 mss/year.** Query by mail with published clips. Submit complete ms on spec only. "Features and articles should speak to young women ages 10-15 looking for new ideas about relationships, family, friends, school, etc. with fresh, savvy advice. Front-of-the-book columns and quizzes are a good place to start." Length: 700-2,000 words. **Pays $350/regular column; $500/feature.**

PHOTOS State availability. Captions, identification of subjects, model releases required. Reviews contact sheets, negatives, transparencies. Negotiates payment individually.

COLUMNS/DEPARTMENTS Buys 20 mss/year. Query with published clips. **Pays $150-450.**

FICTION "We accept short fiction. They should be stand-alone stories and are generally 2,500-3,500 words." Needs short stories.

TIPS "Send thought-out queries with published writing samples and detailed résumé. Have fresh ideas and a voice that speaks to our audience—not down to them. And check out a copy of the magazine or visit girlslife.com before submitting."

JACK AND JILL

U.S. Kids, P.O. Box 88928, Indianapolis IN 46208. (317)634-1100. **E-mail:** jackandjill@saturdayeveningpost.org. **Website:** www.uskidsmags.com. **50% freelance written.** Bimonthly magazine published for children ages 6-12. Jack and Jill is an award-winning magazine for children ages 6-12. It promotes the healthy educational and creative growth of children through interactive activities and articles. The pages are designed to spark a child's curiosity in a wide range of topics through articles, games, and activities. Inside you will find: current real-world topics in articles in stories; challenging puzzles and games; and interactive entertainment through experimental crafts and recipes. Estab. 1938. Circ. 40,000. Byline given. Pays on publication. Publishes ms an average of 8 months after acceptance. Submit seasonal material 8 months in advance. Accepts queries by mail. Accepts simultaneous submissions. Responds to mss in 3 months. Guidelines available online.

Please do not send artwork. We prefer to work with professional illustrators of our own choosing.

NONFICTION Buys 8-10 mss/year. Submit complete ms via postal mail; no e-mail submissions. Queries not accepted. We are especially interested in features or Q&As with regular kids (or groups of kids) in the Jack and Jill age group who are engaged in unusual, challenging, or interesting activities. No celebrity pieces, please. Length: up to 700 words. **Pays 25$ minimum.**

FICTION Submit complete ms via postal mail; no e-mail submissions. The tone of the stories should be fun and engaging. Stories should hook readers right from the get-go and pull them through the story. Humor is very important! Dialogue should be witty instead of just furthering the plot. The story should convey some kind of positive message. Possible themes could include self-reliance, being kind to others, appreciating other cultures, and so on. There are a million positive messages, so get creative! Kids can see preachy coming from a mile away, though, so please focus on telling a good story over teaching a lesson. The message—if there is one—should come organically from the story and not feel tacked on. **Buys 30-35 mss/year.** Length: 600-800 words. **Pays $25 minimum.**

POETRY Submit via postal mail; no e-mail submissions. Wants light-hearted poetry appropriate for the age group. Mss must be typewritten with poet's contact information in upper-right corner of each poem's page. SASE required. Length: up to 30 lines/poem. **Pays $25-50.**

FILLERS Needs puzzles, activities, games. In general, we prefer to use in-house generated material for this category but on occasion we do receive unique and fun puzzles, games, or activities through submissions. Please make sure you are submitting a truly unique activity for our consideration. **Pays $25-40.**

TIPS "We are constantly looking for new writers who can tell good stories with interesting slants—stories that are not full of outdated and time-worn expressions. We like to see stories about kids who are smart and capable but not sarcastic or smug. Problem-solving skills, personal responsibility, and integrity are good topics for us. Obtain current issues of the magazine and study them to determine our present needs and editorial style."

🌎🌎🌎🌎 NATIONAL GEOGRAPHIC KIDS

National Geographic Society, 1145 17th St. NW, Washington DC 20036. **E-mail:** ashaw@ngs.org. **E-mail:** michelle.tyler@natgeo.com. **Website:** www.kids.nationalgeographic.com. **Contact:** Michelle Tyler, editorial assistant. **70% freelance written.** Magazine published 10 times/year. "It's our mission to find fresh ways to entertain children while educating and exciting them about their world." Estab. 1975. Circ. 1.3 million. Byline given. Pays on acceptance. Offers 10% kill fee. Publishes ms an average of 6 months after acceptance. Editorial lead time 6+ months. Submit seasonal material 6+ months in advance. Accepts queries by mail. Accepts simultaneous submissions. Sample copy for #10 SASE. Guidelines online.

💬 "We do not want poetry, sports, fiction, or story ideas that are too young—our audience is between ages 6-14."

NONFICTION Needs general interest, humor, interview, technical. Query with published clips and résumé. Length: 100-1,000 words. **Pays $1/word for assigned articles.**

PHOTOS State availability. Captions, identification of subjects, model releases required. Reviews contact sheets, negatives, transparencies, prints. Negotiates payment individually.

COLUMNS/DEPARTMENTS Freelance columns: Amazing Animals (animal heroes, stories about animal rescues, interesting/funny animal tales), 100 words; Inside Scoop (fun, kid-friendly news items), 50-70 words. Query with published clips. **Pays $1/word.**

TIPS "Submit relevant clips. Writers must have demonstrated experience writing for kids. Read the magazine before submitting."

NATURE FRIEND MAGAZINE

4253 Woodcock Lane, Dayton VA 22821. (540)867-0764. **E-mail:** info@naturefriendmagazine.com; editor@naturefriendmagazine.com; photos@naturefriendmagazine.com. **Website:** www.naturefriendmagazine.com. **Contact:** Kevin Shank, editor. **80% freelance written.** Monthly children's magazine covering creation-based nature. *Nature Friend* includes stories, puzzles, science experiments, and nature experiments. All submissions need to honor God as creator. Estab. 1983. Circ. 8,000. Byline given. Pays on publication. No kill fee. Editorial lead time 4 months. Submit seasonal material 6 months in advance. Accepts simultaneous submissions. Responds in 6 months to mss. Sample copy: $5, postage paid. Guidelines available on website.

💬 Picture-oriented material and conversational material needed.

NONFICTION Needs how-to. No poetry, evolution, animals depicted in captivity, talking animal stories, or evolutionary material. **Buys 50 mss/year.** Send complete ms. Length: 250-900 words. **Pays 5¢/word.**

PHOTOS Send photos. Captions, identification of subjects required. Reviews prints. Offers $20-75/photo. Buys one-time rights.

COLUMNS/DEPARTMENTS Learning By Doing, 500-900 words. **Buys 12 mss/year.** Send complete ms.

FILLERS Needs Facts, puzzles, and short essays on something current in nature. **Buys 35 mss/year.** Length: 150-250 words. **5¢/word.**

TIPS "We want to bring joy and knowledge to children by opening the world of God's creation to them. We endeavor to create a sense of awe about nature's

Creator and a respect for His creation. We'd like to see more submissions on hands-on things to do with a nature theme (not collecting rocks or leaves—real stuff). Also looking for good stories that are accompanied by good photography."

🌕🌕 NEW MOON GIRLS

New Moon Girl Media, P.O. Box 161287, Duluth MN 55816. (218)728-5507. **Fax:** (218)728-0314. **Website:** www.newmoon.com. **25% freelance written.** Bimonthly magazine covering girls ages 8-14, edited by girls ages 8-14. "*New Moon Girls* is for every girl who wants her voice heard and her dreams taken seriously. *New Moon* celebrates girls, explores the passage from girl to woman, and builds healthy resistance to gender inequities. The *New Moon* girl is true to herself, and *New Moon Girls* helps her as she pursues her unique path in life, moving confidently into the world." Estab. 1992. Circ. 30,000. Byline given. Pays on publication. Publishes ms an average of 6 months after acceptance. Editorial lead time 6 months. Submit seasonal material 8 months in advance. Accepts queries by mail, e-mail, fax. Accepts simultaneous submissions. Responds in 2 months to mss. Sample copy: $7.50 or online. Guidelines available at website.

○ In general, all material should be pro-girl and feature girls and women as the primary focus.

NONFICTION Needs essays, general interest, humor, inspirational, interview, opinion, personal experience, photo feature, religious. No fashion, beauty, or dating. **Buys 20 mss/year.** Send complete ms by e-mail. Publishes nonfiction by adults in Herstory and Women's Work departments only. Length: 600 words. **Pays 6-12¢/word.**

PHOTOS State availability. Captions, identification of subjects required. Negotiates payment individually. Buys one-time rights.

COLUMNS/DEPARTMENTS Women's Work (profile of a woman and her job relating the the theme), 600 words; Herstory (historical woman relating to theme), 600 words. **Buys 10 mss/year.** Query. **Pays 6-12¢/word.**

FICTION Prefers girl-written material. All girl-centered. Needs adventure, fantasy, historical, humorous, slice-of-life vignettes. **Buys 6 mss/year.** Send complete ms by e-mail. Length: 900-1,600 words. **Pays 6-12¢/word.**

POETRY No poetry by adults.

TIPS "We'd like to see more girl-written feature articles that relate to a theme. These can be about anything the girl has done personally, or she can write about something she's studied. Please read *New Moon Girls* before submitting to get a sense of our style. Writers and artists who comprehend our goals have the best chance of publication. We love creative articles—both nonfiction and fiction—that are not condescending to our readers. Keep articles to suggested word lengths; avoid stereotypes. Refer to our guidelines and upcoming themes online."

ON COURSE

The General Council of the Assemblies of God, 1445 Boonville Ave., Springfield MO 65802-1894. (417)862-2781. **Fax:** (417)862-1693. **E-mail:** oncourse@ag.org. **Website:** www.oncourse.ag.org. **Contact:** Amber Weigand-Buckley, editor; Josh Carter, art director. *ONCOURSE* is a magazine to empower students to grow in a real-life relationship with Christ. Estab. 1991. Byline given. Pays on acceptance. Accepts simultaneous submissions. Sample copy free for 9x11 SASE. Guidelines on website.

○ *ONCOURSE* no longer uses illustrations, only photos. Works on assignment basis only. Résumés and writing samples will be considered for inclusion in Writer's File to receive story assignments.

NONFICTION "Submit an audition manuscript of less than 1,200 words. *ONCOURSE* evaluates manuscripts to determine if you, as a writer, fit our magazine. We will not print them—we do not purchase unsolicited articles. Article assignments go to writers listed in our Writer's File and focus on scheduled topics. If we approve you for our Writers File, we will also issue you a password for Writers Only, where we post these themes." **Pays $40 for columns, $80 for two-page features, $15 for sidebars/reviews, and $30 for Web-only features.**

FICTION Length: 800 words.

SHINE BRIGHTLY

GEMS Girls' Clubs, 1333 Alger St., SE, Grand Rapids MI 49507. (616)241-5616. **Fax:** (616)241-5558. **E-mail:** shinebrightly@gemsgc.org. **Website:** www.gemsgc.org. **Contact:** Kelli Gilmore, managing editor. **60% freelance written. Works with new and published/established writers.** Monthly magazine (with combined May/June/July/August summer issue). "Our purpose is to lead girls into a living relationship with

Jesus Christ and to help them see how God is at work in their lives and the world around them. Puzzles, crafts, stories, and articles for girls ages 9-14." Estab. 1970. Circ. 14,000. Byline given. Pays on publication. No kill fee. Publishes ms an average of 4 months after acceptance. Submit seasonal material 1 year in advance. Accepts simultaneous submissions. Responds in 2 months to mss. Sample copy with 9x12 SASE with 3 first class stamps and $1. Guidelines available online.

NONFICTION Needs humor, inspirational, interview, personal experience, photo feature, religious, travel. Avoid the testimony approach. **Buys 15 unsolicited mss/year.** Submit complete ms in body of e-mail. No attachments. Length: 100-800 words. **Pays up to $35, plus 2 copies.**

REPRINTS Send typed manuscript with rights for sale noted and information about when and where the material previously appeared.

PHOTOS Purchased with or without ms. Appreciate multicultural subjects. Reviews 5x7 or 8x10 clear color glossy prints. Pays $25-50 on publication.

COLUMNS/DEPARTMENTS How-to (crafts); puzzles and jokes; quizzes. Length: 200-400 words. Send complete ms. **Pay varies.**

FICTION Does not want "unrealistic stories and those with trite, easy endings. We are interested in manuscripts that show how real girls can change the world." Needs ethnic, historical, humorous, mystery, religious, slice-of-life vignettes. Believable only. Nothing too preachy. **Buys 30 mss/year.** Submit complete ms in body of e-mail. No attachments. Length: 700-900 words. **Pays up to $35, plus 2 copies.**

POETRY Needs free verse, haiku, light verse, traditional. **Limited need for poetry. Pays $5-15.**

TIPS Writers: "Please check our website before submitting. We have a specific style and theme that deals with how girls can impact the world. The stories should be current, deal with pre-adolescent problems and joys, and help girls see God at work in their lives through humor as well as problem-solving." Prefers not to see anything on the adult level, secular material, or violence. Writers frequently oversimplify the articles and often write with a Pollyanna attitude. An author should be able to see his/her writing style as exciting and appealing to girls ages 9-14. The style can be fun, but also teach a truth. Subjects should be current and important to *SHINE brightly* readers. Use our theme update as a guide. We would like to receive material with a multicultural slant."

SPARKLE

GEMS Girls' Clubs, 1333 Alger St. SE, Grand Rapids MI 49507. (616)241-5616. **Fax:** (616)241-5558. **E-mail:** sparkle@gemsgc.org. **Website:** www.gemsgc.org. **Contact:** Kelli Gilmore, managing editor; Lisa Hunter, art director/photo editor. **40% freelance written.** Monthly magazine for girls ages 6-9 from October to March. Mission is to prepare young girls to live out their faith and become world-changers. Strives to help girls make a difference in the world. Looks at the application of scripture to everyday life. Also strives to delight the reader and cause the reader to evalute her own life in light of the truth presented. Finally, attempts to teach practical life skills. Estab. 2002. Circ. 9,000. Byline given. Pays on publication. Editorial lead time 3 months. Submit seasonal material 1 year in advance. Accepts queries by e-mail. Accepts simultaneous submissions. Responds 3 months to mss. Sample copy for 9x13 SAE, 3 first-class stamps, and $1 for coverage/publication cost. Guidelines available for #10 SASE or online.

NONFICTION Contact: Kelli Gilmore. Young readers: animal, arts/crafts, biography, careers, cooking, concept, games/puzzles, geography, health, history, hobbies, how-to, humor, inspirational, interview/profile, math, multicultural, music/drama/art, nature/environment, personal experience, photo feature, problem-solving, quizzes, recipes, religious, science, social issues, sports, travel. Looking for inspirational biographies, stories from Zambia, and ideas on how to live a green lifestyle. Constant mention of God is not necessary if the moral tone of the story is positive. **Buys 10 mss/year.** Send complete ms. Length: 100-400 words. **Pays $35 maximum.**

PHOTOS Send photos. Identification of subjects required. Reviews at least 5X7 clear color glossy prints, GIF/JPEG files on CD. Offers $25-50/photo. Buys one-time rights.

COLUMNS/DEPARTMENTS Crafts; puzzles and jokes; quizzes, all 200-400 words. Send complete ms. **Payment varies.**

FICTION Young readers: adventure, animal, contemporary, ethnic/multicultural, fantasy, folktale, health, history, humorous, music and musicians, mystery, nature/environment, problem-solving, religious, recipes, service projects, slice-of-life, sports, suspense/mystery, vignettes, interacting with family and friends. **Buys 10 mss/year.** Send complete ms. Length: 100-400 words. **Pays $35 maximum.**

POETRY Prefers rhyming. "We do not wish to see anything that is too difficult for a first grader to read. We wish it to remain light. The style can be fun but should also teach a truth." No violence or secular material. Buys 4 poems/year. Submit maximum 4 poems.

FILLERS Needs facts, short humor. **Buys 6 mss/year.** Length: 50-150 words. **Pays $10-15.**

TIPS "Keep it simple. We are writing to first to third graders. It must be simple yet interesting. Mss should build girls up in Christian character but not be preachy. They are just learning about God and how He wants them to live. Mss should be delightful as well as educational and inspirational. Writers should keep stories simple but not write with a 'Pollyanna' attitude. Authors should see their writing style as exciting and appealing to girls ages 6-9. Subjects should be current and important to *Sparkle* readers. Use our theme as a guide. We would like to receive material with a multicultural slant."

STONE SOUP

The Magazine by Young Writers & Artists, Children's Art Foundation, P.O. Box 83, Santa Cruz CA 95063-0083. (831)426-5557. **E-mail:** editor@stonesoup.com. **Website:** https://stonesoup.com/. **Contact:** Ms. Gerry Mandel, editor. **100% freelance written.** Bimonthly magazine of writing and art by children age 13 and under, including fiction, poetry, book reviews, and art. *Stone Soup,* available in print and digital formats, is the national magazine of writing and art by kids, founded in 1973. The print edition is 48 pages, 7x10, professionally printed in color on heavy stock, saddle-stapled, with coated cover with full-color illustration. Receives 5,000 poetry submissions/year, accepts about 12. Press run is 12,000. Subscription: $38/year (U.S.). "We have a preference for writing and art based on real-life experiences; no formula stories or poems. We only publish writing by children ages 8 to 13. We do not publish writing by adults." Estab. 1973. Pays on publication. Publishes ms an average of 4 months after acceptance. Submit seasonal material 6 months in advance. View a PDF sample copy at www.stonesoup.com.

Purchase a single copy at www.stonesoupstore.com. Guidelines available at https://stonesoup.com/how-to-submit-writing-and-art-to-stone-soup/.

⭘ Print subscriptions include digital access, including more than 10 years of back issues at stonesoup.com.

NONFICTION Needs historical, humor, memoir, personal experience, reviews. **Buys 12 mss/year.** Submit complete ms; no SASE. **Pays $25, a certificate and 2 contributor's copies, plus discounts.**

FICTION Needs adventure, ethnic, experimental, fantasy, historical, humorous, mystery, science fiction, slice-of-life vignettes, suspense. "We do not like assignments or formula stories of any kind." **Buys 60 mss/year.** Send complete ms; no SASE. Length: 150-2,500 words. **Pays $25 for stories, a certificate and 2 contributor's copies, plus discounts.**

POETRY Needs avant-garde, free verse. Wants free verse poetry. Does not want rhyming poetry, haiku, or cinquain. Buys 12 poems/year. **Pays $25/poem, a certificate, and 2 contributor's copies, plus discounts.**

TIPS "All writing we publish is by young people ages 13 and under. We do not publish any writing by adults. We can't emphasize enough how important it is to read a couple of issues of the magazine. You can read stories and poems from past issues online. We have a strong preference for writing on subjects that mean a lot to the author. If you feel strongly about something that happened to you or something you observed, use that feeling as the basis for your story or poem. Stories should have good descriptions, realistic dialogue, and a point to make. In a poem, each word must be chosen carefully. Your poem should present a view of your subject, and a way of using words that are special and all your own."

LITERARY & LITTLE

💲 AGNI

Boston University, 236 Bay State Rd., Boston MA 02215. **E-mail:** agni@bu.edu. **Website:** www.agnimagazine.org. **Contact:** Sven Birkerts, editor. **90% freelance written.** Eclectic literary magazine publishing first-rate poems, essays, translations, and stories. Estab. 1972. Circ. 3,000 in print, plus more than 60,000 distinct readers online per year. Byline given. Pays on publication. Publishes ms an average of 6 months after acceptance. Accepts queries by online submission form. Accepts simultaneous submissions. Responds in 4 months to mss. No queries please. Sample copy: $10 or online. Guidelines online.

⭘ Reading period is September 1-May 31 only. Online magazine carries original content not found in print edition. All submissions are considered for both. Founding editor Askold Melnyczuk won the 2001 Nora Magid Award for Magazine Editing. Work from *AGNI* has been included and cited regularly in the *Pushcart Prize*, *O. Henry*, and *Best American* anthologies.

NONFICTION Contact: Nonfiction Editor. Needs essays, memoir, reviews. Literary only. "We do not publish journalism or academic work." **Buys 20+ mss/year.** Submit online or by regular mail, no more than one essay at a time. Emailed submissions will not be considered. Include a stamped addressed envelope or your email address if sending by mail. **Pays $20/page up to $300, plus a one-year subscription, and, for print publication, 2 contributor's copies and 4 gift copies.**

FICTION Contact: Fiction Editor. Needs short stories. No genre scifi, horror, mystery, or romance. **Buys 20+ mss/year.** Submit online or by regular mail, no more than 1 story at a time. E-mailed submissions will not be considered. Include a SASE or your e-mail address if sending by mail. **Pays $20/page up to $300, plus a one-year subscription, and, for print publication, 2 contributor's copies and 4 gift copies.**

POETRY Contact: Poetry Editor. Submit online or by regular mail, no more than 5 poems at a time. E-mailed submissions will not be considered. Include a SASE or your e-mail address if sending by mail. Buys 120+ poems/year. Submit maximum 5 poems. **Pays $20/page up to $300, plus a one-year subscription, and, for print publication, 2 contributor's copies and 4 gift copies.**

TIPS "We're also looking for extraordinary translations from little-translated languages. It is important to read work published in *AGNI* before submitting, to see if your own might be compatible."

ALITERATE

Genre, Ltd., P.O. Box 380020, Cambridge MA 02238. **E-mail:** editor@aliterate.org. **E-mail:** submissions@aliterate.org. **Website:** www.aliterate.org. *Aliterate* is a production of Genre, Ltd., a small nonprofit publisher based in Cambridge, Massachusetts. "Much has been said about the gulf between literary and genre literature. *Aliterate* seeks to publish works that span this divide, blending tight prose with the fantastical. *Aliterate* reads during March and April." Estab. 2016. Byline given. Accepts queries by e-mail. Accepts simultaneous submissions. "Our median time to reject

is 6 days, while our median acceptance time is about 70 days."

FICTION *Aliterate* is a publisher of literary genre fiction and publishes only science fiction, fantasy, Westerns, pulps, thrillers, horror, romance, etc. "We consider 'comedy' to be a fairly large genre; if you submit a comedy, please ensure it is also falls within another genre." Submissions should be of a 'literary' character, with an emphasis on character and language over clever plotting. Needs adventure, experimental, fantasy, historical, horror, humorous, mystery, romance, science fiction, short stories, suspense, western. Does not want poetry, inspirational, erotica, gore, polemics, fan fiction, or young adult. **Buys 16 mss/year.** Review is conducted by blind jury. Remove all identifying information from your submission. No need to include a cover letter; we'll solicit biographic information on acceptance. The subject line of your e-mail will be used to track your story in our review system. Submit only 1 ms in each reading period. Submission is open to all writers, apart from residents of Crimea, Cuba, Iran, North Korea, Sudan, and Syria. Length: 3,000-12,000 words. **Pays 6¢/word.**

TIPS "We've been asked for examples of authors who would fit the tone of *Aliterate*; they include Samuel Delany, Margaret Atwood, and Walter J. Miller Jr. While we love writers like Asimov, *Aliterate* doesn't aim to be a venue primarily for hard science fiction."

ALLEGORY

P.O. Box 2714, Cherry Hill NJ 08034. **E-mail:** submissions@allegoryezine.com. **Website:** www.allegoryezine.com. **Contact:** Ty Drago, publisher and managing editor. Biannual online magazine specializing in science fiction, fantasy, and horror. "We are an e-zine by writers for writers. Our articles focus on the art, craft, and business of writing. Our links and editorial policy all focus on the needs of fiction authors." Estab. 1998. Circ. *Allegory* receives upwards of 250,000 hits per year. Pays on publication for one-time, electronic rights. Publishes in May and November. Accepts simultaneous submissions. Responds in 2 months to mss. Guidelines available online.

○ *Allegory* (as Peridot Books) won the Page One Award for Literary Contribution.

NONFICTION Must be related to the craft or business of writing. Length: 1,500 words. **Pays $15/article.**
FICTION Receives 150 unsolicited mss/month. Accepts 12 mss/issue; 24 mss/year. Agented fiction 5%.

Publishes 10 new writers/year. Also publishes literary essays, literary criticism. Often comments on rejected mss. "No media tie-ins (*Star Trek*, *Star Wars*, etc., or space opera, vampires)." "All submissions should be sent by e-mail (no letters or telephone calls) in either text or RTF format. Please place 'Submission [Title]-[first and last name]' in the subject line. Include the following in both the body of the e-mail and the attachment: your name, name to use on the story (byline) if different, your preferred e-mail address, your mailing address, the story's title, and the story's word count." Length: 1,500-7,500 words; average length: 2,500 words. **Pays $15/story.**

TIPS "Give us something original, preferably with a twist. Avoid gratuitous sex or violence. Funny always scores points. Be clever and imaginative, but be able to tell a story with proper mood and characterization. Put your name and e-mail address in the body of the story. Read the site and get a feel for it before submitting."

THE AMERICAN POETRY REVIEW

The University of the Arts, 320 S. Broad St., Hamilton #313, Philadelphia PA 19102. **E-mail:** dbonanno@aprweb.org; escanlon@aprweb.org. **Website:** www.aprweb.org. **Contact:** Elizabeth Scanlon and David Bonanno, editors. "*The American Poetry Review* is dedicated to reaching a worldwide audience with a diverse array of the best contemporary poetry and literary prose. *APR* also aims to expand the audience interested in poetry and literature, and to provide authors, especially poets, with a far-reaching forum in which to present their work." Estab. 1972. Circ. 8,000-10,000. Accepts queries by mail, online submission form. Accepts simultaneous submissions. Responds in 6 months. Sample: $5. Guidelines online.

○ *APR* has included the work of over 1,500 writers, among whom there are 9 Nobel Prize laureates and 33 Pulitzer Prize winners.

NONFICTION Needs essays. Submit complete ms via online submissions manager.

POETRY Submit up to 5 poems via online submissions manager. Has published poetry by D.A. Powell, James Franco, Dean Faulwell, and Caroline Pittman. **Pays $1 per line.**

AMERICAN SHORT FICTION

Badgerdog Literary Publishing, P.O. Box 301209, Austin TX 78703. **E-mail:** editors@americanshortfiction.org. **Website:** www.americanshortfiction.org.

Contact: Rebecca Markovits and Adeena Reitberger, editors. "Issued triannually, *American Short Fiction* publishes work by emerging and established voices: stories that dive into the wreck, that stretch the reader between recognition and surprise, that conjure a particular world with delicate expertise—stories that take a different way home." Estab. 1991. Circ. 2,500. Byline given. Pays on publication. Publishes ms an average of 3 months after acceptance. Accepts queries by online submission form. Accepts simultaneous submissions. Responds in 2 weeks to queries; in 5 months to mss. "Sample copies are available for sale through our publisher's online store." Guidelines online.

○ Stories published by *American Short Fiction* are anthologized in *Best American Short Stories*, *Best American Non-Required Reading*, *The O. Henry Prize Stories*, *The Pushcart Prize: Best of the Small Presses*, and elsewhere.

FICTION "Open to publishing mystery or speculative fiction if we feel it has literary value." Does not want young adult or genre fiction. **Buys 20-25 mss/year.** *American Short Fiction* seeks "short fiction by some of the finest writers working in contemporary literature, whether they are established, new, or lesser-known authors." Also publishes stories under 2,000 words online. Submit 1 story at a time via online submissions manager ($3 fee). No paper submissions. Length: open. **Writers receive $250-500, 2 contributor's copies, free subscription to the magazine. Additional copies $5.**

TIPS "We publish fiction that speaks to us emotionally, uses evocative and precise language, and takes risks in subject matter and/or form. Try to read a few issues of *American Short Fiction* to get a sense of what we like. Also, to be concise is a great virtue."

ANCIENT PATHS

E-mail: skylarburris@yahoo.com. **Website:** www.editorskylar.com/magazine/table.html. **Contact:** Skylar H. Burris, editor. **100% freelance written.** *Ancient Paths* provides "a forum for quality spiritual poetry and short fiction. We consider works from writers of all religions, but poets and authors should be comfortable appearing in a predominantly Christian publication. Works published in *Ancient Paths* explore themes such as redemption, sin, forgiveness, doubt, faith, gratitude for the ordinary blessings of life, spiritual struggle, and spiritual growth. Please, no overly didactic works. Subtlety is preferred." Estab.

1998. Byline given. Pays on publication. Time between acceptance and publication is 1-4 months. Accepts queries by e-mail. Accepts simultaneous submissions. Responds in 8 weeks, usually sooner. Sample copy of printed back issue: $9. Purchase online. Guidelines available on website.

○ New issues of *Ancient Paths* are no longer being produced in print. *Ancient Paths Online* is published as a regularly updated Facebook page with a new poem or piece of flash fiction featured at least once per week. Please send seasonally themed works for Lent and Advent at least 1 month prior to the start of each season. Works on other themes may be sent at any time.

REPRINTS Buys reprints of short fiction and poetry at the regular rate of $1.25/piece.

PHOTOS "We accept submissions of photographs on Christian themes. Send as an attachment." Pays $1.25/published photo. Acquires electronic rights.

FICTION E-mail submissions only. Paste short fiction directly in the e-mail message. Use the subject heading "AP Online Submission (title of your work)." Include name and e-mail address at top of e-mail. Previously published works accepted, provided they are not currently available online. Please indicate if your work has been published elsewhere. Needs humorous, mainstream, novel excerpts, religious, short stories, slice-of-life vignettes, All fiction submissions should be under 2,000 words. Very short submission of under 800 words have a better chance of acceptance. Length: under 800 words preferred; up to 2,000 words. **Pays $1.25/work published. Published authors also receive discount code for $3 off 2 printed back issues.**

POETRY Needs formal verse or free verse on spiritual themes. E-mail all submissions. Paste poems in e-mail message. Use the subject heading "AP Online Submission (title of your work)." Include your name and e-mail address at the top of your e-mail. Poems may be rhymed, unrhymed, free verse, or formal and should have a spiritual theme, which may be explicit or implicit, but which should not be overly didactic. No "preachy" poetry; avoid inconsistent meter and forced rhyme; no stream-of-consciousness or avant-garde work; no esoteric academic poetry; no concrete (shape) poetry; no use of the lowercase *i* for the personal pronoun; do not center poetry. Buys 52 poems/year. Submit maximum 5 poems. Length: 8-60 lines.

Pays $1.25/poem. Published poets also receive discount code for $3 off 2 printed back issues.

TIPS "Read the great religious poets: John Donne, George Herbert, T.S. Eliot, Lord Tennyson. Remember not to preach. This is a literary magazine, not a pulpit. This does not mean you do not communicate morals or celebrate God. It means you are not overbearing or simplistic when you do so."

○ ● THE ANTIGONISH REVIEW

St. Francis Xavier University, P.O. Box 5000, 42 West St., Suite 217, Antigonish NS B2G 2W5 Canada. (902)867-3962. **Fax:** (902)867-5563. **E-mail:** tar@stfx. ca. **Website:** www.antigonishreview.com. **Contact:** Bonnie McIsaac, assistant editor. **100% freelance written.** Quarterly literary magazine for educated and creative readers. *The Antigonish Review*, published quarterly, tries "to produce the kind of literary and visual mosaic that the modern sensibility requires or would respond to." Estab. 1970. Circ. 850. Byline given. Pays on publication. Offers variable kill fee. Publishes ms an average of 8 months after acceptance. Editorial lead time 4 months. Submit seasonal material 8 months in advance. Accepts queries by mail, e-mail, fax, phone. Responds in 1 month to queries; 6 months to mss. Sample copy: $8. Guidelines for #10 SASE or online.

NONFICTION Needs essays, interview, memoir, reviews, book reviews/articles. No academic pieces. **Buys 15-20 mss/year.** Query. Length: 1,500-5,000 words **Pays $50 and 2 contributor's copies.**

FICTION Send complete ms. Accepts submissions by fax. Accepts electronic (disk compatible with WordPerfect/IBM and Windows) submissions. Prefers hard-copy submissions. Needs short stories. No erotica. **Buys 35-40 mss/year.** Send complete ms. Length: 500-5,000 words. **Pays $50 and 2 contributor's copies for stories.**

POETRY Open to poetry on any subject written from any point of view and in any form. However, writers should expect their work to be considered within the full context of old and new poetry in English and other languages. Has published poetry by Andy Wainwright, W.J. Keith, Michael Hulse, Jean McNeil, M. Travis Lane, and Douglas Lochhead. Buys 100-125 poems/year. Submit maximum 8 poems. Submit 6-8 poems at a time. A preferable submission would be 3-4 poems. Lines/poem: not over 80, i.e., 2 pages.

Pays $10/page to a maximum of $50 and 2 contributor's copies.

TIPS "Send for guidelines and/or sample copy. Send ms with cover letter and SASE with submission."

⊛ ANTIOCH REVIEW

P.O. Box 148, Yellow Springs OH 45387-0148. (937)769-1365. **E-mail:** cdunlevy@antiochreview.org. **Website:** www.antiochreview.org. **Contact:** Robert S. Fogarty, editor; Judith Hall, poetry editor. Quarterly magazine for general, literary, and academic audience. Literary and cultural review of contemporary issues and literature for general readership. *The Antioch Review* "is an independent quarterly of critical and creative thought. For well over 70 years, creative authors, poets, and thinkers have found a friendly reception—regardless of formal reputation. We get far more poetry than we can possibly accept, and the competition is keen. Here, where form and content are so inseparable and reaction is so personal, it is difficult to state requirements or limitations. Studying recent issues of *The Antioch Review* should be helpful." Estab. 1941. Circ. 3,000. Byline given. Pays on publication. Publishes ms an average of 10 months after acceptance. Accepts queries by mail. Accepts simultaneous submissions. Responds in 3-6 months to mss. Sample copy: $7. Guidelines online.

NONFICTION Nonfiction submissions are not accepted between June 1-August 31. Length: 2,000-8,000 words. **Pays $20/printed page, plus 2 contributor's copies.**

FICTION Quality fiction only, distinctive in style with fresh insights into the human condition. Needs experimental, contemporary. No science fiction, fantasy, or confessions. Send complete ms with SASE, preferably mailed flat. Fiction submissions are not accepted between June 1-August 31. Length: generally under 8,000 words. **Pays $20/printed page, plus 2 contributor's copies.**

POETRY Has published poetry by Richard Howard, Jacqueline Osherow, Alice Fulton, Richard Kenney, and others. Receives about 3,000 submissions/year. Submit 3-6 poems at a time. No previously published poems or simultaneous submissions. Include SASE with all submissions. No light or inspirational verse. Poetry submissions are not accepted between between May 1-September 1. Submit maximum 6 poems. **Pays $20/printed page, plus 2 contributor's copies.**

◐⊛ ARC POETRY MAGAZINE

Arc Poetry Society, P.O. Box 81060, Ottawa ON K1P 1B1 Canada. **E-mail:** managingeditor@arcpoetry.ca; coordinatingeditor@arcpoetry.ca; arc@arcpoetry.ca. **Website:** www.arcpoetry.ca. **Contact:** Monty Reid, managing editor; Chris Johnson, coordinating editor. Semiannual magazine featuring poetry, poetry-related articles, and criticism. *Arc*'s focus is poetry, and particularly Canadian poetry, although it also publishes writers from elsewhere. Looking for the best poetry from new and established writers. Often publishes special issues. Send a SASE for upcoming special issues and contests. Estab. 1978. Circ. 1,500. Byline given. Pays on publication. Publishes mss an average of 6 months after acceptance. Accepts queries by online submission form. Accepts simultaneous submissions. Responds in 4-6 months. Guidelines available online.

○ Only accepts submissions via online submissions manager. Include a brief biographical note with submission. Accepts unsolicited mss each year from October 15, 2016 to May 31, 2017.

NONFICTION Needs essays, interview, reviews, poetry book reviews. Query first. Length: 500-4,000 words. **Pays $50/printed page (Canadian), and 2 copies.**

PHOTOS **Contact:** Kevin Matthews, the Art Editor; art@arcpoetry.ca. Query first. Pays $50/page upon publication, $100 for art featured on the front cover (CDN). Buys one-time rights.

POETRY Needs Needs contemporary poetry. For over 30 years, *Arc* has been publishing the best in contemporary poetry. *Arc* invites submissions from emerging and established poets. Poets may only submit once each calendar year. Poetry submissions must not exceed 3 poems total. Submissions must be typed and single-spaced (double spaces will be interpreted as blank lines). Include your name, e-mail address, and mailing address on each page. Submit each poem in a separate document with bio. Your submission will be grouped in submission platform. Biographical statements should be 2-3 sentences or approximately 50 words. *Arc* can't promise to respond to inquiries regarding the status of submissions before the completion of an editorial cycle. Buys 60 poems/year. Submit maximum 3 poems. **Pays $50/printed page (Canadian).**

ARTS & LETTERS JOURNAL OF CONTEMPORARY CULTURE

Georgia College & State University, Milledgeville GA 31061. (478)445-1289. **Website:** al.gcsu.edu. **Contact:** Laura Newbern, editor; Abbie Lahmers, managing editor. *Arts & Letters Journal of Contemporary Culture*, published semiannually, is devoted to contemporary arts and literature, featuring ongoing series such as The World Poetry Translation Series and The Mentors Interview Series. Wants work of the highest literary and artistic quality. Estab. 1999. Pays on publication. No kill fee. Accepts simultaneous submissions. Responds in 2-4 months. Guidelines online at artsandletters.gcsu.edu/submit.

◐ Work published in *Arts & Letters Journal* has received the Pushcart Prize.

NONFICTION Submit complete ms via online submissions manager. Length: up to 25 pages typed and double-spaced. **Pays $10/printed page (minimum payment: $50) and 1 contributor's copy.**

FICTION Needs short stories. No genre fiction. Submit complete ms via online submissions manager. Length: up to 25 pages typed and double-spaced. **Pays $10/printed page (minimum payment: $50) and 1 contributor's copy.**

POETRY Submit via online submissions manager. Include cover letter. "Poems are screened, discussed by group of readers. If approved by group, poems are submitted to poetry editor for final approval." Has published poetry by Margaret Gibson, Marilyn Nelson, Stuart Lishan, R.T. Smith, Laurie Lamon, and Miller Williams. No light verse. Submit maximum 6 poems. **Pays $10/printed page (minimum payment: $50) and 1 contributor's copy.**

🅢 ART TIMES

P.O. Box 730, Mount Marion NY 12456. (845)246-6944. **Fax:** (845)246-6944. **E-mail:** info@arttimesjournal.com. **Website:** www.arttimesjournal.com. **Contact:** Raymond J. Steiner, editor. **80% freelance written.** "*Art Times*, now an online-only publication, covers the arts fields with essays about music, dance, theater, film, and art, and includes short fiction and poetry as well as editorials. Our readers are creatives looking for resources and people who appreciate good writing." Estab. 1984. Byline given. Pays on publication for short fiction and essays only. No kill fee. Publishes within 4 months Accepts queries by mail, e-

mail. Accepts simultaneous submissions. Responds in 3 months Guidelines online.

NONFICTION Needs essays, opinion. **Buys 12+ mss/year.** Send complete ms via mail or e-mail. Length: up to 1,000 words. **Pays $25, 6 contributor's copies, and one-year subscription.**

COLUMNS/DEPARTMENTS Open to linking appropriate blogs to arttimesjournal.com

FICTION Contact: Raymond J. Steiner. Looking for quality short fiction that aspires to be literary. Publishes up to 4 stories a month. Needs adventure, ethnic, fantasy, historical, humorous, mainstream, science fiction, contemporary. Nothing violent, sexist, erotic, juvenile, racist, romantic, political, off-beat, or related to sports or juvenile fiction. **Buys 25 mss/year.** Send complete ms. Length: up to 1,000 words. **Pays $25, 6 contributor's copies, and one-year subscription.**

POETRY Needs avant-garde, free verse, haiku, light verse, traditional. Send poems by mail or e-mail. Wants "poetry that strives to express genuine observation in unique language. All topics, all forms. We prefer well-crafted 'literary' poems. No excessively sentimental poetry." Publishes 2-3 poems each month. Nothing violent, sexist, erotic, juvenile, racist, romantic, political, off-beat, or related to sports or juvenile fiction. Buys 30-35 poems/year. Submit maximum 6 poems. Length: up to 20 lines. **Pays 5 contributor's copies and one-year subscription.**

TIPS "Competition is greater (more submissions received), but keep trying. We publish new as well as published writers. Be familiar with *Art Times* and its special audience."

THE BALTIMORE REVIEW

6514 Maplewood Rd., Baltimore MD 21212. **E-mail:** editor@baltimorereview.org. **Website:** www.baltimorereview.org. **Contact:** Barbara Westwood Diehl, senior editor. **100% freelance written.** *The Baltimore Review* publishes poetry, fiction, and creative nonfiction from Baltimore and beyond. Submission periods are August 1-November 30 and February 1-May 31. Estab. 1996. Byline given. Pays on publication No kill fee. Publishes ms 2-6 months after acceptance. Accepts simultaneous submissions. Responds in 4 months or less. Guidelines online.

NONFICTION creative nonfiction. Publishes 2-6 mss per online issue. Length: up to 5,000 words. **Pays $40.**

FICTION literary fiction. Send complete ms using online submission form. Publishes 16-20 mss (combination of poetry, fiction, and creative nonfiction) per online issue. Work published online is also published in annual anthology. Length: 100-5,000 words. **Pays $40.**

POETRY Needs avant-garde, free verse, traditional. Submit 1-3 poems. See editor preferences on submission guidelines on website. **Pays $40.**

TIPS "See editor preferences on staff page of website."

BARRELHOUSE

E-mail: yobarrelhouse@gmail.com. **Website:** www.barrelhousemag.com. **Contact:** Dave Housley, Joe Killiany, and Matt Perez, fiction editors; Tom McAllister, nonfiction editor; Dan Brady, poetry editor. *Barrelhouse* is a biannual print journal featuring fiction, poetry, interviews, and essays about music, art, and the detritus of popular culture. Estab. 2004. Byline given. No kill fee. Accepts queries by online submission form. Accepts simultaneous submissions. Responds in 2-3 months to mss.

> Stories originally published in *Barrelhouse* have been featured in *The Best American Nonrequired Reading, The Best American Science Fiction and Fantasy*, and the Million Writer's Award.

NONFICTION Needs essays. Submit via online submissions manager. DOC or RTF files only. Length: open, but prefers pieces under 8,000 words. **Pays $50 and 2 contributor copies.**

FICTION Needs experimental, humorous, mainstream. Submit complete ms via online submissions manager. DOC or RTF files only. Length: open, but prefers pieces under 8,000. **Pays $50 and 2 contributor copies.**

POETRY Submit up to 5 poems via online submissions manager. DOC or RTF files only. Submit maximum 5 poems. **Pays $50 and 2 contributor's copies.**

BEATDOM

Beatdom Books, 42/R Gowrie St., Dundee Scotland DD2 1AF United Kingdom. **E-mail:** editor@beatdom.com. **Website:** www.beatdom.com. **Contact:** David Wills, editor. **75% freelance written.** Beatdom is a Beat Generation-themed literary journal that publishes essays, short stories, and poems related to the Beats. "We publish studies of Beat texts, figures, and legends; we look at writers and movements related to the Beats; we support writers of the present who take their influ-

ence from the Beats." Estab. 2007. Circ. 1,000. Byline given. Pays on publication. No kill fee. Publishes ms 6 months after acceptance. Accepts queries by e-mail. Accepts simultaneous submissions.

NONFICTION Needs essays, interview, profile, reviews. **Buys 10 mss/year.** Query. Length: 1,000-5,000 words. **Pays $50.**

FICTION Submit complete ms via e-mail. Length: up to 5,000 words. **Pays $50.**

POETRY Needs "Poems should ideally fit the theme of the issue, or display some sort of connection to the Beat Generation."

BIG PULP

Exter Press, P.O. Box 92, Cumberland MD 21501. **E-mail:** editors@bigpulp.com. **Website:** www.bigpulp.com. **Contact:** Bill Olver, editor. Quarterly literary magazine. Submissions accepted by e-mail only. *Big Pulp* defines "pulp fiction" very broadly: It's lively, challenging, thought provoking, thrilling, and fun, regardless of how many or how few genre elements are packed in. It doesn't subscribe to the theory that genre fiction is disposable; a great deal of literary fiction could easily fall under one of their general categories. Places a higher value on character and story than genre elements. Estab. 2008. Byline given. Pays on publication. Offers 100% kill fee. Publishes ms 1 year after acceptance. Accepts queries by e-mail. Accepts simultaneous submissions. Responds in 2 months to mss. Sample copy: $10; excerpts available online at no cost. Guidelines online.

> "Submissions are only accepted during certain reading periods. Our website is updated to reflect when we are and are not reading, and what we are looking for."

FICTION Needs adventure, fantasy, horror, mystery, romance, science fiction, suspense, western, superhero. Does not want generic slice-of-life, memoirs, inspirational, political, pastoral odes. **Buys 70 mss/year.** Submit complete ms. Length: up to 2,500 words. **Pays $5-25.**

POETRY Needs avant-garde, free verse, haiku, light verse, traditional. All types of poetry are considered, but poems should have a genre connection. Buys 20 poems/year. Submit maximum 3 poems. **Pays $5/poem.**

TIPS "We like to be surprised, and we have few boundaries. Fantasy writers may focus on the mundane aspects of a fantastical creature's life or the magic that can happen in everyday life. Romances do not have to be requited or have happy endings, and the object of one's obsession may not be a person. Mysteries need not focus on 'whodunit?' We're always interested in science or speculative fiction focusing on societal issues, but writers should avoid being partisan or shrill. We also like fiction that crosses genre; for example, a science fiction romance or a fantasy crime story. We have an online archive for fiction and poetry and encourage writers to check it out. That said, *Big Pulp* has a strong editorial bias in favor of stories with monkeys. Especially talking monkeys."

🚱 BOMB MAGAZINE

80 Hanson Place, Ste. 703, Brooklyn NY 11217. (718)636-9100. **Fax:** (718)636-9200. **E-mail:** saul@bombsite.com. **Website:** www.bombmagazine.com. **Contact:** Saul Anton, senior editor. Quarterly magazine providing interviews between artists, writers, musicians, directors, and actors. "Written, edited, and produced by industry professionals and funded by those interested in the arts, *BOMB Magazine* publishes work which is unconventional and contains an edge, whether it be in style or subject matter." Estab. 1981. Circ. 36,000. Pays on publication. No kill fee. Publishes ms an average of 3-6 months after acceptance. Editorial lead time 3-4 months. Accepts queries by online submission form. Accepts simultaneous submissions. Responds in 3-5 months to mss. Sample copy: $10. Guidelines by e-mail.

FICTION experimental, novel concepts, contemporary. No genre fiction: romance, science fiction, horror, western. *BOMB Magazine* accepts unsolicited poetry and prose submissions for our literary supplement *First Proof* by online submission manager in January and August. Submissions sent outside these months will not be read. Submit complete ms via online submission manager. E-mailed submissions will not be considered. Length: up to 25 pages. **Pays $100 and contributor's copies.**

POETRY *BOMB Magazine* accepts unsolicited poetry and prose submissions for our literary supplement *First Proof* by online submission manager in January and August. Submissions sent outside these months will not be read. Submit 4-6 poems via online submission manager. E-mailed submissions will not be considered. **Pays $100 and contributor's copies.**

TIPS "Mss should be typed, double-spaced, and proofread, and should be final drafts. Purchase a sample issue before submitting work."

🚱🚱 BOULEVARD

Opojaz, Inc., 6614 Clayton Rd., Box 325, Richmond Heights MO 63117. **E-mail:** editors@boulevardmagazine.org. **Website:** www.boulevardmagazine.org; boulevard.submittable.com/submit. **Contact:** Jessica Rogen, editor. **100% freelance written.** "*Boulevard* is a diverse literary magazine presenting original creative work by well-known authors as well as by writers of exciting promise." Triannual magazine featuring fiction, poetry, and essays. Sometimes comments on rejected mss. *Boulevard* has been called "one of the half-dozen best literary journals" by Poet Laureate Daniel Hoffman in *The Philadelphia Inquirer*. "We strive to publish the finest in poetry, fiction, and nonfiction. We frequently publish writers with previous credits, and we are very interested in publishing less experienced or unpublished writers with exceptional promise. We've published everything from John Ashbery to Donald Hall to a wide variety of styles from new or lesser known poets. We're eclectic. We are interested in original, moving poetry written from the head as well as the heart. It can be about any topic." Estab. 1985. Circ. 11,000. Byline given. Pays on publication. Offers no kill fee. Publishes ms an average of 9 months after acceptance. Accepts queries by mail, e-mail, online submission form. Accepts simultaneous submissions. Responds in 2 weeks to queries; 4-5 months to mss. Sample copy: $10. Subscription: $19 for 3 issues, $29 for 6 issues, $42 for 9 issues. Foreign subscribers, please add $10. Make checks payable to Opojaz, Inc. Subscriptions are available online at www.boulevardmagazine.org/subscribe.html. Guidelines online.

NONFICTION Needs book excerpts, essays, interview, opinion, photo feature. **Buys 10 mss/year.** Submit by mail or Submittable. Accepts multiple submissions. Does not accept mss May 1-October 1. Include SASE for reply. Length: up to 8,000 words. **Pays $100-300.**

FICTION Submit by mail or Submittable. Accepts multiple submissions. Does not accept mss May 1-October 1. SASE for reply. Needs ethnic, experimental, mainstream, novel excerpts, short stories, slice-of-life vignettes. "We do not want erotica, science fiction, romance, western, horror, or children's stories." **Buys 20**

mss/year. Length: up to 8,000 words. **Pays $50-500 (sometimes higher) for accepted work.**

POETRY Needs avant-garde, free verse, haiku, traditional. Submit by mail or Submittable. Accepts multiple submissions. Does not accept poems May 1-October 1. SASE for reply. Does not consider book reviews. "Do not send us light verse." Does not want "poetry that is uninspired, formulaic, self-conscious, unoriginal, insipid." Buys 80 poems/year. Submit maximum 5 poems. Length: up to 200 lines/poem. **Pays $25-250.**

TIPS "Read the magazine first. The work *Boulevard* publishes is generally recognized as among the finest in the country. We continue to seek more good literary or cultural essays. Send only your best work."

☺❸❸ BRICK

Brick, P.O. Box 609, Station P, Toronto ON M5S 2Y4 Canada. **E-mail:** info@brickmag.com. **Website:** www.brickmag.com. **Contact:** Liz Johnston, managing editor. **90% freelance written.** Semiannual magazine covering literature and the arts. "We publish literary nonfiction of a very high quality on a range of arts and culture subjects." Estab. 1977. Circ. 3,000. Byline given. Pays on publication. No kill fee. Publishes ms 3-5 months after acceptance. Editorial lead time 5 months. Accepts simultaneous submissions. Responds in 6 months to mss. Sample copy: $16 plus shipping. Guidelines available online.

NONFICTION Needs essays, interview, opinion, travel. No fiction, poetry, personal memoir, or art. **Buys 30-40 mss/year.** Send complete ms. Length: 250-3,000 words. **Pays $75-500 (Canadian).**

PHOTOS State availability. Reviews transparencies, prints, TIFF/JPEG files. Offers $25-50/photo. Buys one-time rights.

TIPS "*Brick* is interested in polished work by writers who are widely read and in touch with contemporary culture. The magazine is serious but not fusty. We like to feel the writer's personality in the piece, too."

BURNSIDE REVIEW

P.O. Box 1782, Portland OR 97207. **Website:** www.burnsidereview.org. **Contact:** Sid Miller, founder and editor; Dan Kaplan, managing editor. *Burnside Review*, published every 9 months, prints "the best poetry and short fiction we can get our hands on. We tend to publish writing that finds beauty in truly unexpected places; that combines urban and natural imagery; that breaks the heart." Estab. 2004. Pays on publication. Publishes ms 9 months after acceptance.

Submit seasonal material 3-6 months in advance. Accepts queries by online submission form. Accepts simultaneous submissions. Responds in 1-6 months. Single copy: $8; subscription: $13.

○ *Burnside Review* is 80 pages, 6x6, professionally printed, perfect-bound. Charges a $3 submission fee to cover printing costs.

FICTION "We like bright, engaging fiction that works to surprise and captivate us." Needs experimental, short stories. Submit complete ms via online submissions manager. Length: up to 5,000 words. **Pays $25 and 1 contributor's copy.**

POETRY Needs avant-garde, free verse, traditional. Open to all forms. Translations are encouraged. "We like lyric. We like narrative. We like when the two merge. We like whiskey. We like hourglass figures. We like to be surprised. Surprise us." Has published poetry by Linda Bierds, Dorianne Laux, Ed Skoog, Campbell McGrath, Paul Guest, and Larissa Szporluk. Reads submissions year round. "Editors read all work submitted." Seldom comments on rejected work. Submit 3-5 poems via online submissions manager. **Pays $25 and 1 contributor's copy.**

○ THE CAPILANO REVIEW

102-281 Industrial Ave., Vancouver British Columbia V6A 2P2 Canada. **E-mail:** contact@thecapilanoreview.ca. **E-mail:** online through submittable. **Website:** www.thecapilanoreview.ca. **Contact:** Matea Kulic, managing editor. **100% freelance written.** Triannual visual and literary arts magazine that "publishes only what the editors consider to be the very best fiction, poetry, drama, or visual art being produced. *TCR* editors are interested in fresh, original work that stimulates and challenges readers. Over the years, the magazine has developed a reputation for pushing beyond the boundaries of traditional art and writing. We are interested in work that is new in concept and in execution." Estab. 1972. Circ. 800. Byline given. Pays on publication. Publishes work within 1 year after acceptance. Accepts queries by online submission form. Accepts simultaneous submissions. Responds in 4-6 months. Sample copy: $10 (outside of Canada, USD). Review our upcoming issues and submission guidelines on our website: https://www.thecapilanoreview.ca/submissions/.

○ We no longer accept submissions by mail. Please review our submission guidelines on our website and submit online through submittable.

NONFICTION Needs essays, interview, reviews.

PHOTOS Pays $50 for cover and $50/page to maximum of $200 Canadian. Additional payment for electronic rights; negotiable. Pays on publication. Credit line given. Buys first North American serial rights only.

FICTION Needs experimental, literary. No traditional, conventional fiction. Wants to see more innovative, genre-blurring work. **Buys 10-15 mss/year.** Length: up to 5,000 words. **Pays $50-150.**

POETRY Needs Experimental poetry. Submit up to 8 pages of poetry. Buys 40 poems/year. Submit maximum 8 poems. **Pays $50-150.**

💲💲 CHICKEN SOUP FOR THE SOUL PUBLISHING, LLC

Chicken Soup for the Soul Publishing, LLC, P.O. Box 700, Cos Cob CT 06807. **E-mail:** webmaster@chickensoupforthesoul.com (for all inquires). **Website:** www.chickensoup.com. **95% freelance written.** Paperback with 12 publications/year featuring inspirational, heartwarming, uplifting short stories. Estab. 1993. Circ. Over 200 titles; 100 million books in print. Byline given. Pays on publication. No kill fee. Accepts queries by online submission form. Accepts simultaneous submissions. Responds upon consideration. Guidelines available online.

💭 "Stories must be written in the first person."

NONFICTION No sermon, essay, eulogy, term paper, journal entry, political, or controversial issues. **Buys 1,000 mss/year.** Send complete ms. Length: 300-1,200 words. **Pays $200.**

POETRY Needs traditional. No controversial poetry.

TIPS "We no longer accept submissions by mail or fax. Stories and poems can only be submitted on our website. Select the 'Submit Your Story' tab on the left toolbar. The submission form can be found there."

💲 THE CINCINNATI REVIEW

P.O. Box 210069, Cincinnati OH 45221-0069. (513)556-3954. **Fax:** (513)556-3959. **E-mail:** editors@cincinnatireview.com. **Website:** www.cincinnatireview.com. **Contact:** Michael Griffith, fiction editor; Don Bogen, poetry editor; Kristen Iversen, nonfiction editor. **100% freelance written.** Semiannual magazine containing new literary fiction, creative nonfiction, poetry, book reviews, essays, and interviews. A journal devoted to publishing the best new literary fiction, creative nonfiction, and poetry, as well as book reviews, essays, and interviews. Estab. 2003. Byline given. Pays on publication. No kill fee. Publishes ms an average of 6 months after acceptance. Accepts queries by online submission form. Accepts simultaneous submissions. Responds in 4 months to mss. Always sends prepublication galleys. Sample copy: $7 (back issue). Single copy: $9 (current issue). Subscription: $15. Guidelines available on website.

💭 *The Cincinnati Review* is 180-200 pages, digest-sized, perfect-bound, with matte paperback cover with full-color art. Press run is 1,000. Reads submissions August 15-March 15.

NONFICTION Submit complete ms via online submissions manager only. Length: up to 40 double-spaced pages. **Pays $25/page.**

FICTION Needs short stories. Does not want genre fiction. **Buys 13 mss/year.** Submit complete ms via online submissions manager only. Length: up to 40 double-spaced pages. **Pays $25/page.**

POETRY Needs avant-garde, free verse, traditional. Submit up to 10 pages of poetry at a time via submission manager only. Buys 120 poems/year. **Pays $30/page.**

TIPS "Each issue includes a translation feature. For more information on translations, please see our website."

💲 COLORADO REVIEW

Center for Literary Publishing, Colorado State University, 9105 Campus Delivery, Fort Collins CO 80523. (970)491-5449. **E-mail:** creview@colostate.edu. **Website:** coloradoreview.colostate.edu. **Contact:** Stephanie G'Schwind, editor in chief and nonfiction editor; Steven Schwartz, fiction editor; Don Revell, Sasha Steensen, and Matthew Cooperman, poetry editors; Harrison Candelaria Fletcher, nonfiction editor; Dan Beachy-Quick, poetry book review editor; Jennifer Wisner Kelly, fiction and nonfiction book review editor. Literary magazine published 3 times/year. Estab. 1956. Circ. 1,000. Byline given. Pays on publication. No kill fee. Publishes ms an average of 6 months after acceptance. Editorial lead time 1 year. Accepts simultaneous submissions. Responds in 2 months to mss. Sample copy: $10. Guidelines online.

NONFICTION Needs essays, memoir, personal experience. **Buys 6-9 mss/year.** Mss for creative nonfiction are read year round. Send no more than 1 submission at a time. Length: up to 10,000 words. **Pays $200.**

FICTION Needs experimental, literary short fiction. No genre fiction. **Buys 12 mss/year.** Send complete ms. Fiction mss are read August 1-April 30. Mss received May 1-July 31 will be returned unread. Send no more than 1 story at a time. Length: up to 10,000 words. **Pays $200.**

POETRY Considers poetry of any style. Poetry mss are read August 1-April 30. Mss received May 1-July 31 will be returned unread. Has published poetry by Sherman Alexie, Laynie Browne, John Gallaher, Mathias Svalina, Craig Morgan Teicher, Pam Rehm, Elizabeth Robinson, Elizabeth Willis, and Rosmarie Waldrop. Buys 60-100 poems/year. Submit maximum 5 poems. **Pays $30 minimum or $10/page for poetry.**

CONFRONTATION

English Department, LIU Post, Brookville NY 11548. **E-mail:** confrontationmag@gmail.com. **Website:** www.confrontationmagazine.org. **Contact:** Jonna G. Semeiks, editor in chief; Belinda Kremer, poetry editor; Terry Kattleman, publicity director/production editor. **75% freelance written.** "*Confrontation* has been in continuous publication since 1968. Our taste and our magazine is eclectic, but we always look for excellence in style, an important theme, a memorable voice. We enjoy discovering and fostering new talent. Each issue contains work by both well-established and new writers. We read August 16-April 15. Do not send mss or e-mail submissions between April 16 and August 15." Estab. 1968. Circ. 2,000. Byline given. Pays on publication. Offers kill fee. Publishes work in the first or second issue after acceptance. Accepts queries by mail, e-mail. Accepts simultaneous submissions. Responds in 10 weeks to mss. "We prefer single submissions. Clear copy. **No e-mail submissions unless writer resides outside the U.S.** Mail submissions with a SASE."

NONFICTION Needs essays, personal experience. Special issues: "We publish personal, cultural, political, and other kinds of essays as well as self-contained sections of memoirs." **Buys 5-10 mss/year.** Send complete ms. Length: 1,500-5,000 words. **Pays $100-150; more for commissioned work.**

FICTION "We judge on quality of writing and thought or imagination, so we will accept genre fiction. However, it must have literary merit or must transcend or challenge genre." experimental as well

as more traditional fiction, self-contained novel excerpts, slice-of-life vignettes, lyrical or philosophical fiction. No "proselytizing" literature or conventional genre fiction. **Buys 10-15 mss/year.** Send complete ms. Length: up to 7,200 words. **Pays $175-250; more for commissioned work.**

POETRY Needs avant-garde or experimental as well as traditional poems (and forms), lyric poems, dramatic monologues, satiric or philosophical poems. In short, a wide range of verse. "*Confrontation* is interested in all poetic forms. Our only criterion is high literary merit. We think of our audience as an educated, lay group of intelligent readers." Has published poetry by David Ray, T. Alan Broughton, David Ignatow, Philip Appleman, Jane Mayhall, and Joseph Brodsky. Submit no more than 12 pages at a time (up to 6 poems). *Confrontation* also offers the annual Confrontation Poetry Prize. No sentimental verse. No previously published poems. Buys 20 poems/year. Length: up to 2 pages. **Pays $75-100; more for commissioned work.**

TIPS "We look for literary merit. Keep honing your skills, and keep trying."

CONTRARY

The Journal of Unpopular Discontent, P.O. Box 806363, Chicago IL 60616-3299. **E-mail:** chicago@contrarymagazine.com. **Website:** www.contrarymagazine.com. **Contact:** Jeff McMahon, editor; Frances Badgett, fiction editor; Shaindel Beers, poetry editor. **100% freelance written.** *Contrary* publishes fiction, poetry, and literary commentary, and prefers work that combines the virtues of all those categories. Founded at the University of Chicago, it now operates independently and not-for-profit on the South Side of Chicago. Quarterly. Member CLMP. Estab. 2003. Circ. 38,000. Byline given. Pays on publication and receipt of invoice. Publishes ms 90 days after acceptance. Editorial lead time 3 months. Accepts queries by online submission form. Accepts simultaneous submissions. Responds in 2 weeks to queries; 3 months to mss. Rarely comments on/critiques rejected mss. Guidelines available online.

"We like work that is not only contrary in content but contrary in its evasion of the expectations established by its genre. Our fiction defies traditional story form. For example, a story may bring us to closure without ever delivering an ending. We don't insist on the ending, but we do insist on the closure. And we value fiction as poetic as any poem."

NONFICTION Needs book excerpts, essays, general interest, humor, memoir, opinion, personal experience, reviews, lyrical, literary nonfiction. Does not publish expository or argumentative nonfiction. **Buys 4-6 mss/year.** Accepts submissions through website only: www.contrarymagazine.com/contrary/submissions.html. Include estimated word count, brief bio, list of publications.

FICTION Receives 650 mss/month. Accepts 6 mss/issue; 24 mss/year. Publishes 14 new writers/year. Has published Sherman Alexie, Andrew Coburn, Amy Reed, Clare Kirwan, Stephanie Johnson, Laurence Davies, and Edward McWhinney. Needs experimental, mainstream, religious, short stories, slice-of-life vignettes, literary. **Buys 8-12 mss/year.** Accepts submissions through website only: www.contrarymagazine.com/contrary/submissions.html. Include estimated word count, brief bio, list of publications. Length: up to 2,000 words. Average length: 750 words. Publishes short shorts. Average length of short shorts: 750 words. **Pays $20-60.**

POETRY Accepts submissions through website only: www.contrarymagazine.com/contrary/submissions.html. Include estimated word count, brief bio, list of publications. Often comments on rejected poems. Submit maximum 3 poems. **Pays $20 per byline, $60 for featured work.**

TIPS "Beautiful writing catches our eye first. If we realize we're in the presence of unanticipated meaning, that's what clinches the deal. Also, we're not fond of expository fiction. We prefer to be seduced by beauty, profundity, and mystery than to be presented with the obvious. We look for fiction that entrances, that stays the reader's finger above the mouse button. That is, in part, why we favor microfiction, flash fiction, and short shorts. Also, we hope writers will remember that most editors are looking for very particular species of work. We try to describe our particular species in our mission statement and our submission guidelines, but those descriptions don't always convey nuance. That's why many editors urge writers to read the publication itself, in the hope that they will intuit an understanding of its particularities. If you happen to write that particular species of work we favor, your submission may find a happy home with us. If you don't, it does not necessarily reflect on your quality or your ability.

It usually just means that your work has a happier home somewhere else."

COPPER NICKEL

E-mail: wayne.miller@ucdenver.edu. **Website:** copper-nickel.org. **Contact:** Wayne Miller, editor/managing editor; Brian Barker and Nicky Beer, poetry editors; Joanna Luloff, fiction and nonfiction editor; Teague Bohlen, fiction editor. *Copper Nickel*—the national literary journal housed at the University of Colorado Denver—was founded by poet Jake Adam York in 2002. When York died in 2012, the journal went on hiatus until its relaunch in 2014. Estab. 2002. Accepts queries by online submission form. Accepts simultaneous submissions. Responds in 2 months. Guidelines online.

NONFICTION Needs essays. Submit 1 essay at a time through online submissions manager. **Pays $30/printed page, 2 contributor's copies, and a one-year subscription.**

FICTION Submit 1 story or 3 pieces of flash fiction at a time through online submissions manager. **Pays $30/printed page, 2 contributor's copies, and a one-year subscription.**

POETRY Submit 5-10 poems through online submissions manager. **Pays $30/printed page, 2 contributor's copies, and a one-year subscription.**

CRAB ORCHARD REVIEW

Southern Illinois University Carbondale, Department of English, Faner Hall 2380, Mail Code 4503, 1000 Faner Dr., Carbondale IL 62901. (618)453-6833. **Fax:** (618)453-8224. **E-mail:** jtribble@siu.edu. **Website:** www.craborchardreview.siu.edu. **Contact:** Allison Joseph, editor in chief and poetry editor; Carolyn Alessio, prose editor; Jon Tribble, managing editor. "We are a general-interest literary journal published twice/year. We strive to be a journal that writers admire and readers enjoy. We publish fiction, poetry, creative nonfiction, fiction translations, interviews, and reviews." Estab. 1995. Circ. 2,500. No kill fee. Publishes ms an average of 9-12 months after acceptance. Accepts queries by online submission form. Accepts simultaneous submissions. Responds in 3 weeks to queries; 9 months to mss. Sample copy: $12.50. Guidelines online.

NONFICTION Needs essays. Submit through online submissions manager. Length: up to 25 pages double-spaced. **Pays $25/published magazine page**

($100 minimum), 2 contributor's copies, and one-year subscription.

FICTION Needs ethnic, novel excerpts. No science fiction, romance, western, horror, gothic, or children's. Wants more novel excerpts that also stand alone. Submit through online submissions manager. Length: up to 25 pages double-spaced. **Pays $25/published magazine page ($100 minimum), 2 contributor's copies, and one-year subscription.**

POETRY Wants all styles and forms from traditional to experimental. Does not want greeting card verse; literary poetry only. Has published poetry by Luisa A. Igloria, Erinn Batykefer, Jim Daniels, and Bryan Tso Jones. Submit through online submissions manager. Cover letter is preferred. "Indicate stanza breaks on poems of more than 1 page. Poems under serious consideration are discussed and decided on by the managing editor and poetry editor." **Pays $25/published magazine page ($100 minimum), 2 contributor's copies, and one-year subscription.**

CRAZYHORSE

College of Charleston, Department of English, 66 George St., Charleston SC 29424. (843)953-4470. **E-mail:** crazyhorse@cofc.edu. **Website:** crazyhorse.cofc.edu. **Contact:** Jonathan Bohr Heinen, managing editor; Emily Rosko, poetry editor; Anthony Varallo, fiction editor; Bret Lott, nonfiction editor. "We like to print a mix of writing regardless of its form, genre, school, or politics. We're especially on the lookout for original writing that doesn't fit the categories and that engages in the work of honest communication." Estab. 1960. Circ. 1,500. No kill fee. Publishes ms an average of 6-12 months after acceptance. Accepts queries by online submission form. Accepts simultaneous submissions. Responds in 1 week to queries; 3-4 months to mss. Sample copy: $5. Guidelines online.

Reads submissions September 1-May 31.

NONFICTION "*Crazyhorse* publishes 4-6 stories essays year, so we call for the very best writing, period. We believe literary nonfiction can take any form, from the letter to the list, from the biography to the memoir, from the journal to the obituary. All we call for is precision of word and vision, and that the truth of the matter be the flag of the day." Submit 1 essay through online submissions manager. Length: 2,500-8,500 words. **Pays $20/page ($200 maximum) and 2 contributor's copies.**

FICTION "We are open to all narrative styles and forms, and are always on the lookout for something we haven't seen before. Send a story we won't be able to forget." Submit 1 story through online submissions manager. **Buys 12-15 mss/year.** Length: 2,500-8,500 words. **Pays $20/page ($200 maximum) and 2 contributor's copies.**

POETRY "*Crazyhorse* aims to publish work that reflects the multiple poetries of the 21st century. While our taste represents a wide range of aesthetics, from poets at all stages of their writing careers, we read with a discerning eye for poems that demonstrate a rhetorical and formal intelligence—that is, poems that know why they are written in the manner that they are. We seek poems that exhibit how content works symbiotically with form, evidenced in an intentional art of the poetic line or in poems that employ or stretch lyric modes. Along with this, poems that capture our attention enact the lyric utterance through musical textures, tone of voice, vivid language, reticence, and skillful syntax. For us, overall, the best poems do not idly tell the reader how to feel or think, they engender feeling and thought in the reader. " Submit 3-5 poems at a time through online submissions manager. Buys 80 poems/year. Submit maximum 5 poems. **Pays $20/page ($200 maximum) and 2 contributor's copies.**

TIPS "Write to explore subjects you care about. The subject should be one in which something is at stake. Before sending, ask, 'What's reckoned with that's important for other people to read?'"

CREATIVE NONFICTION

Creative Nonfiction Foundation, 5119 Coral Street, Pittsburgh PA 15224. (412) 404-2975. **Fax:** (412) 345-3767. **E-mail:** information@creativenonfiction.org. **Website:** www.creativenonfiction.org. **100% freelance written.** Magazine published 4 times/year covering nonfiction—personal essay, memoir, literary journalism. *Creative Nonfiction* is the voice of the genre. It publishes personal essays, memoirs, and literary journalism on a broad range of subjects. Interviews with prominent writers, reviews, and commentary about the genre also appear in its pages. Estab. 1993. Circ. 7,000. Byline given. Pays on publication. No kill fee. Publishes ms an average of 1 year after acceptance. Editorial lead time 6 months. Accepts queries by mail, online submission form. Accepts simultaneous submissions. Responds in 6 months to mss. Sample copy: $10. Guidelines online.

NONFICTION Needs essays, interview, memoir, personal experience, narrative journalism. No poetry or fiction. Send complete ms. Length: up to 4,000 words. **Pays $50, plus $10/page—sometimes more for theme issues.**

COLUMNS/DEPARTMENTS Contact: Hattie Fletcher. "Have an idea for a literary timeline? An opinion on essential texts for readers and/or writers? An in-depth, working knowledge of a specific type of nonfiction? Pitch us your ideas." Complete guidelines found at www.creativenonfiction.org/submissions/pitch-us-column.

TIPS "Points to remember when submitting to *Creative Nonfiction*: strong reportage; well-written prose, attentive to language, rich with detail and distinctive voice; an informational quality or 'teaching element'; a compelling, focused, sustained narrative that's well-structured and conveys meaning. Mss will not be accepted via fax or e-mail."

CRUCIBLE

Barton College, P.O. Box 5000, Wilson NC 27893. **E-mail:** crucible@barton.edu. **Website:** www.barton.edu/crucible. *Crucible*, published annually in the fall, publishes poetry and fiction as part of its Poetry and Fiction Contest run each year. Deadline for submissions is May 1. Estab. 1964. Circ. 500. Accepts queries by e-mail. Accepts simultaneous submissions. Notifies winners by October each year. Sample: $8. Guidelines online.

    Crucible is under 100 pages, digest-sized, professionally printed on high-quality paper, with matte card cover. Press run is 500.

FICTION Needs ethnic. Submit ms by e-mail. Do not include name on ms. Include separate bio. Length: up to 8,000 words. **Pays $150 for first prize, $100 for second prize, contributor's copies.**

POETRY Submit "poetry that demonstrates originality and integrity of craftsmanship as well as thought. Traditional metrical and rhyming poems are difficult to bring off in modern poetry. The best poetry is written out of deeply felt experience which has been crafted into pleasing form." Wants "free verse with attention paid particularly to image, line, stanza, and voice." Does not want "very long narratives, poetry that is forced." Has published poetry by Robert Grey, R.T. Smith, and Anthony S. Abbott. Submit up to 5 poems by e-mail. Do not include name on poems. Include separate bio. **Pays $150 for first prize, $100 for second prize, contributor's copies.**

THE DARK

Prime Books, P.O. Box 1152, Germantown MD 20875. **E-mail:** thedarkmagazine@gmail.com. **Website:** www.thedarkmagazine.com. **Contact:** Silvia Moreno-Garcia and Sean Wallace, editors. **100% freelance written.** Monthly electronic magazine publishing horror and dark fantasy. Estab. 2013. Byline given. Pays on acceptance. No kill fee. Publishes ms an average of 3 months after acceptance. Editorial lead time 1 month. Accepts queries by e-mail. Responds in 1-2 weeks to mss. Always sends prepublication galleys. Sample: $2.99 (back issue). Guidelines available on website.

REPRINTS See submission guidelines. Pays 1¢/word.

FICTION Needs fantasy, horror, suspense, strange, magic realism, dark fantasy. "Don't be afraid to experiment or to deviate from the ordinary; be different—try us with fiction that may fall out of 'regular' categories. However, it is also important to understand that despite the name, *The Dark* is not a market for graphic, violent horror." **Buys 24 mss/year.** Send complete ms by e-mail attached in Microsoft Word DOC only. No multiple submissions. Length: 2,000-6,000 words. **Pays 3¢/word.**

TIPS "All fiction must have a dark, surreal, fantastical bend to it. It should be out of the ordinary and/or experimental. Can also be contemporary."

DECEMBER

A Literary Legacy Since 1958, December Publishing, P.O. Box 16130, St. Louis MO 63105-0830. (314)301-9980. **E-mail:** editor@decembermag.org. **Website:** decembermag.org. **Contact:** Gianna Jacobson, editor; Jennifer Goldring, managing editor. Committed to distributing the work of emerging writers and artists, and celebrating more seasoned voices through a semi-annual nonprofit literary magazine featuring fiction, poetry, creative nonfiction, and visual art. Estab. 1958. Circ. 1500. Byline given. Pays on publication. Editorial lead time 5 months. Accepts queries by mail, e-mail. Responds in 2 months to mss. Sample copy: $12. Guidelines available online.

NONFICTION Needs essays, general interest, humor, memoir, opinion, personal experience, literary journalism. Not interested in straight journalism (news or features). **Buys 4-10 mss/year.** Submit complete ms. Length: 25-6,000 words. **Pays $10/page (minimum $40; maximum $200).**

PHOTOS Photo and art submissions accepted. Send photos with submission. Reviews GIF/JPEG files. Negotiates payment individually. Purchases one-time rights on photos.

FICTION Needs experimental, humorous, novel excerpts, short stories, slice-of-life vignettes, literary fiction, flash fiction. Does not want genre fiction. **Buys 10-20 mss/year.** Send complete ms. Length: up to 10,000 words. **Pays $10/page (minimum $40; maximum $200).**

POETRY Needs avant-garde, free verse, traditional. Buys 100-150 poems/year. Submit maximum 5 poems. No length requirements. **Pays $10/page (minimum $40; maximum $200).**

DUCTS

P.O. Box 3203, Grand Central Station, New York NY 10163. **E-mail:** vents@ducts.org. **Website:** www.ducts.org. **Contact:** Mary Cool, editor in chief; Tim Tomlinson, fiction editor; Lisa Kirchner, memoir editor; Amy Lemmon, poetry editor; Jacqueline Bishop, art editor. *Ducts* is a semiannual webzine of personal stories, fiction, essays, memoirs, poetry, humor, profiles, reviews, and art. "*Ducts* was founded in 1999 with the intent of giving emerging writers a venue to regularly publish their compelling, personal stories. The site has been expanded to include art and creative works of all genres. We believe that these genres must and do overlap. *Ducts* publishes the best, most compelling stories, and we hope to attract readers who are drawn to work that rises above." Estab. 1999. Circ. 12,000. Pays on publication. Accepts queries by e-mail. Accepts simultaneous submissions. Responds in 1-6 months. Guidelines available on website.

NONFICTION Needs essays, humor, memoir, profile. For essays: "We welcome new and established writers, fresh voices, and original perspectives on both common and uncommon topics. We do not publish research articles; however, we consider for publication essays that include research, as long as this research is connected to a personal narrative." For humor: "Both satire and humorous fiction pieces will be accepted." For memoir: "Please read through some issues to get an idea of what we like. Generally speaking, we're looking for a fresh take on personal experiences. We like quirky, edgy, witty, and smart. Also the heartfelt and moving. But mostly we like great

writing." Submit by e-mail; see online guidelines for appropriate e-mail address. Length: up to 3,000 words for essays; 900-2,000 words for memoirs; 1,000-4,000 words for humor. **Pays $20.**

FICTION Needs experimental, mainstream, short stories. No novel excerpts. Submit by e-mail to julie@ducts.org. **Pays $20.**

POETRY Needs all forms and types. Submit 3-5 poems to poetry@ducts.org. Reads poetry January 1-August 31. **Pays $20.**

TIPS "We prefer writing that tells a compelling story with a strong narrative drive."

⑤ ELLIPSIS

Westminster College, 1840 S. 1300 E., Salt Lake City UT 84105. (801)832-2321. **E-mail:** ellipsis@westminstercollege.edu. **Website:** ellipsis.westminstercollege.edu. *Ellipsis*, published annually in April, needs good literary poetry, fiction, essays, plays, and visual art. Estab. 1965. Byline given. Pays on publication. No kill fee. Publishes ms an average of 3 months after acceptance. Accepts queries by online submission form. Accepts simultaneous submissions. Responds in 6 months to mss. Sample copy: $7.50. Guidelines available online.

○ Reads submissions August 1-November 1. Staff changes each year; check website for an updated list of editors. *Ellipsis* is 120 pages, digest-sized, perfect-bound, with color cover. Accepts about 5% of submissions received. Press run is 2,000; most distributed free through college.

NONFICTION Needs essays, creative nonfiction. Submit complete ms via online submissions manager. Include cover letter. **Pays $50 and 2 contributor's copies.**

FICTION literary fiction, plays. Submit complete ms via online submissions manager. Include cover letter. Length: up to 6,000 words. **Pays $50 and 2 contributor's copies.**

POETRY Submit poems via online submissions manager. Include cover letter. Has published poetry by Allison Joseph, Molly McQuade, Virgil Suaárez, Maurice Kilwein-Guevara, Richard Cecil, and Ron Carlson. Submit maximum 5 poems. **Pays $10/poem and 2 contributor's copies.**

○⑤⑤ EVENT

Douglas College, P.O. Box 2503, New Westminster British Columbia V3L 5B2 Canada. (604)527-5293. **Fax:** (604)527-5095. **E-mail:** event@douglascollege.

ca. **Website:** www.eventmags.com. **100% freelance written.** Magazine published 3 times/year containing fiction, poetry, creative nonfiction, notes on writing, and reviews. "We are eclectic and always open to content that invites involvement. Generally, we like strong narrative." Estab. 1971. Circ. 1,000. Byline given. Pays on publication. Publishes ms an average of 8 months after acceptance. Accepts queries by mail. Accepts simultaneous submissions. Responds in 1 month to queries. Responds in 6 months to mss. Guidelines available online.

○ *EVENT* does not read mss in July, August, December, and January. No e-mail submissions. All submissions must include SASE (Canadian postage, or IRCs, or USD $1).

FICTION "We look for readability, style, and writing that invites involvement." Submit maximum 2 stories. contemporary. No technically poor or unoriginal pieces. **Buys 12-15 mss/year.** Send complete ms. Length: 5,000 words maximum. **Pays $25/page up to $500.**

POETRY Needs free verse. "We tend to appreciate the narrative and sometimes the confessional modes." No light verse. Buys 30-40 poems/year. Submit maximum 10 poems. **Pays $25-500.**

TIPS "Write well and read some past issues of *EVENT*."

○ **THE FIDDLEHEAD**

University of New Brunswick, Campus House, 11 Garland Court, Box 4400, Fredericton NB E3B 5A3 Canada. (506)453-3501. **Fax:** (506)453-5069. **E-mail:** fiddlehd@unb.ca. **Website:** www.thefiddlehead.ca. **Contact:** Kathryn Taglia, managing editor; Ross Leckie, editor; Mark Anthony Jarman and Gerard Beirne, fiction editors; Phillip Crymble, Ian LeTourneau, and Rebecca Salazar, poetry editors; Sabine Campbell and Ross Leckie, reviews editors. "Canada's longest living literary journal, *The Fiddlehead* is published 4 times/year at the University of New Brunswick, with the generous assistance of the University of New Brunswick, the Canada Council for the Arts, and the Province of New Brunswick. It is experienced, wise enough to recognize excellence, and always looking for freshness and surprise. *The Fiddlehead* publishes short stories, poems, book reviews, and a small number of personal essays. Our full-color covers have become collectors' items and feature work by New Brunswick artists and from New Brunswick museums and art galleries. The journal is open to good writing in English from all over the world, looking always for freshness and surprise. Our editors are always happy to see new unsolicited works in fiction and poetry. Work is read on an ongoing basis; the acceptance rate is around 1-2%. Apart from our annual contest, we have no deadlines for submissions." Estab. 1945. Circ. 1,500. Pays on publication. Accepts simultaneous submissions. Responds in 3-9 months to mss. Occasionally comments on rejected mss. Sample copy: $15 U.S. Writer's guidelines online at www.thefiddlehead.ca/submissions.html.

○ "No criteria for publication except quality. For a general audience, including many poets and writers." Has published work by George Elliott Clarke, Kayla Czaga, Daniel Woodrell, and Clea Young. *The Fiddlehead* also sponsors an annual writing contest.

NONFICTION creative nonfiction. Send SASE and *Canadian* stamps or IRCs for return of mss. No e-mail or faxed submissions. Simultaneous submissions only if stated on cover letter; must contact immediately if accepted elsewhere. **Pays up to $40 (Canadian)/published page and 2 contributor's copies.**

FICTION Receives 100-150 unsolicited mss/month. Accepts 4-5 mss/issue; 20-40 mss/year. Agented fiction: small percentage. Publishes high percentage of new writers/year. Needs short stories, literary short fiction, literary novel and play excerpts. Does not want fiction aimed at children. Send SASE and *Canadian* stamps or IRCs for return of mss. No e-mail or faxed submissions. Simultaneous submissions only if stated on cover letter; must contact immediately if accepted elsewhere. Length: up to 6,000 words. Rarely publishes flash fiction. **Pays up to $40 (Canadian)/published page and 2 contributor's copies.**

POETRY Send SASE and *Canadian* stamps or IRCs for return of mss. No e-mail, fax, or disc submissions. Simultaneous submissions only if stated on cover letter; must contact immediately if accepted elsewhere. Submit maximum 10 poems. **Pays up to $40 (Canadian)/published page and 2 contributor's copies.**

TIPS "If you are serious about submitting to *The Fiddlehead*, you should subscribe or read several issues to get a sense of the journal. Contact us if you would like to order sample back issues."

FIELD: CONTEMPORARY POETRY & POETICS

Oberlin College Press, 50 N. Professor St., Oberlin OH 44074. (440)775-8408. **Fax:** (440)775-8124. **E-mail:** oc.press@oberlin.edu. **Website:** www.oberlin.edu/ocpress. **Contact:** Marco Wilkinson, managing editor. **60% freelance written.** Biannual magazine of poetry, poetry in translation, and essays on contemporary poetry by poets. *FIELD: Contemporary Poetry and Poetics*, published semiannually in April and October, is a literary journal with "emphasis on poetry, translations, and essays by poets. See electronic submission guidelines." Estab. 1969. Circ. 1,500. Byline given. Pays on publication. Editorial lead time 4 months. Accepts queries by online submission form. Responds in 6-8 weeks to mss. Sample copy: $8. Subscription: $16/year, $28 for 2 years. Guidelines available online and for #10 SASE.

> *FIELD* is 100 pages, digest-sized, printed on rag stock, flat-spined, with glossy color card cover.

POETRY Needs contemporary, prose poems, free verse, traditional. Submissions are read August 1 through May 31. Submit 2-6 of your best poems through online submissions manager. No e-mail submissions. Has published poetry by Michelle Glazer, Tom Lux, Carl Phillips, Betsy Sholl, Charles Simic, Jean Valentine, and translations by Marilyn Hacker and Stuart Friebert. Buys 120 poems/year. **Pays $15/page and 2 contributor's copies.**

TIPS "Keep trying!"

FILLING STATION

P.O. Box 22135, Bankers Hall RPO, Calgary AB T2P 4J5 Canada. **E-mail:** mgmt@fillingstation.ca. **Website:** www.fillingstation.ca. **Contact:** Paul Zits, managing editor. *filling Station*, published 3 times/year, prints contemporary poetry, fiction, visual art, interviews, reviews, and articles. "We are looking for all forms of contemporary writing, but especially that which is innovative and/or experimental." Estab. 1993. Publishes ms 3-4 months after acceptance. Accepts simultaneous submissions. Responds in 3-6 months. "After your work is reviewed by our Collective, you will receive an e-mail from an editor to let you know if your work has been selected for publication. If selected, you will later receive a second e-mail to let you know which issue your piece has been selected to appear in. Note that during the design phase, we sometimes discover the need to shuffle a piece to a future issue instead. In the event your piece is pushed back, we will inform you." Sample copy: $8. Subscription: $25 for 3 issues. Guidelines online.

> *filling Station* is 64 pages, 8.5x11, perfect-bound, with card cover, includes photos and artwork. Receives about 100 submissions for each issue, accepts approximately 10%. Press run is 700.

NONFICTION Needs essays, interview, reviews. "We encourage you to submit experimental interviews, articles, reviews, and creative nonfiction. Please note that *filling Station* will generally not accept reviews of nonexperimental literature unless the review itself is experimental. We are looking to engage with and draw attention to literature that pushes the boundaries of genre, form, methodology, style, etc. Submit 2 pieces of any such kind via Submittable. If you have concerns about suitability, feel free to send a query to nonfiction@fillingstation.ca. **Pays $25 honorarium and three-issue subscription.**

FICTION Needs experimental, novel excerpts, short stories, flash fiction, postcard fiction. Submit fiction via Submittable. Length: up to 10 pages (submissions at the upper end of this length spectrum will need to be of exceptional quality to be considered). **Pays $25 honorarium and three-issue subscription.**

POETRY Submit up to 6 pages of poetry via Submittable. "If your poem is spaced in a particular way, please make sure to use spaces, never tabs, so we can accurately replicate your layout." Has published poetry by Fred Wah, Larissa Lai, Margaret Christakos, Robert Kroetsch, Ron Silliman, Susan Holbrook, and many more. **Pays $25 honorarium and three-issue subscription.**

TIPS "*filling Station* accepts singular or simultaneous submissions of previously unpublished poetry, fiction, creative nonfiction, nonfiction, or art. We are always on the hunt for great writing!"

THE FIRST LINE

Blue Cubicle Press, LLC, P.O. Box 250382, Plano TX 75025. (972)824-0646. **E-mail:** submission@thefirstline.com. **Website:** www.thefirstline.com. **Contact:** Robin LaBounty, manuscript coordinator. **100% freelance written.** "*The First Line* is an exercise in creativity for writers and a chance for readers to see how many different directions we can take when we start from the same place. The purpose of *The First Line* is to jumpstart the imagination—to help writers break through the block that is the blank page. Each issue contains short stories that stem from a common first line; it also provides a forum for discussing favorite first lines in literature." Estab. 1999. Circ. 2,250. Byline given. Pays on acceptance. Publishes ms 1 month after acceptance. Accepts queries by mail, e-mail. Responds 3 weeks after submission time closes. Sample copy and guidelines available online. All stories must be written with the first line provided. The line cannot be altered in any way, unless otherwise noted by the editors. The story should be between 300 and 5,000 words (this is more like a guideline and not a hardand-fast rule; going over or under the word count won't get your story tossed from the slush pile). The sentences can be found on the home page of *The First Line*'s website, as well as in the prior issue. Note: We are open to all genres. We try to make *TFL* as eclectic as possible.

NONFICTION Needs essays. **Buys 4 mss/year.** Submit complete ms. Length: 300-600 words. **Pays $25.**

FICTION "We only publish stories that start with the first line provided. We are a collection of tales—of different directions writers can take when they start from the same place. " Needs adventure, ethnic, experimental, fantasy, historical, horror, humorous, mainstream, mystery, religious, romance, science fiction, short stories, suspense, western, "No stories that do not start with our first line." **Buys 35-50 mss/year.** Submit complete ms. Length: 300-5,000 words. **Pays $25-50.**

TIPS "Don't just write the first story that comes to mind after you read the sentence. If it is obvious, chances are other people are writing about the same thing. Don't try so hard. Be willing to accept criticism."

💲 FIVE POINTS

Georgia State University, P.O. Box 3999, Atlanta GA 30302-3999. **Website:** www.fivepoints.gsu.edu. **Contact:** David Bottoms, co-editor. *Five Points*, published 3 times/year, is committed to publishing work that compels the imagination through the use of fresh and convincing language. Estab. 1996. Circ. 2,000. No kill fee. Publishes ms an average of 6 months after acceptance. Accepts queries by online submission form. Responds in 2 months. Sample copy: $10. Guidelines available on website.

Magazine: 6x9; 200 pages; cotton paper; glossy cover; photos. Has published Alice Hoffman, Natasha Tretheway, Pamela Painter, Billy Collins, Philip Levine, George Singleton, Hugh Sheehy, and others. All submissions received outside of our reading periods are returned unread.

NONFICTION Needs essays. Submit through online submissions manager. Include cover letter. Reading period: August 15-December 1 and January 11-March 31. Length: up to 7,500 words. **Pays $15/page ($250 maximum), plus free subscription to magazine and 2 contributor's copies; additional copies $4.**

FICTION Receives 250 unsolicited mss/month. Accepts 4 mss/issue; 15-20 mss/year. Reads fiction August 15-December 1 and January 3-March 31. Publishes 1 new writer/year. Sometimes comments on rejected mss. Sponsors awards/contests. Needs short stories. Submit through online submissions manager. Include cover letter. Length: up to 7,500 words. **Pays $15/page ($250 maximum), plus free subscription to magazine and 2 contributor's copies; additional copies $4.**

POETRY Reads poetry August 15-December 1 and January 3-March 31. Submit through online submissions manager. Include cover letter. Submit maximum 2 poems. Length: up to 50 lines/poem.

TIPS "We place no limitations on style or content. Our only criteria is excellence. If your writing has an original voice, substance, and significance, send it to us. We will publish distinctive, intelligent writing that has something to say and says it in a way that captures and maintains our attention."

🌑 FREEFALL MAGAZINE

FreeFall Literary Society of Calgary, 460, 1720 29th Ave. SW, Calgary AB T2T 6T7 Canada. **E-mail:** editors@freefallmagazine.ca. **Website:** www.freefallmagazine.ca. **Contact:** Ryan Stromquist, managing editor. **100% freelance written.** Magazine published triannually containing fiction, poetry, creative nonfiction, essays on writing, interviews, and reviews. "We are looking for exquisite writing with a strong narrative." Estab. 1990. Circ. 1,000. Pays on publication. Accepts queries by online submission form. Accepts simultaneous submissions. Guidelines and submission forms on website.

NONFICTION Needs essays, interview, creative nonfiction, writing-related and general-audience topics. Submit complete ms online submissions manager. Length: up to 4,000 words. **Pays $10/printed page**

in the magazine ($100 maximum) and 1 contributor's copy.

FICTION Needs short stories, slice-of-life vignettes. Submit via online submissions manager. Length: up to 4,000 words. **Pays $10/printed page in the magazine ($100 maximum) and 1 contributor's copy.**

POETRY Submit 2-5 poems via online submissions manager. Accepts any style of poetry. Length: up to 6 pages. **Pays $25/poem and 1 contributor's copy.**

TIPS "Our mission is to encourage the voices of new, emerging, and experienced Canadian writers and provide a platform for their quality work."

THE GEORGIA REVIEW

The University of Georgia, Main Library, Room 706A, 320 S. Jackson St., Athens GA 30602. (706)542-3481. **Fax:** (706)542-0047. **E-mail:** garev@uga.edu. **Website:** thegeorgiareview.com. **Contact:** Stephen Corey, editor. **99% freelance written.** Quarterly journal. "*The Georgia Review* is a literary quarterly committed to the art of editorial practice. We collaborate equally with established and emerging authors of essays, stories, poems, and reviews in the pursuit of extraordinary works that engage with the evolving concerns and interests of intellectually curious readers from around the world. Our aim in curating content is not only to elevate literature, publishing, and the arts, but also to help facilitate socially conscious partnerships in our surrounding communities."

NONFICTION Needs essays. **Buys 12-20 mss/year.** We generally avoid publishing scholarly articles that are narrow in focus and/or overly burdened with footnotes. *The Georgia Review* is interested in provocative, thesis-oriented essays that can engage both the intelligent general reader and the specialist, as well as those that are experimental or lyrical in approach but accessible to a range of readers. **Pays $50/published page.**

PHOTOS Send photos. Reviews 5x7 prints or larger. Offers no additional payment for photos accepted with ms. Buys one-time rights.

FICTION "We seek original, excellent short fiction not bound by type. Ordinarily we do not publish novel excerpts or works translated into English, and we discourage authors from submitting these." Needs short stories. **Buys 12-20 mss/year.** Send complete ms via online submissions manager or postal mail. **Pays $50/published page.**

POETRY We seek original, excellent poetry. Submit 3-5 poems at a time. Buys 60-75 poems/year. **Pays $4/line.**

THE GETTYSBURG REVIEW

Gettysburg College, Gettysburg College, 300 N. Washington St., Gettysburg PA 17325. (717)337-6770. **E-mail:** mdrew@gettysburg.edu. **Website:** www.gettysburgreview.com. **Contact:** Mark Drew, editor; Jess L. Bryant, managing editor. Published quarterly, *The Gettysburg Review* considers unsolicited submissions of poetry, fiction, and essays. "Our concern is quality. Mss submitted here should be extremely well written." Reading period September 1-May 31. Estab. 1988. Circ. 2,000. Byline given. Pays on publication. Publishes ms an average of 6 months after acceptance. Editorial lead time 1 year. Submit seasonal material 9 months in advance. Accepts queries by mail, fax. Accepts simultaneous submissions. Responds in 1 month to queries; in 3-5 months to mss. Sample: $15. Guidelines available online.

NONFICTION Needs book excerpts, essays, general interest, humor, memoir, personal experience, reviews, travel. **Buys 20 mss/year.** Send complete ms. Length: up to 25 pages. **Pays $15/printed page, a one-year subscription, and 1 contributor's copy.**

FICTION Wants high-quality literary fiction. Needs experimental, historical, humorous, mainstream, novel excerpts, short stories, slice-of-life vignettes, literary, contemporary. "We require that fiction be intelligent and aesthetically written." No genre fiction. **Buys 20 mss/year.** Send complete ms with SASE. Length: 2,000-7,000 words. **Pays $15/printed page, a one-year subscription, and 1 contributor's copy.**

POETRY Considers "well-written poems of all kinds on all subjects." Has published poetry by Rita Dove, Alice Friman, Philip Schultz, Michelle Boisseau, Bob Hicok, Linda Pastan, and G.C. Waldrep. Does not want sentimental, clichéd verse. Buys 50 poems/year. Submit maximum 5 poems. **Pays $2/line, a one-year subscription, and 1 contributor's copy.**

GLIMMER TRAIN STORIES

Glimmer Train Press, Inc., P.O. Box 80430, Portland OR 97280. **Fax:** (503)221-0837. **E-mail:** eds@glimmertrain.org. **Website:** www.glimmertrain.org. **Contact:** Susan Burmeister-Brown. **100% freelance written.** Triannual magazine of literary short fiction. "We are interested in literary short stories, particularly by new and emerging writers." Estab. 1991. Circ. 12,000.

Byline given. Pays on acceptance. Publishes ms an average of 15 months after acceptance. Accepts simultaneous submissions. Responds in 2 months to mss. Sometimes comments on rejected mss. Sample: $16 on website. For guidelines and to submit online: www.glimmertrain.org.

FICTION Needs short stories. **Buys 45 mss/year.** Submit via the website at www.glimmertrain.org. In a pinch, send a hard copy and include SASE for response. Receives 36,000 unsolicited mss/year. Accepts 15 mss/issue; 45 mss/year. Agented fiction 1%. Publishes 20 new writers/year. Length: 500-20,000 words. **Pays $700 for standard submissions, up to $3,000 for contest-winning stories.**

TIPS "In the last 2 years, over half of the first-place stories have been their authors' very first publications. See our contest listings in Contests & Awards section."

☉ GRAIN

P.O. Box 3986, Regina SK S4P 3R9 Canada. (306)791-7749. **Fax:** (306)565-8554. **E-mail:** grainmag@skwriter.com. **Website:** www.grainmagazine.ca. Quarterly magazine covering poetry, fiction, creative nonfiction. "*Grain, The Journal of Eclectic Writing* is a literary quarterly that publishes engaging, diverse, and challenging writing and art by some of the best Canadian and international writers and artists. Every issue features superb new writing from both developing and established writers. Each issue also highlights the unique artwork of a different visual artist. *Grain* has garnered national and international recognition for its distinctive, cutting-edge content and design." Estab. 1973. Circ. 1,600. Byline given. Pays on publication. Accepts queries by mail. Responds in 6 months to mss. Sample: $13 CAD. Subscription: $35 CAD/year, $55 CAD for 2 years. (See website for U.S. and foreign postage fees.). Guidelines available online.

○ *Grain* is 112-128 pages, digest-sized, professionally printed. Press run is 1,100. Receives about 3,000 submissions/year. **Submissions are read September 1-May 31 only.** Mss postmarked June 1-August 31 will not be read.

NONFICTION Needs essays. No academic papers or reportage. Postal submissions only. Send typed, unpublished material only (considers work published online to be previously published). Please only submit work in 1 genre at a time. Length: up to 3,500 words. **Pays $50/page ($250 maximum) and 3 contributor's copies.**

FICTION Needs short stories. No romance, confession, science fiction, vignettes, mystery. Postal submissions only. Send typed, unpublished material only (considers work published online to be previously published). Please only submit work in 1 genre at a time. Length: up to 3,500 words. **Pays $50/page ($250 maximum) and 3 contributor's copies.**

POETRY Needs individual poems, sequences, suites. Wants "high-quality, imaginative, well-crafted poetry." Postal submissions only. Send typed, unpublished material only (considers work published online to be previously published). Has published poetry by Lorna Crozier, Don Domanski, Cornelia Haeussler, Patrick Lane, Karen Solie, and Monty Reid. Length: up to 6 pages. **Pays $50/page ($250 maximum) and 3 contributor's copies.**

TIPS "Only work of the highest literary quality is accepted. Read several back issues."

GRASSLIMB

P.O. Box 420816, San Diego CA 92142. **E-mail:** editor@grasslimb.com. **Website:** www.grasslimb.com. **Contact:** Valerie Polichar, editor. **100.** *Grasslimb* publishes literary prose, poetry, and art. Fiction is best when it is short and avant-garde or otherwise experimental. Estab. 2002. Circ. 200. Acceptance $10 Accepts simultaneous submissions. Responds in 4-6 months to mss. Rarely comments on rejected mss. Sample copy: $3. Guidelines for SASE, e-mail, or on website.

FICTION "Fiction in an experimental, avant-garde, or surreal mode is often more interesting to us than a traditional story." Needs experimental. "Although general topics are welcome, we're less likely to select work regarding romance, sex, aging, and children." Send complete ms via e-mail or postal mail with SASE. Length: up to 2,500 words; average length: 1,500 words. **Pays $10-70 and 2 contributor's copies.**

POETRY Submit poems via e-mail or postal mail with SASE. Submit maximum 5 poems. **Pays $5-20/poem.**

TIPS "We publish brief fiction work that can be read in a single sitting over a cup of coffee. Work is generally 'literary' in nature rather than mainstream. Experimental work welcome. Remember to have your work proofread and to send short work. We cannot read over 3,000 words and prefer under 2,000 words. Include word count."

GULF COAST: A JOURNAL OF LITERATURE AND FINE ARTS

4800 Calhoun Rd., Houston TX 77204-3013. (713)743-3223. **E-mail:** editors@gulfcoastmag.org. **Website:** www.gulfcoastmag.org. **Contact:** Luisa Muradyan Tannahill, editor; Michele Nereim, managing editor; Georgia Pearle, digital editor; Henk Rossouw, Dan Chu, and Erika Jo Brown, poetry editors; Alex McElroy, Charlotte Wyatt, and Corey Campbell, fiction editors; Alex Naumann and Nathan Stabenfeldt, nonfiction editors; Jonathan Meyer, online fiction editor; Carolann Madden, online poetry editor; Melanie Brkich, online nonfiction editor. Biannual print magazine covering innovative fiction, nonfiction, poetry, visual art, and critical art writing. GC Online is the companion online journal and publishes unique content. Estab. 1986. Circ. 3,000. No kill fee. Publishes ms 6 months-1 year after acceptance. Accepts queries by mail, e-mail, phone. Accepts simultaneous submissions. Responds in 4-6 months to mss. Sometimes comments on rejected mss. Back issue: $8, plus 7x10 SASE with 4 first-class stamps. Writer's guidelines for #10 SASE or on website.

○ Magazine: 7x9; approximately 300 pages; stock paper, gloss cover; illustrations; photos.

NONFICTION Needs interview, reviews. *Gulf Coast* reads general submissions, submitted by post or through the online submissions manager, September 1-March 1. Submissions e-mailed directly to the editors or postmarked March 1-September 1 will not be read or responded to. "Please visit our contest page for contest submission guidelines." **Pays $100 per review and $200 per interview.**

FICTION "Please do not send multiple submissions; we will read only 1 submission per author at a given time, except in the case of our annual contests." Needs ethnic, multicultural, literary, regional, translations, contemporary. No children's, genre, religious/inspirational. *Gulf Coast* reads general submissions, submitted by post or through the online submissions manager, September 1-March 1. Submissions e-mailed directly to the editors or postmarked March 1-September 1 will not be read or responded to. "Please visit our contest page for contest submission guidelines." Receives 500 unsolicited mss/month. Accepts 6-8 mss/issue; 12-16 mss/year. Agented fiction: 5%. Publishes 2-8 new writers/year. Recently published work by Alan Heathcock, Anne Carson, Bret Anthony Johnston, John D'Agata, Lucie Brock-Broido, Clancy Martin, Steve Almond, Sam Lipsyte, Carl Phillips, Dean Young, and Eula Biss. Publishes short shorts. **Pays $50/page.**

POETRY Submit up to 5 poems at a time. Considers simultaneous submissions with notification; no previously published poems. Cover letter is required. List previous publications and include a brief bio. Reads submissions September-April. **Pays $50/page.**

TIPS "Submit only previously unpublished works. Include a cover letter. Online submissions are strongly preferred. Stories or essays should be typed, double-spaced, and paginated with your name, address, and phone number on the first page and the title on subsequent pages. Poems should have your name, address, and phone number on the first page of each." The Annual Gulf Coast Prizes award publication and $1,500 each in poetry, fiction, and nonfiction; opens in December of each year. Honorable mentions in each category will receive a $250 second prize. Postmark/online entry deadline: March 22 of each year. Winners and honorable mentions will be announced in May. **Entry fee:** $23 (includes one-year subscription). Make checks payable to *Gulf Coast*. Guidelines available on website.

⑤ THE HOLLINS CRITIC

P.O. Box 9538, Hollins University, Roanoke VA 24020-1538. **Website:** www.hollins.edu/who-we-are/news-media/hollins-critic. **100% freelance written.** Magazine published 5 times/year. *The Hollins Critic*, published 5 times/year, presents the first serious surveys of the whole bodies of contemporary writers' work, with complete checklists. In past issues, you'll find essays on such writers as Claudia Emerson (by Allison Seay), Wilma Dykeman (by Casey Clabough), Jerry Mirskin (by Howard Nelson), Sally Mann (by Martha Park), James Alan McPherson (by James Robert Saunders), Elise Partridge (by Nicholas Birns), and Ron Rash (by Jerry Wayne Wells). Estab. 1964. Circ. 400. Byline given. Pays on publication. No kill fee. Publishes ms an average of 1 year after acceptance. Accepts queries by online submission form. Accepts simultaneous submissions. Responds in 2 months to mss. Sample copy: $3. Guidelines for #10 SASE or online.

POETRY Needs avant-garde, free verse, traditional. Submit up to 5 poems at a time using the online submission form at www.hollinscriticsubmissions.com, available September 15-December 1. Submissions received at other times will be returned unread. Publishes 16-20 poems/year. **Pays $25/poem plus 5 contributor's copies.**

TIPS "We accept unsolicited poetry submissions; all other content is by prearrangement."

HOOT

A Postcard Review of (Mini) Poetry and Prose, 4234 Chestnut St., Apt. 1 R, Philadelphia PA 19104. **E-mail:** info@hootreview.com. **Website:** www.hootreview. com. **Contact:** Jane-Rebecca Cannarella, editor in chief; Amanda Vacharat and Dorian Geisler, editors/ co-founders. **100% freelance written.** *HOOT* publishes 1 piece of writing, designed with original art and/or photographs, on the front of a postcard every month, as well as 2-3 pieces online. The postcards are intended for sharing, to be hung on the wall, etc. Therefore, *HOOT* looks for very brief, surprising-yet-gimmick-free writing that can stand on its own, that also follows "The Refrigerator Rule"—something that you would hang on your refrigerator and would want to read and look at for a whole month. This rule applies to online content as well. Estab. 2011. Pays on publication. Publishes ms 2 months after acceptance. Accepts queries by mail, online submission form. Accepts simultaneous submissions. Sample copy: $2. Guidelines available online.

○ Costs $2 to submit up to 2 pieces of work. Submit through online submissions manager or postal mail.

NONFICTION Needs personal experience, creative nonfiction. **Buys 6 mss/year.** Submit complete ms. Length: up to 150 words. **Pays $10-100 for assigned and unsolicited pieces.**

PHOTOS Send photos (GIF/JPEG files) with submission. Buys one-time rights.

FICTION literary, flash/short short. **Buys 14 mss/ year.** Submit complete ms. Length: up to 150 words. **Pays $10-100 for print publication.**

POETRY Needs avant-garde, free verse, haiku, light verse, traditional, prose. Buys 14 poems/year. Submit maximum 2 poems. Length: up to 10 lines. **Pays $10-100 for print publication.**

TIPS "We look for writing with audacity and zest from authors who are not afraid to take risks. We appreciate work that is able to go beyond mere description in its 150 words. We offer free online workshops every other Wednesday for authors who would like feedback on their work from the *HOOT* editors. We

also often give feedback with our rejections. We publish roughly 6-10 new writers each year."

HUBBUB

5344 SE 38th Ave., Portland OR 97202. **E-mail:** lisa. steinman@reed.edu. **Website:** www.reed.edu/hubbub. **Contact:** J. Shugrue and Lisa M. Steinman, co-editors. *Hubbub*, published once/year, is designed "to feature a multitude of voices from interesting, contemporary American poets." Wants "poems that are well crafted, with something to say. We have no single style, subject, or length requirement and in particular will consider long poems." Estab. 1983. Pays on publication. Publishes poems 1-12 months (usually) after acceptance. Accepts queries by mail. Responds in 4 months. Sample: $3.35 (back issues), $7 (current issue). Subscription: $7/year. Guidelines available for SASE or online.

○ *Hubbub* is 50-70 pages, digest-sized, offset-printed, perfect-bound, with cover art. Receives about 1,200 submissions/year, accepts up to 2%. Press run is 350.

POETRY Submit 3-6 typed poems at a time. Include SASE. "We review 2-4 poetry books/year in short (three-page) reviews; all reviews are solicited. We do, however, list books received/recommended." Send materials for review consideration. Has published poetry by Madeline DeFrees, Cecil Giscombe, Carolyn Kizer, Primus St. John, Shara McCallum, and Alice Fulton. Does not want light verse. Buys 40-50 poems/ year. Submit maximum 6 poems. No length requirements. **Pays $20/poem.**

HUNGER MOUNTAIN

Vermont College of Fine Arts, 36 College St., Montpelier VT 05602. (802)828-8517. **E-mail:** hungermtn@ vcfa.edu. **Website:** www.hungermtn.org. Miciah Gault, Editor. **Contact:** Katie Stromme, Assistant Editor. Annual perfect-bound journal covering high-quality fiction, poetry, creative nonfiction, craft essays, writing for children, and artwork. Four contests held annually, one in each genre. Accepts high-quality work from unknown, emerging, or successful writers. Publishing fiction, creative nonfiction, poetry, and young adult & children's writing. Four writing contests annually. Estab. 2002. Circ. 1,000. Byline given. Pays on publication. No kill fee. Publishes ms an average of 1 year after acceptance. General submissions between May 1 and September 15. Accepts queries by online submission form. Accepts simultaneous submissions. Responds in 4 months to mss. Single issue:

$12; subscription: $18 for 2 issues/2 years; back issue: $8. Checks payable to Vermont College of Fine Arts, or purchase online http://hungermtn.org/subscribe. Guidelines online at http://hungermtn.org/submit.

○ *Hunger Mountain* is a print and online journal of the arts. The print journal is about 200 pages, 7x9, professionally printed, perfect-bound, with full-bleed color artwork on cover. Press run is 1,000. Over 10,000 visits online monthly. Uses online submissions manager (Submittable). Member: CLMP.

NONFICTION "We welcome an array of traditional and experimental work, including, but not limited to, personal, lyrical, and meditative essays, memoirs, collages, rants, and humor. The only requirements are recognition of truth, a unique voice with a firm command of language, and an engaging story with multiple pressure points." No informative or instructive articles, no interviews, and no book reviews please. Payment varies. Submit complete ms using online submissions manager at Submittable: https://hungermtn.submittable.com/submit. Length: up to 10,000 words. **$50 for general fiction or creative nonfiction, for both children's lit and general adult lit.**

PHOTOS Send photos. Reviews contact sheets, transparencies, prints, GIF/JPEG files. Slides preferred. Negotiates payment individually. Buys one-time rights.

FICTION "We look for work that is beautifully crafted and tells a good story, with characters that are alive and kicking, storylines that stay with us long after we've finished reading, and sentences that slay us with their precision." Needs experimental, humorous, novel excerpts, short stories, slice-of-life vignettes. No genre fiction, meaning science fiction, fantasy, horror, detective, erotic, etc. Submit ms using online submissions manager: https://hungermtn.submittable.com/submit. Length: up to 10,000 words. **$50 for general fiction.**

POETRY Needs avant-garde, free verse, traditional. Submit 1-5 poems at a time. "We are looking for truly original poems that run the aesthetic gamut: lively engagement with language in the act of pursuit. Some poems remind us in a fresh way of our own best thoughts; some poems bring us to a place beyond language for which there aren't quite words; some poems take us on a complicated language ride that is, itself, its own aim. Complex poem-architectures thrill us

and still-points in the turning world do, too. Send us the best of what you have." Submit using online submissions manager. No light verse, humor/quirky/catchy verse, greeting card verse. Submit maximum 5 poems. **$25 for poetry up to two poems (plus $5 per poem for additional poems);**
$25 for poetry, up to two poems (plus $5 per poem for additional poems).
TIPS "Mss must be typed, prose double-spaced. Poets submit poems as one document. No multiple genre submissions. Fresh viewpoints and human interest are very important, as is originality and diversity. We are committed to publishing an outstanding journal of the arts. Do not send entire novels, mss, or short story collections. Do not send previously published work."

ICONOCLAST

1675 Amazon Rd., Mohegan Lake NY 10547-1804. **Website:** www.iconoclastliterarymagazine.com. **Contact:** Phil Wagner, editor and publisher. *Iconoclast* seeks and chooses the best new writing and poetry available—of all genres and styles and entertainment levels. Its mission is to provide a serious publishing opportunity for unheralded, unknown, but deserving creators, whose work is often overlooked or trampled in the commercial, university, or Internet marketplace. Estab. 1992. Pays on publication. Accepts queries by mail. Responds in 6 weeks to mss. Sample copy: $4. Subscription: $20 for 6 issues.

FICTION "Subjects and styles are completely open (within the standards of generally accepted taste—though exceptions, as always, can be made for unique and visionary works)." Needs adventure, experimental, fantasy, mainstream, short stories. No slice-of-life stories, stories containing alcoholism, incest, and domestic or public violence. Accepts most genres, "with the exception of mysteries." Submit by mail; include SASE. Cover letter not necessary. **Pays 1¢/word and 2 contributor's copies. Contributors get 40% discount on extra copies.**

POETRY "Try for originality; if not in thought than expression. No greeting card verse or noble religious sentiments. Look for the unusual in the usual, parallels in opposites, the capturing of what is unique or often unnoticed in an ordinary or extraordinary moment. What makes us human—and the resultant glories and agonies. The universal usually wins out over the personal. Rhyme isn't as easy as it looks—especially for those unversed in its study." Submit by mail; include SASE. Cover letter not necessary. Length: up to 2 pages. **Pays $2-6/poem and 1 contributor's copy per page or work. Contributors get 40% discount on extra copies.**

TIPS "Please don't send preliminary drafts—rewriting is half the job. If you're not sure about the story, don't truly believe in it, or are unenthusiastic about the subject (we will not recycle your term papers or thesis), then don't send it. This is not a lottery (luck has nothing to do with it)."

THE IDAHO REVIEW

Boise State University, 1910 University Dr., Boise ID 83725. **E-mail:** mwieland@boisestate.edu. **Website:** idahoreview.org. **Contact:** Mitch Wieland, editor. *The Idaho Review* is the literary journal of Boise State University. Estab. 1998. Pays on publication. Publishes ms 1 year after acceptance. Accepts queries by online submission form. Accepts simultaneous submissions. Responds in 3-5 months. Guidelines available online.

Recent stories appearing in *The Idaho Review* have been reprinted in *The Best American Short Stories, The O. Henry Prize Stories, The Pushcart Prize*, and *New Stories from the South*.

NONFICTION Special issues: creative nonfiction. Submit through online submissions manager.

FICTION Needs experimental, literary. No genre fiction of any type. Submit through online submissions manager. Length: up to 25 double-spaced pages. **Pays $100/story and contributor's copies.**

POETRY Submit up to 5 poems using online submissions manager.

TIPS "We look for strongly crafted work that tells a story that needs to be told. We demand vision and intelligence and mystery in the fiction we publish."

ILLUMEN

Alban Lake Publishing, P.O. Box 141, Colo IA 50056-0141. **E-mail:** illumensdp@yahoo.com. **Website:** albanlake.com. **Contact:** Terrie Leigh Relf, editor. **100% freelance written.** "*Illumen* is a print magazine of speculative poetry. It is published quarterly on the first of January, April, July, and October in perfect-bound digest format. It contains speculative poetry, illustrations, articles, and reviews." Estab. 2004. Byline given. Pays on publication. Offers 100% kill fee. About four months between acceptance and publication. Submit seasonal material 6 months in advance. Accepts queries by e-mail. Accepts simultaneous sub-

missions. Responds in 4 months. Guidelines available online.

NONFICTION Needs essays, how-to, interview, opinion, non-fiction must pertain in some way to poetry. Special issues: Wants articles that address some aspect of speculative poetry. Send complete ms by e-mail. Length: 800-2,000 words. **Pays $12 and 1 contributor's copy.**

REPRINTS Pays $3 for reprints.

POETRY Needs avant-garde, free verse, haiku, light verse, traditional. "Speculative poetry is 1 result of the application of imagination to reality. In speculative poetry, one's 'vision' often is taken from a different angle, from another perspective, perhaps even from another time and place. Speculative poetry is usually tinged with 1 or more of the genres. Thus, in speculative poetry you find hints of science fiction, fantasy, folklore, myth, the surreal ... and yes, even horror. Good speculative poetry will awaken a sense of adventure in the reader. That's what we're looking for: good, original speculative poetry." Submit poetry by e-mail. "Speculative horror poetry evokes moods, often dark and spooky ones. It should not make you upchuck. Remember: twisted is an attitude, not an action." Buys 40-50 poems/year. Submit maximum 3 poems. Length: up to 100 lines/poem. **Pays 2¢/word, minimum $3.**

TIPS "*Illumen* publishes beginning writers as well as seasoned veterans. Be sure to read and follow the guidelines before submitting your work. The best advice for beginning writers is to send your best effort, not your first draft."

IMAGE

3307 Third Ave. W., Seattle WA 98119. (206)281-2988. **Fax:** (206)281-2979. **E-mail:** image@imagejournal.org. **Website:** www.imagejournal.org. **Contact:** Gregory Wolfe, publisher and editor. **50% freelance written.** Quarterly magazine covering the intersection between art and faith. "*Image* is a unique forum for the best writing and artwork that is informed by—or grapples with—religious faith. We have never been interested in art that merely regurgitates dogma or falls back on easy answers or didacticism. Instead, our focus has been on writing and visual artwork that embody a spiritual struggle, that seek to strike a balance between tradition and a profound openness to the world. Each issue explores this relationship through outstanding fiction, poetry, painting, sculpture, architecture, film, music, interviews, and dance. *Image* also features 4-color reproductions of visual art." Estab. 1989. Circ. 4,500. Byline given. Pays on acceptance. No kill fee. Publishes ms an average of 8 months after acceptance. Accepts queries by mail, e-mail. Accepts simultaneous submissions. Responds in 1 month to queries; in 5 months to mss. Sample copy: $16 or available online. Guidelines online.

○ Magazine: 7×10; 136 pages; glossy cover stock; illustrations; photos.

NONFICTION Needs essays, interview, profile, religious. No sentimental, preachy, moralistic, or obvious essays. **Buys 10 mss/year.** Send complete ms by postal mail (with SASE for reply or return of ms) or online submissions manager at www.imagejournal.org/journal/submit, or query Mary Mitchell (mkenagy@imagejournal.org). Does not accept e-mail submissions. Length: 3,000-6,000 words. **Pays $10/page ($150 maximum) and 4 contributor's copies.**

FICTION Needs religious, short stories. No sentimental, preachy, moralistic, obvious stories, or genre stories (unless they manage to transcend their genre). **Buys 8 mss/year.** Send complete ms by postal mail (with SASE for reply or return of ms) or online submissions manager. Does not accept e-mail submissions. Length: 3,000-6,000 words. **Pays $10/page ($150 maximum) and 4 contributor's copies.**

POETRY Wants poems that grapple with religious faith, usually Judeo-Christian. Send up to 5 poems by postal mail (with SASE for reply or return of ms) or online submissions manager. Does not accept e-mail submissions. Submit maximum 5 poems. Length: up to 10 pages. **Pays $2/line ($150 maximum) and 4 contributor's copies.**

TIPS "Fiction must grapple with religious faith, though subjects need not be overtly religious."

🟢 INDIANA REVIEW

Ballantine Hall 529, 1020 E. Kirkwood Ave., Indiana University, Bloomington IN 47405. **E-mail:** inreview@indiana.edu. **Website:** indianareview.org. **Contact:** See masthead for current editorial staff. **100% freelance written.** Biannual magazine. "*Indiana Review*, a nonprofit organization run by IU graduate students, is a journal of innovative fiction, nonfiction, and poetry. We're interested in energy, originality, and careful attention to craft. While we publish many well-known writers, we also welcome new and emerging poets and fiction writers." Estab. 1976. Circ.

5,000. Byline given. Pays on publication. Publishes ms an average of 3-6 months after acceptance. Accepts queries by online submission form. Accepts simultaneous submissions. Responds in 4 or more months to mss. Sample copy: $12. Guidelines available online. "We no longer accept hard-copy submissions. All submissions must be made online."

○ See website for open reading periods.

NONFICTION Needs essays. No coming-of-age/slice-of-life pieces or book reviews. **Buys 5-7 mss/year.** Submit complete ms through online submissions manager. Length: up to 8,000 words. **Pays $5/page ($10 minimum), plus 2 contributor's copies.**

FICTION "We look for daring stories which integrate theme, language, character, and form. We like polished writing, humor, and fiction which has consequence beyond the world of its narrator." Needs ethnic, experimental, mainstream, literary, short fictions, translations. No genre fiction. **Buys 14-18 mss/year.** Submit via online submissions manager. Length: up to 8,000 words. **Pays $5/page ($10 minimum), plus 2 contributor's copies.**

POETRY "We look for poems that are skillful and bold, exhibiting an inventiveness of language with attention to voice and sonics." Wants experimental, free verse, prose poem, traditional form, lyrical, narrative. Submit poetry via online submissions manager. Buys 80 poems/year. Submit maximum 6 poems. **Pays $5/page ($10 minimum), plus 2 contributor's copies.**

TIPS "We're always looking for nonfiction essays that go beyond merely autobiographical revelation and utilize sophisticated organization and slightly radical narrative strategies. We want essays that are both lyrical and analytical where confession does not mean nostalgia. Read us before you submit. Often reading is slower in summer and holiday months. Only submit work to journals you would proudly subscribe to, then subscribe to a few. Take care to read the latest 2 issues and specifically mention work you identify with and why. Submit work that 'stacks up' with the work we've published."

THE IOWA REVIEW

308 EPB, The University of Iowa, Iowa City IA 52242. (319)335-0462. **E-mail:** iowa-review@uiowa.edu. **Website:** www.iowareview.org. Lynne Nugent, managing editor. **Contact:** Harilaos Stecopoulos. Triannual magazine covering stories, essays, and poems for a general readership interested in contemporary

literature. *The Iowa Review*, published 3 times/year, prints fiction, poetry, essays, reviews, and, occasionally, interviews. Receives about 5,000 submissions/year, accepts up to 100. Press run is 2,900; 1,500 distributed to stores. Estab. 1970. Circ. 3,500. Pays on publication. Publishes ms an average of 12-18 months after acceptance. Accepts queries by mail, online submission form. Accepts simultaneous submissions. Responds to mss in 4 months. Sample: $8.95 and online. Subscription: $20. Guidelines available online.

This magazine uses the help of colleagues and graduate assistants. Its reading period for unsolicited work is September 1 through December 1. From January through April, the editors read entries to the annual Iowa Review Awards competition. Check the website for further information.

NONFICTION Needs essays, interview. Send complete ms with cover letter. Don't bother with queries. SASE for return of ms. Accepts mss by snail mail (SASE required for response) and online submission form at iowareview.submittable.com/submit; no e-mail submissions. **Pays 8¢/word ($100 minimum), plus 2 contributor's copies.**

FICTION "We are open to a range of styles and voices and always hope to be surprised by work we then feel we need." Receives 600 unsolicited mss/month. Accepts 4-6 mss/issue; 12-18 mss/year. Does not read mss January-August. Publishes ms an average of 12-18 months after acceptance. Agented fiction less than 2%. **Publishes some new writers/year.** Recently published work by Johanna Hunting, Bennett Sims, and Pedro Mairal. Needs experimental, mainstream, novel excerpts, short stories. Send complete ms with cover letter. Don't bother with queries. SASE for return of ms. Accepts mss by snail mail (SASE required for response) and online submission form at iowareview.submittable.com/submit; no e-mail submissions. **Pays 8¢/word ($100 minimum), plus two contributor's copies.**

POETRY Submit up to 8 pages at a time. Online submissions accepted, but no e-mail submissions. Cover letter (with title of work and genre) is encouraged. SASE required. Reads submissions only during the fall semester, September through November, and then contest entries in the spring. Occasionally comments on rejected poems or offers suggestions on accepted poems. "We simply look for poems that, at the time we read and choose, we find we admire. No specifications as to form, length, style, subject matter, or purpose. Though we print work from established writers, we're always delighted when we discover new talent." **Pays $1.50/line, $40 minimum.**

TIPS "We publish essays, reviews, novel excerpts, stories, poems, and photography. We have no set guidelines regarding content but strongly recommend that writers read a sample issue before submitting."

KASMA MAGAZINE

Kasma Publications, **E-mail:** editors@kasmamagazine.com. **Website:** www.kasmamagazine.com. **Contact:** Alex Korovessis, editor. Online magazine. "We publish the best science fiction from promising new and established writers. Our aim is to provide stories that are well written, original, and thought provoking." Estab. 2009. Pays on publication. Publishes mss 2-3 months after acceptance. Editorial lead time 2 months. Submit seasonal material 1 month in advance. Accepts queries by e-mail. Accepts simultaneous submissions. Responds in 1 week to queries; in 3 months to mss. Sample copy available online and by e-mail. Guidelines available online.

FICTION Needs science fiction. No erotica or excessive violence/language. Submit complete ms via e-mail. Length: 1,000-5,000 words. **Pays $25 CAD.**

TIPS "The type of stories I enjoy the most usually come as a surprise: I think I know what is happening, but the underlying reality is revealed to me as I read on. That said, I've accepted many stories that don't fit this model. Sometimes I'm introduced to a new story structure. Sometimes the story I like reminds me of another story, but it introduces a slightly different spin on it. Other times, the story introduces such interesting and original ideas that structure and style don't seem to matter as much."

THE KENYON REVIEW

Finn House, 102 W. Wiggin, Gambier OH 43022. (740)427-5208. **Fax:** (740)427-5417. **E-mail:** kenyonreview@kenyon.edu. **Website:** www.kenyonreview.org. **Contact:** Alicia Misarti. **100% freelance written.** Bimonthly magazine covering contemporary literature and criticism. "An international journal of literature, culture, and the arts, dedicated to an inclusive representation of the best in new writing (fiction, poetry, essays, interviews, criticism) from established and emerging writers." Estab. 1939. Circ. 6,000. Byline given. Pays on publication. No kill fee.

Publishes ms an average of 1 year after acceptance. Editorial lead time 1 year. Submit seasonal material 1 year in advance. Accepts queries by online submission form. Accepts simultaneous submissions. Responds in 4 months to mss. Sample: $10; includes s&h. Call or e-mail to order. Guidelines available online.

NONFICTION Needs essays, interview, criticism. Only accepts mss via online submissions manager; visit website for instructions. Do not submit via e-mail or mail. Receives 130 unsolicited mss/month. Unsolicited mss accepted September 15-November 1 only. Length: 3-15 typeset pages preferred. **Pays 8¢/ published word of prose (minimum payment $80; maximum payment $450); word count does not include title, notes, or citations.**

FICTION Receives 800 unsolicited mss/month. Unsolicited mss accepted September 15-November 1 only. Recently published work by Alice Hoffman, Beth Ann Fennelly, Romulus Linney, John Koethe, Albert Goldbarth, and Erin McGraw. Needs condensed novels, ethnic, experimental, historical, humorous, mainstream, novel excerpts, short stories, contemporary, excerpts from novels, gay/lesbian, literary, translations. Only accepts mss via online submissions manager; visit website for instructions. Do not submit via e-mail or mail. Length: 3-15 typeset pages preferred. **Pays 8¢/published word of prose (minimum payment $80; maximum payment $450); word count does not include title, notes, or citations.**

POETRY Features all styles, forms, lengths, and subject matters. Considers translations. Has published poetry by Billy Collins, D.A. Powell, Jamaal May, Rachel Zucker, Diane di Prima, and Seamus Heaney. Submit up to 6 poems at a time. No previously published poems. Only accepts mss via online submissions program; visit website for instructions. Do not submit via e-mail or snail mail. Accepts submissions September 15-December 15. Submit maximum 6 poems. **Pays 16¢/published word of poetry (minimum payment $40; maximum payment $200); word count does not include title, notes, or citations.**

TIPS "We no longer accept mailed or e-mailed submissions. Work will only be read if it is submitted through our online program on our website. Reading period is September 15 through November 1. We look for strong voice, unusual perspective, and power in the writing."

LADY CHURCHILL'S ROSEBUD WRISTLET

Small Beer Press, 150 Pleasant St., #306, Easthampton MA 01027. **E-mail:** smallbeerpress@gmail.com. **Website:** www.smallbeerpress.com/lcrw. **Contact:** Gavin Grant, editor. *Lady Churchill's Rosebud Wristlet* accepts fiction, nonfiction, poetry, and b&w art. "The fiction we publish tends toward, but is not limited to, the speculative. This does not mean only quietly desperate stories. We will consider items that fall out with regular categories. We do not accept multiple submissions." Estab. 1996. Circ. 1,000. Byline given. Pays on publication. Publishes ms 6-12 months after acceptance. Accepts queries by mail. Responds in 6 months to mss. Sometimes comments on rejected mss. Sample copy: $5. Guidelines available online.

Semiannual.

NONFICTION Needs essays. Send complete ms with a cover letter. Include estimated word count. Send SASE (or IRC) for return of ms, or send a disposable copy of ms and #10 SASE for reply only. **Pays $25.**

FICTION Receives 100 unsolicited mss/month. Accepts 4-6 mss/issue; 8-12 mss/year. Publishes 2-4 new writers/year. Also publishes literary essays, poetry. Has published work by Ted Chiang, Gwenda Bond, Alissa Nutting, and Charlie Anders. Needs experimental, fantasy, science fiction, short stories. "We do not publish gore, sword and sorcery, or pornography. We can discuss these terms if you like. There are places for them all; this is not one of them." Send complete ms with a cover letter. Include estimated word count. Send SASE (or IRC) for return of ms, or send a disposable copy of ms and #10 SASE for reply only. Length: 200-7,000 words. **Pays $25.**

POETRY Send submission with a cover letter. Include estimated word count. Send SASE (or IRC) for return of submission, or send a disposable copy of submission and #10 SASE for reply only. **Pays $5/ poem.**

TIPS "We recommend you read *Lady Churchill's Rosebud Wristlet* before submitting. You can pick up a copy from our website or from assorted book shops."

LINE

6079 Academic Quadrangle, 8888 University Dr., Simon Fraser University, Burnaby BC V5A 1S6 Canada. **E-mail:** wcl@sfu.ca. **Website:** linejournal.tumblr.com/about. "*Line* (formerly *West Coast Line*) is a journal of poetry and critique." Estab. 1990. Circ. 500. Pays on publication. No kill fee. Editorial lead time

4 months. Accepts queries by mail, e-mail. Accepts simultaneous submissions. Responds in 6 months to queries and mss. Sample copy for $15 CAD, $20 U.S. Guidelines for SASE (U.S. must include IRC).

NONFICTION Needs essays, experimental prose. No journalistic articles or articles dealing with non-literary material. **Buys 8-10 mss/year.** Send complete ms. Length: 1,000-5,000 words. **Pays $8/page, 2 contributor's copies, and a one-year subscription.**

FICTION Needs experimental. **Buys 3-6 mss/year.**

POETRY Needs avant-garde. No light verse, traditional. Buys 10-15 poems/year. Submit maximum 5-6 poems. **Pays $8/page.**

TIPS Submissions must be either scholarly or formally innovative. Contributors should be familiar with current literary trends in Canada and the U.S. Scholars should be aware of current schools of theory. All submissions should be accompanied by a brief cover letter; essays should be formatted according to the MLA guide. The publication is not divided into departments. We accept innovative poetry, experimental prose, and scholarly essays.

⚙️💲 THE MALAHAT REVIEW

The University of Victoria, P.O. Box 1700, STN CSC, Victoria BC V8W 2Y2 Canada. (250)721-8524. **E-mail:** malahat@uvic.ca (for queries only). **Website:** www.malahatreview.ca. **Contact:** John Barton, editor. **100% freelance written. Eager to work with new/unpublished writers.** Quarterly magazine covering poetry, fiction, creative nonfiction, and reviews. "We try to achieve a balance of views and styles in each issue. We strive for a mix of the best writing by both established and new writers." Estab. 1967. Circ. 2,000. Byline given. Pays on acceptance. No kill fee. Publishes ms an average of 6 months after acceptance. Accepts queries by online submission form. Accepts simultaneous submissions. Responds in 2 weeks to queries; 3-10 months to mss. Sample: $16.95 (U.S.). Guidelines available online.

NONFICTION Submit via online submissions manager: malahatreview.ca/submission_guidelines. html#submittable. Length: 1,000-3,500 words. **Pays $60/magazine page.**

FICTION Buys 12-14 mss/year. Submit via online submissions manager: malahatreview.ca/submission_guidelines.html#submittable. Length: up to 8,000 words. **Pays $60/magazine page.**

POETRY Needs avant-garde, free verse, traditional. Submit 3-5 poems via online submissions manager: malahatreview.ca/submission_guidelines. html#submittable. Buys 100 poems/year. Length: up to 6 pages. **Pays $60/magazine page.**

TIPS "Please do not send more than 1 submission at a time: 3-5 poems, 1 piece of creative nonfiction, or 1 short story (do not mix poetry and prose in the same submission). See *The Malahat Review*'s Open Season Awards for poetry and short fiction, creative nonfiction, long poem, and novella contests in the Awards section of our website."

💲💲 MĀNOA: A PACIFIC JOURNAL OF INTERNATIONAL WRITING

University of Hawaii at Mānoa, English Department, Honolulu HI 96822. **E-mail:** mjournal-l@lists.hawaii. edu. **Website:** manoajournal.hawaii.edu. **Contact:** Frank Stewart, editor. Semiannual magazine. *Mānoa* is seeking high-quality literary fiction, poetry, essays, and translations for an international audience. In general, each issue is devoted to new work from an area of the Asia-Pacific region. "We recommend that authors and translators who wish to submit work examine a copy of the journal and review our website carefully. Our thanks for doing so." Estab. 1989. Circ. 1,000 print, 10,000 digital. Byline given. Pays on publication. Editorial lead time 9 months. Accepts queries by online submission form. Accepts simultaneous submissions. Responds in 3 weeks to queries. Sample: $20 (U.S.). Guidelines available online.

> *Mānoa* has received numerous awards, and work published in the magazine has been selected for prize anthologies. See website for recently published issues.

NONFICTION No Pacific exotica. Query first. Length: 1,000-5,000 words. **Pays $25/printed page.**

FICTION Query first. Needs mainstream, contemporary, excerpted novel. No Pacific exotica. **Buys 1-2 mss/year.** Send complete ms. Length: 1,000-7,500 words. **Pays $100-500 ($25/printed page).**

POETRY No light verse. Buys 10-20 poems/year. Submit maximum 6 poems. **Pays $25/poem.**

TIPS "Not accepting unsolicited mss at this time because of commitments to special projects. Please query before sending mss as e-mail attachments."

💲💲💲 THE MISSOURI REVIEW

357 McReynolds Hall, University of Missouri, Columbia MO 65211. (573)882-4474. **Fax:** (573)884-4671. **E-**

mail: question@moreview.com. **Website:** www.missourireview.com. **90% freelance written.** Quarterly magazine. Publishes contemporary fiction, poetry, interviews, personal essays, cartoons, special features—such as History as Literature series, Found Text series, and Curio Cabinet art features—for the literary and the general reader interested in a wide range of subjects. Estab. 1978. Circ. 6,500. Byline given. Pays on publication Editorial lead time 4-6 months. Accepts queries by mail, online submission form. Accepts simultaneous submissions. Responds in 2 weeks to queries; in 10-12 weeks to mss. Sample copy: $10 or online. Guidelines available online.

NONFICTION Needs book excerpts, essays. No literary criticism. **Buys 10 mss/year.** Send complete ms. **Pays $40/printed page.**

FICTION Needs ethnic, humorous, mainstream, literary. **Buys 25 mss/year.** Send complete ms. Length: No restrictions, but longer mss (9,000-12,000 words) or flash fiction ms (up to 2,000 words) must be truly exceptional to be published. **Pays $40/printed page.**

POETRY *TMR* publishes poetry features only—6-14 pages of poems by each of 3-5 poets per issue. Keep in mind the length of features when submitting poems. Typically, successful submissions include 8-20 pages of unpublished poetry. (Note: Do not send complete mss—published or unpublished—for consideration.) No inspirational verse. **Pays $40/printed page and 3 contributor's copies.**

TIPS "Send your best work."

MODERN HAIKU

P.O. Box 930, Portsmouth RI 02871. **E-mail:** modernhaiku@gmail.com. **Website:** modernhaiku.org. **Contact:** Paul Miller, editor. **85% freelance written.** Magazine published 3 times/year in February, June, and October covering haiku poetry. *Modern Haiku* is the foremost international journal of English-language haiku and criticism and publishes high-quality material only. Haiku and related genres, articles on haiku, haiku book reviews, and translations comprise its contents. It has an international circulation; subscribers include many university, school, and public libraries. Estab. 1969. Circ. 650. Byline given. No kill fee. Publishes ms an average of 6 months after acceptance. Editorial lead time 4 months. Accepts queries by mail, e-mail. Responds in 1 week to queries; in 6-8 weeks to mss. Sample copy: $15 in North America, $16 in Canada, $20 in Mexico, $22 overseas. Subscription:

$35 ppd by regular mail in the U.S. Payment possible by PayPal on the *Modern Haiku* website. Guidelines available for SASE or on website.

NONFICTION Needs essays, general interest. Send complete ms. **Pays $5/page.**

COLUMNS/DEPARTMENTS Haiku & Senryu; Haibun; Essays (on haiku and related genres); Reviews (books of haiku or related genres). **Buys 40 mss/year.** Send complete ms. **Pays $5/page.**

POETRY Needs haiku, senryu, haibun, haiga. Postal submissions: "Send 5-15 haiku on 1 or 2 letter-sized sheets. Put name and address at the top of each sheet. Include SASE." E-mail submissions: "May be attachments (recommended) or pasted in body of message. Subject line must read: MH Submission. Adhere to guidelines on the website." Publishes 750 poems/year. Has published haiku by Roberta Beary, Billy Collins, Lawrence Ferlinghetti, Carolyn Hall, Sharon Olds, Gary Snyder, John Stevenson, George Swede, and Cor van den Heuvel. Does not want "general poetry, tanka, renku, linked-verse forms. No special consideration given to work by children and teens." **Offers no payment.**

TIPS "Study the history of haiku, read books about haiku, learn the aesthetics of haiku and methods of composition. Write about your sense perceptions of the suchness of entities; avoid ego-centered interpretations. Be sure the work you send us conforms to the definitions on our website."

NARRATIVE MAGAZINE

2443 Fillmore St., #214, San Francisco CA 94115. **E-mail:** contact@narrativemagazine.com. **Website:** www.narrativemagazine.com. **Contact:** Michael Croft, senior editor; Mimi Kusch, managing editor; Michael Wiegers, poetry editor. **100% freelance written.** Online literary journal that publishes American and international literature 3 times/year. "*Narrative* publishes high-quality contemporary literature in a full range of styles, forms, and lengths. Submit poetry, fiction, and nonfiction, including stories, short shorts, novels, novel excerpts, novellas, personal essays, humor, sketches, memoirs, literary biographies, commentary, reportage, interviews, and short audio recordings of short-short stories and poems. We welcome submissions of previously unpublished mss of all lengths, ranging from short-short stories to complete book-length works for serialization. In addition to submissions for issues of *Narrative* itself, we also encourage submissions for our Story of the Week, literary contests, and Readers' Narratives. Please read our Submission Guidelines for all information on mss formatting, word lengths, author payment, and other policies. We accept submissions only through our electronic submission system. We do not accept submissions through postal services or e-mail. You may send us mss for the following submission categories: General Submissions, Narrative Prize, Story of the Week, Readers' Narrative, iPoem, iStory, Six-Word Story, or a specific Contest. Your ms must be in one of the following file forms: DOC, RTF, PDF, DOCX, TXT, WPD, ODF, MP3, MP4, MOV, or FLV." Estab. 2003. Circ. 250,000. Byline given. Accepts queries by e-mail. Accepts simultaneous submissions. Responds in 1 month-14 weeks to queries. Guidelines available online. Charges $23 reading fee except for 2 weeks in April.

NONFICTION Needs book excerpts, essays, general interest, humor, interview, memoir, personal experience, photo feature, travel. Send complete ms.

FICTION Has published work by Alice Munro, Tobias Wolff, Marvin Bell, Jane Smiley, Joyce Carol Oates, E.L. Doctorow, and Min Jin Lee. Publishes new and emerging writers. fiction, cartoons, graphic art, and multimedia content "to entertain, inspire, and engage." Send complete ms. **Pays on publication between $150-1,000, $1,000-5,000 for book length, plus annual prizes of more than $32,000.**

POETRY Needs poetry of all forms.

TIPS "Log on and study our magazine online. Narrative fiction, graphic art, and multimedia are selected, first and foremost, for quality."

🆂 NEW ENGLAND REVIEW

Middlebury College, Middlebury VT 05753. (802)443-5075. **E-mail:** nereview@middlebury.edu. **Website:** www.nereview.com. **Contact:** Marcia Parlow, managing editor. Quarterly literary magazine. *New England Review* is a prestigious, nationally distributed literary journal. Reads September 1 through May 31 (postmarked dates). Estab. 1978. Circ. 2,000. Byline given. Pays on publication. No kill fee. Publishes ms an average of 6 months after acceptance. Accepts simultaneous submissions. Responds in 2 weeks to queries; in 3 months to mss. Sometimes comments on rejected mss. Sample copy: $10 (add $5 for overseas). Subscription: $35. Overseas shipping fees add $25 for subscription, $12 for Canada. Guidelines available online.

NONFICTION **Buys 20-25 mss/year.** Send complete ms via online submission manager. No e-mail submissions. Length: up to 7,500 words, though exceptions may be made. **Pays $20/page ($40 minimum) and 2 contributor's copies.**

FICTION Send 1 story at a time, unless it is very short. Wants only serious literary fiction and novel excerpts. Publishes approximately 10 new writers/year. Has published work by Steve Almond, Christine Sneed, Roy Kesey, Thomas Gough, Norman Lock, Brock Clarke, Carl Phillips, Lucia Perillo, Linda Gregerson, and Natasha Trethewey. **Buys 25 mss/year.** Send complete ms via online submission manager. No e-mail submissions. "Will consider simultaneous submissions, but it must be stated as such and you must notify us immediately if the ms is accepted for publication elsewhere." Length: not strict on word count. **Pays $20/page ($20 minimum), and 2 contributor's copies.**

POETRY Submit up to 6 poems at a time. No previously published or simultaneous submissions for poetry. Accepts submissions by online submission manager only; accepts questions by e-mail. "Cover letters are useful." Address submissions to "Poetry Editor." Buys 75-90 poems/year. Submit maximum 6 poems. **Pays $20/page ($20 minimum), and 2 contributor's copies.**

TIPS "We consider short fiction, including short shorts, novellas, and self-contained extracts from novels in both traditional and experimental forms. In nonfiction, we consider a variety of general and literary but not narrowly scholarly essays; we also publish long and short poems, screenplays, graphics, translations, critical reassessments, statements by artists working in various media, testimonies, and letters from abroad. We are committed to exploration of all forms of contemporary cultural expression in the U.S. and abroad. With few exceptions, we print only work not published previously elsewhere."

🆂 NEW LETTERS

University of Missouri-Kansas City, 5101 Rockhill Rd., Kansas City MO 64110. (816)235-1168. **Fax:** (816)235-2611. **E-mail:** newletters@umkc.edu. **Website:** www.newletters.org. **Contact:** Robert Stewart, editor-in-chief. **100% freelance written.** "*New Letters*, published quarterly, continues to seek the best new writing, whether from established writers or those ready and waiting to be discovered. In addition, it supports those writers, readers, and listeners who want to experience the joy of writing that can both surprise and inspire us all." Estab. 1934. Circ. 5,000. Byline given. Pays on publication. No kill fee. Publishes ms an average of 6 months after acceptance. Editorial lead time 6 months. Submit seasonal material 6 months in advance. Accepts queries by mail. Accepts simultaneous submissions. Responds in 1 month to queries; 5 months to mss. Sample copy: $10; sample articles on website. Guidelines available online.

O Submissions are not read May 1 through October 1.

NONFICTION Needs essays. No self-help, how-to, or nonliterary work. **Buys 8-10 mss/year.** Send complete ms. Length: up to 5,000 words. **Pays $40-100.**

PHOTOS Send photos. Reviews contact sheets, 2x4 transparencies, prints. Pays $10-40/photo. Buys one-time rights.

FICTION Needs ethnic, experimental, humorous, mainstream, contemporary. No genre fiction. **Buys 15-20 mss/year.** Send complete ms. Length: up to 5,000 words. **Pays $30-75.**

POETRY Needs avant-garde, free verse, haiku, traditional. No light verse. Buys 40-50 poems/year. Submit maximum 6 poems. Length: open. **Pays $10-25.**

TIPS "We aren't interested in essays that are footnoted or essays usually described as scholarly or critical. Our preference is for creative nonfiction or personal essays. We prefer shorter stories and essays to longer ones (an average length is 3,500-4,000 words). We have no rigid preferences as to subject, style, or genre, although commercial efforts tend to put us off. Even so, our only fixed requirement is good writing."

NEW OHIO REVIEW

English Department, 360 Ellis Hall, Ohio University, Athens OH 45701. (740)707-3191. **E-mail:** noreditors@ohio.edu. **Website:** www.ohiou.edu/nor. **Contact:** David Wanczyk, editor. *New Ohio Review*, published biannually in spring and fall, publishes fiction, nonfiction, and poetry. Member CLMP. Reading period is September 15-December 15 and January 15-April 15. Annual contests, Jan 15th-Apr 15th ($1000 prizes). Estab. 2007. Byline given. No kill fee. Accepts queries by e-mail, online submission form. Accepts simultaneous submissions. Responds in 2-4 months. Single copy: $9. Subscription: $16. Guidelines available on website.

NONFICTION Needs essays, general interest, memoir. Submit complete ms. **Pays minimum of $30 in addition to 2 contributor's copies and one-year subscription.**

FICTION Considers literary short fiction; no novel excerpts. Send complete ms. **Pays $30 minimum in addition to 2 contributor's copies and one-year subscription.**

POETRY Needs quality free verse, formal, experimental. Please do not submit more than once every 6 months unless requested to do so. Submit maximum 6 poems.

☯ $ $ THE NEW QUARTERLY

St. Jerome's University, 290 Westmount Rd. N., Waterloo ON N2L 3G3 Canada. (519)884-8111, ext. 28290. **E-mail:** editor@tnq.ca; info@tnq.ca. **Website:** www.tnq.ca. **95% freelance written.** Quarterly book covering Canadian fiction and poetry. "Emphasis on emerging writers and genres, but we publish more traditional work as well if the language and narrative structure are fresh." Estab. 1981. Circ. 1,000. Byline given. Pays on publication. No kill fee. Editorial lead time 6 months. Accepts queries by mail. Accepts simultaneous submissions. Responds in early January to submissions received March 1-August 31; in early June to submissions received September 1-February 28. Sample copy: $16.95 (cover price, plus mailing). Guidelines available online.

O Open to Canadian writers only. Reading periods: March 1-August 31; September 1-February 28.

NONFICTION Needs essays. Query with a proposal.

FICTION "*Canadian work only*. We are not interested in genre fiction. We are looking for innovative, beautifully crafted, deeply felt literary fiction." literary. **Buys 20-25 mss/year.** Send complete ms with submission cover sheet and bio. Does not accept submissions by e-mail. Accepts simultaneoues submissions if indicated in cover letter. **Pays $250/story.**

POETRY Needs avant-garde, free verse, traditional. *Canadian work only*. Send with submission cover sheet and bio. Does not accept submissions by e-mail. Accepts simultaneoues submissions if indicated in cover letter. Submit maximum 3 poems. **Pays $40/poem.**

TIPS "Reading us is the best way to get our measure. We don't have preconceived ideas about what we're looking for other than that it must be Canadian work

(Canadian writers, not necessarily Canadian content). We want something that's fresh, something that will repay a second reading, something in which the language soars and the feeling is complexly rendered."

NINTH LETTER

Department of English, University of Illinois, 608 S. Wright St., Urbana IL 61801. **E-mail:** info@ninthletter.com; editor@ninthletter.com; fiction@ninthletter.com; poetry@ninthletter.com; nonfiction@ninthletter.com. **Website:** www.ninthletter.com. **Contact:** Editorial staff rotates; contact genre-specific e-mail address with inquiries. "*Ninth Letter* accepts submissions of fiction, poetry, and essays from September 1-February 28 (postmark dates). *Ninth Letter* is published semiannually at the University of Illinois, Urbana-Champaign. We are interested in prose and poetry that experiment with form, narrative, and nontraditional subject matter, as well as more traditional literary work." Pays on publication. Accepts queries by mail, online submission form. Accepts simultaneous submissions.

NONFICTION "Please send only 1 essay at a time. All mailed submissions must include an SASE for reply." Length: up to 8,000 words. **Pays $25/printed page and 2 contributor's copies.**

FICTION "Please send only 1 story at a time. All mailed submissions must include an SASE for reply." Length: up to 8,000 words. **Pays $25/printed page and 2 contributor's copies.**

POETRY Submit 3-6 poems (no more than 10 pages) at a time. "All mailed submissions must include an SASE for reply." **Pays $25/printed page and 2 contributor's copies.**

NOTRE DAME REVIEW

University of Notre Dame, B009C McKenna Hall, Notre Dame IN 46556. **Website:** ndreview.nd.edu. "The *Notre Dame Review* is an independent, noncommercial magazine of contemporary American and international fiction, poetry, criticism, and art. Especially interested in work that takes on big issues by making the invisible seen, that gives voice to the voiceless. In addition to showcasing celebrated authors like Seamus Heaney and Czelaw Milosz, the *Notre Dame Review* introduces readers to authors they may have never encountered before but who are doing innovative and important work. In conjunction with the *Notre Dame Review*, the online companion to the printed magazine, the *nd[re]view*, engages readers as a

community centered in literary rather than commercial concerns, a community we reach out to through critique and commentary as well as aesthetic experience." Estab. 1995. Circ. 2,000. Pays on publication. Publishes ms an average of 6 months after acceptance. Accepts queries by online submission form. Accepts simultaneous submissions. Responds in 4 or more months to mss. Sample copy: $6. Guidelines online.

Does not accept e-mail submissions. Only reads hardcopy submissions September through November and January through March.

FICTION "We're eclectic. Upcoming theme issues planned. List of upcoming themes or editorial calendar available for SASE." No genre fiction. **Buys 10 mss/year.** Submit complete ms via online submissions manager. Length: up to 3,000 words. **Pays $5-25.**

POETRY Submit 3-5 poems via online submissions manager. Buys 90 poems/year.

TIPS "Excellence is our sole criteria for selection, although we are especially interested in fiction and poetry that take on big issues."

ONE STORY

232 3rd St., #A108, Brooklyn NY 11215. **Website:** www.one-story.com. **Contact:** Maribeth Batcha, publisher. **100% freelance written.** "*One Story* is a literary magazine that contains, simply, 1 story. Approximately every 3-4 weeks, subscribers are sent *One Story* in the mail. *One Story* is artfully designed, lightweight, easy to carry, and ready to entertain on buses, in bed, in subways, in cars, in the park, in the bath, in the waiting rooms of doctor's offices, on the couch, or in line at the supermarket. Subscribers also have access to a website where they can learn more about *One Story* authors and hear about *One Story* readings and events. There is always time to read *One Story*." Estab. 2002. Circ. 3,500. Byline given. Pays on publication. Publishes ms an average of 3-6 months after acceptance. Editorial lead time 3-4 months. Accepts queries by online submission form. Accepts simultaneous submissions. Responds in 2-4 months to mss. Sample copy: $2.50 (back issue). Guidelines available online.

Reading period: September 1-May 31.

FICTION Needs short stories. *One Story* only accepts short stories. Do not send excerpts. Do not send more than 1 story at a time. **Buys 18 mss/year.** Send complete ms using online submission form. Length:

3,000-8,000 words. **Pays $500 and 25 contributor's copies.**

TIPS "*One Story* is looking for stories that are strong enough to stand alone. Therefore they must be very good. We want the best you can give."

ORBIS

17 Greenhow Ave., West Kirby Wirral CH48 5EL United Kingdom. **E-mail:** carolebaldock@hotmail.com. **Website:** www.orbisjournal.com. **Contact:** Carole Baldock, editor; Noel Williams, reviews editor. *Orbis* covers 84 pages of news, reviews, views, letters, features, prose, and a lot of poetry and cover artwork. Each writer is eligible for the Readers Award: £50 (plus £50 divided between the runners-up). Poems are also submitted to the Forward Prize (U.K.) and the Pushcart Prize (U.S.). "*Orbis* has long been considered one of the top 20 small-press magazines in the U.K. We are interested in social inclusion projects and encouraging access to the arts, young people, under 20s, and 20-somethings. Subjects for discussion: 'day in the life,' technical, topical." Estab. 1969. No kill fee. Accepts queries by mail, e-mail. Accepts simultaneous submissions. Responds in 3 months.

Please see guidelines on website before submitting.

NONFICTION Needs essays, reviews, technical, features. Query. **Pays £50.**

PHOTOS Wants artwork for cover.

FICTION Submit by postal mail or e-mail (overseas submissions only). Include cover letter. **Buys 12 mss/year.** Length: up to 1,000 words.

POETRY Submit by postal mail or e-mail (overseas submissions only). Include cover letter. Buys 160 poems/year.

TIPS "Any publication should be read cover to cover because it's the best way to improve your chances of getting published. Enclose SAE with all correspondence. Overseas: 2 IRCs, 3 if work is to be returned."

OVERTIME

Blue Cubicle Press, LLC, P.O. Box 250382, Plano TX 75025. **E-mail:** overtime@workerswritejournal.com. **Website:** www.workerswritejournal.com/overtime.htm. **Contact:** David LaBounty, editor. **100% freelance written.** Quarterly saddle-stitched chapbook covering working-class literature. Estab. 2006. Circ. 500. Byline given. Pays on acceptance of ms. Publishes ms 6 months after acceptance. Accepts queries by mail, e-mail. Accepts simultaneous submissions.

Responds in 1 week to queries; 1 month to mss. Sample copy and writer's guidelines available online at website.

FICTION Needs adventure, condensed novels, ethnic, experimental, historical, humorous, mainstream, novel excerpts, short stories, slice-of-life vignettes, working-class literature. **Buys 4 mss/year.** Query; send complete ms. Length: 5,000-12,000 words. **Pays $35-50.**

PAINTED BRIDE QUARTERLY

Drexel University, Department of English and Philosophy, 3141 Chestnut St., Philadelphia PA 19104. **E-mail:** info@pbqmag.org. **Website:** pbqmag.org. **Contact:** Kathleen Volk Miller and Marion Wrenn, editors. Publishes online each quarter with a print annual each spring. *Painted Bride Quarterly* seeks literary fiction (experimental and traditional), poetry, and artwork and photographs. Estab. 1973. No kill fee. Accepts queries by online submission form. Accepts simultaneous submissions. Responds in 6 months to mss. Guidelines available online and by e-mail.

NONFICTION Needs essays, literary criticism. Submit 1 ms through online submissions manager. Length: up to 3,000 words. **Pays $20.**

FICTION Publishes theme-related work; check website. Holds annual fiction contests. ethnic, experimental, feminist, gay, lesbian, literary, short stories, translations. Send complete ms through online submissions manager. Length: up to 5,000 words. **Pays $20.**

POETRY Submit up to 3 poems through online submissions manager. "We have no specifications or restrictions. We'll look at anything." **Pays $20/poem.**

TIPS "We look for freshness of idea incorporated with high-quality writing. We receive an awful lot of nicely written work with worn-out plots. We want quality in whatever—we hold experimental work to as strict standards as anything else. Many of our readers write fiction; most of them enjoy a good reading. We hope to be an outlet for quality. A good story gives, first, enjoyment to the reader. We've seen a good many of them lately, and we've published the best of them."

PANK

PANK, Department of Humanities, 1400 Townsend Dr., Houghton MI 49931-1200. **Website:** www.pankmagazine.com. **100% freelance written.** Annual literary magazine. "*PANK* Magazine fosters access to emerging and experimental poetry and prose, publishing the brightest and most promising writers for the most adventurous readers. To the end of the road, up country, a far shore, the edge of things, to a place of amalgamation and unplumbed depths, where the known is made and unmade, and where unimagined futures are born, a place inhabited by contradictions, a place of quirk and startling anomaly. *PANK*, no soft pink hands allowed." Estab. 2006. Circ. 1,000/ print; 18,000/online. Publishes ms an average of 3-12 months after acceptance. Accepts queries by online submission form. Accepts simultaneous submissions. Guidelines available on website.

NONFICTION Needs essays, general interest, historical, humor, nostalgic, opinion. Send complete ms through online submissions manager. **Pays $20, a one-year subscription, and a** *PANK* **t-shirt.**

FICTION "Bright, new, energetic, passionate writing, writing that pushes our tender little buttons and gets us excited. Push our tender buttons, excite us, and we'll publish you." Send complete ms through online submissions manager. **Pays $20, a one-year subscription, and a** *PANK* **t-shirt.**

POETRY Submit through online submissions manager. **Pays $20, a one-year subscription, and a** *PANK* **t-shirt.**

TIPS "To read *PANK* is to know *PANK*. Or, read a lot within the literary magazine and small-press universe—there's plenty to choose from. Unfortunately, we see a lot of submissions from writers who have clearly read neither *PANK* nor much else. Serious writers are serious readers. Read. Seriously."

💲💲 PARNASSUS: POETRY IN REVIEW

Poetry in Review Foundation, 205 W. 89th St., #8F, New York NY 10024. (212)787-3569. **E-mail:** info@ parnassus.com. **Website:** www.parnassusreview.com. **Contact:** Herbert Leibowitz, editor and publisher. Annual magazine covering poetry and criticism. "We now publish 1 double issue/year." *Parnassus: Poetry in Review* provides "a forum where poets, novelists, and critics of all persuasions can gather to review new books of poetry, including translations—international poetries have occupied center stage from our very first issue—with an amplitude and reflectiveness that Sunday book supplements and even the literary quarterlies could not afford. Our editorial philosophy is based on the assumption that reviewing is a complex art. Like a poem or a short story, a review essay requires imagination; scrupulous attention to rhythm, pacing, and supple syntax; space in which to build a

persuasive, detailed argument; analytical precision and intuitive gambits; verbal play, wit, and metaphor. We welcome and vigorously seek out voices that break aesthetic molds and disturb xenophobic habits." Estab. 1972. Circ. 1,800. Byline given. Pays on publication. No kill fee. Publishes ms an average of 12-14 months after acceptance. Accepts queries by mail. Accepts simultaneous submissions. Responds in 2 months to mss. Sample copy: $15.

NONFICTION Needs essays, reviews. **Buys 30 mss/ year.** Query with published clips. Length: 1,500-7,500 words. **Pays $200-1,000.**

POETRY Needs avant garde, free verse, traditional. Accepts most types of poetry. Buys 3-4 unsolicited poems/year.

TIPS "Be certain you have read the magazine and are aware of the editor's taste. Blind submissions are a waste of everybody's time. We'd like to see more poems that display intellectual acumen and curiosity about history, science, music, etc., and fewer trivial lyrical poems about the self, or critical prose that's academic and dull. Prose should sing."

THE PEDESTAL MAGAZINE

6815 Honors Court, Charlotte NC 28210. **E-mail:** pedmagazine@carolina.rr.com. **Website:** www.the-pedestalmagazine.com. **Contact:** John Amen, editor in chief. Committed to promoting diversity and celebrating the voice of the individual. Estab. 2000. No kill fee. Accepts queries by online submission form. Accepts simultaneous submissions. Responds in 1-2 months to mss. Guidelines available online.

🗨 See website for reading periods for different forms. Member: CLMP.

NONFICTION Needs essays, interview, reviews. **Pays $40.**

PHOTOS Reviews JPEG, GIF files.

FICTION "We are receptive to all sorts of high-quality literary fiction. Genre fiction is encouraged as long as it crosses or comments upon its genre and is both character-driven and psychologically acute. We encourage submissions of short fiction, no more than 3 flash fiction pieces at a time. There is no need to query prior to submitting; please submit via online submissions manager—no e-mail to the editor." Needs adventure, ethnic, experimental, historical, horror, humorous, mainstream, mystery, romance, science fiction, works that don't fit into a specific category. **Buys 10-25 mss/year.** Length: up to 4,000 words for short stories; up to 1,000 words for flash fiction. **Pays 3¢/word.**

POETRY Open to a wide variety of poetry, ranging from the highly experimental to the traditionally formal. Submit all poems in 1 form. No need to query before submitting. Submit maximum 5 poems. No length restriction.

TIPS "If you send us your work, please wait for a response to your first submission before you submit again."

PLANET: THE WELSH INTERNATIONALIST

Berw Ltd., P.O. Box 44, Aberystwyth Ceredigion SY23 3ZZ United Kingdom. 01970 622408. **E-mail:** submissions@planetmagazine.org.uk. **Website:** www.planet-magazine.org.uk. Lowri Angharad Pearson, Administrative and Marketing Assistant. **Contact:** Emily Trahair, editor. Quarterly journal. A literary/cultural/political journal centered on Welsh affairs but with a strong interest in minority cultures in Europe and elsewhere. *Planet: The Welsh Internationalist*, published quarterly, is a cultural magazine centered on Wales, but with broader interests in arts, sociology, politics, history, and science. Estab. 1970. Circ. 900. Publishes ms 4-6 months after acceptance. Accepts queries by mail, e-mail, phone. Responds in 3 months. Single copy: £6.75; subscription: £22 (£40 overseas). Sample copy: £5. Guidelines online.

   Planet is 96 pages, A5, professionally printed, perfect-bound, with glossy colour card cover. Receives about 500 submissions/year, accepts about 5%. Press run is 1,000 (800 subscribers, about 10% libraries, 200 shelf sales).

NONFICTION Needs essays, general interest, historical, humor, interview, personal experience, reviews, travel. Query. Subscriptions.

FICTION Would like to see more inventive, imaginative fiction that pays attention to language and experiments with form. No magical realism, horror, science fiction. Submit complete ms via mail or e-mail (with attachment). For postal submissions, no submissions returned unless accompanied by an SASE. Writers submitting from abroad should send at least 3 IRCs for return of typescript; 1 IRC for reply only. Length: 1,500-2,750 words. **Pays £50/1,000 words.**

POETRY Wants good poetry in a wide variety of styles. No limitations as to subject matter; length can be a problem. Has published poetry by Nigel Jenkins, Anne Stevenson, and Les Murray. Submit 4-6 poems via mail or e-mail (with attachment). For postal submissions, no submissions returned unless accompanied by an SASE. Writers submitting from abroad should send at least 3 IRCs for return of typescript; 1 IRC for reply only. **Pays £30/poem.**

TIPS "We do not look for fiction that necessarily has a 'Welsh' connection, which some writers assume from our title. We try to publish a broad range of fiction, and our main criterion is quality. Try to read copies of any magazine you submit to. Don't write out of the blue to a magazine which might be completely inappropriate for your work. Recognize that you are likely to have a high rejection rate, as magazines tend to favor writers from their own countries."

PLEIADES: LITERATURE IN CONTEXT

University of Central Missouri, Department of English, Martin 336, 415 E. Clark St., Warrensburg MO 64093. (660)543-4268. **E-mail:** clintoncrockettp@gmail.com (nonfiction inquiries); pnguyen@ucmo.edu (fiction inquiries); pleiadespoetryeditor@gmail.com (poetry inquiries). **Website:** www.pleiadesmag.com. **Contact:** Clint Crockett Peters, nonfiction editor; Phong Nguyen, fiction editor; and Jenny Molberg, poetry editor. **100% freelance written.** "We publish contemporary fiction, poetry, interviews, literary essays, special-interest personal essays, and reviews for a general and literary audience from authors from around the world." Reads in the months of July for the summer issue and December for the winter issue. Estab. 1991. Circ. 3,000. Byline given. Pays on publication. No kill fee. Publishes ms an average of 9 months after acceptance. Editorial lead time 9 months. Accepts queries by mail. Accepts simultaneous submissions. Responds in 2 months to queries; in 1-4 months to mss. Sample copy for $5 (back issue); $6 (current issue). Guidelines available online.

NONFICTION Needs book excerpts, essays, interview, reviews. "Nothing pedantic, slick, or shallow." **Buys 4-6 mss/year.** Send complete ms via online submission manager. Length: 2,000-4,000 words. **Pays $10 and contributor's copies.**

FICTION Reads fiction year-round. Needs ethnic, experimental, humorous, mainstream, magic realism. No science fiction, fantasy, confession, erotica. **Buys 16-20 mss/year.** Send complete ms via online submission manager. Length: 2,000-6,000 words. **Pays $10 and contributor's copies.**

POETRY Needs avant-garde, free verse, haiku, light verse, traditional. Submit 3-5 poems via online submission manager. "Nothing didactic, pretentious, or overly sentimental." Buys 40-50 poems/year. **Pays $3/poem and contributor copies.**

TIPS "Submit only 1 genre at a time to appropriate editors. Show care for your material and your readers—submit quality work in a professional format. Cover art is solicited directly from artists. We accept queries for book reviews."

⬤⬤ PLOUGHSHARES

Emerson College, 120 Boylston St., Boston MA 02116. (617)824-3757. **E-mail:** pshares@pshares.org. **Website:** www.pshares.org. **Contact:** Ladette Randolph, editor in chief/executive director; Ellen Duffer, managing editor. *Ploughshares*, published 3 times/year, is "a journal of new writing guest-edited by prominent poets and writers to reflect different and contrasting points of view. Translations are welcome if permission has been granted. Our mission is to present dynamic, contrasting views on what is valid and important in contemporary literature and to discover and advance significant literary talent. Each issue is guest-edited by a different writer. We no longer structure issues around preconceived themes." Editors have included Carolyn Forché, Gerald Stern, Rita Dove, Chase Twichell, and Marilyn Hacker. "We now accept electronic submissions—there is a $3 fee per submission, which is waived if you are a subscriber." Estab. 1971. Circ. 6,000. Pays on publication. Publishes ms an average of 6 months after acceptance. Accepts queries by mail, online submission form. Accepts simultaneous submissions. Responds in 3-5 months to mss. Sample copy: $14 for current issue, $7 for back issue; please inquire for shipping rates. Subscription: $30 domestic, $30 plus shipping (see website) foreign. Guidelines online.

⬤ *Ploughshares* is 200 pages, digest-sized. Receives about 11,000 poetry, fiction, and essay submissions/year. Reads submissions June 1-January 15 (postmark); mss submitted January 16-May 31 will be returned unread.

NONFICTION Needs essays. Submit complete ms via online submissions form or by mail. Length: up to 6,000 words. **Pays $45/printed page ($90 minimum, $450 maximum); 2 contributor's copies; and one-year subscription.**

FICTION Has published work by ZZ Packer, Antonya Nelson, and Stuart Dybek. "No genre (science fiction, detective, gothic, adventure, etc.), popular formula, or commerical fiction whose purpose is to entertain rather than to illuminate." Submit via online submissions form or by mail. Length: up to 6,000 words **Pays $45/printed page ($90 minimum, $450 maximum); 2 contributor's copies; and one-year subscription.**

POETRY Needs avant-garde, free verse, traditional. Submit up to 5 poems via online submissions form or by mail. Has published poetry by Donald Hall, Li-Young Lee, Robert Pinsky, Brenda Hillman, and Thylias Moss. **Pays $45/printed page ($90 minimum, $450 maximum); 2 contributor's copies; and one-year subscription.**

POETRY

The Poetry Foundation, 61 W. Superior St., Chicago IL 60654. (312)787-7070. **Fax:** (312)787-6650. **E-mail:** editors@poetrymagazine.org. **Website:** www.poetry-magazine.org. Don Share, editor. **Contact:** Don Share, editor. **100% freelance written.** Monthly magazine. *Poetry*, published monthly by The Poetry Foundation (see separate listing in Organizations), "has no special ms needs and no special requirements as to form: We examine in turn all work received and accept that which seems best." Has published poetry by the major voices of our time as well as new talent. Estab. 1912. Circ. 32,500. Byline given. Pays on publication. No kill fee. Publishes ms an average of 9 months after acceptance. Accepts queries by e-mail. Accepts simultaneous submissions. Responds within 6 months to mss and queries. Guidelines available online.

⬤ *Poetry*'s website offers featured poems, letters, reviews, interviews, essays, and web-exclusive features. *Poetry* is elegantly printed, flat-spined. Receives 150,000 submissions/year, accepts about 300-350. Press run is 16,000.

NONFICTION Buys 14 mss/year. Query. No length requirements. **Pays $150/page.**

POETRY Publishes poetry all styles and subject matter. Submit up to 4 poems via Submittable. Reviews books of poetry, most solicited. Buys 180-250 poems/year. Length: up to 10 pages total. **Pays $10 line (minimum payment of $300).**

⬤ POETRY IRELAND REVIEW

Poetry Ireland, 11 Parnell Square East, Dublin 1 Ireland. +353 (0)1 6789815. **E-mail:** publications@poetryireland.ie. **Website:** www.poetryireland.ie. Three times a year covers poetry, reviews, and essays magazine in book form. Estab. 1978. Circ. 2,000. Pays on publication. No kill fee. Accepts queries by mail. Accepts simultaneous submissions. Responds in 1 week to queries. Responds in 3 months to mss. Guidelines available on website: www.poetryireland.ie/writers/submission-to-pir/.

POETRY Needs avant-garde, free verse, haiku, traditional. Buys 120 poems/year. Submit maximum 6 poems. **Pays $32/submission.**

○ THE PRAIRIE JOURNAL

P.O. Box 68073, 28 Crowfoot Terrace NW, Calgary AB T3G 3N8 Canada. **E-mail:** editor@prairiejournal.org (queries only); prairiejournal@yahoo.com. **Website:** www.prairiejournal.org. **Contact:** Anne Burke, literary editor. **100% freelance written.** Semiannual magazine publishing quality poetry, short fiction, drama, literary criticism, reviews, bibliography, interviews, profiles, and artwork. "The audience is literary, university, library, scholarly, and creative readers/writers." Estab. 1983. Circ. 650-750. Byline given. Pays on publication. No kill fee. Publishes ms an average of 4-6 months after acceptance. Editorial lead time 2-6 months. Accepts queries by mail. Responds in 2 weeks to queries; 2-6 months to mss. Sample copy: $5. Guidelines available online.

NONFICTION Needs essays, humor, interview, literary. No inspirational, news, religious, or travel. **Buys 25-40 mss/year.** Query with published clips. Length: 100-3,000 words. **Pays $50-100, plus contributor's copy.**

PHOTOS State availability. Offers additional payment for photos accepted with ms. Rights purchased is negotiable.

COLUMNS/DEPARTMENTS Reviews (books from small presses publishing poetry, short fiction, essays, and criticism), 200-1,000 words. **Buys 5 mss/year.** Query with published clips. **Pays $10-50.**

FICTION Needs mainstream. No genre: romance, horror, western—sagebrush or cowboys—erotic, science fiction, or mystery. **Buys 6 mss/year.** Send complete ms. No e-mail submissions. Length: 100-3,000 words. **Pays $10-75.**

POETRY Needs avant-garde, free verse, haiku. Seeks poetry "of any length; free verse, contemporary themes (feminist, nature, urban, nonpolitical), aesthetic value, a poet's poetry." Does not want to see

"most rhymed verse, sentimentality, egotistical ravings. No cowboys or sage brush." Has published poetry by Liliane Welch, Cornelia Hoogland, Sheila Hyland, Zoe Lendale, and Chad Norman. Receives about 1,000 poems/year, accepts 10%. No heroic couplets or greeting-card verse. Buys 25-35 poems/year. Submit maximum 6-8 poems. Length: 3-50 lines. **Pays $5-50.**

TIPS "We publish many, many new writers and are always open to unsolicited submissions because we are 100% freelance. Do not send U.S. stamps; always use IRCs. We have poems, interviews, stories, and reviews online (query first)."

○ PRISM INTERNATIONAL

Dept. of Creative Writing, Buch E462, 1866 Main Mall, University of British Columbia, Vancouver British Columbia V6T 1Z1 Canada. (604)822-2514. **Fax:** (604)822-3616. **E-mail:** prismcirculation@gmail.com. **Website:** www.prismmagazine.ca. **100% freelance written. Works with new/unpublished writers.** A quarterly international journal of contemporary writing—fiction, poetry, drama, creative nonfiction and translation. *PRISM international* is digest-sized, elegantly printed, flat-spined, with original colour artwork on a glossy card cover. Readership: public and university libraries, individual subscriptions, bookstores—a world-wide audience concerned with the contemporary in literature. "We have no thematic or stylistic allegiances: Excellence is our main criterion for acceptance of manuscripts." Receives 1,000 submissions/year, accepts about 80. Circulation is for 1,200 subscribers. Subscription: $35/year for Canadian subscriptions, $40/year for US subscriptions, $45/year for international. Sample: $13. Estab. 1959. Circ. 1,200. Pays on publication. No kill fee. Publishes ms an average of 4 months after acceptance. Accepts queries by mail, e-mail, online submission form. Accepts simultaneous submissions. Responds in 4 months to queries. Responds in 3-6 months to mss. Sample copy for $13, more info online. Guidelines available online.

NONFICTION No reviews, tracts, or scholarly essays. **Prose pays $30/printed page, and 2 copies of issue.**

PHOTOS PRISM international buys photography for covers only. Sample copies available for $13 each; art guidelines free for SASE with first-class Canadian postage. Portfolio review not required. Buys first rights. "Image may also be used for promotional purposes related to the magazine." Pays on publication:

$300 Canadian and 2 copies of magazine. Portfolio review not required. Buys first rights. "Image may also be used for promotional purposes related to the magazine." Pays on publication: $300 Canadian and 2 copies of magazine.

FICTION For Drama: one-acts/excerpts of no more than 1500 words preferred. Also interested in seeing dramatic monologues. Needs experimental, traditional. "New writing that is contemporary and literary. Short stories and self-contained novel excerpts. Works of translation are eagerly sought and should be accompanied by a copy of the original. Would like to see more translations. No gothic, confession, religious, romance, pornography, or science fiction." **Buys 12-16 mss/year.** Send complete ms. Length: 25 pages maximum. **Pays $30/printed page, and 2 copies of issue.**

POETRY Needs avant-garde, traditional. Wants "fresh, distinctive poetry that shows an awareness of traditions old and new. We read everything." Considers poetry by children and teens. "Excellence is the only criterion." Has published poetry by Margaret Avison, Elizabeth Bachinsky, John Pass, Warren Heiti, Don McKay, Bill Bissett, and Stephanie Bolster. Submit maximum up to 6 poems. **Pays $40/printed page, and 2 copies of issue.**

TIPS "We are looking for new and exciting fiction. Excellence is still our No. 1 criterion. As well as poetry, imaginative nonfiction and fiction, we are especially open to translations of all kinds, very short fiction pieces and drama which work well on the page. Translations must come with a copy of the original language work."

THE RAG

P.O. Box 17463, Portland OR 97217. **E-mail:** submissions@raglitmag.com; seth@raglitmag.com. **Website:** raglitmag.com. **Contact:** Seth Porter, managing editor; Dan Reilly, editor. **90% freelance written.** *The Rag* focuses on the grittier genres that tend to fall by the wayside at more traditional literary magazines. *The Rag's* ultimate goal is to put the literary magazine back into the entertainment market while rekindling the social and cultural value short fiction once held in North American literature. Estab. 2011. Byline given. Pays prior to publication. Editorial lead time 1-2 months. Accepts queries by e-mail. Accepts simultaneous submissions. Responds in 1 month or less for queries; in 1-2 months for mss. Guidelines available online.

○ Fee to submit online ($3) is waived if you subscribe or purchase a single issue.

PHOTOS Reviews GIF/JPEG files. Negotiates payment individually. Purchases one-time rights.

FICTION Accepts all styles and themes. Needs humorous, transgressive. **Buys 12 mss/year.** Send complete ms. Length: up to 10,000 words. **Pays 5¢/word, $250 average/story.**

FILLERS Length: 150-1,000 words. **Pays $20-100.**

TIPS "We like gritty material: material that is psychologically believable and that has some humor in it, dark or otherwise. We like subtle themes, original characters, and sharp wit."

RALEIGH REVIEW LITERARY & ARTS MAGAZINE

Box 6725, Raleigh NC 27628-6725. **E-mail:** info@raleighreview.org. **Website:** www.raleighreview.org. Rob Greene, editor. **Contact:** Rob Greene, editor; Landon Houle, fiction editor; Bryce Emley, poetry editor. **90% freelance written.** Semiannual literary magazine. "*Raleigh Review* is a national nonprofit magazine of poetry, short fiction (including flash), and art. We believe that great literature inspires empathy by allowing us to see the world through the eyes of our neighbors, whether across the street or across the globe. Our mission is to foster the creation and availability of accessible yet provocative contemporary literature. We look for work that is emotionally and intellectually complex. Estab. 2010. Pays on publication. Publishes ms 3-6 months after acceptance. Accepts simultaneous submissions. Responds typically in 1-3 months, though sometimes up to 3-6 months. "Poetry and fiction submissions through Tell It Slant online system; no prior query required." Sample copy: $13.50 hardcopy or $4.95 on Kindle. "Sample work also online at website." Guidelines available online at www.raleighreview.org.

FICTION Needs confessions, ethnic, mainstream, novel excerpts, slice-of-life vignettes. "We prefer work that is physically grounded and accessible, though complex and rich in emotional or intellectual power. We delight in stories from unique voices and perspectives. Any fiction that is born from a relatively unknown place grabs our attention. We are not opposed to genre fiction, so long as it has real, human characters and is executed artfully." **Buys 10-15 mss/**

year. Submit complete ms. Length: 250-7,500 words. "While we accept fiction up to 7,500 words, we are more likely to publish work in the 4,500- to 5,000-word range." **Pays $10 maximum.**

POETRY Needs free verse, traditional, lyric, narrative poems of experience. Submit up to 5 poems. "If you think your poems will make a perfect stranger's toes tingle, heart leap, or brain sizzle, then send them our way. We typically do not publish avant garde, experimental, or language poetry. We *do* like a poem that causes—for a wide audience—a visceral reaction to intellectually and emotionally rich material." Buys 30-40 poems/year. Submit maximum 5 poems. Length: open. **Pays $10 maximum.**

TIPS "Please be sure to read the guidelines and look at sample work on our website. Every piece is read for its intrinsic value, so new/emerging voices are often published alongside nationally recognized, award-winning authors."

RATTLE

12411 Ventura Blvd., Studio City CA 91604. (818)505-6777. **E-mail:** tim@rattle.com. **Website:** www.rattle.com. **Contact:** Timothy Green, editor. *Rattle* publishes unsolicited poetry and translations of poetry. Estab. 1994. Accepts queries by mail, online submission form. Accepts simultaneous submissions. Responds in 1-6 months. Guidelines available online.

POETRY "We're looking for poems that move us, that might make us laugh or cry, or teach us something new. We like both free verse and traditional forms—we try to publish a representative mix of what we receive. We read a lot of poems, and only those that are unique, insightful, and musical stand out—regardless of style." Submit up to 4 poems via online submissions manager or postal mail. Buys 200 poems/year. **Pays $100/poem and a one-year subscription for print contributors; $50/poem for online contributors.**

♻ ROOM

West Coast Feminist Literary Magazine Society, P.O. Box 46160, Station D, Vancouver BC V6J 5G5 Canada. **E-mail:** contactus@roommagazine.com. **Website:** www.roommagazine.com. "*Room* is Canada's oldest feminist literary journal. Published quarterly by a collective based in Vancouver, *Room* showcases fiction, poetry, reviews, artwork, interviews, and profiles by writers and artists who identify as women or genderqueer. Many of our contributors are at the beginning of their writing careers, looking for an opportunity to get published for the first time. Some later go on to great acclaim. *Room* is a space where women can speak, connect, and showcase their creativity. Each quarter we publish original, thought-provoking works that reflect women's strength, sensuality, vulnerability, and wit." Estab. 1975. Circ. 1,400. Byline given. Pays on publication. Offers kill fee if work is accepted but cannot be published. Accepts queries by online submission form. Accepts simultaneous submissions. Responds in 6 months. Sample copy: $12 or online at website.

NONFICTION Buys 1-2 mss/year. Submit complete ms via online submissions manager. Length: up to 3,500 words. **Pays $50-120 CAD, 2 contributor's copies, and a one-year subscription.**

FICTION Accepts literature that illustrates the female experience—short stories, creative nonfiction, poetry—by, for, and about women. Submit complete ms via online submissions manager. **Pays $50-120 CAD, 2 contributor's copies, and a one-year subscription.**

POETRY *Room* uses "poetry by women, including trans and genderqueer writers, written from a feminist perspective. Nothing simplistic, clichéd. We prefer to receive up to 5 poems at a time, so we can select a pair or group." Submit via online submissions manager. Pays $50-120 CAD, 2 contributor's copies, and a one-year subscription.

SEQUESTRUM

Sequestrum Publishing, 1023 Garfield Ave., Ames IA 50014. **E-mail:** sequr.info@gmail.com. **Website:** www.sequestrum.org. **Contact:** R.M. Cooper, managing editor. Biweekly literary magazine in tabloid and online formats. All publications are paired with a unique visual component. Regularly holds contests and features well-known authors, as well as promising new and emerging voices. Estab. 2014. Circ. 2,000 monthly. Byline given. Pays on acceptance. 100% kill fee. Publishes ms 2-6 months after acceptance. Editorial lead time: 3 months. Accepts queries by online submission form. Accepts simultaneous submissions. Sample copy available for free online. Guidelines available for free online.

NONFICTION Needs book excerpts, essays, general interest, humor, memoir, opinion, personal experience, photo feature, narrative, experimental. Special issues: Two contests yearly: Editor's Reprint Award (for previously published material) and New Writer Awards (for writers yet to publish a book-length manuscript). **Buys 3-5 mss/year.** Submit complete ms via online submissions manager. Length: 500-12,000 words. **Pays $10/article.**

PHOTOS Send photos with submission (GIF/JPEG files). Pays $10/photo. Buys one-time rights.

FICTION Needs adventure, confessions, experimental, fantasy, horror, humorous, mainstream, mystery, novel excerpts, science fiction, short stories, suspense, western, Slipstream. **Buys 20-36 mss/year.** Submit complete ms via online submissions manager. Length: 12,000 words max. **Pays $10-15/story.**

POETRY Needs avant-garde, free verse, light verse, traditional, cross-genre. Buys 20 poems/year. Submit maximum 4 poems. Length: 40 lines. **Pays $10/set of poems.**

TIPS "Reading a past issue goes a long way; there's little excuse not to. Our entire archive is available online to preview, and subscription rates are variable. Send your best, most interesting work. General submissions are always open, and we regularly hold contests and offer awards which are themed."

THE SEWANEE REVIEW

735 University Ave., Sewanee TN 37383. (931)598-1246. **E-mail:** sewaneereview@sewanee.edu. **Website:** thesewaneereview.com. **Contact:** Adam Ross, editor. *The Sewanee Review* is America's oldest continuously published literary quarterly. Publishes original fiction, poetry, essays on literary and related subjects, and book reviews for well-educated readers who appreciate good American and English literature. Only erudite work representing depth of knowledge and skill of expression is published. Estab. 1892. Circ. 2,200. Pays on publication. Accepts queries by online submission form. Responds in 4 months to mss. Sample copy: $8.50 ($9.50 outside U.S.). Guidelines available online.

Does not read mss June 1-August 31.

NONFICTION Submit complete ms via online submissions manager. Queries accepted but not preferred. Rarely accepts unsolicited reviews. Length: up to 10,000 words. **Pays $10-12/printed page, plus 2 contributor's copies.**

FICTION literary, contemporary. No erotica, science fiction, fantasy, or excessively violent or profane material. **Buys 10-15 mss/year.** Submit complete ms via online submissions manager. Length: up to 10,000 words. No short-short stories. **Pays $10-12/printed page, plus 2 contributor's copies.**

POETRY Submit up to 6 poems via online submissions manager. Keep in mind that for each poem published in *The Sewanee Review*, approximately 250 poems are considered. Length: up to 40 lines/poem. **Pays $2.50/line, plus 2 contributor's copies (and reduced price for additional copies).**

SHENANDOAH

Washington and Lee University, Lexington VA 24450. (540)458-8908. **E-mail:** shenandoah@wlu.edu. **Website:** shenandoahliterary.org. **Contact:** R.T. Smith, editor; William Wright, assistant editor. Semiannual digital-only literary journal. For more than half a century, *Shenandoah* has been publishing splendid poems, stories, essays, and reviews which display passionate understanding, formal accomplishment, and serious mischief. Estab. 1950. Circ. 2,000. Byline given. Pays on publication. No kill fee. Publishes ms an average of 10 months after acceptance. Accepts queries by online submission form. Accepts simultaneous submissions. Responds in 4-6 weeks to mss. Sample copy: $12. Guidelines online.

NONFICTION Needs essays, interview, reviews. **Buys 6 mss/year.** Send complete ms via online submissions manager. Query for reviews and interviews. Length: up to 20 pages. **Pays $25/page ($250 maximum), one-year subscription, and 1 contributor's copy.**

FICTION Needs mainstream, novel excerpts. No sloppy, hasty, slight fiction. **Buys 15 mss/year.** Send complete ms via online submissions manager. Length: up to 20 pages. **Pays $25/page ($250 maximum), one-year subscription, and 1 contributor's copy.**

POETRY Submit 3-5 poems via online submissions manager. No inspirational, confessional poetry. Buys 70 poems/year. Submit maximum 5 poems. **Pays $2.50/line, one-year subscription, and 1 contributor's copy.**

STAR*LINE

Science Fiction Poetry Association, Science Fiction Poetry Association, W5679 State Rd. 60, Poynette WI 53955 USA. **E-mail:** starlineeditor@gmail.com. **E-mail:** starlineeditor@gmail.com. **Website:** www.sfpoetry.com. **Contact:** F.J. Bergmann, editor. **All freelance.** *Star*Line*, published quarterly in print and .pdf format by the Science Fiction Poetry Association (see separate listing in Organizations), is a speculative poetry magazine. "Open to all forms as long as your poetry uses speculative motifs: science fiction, fantasy, or horror." Estab. 1978. Circ. 300. Byline given. After publication. No kill fee. No more than 6 months. Accepts queries by e-mail. Accepts simultaneous submissions. Responds in 3 days. Guidelines available online.

NONFICTION Needs reviews.

POETRY Submit 3-5 poems at a time. Accepts e-mail submissions (preferred; pasted into body of message, no attachments). Submit maximum 5 poems. **Pays 3¢/word rounded to the next dollar; minimum $3, maximum $25.**

STORIE

Via Suor Celestina Donati 13/E, Rome 00167 Italy. **E-mail:** info@storie.it. **Website:** www.storie.it/english. *Storie* is one of Italy's leading cultural and literary magazines. Committed to a truly crossover vision of writing, the bilingual (Italian/English) review publishes high-quality fiction and poetry, interspersed with the work of alternative wordsmiths such as filmmakers and musicians. Through writings bordering on narratives and interviews with important contemporary writers, it explores the culture and craft of writing. Estab. 1986.

FICTION "Manuscripts may be submitted directly by regular post without querying first; however, we do not accept unsolicited manuscripts via e-mail. Please query via e-mail first. We only contact writers if their work has been accepted. We also arrange for and oversee a high-quality, professional translation of the piece." **Pays $30-600 and 2 contributor's copies.**

TIPS "More than erudite references or a virtuoso performance, we're interested in a style merging news writing with literary techniques in the manner of new journalism. *Storie* reserves the right to include a brief review of interesting submissions not selected for publication in a special column of the magazine."

THE STRAND MAGAZINE

P.O. Box 1418, Birmingham MI 48012-1418. (800)300-6652. **E-mail:** strandmag@strandmag.com. **Website:** www.strandmag.com. Quarterly magazine covering mysteries, short stories, essays, book reviews. "After an absence of nearly half a century, the magazine known to millions for bringing Sir Arthur Conan Doyle's ingenious detective, Sherlock Holmes, to the world has once again appeared on the literary scene. First launched in 1891, *The Strand* included in its

pages the works of some of the greatest writers of the 20th century: Agatha Christie, Dorothy Sayers, Margery Allingham, W. Somerset Maugham, Graham Greene, P.G. Wodehouse, H.G. Wells, Aldous Huxley, and many others. In 1950, economic difficulties in England caused a drop in circulation, which forced the magazine to cease publication." Estab. 1998. Circ. 50,000. Byline given. Pays on acceptance. No kill fee. Publishes ms an average of 4 months after acceptance. Accepts queries by e-mail. Accepts simultaneous submissions. Responds in 1 month to queries; in 4-10 months to mss. Sample copy: $10. Guidelines online.

NONFICTION Query.

FICTION "We are interested in mysteries, detective stories, tales of terror and the supernatural as well as short stories. Stories can be set in any time or place, provided they are well written, the plots interesting and well thought." Occasionally accepts short shorts and short novellas. Needs horror, humorous, mystery, suspense. "We are not interested in submissions with any sexual content." Submit complete ms by postal mail. Include SASE. No e-mail submissions. Length: 2,000-6,000 words. **Pays $25-150.**

TIPS "No gratuitous violence, sexual content, or explicit language, please."

SUBTERRAIN

Strong Words for a Polite Nation, P.O. Box 3008, MPO, Vancouver British Columbia V6B 3X5 Canada. (604)876-8710. **Fax:** (604)879-2667. **E-mail:** subter@portal.ca. **Website:** www.subterrain.ca. **Contact:** Brian Kaufman, editor-in-chief; Natasha Sanders-Kay, managing editor. "*subTerrain* magazine is published 3 times/year from modest offices just off of Main Street in Vancouver, BC. We strive to produce a stimulating fusion of fiction, poetry, photography, and graphic illustration from uprising Canadian, U.S., and international writers and artists." Estab. 1988. Circ. 3,500. Pays on publication for first North American serial rights. Publishes ms 4-9 months after acceptance. Accepts queries by mail, online submission form. Accepts simultaneous submissions. Responds in 6-9 months to mss. Rarely comments on rejected mss. Sample copy: $5 (subterrain.ca/subscriptions). Writer's guidelines online (subterrain.ca/about/35/sub-terrain-writer-s-guidelines).

Magazine: 8.5×11; 80 pages; colour matte stock paper; colour matte cover stock; illustrations; photos. "Strong words for a polite nation."

NONFICTION Needs book excerpts, essays, expose, general interest, humor, memoir, nostalgic, opinion, personal experience, travel, literary essays, literary criticism. Send complete ms. Include disposable copy of the ms and SASE for reply only. Accepts multiple submissions. Receives 100 unsolicited mss/month. Accepts 4 mss/issue; 10-15 mss/year. **Pays $50/page for prose & $50 per poem**

PHOTOS Uses colour and/or b&w prints. *No unsolicited material.* "We are now featuring 1 artist (illustration or photography) per issue and are generally soliciting that work."

FICTION Receives 100 unsolicited mss/month. Accepts 4 mss/issue; 10-15 mss/year. Recently published work by J.O. Bruday, Lisa Pike, and Peter Babiak. Needs confessions, erotica, ethnic, experimental, humorous, novel excerpts, short stories, slice-of-life vignettes. Does not want genre fiction or children's fiction. Send complete ms. Include disposable copy of the ms and SASE for reply only. Accepts multiple submissions. **3,000 words max. Pays $50/page for prose.**

POETRY "We accept poetry, but we no longer accept unsolicited submissions, except when related to 1 of our theme issues." "We no longer accept unsolicited poetry submissions (unless specifically related to one of our theme issues)." Poems unrelated to any theme issues may be submitted to the annual "General" issue (usually the summer/fall issue). **Pays $50/poem.**

TIPS "Read the magazine first. Get to know what kind of work we publish."

🜂🜂🜂 SUBTROPICS

University of Florida, P.O. Box 112075, 4008 Turlington Hall, Gainesville FL 32611-2075. **E-mail:** subtropics@english.ufl.edu. **Website:** www.english.ufl.edu/subtropics. **Contact:** David Leavitt, editor. **100% freelance written.** Magazine published twice/year through the University of Florida's English department. *Subtropics* seeks to publish the best literary fiction, essays, and poetry being written today, both by established and emerging authors. Will consider works of fiction of any length, from short shorts to novellas and self-contained novel excerpts. Gives the same latitude to essays. Appreciates work in translation and, from time to time, republishes important and compelling stories, essays, and poems that have lapsed out of print by writers no longer living. Member: CLMP. Estab. 2005. Circ. 1,500. Byline given. Pays on acceptance for prose; pays on publication of

the issue preceding the issue in which the author's work will appear for poetry. Publishes ms an average of 6 months after acceptance. Accepts simultaneous submissions. Responds in 1 month to queries and mss. Rarely comments on/critiques rejected mss Sample copy: $12.95. Guidelines online.

◯ Literary magazine/journal: 9x6, 160 pages. Includes photographs. Submissions accepted from September 1-April 15.

NONFICTION No book reviews. **Buys 4-5 mss/year.** Send complete ms via online submissions manager. Length: up to 15,000 words. Average length: 5,000 words. **Pays $1,000.**

FICTION Does not read May 1-August 31. Agented fiction 33%. **Publishes 1-2 new writers/year.** Has published John Barth, Ariel Dorfman, Tony D'Souza, Allan Gurganus, Frances Hwang, Kuzhali Manickavel, Eileen Pollack, Padgett Powell, Nancy Reisman, Jarret Rosenblatt, Joanna Scott, and Olga Slavnikova. No genre fiction. **Buys 10-12 mss/year.** Submit complete ms via online submissions manager. Length: up to 15,000 words. Average length: 5,000 words. Average length of short shorts: 400 words. **Pays $500 for short shorts; $1,000 for full stories; 2 contributor's copies.**

POETRY Submit up to 4 poems via online submissions manager. Buys 50 poems/year. **Pays $100 per poem.**

TIPS "We publish longer works of fiction, including novellas and excerpts from forthcoming novels. Each issue includes a short-short story of about 250 words on the back cover. We are also interested in publishing works in translation for the magazine's English-speaking audience."

THEMA

Thema Literary Society, P.O. Box 8747, Metairie LA 70011-8747. **E-mail:** thema@cox.net. **E-mail:** Only for writers living outside the U.S.. **Website:** themaliterarysociety.com. **Contact:** Virginia Howard, editor; Gail Howard, poetry editor. **100% freelance written.** "*THEMA* is designed to stimulate creative thinking by challenging writers with unusual themes, such as 'Drop the Zucchini and Run!' and 'Second Thoughts.' Appeals to writers, teachers of creative writing, artists, photographers, and general reading audience." Estab. 1988. Byline given. Pays on acceptance. No kill fee. Publishes ms, on average, within 6 months after acceptance. Accepts queries by mail, e-mail. Accepts simultaneous submissions. Responds in 1 week to queries. Responds in 5 months to mss. Sample $15 U.S./$25 foreign. Upcoming themes and guidelines available in magazine, for SASE, by e-mail, or on website.

○ THEMA is 100 pages, digest-sized professionally printed, with glossy card cover. Receives about 400 poems/year, accepts about 8%. Press run is 400 (230 subscribers, 30 libraries). Subscription: $30 U.S./$40 foreign. Has published poetry by John Grey, Carol Louis Munn, James B. Nicola, and Dennis Trujillo.

NONFICTION Contact: Virginia Howard, Editor. Needs book excerpts, essays, historical, humor, memoir, nostalgic, personal experience, *NOTE:* Nonfiction must relate to one of the upcoming themes. Special issues: *NOTE:* Nonfiction must relate to one of the upcoming themes. No salacious subject matter. Length: 300 to 6,000 words (one to twenty double-spaced pages). **Pays $10 for under 1,000 words; $25 for articles over 1,000 words.**

PHOTOS Contact: Virginia Howard, Editor. *NOTE:* Submitted photograph must relate to one of the upcoming themes. high resolution; portrait orientation. Payment: $10 for interior black-and-white photo; $25 for full-color cover photo. one time only.

FICTION Contact: Virginia Howard, Editor. All stories must relate to one of *THEMA*'s upcoming themes **(indicate the target theme on submission of manuscript).** See website for themes. Needs adventure, ethnic, experimental, fantasy, historical, humorous, mainstream, mystery, religious, science fiction, short stories, slice-of-life vignettes, suspense, Fiction **must** relate to a target theme. No erotica. Send complete ms with SASE, cover letter; include "name and address, brief introduction, **specifying the intended target issue for the mss.**" SASE. Accepts simultaneous, multiple submissions, and reprints. Does not accept e-mailed submissions except from non-USA addresses. Length: 300 to 6,000 words (one to twenty double-spaced pages). **Payment: $10 for under 1,000 words; $25 for stories over 1,000 words, plus one contributor copy.**

POETRY Contact: Gail Howard, Poetry Editor. Needs All poetry must relate to one of *THEMA*'s upcoming themes **(indicate the target theme on submission of manuscript).** See website for themes. Submit up to 3 poems at a time. Include SASE. All submissions should be typewritten on standard $8\frac{1}{2}$x11 pa-

per. Submissions are accepted all year, but evaluated after specified deadlines. **Specify target theme.** Editor comments on submissions. Each issue is based on an unusual premise. Please send SASE for guidelines before submitting poetry to find out the upcoming themes. Does not want scatologic language or explicit love poetry. Buys 24 published out of 250 submitted poems/year. Submit maximum 3 poems. Length: 1 - 3 pages. **Payment: $10/poem and 1 contributor's copy.**

⊛⊛ THE THREEPENNY REVIEW

P.O. Box 9131, Berkeley CA 94709. (510)849-4545. **E-mail:** wlesser@threepennyreview.com. **Website:** www.threepennyreview.com. **Contact:** Wendy Lesser, editor. **100% freelance written. Works with small number of new/unpublished writers each year.** Quarterly tabloid. "We are a general-interest, national literary magazine with coverage of politics, the visual arts, and the performing arts." Reading period: January 1-June 30. Estab. 1980. Circ. 6,000-9,000. Byline given. Pays on acceptance. Publishes ms an average of 1 year after acceptance. Accepts queries by mail, online submission form. Responds in 1 month to queries; in 2 months to mss. Sample copy: $12, or online. Guidelines available online.

NONFICTION Needs essays, historical, memoir, personal experience, reviews, book, film, theater, dance, music, and art reviews. **Buys 40 mss/year.** Send complete ms. Length: 1,500-4,000 words. **Pays $400.**

FICTION No fragmentary, sentimental fiction. **Buys 8 mss/year.** Send complete ms. Length: 800-4,000 words. **Pays $400.**

POETRY Needs free verse, traditional. No poems without capital letters or poems without a discernible subject. Buys 30 poems/year. Submit maximum 5 poems. Length: up to 100 lines/poem. **Pays $200.**

TIPS "Nonfiction (political articles, memoirs, reviews) is most open to freelancers."

⊛⊛⊛ TIN HOUSE

McCormack Communications, P.O. Box 10500, Portland OR 97296. (503)219-0622. **E-mail:** info@tinhouse.com. **Website:** www.tinhouse.com. **Contact:** Cheston Knapp, managing editor; Holly MacArthur, founding editor. **90% freelance written.** "We are a general-interest literary quarterly. Our watchword is quality. Our audience includes people interested in literature in all its aspects, from the mundane to the exalted." Estab. 1999. Circ. 11,000. Byline given. Pays on publication. No kill fee. Publishes ms an average of 6 months after acceptance. Editorial lead time 6 months. Submit seasonal material 6 months in advance. Accepts queries by mail, online submission form. Accepts simultaneous submissions. Responds in 6 weeks to queries; in 4 months to mss. Sample copy: $15. Guidelines online.

Reading period: September 1-May 31.

NONFICTION Needs book excerpts, essays, interview, personal experience. Special issues: Check website for upcoming theme issues. Submit via online submissions manager or postal mail. Include cover letter with word count. Length: up to 10,000 words. **Pays $50-800 for assigned articles. Pays $50-500 for unsolicited articles.**

FICTION Needs experimental. Submit via online submissions manager or postal mail. Include cover letter with word count. Length up to 10,000 words. **Pays $200-800.**

POETRY Needs avant-garde, free verse, traditional. Submit via online submissions manager or postal mail. Include cover letter. Submit maximum 5 poems. **Pays $50-150.**

WESTERLY MAGAZINE

University of Western Australia, The Westerly Centre (M202), Crawley WA 6009 Australia. (61)(8)6488-3403. **Fax:** (61)(8)6488-1030. **E-mail:** westerly@uwa.edu.au. **Website:** westerlymag.com.au. **Contact:** Catherine Noske, editor. *Westerly*, published in July and November, prints quality short fiction, poetry, literary criticism, socio-historical articles, and book reviews with special attention given to Australia, Asia, and the Indian Ocean region. "We assume a reasonably well-read, intelligent audience. Past issues of *Westerly* provide the best guides. Not consciously an academic magazine." Estab. 1956. Time between acceptance and publication may be up to 1 year, depending on when work is submitted. Accepts queries by online submission form. "Please wait for a response before forwarding any additional submissions for consideration."

Westerly is about 200 pages, digest-sized. Online Special Issues complement the print publication. Subscription information available on website. Deadline for July edition: March 31; deadline for November edition: August 31.

NONFICTION Submit complete ms by postal mail, e-mail, or online submissions form. Length: up to 5,000 words for essays; up to 3,500 words for creative nonfiction. **Pays $150 and contributor's copies.**

FICTION Submit complete ms by mail, e-mail, or online submissions form. Length: up to 3,500 words. **Pays $150 and contributor's copies.**

POETRY "We don't dictate to writers on rhyme, style, experimentation, or anything else. We are willing to publish short or long poems." Submit up to 3 poems by mail, e-mail, or online submissions form. **Pays $75 for 1 page or 1 poem, or $100 for 2 or more pages/poems, and contributor's copies.**

WORKERS WRITE!

Blue Cubicle Press, LLC, P.O. Box 250382, Plano TX 75025. **E-mail:** info@workerswritejournal.com. **Website:** www.workerswritejournal.com. **Contact:** David LaBounty, managing editor. **100% freelance written.** Covers working-class literature. "*Workers Write!* is an annual print journal published by Blue Cubicle Press, an independent publisher dedicated to giving voice to writers trapped in the daily grind. Each issue focuses on a particular workplace; check website for details. Submit your stories via e-mail or send a hard copy." Estab. 2005. Circ. 750. Byline given. Pays on acceptance. Publishes mss 6 months after acceptance. Accepts queries by mail, e-mail. Accepts simultaneous submissions. Responds in 1 week to queries; in 3 months to mss. Sample copy available on website. Writer's guidelines free for #10 SASE and on website.

FICTION "We need your stories (5,000-12,000 words) about the workplace from our Overtime series. Every 3 months, we'll release a chapbook containing 1-2 related stories that center on work." Needs experimental, historical, humorous, mainstream, short stories, slice-of-life vignettes. **Buys Buys 10-12 mss/year mss/year.** Send complete ms. Length: 500-5,000 words. **Payment: $5-50 (depending on length and rights requested).**

POETRY Needs free verse and traditional. Buys 3-5 poems/year. **Pays $5-10.**

THE YALE REVIEW

The Yale Review, P.O. Box 208243, New Haven CT 06520-8243. (203)432-0499. **Fax:** (203)432-0510. **Website:** www.yale.edu/yalereview. **Contact:** J.D. McClatchy, editor. **20% freelance written.** Quarterly magazine. "Like Yale's schools of music, drama, and architecture, like its libraries and art galleries, *The Yale Review* has helped give the University its leading place in American education. In a land of quick fixes and short view and in a time of increasingly commercial publishing, the journal has an authority that derives from its commitment to bold established writers and promising newcomers, to both challenging literary work and a range of essays and reviews that can explore the connections between academic disciplines and the broader movements in American society, thought, and culture. With independence and boldness, with a concern for issues and ideas, with a respect for the mind's capacity to be surprised by speculation and delighted by elegance, *The Yale Review* proudly continues into its third century." Estab. 1911. Circ. 7,000. Pays prior to publication. No kill fee. Publishes ms an average of 6 months after acceptance. Accepts simultaneous submissions. Responds in 1-3 months to mss. Sample copy online. Guidelines available online.

NONFICTION Send complete ms with cover letter and SASE. **Pays $400-500.**

FICTION Submit complete ms with SASE. All submissions should be sent to the editorial office. **Pays $400-500.**

POETRY Submit with SASE. All submissions should be sent to the editorial office. **Pays $100-250.**

🆂🆂🆂 ZOETROPE: ALL-STORY

Zoetrope: All-Story, The Sentinel Bldg., 916 Kearny St., San Francisco CA 94133. (415)788-7500. **Website:** www.all-story.com. **Contact:** fiction editor. Quarterly magazine specializing in the best of contemporary short fiction. *Zoetrope: All Story* presents a new generation of classic stories. Estab. 1997. Circ. 20,000. Byline given. No kill fee. Publishes ms an average of 5 months after acceptance. Accepts queries by mail. Accepts simultaneous submissions. Responds in 8 months (if SASE included). Sample copy: $8. Guidelines available online.

FICTION Buys 25-35 mss/year. "Writers should submit only 1 story at a time and no more than 2 stories a year. We do not accept artwork or design submissions. We do not accept unsolicited revisions nor respond to writers who don't include an SASE." Send complete ms by mail. Length: up to 7,000 words. "Excerpts from larger works, screenplays, treatments, and poetry will be returned unread." **Pays up to $1,000.**

TIPS "Before submitting, nonsubscribers should read several issues of the magazine to determine if their works fit with *All-Story*. Electronic versions of the magazine are available to read, in part, at the website,

and print versions are available for purchase by single-issue order and subscription."

🆂 ZYZZYVA

57 Post St., Suite 604, San Francisco CA 94104. (415)757-0465. **E-mail:** editor@zyzzyva.org. **Website:** www.zyzzyva.org. **Contact:** Laura Cogan, editor; Oscar Villalon, managing editor. **100% freelance written. Works with a small number of new/unpublished writers each year.** "Every issue is a vibrant mix of established talents and new voices, providing an elegantly curated overview of contemporary arts and letters with a distinctly San Francisco perspective." Estab. 1985. Circ. 2,500. Byline given. Pays on acceptance. No kill fee. Publishes ms an average of 3 months after acceptance. Accepts queries by mail. Accepts simultaneous submissions. Responds in 1 week to queries; in 1 month to mss. Sample copy: $12. Guidelines available online.

○ Accepts submissions January 1-May 31 and August 1-November 30. Does not accept online submissions.

NONFICTION Needs book excerpts, general interest, historical, humor, personal experience. **Buys 50 mss/year.** Submit by mail. Include SASE and contact information. Length: no limit. **Pays $50.**

PHOTOS Reviews scans only at 300 dpi, 5.5.

FICTION Needs ethnic, experimental, humorous, mainstream. **Buys 60 mss/year.** Send complete ms by mail. Include SASE and contact information. Length: no limit. **Pays $50.**

POETRY Submit by mail. Include SASE and contact information. Buys 20 poems/year. Submit maximum 5 poems. Length: no limit. **Pays $50.**

TIPS "We are not currently seeking work about any particular theme or topic; that said, reading recent issues is perhaps the best way to develop a sense for the length and quality we are looking for in submissions."

MEN'S

🆂🆂🆂🆂 ESQUIRE

Hearst Media, 300 W. 57th St., New York NY 10019. (212)649-4158. **E-mail:** editor@esquire.com. **Website:** www.esquire.com. Monthly magazine covering the ever-changing trends in American culture. *Esquire* is geared toward smart, well-off men. General readership is college educated and sophisticated, between ages 30 and 45. Written mostly by contributing editors on contract. Rarely accepts unsolicited mss. Estab. 1933. Circ. 720,000. Publishes ms an average of 2-6 months after acceptance. Editorial lead time at least 2 months. Accepts queries by mail, e-mail. Accepts simultaneous submissions. Guidelines on website.

NONFICTION Query. Length: 5,000 words average. **Payment varies.**

PHOTOS Uses mostly commissioned photography. Payment depends on size and number of photos.

TIPS "A writer has the best chance of breaking in at *Esquire* by querying with a specific idea that requires special contacts and expertise. Ideas must be timely and national in scope."

GQ

Condé Nast, 1 World Trade Center, New York NY 10007. (212)286-2860. **E-mail:** letters@gq.com. **Website:** www.gq.com. Monthly magazine covering subjects ranging from finance, food, entertainment, technology, celebrity profiles, sports, and fashion. *Gentleman's Quarterly* is devoted to men's personal style and taste, from what he wears to the way he lives his life. Estab. 1957. Circ. 964,264. No kill fee. Accepts queries by e-mail. Accepts simultaneous submissions.

Query before submitting.

NONFICTION Needs interview.

MAXIM

Alpha Media Group, 1040 Avenue of the Americas, 16th Floor, New York NY 10018-3703. (212)302-2626. **Fax:** (212)302-2635. **E-mail:** editors@maximmag. com. **Website:** www.maximonline.com. Monthly magazine covering relationships, sex, women, careers and sports. Written for young, professional men interested in fun and informative articles. Circ. 2.5 million. No kill fee. Editorial lead time 5 months. Accepts simultaneous submissions. Sample copy for $3.99 at newsstands.

Query before submitting.

MEN'S HEALTH

Rodale, Inc., 400 S. 10th St., Emmaus PA 18098. (212)697-2040. **E-mail:** mhonline@rodale.com. **Website:** www.menshealth.com. **Contact:** Kevin Donahue, senior managing editor. Covers various men's lifestyles topics, such as fitness, nutrition, fashion, and sexuality. The world's largest men's magazine brand, with 40 editions in 47 countries. Estab. 1987. Circ. 1,918,387. Accepts simultaneous submissions.

Query before submitting.

MILITARY

AIRFORCE

Royal Canadian Air Force Association, P.O Box 2460, Station D, Ottawa ON K1P 5W6 Canada. (613)232-2303. **Fax:** (613)232-2156. **E-mail:** editor@airforce. ca. **Website:** rcafassociation.ca. **5% freelance written.** Quarterly magazine covering Canada's air force heritage. Stories center on Canadian military aviation—past, present, and future. Estab. 1977. Circ. 16,000. Byline given. Pays on publication. Publishes ms an average of 6 months after acceptance. Editorial lead time 3 months. Submit seasonal material 3 months in advance. Accepts queries by mail, e-mail. Accepts simultaneous submissions. Responds in 2 weeks to queries; in 1 month to mss. Sample copy free. Guidelines by e-mail.

NONFICTION Needs historical, interview, personal experience, photo feature. **Buys 2 mss/year.** Query with published clips. Length: 1,500-3,500 words. Limit agreed upon in advance.

PHOTOS Send photos. Captions, identification of subjects required. Reviews prints, GIF/JPEG files. Buys one-time rights.

FILLERS Needs anecdotes, facts. Length: about 800 words. **Pay negotiable.**

TIPS "Writers should have a good background in Canadian military history."

AIR FORCE TIMES

Sightline Media Group, 1919 Gallows Road, 4th Floor, Vienna VA 22182. (703)750-8646. **Fax:** (703)750-8601. **Website:** www.airforcetimes.com. **Contact:** Michelle Tan, editor. "Weeklies edited separately for Army, Navy, Marine Corps, and Air Force military personnel and their families. They contain career information such as pay raises, promotions, news of legislation affecting the military, housing, base activities, and features of interest to military people." Estab. 1940. Byline given. Pays on acceptance. Offers kill fee. Accepts queries by mail, e-mail, phone. Accepts simultaneous submissions. Responds in 1 month to queries. Sample copy for #10 SASE. Guidelines for #10 SASE.

NONFICTION No advice pieces. **Buys 150-175 mss/ year.** Query. Length: 750-2,000 words. **Pays $100-500.**

COLUMNS/DEPARTMENTS Length: 500-900 words. **Buys 75 mss/year. Pays $75-125.**

TIPS "Looking for stories on active duty, reserve and retired military personnel; stories on military matters and localized military issues; stories on successful civilian careers after military service."

⑤⑤ MARINE CORPS TIMES

Sightline Media Group, 1919 Gallows Rd., 4th Floor, Vienna VA 22182. **Website:** www.marinecorpstimes. com. **Contact:** Andrew Tilghman, editor. Weeklies edited separately for Army, Navy, Marine Corps, and Air Force military personnel and their families. They contain career information such as pay raises, promotions, news of legislation affecting the military, housing, base activities and features of interest to military people. Estab. 1940. Circ. 230,000 (combined). Byline given. Pays on publication. Offers kill fee. Accepts simultaneous submissions. Responds in 1 month.

NONFICTION No advice pieces. **Buys 150-175 mss/year.** Query. Length: 750-2,000 words. **Pays $100-500.**

COLUMNS/DEPARTMENTS Length: 500-900 words. **Buys 75 mss/year. Pays $75-125.**

TIPS Looking for stories on active duty, reserve and retired military personnel; stories on military matters and localized military issues; stories on successful civilian careers after military service.

⑤⑤⑤ MILITARY OFFICER

201 N. Washington St., Alexandria VA 22314-2539. **E-mail:** editor@moaa.org; msc@moaa.org. **Website:** www.moaa.org. **60% freelance written. Prefers to work with published/established writers.** Monthly magazine for officers of the 7 uniformed services and their families. Estab. 1945. Circ. 325,000. Byline given. Pays on acceptance. Publishes ms an average of 1 year after acceptance. Accepts queries by e-mail. Accepts simultaneous submissions. Responds in 3 months to queries. Sample copy and guidelines available online.

NONFICTION "We rarely accept unsolicited mss." **Buys 50 mss/year.** Query with résumé, sample clips. Length: 1,000-2,000 words (features). **Pays 80¢/word (features).**

PHOTOS Query with list of stock photo subjects. Images should be 300 dpi or higher. Pays $75-250 for inside color; $300 for cover.

MUSIC CONSUMER

AMERICAN SONGWRITER MAGAZINE

P.O. Box 330249, Nashville TN 37203. (615)321-6096. **Fax:** (615)321-6097. **E-mail:** info@americansongwriter.com. **Website:** www.americansongwriter.com. **90% freelance written.** Bimonthly magazine about songwriters and the craft of songwriting for many types of music, including pop, country, rock, metal, jazz, gospel, and r&b. Estab. 1984. Circ. 5,000. Pays on publication. Offers 25% kill fee. Publishes ms an average of 2 months after acceptance. Accepts simultaneous submissions. Responds in 2 months to queries. Sample copy for $4. Guidelines for #10 SASE or by e-mail.

NONFICTION Needs general interest, interview, new product, technical, home demo studios, movie and TV scores, performance rights organizations. **Buys 20 mss/year.** Query with published clips. Length: 300-1,200 words. **Pays $25-60.**

REPRINTS Send tearsheet or photocopy and information about when and where the material previously appeared. Pays same amount as paid for an original article

PHOTOS Send photos. Identification of subjects required. Reviews 3x5 prints. Offers no additional payment for photos accepeted with ms. Buys one time rights.

TIPS *American Songwriter* strives to present articles which can be read a year or 2 after they were written and still be pertinent to the songwriter reading them.

⑤⑤ GUITAR PLAYER

New Bay Media, LLC, 28 E. 28th St., 12th Floor, New York NY 10016. **E-mail:** etrabb@nbmedia.com. **Website:** www.guitarplayer.com. **50% freelance written.** Monthly magazine for persons interested in guitars, guitarists, manufacturers, guitar builders, equipment, careers, etc. Circ. 150,000. Byline given. Pays on acceptance. No kill fee. Publishes ms an average of 3 months after acceptance. Accepts simultaneous submissions. Responds in 6 weeks to queries.

NONFICTION Buys 30-40 mss/year. Query. Open **Pays $250-450.**

PHOTOS Reviews 35 mm color transparencies, b&w glossy prints. Payment varies. Buys one time rights.

MUSIC CONNECTION

Music Connection, Inc., 3441 Ocean View Blvd., Glendale CA 91208. (818)995-0101. **Fax:** (818)995-9235. **E-mail:** markn@musicconnection.com; contactmc@musicconnection.com. **Website:** www.musicconnection.com. **Contact:** Mark Nardone, associate publisher/senior editor. **40% freelance written.** Monthly magazine geared toward working musicians and/or other industry professionals, including producers/engineers/studio staff, managers, agents, publicists, music publishers, record company staff, concert promoters/bookers, etc. Found in select major booksellers and all Guitar Centers in America. Estab. 1977. Circ. 75,000. Byline given. Pays after publication. Kill fee varies. Publishes ms an average of 2 months after acceptance. Editorial lead time 2 months. Submit seasonal material 2 months in advance. Accepts simultaneous submissions. Sample copy: $5. Online copy also available.

NONFICTION Needs how-to, interview, new product, technical. Query with published clips. Length: 1,000-5,000 words. **Payment varies.**

TIPS "Articles must be informative 'how-to' music/music industry-related pieces, geared toward a trade-reading audience comprised mainly of musicians. No fluff."

ROLLING STONE

Wenner Media, 1290 Avenue of the Americas, New York NY 10104. (212)484-1616. **Fax:** (212)484-1664. **E-mail:** rseditors@rollingstone.com. **Website:** www.rollingstone.com. **Contact:** Caryn Ganz, editorial director. Biweekly magazine geared towards young adults interested in news of popular music, entertainment, and the arts; current news events; politics; and American culture. Circ. 1.46 million. No kill fee. Editorial lead time 1 month. Accepts simultaneous submissions.

○ Query before submitting.

MYSTERY

ALFRED HITCHCOCK'S MYSTERY MAGAZINE

Dell Magazines, 44 Wall St., Suite 904, New York NY 10005. **E-mail:** alfredhitchcockmm@dellmagazines.com. **Website:** www.themysteryplace.com/ahmm. **100% freelance written.** Monthly magazine featuring new mystery short stories. Estab. 1956. Circ. 90,000. Byline given. Pays on publication. No kill fee. Submit seasonal material 7 months in advance. Accepts queries by mail, online submission form. Responds in 3-5 months to mss. Sample copy: $5. Guidelines for SASE or on website.

FICTION Wants "original and well-written mystery and crime fiction. Because this is a mystery magazine, the stories we buy must fall into that genre in some sense or another. We are interested in nearly every kind of mystery: stories of detection of the classic kind, police procedurals, private eye tales, suspense, courtroom dramas, stories of espionage, and so on. We ask only that the story be about crime (or the threat or fear of one). We sometimes accept ghost stories or supernatural tales, but those also should involve a crime." Needs mystery, suspense. No sensationalism. Send complete ms. Length: up to 12,000 words. **Payment varies.**

TIPS "No simultaneous submissions, please. Submissions sent to *Alfred Hitchcock's Mystery Magazine* are not considered for or read by *Ellery Queen's Mystery Magazine*, and vice versa."

NATURE, CONSERVATION & ECOLOGY

○$ ALTERNATIVES JOURNAL

Alternatives Inc., 195 King St., Kitchener Ontario N2H 3X7 Canada. (519)588-4505. **E-mail:** david@alternativesjournal.ca, megan@alternativesjournal.ca. **Website:** www.alternativesjournal.ca. **Contact:** David McConnachie, publisher. **90% freelance written.** Magazine published 4 times/year with special issue(s) covering international environmental issues. "*Alternatives Journal*, Canada's national environmental magazine, delivers thoughtful analysis and intelligent debate on Canadian and world environmental issues, the latest news and ideas, as well as profiles of environmental leaders who are making a difference. *A/J* is a quarterly+ magazine featuring bright, lively writing by the nation's foremost environmental thinkers and researchers. *A/J* offers a vision of a more sustainable future as well as the tools needed to take us there." Estab. 1971. Circ. 5,000. Byline given. Pays on publication. Offers 50% kill fee. Publishes ms an average of 5 months after acceptance. Editorial lead time 7 months. Submit seasonal material 5 months in advance. Accepts queries by e-mail, online submission form. Accepts simultaneous submissions. Sample copy free for Canadian writers only. Guidelines available on website.

NONFICTION Needs book excerpts, essays, expose, how-to, humor, interview, opinion, photo feature, profile, reviews, technical. **Buys 50 mss/year.** Query with published clips. Length: 800-3,000 words. **Pays 10¢/word (Canadian).**

PHOTOS State availability. Identification of subjects required. Pays $35-75/photo. Buys one-time rights.

TIPS "Before responding to this call for submissions, please read several back issues of the magazine so that you understand the nature of our publication. We also suggest you go through our detailed submission procedures to understand the types and lengths of articles we accept. Queries should explain, in less than 300 words, the content and scope of your article, and should convey your intended approach, tone, and style. Please include a list of people you will interview, potential images or sources for images, and the number of words you propose to write. We would also like to receive a very short bio. And if you have not written for *Alternatives* before, please include other examples of your writing. Articles range from about 500-3,000 words in length. Keep in mind that our lead time is several months. Articles should not be so time-bound that they will seem dated once published. *Alternatives* has a limited budget of 10¢ per word for several articles. This stipend is available to professional and amateur writers and students only. Please indicate your interest in this funding in your submission."

BIRD WATCHER'S DIGEST

P.O. Box 110, Marietta OH 45750. (740)373-5285; (800)879-2473. **E-mail:** submissions@birdwatchers-digest.com. **Website:** www.birdwatchersdigest.com. **Contact:** Bill Thompson III, editor; Dawn Hewitt, managing editor. **30% freelance written.** Bimonthly, digest-sized magazine covering birds, bird watching, travel for birding, and natural history. *Bird Watcher's Digest* is a nontechnical magazine interpreting ornithological material for amateur observers, including the knowledgeable birder, the serious novice, and the backyard bird watcher; strives to provide good reading and good ornithology. Works with a small number of new/unpublished writers each year. Estab. 1978. Circ. 42,000. Byline given. Pays after publication. Publishes ms an average of 2 years after acceptance. Submit seasonal material 6 months in advance. Responds in 4 weeks to queries. Sample copy for $4.99 plus shipping, or access online. Guidelines online.

○ "We take pride in sharing wonderful stories about birds, bird watching, birders, and places to travel to enjoy birds. On rare occasion, we publish short poems; we do not publish fiction."

NONFICTION Needs book excerpts, essays, how-to, humor, new product, personal experience, reviews, travel, Only stories about wild birds, bird watching, bird watchers, birding gear, or birding hot spots are considered. No articles on domestic, pet or caged birds, or raising a baby bird. **Buys 30-40 mss/year.** "We gladly accept e-mail queries and ms submissions. When submitting by e-mail, please use the subject line 'Submission—[your topic].' Attach your submission to your e-mail in either MS Word (DOC) or RichText Format (RTF). Please include full contact information on every page." Length: 600-2,500 words. **Pays up to $200.**

PHOTOS Reviews digital photos only. "Our payment schedule is $75 per image used, regardless of size. Images reused on our table of contents page or on our website will be paid an additional $25. There is no payment or contract for photos used in 'My Way,' or for photos that have been loaned for courtesy use." Buys one-time rights for simultaneous print and digital publication.

POETRY Prints short poems about birds or bird watching only on rare occasion. **Pays $10-25, or complimentary subscription.**

TIPS "Obtain a sample copy of *BWD* from us or at your local newsstand, bird store, or bookstore, and familiarize yourself with the type of material we regularly publish. We rarely repeat coverage of a topic within a period of 2-3 years. We aim at an audience ranging from the backyard bird watcher to the very knowledgeable birder; we include in each issue material that will appeal at various levels. We always strive for a good geographical spread, with material from every section of the country. We leave very technical matters to others, but we want facts and accuracy, depth and quality, directed at the veteran bird watcher and at the enthusiastic novice. We stress the joys and pleasures of bird watching, its environmental contribution, and its value for the individual and society."

○ GREEN TEACHER

Green Teacher, 95 Robert St., Toronto ON M5S 2K5 Canada. (416)960-1244. **Fax:** (416)925-3474. **E-mail:** tim@greenteacher.com; info@greenteacher.com. **E-mail:** tim@greenteacher.com. **Website:** www.greenteacher.com. **Contact:** Tim Grant, co-editor; Amy Stubbs, editorial assistant. "We're a nonprofit organization dedicated to helping educators, both inside and outside of schools, promote environmental awareness among young people aged 6-19." Estab. 1991. Circ. 15,000. Publishes ms 8 months after acceptance. Ac-

cepts queries by mail, e-mail. Accepts simultaneous submissions. Responds to queries in 1 week.
NONFICTION multicultural, nature, environment. Query. Submit one-page summary or outline. Length: 1,500-3,500 words.

💲💲 HIGH COUNTRY NEWS

119 Grand Ave., P.O. Box 1090, Paonia CO 81428. (970)527-4898. **E-mail:** brianc@hcn.org; cindy@hcn.org. **E-mail:** editor@hcn.org; photos@hcn.org. **Website:** www.hcn.org. **Contact:** Brian Calvert, managing editor; Cindy Wehling, art director. **70% freelance written.** Biweekly nonprofit magazine covering environment, rural communities, and natural resource issues in 11 western states and Alaska, for environmentalists, politicians, companies, college classes, government agencies, grass roots activists, public land managers, etc. Estab. 1970. Circ. 30,000. Byline given. Pays on publication. Offers kill fee of 1/3 of agreed rate. Publishes ms an average of 2 months after acceptance. Accepts queries by e-mail. Accepts simultaneous submissions. Responds in 2 weeks to queries. Sample copy available online. Guidelines available online.

NONFICTION Needs book excerpts, essays, expose, humor, personal experience, travel. **Buys 100 mss/year.** Query. Length: up to 4,900 words. **Pays 50¢-$1.50/word.**

PHOTOS Send photos. Captions, identification of subjects required. Reviews b&w or color prints.

COLUMNS/DEPARTMENTS Back-Page Essay, 700-900 words; Writers on the Range (taut and pithy opinion pieces). Submit back-page essay queries to Michelle Nijhuis (michelle@hcn.org); submit Writers on the Range pieces to Betsy Marston (betsym@hsn.org).

TIPS "We use a lot of freelance material. Familiarity with the newsmagazine is a must. Start by writing a query letter. We define 'resources' broadly to include people, culture, and aesthetic values, not just coal, oil, and timber."

💲💲💲⊘ NATIONAL PARKS MAGAZINE

National Parks Conservation Association, 777 Sixth St. NW, Suite 700, Washington DC 20001. (202)223-6722; (800)628-7275. **Fax:** (202)454-3333. **E-mail:** npmag@npca.org. **Website:** www.npca.org/magazine. **Contact:** Scott Kirkwood, editor-in-chief. **60% freelance written. Prefers to work with published/established writers.** Quarterly magazine for a largely

unscientific but highly educated audience interested in preservation of National Park System units, natural areas, and protection of wildlife habitat. "*National Parks* magazine publishes articles about areas in the National Park System, proposed new areas, threats to parks or park wildlife, scientific discoveries, legislative issues, and endangered species of plants or animals relevant to national parks. We do not publish articles on general environmental topics, nor do we print articles about land managed by the Fish and Wildlife Service, Bureau of Land Management, or other federal agencies." Estab. 1919. Circ. 340,000. Pays on acceptance. Offers 33% kill fee. Publishes ms an average of 2 months after acceptance. Accepts simultaneous submissions. Responds in 3-4 months to queries. Sample copy for $3 and 9x12 SASE or online. Guidelines available online.

NONFICTION Needs expose, descriptive articles about new or proposed national parks and wilderness parks. No poetry, philosophical essays, or first-person narratives. No unsolicited mss. Length: 1,500 words. **Pays $1,300 for 1,500-word features and travel articles.**

PHOTOS Not looking for new photographers. Send photos.

TIPS "Articles should have an original slant or news hook and cover a limited subject, rather than attempt to treat a broad subject superficially. Specific examples, descriptive details, and quotes are always preferable to generalized information. The writer must be able to document factual claims, and statements should be clearly substantiated with evidence within the article. *National Parks* does not publish fiction, poetry, personal essays, or 'My trip to ..' stories."

💲 NATURE

Nature Publishing Group, The Macmillan Building, 4 Crinan St., London N1 9XW United Kingdom. (44)(207)833-4000. **Fax:** (44)(207)843-4596. **E-mail:** nature@nature.com. **Website:** www.nature.com/nature. **5% freelance written.** Weekly magazine covering multidisplinary science. *Nature* is the number one multidisciplinary journal of science, publishing News, Views, Commentary, Reviews, and ground-breaking research. Estab. 1869. Circ. 60,000. Byline given. No kill fee. Publishes ms an average of 2 months after acceptance. Accepts simultaneous submissions. Responds to ms in 1 week. Guidelines available on website.

PERSONAL COMPUTERS

⊘ BASELINE

QuinStreet Enterprise, 28 E. 28th St., New York NY 10016. **Website:** www.baselinemag.com. **Contact:** Eileen Feretic, editor. "Baseline - the Fusion of Business and Technology - is a handbook for the IT and business leaders who put technology to work for their enterprise. The magazine is dedicated to helping these executives, managers and professionals effectively execute technology initiatives in order to achieve a solid return on those investments. Baseline offers lessons learned in the form of real-world business case studies from a variety of organizations across a wide array of industries." Circ. 125,000. No kill fee. Editorial lead time 3 months. Accepts simultaneous submissions.

○ Most of the reporting and writing is done by staff writers and editors.

INFOWORLD

InfoWorld Media Group, 501 2nd St., 6F, San Francisco CA 94107. (415)243-0500. **E-mail:** jason_snyder@infoworld.com; doug_dineley@infoworld.com; eric_knorr@infoworld.com. **Website:** www.infoworld.com. **Contact:** Jason Snyder, features; Doug Dineley, reviews; Eric Knorr, news analysis. *InfoWorld* provides in-depth technical analysis on key products, solutions, and technologies for sound buying decisions and business gain. Contact specific editor. Circ. 220,000. No kill fee. Editorial lead time 2 months. Accepts queries by e-mail. Accepts simultaneous submissions.

WIRED

Condé Nast Publications, 520 Third St., 3rd Floor, San Francisco CA 94107-1815. **E-mail:** submit@wired.com. **Website:** www.wired.com. **95% freelance written.** Monthly magazine covering technology and digital culture. Covers the digital revolution and related advances in computers, communications, and lifestyles. Estab. 1993. Circ. 500,000. Byline given. Pays on publication. Offers 25% kill fee. Publishes ms an average of 3 months after acceptance. Editorial lead time 3 months. Accepts queries by e-mail. Accepts simultaneous submissions. Responds in 3 weeks to queries. Sample copy: $4.95. Guidelines by e-mail.

○ Query before submitting.

NONFICTION Needs essays, interview, opinion. No poetry or trade articles. Query.

TIPS "Read the magazine. We get too many inappropriate queries. We need quality writers who understand our audience and who understand how to query."

PHOTOGRAPHY

APOGEE PHOTO MAGAZINE

24 Holborn Viaduct, City of London EC1A 2BN UK. (0)(333)360-1054. **E-mail:** editor.sales@apogeephoto.com. **Website:** apogeephoto.com. **Contact:** Marla Meier, owner. A free online magazine designed to inspire, educate and inform photographers of all ages and levels. Hundreds of articles, columns and tips covering a wide range of photo topics. Find listings of photo workshops and tours, camera clubs, and books. Submit your articles for publication." Accepts queries by e-mail. Accepts simultaneous submissions.

NONFICTION Needs essays, general interest, how-to, inspirational, interview, new product, photo feature, profile, reviews, technical, travel. Accepts well-written articles with 600-1,200 words on any photography related subject geared towards the beginner to advanced photographer. Articles must be accompanied by a minimum of 6 high quality photographs. Format and photo details will be given via email upon acceptance of terms.

PHOTOS "*Apogee Photo* is interested in providing an electronic forum for high quality work from photographic writers and photographers. We will accept articles up to 1,200 words on any photographic subject geared towards the beginning to advanced photographer. Articles must have a minimum of 4-6 photographs accompanying them. You must hold the copyright and/or have a copyright release from a 3rd party and you must have signed model releases where applicable for any identifiable person or persons which appear in your photographs." Accepts reviews of new products, 800/words max.

TIPS "Please do a search by subject before submitting your article to see if your article covers a new subject or brings a new perspective on a particular subject or theme."

POLITICS & WORLD AFFAIRS

THE AMERICAN SPECTATOR

933 N. Kenmore St., Suite 405, Arlington VA 22201. **Website:** www.spectator.org. Monthly conservative magazine covering U.S. politics. "For many years, one ideological viewpoint dominated American print and broadcast journalism. Today, that viewpoint still controls the entertainment and news divisions of the television networks, the mass-circulation news magazines, and the daily newspapers. *The American Spectator* has attempted to balance the Left's domination of the media by debunking its perceived wisdom and advancing alternative ideas through spirited writing, insightful essays, humor, and, most recently, through well-researched investigative articles that have themselves become news." Estab. 1967. Circ. 50,000. No kill fee. Accepts queries by online submission form. Accepts simultaneous submissions. Responds only if interested in 3-4 weeks.

NONFICTION Special issues: "Our preference is for reported pieces that provide new information or draw upon rare expertise." No unsolicited poetry, fiction, satire, or crossword puzzles. Reviews unsolicited mss for online publication. Submit via online submission form. Length: 700-1,000 words.

🚫 COMMONWEAL

Commonweal Foundation, 475 Riverside Dr., Room 405, New York NY 10115. (212)662-4200. **Fax:** (212)662-4183. **E-mail:** editors@commonwealmagazine.org. **Website:** www.commonwealmagazine.org. **Contact:** Paul Baumann, editor; Tiina Aleman, production editor. Biweekly journal of opinion edited by Catholic lay people, dealing with topical issues of the day on public affairs, religion, literature, and the arts. Estab. 1924. Circ. 20,000. Byline given. Pays on publication. No kill fee. Submit seasonal material 4 months in advance. Accepts simultaneous submissions. Responds in 2 months to queries. Sample copy free. Guidelines available online.

NONFICTION Needs essays, general interest, interview, personal experience, religious. **Buys 30 mss/year.** Query with published clips. *Commonweal* welcomes original manuscripts dealing with topical issues of the day on public affairs, religion, literature, and the arts. Looks for articles that are timely, ac-

curate, and well written. Length: 2,000-3,000 words for features. **Pays $200-300 for longer mss; $100-200 for shorter pieces.**

COLUMNS/DEPARTMENTS Upfronts: (750-1,000 words) brief, newsy reportorials, giving facts, information and some interpretation behind the headlines of the day; Last Word: (750 words) usually of a personal nature, on some aspect of the human condition: spiritual, individual, political, or social.

POETRY Needs free verse, traditional. *Commonweal*, published every 2 weeks, is a Catholic general interest magazine for college-educated readers. Does not publish inspirational poems. Buys 20 poems/year. Length: no more than 75 lines. **Pays 75¢/line plus 2 contributor's copies. Acquires all rights. Returns rights when requested by the author.**

TIPS "Articles should be written for a general but well-educated audience. While religious articles are always topical, we are less interested in devotional and churchy pieces than in articles which examine the links between 'worldly' concerns and religious beliefs."

💲💲 THE FREEMAN: IDEAS ON LIBERTY

1819 Peachtree Road NE, Suite 300, Atlanta GA 30309 United States. (404)554-9980. **Fax:** (404)393-3142. **E-mail:** freeman@fee.org. **E-mail:** editor@fee.org. **Website:** fee.org. James Anderson, deputy publisher. **Contact:** Dan Sanchez, managing editor. **85% freelance written.** Monthly publication for the layman and fairly advanced students of liberty. Estab. 1946. Byline given. Pays on publication. No kill fee. Publishes online within weeks. Some online articles are also published in the quarterly print edition. Accepts queries by e-mail. Guidelines available on website.

Eager to work with new/unpublished writers.

NONFICTION **Buys 100 mss/year.** Query with SASE. Length: 3,500 words. **Pays 10¢/word.**

TIPS "It's most rewarding to find freelancers with new insights and fresh points of view. Facts, figures, and quotations cited should be fully documented, to their original source, if possible."

THE NATION

520 Eighth Avenue, 8th Flo, New York NY 10018. **E-mail:** submissions@thenation.com. **Website:** www.thenation.com. Steven Brower, art director. **Contact:** Roane Carey, managing editor; Ange Mlinko, poetry editor. *The Nation*, published weekly, is a journal of left/liberal opinion, with arts coverage that includes poetry. The only requirement for poetry is excellence.

Estab. 1865. Circ. 100,000. Guidelines available on-line.

O Poetry published by *The Nation* has been included in *The Best American Poetry*. Has published poetry by W.S. Merwin, Maxine Kumin, James Merrill, May Swenson, Edward Hirsch, and Charles Simic.

NONFICTION civil liberties, civil rights, labor, economics, environmental, feminist issues, politics, the arts. Queries accepted via online form. Length: 750-2,500 words. **Pays $150-500, depending on length.**

POETRY Contact: Ange Mliko, poetry editor.. "Please email poems in a single PDF attachment to PoemNationSubmit@gmail.com. Submissions are not accepted from June 1-September 15." Buys 6 poems/year. Submit maximum 3 poems.

NATIONAL REVIEW

215 Lexington Ave., New York NY 10016. (212)679-7330. **E-mail:** submissions@nationalreview.com. **Website:** www.nationalreview.com. Accepts simultaneous submissions. Guidelines available on website.

O Query before submitting.

PROGRESSIVE POPULIST

Ampersand Publishing Co., P.O. Box 819, Manchaca TX 78652. (512)828-7245. **E-mail:** populist@usa.net. **Website:** www.populist.com. **90% freelance written.** Biweekly tabloid covering politics and economics. "We cover political and economic issues of interest to workers, small businesses, and family farmers and ranchers." Estab. 1995. Circ. 15,000. Byline given. Pays quarterly. No kill fee. Publishes ms an average of 1 month after acceptance. Editorial lead time 3 weeks. Submit seasonal material 1 month in advance. Accepts queries by mail, e-mail, fax, phone. Accepts simultaneous submissions. Sample copy and writer's guidelines free.

NONFICTION Needs essays, general interest, historical, humor, interview, opinion. "We are not much interested in 'sound-off' articles about state or national politics, although we accept letters to the editor. We prefer to see more 'journalistic' pieces in which the writer does enough footwork to advance a story beyond the easy realm of opinion." **Buys 400 mss/year.** Query. Length: 600-1,000 words. **Pays $15-50.** Pays writers with contributor copies or other premiums if preferred by writer.

REPRINTS Send photocopy with rights for sale noted and information about when and where the material previously appeared.

PHOTOS State availability. Identification of subjects required. Negotiates payment individually. Buys one-time rights.

TIPS "We do prefer submissions by e-mail. I find it's easier to work with e-mail, and for the writer it probably increases the chances of getting a response."

⊘ U.S. NEWS & WORLD REPORT

U.S. News & World Report, Inc., 1050 Thomas Jefferson St. NW, 4th Floor, Washington DC 20007. (202)955-2630. **Fax:** (202)955-2056. **Website:** www.usnews.com. Weekly magazine devoted largely to reporting and analyzing national and international affairs, politics, business, health, science, technology, and social trends. Circ. 2,000,000. No kill fee. Editorial lead time 10 days. Accepts simultaneous submissions.

O Query before submitting.

WORLD POLICY JOURNAL

World Policy Institute, 108 W. 39th St., Suite 1000, New York NY 10018. (212)481-5005. **Fax:** (212)481-5009. **E-mail:** fredrick@worldpolicy.org. **Website:** www.worldpolicy.org. **Contact:** Yaffa Frederick, managing editor. **10% freelance written.** Quarterly journal covering international politics, economics, and security isssues, as well as historical and cultural essays, book reviews, profiles, and first-person reporting from regions not covered in the general media. "We hope to bring principle and proportion, as well as a sense of reality and direction to America's discussion of its role in the world." Circ. 8,000. Byline given. Pays on publication. No kill fee. Publishes ms an average of 3 months after acceptance. Accepts queries by mail. Accepts simultaneous submissions. Responds in 3 months to queries. Guidelines available online.

NONFICTION Query. Length: 4,000-5,000 words. **Pays variable commission rate.**

TIPS "In selecting pieces for publication, we look for a strong point of view expressed in a lively, non-academic style. Each issue has a cover theme chosen by the editors, though at least half of each issue is given to topical articles on a broad array of subjects."

PSYCHOLOGY & SELF-IMPROVEMENT

⑤⑤⑤⑤ GRADPSYCH

American Psychological Association, 750 First St. NE, Washington DC 20009. **Fax:** (202)336-6103. **Website:** www.apa.org/gradpsych. **50% freelance written.** Quarterly magazine. "We cover issues of interest to psychology graduate students, including career outlook, tips for success in school, profiles of interesting students, and reports on student research. We aim for our articles to be readable, informative, and fun. Grad students have enough dry, technical reading to do at school; we don't want to add to it." Estab. 2003. Circ. 60,000. Byline given. Pays on acceptance. Offers $200 kill fee. Publishes ms an average of 4 months after acceptance. Editorial lead time 3-5 months. Submit seasonal material 4 months in advance. Accepts queries by e-mail. Accepts simultaneous submissions. Responds in 2 weeks to queries. Sample copy online.

NONFICTION Needs general interest, how-to, interview, journalism for grad students. **Buys 25 mss/year.** Query with published clips. Length: 300-2,000 words. **Pays $300-2,000 for assigned articles.**

PHOTOS State availability. Identification of subjects, model releases required. Reviews GIF/JPEG files. Negotiates payment individually. Buys one-time rights.

TIPS "Check out our website and pitch a story on a topic we haven't written on before or that gives an old topic a new spin. Also, have quality clips."

REGIONAL

ALABAMA

⑤⑤ ALABAMA HERITAGE

University of Alabama, Box 870342, Tuscaloosa AL 35487-0342. (205)348-7467. **Fax:** (205)348-7473. **E-mail:** reyno031@bama.ua.edu. **Website:** www.alabamaheritage.com. **Contact:** Susan Reynolds, associate editor. **90% freelance written.** *Alabama Heritage* is a nonprofit historical quarterly published by the University of Alabama and the Alabama Department of Archives and History for the intelligent lay reader. "We are interested in lively, well-written, and thoroughly researched articles on Alabama/Southern history and culture. Readability and accuracy are es-

sential." Estab. 1986. Byline given. Pays on publication. No kill fee. Accepts queries by mail, e-mail. Accepts simultaneous submissions. Guidelines online.

NONFICTION "We do not publish fiction, poetry, articles on current events or living artists, or personal/family reminiscences." Query. Length: 750-4,000 words. **Pays $50-350.**

PHOTOS Identification of subjects required. Reviews contact sheets. Buys one-time rights.

TIPS "Authors need to remember that we regard history as a fascinating subject, not as a dry recounting of dates and facts. Articles that are lively and engaging, in addition to being well researched, will find interested readers among our editors. No term papers, please. All areas are open to freelance writers. Best approach is a written query."

ALABAMA LIVING

Alabama Rural Electric Association, 340 TechnaCenter Dr., Montgomery AL 36117. (800)410-2737. **E-mail:** agriffin@areapower.com. **Website:** areapower.coop. **Contact:** Allison Griffin, editor. **80% freelance written.** Monthly magazine covering topics of interest to rural and suburban Alabamians. "Our magazine is an editorially balanced, informational and educational service to members of rural electric cooperatives. Our mix regularly includes Alabama history, Alabama features, gardening, outdoor, and consumer pieces." Estab. 1948. Circ. 400,000. Byline given. Pays on acceptance. No kill fee. Editorial lead time 4 months. Submit seasonal material 4 months in advance. Accepts queries by mail, e-mail. Accepts simultaneous submissions. Responds in 1 month to queries. Sample copy free.

NONFICTION Needs historical. Special issues: Gardening (March); Travel (April); Home Improvement (May); Holiday Recipes (December). **Buys 20 mss/year.** Send complete ms. Length: 500-750 words. **Pays $250 minimum for assigned articles. Pays $150 minimum for unsolicited articles.**

REPRINTS Send typed manuscript with rights for sale noted. Pays $100.

PHOTOS Buys 1-3 photos from freelancers/issue; 12-36 photos/year. Pays $100 for color cover; $50 for color inside; $60-75 for photo/text package. **Pays on acceptance.** Credit line given. Buys one-time rights for publication and website; negotiable.

TIPS "Preference given to submissions with accompanying art."

ALASKA

🟢🟢 ALASKA

Morris Communications, 301 Arctic Slope Ave., Ste. 300, Anchorage AK 99518-3035. **E-mail:** editor@alaskamagazine.com. **Website:** www.alaskamagazine.com. **Contact:** Michelle Theall, editor; Corrynn Cochran, photo editor. **70% freelance written. Eager to work with new/unpublished writers.** Magazine published 10 times/year covering topics uniquely Alaskan. Estab. 1935. Circ. 180,000. Byline given. Pays on publication. No kill fee. Publishes ms an average of 6 months after acceptance. Submit seasonal material 1 year in advance. Accepts queries by e-mail. Accepts simultaneous submissions. Responds in 2 months to queries and mss. Sample copy: $4.99 plus 9x12 SASE with 7 first-class stamps. Guidelines online.

NONFICTION Needs book excerpts, essays, historical, humor, interview, personal experience, photo feature, travel. No fiction or poetry. **Buys 40 mss/year.** Query. Length: 700-2,000 words **Pays $100-1,250.**

PHOTOS *Alaska* is dedicated to depicting life in Alaska through high-quality images of its people, places, and wildlife. Color photographs from professional freelance photographers are used extensively and selected according to their creative and technical merits. Send photos. Captions, identification of subjects required. Reviews 35mm or larger transparencies, slides labeled with your name. Pays $50 maximum for b&w photos; $75-500 for color photos; $300 maximum/day; $2,000 maximum/complete job; $300 maximum/full page; $500 maximum/cover. Buys limited rights, first North American serial rights, and electronic rights. "Each issue of *Alaska* features a 4-, 6-, and/or 8-page feature. We're looking for themes and photos to show the best of Alaska. We want sharp, artistically composed pictures. Cover photo always relates to stories inside the issue." Photographers on assignment are paid a competitive day rate and reimbursed for approved expenses. All assignments are negotiated in advance.

COLUMNS/DEPARTMENTS Escape (gives readers a reason to get out and explore the Last Frontier); Adventure (features a variety of Alaskan outdoor subjects, including fishing, hunting, hiking, camping, birding, adventure sports, and extreme activities); Alaska History; Alaska Native Culture; all 800-1,000 words. Query.

TIPS "We're looking for top-notch writing—original, well researched, lively. Subjects must be distinctly Alaskan. A story on a mall in Alaska, for example, won't work for us; every state has malls. If you've got a story about a Juneau mall run by someone who is also a bush pilot and part-time trapper, maybe we'd be interested. The point is that *Alaska* stories need to be vivid, focused, and unique. Alaska is like nowhere else—we need our stories to be the same way."

ARIZONA

🟢🟢 ARIZONA FOOTHILLS MAGAZINE

8132 N. 87th Place, Scottsdale AZ 85258. (480)460-5203. **Fax:** (480)443-1517. **Website:** www.azfoothillsmag.com. **10% freelance written.** Monthly magazine covering Arizona lifestyle. Estab. 1996. Circ. 60,000. Byline given. Pays on publication. No kill fee. Publishes ms an average of 6 months after acceptance. Editorial lead time 6 months. Submit seasonal material at least 4 months in advance. Accepts queries by mail, e-mail. Accepts simultaneous submissions. Responds in 1 month to queries. Sample copy for #10 SASE.

NONFICTION Needs general interest, photo feature, travel, fashion, decor, arts, interview. **Buys 10 mss/year.** Query with published clips. Length: 900-2,000 words. **Pays 35-40¢/word for assigned articles.**

PHOTOS Photos may be requested. Captions, identification of subjects, model releases required. Reviews contact sheets, transparencies. Negotiates payment individually. Occasionally buys one-time rights.

COLUMNS/DEPARTMENTS Travel, dining, fashion, home decor, design, architecture, wine, shopping, golf, performance & visual arts.

TIPS "We prefer stories that appeal to our affluent audience written with an upbeat, contemporary approach and reader service in mind."

🟢🟢🟢🟢 ARIZONA HIGHWAYS

2039 W. Lewis Ave., Phoenix AZ 85009. (602)712-2200. **Fax:** (602)254-4505. **E-mail:** kkramer@azdot.gov. **Website:** www.arizonahighways.com. **Contact:** Kelly Kramer, managing editor. **100% freelance written.** Magazine that is state-owned, designed to help attract tourists into and through Arizona. Estab. 1925. Circ. 425,000. Pays on acceptance. No kill fee. Accepts queries by mail, e-mail, fax. Accepts simultaneous submissions. Responds in 1 month. Guidelines online.

NONFICTION Buys 50 mss/year. Query with a lead paragraph and brief outline of story. Length: 600-1,800 words. **Pays up to $1/word.**

PHOTOS Contact: Peter Ensenberger, director of photography. For digital requirements, contact the photography department. Pays $125-600. Buys one-time rights.

COLUMNS/DEPARTMENTS Focus on Nature (short feature in first or third person dealing with the unique aspects of a single species of wildlife), 800 words; Along the Way (short essay dealing with life in Arizona, or a personal experience keyed to Arizona), 750 words; Back Road Adventure (personal back-road trips, preferably off the beaten path and outside major metro areas), 1,000 words; Hike of the Month (personal experiences on trails anywhere in Arizona), 500 words. **Pays $50-1,000, depending on department.**

TIPS "Writing must be of professional quality, warm, sincere, in-depth, well peopled, and accurate. Avoid themes that describe first trips to Arizona, the Grand Canyon, the desert, Colorado River running, etc. Emphasis is to be on Arizona adventure and romance as well as flora and fauna, when appropriate, and themes that can be photographed. Double check your manuscript for accuracy. Our typical reader is a 50-something person with the time, the inclination, and the means to travel."

CALIFORNIA

💲💲 ORANGE COAST MAGAZINE

Orange Coast Kommunications, Inc., 3701 Birch St., Suite 100, Newport Beach CA 92660. (949)862-1133. **Fax:** (949)862-0133. **E-mail:** editorial@orangecoast. com; agibbons@orangecoastmagazine.com. **Website:** www.orangecoast.com. **Contact:** Martin J. Smith, editor-in-chief. **90% freelance written.** Monthly magazine designed to inform and enlighten the educated, upscale residents of Orange County, California; highly graphic and well researched. Estab. 1974. Circ. 52,000. Byline given. Pays on publication. Offers 20% kill fee. Publishes ms an average of 4 months after acceptance. Editorial lead time 5 months. Submit seasonal material 6 months in advance. Accepts queries by mail, e-mail. Accepts simultaneous submissions. Responds in 3 months to queries; 3 months to mss. Guidelines online.

NONFICTION Needs general interest, inspirational, interview, personal experience, celebrity profiles, guides to activities and services. Special issues: Health, Beauty, and Fitness (January); Dining (March and August); International Travel (April); Home Design (June); Arts (September); Local Travel (October). We do not accept stories that do not have specific Orange County angles. We want profiles on local people, stories on issues going on in our community, informational stories using Orange County-based sources. We cannot emphasize the local angle enough. **Buys up to 65 mss/year.** Query with published clips. Length: 1,000-2,000 words. **Negotiates payment individually.**

PHOTOS State availability. Captions, identification of subjects required. Negotiates payment individually. Buys one time rights.

COLUMNS/DEPARTMENTS Short Cuts (stories for the front of the book that focus on Orange County issues, people, and places), 150-250 words. **Buys up to 25 mss/year.** Query with published clips. **Negotiates payment individually.**

TIPS We're looking for more local personality profiles, analysis of current local issues, local takes on national issues. Most features are assigned to writers we've worked with before. Don't try to sell us 'generic' journalism. *Orange Coast* prefers articles with specific and unusual angles focused on Orange County. A lot of freelance writers ignore our Orange County focus. We get far too many generalized manuscripts.

CANADA/ INTERNATIONAL

🌐 ALBERTA VIEWS

Alberta Views, Ltd., Suite 208, 320 23rd Ave. SW, Calgary AB T2S 0J2 Canada. (403)243-5334; (877)212-5334. **Fax:** (403)243-8599. **E-mail:** queries@alberta-views.ab.ca. **Website:** www.albertaviews.ab.ca. **Contact:** Evan Osenton, editor. **50% freelance written.** Bimonthly magazine covering Alberta culture: politics, economy, social issues, and art. "We are a regional magazine providing thoughtful commentary and background information on issues of concern to Albertans. Most of our writers are Albertans." Estab. 1997. Circ. 30,000. Byline given. Pays on publication. Offers 50% kill fee. Publishes ms an average of 3 months after acceptance. Editorial lead time 4 months. Submit seasonal material 3 months in advance. Accepts queries by e-mail. Accepts simultaneous submissions. Responds in 6 weeks to queries; 2 months to mss. Sample copy free. "If you are a writer, illustrator, or photographer interested in contributing to *Alberta Views*, please see our contributor's guidelines online."

○ No phone queries.

NONFICTION Needs essays. **Buys 18 mss/year.** "Query with written proposal of 300–500 words outlining your intended contribution to *Alberta Views*, why you are qualified to write about your subject, and what sources you intend to use; a résumé outlining your experience and education; recent examples of your published work (tear sheets)." Length: 3,000-5,000 words. **Pays $1,000-1,500 for assigned articles; $350-750 for unsolicited articles.**

PHOTOS State availability. Negotiates payment individually. Buys one-time rights, Web rights.

FICTION Only fiction by Alberta writers via the annual *Alberta Views* fiction contest. **Buys 6 mss/year.** Send complete ms. Length: 2,500-4,000 words. **Pays up to $1,000.**

POETRY Accepts unsolicited poetry. Submit complete ms.

○ EDGE YK

Verge Communications Ltd., P.O. Box 2451, 5112 52 St., Yellowknife NT X1A 2P8 Canada. (867)445-8360. **E-mail:** editor@edgeyk.ca. **Website:** www.edgenorth.ca/edge-yk-magazine/. **Contact:** Laurie Sarkadi, editor. Magazine published 6 times/year covering life in Yellowknife, NT, Canada. "*EDGE YK* magazine is a free publication dedicated to showcasing some of the vast creative talent within Yellowknife, Northwest Territories. We're interested in well-told first-person narrative stories, as well as pieces on the issues, ideas, and people affecting the city's past, present, and future." Estab. 2011. Circ. 7,000. Byline given. Pays on publication. Offers 50% kill fee. Publishes ms 1 month after acceptance. Editorial lead time 3 months. Submit seasonal material 3 months in advance. Accepts queries by mail, e-mail. Accepts simultaneous submissions. Responds in 1 month to queries; in 2 months to mss.

NONFICTION Needs book excerpts, essays, general interest, historical, how-to, humor, interview, nostalgic, opinion, personal experience, photo feature, profile, travel. No fiction. Query. Length: 300-2,000 words. **Pays minimum of $100 for assigned and unsolicited articles.**

PHOTOS State availability of photos with submission. Reviews GIF/JPEG files. Offers payment for photos accepted with ms; negotiates payment individually.

COLUMNS/DEPARTMENTS On EDGE Opinion, any topic/slant, approximately 400-600 words. Query. **Pays $100.**

FICTION "We rarely publish fiction."

POETRY Needs free verse. "We rarely publish poetry submissions." Buys 4 poems/year. Submit maximum 1 poems. No minimum or maximum length.

○ⓈⓈ MONDAY MAGAZINE

Black Press Ltd., 818 Broughton St., Victoria British Columbia V8W 1E4 Canada. (250)382-6188. **E-mail:** editor@mondaymag.com. **Website:** www.mondaymag.com. **Contact:** Sarah Wilson, editor. **10% freelance written.** Weekly tabloid covering local news. "*Monday Magazine* is Victoria's only alternative newsweekly. For more than 35 years, we have published fresh, informative, and alternative perspectives on local events. We prefer lively, concise writing with a sense of humor and insight." Estab. 1975. Circ. 20,000. Byline given. **Currently not accepting freelance articles requiring payment.** Pays 1 month after publication. No kill fee. Publishes ms an average of 1 month after acceptance. Editorial lead time 1-2 months. Submit seasonal material 2 months in advance. Accepts queries by e-mail. Accepts simultaneous submissions. Responds in 6-8 weeks to queries; 3 months to mss. Guidelines online.

NONFICTION Needs expose, general interest, humor, interview, personal experience. Special issues: Body, Mind, Spirit (October); Student Survival Guide (August). Does not want fiction, poetry, or conspiracy theories. Send complete ms. Length: 300-1,000 words. **Pays $25-50. Currently not accepting freelance articles requiring payment.**

PHOTOS Send photos. Captions, identification of subjects required. Reviews GIF/JPEG files (300 dpi at 4x6). Offers no additional payment for photos accepted with ms. Buys one-time rights.

TIPS "Local writers tend to have an advantage, as they are familiar with the issues and concerns of interest to a Victoria audience."

DELAWARE

ⓈⓈⓈ DELAWARE BEACH LIFE

Endeavours LLC, P.O. Box 417, Rehoboth Beach DE 19971. (302)227-9499. **E-mail:** info@delaware-beachlife.com. **Website:** www.delawarebeachlife.com. **Contact:** Terry Plowman, publisher/editor.

Magazine published 8 times/year covering coastal Delaware. "*Delaware Beach Life* focuses on coastal Delaware: Fenwick to Lewes. You can go slightly inland as long as there's water and a natural connection to the coast, e.g., Angola or Long Neck." Estab. 2002. Circ. 15,000. Byline given. Pays on acceptance. 50% kill fee. Publishes ms 4 months after acceptance. Editorial lead time 6 months. Submit seasonal material 1 year in advance. Accepts queries by e-mail. Responds in 2 months to queries; in 6 months to mss. Sample copy available online at website. Guidelines free and by e-mail.

○ "*Delaware Beach Life* is the only full-color glossy magazine focused on coastal Delaware's culture and lifestyle. Created by a team of the best freelance writers, the magazine takes a deeper look at the wealth of topics that interest coastal residents. *Delaware Beach Life* features such top-notch writing and photography that it inspires 95% of its readers to save it as a 'coffee-table' magazine."

NONFICTION Needs book excerpts, essays, general interest, humor, interview, opinion, photo feature. Does not want anything not focused on coastal Delaware. Query with published clips. Length: 1,200-3,000 words. **Pays $400-1,000 for assigned articles.**

PHOTOS Send photos. Photos require captions, identification of subjects. Reviews GIF/JPEG files. Pays $25-100 per photo. Purchases one-time rights.

COLUMNS/DEPARTMENTS Profiles, History, Opinion (focused on coastal DE), all 1,200 words. **Buys 32 mss/year.** Query with published clips. **Pays $150-350.**

FICTION Needs adventure, condensed novels, historical, humorous, novel excerpts, Must have coastal theme. Does not want anything not coastal. **Buys 3 mss/year.** Query with published clips. Length: 1,000-2,000 words.

POETRY Needs avant-garde, free verse, haiku, light verse, traditional. Does not want anything not coastal. No erotic poetry. Buys 6 poems/year. Submit maximum 3 poems. Length: 6-15 lines/poem. **Pays up to $50.**

FLORIDA

FT. MYERS MAGAZINE

And Pat llc, 52 Park Avenue E., Merrick NY 11566 United States of America. (516)652-6072. **E-mail:** ftmyers@optonline.net. **E-mail:** ftmyers2@optonline.net. **Website:** www.ftmyersmagazine.com. **Contact:** Andrew Elias. **90% freelance written.** Bimonthly magazine covering regional arts and living for educated, active, successful, and creative residents of Lee & Collier counties (FL) and guests at resorts and hotels in Lee County. Content: Arts, entertainment, media, culture, travel, sports, health, home, garden, environmental issues. Estab. 2001. Circ. 20,000. Byline given. 30 days after publication. No kill fee. Publishes ms an average of 2-6 months after acceptance. Editorial lead time 2-6 months. Submit seasonal material 2-6 months in advance. Accepts queries by e-mail. Accepts simultaneous submissions. Responds in 3 months to queries and to mss. Guidelines available online on 'Contact Us' page of website.

NONFICTION Needs essays, general interest, historical, how-to, humor, interview, personal experience, profile, travel, reviews, previews, news, informational. **Buys 10-25 mss/year.** Send complete ms. Length: 750-1,500 words. **Pays $50-150 or approximately 10¢/word.**

PHOTOS Contact: Andrew Elias. State availability of or send photos. Captions, identification of subjects required. Negotiates payment individually; generally offers $10-100/photo or art. Buys one-time rights.

WHERE (WHERE GUESTBOOK, WHERE MAP, WHERE NEWSLETTER)

Morris Visitor Publications, 699 Broad St., Suite 500, Augusta GA 30901. **E-mail:** editorial@wheretraveler.com. **Website:** www.wheretraveler.com. **Contact:** Geoff Kohl, chief travel editor. **40% freelance written.** Monthly magazine covering tourism in U.S. cities, certain European cities, and Singapore. Estab. 1936. Circ. 30,000. Byline for features only, but all writers listed on masthead. Pays on publication. Editorial lead time 3 months. Submit seasonal material 3 months in advance. Accepts queries by mail, e-mail. Responds in 1 week to queries Sample copy available online. Guidelines available by e-mail.

○ Query before submitting.

NONFICTION Needs new product, photo feature, travel. Query. Length: 500 words.

PHOTOS Send photos. Captions, identification of subjects, model releases required. Reviews GIF/JPEG files. Negotiates payment individually. Buys all rights.

COLUMNS/DEPARTMENTS Columns (all 50 words): Dining; Entertainment; Museums & Attractions; Art Galleries; Shops & Services. Queries for writer clips only per page of 1 blurbs per page.

TIPS "We look for a new slant on a 'where to go' or 'what to do' in each location."

GENERAL

FLUENT MAGAZINE

245 Timber Lane, Harpers Ferry WV 25425. **E-mail:** info@fluent-magazine.com. **E-mail:** poetry@fluent-magazine.com; fiction@fluent-magazine.com; nonfiction@fluent-magazine.com. **Website:** www.fluent-magazine.com. **Contact:** Nancy McKeithen. *FLUENT Magazine*, headquartered in West Virginia's Eastern Panhandle, is a free-subscription quarterly online magazine covering arts and culture in West Virginia, Pennsylvania, Maryland, Virginia, and the Washington DC area. "We reach an audience in four states plus other subscribers around the world. Each issue features a two-page spread by an individual poet. *FLUENT*'s broader arts and culture coverage emphasizes visual arts, and includes fiction, music, personal essays, humor and interviews drawn from the four-state region." Estab. 2012. Accepts simultaneous submissions.

POETRY Contact: Stephen Altman, poetry editor. Needs Intriguing poetry, traditional or otherwise, that grabs the attention and reaches the emotions. Long-form poems should not exceed 50 lines. "We prefer material that has never been published. We will consider poems excerpted from previously published books and chapbooks. Explicitly sexual or violent material will likely not work for us. We feature four poets a year, devoting a two-page spread to each. We'll need your home address and phone. Brief biographical material if you care to provide it. We read all poetry with names covered-up." Submit maximum 6 poems.

MIDWEST LIVING

Meredith Corp., 1716 Locust St., Des Moines IA 50309. **E-mail:** midwestliving@meredith.com. **Website:** www.midwestliving.com. **Contact:** Query Editor. Bimonthly magazine covering Midwestern families. Regional service magazine that celebrates the interest, values, and lifestyles of Midwestern families. Estab. 1987. Circ. 925,000. Pays 2-3 weeks after acceptance. No kill fee. Editorial lead time 1 year. Accepts queries by mail. Accepts simultaneous submissions. Sample copy: $3.95. Guidelines available online.

○ Query before submitting.

NONFICTION Needs general interest, historical, interview, travel. Does not want personal essays, stories about vacations, humor, nostalgia/reminiscent pieces, celebrity profiles, routine pieces on familiar destinations such as the dells, the Black Hills, or Navy Pier. Query with published clips.

PHOTOS State availability.

TIPS "As a general rule of thumb, we're looking for stories that are useful to the reader with information of ideas they can act on in their own lives. Most important, we want stories that have direct relevance to our Midwest audience."

SOUTHERN LIVING

Time Inc. Lifestyle Group, Editorial Offices, 4100 Old Montgomery Hwy., Birmingham AL 35209. (205)445-6000. **E-mail:** sl_online@timeinc.com. **Website:** www.southernliving.com. **Contact:** Claire Machamer, online editor. Monthly magazine covering southern lifestyle. Publication addressing the tastes and interests of contemporary southerners. Estab. 1966. Circ. 2.8 million. No kill fee. Editorial lead time 3 months. Accepts queries by mail. Accepts simultaneous submissions. Sample copy for $4.99 at newsstands. Guidelines by e-mail.

○ Accepts submissions for their Southern Journal column. Article must be southern, commenting on life in this region. "Make it personal, contemporary in the author's point of view; original, not published."

NONFICTION Needs essays. Send ms (typed, double-spaced) by postal mail. *Southern Living* column: Above all, it must be southern. Need comments on life in this region, written from the standpoint of a person who is intimately familiar with this part of the world. It's personal, almost always involving something that happened to the writer or someone he or she knows very well. Takes special note of stories that are contemporary in their point of view. Length: 500-600 words.

TIPS "The easiest way to break into the magazine for writers new to us is to propose short items."

SUNSET MAGAZINE

Sunset Publishing Corp., 55 Harrison St., Ste. 200, Oakland CA 94607. (510)858-3400. **Fax:** (650)327-7537. **E-mail:** readerletters@sunset.com. **Website:** www.sunset.com. Monthly magazine covering the lifestyle of the Western states. *Sunset* is a Western lifestyle publication for educated, active consumers. Editorial provides localized information on gardening and travel, food and entertainment, home building and remodeling. Byline given. Pays on acceptance. No kill fee. Accepts simultaneous submissions. Guidelines available online.

NONFICTION Needs travel. **Buys 50-75 mss/year.** Query before submitting. Freelance articles should be timely and only about the 13 Western states. Garden section accepts queries by mail. Travel section prefers queries by e-mail. Length: 550-750 words. **Pays $1/word.**

COLUMNS/DEPARTMENTS Building & Crafts, Food, Garden, Travel. Travel Guide length: 300-350 words. Direct queries to specific editorial department.

YANKEE

Yankee Publishing, Inc., P.O. Box 520, Dublin NH 03444-0520. (603)563-8111. **Fax:** (603)563-8298. **E-mail:** editors@yankeepub.com. **Website:** www.yankeemagazine.com. **Contact:** Joe Bills, associate editor; Heather Marcus, photo editor. **60% freelance written.** Monthly magazine covering the New England states of Connecticut, Massachusetts, Maine, New Hampshire, Rhode Island, and Vermont. "Our feature articles, as well as the departments of Home, Food, and Travel, reflect what is happening currently in these New England states. Our mission is to express and perhaps, indirectly, preserve the New England culture—and to do so in an entertaining way. Our audience is national and has one thing in common—it loves New England." Estab. 1935. Circ. 317,000. Byline given. Pays on acceptance. Offers kill fee. Editorial lead time 12 months. Submit seasonal material 1 year in advance. Accepts simultaneous submissions. Responds in 2 months to queries. Guidelines available online.

NONFICTION Needs essays, general interest, interview. Does not want "good old days" pieces or dialect, humor, or anything outside New England. **Buys 30 mss/year.** Query or submit complete ms with published clips and SASE. Length: up to 2,500 words. **Pays per assignment.** Pays expenses of writers on assignment when appropriate.

PHOTOS All photos and art are assigned to experienced professionals. If interested, send a portfolio with 35mm, 2.25, or 4x5 color transparencies. Do not send any unsolicited original photos or artwork.

TIPS "Submit lots of ideas. Don't censor yourself—let us decide whether an idea is good or bad. We might surprise you. Remember that we've been publishing since 1935, so chances are we've already done every 'classic' New England subject. Try to surprise us—it isn't easy. Study the ones we publish—the format should be apparent. It is to your advantage to read several issues of the magazine before sending us a query or a ms. *Yankee* does not publish fiction, poetry, humor, history, memoir, or cartoons as a routine format, nor do we solicit submissions."

GEORGIA

⑤⑤ ATLANTA TRIBUNE: THE MAGAZINE
875 Old Roswell Rd, Suite C-100, Roswell GA 30076. (770)587-0501. **Fax:** (770)642-6501. **E-mail:** info@atlantatribune.com. **Website:** www.atlantatribune.com. **30% freelance written.** Monthly magazine covering African-American business, careers, technology, wealth-building, politics, and education. The *Atlanta Tribune* is written for Atlanta's black executives, professionals and entrepreneurs with a primary focus of business, careers, technology, wealth-building, politics, and education. Our publication serves as an advisor that offers helpful information and direction to the black entrepreneur. Estab. 1987. Circ. 30,000. Byline given. Pays on publication. Offers 10% kill fee. Editorial lead time 3 months. Submit seasonal material 4 months in advance. Accepts queries by e-mail. Accepts simultaneous submissions. Responds in 6 weeks to queries. Sample copy online or mail a request. Guidelines available online.

NONFICTION Needs book excerpts, how-to, interview, new product, opinion, technical. **Buys 100 mss/year.** Query with published clips. Length: 1,400-2,500 words. **Pays $250-600.**

PHOTOS State availability. Identification of subjects, model releases required. Reviews 21/4x21/4 transparencies. Negotiates payment individually. Buys one time rights.

COLUMNS/DEPARTMENTS Business; Careers; Technology; Wealth-Building; Politics and Education; all 400-600 words. **Buys 100 mss/year.** Query with published clips. **Pays $100-200.**

TIPS Send a well-written, convincing query by e-mail that demonstrates that you have thoroughly read previous issues and reviewed our online writer's guidelines.

💲 FLAGPOLE MAGAZINE

P.O. Box 1027, Athens GA 30603. (706)549-9523. **Fax:** (706)548-8981. **E-mail:** editor@flagpole.com. **Website:** www.flagpole.com. **Contact:** Pete McCommons, editor and publisher. **75% freelance written.** Local alternative weekly with a special emphasis on popular (and unpopular) music. Will consider stories on national, international musicians, authors, politicians, etc., even if they don't have a local or regional news peg. However, those stories should be original and irreverent enough to justify inclusion. Of course, local/Southern news/feature stories are best. We like reporting and storytelling more than opinion pieces. Estab. 1987. Circ. 16,000. Byline given. Pays on publication. No kill fee. Publishes ms an average of 1 month after acceptance. Editorial lead time 2 months. Submit seasonal material 2 months in advance. Accepts simultaneous submissions. Responds in 2 weeks to queries. Responds in 1 month to mss. Sample copy online.

NONFICTION Needs book excerpts, essays, expose, interview, new product, personal experience. **Buys 50 mss/year.** Query by e-mail Length: 600-2,000 words.

REPRINTS Send tearsheet, photocopy or typed ms with rights for sale noted and information about when and where the material previously appeared.

PHOTOS State availability. Captions required. Reviews prints. Negotiates payment individually. Buys one time rights.

TIPS "Read our publication online before querying, but don't feel limited by what you see. We can't afford to pay much, so we're open to young/inexperienced writer-journalists looking for clips. Fresh, funny/insightful voices make us happiest, as does reportage over opinion. If you've ever succumbed to the temptation to call a pop record 'ethereal' we probably won't bother with your music journalism. No faxed submissions, please."

GEORGIA MAGAZINE

Georgia Electric Membership Corp., P.O. Box 1707, 2100 E. Exchange Place, Tucker GA 30085. (770)270-6500. **E-mail:** laurel.george@georgiaemc.com; magazine@georgiamc.com. **Website:** www.georgiamagazine.org. **Contact:** Laurel George, editor. **50% freelance written.** "We are a monthly magazine for and about Georgians, with a friendly, conversational tone and human interest topics." Estab. 1945. Circ. 500,000. Byline given. Pays on acceptance. No kill fee. Publishes ms an average of 6 months after acceptance. Editorial lead time 2 months. Submit seasonal material 6 months in advance. Accepts queries by mail, e-mail. Accepts simultaneous submissions. Responds in 1 month to subjects of interest. Sample copy: $2. Guidelines for #10 SASE, or by e-mail.

NONFICTION Needs general interest, historical, how-to, humor, inspirational, interview, photo feature, travel. Query with published clips. Length: 1,000-1,200 words; 800 words for smaller features and departments. **Pays $350-500.**

PHOTOS State availability. Identification of subjects, model releases required. Reviews digital images, websites, and prints. Negotiates payment individually. Buys one-time rights.

💲💲 KNOWATLANTA MAGAZINE

New South Publishing, Inc., 9040 Roswell Rd., Suite 210, Atlanta GA 30350. (770)650-1102. **Fax:** (770)650-2848. **E-mail:** lindsay@knowatlanta.com. **Website:** www. knowatlanta.com. **Contact:** Lindsay Penticuff, editor. **80% freelance written.** Quarterly magazine covering the Atlanta area. *KNOWAtlanta* is metro Atlanta's premier relocation guide. The magazine provides valuable information to people relocating to the area with articles on homes, healthcare, jobs, finances, temporary housing, apartments, education, county-by-county guides, and so much more. *KNOWAtlanta* puts Atlanta at its readers' fingertips. The magazine is used by executives relocating their companies, realtors working with future Atlantans, and individuals moving to the "capital of the Southeast." Estab. 1986. Circ. 192,000. Byline given. Pays on publication. Offers 100% kill fee. Editorial lead time 2 months. Submit seasonal material 2 months in advance. Accepts queries by e-mail. Accepts simultaneous submissions. Sample copy free.

NONFICTION Needs general interest, how-to, interview, personal experience, photo feature. No fiction. **Buys 20 mss/year.** Query with published clips. Length: 800-1,500 words. **Pays $100-500 for assigned articles. Pays $100-300 for unsolicited articles.**

PHOTOS Send photos with submission, if available. Captions, identification of subjects required. Reviews contact sheets. Negotiates payment individually. Buys one-time rights.

HAWAII

💲💲💲 HONOLULU MAGAZINE

PacificBasin Communications, 1000 Bishop Street, Suite 405, Honolulu HI 96813. (808)537-9500. **Fax:**

(808)537-6455. **E-mail:** kristinl@honolulumagazine. com. **Website:** www.honolulumagazine.com. Michael Keany, managing editor. **Contact:** Kristin Lipman, creative director. Monthly magazine covering general-interest topics relating to Hawaii residents. Estab. 1888. Circ. 30,000. Byline given. Pays about 30 days after publication. Where appropriate, offers 50% kill fee. Prefers to work with published/established writers. Accepts queries by mail, e-mail. Accepts simultaneous submissions. Guidelines available online. **NONFICTION** Needs historical, interview, sports, politics, lifestyle trends, all Hawaii-related. "We write for Hawaii residents, so travel articles about Hawaii are not appropriate." Send complete ms. Length determined when assignments discussed. **Pays $250-1,200.**
PHOTOS State availability. Captions, identification of subjects, model releases required. Pays $100 for stock, $200 for assigned shot. Package rates also negotiated.
COLUMNS/DEPARTMENTS Length determined when assignments discussed. Query with published clips or send complete ms. **Pays $100-300.**

ILLINOIS

💲 ILLINOIS ENTERTAINER

4223 W. Lake St., Suite 490, Chicago IL 60624. (773)717-5665. **Fax:** (773)717-5666. **E-mail:** service@illinoisentertainer.com. **Website:** www.illinoisentertainer.com. **80% freelance written.** Monthly free magazine covering popular and alternative music, as well as other entertainment (film, media) in Illinois. Estab. 1974. Circ. 55,000. Byline given. Pays on publication. Offers 50% kill fee. Publishes ms an average of 2 months after acceptance. Editorial lead time 2 months. Submit seasonal material 2 months in advance. Accepts queries by mail. Accepts simultaneous submissions. Responds in 2 months to queries. Sample copy: $5.
NONFICTION Needs expose, how-to, humor, interview, new product, reviews. No personal, confessional, or inspirational articles. **Buys 75 mss/year.** Query with published clips. Length: 600-2,600 words. **Pays $15-160.**
REPRINTS Send typed ms with rights for sale noted and information about when and where the material previously appeared. Pays 100% of amount paid for an original article.

PHOTOS Send photos. Captions, identification of subjects, model releases required. Reviews contact sheets, transparencies, 5x7 prints. Offers $20-200/photo. Buys one-time rights.
COLUMNS/DEPARTMENTS Spins (LP reviews), 100-400 words. **Buys 200-300 mss/year.** Query with published clips. **Pays $8-25.**
TIPS "Send clips, résumé, etc. and be patient. Also, sending queries that show you've seen our magazine and have a feel for it greatly increases your publication chances. Don't send unsolicited material. No e-mail solicitations or queries of any kind."

NORTHWEST QUARTERLY MAGAZINE

Hughes Media Corp., 222 Seventh St., Rockford IL 61104. (815)316-2300. **E-mail:** clinden@northwestquarterly.com. **Website:** www.northwestquarterly.com. **Contact:** Chris Linden, editor. **20% freelance written.** Quarterly magazine covering regional lifestyle of Northern Illinois and Southern Wisconsin, and also Kane and McHenry counties (Chicago collar counties), highlighting strengths of living and doing business in the area. Estab. 2004. Circ. 42,000. Byline given. Pays on publication. Publishes ms an average of 4-6 months after acceptance. Editorial lead time 6 months. Submit seasonal material 6 months in advance. Accepts queries by mail, e-mail. Accepts simultaneous submissions. Responds in 2 weeks to queries; in 2 months to mss. Sample copy and guidelines available by e-mail.
NONFICTION Needs historical, interview, photo feature, regional features. Does not want opinion, fiction, or "anything unrelated to our geographic region." **Buys 150 mss/year.** Query. Length: 700-2,500 words. **Pays $25-500.**
PHOTOS State availability. Captions required. Reviews GIF/JPEG files. Negotiates payment individually. Buys one-time rights.
COLUMNS/DEPARTMENTS Health & Fitness, 1,000-2,000 words; Home & Garden, 1,500 words; Destinations & Recreation, 1,000-2,000 words; Environment & Nature, 2,000-3,000 words. **Buys 120 mss/year.** Query. **Pays $100-500.**
FILLERS Needs short humor. **Buys 24 mss/year.** Length: 100-200 words. **Pays $30-50.**
TIPS "Any interesting, well-documented feature relating to the 16-county area we cover may be considered. Nature, history, geography, culture, and destinations are favorite themes."

🟢🟢 WEST SUBURBAN LIVING

C2 Publishing, Inc., P.O. Box 111, Elmhurst IL 60126. (630)834-4995. **Fax:** (630)834-4996. **E-mail:** wsl@ westsuburbanliving.net. **Website:** www.westsuburbanliving.net. **80% freelance written.** Bimonthly magazine focusing on the western suburbs of Chicago. Estab. 1996. Circ. 25,000. Byline given. Pays on publication. Publishes ms an average of 2-4 months after acceptance. Accepts queries by mail, e-mail, fax. Sample copy available online.

NONFICTION Needs general interest, how-to, travel. "Does not want anything that does not have an angle or tie-in to the area we cover—Chicago's western suburbs." **Buys 15 mss/year. Pays $100-500.**

PHOTOS State availability. Model releases required. Offers $50-700/photo; negotiates payment individually.

INDIANA

🟢🟢 EVANSVILLE LIVING

Tucker Publishing Group, 223 NW Second St., Suite 200, Evansville IN 47708. (812)426-2115. **E-mail:** ktucker@evansvilleliving.com. **Website:** www.evansvilleliving.com. **Contact:** Kristen Tucker, publisher and editor. **80-100% freelance written.** Bimonthly magazine covering Evansville, Indiana, and the greater area. *Evansville Living* is the only full-color, glossy, 100+ page city magazine for the Evansville, Indiana, area. Regular departments include: Home Style, Garden Style, Day Tripping, Sporting Life, and Local Flavor (menus). Estab. 2000. Circ. 50,000. Byline given. Pays on acceptance. No kill fee. Publishes ms an average of 3 months after acceptance. Editorial lead time 6 months. Submit seasonal material 6 months in advance. Accepts queries by mail, e-mail. Accepts simultaneous submissions. Sample copy for $5 or online. Guidelines by e-mail.

NONFICTION Needs essays, general interest, historical, photo feature, travel. **Buys 60-80 mss/year.** Query with published clips. Length: 200-2,000 words. **Pays $100-300.**

PHOTOS State availability. Captions, identification of subjects required. Reviews contact sheets, negatives, transparencies, prints. Negotiates payment individually. Buys all rights.

COLUMNS/DEPARTMENTS Home Style (home); Garden Style (garden); Sporting Life (sports); Local Flavor (menus), all 1,500 words. Query with published clips. **Pays $100-300.**

IOWA

THE IOWAN

Pioneer Communications, Inc., 300 Walnut St., Suite 6, Des Moines IA 50309. (515)246-0402. **E-mail:** editor@iowan.com. **Website:** www.iowan.com. **Contact:** Erich Gaukel, editor. **75% freelance written.** Bimonthly magazine covering the state of Iowa. *The Iowan* is a bimonthly magazine exploring everything Iowa has to offer. Each issue travels into diverse pockets of the state to discover the sights, meet the people, learn the history, taste the cuisine, and experience the culture. Estab. 1952. Circ. 20,000. Byline given. Pays 60 days from invoice approval or publication date, whichever comes first. Offers $100 kill fee. Publishes ms an average of 3 months after acceptance. Editorial lead time 9-10 months. Submit seasonal material 6-12 months in advance. Accepts queries by mail, e-mail. Accepts simultaneous submissions. Sample copy for $4.95, plus s&h. Guidelines available online.

NONFICTION Needs essays, general interest, historical, interview, photo feature, travel. Special issues: Each issue offers readers a collection of "shorts" that cover timely issues, current trends, interesting people, noteworthy work, enticing food, historical and historic moments, captivating arts and culture, beckoning recreational opportunities, and more. Features cover every topic imaginable with only 2 primary rules: (1) solid storytelling and (2) great photography potential. **Buys 30 mss/year.** Query with published clips. Length: 500-750 words for "shorts"; 1,000-1,500 words for features. **Pays $150-450.**

PHOTOS Send photos. Captions, identification of subjects, model releases required. Reviews contact sheets, GIF/JPEG files (8x10 at 300 dpi minimum). Negotiates payment individually, according to space rates. Buys one-time rights.

COLUMNS/DEPARTMENTS Last Word (essay), 800 words. **Buys 6 mss/year.** Query with published clips. **Pays $100.**

TIPS "Must have submissions in writing, either via e-mail or snail mail. Submitting published clips is preferred."

KANSAS

🖒🖒 KANSAS!

1020 S. Kansas Ave., Suite 200, Topeka KS 66612-1354. (785)296-8478. **Fax:** (785)296-6988. **E-mail:** ksmagazine@sunflowerpub.com. **Website:** www.travelks.com/ks-mag. **Contact:** Andrea Etzel, editor. **90% freelance written.** Quarterly magazine emphasizing Kansas travel attractions and events. Estab. 1945. Circ. 45,000. Byline and courtesy bylines are given to all content. Pays on acceptance. No kill fee. Publishes ms an average of 1 year after acceptance. Submit seasonal material 8 months in advance. Accepts queries by mail, e-mail. Accepts simultaneous submissions. Responds in 2 months to queries. Guidelines available on website.

NONFICTION Needs general interest, photo feature, travel. Query. Length: 750-1,250 words. **Pays $200-350.** Mileage reimbursement is available for writers on assignment in the state of Kansas, TBD by assignment editor.

PHOTOS "We are a full-color photograph/ms publication. Send digital photos (original transparencies only or CD with images available in high resolution) with query." Captions and location of the image (county and city) are required. Pays $25-75 for gallery images, $150 for cover. Assignments also available, welcomes queries.

TIPS "History and nostalgia or essay stories do not fit into our format because they can't be illustrated well with color photos. Submit a query letter describing 1 appropriate idea with outline for possible article and suggestions for photos. Do not send unsolicited mss."

KENTUCKY

🖒🖒 KENTUCKY LIVING

Kentucky Association of Electric Co-Ops, P.O. Box 32170, Louisville KY 40232. (502)451-2430. **Fax:** (502)459-1611. **E-mail:** email@kentuckyliving.com. **Website:** www.kentuckyliving.com. **Contact:** Anita Travis Richter, editor. **Mostly freelance written. Prefers to work with published/established writers.** Monthly feature magazine primarily for Kentucky residents. Estab. 1948. Circ. 500,000. Byline given. Pays on acceptance. No kill fee. Publishes ms an average of 12 months after acceptance. Submit seasonal material at least 6 months in advance. Accepts queries by e-mail, online submission form. Accepts simultaneous submissions. Responds in 1 month to queries. Sample copy with SASE (9x12 envelope and 4 first-class stamps). Guidelines available online.

NONFICTION Needs general interest, historical, profile. Special issues: Stories of interest include: Kentucky-related profiles (people, places, or events), business and social trends, history, biography, recreation, travel, leisure or lifestyle articles/book excerpts, articles on contemporary subjects of general public interest, and general consumer-related features. **Buys 18-24 mss/year.** Prefers queries rather than submissions. Length: 500-1,500 words. **Pays $75-935**

PHOTOS State availability of or send photos. Identification of subjects required. Reviews photo e-files at online link or sent CD. Payment for photos included in payment for ms.

COLUMNS/DEPARTMENTS Accepts queries for Worth the Trip column. Other columns have established columnists.

TIPS "The quality of writing and reporting (factual, objective, thorough) is considered in setting payment price. We prefer general interest pieces filled with quotes and anecdotes. Avoid boosterism. Well-researched, well-written feature articles are preferred. All articles must have a strong Kentucky connection."

🖒🖒 KENTUCKY MONTHLY

Vested Interest Publications, P.O. Box 559, 100 Consumer Lane, Frankfort KY 40602-0559. (502)227-0053; (888)329-0053. **Fax:** (502)227-5009. **E-mail:** kymonthly@kentuckymonthly.com; steve@kentuckymonthly.com. **E-mail:** patty@kentuckymonthly.com. **Website:** www.kentuckymonthly.com. **Contact:** Stephen Vest, editor; Patricia Ranft, associate editor. **60% freelance written.** Monthly magazine. "We publish stories about Kentucky and by Kentuckians, including stories written by those who live elsewhere." Estab. 1998. Circ. 40,000. Byline given. Pays within 3 months of publication. Offers kill fee. Publishes ms an average of 3 months after acceptance. Editorial lead time 4-12 months. Submit seasonal material 4-10 months in advance. Accepts queries by e-mail. Accepts simultaneous submissions. Responds in 1-3 months to queries; in 1 month to mss. Sample copy and writer's guidelines online.

NONFICTION Needs book excerpts, essays, general interest, historical, how-to, humor, interview, photo feature, profile, religious, reviews, travel, All pieces should have a Kentucky angle. Special issues: Kentucky Derby Festival Guide (April); Kentucky Gift Guide (November). **Buys 50 mss/year.** Query. Length: 300-2,000 words. **Pays $45-300 for assigned articles; $50-200 for unsolicited articles.**

PHOTOS State availability. Captions required. Reviews negatives. Buys first rights.

FICTION We publish stories about Kentucky and by Kentuckians, including stories written by those who live elsewhere." Needs adventure, historical, mainstream, slice-of-life vignettes, Wants Kentucky-related stories. **Buys 30 mss/year.** Query with published clips. Accepts submissions by e-mail. Length: 1,000-5,000 words. **Pays $50-500.**

TIPS "Please read the magazine to get the flavor of what we're publishing each month. We accept articles via e-mail. Approximately 70% of articles are assigned."

MASSACHUSETTS

CAPE COD LIFE PUBLICATIONS

13 Steeple St., Suite 204, P.O. Box 1439, Mashpee MA 02649. (508)419-7381. **Fax:** (508)477-1225. **Website:** www.capecodlife.com. **Contact:** Jen Dow, Creative Director; Matthew Gill, *Cape Cod LIFE* Editor, Julie Wagner, *Cape Cod HOME* Editor. **80% freelance written.** Cape Cod LIFE Magazine published 7 times/year focusing on area lifestyle, history and culture, people and places, business and industry, and issues and answers for year-round and summer residents of Cape Cod, Nantucket, and Martha's Vineyard as well as nonresidents who spend their leisure time here. Cape Cod Life Magazine has become the premier lifestyle magazine for the Cape & Islands, featuring topics ranging from arts and events, history and heritage, beaches and boating as well as a comprehensive resource for planning the perfect vacation. Cape Cod ART is published annually. Cape Cod HOME is published 6 times per year. Estab. 1979. Circ. 45,000. Byline given. Pays 90 days after published. Submit seasonal material 6 months in advance. Accepts queries by mail, e-mail. Accepts simultaneous submissions. Responds in 3 months to queries. Responds in 3 months to mss. Sample copy for $5. Guidelines for #10 SASE.

NONFICTION Needs book excerpts, general interest, historical, interview, photo feature, travel, outdoors, gardening, nautical, nature, arts, antiques, history, housing. **Buys 20 mss/year.** Query. Length: 800-1,500 words. **Pays $200-400.**

PHOTOS Photo guidelines for #10 SASE. Captions, identification of subjects required. Pays $25-225. Buys first rights with right to reprint.

TIPS "Freelancers submitting *quality* spec articles with a Cape Cod and Islands angle have a good chance at publication. We like to see a wide selection of writer's clips before giving assignments. We also publish *Cape Cod HOME* covering architecture, landscape design, and interior design with a Cape and Islands focus. Also publish Cape Cod ART annually."

WORCESTER MAGAZINE

72 Shrewbury St., Worcester MA 01604. (508)749-3166. **E-mail:** editor@worcestermag.com; wbird@worcestermag.com. **Website:** www.worcestermag.com. **Contact:** Walter Bird, Jr., editor; Kathy Real, publisher. **10% freelance written.** Weekly tabloid emphasizing the central Massachusetts region, especially the city of Worcester. Estab. 1976. Circ. 40,000. Byline given. Pays on publication. No kill fee. Publishes ms an average of 3 weeks after acceptance. Submit seasonal material 2 months in advance. Accepts queries by mail, e-mail, fax. Accepts simultaneous submissions. Does not respond to unsolicited material.

NONFICTION Needs essays, expose, general interest, historical, humor, opinion, personal experience, photo feature. **Buys less than 75 mss/year.** Length: 500-1,500 words. **Pays 10¢/word.**

MICHIGAN

ANN ARBOR OBSERVER

Ann Arbor Observer Co., 2390 Winewood, Ann Arbor MI 48103. (734)769-3175. **Fax:** (734)769-3375. **E-mail:** editor@aaobserver.com. **Website:** www.annarborobserver.com. **Contact:** John Hilton, editor. **50% freelance written.** Monthly magazine. "We depend heavily on freelancers, and we're always glad to talk to new ones. We look for the intelligence and judgment to fully explore complex people and situations, and the ability to convey what makes them interesting." Estab. 1976. Circ. 60,000. Byline given in some sections. Pays on publication. No kill fee. Publishes ms an average of 2 months after acceptance. Accepts queries by mail, e-mail, phone. Responds in 3 weeks to queries; several months to mss. Sample copy for

12.5x15 SAE with $3 postage. Guidelines by e-mail or mail for #10 SASE.

NONFICTION Buys 75 mss/year. Length: 100-2,500 words. **Pays up to $1,000.**

COLUMNS/DEPARTMENTS Up Front (short, interesting tidbits), 150 words, pays $150; Inside Ann Arbor (concise stories), 300-500 words, pays $250; Around Town (unusual, compelling anecdotes), 750-1,500 words; pays $250-300.

TIPS "If you have an idea for a story, write a 100- to 200-word description telling us why the story is interesting. We are open most to intelligent, insightful features about interesting aspects of life in Ann Arbor—all stories must have a strong Ann Arbor tie."

⊕⊛ MICHIGAN HISTORY

The Historical Society of Michigan, 5815 Executive Dr., Lansing MI 48911. (517)332-1828. **Fax:** (517)324-4370. **E-mail:** mhmeditor@hsmichigan.org; hsm@hsmichigan.org. **E-mail:** majher@hsmichigan.org. **Website:** www.hsmichigan.org. **Contact:** Patricia Majher, editor. Covers exciting stories of Michigan people and their impact on their communities, the nation and the world. *Michigan History* overflows with intriguing feature articles, bold illustrations and departments highlighting history-related books, travel and events 6 times each year. Bimonthly magazine, 64 colorful pages. "A thoroughly entertaining read, *Michigan History* specializes in stories from Michigan's colorful past. Within its pages, you'll learn about logging, mining, manufacturing, and military history as well as art and architecture, music, sports, shipwrecks, and more. Requires idea queries first." In addition to payment, authors receive 5 free copies of issues in which their work appears. Estab. 1917. Circ. 22,000. Byline given. Pays on publication. Publishes ms 6 months after acceptance. Editorial lead time 1 year. Accepts queries by mail, e-mail. Accepts simultaneous submissions. Guidelines for authors at www.hsmichigan.org/michiganhistory/contribute.

NONFICTION Remember the Time features (first-person, factual, personal experiences that happened in Michigan—750 words) pay $100. Other features pay $200-$400, depending on word length and cooperation in gathering photos. "We are not a scholarly journal and do not accept academic papers." **Buys 50-55/mss/year mss/year.** "When you are ready to submit a manuscript, please provide a digital copy of the text, and also list your research sources for fact-checking

purposes. Include with your ms a summary of your writing experience and "in the interest of full disclosure" any relationship you have to your subject. You are expected to gather your own graphics (provided digitally and with captions, if possible) or at least suggest possible graphics." Length: 1,500-2,500 words. **Pays $150-400.**

PHOTOS Expects writers to provide photos or recommend their source; will pay for photo permissions.

TIPS "All stories must be well-researched, well-written, interesting, and accurate. Most of our authors are seasoned journalists, graduate students, academics, or published book authors—not first-time writers. You can save yourself time if you present your idea first; if approved, you can proceed to produce a manuscript. When you query, list your writing credentials and attach published clips. We do not publish fiction."

MINNESOTA

⊕⊛ LAKE COUNTRY JOURNAL

1480 Northern Pacific Road, #2A, Brainerd MN 56401. (218)828-6424, ext. 14. **Fax:** (218)825-7816. **E-mail:** editor@lakecountryjournal.com; info@lakecountry-journal.com. **Website:** www.lakecountryjournal.com. **90% freelance written.** Bimonthly magazine covering central Minnesota's lake country. "Lake Country is one of the fastest-growing areas in the midwest. Each bimonthly issue of *Lake Country Journal* captures the essence of why we work, play, and live in this area. Through a diverse blend of articles from features and fiction, to recreation, recipes, gardening, and nature, this quality lifestyle magazine promotes positive family and business endeavors, showcases our natural and cultural resources, and highlights the best of our people, places, and events." Estab. 1996. Circ. 14,500. Byline given. Pays on publication. Offers 25% kill fee. Publishes ms an average of 6 months after acceptance. Submit seasonal material 1 year in advance. Accepts queries by mail, e-mail. Accepts simultaneous submissions. Responds in 2 months to queries. Responds in 3 months to mss. Sample copy for $6. Guidelines available online.

⊕ Break in by "submitting department length first—they are not scheduled as far in advance as features. Always in need of original fillers."

NONFICTION Needs essays, general interest, how-to, humor, interview, personal experience, photo feature. "No articles that come from writers who are not familiar with our target geographical location." **Buys 30 mss/year.** Query with or without published clips. Length: 1,000-1,500 words. **Pays $100-200.**

PHOTOS State availability. Identification of subjects, model releases required. Reviews transparencies. Negotiates payment individually. Buys one-time rights.

COLUMNS/DEPARTMENTS Profile-People from Lake Country, 800 words; Essay, 800 words; Health (topics pertinent to central Minnesota living), 500 words. **Buys 40 mss/year.** Query with published clips. **Pays $50-75.**

FICTION Needs adventure, humorous, mainstream. **Buys 6 mss/year.** Length: 1,500 words. **Pays $100-200.**

POETRY Needs free verse. "Never use rhyming verse, avant-garde, experimental, etc." Buys 6 poems/year. Submit maximum 4 poems. Length: 8-32 lines. **Pays $25.**

FILLERS Needs anecdotes, short humor. **Buys 20 mss/year.** Length: 100-300 words. **Pays $25/filler.**

TIPS "Most of the people who will read your articles live in the north central Minnesota lakes area. All have some significant attachment to the area. We have readers of various ages, backgrounds, and lifestyles. After reading your article, we hope to have a deeper understanding of some aspect of our community, our environment, ourselves, or humanity in general."

🌣🌣 LAKE SUPERIOR MAGAZINE

Lake Superior Port Cities, Inc., P.O. Box 16417, Duluth MN 55816-0417. (218)722-5002. **Fax:** (218)722-4096. **E-mail:** edit@lakesuperior.com. **Website:** www.lakesuperior.com. **Contact:** Konnie LeMay, editor. **40% freelance written. Works with a small number of new/unpublished writers each year. Please include phone number and address with e-mail queries.** Bimonthly magazine covering contemporary and historic people, places, and current events around Lake Superior. Estab. 1979. Circ. 20,000. Byline given. Pays on publication. No kill fee. Publishes ms an average of 10 months after acceptance. Submit seasonal material 1 year in advance. Accepts queries by mail, e-mail. Accepts simultaneous submissions. Responds in 3 months to queries. Sample copy: $4.95 plus 6 first-class stamps. Guidelines available online.

NONFICTION Needs book excerpts, general interest, historical, humor, interview, personal experience, photo feature, travel, city profiles, regional business, some investigative. **Buys 15 mss/year.** Prefers mss,

but accepts short queries via mail or e-mail. Length: 1,600-2,000 words for features. **Pays $200-400.**

PHOTOS "Quality photography is our hallmark." Send photos. Captions, identification of subjects, model releases required. Reviews electronically only. Offers $50/image; $150 for covers.

COLUMNS/DEPARTMENTS Shorter articles on specific topics of interest: Homes, Health & Wellness, Lake Superior Journal, Wild Superior, Heritage, Destinations, Profile, all 800-1,200 words. **Buys 20 mss/year.** Query with published clips. **Pays $75-200.**

FICTION Must be targeted regionally. Needs historical, humorous, mainstream, novel excerpts. Wants stories that are Lake Superior related. Rarely uses fiction stories. **Buys 2-3 mss/year.** Query with published clips. Length: 300-2,500 words. **Pays $50-125.**

TIPS "Well-researched queries are attended to. We actively seek queries from writers in Lake Superior communities. We prefer mss to queries. Provide enough information on why the subject is important to the region and our readers, or why and how something is unique. We want details. The writer must have a thorough knowledge of the subject and how it relates to our region. We prefer a fresh, unused approach to the subject that provides the reader with an emotional involvement. Almost all of our articles feature quality photography in color or b&w. It is a prerequisite of all nonfiction. All submissions should include a *short* biography of author/photographer; mug shot sometimes used. Blanket submissions need not apply."

🌣🌣🌣 MPLS. ST. PAUL MAGAZINE

MSP Communications, 220 S. Sixth St., Suite 500, Minneapolis MN 55402. **E-mail:** edit@mspmag.com. **Website:** www.mspmag.com. **Contact:** Kelly Ryan Kegans, executive editor. Monthly magazine covering the Minneapolis-St. Paul area. *Mpls. St. Paul Magazine* is a city magazine serving upscale readers in the Minneapolis-St. Paul metro area. Circ. 80,000. Pays on publication. Editorial lead time 3 months. Accepts queries by mail, e-mail. Accepts simultaneous submissions. Sample copy: $10.

NONFICTION Needs book excerpts, essays, general interest, historical, interview, personal experience, photo feature, travel. **Buys 150 mss/year.** Query with published clips. Length: 500-4,000 words. **Pays 50-75¢/word for assigned articles.**

MISSOURI

🟡🟡 417 MAGAZINE

Whitaker Publishing, 2111 S. Eastgate Ave., Springfield MO 65809. (417)883-7417. **Fax:** (417)889-7417. **E-mail:** editor@417mag.com. **Website:** www.417mag.com. **Contact:** Katie Pollock Estes, editor. **50% freelance written.** Monthly magazine. *"417 Magazine* is a regional title serving southwest Missouri. Our editorial mix includes service journalism and lifestyle content on home, fashion and the arts; as well as narrative and issues pieces. The audience is affluent, educated, mostly female." Estab. 1998. Circ. 20,000. Byline given. Pays on acceptance. Publishes ms an average of 2-3 months after acceptance. Editorial lead time 6 months. Accepts queries by e-mail. Accepts simultaneous submissions. Responds in 1-2 months to queries. Sample copy by e-mail. Guidelines online.

NONFICTION Needs essays, expose, general interest, how-to, humor, inspirational, interview, new product, personal experience, photo feature, travel, local book reviews. "We are a local magazine, so anything not reflecting our local focus is something we have to pass on." **Buys 175 mss/year.** Query with published clips. Length: 300-3,500 words. **Pays $30-500, sometimes more.**

TIPS "Read the magazine before contacting us. Send specific ideas with your queries. Submit story ideas of local interest. Send published clips. Be a curious reporter, and ask probing questions."

KC MAGAZINE

Anthem Publishing, P.O. Box 26206, Shawnee Mission KS 66225. (913)894-6923. **Website:** www.kcmag.com. **75% freelance written.** Monthly magazine covering life in Kansas City, Kansas. "Our mission is to celebrate living in Kansas City. We are a consumer lifestyle/general-interest magazine focused on Kansas City, its people, and places." Estab. 1994. Circ. 31,000. Byline given. Pays on acceptance. Offers 10% kill fee. Publishes ms an average of 3 months after acceptance. Editorial lead time 4 months. Submit seasonal material 6 months in advance. Accepts queries by mail, e-mail. Accepts simultaneous submissions. Sample copy for 8.5x11 SAE or online.

NONFICTION Needs general interest, interview, photo feature. **Buys 15-20 mss/year.** Query with published clips. Length: 250-3,000 words.

PHOTOS Negotiates payment individually. Buys one-time rights.

COLUMNS/DEPARTMENTS Entertainment (Kansas City only), 1,000 words; Food (Kansas City food and restaurants only), 1,000 words. **Buys 12 mss/year.** Query with published clips.

🟡🟡 MISSOURI LIFE

501 High St., Suite A, Boonville MO 65233. (660)882-9898. **Fax:** (660)882-9899. **E-mail:** dcawthon@missourilife.com. **Website:** www.missourilife.com. **Contact:** David Cawthon, associate editor. **85% freelance written.** Bimonthly magazine covering the state of Missouri. *"Missouri Life*'s readers are mostly college-educated people with a wide range of travel and lifestyle interests. Our magazine discovers the people, places, and events—both past and present—that make Missouri a great place to live and/or visit." Estab. 1973. Circ. 96,800. Byline given. Pays on publication. Editorial lead time 6 months. Submit seasonal material 6 months in advance. Accepts queries by mail, e-mail, fax. Accepts simultaneous submissions. Responds in approximately 2 months to queries. Sample copy available for $4.95 and SASE with $2.44 first-class postage (or a digital version can be purchased online). Guidelines available online.

NONFICTION Needs general interest, historical, travel, all Missouri related. Length: 300-2,000 words. **No set amount per word.**

PHOTOS Contact: Sarah Herrera, associate art director. E-mail: sarah@missourilife.com. (Also contact for art/illustration.). State availability in query; buys all rights nonexclusive. Captions, identification of subjects, model releases required. Offers $50-150/photo.

COLUMNS/DEPARTMENTS "All Around Missouri (people and places, past and present, written in an almanac style); Missouri Artist (features a Missouri artist), 500 words; Made in Missouri (products and businesses native to Missouri), 500 words. Contact assistant manager for restaurant review queries.

NEVADA

🟡🟡 NEVADA MAGAZINE

401 N. Carson St., Carson City NV 89701. (775)687-0602. **Fax:** (775)687-6159. **E-mail:** editor@nevadamagazine.com. **Website:** www.nevadamagazine.com. **25% freelance written. Works with a small**

number of new/unpublished writers each year. Bi-monthly magazine published by the state of Nevada to promote tourism. Estab. 1936. Circ. 20,000. Byline given. Pays on publication. No kill fee. Publishes ms an average of 6 months after acceptance. Submit seasonal material 6 months in advance. Accepts simultaneous submissions. Responds in 1 month to queries. Sample copy available by request. Guidelines available online.

NONFICTION Prefers a well-written query or outline with specific story elements before receiving the actual story. Write, e-mail, or call if you have a story that might work. Length: 500-1,500 words. **Pays flat rate of $250 or less. For web stories, pays $100 or $200 depending on the assignment.**

PHOTOS Contact: Query art director Sean Nebeker (snebeker@nevadamagazine.com). Reviews digital images. Pays $25-250; cover, $250. Buys one-time rights.

COLUMNS/DEPARTMENTS Columns include: Up Front (the latest Nevada news), Visions (emphasizes outstanding photography with extended captions), City Limits (features destination stories for Nevada's larger cities), Wide Open (features destination stories for Nevada's rural towns and regions), Cravings (stories centered on food and drink), Travels (people traveling Nevada, sharing their adventures), History, and Events & Shows.

TIPS "Keep in mind the magazine's purpose is to promote Nevada tourism."

NEW JERSEY

$$$$ NEW JERSEY MONTHLY

55 Park Place, P.O. Box 920, Morristown NJ 07963-0920. (973)539-8230. **Fax:** (973)538-2953. **E-mail:** kschlager@njmonthly.com. **Website:** www.njmonthly.com. **Contact:** Ken Schlager, editor. **75-80% freelance written.** Monthly magazine covering just about anything to do with New Jersey, from news, politics, and sports to decorating trends and lifestyle issues. Our readership is well-educated, affluent, and on average our readers have lived in New Jersey 20 years or more. Estab. 1976. Circ. 92,000. Byline given. Pays on completion of fact-checking. Offers 20% kill fee. Publishes ms an average of 3 months after acceptance. Editorial lead time 3 months. Submit seasonal material 6 months in advance. Accepts queries by mail, e-mail, fax, phone. Accepts simultaneous submissions.

Responds in 2-3 months to queries. Guidelines available online.

○ This magazine continues to look for strong investigative reporters with novelistic style and solid knowledge of New Jersey issues.

NONFICTION Needs book excerpts, essays, expose, general interest, historical, humor, interview, personal experience, photo feature, travel, arts, sports, politics. No experience pieces from people who used to live in New Jersey or general pieces that have no New Jersey angle. **Buys 90-100 mss/year.** Query with published magazine clips via e-mail. Length: 250-3,000 words. **Payment varies.** Pays reasonable expenses of writers on assignment with prior approval.

PHOTOS Contact: Donna Panagakos, art director.. State availability. Identification of subjects, model releases required. Reviews transparencies, prints. Payment negotiated. Buys one time rights.

COLUMNS/DEPARTMENTS Exit Ramp (back page essay usually originating from personal experience but written in a way that tells a broader story of statewide interest), 500 words; front-of-the-book Garden Variety (brief profiles or articles on local life, 250-350 words; restaurant reviews. **Buys 12 mss/year.** Query with published clips. **Payment varies.**

FILLERS Needs anecdotes, for front-of-book. **Buys 12-15 mss/year.** Length: 200-250 words. **Payment varies.**

TIPS "The best approach: Do your homework! Read the past year's issues to get an understanding of our well-written, well-researched articles that tell a tale from a well-established point of view."

NEW MEXICO

$$ NEW MEXICO MAGAZINE

Lew Wallace Bldg., 495 Old Santa Fe Trail, Santa Fe NM 87501-2750. (505)827-7447. **E-mail:** artdirector@nmmagazine.com. **Website:** www.nmmagazine.com. **70% freelance written.** Covers areas throughout the state. "We want to publish a lively editorial mix, covering both the down-home (like a diner in Tucumcari) and the upscale (a new bistro in world-class Santa Fe)." Explore the gamut of the Old West and the New Age. "Our magazine is about the power of place—in particular more than 120,000 square miles of mountains, desert, grasslands, and forest inhabited by a culturally rich mix of individuals. It is an enterprise of the

New Mexico Tourism Department, which strives to make potential visitors aware of our state's multicultural heritage, climate, environment, and uniqueness." Estab. 1923. Circ. 100,000. Pays on acceptance. 20% kill fee. Publishes ms an average of 3 months after acceptance. Submit seasonal material 1 year in advance. Accepts queries by mail. Accepts simultaneous submissions. Responds to queries if interested. Sample copy for $5. Guidelines available online.

Ⓞ Does not return unsolicited material.

NONFICTION Submit story idea along with a working head and subhead and a paragraph synopsis. Include published clips and a short sum-up about your strengths as a writer. Considers proposal as well as writer's potential to write the conceptualized stories.

REPRINTS Rarely publishes reprints, but sometimes publishes excerpts from novels and nonfiction books.

PHOTOS "Purchased as portfolio or on assignment. Photographers interested in photo assignments should reference submission guidelines on the contributors' page of our website."

NEW YORK

ADIRONDACK LIFE

P.O. Box 410, Rt. 9N, Jay NY 12941-0410. (518)946-2191. **Fax:** (518)946-7461. **E-mail:** astoltie@adirondacklife.com; khofschneider@adirondacklife.com. **Website:** adirondacklifemag.com. **Contact:** Annie Stoltie, editor; Kelly Hofschneider, photo editor. **70% freelance written. Prefers to work with published/established writers.** Magazine, published bimonthly, that emphasizes the Adirondack region and the North Country of New York State in articles covering outdoor activities, history, and natural history directly related to the Adirondacks. Estab. 1970. Circ. 50,000. Byline given. Pays 30 days after publication. No kill fee. Publishes ms an average of 10 months after acceptance. Submit seasonal material 1 year in advance. Accepts queries by mail, e-mail. Accepts simultaneous submissions. Responds in 1 month to queries. Sample copy for $3 and 9x12 SAE. Guidelines available online.

Ⓞ "For new contributors, the best way to break into the magazine is through departments."

NONFICTION Special issues: Special issues: Annual Guide to the Great Outdoors (how-to and where-to articles that offer in-depth information about recreational offerings in the park); At Home in the Adiron-

dacks (focuses on the region's signature style). Does not want poetry, fiction, or editorial cartoons. **Buys 20-25 unsolicited mss/year.** Query with published clips. Accepts queries, but not unsolicited mss, via e-mail. Length: 1,500-3,000 words. **Pays 30¢/word.**

PHOTOS "All photos must have been taken in the Adirondacks. Each issue contains a photo feature. Purchased with or without ms on assignment. All photos must be individually identified as to the subject or locale and must bear the photographer's name." Send photos. Reviews hi-res (300 dpi) TIFF/JPEG/PSD files via e-mail, or raw files on CD. Pays $150 for full page, b&w, or color; $400 for cover (color only, vertical in format). Credit line given.

COLUMNS/DEPARTMENTS Short Carries; Northern Lights; Special Places (unique spots in the Adirondack Park); Skills; Working (careers in the Adirondacks); The Scene; Back Page. Length: 1,000-1,800 words. Query with published clips. **Pays 30¢/word.**

FICTION Considers first-serial novel excerpts in its subject matter and region.

TIPS "Do not send a personal essay about your meaningful moment in the mountains. We need factual pieces about regional history, sports, culture, and business. We are looking for clear, concise, well-organized mss that are strictly Adirondack in subject. Check back issues to be sure we haven't already covered your topic. Check out our guidelines online."

IN NEW YORK

Morris Media Network, 79 Madison Ave., 8th Floor, New York NY 10016. (212)716-8562. **E-mail:** lois.levine@morris.com. **Website:** www.innewyork.com. **Contact:** Lois Levine, editor-in-chief. Monthly full-color magazine covering shopping, dining, attractions, museums, tours, galleries, nightlife, theater, and special events, created exclusively for sophisticated travelers to the New York Metropolitan area and distributed at most hotels, tourist centers, VIP lounges of Amtrak Acela, airlines, and popular sights. Circ. 146,000. Kill fee 20% Accepts simultaneous submissions. Sample copy for free in upscale hotels at concierge desk.

TIPS "No unsolicited manuscripts, please. All queries should be snail mail only."

WESTCHESTER MAGAZINE

Today Media, 2 Clinton Ave., Rye NY 10580. (914)345-0601. **Website:** www.westchestermagazine.com. **35% freelance written.** Monthly magazine covering culture and lifestyle of Westchester County, New York. *Westchester Magazine* is an upscale, high-end regional lifestyle publication covering issues specific to Westchester County, New York. All stories must have a local slant. Estab. 2001. Circ. 65,475. Byline given. Pays on publication. Offers 25% kill fee. Publishes ms an average of 3 months after acceptance. Editorial lead time 3 months. Submit seasonal material 3 months in advance. Accepts queries by mail. Sample copy available online.

NONFICTION Needs expose, general interest, interview, local service. Does not want personal essays, reviews, stories not specific to Westchester. **Buys 36 mss/year.** Query with published clips. Length: 150-5,000 words. **Pays $50-$1000.**

PHOTOS Contact: Contact Aiko Masazumi, creative director.. State availability. Captions, identification of subjects required. Reviews GIF/JPEG files. Negotiates payment individually. Negotiates rights individually.

COLUMNS/DEPARTMENTS Our Neighbor (profile of a local celebrity), 500 words; Westchester Chronicles (short items of local interest), 300 words; County Golf (articles about the local golf scene), 500 words. **Buys 36 mss/year.** Query with published clips. **Pays $30-200.**

TIPS "Be sure to query ideas applicable *only* to Westchester County that we have not written about before."

NORTH CAROLINA

💲💲 CHARLOTTE MAGAZINE

Morris Visitor Publications, 214 W. Tremont Ave., Suite 303, Charlotte NC 28203. (704)335-7181. **Fax:** (704)335-3757. **E-mail:** michael.graff@charlottemagazine.com. **Website:** www.charlottemagazine.com. **Contact:** Michael Graff, publisher. **75% freelance written.** Monthly magazine covering Charlotte life. This magazine tells its readers things they didn't know about Charlotte in an interesting, entertaining, and sometimes provocative style. Circ. 40,000. Byline given. Pays within 30 days of acceptance. Offers 25% kill fee. Publishes ms an average of 3 months after acceptance. Editorial lead time 3 months. Submit seasonal material 6 months in advance. Accepts queries by mail, e-mail. Accepts simultaneous submissions. Responds in 6 months to mss. Sample copy for $6.

NONFICTION Needs book excerpts, expose, general interest, interview, photo feature, travel. **Buys 35-50 mss/year.** Query with published clips. Length: 200-3,000 words. **Pays 20-40¢/word.**

PHOTOS State availability. Identification of subjects required. Negotiates payment individually. Buys one-time rights.

COLUMNS/DEPARTMENTS Buys 35-50 mss/year. **Pays 20-40¢/word**

TIPS "A story for *Charlotte* magazine could only appear in *Charlotte* magazine. That is, the story and its treatment are particularly germane to this area. Because of this, we rarely work with writers who live outside the Charlotte area."

💲💲 FIFTEEN 501

Weiss and Hughes Publishing, 189 Wind Chime Court, Suite 104, Raleigh NC 27615. (919)870-1722. **Fax:** (919)719-5260. **E-mail:** djackson@whmags.com. **Website:** www.fifteen501.com. **Contact:** Danielle Jackson, editor. **50% freelance written.** Quarterly magazine covering lifestyle issues relevant to residents in the U.S. 15/501 corridor of Durham, Orange, and Chatham counties in North Carolina. "We cover issues important to residents of Durham, Orange and Chatham counties. We're committed to improving our readers' overall quality of life and keeping them informed of the lifestyle amenities there." Estab. 2006. Circ. 30,000. Byline given. Pays within 30 days of publication. Offers 25% kill fee. Publishes ms an average of 2 months after acceptance. Editorial lead time 2-3 months. Submit seasonal material 6 months in advance. Accepts queries by mail, e-mail. Accepts simultaneous submissions. Responds in 2-4 weeks to queries. Sample copy available online. Guidelines by e-mail.

NONFICTION Needs general interest, historical, how-to, inspirational, interview, personal experience, photo feature, technical, travel. Does not want opinion pieces or political or religious topics. Query. Length: 600-1,200 words. **Pays 35¢/word.**

PHOTOS State availability. Captions, identification of subjects required. Reviews transparencies, GIF/JPEG files. Offers no additional payment for photos accepted with ms. Rights are negotiable.

COLUMNS/DEPARTMENTS Around Town (local lifestyle topics), 1,000 words; Hometown Stories, 600 words; Travel (around North Carolina), 1,000 words;

Home Interiors/Landscaping (varies), 1,000 words; Restaurants (local, fine dining), 600-1,000 words. **Buys 20-25 mss/year.** Query. **Pays 35¢/word.**

TIPS "All queries must be focused on the issues that make Durham, Chapel Hill, Carrboro, Hillsborough, and Pittsboro unique and wonderful places to live."

OHIO

AKRON LIFE

Baker Media Group, 1653 Merriman Rd., Suite 116, Akron OH 44313. (330)253-0056. **Fax:** (330)253-5868. **E-mail:** editor@bakermediagroup.com; acymerman@bakermediagroup.com; dbakerjr@bakermediagroup.com. **Website:** www.akronlife.com. **Contact:** Abby Cymerman, managing editor. **10% freelance written.** Monthly regional magazine covering Summit, Stark, Portage and Medina counties. "*Akron Life* is a monthly lifestyles publication committed to providing information that enhances and enriches the experience of living in or visiting Akron and the surrounding region of Summit, Portage, Medina and Stark counties. Each colorful, thoughtfully designed issue profiles interesting places, personalities and events in the arts, sports, entertainment, business, politics and social scene. We cover issues important to the Greater Akron area and significant trends affecting the lives of those who live here." Estab. 2002. Circ. 15,000. Byline given. Pays on publication. Offers 50% kill fee. Publishes ms an average of 4-6 months after acceptance. Editorial lead time 2+ months. Submit seasonal material 6 months in advance. Accepts queries by mail, e-mail, fax. Accepts simultaneous submissions. Sample copy free. Guidelines free.

NONFICTION Needs essays, general interest, historical, how-to, humor, interview, photo feature, travel. Query with published clips. Length: 300-2,000 words. **Pays $0.10 max/word for assigned and unsolicited articles.**

PHOTOS State availability. Captions, identification of subjects, model releases required. Reviews GIF/JPEG files. Negotiates payment individually. Buys all rights.

TIPS "It's best to submit a detailed query along with samples of previously published works. Include why you think the story is of interest to our readers, and be sure to have a fresh approach."

💲💲💲 CINCINNATI MAGAZINE

Emmis Publishing Corp., 441 Vine St., Suite 200, Cincinnati OH 45202-2039. (513)421-4300. **E-mail:** jwilliams@cincinnatimagazine.com. **Website:** www.cincinnatimagazine.com. **Contact:** Jay Stowe, editor in chief; Amanda Boyd Walters, director of editorial operations. Monthly magazine emphasizing Cincinnati living. Circ. 38,000. Byline given. Pays on publication. Offers kill fee only on assigned pieces. Accepts queries by mail, e-mail. Accepts simultaneous submissions. Send SASE for guidelines; view content on magazine website.

NONFICTION Buys 12 mss/year. Query. Length: 2,500-3,500 words. **Pays $500-1,000.**

COLUMNS/DEPARTMENTS Cincinnati media, arts and entertainment, people, politics, sports, business, regional. Length: 1,500-2,000 words. **Buys 10-15 mss/year.** Query. **Pays $300-400.**

TIPS "It's most helpful on us if you query in writing with clips. All articles have a local focus. No generics, please. Also: No movie, book, theater reviews, poetry, or fiction. For special advertising sections, query special sections editor Sue Goldberg; for *Cincinnati Wedding*, query custom publishing editor Kara Renee Hagerman."

HYDE PARK LIVING

Community Publications, Inc., 179 Fairfield Ave., Bellevue KY 41073. (859)291-1412. **E-mail:** hydepark@livingmagazines.com. **Website:** www.livingmagazines.com. **Contact:** Grace DeGregorio. Monthly magazine covering Hyde Park community. Estab. 1983. Circ. 6,800. Byline given. Pays on publication. Editorial lead time 2 months. Submit seasonal material 3 months in advance. Accepts queries by mail, e-mail, fax. Accepts simultaneous submissions. Guidelines by e-mail.

NONFICTION Needs essays, general interest, historical, humor, inspirational, interview, new product, personal experience, travel. "Does not want anything unrelated to Hyde Park, Ohio." Query.

PHOTOS State availability. Captions, identification of subjects, model releases required. Reviews contact sheets, negatives, transparencies, prints, GIF/JPEG files. Negotiates payment individually. Buys all rights.

COLUMNS/DEPARTMENTS Financial; Artistic (reviews, etc.); Historic; Food. Query.

POETRY Needs free verse, light verse, traditional. Please query.

FILLERS Needs anecdotes, short humor. Please query.

WYOMING LIVING

Community Publications, Inc., 179 Fairfield Ave., Bellevue KY 41073. (859)291-1412. **Fax:** (859)291-1417. **E-mail:** wyoming@livingmagazines.com. **Website:** www.livingmagazines.com. **Contact:** Amy Elliot, editor. Monthly magazine covering Wyoming community. Estab. 1983. Circ. 3,400. Byline given. Pays on publication. Editorial lead time 2 months. Submit seasonal material 3 months in advance. Accepts queries by mail, e-mail, fax. Accepts simultaneous submissions. Guidelines by e-mail.

NONFICTION Needs book excerpts, essays, expose, general interest, historical, humor, inspirational, interview, new product, personal experience, photo feature, travel. Does not want anything unrelated to Wyoming, Ohio. Query.

PHOTOS State availability. Captions, identification of subjects, model releases required. Reviews contact sheets, negatives, transparencies, prints, GIF/JPEG files. Negotiates payment individually. Buys all rights.

COLUMNS/DEPARTMENTS Financial; Artistic (reviews, etc.); Historic; Food. Query.

FICTION Needs adventure, historical, humorous, mainstream, slice-of-life vignettes. Query.

POETRY Needs free verse, light verse, traditional. Please query.

FILLERS Please query. Needs anecdotes, short humor.

OKLAHOMA

💲💲 INTERMISSION

Langdon Publishing, 110 E. 2nd St., Tulsa OK 74103. **E-mail:** nbizjack@cityoftulsa.org. **Website:** www.tulsapac.com. **Contact:** Nancy Bizjack, editor. **30% freelance written.** Monthly magazine covering events held at the Tulsa Performing Arts Center. "We feature profiles of entertainers appearing at our center, Q&As, stories on the events, and entertainers slated for the Tulsa PAC." Byline given. Pays on publication. Offers 50% kill fee. Publishes ms an average of 1 month after acceptance. Editorial lead time 2 months. Submit seasonal material 2 months in advance. Accepts queries by mail, e-mail. Accepts simultaneous submissions. Responds in 2 weeks to queries. Sample copy available online. Guidelines by e-mail.

NONFICTION Needs general interest, interview. Does not want personal experience articles. **Buys 35 mss/year.** Query with published clips. Length: 600-1,400 words. **Pays $100-200.**

COLUMNS/DEPARTMENTS Q&A (personalities and artists tied in to the events at the Tulsa PAC), 1,100 words. **Buys 12 mss/year.** Query with published clips. **Pays $100-150.**

TIPS "Look ahead at our upcoming events, and find an interesting slant on an event. Interview someone who would be of general interest."

OREGON

💲💲 OREGON COAST

4969 Hwy. 101 N, Suite 2, Florence OR 97439. (800)348-8401. **E-mail:** alispooner@gmail.com. **Website:** www.northwestmagazines.com. **Contact:** Alicia Spooner. **65% freelance written.** Bimonthly magazine covering the Oregon Coast. Estab. 1982. Circ. 50,000. Byline given. Pays after publication. Offers 33% (on assigned stories only, not on stories accepted on spec) kill fee. Publishes ms an average of up to 1 year after acceptance. Submit seasonal material 6 months in advance. Accepts queries by mail, e-mail. Accepts simultaneous submissions. Responds in 3 months to queries. Sample copy for $4.50. Guidelines available on website.

NONFICTION **Buys 55 mss/year.** Query with published clips. Length: 500-1,500 words. **Pays $75-350, plus 2 contributor copies.**

REPRINTS Send tearsheet or photocopy and information about when and where the material previously appeared. Pays an average of 60% of the amount paid for an original article.

PHOTOS Photo submissions with no ms or stand alone or cover photos. Send photos. Captions, identification of subjects, True required. Slides or high-resolution digital. Buys one time rights.

TIPS "Slant article for readers who do not live at the Oregon Coast. At least 1 historical article is used in each issue. Manuscript/photo packages are preferred over manuscripts with no photos. List photo credits and captions for each photo. Check all facts, proper names, and numbers carefully in photo/manuscript packages. Must pertain to Oregon Coast somehow.

PENNSYLVANIA

PENNSYLVANIA HERITAGE

Pennsylvania Heritage Foundation/Pennsylvania Historical & Museum Commission, Commonwealth Keystone Bldg., Plaza Level, 400 North St., Harrisburg PA 17120. **E-mail:** kyweaver@pa.gov. **Website:** www.paheritage.org. **Contact:** Kyle Weaver, editor. **65% freelance written. Prefers to work with published/established writers.** History and culture in Pennsylvania. *Pennsylvania Heritage* introduces readers to Pennsylvania's rich culture and historic legacy; educates and sensitizes them to the value of preserving that heritage; and entertains and involves them in such a way as to ensure that Pennsylvania's past has a future. The magazine is intended for intelligent lay readers. Estab. 1974. Byline given. Pays on publication. Publishes ms 1-2 years after acceptance. Accepts queries by mail, e-mail. Accepts simultaneous submissions. Responds in 10 weeks to queries. Responds in 8 months to mss. Send e-mail for guidelines.

NONFICTION Buys 20-24 mss/year. Prefers to see mss with suggested illustrations. Considers freelance submissions that are shorter in length; pictorial/photographic essays; biographies of notable Pennsylvanians; and interviews with individuals who have helped shape, make, and preserve the Keystone State's history and heritage. Length: 2,000-3,500 words. **Pays $100-500.**

PHOTOS State availability of or send photos. Captions, identification of subjects required. Buys one-time rights.

TIPS "We are looking for well-written, interesting material that pertains to any aspect of Pennsylvania history or culture. Potential contributors should realize that, although our articles are popularly styled, they are not light, puffy, or breezy; in fact they demand strident documentation and substantiation (sans footnotes). The most frequent mistake made by writers in completing articles for us is making them either too scholarly or too sentimental or nostalgic. We want material which educates, but also entertains. Authors should make history readable and enjoyable. Our goal is to make the Keystone State's history come to life in a meaningful, memorable way."

SOUTH CAROLINA

💲💲 HILTON HEAD MONTHLY

Monthly Media LLC, P.O. Box 5926, Hilton Head Island SC 29938. (843)842-6988, ext. 230. **E-mail:** lance@hiltonheadmonthly.com. **Website:** www.hiltonheadmonthly.com. **Contact:** Lance Hanlin, editor in chief. **75% freelance written.** Monthly magazine covering the people, business, community, environment, and lifestyle of Hilton Head, SC, and the surrounding Lowcountry. "Our mission is to offer lively, fresh writing about Hilton Head Island, an upscale, environmentally conscious, and intensely proactive resort community on the coast of South Carolina." Circ. 35,000. Byline given. Pays on publication. Offers 50% kill fee. Publishes ms an average of 6 months after acceptance. Editorial lead time 3 months. Submit seasonal material 4 months in advance. Accepts queries by mail, e-mail. Accepts simultaneous submissions. Responds in 1 week to queries; in 4 months to mss. Sample copy: $3.

NONFICTION Needs general interest, how-to, humor, opinion, personal experience, travel. "Everything is local, local, local, so we're especially interested in profiles of notable residents (or those with Lowcountry ties) and original takes on home design/maintenance, environmental issues, entrepreneurship, health, sports, arts and entertainment, humor, travel, and volunteerism. We like to see how national trends/issues play out on a local level." **Buys 225-250 mss/year.** Query with published clips.

PHOTOS State availability. Reviews contact sheets, prints, digital samples. Negotiates payment individually. Buys one-time rights.

COLUMNS/DEPARTMENTS News; Business; Lifestyles (hobbies, health, sports, etc.); Home; Around Town (local events, charities, and personalities); People (profiles, weddings, etc.). Query with synopsis. **Pays 20¢/word.**

TIPS "Sure, Hilton Head is known primarily as an affluent resort island, but there's plenty more going on than just golf and tennis; this is a lively community with a strong sense of identity and decades-long tradition of community, volunteerism, and environmental preservation. We don't need any more tales of why you chose to retire here or how you fell in love with the beaches, herons, or salt marshes. Seek out lively, surprising characters—there are plenty—and offer fresh (but not trendy) takes on local personalities, Southern living, and green issues."

TENNESSEE

MEMPHIS DOWNTOWNER MAGAZINE

Downtown Productions, Inc., 408 S. Front St., Suite 109, Memphis TN 38103. (901)525-7118. **Fax:** (901)525-7128. **E-mail:** editor@memphisdowntowner. com. **Website:** www.memphisdowntowner.com. **Contact:** Terre Gorham, editor. **50% freelance written.** Bi-monthly magazine covering features on positive aspects with a Memphis tie-in, especially to downtown. "We feature people, companies, nonprofits, and other issues that the general Memphis public would find interesting, entertaining, and informative. All editorial focuses on the positives Memphis has. No negative commentary or personal judgements. Controversial subjects should be treated fairly and balanced without bias." Estab. 1991. Circ. 30,000. Byline given. Pays on 15th of month in which assignment is published. Offers 25% kill fee. Publishes ms an average of 2-6 months after acceptance. Editorial lead time 3-6 months. Submit seasonal material 3-6 months in advance. Accepts queries by mail, e-mail. Responds in 2 weeks to queries. Sample copy free. Guidelines by e-mail.

NONFICTION Needs general interest, historical, how-to, humor, interview, personal experience, photo feature. **Buys 40-50 mss/year.** Query with published clips. Length: 600-2,000 words. **Pays scales vary depending on scope of assignment, but typically runs 15¢/word.**

PHOTOS State availability. Identification of subjects required. Reviews GIF/JPEG files (300 DPI). Negotiates payment individually.

COLUMNS/DEPARTMENTS So It Goes (G-rated humor), 600-800 words; Discovery 901 (Memphis one-of-a-kinds), 1,000-1,200 words. **Buys 6 mss/year.** Query with published clips. **Pays $100-150.**

FILLERS Unusual, interesting, or how-to or what to look for appealing to a large, general audience.

TIPS "Always pitch an actual story idea. E-mails that simply let us know you're a freelance writer mysteriously disappear from our inboxes. Actually read the magazine before you pitch. Get to know the regular columns and departments. In your pitch, explain where in the magazine you think your story idea would best fit. See website for magazine samples and past issues."

TEXAS

💲 HILL COUNTRY SUN

TD Austin Lane, Inc., 100 Commons Rd., Suite 7, #319, Dripping Springs TX 78620. (512)484-9716. **E-mail:** melissa@hillcountrysun.com. **Website:** www.hillcountrysun.com. **Contact:** Melissa Maxwell Ball, editor. **75% freelance written.** Monthly tabloid covering traveling in the Central Texas Hill Country. Publishes stories of interesting people, places, and events in the Central Texas Hill Country. Estab. 1990. Circ. 34,000. Byline given. Pays on acceptance. Publishes ms an average of 2 months after acceptance. Editorial lead time 1 month. Submit seasonal material 2 months in advance. Accepts queries by e-mail. Accepts simultaneous submissions. Responds in 1 week to queries. Sample copy free. Guidelines available online.

NONFICTION Needs interview, travel. No first-person articles. **Buys 50 mss/year.** Query. Length: 600-800 words. **Pays $60 minimum.**

PHOTOS State availability of or send photos. Identification of subjects required. No additional payment for photos accepted with ms. Buys one-time rights.

TIPS "Writers must be familiar with both the magazine's style and the Texas Hill Country."

TEXAS PARKS & WILDLIFE

4200 Smith School Rd., Bldg. D, Austin TX 78744. (800)937-9393. **Fax:** (512)389-8397. **E-mail:** magazine@tpwd.texas.gov. **Website:** www.tpwmagazine. com. **20% freelance written.** Monthly magazine featuring articles about "Texas hunting, fishing, birding, outdoor recreation, game and nongame wildlife, state parks, environmental issues." All articles must be about Texas. Estab. 1942. Circ. 150,000. Byline given. Pays on acceptance. Offers kill fee. Negotiable. Publishes ms an average of 4 months after acceptance. Accepts queries by e-mail. Accepts simultaneous submissions. Responds in 1 month to queries; 3 months to mss. Sample copy and guidelines available online.

○ *Texas Parks & Wildlife* needs more short items for front-of-the-book section and wildlife articles written from a natural history perspective (not for hunters).

NONFICTION Needs general interest, how-to, photo feature, travel, Texas outdoors, hunting, fishing, camping, etc. **Buys 20 mss/year.** Query with published clips; follow up by e-mail 1 month after submitting query. Length: 500-2,500 words. **Pays per article content.**

PHOTOS Send photos to photo editor. Captions, identification of subjects required. Digital submissions preferred. Offers $65-500/photo. Buys rights for print and digital versions.

TIPS "Queries with a strong seasonal peg are preferred. Our planning progress begins 7-8 months (or longer) before the date of publication. That means you have to think ahead: *What will Texas outdoor enthusiasts want to read about 7-12 months from today?*"

VIRGINIA

ALBEMARLE

Carden Jennings Publishing, 375 Greenbrier Dr., Suite 100, Charlottesville VA 22901. (434)817-2010. **Fax:** (434)817-2020. **E-mail:** info@albemarlemagazine.com. **E-mail:** editorial@albemarlemagazine.com. **Website:** www.albemarlemagazine.com. **80% freelance written.** Bimonthly magazine covering lifestyle for central Virginia. "*albemarle* is a lifestyle magazine originating from the birthplace of Thomas Jefferson. We are committed to Jeffersonian ideals: intellectual depth, love for the land, historic and cultural significance, humor, and celebration of life. Much of the content is regional and seeks to enlighten, educate, and entertain readers who are longtime residents, newcomers, and visitors to Charlottesville and Albemarle County." Estab. 1987. Circ. 10,000. Byline given. Pays on publication. Offers 30% kill fee. Publishes ms an average of 4 months after acceptance. Editorial lead time 6-8 months. Submit seasonal material 6 months in advance. Accepts queries by e-mail. Accepts simultaneous submissions. Responds in 1 month to queries; in 2 months to mss. Sample copy for $6; e-mail eden@cjp.com. Guidelines online.

NONFICTION Needs essays, historical, interview, photo feature, travel. No fiction, poetry, or anything without a direct tie to central Virginia. **Buys 30-35 mss/year.** Query with published clips. Length: 900-3,500 words. **Payment varies based on type of article.**

PHOTOS State availability. Captions, identification of subjects, model releases required. Reviews transparencies. Negotiates payment individually. Buys one-time rights.

COLUMNS/DEPARTMENTS Etcetera (personal essay), 900-1,200 words; Leisure (travel, sports), 3,000 words. **Buys 20 mss/year.** Query with published clips. **Pays $75-150.**

TIPS "Be familiar with the central Virginia area and lifestyle. We prefer a regional slant, which should include a focus on someone or something located in the region, or a focus on someone or something from the region making an impact in other parts of the world. Quality writing is a must. Story ideas that lend themselves to multiple sources will give you a leg up on the competition."

WISCONSIN

$$$$ MILWAUKEE MAGAZINE

Quad Graphics, Inc., 126 N. Jefferson St., Ste. 100, Milwaukee WI 53202. (414)287-4394. **Fax:** (414)273-0016. **E-mail:** daniel.simmons@milwaukeemag.com; claire.hanan@milwaukeemag.com. **Website:** www.milwaukeemag.com. **Contact:** Daniel Simmons, managing editor; Claire Hanan, senior editor, arts and culture. **40% freelance written.** Monthly magazine covering the people, issues, and places of the Milwaukee, Wisconsin, area. "We publish stories about Milwaukee, of service to Milwaukee-area residents, and exploring the area's changing lifestyle, business, arts, politics, and dining. Our goal has always been to create an informative, literate, and entertaining magazine that will challenge Milwaukeeans with in-depth reporting and analysis of issues of the day, provide useful service features, and enlighten readers with thoughtful stories, essays, and columns. Underlying this mission is the desire to discover what is unique about Wisconsin and its people, to challenge conventional wisdom when necessary, criticize when warranted, heap praise when deserved, and season all with affection and concern for the place we call home." Circ. 35,000. Byline given. Pays on publication. Offers 20% kill fee. Publishes ms an average of 2 months after acceptance. Submit seasonal material 6 months in advance. Accepts queries by e-mail. Accepts simultaneous submissions. Responds in 6 weeks to queries. Sample copy: $6. Guidelines online.

"The department most open is Insider. Think short, lively, offbeat, fresh, people-oriented."

NONFICTION Needs essays, expose, general interest, historical, interview, photo feature, travel, food and dining, other services. Special issues: Health, Weddings (one each per year). No articles without a strong Milwaukee or Wisconsin angle; writers from outside the area are welcome, but please only pitch stories that have a connection to this place. **Buys 30-50 mss/year.** Query with published clips. Length: 2,500-5,000 words for full-length features; 800 words for two-page breaker features (short on copy, long on visuals). **Payment varies.**

COLUMNS/DEPARTMENTS Insider (inside information on Milwaukee, exposé, slice-of-life, unconventional angles on current scene), up to 500 words; Mini Reviews for Insider, 125 words. Query with published clips.

TIPS "Pitch something for the Insider, or suggest a compelling profile we haven't already done. Submit clips that prove you can do the job. We are actively seeking freelance writers who can deliver lively, readable copy that helps our readers make the most of the Milwaukee area. Because we're only human, we'd like writers who can deliver copy on deadline that fits the specifications of our assignment. If you fit this description, we'd love to work with you."

WYOMING

💲 WYOMING RURAL ELECTRIC NEWS (WREN)

2710 Thomas Ave., Cheyenne WY 82001. (307)772-1986. **Fax:** (307)634-0728. **E-mail:** wren@wyomingrea.org. **Website:** wyomingrea.org/community/wren-magazine. **40% freelance written.** Monthly magazine (except in January) for audience of rural residents, vacation-home owners, farmers, ranchers and business owners in Wyoming. Estab. 1954. Circ. 39,100. Byline given. Pays on publication. No kill fee. Publishes ms an average of 2 months after acceptance. At least 3 months. Submit seasonal material 2 months in advance. Accepts queries by mail, e-mail. Accepts simultaneous submissions. Responds in 1 month to queries. Sample copy for $2.50 and 9x12 SASE. Guidelines for #10 SASE.

NONFICTION No nostalgia, sarcasm, or tongue-in-cheek. **Buys 4-10 mss/year.** Send complete ms. Length: 600-800 words. **Pays up to $150, plus 3 copies.**

REPRINTS Send tearsheet or photocopy and information about when and where the material previously appeared.

PHOTOS Color only.

TIPS "Always looking for fresh, new writers. Submit entire ms. Don't submit a regionally set story from some other part of the country. Photos and illustrations (if appropriate) are always welcomed. We want factual articles that are to the point, accurate."

RELIGIOUS

ALIVE NOW

1908 Grand Ave., P.O. Box 340004, Nashville TN 37203. (615)340-7254. **E-mail:** alivenow@upperroom. org. **Website:** www.alivenow.org; alivenow.upperroom.org. **Contact:** Beth A. Richardson, editor. *Alive Now*, published bimonthly, is a devotional magazine that invites readers to enter an ever-deepening relationship with God. "*Alive Now* seeks to nourish people who are hungry for a sacred way of living. Submissions should invite readers to see God in the midst of daily life by exploring how contemporary issues impact their faith lives. Each word must be vivid and dynamic and contribute to the whole. We make selections based on a list of upcoming themes. Mss which do not fit a theme will be returned." Estab. 1971. Circ. 70,000. Pays on acceptance. Accepts queries by mail, e-mail. Accepts simultaneous submissions. Subscription: $17.95/year (6 issues); $26.95 for 2 years (12 issues). Additional subscription information, including foreign rates, available on website. Guidelines available online.

NONFICTION meditations. Prefers electronic submissions attached as Word document. Postal submissions should include SASE. Include name, address, theme on each sheet. Length: 400-500 words. **Pays $35 minimum.**

FICTION Needs religious. Prefers electronic submissions attached as Word document. Postal submissions should include SASE. Include name, address, theme on each sheet. Length: 400-500 words. **Pays $35 minimum.**

POETRY Prefers electronic submissions attached as Word document. Postal submissions should include SASE. Include name, address, theme on each sheet. **Pays $35 minimum.**

BREAD FOR GOD'S CHILDREN

Bread Ministries, INC., P.O. Box 1017, Arcadia FL 34265. (863)494-6214. **E-mail:** bread@breadministries.org. **E-mail:** Do not accept. **Website:** www. breadministries.org. **Contact:** Judith M. Gibbs, editor. **10% freelance written.** An interdenominational Christian teaching publication published 4-6 times/year written to aid children and youth in leading a Christian life. Estab. 1972. Circ. 10,000 (U.S. and Canada). Byline given. Publication No kill fee. Publishes ms an average of 6 months after acceptance. Accepts queries by mail. Accepts simultaneous submissions. Responds in 6 months to mss. Sample copy for 9x12 SAE and 5 first-class stamps. Guidelines for #10 SASE.

NONFICTION Needs inspirational, All levels: how-to. "We do not want anything detrimental to solid family values. Most topics will fit if they are slanted to our basic needs." **Buys 3-4 mss/year.** Send complete ms. Length: 500-800 words **On publication**

REPRINTS Send tearsheet and information about when and where the material previously appeared.

COLUMNS/DEPARTMENTS Freelance columns: Let's Chat (children's Christian values), 500-700 words; Teen Page (youth Christian values), 600-800 words; Idea Page (games, crafts, Bible drills). **Buys 5-8 mss/year.** Send complete ms. **Pays $30.**

FICTION "We are looking for writers who have a solid knowledge of Biblical principles and are concerned for the youth of today living by those principles. Stories must be well written, with the story itself getting the message across—no preaching, moralizing, or tag endings." Needs historical, religious, Young readers, middle readers, young adult/teen: adventure, religious, problem-solving, sports. Looks for "teaching stories that portray Christian lifestyles without preaching." **Buys 10-15 mss/year.** Send complete ms. Length: 600-800 words for young children; 900-1,500 words for older children. **Pays $40-50.**

TIPS "We want stories or articles that illustrate overcoming obstacles by faith and living solid, Christian lives. Know our publication and what we have used in the past. Know the readership and publisher's guidelines. Stories should teach the value of morality and honesty without preaching. Edit carefully for content and grammar."

EVANGELICAL MISSIONS QUARTERLY

Billy Graham Center at Wheaton College, 500 College Ave., Wheaton IL 60187. (630)752-7158. **E-mail:** emq@wheaton.edu. **Website:** www.emqonline.com. **Contact:** Laurie Fortunak Nichols, managing editor; A. Scott Moreau, editor. **67% freelance written.** Quarterly magazine covering evangelical missions. *Evangelical Missions Quarterly* is a professional jour-

nal serving the worldwide missions community. *EMQ* articles reflect missionary life, thought, and practice. Each issue includes articles, book reviews, editorials, and letters. Subjects are related to worldwide mission and evangelism efforts and include successful ministries, practical ideas, new tactics and strategies, trends in world evangelization, church planting and discipleship, health and medicine, literature and media, education and training, relief and development, missionary family life, and much more. Estab. 1964. Circ. 7,000. Byline given. Pays on publication. Offers negotiable kill fee. Publishes ms an average of 18 months after acceptance. Editorial lead time 1 year. Accepts queries by e-mail. Accepts simultaneous submissions. Responds in 2 weeks to queries. Sample copy free. Guidelines available online.

NONFICTION Needs interview, opinion, personal experience, religious. No sermons, poetry, or straight news. **Buys 24 mss/year.** Query. Length: 3,000 words. **Pays $25-100.**

PHOTOS Send photos. Identification of subjects required. Offers no additional payment for photos accepted with ms. Buys first rights.

COLUMNS/DEPARTMENTS In the Workshop (practical how tos), 800-2,000 words; Perspectives (opinion), 800 words. **Buys 8 mss/year.** Query. **Pays $50-100.**

TIPS "We prefer articles about deeds done, showing the why and the how, not only claiming success but also admitting failure. Principles drawn from 1 example must be applicable to missions more generally. *EMQ* does not include articles which have been previously published in journals, books, websites, etc."

FAITH TODAY

Evangelical Fellowship of Canada, P.O. Box 5885, West Beaver Creek Post Office, Richmond Hill ON L4B 0B8 Canada. (905)479-5885. **Fax:** (905)479-4742. **E-mail:** editor@faithtoday.ca. **Website:** www.faithtoday.ca. **Over 80% freelance written.** Bimonthly magazine. *Faith Today* is the magazine of an association of more than 40 evangelical denominations but serves evangelicals in all denominations. In January 2016 it added a sister magazine for youth and young adults, called *Love Is Moving*. Estab. 1983. Circ. 20,000. Byline given. Pays on publication. Offers 30-50% kill fee. Publishes ms an average of 4 months after acceptance. Editorial lead time 4 months. Accepts queries by mail, e-mail. Accepts simultaneous submissions. Responds in 6 weeks to queries. Sample copy for SASE in Canadian postage. Guidelines available online at www.faithtoday.ca/writers. "View complete back issues at www.faithtoday.ca/digital. Or download 1 of our free apps from www.faithtoday.ca/mobile."

○ *Faith Today* focuses on church issues, social issues, and personal faith as they are tied to the Canadian context. Writing should explicitly acknowledge that Canadian evangelical context.

NONFICTION Needs book excerpts, essays, expose, general interest, historical, how-to, humor, interview, opinion, religious, reviews, news feature. Does not want Bible studies, poetry, serialized articles, seasonal material, generic or U.S.-focused Christian-living material. **Buys 75 mss/year.** Query. Length: 400-2,000 words. **Pays $100-500 Canadian.**

REPRINTS Pays 50% of amount paid for an original article.

PHOTOS State availability. Buys one-time rights.

TIPS "Query should include brief outline and names of the sources you plan to interview in your research. Use Canadian postage on SASE."

⊙⊙ FCA MAGAZINE

Fellowship of Christian Athletes, 8701 Leeds Rd., Kansas City MO 64129. (816)921-0909; (800)289-0909. **Fax:** (816)921-8755. **E-mail:** mag@fca.org. **Website:** www.fca.org/mag. **Contact:** Clay Meyer, editor; Matheau Casner, creative director. **50% freelance written. Prefers to work with published/established writers, but works with a growing number of new/unpublished writers each year.** Published 6 times/year. *FCA Magazine*'s mission is to serve as a ministry tool of the Fellowship of Christian Athletes by informing, inspiring and involving coaches, athletes and all whom they influence, that they may make an impact for Jesus Christ. Estab. 1959. Circ. 75,000. Byline given. Pays on publication. No kill fee. Publishes ms an average of 4 months after acceptance. Submit seasonal material 6 months in advance. Accepts simultaneous submissions. Responds to queries/mss in 3 months. Sample copy for $2 and 9x12 SASE with 3 first-class stamps. Guidelines available at www.fca.org/mag/media-kit.

NONFICTION Needs inspirational, personal experience, photo feature. **Buys 5-20 mss/year.** Articles should be accompanied by at least 3 quality photos. Query and submit via e-mail. Length: 1,000-2,000 words. **Pays $150-400 for assigned and unsolicited articles.**

PHOTOS State availability. Reviews contact sheets. Payment based on size of photo. Buys one-time rights.

TIPS "Profiles and interviews of particular interest to coed athlete, primarily high school and college age. Our graphics and editorial content appeal to youth. The area most open to freelancers is profiles on or interviews with well-known athletes or coaches (male, female, minorities) who have been or are involved in some capacity with FCA."

KEYS FOR KIDS DEVOTIONAL

Keys for Kids Ministries, 2060 43rd St. SE, Grand Rapids MI 49508. **E-mail:** editorial@keysforkids.org. **Website:** www.keysforkids.org. **Contact:** Courtney Lasater, editor. **95% freelance.** Quarterly devotional featuring daily stories and Scripture verses for children ages 6-12 that ignite a passion for Christ in kids and their families. Estab. 1982. Circ. 60,000 print (not including digital circulation). Byline given. Pays on acceptance. Typically publishes stories 6-9 months after acceptance. Editorial lead time 6-8 months. Accepts queries by e-mail. Responds in 2-4 months. Sample copy online. Guidelines online: www.keysforkids.org/writersguidelines.

FICTION Needs short contemporary stories with spiritual applications for kids. Please suggest a key verse and an appropriate Scripture passage, generally 3-10 verses, to reinforce the theme of your story. Up to 375 words. **Pays $30.**

TIPS "Please follow writer's guidelines at www.keysforkids.org/writersguidelines."

LIGHT + LIFE MAGAZINE

Free Methodist Church – USA, 770 N. High School Rd., Indianapolis IN 46214. (317)616-4776. **Fax:** (317)244-1247. **E-mail:** jeff.finley@fmcusa.org. **Website:** lightandlifemagazine.com. **Contact:** Jeff Finley, managing editor. **50% freelance written.** *Light and Life Magazine* is a monthly magazine published by Light + Life Communications, the publishing arm of the Free Methodist Church–USA. Each issue focuses on a specific theme with a cohesive approach in which the articles complement each other. The magazine has a flip format with articles in English and Spanish. Estab. 1868. Circ. 38,000. Byline given. Pays on publication. No kill fee. Accepts queries by e-mail. Accepts simultaneous submissions. Responds in 2 months.

Guidelines available at fmcusa.org/lightandlifemag/ writers.

NONFICTION Needs religious. Query. Length: 2,100 words for feature articles, 800 words for print discipleship articles, 500-1,000 words for online discipleship articles, 500-1,000 words for online articles not published in the magazine. **Pays $50 per article.**

LIVE

Gospel Publishing House, 1445 N. Boonville Ave., Springfield MO 65802-1894. (417)862-1447. **E-mail:** rl-live@gph.org. **Website:** www.gospelpublishing. com. **100% freelance written.** Weekly magazine for weekly distribution covering practical Christian living. "*LIVE* is a take-home paper distributed weekly in young adult and adult Sunday school classes. We seek to encourage Christians in living for God through fiction and true stories which apply Biblical principles to everyday problems." Estab. 1928. Circ. 18,000. Byline given. Pays on acceptance. No kill fee. Publishes ms an average of 18 months after acceptance. Editorial lead time 12 months. Submit seasonal material 18 months in advance. Accepts queries by mail, e-mail. Accepts simultaneous submissions. Responds in 6 weeks to queries; in 8 weeks to mss. Sample copy for #10 SASE. Guidelines for #10 SASE or on website: www.gospel-publishing.com/store/startcat.cfm?cat=tWRITGUID.

NONFICTION Needs inspirational, religious. No preachy articles or stories that refer to religious myths (e.g., Santa Claus, Easter Bunny, etc.). **Buys 50-100 mss/year.** Send complete ms. Length: 550-1,100 words. **Pays 7-10¢/word.**

REPRINTS Send tearsheet, photocopy, or typed ms with rights for sale noted and information about when and where the material previously appeared. Pays 7¢/ word.

PHOTOS Send photos. Identification of subjects required. Reviews 35mm transparencies and 3x4 prints or larger. Higher-resolution digital files also accepted. Offers $35-60/photo. Buys one-time rights.

FICTION Needs religious, inspirational, prose poem. No preachy fiction, fiction about Bible characters, or stories that refer to religious myths (e.g., Santa Claus, Easter Bunny, etc.). No science or Bible fiction. No controversial stories about such subjects as feminism, war, or capital punishment. **Buys 20-50 mss/ year.** Send complete ms. Length: 800-1,200 words. **Pays 7-10¢/word.**

POETRY Needs free verse, haiku, light verse, traditional. Buys 15-24 poems/year. Submit maximum 3 poems. Length: 12-25 lines. **Pays $35-60.**

TIPS "Don't moralize or be preachy. Provide human interest articles with Biblical life application. Stories should consist of action, not just thought-life, interaction, or insight. Heroes and heroines should rise above failures, take risks for God, prove that scriptural principles meet their needs. Conflict and suspense should increase to a climax! Avoid pious conclusions. Characters should be interesting, believable, and realistic. Avoid stereotypes. Characters should be active, not just pawns to move the plot along. They should confront conflict and change in believable ways. Describe the character's looks and reveal his personality through his actions to such an extent that the reader feels he has met that person. Readers should care about the character enough to finish the story. Feature racial, ethnic, and regional characters in rural and urban settings."

☻ LIVE

Canadian Baptist Women of Ontario and Quebec, 5 International Blvd., Etobicoke ON M9W 6H3 Canada. (416)651-8967. **Website:** www.baptistwomen.com. **Contact:** Renee James, editor/director of communications. **50% freelance written.** Magazine published 6 times/year designed to help women grow in their authentic experience of God and in their intimate connection to mission. Vision: evangelical, egalitarian, Canadian. Estab. 1878. Circ. 3,500. Byline given. Pays on publication. No kill fee. Publishes ms an average of 6 months after acceptance. Editorial lead time 2 months. Submit seasonal material 4 months in advance. Accepts simultaneous submissions. Sample copy for 9x12 SAE with 2 first-class Canadian stamps.

○ Canadian writers only.

NONFICTION Needs inspirational, interview, personal experience, religious. **Buys 30-35 mss/year.** Query first. Unsolicited mss not accepted. Length: 650-800 words. **Pays 5-12¢/word (Canadian).**

PHOTOS State availability. Captions required. Offers no additional payment for photos accepted with ms. Buys one-time rights.

TIPS "We cannot use unsolicited mss from non-Canadian writers. When submitting by e-mail, please send stories as messages, not as attachments."

⊖⊕ THE LOOKOUT

Christian Standard Media, 8805 Governor's Hill Dr., Ste. 400, Cincinnati OH 45249. (513)931-4050. **Fax:** (513)931-0950. **E-mail:** lookout@christianstandard-media.com. **Website:** www.lookoutmag.com. **Contact:** Kelly Carr, editor. **80% freelance written.** Weekly magazine for Christian adults, with emphasis on spiritual growth, family life, and topical issues. "Our purpose is to provide Christian adults with practical, Biblical teaching and current information that will help them mature as believers." Estab. 1894. Circ. 30,000. Byline given. Pays on acceptance. Offers 33% kill fee. Publishes ms an average of 3-6 months after acceptance. Editorial lead time 6-9 months. Chooses by theme list. Accepts queries by e-mail. Accepts simultaneous submissions. Sample on website. Guidelines and theme list online.

○ Audience is mainly conservative Christians. Send mss only on request.

NONFICTION Needs inspirational, interview, opinion, personal experience, religious. No fiction or poetry. **Buys 200 mss/year.** Query article first. Length: 1,200-1,400 words. **Pays 11¢/word.**

PHOTOS State availability. Identification of subjects required. Offers no additional payment for photos accepted with ms.

TIPS "*The Lookout* publishes from a theologically conservative, nondenominational, and noncharismatic perspective. We aim primarily for those aged 30-55. Most readers are married and have elementary to young adult children. Our emphasis is on the needs of ordinary Christians who want to grow in their faith. We value well-informed articles that offer lively and clear writing as well as strong application. We often address tough issues and seek to explore fresh ideas or recent developments affecting today's Christians."

⊕ THE LUTHERAN DIGEST

The Lutheran Digest, Inc., 6160 Carmen Ave., Inver Grove Heights MN 55076. (651)451-9945. **E-mail:** editor@lutherandigest.com. **Website:** www.lutherandigest.com. **Contact:** Nick Skapyak, editor. **95% freelance written.** Quarterly magazine covering Christianity from a Lutheran perspective. Publishes articles, humor, and poetry. Articles frequently reflect a Lutheran Christian perspective but are not intended to be sermonettes. Popular stories show how God has intervened in a person's life to help solve a problem. Estab. 1953. Circ. 20,000. No byline given.

Pays on publication. No kill fee. Publishes ms an average of 6 months after acceptance. Editorial lead time 9 months. Submit seasonal material 9 months in advance. "No queries, please." Accepts simultaneous submissions. Responds in 4 months to mss. No response to e-mailed mss unless selected for publication. Sample copy: $3.50. Subscription: $16/year, $22 for 2 years. Guidelines available online.

NONFICTION Needs general interest, historical, how-to, humor, inspirational, personal experience. Does not want to see personal tributes to deceased relatives or friends. These are seldom used unless the subject of the article is well known. Avoids articles about the moment a person finds Christ as his or her personal savior. **Buys 50-60 mss/year.** Send complete ms. Length: up to 1,500 words. **Pays $25-50.**

REPRINTS Accepts previously published submissions. "We prefer this as we are a digest and 70-80% of our articles are reprints."

PHOTOS "We never print photos from outside sources."

POETRY Submit up to 3 poems at a time. Prefers e-mail submissions but also accepts mailed submissions. Cover letter is preferred. Include SASE only if return is desired. Poems are selected by editor and reviewed by publication panel. Length: up to 25 lines/poem. **Pays 1 contributor's copy.**

TIPS "Reading our writers' guidelines and sample articles online is encouraged and is the best way to get a feel for the type of material we publish."

⊖⊕ MESSAGE MAGAZINE

North American Division of Seventh-day Adventists, 12501 Old Columbia Pike, Silver Spring MD 20904. (301)680-6598. **E-mail:** editor@messagemagazine.com; associateeditor@messagemagazine.com. **Website:** www.messagemagazine.com. **Contact:** Carmela Monk Crawford, editor. **10-20% freelance written.** Bimonthly magazine. "*Message* is the oldest religious journal addressing ethnic issues in the country. Our audience is predominantly Black and Seventh-day Adventist; however, *Message* is an outreach magazine for the churched and unchurched across cultural lines." Estab. 1898. Circ. 110,000. Byline given. Pays on acceptance. No kill fee. Publishes ms an average of 12 months after acceptance. Editorial lead time 6 months. Submit seasonal material 6 months in advance. Accepts simultaneous submissions. Responds in 9 months to queries. Sample copy by e-mail. Guidelines by e-mail and online.

NONFICTION Send complete ms. Length: 300-900 words. **Pays $75-300 for features.**

PHOTOS State availability. Identification of subjects required. Buys one time rights.

COLUMNS/DEPARTMENTS Eye on the Times: religious liberty, public affairs, human rights, and news (300 words); Optimal Health: health news, how-tos, and healthy habits (550 words). **Pays $75-150.**

TIPS "Please look at the magazine before submitting mss. *Message* publishes a variety of writing styles as long as the writing style is easy to read and flows. Please avoid highly technical writing styles."

⑤⑤ ONE

1011 First Ave., New York NY 10022-4195. (212)826-1480. **Fax:** (212)838-1344. **E-mail:** cnewa@cnewa.org; editorial@cnewa.org. **Website:** www.cnewa.org. **Contact:** Deacon Greg Kandra, executive editor. **75% freelance written.** Bimonthly magazine for a Catholic audience with interest in the Near East, particularly its current religious, cultural, and political aspects. Estab. 1974. Circ. 100,000. Byline given. Pays on publication. No kill fee. Publishes ms an average of 6 months after acceptance. Accepts queries by mail, fax. Accepts simultaneous submissions. Responds in 1 month to queries. Sample copy and writer's guidelines for 7½×10½ SAE with 2 first-class stamps.

NONFICTION Query. Length: 1,200-1,800 words. **Pays 20¢/edited word.**

PHOTOS "Photographs to accompany ms are welcome; they should illustrate the people, places, ceremonies, etc. which are described in the article. We prefer color transparencies but occasionally use b&w." Pay varies depending on use—scale from $50-300.

TIPS "We are interested in current events in the Near East as they affect the cultural, political, and religious lives of the people."

⑤⑤ POINT

Converge (Baptist General Conference), 11002 Lake Hart Dr., Mail Code 200, Orlando FL 32832. (407)563-6083. **Fax:** (866)990-8980. **E-mail:** bob.putman@converge.org. **Website:** www.converge.org. **Contact:** Bob Putman, editor. **15% freelance written.** Nonprofit, religious, evangelical Christian magazine published 4 times/year covering Converge. *Point* is the official magazine of Converge (BGC). Almost exclusively uses articles related to Converge, their churches, or

by/about Converge people. Circ. 43,000. Byline given. Pays on publication. Offers 50% kill fee. Editorial lead time 6 months. Submit seasonal material 6 months in advance. Accepts queries by e-mail. Accepts simultaneous submissions. Responds in 1 month to queries; in 3 months to mss. Sample upon request. Guidelines available free.

NONFICTION Buys 6-8 mss/year. Query with published clips. Wants "articles about our people, churches, missions. View online at www.converge.org before sending anything." Length: 300-1,500 words. **Pays $60-280.**

PHOTOS State availability. Captions, identification of subjects, model releases required. Reviews prints, some high-resolution digital. Offers $15-60/photo. Buys one-time rights.

COLUMNS/DEPARTMENTS Converge Connection (blurbs of news happening in Converge Worldwide), 50-150 words. Send complete ms and photos. **Pays $30.**

POETRY Needs We do not publish poetry.

TIPS "Please study the magazine and the denomination. We will send sample copies to interested freelancers and give further information about our publication needs upon request. Freelancers from our churches who are interested in working on assignment are especially welcome."

⑤⑤ PRAIRIE MESSENGER

Benedictine Monks of St. Peter's Abbey, P.O. Box 190, 100 College Dr., Muenster Saskatchewan S0K 2Y0 Canada. (306)682-1772. **Fax:** (306)682-5285. **E-mail:** pm.canadian@stpeterspress.ca. **Website:** www.prairiemessenger.ca. **Contact:** Maureen Weber, associate editor. **30% freelance written.** Weekly Catholic publication published by the Benedictine Monks of St. Peter's Abbey. Has a strong focus on ecumenism, social justice, interfaith relations, aboriginal issues, arts, and culture. Estab. 1904. Circ. 4,000. Byline given. Pays on publication. No kill fee. Publishes ms an average of 4 months after acceptance. Submit seasonal material 3 months in advance. Accepts queries by mail, e-mail. Accepts simultaneous submissions. Responds only if interested; send nonreturnable samples. Sample copy for 9x12 SASE with $1 Canadian postage or IRCs. Guidelines available online. "Because of government subsidy regulations, we are no longer able to accept non-Canadian freelance material."

NONFICTION Needs book excerpts, essays, interview, opinion, religious. Special issues: Christmas, Easter. **Buys 15 mss/year.** Send complete ms. Length: 500-800 words. **Pays $70/article.**

PHOTOS Send photos. Captions required. Reviews 3x5 prints. Offers $25/photo. Buys all rights.

POETRY Needs Shorter poems preferred. Buys 45 poems/year. Length: up to 35 lines. **Pays $30/published poem.**

PURPOSE

1251 Virginia Ave, Harrisonburg VA 22801. **E-mail:** PurposeEditor@MennoMedia.org. **Website:** www.mennomedia.org/purpose. **20% freelance written.** Magazine focuses on Christian discipleship—how to be a faithful Christian in the midst of everyday life situations. Uses personal story form to present models and examples to encourage Christians in living a life of faithful discipleship. Each issue follows a designated theme. *Purpose* is published monthly by Mennomedia, the publisher for Mennonite Church Canada and Mennonite Church USA. It is a faith-based adult monthly magazine that focuses on discipleship-living, simplicity, and the Christian faith. Estab. 1968. Circ. 4,400. Pays upon publication. Submit material according to writer guidelines and theme deadlines posted on the website. Accepts queries by e-mail. Guidelines available online at www.mennomedia.org/purpose.

NONFICTION Buys 140 mss/year. E-mail submissions preferred. Length: 500-700 words. **Pays $25-50/story.**

POETRY Needs free verse, light verse, traditional. Poetry must address monthly themes. Buys 12 poems/year. Length: 12 lines maximum. **Pays $10-20/poem.**

TIPS "We seek true stories that follow monthly themes. Be sure to look at the website for the theme list and deadlines, as we only consider stories that are tied to the themes. Follow the writer guidelines on the website for the latest submission information."

THE SECRET PLACE

P.O. Box 851, Valley Forge PA 19482. (610)768-2434. **Fax:** (610)768-2441. **E-mail:** thesecretplace@abc-usa.org. **E-mail:** thesecretplace@abc-usa.org. **Website:** www.judsonpress.com/catalog_secretplace.cfm. **100% freelance written.** Quarterly devotional covering Christian daily devotions. Estab. 1937. Circ. 250,000. Byline given. Pays on acceptance. No kill fee. Editorial lead time 1 year. Submit seasonal material 9 months in advance. Guidelines online.

NONFICTION Needs inspirational, religious. **Buys 400 mss/year.** Send complete ms. Length: 100-200 words. **Pays $20.**

POETRY Needs avant-garde, free verse, light verse, traditional. Submit up to 6 poems by mail or e-mail. E-mail preferred. Buys 12-15 poems/year. Submit maximum 6 poems. Length: 4-30 lines/poem. **Pays $20.**

TIPS "Prefers submissions via e-mail."

U.S. CATHOLIC

Claretian Publications, 205 W. Monroe St., Chicago IL 60606. (312)236-7782. **Fax:** (312)236-8207. **E-mail:** literaryeditor@uscatholic.org. **E-mail:** submissions@claretians.org. **Website:** www.uscatholic.org. **Mostly freelance written.** Monthly magazine covering contemporary issues from a Catholic perspective. "*U.S. Catholic* puts faith in the context of everyday life. With a strong focus on social justice, we offer a fresh and balanced take on the issues that matter most in our world, adding a faith perspective to such challenges as poverty, education, family life, the environment, and even pop culture." Estab. 1935. Circ. 25,000. Byline given. Pays on acceptance. No kill fee. Publishes ms an average of 6 months after acceptance. Editorial lead time 8 months. Submit seasonal material 6 months in advance. Accepts queries by mail, e-mail. Responds in 1 month to queries; in 2 months to mss. Guidelines on website.

Please include SASE with written ms.

NONFICTION Needs essays, inspirational, opinion, personal experience, religious. **Buys 100 mss/year.** Send complete ms. Length: 700-1,400 words. **Pays minimum $200.**

PHOTOS State availability.

FICTION Accepts short stories. "Topics vary, but unpublished fiction should be no longer than 1,500 words and should include strong characters and cause readers to stop for a moment and consider their relationships with others, the world, and/or God. Specifically religious themes are not required; subject matter is not restricted. E-mail submissions@uscatholic.org." Needs ethnic, mainstream, religious, slice-of-life vignettes. **Buys 4-6 mss/year.** Send complete ms. Length: 700-1,500 words. **Pays minimum $200.**

POETRY Needs free verse. Submit 3-5 poems at a time. Accepts e-mail submissions (pasted into body of message or as attachments). Cover letter is preferred.

No light verse. Buys 12 poems/year. Length: up to 50 lines/poem. **Pays $75.**

RETIREMENT

AARP BULLETIN

AARP, c/o Editorial Submissions, 601 E. St. NW, Washington DC 20049. **E-mail:** member@aarp.org. **Website:** www.aarp.org/bulletin. *AARP Bulletin* provides timely insights and news on health, healthy policy, Social Security, consumer protection, and more from an award-winning source. Accepts simultaneous submissions.

○ Query before submitting. Does not accept unsolicited mss. Difficult market to break into.

NONFICTION Needs essays, general interest, personal experience.

◐◐◐◐ AARP THE MAGAZINE

AARP, c/o Editorial Submissions, 601 E. St. NW, Washington DC 20049. **E-mail:** aarpmagazine@aarp.org. **Website:** www.aarp.org/magazine. **50% freelance written. Prefers to work with published/established writers.** Bimonthly magazine covering issues that affect people over the age of 50. *AARP The Magazine* is devoted to the varied needs and active life interests of AARP members, age 50 and over, covering such topics as financial planning, travel, health, careers, retirement, relationships, and social and cultural change. Its editorial content serves the mission of AARP, seeking through education, advocacy, and service to enhance the quality of life for all by promoting independence, dignity, and purpose. Circ. 22,721,661. Byline given. Pays on acceptance. Offers 25% kill fee. Publishes ms an average of 6 months after acceptance. Submit seasonal material 6 months in advance. Accepts queries by mail, e-mail. Accepts simultaneous submissions. Responds in 3 months to queries. Sample copy free. Guidelines available online.

NONFICTION No previously published articles. Query for features, or submit complete ms for personal essays. Submit queries and mss via e-mail or mail. "Story pitches for specific features and departments should be 1 page in length and accompanied by recent writing samples. The pitch should explain the idea for the piece, tell how you would approach it as a writer, give some sense of your writing style, and mention the section of the magazine for which the piece is intended. Your samples should not include the actual story that you are proposing, except in the case of personal essays, which should be submitted in full. Features and departments cover the following categories: Money (investments, savings, retirement, and work issues); Health and Fitness (tips, trends, studies); Food and Nutrition (recipes, emphasis on healthy eating); Travel (tips and trends on how and where to travel); Consumerism (practical information and advice); General Interest (new thinking, research, information on timely topics, trends); Relationships (family matters, caregiving, living arrangements, grandparents); Personal Essay (thoughtful, timely, new takes on matters of importance to people over 50); Personal Best (first-person essays on leisure-time pursuits). Length: up to 2,000 words. **Pays $1/word.**

PHOTOS Photos purchased with or without accompanying mss. Pays $250 and up for color; $150 and up for b&w.

TIPS "The most frequent mistake made by writers in completing an article for us is poor follow-through with basic research. The outline is often more interesting than the finished piece. We do not accept unsolicited mss."

◐ CHRISTIAN LIVING IN THE MATURE YEARS

The United Methodist Publishing House, 2222 Rosa L. Parks Blvd., P.O. Box 17890, Nashville TN 37228-7890. (615)749-6474. **E-mail:** matureyears@umpublishing.org. **Website:** matureyears.submittable.com. **80% freelance written. Prefers to work with published/established writers.** Quarterly magazine designed to help persons in and nearing the retirement years understand and appropriate the resources of the Christian faith in dealing with specific problems and opportunities related to aging. Estab. 1954. Circ. 35,000. Byline given. Pays on acceptance. No kill fee. Publishes ms an average of 1 year after acceptance. Submit seasonal material 14 months in advance. Accepts queries by e-mail. Responds in 6-7 months to mss. Sample copy: Available for purchase online at cokesbury.com. Writer's guidelines by e-mail.

NONFICTION Needs how-to, inspirational, religious, travel, older adult health, life, faith, travel, finance issues. **Buys 75-80 mss/year.** Send complete ms to matureyears.submittable.com. No longer accepts e-mailed or hard-copy submissions. Length: 900-2,000 words. **Pays 7¢/word.**

REPRINTS Submit original ms with rights for sale noted and information about when and where the material previously appeared. Pays 7¢/word.

PHOTOS Send high-resolution photos. Captions, model releases required. Negotiates pay individually. Typically buys one-time rights.

COLUMNS/DEPARTMENTS Assignment only. "We are not currently accepting unsolicited columns." **Buys 4-8 mss/year.**

POETRY Needs free verse, haiku, light verse, traditional. Wants upbeat poetry. Must express hope; strong imagery preferred. Buys 12-16 poems/year. Submit maximum 6 poems. Length: 3-16 lines; up to 50 characters/line. **Pays $1.00 per line.**

○⑤ INSPIRED SENIOR LIVING

Stratis Publishing Ltd., 3, 3948 Quadra St., Victoria BC V8X 1J6 Canada. (250)479-4705. **E-mail:** editor@seniorlivingmag.com. **Website:** www.seniorliving-mag.com. **Contact:** Bobbie Jo Reid, managing editor. **100% freelance written.** Magazine published 12 times/year covering active 55+ living. Inspiration for people over 55. Monthly magazine distributed throughout British Columbia, extensive website, 2 annual 55+ Lifestyle Shows. Estab. 2004. Circ. 50,000. Byline given. Pays quarterly. No kill fee. Publishes an average of 2-3 months after acceptance. Editorial lead time 3 months. Submit seasonal material 6 months in advance. Accepts queries by e-mail. Sample copy available online. Guidelines available.

NONFICTION Needs historical, how-to, humor, inspirational, interview, personal experience, travel, profiles of inspiring people age 55+ who live in British Columbia. Special issues: Special issues: housing, travel, charitable giving, fashion. Does not want politics; religion; promotion of business, service, or products; humor that demeans senior demographic or aging process. Query. Does not accept previously published material. Length: 500-1,200 words. **Pays $35-150 for assigned articles; $35-150 for unsolicited articles.** Sometimes pays expenses (limit agreed upon in advance).

PHOTOS Send photos. Identification of subjects, model releases required. Reviews GIF/JPEG files. Offers $10-75 per photo. Buys all rights.

COLUMNS/DEPARTMENTS Buys 5-6 mss/year. Query with published clips. **Pays $25-$50.**

TIPS "Editorial must be about or reflect the lifestyles of people age 55+ living in British Columbia."

⑤ MATURE LIVING

Lifeway Christian Resources, 1 Lifeway Plaza, Nashville TN 37234. (615)251-2000. **E-mail:** matureliving@lifeway.com. **Website:** www.lifeway.com. **Contact:** Debbie Dickerson, managing editor. **10% freelance written.** "Monthly leisure reading magazine for senior adults 55 and older. *Mature Living* is Christian in content, and the material required is what would appeal to the 55-and-over age group: inspirational, informational, nostalgic, humorous. Our magazine is distributed mainly through churches (especially Southern Baptist churches) that buy the magazine in bulk and distribute it to members in this age group." Estab. 1977. Circ. 320,000. Byline given. Pays on acceptance. No kill fee. Publishes ms an average of 7-8 weeks after acceptance. Submit seasonal material 1 year in advance. Accepts queries by mail, e-mail. Accepts simultaneous submissions. Responds in 6-8 weeks for mss that are accepted only. Sample copy: $4.

NONFICTION Needs historical, how-to, humor, inspirational, interview, personal experience, religious, travel. No pornography, profanity, occult, liquor, dancing, drugs, gambling. **Buys 100 mss/year.** Query. Length: 600-1,200 words. **Pays $85-115**

PHOTOS State availability.

COLUMNS/DEPARTMENTS Cracker Barrel (brief, humorous, original quips and verses); Grandparents' Brag Board (something humorous or insightful said or done by your grandchild or great-grandchild); Inspirational (devotional items); Food (introduction and 4-6 recipes); Crafts (step-by-step procedures); Game Page (crossword or word-search puzzles and quizzes). **Pays $15-40.**

RURAL

⑤⑤ BACKWOODS HOME MAGAZINE

P.O. Box 712, Gold Beach OR 97444. (541)247-8900. **Fax:** (541)247-8600. **E-mail:** lisa@backwoodshome.com. **E-mail:** article-submission@backwoodshome.com. **Website:** www.backwoodshome.com. **Contact:** Lisa Nourse, editorial coordinator. **90% freelance written.** Bimonthly magazine covering self-reliance. *Backwoods Home Magazine* is written for people who have a desire to pursue personal independence, self-sufficiency, and their dreams. Offers how-to articles on self-reliance. Estab. 1989. Circ. 38,000. Byline given. Pays on acceptance. Editorial lead time

4-6 months. Submit seasonal material 4-6 months in advance. Accepts queries by mail, e-mail. Sample copy for 9x10 SAE and 6 first-class stamps. Guidelines available online.

NONFICTION Needs general interest, how-to, humor, personal experience, technical. **Buys 120 mss/year.** Send complete ms via e-mail (no attachments) or postal mail. Looking for straightforward, clear writing similar to what you would find in a good newspaper. Length: 500 words. **Pays $40-200.**

PHOTOS Send photos. Captions, identification of subjects, model releases required. Offers no additional payment for photos accepted with ms.

FARM & RANCH LIVING

Trusted Media Brands, Inc., 1610 N. Second St., Suite 102, Milwaukee WI 53212-3906. (414)423-0100. **Fax:** (414)423-8463. **E-mail:** submissions@farmandranchliving.com. **Website:** farmandranchliving.com. **30% freelance written. Eager to work with new/unpublished writers.** Bimonthly magazine aimed at families that live on, work on, or have ties to a farm or ranch. FRL focuses on people who celebrate the pleasures of living off the land rather than production and profits. Estab. 1978. Byline given. Pays on publication. No kill fee. Publishes ms an average of 6 months after acceptance. Submit seasonal material 6 months in advance. Accepts queries by e-mail. Accepts simultaneous submissions. "We are unable to respond to queries." To purchase a single copy, contact customercare@farmandranchliving.com.

NONFICTION Needs humor, inspirational, interview, personal experience, photo feature, nostalgia, prettiest place in the country (photo/text tour of ranch or farm). No issue-oriented stories (pollution, animal rights, etc.). **Buys 30 mss/year.** Send complete ms. Length: 600-1,200 words. **Pays up to $400 for text/photo package.**

REPRINTS Send photocopy with rights for sale noted. Payment negotiable.

PHOTOS "We no longer accept slides. We look for photos of farm animals, people, and rural scenery." State availability. Buys one-time rights.

TIPS "Our readers enjoy stories and features that are upbeat and positive. A freelancer must see *F&RL* to fully appreciate how different it is from other farm publications—ordering a sample is strongly advised. Photo features (about interesting farm or ranch families) and personality profiles are most open to freelancers."

💲💲 HOBBY FARMS

I-5 Publishing, 470 Conway Court, Suite B6, Lexington KY 40511. **E-mail:** hobbyfarms@luminamedia.com. **Website:** www.hobbyfarms.com. **85% freelance written.** Bimonthly magazine covering small farms and rural lifestyle. "*Hobby Farms* is the magazine for rural enthusiasts. Whether you have a small garden or 100 acres, there is something in *Hobby Farms* to educate, enlighten, or inspire you." Estab. 2001. Circ. 252,801. Byline given. Pays on publication. Publishes ms an average of 6 months after acceptance. Editorial lead time 4 months. Submit seasonal material 6 months in advance. Accepts queries by mail, e-mail. Accepts simultaneous submissions. Responds in 2 months to queries and mss. Guidelines free.

💬 "Writing tone should be conversational but authoritative."

NONFICTION Needs historical, how-to, interview, personal experience, technical, breed or crop profiles. **Buys 10 mss/year.** Send complete ms. Length: 1,000-1,500 words. Limit agreed upon in advance.

PHOTOS State availability of or send photos. Identification of subjects, model releases required. Reviews GIF/JPEG files. Negotiates payment individually. Buys one-time rights.

TIPS "Please state your specific experience with any aspect of farming (livestock, gardening, equipment, marketing, etc.)."

💲 MOTHER EARTH NEWS

Ogden Publications, 1503 SW 42nd St., Topeka KS 66609-1265. (785)274-4300. **E-mail:** letters@motherearthnews.com. **Website:** www.motherearthnews.com. **Contact:** Oscar "Hank" Will III, editor; Rebecca Martin, managing editor. **Mostly written by staff and team of established freelancers.** Bimonthly magazine emphasizing country living, country skills, natural health, and sustainable technologies for both long-time and would-be ruralists. "*Mother Earth News* promotes self-sufficient, financially independent, and environmentally aware lifestyles. Many of our feature articles are written by our Contributing Editors, but we also assign articles to freelance writers, particularly those who have experience with our subject matter (both firsthand and writing experience)." Circ. 350,000. Byline given. Pays on publication. No kill fee. Submit seasonal material 5 months in advance. Accepts queries by mail, e-mail. Accepts simultaneous submissions. Responds in 6 months to mss. Sample copy: $5. Guidelines available online.

NONFICTION Needs how-to, green building, do-it-yourself, organic gardening, whole foods and cooking, natural health, livestock and sustainable farming, renewable energy, 21st-century homesteading, nature-environment-community, green transportation. No fiction, please. **Buys 35-50 mss/year.** "Query. Please send a short synopsis of the idea, a one-page outline, and any relevant digital photos and samples. If available, please send us copies of 1 or 2 published articles, or tell us where to find them online." **Pays $25-150.**

PHOTOS "We welcome quality photographs for our 2 departments."

COLUMNS/DEPARTMENTS Country Lore (helpful how-to tips); 100-300 words; Firsthand Reports (first-person stories about sustainable lifestyles of all sorts), 1,500-2,000 words.

TIPS "Read our magazine, and take a close look at previous issues to learn more abut the various topics we cover. We assign articles about 6-8 months ahead of publication date, so keep in mind timing and the seasonality of some topics. Our articles provide hands-on, useful information for people who want a more fun, conscientious, sustainable, secure, and satisfying lifestyle. Practicality is critical; freelance articles must be informative, well-documented, and tightly written in an engaging and energetic voice. For how-to articles, complete, easy-to-understand instructions are essential."

RURALITE

5605 N.E. Elam Young Pkwy., Hillsboro OR 97124. (503)357-2105. **E-mail:** editor@ruralite.org. **E-mail:** curtisc@ruralite.org. **Website:** www.ruralite.org. **Contact:** Curtis Condon, editor. **80% freelance written. Works with new, unpublished writers.** Monthly magazine aimed at members of consumer-owned electric utilities throughout 7 western states. General-interest publication used by 48 rural electric cooperatives and PUDs. Readers are predominantly rural and small-town residents interested in stories about people and issues that affect Northwest lifestyles. Estab. 1954. Circ. 330,000. Byline given. Pays on acceptance. No kill fee. Accepts queries by mail. Accepts simultaneous submissions. Responds within 2 months to queries. Sample copy for 9x12 SAE with $1.61 of postage affixed. Guidelines available online.

NONFICTION Buys 50-60 mss/year. Length: 100-2,000 words. **Pays $50-800.**

REPRINTS Send typed ms with rights for sale noted and information about when and where the material previously appeared.

PHOTOS Illustrated stories are the key to a sale. Stories without art rarely make it. Color prints/negatives, color slides, all formats accepted. No b&w. Inside color is $25-100; cover photo is $250-350.

TIPS "Study recent issues. Follow directions when given an assignment. Be able to deliver a complete package (story and photos). We're looking for regular contributors to whom we can assign topics from our story list after they've proven their ability to deliver quality mss."

SCIENCE

⑤⑤ AD ASTRA

National Space Society, P.O. Box 98106, Washington DC 20090. (202)429-1600. **Fax:** (703)435-4390. **E-mail:** adastra@nss.org. **Website:** www.nss.org/adastra. **Contact:** Katherine Brick, editor. **90% freelance written.** *Ad Astra* ("to the stars") is the award-winning magazine of the National Space Society, featuring the latest news in space exploration and stunning full-color photography. Published quarterly. "We publish nontechnical, lively articles about all aspects of international space programs, from shuttle missions to planetary probes to plans for the future and commercial space." Estab. 1989. Circ. 25,000. Byline given. Pays on publication. No kill fee. Publishes ms 3-6 months after acceptance. Accepts queries by e-mail. Accepts simultaneous submissions. Responds only when interested. Sample copy for 9x12 SASE.

NONFICTION Needs book excerpts, essays, general interest, interview, opinion, photo feature, technical. No science fiction or UFO stories. Query with published clips. Length: 1,200-2,000 words with 2-8 full-size (8.5x11) color images at 300 dpi; 100-600 words for sidebars; 600-750 words for book reviews. **Pays 25¢/word.**

PHOTOS State availability. Identification of subjects required. Reviews color prints, digital, JPEG-IS, GISS. Negotiates pay. Buys one-time rights.

TIPS "We require mss to be in Word or text file formats. Know the field of space technology, programs, and policy. Know the players. Look for fresh angles. And please know how to write!"

AMERICAN ARCHAEOLOGY

The Archaeological Conservancy, 1717 Girard Blvd. NE, Albuquerque NM 87106. (505)266-9668. **Fax:** (505)266-0311. **E-mail:** tacmag@nm.net. **Website:** www.americanarchaeology.org. **Contact:** Michael Bawaya, editor; Vicki Singer, art director. **60% freelance written.** Quarterly magazine. "We're a popular archaeology magazine. Our readers are very interested in this science. Our features cover important digs, prominent archaeologists, and most any aspect of the science. We only cover North America." Estab. 1997. Circ. 35,000. Byline given. Pays on acceptance. Offers 20% kill fee. Publishes ms an average of 3 months after acceptance. Editorial lead time 3 months. Accepts queries by mail, e-mail, fax. Accepts simultaneous submissions. Responds in 3 weeks to queries; in 1 month to mss.

NONFICTION No fiction, poetry, humor. **Buys 15 mss/year.** Query with published clips. Length: 1,500-3,000 words. **Pays $1,000-2,000.**

PHOTOS State availability. Identification of subjects required. Reviews transparencies, prints. Pays $50 and up for occasional stock images; assigns work by project (pay varies); negotiable. **Pays on acceptance.** Credit line given. Buys one-time rights. Offers $400-600/photo shoot. Negotiates payment individually. Buys one-time rights.

TIPS "Read the magazine. Features must have a considerable amount of archaeological detail."

ARCHAEOLOGY

Archaeological Institute of America, 36-36 33rd St., Suite 301, Long Island City NY 11106 USA. (718)472-3050. **Fax:** (718)472-3051. **E-mail:** cvalentino@archaeology.org; editorial@archaeology.org. **Website:** www.archaeology.org. **Contact:** Editor-in-chief. **50% freelance written.** *ARCHAEOLOGY* covers current excavations and recent discoveries, and includes technology updates and studies of ancient cultures. *ARCHAEOLOGY* magazine has been published continuously for nearly 70 years. It has a total print audience of nearly 750,000, mostly in the United States and Canada, over half a million unique views, and over 2 million Facebook fans. The magazine is edited for general audiences and enthusiasts. Published bimonthly, news and features bring archaeology home to its readers—along with the adventure, discovery,

culture, history, technology, and travel of the discipline. Stories are written by both staff and freelance journalists. For writers guidelines visit archaeology.org. Estab. 1948. Circ. 750,000. Byline given. Pays on publication. Offers 25% kill fee. Submit seasonal material 6 months in advance. Accepts queries by e-mail. Accepts simultaneous submissions. Sample copy and writer's guidelines free. Guidelines online.

> If considering proposing a story to Archaeology's editors, pay close attention to the length and form of stories currently being published in the magazine. That, and the writers guidelines found at archaeology.org, should guide you.

NONFICTION Buys 6 mss/year. Query preferred. "Preliminary queries should be no more than 1 or 2 pages (500 words max.) in length and may be sent to the Editor-in-Chief by mail or via e-mail to editorial@archaeology.org. We do not accept telephone queries. Check our online index and search to make sure that we have not already published a similar article. Your query should tell us the following: who you are, why you are qualified to cover the subject, how you will cover the subject (with an emphasis on narrative structure, new knowledge, etc.), and why our readers would be interested in the subject." Length: 1,000-3,000 words.

PHOTOS We do not commission photography and most photos published are contributed by archaeologists themselves.

TIPS "We reach nonspecialist readers interested in art, science, history, and culture. Our reports, regional commentaries, and feature-length articles introduce readers to recent developments in archaeology worldwide."

$ $ ASTRONOMY

Kalmbach Publishing, 21027 Crossroads Circle, P.O. Box 1612, Waukesha WI 53187-1612. (800)533-6644. **Fax:** (262)798-6468. **Website:** www.astronomy.com. **Contact:** David J. Eicher, editor; LuAnn Williams Belter, art director (for art and photography). **50% of articles submitted and written by science writers; includes commissioned and unsolicited.** Monthly magazine covering the science and hobby of astronomy. "Half of our magazine is for hobbyists (who are active observers of the sky); the other half is directed toward armchair astronomers who are intrigued by the science." Estab. 1973. Circ. 108,000. Byline given. Pays on acceptance. Does pay a kill fee, although rarely used. Accepts simultaneous submissions. Responds in 1 month to queries. Responds in 3 months to mss. on website.

"We are governed by what is happening in astronomical research and space exploration. It can be up to a year before we publish a ms. Query for electronic submissions."

NONFICTION Needs book excerpts, new product, photo feature, technical, space, astronomy. **Buys 75 mss/year.** Please query on all article ideas Length: 500-3,000 words. **Pays $100-1,000.**

TIPS "Submitting to *Astronomy* could be tough—take a look at how technical astronomy is. But if someone is a physics teacher or an amateur astronomer, he or she might want to study the magazine for a year to see the sorts of subjects and approaches we use, and then submit a proposal. Submission guidelines available online."

INVENTORS DIGEST

520 Elliot St., Suite 200, Charlotte NC 28202. (800)838-8808. **Fax:** (704)333-5115. **E-mail:** info@inventorsdigest.com. **Website:** www.inventorsdigest.com. **50% freelance written.** Monthly magazine covering inventors, inventions, technology, engineering, and intellectual property issues. *Inventors Digest* is committed to educating and inspiring entry- and enterprise-level inventors and professional innovators. As the leading print and online publication for the innovation culture, *Inventors Digest* delivers useful, entertaining, and cutting-edge information to help its readers succeed. Estab. 1985. Circ. 40,000. Byline given. Pays on publication. No kill fee. Publishes an average of 2 months after acceptance. Editorial lead time 2 months. Submit seasonal material 4 months in advance. Accepts queries by mail, e-mail. Accepts simultaneous submissions. Responds in 3 weeks to queries; in 1 month to mss. Sample copy available online. Guidelines free.

NONFICTION Needs book excerpts, historical, how-to, humor, inspirational, interview, new product, opinion, personal experience, technical. Special issues: Editorial calendar available online. "We don't want poetry or fiction. Nothing that duplicates what you can read elsewhere." **Buys 4 mss/year.** Query. Length varies. For any piece more than 2,000 words, send a 300-word synopsis first. **Payment varies.**

PHOTOS State availability. Identification of subjects required. Reviews GIF/JPEG files. Negotiates payment individually. Rights subject to negotiation.
COLUMNS/DEPARTMENTS Cover, 2,000 words; American Inventors, 1,200 words. Query about column submission. **Negotiable column payment.**
TIPS "We prefer e-mail queries. If it's a long piece (more than 2,000 words), send a synopsis, captivating us in 300 words. Put 'Article Query' in the subject line. A great story should have relevance to a wide audience, with either compelling anecdotes, conflict or obstacles to overcome. Show us something surprising and why we should care, and put it in context."

POPULAR SCIENCE

Bonnier Corporation, 2 Park Ave., 9th Floor, New York NY 10016. **E-mail:** queries@popsci.com; bown@bonniercorp.com. **Website:** www.popsci.com. **Contact:** Jill C. Shomer, managing editor. **50% freelance written.** Monthly magazine for the well-educated adult, interested in science, technology, new products. *Popular Science* is devoted to exploring (and explaining) to a nontechnical, but knowledgeable, readership the technical world around us. Covers all of the sciences, engineering, and technology, and above all, products. Especially focused on the new, the ingenious, and the useful. Contributors should be as alert to the possibility of selling pictures and short features as they are to major articles. Estab. 1872. Circ. 1,450,000. Byline given. Pays on acceptance. Offers 25% kill fee. Editorial lead time 3 months. Accepts queries by mail, e-mail, fax. Accepts simultaneous submissions. Responds in 1 month to queries. Guidelines available online.

NONFICTION *Popular Science* welcomes pitches from writers who want to tell amazing stories about scientific and technological advances in every realm. Query should include a brief summary of the proposed article and provide some indication of a plan to execute the reporting. Links to past work might also be helpful. Reads every query but will respond only to those that are under serious consideration.
TIPS "Probably the easiest way to break in here is by covering a news story in science and technology that we haven't heard about yet. We need people to be acting as scouts for us out there, and we are willing to give the most leeway on these performances. We are interested in good, sharply focused ideas in all areas we cover. We prefer a vivid, journalistic style of

writing, with the writer taking the reader along with him, showing the reader what he saw, through words."

STARDATE

University of Texas, 2515 Speedway, Stop C1402, Austin TX 78712. (512)475-6763. **Fax:** (512)471-5060. **E-mail:** rjohnson@stardate.org. **Website:** http://stardate. org. **Contact:** Rebecca Johnson, editor. **80% freelance written.** Bimonthly magazine covering astronomy and skywatching. *StarDate* is written for people with an interest in astronomy and what they see in the night sky, but no special astronomy training or background. Estab. 1975. Circ. 10,000. Byline given. Pays on acceptance. Offers 25% kill fee. Publishes ms an average of 4 months after acceptance. Editorial lead time 6 months. Submit seasonal material 6 months in advance. Accepts queries by mail, e-mail, fax. Accepts simultaneous submissions. Responds in 6 weeks to queries. Sample copy and writer's guidelines free.

- Query with published quips, by email or regular mail. No unsolicited mss.

NONFICTION Needs general interest, historical, interview, photo feature, technical, travel. No first-person, first stargazing experiences, or paranormal. **Buys 8 mss/year.** Query with published clips. Length: 1,500-3,000 words. **Pays $500-1,500.**

PHOTOS Send photos. Identification of subjects required. Reviews transparencies, prints. Negotiates payment individually. Buys one time rights.

COLUMNS/DEPARTMENTS Astro News (short astronomy news item), 250 words. **Buys 6 mss/year.** Query with published clips. **Pays $100-200.**

TIPS "Keep up to date with current astronomy news and space missions. No technical jargon."

SCIENCE FICTION, FANTASY & HORROR

ANALOG SCIENCE FICTION & FACT

Dell Magazines, 44 Wall St., Suite 904, New York NY 10005-2401. **E-mail:** analogsf@dellmagazines.com. **Website:** www.analogsf.com. **Contact:** Trevor Quachri, editor. **100% freelance written. Eager to work with new/unpublished writers.** *Analog* seeks "solidly entertaining stories exploring solidly thought-out speculative ideas. But the ideas, and consequently the stories, are always new. Real science and technology have always been important in *ASF,* not only as the foundation of its fiction but as the subject of articles

about real research with big implications for the future." Estab. 1930. Circ. 50,000. Byline given. Pays on acceptance. No kill fee. Publishes ms an average of 10 months after acceptance. Accepts queries by mail, online submission form. Accepts simultaneous submissions. Responds in 2-3 months to mss. Sample copy: $5 and SASE. Guidelines online.

- Fiction published in *Analog* has won numerous Nebula and Hugo Awards.

NONFICTION Special issues: Articles should deal with subjects of not only current but future interest, i.e., with topics at the present frontiers of research whose likely future developments have implications of wide interest. **Buys 11 mss/year.** Send complete ms via online submissions manager (preferred) or postal mail. Does not accept e-mail submissions. Length: up to 4,000 words. **Pays 9¢/word.**

FICTION "Basically, we publish science fiction stories. That is, stories in which some aspect of future science or technology is so integral to the plot that, if that aspect were removed, the story would collapse. The science can be physical, sociological, psychological. The technology can be anything from electronic engineering to biogenetic engineering. But the stories must be strong and realistic, with believable people (who needn't be human) doing believable things—no matter how fantastic the background might be." Needs science fiction. No fantasy or stories in which the scientific background is implausible or plays no essential role. Send complete ms via online submissions manager (preferred) or postal mail. Does not accept e-mail submissions. Length: 2,000-7,000 words for short stories, 10,000-20,000 words for novelettes and novellas, and 40,000-80,000 for serials. **Analog pays 8-10¢/word for short stories up to 7,500 words, 8-8.5¢ for longer material, 6¢/word for serials.**

POETRY Send poems via online submissions manager (preferred) or postal mail. Does not accept e-mail submissions. Length: up to 40 lines/poem. **Pays $1/line.**

TIPS "I'm looking for irresistibly entertaining stories that make me think about things in ways I've never done before. Read several issues to get a broad feel for our tastes, but don't try to imitate what you read."

APEX MAGAZINE

Apex Publications, LLC, P.O. Box 24323, Lexington KY 40524. **E-mail:** lesley@apex-magazine.com. **Website:** www.apexbookcompany.com. **Contact:** Lesley

Conner, managing editor. **100% freelance written.** Monthly e-zine publishing dark speculative fiction. "An elite repository for new and seasoned authors with an other-worldly interest in the unquestioned and slightly bizarre parts of the universe." Estab. 2004. Circ. 28,000 unique visits per month. Byline given. Pays 30 days after publication. Offers 30% kill fee. Publishes mss an average of 6 months after acceptance. Editorial lead time 2 weeks. Submit seasonal material 6 months in advance. Accepts queries by e-mail. Responds in 20-30 days to queries and mss. Sample content available online. Guidelines available online.

○   "We want science fiction, fantasy, horror, and mash-ups of all three of the dark, weird stuff down at the bottom of your little literary heart."

NONFICTION Buys 36 mss/year. Send complete ms. Length: 100-7,500 words. **Pays 6¢/word.**

FICTION Needs fantasy, horror, science fiction, short stories. **Buys 36 mss/year.** Send complete ms. Length: 100-7,500 words. **Pays 6¢/word.**

POETRY Submit up to 5 poems. Length: up to 200 lines/poem. **Pays 25¢/line.**

🆂 ASIMOV'S SCIENCE FICTION

Dell Magazines, 44 Wall St., Suite 904, New York NY 10005. **E-mail:** asimovs@dellmagazines.com. **Website:** www.asimovs.com. **Contact:** Sheila Williams, editor; Victoria Green, senior art director. **98% freelance written. Works with a small number of new/unpublished writers each year.** *Asimov's*, published 10 times/year, including 2 double issues, is 5.875x8.625 (trim size); 112 pages; 30 lb. newspaper; 70 lb. to 8 pt. C1S cover stock; illustrations; rarely has photos. "Magazine consists of science fiction and fantasy stories for adults and young adults. Publishes the best short science fiction available." Estab. 1977. Circ. 50,000. Pays on acceptance. No kill fee. Publishes ms an average of 6-12 months after acceptance. Accepts queries by mail. Responds in 2 months to queries; in 3 months to mss. Sample copy: $5. Guidelines online or for #10 SASE.

○   Named for a science fiction "legend," *Asimov's* regularly receives Hugo and Nebula Awards.

FICTION Wants "science fiction primarily. Some fantasy and humor. It is best to read a great deal of material in the genre to avoid the use of some very old ideas." Submit ms via online submissions manager

or postal mail; no e-mail submissions. Needs fantasy, science fiction. No horror or psychic/supernatural, sword and sorcery, explicit sex or violence that isn't integral to the story. Would like to see more hard science fiction. Length: 750-15,000 words. **Pays 8-10¢/word for short stories up to 7,500 words; 8-8.5¢/word for longer material. Works between 7,500-10,000 words by authors who make more than 8¢/word for short stories will receive a flat rate that will be no less than the payment would be for a shorter story.**

TIPS "In general, we're looking for 'character-oriented' stories, those in which the characters, rather than the science, provide the main focus for the reader's interest. Serious, thoughtful, yet accessible fiction will constitute the majority of our purchases, but there's always room for the humorous as well."

LEADING EDGE MAGAZINE

4087 JKB, Provo UT 84602. **E-mail:** editor@leadingedgemagazine.com; fiction@leadingedgemagazine.com; art@leadingedgemagazine.com; poetry@leadingedgemagazine.com; nonfiction@leadingedgemagazine.com. **Website:** www.leadingedgemagazine.com. **Contact:** Hayley Brooks, editor in chief. **90% freelance written.** Semiannual magazine covering science fiction and fantasy. "*Leading Edge* is a magazine dedicated to new and upcoming talent in the fields of science fiction and fantasy. We strive to encourage developing and established talent and provide high-quality speculative fiction to our readers." Does not accept mss with sex, excessive violence, or profanity. Estab. 1981. Circ. 200. Byline given. Pays on publication. No kill fee. Publishes ms an average of 2-4 months after acceptance. Accepts queries by mail, e-mail. Responds within 12 months to mss. Single copy: $5.95. "We no longer provide subscriptions, but *Leading Edge* is now available on Amazon Kindle, as well as print-on-demand." Guidelines available online.

○   Accepts unsolicited submissions.

NONFICTION Needs essays, expose, interview, reviews. Send complete ms with cover letter and SASE. Include estimated word count. Length: up to 15,000 words. **Pays 1¢/word; $50 maximum.**

FICTION Needs fantasy, science fiction. **Buys 14-16 mss/year.** Send complete ms with cover letter and SASE. Include estimated word count. Length: up to 15,000 words. **Pays 1¢/word; $50 maximum.**

POETRY Needs avant-garde, haiku, light verse, traditional. Publishes 2-4 poems per issue. Poetry should reflect both literary value and popular appeal and should deal with science fiction- or fantasy-related themes. No e-mail submissions. Cover letter is preferred. Include name, address, phone number, length of poem, title, and type of poem at the top of each page. Please include SASE with every submission. Submit maximum 10 poems. Pays $10 for first 4 pages; $1.50/each subsequent page.

TIPS "Buy a sample issue to know what is currently selling in our magazine. Also, make sure to follow the writer's guidelines when submitting."

THE MAGAZINE OF FANTASY & SCIENCE FICTION

P.O. Box 3447, Hoboken NJ 07030. (201)876-2551. **E-mail:** fandsf@aol.com. **Website:** www.fandsf.com; submissions.ccfinlay.com/fsf. **Contact:** C.C. Finlay, editor. **100% freelance written.** *The Magazine of Fantasy & Science Fiction* publishes various types of science fiction and fantasy short stories and novellas, making up about 80% of each issue. The balance of each issue is devoted to articles about science fiction, a science column, book and film reviews, cartoons, and competitions. Bimonthly. Estab. 1949. Circ. 40,000. Byline given. Pays on acceptance. No kill fee. Publishes ms an average of 9-12 months after acceptance. Submit seasonal material 8 months in advance. Accepts queries by mail, e-mail. Accepts simultaneous submissions. Responds in 2 months to queries. Sample: $7 ($15 international). Guidelines on website at www.sfsite.com/fsf/glines.htm and on the online submission form at submissions.ccfinly.com/fsf. Send a SASE to receive the guidelines by mail.

Ⓠ *The Magazine of Fantasy & Science Fiction* is one of the oldest and most prestigious magazines in the field, having published Isaac Asimov, Ray Bradbury, Shirley Jackson, Robert Heinlein, Kurt Vonnegut, Joyce Carol Oates, Harlan Ellison, Samuel R. Delany, James Tiptree Jr., Ursula K. Le Guin, Karen Joy Fowler, Ted Chiang, and many others. Many stories published by *F&SF* receive award nominations and are reprinted in Year's Best anthologies. Alaya Dawn Johnson's "A Guide to the Fruits of Hawai'i" won the Nebula Award for Best Novelet in 2015.

NONFICTION Needs memoir. Send complete ms.

REPRINTS Submit potential reprints in the same manner as new work, but be sure to indicate with the submission where it first was published. Pays 5¢/word.

COLUMNS/DEPARTMENTS Curiosities (reviews of odd and obscure books), up to 270 words. **Buys 6 mss/year.** Query. **Pays $75.**

FICTION *F&SF* has no formula for fiction. The speculative element may be slight, but it should be present. We prefer character-oriented stories, whether it's fantasy, science fiction, horror, humor, or another genre. *F&SF* is open to diverse voices and perspectives, and has published writers from all over the world. Needs adventure, fantasy, horror, humorous, science fiction, short stories, space fantasy, sword & sorcery, dark fantasy, futuristic, psychological, supernatural, science fiction, hard science/technological, soft/sociological. **Buys 60-70 mss/year.** Send complete ms. Length: up to 25,000 words. **Pays 7-12¢/word.**

POETRY *F&SF* buys only a few poems per year. We want only poetry that deals with the fantastic or the science fictional. In the past, we've published poetry by Rebecca Kavaler, Elizabeth Bear, Sophie M. White, and Robert Frazier. Poetry may be submitted using the same online form for fiction. Buys 4-6 poems/year. Submit maximum 5 poems. Length: up to 40 lines/poem, including blank lines. **Pays $50/poem and 2 contributor's copies.**

TIPS Good storytelling makes a submission stand out. We like to be surprised by stories, either by the character insights, ideas, plots, or prose. Even though we prefer electronic submissions, we need stories in standard mss format (like that described here: www.sfwa.org/writing/vonda/vonda.htm). Read an issue of the magazine before submitting to get a sense of the range of our tastes and interests.

🌀 MORPHEUS TALES

E-mail: morpheustales@gmail.com. **Website:** morpheustales.wixsite.com/morpheustales. **Contact:** Adam Bradley, publisher. **100% freelance written.** Quarterly magazine covering horror, science fiction, and fantasy. "We publish the best in horror, science fiction, and fantasy—both fiction and nonfiction." Estab. 2008. Circ. 1,000. No kill fee. Publishes ms an average of 18 months after acceptance. Editorial lead time 3 months. Submit seasonal material 6 months in advance. Accepts queries by e-mail. Responds in 4 week to queries; 3 month to mss. Sample: $7. Guidelines online.

NONFICTION Needs book excerpts, essays, general interest, how-to, inspirational, interview, new product, opinion, photo feature, letters to the editor. All material must be based in the horror, science fiction, or fantasy genres. **Buys 6 mss/year.** Query. Length: 1,000-3,000 words.

PHOTOS Model and property release are required. Buys first rights, electronic rights, which may vary according to the project.

FICTION Needs experimental, fantasy, horror, mystery, science fiction, suspense. **Buys 20 mss/year.** Send complete ms. Length: 800-3,000 words.

💲 MYTHIC DELIRIUM

3514 Signal Hill Ave. NW, Roanoke VA 24017-5148. **E-mail:** mythicdelirium@gmail.com. **Website:** www.mythicdelirium.com. **Contact:** Mike Allen, editor. "*Mythic Delirium* is an online and e-book venue for fiction and poetry that ranges through science fiction, fantasy, horror, interstitial, and cross-genre territory—we love blurred boundaries and tropes turned on their heads. We are interested in work that demonstrates ambition, that defies traditional approaches to genre, that introduces readers to the legends of other cultures, that re-evaluates the myths of old from a modern perspective, that twists reality in unexpected ways. We are committed to diversity and are open to and encourage submissions from people of every race, gender, nationality, sexual orientation, political affiliation, and religious belief. We publish 12 short stories and 24 poems a year. Our quarterly e-books in PDF, EPUB, and MOBI formats, published in July, October, January, and April, each contain 3 stories and 6 poems. We also publish 1 story and 2 poems on our website each month. Check our website for our next reading period." Estab. 1998. Responds in 2 months. Accepts electronic submissions only to mythicdelirium@gmail.com.

FICTION "No unsolicited reprints or multiple submissions. Please use the words 'fiction submission' in the e-mail subject line. Stories should be sent in standard manuscript format as RTF or DOC attachments." Length: up to 4,000 words (firm). **Pays 2¢/word.**

POETRY "No unsolicited reprints. Please use the words 'poetry submission' in the e-mail subject line. Poems may be included in the e-mail as RTF or DOC attachments." Submit maximum 6 poems. Length: open. **Pays $5 flat fee.**

TIPS "*Mythic Delirium* isn't easy to get into, but we publish newcomers in every issue. Show us how ambitious you can be, and don't give up."

💲💲 ON SPEC

P.O. Box 4727, Station South, Edmonton AB T6E 5G6 Canada. (780)628-7121. **E-mail:** onspec@onspec.ca. **Website:** www.onspec.ca. **95% freelance written.** Quarterly magazine covering Canadian science fiction, fantasy, and horror. "We publish speculative fiction and poetry by new and established writers, with a strong preference for Canadian-authored works." Estab. 1989. Circ. 2,000. Byline given. Pays on acceptance. No kill fee. Publishes ms an average of 6-18 months after acceptance. Editorial lead time 6 months. Accepts queries by mail. Accepts simultaneous submissions. Responds in 2 weeks to queries; in 6 months after deadline to mss. Sample copy: $8. Guidelines on website.

💭 See website guidelines for submission announcements. "Please refer to website for information regarding submissions, as we are not open year round."

FICTION Needs fantasy, horror, science fiction, magic realism, ghost stories, fairy stories. No media tie-in or shaggy-alien stories. No condensed or excerpted novels, religious/inspirational stories, fairy tales. **Buys 50 mss/year.** Send complete ms. Electronic submissions preferred. Length: 1,000-6,000 words.

POETRY Needs avant-garde, free verse. No rhyming or religious material. Buys 6 poems/year. Submit maximum 10 poems. Length: 4-100 lines. **Pays $50 and 1 contributor's copy.**

TIPS "We want to see stories with plausible characters, a well-constructed, consistent, and vividly described setting, a strong plot, and believable emotions; characters must show us (not tell us) their emotional responses to each other and to the situation and/or challenge they face. Also: Don't send us stories written for television. We don't like media tie-ins, so don't watch TV for inspiration! Read instead! Strong preference given to submissions by Canadians."

QUANTUM FAIRY TALES

E-mail: editorqft@gmail.com. **Website:** quantumfairytales.org. **Contact:** The Gnomies. Quantum Fairy Tales is a nonprofit, all-volunteer, all-donation, quarterly e-zine showcasing art, poetry and literature with elements of science fiction, fantasy, and the supernatural, with weekly website articles and author/artist highlights. "The best part about QFT is that real, live gnomies reply with feedback to every submission." Estab. October 2012. Accepts queries by e-mail. Accepts simultaneous submissions. Guidelines online. http://www.quantumfairytales.org/submissions/.

NONFICTION "Want to write a column? Want to write a nonfiction article, interview, book review, or exegesis? If it's pertinent to the interests of speculative fiction fans, we'll consider it." E-mail submission with title, type of submission, and word count in submission line.

FICTION Prose fiction submissions should be 7,000 words or less. Seeking all varieties of speculative fiction. Needs fantasy, horror, science fiction, serialized novels, short stories, Steampunk, Cyberpunk - anything under the speculative umbrella. E-mail fiction submissions with type of submission, title, author name, and word count in subject line.

POETRY E-mail poetry submission with title, type of submission, and word count in submission line. Poetry submissions should be 50 lines or less and should fit into a speculative fiction category, such as: scifi, horror, fantasy, steampunk, etc.

TIPS "Your writing and art work must fall in the category of speculative fiction for us to consider it. Every submission gets a free critique whether published or not. If you do not hear from us within three months, please give us a nudge. Thank you!"

SCIFAIKUEST

Alban Lake Publishing, P.O. Box 782, Cedar Rapids IA 52406. **E-mail:** gatrix65@yahoo.com. **Website:** albanlake.com/scifaikuest. **Contact:** Tyree Campbell, managing editor; Teri Santitoro, editor. *Scifaikuest*, published quarterly both online and in print, features "science fiction/fantasy/horror minimalist poetry, especially scifaiku, and related forms. We also publish articles about various poetic forms and reviews of poetry collections. The online and print versions of *Scifaikuest* are different." Estab. 2003. Time between acceptance and publication is 1-2 months. Submit seasonal poems 6 months in advance. Responds in 6-8 weeks. Single copy: $7; subscription: $20/year, $37 for 2 years. Make checks payable to Tyree Campbell/Alban Lake Publishing. Guidelines available on website.

○ *Scifaikuest* (print edition) is 32 pages, digest-sized, offset-printed, perfect-bound, with color cardstock cover, includes ads. Receives about

500 poems/year, accepts about 160 (32%). Press run is 100/issue; 5 distributed free to reviewers. Member: The Speculative Literature Foundation. *Scifaikuest* was voted #1 poetry magazine in the 2004 Preditors & Editors poll.

NONFICTION "We're looking for articles related in some way to one or more of the poetry forms we publish, or related to similar forms such as sijo." Length: under 1,000 words but considers longer essays. **Pays $6/article and 1 contributor's copy.**

POETRY Wants artwork, scifaiku, and speculative minimalist forms such as tanka, haibun, ghazals, senryu. Submit 10 poems at a time. Accepts e-mail submissions (pasted into body of message). No disk submissions; artwork as e-mail attachment or inserted body of e-mail. Submission should include snail-mail address and a short (1-2 lines) bio. Reads submissions year round. Editor Teri Santitoro makes all decisions regarding acceptances. Often comments on rejected poems. Has published poetry by Tom Brinck, Oino Sakai, Deborah P. Kolodji, Aurelio Rico Lopez III, Joanne Morcom, and John Dunphy. No 'traditional' poetry. Length: varies, depending on poem type. **Pays $1/poem, $6/review or article, and 1 contributor's copy.**

SPACE AND TIME

458 Elizabeth Ave., Somerset NJ 08873. **Website:** www.spaceandtimemagazine.com. **Contact:** Hildy Silverman, publisher. **100% freelance written.** *Space and Time* is the longest continually published small-press genre fiction magazine still in print. We pride ourselves in having published the first stories of some of the great writers in science fiction, fantasy, and horror. Estab. 1966. Circ. 2,000. Byline given. Pays on publication. No kill fee. Publishes stories/poems 6-12 months after acceptance. Accepts queries by e-mail. Sample copy: $6. Guidelines available only on website. Only opens periodically—announcements of open reading periods appear on Facebook page and website. No fiction or poetry considered outside of open reading periods.

○ We love stories that blend elements—horror and science fiction, fantasy with science fiction elements, etc. We challenge writers to try something new and send us their hard to classify works-—what other publications reject because the work doesn't fit in their "pigeonholes."

FICTION "We are looking for creative blends of science fiction, fantasy, and/or horror." Needs fantasy, horror, science fiction, short stories. "Do not send children's stories." Submit electronically as a Word doc or .rtf attachment ONLY during open reading periods. Anything sent outside those period will be rejected out of hand. Length: 1,000-10,000 words. Average length: 6,500 words. Average length of short shorts: 1,000 words. **Pays 1¢/word.**

POETRY Contact: Linda Addison. Needs speculative nature—science fiction, fantasy, horror themes and imagery. "Multiple submissions are okay within reason (no more than 3 at a time). Submit embedded in an e-mail, a Word doc, or .rtf attachment. ONLY submit during open poetry reading periods, which are announced via the Facebook page and on the website. All other poetry submitted outside these reading periods will be rejected out of hand." Poetry without any sort of genre or speculative element. Buys average of 15 per year poems/year. Submit maximum 3 poems. No longer than a single standard page. **Pays $5/poem.**

STRANGE HORIZONS

Strange Horizons, Inc., P.O. Box 1693, Dubuque IA 52004-1693. **E-mail:** editor@strangehorizons.com; fiction@strangehorizons.com. **Website:** strangehorizons.com. **Contact:** Niall Harrison, editor-in-chief. "*Strange Horizons* is a magazine of and about speculative fiction and related nonfiction. Speculative fiction includes science fiction, fantasy, horror, slipstream, and other flavors of fantastica." Estab. 2000. Accepts simultaneous submissions. Responds in 1-3 month to mss. Only responds if interested.

○ Work published in *Strange Horizons* has been shortlisted for or won Hugo, Nebula, Rhysling, Theodore Sturgeon, James Tiptree Jr., and World Fantasy Awards.

NONFICTION Contact: articles@strangehorizons. com. Needs essays. Special issues: "Nonfiction published in *Strange Horizons* should provide an original contribution to the field's discussion." Query (with the word QUERY in subject line) or submit complete ms (with the word SUB in subject line) by e-mail. Length: 3,000-5,000 words. **Pays $20-50.**

REPRINTS Wants reprints of essays that represent significant contributions to SF criticism. Pays $25.

COLUMNS/DEPARTMENTS Contact: columns@ strangehorizons.com. "We publish 1 column per week. Columns are standalone personal essays of 1,000-2,000 words on topics of interest to *Strange Horizons* readers. In the past we have published columns on SF in a wide range of media, from theatre to video games to comics to literature; debates within the SF community, and about the history of the community; and broader cultural, political, and technological issues of interest to the SF community." Submit complete ms (with the word SUB in subject line) by e-mail. **Pays $40.**

FICTION Contact: fiction@strangehorizons.com (questions only). "We love, or are interested in, fiction from or about diverse perspectives and traditionally under-represented groups, settings, and cultures, written from a nonexoticizing and well-researched position; unusual yet readable styles and inventive structures and narratives; stories that address political issues in complex and nuanced ways, resisting oversimplification; and hypertext fiction." speculative fiction, broadly defined. No excessive gore. Submit via online submissions manager; no e-mail or postal submission accepted. Length: up to 10,000 words (under 5,000 words preferred). **Pays 8¢/word, $50 minimum.**

POETRY Contact: poetry@strangehorizons.com. "We're looking for high-quality SF, fantasy, horror, and slipstream poetry. We're looking for modern, exciting poems that explore the possible and impossible: stories about human and nonhuman experiences, dreams and reality, past and future, the here-and-now and otherwhere-and-elsewhen. We want poems from imaginative and unconventional writers; we want voices from diverse perspectives and backgrounds." Submit up to 6 poems within 2 calendar months via e-mail; 1 poem per e-mail. Include "POETRY SUB: Your Poem Title" in subject line. **Pays $30 per poem.**

SPORTS

ARCHERY & BOWHUNTING

PETERSEN'S BOWHUNTING

Outdoor Sportsman Group, 6385 Flank Dr., Ste. 800, Harrisburg PA 17112. (717)695-8085. **Fax:** (717)545-2527. **E-mail:** bowhunting@outdoorsg.com. **Website:** www.bowhuntingmag.com. **Contact:** Christian Berg, editor; Emily Kantner, associate editor; David Siegfried, art director. **70% freelance written.** Magazine published 9 times/year covering bowhunting. "Our readers are 'superenthusiasts,' therefore our writers must have an advanced knowledge of bowhunting." Estab. 1989. Circ. 126,000. Byline given. Pays on acceptance. No kill fee. Editorial lead time 6 months. Submit seasonal material 6 months in advance. Accepts queries by mail, e-mail. Accepts simultaneous submissions. Responds in 3 months to queries. Guidelines free.

NONFICTION Needs how-to, humor, interview, new product, opinion, personal experience, photo feature. **Buys 50 mss/year.** Query. Length: 1,500-2,000 words.

PHOTOS Send photos. Captions, model releases required. Digital submissions only. Buys one-time rights.

COLUMNS/DEPARTMENTS Query.

BASEBALL

BASEBALL AMERICA

Baseball America, Inc., P.O. Box 2089, Durham NC 27702. **Website:** www.baseballamerica.com. **10% freelance written.** Biweekly tabloid covering baseball. *Baseball America* is read by industry insiders and passionate, knowledgeable fans. Writing should go beyond routine baseball stories to include more depth or a unique angle. Estab. 1981. Circ. 80,000. Byline given. Pays on publication. No kill fee. Publishes ms an average of 2 months after acceptance. Editorial lead time 1 month. Submit seasonal material 2 months in advance. Accepts simultaneous submissions. Sample copy for $3.25.

NONFICTION Needs historical, interview, theme or issue-oriented baseball features. No major league player features that don't cover new ground or superficial treatments of baseball subjects. Send complete ms. Length: 100-2,000 words.

PHOTOS State availability. Identification of subjects required. Negotiates payment individually. Buys one time rights.

BICYCLING

💲💲💲 ADVENTURE CYCLIST

Adventure Cycling Association, P.O. Box 8308, Missoula MT 59807. **Fax:** (406)721-8754. **E-mail:** magazine@adventurecycling.org. **Website:** www.adventu-

recycling.org/adventure-cyclist. **Contact:** Alex Strickland. **75% freelance written.** Published 9 times/year for Adventure Cycling Association members, emphasizing bicycle tourism and travel. Estab. 1975. Circ. 51,000. Byline given. Pays on publication. Kill fee 25%. Publishes ms 8-12 months after acceptance. Submit seasonal material 12 months in advance. Accepts queries by online submission form. Accepts simultaneous submissions. Sample copy and guidelines for 9x12 SAE with 4 first-class stamps. Guidelines online.

NONFICTION Needs essays, historical, how-to, humor, inspirational, memoir, opinion, personal experience, photo feature, reviews, travel, U.S. or foreign tour accounts. **Buys 20-25 mss/year.** Length: 1,400-3,000 words. **Inquiries requested prior to complete mss. Pays sliding scale per word.** Expenses must be agreed on before final contract is signed.

PHOTOS State availability. Guidelines online: adventurecycling.org/adventure-cyclist/adventure-cyclist-submissions/photography-guidelines. Photo rates available online.

FICTION We rarely publish fiction but are interested if it's well written and appropriate for our audience. Needs adventure. 1500-3000 **$.30-$.45 per word.**

CYCLE CALIFORNIA! MAGAZINE

1702 Meridian Ave. Suite L, #289, San Jose CA 95125. (408)924-0270. **E-mail:** tcorral@cyclecalifornia.com; bmack@cyclecalifornia.com. **Website:** www.cycle-california.com. **Contact:** Tracy L. Corral, publisher. **75% freelance written.** Magazine published 11 times/year covering Northern California bicycling events, races, people. Issues (topics) covered include bicycle commuting, bicycle politics, touring, racing, nostalgia, history—anything at all to do with riding a bike. Magazine published 11 times/year covering Northern California bicycling events, races, people. Issues (topics) covered include bicycle commuting, bicycle politics, touring, racing, nostalgia, history—anything at all to do with riding a bike. Estab. 1995. Circ. 32,000 print; 2,800 digital subscribers. Byline given. Pays on publication. No kill fee. Publishes ms an average of 3 months after acceptance. Editorial lead time 6 weeks. Submit seasonal material 3-6 months in advance. Accepts queries by e-mail. Accepts simultaneous submissions. Responds in 1 month to queries. Sample copy with 9x12 SASE and $1.50 first-class postage. Guidelines with #10 SASE.

⬤ Use e-mail (tcorral@cyclecalifornia.com) or Twitter (@Tlynn48) to query editor.

NONFICTION Needs historical, how-to, humor, interview, memoir, opinion, personal experience, profile, technical, travel. Special issues: Bicycle Tour & Travel (January issue). No articles about any sport that doesn't relate to bicycling. No product reviews. **Buys 36 mss/year.** Query. Length: 500-1,000 words. **Pays 10-15¢/word.**

PHOTOS Send photos. Identification of subjects preferred. Identification of location or event required. Negotiates payment individually. Buys one-time rights.

COLUMNS/DEPARTMENTS Buys 2-3 mss/year. Query with links to published stories. **Pays 10-15¢/word.**

FICTION Needs humorous.

POETRY Needs Poetry as it relates to bike riding. Buys 1-2 poems/year.

TIPS "E-mail us with good ideas. While we don't exclude writers from other parts of the country, articles really should reflect a West Coast slant or be of general interest to bicyclists. We prefer stories written by people who like and use their bikes."

BOATING

CHESAPEAKE BAY MAGAZINE

601 Sixth St., Annapolis MD 21403. (410)263-2662. **Fax:** (410)267-6924. **E-mail:** joe@chesapeakebaymagazine.com. **E-mail:** editor@chesapeakebaymagazine.com. **Website:** www.chesapeakebaymagazine.com. **Contact:** Ann Levelle, managing editor; Joe Evans, editor. **70% freelance written.** Monthly magazine covering boating and the Chesapeake Bay. "Our readers are boaters - sailors, paddlers, power boaters, anglers, conservationists, and foodies. Read the magazine before submitting." Estab. 1972. Circ. 25,000. Byline given. Pays on publication. No kill fee. Publishes ms an average of 6 months after acceptance. Editorial lead time 1 year. Submit seasonal material 1 year in advance. Accepts queries by mail, e-mail, fax, phone. Accepts simultaneous submissions. Responds in 2 months to queries; 3 months to mss. Sample copy for $5.19 prepaid and SASE.

NONFICTION Needs book excerpts, new product. **Buys 30 mss/year.** Query with published clips. Length: 300-3,000 words. **Pays $100-1,000.**

PHOTOS Captions, identification of subjects required. Offers $75-250/photo, $400/day rate for assignment photography. Pays $275 for color cover; $75-250 for color *stock* inside, depending on size; $200-1,200 for *assigned* photo package. Pays on publication. Credit line given. Buys one-time rights. Buys one-time rights.

TIPS "Send us unedited writing samples (not clips) that show the writer can write, not just string words together. We look for well-organized, lucid, lively, intelligent writing."

GOOD OLD BOAT

The Sailing Magazine for the Rest of Us, Partnership for Excellence, Inc., 7340 Niagara Lane N., Maple Grove MN 55311-2655 United States of America. (701)952-9433. **Fax:** (701)952-9434. **E-mail:** karen@goodoldboat.com. **E-mail:** karen@goodoldboat.com. **Website:** www.goodoldboat.com. **Contact:** Karen Larson, editor. **90% freelance written.** Bimonthly magazine covering sailing. *Good Old Boat* magazine focuses on maintaining, upgrading, and loving fiberglass cruising sailboats from the 1960s and well into the 2000s. Readers see themselves as part of a community of sailors who share similar maintenance and replacement concerns not generally addressed in the other sailing publications. Readers do much of the writing about projects they have done on their boats and the joy they receive from sailing them. Estab. 1998. Circ. 25,000. Byline given. Pays 2 months in advance of publication. No kill fee. Publishes ms an average of 12-18 months after acceptance. Editorial lead time 4-6 months. Submit seasonal material 12-15 months in advance. Accepts queries by mail, e-mail. Accepts simultaneous submissions. Responds in 1 week to queries; in 1 month to mss. Downloadable sample copy free. Guidelines available online.

NONFICTION Needs general interest, historical, how-to, interview, personal experience, photo feature, technical. "Articles written by nonsailors serve no purpose for us." **Buys 150 mss/year.** Query or send complete ms. Length: up to 3,000 words. **Payment varies.**

PHOTOS Contact: Karen Larson. State availability of or send photos. "We do not pay additional fees for photos except when they run as covers, or are specifically requested to support an article."

TIPS "Our shorter pieces are the best way to break into our magazine. We publish many Simple Solutions and Quick & Easy pieces. These are how-to tips that have worked for sailors on their boats. In addition, our readers send lists of projects which they've done on their boats and which they could write for publication. We respond to these queries with a thumbs up or down by project. Articles are submitted on speculation, but they have a better chance of being accepted once we have approved of the suggested topic."

HEARTLAND BOATING

The Waterways Journal, Inc., 319 N. Fourth St., Suite 650, St. Louis MO 63102. (314)241-4310. **Fax:** (314)241-4207. **E-mail:** brad@heartlandboating.com. **Website:** www.heartlandboating.com. Zac Metcalf, regional sales manager. **Contact:** Brad Kovach, editor. **75% freelance written.** Magazine published 5 times/year covering recreational boating on the inland waterways of mid-America, from the Great Lakes south to the Gulf of Mexico. "Our writers must have experience with, and a great interest in, boating in mid-America. *HeartLand Boating*'s content is both informative and inspirational—describing boating life as the heartland boater knows it. The content reflects the challenge, joy, and excitement of our way of life. We are devoted to both power and sailboating enthusiasts throughout America's inland waterways." Estab. 1989. Circ. 10,000. Byline given. Pays on publication. No kill fee. Editorial lead time two months. Accepts queries by mail. Responds only if interested. Sample copy upon request. Guidelines for #10 SASE.

NONFICTION Needs book excerpts, how-to, humor, inspirational, new product, personal experience, profile, reviews, technical, travel. **Buys 100 mss/year.** Send complete ms. Length: 850-1,500 words. **Pays $150-350.**

REPRINTS Send tearsheet, photocopy or typed ms and information about when and where the material previously appeared.

PHOTOS Magazine published five times/year covering recreational boating on the inland waterways of mid-America, from the Great Lakes south to the Gulf of Mexico and over to the east. Send photos. Model release is required, property release is preferred, photo captions are required. Include names and locations. Reviews prints, digital images. Offers no additional payment for photos accepted with ms. Buys one-time print rights and Web rights of photos.

COLUMNS/DEPARTMENTS Query with published clips or send complete ms.

TIPS "We begin planning the next year's schedule starting in August. So submitting material between August 1 and October 15 is the best way to proceed."

HOUSEBOAT MAGAZINE

Harris Publishing, Inc., 360 B St., Idaho Falls ID 83402. (208)524-7000. **Fax:** (208)522-5241. **E-mail:** blk@houseboatmagazine.com. **Website:** www.houseboatmagazine.com. **Contact:** Brady L. Kay, executive editor. **15% freelance written.** Bi-monthly magazine for houseboaters who enjoy reading everything that reflects the unique houseboating lifestyle. If it is not a houseboat-specific article, please do not query. Estab. 1990. Circ. 25,000. Byline given. Pays on acceptance. Offers 25% kill fee. Publishes ms an average of 3 months after acceptance. Editorial lead time 2 months. Submit seasonal material 6 months in advance. Accepts simultaneous submissions. Responds in 1 week to queries. Sample copy for $5. Guidelines by e-mail.

No unsolicited mss. Accepts queries by mail and fax, but e-mail strongly preferred.

NONFICTION Needs how-to, interview, new product, personal experience, travel. **Buys 36 mss/year.** Query before submitting. Length: 1,500-2,200 words. **Pays $200-500.**

PHOTOS Often required as part of submission package. Color prints discouraged. Digital prints are unacceptable. Seldom purchases photos without ms, but occasionally buys cover photos. Captions, model releases required. Reviews transparencies, high-resolution electronic images. Offers no additional payment for photos accepted with ms. Buys one-time rights.

COLUMNS/DEPARTMENTS Pays $150-300.

TIPS "As a general rule, how-to articles are always in demand. So are stories on unique houseboats or houseboaters. You are less likely to break in with a travel piece that does not revolve around specific people or groups. Personality profile pieces with excellent supporting photography are your best bet."

LAKELAND BOATING

O'Meara-Brown Publications, Inc., 630 Davis St., Suite 301, Evanston IL 60201. **E-mail:** info@lakelandboating.com. **Website:** www.lakelandboating.com. **50% freelance written.** Magazine covering Great Lakes boating. Estab. 1946. Circ. 60,000. Byline given. Pays on publication. No kill fee. Accepts queries by e-mail. Accepts simultaneous submissions. Responds in 4 months to queries. Sample copy for $5.50 and 9x12 SAE with 6 first-class stamps. Guidelines free.

NONFICTION Needs book excerpts, historical, how-to, interview, personal experience, photo feature, technical, travel, must relate to boating in Great Lakes. No inspirational, religious, expose, or poetry. **Buys 20-30 mss/year.** Length: 300-1,500 words. **Pays $100-600.**

PHOTOS State availability. Captions required. Reviews prefers 35mm transparencies, high-res digital shots. Buys one time rights.

COLUMNS/DEPARTMENTS Bosun's Locker (technical or how-to pieces on boating), 100-1,000 words. **Buys 40 mss/year.** Query. **Pays $25-200.**

PONTOON & DECK BOAT

PDB Magazine, Harris Publishing, Inc., 360 B. St., Idaho Falls ID 83402. (208)524-7000. **Fax:** (208)522-5241. **E-mail:** blk@pdbmagazine.com. **Website:** www.pdbmagazine.com. **Contact:** Brady L. Kay, editor. **15% freelance written.** Magazine published 11 times/year covering boating. A boating niche publication geared toward the pontoon and deck boating lifestyle and consumer market. Audience is comprised of people who utilize these boats for varied family activities and fishing. Magazine is promotional of the PDB industry and its major players. Seeks to give the reader a twofold reason to read publication: to celebrate the lifestyle, and to do it aboard a first-class craft. Estab. 1995. Circ. 84,000. Byline given. Pays on publication. No kill fee. Editorial lead time 2 months. Submit seasonal material 3 months in advance. Accepts queries by mail, e-mail. Accepts simultaneous submissions. Responds in 3 weeks to queries; in 3 months to mss. Sample copy and writer's guidelines available.

NONFICTION Needs how-to, personal experience. "No general boating (must be pontoon or deck boat specific), no humor, fiction, or poetry." **Buys 15 mss/year.** Send complete ms. Length: 600-2,000 words. **Pays $50-300.**

PHOTOS State availability. Captions, model releases required. Reviews transparencies. Rights negotiable.

COLUMNS/DEPARTMENTS No Wake Zone (short, fun quips); Better Boater (how-to). **Buys 6-12 mss/year.** Query with published clips. **Pays $50-150.**

TIPS "Be specific to pontoon and deck boats. Any general boating material goes to the slush pile. The more you can tie together the lifestyle, attitudes, and the PDB industry, the more interest we'll take in what you send us."

SAILING BREEZES ONLINE MAGAZINE

Northern Breezes, Inc., 3949 Winnetka Ave. N, Minneapolis MN 55427 USA. (763)542-9707. **Fax:** (763)542-8998. **E-mail:** info@sailingbreezes.com. **Website:** www.sailingbreezes.com. **20% freelance written.** Magazine published 8 times/year for the Great Lakes and Midwest sailing community. Focusing on regional cruising, racing, and day sailing. Digital publication only. Estab. 1989. Circ. 22,300. Byline given. Does not offer payment. No kill fee. Editorial lead time 1 month. Submit seasonal material 3 months in advance in a digital format. Accepts queries by mail, e-mail, fax. Accepts simultaneous submissions. Responds in 1 month to queries. Responds in 2 months to mss. Sample copy free.

NONFICTION Needs book excerpts, historical, how-to, humor, inspirational, interview, new product, personal experience, photo feature, technical, travel. **Buys 24 mss/year.** Query with published clips. Length: 300-3,500 words.

PHOTOS Send photos. Captions required. Reviews negatives, 35 mm slides, 3x5 or 4x6 prints. "Digital submission preferred." Offers no payment for photos accepted with ms. Buys one-time rights.

COLUMNS/DEPARTMENTS This Old Boat (sailboat), 500-1,000 words; Surveyor's Notebook, 500-800 words. **Buys 8 mss/year.** Query with published clips.

TIPS "Query with a regional connection already in mind."

🅢🅢🅢 YACHTING

Bonnier Corporation, 55 Hammarlund Way, Middletown RI 02842. **Website:** www.yachtingmagazine.com. **30% freelance written.** Monthly magazine covering yachts, boats. Monthly magazine written and edited for experienced, knowledgeable yachtsmen. Estab. 1907. Circ. 132,000. Byline given. Pays on acceptance. No kill fee. Editorial lead time 2 months. Submit seasonal material 6 months in advance. Accepts queries by mail, e-mail, fax. Accepts simultaneous submissions. Responds in 1 month to queries. Responds in 3 months to mss. Sample copy free.

NONFICTION Needs personal experience, technical. **Buys 50 mss/year.** Query with published clips. Length: 750-800 words. **Pays $150-1,500.**

PHOTOS Send photos. Captions, identification of subjects, model releases required. Reviews transparencies. Negotiates payment individually.

TIPS "We require considerable expertise in our writing because our audience is experienced and knowledgeable. Vivid descriptions of quaint anchorages and quainter natives are fine, but our readers want to know how the yachtsmen got there, too. They also want to know how their boats work. *Yachting* is edited for experienced, affluent boatowners—power and sail—who don't have the time or the inclination to read sub-standard stories. They love carefully crafted stories about places they've never been or a different spin on places they have, meticulously reported pieces on issues that affect their yachting lives, personal accounts of yachting experiences from which they can learn, engaging profiles of people who share their passion for boats, insightful essays that evoke the history and traditions of the sport and compelling photographs of others enjoying the game as much as they do. They love to know what to buy and how things work. They love to be surprised. They don't mind getting their hands dirty or saving a buck here and there, but they're not interested in learning how to make a masthead light out of a mayonnaise jar. If you love what they love and can communicate like a pro (that means meeting deadlines, writing tight, being obsessively accurate and never misspelling a proper name), we'd love to hear from you."

YACHTING MONTHLY

IPC Media Ltd, Pinehurst 2, Stamford Street, London England SE1 9LS United Kingdom. **E-mail:** yachtingmonthly@timeinc.com; Leeanne.Wright@timeinc.com. **Website:** www.yachtingmonthly.com. Monthly magazine covering practical and technical articles on all aspects of seamanship, navigation, and the handling of small craft and their design, construction and equipment. Also accepts cruising narratives about sailing almost anywhere in the world and carefully researched pilotage articles on anchorages and cruising areas. No kill fee. Accepts queries by mail, e-mail. Accepts simultaneous submissions. Guidelines available online.

NONFICTION Needs humor, technical, cruising narratives, lessons learned from mistakes/mishaps. Submit 150-word synopsis or complete ms. Length: 450-1,800 words. **Fees are quoted on acceptance.**

PHOTOS Send photos. Captions, identification of subjects required. Reviews transparencies, prints, 300 dpi digital images, original artwork/sketches.

GENERAL INTEREST

ESPN THE MAGAZINE

ESPN Inc. (The Walt Disney Company/Hearst Corporation), 19 E. 34th St., New York NY 10016. **E-mail:** post@espnmag.com. **Website:** www.espn.go.com/magazine. **Contact:** Craig Winston, managing editor. Biweekly sports magazine published by ESPN. *ESPN The Magazine* covers Major League Baseball, National Basketball Association, National Football League, National Hockey League, college basketball, and college football. The magazine typically takes a more lighthearted and humorous approach to sporting news. Estab. 1998. Circ. 2.1 million. Accepts simultaneous submissions.

○ Query before submitting. Difficult market to break into.

SPORTS ILLUSTRATED

Time, Inc., 1271 Avenue of the Americas, New York NY 10020. (212)522-1212. **E-mail:** story_queries@simail.com. **Website:** www.si.com. Weekly magazine covering sports. *Sports Illustrated* reports and interprets the world of sport, recreation, and active leisure. It previews, analyzes, and comments on major games and events, as well as those noteworthy for character and spirit alone. It features individuals connected to sport and evaluates trends concerning the part sport plays in contemporary life. In addition, the magazine has articles on such subjects as sports gear and swim suits. Special departments deal with sports equipment, books, and statistics. Estab. 1954. Circ. 3 million. No kill fee. Accepts queries by mail. Accepts simultaneous submissions. Responds in 4-6 weeks to queries.

○ Query before submitting. Do not send photos or graphics. Include a SASE for return of materials.

NONFICTION Query.

GOLF

AFRICAN AMERICAN GOLFER'S DIGEST

80 Wall St., Suite 720, New York NY 10005. (212)571-6559. **E-mail:** debertcook@aol.com. **Website:** www.africanamericangolfersdigest.com. **Contact:** Debert Cook, publisher. **100% freelance written.** Quarterly. Covering golf lifestyle, health, travel destinations

and reviews, golf equipment, golfer profiles. "Editorial should focus on interests of our market demographic of African Americans with historical, artistic, musical, educational (higher learning), automotive, sports, fashion, entertainment, and other categories of high interest to them." Estab. 2003. Circ. 20,000. Byline given. No kill fee. Publishes ms an average of 3 months after acceptance. Editorial lead time 3-6 months. Submit seasonal material 3-6 months in advance. Accepts queries by e-mail. Accepts simultaneous submissions. Responds in 3 weeks to queries; 3 months to mss. Sample copy for $8. Guidelines by e-mail.

NONFICTION Needs how-to, interview, new product, opinion, personal experience, photo feature, reviews, technical, travel, golf-related. **Buys 3 mss/year.** Query. Length: 250-1,500 words. **Pays 0.03-0.5¢/word.**

PHOTOS State availability. Captions, identification of subjects, model releases required. Reviews GIF/JPEG files (300 dpi or higher at 4x6). Negotiates payment individually. Credit line given. Buys all rights.

COLUMNS/DEPARTMENTS Profiles (celebrities, national leaders, entertainers, corporate leaders, etc., who golf); Travel (destination/golf course reviews); Golf Fashion (jewelry, clothing, accessories). **Buys 3 mss/year.** Query. **Pays 10-50¢/word.**

FILLERS Needs anecdotes, facts, gags, newsbreaks, short humor. **Buys 3 mss/year. mss/year.** Length: 20-125 words. **Pays 10-50¢/word.**

TIPS "Emphasize golf and African American appeal."

EXECUTIVE GOLFER

Pazdur Publishing, 2171 Campus Dr., Suite 330, Irvine CA 92612. (949)752-6474. **Fax:** (949)752-0398. **Website:** www.executivegolfermagazine.com. **20% freelance written.** Bimonthly magazine covering golf. Estab. 1972. Circ. 100,000. Byline sometimes given. Pays on acceptance. Accepts queries by fax, phone. Accepts simultaneous submissions. Sample copy and writer's guidelines for SASE.

NONFICTION Needs general interest, humor, travel. Query.

GOLF DIGEST

Condé Nast, 1 World Trade Center, New York NY 10007. (212)286-2860. **Fax:** (212)286-3147. **E-mail:** contact@golfdigest.com. **Website:** www.golfdigest.com. **Contact:** Jerry Tarde, editor in chief. Monthly magazine covering the sport of golf. Written for all golf enthusiasts, whether recreational, amateur, or professional. Estab. 1950. Circ. 1.6 million. No kill fee. Editorial lead time 6 months. Accepts queries by mail. Accepts simultaneous submissions. Sample copy: $3.95.

Query before submitting.

NONFICTION Query.

GOLF MAGAZINE

Time4 Media, Inc., 1271 Avenue of the Americas, New York NY 10020. **Website:** www.golfonline.com. Monthly magazine written for all levels of golf enthusiasts, including beginners, experts and pros. Estab. 1954. Circ. 1,403,685. No kill fee. Editorial lead time 6 weeks. Accepts simultaneous submissions.

Query before submitting.

GOLF TIPS

Madavor Media, 25 Braintree Hill Office Park, Suite 404, Braintree MA 02184. (617)706-9110. **Fax:** (617)536-0102. **E-mail:** editors@golftipsmag.com; vwilliams@madavor.com. **Website:** www.golftipsmag.com. **Contact:** Vic Williams, editor. **95% freelance written.** Magazine published 9 times/year covering golf instruction and equipment. "We provide mostly concise, very clear golf instruction pieces for the serious golfer." Estab. 1986. Circ. 300,000. Byline given. Pays on publication. Offers 33% kill fee. Publishes ms an average of 2 months after acceptance. Editorial lead time 3 months. Submit seasonal material 4 months in advance. Accepts queries by e-mail. Accepts simultaneous submissions. Responds in 1 month to queries. Sample copy free. Guidelines on website.

NONFICTION Needs book excerpts, how-to, interview, new product, photo feature, technical. "Generally, golf essays rarely make it." **Buys 125 mss/year.** Query. Length: 250-2,000 words. **Pays $300-1,000 for assigned articles. Pays $300-800 for unsolicited articles.**

PHOTOS State availability. Captions, identification of subjects required. Reviews 2¼×2¼, 4×5, or 35mm transparencies. Negotiates payment individually. Buys all rights.

COLUMNS/DEPARTMENTS Stroke Saver (very clear, concise instruction), 350 words; Lesson Library (book excerpts—usually in a series), 1,000 words; Travel Tips (formatted golf travel), 2,500 words. **Buys 40 mss/year.** Query. **Pays $300-850.**

TIPS "Contact a respected PGA professional and find out if they're interested in being published. A good writer can turn an interview into a decent instruction piece."

GUNS

AMERICAN RIFLEMAN

National Rifle Association, 11250 Waples Mill Rd., Fairfax VA 22030. **E-mail:** publications@nrahq.org. **E-mail:** armedcitizen@nrahq.org. **Website:** www.americanrifleman.org. Monthly magazine. *American Rifleman* is a shooting and firearms interest publication, owned by the National Rifle Association. Query before submitting for anything other than the Armed Citizen column. Estab. 1923. Circ. 2.1 million. Accepts queries by e-mail. Accepts simultaneous submissions.

COLUMNS/DEPARTMENTS Accepts articles for the Armed Citizen column. Send via e-mail.

👀 💲 MUZZLE BLASTS

P.O. Box 67, Friendship IN 47021. (812)667-5131. **Fax:** (812)667-5136. **E-mail:** llarkin@nmlra.org. **Website:** www.nmlra.org. **Contact:** Lee A. Larkin, editor. **65% freelance written.** Monthly magazine. "Articles must relate to muzzleloading or the muzzleloading era of American history." Estab. 1939. Circ. 17,500. Byline given. Pays on publication. Offers $50 kill fee. Publishes ms an average of 6 months after acceptance. Editorial lead time 4 months. Submit seasonal material 6 months in advance. Accepts queries by mail, e-mail. Responds in 1 month to mss. Sample copy and writer's guidelines free.

NONFICTION Needs general interest, historical, how-to, humor, interview, new product, personal experience, photo feature, technical, travel. No subjects that do not pertain to muzzleloading. **Buys 80 mss/year.** Query. Length: 2,000-2,500 words. **Pays $150 minimum for assigned articles. Pays $50 minimum for unsolicited articles.**

PHOTOS Send photos. Captions, model releases required. Reviews prints and digital images. Negotiates payment individually. Buys one-time rights.

COLUMNS/DEPARTMENTS Buys 96 mss/year. Query. **Pays $50-200.**

FICTION Must pertain to muzzleloading. Needs adventure, historical, humorous. **Buys 6 mss/year.** Query. Length: 2,500 words. **Pays $50-300.**

FILLERS Needs facts. **Pays $50.**

HIKING & BACKPACKING

A.T. JOURNEYS

Appalachian Trail Conservancy, P.O. Box 807, 799 Washington St., Harpers Ferry WV 25425-0807. (304)535-6331. **Fax:** (304)535-2667. **E-mail:** editor@appalachiantrail.org. **Website:** www.appalachiantrail.org. Estab. 1925. Accepts queries by mail, e-mail. Accepts simultaneous submissions. Responds in 2 months to queries. Guidelines available online.

NONFICTION Needs general interest, historical, how-to, interview, profile, travel. **Buys 5-10 mss/year.** Query with or without published clips, or send complete ms. Prefers e-mail queries. Length: 250-3,000 words. **Pays $25-300.**

REPRINTS Send photocopy with rights for sale noted and information about when and where the material previously appeared.

PHOTOS State availability. Identification of subjects, model releases required. Reviews contact sheets, 5x7 prints, slides, digital images. Offers $25-150/photo; $200/cover.

TIPS "Contributors should display a knowledge of or interest in the Appalachian Trail. Those who live in the vicinity of the Trail may opt for an assigned story and should present credentials and subject of interest to the editor."

💲💲💲💲 BACKPACKER MAGAZINE

Cruz Bay Publishing, Inc., Active Interest Media Co., 5720 Flatiron Pkwy., Boulder CO 80301. **E-mail:** dlewon@backpacker.com; mhorjus@aimmedia.com; caseylyons@aimmedia.com; mleister@aimmedia.com. **Website:** www.backpacker.com. **Contact:** Dennis Lewon, editor-in-chief; Casey Lyons, deputy editor; Maren Horjus, destinations editor; Mike Leister, art director; Giovanni C. Leone, assistant art director Louisa Albanese, photo assistant, Genny Fullerton, photography director. **50% freelance written.** Magazine published 9 times/year covering wilderness travel for backpackers. "*Backpacker* is the source for backpacking gear reviews, outdoor skills information and advice, and destinations for backpacking, camping, and hiking." Estab. 1973. Circ. 340,000. Byline given. Pays on acceptance. Offers 25% kill fee. Editorial lead time 6 months. Accepts queries by e-mail. Accepts simultaneous submissions. Responds in 2-4 weeks to queries. Sample copy free. Guidelines available online.

○ E-mail the appropriate editor when querying; list can be found on website.

NONFICTION Needs inspirational, interview, new product, personal experience, technical, "Features usually fall into a distinct category: destinations, personality, skills, or gear. Gear features are generally staff written. In order to make the grade, a potential feature needs an unusual hook, a compelling story, a passionate sense of place, or unique individuals finding unique ways to improve or enjoy the wilderness." Special issues: See website for upcoming issue themes. "Journal-style articles are generally unacceptable." Query with published clips before sending complete ms. Length: 1,500-5,000 words. **Pays 10¢-$1/word.**

PHOTOS Contact: Genny Fullerton, photo editor: gfullerton@backpacker.com. Buys 80 photos from freelancers/issue; 720 photos/year. Needs transparencies or hi-res digital of people backpacking, camping, landscapes/scenics. Reviews photos with or without a ms. Model/property release required (if necessary). Accepts images in digital format. Send via ZIP; e-mail as JPEG files at 72 dpi for review (300 dpi needed to print). State availability. Payment varies. Buys one-time rights.

COLUMNS/DEPARTMENTS Life List (personal essay telling a story about a premier wilderness destination or experience), 300-400 words; Done in a Day (a hike that can be finished in a day), 500 words; Weekend (a trip of 1-2 nights, 6-10 miles/day, within striking distance of a major city, and seasonally appropriate for the month in which they run); Skills (the advice source for all essential hiking and adventure skills, with information targeted to help both beginners and experts); Gear (short reviews of gear that has been field-tested; unlike other departments, Gear is done by assignment only). **Buys 50-75 mss/year.** Query with published clips. **Pays 10¢-$1/word.**

HOCKEY

⑤⑤⑤ USA HOCKEY MAGAZINE

Touchpoint Sports, 1775 Bob Johnson Dr., Colorado Springs CO 80906. (719)576-8724. **Fax:** (763)538-1160. **E-mail:** usah@usahockey.org. **Website:** www. usahockeymagazine.com. **Contact:** Harry Thompson, editor-in-chief. **60% freelance written.** Maga-

zine published 10 times/year covering amateur hockey in the U.S. The world's largest hockey magazine, *USA Hockey Magazine* is the official magazine of USA Hockey, Inc., the national governing body of hockey. Estab. 1980. Circ. 444,000. Byline given. Pays on acceptance or publication. No kill fee. Editorial lead time 6 months. Submit seasonal material 4 months in advance. Accepts simultaneous submissions. Sample copy and writer's guidelines free.

NONFICTION Needs essays, general interest, historical, how-to, humor, inspirational, interview, new product, opinion, personal experience, photo feature, hockey camps, pro hockey, juniors, college, NCAA hockey championships, Olympics, youth, etc. **Buys 20-30 mss/year.** Query. Length: 500-5,000 words. **Pays $50-750.**

PHOTOS State availability. Captions, identification of subjects required. Reviews contact sheets. Negotiates payment individually. Rights purchased varies.

COLUMNS/DEPARTMENTS Short Cuts (news and notes); Coaches' Corner (teaching tips); USA Hockey; Inline Notebook (news and notes). **Pays $150-250.**

FICTION Needs adventure, humorous, slice-of-life vignettes. **Buys 10-20 mss/year. Pays $150-1,000.**

FILLERS Needs anecdotes, facts, gags, newsbreaks, short humor. **Buys 20-30 mss/year.** Length: 10-100 words. **Pays $25-250.**

TIPS "Writers must have a general knowledge and enthusiasm for hockey, including ice, inline, street, and other. The primary audience is youth players in the U.S."

HORSE RACING

AMERICAN TURF MONTHLY

747 Middle Neck Rd., Great Neck NY 11024. (516)773-4075. **Fax:** (516)773-2944. **E-mail:** jcorbett@americanturf.com; editor@americanturf.com. **Website:** www.americanturf.com. **Contact:** Joe Girardi, editor. **90% freelance written.** Monthly magazine squarely focused on Thoroughbred racing, handicapping and wagering. *ATM* is a magazine for horseplayers, not owners, breeders, or 12-year-old girls enthralled with ponies. Estab. 1946. Circ. 30,000. Byline given. Pays on publication. No kill fee. Publishes ms an average of 4 months after acceptance. Editorial lead time 2 months. Submit seasonal material 2 months in ad-

vance. Accepts queries by mail, e-mail. Accepts simultaneous submissions. Responds in 1 month to queries. Sample copy and writer's guidelines free.

○ "*American Turf Monthly*, the only handicapping magazine sold on news stands within the U.S. and Canada, has been entertaining horse racing enthusiasts since 1946. Each issue draws the reader into the exhilarating world of horse racing with features written by premier handicapping authors in the sport. The photography and creative design capture the spellbinding highlights of the race tracks to satiate the thrill seeking desire of the wagering player."

NONFICTION No historical essays, bilious 'guest editorials,' saccharine poetry, fiction. Special issues: Triple Crown/Kentucky Derby (May); Saratoga/Del Mar (August); Breeder's Cup (November). **Buys Length: 800-2,000 words. Pays $75-300 for assigned articles. Pays $100-500 for unsolicited articles. mss/year.** Query. Length: 800-2,000 words. **Pays $75-300 for assigned articles. Pays $100-500 for unsolicited articles.** No.

PHOTOS Send photos. Identification of subjects required. Reviews 3 x 5 transparencies, prints, 300 dpi TIFF images on CD. Offers $25 for b&w or color interior; $150 min. for color cover. Pays on publication. Credit line given. Buys one-time rights.

FILLERS newsbreaks, short humor Needs newsbreaks, short humor. **Buys 5 mss/year.** Length: 400 words. **Pays $25.**

TIPS "Like horses and horse racing."

HOOF BEATS

U.S. Trotting Association, 6130 S. Sunbury Rd., Westerville OH 43081-9309. **E-mail:** hoofbeats@ ustrotting.com. **Website:** www.hoofbeatsmagazine. com. **Contact:** T.J. Burkett. **60% freelance written.** Monthly magazine covering harness racing and standardbred horses. "Articles and photos must relate to harness racing or Standardbreds. We do not accept any topics that do not touch on these subjects." Estab. 1933. Circ. 7,000. Byline given. Pays on publication. Offers 25% kill fee. Publishes ms an average of 2-4 months after acceptance. Editorial lead time 6 months. Submit seasonal material 6 months in advance. Accepts queries by mail, e-mail, fax. Accepts simultaneous submissions. Responds in 2 weeks to queries. Responds in 1 month to mss. Sample copy available online. Guidelines free.

NONFICTION Needs general interest, how-to, interview, personal experience, photo feature, technical. "We do not want any fiction or poetry." **Buys 48-72 mss/year.** Query. Length: 750-3,000 words. **Pays $100-500. Pays $100-500 for unsolicited articles.**

PHOTOS State availability. Identification of subjects required. Reviews contact sheets. We offer $25-100 per photo. Buys one-time rights.

COLUMNS/DEPARTMENTS Equine Clinic (Standardbreds who overcame major health issues), 900-1,200 words; Profiles (short profiles on people or horses in harness racing), 600-1,000 words; Industry Trends (issues impacting Standardbreds & harness racing), 1,000-2,000 words. **Buys 60 mss/year mss/year.** Query for column submissions. **Pays $100-500.**

TIPS "We welcome new writers who know about harness racing or are willing to learn about it. Make sure to read *Hoof Beats* before querying to see our slant & style. We look for informative/promotional stories on harness racing—not exposés on the sport."

HUNTING & FISHING

⑤⑤ AMERICAN ANGLER

Morris Communications Company, LLC, 735 Broad St., Augusta GA 30904. (706)828-3971. **E-mail:** editor@americanangler.com. **Website:** www.americanangler.com. **Contact:** Ben Romans, editor; Wayne Knight, art director. **95% freelance written.** Bimonthly magazine covering fly fishing. "*American Angler* is devoted exclusively to fly fishing. We focus mainly on coldwater fly fishing for trout, steelhead, and salmon, but we also run articles about warmwater and saltwater fly fishing. Our mission is to supply our readers with well-written, accurate articles on every aspect of the sport—angling techniques and methods, reading water, finding fish, selecting flies, tying flies, fish behavior, places to fish, casting, managing line, rigging, tackle, accessories, entomology, and any other relevant topics. Each submission should present specific, useful information that will increase our readers' enjoyment of the sport and help them catch more fish." Estab. 1976. Circ. 32,000. Byline given. Pays on publication. No kill fee. Publishes ms an average of 6 months after acceptance. Editorial lead time 3 months. Submit seasonal material 5 months in advance. Accepts queries by e-mail. Accepts simultaneous submissions. Responds in 6 weeks to queries; in 2 months to mss.

NONFICTION Needs general interest, historical, how-to, interview, personal experience, photo feature, profile, technical, travel. "No superficial, broadbrush coverage of subjects. We're interested in queries created with the magazine in mind; not shotgunned ideas. The more specific and unique, the better. Not interested in concepts that don't have a solid structure or are one-sided opinions. The more journalistic the approach (the inclusion of interviews, data, or other supporting evidence and information), the better. We're interested in someone who's willing to chase a story angle, beat the pavement, and put together a strong package more than we're interested in how well you can write a sentence." **Buys 45-60 mss/year.** Query with published clips. Length: 800-2,200 words. **Pays $200-600.**

REPRINTS Send information about when and where the material previously appeared. Pay negotiable.

PHOTOS "How-to pieces—those that deal with tactics, rigging, fly tying, and the like—must be accompanied by appropriate photography or rough sketches for our illustrator. Naturally, where-to stories must be illustrated with shots of scenery, people fishing, anglers holding fish, and other pictures that help flesh out the story and paint the local color. Do not bother sending subpar photographs. We only accept photos that are well lit, tack sharp, and correctly framed. A fly-tying submission should always include samples of flies to send to our staff photographer, even if photos of the flies are included. Send photos. Captions, identification of subjects required. Digital photos only. Offers no additional payment for photos accepted with ms. Pays $600-700 for color cover; $30-350 for color inside. Pays on publication. Credit line given. Buys one-time rights, first rights for covers. "Payment is made just prior to publication. "We don't pay by the word, and length is only one of the variables considered. The quality and completeness of a submission may be more important than its length in determining rates, and articles that include good photography are usually worth more. As a guideline, the following rates generally apply: Feature articles pay $450 (and perhaps a bit more if we're impressed), while short features pay $200-400. Generally, these rates assume that useful photos, drawings, or sketches accompany the words. Buys first rights along with nonexclusive perpetual rights, shared with the author after publication. "Tell us in your query or when you submit your ms that you have no good photo support; if the story is good enough, we'll find photos elsewhere. We buy first North American serial print, electronic, and in-house marketing rights to articles and photos."

COLUMNS/DEPARTMENTS One-page shorts (problem solvers), 350-750 words. Query with published clips. **Pays $100-300.**

TIPS "If you are submitting for the first time, please submit complete queries."

AMERICAN HUNTER

11250 Waples Mill Rd., Fairfax VA 22030-9400. (800)672-3888. **E-mail:** Publications@nrahq.org; americanhunter@nrahq.org; EmediaHunter@nrahq.org. **Website:** www.americanhunter.org. **Contact:** editor-in-chief. Monthly magazine for hunters who are members of the National Rifle Association (NRA). *American Hunter*, the official journal of the National Rifle Association, contains articles dealing with various sport hunting and related activities both at home and abroad. With the encouragement of the sport as a prime game management tool, emphasis is on technique, sportsmanship, and safety. In each issue, hunting equipment and firearms are evaluated, legislative happenings affecting the sport are reported, lore and legend are retold, and the business of the Association is recorded in the Official Journal section. Circ. 1,000,000. Byline given. Pays on publication. No kill fee. Accepts queries by mail, e-mail. Accepts simultaneous submissions. Responds in 6 months to queries. Guidelines online at www.professionaloutdoormedia.org/sites/all/downloads/American%20Hunter%20Writer%27s%20Guidelines.pdf.

NONFICTION Special issues: Special issues: pheasants, whitetail tactics, black bear feed areas, mule deer, duck hunters' transport by land and sea, tech topics to be decided, rut strategies, muzzleloader moose and elk, fall turkeys, staying warm, goose talk, long-range muzzleloading. Not interested in material on fishing, camping, or firearms knowledge. Query (preferred) or submit complete ms by mail or e-mail. Length: 2,000-3,000 words. **Pays up to $1,500 for full-length features with complete photo packages.**

REPRINTS Copies for author will be provided upon publication. No reprints possible.

PHOTOS Captions preferred. Accepts images in digital format only, no slides. Model release required "for every recognizable human face in a photo." Pays $125-600/image; $1,000 for color cover; $400-1,400 for text/photo package. Pays on publication. Credit line given. No additional payment made for photos used with ms. Photos purchased with or without accompanying mss. Buys one-time rights.

COLUMNS/DEPARTMENTS Build Your Skills (technical how-to column on hunting-related procedure); Hardware (covers new firearms, ammunition, and optics used for hunting), 800-1,200 words. **Pays $500-1,000.**

TIPS "Although unsolicited mss are accepted, detailed query letters outlining the proposed topic and approach are appreciated and will save both writers and editors a considerable amount of time. If we like your story idea, you will be contacted by mail or phone and given direction on how we'd like the topic covered."

ARIZONA WILDLIFE VIEWS

5000 W. Carefree Hwy., Phoenix AZ 85086. (800)777-0015. **E-mail:** awv@azgfd.gov; hrayment@azgfd.gov. **Website:** www.azgfd.gov/magazine. **Contact:** Heidi Rayment. **50% freelance written.** Bimonthly magazine covering Arizona wildlife, wildlife management, and outdoor recreation (specifically hunting, fishing, wildlife watching, boating and off-highway vehicle recreation). "*Arizona Wildlife Views* is a general interest magazine about Arizona wildlife, wildlife management and outdoor recreation. We publish material that conforms to the mission and policies of the Arizona Game and Fish Department. In addition to Arizona wildlife and wildlife management, topics include habitat issues, outdoor recreation involving wildlife, boating, fishing, hunting, bird-watching, animal observation, off-highway vehicle use, etc., and historical articles about wildlife and wildlife management." Circ. 22,000. Byline given. Pays on publication. No kill fee. Publishes ms an average of 10 months after acceptance. Editorial lead time 1 year. Submit seasonal material 2 months in advance. Accepts queries by mail. Accepts simultaneous submissions. Responds in 1 month to queries. Responds in 2 months to mss. Sample copy free. Guidelines available online.

NONFICTION Needs general interest, historical, how-to, interview, photo feature, technical. Does not want "Me and Joe" articles, anthropomorphism of wildlife, or opinionated pieces not based on confirmable facts. **Buys 20 mss/year.** Query. Length: 1,000-2,500 words. **Pays $450-800.**

TIPS "Unsolicited material without proper identification will be returned immediately."

✿❸❸❸ THE ATLANTIC SALMON JOURNAL

The Atlantic Salmon Federation, P.O. Box 5200, St. Andrews New Brunswick E5B 3S8 Canada. (514)457-8737. **Fax:** (506)529-1070. **E-mail:** savesalmon@asf.ca; martinsilverstone@videotron.ca. **Website:** www.asf.ca. **Contact:** Martin Silverstone, editor. **50-68% freelance written.** Quarterly magazine covering conservation efforts for the Atlantic salmon, catering to the dedicated angler and conservationist. Circ. 11,000. Byline given. Pays on publication. No kill fee. Publishes ms an average of 6 months after acceptance. Submit seasonal material 3 months in advance. Accepts simultaneous submissions. Responds in 2 months to queries. Sample copy for 9x12 SAE with $1 (Canadian), or IRC. Guidelines free.

NONFICTION Needs historical, how-to, humor, interview, new product, opinion, personal experience, photo feature, technical. **Buys 15-20 mss/year.** Query with published clips. Length: 2,000 words. **Pays $400-800 for articles with photos.**

PHOTOS State availability. Captions, identification of subjects required. Pays $50 minimum; $350-500 for covers; $300 for 2-page spread; $175 for full page photo; $100 for 1/2-page photo.

COLUMNS/DEPARTMENTS Fit To Be Tied (conservation issues and salmon research; the design, construction, and success of specific flies); interesting characters in the sport and opinion pieces by knowledgeable writers, 900 words; Casting Around (short, informative, entertaining reports, book reviews, and quotes from the world of Atlantic salmon angling and conservation). Query. **Pays $50-300.**

TIPS "Articles must reflect informed and up-to-date knowledge of Atlantic salmon. Writers need not be authorities, but research must be impeccable. Clear, concise writing is essential, and submissions must be typed."

❸ BACON BUSTERS

Yaffa Publishing, 17-21 Bellevue St., Surry Hills NSW 2010 Australia. (02)9213-8258. **E-mail:** marcusodean@yaffa.com.au. **Website:** www.yaffa.com.au. **Contact:** Marcus O'Dean, editor. Bimonthly magazine covering the hog hunting scene in Australia. "*Bacon Busters* content includes readers' short stories, how-to articles, pig hunting features, technical advice, pig dog profiles, and Australia's biggest collection of pig hunting photos. Not to mention the famous Babes &

Boars section!" Estab. 1995. Accepts queries by e-mail. Accepts simultaneous submissions.

NONFICTION Needs expose, general interest, how-to, interview. Query by e-mail with image, short bio, and contact info.

🟡🟡 BASSMASTER MAGAZINE

B.A.S.S. Publications, 1170 Celebration Blvd., Suite 200, Celebration FL 32830. (407)566-2277. **Fax:** (407)566-2072. **Website:** www.bassmaster.com. **80% freelance written.** Magazine published 11 times/year about largemouth, smallmouth, and spotted bass, offering how-to articles for dedicated beginning and advanced bass fishermen, including destinations and new product reviews. Estab. 1968. Circ. 600,000. Byline given. Pays on acceptance. No kill fee. Publishes ms an average of less than 1 year after acceptance. Editorial lead time 2 months. Submit seasonal material 6 months in advance. Accepts queries by mail, e-mail. Accepts simultaneous submissions. Responds in 2 months to queries. Sample copy upon request. Guidelines for #10 SASE.

🔵 Needs destination stories (how to fish a certain area) for the Northwest and Northeast.

NONFICTION Needs historical, how-to, interview, new product, travel, conservation related to bass fishing. No first-person, personal experience-type articles. **Buys 100 mss/year.** Query. Length: 500-1,500 words. **Pays $100-300.**

PHOTOS Send photos. Captions, model releases required. Reviews transparencies. Offers no additional payment for photos accepted with ms, but pays $800 for color cover transparencies. Buys all rights.

COLUMNS/DEPARTMENTS Short Cast/News/Views/Notes/Briefs (upfront regular feature covering news-related events such as new state bass records, unusual bass fishing happenings, conservation, new products, and editorial viewpoints). Length: 250-400 words. **Pays $100-300.**

TIPS "Editorial direction continues in the short, more direct how-to article. Compact, easy-to-read information is our objective. Shorter articles with good graphics, such as how-to diagrams, step-by-step instruction, etc., will enhance a writer's articles submitted to *Bassmaster Magazine*. The most frequent mistakes made by writers in completing an article for us are poor grammar, poor writing, poor organization, and superficial research. Send in detailed queries

outlining specific objectives of article, obtain writer's guidelines. Be as concise as possible."

BUGLE

Rocky Mountain Elk Foundation, 5705 Grant Creek, Missoula MT 59808. (406)523-4500. **Fax:** (800)225-5355. **E-mail:** bugle@rmef.org. **E-mail:** conservationeditor@rmef.org; huntingeditor@rmef.org; assistanteditor@rmef.org; photos@rmef.org. **Website:** www.rmef.org. **50% freelance.** *Bugle* is the membership publication of the Rocky Mountain Elk Foundation, a nonprofit wildlife conservation group. "Our readers are predominantly hunters, many of them conservationists who care deeply about protecting wildlife habitat." Bimonthly. Estab. 1984. Circ. 220,000. Byline given. Pays on acceptance. Kill fee. 3-9 months between acceptance and publication. Accepts queries by mail, e-mail. Accepts simultaneous submissions. Responds in 1 month to queries; 3 months to mss. Sample copy for $5. Writer's guidelines online.

🔵 Magazine: 114-212 pages; 55 lb. Escanaba paper; 80 lb. Sterling cover, b&w, 4-color illustrations; photos.

NONFICTION Needs essays, personal experience. Special issues: July/August Bowhunting section. Query or submit complete ms to appropriate e-mail address; see website for guidelines. Length: 750-4,500 words, depending on type of piece. **Pays 30¢/word and 3 contributor's copies.**

PHOTOS Digital files only unless specified. Reviews low-res digital photos, CDs. Pays $600 for cover, $200 for full-page spread, $150 for full page, $100 for half-page, $75 for third-page or smaller. Busy one-time North American rights.

FICTION "We accept fiction and nonfiction stories pertaining in some way to elk, other wildlife, hunting, habitat conservation, and related issues. We would like to see more humor." Needs adventure, historical, humorous, novel excerpts, slice-of-life vignettes, western, children's/juvenile, satire, human interest, natural history, conservation—as long as they related to elk. Query or submit complete ms to appropriate e-mail address; see website for guidelines. Length: 1,500-4,500 words; average length: 2,500 words. **Pays 20¢/word and 3 contributor's copies.**

TIPS "Hunting stories and essays should celebrate the hunting experience, demonstrating respect for wildlife, the land, and the hunt. Articles on elk behavior or elk habitat should include personal observations and should entertain as well as educate. No freelance product reviews or formulaic how-to articles accepted. Straight action-adventure hunting stories are in short supply, as are 'Situation Ethics' mss."

FIELD & STREAM

2 Park Ave., New York NY 10016. (212)779-5296. **Fax:** (212)779-5114. **E-mail:** fsletters@bonniercorp.com. **Website:** www.fieldandstream.com. **50% freelance written.** Broad-based monthly service magazine for the hunter and fisherman. Editorial content consists of articles of penetrating depth about national hunting, fishing, and related activities. Also humor, personal essays, profiles on outdoor people, conservation, sportsmen's insider secrets, tactics and techniques, and adventures. Estab. 1895. Circ. 1,500,000. Byline given. Pays on acceptance for most articles. No kill fee. Accepts queries by mail. Accepts simultaneous submissions. Responds in 1 month to queries. Guidelines available online.

PHOTOS Contact: Photo editor. Send photos. Reviews slides (prefers color). When purchased separately, pays $450 minimum for color. Buys first rights.

TIPS "Writers are encouraged to submit queries on article ideas. These should be no more than a paragraph or 2, and should include a summary of the idea, including the angle you will hang the story on, and a sense of what makes this piece different from all others on the same or a similar subject. Many queries are turned down because we have no idea what the writer is getting at. Be sure that your letter is absolutely clear. We've found that if you can't sum up the point of the article in a sentence or 2, the article doesn't have a point. Pieces that depend on writing style, such as humor, mood, and nostalgia or essays often can't be queried and may be submitted in ms form. The same is true of short tips. All submissions to *Field & Stream* are on an on-spec basis. Before submitting anything, however, we encourage you to *study*, not simply read, the magazine. Many pieces are rejected because they do not fit the tone or style of the magazine, or fail to match the subject of the article with the overall subject matter of *Field & Stream*."

FUR-FISH-GAME

2878 E. Main St., Columbus OH 43209-9947. **E-mail:** ffgcox@ameritech.net; subs@furfishgame.com. **Website:** www.furfishgame.com. **Contact:** Mitch Cox, editor. **65% freelance written.** Monthly magazine for outdoorsmen of all ages who are interested in hunting, fishing, trapping, dogs, camping, conservation, and related topics. Estab. 1900. Circ. 118,000. Byline given. Pays on acceptance. No kill fee. Publishes ms an average of 4 months after acceptance. Accepts simultaneous submissions. Responds in 2 months to queries. Sample copy for $1 and 9x12 SASE. Guidelines with #10 SASE.

NONFICTION Query. Length: 500-3,000 words. **Pays $50-250 or more for features depending upon quality, photo support, and importance to magazine.**

PHOTOS Send photos. Captions, True required. Reviews transparencies, color 5×7 or 8×10 prints, digital photos on CD only with thumbnail sheet of small images and a numbered caption sheet. Pays $35 for separate freelance photos.

TIPS "We are always looking for quality how-to articles about fish, game animals, or birds that are popular with everyday outdoorsmen but often overlooked in other publications, such as catfish, bluegill, crappie, squirrel, rabbit, crows, etc. We also use articles on standard seasonal subjects such as deer and pheasant, but like to see a fresh approach or new technique. Instructional trapping articles are useful all year. Articles on gun dogs, ginseng, and do-it-yourself projects are also popular with our readers. An assortment of photos and/or sketches greatly enhances any manuscript, and sidebars, where applicable, can also help. No phone queries, please."

🖲 MIDWEST OUTDOORS

MidWest Outdoors, Ltd., 111 Shore Dr., Burr Ridge IL 60527. (630)887-7722. **Fax:** (630)887-1958. **Website:** www.midwestoutdoors.com. **100% freelance written.** Monthly tabloid emphasizing fishing, hunting, camping, and boating. Estab. 1967. Byline given. Pays on publication. No kill fee. Publishes ms an average of 3 months after acceptance. Submit seasonal material 2 months in advance. Accepts simultaneous submissions. Responds in 3 weeks to queries. Sample copy for $1 or online. Guidelines available online.

NONFICTION Needs how-to. "We do not want to see any articles on 'my first fishing, hunting, or camping experiences,' 'cleaning my tackle box,' 'tackle tune-up,' 'making fishing fun for kids,' or 'catch and release.'" **Buys 1,800 unsolicited mss/year.** Send complete ms. Submissions should be submitted via website's online form as a Microsoft Word doc. Length: 600-1,500 words. **Pays $15-30.**

PHOTOS Captions required. Reviews slides and b&w prints. Offers no additional payment for photos accompanying ms. Buys all rights.

COLUMNS/DEPARTMENTS Fishing; Hunting. Send complete ms. **Pays $30.**

TIPS "Break in with a great unknown fishing hole or new technique within 500 miles of Chicago. Where, how, when, and why. Know the type of publication you are sending material to."

⑤⑤ MUSKY HUNTER MAGAZINE

P.O. Box 340, 7978 Hwy. 70 E., St. Germain WI 54558. (715)477-2178. **Fax:** (715)477-8858. **E-mail:** editor@ muskyhunter.com. **Website:** www.muskyhunter.com. **Contact:** Jim Saric, editor. **90% freelance written.** Bimonthly magazine on musky fishing. Serves the vertical market of musky fishing enthusiasts. "We're interested in how-to, where-to articles." Estab. 1988. Circ. 37,000. Byline given. Pays on publication. No kill fee. Publishes ms an average of 4 months after acceptance. Submit seasonal material 4 months in advance. Accepts simultaneous submissions. Responds in 2 months to queries. Sample copy for 9x12 SASE and $2.79 postage. Guidelines for #10 SASE.

NONFICTION Needs historical, how-to, travel. **Buys 50 mss/year.** Send complete ms. Length: 1,000-2,500 words. **Pays $100-300 for assigned articles. Pays $50-300 for unsolicited articles.**

PHOTOS Send photos. Identification of subjects required. Reviews 35mm transparencies, 3x5 prints, high-res digital images preferred. Offers no additional payment for photos accepted with ms. Buys one-time rights.

MARTIAL ARTS

KUNG FU TAI CHI

TC Media International, 40748 Encyclopedia Circle, Fremont CA 94538. (510)656-5100. **Fax:** (510)656-8844. **E-mail:** gene@kungfumagazine.com. **Website:** www.kungfumagazine.com. **Contact:** Gene Ching. **70% freelance written.** Bimonthly magazine covering Chinese martial arts and culture. *Kung Fu Tai Chi* covers the full range of Kung Fu culture, including healing, philosophy, meditation, Fengshui, Buddhism, Taoism, history, and the latest events in art and culture, plus insightful features on the martial arts. Es-

tab. 1992. Circ. 10,000. Byline given. Pays on publication. No kill fee. Publishes ms 3 or more months after acceptance. Editorial lead time 4 months. Submit seasonal material 4 months in advance. Accepts queries by mail, e-mail, fax, phone. Accepts simultaneous submissions. Responds in 2 months to queries; in 3 months to mss. Sample copy for $4.99 or online. Guidelines available online.

NONFICTION Needs general interest, historical, interview, personal experience, religious, technical, travel, cultural perspectives. No poetry or fiction. **Buys 70 mss/year.** Query. Length: 500-2,500 words. **Pays $35-125.**

PHOTOS Send photos. Captions, identification of subjects required. Reviews 5x7 prints, GIF/JPEG files. Offers no additional payment for photos accepted with ms. Buys one-time rights.

TIPS "Check out our website and get an idea of past articles."

SKIING & SNOW SPORTS

AMERICAN SNOWMOBILER

Kalmbach Publishing Co., 21027 Crossroads Circle, P.O. Box 1612, Waukesha WI 53187-1612. **E-mail:** editor@amsnow.com. **Website:** www.amsnow.com. **Contact:** Mark Savage, executive editor. **30% freelance written.** Magazine published 6 times seasonally covering snowmobiling. Estab. 1985. Circ. 54,000. Byline given. Pays on acceptance. No kill fee. Publishes an average of 4 months after acceptance. Editorial lead time 4 months. Submit seasonal material 6 months in advance. Accepts queries by mail, e-mail, fax. Accepts simultaneous submissions. Responds in 1 month to queries. Responds in 2 months to mss. Guidelines available online.

NONFICTION Needs general interest, historical, how-to, interview, personal experience, photo feature, travel. **Buys 10 mss/year.** Query with published clips. Length: 500-1,200 words. **Pay varies for assigned articles. Pays $100 minimum for unsolicited articles.**

PHOTOS State availability. Captions, identification of subjects, model releases required. Offers no additional payment for photos accepted with ms. Buys all rights.

⑤⑤ MUSHING MAGAZINE

2300 Black Spruce Ct., Fairbanks AK 99709. (907)495-2468. **E-mail:** editor@mushing.com; jake@mushing. com. **Website:** www.mushing.com. **Contact:** Greg

Sellentin, publisher and executive editor. Bimonthly magazine covering "all aspects of the growing sports of dogsledding, skijoring, carting, dog packing, and weight pulling. *Mushing* promotes responsible dog care through feature articles and updates on working animal health care, safety, nutrition, and training." Estab. 1987. Circ. 10,000. Byline given. Pays within 3 months of publication. No kill fee. Publishes ms an average of 4 months after acceptance. Submit seasonal material 4 months in advance. Accepts queries by mail, e-mail, fax, phone. Accepts simultaneous submissions. Responds in 8 months to queries. Sample copy: $5 ($6 U.S. to Canada). Guidelines online.

NONFICTION Needs historical, how-to. Special issues: Iditarod (January/February); Skijor/Sprint/Peak of Season (March/April); Health and Nutrition (May/June); Meet the Mushers/Tour Business Directory (July/August); Equipment (September/October); Races and Places/Sled Dog Events Calendar (November/December). See website for current editorial calendar. Query with or without published clips. "We prefer detailed queries but also consider unsolicited mss. Please make proposals informative yet to the point. Spell out your qualifications for handling the topic. We like to see clips of previously published material but are eager to work with new and unpublished authors, too." Considers complete ms by postal mail (with SASE) or e-mail (as attachment or part of message). Also accepts disk submissions. Length: 1,000-2,500 words. **Pays $50-250.**

PHOTOS "We look for good-quality color for covers and specials." Send photos. Captions, identification of subjects. Reviews digital images only. Pays $20-165/photo. Buys one-time and second reprint rights.

COLUMNS/DEPARTMENTS Query with or without published clips or send complete ms. Length: 150-500 words.

FILLERS Needs anecdotes, facts, newsbreaks, short humor, cartoons, puzzles. Length: 100-250 words. **Pays $20-35.**

TIPS "Read our magazine. Know something about dog-driven, dog-powered sports."

TEEN & YOUNG ADULT

Ⓐ SEVENTEEN MAGAZINE

300 W. 57th St., 17th Floor, New York NY 10019. (917)934-6500. **Fax:** (917)934-6574. **E-mail:** mail@

seventeen.com. **Website:** www.seventeen.com. **Contact:** Consult masthead to contact appropriate editor. Monthly magazine covering topics geared toward young adult American women. "We reach 14.5 million girls each month. Over the past 6 decades, *Seventeen* has helped shape teenage life in America. We represent an important rite of passage, helping to define, socialize, and empower young women. We create notions of beauty and style, proclaim what's hot in popular culture, and identify social issues." Estab. 1944. Circ. 2,000,000. Byline sometimes given. Pays on publication. Accepts queries by mail. Accepts simultaneous submissions. Writer's guidelines for SASE.

💬 *Seventeen* no longer accepts fiction submissions.

NONFICTION Buys 7-12 mss/year. Query by mail. Consult masthead to pitch appropriate editor. Length: 200-2,000 words.

TIPS "Send for guidelines before submitting."

TEEN VOGUE

Condè Nast Publications, One World Trade Center, 40th Floor, New York NY 10007. (212)286-2860. **Fax:** (212)286-2378. **E-mail:** web@teenvogue.com. **Website:** www.teenvogue.com. Magazine published 10 times/year. Written for sophisticated teenage girls age 12-17 years old. Circ. 450,000. No kill fee. Editorial lead time 2 months. Accepts simultaneous submissions.

💬 Query before submitting.

TRAVEL, CAMPING & TRAILER

BACKROADS

P.O. Box 317, Branchville NJ 07826. (973)948-4176. **Fax:** (973)948-0823. **E-mail:** editor@backroadsusa. com. **Website:** www.backroadsusa.com. **50% freelance written.** Monthly tabloid covering motorcycle touring. "*Backroads* is a motorcycle tour magazine geared toward getting motorcyclists on the road and traveling. We provide interesting destinations, unique roadside attractions and eateries, plus Rip & Ride Route Sheets. We cater to all brands. Although *Backroads* is geared towards the motorcycling population, it is not by any means limited to just motorcycle riders. Non-motorcyclists enjoy great destinations, too. As time has gone by, *Backroads* has developed more and more into a cutting-edge touring publication. We like to see submissions that give the reader the distinct impression of being part of the ride they're reading. Words describing the feelings and emotions brought on by partaking in this great and exciting lifestyle are encouraged." Estab. 1995. Circ. 50,000. Byline given. Pays 1 month after publication. Editorial lead time 1 month. Submit seasonal material 3 months in advance. Accepts queries by mail, e-mail. Responds in 1 month. Sample copy: $4. Guidelines online.

NONFICTION "What *Backroads* does not want is any 'us vs. them' submissions. We are decidedly non-political and secular. *Backroads* is about getting out and riding, not getting down on any particular group, nor do we feel this paper should be a pulpit for a writer's beliefs .. be they religious, political, or personal." Query. Needs travel features: "This type of story offers a good opportunity for prospective contributors. They must feature spectacular photography, color preferably, and may be used as a cover story, if of acceptable quality. **All submissions must be accompanied by images**, with an SASE of adequate size (10x13) to return all material sent, as well as a copy of the issue in which they were published, and a hard copy printout of the article, including your name, address, and phone number. If none is enclosed, the materials will not be returned. Text submissions are accepted via U.S. mail or e-mail. We can usually convert most file types, although it is easier to submit in plain text format, sometimes called ASCII." **Pays $75 and up; varies.**

PHOTOS Digital photos may be sent via U.S. mail on CD or via e-mail if they are in a stuffed file or Drop Box. All images must be no smaller then 300 dpi and at least 4x6. If you are sending images at 72 dpi, they MUST BE NO SMALLER THAN 20x30 FOR PROPER RESIZING. We do not accept photographs, slides, or negatives. Send photos. Offers no additional payment for photos accepted with ms.

COLUMNS/DEPARTMENTS We're Outta Here (weekend destinations), 500-750 words; Great All-American Diner Run (good eateries with great location), 500-750 words; Thoughts from the Road (personal opinion/insights), 400-600 words; Mysterious America (unique and obscure sights), 500-750 words; Big City Getaway (day trips), 500-750 words. **Buys 20-24 mss/year.** Query. **Pays $75/article.**

CONDE NAST TRAVELER

4 Times Square, 14th Floor, New York NY 10036. (800)777-0700. **E-mail:** web@condenasttraveler.com; letters@condenasttraveler.com. **Website:** www.cntraveler.com. **Contact:** Laura Garvey and Maeve Nicholson, editorial assistant; Greg Ferro, managing editor.. Monthly magazine. Condè Nast Traveler is a luxury and lifestyle magazine. Estab. 1987. Circ. 800,000.

Query before submitting. Difficult market to break into.

PHOTOS Contact: Leonor Mamanna, senior photo editor.

ESCAPEES

Sharing the RV Lifestyle, Roving Press, 100 Rainbow Dr., Livingston TX 77351. (888)757-2582. **Fax:** (409)327-4388. **E-mail:** editor@escapees.com. **Website:** escapees.com. **Contact:** Kelly Evans-Hill, editorial assistant. *Escapees* magazine's contributors are RVers interested in sharing the RV lifestyle. Audience includes full-time RVers, snowbirds, and those looking forward to traveling extensively. *Escapees* members have varying levels of experience; therefore, the magazine looks for a wide variety of material, beyond what is found in conventional RV magazines, and welcomes submissions on all phases of RV life, especially relevant mechanical/technical information. About 65% of the club members are retired, and about 45% live in their motorhomes, fifth-wheels, or travel trailers on a full-time basis. RVing families traveling with children full time is heavily on the rise. A bimonthly magazine that provides a total support network to RVers and shares the RV lifestyle. Estab. 1979. Circ. 25,000. Byline given. Pays on publication. Publishes ms an average of 3-6 months after acceptance. Editorial lead time 3 months. Submit seasonal material 6 months in advance. Accepts simultaneous submissions. Responds in 2 weeks to queries; in 3 months to mss. Sample copy available free online. Guidelines available online and by e-mail at departmentseditor@escapees.com. Editor does not accept articles based on queries alone. Decisions for use of material are based on the full article with any accompanying photos, graphics, or diagrams. Only complete articles are considered.

NONFICTION Needs general interest, historical, how-to, humor, inspirational, new product, nostalgic, personal experience, photo feature, profile, technical, travel. Do not send anything religious, political, or unrelated to RVs. Submit complete ms. When submitting an article via e-mail as an attachment, please include the text in the body of the e-mail. Length: 300-1,500 words. Please include word count on first page of article. **Pays $50-150 for unsolicited articles.** Publication sometimes "pays" writers with contributor copies rather than a cash payment, often in exchange for company bio/company product-themed photos.

PHOTOS Contact: Cole Carter, graphic artist. Freelancers should send photos with submissions. Captions, model releases, and identification of subjects required. Reviews GIF/JPEG files. Negotiates payment individually. Purchases one-time rights.

COLUMNS/DEPARTMENTS SKP Stops (short blurbs with photos on unique travel destination stops for RVers), 300-500 words. **Buys 10-15 mss/year.** Submit complete ms. **Pays $25-75.**

TIPS "Use an engaging, conversational tone. Well-placed humor is refreshing. Eliminate any fluff and verbosity. Avoid colloquialisms."

⊗⊗ FAMILY MOTOR COACHING

Family Motor Coach Association, 8291 Clough Pike, Cincinnati OH 45244. (513)474-3622; (800)543-3622. **Fax:** (513)474-2332. **E-mail:** rgould@fmca.com; magazine@fmca.com. **Website:** www.fmca.com. **Contact:** Robbin Gould, editor. **80% freelance written. "We prefer that writers/photographers be experienced RVers or at least knowledgeable of the RV lifestyle."** Monthly magazine covers all aspects of motorhome travel and lifestyle. Includes travel/destination topics; mechanics, maintenance, and other technical information; new RV products; hobbies; personality profiles of motorhome travelers; and more. *Family Motor Coaching* is the official publication of Family Motor Coach Association, an international organization serving motorhome owners and enthusiasts. The magazine is distributed to association members who own motorhomes as a requirement of membership—specifically, self-contained, motorized recreation vehicles—and is also read by prospective members who may or may not own a motorhome. Articles focus on RV travel, recreation, and related lifestyle topics; association news and activities; motorhome maintenance, repair, and DIY projects; new motorhome models; and motorhome components and accessories. Approximately one-third of editorial content is devoted to travel and entertainment, one-third to association news, and one-third to new products, industry news, and motorhome maintenance/technical topics. Estab. 1963. Circ. 75,000. Byline given. Pays on acceptance. Publishes ms an average of 8-12 months after acceptance. Submit seasonal material 4-6 months in advance. Accepts queries by mail, e-mail, fax. Responds in approximately 1-2 months to queries/submissions. Sample copy: $3.99; $5 if paying by credit card. Guidelines with #10 SASE, or request PDF by e-mail.

○ As the official publication of the largest motorhome owners' association, *Family Motor Coaching* is dedicated to the motorized RV category. Other than featuring general aspects of the RV lifestyle, we do not focus on towable RVs.

NONFICTION Needs general interest, how-to, humor, interview, new product, nostalgic, profile, technical, travel, motorhome travel (various areas of North America accessible by motorhome), bus conversions. **Buys approximately 50-75 mss/year.** Query with published clips or description of writing background/credits. Clearly state proposed article subject, length, photo availability, why article would interest motorhomers. Plan to send photos (high-resolution digital images preferred). Submissions are requested on speculation. Length: 1,000-2,000 words. **Pays $100-500, depending on article category.** Expenses paid in select cases if discussed in advance.

PHOTOS Hi-res digital images preferred (minimum 300 dpi, 4x6). Typically included in ms payment. In select instances, images are purchased independently. Prefers first North American serial and electronic rights to editorial but will consider one-time rights on photos only.

TIPS "One of our biggest freelance needs are travel articles that focus on North American destinations, routes, regions, attractions, etc. Articles should be oriented toward those traveling via motorhome. Featured sites must be accessible by motorized RV, and road conditions impacting motorhome travel should be noted. No articles focusing on towable RVs (e.g., trailers, fifth-wheels), please. Another need: activities, hobbies, and sports that can be enjoyed during motorhome trips. Queries are preferred over article submissions."

●⊗⊗ INTERNATIONAL LIVING

International Living Publishing, Ltd., Elysium House, Ballytruckle, Waterford Ireland (800)643-2479. **Fax:**

353-51-304-561. **E-mail:** submissions@internationalliving.com; editor@internationalliving.com. **Website:** www.internationalliving.com. **Contact:** Eoin Bassett, editorial director. **50% freelance written.** "*International Living* magazine aims at providing a scope and depth of information about global travel, living, retiring, investing, and real estate that is not available anywhere else at any price." Estab. 1981. Circ. 500,000. Byline given. Pays on publication. Offers 25-50% kill fee. Publishes ms an average of 3 months after acceptance. Editorial lead time 2 months. Submit seasonal material 3 months in advance. Accepts queries by e-mail. Accepts simultaneous submissions. Responds in 2 months to mss. Sample copy available online. Guidelines available online.

NONFICTION Needs how-to, interview, new product, personal experience, travel, health care. No descriptive, run-of-the-mill travel articles. **Buys 100 mss/year.** Query. Length: 840-1,400 words. **Pays $250-400.**

PHOTOS State availability. Identification of subjects required. Reviews contact sheets, negatives, transparencies, prints. Offers $50/photo. Buys all rights.

TIPS "Make recommendations in your articles. We want first-hand accounts. Tell us how to do things: how to catch a cab, order a meal, buy a souvenir, buy property, start a business, etc. *International Living*'s philosophy is that the world is full of opportunities to do whatever you want, whenever you want. We will show you how."

☺☺ MOTORHOME

2750 Park View Court, Suite 240, Oxnard CA 93036. **E-mail:** info@motorhomemagazine.com. **Website:** www.motorhome.com. **Contact:** Eileen Hubbard, editor. **60% freelance written.** Monthly magazine covering topics for RV enthusiasts. "*MotorHome* is a magazine for owners and prospective buyers of motorized recreational vehicles who are active outdoorsmen and wide-ranging travelers. We cover all aspects of the RV lifestyle; editorial material is both technical and non-technical in nature. Regular features include tests and descriptions of various models of motorhomes, travel adventures, and hobbies pursued in such vehicles, objective analysis of equipment and supplies for such vehicles, and do-it-yourself articles. Guides within the magazine provide listings of manufacturers, rentals, and other sources of equipment and accessories of interest to enthusiasts. Articles must have an RV slant

and excellent photography accompanying text." Estab. 1968. Circ. 150,000. Byline given. Pays on acceptance. Offers 30% kill fee. Publishes ms an average of 1 year after acceptance. Editorial lead time 4 months. Submit seasonal material 6 months in advance. Accepts queries by mail, fax. Accepts simultaneous submissions. Responds in 1 month to queries; in 2 months to mss. Sample copy free. Guidelines available online.

NONFICTION Needs general interest, historical, how-to, humor, interview, new product, personal experience, photo feature, technical. No diaries of RV trips or negative RV experiences. **Buys 120 mss/year.** Query with published clips. Length: 800-2,500 words. **Pays $400-900.**

PHOTOS Digital photography accepted. Send photos. Captions, identification of subjects, model releases required. Reviews hi-res photos at 300 dpi. Offers no additional payment for art accepted with ms. Pays $500 for covers. Buys one-time rights.

COLUMNS/DEPARTMENTS Crossroads (offbeat briefs of people, places, and events of interest to travelers), 100-200 words; Keepers (tips, resources). Query with published clips, or send complete ms. **Pays $100.**

TIPS "If a freelancer has an idea for a good article, it's best to send a query and include possible photo locations to illustrate the article. We prefer to assign articles and work with the author in developing a piece suitable to our audience. We are in a specialized field with very enthusiastic readers who appreciate articles by authors who actually enjoy motorhomes."

TRAVEL + LEISURE

American Express Publishing Corp., 1120 Avenue of the Americas, 9th Floor, New York NY 10036. (212)382-5600. **Website:** www.travelandleisure.com. **Contact:** Laura Teusink, managing editor. **95% freelance written.** *Travel + Leisure* is a monthly magazine edited for affluent travelers. It explores the latest resorts, hotels, fashions, foods, and drinks, as well as political, cultural, and economic issues affecting travelers. Circ. 950,000. Byline given. Pays on acceptance. Offers 25% kill fee. Accepts queries by mail, online submission form. Accepts simultaneous submissions. Responds in 6 weeks to queries and mss. Sample copy for $5.50 from (800)888-8728. Guidelines available online.

NONFICTION Needs travel. **Buys 40-50 feature (3,000-5,000 words) and 200 short (125-500 words) mss/year.** Query online or by postal mail. An online

query will receive a faster response. Editors are looking for a compelling reason to assign an article: a specific angle, news that makes the subject fresh, a writer's enthusiasm for and familiarity with the topic. **Pays $4,000-6,000/feature; $100-500/short piece.**
PHOTOS Contact: Photo Dept.. Discourages submission of unsolicited transparencies. Captions required. Payment varies. Buys one time rights.
COLUMNS/DEPARTMENTS Length: 2,500-3,500 words. **Buys 125-150 mss/year. Pays $2,000-3,500.**
TIPS "Queries should not be generic, but should specify what is new or previously uncovered in a destination or travel-related subject area."

WESTERN JOURNEY MAGAZINE

AAA Washington, 3605 132nd Ave S.E.1745 114th Ave. SE, Bellevue WA 98004. **E-mail:** robbhatt@aaawa.com; sueboylan@aaawa.com. **Website:** www.wa.aaa.com/journey. Sue Boylan, art director. **Contact:** Rob Bhatt, editor. Bimonthly magazine. "The magazine for AAA members in Washington state and North Idaho combines regional and international travel coverage with articles on auto technology, traffic safety, insurance and other AAA-centric topics." Circ. 670,000. Pays on acceptance. Accepts queries by e-mail. Response time varies.
NONFICTION "We consider all pitches and assign stories based on need. We look for writers who combine sound research and reporting skills with a strong voice and excellent storytelling ability. We adhere to AP style. Each spring, we create our features calendar for the following calendar year. We encourage you to read several issues of the magazine to familiarize yourself with our publication before you submit article ideas. We run all articles with high-quality photographs and illustrations. If you are a published photographer, let us know—but please do not submit any photos unless requested. To be considered for an assignment, submit a query by e-mail with 3 samples of published work (or links to websites where your work can be found)." Length: 200-1,500 words. **Pay negotiable, based on experience.** Travel expenses must be approved ahead of time.
PHOTOS Contact: Sue Boylan, art director.

WOMEN'S

ALLURE

Condé Nast Publications, 1 World Trade Center, New York NY 10007. (212)286-2860. **Website:** www.allure.com. **Contact:** Michelle Lee, editor-in-chief. Monthly magazine covering fashion, beauty, fitness, etc. Geared toward the professional, modern woman, *Allure* offers the most comprehensive understanding of trends, science, and service information, as well as the most valued product recommendations in the field. Circ. 1,157,024. Accepts simultaneous submissions. Query before submitting.

ALL YOU

Time Inc., 135 W. 50th St., 2nd Floor, New York NY 10020. **Website:** www.allyou.com. Monthly magazine that focuses on realistic and affordable ideas, budget-friendly recipes, candid health information, smart shopping strategies, high-value coupons on products, hair and beauty ideas, fashion for real women's bodies, and real-life advice for women from women. *All You* speaks directly to value-minded women helping them to live well for less in every area of their life. Mission is to help readers save money, save time, get food on the table faster, and prepare for the holidays with ease. No kill fee. Accepts simultaneous submissions. Query before submitting.

COSMOPOLITAN

Hearst Corporation, 300 W. 57th St., New York NY 10019-3791. **E-mail:** inbox@cosmopolitan.com. **Website:** www.cosmopolitan.com. *Cosmopolitan* is an international magazine for women that includes articles on women's issues, relationships, sex, health, careers, self-improvement, celebrities, fashion, and beauty. Estab. 1886. Circ. 3 million. Accepts queries by online submission form. Accepts simultaneous submissions.
NONFICTION Submit 800-word essay through online submission form. If essay is selected, you will be considered for future assignments.

ELLE

Hearst Communications, Inc., 300 W. 57th St., 24th Floor, New York NY 10019. (212)903-5000. **E-mail:** editors@elle.com. **Website:** www.elle.com. Monthly magazine. Edited for the modern, sophisticated, affluent, well-traveled woman in her twenties to early thirties. Circ. 1,100,000. No kill fee. Editorial lead time 3 months. Accepts queries by e-mail. Accepts simultaneous submissions.
NONFICTION Query before submitting.

ESSENCE

225 Liberty Street, 9th Flor, New York NY 10048. **Website:** www.essence.com. Monthly magazine. *Es-

sence is the magazine for today's black women. Edited for career-minded, sophisticated, and independent achievers, *Essence*'s editorial is dedicated to helping its readers attain their maximum potential in various lifestyles and roles. The editorial content includes career and educational opportunities, fashion and beauty, investing and money management, health and fitness, parenting, information on home decorating and food, travel, cultural reviews, and profiles of achievers and celebrities. Estab. 1970. Circ. 1 million. Byline given. Pays on acceptance. Offers 25% kill fee. Editorial lead time 6 months. Submit seasonal material 6 months in advance. Accepts queries by mail, fax. Accepts simultaneous submissions. Responds in 2 months to queries; in 2 months to mss. Sample copy: $3.25. Guidelines available online.

NONFICTION Needs book excerpts. **Buys 200 mss/year.** Query with published clips. Address to specific editor. Departments include Arts and Entertainment; Books and Poetry; Beauty and Style; Health, Relationships, and Food; Personal Essays; News; Money and Power; Feature Articles/Personal Growth. See online guidelines for specific editors. Length is given upon assignment. **Pays competitive rate.**

REPRINTS Send tearsheet and information about when and where the material previously appeared. Pays 50% of the amount paid for the original article.

PHOTOS "Would like to see photographs for our travel section that feature Black travelers". State availability. Model releases required. Pays $200 minimum depending on the size of the image.

FIRST FOR WOMEN

Bauer Media Group, 270 Sylvan Ave., Englewood Cliffs NJ 07632. (201)569-6699. **E-mail:** contactus@firstforwomen.com. **Website:** www.firstforwomen.com. *First for Women*, published 17 times/year, covers everything from beauty, health, nutrition, cooking, decor, and fun. Every issue also includes a 24-page cookbook that pulls out from the center of the magazine. Magazine is visual with a lot of quick tips. Estab. 1989. Circ. 1.3 million. Accepts simultaneous submissions.

 Query before submitting. Difficult market to break into.

🄢🄢🄢🄢 GLAMOUR

Condé Nast, 4 Times Square, 16th Floor, New York NY 10036. (212)286-2860. **Fax:** (212)286-8336. **Website:** www.glamour.com. **Contact:** Cyndi Leive, editor-in-chief. Monthly magazine covering subjects ranging from fashion, beauty, health, personal relationships, career, travel, food, and entertainment. *Glamour* is edited for the contemporary woman. It informs her of current trends, recommends how she can adapt them to her needs, and motivates her to take action. Estab. 1939. Circ. 2.3 million. No kill fee. Accepts queries by mail. Accepts simultaneous submissions.

NONFICTION Needs personal experience, travel.

PHOTOS Only uses professional photographers.

🄢🄢 HOPE FOR WOMEN

P.O. Box 3241, Muncie IN 47307. **E-mail:** hope@hopeforwomenmag.org. **Website:** www.hopeforwomenmag.com. **90% freelance written.** Bimonthly lifestyle magazine that offers faith, love, and virtue for the modern Christian Woman. *Hope for Women* presents refreshing, inspirational articles in an engaging and authentic tone to women from various walks of life. The magazine encourages readers and deals with real-world issues—all while adhering to Christian values and principles. Estab. 2005. Circ. 10,000. Byline given. Pays on publication. Publishes ms an average of 4-6 months after acceptance. Editorial lead time 4-6 months. Accepts queries by mail, e-mail. Accepts simultaneous submissions. Guidelines by email.

NONFICTION Needs book excerpts, essays, general interest, how-to, humor, inspirational, interview, new product, opinion, personal experience, photo feature, religious, travel. Query. Length: 500 words minimum. **Pays 10-20¢/word.**

COLUMNS/DEPARTMENTS Relationships (nurturing positive relationships—marriage, dating, divorce, single life), 800-1,200 words; Light (reports on issues such as infidelity, homosexuality, addiction, and domestic violence), 500-800 words; Journey (essays on finding your identity with Christ), 500-800 words; Marketplace (finance/money management), 800-1,200 words); E-Spot (book, music, TV, and film reviews), 500-800 words; Family First (parenting encouragement and instruction), 800-1,500 words; Health/Fitness (nutrition/exercise), 800-1,200 words; The Look (fashion/beauty tips), 500-800 words; Home Essentials (home/garden how-to), 500-800 words. Query. **Pays 10-20¢/word.**

TIPS "Our readers are a diverse group of women, ages 25-54. They want to read articles about real women dealing with real problems. Because our readers are balancing work and family, they want information presented in a no-nonsense fashion that is relevant and readable."

INSTYLE

Time, Inc., 1271 Avenue of the Americas, 18th Floor, New York NY 10020. (212)522-1212. **Fax:** (212)522-0867. **E-mail:** letters@instylemag.com. **Website:** www.instyle.com. **Contact:** Laura Brown, editorial director. Monthly magazine. Written to be the most trusted style adviser and lifestyle resource for women. Circ. 1,670,000. No kill fee. Editorial lead time 4 months. Accepts simultaneous submissions.

 ⚪ Query before submitting.

❺❺❺❺ LADIES' HOME JOURNAL

Meredith Corp., P.O. Box 37508, Boone IA 50037. 212-499-2087. **E-mail:** lhjcustserv@cdsfulfillment.com. **Website:** www.divinecaroline.com/ladies-home-journal. **50% freelance written.** Monthly magazine focusing on issues of concern to women 30-45. *Ladies' Home Journal* is for active, empowered women who are evolving in new directions. It addresses informational needs with highly focused features and articles on a variety of topics: self, style, family, home, world, health, and food. Estab. 1882. Circ. 4.1 million. Pays on acceptance. Offers 25% kill fee. Publishes ms an average of 4-12 months after acceptance. Editorial lead time 4 months. Accepts queries by mail, e-mail. Accepts simultaneous submissions. Responds in 3 months to queries. Guidelines available online.

NONFICTION Send 1-2 page query, SASE, résumé, and clips via mail or e-mail (preferred). Length: 2,000-3,000 words. **Pays $2,000-4,000.**

PHOTOS *LHJ* arranges for its own photography almost all the time. State availability. Captions, identification of subjects, model releases required. Offers variable payment for photos accepted with ms. Rights bought vary with submission.

FICTION Only short stories and novels submitted by an agent or publisher will be considered. No poetry of any kind. **Buys 12 mss/year.** Send complete ms. Length: 2,000-2,500 words.

LONG ISLAND WOMAN

P.O. Box 176, Malverne NY 11565. **E-mail:** editor@liwomanonline.com. **E-mail:** editor@liwomanonline.com. **Website:** www.liwomanonline.com. **30%**

freelance written. Monthly magazine covering issues of importance to women (age 35-65) in Nassau and Suffolk counties in New York—health, finance, arts, entertainment, fitness, travel, home. Estab. 2001. Circ. 32,000. Byline given. Pays within 1 month of publication. Offers 20% kill fee. Publishes an average of 3 months after acceptance. Editorial lead time 3 months. Submit seasonal material 3 months in advance. Accepts queries by e-mail. Accepts simultaneous submissions. Auto response and response when/if interested Sample copy for $5. Guidelines at www.liwomanonline.com/guidelines.

 ⚪ Responds if interested in using reprints that were submitted.

NONFICTION Needs book excerpts, essays, how-to, humor, interview, new product, nostalgic, reviews, travel. **Buys 12-20 mss/year.** Send complete ms. Length: 500-2,250 words. **Pays $70-200.**

REPRINTS Length: 500-2,250 words. Pays $40-100.

PHOTOS State availability of or send photos. Captions, identification of subjects, model releases required.

COLUMNS/DEPARTMENTS Humor; Health Issues; Family Issues; Financial and Business Issues; Book Reviews and Books; Arts and Entertainment; Travel and Leisure; Home and Garden; Fitness.

MORE

Meredith Corp., 805 Third Avenue, New York NY 10022. **E-mail:** more@meredith.com. **Website:** www.more.com. **Contact:** Ila Stanger, managing editor. Magazine published 10 times/year. *More* celebrates women of style and substance. The magazine is the leading voice for the woman who lives in a constant state of possibility. Estab. 1998. Circ. 1.8 million. Byline given. Editorial lead time 4 months. Accepts queries by mail. Accepts simultaneous submissions. Guidelines online.

 ⚪ Query before submitting.

NONFICTION *More* only accepts queries, before submissions. Keep query brief (1-2 pages), citing lead and describing how you will research and develop story. Be specific, and direct query to the appropriate editor, as listed on the masthead of the magazine. Send published clips, credits, and a résumé. Does not respond unless a SASE is enclosed. Word length is discussed upon assignment. Average story length is 2,000 words. **Payment is discussed upon assignment.**

🖉🖉 NA'AMAT WOMAN

21515 Vanowen Street, Suite 102, Canoga Park CA 91303. (818)431-2200. **E-mail:** naamat@naamat.org; judith@naamat.org. **Website:** www.naamat.org. **Contact:** Judith Sokoloff, editor. **80% freelance written.** Published 3 times per year, covering Jewish issues/subjects. "Magazine covering a wide variety of subjects of interest to the Jewish community— including political and social issues, arts, profiles; many articles about Israel and women's issues. Fiction must have a Jewish theme. Readers are the American Jewish community." Estab. 1926. Circ. 10,000. Byline given. Pays on publication. No kill fee. Publishes ms an average of 6 months after acceptance. Submit seasonal material 6 months in advance. Accepts queries by e-mail. Accepts simultaneous submissions. Responds in 4 weeks to queries. Responds in 3 months to mss. Sample copy for $2. Guidelines by e-mail.

NONFICTION Needs book excerpts, essays, historical, interview, personal experience, photo feature, travel, Jewish topics & issues, political & social issues & women's issues. **Buys 16-20 mss/year.** Send complete ms. **Pays 10-20¢/word for assigned and unsolicited articles.**

PHOTOS State availability. Reviews GIF/JPEG files. Negotiates payment individually. Buys one-time rights.

FICTION "We want serious fiction, with insight, reflection and consciousness." Needs novel excerpts, literary with Jewish content. "We do not want fiction that is mostly dialogue. No corny Jewish humor. No Holocaust fiction." **Buys 1-2 mss/year. mss/year.** Query with published clips or send complete ms. Length: 2,000-3,000 words. **Pays 10-20¢/word for assigned articles and for unsolicited articles.**

TIPS "No maudlin nostalgia or romance; no hackneyed Jewish humor."

O, THE OPRAH MAGAZINE

Hearst Corporation, 300 W. 57th St., New York NY 10019-5915. (212)903-5187. **Fax:** (212)977-1947. **Website:** www.oprah.com. **Contact:** Katie Arnold-Ratliff, articles editor. Monthly magazine founded by Oprah Winfrey and Hearst Corporation, primarily marketed at women. With lush photography gracing oversize pages, each issue of O, *The Oprah Magazine* offers compelling stories and empowering ideas stamped with Oprah's unique vision. Circ. 2.3 million. No kill fee. Accepts queries by mail. Accepts simultaneous submissions.

🖉 Query before submitting.

REAL SIMPLE

Time Inc., 1271 Avenue of the Americas, New York NY 10020. (212)522-1212. **Fax:** (212)467-1392. **Website:** www.realsimple.com. *Real Simple* is a monthly women's interest magazine. *Real Simple* features articles and information related to homekeeping, childcare, cooking, and emotional wellbeing. The magazine is distinguished by its clean, uncluttered style of layout and photos. Estab. 2000. Circ. 1.97 million. Accepts simultaneous submissions.

🖉 Query before submitting.

🖉🖉🖉 REDBOOK MAGAZINE

Hearst Corporation, Articles Department, Redbook, 300 W. 57th St., 22nd Floor, New York NY 10019. **Website:** www.redbookmag.com. Monthly magazine covering women's issues. *Redbook* is targeted to women between the ages of 25-45 who define themselves as smart, capable, and happy with their lives. Many, but not all, readers are going through 1 of 2 key life transitions: single to married and married to mom. Each issue is a provocative mix of features geared to entertain and inform them, including: news stories on contemporary issues that are relevant to the reader's life and experience and that explore the emotional ramifications of cultural and social changes; first-person essays about dramatic pivotal moments in a woman's life; marriage articles with an emphasis on strengthening the relationship; short parenting features on how to deal with universal health and behavioral issues; and reporting on exciting trends in women's lives. Estab. 1903. Circ. 2.2 million. Pays on acceptance. No kill fee. Publishes ms an average of 6 months after acceptance. Accepts queries by mail. Accepts simultaneous submissions. Responds in 3 months to queries and mss. Guidelines available online.

NONFICTION Query with published clips and SASE. Length: 2,500-3,000 words for features; 1,000-1,500 words for short articles.

TIPS "Most *Redbook* articles require solid research, well-developed anecdotes from on-the-record sources, and fresh, insightful quotes from established experts in a field that pass our 'reality check' test. Articles must apply to women in our demographics. Writers are advised to read at least the last 6 issues of the magazine (available in most libraries) to get a better understanding of appropriate subject matter and treatment. We prefer to see detailed queries rather than completed mss, and we suggest that you provide us with some ideas for sources/experts. Please enclose 2 or more samples of your writing, as well as a SASE."

SELF

Conde Nast, One World Trade Center, New York NY 10007. (212)286-2860. **Fax:** (212)286-6174. **E-mail:** comments@self.com. **Website:** www.self.com. Monthly magazine for women ages 20-45. Self-confidence, self-assurance, and a healthy, happy lifestyle are pivotal to *Self* readers. This healthy lifestyle magazine delivers by addressing real-life issues from the inside out, with unparalleled energy and authority. From beauty, fitness, health and nutrition to personal style, finance, and happiness, the path to total well-being begins with *Self*. Circ. 1.3 million. Byline given on features and most short items. Pays on acceptance. No kill fee. Accepts queries by online submission form. Accepts simultaneous submissions. Responds in 1 month to queries. Guidelines for #10 SASE.

Query before submitting.

NONFICTION Buys 40 mss/year. Query with published clips. Length: 1,500-5,000 words. **Pays $1-2/word.**

COLUMNS/DEPARTMENTS Uses short, news-driven items on health, fitness, nutrition, money, jobs, love/sex, psychology and happiness, travel. Length: 300-1,000 words. **Buys 50 mss/year.** Query with published clips. **Pays $1-2/word.**

10007. (212)286-2860. **Website:** www.vogue.com. Monthly magazine. *Vogue* mirrors the changing roles and concerns of women, covering not only evolutions in fashion, beauty and style, but the important issues and ideas of the arts, health care, politics, and world affairs. Estab. 1892. Circ. 1.1 million. Byline sometimes given. Pays on acceptance. Offers 25% kill fee. Accepts simultaneous submissions. Responds in 3 months to queries. Guidelines for #10 SASE.

WOMAN'S DAY

Hearst Communications, 300 W. 57th St., 28th Floor, New York NY 10019. (212)649-2000. **E-mail:** womansday@hearst.com. **Website:** www.womansday.com. **Contact:** Sue Kakstys, managing editor. Monthly magazine. "*Woman's Day* is an indispensable resource to 20 million women. The brand speaks to our reader's values and focuses on what's important. We empower her with smart solutions for her core concerns—health, home, food, style, and money—and celebrate the connection she cherishes with family, friends, and community. Whether in-book, online, mobile, or through social outlets, we provide inspiring insight and fresh ideas on how to get the most of everything." Estab. 1937. Circ. 3.2 million. Accepts queries by e-mail. Accepts simultaneous submissions. Guidelines available online.

NONFICTION Editors work almost exclusively with experienced writers who have clips from major national magazines. Accepts unsolicited mss only from writers with such credentials. There are no exceptions. E-mail an idea or mss that might be of interest and include recent, published clips. Will respond only if interested. Does not accept hard copy submissions.

WOMAN'S WORLD

Bauer Publishing, 270 Sylvan Ave., Englewood Cliffs NJ 07632. (201)569-6699. **Fax:** (201)569-3584. **E-mail:** dearww@womansworldmag.com. **E-mail:** wwfeatures@womansworldmag.com; circleofkindness@womansworldmag.com; moneysavingrecipe@womansworldmag.com; angels@womansworldmag.com; happiness@womansworldmag.com; loveandlaughter@womansworldmag.com. **Website:** www.womansworldmag.com. Weekly magazine covering human interest and service pieces of interest to family-oriented women across the nation. *Woman's World* is a women's service magazine. It offers a blend of fashion, food, parenting, beauty, and relationship features coupled with the true-life human interest stories. Publishes short romances and mini-mysteries for all women, ages 18-68. Estab. 1980. Circ. 1.6 million. Pays on acceptance. No kill fee. Publishes ms an average of 4 months after acceptance. Submit seasonal material 4 months in advance. Accepts queries by mail. Accepts simultaneous submissions. Responds in 2 months to mss. Guidelines for #10 SASE.

Woman's World is not looking for freelancers to take assigments generated by the staff, but it will assign stories to writers who have made a successful pitch.

NONFICTION Query.

FICTION Wants romance and mainstream short stories of 800 words and mini-mysteries of 1,000 words. Each of story should have a light romantic theme and can be written from either a masculine or feminine point of view. Women characters may be single, married, or divorced. Plots must be fast moving with vivid dialogue and action. The problems and dilemmas inherent in them should be contemporary and realistic, handled with warmth and feeling. The stories must have a positive resolution. Specify Fiction on envelope. Always enclose SASE. Mini-mysteries may revolve around anything from a theft to murder. Not interested in sordid or grotesque crimes. Emphasis should be on intricacies of plot rather than gratuitous violence. The story must include a resolution that clearly states the villain is getting his or her come-uppance. Submit complete mss. Specify Mini-Mystery on envelope. Needs mystery, romance. Not interested in science fiction, fantasy, historical romance, or foreign locales. No explicit sex, graphic language, or steamy settings. Send complete ms. Romances: 800 words; mysteries: 1,000 words. **Pays $1,000.**

TIPS The whole story should be sent when submitting fiction. Stories slanted for a particular holiday should be sent at least 6 months in advance. "Familiarize yourself totally with our format and style. Read at least a year's worth of *Woman's World* fiction. Analyze and dissect it. Regarding romances, scrutinize them not only for content but tone, mood, and sensibility."

WOMEN'S HEALTH

Rodale Inc., 400 South 10th St., Emmaus PA 18098. **E-mail:** womenshealth@rodale.com; whonline@womenshealthmag.com. **Website:** www.womenshealthmag.com. Magazine published 10 times/year for the woman who wants to reach a healthy, attractive weight. *Women's Health* reaches a new generation of women who don't like the way most women's magazines make them feel. Estab. 2005. Circ. 1.5 million. Accepts queries by e-mail. Accepts simultaneous submissions.

 Query before submitting.

ZINK

244 5th Ave., Suite 2205, New York NY 10001. (212)260-9725. **E-mail:** constance.white@zinkmediagroup.com. **Website:** www.zinkmagazine.com. **Contact:** Constance C.R. White, editor. *Zink* is a monthly fashion magazine catering to a savvy, well-cultured, and upscale audience. Accepts queries by e-mail. Accepts simultaneous submissions.

NONFICTION Query first. Guidelines available at www.zinkmagazine.com/submissions/.

TRADE JOURNALS

//

Many writers who pick up *Writer's Market* for the first time do so with the hope of selling an article to one of the popular, high-profile consumer magazines found on newsstands and in bookstores. Many of those writers are surprised to find an entire world of magazine publishing exists outside the realm of commercial magazines—trade journals. Writers who *have* discovered trade journals have found a market that offers the chance to publish regularly in subject areas they find interesting, editors who are typically more accessible than their commercial counterparts, and pay rates that rival those of the big-name magazines.

Trade journal is the general term for any publication focusing on a particular occupation or industry. Other terms used to describe the different types of trade publications are business, technical, and professional journals. They are read by truck drivers, bricklayers, farmers, fishermen, heart surgeons, and just about everyone else working in a trade or profession. Trade periodicals are sharply angled to the specifics of the professions on which they report. They offer business-related news, features, and service articles that will foster their readers' professional development.

Writers for trade journals have to either possess knowledge about the field in question or be able to report it accurately from interviews with those who do. Writers who have or can develop a good grasp of a specialized body of knowledge will find trade magazine editors who are eager to hear from them.

An ideal way to begin your foray into trade journals is to write for those that report on your present profession. If you don't have experience in a profession but can demonstrate an ability to understand (and write about) the intricacies and issues of a particular trade that interests you, editors will still be willing to hear from you.

ADVERTISING, MARKETING & PR

BRAND PACKAGING

BNP Media, 2401 W. Big Beaver Rd., Suite 700, Troy MI 48084. (248)362-3700. **Fax:** (847)362-0317. **E-mail:** kalkowskij@bnpmedia.com. **Website:** www.brandpackaging.com. **Contact:** John Kalkowski, editor-in-chief. **15% freelance written.** Magazine published 10 times/year covering how packaging can be a marketing tool. Publishes strategies and tactics to make products stand out on the shelf. Market is brand managers who are marketers but need to know something about packaging. Estab. 1997. Circ. 33,000. Byline given. Pays on acceptance. Publishes ms an average of 2 months after acceptance. Editorial lead time 3 months. Submit seasonal material 3 months in advance. Accepts queries by mail, fax. Accepts simultaneous submissions. Sample copy free.

NONFICTION Needs how-to, interview, new product. **Buys 10 mss/year.** Send complete ms. Length: 600-2,400 words. **Pays 40-50¢/word.**

PHOTOS State availability. Identification of subjects required. Reviews contact sheets, 35mm transparencies, 4x5 prints. Negotiates payment individually. Buys one-time rights.

COLUMNS/DEPARTMENTS Emerging Technology (new packaging technology), 600 words. **Buys 10 mss/year.** Query. **Pays $150-300.**

TIPS "Be knowledgeable on marketing techniques and be able to grasp packaging techniques. Be sure you focus on packaging as a marketing tool. Use concrete examples. We are not seeking case histories at this time."

DECA DIRECT

1908 Association Dr., Reston VA 20191. (703)860-5000. **E-mail:** info@deca.org. **E-mail:** christopher_young@deca.org. **Website:** www.decadirect.org. **Contact:** Christopher Young, editor in chief. **30% freelance written.** Quarterly magazine covering marketing, professional development, business, and career training during school year (no issues published May-August). *DECA Direct* is the membership magazine for DECA—The Association of Marketing Students, primarily ages 15-19 in all 50 states, the U.S. territories, Germany, and Canada. The magazine is delivered through the classroom. Students are interested in developing professional, leadership, and career skills.

Estab. 1947. Circ. 160,000. Byline given. Pays on publication. No kill fee. Editorial lead time 3 months. Submit seasonal material 4 months in advance. Accepts queries by e-mail. Accepts simultaneous submissions. Sample copy free online.

NONFICTION Needs essays, general interest, how-to, interview, personal experience. **Buys 10 mss/year.** Submit a paragraph description of your article by e-mail. Length: 500-1,000 words. **Pays $125 for assigned articles. Pays $100 for unsolicited articles.**

REPRINTS Send typed ms and information about when and where the material previously appeared. Pays 85% of amount paid for an original article.

COLUMNS/DEPARTMENTS Professional Development; Leadership, 500-1,000 words. **Buys 6 mss/year.** Send complete ms. **Pays $75-100.**

TIPS "Articles can be theme specific, but we accept a variety of articles that are appropriate for our readership on topics such as community service, leadership development, or professionalism. The primary readership of the magazine is compromised of high school students, and articles should be relevant to their needs and interests. In most cases, articles should not promote the products or services of a specific company or organization; however, you may use examples to convey concepts or principles."

FORMAT MAGAZINE

315 5th Ave. NW, St. Paul MN 55112. **Website:** www.formatmag.com. **90% freelance written.** Estab. 1954. Circ. 6,000. Byline given. Pays on publication. No kill fee. Editorial lead time 1 months. Accepts simultaneous submissions.

NONFICTION Needs general interest, historical, humor, interview, photo feature. **Buys 2 mss/year.** Length: 300-800 words. **Pays $25-50.**

PHOTOS Send photos. Identification of subjects required. Negotiates payment individually. Buys one-time rights.

COLUMNS/DEPARTMENTS Advertising (ad humor), 400 words. **Buys 12 mss/year. Pays $25-50.**

FILLERS Needs anecdotes, facts, gags, newsbreaks, short humor. **Buys 12 mss/year.** Length: 100-300 words. **Pays $10-25.**

MEDIA INC.

P.O. Box 24365, Seattle WA 98124-0365. (206)382-9220. **Fax:** (206)382-9437. **E-mail:** media@media-inc.com. **E-mail:** ksauro@media-inc.com. **Website:** www.media-inc.com. **Contact:** Katie Sauro. **30% free-**

lance written. Bimonthly magazine covering Northwest U.S. media, advertising, marketing, and creative-service industries. Audience is Northwest ad agencies, marketing professionals, media, and creative-service professionals. Estab. 1987. Circ. 10,000. Byline given. No kill fee. Accepts simultaneous submissions. Responds in 1 month to queries. Sample copy free online.

NONFICTION Special issues: *"Media Inc.* is always accepting new story ideas and article submissions for inclusion in the magazine and online. Help us stay up to date with what's going on around the Northwest by sending us your ideas, as well as editorial on your new campaign, new faces at your company, and recent awards or accomplishments." Query or send complete ms.

TIPS "It is best if writers live in the Pacific Northwest and can report on local news and events in Media Inc.'s areas of business coverage."

O'DWYER'S PR REPORT

271 Madison Ave., #600, New York NY 10016. (212)679-2471; (866)395-7710. **Fax:** (212)683-2750. **E-mail:** john@odwyerpr.com. **Website:** www.odwyerpr.com. **Contact:** John O'Dwyer, associate publisher/editor. Monthly magazine providing PR articles. *O'Dwyer's* has been covering public relations, marketing communications, and related fields for over 40 years. The company provides the latest news and information about PR firms and professionals, the media, corporations, legal issues, jobs, technology, and much more through its website, weekly newsletter, monthly magazine, directories, and guides. Many of the contributors are PR people publicizing themselves while analyzing something. Byline given. No kill fee. Accepts queries by mail. Accepts simultaneous submissions.

NONFICTION Needs opinion. Query. **Pays $250.**

PROMO MAGAZINE

Access Intelligence, 761 Main Avenue, Norwalk CT 06851. (203)899-8442. **E-mail:** podell@accessintel.com. **Website:** www.chiefmarketer.com/promotional-marketing. **Contact:** Patricia Odell, senior editor. **5% freelance written.** Monthly magazine covering promotion marketing. *Promo* serves marketers, and stories must be informative, well written, and familiar with the subject matter. Estab. 1987. Circ. 25,000. Byline given. Pays on publication. Offers 25% kill fee. Publishes ms an average of 2 months after acceptance. Editorial lead time 3 months. Submit seasonal material 3 months in advance. Accepts simultaneous submissions. Responds in 1 month to queries. Sample copy for $5.

NONFICTION Needs general interest, how-to, interview, new product. No general marketing stories not heavily involved in promotions. Generally does not accept unsolicited mss; query first. **Buys 6-10 mss/year.** Query with published clips. **Pays $1,000 maximum for assigned articles. Pays $500 maximum for unsolicited articles.**

PHOTOS State availability. Captions, identification of subjects, model releases required. Reviews contact sheets, negatives. Negotiates payment individually.

TIPS "Understand that our stories aim to teach marketing professionals about successful promotion strategies. Case studies or new promos have the best chance."

SIGN BUILDER ILLUSTRATED

Simmons-Boardman Publishing Corp., 55 Broad St., 26th Floor, New York NY 10004. (252)355-5806. **E-mail:** jwooten@sbpub.com; abray@sbpub.com. **Website:** www.signshop.com. **Contact:** Jeff Wooten, editor; Ashley Bray, associate editor. **40% freelance written.** Monthly magazine covering sign and graphic industry. *Sign Builder Illustrated* targets sign professionals where they work: on the shop floor. Topics cover the broadest spectrum of the sign industry, from design to fabrication, installation, maintenance, and repair. Readers own a similarly wide range of shops, including commercial, vinyl, sign erection and maintenance, electrical and neon, architectural, and awnings. Estab. 1987. Circ. 14,500. Byline given. Pays on acceptance. Offers 10% kill fee. Publishes ms an average of 3 months after acceptance. Editorial lead time 3 months. Submit seasonal material 4 months in advance. Accepts queries by mail, e-mail, fax, phone. Accepts simultaneous submissions. Responds in 1 month to queries. Sample copy and writer's guidelines free.

NONFICTION Needs historical, how-to, humor, interview, photo feature, technical. **Buys 50-60 mss/year.** Query. Length: 1,000-1,500 words. **Pays $250-550 for assigned articles.**

PHOTOS Send photos. Captions, identification of subjects required. Reviews 3x5 prints. Negotiates payment individually,. Buys all rights.

TIPS "Be very knowledgeable about a portion of the sign industry you are covering. We want our readers to come away from each article with at least 1 good idea, 1 new technique, or 1 more 'trick of the trade.' At the same time, we don't want a purely textbook listing of 'do this, do that.' Our readers enjoy *Sign Builder Illustrated* because the publication speaks to them in a clear and lively fashion, from 1 sign professional to another. We want to engage the reader who has been in the business for some time. While there might be a place for basic instruction in new techniques, our average paid subscriber has been in business over 20 years, employs over 7 people, and averages $800,000 in annual sales. These people aren't neophytes content with retread articles they can find anywhere. It's important for our writers to use anecdotes and examples drawn from the daily sign business."

SOCAL MEETINGS + EVENTS MAGAZINE

Tiger Oak Publications, One Tiger Oak Plaza, 900 S. Third St., Minneapolis MN 55415. **Fax:** (612)338-0532. **E-mail:** bobby.hart@tigeroak.com. **Website:** http://meetingsmags.com. **Contact:** Bobby Hart, managing editor. **80% freelance written.** Meetings + Events Media Group, including Minnesota Meetings + Events, Illinois Meetings + Events, Colorado Meetings & Events, Michigan Meetings + Events, California Meetings + Events, Texas Meetings + Events, Northwest Meetings + Events, Mountain Meetings, Pennsylvania Meetings + Evens and New Jersey Meetings + Events is a group of premier quarterly trade magazines for meetings planners and hospitality service providers throughout the US. Thesemagazines aim to report on and promote businesses involved in the meetings and events industry, covering current and emerging trends, people and venues in the meetings and events industry in their respective regions. Estab. 1993. Circ. approximately 20,000 per title. Byline given. Pays on acceptance. Offers 20% kill fee. Publishes ms an average of 4 months after acceptance. Editorial lead time 4-6 months. Submit seasonal material 6 months in advance. Accepts queries by mail. Accepts simultaneous submissions. Responds in 1-2 weeks to queries.

NONFICTION Needs general interest, historical, interview, new product, opinion, personal experience, photo feature, technical, travel. **Buys 30 mss/ year.** "Each query should tell us: What the story will be about; how you will tell the story (what sources you will use, how you will conduct research, etc.); why is the story pertinent to the market audience. Please

also attach PDFs of 3 published magazine articles." Length: 600-1,500 words. **The average department length story (4-700 words) pays about $2-300 and the average feature length story (1,000-1,200 words) pays up to $800, depending on the story. These rates are not guaranteed and vary.**

PHOTOS State availability. Identification of subjects, model releases required. Negotiates payment individually. Buys one-time rights.

COLUMNS/DEPARTMENTS Meet + Eat (restaurant reviews); Facility Focus (venue reviews); Regional Spotlight (city review), 1,000 words. **Buys 30 mss/ year.** Query with published clips. **Pays $400-600.**

TIPS "Familiarization with the meetings and events industry is critical, as well as knowing how to write for a trade magazine. Writers experienced in writing for the trade magazine business industry are preferred."

TEXAS MEETINGS + EVENTS

Tiger Oak Publications, One Tiger Oak Plaza, 900 S. 3rd St., Minneapolis MN 55401. (612)548-3180. **Fax:** (612)548-3181. **E-mail:** bobby.hart@tigeroak. com. **Website:** http://tx.meetingsmags.com. **Contact:** Bobby Hart, managing editor. **80% freelance written.** Quarterly magazine covering meetings and events industry. *Texas Meetings & Events* magazine is the premier trade publication for meetings planners and hospitality service providers in the state. This magazine aims to report on and promote businesses involved in the meetings and events industry. The magazine covers current and emerging trends, people and venues in the meetings and events industry in the state. Estab. 1993. Circ. 20,000. Byline given. Pays on acceptance. Offers 20% kill fee. Publishes ms an average of 4 months after acceptance. Editorial lead time 4-6 months. Submit seasonal material 6 months in advance. Accepts queries by mail. Accepts simultaneous submissions. Responds in 1-2 weeks to queries. Guidelines online.

NONFICTION Needs general interest, historical, interview, new product, opinion, personal experience, photo feature, technical, travel. **Buys 30 mss/year.** Query with published clips of 3 magazine articles. Length: 600-1,500 words. **Pays $400-800.**

PHOTOS State availability. Identification of subjects, model releases required. Negotiates payment individually. Buys one-time rights.

COLUMNS/DEPARTMENTS Meet + Eat (restaurant reviews); Facility Focus (venue reviews); Regional Spotlight (city review), 1,000 words. **Buys 30 mss/year.** Query with published clips. **Pays $400-600.**

TIPS "Familiarization with the meetings and events industry is critical, as well as knowing how to write for a trade magazine. Writers experienced in writing for the trade magazine business industry are preferred."

ART, DESIGN & COLLECTIBLES

AIRBRUSH ACTION MAGAZINE

Action, Inc., P.O. Box 438, Allenwood NJ 08720. (732)223-7878; (800)876-2472. **E-mail:** ceo@airbrushaction.com. **Website:** www.airbrushaction.com. **Contact:** Cliff Stieglitz, publisher. **80% freelance written.** Bimonthly magazine covering the spectrum of airbrush applications: automotive and custom paint applications, illustration, T-shirt airbrushing, fine art, automotive and sign painting, hobby/craft applications, wall murals, fingernails, temporary tattoos, artist profiles, reviews, and more. Estab. 1985. Circ. 35,000. Byline given. Pays 1 month after publication. Publishes ms an average of 6 months after acceptance. Editorial lead time 6 months. Submit seasonal material 6 months in advance. Accepts queries by mail, e-mail. Accepts simultaneous submissions.

NONFICTION Needs how-to, humor, inspirational, interview, new product, personal experience, technical. Doesn't want anything unrelated to airbrush. Query with published clips. **Pays 15¢/word.**

PHOTOS Digital images preferred. Send photos. Captions, identification of subjects, model releases required. Negotiates payment individually. Buys all rights.

COLUMNS/DEPARTMENTS Query with published clips.

TIPS "Send bio and writing samples. Send well-written technical information pertaining to airbrush art. We publish a lot of artist profiles—they all sound the same. Looking for new pizzazz!"

ANTIQUEWEEK

MidCountry Media, 27 N. Jefferson St., P.O. Box 90, Knightstown IN 46148. (800)876-5133, ext. 188. **Fax:** (800)695-8153. **E-mail:** rshallenberg@antiqueweek.com; tony@antiqueweek.com. **Website:** www.antiqueweek.com. **Contact:** Rachel Shallenberg, editor; Tony Gregory, publisher. **80% freelance written.** Weekly tabloid covering antiques and collectibles

with 3 editions: Eastern, Central, and National, plus the monthly *AntiqueWest. AntiqueWeek* has a wide range of readership from dealers and auctioneers to collectors, both advanced and novice. Readers demand accurate information presented in an entertaining style. Estab. 1968. Circ. 50,000. Byline given. Pays on publication. Offers 10% kill fee or $25. Submit seasonal material 1 month in advance. Accepts queries by mail, e-mail. Accepts simultaneous submissions. Sample copy free. Guidelines by e-mail.

NONFICTION Needs historical, how-to, interview, opinion, personal experience, antique show and auction reports, feature articles on particular types of antiques and collectibles. **Buys 400-500 mss/year.** Query. Length: 1,000-2,000 words. **Pays $50-250.**

REPRINTS Send electronic copy with rights for sale noted and information about when and where the material previously appeared.

PHOTOS All material must be submitted electronically via e-mail or on CD. Send photos. Identification of subjects required.

TIPS "Writers should know their topics thoroughly. Feature articles must be well researched and clearly written. An interview and profile article with a knowledgeable collector might be the break for a first-time contributor. We seek a balanced mix of information on traditional antiques and 20th-century collectibles."

THE APPRAISERS STANDARD

New England Appraisers Association, 6973 Crestridge Dr., Memphis TN 38119. (901)758-2659. **E-mail:** etuten551@aol.com. **Website:** www.newenglandappraisers.org. **Contact:** Edward Tuten, editor. **50% freelance written. Works with a small number of new/unpublished writers each year.** Quarterly publication covering the appraisals of antiques, art, collectibles, jewelry, coins, stamps, and real estate. Estab. 1980. Circ. 1,000. Short bio and byline given. Pays on publication. No kill fee. Publishes ms an average of 1 year after acceptance. Submit seasonal material 2 months in advance. Accepts queries by mail, e-mail. Accepts simultaneous submissions. Responds in 1 month to queries. Responds in 2 months to mss. Sample copy for 9x12 SAE with $1 postage. Guidelines for #10 SASE.

NONFICTION Needs interview, personal experience, technical, travel. Send complete ms. Length: 700 words. **Pays $60.**

REPRINTS "Send typed manuscript with rights for sale noted and information about when and where the material previously appeared."

PHOTOS Send photos. Identification of subjects required. Reviews negatives, prints. Offers no additional payment for photos accepted with ms. Buys one time rights.

TIPS "Interviewing members of the association for articles, reviewing, shows, and large auctions are all ways for writers who are not in the field to write articles for us. Articles should be geared to provide information which will help the appraisers with ascertaining value, detecting forgeries or reproductions, or simply providing advice on appraising the articles. I would like writers to focus on particular types of antiques: i.e. types of furniture, glass, artwork, etc., giving information on the history of this type of antique, good photos, recent sale prices, etc."

ART MATERIALS RETAILER

Fahy-Williams Publishing, Inc., 171 Reed St., P.O. Box 1080, Geneva NY 14456. (315)789-0458. **Fax:** (315)789-4263. **E-mail:** tmanzer@fwpi.com. **Website:** www.artmaterialsretailer.com. Publisher: J. Kevin Fahy (kfahy@fwpi.com). **Contact:** Tina Manzer, editorial director. **10% freelance written.** Quarterly magazine covering retail stores that sell art materials. Offers book reviews, retailer-recommended products, and profiles of stores from around the country. Estab. 1998. Byline given. Pays on publication. No kill fee. Editorial lead time 2 months. Submit seasonal material 3 months in advance. Accepts simultaneous submissions. Responds in 3 weeks to queries. Responds in 3 months to mss. Sample copy and writer's guidelines free.

NONFICTION Needs book excerpts, how-to, interview, personal experience. **Buys 2 mss/year.** Send complete ms. Length: 1,500-3,000 words. **Pays $50-250.**

PHOTOS State availability. Identification of subjects required. Reviews transparencies. Offers no additional payment for photos accepted with ms. Buys one-time rights.

FILLERS Needs anecdotes, facts, newsbreaks. **Buys 5 mss/year.** Length: 500-1,500 words. **Pays $50-125.**

TIPS "We like to review mss rather than queries. Artwork (photos, drawings, etc.) is a real plus. We (and our readers) enjoy practical, nuts-and-bolts, news-you-can-use articles."

HOW

F+W, a Content + eCommerce Company, 10151 Carver Rd., Suite 200, Blue Ash OH 45242. (513)531-2690. **Fax:** (513)531-2902. **E-mail:** editorial@howdesign.com. **Website:** www.howdesign.com. **75% freelance written.** Bi-monthly magazine covering graphic design profession. *HOW: Design Ideas at Work* strives to serve the business, technological and creative needs of graphic-design professionals. The magazine provides a practical mix of essential business information, up-to-date technological tips, the creative whys and hows behind noteworthy projects, and profiles of professionals who are impacting design. The ultimate goal of *HOW* is to help designers, whether they work for a design firm or for an inhouse design department, run successful, creative, profitable studios. Estab. 1985. Circ. 40,000. Byline given. Pays on acceptance. No kill fee. Accepts simultaneous submissions. Responds in 6 weeks to queries.

NONFICTION Special issues: Self-Promotion Annual (September/October); Business Annual (November/December); In-House Design Annual (January/February); International Annual of Design (March/April); Creativity/Paper/Stock Photography (May/June); Digital Design Annual (July/August). No how-to articles for beginning artists or fine-art-oriented articles. **Buys 40 mss/year.** Query with published clips and samples of subject's work, artwork, or design. Length: 1,500-2,000 words. **Pays $700-900.**

PHOTOS State availability. Captions required. Reviews information updated and verified. Buys one-time rights.

COLUMNS/DEPARTMENTS Creativity (focuses on creative exercises and inspiration) 1,200-1,500 words. In-House Issues (focuses on business and creativity issues for corporate design groups), 1,200-1,500 words. Business (focuses on business issue for design firm owners), 1,200-1, 500 words. **Number of columns: 35.** Query with published clips. **Pays $250-400.**

TIPS "We look for writers who can recognize graphic designers on the cutting-edge of their industry, both creatively and business-wise. Writers must have an eye for detail, and be able to relay *HOW*'s editorial style in an interesting, concise manner—without omitting any details. Showing you've done your homework on a subject—and that you can go beyond asking those same old questions—will give you a big advantage."

THE PASTEL JOURNAL

F+W, 10151 Carver Rd., Suite 200, Cincinnati OH 45242. (513)531-2690. **Fax:** (513)891-7153. **E-mail:** pjedit@fwcommunity.com. **Website:** www.pastel-journal.com. **Contact:** Anne Hevener, editor; Jessica Canterbury, managing editor. Bimonthly magazine covering pastel art. *Pastel Journal* is the only national magazine devoted to the medium of pastel. Addressing the working professional as well as passionate amateurs, *Pastel Journal* offers inspiration, information, and instruction to our readers. Estab. 1999. Circ. 22,000. Byline given. Pays on acceptance. Offers 25% kill fee. Publishes ms an average of 3-6 months after acceptance. Editorial lead time 6 months. Submit seasonal material 6 months in advance. Accepts queries by mail, e-mail. Accepts simultaneous submissions. Responds in 4-6 weeks to queries. Guidelines online.

NONFICTION Needs how-to, interview, new product, profile. Does not want articles that aren't art-related. Review magazine before submitting. Query with or without published clips. Length: 500-2,000 words. **Payment does not exceed $600.**

PHOTOS State availability of or send photos. Captions required. Reviews transparencies, prints, GIF/JPEG files. Offers no additional payment for photos accepted with ms. Buys all rights.

PRINT

F+W, a Content + eCommerce Company, 10151 Carver Rd., Suite 200, Blue Ash OH 45242. (513)531-2690. **E-mail:** info@printmag.com. **Website:** www.printmag.com. **Contact:** Zachary Petit, editor. **75% freelance written.** Quarterly magazine covering graphic design and visual culture. *PRINT*'s articles, written by design specialists and cultural critics, focus on the social, political and historical context of graphic design, and on the places where consumer culture and popular culture meet. Aims to produce a general interest magazine for professionals with engagingly written text and lavish illustrations. By covering a broad spectrum of topics, both international and local, *Print* tries to demonstrate the significance of design in the world at large. Estab. 1940. Circ. 45,000. Byline given. Pays on acceptance. Offers 25% kill fee. Publishes ms an average of 2 months after acceptance. Editorial lead time 3 months. Submit seasonal material 3 months in advance. Accepts queries by e-mail. Accepts simultaneous submissions. Responds in 2 weeks to queries. Responds in 1 month to mss.

NONFICTION Needs book excerpts, essays, interview, opinion, photo feature, profile, reviews. **Buys 35-40 mss/year.** Query with published clips. Length: 500-3,500 words. **Pays 50¢/word.**

COLUMNS/DEPARTMENTS Query with published clips. **Pays 50¢/word.**

TIPS "Be well versed in issues related to the field of graphic design; don't submit ideas that are too general or geared to nonprofessionals."

PROFESSIONAL ARTIST

Turnstile Media Group, 1500 Park Center Dr., Orlando FL 32835. (407)563-7000. **Fax:** (407)563-7099. **E-mail:** nhassanein@professionalartistmag.com. **Website:** www.professionalartistmag.com. **Contact:** Nada Hassanein, associate editor. **75% freelance written.** Monthly magazine. *Professional Artist* is dedicated to providing independent visual artists from all backgrounds with the insights, encouragement and business strategies they need to make a living with their artwork. Estab. 1986. Circ. 20,000. Pays on publication. No kill fee. Accepts simultaneous submissions. Sample print copy for $5. Guidelines online.

NONFICTION Needs essays, how-to, interview, cartoons, art law, including pending legislation that affects artists (copyright law, Internet regulations, etc.). Does not run reviews or art historical pieces, nor writing characterized by "critic-speak," philosophical hyperbole, psychological arrogance, politics, or New Age religion. Also, does not condone a get-rich-quick attitude. Send complete ms. **Pays $150-350.**

REPRINTS Send photocopy or typed ms and information about when and where the material previously appeared. Pays $50.

COLUMNS/DEPARTMENTS "If an artist or freelancer sends us good articles regularly, and based on results we feel that he is able to produce a column at least 3 times per year, we will invite him to be a contributing writer. If a gifted artist-writer can commit to producing an article on a monthly basis, we will offer him a regular column and the title contributing editor." Send complete ms.

TIPS "We strongly suggest that you read a copy of the publication before submitting a proposal. Most queries are rejected because they are too general for our audience."

TEXAS ARCHITECT

Texas Society of Architects, 500 Chicon St., Austin TX 78702. (512)478-7386. **Fax:** (512)478-0528. **Web-**

site: www.texasarchitect.org. **Contact:** Aaron Seward, editor. **30% freelance written. Mostly written by unpaid members of the professional society.** Bimonthly journal covering architecture and architects of Texas. *Texas Architect* is a highly visually-oriented look at Texas architecture, design, and urban planning. Articles cover varied subtopics within architecture. Readers are mostly architects and related building professionals. Estab. 1951. Circ. 12,500. Byline given. Pays on publication. No kill fee. Publishes ms an average of 3 months after acceptance. Submit seasonal material 4 months in advance. Accepts queries by mail, e-mail. Accepts simultaneous submissions. Responds in 6 weeks to queries. Guidelines online.

NONFICTION Needs interview, photo feature, technical, book reviews. Query with published clips. Length: 100-2,000 words. **Pays $50-100 for assigned articles.**

PHOTOS Send photos. Identification of subjects required. Reviews contact sheets, 35mm or 4x5 transparencies, 4x5 prints. Offers no additional payment for photos accepted with ms. Buys one-time rights.

COLUMNS/DEPARTMENTS News (timely reports on architectural issues, projects, and people), 100-500 words. **Buys 10 articles/year mss/year.** Query with published clips. **Pays $50-100.**

WATERCOLOR ARTIST

F+W, a Content + eCommerce Company, 10151 Carver Rd., Suite 200, Blue Ash OH 45242. (513)531-2690. **Fax:** (513)891-7153. **E-mail:** wcamag@fwmedia.com. **Website:** www.watercolorartistmagazine.com. **Contact:** Jennifer Hoffman, art director; Kelly Kane, editor. Bimonthly magazine covering water media arts. Estab. 1984. Circ. 44,000. Byline given. Pays on acceptance. Publishes ms an average of 3-6 months after acceptance. Editorial lead time 6 months. Submit seasonal material 6 months in advance. Accepts queries by mail. Accepts simultaneous submissions. Writer's guidelines available at www.artistsnetwork.com/contactus.

NONFICTION Needs book excerpts, essays, how-to, inspirational, interview, new product, personal experience. Does not want articles that aren't art-related. Review magazine before submitting. **Buys 36 mss/year.** Send query letter with images. Length: 350-2,500 words. **Pays $150-600.**

PHOTOS State availability of or send photos. Captions required. Reviews transparencies, prints, slides, GIF/JPEG files. Buys one-time rights.

AUTO & TRUCK

AUTO RESTORER

i5 Publishing, Inc., 3 Burroughs, Irvine CA 92618. (213)385-2222. **Fax:** (213)385-8565. **E-mail:** tkade@i5publishing.com. **Website:** www.autorestorermagazine.com. **Contact:** Ted Kade, editor. **85% freelance written.** Monthly magazine covering auto restoration. "Our readers own old cars, and they work on them. We help our readers by providing as much practical, how-to information as we can about restoration and old cars." Estab. 1989. Circ. 60,000. Pays on publication. Publishes mss 3 months after acceptance. Submit seasonal material 4 months in advance. Accepts queries by mail, e-mail, fax. Accepts simultaneous submissions. Responds in 2 months to queries. Sample copy: $7. Guidelines free.

NONFICTION Needs how-to, new product, photo feature. **Buys 60 mss/year.** Query first. Length: 250-2,000 words. **Pays $150/published page, including photos and illustrations.**

PHOTOS Emphasizes restoration of collector cars and trucks. Readers are 98% male, professional/technical/managerial, ages 35-65. Buys 47 photos from freelancers/issue; 564 photos/year. Send photos. Model/property release preferred. Photo captions required; include year, make, and model of car; identification of people in photo. Reviews photos with accompanying ms only. Reviews contact sheets, transparencies, 5x7 prints. Looks for "technically proficient or dramatic photos of various automotive subjects, auto portraits, detail shots, action photos, good angles, composition, and lighting. We're also looking for photos to illustrate how-to articles such as how to repair a damaged fender or how to repair a carburetor." Pays $50 for b&w cover; $35 for b&w inside. Pays on publication. Credit line given. Buys first North American serial rights.

TIPS "Interview the owner of a restored car. Present advice to others on how to do a similar restoration. Seek advice from experts. Go light on history and nonspecific details. Make it something that the magazine regularly uses. Do automotive how-tos."

BUSINESS FLEET

Bobit Publishing, 3520 Challenger St., Torrance CA 90503. (310)533-2400. **E-mail:** chris.brown@bobit. com. **Website:** www.businessfleet.com. **Contact:** Chris Brown, executive editor. **10% freelance written.** Bimonthly magazine covering businesses which operate 10-50 company vehicles. Estab. 2000. Circ. 100,000. Byline given. Pays on publication. Offers 25% kill fee. Publishes ms an average of 3 months after acceptance. Editorial lead time 2 months. Submit seasonal material 2 months in advance. Accepts queries by mail, e-mail, fax. Accepts simultaneous submissions. Responds in 3 weeks to queries; 2 months to mss. Sample copy and guidelines free.

NONFICTION Needs how-to, interview, new product, personal experience, photo feature, technical. **Buys 16 mss/year.** Query with published clips. Length: 500-2,000 words. **Pays $100-400.**

PHOTOS State availability. Captions required. Reviews 3x5 prints. Negotiates payment individually. Buys one-time, reprint, and electronic rights.

TIPS "Our mission is to educate our target audience on more economical and efficient ways of operating company vehicles, and to inform the audience of the latest vehicles, products, and services available to small commercial companies. Be knowledgeable about automotive and fleet-oriented subjects."

FENDERBENDER

DeWitt Publishing, 571 Snelling Avenue North, St. Paul MN 55104. (651)224-6207. **Fax:** (651)224-6212. **E-mail:** news@fenderbender.com; jweyer@fenderbender.com. **Website:** www.fenderbender.com. **Contact:** Jake Weyer, editor. **50% freelance written.** Monthly magazine covering automotive collision repair. Estab. 1999. Circ. 58,000. Byline given. Pays on publication. Offers 20% kill fee. Publishes ms an average of 2 months after acceptance. Editorial lead time 3 months. Submit seasonal material 6 months in advance. Accepts queries by e-mail. Accepts simultaneous submissions. Responds in 1-2 months to queries; 2-3 months to mss. Sample copy for SAE with 10x13 envelope and 6 first-class stamps. Guidelines online.

NONFICTION Needs expose, how-to, inspirational, interview, technical. Does not want personal narratives or any other first-person stories. No poems or creative writing mss. Query with published clips. Length: 1,800-2,500 words. **Pays 25-60¢/word.**

PHOTOS Send photos. Captions, identification of subjects, model releases required. Reviews PDF, GIF/JPEG files. Offers no additional payment for photos accepted with ms. Buys one-time rights.

COLUMNS/DEPARTMENTS Q&A, 600 words; Shakes, Rattles & Rollovers; Rearview Mirror. Query with published clips. **Pays 25-35¢/word.**

TIPS "Potential writers need to be knowledgeable about the auto collision repair industry. They should also know standard business practices and be able to explain to shop owners how they can run their businesses better."

FLEETSOLUTIONS

NAFA Fleet Management Association, 125 Village Blvd., Suite 200, Princeton NJ 08540. (609)986-1063; (609)720-0882. **Fax:** (609)452-8004. **E-mail:** publications@nafa.org; ddunphy@nafa.org. **Website:** www.nafa.org. **Contact:** Donald W. Dunphy, communications manager/editor. **10% freelance written.** Magazine published 6 times/year covering automotive fleet management. Generally focuses on car, van, and light-duty truck management in US and Canadian corporations, government agencies, and utilities. Editorial emphasis is on general automotive issues; improving jobs skills, productivity, and professionalism; legislation and regulation; alternative fuels; safety; interviews with prominent industry personalities; technology; association news; public service fleet management; and light-duty truck fleet management. Estab. 1957. Circ. 4,000. Bylines provided. Pays on publication. No kill fee. Publishes ms an average of 4 months after acceptance. Editorial lead time 2 months. Accepts queries by mail. Accepts simultaneous submissions. Responds in 1 month to queries. Sample copy online.

NONFICTION Needs interview, technical. **Buys 24 mss/year.** Query with published clips. Length: 500-3,000 words. **Pays $500 maximum.**

PHOTOS State availability. Reviews electronic images.

OVERDRIVE

Randall-Reilly Publishing, 3200 Rice Mine Rd. NE, Tuscaloosa AL 35406. (205)349-2990. **Fax:** (205)750-8070. **E-mail:** mheine@rrpub.com. **Website:** www.etrucker.com. **Contact:** Max Heine, editorial director. **5% freelance written.** Monthly magazine for independent truckers. Estab. 1961. Circ. 100,000. Byline given. Pays on publication. Offers 10% kill fee.

Publishes ms an average of 2 months after acceptance. Accepts simultaneous submissions. Responds in 2 months to queries. Sample copy for 9x12 SASE. Digital copy online.

NONFICTION Needs essays, expose, how-to, interview, personal experience, photo feature, technical. Send complete ms. Length: 500-2,500 words. **Pays $300-1,500 for assigned articles.**

PHOTOS Photo fees negotiable. Buys all rights.

TIPS "Talk to independent truckers. Develop a good knowledge of their concerns as small-business owners, truck drivers, and individuals. We prefer articles that quote experts, people in the industry, and truckers, to first-person expositions on a subject. Get straight facts. Look for good material on truck safety, on effects of government regulations, and on rates and business relationships between independent truckers, brokers, carriers, and shippers."

RVBUSINESS

G&G Media Group, 2901 E. Bristol St., Suite B, Elkhart IN 46514. (574)266-7980, ext. 13. **Fax:** (574)266-7984. **E-mail:** bhampson@rvbusiness.com; bhampson@g-gmediagroup.com. **Website:** www.rv-business.com. **Contact:** Bruce Hampson, editor. **50% freelance written.** Bimonthly magazine. *RVBusiness* caters to a specific audience of people who manufacture, sell, market, insure, finance, service and supply, components for recreational vehicles. Estab. 1972. Circ. 21,000. Byline given. Pays on acceptance. Offers kill fee. Publishes ms an average of 2 months after acceptance. Editorial lead time 2 months. Accepts simultaneous submissions. Sample copy free.

NONFICTION Needs new product, photo feature, industry news and features. No general articles without specific application to market. **Buys 50 mss/year.** Query with published clips. Length: 125-2,200 words. **Pays $50-1,000.**

COLUMNS/DEPARTMENTS Top of the News (RV industry news), 75-400 words; Business Profiles, 400-500 words; Features (indepth industry features), 800-2,000 words. **Buys 50 mss/year.** Query. **Pays $50-1,000.**

TIPS "Query. Send 1 or several ideas and a few lines letting us know how you plan to treat it/them. We are always looking for good authors knowledgeable in the RV industry or related industries. We need more articles that are brief, factual, hard hitting, and business oriented. Review other publications in the field, including enthusiast magazines."

⊙ TIRE NEWS

Rousseau Automotive Communication, 455, Notre-Dame East, Suite 311, Montreal QC H2Y 1C9 Canada. (514)289-0888; 1-877-989-0888. **Fax:** (514)289-5151. **E-mail:** info@autosphere.ca. **E-mail:** news@autosphere.ca. **Website:** www.autosphere.ca. Bimonthly magazine covering the Canadian tire industry. *Tire News* focuses on education/training, industry image, management, new tires, new techniques, marketing, HR, etc. Estab. 2004. Circ. 18,725. Byline given. Pays on publication. Publishes ms an average of 2 months after acceptance. Editorial lead time 2 months. Submit seasonal material 2 months in advance. Accepts simultaneous submissions. Responds in 2 weeks to queries. Responds in 2 months to mss. Sample copy free. Guidelines by e-mail.

NONFICTION Needs general interest, how-to, inspirational, interview, new product, technical. Does not want opinion pieces. **Buys 5 mss/year.** Query with published clips. Length: 550-610 words. **Pays up to $200 (Canadian).**

PHOTOS Send photos. Captions required. Reviews GIF/JPEG files. Offers no additional payment for photos accepted with ms. Buys all rights.

FILLERS Needs facts. **Buys 2 mss/year.** Length: 550-610 words. **Pays $0-200.**

⊙ WESTERN CANADA HIGHWAY NEWS

Craig Kelman & Associates, 2020 Portage Ave., 3rd Floor, Winnipeg MB R3J 0K4 Canada. (204)985-9785. **Fax:** (204)985-9795. **E-mail:** terry@kelman.ca. **Website:** highwaynews.ca. **Contact:** Terry Ross, editor. **30% freelance written.** Quarterly magazine covering trucking. The official magazine of the Alberta, Saskatchewan, and Manitoba trucking associations. As the official magazine of the trucking associations in Alberta, Saskatchewan and Manitoba, *Western Canada Highway News* is committed to providing leading edge, timely information on business practices, technology, trends, new products/services, legal and legislative issues that affect professionals in Western Canada's trucking industry. Estab. 1995. Circ. 4,500. Byline given. Pays on publication. No kill fee. Publishes ms an average of 2 months after acceptance. Editorial lead time 3 months. Submit seasonal material 3 months in advance. Accepts simultaneous submissions. Responds in 1 month. Sample copy for 10x13 SAE with 1 IRC. Guidelines for #10 SASE.

NONFICTION Needs essays, general interest, how-to, interview, new product, opinion, personal experience, photo feature, technical, profiles in excellence (bios of trucking or associate firms enjoying success). **Buys 8-10 mss/year.** Query. Length: 500-3,000 words. **Pays 18-25¢/word.**

PHOTOS State availability. Identification of subjects required. Reviews 4x6 prints. Buys one-ime rights.

COLUMNS/DEPARTMENTS Safety (new safety innovation/products), 500 words; Trade Talk (new products), 300 words. Query. **Pays 18-25¢/word.**

TIPS "Our publication is fairly time sensitive regarding issues affecting the trucking industry in Western Canada. Current 'hot' topics are international trucking, security, driver fatigue, health and safety, emissions control, and national/international highway systems."

AVIATION & SPACE

AEROSAFETY WORLD MAGAZINE

Flight Safety Foundation, 701 N. Fairfax St., Suite 4250, Alexandria VA 22314-2058. (703)739-6700. **Fax:** (703)739-6708. **E-mail:** jackman@flightsafety.org. **Website:** www.flightsafety.org. **Contact:** Frank Jackman, vice president of communications. Monthly newsletter covering safety aspects of airport operations. Full-color monthly magazine offers in-depth analysis of important safety issues facing the industry, with emphasis on timely news coverage in a convenient format and eye-catching contemporary design. Estab. 2006. Pays on publication. Accepts queries by mail, e-mail. Guidelines available online.

NONFICTION Needs technical. Query. **Pays $300-1,500.**

PHOTOS Pays $75 for each piece of original art.

TIPS "Few aviation topics are outside its scope."

AVIATION INTERNATIONAL NEWS

AIN Publications, 214 Franklin Ave., Midland Park NJ 07432. (201)444-5075. **Fax:** (201)251-2106. **E-mail:** nmoll@ainonline.com. **E-mail:** nmoll@ainonline.com. **Website:** www.ainonline.com. **Contact:** Nigel Moll, editor. **30% freelance written.** Monthly magazine covering business and commercial aviation with news features, special reports, aircraft evaluations and surveys on business aviation worldwide, written for business pilots and industry professionals. Sister print products include daily onsite issues published at 6 conventions and 4 international air shows. Electronic products include four-times-weekly AINalerts, once-weekly AIN Air Transport Perspective and AIN Defense Perspective, and AINonline website. "While the heartbeat of *AIN* is driven by the news it carries, the human touch is not neglected. We pride ourselves on our people stories about the industry's 'movers and shakers' and others in aviation who make a difference." Estab. 1972. Circ. 40,000. Byline given. Pays on acceptance and upon receipt of writer's invoice. Offers variable kill fee. Publishes ms an average of 2 months after acceptance. Editorial lead time 2 months. Submit seasonal material 3 months in advance. Accepts queries by mail, e-mail, fax. Responds in 6 weeks to queries; 2 months to mss. Sample copy for $10.

NONFICTION Needs how-to, interview, new product, opinion, personal experience, photo feature, technical. No place for puff pieces. "Our readers expect serious, real news. We don't pull any punches. *AIN* is not a 'good news' publication; it tells the story, both good and bad." **Buys 150-200 mss/year.** Query with published clips. Do not send mss by e-mail unless requested. Length: 200-3,000 words. **Pays 45¢/word to first timers, higher rates to proven *AIN* freelancers.**

PHOTOS Send photos. Captions required. Digital photos must be high-res (300 dpi). Reviews contact sheets, transparencies, prints, TIFF files (300 dpi). Negotiates payment individually. Buys one-time rights.

TIPS "Our core freelancers are professional pilots with good writing skills, or good journalists and reporters with an interest in aviation (some with pilot certificates) or technical experts in the aviation industry. The ideal *AIN* writer has an intense interest in and strong knowledge of aviation, a talent for writing news stories, and journalistic cussedness. Hit me with a strong news story relating to business aviation that takes me by surprise—something from your local area or area of expertise. Make it readable, fact-filled and in the inverted-pyramid style. Double-check facts and names. Interview the right people. Send me good, clear photos and illustrations. Send me well written, logically ordered copy. Do this for me consistently and we may take you along on our staff to 1 of the conventions in the U.S. or an airshow in Paris, Singapore, London or Dubai."

PROFESSIONAL PILOT

Queensmith Communications Corp., 5290 Shawnee Road, Suite 201, Alexandria VA 22312. (703)370-0606. **Fax:** (703)370-7082. **E-mail:** editor@propilotmag.com; editorial@propilotmag.com. **E-mail:** rafael@propilotmag.com. **Website:** www.propilotmag.com. **Contact:** Murray Smith, editor/publisher; Rafael Henriquez, associate editor. **75% freelance written.** Monthly magazine covering corporate, noncombat government, law enforcement, and various other types of professional aviation. The typical reader of *Professional Pilot* has a sophisticated grasp of piloting/aviation knowledge and is interested in articles that help him/her do the job better or more efficiently. Estab. 1967. Circ. 40,000. Byline given. Pays on publication. Offers kill fee. Kill fee negotiable. Publishes ms an average of 2-3 months after acceptance. Accepts queries by mail, e-mail. Accepts simultaneous submissions.

NONFICTION Buys 40 mss/year. Query. Length: 750-2,500 words. **Pays $200-1,000, depending on length. A fee for the article will be established at the time of assignment.**

PHOTOS Prefers transparencies or high resolution 300 JPEG digital images. Send photos. Captions, identification of subjects required. Additional payment for photos negotiable. Buys all rights.

TIPS "Query first. Freelancer should be a professional pilot or have background in aviation. Authors should indicate relevant aviation experience and pilot credentials (certificates, ratings and hours). We place a greater emphasis on corporate operations and pilot concerns."

BEAUTY & SALON

ASCP SKIN DEEP

Associated Skin Care Professionals, 25188 Genesee Trail Rd., Suite 200, Golden CO 80401. (800)789-0411. **E-mail:** editor@ascpskincare.com; getconnected@ascpskincare.com. **Website:** www.ascpskincare.com. **Contact:** Mary Abel, editor. **80% freelance written.** Bimonthly member magazine of Associated Skin Care Professionals (ASCP), covering technical, educational, and business information for estheticians with an emphasis on solo practitioners and spa/salon employees or independent contractors. Audience is the U.S. individual skin care practitioner who may work on her own and/or in a spa or salon setting. Magazine keeps her up to date on skin care trends and techniques and ways to earn more income doing waxing, facials, peels, microdermabrasion, body wraps, and other skin treatments. Product-neutral stories may include novel spa treatments within the esthetician scope of practice. Does not cover mass-market retail products, hair care, nail care, physician-only treatments/products, cosmetic surgery, or invasive treatments like colonics or ear candling. Successful stories have included how-tos on paraffin facials, aromatherapy body wraps, waxing tips, how to read ingredient labels, how to improve word-of-mouth advertising, and how to choose an online scheduling software package. Estab. 2003. Circ. 14,000+. Byline given. Pays on acceptance. No kill fee. Publishes ms an average of 4-6 months after acceptance. Editorial lead time 4-5 months. Submit seasonal material 7 months in advance. Accepts queries by e-mail. Accepts simultaneous submissions. Responds in 2-4 weeks to queries. Sample copy online at www.ascp-skindeepdigital.com.

NONFICTION Needs how-to. "We don't run general consumer beauty material or products, and very rarely run a new product that is available through retail outlets. 'New' products means introduced in the last 12 months. We do not run industry personnel announcements or stories on individual spas/salons or getaways. We don't cover hair or nails." **Buys 12 mss/year.** Query. Length: 1,200-1,600 words. **Pays $75-300 for assigned articles.**

TIPS "Visit website to read previous issues and learn about what we do. Submit a brief query with an idea to determine if you are on the right track. State specifically what value this has to estheticians and their work/income. Please note that we do not publish fashion, nails, hair, or consumer-focused articles."

BEAUTY STORE BUSINESS

Creative Age Communications, 7628 Densmore Ave., Van Nuys CA 91406. (818)782-7328 or (800)442-5667. **E-mail:** khenderson@creativeage.com. **Website:** www.beautystorebusiness.com. **Contact:** Kim Henderson, executive editor; Breanna Armstrong, managing editor. **50% freelance written.** Monthly magazine covering beauty store business management, news, and beauty products. The primary readers of the publication are owners, managers, and buyers at open-to-the-public beauty stores, including general-market and multicultural market-oriented ones with or without salon services. Secondary readers are those at beauty stores only open to salon industry professionals. Also goes to beauty distributors. Estab. 1994. Circ. 15,000. Byline given. Pays on acceptance. Offers negotiable kill fee. Publishes ms an average of 3 months after acceptance. Editorial lead time 3 months. Submit seasonal material 4 months in advance. Accepts queries by mail, e-mail. Accepts simultaneous submissions. Responds in 2 weeks, if interested. Sample copy free.

NONFICTION Needs how-to, interview. **Buys 20-30 mss/year.** Query. Length: 1,800-2,200 words. **Pays $250-525 for assigned articles.**

PHOTOS Do not send computer art electronically. State availability. Captions, identification of subjects required. Reviews transparencies, computer art (artists work on Macs, request 300 dpi, on CD or Zip disk, saved as JPEG, TIFF, or EPS). Negotiates payment individually. Buys all rights.

✪ COSMETICS

Rogers Publishing Limited, 420 Britannia Road East, Suite 102, Mississauga ON L4Z 3L5 Canada. (905)890-5161. **E-mail:** jhicks@cctfa.com. **Website:** www.cosmeticsmag.com. **Contact:** Jim Hicks. **10% freelance written.** Bimonthly magazine covering cosmetics for industry professionals. Estab. 1972. Circ. 13,000. Byline given. Pays on acceptance. Offers 50% kill fee. Publishes ms an average of 3 months after acceptance. Editorial lead time 4 months. Submit seasonal material 4 months in advance. Accepts queries by mail. Accepts simultaneous submissions. Responds in 1 month to queries. Sample copy for $6 (Canadian) and 8% GST.

NONFICTION Needs general interest, interview, photo feature. **Buys 1 mss/year.** Query. Length: 250-1,200 words. **Pays 25¢/word.**

PHOTOS Send photos. Captions, identification of subjects, model releases required. Reviews 2 1/2 up to 8x10 transparencies, 4x6 up to 8x10 prints, 35mm slides; e-mail pictures in 300 dpi JPEG format. Offers no additional payment for photos accepted with ms. Buys all rights.

COLUMNS/DEPARTMENTS "All articles assigned on a regular basis from correspondents and columnists that we know personally from the industry."

TIPS "Must have broad knowledge of the Canadian cosmetics, fragrance, and toiletries industry and retail business. 99.9% of freelance articles are assigned

by the editor to writers involved with the Canadian cosmetics business."

DAYSPA

Creative Age Publications, 7628 Densmore Ave., Van Nuys CA 91406. (818)782-7328, ext. 301. **Fax:** (818)782-7450. **Website:** www.dayspamagazine.com. **Contact:** Lesley McCave, executive editor. **50% freelance written.** Monthly magazine covering the business of day spas, multiservice/skincare salons, and resort/hotel spas. *Dayspa* includes only well-targeted business and trend articles directed at the owners and managers. It serves to enrich, enlighten, and empower spa/salon professionals. Estab. 1996. Circ. 31,000. Byline given. Pays on acceptance. No kill fee. Publishes ms an average of 4 months after acceptance. Editorial lead time 4 months. Submit seasonal material 4 months in advance. Accepts queries by online submission form. Accepts simultaneous submissions. Responds in 2 months to queries. Sample copy: $5.

NONFICTION **Buys 40 mss/year.** Query. Length: 1,500-1,800 words. **Pays $150-500.**

PHOTOS Send photos. Identification of subjects, model releases required. Negotiates payment individually. Buys one-time rights.

COLUMNS/DEPARTMENTS Legal Pad (legal issues affecting salons/spas); Money Matters (financial issues); Management Workshop (spa management issues); Health Wise (wellness trends), all 1,200-1,500 words. **Buys 20 mss/year.** Query. **Pays $150-400.**

MASSAGE MAGAZINE

820 A1A N. Highway, Suite W18, Ponte Vedra Beach FL 32082. **E-mail:** kmenehan@massagemag.com. **E-mail:** kmenehan@massagemag.com. **Website:** www.massagemag.com. **Contact:** Karen Menehan. **20% freelance written.** Magazine about massage and other touch therapies published 10-12 times/year. Readers are professional therapists who have been in practice for several years. About 80% are self-employed; 95% live in the U.S. The techniques they practice include Swedish, sports, and geriatric massage and energy work. Readers work in settings ranging from home-based studios to spas to integrated clinics. Readers care deeply that massage is portrayed in a professional manner. Estab. 1985. Circ. 50,000. Byline given. Pays the month of publication. Offers kill fee. Publishes ms an average of 1-3 months after submission. Editorial lead time 1 month. Advance time 1 month. Accepts queries by e-mail. Responds in 2 weeks to queries.

Do not send ms without querying first. Sample copy: $6.95; however; sample articles available via e-mail. Guidelines available by request.

NONFICTION Needs general interest, interview, profile, News: hard news, features and profiles. "We do not publish humorous travel pieces about unusual massage experiences." **Buys 12 mss/year.** Length: 700-1,500 words for news; 1,600 words for features. **Pays $80-200.**

PHOTOS Send photos with submission via e-mail. Identification of subjects. Identification of photographer. Buys one-time rights.

COLUMNS/DEPARTMENTS Profiles; News and Current Events; Practice Building (business); Technique; Mind/Body/Spirit. Length: 200-2,500 words. See website for details.

FILLERS Needs facts, newsbreaks.

TIPS "Our readers seek practical information on how to help their clients and make their businesses more successful, as well as feature articles that place massage therapy in a positive or inspiring light. Since most of our readers are professional therapists, we do not publish articles on topics like 'How Massage Can Help You Relax'; nor do we publish humorous essays or travel essays."

NAILPRO

Creative Age Publications, 7628 Densmore Ave., Van Nuys CA 91406. (800)442-5667; (818)782-7328. **Fax:** (818)782-7450. **E-mail:** nailpro@creativeage.com. **Website:** www.nailpro.com. **Contact:** Stephanie Lavery, executive editor. **20% freelance written.** Monthly magazine written for manicurists and salon owners working as an independent contractor or in a full-service salon or nails-only salons. Estab. 1989. Circ. 65,000. Byline given. Pays on acceptance. 25% kill fee. Publishes ms an average of 6 months after acceptance. Editorial lead time 3 months. Submit seasonal material 3 months in advance. Accepts queries by e-mail. Accepts simultaneous submissions. Responds in 6 weeks to queries only if interested. Sample copy: $2 and 9x12 SASE.

NONFICTION Needs book excerpts, how-to, humor, inspirational, interview, personal experience, photo feature, profile, technical. No general interest articles or business articles not geared to the nail-care industry. **Buys 50 mss/year.** Query. Length: 1,000-3,000 words. **Pays $150-450.**

PHOTOS Send photos. Identification of subjects, model releases required. Reviews transparencies, prints. Negotiates payment individually. Pays on acceptance. Buys one-time rights for print and web.

COLUMNS/DEPARTMENTS Business (articles on building salon business, marketing and advertising, dealing with employees), 1,500-2,500 words; Attitudes (aspects of operating a nail salon and trends in the nail industry), 1,200-2,500 words. **Buys 50 mss/year.** Query. **Pays $250-350.**

$ $ $ ⊘ NAILS

Bobit Business Media, 3520 Challenger St., Torrance CA 90503. (310)533-2457. **Fax:** (310)533-2507. **E-mail:** judy.lessin@bobit.com. **Website:** www.nailsmag.com. **Contact:** Judy Lessin, features editor. **10% freelance written.** Monthly magazine. *NAILS* seeks to educate its readers on new techniques and products, nail anatomy and health, customer relations, working safely and ergonomically, salon sanitation, and the business aspects of running a salon. Estab. 1983. Circ. 55,000. Byline given. Pays on acceptance. No kill fee. Editorial lead time 3 months. Submit seasonal material 4 months in advance. Accepts queries by e-mail. Accepts simultaneous submissions. Responds in 1 month to queries. Visit website to view past issues.

NONFICTION Needs historical, how-to, inspirational, interview, personal experience, photo feature, profile, technical. No articles on one particular product, company profiles, or articles slanted toward a particular company or manufacturer. **Buys 20 mss/year.** Query with published clips. Length: 750-1,600 words. **Pays $100-350.**

PHOTOS State availability. Captions, identification of subjects, model releases required. Reviews contact sheets, transparencies, prints (any standard size acceptable). Rarely buys unsolicited photos. Buys all rights.

TIPS "Send clips and query; *do not send unsolicited manuscripts*. We would like to see fresh and unique angles on business, health, or technical topics. Topics must be geared specifically to salon owners and nail technicians. Focus on an innovative business idea or unique point of view. Articles from experts on specific business issues—insurance, handling difficult employees, cultivating clients, navigating social media—are encouraged."

PULSE MAGAZINE

HOST Communications Inc., 2365 Harrodsburg Rd., Suite A325, Lexington KY 40504. (859)226-4326. **Fax:** (859)226-4445. **E-mail:** mae.manacap-johnson@ispastaff.com. **Website:** www.experienceispa.com/media/pulse-magazine. **Contact:** Mae Manacap-Johnson, editor. **20% freelance written.** Magazine published 10 times/year covering spa industry. *Pulse* is the magazine for the spa professional. As the official publication of the International SPA Association, its purpose is to advance the business of the spa professionals by informing them of the latest trends and practices and promoting the wellness aspects of spa. *Pulse* connects people, nurtures their personal and professional growth, and enhances their ability to network and succeed in the spa industry. Estab. 1991. Circ. 5,300. Byline given. Pays on publication. Publishes ms an average of 1 month after acceptance. Editorial lead time 3 months. Submit seasonal material 4 months in advance. Accepts queries by e-mail. Accepts simultaneous submissions. Sample copy for #10 SASE. Guidelines by e-mail.

NONFICTION Needs general interest, how-to, interview, new product. Does not want articles focused on spas that are not members of ISPA, consumer-focused articles (market is the spa industry professional), or features on hot tubs ("not *that* spa industry"). **Buys 8-10 mss/year.** Query with published clips. Length: 800-2,000 words. **Pays $250-500.**

PHOTOS Send photos. Captions required. Reviews GIF/JPEG files. Negotiates payment individually. Buys one-time rights.

TIPS "Understand the nuances of association publishing (different than consumer and B2B). Send published clips, not Word documents. Experience in writing for health and wellness market is helpful. Only feature ISPA member companies in the magazine; visit our website to learn more about our industry and to see if your pitch includes member companies before making contact."

SKIN INC. MAGAZINE

Allured Business Media, P.O. Box 3009, Northbrook IL 60065. (1-800)362-2192. **Fax:** (1-847)291-4816. **E-mail:** kanderson@allured.com. **Website:** www.skininc.com. **Contact:** Katie Anderson, managing editor. **30% freelance written.** Magazine published 12 times/year as an educational resource for skin care professionals interested in business solutions, treat-ment techniques, and skin science. Estab. 1988. Circ. 30,000. Byline given. Pays on publication. No kill fee. Publishes ms an average of 6 months after acceptance. Editorial lead time 6 months. Submit seasonal material 1 year in advance. Accepts queries by mail, e-mail, fax, phone. Accepts simultaneous submissions. Responds in 3 weeks to queries; 1 month to mss. Sample copy and guidelines free.

NONFICTION Needs general interest, how-to, interview, personal experience, technical. **Buys 6 mss/year.** Query with published clips. Length: 2,000 words. **Pays $100-300 for assigned articles. Pays $50-200 for unsolicited articles.**

PHOTOS State availability. Captions, identification of subjects, model releases required. Reviews 3x5 prints. Offers no additional payment for photos accepted with ms. Buys one-time rights.

COLUMNS/DEPARTMENTS Finance (tips and solutions for managing money), 2,000-2,500 words; Personnel (managing personnel), 2,000-2,500 words; Marketing (marketing tips for salon owners), 2,000-2,500 words; Retail (retailing products and services in the salon environment), 2,000-2,500 words. Query with published clips. **Pays $50-200.**

FILLERS Needs facts, newsbreaks. **Buys Buys 6 mss/year. mss/year.** Length: 250-500 words. **Pays $50-100.**

TIPS "Have an understanding of the professional spa industry."

BEVERAGES & BOTTLING

⚙ BAR & BEVERAGE BUSINESS MAGAZINE

Mercury Publications, 1313 Border St., Unit 16, Winnipeg MB R3H 0X4 Canada. (204)954-2085, ext. 213. **Fax:** (204)954-2057. **E-mail:** edufault@mercurypublications.ca. **Website:** www.barandbeverage.com. **Contact:** Elaine Dufault, associate publisher and national account manager. **33% freelance written.** Bimonthly magazine providing information on the latest trends, happenings, and buying/selling of beverages and product merchandising. Estab. 1998. Circ. 15,000+. Byline given. Pays 30-45 days from receipt of invoice. Offers 33% kill fee. Submit seasonal material 3 months in advance. Accepts simultaneous submissions. Sample copy and writer's guidelines free or by e-mail.

○ Does not accept queries for specific stories. Assigns stories to Canadian writers.

NONFICTION Needs how-to, interview. Does not want industry reports, profiles on companies. Query with published clips. Length: 500-9,000 words. **Pays 25-35¢/word.**

PHOTOS State availability. Captions required. Reviews negatives; transparencies; 3x5 prints; JPEG, EPS, or TIFF files. Negotiates payment individually. Buys all rights.

COLUMNS/DEPARTMENTS Out There (bar and beverage news in various parts of the country), 100-500 words. Query. **Pays up to $100.**

MICHIGAN HOSPITALITY REVIEW

Michigan Licensed Beverage Association, 101 S. Washington Sq., Suite 800, Lansing MI 48933. (800)292-2896; (517)374-9611. **Fax:** (517)374-1165. **E-mail:** editor@mlba.org; mdoerr@mlba.org. **Website:** www.mlba.org. **Contact:** Mason Doerr, editor. **40-50% freelance written.** Monthly trade magazine devoted to the beer, wine, and spirits industry in Michigan. It is dedicated to serving those who make their living serving the public and the state through the orderly and responsible sale of beverages. Estab. 1983. Circ. 4,200. Pays on publication. No kill fee. Editorial lead time 3 months. Submit seasonal material 3 months in advance. Accepts queries by mail, e-mail. Accepts simultaneous submissions. Responds in 2 weeks to queries. Responds in 1 month to mss. Sample copy for $5 or online.

NONFICTION Needs essays, general interest, historical, how-to, humor, interview, new product, opinion, personal experience, photo feature, technical. **Buys 24 mss/year.** Send complete ms. Length: 1,000 words. **Pays $20-200.**

COLUMNS/DEPARTMENTS Open to essay content ideas. Interviews (legislators, others), 750-1,000 words; personal experience (waitstaff, customer, bartenders), 500 words. **Buys 12 mss/year.** Send complete ms. **Pays $25-100.**

TIPS "We are particularly interested in nonfiction concerning responsible consumption/serving of alcohol. We are looking for product reviews, company profiles, personal experiences, and news articles that would benefit our audience. Our audience is a busy group of business owners and hospitality professionals striving to obtain pertinent information that is not too wordy."

SANTÉ MAGAZINE

On-Premise Communications, 160 Benmont Ave., Suite 92, Third Floor, West Wing, Bennington VT 05201. (802)442-6771. **Fax:** (802)442-6859. **E-mail:** mvaughan@santemagazine.com. **Website:** www.isantemagazine.com. **Contact:** Mark Vaughan, editor. **75% freelance written.** Four issues/year magazine covering food, wine, spirits, and management topics for restaurant professionals. Information and specific advice for restaurant professionals on operating a profitable food and beverage program. Writers should "speak" to readers on a professional-to-professional basis. Estab. 1996. Circ. 45,000. Byline given. Pays on publication. Offers 50% kill fee. Publishes ms an average of 2 months after acceptance. Editorial lead time 3 months. Submit seasonal material 6 months in advance. Accepts queries by e-mail. Accepts simultaneous submissions. Responds in 2 weeks to queries. Does not accept mss. Sample copy available. Guidelines by e-mail.

NONFICTION Needs interview, restaurant business news. Does not want consumer-focused pieces. **Buys 20 mss/year.** Query with published clips. Length: 650-1,800 words.

PHOTOS State availability. Captions required. Reviews PDF/GIF/JPEG files 500kb-10mb. Offers no additional payment for photos accepted. Buys one-time rights.

COLUMNS/DEPARTMENTS Due to a Redesign, 650 words; Bar Tab (focuses on 1 bar's unique strategy for success), 1,000 words; Restaurant Profile (a business-related look at what qualities make 1 restaurant successful), 1,000 words; Maximizing Profits (covers 1 great profit-maximizing strategy per issue from several sources), Signature Dish (highlights 1 chef's background and favorite dish with recipe), Sommeliers Choice (6 top wine managers recommend favorite wines; with brief profiles of each manager), Distillations (6 bar professionals offer their favorite drink for a particular type of spirit; with brief profiles of each manager), 1,500 words; Provisions (like The Goods only longer; an in-depth look at a special ingredient), 1,500 words. **Buys 20 mss/year.** Query with published clips. **Pays $300-800.**

TIPS "Present 2 or 3 of your best ideas via e-mail. Include a brief statement of your qualifications. Attach your resumé and 3 electronic clips. The same format may be used to query via postal mail if necessary."

VINEYARD & WINERY MANAGEMENT

P.O. Box 14459, Santa Rosa CA 95402-6459. (707)577-7700. **Fax:** (707)577-7705. **E-mail:** jfpowers@vwmmedia.com. **Website:** www.vwmmedia.com. **Contact:** Julie Fadda Powers, editor in chief. **80% freelance written.** Bimonthly magazine of professional importance to grape growers, winemakers, and winery sales and business people. Headquartered in Sonoma County, California, *Vineyard & Winery Management* proudly remains a leading independent wine trade magazine serving all of North America. Estab. 1975. Circ. 6,500. Byline given. Pays on publication. 20% kill fee. Accepts queries by e-mail. Accepts simultaneous submissions. Responds in 3 weeks to queries. Responds in 1 month to mss. Sample copy free. Guidelines available by e-mail.

NONFICTION Needs how-to, interview, new product, technical. **Buys 30 mss/year.** Query. Length: 1,500-2,000 words. **Pays approximately $500/feature.**

PHOTOS State availability. Captions, identification of subjects required. Digital photos preferred, JPEG or TIFF files 300 pixels/inch resolution at print size. Pays $20/each photo published.

TIPS "We're looking for long-term relationships with authors who know the business and write well. Electronic submissions required; query for formats."

WINES & VINES

Wine Communications Group, 65 Mitchell Blvd., Suite A, San Rafael CA 94903. (415)453-9700; (866)453-9701. **Fax:** (415)453-2517. **E-mail:** edit@winesandvines.com; info@winesandvines.com. **Website:** www.winesandvines.com. **Contact:** Jim Gordon, editor; Kate Lavin, managing editor. **50% freelance written.** Monthly magazine covering the North American winegrape and winemaking industry. "Since 1919, *Wines & Vines Magazine* has been the authoritative voice of the wine and grape industry—from prohibition to phylloxera, we have covered it all. Our paid circulation reaches all 50 states and many foreign countries. Because we are intended for the trade—including growers, winemakers, winery owners, wholesalers, restauranteurs, and serious amateurs—we accept more technical, informative articles. We do not accept wine reviews, wine country tours, or anything of a wine consumer nature." Estab. 1919. Circ. 5,000. Byline given. Pays 30 days after acceptance. No kill fee. Publishes ms an average of 3 months after acceptance. Editorial lead time 2 months.

Submit seasonal material 4 months in advance. Accepts queries by e-mail. Accepts simultaneous submissions. Responds in 2-3 weeks to queries. Sample copy: $5. Guidelines free.

NONFICTION Needs interview, new product, technical. "No wine reviews, wine country travelogues, 'lifestyle' pieces, or anything aimed at wine consumers. Our readers are professionals in the field." **Buys 60 mss/year.** Query with published clips. Length: 1,000-2,000 words. **Pays flat fee of $500 for assigned articles.**

PHOTOS Prefers JPEG files (JPEG, 300 dpi minimum). Can use high-quality prints. State availability of or send photos. Captions, identification of subjects required. Does not pay for photos submitted by author, but will give photo credit.

BOOK & BOOKSTORE

AMERICAN BOOK REVIEW

The Writer's Review, Inc., School of Arts & Sciences, Univ. of Houston-Victoria, 3007 N. Ben Wilson, Victoria TX 77901. (361)570-4848. **E-mail:** americanbookreview@uhv.edu. **Website:** www.americanbookreview.org. Bimonthly magazine covering book reviews. "We specialize in reviewing books published by independent presses." Estab. 1977. Circ. 15,000. Byline given. Pays on publication. Offers $50 kill fee. Publishes ms an average of 2-4 months after acceptance. Editorial lead time 1 month. Accepts queries by mail, e-mail, fax, phone. Accepts simultaneous submissions. Responds in 2 weeks to queries; 1-2 months to mss. Sample copy for $4. Guidelines online.

NONFICTION Does not want fiction, poetry, or interviews. Query with published clips. Length: 750-1,250 words. **Pays $50.**

TIPS "Most of our reviews are assigned, but we occasionally accept unsolicited reviews. Send query and samples of published reviews."

FOREWORD REVIEWS

FOREWORD MAGAZINE INC., 425 Boardman Ave., Suite B, Traverse City MI 49684. (231)933-3699. **Fax:** (231)933-3899. **E-mail:** howard@forewordreviews.com; victoria@forewordreviews.com. **E-mail:** mschingler@forewordreviews.com. **Website:** www.forewordreviews.com. **Contact:** Michelle Schingler, book review editor; Howard Lovy, executive editor. **75% freelance written.** Quarterly magazine cover-

TRADE JOURNALS

ing reviews of good books independently published. In each issue of the magazine, there are 3 to 4 feature *ForeSight* articles focusing on trends in popular categories. These are in addition to the 100 or more critical reviews of forthcoming titles from independent and university presses in the *Review* section. Look online for review submission guidelines or view editorial calendar. Estab. 1998. Circ. 10,000 (about 80% librarians, 10% bookstores, 10% publishing professionals). Byline given. Pays 1 months after submissions. $20 kill fee. Publishes ms an average of 2-3 months after acceptance. Editorial lead time 2-3 months. Submit seasonal material 5 months in advance. Accepts queries by mail, e-mail. Accepts simultaneous submissions. Responds in 1 month. Sample copy for $5.99 and 8 ½ x11 SASE with $1.50 postage.

NONFICTION Contact: Matt Sutherland. Needs book excerpts, interview, profile. **Buys 4 mss/year.** Query with published clips. All review submissions should be sent to the book review editor. Submissions should include a fact sheet or press release. Length: 400-1,500 words. **Pays $50-250 for assigned articles.**

TIPS "Be knowledgeable about the needs of book-sellers and librarians—remember we are an industry trade journal, not a how-to or consumer publication. We review books prior to publication, so book reviews are always assigned—but send us a note telling subjects you wish to review, as well as a résumé."

VIDEO LIBRARIAN

3435 NE Nine Boulder Dr., Poulsbo WA 98370. (360)626-1259. **Fax:** (360)626-1260. **E-mail:** vidlib@videolibrarian.com. **Website:** www.videolibrarian.com. **75% freelance written.** Bimonthly magazine covering DVD/Blu-ray reviews for librarians. "*Video Librarian* reviews approximately 225 titles in each issue: children's, documentaries, how-to's, movies, TV, music and anime." Estab. 1986. Circ. 2,000. Byline given. Pays on publication. Publishes ms an average of 2 months after acceptance. Editorial lead time 2 months. Accepts queries by e-mail. Accepts simultaneous submissions. Responds in 1 week to queries. Sample copy: $11.

NONFICTION Buys 500+ mss/year. Query with published clips. Length: 200-300 words. **Pays $10-20/review.**

TIPS "We are looking for DVD/Blu-ray reviewers with a wide range of interests, good critical eye, and strong writing skills."

BRICK, GLASS & CERAMICS

STAINED GLASS

Stained Glass Association of America, 9313 East 63rd St., Raytown MO 64133. (800)438-9581. **Fax:** (816)737-2801. **E-mail:** webmaster@sgaaonline.com. **Website:** www.stainedglassquarterly.com. **Contact:** Richard Gross, editor and media director. **70% freelance written.** Quarterly magazine. *Stained Glass* is the official voice of the Stained Glass Association of America. As the oldest, most respected stained glass publication in North America, *Stained Glass* preserves the techniques of the past as well as illustrates the trends of the future. This vital information, of significant value to the professional stained glass studio, is also of interest to those for whom stained glass is an avocation or hobby. Estab. 1906. Circ. 8,000. Byline given. Pays on publication. No kill fee. Publishes ms an average of 1 year after acceptance. Editorial lead time 6 months. Submit seasonal material 8 months in advance. Accepts queries by mail, e-mail, fax. Accepts simultaneous submissions. Responds in 3 months to queries. Sample copy free. Guidelines on website.

NONFICTION Needs how-to, humor, interview, new product, opinion, photo feature, technical. **Buys 9 mss/year.** Query or send complete ms, but must include photos or slides—very heavy on photos. Length: 2,500-3,500 words. **Pays $125/illustrated article; $75/nonillustrated.**

REPRINTS Accepts previously published submissions from stained glass publications only. Send tearsheet of article. Payment negotiable.

PHOTOS Send photos. Identification of subjects required. Reviews 4x5 transparencies, send slides with submission. Pays $75 for non-illustrated. Pays $125, plus 3 copies for line art or photography. Buys one-time rights.

COLUMNS/DEPARTMENTS Columns must be illustrated. Teknixs (technical, how-to, stained and glass art), word length varies by subject. **Buys 4 mss/year.** Query or send complete ms, but must be illustrated.

TIPS "We need more technical articles. Writers should be extremely well versed in the glass arts. Photographs are extremely important and must be of very high quality. Submissions without photographs or illustrations are seldom considered unless something special and writer states that photos are available. However, prefer to see with submission."

US GLASS, METAL & GLAZING

Key Communications, Inc., 20 PGA Dr., Suite 201, Stafford VA 22554. (540)720-5584, ext.118. **Fax:** (540)720-5687. **E-mail:** info@usglassmag.com. **E-mail:** erogers@glass.com. **Website:** www.usglass-mag.com. **Contact:** Ellen Rogers, editor. **25% freelance written.** Monthly magazine for companies involved in the flat glass trades. Estab. 1966. Circ. 27,000. Byline given. Pays on publication. No kill fee. Publishes ms an average of 3 months after acceptance. Editorial lead time 3 months. Submit seasonal material 2 months in advance. Accepts queries by mail, e-mail. Accepts simultaneous submissions. Responds in 1 month to queries. Responds in 2 months to mss. Sample copy online.

NONFICTION Buys 12 mss/year. Query with published clips. **Pays $300-600 for assigned articles.**

PHOTOS State availability. Captions, identification of subjects required. Reviews contact sheets. Offers no additional payment for photos accepted with ms. Buys first North American rights.

BUILDING INTERIORS

FABRICS + FURNISHINGS INTERNATIONAL

SIPCO Publications + Events, 3 Island Ave., Suite 6i, Miami Beach FL 33139. **E-mail:** eric@sipco.net. **Website:** www.fandfi.com. **Contact:** Eric Schneider, editor/publisher. **10% freelance written.** Bimonthly magazine covering commercial, hospitality interior design, and manufacturing. *F+FI* covers news from vendors who supply the hospitality interiors industry. Estab. 1990. Circ. 11,000+. Byline given. Pays on publication. Offers $100 kill fee. Editorial lead time 3 months. Submit seasonal material 3 months in advance. Accepts queries by e-mail. Accepts simultaneous submissions. Sample copy available online.

NONFICTION Needs interview, technical. Does not want opinion or consumer pieces. Readers must learn something from our stories. Query with published clips. Length: 500-1,000 words. **Pays $250-350.**

PHOTOS Send photos. Captions, identification of subjects required. Reviews GIF/JPEG files. Offers no additional payment for photos accepted with ms.

TIPS "Give us a lead on a new project that we haven't heard about. Have pictures of space and ability to interview designer on how they made it work."

KITCHEN & BATH DESIGN NEWS

SOLA Group Inc., 724 12th St., Suite 1W, Wilmette IL 60091. (631)581-2029 or (516)605-1426. **E-mail:** anita@solabrands.com; janice@solabrands.com. **Website:** www.kitchenbathdesign.com. **15% freelance written.** Monthly tabloid for kitchen and bath dealers and design professionals, offering design, business, and marketing advice to help readers be more successful. It is not a consumer publication about design, a book for do-it-yourselfers, or a magazine created to showcase pretty pictures of kitchens and baths. Rather, the magazine covers the professional kitchen and bath design industry in depth, looking at the specific challenges facing these professionals, and how they address these challenges. Estab. 1983. Circ. 51,000. Byline given. Pays on publication. Publishes ms an average of 2-3 months after acceptance. Editorial lead time 2 months. Accepts queries by mail, e-mail. Accepts simultaneous submissions. Responds in 2-4 weeks to queries. Sample copy available online. Guidelines by e-mail.

NONFICTION Needs how-to, interview. Does not want consumer stories, generic business stories, or "I remodeled my kitchen and it's so beautiful" stories. This is a magazine for trade professionals, so stories need to be both slanted for these professionals, as well as sophisticated enough that people who have been working in the field 30 years can still learn something from them. **Buys 16 mss/year.** Query with published clips. Length: 1,100-3,000 words. **Pays $200-650.**

PHOTOS Send photos. Identification of subjects required. Offers no additional payment for photos accepted with ms.

TIPS "This is a trade magazine for kitchen and bath dealers and designers, so trade experience and knowledge of the industry are essential. We look for writers who already know the unique challenges facing this industry, as well as the major players, acronyms, etc. This is not a market for beginners, and the vast majority of our freelancers are either design professionals or experienced in the industry."

QUALIFIED REMODELER

SOLA Group, Inc., 1880 Oak Ave., Suite 350, Evanston IL 60201. (847)920-9513. **Website:** www.forresidentialpros.com. Publisher/Editorial Director: Patrick L.

O'Toole. **5% freelance written.** Monthly magazine covering residential remodeling. Estab. 1975. Circ. 83,500. Byline given. Pays on acceptance. No kill fee. Publishes ms an average of 1 month after acceptance. Editorial lead time 3 months. Submit seasonal material 2 months in advance. Accepts queries by mail, e-mail, fax, phone. Accepts simultaneous submissions. Sample copy available online.

NONFICTION Needs how-to, new product. **Buys 12 mss/year.** Query with published clips. Length: 1,200-2,500 words. **Pays $300-600 for assigned articles. Pays $200-400 for unsolicited articles.**

PHOTOS Send photos. Reviews negatives, transparencies. Negotiates payment individually. Buys one-time rights.

COLUMNS/DEPARTMENTS Query with published clips. **Pays $400.**

TIPS "We focus on business management issues faced by remodeling contractors. For example, sales, marketing, liability, taxes, and just about any matter addressing small business operation."

REMODELING

HanleyWood, LLC, One Thomas Circle NW, Suite 600, Washington DC 20005. (202)452-0800. **Fax:** (202)785-1974. **E-mail:** cwebb@hanleywood.com. **Website:** www.remodelingmagazine.com. **Contact:** Craig Webb, editor. **10% freelance written.** Monthly magazine covering residential and light commercial remodeling. "We cover the best new ideas in remodeling design, business, construction and products." Estab. 1985. Circ. 80,000. Byline given. Pays on publication. Offers 5¢/word kill fee. Publishes ms an average of 3 months after acceptance. Accepts queries by mail, e-mail, fax. Accepts simultaneous submissions. Sample copy free.

NONFICTION Needs interview, new product, technical, small business trends. **Buys 6 mss/year.** Query with published clips. Length: 250-1,000 words. **Pays $1/word.**

PHOTOS State availability. Captions, identification of subjects, model releases required. Reviews 4x5 transparencies, slides, 8x10 prints. Offers $25-125/photo. Buys one-time rights.

TIPS "We specialize in service journalism for remodeling contractors. Knowledge of the industry is essential."

WALLS & CEILINGS

2401 W. Big Beaver Rd., Suite 700, Troy MI 48084. **Fax:** (248)362-5103. **E-mail:** wyattj@bnpmedia.com; mark@wwcca.org. **Website:** www.wconline.com. **Contact:** John Wyatt, editor; Mark Fowler, editorial director. **20% freelance written.** Monthly magazine for contractors involved in lathing and plastering, drywall, acoustics, fireproofing, curtain walls, and movable partitions, together with manufacturers, dealers, and architects. Estab. 1938. Circ. 30,000. Byline given. Pays on publication. No kill fee. Publishes ms an average of 6 months after acceptance. Submit seasonal material 4 months in advance. Accepts queries by mail, e-mail. Accepts simultaneous submissions. Responds in 6 months to queries. Sample copy for 9x12 SAE with $2 postage. Guidelines for #10 SASE.

NONFICTION Needs how-to, technical. **Buys 20 mss/year.** Query or send complete ms. Length: 1,000-1,500 words. **Pays $50-500.**

REPRINTS Send tearsheet or photocopy with rights for sale noted and information about when and where the material previously appeared. Pays 50% of the amount paid for an original article.

PHOTOS Send photos. Captions, identification of subjects required. Reviews contact sheets, negatives, transparencies, prints. Buys one-time rights.

BUSINESS MANAGEMENT

BUSINESS TRAVEL EXECUTIVE

5768 Remington Dr., Winston-Salem NC 27104. (336)766-1961. **E-mail:** dbooth@askbte.com. **Website:** www.askbte.com. **Contact:** Dan Booth, managing editor. **90% freelance written.** Monthly magazine covering corporate procurement of travel services. Byline given. Pays on publication. No kill fee. Publishes ms an average of 2 months after acceptance. Editorial lead time 0-3 months. Accepts queries by e-mail. Accepts simultaneous submissions.

NONFICTION Needs how-to, technical. **Buys 48 mss/year.** Please send unsolicited submissions, at your own risk. Please enclose a SASE for return of material. Submission of letters implies the right to edit and publish all or in part. Length: 800-2,000 words. **Pays $200-800.**

COLUMNS/DEPARTMENTS Meeting Place (meeting planning and management); Hotel Pulse (hotel negotiations, contracting and compliance); Security Watch (travel safety); all 1,000 words. **Buys 24 mss/year.** Query. **Pays $200-400.**

TIPS "We are not a travel magazine. We publish articles designed to help corporate purchasers of travel negotiate contracts, enforce policy, select automated services, track business travelers, and account for their safety and expenditures, understand changes in the various industries associated with travel. Do not submit mss without an assignment. Look at the website for an idea of what we publish."

CBA RETAILERS+RESOURCES

CBA, the Association for Christian Retail, 1365 Garden of the Gods Rd., Suite 105, Colorado Springs CO 80907. **Fax:** (719)272-3510. **E-mail:** cellis@cbaonline.org; info@cbaonline.org. **Website:** www.cbaonline.org. **Contact:** Cathy Ellis. **80% freelance written.** Monthly magazine covering the Christian products industry. Writers must have knowledge of and direct experience in the Christian products industry. Subject matter must specifically pertain to the Christian products audience. Estab. 1968. Byline given. Pays on publication. No kill fee. Publishes ms an average of 3 months after acceptance. Editorial lead time 3 months. Submit seasonal material 6 months in advance. Accepts queries by e-mail. Accepts simultaneous submissions. Responds in 2 months to queries. Sample copy for $9.50 or online.

◯ "Please use AP style."

NONFICTION Buys 24 mss/year. Query. Length: 650-1,500 words. **Pays 25¢/word.**

TIPS "Only experts on Christian retail industry, completely familiar with supplier and retail audience and their needs and considerations, should submit a query. Do not submit articles unless requested."

CONTRACTING PROFITS

Trade Press Publishing, 2100 W. Florist Ave., Milwaukee WI 53209. (414)228-7701; (800)727-7995. **Fax:** (414)228-1134. **E-mail:** dan.weltin@tradepress.com. **Website:** www.cleanlink.com/cp. **Contact:** Dan Weltin, editor-in-chief. **40% freelance written.** Magazine published 10 times/year covering building service contracting and business management advice. The pocket MBA for this industry—focusing not only on cleaning-specific topics, but also discussing how to run businesses better and increase profits through a variety of management articles. Estab. 1995. Circ. 32,000. Byline given. Pays within 30 days of acceptance. No kill fee. Editorial lead time 2 months. Submit seasonal material 3 months in advance. Accepts queries by mail, e-mail. Accepts simultaneous submissions. Responds in weeks to queries. Sample copy available online. Guidelines free.

NONFICTION Needs expose, how-to, interview, technical. No product-related reviews or testimonials. **Buys 30 mss/year.** Query with published clips. Length: 1,000-1,500 words. **Pays $100-500.**

COLUMNS/DEPARTMENTS Query with published clips.

TIPS "Read back issues on our website and be able to understand some of those topics prior to calling."

CONTRACT MANAGEMENT

National Contract Management Association, 21740 Beaumeade Circle, Suite 125, Ashburn VA 20147. (571)382-0082. **Fax:** (703)448-0939. **E-mail:** khansen@ncmahq.org. **Website:** www.ncmahq.org. **Contact:** Kerry McKinnon Hansen, director of publications and editor-in-chief. **10% freelance written.** Monthly magazine covering contract and business management. Most of the articles published in *Contract Management (CM)* are written by NCMA members, although one does not have to be an NCMA member to be published in the magazine. Articles should concern some aspect of the contract management profession, whether at the level of a beginner or that of the advanced practitioner. Estab. 1960. Circ. 23,000. Byline given. Pays on publication. No kill fee. Publishes ms an average of 3 months after acceptance. Editorial lead time 10 weeks. Submit seasonal material 3 months in advance. Accepts queries by mail, e-mail, fax, phone. Accepts simultaneous submissions. Responds in 2 weeks to queries. Responds in 1 month to mss. Sample copy and writer's guidelines available online.

NONFICTION Needs essays, general interest, how-to, humor, inspirational, new product, opinion, technical. No company or CEO profiles. Read a copy of publication before submitting. **Buys 6-10 mss/year.** Query with published clips. Send an inquiry including a brief summary (150 words) of the proposed article to the managing editor before writing the article. Length: 1,800-4,000 words. **Pays $300.**

PHOTOS State availability. Captions, identification of subjects required. Offers no additional payment for photos accepted with ms. Buys one-time rights.
COLUMNS/DEPARTMENTS Professional Development (self-improvement in business), 1,000-1,500 words; Back to Basics (basic how-tos and discussions), 1,500-2,000 words. **Buys 2 mss/year.** Query with published clips. **Pays $300.**
TIPS "Query and read at least 1 issue. Visit website to better understand our audience."

INTENTS

Industrial Fabrics Association International, 1801 County Rd. B W, Roseville MN 55113. (651)222-2508. **Fax:** (651)631-9334. **E-mail:** generalinfo@ifai.com. **Website:** intentsmag.com. **50% freelance written.** Bimonthly magazine covering tent-rental and special-event industries. *InTents* is the official publication of IFAI's Tent Rental Division, delivering "the total tent experience." *InTents* offers focused, credible information needed to stage and host safe, successful tented events. Issues of the magazine include news, trends and behind-the-scenes coverage of the latest events in tents. Estab. 1995. Circ. 12,000. Byline given. Pays on acceptance. No kill fee. Publishes ms an average of 2 months after acceptance. Editorial lead time 3 months. Accepts queries by mail, e-mail, fax. Accepts simultaneous submissions. Sample copy and writer's guidelines free.
NONFICTION Needs how-to, interview, new product, photo feature, technical. **Buys 12-18 mss/year.** Query. Length: 800-2,000 words. **Pays $300-500.**
PHOTOS State availability. Captions, identification of subjects, model releases required. Reviews contact sheets, negatives, prints, digital images. Negotiates payment individually.
TIPS "We look for lively, intelligent writing that makes technical subjects come alive."

MAINEBIZ

Mainebiz Publications, Inc., 48 Free St., Portland ME 04101. (207)761-8379. **Fax:** (207)761-0732. **E-mail:** pvanallen@mainebiz.biz; editorial@mainebiz.biz. **Website:** www.mainebiz.biz. **Contact:** Peter Van Allen, editor. **25% freelance written.** Biweekly tabloid covering business in Maine. *Mainebiz* is read by business decision makers across the state. Readers look to the publication for business news and analysis. Estab. 1994. Circ. 13,000. Byline given. Pays on publication. Offers 10% kill fee. Publishes ms an average of 1 month after acceptance. Editorial lead time 1 month. Submit seasonal material 2 months in advance. Accepts queries by mail, e-mail. Accepts simultaneous submissions. Responds in 3 weeks to queries. Sample copy online.
NONFICTION Needs essays, expose, interview, business trends. Special issues: See website for editorial calendar. **Buys 50+ mss/year.** Query with published clips. Length: 500-2,500 words. **Pays $75-350.**
PHOTOS State availability. Identification of subjects required. Reviews GIF/JPEG files. Negotiates payment individually. Buys one-time rights.
TIPS "If you wish to contribute, please spend some time familiarizing yourself with *Mainebiz*. Tell us a little about yourself, your experience and background as a writer and qualifications for writing a particular story. If you have clips you can send us via e-mail, or web addresses of pages that contain your work, please send us a representative sampling (no more than 3 or 4, please). Stories should be well thought out with specific relevance to Maine. Arts and culture-related queries are welcome, as long as there is a business angle. We appreciate unusual angles on business stories and regularly work with new freelancers. Send the text of your query or submission in plain text in the body of your e-mail, rather than as an attached file, as we may not be able to read the format of your file. We do our best to respond to all inquiries, but be aware that we are sometimes inundated."

RETAIL INFO SYSTEMS NEWS

Edgell Communications, 4 Middlebury Blvd., Randolph NJ 07869. (973)607-1300. **Fax:** (973)607-1395. **E-mail:** ablair@edgellmail.com; jskorupa@edgellmail.com. **Website:** www.risnews.com. **Contact:** Adam Blair, editor; Joe Skorupa, group editor-in-chief. **65% freelance written.** Monthly magazine covering retail technology. Estab. 1988. Circ. 22,000. Byline sometimes given. Pays on publication. No kill fee. Publishes ms an average of 2 months after acceptance. Editorial lead time 3 months. Submit seasonal material 3 months in advance. Accepts queries by mail. Accepts simultaneous submissions. Sample copy available online.
NONFICTION Needs essays, how-to, humor, interview, technical. **Buys 80 mss/year.** Query with published clips. Length: 700-1,900 words. **Pays $600-1,200 for assigned articles.**

PHOTOS State availability of or send photos. Identification of subjects required. Negotiates payment individually. Buys one-time rights plus reprint, if applicable.

COLUMNS/DEPARTMENTS News/trends (analysis of current events), 150-300 words. **Buys 4 articles/year mss/year.** Query with published clips. **Pays $100-300.**

TIPS "Case histories about companies achieving substantial results using advanced management practices and/or advanced technology are best."

RTOHQ: THE MAGAZINE

1504 Robin Hood Trail, Austin TX 78703. (800)204-2776. **Fax:** (512)794-0097. **E-mail:** nferguson@rtohq.org; bkeese@rtohq.org. **Website:** www.rtohq.org. **Contact:** Neil Ferguson, art director; Bill Keese, executive editor. **50% freelance written.** Bimonthly magazine covering the rent-to-own industry. *RTOHQ: The Magazine* is the only publication representing the rent-to-own industry and members of APRO. The magazine covers timely news and features affecting the industry, association activities, and member profiles. Awarded best 4-color magazine by the American Society of Association Executives in 1999. Estab. 1980. Circ. 5,500. Byline given. Pays on acceptance. Offers 25% kill fee. Publishes ms an average of 2 months after acceptance. Editorial lead time 2 months. Submit seasonal material 4 months in advance. Accepts queries by mail, e-mail, fax, phone, online submission form. Accepts simultaneous submissions. Responds in 1 month to queries. Responds in 2 months to mss. Sample copy free.

NONFICTION Needs expose, general interest, how-to, inspirational, interview, technical, industry features. **Buys 12 mss/year.** Query with published clips. Length: 1,200-2,500 words. **Pays $150-700.**

SECURITY DEALER & INTEGRATOR

Southcomm, 12735 Morris Road Bldg. 200 Suite 180, Alpharetta GA 30004. (800)547-7377, ext 2226. **E-mail:** paul.rothman@cygnus.com. **Website:** www.securityinfowatch.com/magazine. **Contact:** Paul Rothman, editor-in-chief. **25% freelance written.** Circ. 25,000. Byline sometimes given. Pays 3 weeks after publication. No kill fee. Publishes ms an average of 3 months after acceptance. Accepts queries by e-mail. Accepts simultaneous submissions.

NONFICTION Needs how-to, interview, technical. No consumer pieces. Query by e-mail. Length: 1,000-3,000 words. **Pays $250.**

PHOTOS State availability. Captions, identification of subjects required. Reviews contact sheets, transparencies. Offers $25 additional payment for photos accepted with ms.

COLUMNS/DEPARTMENTS Query by mail only.

TIPS "The areas of our publication most open to freelancers are technical innovations, trends in the alarm industry, and crime patterns as related to the business as well as business finance and management pieces."

SMART BUSINESS

Smart Business Network, Inc., 835 Sharon Dr., Suite 200, Cleveland OH 44145. (440)250-7000. **Fax:** (440)250-7001. **E-mail:** mscott@sbnonline.com. **Website:** www.sbnonline.com. **Contact:** Mark Scott, senior associate editor. **5% freelance written.** Monthly business magazine with an audience made up of business owners and top decision makers. *Smart Business* is one of the fastest growing national chains of regional management journals for corporate executives. Every issue delves into the minds of the most innovative executives in each of our regions to report on how market leaders got to the top and what strategies they use to stay there. Estab. 1989. Byline given. Pays on publication. Offers 50% kill fee. Publishes ms an average of 2 months after acceptance. Editorial lead time 3 months. Submit seasonal material 3 months in advance. Accepts queries by mail, e-mail. Accepts simultaneous submissions. Responds in 2 weeks to queries. Responds in 1 month to mss. Sample copy available online. Guidelines by e-mail.

NONFICTION Needs how-to, interview. No breaking news or news features. **Buys 10-12 mss/year.** Query with published clips. Length: 1,150-2,000 words. **Pays $200-500.**

PHOTOS State availability. Identification of subjects required. Reviews negatives, prints. Offers no additional payment for photos accepted with ms. Buys one-time, reprint, and Web rights.

TIPS "The best way to submit to *Smart Business* is to read us—either online or in print. Remember, our audience is made up of top level business executives and owners."

STAMATS MEETINGS MEDIA

615 5th St. SE, Cedar Rapids IA 52401. **Fax:** (319)364-4278. **E-mail:** tyler.davidson@meetingsfocus.com.

Website: www.meetingsfocus.com. **Contact:** Tyler Davidson, chief content director. **75% freelance written.** Monthly tabloid covering meeting, event, and conference planning. Estab. 1986. Circ. *Meetings East* and *Meetings South* 22,000; *Meetings West* 26,000. Byline given. Pays 1 month after publication. No kill fee. Publishes ms an average of 1 month after acceptance. Editorial lead time 3 months. Submit seasonal material 3 months in advance. Accepts queries by mail, e-mail, fax. Accepts simultaneous submissions. Responds in 3 weeks to queries. Sample copy for DSR with 9x13 envelope and 5 first-class stamps.

NONFICTION Needs how-to, travel. "No first-person fluff—this is a business magazine." **Buys 150 mss/year.** Query with published clips. Length: 1,200-2,000 words. **Pays $500 flat rate/package.**

PHOTOS State availability. Identification of subjects required. Offers no additional payment for photos accepted with ms. Buys one-time rights.

TIPS "We're always looking for freelance writers who are local to our destination stories. For Site Inspections, get in touch in late September or early October, when we usually have the following year's editorial calendar available."

SUPERVISION MAGAZINE

National Research Bureau, 320 Valley St., Burlington IA 52601. (319)752-5415. **E-mail:** articles@supervisionmagazine.com. **Website:** www.supervisionmagazine.com/. **Contact:** Todd Darnall. **80% freelance written.** Monthly magazine covering management and supervision. *Supervision Magazine* explains complex issues in a clear and understandable format. Articles written by both experts and scholars provide practical and concise answers to issues facing today's supervisors and managers. Estab. 1939. Circ. 500. Byline given. Pays on acceptance. Publishes ms an average of 1 month after acceptance. Editorial lead time 1 month. Submit seasonal material 2 months in advance. Accepts queries by e-mail. Accepts simultaneous submissions. Sample copy free. Guidelines available online.

NONFICTION Needs personal experience, "We can use articles dealing with motivation, leadership, human relations and communication." Send complete ms. Length: 1,500-2,000 words. **Pays 4¢/word.**

CHURCH ADMINISTRATION & MINISTRY

CHRISTIAN COMMUNICATOR

American Christian Writers, 9118 W. Elmwood Dr., Suite 1G, Niles IL 60714-5820. (847)296-3964. **E-mail:** ljohnson@wordprocommunications.com. **Website:** acwriters.com. **Contact:** Lin Johnson, managing editor; Sally Miller, poetry editor (sallymiller@ameritech.net). **50% freelance written.** Bimonthly magazine covering Christian writing and speaking. Estab. 1988. Circ. 1,000. Byline given. Pays on publication. No kill fee. Publishes ms an average of 6-12 months after acceptance. Editorial lead time 3 months. Submit seasonal material 9 months in advance. Accepts queries by e-mail. Responds in 6-8 weeks to queries; in 8-12 weeks to mss. Sample copy for SAE and 4 first-class stamps. Writers guidelines by email or on website.

NONFICTION Needs essays, how-to, interview, reviews, "Articles on writing nonfiction, research, creativity." **Buys 24 mss/year.** Query or send complete ms only by e-mail. Length: 700-1,000 words. **Pays $10. $5 for reviews. ACW CD for anecdotes.**

REPRINTS Same as first rights.

POETRY Needs free verse, light verse, traditional. Buys Publishes 12 poems/year. poems/year. Submit maximum 2 poems. Length: 4-20 lines. **Pays $5.**

FILLERS Needs anecdotes, short humor.

TIPS "Everything, including poetry, must be related to writing, publishing, or speaking. We primarily use how-to articles but are willing to look at other types of manuscripts."

GROUP MAGAZINE

Simply Youth Ministry, 1515 Cascade Ave., Loveland CO 80538. **E-mail:** PuorgBus@group.com. **Website:** www.youthministry.com/group-magazine. **Contact:** Scott Firestone IV, associate editor. **50% freelance written.** Bimonthly magazine for Christian youth workers. *Group* is the interdenominational magazine for leaders of Christian youth groups. *Group's* purpose is to supply ideas, practical help, inspiration, and training for youth leaders. Estab. 1974. Circ. 55,000. Byline sometimes given. Pays on acceptance. No kill fee. Editorial lead time 4 months. Submit seasonal material 5 months in advance. Accepts queries by mail, e-mail, fax. Accepts simultaneous submissions. Responds in 8-10 weeks to queries. Responds in 2 months to mss. Sample copy for $2, plus 10x12 SAE and 3 first-class stamps.

NONFICTION Needs inspirational, personal experience, religious. No fiction, prose, or poetry. **Buys 30 mss/year.** Query. Submit online, through website. Length: 200-2,000 words. **Pays $50-250.**

COLUMNS/DEPARTMENTS "Try This One" section needs short ideas (100-250 words) for youth group use. These include games, fundraisers, crowdbreakers, Bible studies, helpful hints, outreach ideas, and discussion starters. "Hands-on Help" section needs mini-articles (100-350 words) that feature practical tips for youth leaders on working with students, adult leaders, and parents. **Pays $50.**

TIPS "We are always looking for submissions for short, novel, practical ideas that have worked in actual youth ministry settings. It's best to familiarize yourself with *Group Magazine* before sending in ideas for our departments."

THE JOURNAL OF ADVENTIST EDUCATION

General Conference of SDA, 12501 Old Columbia Pike, Silver Spring MD 20904. (301) 680-5069. **Fax:** (301) 622-9627. **E-mail:** mcgarrellf@gc.adventist.org; goffc@gc.adventist.org. **E-mail:** http://www.editorialmanager.com/jae/default.aspx. **Website:** jae.adventist.org. **Contact:** Faith-Ann McGarrell, editor; Chandra Goff, admin assistant. A quarterly professional journal for Christian teachers, administrators, and stakeholders, with specific emphasis on educators in Seventh-day Adventist schools. Published 4 times per year in English, French, Spanish, and Portuguese. Emphasizes procedures, philosophy, and subject matter of Christian education. Estab. 1939. Circ. 14,000 in English; 13,000 in other languages. Byline given. Pays on publication. No kill fee. Publishes ms an average of 1 year after acceptance. Editorial lead time 1 year. Accepts queries by mail, e-mail, fax, phone. Accepts simultaneous submissions. Responds in 6 weeks to queries; 4 months to mss. Sample copy for SAE with 10x12 envelope and 5 first-class stamps. Guidelines available online at http://jae.adventist.org/authors.htm and http://www.editorialmanager.com/jae/default.aspx.

NONFICTION Needs book excerpts, essays, how-to, personal experience, photo feature, religious. "No brief first-person stories about Sunday Schools." Query. All articles must be submitted in electronic format. Store in Word or .rtf format. If you submit a CD, include a printed copy of the article with the CD. Articles should be 6-8 pages long, with a max of 10 pages, including references. Two-part articles will be considered. Length: 1,000-1,500 words. **Pays $25-$300.**

REPRINTS Send tearsheet or photocopy and information about when and where the material previously appeared.

PHOTOS Buys 5-15 photos from freelancers/issue; up to 75 photos/year. Photos of children/teens, multicultural, parents, education, religious, health/fitness, technology/computers with people, committees, offices, school photos of teachers, students, parents, activities at all levels, elementary though graduate school. Reviews photos with or without a ms. Model release preferred. Photo captions preferred. Uses mostly digital color images but also accepts color prints; 35mm, 21/4x21/4, 4x5 transparencies. Send digital photos via ZIP, CD, or DVD (preferred); e-mail as TIFF, GIF, JPEG files at 300 DPI. Do not send large numbers of photos as e-mail attachments, instead use file sharing products such as Dropbox or WeTransfer. Send query letter with prints, photocopies, transparencies. Provide self-promotion piece to be kept on file for possible future assignments. Responds in 1 month to queries. Simultaneous submissions and previously published work OK. State availability of or send photos. Pays $100-350 for color cover; $50-100 for color inside. Willing to negotiate on electronic usage of photos. Pays on publication. Credit line given. Buys one-time rights for use in magazine and on website.

TIPS "Articles may deal with educational theory or practice, although the *Journal* seeks to emphasize the practical. Articles dealing with the creative and effective use of methods to enhance teaching skills or learning in the classroom are especially welcome. Whether theoretical or practical, such essays should demonstrate the skillful integration of Seventh-day Adventist faith/values and learning."

LEADERSHIP JOURNAL

Christianity Today International, 465 Gundersen Dr., Carol Stream IL 60188. (630)260-6200. **Fax:** (630)260-0114. **E-mail:** ljeditor@leadershipjournal.net. **Website:** www.christianitytoday.com/le. Skye Jethani, managing editor. **Contact:** Marshall Shelley, editor-in-chief. **75% freelance written. Works with a small number of new/unpublished writers each year.** Quarterly magazine. Writers must have a knowledge of and sympathy for the unique expectations placed on pastors and local church leaders. Each article must support points by illustrating from real life experiences in local churches. Estab. 1980. Circ. 48,000. Byline given. Pays on acceptance. Offers 33% kill fee. Publishes ms an average of 6 months after acceptance. Editorial lead time 6 months. Submit seasonal material 6 months in advance. Accepts queries by mail, e-mail, fax. Accepts simultaneous submissions. Responds in 2 weeks to queries. Responds in 2 months to mss. Sample copy for free or online.

NONFICTION Needs how-to, humor, interview, personal experience, sermon illustrations. No articles from writers who have never read our journal. No unsolicited ms. **Buys 60 mss/year.** Query with proposal. Send a brief query letter describing your idea and how you plan to develop it. Length: 300-3,000 words. **Pays $35-400.**

COLUMNS/DEPARTMENTS Contact: Skye Jethanis, managing editor. Toolkit (book/software reviews), 500 words. **Buys 8 mss/year. mss/year.** Query.

TIPS "Every article in *Leadership* must provide practical help for problems that church leaders face. *Leadership* articles are not essays expounding a topic or editorials arguing a position or homilies explaining Biblical principles. They are how-to articles, based on first-person accounts of real-life experiences in ministry. They allow our readers to see `over the shoulder' of a colleague in ministry who then reflects on those experiences and identifies the lessons learned. As you know, a magazine's slant is a specific personality that readers expect (and it's what they've sent us their subscription money to provide). Our style is that of friendly conversation rather than directive discourse—what I learned about local church ministry rather than what you need to do."

MOMENTUM

National Catholic Educational Association, 1005 N. Glebe Rd., Suite 525, Arlington VA 22201. (800)711-6232. **Fax:** (703)243-0025. **E-mail:** momentum@ncea.org. **Website:** www.ncea.org/publications/momentum. **Contact:** Gabrielle Gallagher, editor. **65% freelance written.** Quarterly educational journal covering educational issues in Catholic schools and parishes. *Momentum* is a membership journal of the National Catholic Educational Association. The audience is educators and administrators in Catholic schools K-12, and parish programs. Estab. 1970. Circ. 19,000. Byline given. Pays on publication. No kill fee. Publishes ms an average of 3 months after acceptance. Accepts queries by e-mail. Accepts simultaneous submissions. Sample copy for $5 SASE and 8 first-class stamps. Guidelines online.

NONFICTION No articles unrelated to educational and catechesis issues. **Buys 40-60 mss/year.** Query and send complete ms. Length: 1,500 words for feature articles; 700-1,000 words for columns, "From the Field," and opinion pieces or essays; 500-750 words for book reviews. **Pays $75 maximum.**

PHOTOS State availability of photos. Captions, identification of subjects required. Reviews prints. Offers no additional payment for photos accepted with ms.

THE PRIEST

Our Sunday Visitor, Inc., 200 Noll Plaza, Huntington IN 46750. (800)348-2440. **Fax:** (260)356-8472. **E-mail:** tpriest@osv.com. **Website:** www.osv.com. **Contact:** Editorial Department. **40% freelance written.** Monthly magazine that publishes articles to aid priests in their day-to-day parish ministry. Includes items on spirituality, counseling, administration, theology, personalities, the saints, etc. Byline given. Pays on acceptance. No kill fee. Editorial lead time 3 months. Submit seasonal material 4 months in advance. Accepts queries by mail, e-mail, fax, phone, online submission form. Accepts simultaneous submissions. Responds in 5 weeks to queries; 3 months to mss. Sample copy free. Guidelines available online.

NONFICTION Needs essays, historical, humor, inspirational, opinion, personal experience, photo feature, religious. **Buys 96 mss/year.** Send complete ms. Length: 2,500 words maximum. **Pays $200 minimum for assigned articles; $50 minimum for unsolicited articles.**

PHOTOS Send photos. Captions, identification of subjects required. Reviews prints. Negotiates payment individually. Buys one-time rights.

TIPS "Please do not stray from the magisterium of the Catholic Church."

RTJ'S CREATIVE CATECHIST

Twenty-Third Publications, P.O. Box 6015, New London CT 06320. (800)321-0411, ext. 188. **Fax:** (860)437-6246. **E-mail:** creativesubs@rtjscreativecatechist.com; editor@rtjscreativecatechist.com; pat.gohn@bayard-inc.com. **Website:** www.rtjscreativecatechist.com. **Contact:** Pat Gohn, editor. Monthly magazine for Catholic catechists and religion teachers. The mission of *RTJ's Creative Catechist* is to encourage and assist Catholic DREs and catechists in their vocation to proclaim the gospel message and lead others to the joy of following Jesus Christ. *RTJ* provides professional support, theological content, age appropriate methodology, and teaching tools. Estab. 1966. Circ. 30,000. Byline given. Pays on acceptance. Publishes ms an average of 3-20 months after acceptance. Editorial lead time 4 months. Submit seasonal material 6 months in advance. Accepts queries by mail, e-mail. Accepts simultaneous submissions. Responds in 1-2 weeks to queries. Responds in 1-2 months to mss. Sample copy for SAE with 9x12 envelope and 3 first-class stamps. Guidelines free.

NONFICTION Needs how-to, inspirational, personal experience, religious, articles on celebrating church seasons, sacraments, on morality, on prayer, on saints. Special issues: Sacraments; Prayer; Advent/Christmas; Lent/Easter. All should be written by people who have experience in religious education, or a good background in Catholic faith. Does not want fiction, poems, plays, articles written for Catholic school teachers (i.e., math, English, etc.), or articles that are academic rather than catechetical in nature. **Buys 35-40 mss/year.** Send complete ms. Length: 600-1,300 words. **Pays $100-125 for assigned articles. Pays $75-125 for unsolicited articles.**

COLUMNS/DEPARTMENTS Catechist to Catechist (brief articles on crafts, games, etc., for religion lessons); Faith and Fun (full-page religious word games, puzzles, mazes, etc., for children). **Buys 30 mss/year.** Send complete ms. **Pays $20-125.**

TIPS "We look for clear, concise articles written from experience. Articles should help readers move from theory/doctrine to concrete application. Unsolicited mss not returned without SASE. No fancy formatting; no handwritten mss. Author should be able to furnish article on disk or via e-mail if possible."

TODAY'S CATHOLIC TEACHER

Peter Li Education Group, 3055 Kettering Blvd., Suite 100, Dayton OH 45439. (937)293-1415; (800)523-4625, x1139. **Fax:** (937)293-1310. **E-mail:** bshepard@peterli.com; danielle.bean@bayard-inc.com. **E-mail:** bshepard@peterli.com. **Website:** www.catholicteacher.com. **Contact:** Dr. Lisa D'Souza, editor; Danielle Bean, publisher. **60% freelance written.** Magazine published 6 times/year during school year covering Catholic education for grades K-12. Looks for topics of interest and practical help to teachers in Catholic elementary schools in all curriculum areas including religion technology, discipline, and motivation. Estab. 1972. Circ. 50,000. Byline given. Pays on publication. No kill fee. Publishes ms an average of 2 months after acceptance. Editorial lead time 3 months. Submit seasonal material 6 months in advance. Accepts queries by mail, e-mail, fax. Accepts simultaneous submissions. Responds in 1 month to queries. Responds in 3 months to mss. Sample copy for $3 or on website. Guidelines available online.

NONFICTION Needs essays, how-to, humor, interview, personal experience. No articles pertaining to public education. **Buys 15 mss/year.** Query or send complete ms. Query letters are encouraged. E-mail, write, call, or fax the editor for editorial calendar. Articles may be submitted as hard copy; submission by e-mail with accompanying hard copy is appreciated. Length: 600-1,500 words. **Pays $100-250.**

PHOTOS State availability. Captions, identification of subjects, model releases required. Reviews transparencies, prints. Offers $20-50/photo. Buys one-time rights.

TIPS "Although our readership is primarily classroom teachers, *Today's Catholic Teacher* is also read by principals, supervisors, superintendents, boards of education, pastors, and parents. *Today's Catholic Teacher* aims to be for Catholic educators a source of information not available elsewhere. The focus of articles should span the interests of teachers from early childhood through junior high. Articles may be directed to just 1 age group, yet have wider implications. Preference is given to material directed to teachers in grades 4-8. The desired magazine style is direct, concise, informative, and accurate. Writing should be enjoyable to read, informal rather than scholarly, lively, and free of educational jargon."

YOUTHWORKER JOURNAL

Salem Publishing/CCM Communications, 402 BNA Dr., Suite 400, Nashville TN 37217-2509. **E-mail:** ALee@SalemPublishing.com. **Website:** www.youthworker.com. **Contact:** Steve Rabey, editor; Amy L. Lee, managing editor. **100% freelance written.** Website and bimonthly magazine covering professional youth ministry in the church and parachurch. Estab. 1984. Circ. 20,000. Byline given. Pays on publication. No kill fee. Publishes ms an average of 3 months after acceptance for print; immediately online. Editorial lead time 6 months for print; immediately online. Submit seasonal material 6 months in advance for print. Accepts queries by e-mail, online submission form. Accepts simultaneous submissions. Responds within 6 weeks to queries. Sample copy for $5. Guidelines available online.

NONFICTION Needs essays, new product, personal experience, photo feature, religious. Special issues: See website for themes in upcoming issues. Query. Length: 250-3,000 words. **Pays $15-200.**

PHOTOS Send photos. Reviews GIF/JPEG files. Negotiates payment individually.

TIPS "We exist to help meet the personal and professional needs of career, Christian youth workers in the church and parachurch. Proposals accepted on the posted theme, according to the writer's guidelines on our website. It's not enough to write well—you must know youth ministry."

CLOTHING

FOOTWEAR PLUS

9 Threads, 135 West 20th Street, 4th Floor, New York NY 10011. (646)278-1550. **Fax:** (646)278-1553. **E-mail:** editorialrequests@9threads.com. **Website:** www.footwearplusmagazine.com. **Contact:** Brittany Leitner, assistant editor. **20% freelance written.** Monthly magazine covering footwear fashion and business. A business-to-business publication targeted at footwear retailers. Covers all categories of footwear and age ranges with a focus on new trends, brands and consumer buying habits, as well as retailer advice on operating the store more effectively. Estab. 1990. Circ. 18,000. Byline given. Pays on publication. No kill fee. Publishes ms an average of 1-2 months after acceptance. Editorial lead time 1-2 months. Accepts simultaneous submissions. Sample copy for $5.

NONFICTION Needs interview, new product, technical. Does not want pieces unrelated to footwear/fashion industry. **Buys 10-20 mss/year.** Query. Length: 500-2,500 words. **Pays $1,000 maximum.**

IMPRESSIONS

Emerald Expositions, 1145 Sanctuary Pkwy., Suite 355, Alpharetta GA 30009-4772. (800)241-9034; (770)291-5412. **Fax:** (770)777-8733. **E-mail:** mderryberry@impressionsmag.com; jlaster@impressionsmag.com; michelle.havich@emeraldexpo.com. **Website:** www.impressionsmag.com. **Contact:** Marcia Derryberry, editor in chief; Jamar Laster, senior editor; Michelle Havich, managing editor. **30% freelance written.** Magazine, published 13 times/year, covering computerized embroidery and digitizing design. Features authoritative, up-to-date information on screen printing, embroidery, heat-applied graphics, and ink-jet-to-garment printing. Readable, practical business and/or technical articles show readers how to succeed in their profession. Estab. 1994. Circ. 20,000. Byline given. Pays on publication. No kill fee. Publishes ms an average of 3 months after acceptance. Editorial lead time 3 months. Submit seasonal material 6 months in advance. Accepts queries by mail, e-mail. Accepts simultaneous submissions. Sample copy: $10.

NONFICTION Needs how-to, interview, new product, photo feature, technical. **Buys 40 mss/year.** Query. Length: 800-2,000 words. **Pays $200 and up for assigned articles.**

PHOTOS Send photos. Reviews transparencies, prints. Negotiates payment individually.

TIPS "Show us you have specified knowledge, experience, or contacts in the embroidery industry or a related field."

TEXTILE WORLD

Billian Publishing Co., P.O. Box 683155, Marietta GA 30068. (678)483-6102; (404)518-9599. **Fax:** (770)952-0669. **E-mail:** editor@textileworld.com; rsdavis@textileworld.com. **Website:** www.textileworld.com. **Contact:** editor. **5% freelance written.** Bimonthly magazine covering the business of textile, apparel, and fiber industries with considerable technical focus on products and processes. Estab. 1868. Byline given. Pays on publication. No kill fee. Accepts simultaneous submissions.

NONFICTION No puff pieces pushing a particular product. **Buys 10 mss/year.** Query. Length: 500 words minimum. **Pays $200/published page.**

PHOTOS Send photos. Captions required. Reviews prints. Offers no additional payment for photos accepted with ms. Buys one-time rights.

CONSTRUCTION & CONTRACTING

AUTOMATED BUILDER

CMN Associates, Inc., 2401 Grapevine Dr., Oxnard CA 93036. (805)351-5931. **Fax:** (805)351-5755. **E-mail:** cms03@pacbell.net. **Website:** www.automatedbuild-

TRADE JOURNALS

er.com. **Contact:** Don O. Carlson, editor/publisher. **5% freelance written.** *"Automated Builder* covers management, production and marketing information on all 7 segments of home, apartment and commercial construction. These include: (1) production (site) builders, (2) panelized home manufacturers, (3) HUD-code (mobile) home manufacturers, (4) modular home manufacturers, (5) component manufacturers, (6) special unit (commercial) manufacturers, and (7) all types of builders and builders/dealers. The in-plant material is technical in content and covers new machine technologies and improved methods for in-plant building and erecting. Home and commercial buyers will see the latest in homes and commercial structures." Estab. 1964. Circ. 75,000 when printed. Byline given if desired. Pays on acceptance. Publishes ms an average of 2 months after acceptance. Editorial lead time 2 months. Accepts queries by mail, e-mail, fax. Accepts simultaneous submissions. Responds in 2 weeks to queries.

NONFICTION "No fiction and no planned 'dreams.' Housing projects must be built or under construction. Same for commercial structures." **Buys 6-8 mss/year.** Phone queries OK. Length: 500-750 words. **Pays $250 for stories including photos.**

PHOTOS Captions are required for each photo. Offers no additional payment for photos accepted with ms. Payment is on acceptance.

TIPS "Stories often are too long, too loose; we prefer 500-750 words plus captions. We prefer a phone query on feature articles. If accepted on query, articles will rarely be rejected later. It is required that every story and photos are cleared with the source before sending to *Automated Builder*. At-Home segment will contain details and photos of newest residential and commercial buildings sold or ready for sale. At-Home segment also will welcome stories and photos of new units added to existing homes or commercial structures. Ideal layout would be one page of photos with exterior and/or interior photos of the structures and an adjoining page for text."

THE CONCRETE PRODUCER

Hanley-Wood, LLC, 8725 W. Higgins Rd., Suite 600, Chicago IL 60631. (773)824-2400 or (773)824-2496. **E-mail:** tbagsarian@hanleywood.com; ryelton@hanleywood.com; tcpeditor@hanleywood.com. **Website:** www.theconcreteproducer.com. **Contact:** Tom Bagsarian, group managing editor; Richard Yelton, editor-at-large. **25% freelance written.** Monthly magazine covering concrete production. Audience consists of producers who have succeeded in making concrete the preferred building material through management, operating, quality control, use of the latest technology, or use of superior materials. Estab. 1982. Circ. 18,000. Byline given. Pays on acceptance. No kill fee. Publishes ms an average of 2 months after acceptance. Editorial lead time 4 months. Accepts queries by mail, e-mail, fax, phone. Accepts simultaneous submissions. Responds in 1 week to queries; in 2 months to mss. Sample copy: $4. Guidelines free.

NONFICTION Needs how-to, new product, technical. **Buys 10 mss/year.** Send complete ms. Length: 500-2,000 words. **Pays $200-1,000.**

PHOTOS Scan photos at 300 dpi. State availability. Captions, identification of subjects required. Reviews transparencies, prints. Offers no additional payment for photos accepted with ms.

HARD HAT NEWS

Lee Publications, Inc., 6113 State Highway 5, P.O. Box 121, Palatine Bridge NY 13428. (518)673-3763 or (800)218-5586. **Fax:** (518)673-2381. **E-mail:** jcasey@leepub.com. **Website:** www.hardhat.com. **Contact:** Jon Casey, editor. **50% freelance written.** Biweekly tabloid covering heavy construction, equipment, road, and bridge work. "Our readers are contractors and heavy construction workers involved in excavation, highways, bridges, utility construction, and underground construction." Estab. 1980. Circ. 15,000. Byline given. No kill fee. Editorial lead time 2 weeks. Submit seasonal material 2 weeks in advance. Accepts queries by mail, e-mail, fax, phone. Sample copy and writer's guidelines free.

NONFICTION Needs interview, new product, opinion, photo feature, technical. Send complete ms. Length: 800-2,000 words. **Pays $2.50/inch.**

PHOTOS Send photos. Captions, identification of subjects required. Reviews prints, digital preferred. Offers $15/photo.

COLUMNS/DEPARTMENTS Association News; Parts and Repairs; Attachments; Trucks and Trailers; People on the Move.

TIPS "Every issue has a focus—see our editorial calendar. Special consideration is given to a story that coincides with the focus. A color photo is necessary for the front page. Vertical shots work best. We need more writers in the metro New York area. Also, we are expanding our distribution into the Mid-Atlantic states and need writers in New York, Massachusetts, Vermont, Connecticut, and New Hampshire."

HOME ENERGY MAGAZINE

Energy Auditor & Retrofitter, 1250 Addison St., Suite 211B, Berkeley CA 94702. (510) 524-5405. **Fax:** (510) 981-1406. **E-mail:** contact@homeenergy.org; jpgunshinan@homeenergy.org. **Website:** www.homeenergy.org. **Contact:** Jim Gunshinan, editor. **10% freelance written.** Quarterly print and digital magazine plus online articles and blog covering green home building and renovation. Readers are building contractors, energy auditors, and weatherization professionals. They expect technical detail, accuracy, and brevity. Estab. 1984. Circ. 5,000. Byline given. Pays on publication. Offers 10% kill fee. Publishes ms an average of 4 months after acceptance. Editorial lead time 4 months. Accepts queries by e-mail. Accepts simultaneous submissions. Responds in 2 weeks to queries; 2 months to mss. Guidelines online.

NONFICTION Needs interview, technical. Does not want articles for consumers/general public. **Buys 6 mss/year.** Query with published clips. Submit article via e-mail. Length: 400-2,500 words. **Pays 20¢/word; $400 maximum for both assigned and unsolicited articles.**

COLUMNS/DEPARTMENTS "Trends" are short stories explaining a single advance or research result (400-1,500 words). "Features" are longer pieces that provide more in-depth information (1,500-2,500 words). "Field Notes" provide readers with first-person testimonials (1,500-2,500 words). "Columns" provide readers with direct answers to their specific questions (400-1,500 words). Submit columns via e-mail. Accepts Word, RTF documents, Text documents, and other common formats.

INTERIOR CONSTRUCTION

Ceilings & Interior Systems Construction Association, 1010 Jorie Blvd., Suite 30, Oak Brook IL 60523. (630)584-1919. **Fax:** (866)560-8537. **E-mail:** cisca@cisca.org; csmith@naylor.com. **Website:** www.cisca.org. **Contact:** Cody Smith. Quarterly magazine on acoustics and commercial specialty ceiling construction. The resource for the Ceilings & Interior Systems Construction Industry. Features examine leading industry issues and trends like specialty ceilings, LEED, acoustics, and more. Each issue features industry news, new products, columns from industry experts, and CISCA news and initiatives. Estab. 1950. Circ. 3,000. Byline given. Pays on publication. No kill fee. Publishes ms an average of 1 1/2 months after acceptance. Editorial lead time 2-3 months. Accepts queries by e-mail. Accepts simultaneous submissions. Sample copy by e-mail. Guidelines available.

NONFICTION Needs new product, technical. Query with published clips. Publishes 1-2 features per issue. Length: 700-1,700 words. **Pays $400 minimum, $800 maximum for assigned articles.**

METAL ROOFING MAGAZINE

a Division of F+W Media, Inc., 700 E. Iola St., Iola WI 54990-0001. (715)445-4612. **Fax:** (715)445-4087. **E-mail:** sharon.glorioso@fwmedia.com. **Website:** www.constructionmagnet.com/metal-roofing. **10% freelance written.** Bimonthly magazine covering roofing. *Metal Roofing Magazine* offers contractors, designers, suppliers, architects, and others in the construction industry a wealth of information on metal roofing—a growing segment of the roofing trade. Estab. 2000. Circ. 26,000. Byline given. Pays on publication. Publishes ms an average of 3 months after acceptance. Editorial lead time 3 months. Submit seasonal material 3 months in advance. Accepts queries by mail. Accepts simultaneous submissions. Sample copy free.

NONFICTION Needs book excerpts, historical, how-to, interview, new product, opinion, photo feature, technical. No advertorials. **Buys 15 mss/year.** Query with published clips. Length: 750 words minimum. **Pays $100-500 for assigned articles.**

PHOTOS Send photos. Captions, identification of subjects required. Reviews GIF/JPEG files. Negotiates payment individually. Buys all rights.

COLUMNS/DEPARTMENTS Gutter Opportunities; Stay Cool; Metal Roofing Details; Spec It. **Buys 15 mss/year.** Send complete ms. **Pays $0-500.**

TIPS "Read our magazine online for a sense of our typical subject matter and audience. Contact by regular mail is best."

◑ NETCOMPOSITES

4a Broom Business Park, Bridge Way Chesterfield S41 9QG UK. **E-mail:** info@netcomposites.com. **Website:** www.netcomposites.com. **1% freelance written.** Bimonthly newsletter covering advanced materials and fiber-reinforced polymer composites, plus a weekly electronic version called *Composite eNews*. *Advanced Materials & Composites News* covers markets, applications, materials, processes, and organizations for all sectors of the global hi-tech materials world. Audience is management, academics, researchers, government, suppliers, and fabricators. Focus on news about growth opportunities. Estab. 1978. Circ. 15,000+. Byline sometimes given. Pays on publication. No kill fee. Publishes ms an average of 1 month after acceptance. Editorial lead time 2 weeks. Submit seasonal material 1 month in advance. Accepts queries by e-mail. Accepts simultaneous submissions. Responds in 1 week to queries. Responds in 1 month to mss. Sample copy for #10 SASE.

NONFICTION Needs new product, technical, industry information. **Buys 4-6 mss/year.** Query. 300 words. **Pays $200/final printed page.**

PHOTOS State availability. Captions, identification of subjects, model releases required. Reviews 4x5 transparencies, prints, 35mm slides, JPEGs (much preferred). Offers no additional payment for photos accepted with ms. Buys all rights.

POB MAGAZINE

BNP Media, 2401 W. Big Beaver Rd., Suite 700, Troy MI 48084. (248)362-3700. **E-mail:** trunickp@bnpmedia.com. **Website:** www.pobonline.com. **Contact:** Perry Trunick, editor. **5% freelance written,.** Monthly magazine covering surveying, mapping, and geomatics. Estab. 1975. Circ. 39,000. Byline given. Pays on publication. Publishes ms an average of 3 months after acceptance. Editorial lead time 3 months. Accepts queries by e-mail, phone. Accepts simultaneous submissions. Sample copy and guidelines available online.

NONFICTION Query. Document should be saved in Microsoft Word or text-only format. Also include an author byline and biography. Length: 1,700-2,200 words, with 2 graphics included. **Pays $400.**

PHOTOS State availability. Captions, identification of subjects required. Reviews GIF/JPEG files. Offers no additional payment for photos accepted with ms. Buys one-time rights.

TIPS "Authors must know our profession and industry."

PRECAST INC.

National Precast Concrete Association, 1320 City Center Dr., Suite 200, Carmel IN 46032. (317)571-9500. **Fax:** (317)571-0041. **E-mail:** npca@precast.org; sgreer@precast.org. **Website:** www.precast.org. **Contact:** Sara Greer, managing editor. **75% freelance written.** Bimonthly magazine covering manufactured concrete products. *Precast Inc.* is a publication for

owners and managers of factory-produced concrete products used in construction. Publishes business articles, technical articles, company profiles, safety articles, and project profiles, with the intent of educating our readers in order to increase the quality and use of precast concrete. Estab. 1995. Circ. 8,500. Byline given. Pays on acceptance. No kill fee. Publishes ms an average of 6 months after acceptance. Editorial lead time 3 months. Accepts queries by mail, e-mail, fax. Accepts simultaneous submissions. Responds in 1 month to queries. Responds in 2 months to mss. Sample copy available online. Guidelines available online.

NONFICTION Needs how-to, interview, technical. No humor, essays, fiction, or fillers. **Buys 8-14 mss/year.** Query or send complete ms. Length: 1,500-2,500 words. **Pays $250-750.**

PHOTOS State availability. Captions required. Offers no additional payment for photos accepted with ms. Buys all rights.

TIPS "Understanding audience interests and needs is important and expressing a willingness to tailor a subject to get the right slant is critical. Our primary freelance needs are about general business or technology topics. Of course, if you are an engineer or a writer specializing in industry, construction, or manufacturing technology, other possibilities may exist. Writing style should be concise, yet lively and entertaining. Avoid clichés. We require a third-person perspective, and encourage a positive tone and active voice. For stylistic matters, follow the *AP Style Book*."

RURAL BUILDER

F+W Media, Inc., 700 E. State St., Iola WI 54990-0001. (715)445-4612, ext. 13644. **Fax:** (715)445-4087. **E-mail:** sharon.thatcher@fwcommunity.com. **Website:** www.ruralbuilder.com. **10% freelance written.** Magazine published 8 times/year covering rural building. "*Rural Builder* serves diversified town and country builders, offering them help managing their businesses through editorial and advertising material about metal, wood, post-frame, and masonry construction." Estab. 1967. Circ. 29,000. Byline given. Pays on publication. Publishes ms an average of 3 months after acceptance. Editorial lead time 3 months. Submit seasonal material 3 months in advance. Accepts queries by mail, e-mail. Accepts simultaneous submissions. Sample copy free.

NONFICTION Needs how-to, photo feature, technical. No advertorials. **Buys 10 mss/year.** Query with published clips. Length: 750 words minimum. **Pays $100-300.**

PHOTOS Send photos. Captions, identification of subjects required. Reviews GIF/JPEG files. Negotiates payment individually. Buys all rights.

COLUMNS/DEPARTMENTS Money Talk (taxes for business); Tech Talk (computers for builders); Tool Talk (tools); Management Insights (business management); all 1,000 words. **Buys 10 mss/year.** Send complete ms. **Pays $0-250.**

TIPS "Read our magazine online for a sense of our typical subject matter and audience. Contact by e-mail is best. No advertorials, please."

UNDERGROUND CONSTRUCTION

Oildom Publishing Company of Texas, Inc., P.O. Box 941669, Houston TX 77094-8669. (281)558-6930, ext. 220. **Fax:** (281)558-7029. **E-mail:** rcarpenter@oildom.com; efitzpatrick@oildom.com. **Website:** www.undergroundconstructionmagazine.com. **Contact:** Robert Carpenter, editor-in-chief; Cleve Hogarth, publisher; Elizabeth Fitzpatrick, art director. **35% freelance written.** Monthly magazine covering underground oil and gas pipeline, water and sewer pipeline, cable construction for contractors, and owning companies. Circ. 40,000. No kill fee. Publishes ms an average of 6 months after acceptance. Accepts queries by mail, e-mail, fax, phone. Accepts simultaneous submissions. Responds in 1 month to mss. Sample copy for SAE.

NONFICTION Needs how-to, job stories and industry issues. Query with published clips. Length: 1,000-2,000 words. **Pays $3-500.**

PHOTOS Send photos. Captions required. Reviews color prints and slides. Buys one-time rights.

EDUCATION & COUNSELING

ARTS & ACTIVITIES

Publishers' Development Corp., 12345 World Trade Dr., San Diego CA 92128. (858)605-0242. **Fax:** (858)605-0247. **E-mail:** ed@artsandactivities.com. **Website:** www.artsandactivities.com. **Contact:** Maryellen Bridge, editor-in-chief. **95% freelance written. Eager to work with new/unpublished writers.** Monthly (except July and August) magazine covering art education at levels from preschool through college for educators and therapists engaged in arts and crafts education and training. Estab. 1932. Circ. 20,000. Byline given. Pays on publication. No kill fee. Publishes ms 6 months to 3 years after acceptance. Submit seasonal material 6 months in advance. Accepts queries by mail, e-mail. Responds in 3 months to queries. Sample copy for SAE with 9x12 envelope and 8 first-class stamps. Guidelines available on website.

NONFICTION Needs historical, how-to. **Buys 80-100 mss/year.** Length: 500-1,500 words. **Pays $35-150.**

TIPS "Frequently in unsolicited mss, writers obviously have not studied the magazine to see what style of articles we publish. Send for a sample copy to familiarize yourself with our style and needs. The best way to find out if his/her writing style suits our needs is for the author to submit a ms on speculation. We prefer an anecdotal style of writing so that readers will feel as though they are there in the art room as the lesson/project is taking place. Also, good quality photographs of student artwork are important. We are a visual art magazine!"

✪ THE ATA MAGAZINE

11010 142nd St. NW, Edmonton Alberta T5N 2R1 Canada. (780)447-9400. **Fax:** (780)455-6481. **E-mail:** government@teachers.ab.ca. **Website:** www.teachers.ab.ca. Quarterly magazine covering education. Estab. 1920. Circ. 42,100. Byline given. Pays on publication. No kill fee. Publishes ms an average of 4 months after acceptance. Editorial lead time 2 months. Submit seasonal material 2 months in advance. Accepts queries by mail, e-mail, fax, phone. Accepts simultaneous submissions. Responds in 2 months to queries. Previous articles available for viewing online. Guidelines available online.

NONFICTION Query with published clips. Length: 500-1,500 words. **Pays $100 (Canadian).**

PHOTOS Send photos. Captions required. Reviews 4x6 prints. Negotiates payment individually. Negotiates rights.

THE FORENSIC TEACHER MAGAZINE

Wide Open Minds Educational Services, P.O. Box 5263, Wilmington DE 19808. **E-mail:** admin@theforensicteacher.com. **Website:** www.theforensicteacher.com. **Contact:** Dr. Mark R. Feil, editor. **70% freelance written.** Quarterly magazine covering forensic education. Readers are middle, high and post-secondary teachers who are looking for better, easier and more engaging ways to teach forensics as well as law enforcement and scientific forensic experts. Writers understand this and are writing from a forensic or educational background, or both. Prefers a first-person writing style. Estab. 2006. Circ. 30,000. Byline given. Pays 60 days after publication. No kill fee. Publishes ms an average of 6 months after acceptance. Editorial lead time 6 months. Submit seasonal material 6 months in advance. Accepts queries by e-mail. Accepts simultaneous submissions. Responds in 2 weeks to queries; 2 months to mss. Sample copy available at website. Guidelines available online.

NONFICTION Needs general interest, historical, how-to, personal experience, photo feature, technical. Does not want poetry, fiction, or anything unrelated to medicine, law, forensics or teaching. **Buys 18 mss/year.** Send complete ms. Length: 400-3,000 words. **Pays 2¢/word.**

PHOTOS State availability. Captions required. Reviews GIF/JPEG files/pdf. Send photos separately in e-mail, not in the article. Negotiates payment individually. Buys electronic rights.

COLUMNS/DEPARTMENTS Needs lesson experiences or ideas, personal or professional experiences with a branch of forensics. "If you've done it in your classroom please share it with us. Also, if you're a professional, please tell our readers how they can duplicate the lesson/demo/experiment in their classrooms. Please share what you know."

FILLERS Needs Needs facts, newsbreaks. **Buys 15 mss/year.** Length: 50-200 words. **Pays 2¢/word.**

TIPS "Your article will benefit forensics teachers and their students. It should inform, entertain and enlighten the teacher and the students. Would you read it if you were a busy forensics teacher? Also, don't send a rèsumè and tell us how much experience you have and ask for an assignment; query via e-mail with an outline of your proposed piece."

THE HISPANIC OUTLOOK IN HIGHER EDUCATION

299 Market Street, Suite 145, Saddle Brook NJ 07663. (800)587-8800. **Fax:** (201)587-9105. **Website:** www. hispanicoutlook.com. **Contact:** Mary Ann Cooper, editor in chief. **50% freelance written.** Biweekly magazine (except during the summer) covering higher education of Hispanics. Looking for higher education story articles, with a focus on Hispanics and the advancements made by and for Hispanics in higher education. Circ. 28,000. Byline given. Pays on publication.

No kill fee. Publishes ms an average of 2 months after acceptance. Editorial lead time 2 months. Submit seasonal material 3 months in advance. Accepts queries by mail, e-mail, fax. Accepts simultaneous submissions. Sample copy free.

NONFICTION Needs historical. **Buys 20-25 mss/year.** Query with published clips. Length: 1,800-2,200 words. **Pays $400 minimum for print articles, and $300 for online articles when accepted.**

PHOTOS Send photos. Reviews color or b&w prints, digital images must be 300 dpi (call for e-mail photo address). Offers no additional payment for photos accepted with ms.

TIPS "Articles explore the Hispanic experience in higher education. Special theme issues address sports, law, health, corporations, heritage, women, and a wide range of similar issues; however, articles need not fall under those umbrellas."

PTO TODAY

PTO Today, Inc., 100 Stonewall Blvd., Suite 3, Wrentham MA 02093. (800)644-3561. **Fax:** (508)384-6108. **E-mail:** queries@ptotoday.com. **Website:** www.ptotoday.com. **Contact:** Craig Bystrynski, editor-in-chief. **50% freelance written.** Magazine published 6 times during the school year covering the work of school parent-teacher groups. Celebrates the work of school parent volunteers and provide resources to help them do that work more effectively. Estab. 1999. Circ. 80,000. Byline given. Pays on acceptance. Offers 30% kill fee. Publishes ms an average of 4-6 months after acceptance. Editorial lead time 4 months. Submit seasonal material 4 months in advance. Accepts queries by e-mail. Accepts simultaneous submissions. Guidelines by e-mail.

NONFICTION Needs general interest, how-to, interview, personal experience. **Buys 20 mss/year.** Query. "We review but do not encourage unsolicited submissions." Features are roughly 1,200-2,200 words. Average assignment is 1,200 words. Department pieces are 600-1,200 words. **Payment depends on the difficulty of the topic and the experience of the writer. "We pay by the assignment, not by the word; our pay scale ranges from $200 to $700 for features and $150 to $400 for departments. We occasionally pay more for high-impact stories and highly experienced writers. We buy all rights, and we pay on acceptance (within 30 days of invoice)."**

PHOTOS State availability. Identification of subjects required. Negotiates payment individually. Permission for print and web publishing.

TIPS "It's difficult for us to find talented writers with strong experience with parent groups. This experience is a big plus. Also, it helps to review our writer's guidelines before querying. All queries must have a strong parent group angle."

SCHOOLARTS MAGAZINE

Davis Art, 50 Portland St., Worcester MA 01608. **E-mail:** lmarkey@schoolartsmagazine.com. **E-mail:** sa-submissions@davisart.com. **Website:** schoolartsmagazine.com. **Contact:** Lorraine Markey. **85% freelance written.** Monthly magazine (September-July), serving arts and craft education profession, K-12, higher education, and museum education programs written by and for art teachers. Estab. 1901. Pays on publication (honorarium and 6 copies). No kill fee. Publishes ms an average of 24 months after acceptance. Accepts queries by mail. Responds in 2-4 months to queries. Guidelines available online.

NONFICTION Query or send complete ms and SASE. E-mail submissions are also accepted. See website for details. Length: 800 words maximum. **Pays $30-150.**

TIPS "We prefer articles on actual art projects or techniques done by students in actual classroom situations. Philosophical and theoretical aspects of art and art education are usually handled by our contributing editors. Our articles are reviewed and accepted on merit and each is tailored to meet our needs. Keep in mind that art teachers want practical tips above all—more hands-on information than academic theory. Write your article with the accompanying photographs in hand. The most frequent mistakes made by writers are bad visual material (photographs, drawings) submitted with articles, a lack of complete descriptions of art processes, and no rationale behind programs or activities. Familiarity with the field of art education is essential. Review recent issues of *SchoolArts*."

TEACHERS & WRITERS MAGAZINE

Teachers & Writers Collaborative, 540 President Street, 3rd Floor, Brooklyn NY 11215. (212)691-6590. **Fax:** (212)675-0171. **E-mail:** editors@twc.org. **Website:** http://teachersandwritersmagazine.org/. **Contact:** Amy Swauger. **30% freelance written.** *Teachers & Writers Magazine* covers a cross-section of contemporary issues and innovations in education and writing, and engages writers, educators, critics, and students in a conversation on the nature of creativity and the imagination. Estab. 1967. Circ. 6,500. Byline given. Pays on publication. No kill fee. Publishes ms an average of 4-6 months after acceptance. Editorial lead time 2-4 months. Submit seasonal material 4-6 months in advance. Accepts queries by e-mail. Accepts simultaneous submissions. Responds in 1-2 months to queries and submissions. Guidelines available online: www.teachersandwritersmagazine.org/about-us/submission-guidelines.

NONFICTION Needs book excerpts, essays, how-to, interview, opinion, personal experience, creative writing exercises. Length: 500-2,500 words. **Pays $50-150.**

TEACHERS OF VISION

A Publication of Christian Educators Association, P.O. Box 45610, Westlake OH 44145. (888)798-1124. **E-mail:** TOV@ceai.org. **Website:** www.ceai.org. **70% freelance written.** Magazine published 3 times/year for Christians in public education. *Teachers of Vision*'s articles inspire, inform, and equip teachers and administrators in the educational arena. Readers look for teacher tips, integrating faith and work, and general interest education articles. Topics include subject matter, religious expression and activity in public schools, and legal rights of Christian educators. Audience is primarily public school educators. Other readers include teachers in private schools, university professors, school administrators, parents, and school board members. Estab. 1953. Circ. 10,000. Byline given. Pays on publication. No kill fee. Publishes ms an average of 6 months after acceptance. Editorial lead time 4 months. Submit seasonal material 4 months in advance. Accepts queries by mail, e-mail. Accepts simultaneous submissions. Responds in 1 month to queries; 3-4 months to mss. Sample copy for SAE with 9x12 envelope and 4 first-class stamps. Guidelines available online.

NONFICTION Needs how-to, humor, inspirational, interview, opinion, personal experience, religious. No preaching. **Buys 30-50 mss/year.** Query or send complete ms if 2,000 words or less. Length: 1,500 words. **Pays $25-50.**

REPRINTS Buys reprints.

PHOTOS State availability of photos. Offers no additional payment for photos accepted with ms. Buys one-time, web, and reprint rights by members for educational purposes.

COLUMNS/DEPARTMENTS Query. **Pays $25-50.**

POETRY Will accept poetry if it pertains to education.

FILLERS Send with SASE—must relate to public education.

TIPS "We are looking for material on living out one's faith in appropriate, legal ways in the public school setting."

TEACHING THEATRE

Educational Theatre Association, 2343 Auburn Ave., Cincinnati OH 45219-2815. (513)421-3900. **E-mail:** gbossler@schooltheatre.org; publicationsdept@ schooltheatre.org. **Website:** www.schooltheatre.org. **Contact:** Gregory Bossler, managing editor. **65% freelance written.** Quarterly magazine covering education theater K-12; primary emphasis on middle and secondary level education. Estab. 1989. Circ. 5,000. Byline given. Pays on acceptance. No kill fee. Publishes ms an average of 3 months after acceptance. Editorial lead time 2 months. Accepts queries by mail, e-mail. Accepts simultaneous submissions. Responds in 4-6 weeks to queries. Responds in 3 months to mss. Sample copy available online. Guidelines available online.

NONFICTION Needs book excerpts, essays, how-to, interview. **Buys 12-15 mss/year.** Query. A typical issue might include: an article on theatre curriculum development; a profile of an exemplary theatre education program; a how-to teach piece on acting, directing, or playwriting; and a news story or 2 about pertinent educational theatre issues and events. Once articles are accepted, authors are asked to supply their work electronically via e-mail. Length: 750-4,000 words. **Pays $150-500.**

PHOTOS State availability. Reviews digital images (300 dpi minimum), prints. Unless other arrangements are made, payment for articles includes payment for the photos and illustrations.

TIPS Wants "articles that address the needs of the busy but experienced high school theater educators. Fundamental pieces on the value of theater education are not of value to us—our readers already know that."

TEACHING TOLERANCE

A Project of The Southern Poverty Law Center, 400 Washington Ave., Montgomery AL 36104. (334)956-8374. **Fax:** (334)956-8488. **E-mail:** editor@teaching-tolerance.org. **Website:** www.teachingtolerance.org.

Contact: Adrienne van der Valk, managing editor. **30% freelance written.** Semiannual magazine. Estab. 1991. Circ. 400,000. Byline given. Pays on acceptance. No kill fee. Editorial lead time 6 months. Submit seasonal material 6 months in advance. Accepts queries by mail, fax, online submission form. Accepts simultaneous submissions. Sample copy avialble online. Guidelines available online.

NONFICTION Needs essays, how-to, personal experience, photo feature. No jargon, rhetoric or academic analysis. No theoretical discussions on the pros/cons of multicultural education. **Buys 2-4 mss/year.** Submit outlines or complete mss. Length: 400-1,600 words. **Pays $1/word.**

PHOTOS State availability. Captions, identification of subjects required. Reviews contact sheets, transparencies. Buys one-time rights.

COLUMNS/DEPARTMENTS Features (stories and issues related to anti-bias education), 800-1,600 words; Why I Teach (personal reflections about life in the classroom), 600 words or less; Story Corner (designed to be read by or to students and must cover topics that are appealing to children), 600 words; Activity Exchange (brief descriptions of classroom lesson plans, special projects or other school activities that can be used by others to promote tolerance), 400 words. **Buys 8-12 mss/year.** Query with published clips. Does not accept unsolicited mss. **Pays $1/ word.**

TIPS "We want lively, simple, concise writing. Be descriptive and reflective, showing the strength of programs dealing successfully with diversity by employing clear descriptions of real scenes and interactions, and by using quotes from teachers and students. Study previous issues of the magazine before submitting. Most open to articles that have a strong classroom focus. We are interested in approaches to teaching tolerance and promoting understanding that really work that we might not have heard of. We want to inform, inspire and encourage our readers. We know what's happening nationally; we want to know what's happening in your neighborhood classroom."

ELECTRONICS & COMMUNICATION

THE ACUTA JOURNAL

Information Communications Technology in Higher Education, 152 W. Zandale Dr., Suite 200, Lexington KY 40503. (859)278-3338. **Fax:** (859)278-3268. **E-mail:** pscott@acuta.org. **Website:** www.acuta.org. **Contact:** Pat Scott, director of communications. **20% freelance written.** Quarterly professional association journal covering information communications technology (ICT) in higher education. Audience includes, primarily, middle to upper management in the IT/telecommunications department on college/university campuses. They are highly skilled, technology-oriented professionals who provide data, voice, and video communications services for residential and academic purposes. Estab. 1997. Circ. 2,200. Byline given. Pays on publication. No kill fee. Publishes ms an average of 6 months after acceptance. Editorial lead time 6 months. Accepts queries by mail, e-mail, fax, phone. Accepts simultaneous submissions. Responds in 2 weeks to queries. Request a sample copy by calling (859)721-1659. Guidelines online.

NONFICTION Needs how-to, technical, case study, college/university application of technology. **Buys 6-8 mss/year.** Query. Length: 1,200-4,000 words. **Pays 8-10¢/word.**

PHOTOS State availability. Captions, model releases required. Reviews prints. Offers no additional payment for photos accepted with ms.

TIPS "Our audience expects every article to be relevant to information communications technology on the college/university campus, whether it is related to technology, facilities, or management. Writers must read back issues to understand this focus and the level of technicality we expect."

COMPUTERWORLD

IDG, Inc., P.O. Box 9208, Framingham MA 01701. (508)879-0700. **Website:** www.computerworld.com. **Contact:** Ellen Fanning, editor. Weekly magazine. We provide readers with a lively variety of everything from the latest IT news, in-depth analysis and feature stories, to special reports, case studies, industry updates, product information, advice and opinion. Estab. 1967. Circ. 180,000. No kill fee. Accepts simultaneous submissions.

🖵 Contact specific editor.

NONFICTION Needs how-to, opinion. Query.

DIGITAL OUTPUT

Rockport Custom Publishing, LLC, 100 Cummings Center, Suite 321E, Beverly MA 01915. (978)921-7850, ext. 13. **E-mail:** mdonovan@rdigitaloutput.net; edit@rockportpubs.com. **Website:** www.digitaloutput.net.

Contact: Melissa Donovan, editor. **70% freelance written.** Monthly magazine covering electronic prepress, desktop publishing, and digital imaging, with articles ranging from digital capture and design to electronic prepress and digital printing. *Digital Output* is a national business publication for electronic publishers and digital imagers, providing monthly articles which examine the latest technologies and digital methods and discuss how to profit from them. Readers include service bureaus, prepress and reprographic houses, designers, commercial printers, wide-format printers, ad agencies, corporate communications, sign shops, and others. Estab. 1994. Circ. 25,000. Byline given. Pays on publication. Offers 10-20% kill fee. Publishes ms an average of 2 months after acceptance. Editorial lead time 3 months. Submit seasonal material 3 months in advance. Accepts queries by mail, e-mail. Accepts simultaneous submissions. Responds in 3 weeks to queries. Responds in 1 month to mss. Sample copy for $4.50 or online.

NONFICTION Needs how-to, interview, technical, case studies. **Buys 36 mss/year.** Query with published clips or hyperlinks to posted clips. Length: 1,500-4,000 words. **Pays $250-600.**

PHOTOS Send photos.

TIPS "Our readers are graphic arts professionals. The freelance writers we use are deeply immersed in the technology of commercial printing, desktop publishing, digital imaging, color management, PDF workflow, inkjet printing, and similar topics."

SOUND & VIDEO CONTRACTOR

NewBay Media, LLC, 28 E. 28th St., 12th Floor, New York NY 10016. (818)236-3667. **Fax:** (913)514-3683. **E-mail:** cwisehart@nbmedia.com; jgutierrez@nbmedia.com. **Website:** www.svconline.com. Cynthia Wisehart, editor. **Contact:** Cynthia Wisehart, editor; Jessaca Gutierrez, managing and online editor. **60% freelance written.** Monthly magazine covering professional audio, video, security, acoustical design, sales, and marketing. Estab. 1983. Circ. 24,000. Byline given. Pays on acceptance. No kill fee. Publishes ms an average of 3 months after acceptance. Editorial lead time 3 months. Accepts queries by mail, e-mail, fax, phone. Accepts simultaneous submissions. Responds ASAP to queries. Sample copy and writer's guidelines free.

NONFICTION Needs historical, how-to, photo feature, technical, professional audio/video applications, installations, product reviews. No opinion pieces, advertorial, interview/profile, expose/gossip. **Buys 60 mss/year.** Query. Length: 1,000-2,500 words. **Pays $200-1,200 for assigned articles. Pays $200-650 for unsolicited articles.**

REPRINTS Accepts previously published submissions.

PHOTOS Send photos. Identification of subjects required. Reviews transparencies, prints. Offers no additional payment for photos accepted with ms.

COLUMNS/DEPARTMENTS Security Technology Review (technical install information); Sales & Marketing (techniques for installation industry); Video Happenings (Pro video/projection/storage technical info), all 1,500 words. **Buys 30 mss/year.** Query. **Pays $200-350.**

TIPS "We want materials and subject matter that would be of interest to audio/video/security/low-voltage product installers/contractors/designers professionals. If the piece allows our readers to save time, money and/or increases their revenues, then we have reached our goals. Highly technical is desirable."

SQL SERVER MAGAZINE

Penton Media, 221 E. 29th St., Loveland CO 80538. (970)663-4700. **Fax:** (970)667-2321. **E-mail:** Debra.Donston-Miller@penton.com. **Website:** www.sqlmag.com. **Contact:** Deb Donston-Miller, editor. **35% freelance written.** Monthly magazine covering Microsoft SQL Server. *SQL Server Magazine* is the only magazine completely devoted to helping developers and DBAs master new and emerging SQL Server technologies and issues. It provides practical advice and lots of code examples for SQL Server developers and administrators, and includes how-to articles, tips, tricks, and programming techniques offered by SQL Server experts. Estab. 1999. Circ. 20,000. Byline given. "Penton Media pays for articles upon publication. Payment rates are based on the author's writing experience and the quality of the article submitted. We will discuss the payment rate for your article when we notify you of its acceptance." Offers $100 kill fee. Publishes ms an average of 6 months after acceptance. Editorial lead time 4+ months. Accepts queries by mail, e-mail. Accepts simultaneous submissions. Responds in 6 weeks to queries. Responds in 2-3 months to mss. Sample copy available online. Guidelines available online.

NONFICTION Needs how-to, technical, SQL Server administration and programming. Nothing promot-

ing third-party products or companies. **Buys 25-35 mss/year.** Send complete ms. Length: 1,800-2,500 words. **Pays $200 for feature articles; $500 for Focus articles.**

COLUMNS/DEPARTMENTS Contact: R2R Editor. Reader to Reader (helpful SQL Server hints and tips from readers), 200-400 words. **Buys 6-12 mss/year.** Send complete ms. **Pays $50**

TIPS "Read back issues and make sure that your proposed article doesn't overlap previous coverage. When proposing articles, state specifically how your article would contain new information compared to previously published information, and what benefit your information would be to *SQL Server Magazine*'s readership."

ENERGY & UTILITIES

⑤⑤ ELECTRICAL APPARATUS

Barks Publications, Inc., Suite 901, 500 N. Michigan Ave., Chicago IL 60611. (312)321-9440. **Fax:** (312)321-1288. **E-mail:** eamagazine@barks.com. **Website:** www.barks.com. **Contact:** Elizabeth Van Ness, publisher; Kevin N. Jones, senior editor. Monthly magazine for persons working in electrical and electronic maintenance, in industrial plants and service and sales centers, who install and service electric motors, transformers, generators, controls, and related equipment. Contact staff members by telephone for their preferred e-mail addresses. Estab. 1967. Circ. 16,000. Byline given. Pays on publication. No kill fee. Publishes ms an average of 1 month after acceptance. Accepts queries by mail, e-mail, fax. Accepts simultaneous submissions. Responds in 1 week to queries sent by US mail.

NONFICTION Needs technical. Length: 1,500-2,500 words. **Pays $250-500 for assigned articles.**

TIPS "We welcome queries re: technical columns on electro-mehanical subjects as pump repari, automation, drives, etc. All feature articles are assigned to staff and contributing editors and correspondents. Professionals interested in appointments as contributing editors and correspondents should submit résumé and article outlines, including illustration suggestions. Writers should be competent with a camera, which should be described in résumé. Technical expertise is absolutely necessary, preferably an E.E. degree, or practical experience. We are also book publishers and some of the material in *EA* is now in book form, bringing the authors royalties. Also publishes an annual directory, subtitled *ElectroMechanical Bench Reference.*"

✪ ELECTRICAL BUSINESS

CLB Media, Inc., 222 Edward St., Aurora ON L4G 1W6 Canada. (905)727-0077; (905)713-4391. **Fax:** (905)727-0017. **E-mail:** acapkun@annexweb.com. **Website:** www.ebmag.com. **Contact:** Anthony Capkun, editor. **35% freelance written.** Tabloid published 10 times/year covering the Canadian electrical industry. *Electrical Business* targets electrical contractors and electricians. It provides practical information readers can use right away in their work and for running their business and assets. Estab. 1964. Circ. 18,097. Byline given. Pays on acceptance. Offers 50% kill fee. Publishes ms an average of 1-2 months after acceptance. Editorial lead time 3 months. Submit seasonal material 6 months in advance. Accepts queries by e-mail, phone. Accepts simultaneous submissions. Responds in 1 month. Sample copy online. Guidelines online.

NONFICTION Needs how-to, technical. Special issues: Summer Blockbuster issue (June/July); Special Homebuilders' issue (November/December). **Buys 15 mss/year.** Query. Length: 800-1,200 words. **Pays 40¢/word.**

PHOTOS State availability. Captions, identification of subjects, model releases required. Reviews GIF/JPEG files. Negotiates payment individually. Buys simultaneous rights.

COLUMNS/DEPARTMENTS Atlantic Focus (stories from Atlantic Canada); Western Focus (stories from Western Canada, including Manitoba); Trucks for the Trade (articles pertaining to the vehicles used by electrical contractors); Tools for the Trade (articles pertaining to tools used by contractors); all 800 words. **Buys 6 mss/year.** Query. **Pays 40¢/word.**

TIPS "Call me, and we'll talk about what I need, and how you can provide it. Stories must have Canadian content."

PUBLIC POWER

2451 Crystal Dr., Suite 1000, Arlington VA 22202-4804. (202)467-2900. **Fax:** (202)467-2910. **E-mail:** news@publicpower.org; ldalessandro@publicpower.org; rthomas@publicpower.org. **Website:** www.publicpower.org. **Contact:** Laura D'Alessandro, editor; Robert Thomas, art director. **60% freelance written.** Prefers to work with published/established writers. Publication of the American Public Power Association, published 6 times a year. Emphasizes electric power provided by cities, towns, and utility districts. Estab. 1942. Circ. 14,000. Byline given. Pays on acceptance. No kill fee. Publishes ms an average of 3 months after acceptance. Accepts queries by mail, e-mail, fax. Accepts simultaneous submissions. Responds in 6 months to queries. Sample copy and writer's guidelines free.

NONFICTION Pays $500 and up.

PHOTOS Reviews electronic photos (minimum 300 dpi at reproduction size).

TIPS "We look for writers who are familiar with energy policy issues."

ENGINEERING & TECHNOLOGY

✪ CANADIAN CONSULTING ENGINEER

Business Information Group, 80 Valleybrook Dr., Toronto ON M3B 2S9 Canada. (416)510-5119. **Fax:** (416)510-5134. **E-mail:** dpicklyk@ccemag.com. **Website:** www.canadianconsultingengineer.com. **Contact:** Doug Picklyk, editor. **20% freelance written.** Bimonthly magazine covering consulting engineering in private practice. Estab. 1958. Circ. 8,900. Byline given depending on length of story. Pays on publication. Offers 50% kill fee. Publishes ms an average of 4 months after acceptance. Editorial lead time 6 months. Accepts simultaneous submissions. Responds in 3 months to mss. Sample copy free.

   ◑   Canadian content only. Impartial editorial required.

NONFICTION Needs historical, new product. **Buys 8-10 mss/year.** Query with published clips. Length: 300-1,500 words. **Pays $200-1,000 (Canadian).**

PHOTOS State availability. Negotiates payment individually. Buys one-time rights.

COLUMNS/DEPARTMENTS Export (selling consulting engineering services abroad); Management (managing consulting engineering businesses); On-Line (trends in CAD systems); Employment; Business; Construction and Environmental Law (Canada); all 800 words. **Buys 4 mss/year.** Query with published clips. **Pays $250-400.**

COMPOSITES MANUFACTURING MAGAZINE

American Composites Manufacturers Association, 3033 Wilson Blvd., Suite 420, Arlington VA 22201. (703)525-0511. **E-mail:** communications@acmanet.org; info@acmanet.org. **Website:** www.acmanet.org. Monthly magazine covering any industry that uses reinforced composites: marine, aerospace, infrastructure, automotive, transportation, corrosion, architecture, tub and shower, sports, and recreation. Primarily publishes educational pieces, the how-to of the shop environment. Also publishes marketing, business trends, and economic forecasts relevant to the composites industry. Estab. 1979. Circ. 12,000. Byline given. Pays on acceptance. No kill fee. Publishes ms an average of 2-3 months after acceptance. Editorial lead time 2 months. Accepts queries by e-mail. Accepts simultaneous submissions. Responds in 1 week to queries. Responds in 1 month to mss. Sample copy free. Guidelines by e-mail and online. Specific details on submission types available online.

NONFICTION Needs how-to, new product, technical, marketing, related business trends and forecasts. Special issues: "Each January we publish a World Market Report where we cover all niche markets and all geographic areas relevant to the composites industry. Freelance material will be considered strongly for this issue." No need to query company or personal profiles unless there is an extremely unique or novel angle. **Buys 5-10 mss/year.** Query. *Composites Manufacturing* invites freelance feature submissions, all of which should be sent via e-mail as a Microsoft Word attachment. A query letter is required. Length: 1,500-2,000 words. **Pays 20-40¢/word (negotiable).**

COLUMNS/DEPARTMENTS "We publish columns on HR, relevant government legislation, industry lessons learned, regulatory affairs, and technology. Average word length for columns is 500 words. We would entertain any new column idea that hits hard on industry matters." Query. **Pays $300-350.**

TIPS "The best way to break into the magazine is to empathize with the entrepreneurial and technical background of readership, and come up with an exclusive, original, creative story idea. We pride ourselves on not looking or acting like any other trade publication (composites industry or otherwise). Our editor is very open to suggestions, but they must be unique. Don't waste his time with canned articles dressed up to look exclusive. This is the best way to get on the 'immediate rejection list.'"

✪ CONNECTIONS+

The Magazine for ICT Professionals, Business Information Group, 80 Valleybrook Dr., Toronto ON M3B 2S9 Canada. (416)510-6752. **Fax:** (416)510-5134. **E-mail:** pbarker@connectionsplus.ca. **Website:** www.connectionsplus.ca. **Contact:** Paul Barker, editor. **50% freelance written.** Magazine published 6 times/year covering the structured cabling/telecommunications industry. Estab. 1998. Circ. 15,000 print; 45,000 electronic. Byline given. Pays on publication. No kill fee. Publishes ms an average of 1 month after acceptance. Editorial lead time 3 months. Submit seasonal material 1 month in advance. Accepts queries by mail, e-mail, phone. Accepts simultaneous submissions. Sample copy available online. Guidelines free.

NONFICTION Needs technical. No reprints or previously written articles. All articles are assigned by editor based on query or need of publication. **Buys 12 mss/year.** Query with published clips. Length: 1,500-2,500 words. **Pays 40-50¢/word.**

PHOTOS State availability. Captions, identification of subjects required. Reviews contact sheets, prints. Negotiates payment individually.

COLUMNS/DEPARTMENTS Focus on Engineering/Design; Focus on Installation; Focus on Maintenance/Testing; all 1,500 words. **Buys 7 mss/year.** Query with published clips. **Pays 40-50¢/word.**

TIPS "Visit our website to see back issues, and visit links on our website for background."

ENTERPRISE MINNESOTA MAGAZINE

Enterprise Minnesota, Inc., 310 Fourth Ave. S., Suite 7050, Minneapolis MN 55415. (612)373-2900. **Fax:** (612)373-2901. **E-mail:** editor@enterpriseminnesota.org. **Website:** www.enterpriseminnesota.org. **90% freelance written.** Magazine published 5 times/year. *Enterprise Minnesota Magazine* is for the owners and top management of Minnesota's technology and manufacturing companies. The magazine covers technology trends and issues, global trade, management techniques, and finance. Profiles new and growing companies, new products, and the innovators and entrepreneurs of Minnesota's technology sector. Estab. 1991. Circ. 16,000. Byline given. Pays on publication. Offers 10% kill fee. Publishes ms an average of 3 months after acceptance. Editorial lead time 1 month. Submit seasonal material 1 year in advance. Accepts queries by mail, e-mail. Accepts simultaneous submissions. Guidelines free.

NONFICTION Needs general interest, how-to, interview. **Buys 60 mss/year.** Query with published clips. **Pays $150-1,000.**

COLUMNS/DEPARTMENTS Feature Well (Q&A format, provocative ideas from Minnesota business and industry leaders), 2,000 words; Up Front (mini profiles, anecdotal news items), 250-500 words. Query with published clips.

EROSION CONTROL

Forester Media Inc., P.O. Box 3100, Santa Barbara CA 93130. (805)679-7629. **E-mail:** asantiago@forester.net. **Website:** www.erosioncontrol.com. **Contact:** Arturo Santiago. **60% freelance written.** Magazine published 7 times/year covering all aspects of erosion prevention and sediment control. *Erosion Control* is a practical, hands-on, how-to professional journal. Readers are civil engineers, landscape architects, builders, developers, public works officials, road and highway construction officials and engineers, soils specialists, farmers, landscape contractors, and others involved with any activity that disturbs significant areas of surface vegetation. Estab. 1994. Circ. 23,000. Byline given. Pays 1 month after acceptance. No kill fee. Publishes ms an average of 3 months after acceptance. Editorial lead time 4 months. Submit seasonal material 4 months in advance. Accepts queries by e-mail, phone. Responds in 3 weeks to queries. Sample copy and writer's guidelines free.

NONFICTION Needs photo feature, technical. **Buys 15 mss/year.** Query with published clips. Length: 2,000-4,000 words. **Pays $700-850.**

PHOTOS Send photos. Captions, identification of subjects, model releases required. Reviews transparencies, prints. Offers no additional payment for photos accepted with ms. Buys all rights.

TIPS "Writers should have a good grasp of technology involved and good writing and communication skills. Most of our freelance articles include extensive interviews with engineers, contractors, developers, or project owners, and we often provide contact names for articles we assign."

MFRTECH EJOURNAL

Manufacturers Group Inc., P.O. Box 4310, Lexington KY 40544. **E-mail:** editor@mfrtech.com. **Website:** www.mfrtech.com. **40% freelance written.** Magazine published daily online covering manufacturing and technology from news throughout the U.S. Editorial includes anufacturing news, expansions, acquisition white papers, case histories, new product announcements, feature submissions, book synopsis. Estab. 1976 (print). Circ. 60,000+ weekly subscribers (e-mail); 750,000 monthly online visitors. Byline given. Pays 30 days following publication. Offers 25% kill fee. Publishes ms 3-4 days after acceptance. Editorial lead time 2 weeks. Submit seasonal material 2 weeks in advance. Accepts simultaneous submissions. Sample copy online. Guidelines by e-mail.

NONFICTION Needs new product, opinion, technical. Does not want general interest, inspirational, personal, travel, book excerpts. Length: 750-1,500 words; byline: 75 words. **Pays $0.20/word published (prior to approval from editor).**

PHOTOS Up to 3 photo or graphic images permitted; must come as an attachment to ms submissions via e-mail as JPEGs and no larger than 300x300 pixels each.

COLUMNS/DEPARTMENTS New Plant Announcement, Acquisitions, Expansions, New Technology, Federal, Case Histories, Human Resources, Marketing. Query. **Pays $0.20/word (prior to approval from editor).**

MINORITY ENGINEER

Equal Opportunity Publications, Inc., 445 Broad Hollow Rd., Suite 425, Melville NY 11747. (631)421-9421. **Fax:** (516)421-0359. **E-mail:** bloehr@eop.com; info@eop.com. **Website:** www.eop.com. **Contact:** Barbara Capella Loehr, editor. **60% freelance written. Prefers to work with published/established writers.** Triannual magazine covering career guidance for minority engineering students and minority professional engineers. Estab. 1969. Circ. 15,000. Byline given. Pays on publication. No kill fee. Publishes ms an average of 3 months after acceptance. Editorial lead time 3 months. Accepts queries by mail, e-mail, fax, phone. Accepts simultaneous submissions. Responds in 2 weeks to queries. Responds in 2 months to mss. Sample copy and writer's guidelines for 9x12 SAE with 5 first-class stamps. Guidelines free.

NONFICTION Needs book excerpts, general interest, how-to, interview, opinion, personal experience, technical, articles on job search techniques, role models. No general information. Query. Length: 1,500-2,500 words. **Pays $350 for assigned articles.**

REPRINTS Send typed ms with rights for sale noted and information about when and where the material previously appeared. Pays 100% of amount paid for an original article.

PHOTOS State availability.

TIPS Articles should focus on career guidance, role model and industry prospects for minority engineers. Prefers articles related to careers, not politically or socially sensitive.

RAILWAY TRACK AND STRUCTURES

Simmons-Boardman Publishing, 55 Broad St., 26th Floor, New York NY 10004. (212)620-7200. **Fax:** (212)633-1165. **E-mail:** Mischa@sbpub-chicago.com; ksenese@sbpub.com. **Website:** www.rtands.com. **Contact:** Mischa Wanek-Libman, editor; Kyra Senese, assistant editor. **1% freelance written.** Monthly magazine covering railroad civil engineering. *RT&S* is a nuts-and-bolts journal to help railroad civil engineers do their jobs better. Estab. 1904. Circ. 9,500. Byline given. Pays on publication. Offers 90% kill fee. Publishes ms an average of 1 month after acceptance. Editorial lead time 2 months. Submit seasonal material 3 months in advance. Accepts queries by mail, fax, phone. Accepts simultaneous submissions. Responds in 1 month to queries and to mss. Sample copy available online.

NONFICTION Needs how-to, new product, technical. Does not want nostalgia or "railroadiana." **Buys 1 mss/year.** Query. Length: 900-2,000 words. **Pays $500-1,000.**

PHOTOS State availability. Captions, identification of subjects, model releases required. Reviews GIF/JPEG files. Negotiates payment individually. Buys one-time rights.

TIPS "We prefer writers with a civil engineering background and railroad experience."

TECH DIRECTIONS

Prakken Publications, Inc., P.O. Box 8623, Ann Arbor MI 48107-8623. (734)975-2800. **Fax:** (734)975-2787. **E-mail:** vanessa@techdirections.com. **Website:** www.techdirections.com. **Contact:** Vanessa Revelli, managing editor. **100% freelance written. Eager to work with new/unpublished writers.** Monthly (except June and July) magazine covering issues, trends, and activities of interest to science, technical, and technology educators at the elementary through post-secondary school levels. Estab. 1934. Circ. 40,000. Byline given. Pays on publication. No kill fee. Publishes ms an average of 1 year after acceptance. Responds in 1 month to queries. Sample copy for $5. Guidelines available online.

NONFICTION Needs general interest, how-to, personal experience, technical, think pieces. **Buys 50 un-** solicited mss/year. Length: 2,000 words. **Pays $50-150.**

PHOTOS Send photos. Reviews color prints. Payment for photos included in payment for ms. Will accept electronic art as well.

COLUMNS/DEPARTMENTS Direct from Washington (education news from Washington, DC); Technology Today (new products under development); Technologies Past (profiles the inventors of last century); Mastering Computers, Technology Concepts (project orientation).

TIPS "We are mostly interested in articles written by technology and science educators about their class projects and their ideas about the field. We need more and more technology-related articles, especially written for the community college level."

WOMAN ENGINEER

Equal Opportunity Publications, Inc., 445 Broad Hollow Rd., Suite 425, Melville NY 11747. (631)421-9421. **Fax:** (631)421-1352. **E-mail:** info@eop.com; bloehr@eop.com. **Website:** www.eop.com. **Contact:** Barbara Capella Loehr, editor. **60% freelance written. Works with a small number of new/unpublished writers each year.** Triannual magazine aimed at advancing the careers of women engineering students and professional women engineers. Estab. 1968. Circ. 16,000. Byline given. Pays on publication. No kill fee. Publishes ms an average of 3 months after acceptance. Editorial lead time 3 months. Accepts queries by mail, e-mail, fax, phone. Accepts simultaneous submissions. Responds in 2 weeks to queries. Responds in 2 months to mss. Sample copy and writer's guidelines free.

NONFICTION Needs how-to, interview, personal experience. Query. Length: 1,500-2,500 words. **Pays $350 for assigned articles.**

PHOTOS Captions, identification of subjects required. Reviews color slides but will accept b&w. Buys all rights.

TIPS "We are looking for first-person 'As I See It' personal perspectives. Gear it to our audience."

ENTERTAINMENT & THE ARTS

AMERICAN CINEMATOGRAPHER

American Society of Cinematographers, 1782 N. Orange Dr., Hollywood CA 90028. (800)448-0145; outside US: (323)969-4333. **Fax:** (323)876-4973. **E-mail:** stephen@ascmag.com. **E-mail:** jon@ascmag.com.

Website: www.theasc.com. **Contact:** Stephen Pizzello, editor-in-chief and publisher; Jon Witmer, Jon Witmer, managing editor (jon@ascmag.com). **90% freelance written.** Monthly magazine covering cinematography (motion picture, TV, music video, commercial). "*American Cinematographer* is a trade publication devoted to the art and craft of cinematography. Our readers are predominantly film industry professionals." Estab. 1919. Circ. 33,000. Byline given. Pays on publication. Offers 50% kill fee. Publishes ms an average of 2-3 months after acceptance. Editorial lead time 2 months. Submit seasonal material 3 months in advance. Accepts queries by mail, e-mail, phone. Responds in 2 weeks to queries; 2 months to mss. Sample copy and guidelines free.

NONFICTION Needs interview, new product, technical. No reviews or opinion pieces. **Buys 20-25 mss/year.** Query with published clips. Length: 1,000-4,000 words. **Pays $400-1,500.**

TIPS "Familiarity with the technical side of film production and the ability to present that information in an articulate fashion to our audience are crucial."

AMERICAN THEATRE

Theatre Communications Group, 520 Eighth Ave., 24th Floor, New York NY 10018. (212)609-5900. **Fax:** (212)609-5902. **E-mail:** rwkendt@tcg.org. **Website:** www.tcg.org. **Contact:** Rob Weinert-Kendt, editor-in-chief. **60% freelance written.** Monthly magazine covering theatre. Focus is on American regional non-profit theatre. *American Theatre* typically publishes 2-3 features and 4-6 back-of-the-book articles covering trends and events in all types of theatre, as well as economic and legislative developments affecting the arts. *American Theatre* rarely publishes articles about commercial, amateur, or university theatre, nor about works that would widely be classified as dance or opera, except at the editors' discretion. While significant productions may be highlighted in the Critic's Notebook section, *American Theatre* does not review productions (but does review theatre-related books). Estab. 1982. Circ. 100,000. Byline given. Pays on publication. Editorial lead time 2 months. Submit seasonal material 3 months in advance. Accepts queries by mail, e-mail, online submission form. Accepts simultaneous submissions. Responds in 2 months to queries. Sample copy and guidelines available online.

NONFICTION Needs book excerpts, essays, general interest, historical, how-to, humor, inspirational, interview, opinion, personal experience, photo feature, travel. Special issues: Training (January); International (May/June); Season Preview (October). No unsolicited submissions (rarely accepted). No reviews. Writers wishing to submit articles to *American Theatre* should mail or e-mail a query to editor-in-chief Rob Weinert-Kendt outlining a particular proposal; unsolicited material is rarely accepted. Include a brief résumé and sample clips. Planning of major articles usually occurs at least 3 months in advance of publication. All mss are subject to editing. Length: 200-2,000 words. **"While fees are negotiated per ms, we pay an average of $350 for full-length (2,500-3,500 words) features, and less for shorter pieces."**

PHOTOS Contact: Kitty Suen, creative director: atphoto@tcg.com. Send photos. Captions required. Reviews JPEG files. Negotiates payment individually.

TIPS "The main focus is on professional American nonprofit theatre. Don't pitch music or film festivals. Must be about theatre."

DANCE TEACHER

McFadden Performing Arts Media, 333 Seventh Ave., 11th Floor, New York NY 10001. **E-mail:** khildebrand@dancemedia.com; jsullivan@dancemedia.com. **Website:** www.dance-teacher.com. **Contact:** Karen Hildebrand, editor in chief; Joe Sullivan, managing editor. **60% freelance written.** Monthly magazine. Estab. 1979. Circ. 25,000. Byline given. Pays on publication. No kill fee. Publishes ms an average of 3 months after acceptance. Submit seasonal material 6 months in advance. Accepts queries by e-mail. Accepts simultaneous submissions. Responds in 3 months to mss. Sample copy for SAE with 9x12 envelope and 6 first-class stamps. Guidelines available for free.

NONFICTION Needs how-to. Special issues: Summer Programs (January); Music & More (May); Costumes and Production Preview (November); College/Training Schools (December). No PR or puff pieces. All articles must be well researched. **Buys 50 mss/year.** Query. Length: 700-2,000 words. **Pays $100-300.**

PHOTOS Send photos. Reviews contact sheets, negatives, transparencies, prints. Limited photo budget.

TIPS "Read several issues—particularly seasonal. Stay within writer's guidelines."

DRAMATICS MAGAZINE

Educational Theatre Association, 2343 Auburn Ave., Cincinnati OH 45219. (513)421-3900. **E-mail:** gbossler@schooltheatre.org. **Website:** schooltheatre.

org. **Contact:** Gregory Bossler, editor-in-chief. *Dramatics* is for students (mainly high school age) and teachers of theater. The magazine wants student readers to grow as theater artists and become a more discerning and appreciative audience. Material is directed to both theater students and their teachers, with strong student slant. Tries to portray the theater community in all its diversity. Estab. 1929. Circ. 45,000. Byline given. Pays on acceptance. Publishes ms 3 months after acceptance. Accepts queries by mail, e-mail. Accepts simultaneous submissions. Sample copy available for 9x12 SAE with 4-ounce first-class postage. Guidelines available for SASE.

NONFICTION Needs how-to, profile, practical articles on acting, directing, design, production, and other facets of theater; career-oriented profiles of working theater professionals. Special issues: College Theater Programs (November); Summer Theater Work and Study Opportunities (January). Does not want academic treatises. **Buys 50 mss/year.** Submit complete ms. Length: 750-3,000 words. **Pays $50-500 for articles.**

FICTION Young adults: drama (one-act and full-length plays). "We prefer unpublished scripts that have been produced at least once." Does not want to see plays that show no understanding of the conventions of the theater. No plays for children, no Christmas or didactic "message" plays. Submit complete ms. Buys 5-9 plays/year. Emerging playwrights have better chances with résumé of credits. Length: 10 minutes to full length. **Pays $100-500 for plays.**

TIPS "Obtain our writer's guidelines and look at recent back issues. The best way to break in is to know our audience—drama students, teachers, and others interested in theater—and write for them. Writers who have some practical experience in theater, especially in technical areas, have an advantage, but we'll work with anybody who has a good idea. Some freelancers have become regular contributors."

EMMY

Television Academy, 5220 Lankershim Blvd., North Hollywood CA 91601. (818)754-2800. **E-mail:** emmymag@emmys.org. **Website:** www.emmys.com/emmymagazine. **Contact:** Editor. **90% freelance written. Prefers to work with published/established writers.** Bimonthly magazine on television for TV professionals. "From the executive suite to the editing bay, *emmy* magazine goes behind the scenes of television and digital entertainment to cover the people who make the magic happen. *Emmy*'s core readers include the members of the Television Academy and other television industry professionals. Articles must appeal to the television and digital entertainment professional while being understandable to the enthusiast." Circ. 14,000. Byline given. Pays on publication or within 6 months. Offers 25% kill fee. Publishes ms an average of 4 months after acceptance. Accepts queries by mail. Accepts simultaneous submissions. Responds in 1 month to queries. Sample copy for SAE with 9x12 envelope and 6 first-class stamps. Guidelines available online.

NONFICTION "We do not run highly technical articles, nor do we accept academic or fan-magazine approaches." Query with published clips. Length: 1,500-2,000 words. **Pays $1,000-1,200.**

COLUMNS/DEPARTMENTS Mostly written by regular contributors, but newcomers can break in with filler items with In the Mix or short profiles in Labors of Love. Length: 250-500 words, depending on department. Query with published clips. **Pays $250-500.**

TIPS "Demonstrate experience in covering the business of television and your ability to write in a lively and compelling manner about programming trends and new technology. Identify fascinating people behind the scenes, not just in the executive suites, but in all ranks of the industry."

MAKE-UP ARTIST MAGAZINE

12808 NE 95th St., Vancouver WA 98682. (360)882-3488. **E-mail:** heatherw@kpgmedia.com. **Website:** www.makeupmag.com; www.makeup411.com; www.imats.net. **Contact:** Heather Wisner, managing editor. **90% freelance written.** Bimonthly magazine covering all types of professional make-up artistry. Audience is a mixture of high-level make-up artists, make-up students, fashion and movie buffs. Writers should be comfortable with technical writing, and should have substantial knowledge of at least one area of make-up, such as effects or fashion. This is an entertainment-industry magazine, so writing should have an element of fun and storytelling. Good interview skills required. Estab. 1996. Circ. 16,000. Byline given. Pays within 30 days of publication. No kill fee. Editorial lead time 6 weeks. Submit seasonal material 2 months in advance. Accepts queries by e-mail. Accepts simultaneous submissions. Sample copy for $7. Guidelines available via e-mail.

NONFICTION "Does not want fluff pieces about consumer beauty products." **Buys 20+ mss/year.** Query with published clips. Length: 500-3,000 words. **Pays 20-50¢/word.**

PHOTOS Send photos. Captions, identification of subjects required. Reviews prints, GIF/JPEG files. Negotiates payment individually. Buys all rights.

COLUMNS/DEPARTMENTS Lab Tech, how-to advice for effects artists, written by a current make-up artist working in a lab (700 words + photos); Backstage (behind the scenes info on a theatrical production's make-up (700 words + photos): Out of the Kit, written by make-up artists working on sets (700 words + photos); Industry Buzz (industry news), length varies. Query with published clips. .

TIPS "Read books about professional make-up artistry (see http://makeupmag.com/shop). Read online interviews with make-up artists. Read make-up oriented mainstream magazines, such as *Allure*. Read *Cinefex* and other film-industry publications. Meet and talk to make-up artists and make-up students."

SCREEN MAGAZINE

Screen Enterprises, Inc., 676 N. LaSalle Blvd., #501, Chicago IL 60654. (312)640-0800. **Fax:** (312)640-1928. **E-mail:** editor@screenmag.com. **Website:** www.screenmag.com. **Contact:** Andrew Schneider, editor. **5% freelance written.** Biweekly Chicago-based trade magazine covering advertising and film production in the Midwest and national markets. *Screen* is written for Midwest producers (and other creatives involved) of commercials, AV, features, independent corporate, and multimedia. Estab. 1979. Circ. 15,000. Byline given. Pays on publication. No kill fee. Accepts queries by e-mail. Accepts simultaneous submissions. Responds in 3 weeks to queries. Sample copy available online.

NONFICTION Needs interview, new product, technical. No general AV; nothing specific to other markets; no no-brainers or opinion. **Buys 26 mss/year.** Query with published clips. Length: 750-1,500 words. **Pays $50.**

PHOTOS Send photos. Captions required. Reviews prints. Offers no additional payment for photos accepted with ms.

TIPS "Our readers want to know facts and figures. They want to know the news about a company or an individual. We provide exclusive news of this market,

in as much depth as space allows without being boring, with lots of specific information and details. We write knowledgably about the market we serve. We recognize the film/video-making process is a difficult one because it 1) is often technical, 2) has implications not immediately discerned."

SOUTHERN THEATRE

Southeastern Theatre Conference, 1175 Revolution Mill Drive, Studio 14, Greensboro NC 27405. (336)272-3645. **E-mail:** kim@setc.org. **Website:** www.setc.org/southern-theatre. **Contact:** Kim Doty. **100% freelance written.** Quarterly magazine covering all aspects of theater in the Southeast, from innovative theater companies, to important trends, to people making a difference in the region. All stories must be written in a popular magazine style but with subject matter appropriate for theater professionals (not the general public). The audience includes members of the Southeastern Theatre Conference, founded in 1949 and the nation's largest regional theater organization. These members include individuals involved in professional, community, college/university, children's, and secondary school theater. The magazine also is purchased by more than 100 libraries. Estab. 1962. Circ. 4,200. Byline given. Pays on publication. No kill fee. Publishes ms an average of 3 months after acceptance. Editorial lead time 3 months. Submit seasonal material 6 months in advance. Accepts queries by mail, e-mail. Accepts simultaneous submissions. Responds in 3 months to queries. Responds in 6 months to mss. Sample copy for $10. Guidelines available online.

NONFICTION Needs general interest, interview. Special issues: Playwriting (Fall issue, all stories submitted by January 1). No scholarly articles. **Buys 15-20 mss/year.** Send complete ms. Length: 1,000-3,000 words. **Pays $50 for feature stories.**

PHOTOS State availability of or send photos. Captions, identification of subjects, model releases required. Reviews transparencies, prints. Offers no additional payment for photos accepted with ms.

COLUMNS/DEPARTMENTS *Outside the Box* (innovative solutions to problems faced by designers and technicians), 800-1,000 words; *400 Words* (column where the theater professionals can sound off on issues), 400 words; 800-1,000 words; *Words, Words, Words* (reviews of books on theater), 400 words. Query or send complete ms **No payment for columns.**

TIPS "Look for a theater or theater person in your area that is doing something different or innovative that would be of interest to others in the profession, then write about that theater or person in a compelling way. We also are looking for well-written trend stories (talk to theaters in your area about trends that are affecting them), and we especially like stories that help our readers do their jobs more effectively. Send an e-mail detailing a well-developed story idea, and ask if we're interested."

VENUES TODAY

4952 Warner Ave., Suite 201, Huntington Beach CA 92649. (714)378-5400. **Fax:** (714)378-0040. **E-mail:** linda@venuestoday.com; dave@venuestoday.com. **Website:** www.venuestoday.com. **Contact:** Linda Deckard, publisher and editor in chief. **70% freelance written.** Weekly magazine covering the live entertainment industry and the buildings that host shows and sports. Needs writers who can cover an exciting industry from the business side, not the consumer side. Readers are venue managers, concert promoters, those in the concert and sports business, not the audience for concerts and sports. Need business journalists who can cover the latest news and trends in the market. Estab. 2002. Byline given. Pays on publication. Publishes ms an average of 1 month after acceptance. Editorial lead time 1-2 months. Submit seasonal material 1-2 months in advance. Accepts queries by mail, e-mail, fax. Accepts simultaneous submissions. Responds in 1 week to queries. Sample copy available online. Guidelines free.

NONFICTION Needs interview, photo feature, technical, travel. Does not want customer slant, marketing pieces. Query with published clips. Length: 500-1,500 words. **Pays $100-250.**

PHOTOS State availability. Captions, identification of subjects required. Reviews GIF/JPEG files. Negotiates payment individually. Buys one-time rights.

COLUMNS/DEPARTMENTS Venue News (new buildings, trend features, etc.); Bookings (show tours, business side); Marketing (of shows, sports, convention centers); Concessions (food, drink, merchandise). Length: 500-1,200 words. **Buys 250 mss/year. mss/year.** Query with published clips. **Pays $100-250.**

FILLERS Needs gags. **Buys 6 mss/year. Pays $100-300.**

FARM

💲💲 **ACRES U.S.A.**

P.O. Box 301209, Austin TX 78703. (512)892-4400. **Fax:** (512)892-4448. **E-mail:** editor@acresusa.com.

Website: www.acresusa.com. **Contact:** Tara Maxwell. "Monthly trade journal written by people who have a sincere interest in the principles of organic and sustainable agriculture." Estab. 1970. Circ. 25,000. Byline given. Pays on publication. No kill fee. Editorial lead time 3 months. Submit seasonal material 6 months in advance. Accepts queries by mail, e-mail. Accepts simultaneous submissions. Sample copy and writer's guidelines free.

NONFICTION Needs book excerpts, expose, how-to, interview, new product, personal experience, photo feature, profile, technical. Special issues: Seeds (January), Poultry (March), Permaculture (May), Livestock (June), Homesteading (August), Soil Fertility & Testing (October). Does not want poetry, fillers, product profiles, or anything with an overly promotional tone. **Buys about 50 mss/year.** Send complete ms. Length: 500-3,000 words. **Pays 10¢/word.**

PHOTOS State availability of or send photos. Captions, identification of subjects required. Reviews JPEG/TIFF files. Negotiates payment individually. Buys one-time rights.

AG JOURNAL

Gatehouse Media, Inc., 422 Colorado Ave., (P.O. Box 500), La Junta CO 81050. (719)384-1453. **E-mail:** publisher@ljtdmail.com; bcd@ljtdmail.com. **Website:** www.agjournalonline.com. **Contact:** Candi Hill, publisher/editor; Jennifer Justice, assistant editor. **20% freelance written.** Weekly journal covering agriculture. Estab. 1949. Circ. 11,000. Byline given. Pays on publication. No kill fee. Publishes ms an average of 2 weeks after acceptance. Editorial lead time 1 month. Submit seasonal material 1 month in advance. Accepts queries by e-mail. Accepts simultaneous submissions. Responds in 2 weeks to queries. Sample copy and writer's guidelines free.

> The *Ag Journal* covers people, issues, and events relevant to agriculture producers in a seven-state region (Colorado, Kansas, Oklahoma, Texas, Wyoming, Nebraska, New Mexico).

NONFICTION Needs how-to, interview, new product, opinion, photo feature, technical. Query by e-mail only. **Pays 4¢/word.**

PHOTOS State availability. Captions, identification of subjects required. Offers $8/photo. Buys one-time rights.

AG WEEKLY

Lee Agri-Media, P.O. Box 918, Bismarck ND 58501. (701)255-4905. **Fax:** (701)255-2312. **E-mail:** editor@

theprairiestar.com. **Website:** www.agweekly.com. **40% freelance written.** *Ag Weekly* is an agricultural publication covering production, markets, regulation, politics. Writers need to be familiar with Idaho agricultural commodities. No printed component; website with 6,000 monthly unique visitors; weekly email newsletter with 3,000 subscribers. Byline given. Pays on publication. Publishes ms an average of 1 month after acceptance. Editorial lead time 1 month. Submit seasonal material 1 month in advance. Accepts queries by e-mail. Accepts simultaneous submissions. Responds in 2 weeks to queries. Responds in 1 month to mss. Sample copy available online. Guidelines with #10 SASE.

NONFICTION Needs interview, new product, opinion, travel, ag-related. Does not want anything other than local/regional ag-related articles. No cowboy poetry. **Buys 100 mss/year.** Query. Length: 250-700 words. **Pays $40-70.**

PHOTOS State availability. Captions required. Reviews GIF/JPEG files. Offers $10/photo. Buys one-time rights.

AMERICAN AGRICULTURIST

1166 Avenue of the Americas, 10th Floor, New York NY 10036. (717)359-0150. **Fax:** (717)359-0250. **E-mail:** john.vogel@penton.com. **Website:** http://www.americanagriculturist.com/. **Contact:** John Vogel, editor. **20% freelance written.** Monthly magazine covering cutting-edge technology and news to help farmers improve their operations. Publishes cutting-edge technology with ready on-farm application. Estab. 1842. Circ. 32,000. Pays on publication. No kill fee. Publishes ms an average of 3 months after acceptance. Editorial lead time 3 months. Submit seasonal material 3 months in advance. Accepts queries by e-mail, fax. Responds in 2 weeks to queries; in 1 month to mss. Guidelines for #10 SASE.

NONFICTION Needs how-to, humor, inspirational, interview, new product, technical. No stories without a strong tie to Mid-Atlantic farming. **Buys 20 mss/year.** Query. Length: 500-1,000 words. **Pays $250-500.**

PHOTOS Send photos. Captions, identification of subjects, model releases required. Reviews transparencies, JPEG files. Offers $75-200/photo. Buys one-time rights.

COLUMNS/DEPARTMENTS Country Air (humor, nostalgia, inspirational), 300-400 words. **Buys 12 mss/year.** Send complete ms. **Pays $100.**

AMERICAN FRUIT GROWER AND WESTERN FRUIT GROWER

Meister Media Worldwide, 37733 Euclid Ave., Willoughby OH 44094. (290)573-8740. **E-mail:** deddy@meistermedia.com. **Website:** www.fruitgrower.com. **Contact:** David Eddy, editor. **3% freelance written.** Annual magazines covering commercial fruit growing. "Founded in 1880, *American Fruit Grower* and *Western Fruit Grower* magazines reaches producers, shippers, and other influencers who serve the fresh and processing markets for deciduous fruits, citrus, grapes, berries, and nuts. *Western Fruit Grower* has additional reach to producers and others who work with unique varieties and climate and market conditions in the American West." Estab. 1880. Circ. 44,000. Byline given. Pays on publication. No kill fee. Publishes ms an average of 4 months after acceptance. Editorial lead time 2 months. Submit seasonal material 4 months in advance. Accepts queries by mail, e-mail, fax, phone. Accepts simultaneous submissions. Responds in 2 weeks to queries; in 2 months to mss. Sample copy and writer's guidelines free.

NONFICTION Needs how-to. **Buys 6-10 mss/year.** Send complete ms. Length: 800-1,200 words. **Pays $200-250.**

PHOTOS Send photos. Reviews prints, slides. Negotiates payment individually. Buys one-time rights.

TIPS "How-to articles are best."

ANGUS JOURNAL

Angus Productions, Inc., 3201 Frederick Ave., St. Joseph MO 64506-2997. (816)383-5270. **E-mail:** shermel@angusjournal.com. **Website:** www.angusjournal.com. **40% freelance written.** Monthly magazine covering Angus cattle. *Angus Journal* is the official magazine of the American Angus Association. Its primary function as such is to report to the membership association activities and information pertinent to raising Angus cattle. Estab. 1919. Circ. 13,500. Byline given. Pays on publication. No kill fee. Publishes ms an average of 3 months after acceptance. Editorial lead time 2 months. Submit seasonal material 3 months in advance. Accepts queries by mail, e-mail. Accepts simultaneous submissions. Responds in 3 weeks to queries; in 2 months to mss. Sample copy: $5. Guidelines with #10 SASE.

NONFICTION Needs how-to, interview, technical. **Buys 20-30 mss/year.** Query with published clips. Length: 800-3,500 words. **Pays $50-1,000.**

PHOTOS Send photos. Identification of subjects required. Reviews 5×7 glossy prints. Offers $25-400/ photo. Buys all rights.

TIPS "Have a firm grasp of the cattle industry."

BEE CULTURE

623 W Liberty St., Medina OH 44256-0706. (330)725-6677; (800)289-7668. **Fax:** (330)725-5624. **E-mail:** kim@beeculture.com; info@beeculture.com. **Website:** www.beeculture.com. **Contact:** Mr. Kim Flottum, editor. **50% freelance written.** Covers the natural science of honey bees, and honey bee management. "Monthly magazine for beekeepers and those interested in the natural science of honey bees, with environmentally-oriented articles relating to honey bees or pollination." Estab. 1873. Pays on publication. No kill fee. Publishes ms an average of 4 months after acceptance. Accepts queries by mail, e-mail. Accepts simultaneous submissions. Responds in 1 month to mss. Sample copy with 9x12 SASE and 5 first-class stamps. Guidelines and sample copy available online.

NONFICTION Needs interview, personal experience, photo feature. No "How I Began Beekeeping" articles. Length: 2,000 words average. **Pays $200-250.**

REPRINTS Send photocopy and information about when and where the material previously appeared. Pays about the same as for an original article, on negotiation.

PHOTOS Electronic images encouraged. Digital JPEG, color only, at 300 dpi best,. Model release required. Photo captions preferred. Pays $50 for cover photos. Photos payment included with article payment. Buys first rights.

TIPS "Do an interview story on commercial beekeepers who are cooperative enough to furnish accurate, factual information on their operations. Frequent mistakes made by writers in completing articles are that they are too general in nature and lack management knowledge."

THE BRAHMAN JOURNAL

Carl and Victoria Lambert, 915 12th St., Hempstead TX 77445. (979)826-4347. **Fax:** (979)826-2007. **E-mail:** info@brahmanjournal.com; vlambert@brahmanjournal.com. **Website:** www.brahmanjournal. com. **Contact:** Victoria Lambert, editor. **10% freelance written.** Monthly magazine promoting, supporting, and informing the owners and admirers of American Brahman Cattle through honest and forthright journalism. *The Brahman Journal* provides timely and useful information about one of the largest and most dynamic breeds of beef cattle in the world. In each issue, *The Brahman Journal* reports on Brahman shows, events, and sales as well as technical articles and the latest research as it pertains to the Brahman Breed. Estab. 1971. Circ. 4,000. Byline given. Pays on publication. No kill fee. Publishes ms an average of 2 months after acceptance. Submit seasonal material 3 months in advance. Accepts simultaneous submissions. Sample copy for SAE with 9x12 envelope and 5 first-class stamps.

NONFICTION Needs general interest, historical, interview. Special issues: See the Calendar online for special issues. **Buys 3-4 mss/year.** Query with published clips. Length: 1,200-3,000 words. **Pays $100-250.**

REPRINTS Send typed ms with rights for sale noted. Pays 50% of amount paid for an original article.

PHOTOS Photos needed for article purchase. Send photos. Captions required. Reviews 4x5 prints. Offers no additional payment for photos accepted with ms. Buys one-time rights.

TIPS "Since *The Brahman Journal* is read around the world, being sent to 48 different countries, it is important that the magazine contain a wide variety of information. *The Brahman Journal* is read by seed stock producers, show ring competitors, F-1 breeders and Brahman lovers from around the world."

THE CATTLEMAN

Texas and Southwestern Cattle Raisers Association, 1301 W. Seventh St., Suite 201, Fort Worth TX 76102. (817)332-7064. **Fax:** (817)332-6441. **E-mail:** ehbrisendine@tscra.org. **Website:** www.tscra.org. **Contact:** Ellen H. Brisendine, editor. **25% freelance written.** Monthly magazine covering the Texas/Oklahoma beef cattle industry. Specializes in in-depth, management-type articles related to range and pasture, beef cattle production, animal health, nutrition, and marketing. Wants "how-to" articles. Estab. 1914. Circ. 18,000. Byline given. Pays on acceptance. No kill fee. Publishes ms an average of 2 months after acceptance. Editorial lead time 2 months. Submit seasonal material 6 months in advance. Accepts queries by e-mail. Accepts simultaneous submissions. Sample copy free. Guidelines online.

NONFICTION Needs how-to, interview, new product, personal experience, technical. Does not want to see anything not specifically related to beef production in the Southwest. **Buys 20 mss/year.** Query with published clips. Length: 1,500-2,000 words. **Pays $350-500 for assigned articles. Pays $100-350 for unsolicited articles.**

PHOTOS Identification of subjects required. Reviews digital files. Offers no additional payment for photos accepted with ms. Buys one-time rights.

TIPS "Subscribers said they were most interested in the following topics, in this order: range/pasture, property rights, animal health, water, new innovations, and marketing. *The Cattleman* prefers to work on an assignment basis. However, prospective contributors are urged to write the managing editor of the magazine to inquire of interest on a proposed subject. Occasionally, the editor will return a ms to a potential contributor for cutting, polishing, checking, rewriting, or condensing. Be able to demonstrate background/knowledge in this field. Include tearsheets from similar magazines."

COTTON GROWER MAGAZINE

Meister Media Worldwide, Cotton Media Group, 8000 Centerview Pkwy., Suite 114, Cordova TN 38018-4246. (901)756-8822. **E-mail:** mccue@meister-media.com. **Website:** www.cotton247.com. **Contact:** Mike McCue, editor. **5% freelance written.** Monthly magazine covering cotton production, cotton markets, and related subjects. Circ. 43,000. Byline given. Pays on acceptance. No kill fee. Publishes ms an average of 2 months after acceptance. Editorial lead time 2 months. Submit seasonal material 2 months in advance. Accepts queries by mail, e-mail, fax, phone. Accepts simultaneous submissions. Sample copy free.

Ⓞ   Readers are mostly cotton producers who seek information on production practices, equipment, and products related to cotton.

NONFICTION Needs interview, new product, photo feature, technical. No fiction or humorous pieces. **Buys 5-10 mss/year.** Query with published clips. Length: 500-800 words. **Pays $200-400.**

PHOTOS State availability. Captions, identification of subjects required. Reviews transparencies. Offers no additional payment for photos accepted with ms. Buys all rights.

FEED LOT MAGAZINE

Feed Lot Magazine, Inc., P.O. Box 850, Dighton KS 67839. (800)798-9515. **Fax:** (620)397-2839. **E-mail:** feedlot@st-tel.net. **Website:** www.feedlotmagazine.com. Annita Lorimor. **Contact:** Jill Dunkel, editor. **80% freelance written.** Published 8 times/year. Magazine provides readers with the most up-to-date information on the beef industry in concise, easy-to-read articles designed to increase overall awareness among the feedlot community. "The editorial information content fits a dual role: large feedlots and their related cow/calf operations, and large 500+ cow/calf, 100+ stocker operations. The information covers all phases of production from breeding, genetics, animal health, nutrition, equipment design, research through finishing fat cattle. *Feed Lot* publishes a mix of new information and timely articles which directly affect the cattle industry." Estab. 1992. Circ. 12,000. Byline given. Pays on publication. Offers 50% kill fee. Publishes ms an average of 2 months after acceptance. Editorial lead time 2 months. Submit seasonal material 6 months in advance. Accepts queries by mail, e-mail, fax. Accepts simultaneous submissions. Responds in 1 month to queries. Sample copy and writer's guidelines by e-mail.

NONFICTION Needs interview, new product, photo feature. Send complete ms; original material only. Length: 100-700 words. **Pays 30¢/word.**

PHOTOS State availability or send photos. Captions, model releases required. Reviews contact sheets. Negotiates payment individually. Buys all rights.

TIPS "Know what you are writing about—have a good knowledge of the subject."

FLORIDA GROWER

Meister Media Worldwide, 37733 Euclid Ave., Willoughby OH 44094. (440)942-2000. **E-mail:** fgiles@meistermedia.com; pprusnak@meistermedia.com. **Website:** www.growingproduce.com/magazine/florida-grower; www.meistermedia.com/publications/florida-grower. **Contact:** Frank Giles, editor; Paul Rusnak, managing editor. **10% freelance written.** Monthly magazine edited for the Florida farmer with commercial production interest primarily in citrus, vegetables, and other ag endeavors. Goal is to provide articles that update and inform on such areas as production, ag financing, farm labor relations, technology, safety, education, and regulation. Estab. 1907. Circ. 12,200. Byline given. Pays on publication. No kill fee. Editorial lead time 2 months. Submit seasonal material 3 months in advance. Accepts queries by mail, e-mail, fax, phone. Accepts simultaneous submissions. Responds in 1 month to queries. Sample copy for SAE with 9x12 envelope and 5 First-Class stamps. Guidelines free.

NONFICTION Needs interview, photo feature, technical. Query with published clips. Length: 700-1,000 words. **Pays $150-250.**

PHOTOS Send photos.

FRUIT GROWERS NEWS

Great American Publishing, P.O. Box 128, Sparta MI 49345. (616)887-9008. **Fax:** (616)887-2666. **E-mail:** fgnedit@fruitgrowersnews.com. **Website:** www.fruit-growersnews.com. **Contact:** Matt Milkovich, managing editor; Lee Dean, editorial director. **10% freelance written.** Monthly tabloid covering agriculture. "Our objective is to provide commercial fruit growers of all sizes with information to help them succeed." Estab. 1961. Circ. 16,429. Pays on publication. No kill fee. Publishes ms an average of 2 months after acceptance. Editorial lead time 1-2 months. Submit seasonal material 3 months in advance. Accepts queries by mail, e-mail, fax. Accepts simultaneous submissions. Responds in 2 weeks to queries. Responds in 1 month to mss. Sample copy free.

NONFICTION Needs general interest, interview, new product. No advertorials or other puff pieces. **Buys 25 mss/year.** Query with published clips and résumé. Length: 600-1,000 words. **Pays $150-250.**

PHOTOS Send photos. Captions required. Reviews prints. Offers $15/photo. Buys one-time rights.

GOOD FRUIT GROWER

Washington State Fruit Commission, 105 S. 18th St., Suite 217, Yakima WA 98901. (509)853-3520. **Fax:** (509)853-3521. **E-mail:** casey.corr@goodfruit.com. **Website:** www.goodfruit.com. **Contact:** O. Casey Corr, managing editor. **10% freelance written.** Semi-monthly magazine covering tree fruit/grape growing. Estab. 1946. Circ. 11,000. Byline given. Pays on acceptance. Publishes ms an average of 2 months after acceptance. Accepts queries by mail, e-mail. Accepts simultaneous submissions. Responds in 1 week to queries; in 1 month to mss. Sample copy free. Guidelines free.

NONFICTION Buys 20 mss/year. Query. Length: 500-1,500 words. **Pays 40-50¢/word.**

PHOTOS Contact: Jim Black. Reviews GIF/JPEG files. Negotiates payment individually. Buys one-time rights.

TIPS "We want well-written, accurate information. We deal with our writers honestly and expect the same in return."

GRAIN JOURNAL

Country Journal Publishing Co., 3065 Pershing Court, Decatur IL 62526. (800)728-7511. **E-mail:** ed@grain-net.com. **Website:** www.grainnet.com. **Contact:** Ed Zdrojewski, editor. **5% freelance written.** Bimonthly magazine covering grain handling and merchandising. *Grain Journal* serves the North American grain industry, from the smallest country grain elevators and feed mills to major export terminals. Estab. 1972. Circ. 12,000. Byline sometimes given. Pays on publication. No kill fee. Publishes ms an average of 2 months after acceptance. Editorial lead time 2 months. Submit seasonal material 2 months in advance. Accepts simultaneous submissions. Sample copy free.

NONFICTION Needs how-to, interview, new product, technical. Query. 750 words maximum. **Pays $100.**

PHOTOS Send photos. Captions, identification of subjects required. Reviews contact sheets, negatives, transparencies, 3x5 prints, electronic files. Offers $50-100/photo. Buys one time rights.

TIPS "Call with your idea. We'll let you know if it is suitable for our publication."

THE LAND

Free Press Co., P.O. Box 3169, Mankato MN 56002-3169. (507)345-4523. **E-mail:** editor@thelandonline.com. **Website:** www.thelandonline.com. **40% freelance written.** Weekly tabloid covering farming and rural life in Minnesota and Northern Iowa. "Although we're not tightly focused on any one type of farming, our articles must be of interest to farmers. In other words, will your article topic have an impact on people who live and work in rural areas?" Prefers to work with Minnesota or Iowa writers. Estab. 1976. Circ. 33,000. Byline given. Pays on acceptance. No kill fee. Publishes ms an average of 2 months after acceptance. Editorial lead time 2 months. Submit seasonal material 2 months in advance. Accepts queries by mail, e-mail. Accepts simultaneous submissions. Responds in 3 weeks to queries; in 2 months to mss. Sample copy free. Guidelines with #10 SASE.

NONFICTION Needs general interest, how-to. **Buys 80 mss/year.** Query. Length: 500-750 words. **Pays $50-70 for assigned articles.**

PHOTOS Send photos. Reviews contact sheets. Negotiates payment individually. Buys one-time rights.
COLUMNS/DEPARTMENTS Query. **Pays $10-50.**
TIPS "Be enthused about rural Minnesota and Iowa life and agriculture, and be willing to work with our editors. We try to stress relevance. When sending me a query, convince me the story belongs in a Minnesota farm publication."

MAINE ORGANIC FARMER & GARDENER

Maine Organic Farmers & Gardeners Association, P.O. Box 170, Unity ME 04988. (207)568-4142. **Fax:** (207)568-4141. **E-mail:** jenglish@tidewater.ne. **Website:** www.mofga.org. **40% freelance written. Prefers to work with published/established local writers.** Quarterly newspaper. "The *MOF&G* promotes and encourages sustainable agriculture and environmentally sound living. Our primary focus is organic farming, gardening, and forestry, but we also deal with local, national, and international agriculture, food, and environmental issues." Estab. 1976. Circ. 10,000. Byline and bio offered. Pays on publication. No kill fee. Publishes ms an average of 8 months after acceptance. Submit seasonal material 1 year in advance. Accepts queries by mail, e-mail. Accepts simultaneous submissions. Responds in 2 months to queries. Sample copy for $2 and SAE with 7 first-class stamps; from MOFGA, P.O. Box 170, Unity ME 04988. Guidelines available at www.mofga.org.
NONFICTION **Buys 30 mss/year.** Send complete ms. Length: 250-3,000 words. **Pays $25-300.**
REPRINTS E-mail manuscript with rights for sale noted and information about when and where the material previously appeared. Pays 50% of amount paid for an original article.
PHOTOS State availability of photos with query. Captions, identification of subjects, model releases required. Buys one time rights. We rarely buy photos without an accompanying article.
TIPS "We are a nonprofit organization. Our publication's primary mission is to inform and educate, but we also want readers to enjoy the articles. Most of our articles are written by our staff or by freelancers who have been associated with the publication for several years."

⑤ ONION WORLD

Columbia Publishing, P.O. Box 333, Roberts ID 83444. (208)520-6461. **Fax:** (509)248-4056. **E-mail:** dkeller@columbiapublications.com. **Website:** www. onionworld.net. **Contact:** Denise Keller, editor. **25% freelance written.** Monthly magazine covering the world of onion production and marketing for onion growers and shippers. Estab. 1985. Circ. 5,500. Byline given. Pays on publication. No kill fee. Publishes ms an average of 1 month after acceptance. Submit seasonal material 1 month in advance. Accepts simultaneous submissions. Responds in 1 month to queries. Sample copy for SAE with 9x12 envelope and 5 first-class stamps.
NONFICTION Needs general interest, historical, interview. Special issues: Editorial calendar available online. **Buys 30 mss/year.** Query. Length: 1,200-1,250 words. **Pays $100-250 per article, depending upon length. Mileage paid, but query first.**
REPRINTS Send photocopy and information about when and where the material previously appeared. Pays 50% of amount paid for an original article.
PHOTOS Send photos. Captions, identification of subjects required. Offers no additional payment for photos accepted with ms, unless it's a cover shot. Buys all rights.
TIPS "Writers should be familiar with growing and marketing onions. We use a lot of feature stories on growers, shippers, and others in the onion trade—what they are doing, varieties grown, their problems, solutions, marketing plans, etc."

PRODUCE BUSINESS

Phoenix Media Network Inc., P.O. Box 810425, Boca Raton FL 33481. (561)994-1118. **E-mail:** kwhitacre@ phoenixmedianet.com; info@producebusiness.com. **Website:** www.producebusiness.com. **Contact:** Ken Whitacre, publisher/editorial director. **90% freelance written.** Monthly magazine covering produce and floral marketing. Addresses the buying end of the produce/floral industry, concentrating on supermarkets, chain restaurants, etc. Estab. 1985. Circ. 16,000. Byline given. Pays 30 days after publication. Offers $50 kill fee. Editorial lead time 2 months. Accepts queries by e-mail. Sample copy and guidelines free.
NONFICTION Does not want unsolicited articles. **Buys 150 mss/year.** Query with published clips. Length: 1,200-10,000 words. **Pays $240-1,200.**

⑤ SHEEP! MAGAZINE

Countryside Publications, Ltd., 145 Industrial Dr., Medford WI 54451. (715)785-7979; (800)551-5691. **Fax:** (715)785-7414. **E-mail:** sheepmag@tds.net; singersol@countrysidemag.com. **Website:** www.sheep-magazine.com. **Contact:** Nathan Griffith, editor. **35% freelance written. Prefers to work with published/ established writers.** Bimonthly magazine published in north-central Wisconsin. Estab. 1980. Circ. 11,000. Byline given. Pays on publication. Offers $30 kill fee. Submit seasonal material 3 months in advance. Accepts simultaneous submissions.

○   Looking for clear, concise, useful information for sheep raisers who have a few sheep to a 1,000 ewe flock.

NONFICTION Needs book excerpts, how-to, interview, new product, technical. **Buys 80 mss/year.** Send complete ms. Length: 750-2,500 words. **Pays $45-150.**

PHOTOS Color photos (vertical compositions of sheep and/or people) for cover. 35mm photos or other visuals improve chances of a sale. Identification of subjects required. Buys all rights.

TIPS "Send us your best ideas and photos! We love good writing!"

SMALLHOLDER MAGAZINE

Newsquest Media Group, 3 Falmouth Business Park, Bickland Water Rd., Falmouth Cornwall TR11 4SZ United Kingdom. (01)326-213338. **Fax:** (01)326-212084. **E-mail:** editorial@smallholder.co.uk. **Website:** www.smallholder.co.uk. **Contact:** Paul Armstrong, editor. *Smallholder* magazine is the leading monthly publication for the small producer and self-reliant household and has a publishing history spanning more than 100 years. The magazine has a reputation for quality and informed editorial content, and back issues are highly collectable. It is available nationally, through newsagent sales, specialist retail outlets and by subscription. No kill fee. Accepts queries by e-mail. Accepts simultaneous submissions. Sample copy available online. Guidelines by e-mail.

NONFICTION Length: 700-1,400 words. **Pays 4£/ word.**

PHOTOS Send photos. Reviews 300 dpi digital images. Pays £5-50.

THE VEGETABLE GROWERS NEWS

Great American Publishing, P.O. Box 128, Sparta MI 49345. (616)887-9008, ext. 102. **Fax:** (616)887-2666. **E-mail:** vgnedit@vegetablegrowersnews.com. **Website:** www.vegetablegrowersnews.com. **Contact:** Matt Milkovich, managing editor. **10% freelance written.** Monthly tabloid covering agriculture. Estab. 1970. Circ. 16,000. Pays on publication. No kill fee. Publishes ms an average of 2 months after acceptance. Ed-

itorial lead time 1-2 months. Submit seasonal material 3 months in advance. Accepts queries by mail, e-mail, fax. Accepts simultaneous submissions. Responds in 2 weeks to queries. Responds in 1 month to mss. Sample copy free.

NONFICTION Needs general interest, interview, new product. No advertorials, other puff pieces. **Buys 25 mss/year.** Query with published clips and résumé. Length: 800-1,200 words. **Pays $100-125.**

PHOTOS Send photos. Captions required. Reviews prints. Offers $15/photo. Buys one-time rights.

FINANCE

ADVISOR'S EDGE

Rogers Media, Inc., 333 Bloor St. E., 6th Floor, Toronto ON M4W 1G6 Canada. **E-mail:** melissa.shin@rci.rogers.com. **Website:** www.advisor.ca. **Contact:** Melissa Shin, editor. Monthly magazine covering the financial industry (financial advisors and investment advisors). *Advisor's Edge* focuses on sales and marketing opportunities for the financial advisor (how they can build their business and improve relationships with clients). Estab. 1998. Circ. 36,000. Byline given. Pays on publication. Offers 25% kill fee. Publishes ms an average of 3 months after acceptance. Editorial lead time 3 months. Accepts queries by e-mail. Accepts simultaneous submissions. Sample copy available online.

NONFICTION Needs how-to, interview. No articles that aren't relevant to how a financial advisor does his/ her job. **Buys 12 mss/year.** Query with published clips. Length: 1,500-2,000 words. **Pays $900 (Canadian).**

AFP EXCHANGE

Association for Financial Professionals, 4520 East West Hwy., Suite 750, Bethesda MD 20814. (301)907-2862. **E-mail:** exchange@afponline.org. **Website:** www.afponline.org/exchange. **20% freelance written.** Monthly magazine covering corporate treasury, corporate finance, B2B payments issues, corporate risk management, accounting, and regulatory issues from the perspective of corporations. Welcomes interviews with CFOs and senior-level practitioners. Best practices and practical information for corporate CFOs and treasurers. Tone is professional, intended to appeal to financial professionals on the job. Most accepted articles are written by professional journalists and editors, many featuring high-level AFP members in profile and case studies. Estab. 1979. Circ. 25,000.

TRADE JOURNALS

Byline given. Pays on publication. Offers kill fee. Pays negotiable kill fee in advance. Editorial lead time 2 months. Submit seasonal material 3 months in advance. Accepts queries by e-mail. Accepts simultaneous submissions. Responds in 1 week to queries; in 1 month to mss.

NONFICTION Needs book excerpts, how-to, interview, personal experience, technical. No PR-type articles pointing to any type of product or solution. **Buys 3-4 mss/year.** Query. Length: 1,100-1,800 words. **Pays 75¢-$1/word for assigned articles.**

COLUMNS/DEPARTMENTS Cash Flow Forecasting (practical tips for treasurers, CFOs); Financial Reporting (insight, practical tips); Risk Management (practical tips for treasurers, CFOs); Corporate Payments (practical tips for treasurers), all 1,000-1,300 words. Professional Development (success stories, career related, about high-level financial professionals), 1,100 words. **Buys 10 mss/year.** Query. **Pays $75¢-$1/word.**

FILLERS Needs anecdotes. Length: 400-700 words. **Pays 75¢/word.**

TIPS "Accepted submissions deal with high-level issues relevant to today's corporate CFO or treasurer, including issues of global trade, global finance, accounting, M&A, risk management, corporate cash management, international regulatory issues, communications issues with corporate boards and shareholders, and especially new issues on the horizon. Preference given to articles by or about corporate practitioners in the finance function of mid- to large-size corporations in the U.S. or abroad. We also purchase articles by accomplished financial writers. We cannot accept content that points to any product, 'solution,' or that promotes any vendor. We should not be considered a PR outlet. Authors may be required to sign agreement."

CREDIT TODAY

P.O. Box 20091, Roanoke VA 24018. (540)343-7500. **E-mail:** robl@credittoday.net; editor@credittoday.net. **Website:** www.credittoday.net. **Contact:** Rob Lawson, publisher. **10% freelance written.** Web-based publication covering business or trade credit. Estab. 1997. No byline given. Pays on acceptance. Publishes ms an average of 1 week after acceptance. Editorial lead time 1-2 months. Accepts queries by e-mail. Sample copy free. Guidelines free.

NONFICTION Needs how-to, interview, technical. Does not want "puff" pieces promoting a particular product or vendor. **Buys 20 mss/year.** Send complete ms. Length: 700-1,800 words. **Pays $200-1,400.**

TIPS "Make pieces actionable, personable, and a quick read."

⑤⑤ CREDIT UNION MANAGEMENT

Credit Union Executives Society, 5710 Mineral Point Road, Madison WI 53705. (800)231-4211. **E-mail:** apeterson@cuna.com. **Website:** www.cuna.org. **Contact:** Ann Hayes Peterson, editor in chief. **44% freelance written.** Monthly magazine covering credit union, banking trends, management, HR, and marketing issues. "Our philosophy mirrors the credit union industry of cooperative financial services." Estab. 1978. Circ. 7,413. Pays on acceptance. No kill fee. Publishes ms an average of 2 months after acceptance. Editorial lead time 3 months. Submit seasonal material 4 months in advance. Accepts queries by mail. Accepts simultaneous submissions. Responds in 2 weeks to queries; 1 month to mss. Sample copy and writer's guidelines free.

NONFICTION Needs book excerpts, how-to, interview, technical. **Buys 74 mss/year.** Query with published clips. Length: 700-2,400 words. **$250-350 for assigned features.**

COLUMNS/DEPARTMENTS Management Network (book/Web reviews, briefs), 300 words; e-marketing, 700 words; Point of Law, 700 words; Best Practices (new technology/operations trends), 700 words. Query with published clips.

TIPS "The best way is to e-mail an editor; include rèsumè, cover letter and clips. Knowledge of financial services is very helpful."

THE FEDERAL CREDIT UNION

National Association of Federal Credit Unions, 3138 10th St. N., Arlington VA 22201. (703)522-4770; (800)336-4644. **Fax:** (703)524-1082. **E-mail:** msc@nafcu.org; sbroaddus@nafcu.org. **Website:** www.nafcu.org/tfcuonline. **Contact:** Susan Broaddus, managing editor. **30% freelance written.** Published bimonthly, *The Federal Credit Union* is the official publication of the National Association of Federal Credit Unions. The magazine is dedicated to providing credit union management, staff, and volunteers with in-depth information (HR, technology, security, board management, etc.) they can use to fulfill their duties and better serve their members. The editorial focus includes coverage of management issues, operations, and technology as well as volunteer-related issues. Looking for writers with financial, banking, or credit union experience, but will work with inexperienced (unpublished) writers based on writing skill. Estab. 1967. Circ. 8,000. Byline given. Pays on publication. No kill fee. Publishes ms an average of 3 months after acceptance. Submit seasonal material 5 months in advance. Accepts queries by mail, e-mail, fax. Accepts simultaneous submissions. Responds in 2 months to queries. Sample copy for SAE with 10x13 envelope and 5 first-class stamps. Guidelines for #10 SASE.

NONFICTION Needs humor, inspirational, interview. Query with published clips and SASE. Length: 1,200-2,000 words. **Pays $400-1,000.**

PHOTOS Send photos. Identification of subjects, model releases required. Reviews 35mm transparencies, 5x7 prints, high-resolution photos. Offers no additional payment for photos accepted with ms. Pays $50-500. Buys all rights.

TIPS "We would like more articles on how credit unions are using technology to serve their members and more articles on leading-edge technologies they can use in their operations. If you can write on current trends in technology, human resources, or strategic planning, you stand a better chance of being published than if you wrote on other topics."

SERVICING MANAGEMENT

Zackin Publications, P.O. Box 2180, Waterbury CT 06722. (800)325-6745. **Fax:** (203)262-4680. **E-mail:** pbarnard@sm-online.com. **Website:** www.sm-online.com. **Contact:** Patrick Barnard, editor. **15% freelance written.** Monthly magazine covering residential mortgage servicing. Estab. 1989. Circ. 20,000. Byline given. Pays on acceptance. No kill fee. Publishes ms an average of 2 months after acceptance. Accepts queries by mail, e-mail, fax, phone. Accepts simultaneous submissions. Responds in 2 weeks to queries. Sample copy free. Guidelines available online.

NONFICTION Needs how-to, interview, new product, technical. **Buys 10 mss/year.** Query. Length: 1,500-2,500 words.

PHOTOS State availability. Identification of subjects required. Reviews contact sheets. Offers no additional payment for photos accepted with ms. Buys all rights.

COLUMNS/DEPARTMENTS Buys 5 mss/year. Query. **Pays $200.**

FLORISTS, NURSERIES & LANDSCAPERS

DIGGER

Oregon Association of Nurseries, 29751 SW Town Center Loop W., Wilsonville OR 97070. (503)682-5089. **Fax:** (503)682-5099. **E-mail:** ckipp@oan.org; info@oan.org. **Website:** www.diggermagazine.com. **Contact:** Curt Kipp, editor. **50% freelance written.** Monthly magazine covering the nursery and greenhouse industry. *Digger* is a monthly magazine that focuses on industry trends, regulations, research, marketing, and membership activities. In August the magazine becomes *Digger Farwest Edition*, with all the features of *Digger* plus a complete guide to the annual Farwest Show, one of North America's top-attended nursery industry trade shows. Circ. 8,000. Byline given. Pays on receipt of copy. Offers 100% kill fee. Publishes ms an average of 2 months after acceptance. Editorial lead time 6 weeks. Submit seasonal material 2 months in advance. Accepts queries by mail, e-mail, fax, phone. Accepts simultaneous submissions. Sample copy and writer's guidelines free.

NONFICTION Needs general interest, how-to, interview, personal experience, technical. Special issues: Farwest Edition (August): "This is a triple-size issue that runs in tandem with our annual trade show (14,500 circulation for this issue)." No articles not related or pertinent to nursery and greenhouse industry. **Buys 20-30 mss/year.** Query. Length: 800-2,000 words. **Pays $125-400 for assigned articles. Pays $100-300 for unsolicited articles.**

PHOTOS State availability. Captions, identification of subjects required. Reviews high-res digital images sent by e-mail or on CD. Offers $25-150/photo. Buys one-time rights, which includes Web posting.

TIPS "Our best freelancers are familiar with or have experience in the horticultural industry. Some 'green' knowledge is a definite advantage. Our readers are mainly nursery and greenhouse operators and owners who propagate nursery stock/crops, so we write with them in mind."

GROWERTALKS

Ball Publishing, 622 Town Rd., P.O. Box 1660, West Chicago IL 60186. (630)231-3675; (630)588-3401. **Fax:** (630)231-5254. **E-mail:** info@ballpublishing.com. **E-mail:** cbeytes@ballpublishing.com. **Website:** www.growertalks.com. **Contact:** Chris Beytes, editor. **50%**

freelance written. Monthly magazine covering horticulture. *GrowerTalks* serves the commercial greenhouse grower. Editorial emphasis is on floricultural crops: bedding plants, potted floral crops, foliage, and fresh cut flowers. Readers are growers, managers, and owners. Looking for writers who've had experience in the greenhouse industry. Estab. 1937. Circ. 9,500. Byline given. Pays on publication. No kill fee. Publishes ms an average of 3 months after acceptance. Editorial lead time 4 months. Submit seasonal material 3 months in advance. Accepts queries by mail, e-mail, fax. Accepts simultaneous submissions. Responds in 1 month to queries. Sample copy and writer's guidelines free.

NONFICTION Needs how-to, interview, personal experience, technical. No articles that promote only 1 product. **Buys 36 mss/year.** Query. Length: 1,200-1,600 words. **Pays $125 minimum for assigned articles. Pays $75 minimum for unsolicited articles.**

PHOTOS State availability. Captions, identification of subjects, model releases required. Reviews 2 1/2x2 1/2 slides and 3x5 prints. Negotiates payment individually. Buys one-time rights.

TIPS "Discuss magazine with ornamental horticulture growers to find out what topics that have or haven't appeared in the magazine interest them."

TREE CARE INDUSTRY MAGAZINE

Tree Care Industry Association, 136 Harvey Rd., Suite 101, Londonderry NH 03053. (800)733-2622 or (603)314-5380. **Fax:** (603)314-5386. **E-mail:** editor@tcia.org; dstaruk@TCIA.org. **Website:** www.tcia.org. **Contact:** Don Staruk, editor. **50% freelance written.** Monthly magazine covering tree care and landscape maintenance. Estab. 1990. Circ. 24,000. Byline given. Pays within 1 month of publication. No kill fee. Publishes ms an average of 3 months after acceptance. Editorial lead time 10 weeks. Submit seasonal material 3 months in advance. Accepts queries by e-mail. Accepts simultaneous submissions. Responds within 2 days to queries; 2 months to mss. Sample copies online. Guidelines free.

NONFICTION Needs book excerpts, historical, interview, new product, technical. **Buys 60 mss/year.** Query with published clips. Length: 900-3,500 words. **Pays negotiable rate.**

PHOTOS Send photos with submission by e-mail or FTP site. Captions, identification of subjects required. Reviews prints. Negotiates payment individually. Buys one-time and online rights.

COLUMNS/DEPARTMENTS Buys 40 mss/year. Send complete ms. **Pays $100 and up.**

TIPS "Preference is given to writers with background and knowledge of the tree care industry; our focus is relatively narrow."

GOVERNMENT & PUBLIC SERVICE

AMERICAN CITY & COUNTY

Penton Media, 6151 Powers Ferry Rd. NW, Suite 200, Atlanta GA 30339. (770)618-0401. **E-mail:** bill.wolpin@penton.com; derek.prall@penton.com. **Website:** www.americancityandcounty.com. **Contact:** Bill Wolpin, editorial director; Derek Prall, managing editor. **40% freelance written.** Monthly magazine covering local and state government in the U.S. Estab. 1909. Circ. 65,000. Byline given. Pays on publication. Offers 25% kill fee. Publishes ms an average of 2 months after acceptance. Editorial lead time 3 months. Accepts queries by e-mail. Accepts simultaneous submissions. Sample copy available online. Guidelines by e-mail.

NONFICTION Needs new product. **Buys 36 mss/year.** Query. Length: 600-2,000 words. **Pays 30¢/published word.**

PHOTOS State availability. Captions required. Reviews GIF/JPEG files. Negotiates payment individually. Buys all rights.

COLUMNS/DEPARTMENTS Issues & Trends (local and state government news analysis), 500-700 words. **Buys 24 mss/year.** Query. **Pays $150-250.**

TIPS "We use only third-person articles. We do not tell the reader what to do; we offer the facts and assume the reader will make his or her own informed decision. We cover city and county government and state highway departments. We do not cover state legislatures or the federal government, except as they affect local government."

COUNTY

Texas Association of Counties, 1210 San Antonio St., Austin TX 78701. (512)478-8753. **Fax:** (512)481-1240. **E-mail:** marias@county.org. **Website:** www.county.org. **Contact:** Maria Sprow, managing editor. **15% freelance written.** Bimonthly magazine covering county and state government in Texas. Provides elected and appointed county officials with insights and information that help them do their jobs and enhances communications among the independent office-holders in the courthouse. Estab. 1988. Circ. 5,500. Byline given. Pays on acceptance. No kill fee. Publishes ms an average of 2 months after acceptance. Editorial lead time 2 months. Submit seasonal material 4 months in advance. Accepts queries by mail, e-mail, phone. Accepts simultaneous submissions. Responds in 2 weeks to queries. Responds in 1 month to mss. Sample copy and writer's guidelines for 8x10 SAE with 3 first-class stamps.

NONFICTION Needs historical. **Buys 5 mss/year.** Query with published clips. Length: 1,000-3,000 words. **Pays $500-700.**

PHOTOS State availability. Captions, identification of subjects, model releases required. Negotiates payment individually. Buys all rights.

COLUMNS/DEPARTMENTS Safety; Human Resources; Risk Management (all directed toward education of Texas county officials), maximum length 1,000 words. **Buys Buys 2 mss/year. mss/year.** Query with published clips. **Pays $500.**

TIPS "Identify innovative practices or developing trends that affect Texas county officials, and have the basic journalism skills to write a multi-sourced, informative feature."

FIRE CHIEF

Primedia Business, 330 N. Wabash Ave., Suite 2300, Chicago IL 60611. (312)595-1080. **Fax:** (312)595-0295. **E-mail:** Rick.Markley@praetoriangroup.com. **Website:** www.firechief.com. **Contact:** Rick Markley, editor in chief. **60% freelance written.** Monthly magazine covering the fire chief occupation. "*Fire Chief* is the management magazine of the fire service, addressing the administrative, personnel, training, prevention/education, professional development, and operational issues faced by chiefs and other fire officers, whether in paid, volunteer, or combination departments. We're potentially interested in any article that can help them do their jobs better, whether that's as incident commanders, financial managers, supervisors, leaders, trainers, planners, or ambassadors to municipal officials or the public." Estab. 1956. Circ. 53,000. Byline given. Pays on publication. Offers kill fee. Kill fee negotiable. Publishes ms an average of 6 months after acceptance. Editorial lead time 2 months. Submit seasonal material 4 months in advance. Accepts queries by mail, e-mail, fax. Responds in 1 month to queries. Responds in 2 months to mss. Sample copy and submission guidelines free.

NONFICTION Needs how-to, technical. "We do not publish fiction, poetry, or historical articles. We also aren't interested in straightforward accounts of fires or other incidents, unless there are one or more specific lessons to be drawn from a particular incident, especially lessons that are applicable to a large number of departments." **Buys 50-60 mss/year.** Query first with published clips. Length: 1,000-10,000 words. **Pays $50-400.**

PHOTOS State availability. Captions, identification of subjects required. Reviews transparencies, prints. Buys one-time or reprint rights.

COLUMNS/DEPARTMENTS Training Perspectives; EMS Viewpoints; Sound Off; Volunteer Voice; all 1,000-1,800 words.

TIPS "Writers who are unfamiliar with the fire service are very unlikely to place anything with us. Many pieces that we reject are either too unfocused or too abstract. We want articles that help keep fire chiefs well informed and effective at their jobs."

FIREHOUSE MAGAZINE

Cygnus Business Media, 1233 Janesville Ave., Fort Atkinson WI 53538. (800)547-7377. **E-mail:** janelle@firehouse.com. **Website:** www.firehouse.com. **Contact:** Janelle Foskett, executive editor. **85% freelance written. Works with a small number of new/unpublished writers each year.** Monthly magazine. *Firehouse* covers major fires nationwide, controversial issues and trends in the fire service, the latest firefighting equipment and methods of firefighting, historical fires, firefighting history and memorabilia. Fire-related books, fire safety education, hazardous-materials incidents, and the emergency medical services are also covered. Estab. 1976. Circ. 83,538 (print). Byline given. Pays on publication. No kill fee. Accepts queries by mail, e-mail, fax, online submission form. Sample copy for SAE with 9x12 envelope and 8 first-class stamps.

NONFICTION Needs book excerpts, historical, how-to, trends in the fire service. No profiles of people or departments that are not unusual or innovative, reports of nonmajor fires, articles not slanted toward firefighters' interests. No poetry. **Buys 100 mss/year.** Query. "If you have any story ideas, questions, hints, tips, etc., please do not hesitate to call." Length: 500-3,000 words. The average length of each article is between 2-3 pages, including visuals. **Pays $50-400 for assigned articles.**

PHOTOS *Firehouse* is a visually-oriented publication. Please include photographs (color preferred) with captions (or a description of what is taking place in the photo), illustrations, charts or diagrams that support your ms. The highest priority is given to those submissions that are received as a complete package. Pays $25-200 for transparencies and color prints. Cannot accept negatives.

COLUMNS/DEPARTMENTS Training (effective methods); Book Reviews; Fire Safety (how departments teach fire safety to the public); Communicating (PR, dispatching); Arson (efforts to combat it). Length: 750-1,000 words. **Buys 50 mss/year.** Query or send complete ms. **Pays $100-300.**

TIPS "Have excellent fire service credentials and be able to offer our readers new information. Read the magazine to get a full understanding of the subject matter, the writing style, and the readers before sending a query or ms. Indicate sources for photos. Be sure to focus articles on firefighters."

FIRERESCUE

PennWell Corporation, 21-00 Route 208 South, Fair Lawn NJ 07410. (973)251-5055. **E-mail:** frm.editor@pennwell.com; dianer@pennwell.com. **Website:** www.firefighternation.com. **Contact:** Diane Rothschild, executive editor. "FireRescue covers the fire and rescue markets. Our 'Read It Today, Use It Tomorrow' mission weaves through every article and image we publish. Our readers consist of fire chiefs, company officers, training officers, firefighters, and technical rescue personnel." Estab. 1997. Circ. 50,000. Pays on publication. Accepts queries by mail, e-mail. Responds in 1 month to mss. Guidelines available online.

NONFICTION Needs general interest, how-to, interview, new product, technical. "All story ideas must be submitted with a cover letter that outlines your qualifications and includes your name, full address, phone, and e-mail address. We accept story submissions in 1 of the following 2 formats: query letters and mss." Length: 800-2,200 words. **Pays $100—$200 for features.**

PHOTOS Looks for "photographs that show firefighters in action, using proper techniques and wearing the proper equipment. Submit timely photographs that show the technical aspects of firefighting and rescue. ". Digital images in JPEG, TIFF, or EPS format at

72 dpi for initial review. We require 300 dpi resolution for publication. If you send images as attachments via e-mail, compress your files first.

TIPS "Read back issues of the magazine to learn our style. Research back issues to ensure we haven't covered your topic within the past three years. Read and follow the instructions on our guidelines page."

LAW ENFORCEMENT TECHNOLOGY MAGAZINE

Cygnus Business Media, 1233 Janesville Ave., Fort Atkinson WI 53538. (800)547-7377. **E-mail:** sara.scullin@cygnus.com. **Website:** www.officer.com. **Contact:** Sara Scullin, editor. **40% freelance written.** Monthly magazine covering police management and technology. Estab. 1974. Circ. 30,000. Byline given. Pays on publication. No kill fee. Publishes ms an average of 4 months after acceptance. Editorial lead time 6 months. Accepts simultaneous submissions. Responds in 1 month to queries; 2 months to mss. Guidelines free.

NONFICTION Needs how-to, interview, photo feature, police management and training. **Buys 30 mss/year.** Query. Length: 1,200-2,000 words. **Pays $75-400 for assigned articles.**

REPRINTS Send typed ms with rights for sale noted and information about when and where the material previously appeared. Payment negotiable.

PHOTOS Send photos. Captions required. Reviews contact sheets, negatives, 5x7 or 8x10 prints. Offers no additional payment for photos accepted with ms. Buys one-time rights.

TIPS "Writer should have background in police work or currently work for a police agency. Most of our articles are technical or supervisory in nature. Please query first after looking at a sample copy. Prefers mss, queries, and images be submitted electronically."

PLANNING

American Planning Association, 205 N. Michigan Ave., Suite 1200, Chicago IL 60601. (312)431-9100. **Fax:** (312)786-6700. **E-mail:** mstromberg@planning.org. **Website:** www.planning.org. **Contact:** Meghan Stromberg, executive editor; Sylvia Lewis, editor; Joan Cairney, art director. **30% freelance written.** Monthly magazine emphasizing urban planning for adult, college-educated readers who are regional and urban planners in city, state, or federal agencies or in private business, or university faculty or students. Estab. 1972. Circ. 44,000. Byline given. Pays on publication.

No kill fee. Publishes ms an average of 2 months after acceptance. Accepts queries by mail, e-mail. Accepts simultaneous submissions. Responds in 5 weeks to queries. Guidelines available online.

NONFICTION Special issues: Transportation issue. Also needs news stories up to 500 words. **Buys 44 features and 33 news stories mss/year.** Length: 500-3,000 words. **Pays $150-1,500.**

PHOTOS "We prefer authors supply their own photos, but we sometimes take our own or arrange for them in other ways." State availability. Captions required. Pays $100 minimum for photos used on inside pages and $300 for cover photos. Buys one-time rights.

POLICE AND SECURITY NEWS

DAYS Communications, Inc., 1208 Juniper St., Quakertown PA 18951-1520. (215)538-1240. **Fax:** (215)538-1208. **E-mail:** amenear@policeandsecuritynews.com. **Website:** www.policeandsecuritynews.com. **Contact:** Al Menear, publisher. **40% freelance written.** Bi-monthly periodical on public law enforcement and homeland security. "Our publication is designed to provide educational and entertaining information directed toward management level. Technical information written for the expert in a manner the nonexpert can understand." Estab. 1984. Circ. 24,000. Byline given. Pays on publication. No kill fee. Publishes ms an average of 2 months after acceptance. Accepts queries by mail, e-mail, fax, phone, online submission form. Accepts simultaneous submissions. Sample copy and writer's guidelines with 10x13 SASE with $2.53 postage.

NONFICTION Contact: Al Menear, articles editor. Needs historical, how-to, humor, interview, opinion, personal experience, photo feature, technical. **Buys 12 mss/year.** Query. Length: 200-2,500 words. **Pays 10¢/word. Sometimes pays in trade-out of services.**

REPRINTS Send tearsheet, photocopy or typed ms with rights for sale noted and information about when and where the material previously appeared.

PHOTOS State availability. Reviews 3x5 prints. Offers $10-50/photo. Buys one-time rights.

FILLERS Needs facts, newsbreaks, short humor. **Buys 6 mss/year.** Length: 200-2,000 words. **10¢/word.**

YOUTH TODAY

Kennesaw State University, 1000 Chastain Rd., MD 2212, Bldg. 22, Kennesaw GA 30144. (678)797-2899. **E-mail:** jfleming@youthtoday.org. **Website:** www.youthtoday.org. **Contact:** John Fleming, editor. **50% freelance written.** Bi-monthly newspaper covering businesses that provide services to youth. Audience is people who run youth programs—mostly nonprofits and government agencies—who want help in providing services and getting funding. Estab. 1994. Circ. 9,000. Byline given. Pays on publication. Offers $200 kill fee for features. Editorial lead time 2 months. Accepts queries by mail. Accepts simultaneous submissions. Responds in 2 weeks to queries. Responds in 1 month to mss. Sample copy for $5. Guidelines available on website.

NONFICTION Needs general interest, technical. "No feel-good stories about do-gooders. We examine the business of youth work." **Buys 5 mss/year.** Query. Send rèsumè, short cover letter, clips. Length: 600-2,500 words. **Pays $150-2,000 for assigned articles.**

PHOTOS Identification of subjects required. Offers no additional payment for photos accepted with ms. Buys one-time and Internet rights.

COLUMNS/DEPARTMENTS "*Youth Today* also publishes 750-word guest columns, called Viewpoints. These pieces can be based on the writer's own experiences or based on research, but they must deal with an issue of interest to our readership and must soundly argue an opinion, or advocate for a change in thinking or action within the youth field."

TIPS "Business writers have the best shot. Focus on evaluations of programs, or why a program succeeds or fails. Please visit online."

GROCERIES & FOOD PRODUCTS

CONVENIENCE DISTRIBUTION

American Wholesale Marketers Association, 11311 Sunset Hills Road, Reston VA 20190. (703)208-3358. **Fax:** (703)573-5738. **E-mail:** info@awmanet.org; joanf@awmanet.org. **Website:** www.cdaweb.net. **Contact:** Joan Fay, associate publisher and editor. **70% freelance written.** Magazine published 10 times/year. See website for editorial calendar. Covers trends in candy, tobacco, groceries, beverages, snacks, and other product categories found in convenience stores, grocery stores, and drugstores, plus distribution topics. Contributors should have prior experience writing about the food, retail, and/or distribution industries. Editorial includes a mix of columns, departments, and features (2-6 pages). Also covers

AWMA programs. Estab. 1948. Circ. 11,000. Byline given. Pays on acceptance. No kill fee. Publishes ms an average of 2 months after acceptance. Editorial lead time 3-4 months. Accepts simultaneous submissions. Guidelines available online.

NONFICTION Needs how-to, technical, industry trends, also profiles of distribution firms. No comics, jokes, poems, or other fillers. **Buys 40 mss/year.** Query with published clips. Length: 1,200-3,600 words. **Pays 50¢/word.**

PHOTOS Authors must provide artwork (with captions) with articles.

TIPS "We're looking for reliable, accurate freelancers with whom we can establish a long-term working relationship. We need writers who understand this industry. We accept very few articles on speculation. Most are assigned. To consider a new writer for an assignment, we must first receive his or her résumé at least 2 writing samples, and references."

FRESH CUT MAGAZINE

Great American Publishing, P.O. Box 128, 75 Applewood Dr., Suite A, Sparta MI 49345. (616)887-9008. **Fax:** (616)887-2666. **E-mail:** fcedit@freshcut.com. **Website:** www.freshcut.com. **Contact:** Lee Dean, editorial director. **20% freelance written.** Monthly magazine covering the value-added and pre-cut fruit and vegetable industry. Interested in articles that focus on what different fresh-cut processors are doing. Estab. 1993. Circ. 16,000. Byline given. Pays on publication. No kill fee. Publishes ms an average of 2 months after acceptance. Editorial lead time 2 months. Accepts queries by mail, e-mail, fax, phone, online submission form. Accepts simultaneous submissions. Responds in 1 month to queries. Responds in 2 months to mss. Sample copy for SAE with 9x12 envelope. Guidelines for #10 SASE.

NONFICTION Needs historical, new product, opinion, technical. **Buys 2-4 mss/year.** Query with published clips.

REPRINTS Send tearsheet with rights for sale noted and information about when and where the material previously appeared. Pays 50% of amount paid for an original article.

PHOTOS Send photos. Identification of subjects required. Reviews transparencies. Offers no additional payment for photos accepted with ms. Buys one-time rights.

COLUMNS/DEPARTMENTS Packaging; Food Safety; Processing/Engineering. **Buys 20 mss/year.** Query. **Pays $125-200.**

THE PRODUCE NEWS

800 Kinderkamack Rd., Suite 100, Oradell NJ 07649. (201)986-7990. **Fax:** (201)986-7996. **E-mail:** groh@theproducenews.com. **Website:** www.theproducenews.com. **Contact:** John Groh, editor/publisher. **10% freelance written. Works with a small number of new/unpublished writers each year.** Weekly magazine for commercial growers and shippers, receivers, and distributors of fresh fruits and vegetables, including chain store produce buyers and merchandisers. Estab. 1897. Pays on publication. No kill fee. Publishes ms an average of 2 weeks after acceptance. Accepts queries by mail, e-mail. Accepts simultaneous submissions. Responds in 1 month to queries. Sample copy and writer's guidelines for 10x13 SAE and 4 first-class stamps.

NONFICTION Query. **Pays $1/column inch minimum.**

PHOTOS B&W glossies or color prints. Pays $8-10/photo.

TIPS "Stories should be trade oriented, not consumer oriented. As our circulation grows, we are interested in stories and news articles from all fresh-fruit-growing areas of the country."

○ WESTERN GROCER MAGAZINE

Mercury Publications Ltd., 1313 Border Ave., Unit 16, Winnipeg MB R3H 0X4 Canada. (204)954-2085, ext. 219; (800)337-6372. **Fax:** (204)954-2057. **E-mail:** rbradley@mercurypublications.ca. **Website:** www.westerngrocer.com. **Contact:** Robin Bradley, associate publisher and national account manager. **75% freelance written.** Bimonthly magazine covering the grocery industry. Reports for the Western Canadian grocery, allied non-food and institutional industries. Each issue features a selection of relevant trade news and event coverage from the West and around the world. Feature reports offer market analysis, trend views, and insightful interviews from a wide variety of industry leaders. *The Western Grocer* target audience is independent retail food stores, supermarkets, manufacturers and food brokers, distributors and wholesalers of food, and allied non-food products, as well as bakers, specialty and health food stores, and convenience outlets. Estab. 1916. Circ. 15,500. Byline given. Pays 30-45 days from receipt of invoice. Offers 33% kill fee. Submit seasonal material 3 months in advance. Sample copy and writer's guidelines free.

NONFICTION Needs how-to, interview. Does not want industry reports and profiles on companies. Query with published clips. Length: 500-9,000 words. **Pays 25-35¢/word.**

PHOTOS State availability. Captions required. Reviews negatives, transparencies, 3x5 prints, JPEG, EPS, or TIF files. Negotiates payment individually. Buys all rights.

TIPS "E-mail, fax, or mail a query outlining your experience, interest, and pay expectations. Include clippings."

HOME FURNISHINGS & HOUSEHOLD GOODS

HOME FURNISHINGS RETAILER

National Home Furnishings Association (NHFA), 500 Giuseppe Ct., Suite 6, Roseville CA 95678. (336)801-6156; (800)422-3778. **E-mail:** wynnryan@rcn.com. **Website:** www.nhfa.org. **Contact:** Mary Wynn Ryan, editor-in-chief. **75% freelance written.** Monthly magazine published by NHFA covering the home furnishings industry. "We hope home furnishings retailers view our magazine as a profitability tool. We want each issue to help them make or save money." Estab. 1927. Circ. 15,000. Byline given. Pays on acceptance. No kill fee. Publishes ms an average of 6 weeks after acceptance. Editorial lead time 3 months. Accepts queries by mail, e-mail. Accepts simultaneous submissions. Responds in 1 month to queries. Sample copy available with proper postage. Guidelines available.

NONFICTION Query. "When submitting a query or requesting a writing assignment, include a résumé, writing samples, and credentials. When articles are assigned, *Home Furnishings Retailer* will provide general direction along with suggestions for appropriate artwork. The author is responsible for obtaining photographs or other illustrative material. Assigned articles should be submitted via e-mail or on disc along with a list of sources with telephone numbers, fax numbers, and e-mail addresses." Length: 3,000-5,000 words (features). **Pays $350-500.**

PHOTOS Author is responsible for obtaining photos or other illustrative material. State availability. Identification of subjects required. Reviews transparen-

cies. Negotiates payment individually. Buys one-time rights.

COLUMNS/DEPARTMENTS Columns cover business and product trends that shape the home furnishings industry. Advertising and Marketing; Finance; Technology; Training; Creative Leadership; Law; Style and Operations. Length: 1,200-1,500 words. Query with published clips.

TIPS "Our readership includes owners of small 'ma and pa' furniture stores, executives of medium-sized chains (2-10 stores), and executives of big chains. Articles should be relevant to retailers and provide them with tangible information, ideas, and products to better their business."

HOSPITALS, NURSING & NURSING HOMES

CURRENT NURSING IN GERIATRIC CARE

Freiberg Press Inc., P.O. Box 612, Cedar Falls IA 50613. (319)553-0642; (800)354-3371. **Fax:** (319)553-0644. **E-mail:** bfreiberg@cfu.net. **Website:** www.care4elders.com. **Contact:** Bill Freiberg. **25% freelance written.** Bimonthly trade journal covering medical information and new developments in research for geriatric nurses and other practitioners. Estab. 2006. Byline sometimes given. Pays on acceptance. No kill fee. Accepts queries by e-mail. Accepts simultaneous submissions. Sample copy free; send e-mail to Kathy Freiderg at kfreiberg@cfu.net.

NONFICTION Query. Length: 500-1,500 words. **Pays 15¢/word for assigned articles.**

PHOTOS State availability.

NURSEWEEK

Gannett Healthcare Group, 1721 Moon Lake Blvd., Suite 540, Hoffman Estates IL 60169. **E-mail:** editor@nurse.com. **Website:** www.nurse.com. **Contact:** Nick Hut, editor. **98% freelance written.** Biweekly magazine covering nursing news. Covers nursing news about people, practice, and the profession. Review several issues for content and style. Also consider e-mailing your idea to the editorial director in your region (see list online). The editorial director can help you with the story's focus or angle, along with the organization and development of ideas. Estab. 1999. Circ. 155,000. Byline given. Pays on publication. Offers $200 kill fee. Publishes ms an average of 2 months after acceptance. Editorial lead time 2-3 months. Submit seasonal material 4 months in advance. Accepts queries by e-mail. Accepts simultaneous submissions. Sample copy free. Guidelines on website.

NONFICTION Needs interview, personal experience, articles on innovative approaches to clinical care and evidence-based nursing practice, health-related legislation and regulation, community health programs, healthcare delivery systems, and professional development and management, advances in nursing specialties such as critical care, geriatrics, perioperative care, women's health, home care, long-term care, emergency care, med/surg, pediatrics, advanced practice, education, and staff development. **Buys 20 mss/year mss/year.** Query with a 50-word summary of story and a list of RN experts you plan to interview. Length: 900 words. **Pays $200-800 for assigned or unsolicited articles.**

PHOTOS Send photos. Captions, model releases required. Reviews contact sheets, GIF/JPEG files. Offers no additional payment for photos accepted with ms. Buys all rights.

TIPS "Pitch us nursing news, AP style, minimum 3 sources, incorporate references. The stories we publish are short and written in a conversational, magazine-style rather than a scholarly tone. In keeping with any article appearing in a nursing publication, clinical accuracy is essential."

NURSING

Lippincott Williams & Wilkins, 323 Norristown Rd., Suite 200, Ambler PA 19002-2758. (215)646-8700. **Fax:** (215)654-1328. **E-mail:** nursingeditor@ wolterskluwer.com. **Website:** http://journals.lww. com/nursing/pages/default.aspx. **Contact:** Linda Laskowski-Jones, RN, ACNS-BC, CCRN, CEN, MS, FAWM. **100% freelance written.** Monthly magazine written by nurses for nurses. Looks for practical advice for the direct caregiver that reflects the author's experience. Any form acceptable, but focus must be nursing. Published monthly, *Nursing2014* is widely regarded as offering current, practical contents to its readers, and has won many editorial awards testifying to the quality of its copy and graphics. The editorial and clinical staff, a 18-member editorial board of distinguished clinicians and practitioners, and over 100 invited reviewers help ensure the quality of this publication. Estab. 1971. Circ. over 300,000. Byline given. Pays on publication. Offers 50% kill fee. Publishes ms an average of 18 months after acceptance.

Submit seasonal material 8 months in advance. Accepts simultaneous submissions. Responds in 2 weeks to queries. Responds in 3 months to mss. Sample copy for $5. Guidelines available online.

NONFICTION Needs book excerpts, how-to, inspirational, opinion, personal experience, photo feature. No articles from patients' point of view, poetry, etc. **Buys 100 mss/year.** Query. All mss can be submitted online through the journal's submission website. Using this process will expedite review and feedback, and allows the the author to see where the ms is in the editorial process at any time after it's accepted. Encourages authors to register there and follow the directions. Length: 3,500 words (continuing ed feature); 2,100 words (features); short features/departments, 700 words. **Pays $50-400 for assigned articles.**

REPRINTS Send photocopy and information about when and where the material previously appeared. Pays 50% of amount paid for an original articles.

PHOTOS State availability. Model releases required. Offers no additional payment for photos accepted with ms. Buys all rights.

SCHOOL NURSE NEWS

Franklin Communications, Inc., 767 Buena Vista Ave. W., #101, San Francisco CA 94117. (415)670-0436. **Fax:** (415)663-4768. **E-mail:** editor@schoolnursenews.org. **Website:** www.schoolnursenews.org. **Contact:** Deb Ilardi. **10% freelance written.** Magazine published 5 times/year covering school nursing. *School Nurse News* focuses on topics related to the health issues of school-aged children and adolescents (grades K-12), as well as the health and professional issues that concern school nurses. This is an excellent opportunity for both new and experienced writers. *School Nurse News* publishes feature articles as well as news articles and regular departments, such as Asthma & Allergy Watch, Career & Salary Survey, Oral Health, Nursing Currents, and Sights & Sounds. Estab. 1982. Circ. 7,500. Byline given. Pays on publication. Publishes ms an average of 3-6 months after acceptance. Editorial lead time 3-6 months. Submit seasonal material 6 months in advance. Accepts queries by e-mail, fax, phone. Accepts simultaneous submissions. Sample copy free. Guidelines available on website.

NONFICTION Needs how-to, interview, new product, personal experience. **Buys 1-2 mss/year.** Query. Send via e-mail or forward ms with disk. Mss can include case histories, scenarios of health office situations, updates on diseases, reporting of research, and discussion of procedures and techniques, among others. The author is responsible for the accuracy of content. References should be complete, accurate, and in APA format. Tables, charts and photographs are welcome. Authors are responsible for obtaining permission to reproduce any material that has a pre-existing copyright. The feature article, references, tables, and charts should total 8-10 typewritten pages, double-spaced. The author's name should be included only on the top sheet. The top sheet should also include the title of the article, the author's credentials, current position, address, and phone. **Pays $100.**

HOTELS, MOTELS, CLUBS, RESORTS & RESTAURANTS

BARTENDER® MAGAZINE

Foley Publishing, P.O. Box 157, Spring Lake NJ 07762. (732)449-4499. **E-mail:** info@bartender.com. **Website:** bartender.com/mixologist.com. **Contact:** Jackie Foley, editor. **75% freelance written. Prefers to work with published/established writers; eager to work with new/unpublished writers.** Quarterly publication for full-service on-premise establishments able to serve a mixed drink on-premise. Features bartenders, bars, creative cocktails, signature drinks, jokes, cartoons, wine, beer, liquor, new products and those products aligned to the field. Estab. 1979. Circ. 150,000. Byline given. Pays on publication. No kill fee. Publishes ms an average of 3 months after acceptance. Submit seasonal material 3 months in advance. Accepts simultaneous submissions. Responds in 2 months to mss. Sample copy with 9x12 SAE and 4 first-class stamps.

NONFICTION Needs general interest, historical, how-to, humor, new product, opinion, personal experience, photo feature. Special issues: Special issues: Annual Calendar and Daily Cocktail Recipe Guide. Send complete ms and SASE. Length: 100-1,000 words.

REPRINTS Send tearsheet and information about when and where the material previously appeared. Pays 25% of amount paid for an original article.

PHOTOS Send photos. Captions, model releases required. Pays $7.50-50 for 8x10 b&w glossy prints; $10-75 for 8x10 color glossy prints.

COLUMNS/DEPARTMENTS Bar of the Month; Bartender of the Month; Creative Cocktails; Bar Sports; Quiz; Bar Art; Wine Cellar; Tips from the Top (from prominent figures in the liquor industry); One For the Road (travel); Collectors (bar or liquor-related items); Photo Essays. Length: 200-1,000 words. Query by mail only with SASE. **Pays $50-200.**

FILLERS Needs anecdotes, newsbreaks, short humor, clippings, jokes, gags. Length: 25-100 words. **Pays $5-25.**

TIPS "To break in, absolutely make sure your work will be of interest to all bartenders across the country. Your style of writing should reflect the audience you are addressing. The most frequent mistake made by writers in completing an article for us is using the wrong subject."

EL RESTAURANTE

P.O. Box 2249, Oak Park IL 60303-2249. (708)267-0023. **E-mail:** kfurore@comcast.net. **Website:** www.restmex.com. **Contact:** Kathleen Furore, editor. Bi-monthly magazine covering Mexican and other Latin cuisines. "*el Restaurante* offers features and business-related articles that are geared specifically to owners and operators of Mexican, Tex-Mex, Southwestern, and Latin cuisine restaurants and other foodservice establishments that want to add that type of cuisine." Estab. 1997. Circ. 25,000. Byline given. Pays on publication. No kill fee. Publishes ms an average of 3 months after acceptance. Accepts simultaneous submissions. Responds in 2 months to queries. Sample copy free.

NONFICTION "No specific knowledge of food or restaurants is needed; the key qualification is to be a good reporter who knows how to slant a story toward the Mexican restaurant operator." **Buys 2-4 mss/year.** Query with published clips. Length: 800-1,200 words. **Pays $250-300.**

TIPS "Query with a story idea, and tell how it pertains to Mexican restaurants."

HOSPITALITY TECHNOLOGY

Edgell Communications, 4 Middlebury Blvd., Randolph NJ 07869. (973)607-1300. **E-mail:** alorden@edgellmail.com; dcreamer@edgellmail.com. **Website:** www.htmagazine.com. **Contact:** Abigail Lorden, editor-in-chief; Dorothy Creamer, managing editor. **70% freelance written.** Magazine published 9 times/year covering restaurant and lodging executives who manage hotels, casinos, cruise lines, quick service restaurants, etc. Covers the technology used in food-service and lodging. Readers are the operators, who have significant IT responsibilities. Estab. 1996. Circ. 16,000. Byline given. Pays on acceptance. No kill fee. Publishes ms an average of 1 month after acceptance. Editorial lead time 2 months. Accepts queries by mail, e-mail. Accepts simultaneous submissions. Responds in 2 weeks to queries.

This publication will not respond to all inquiries, due to the number of submissions—only those that are of particular interest to the editor.

NONFICTION Needs how-to, interview, new product, technical. Special issues: Publishes 2 studies each year: the Restaurant Industry Technology Study and the Lodging Industry Technology Study. No unsolicited mss. **Buys 40 mss/year.** Query with published clips. Length: 800-1,200 words. **Pays $1/word.**

HOTELIER

Kostuch Media Ltd., 101-23 Lesmill Rd., Toronto ON M3B 3P6 Canada. (416)447-0888. Fax: (416)447-5333. **E-mail:** rcaira@foodservice.ca. **Website:** www.hoteliermagazine.com. **Contact:** Rosanna Caira, editor & publisher. **40% freelance written.** Magazine published 8 times/year covering the Canadian hotel industry. Canada's leading hotel publication. Provides comprehensive and insightful content focusing on business developments, trend analysis, and profiles of the industry's movers and shakers. Estab. 1989. Circ. 9,000. Byline given. Pays on publication. No kill fee. Editorial lead time 3 months. Submit seasonal material 2 months in advance. Accepts queries by mail, fax. Accepts simultaneous submissions. Query for free sample copy. Query for free guidelines.

NONFICTION Needs how-to, new product. No case studies. **Buys 30-50 mss/year.** Query. Length: 700-1,500 words. **Pays 35¢/word (Canadian) for assigned articles.**

PHOTOS Send photos. Offers $30-75/photo.

PIZZA TODAY

Macfadden Protech, LLC, 908 S. 8th St., Suite 200, Louisville KY 40203. (502)736-9500. **Fax:** (502)736-9502. **E-mail:** jwhite@pizzatoday.com. **Website:** www.pizzatoday.com. **Contact:** Jeremy White, editor-in-chief. **30% freelance written. Works with published/established writers; occasionally works with new writers.** Monthly magazine for the pizza industry, covering trends, features of successful pizza op-

erators, business and management advice, etc. Estab. 1984. Circ. 44,000. Byline given. Pays on acceptance. No kill fee. Publishes ms an average of 2 months after acceptance. Submit seasonal material 3 months in advance. Accepts queries by mail, e-mail, fax. Accepts simultaneous submissions. Responds in 2 months to queries. Responds in 3 weeks to mss. Sample copy for sae with 10x13 envelope and 6 first-class stamps. Guidelines for #10 SASE and online.

NONFICTION Needs interview, entrepreneurial slants, pizza production and delivery, employee training, hiring, marketing, and business management. No fillers, humor, or poetry. **Buys 85 mss/year.** Length: 1,000 words. **Pays 50¢/word, occasionally more.**

PHOTOS Captions required. Reviews contact sheets, negatives, transparencies, color slides, 5x7 prints.

TIPS "Our most pressing need is for articles that would fall within our Front of the House section. Review the magazine before sending in your query."

WESTERN HOTELIER MAGAZINE

Mercury Publications, Ltd., 1313 Border St., Unit 16, Winnipeg MB R3H 0X4 Canada. (800)337-6372 ext. 221. **Fax:** (204)954-2057. **E-mail:** dbastable@mercurypublications.ca. **Website:** www.westernhotelier.com. **Contact:** David Bastable, associate publisher and national accounts manager. **33% freelance written.** Quarterly magazine covering the hotel industry. *Western Hotelier* is dedicated to the accommodation industry in Western Canada and U.S. western border states. *WH* offers the West's best mix of news and feature reports geared to hotel management. Feature reports are written on a sector basis and are created to help generate enhanced profitability and better understanding. Circ. 4,342. Byline given. Pays 30-45 days from receipt of invoice. Offers 33% kill fee. Submit seasonal material 3 months in advance. Accepts queries by mail, fax. Accepts simultaneous submissions. Responds in 2 weeks to queries. Sample copy and writer's guidelines free.

NONFICTION Needs how-to, interview. Industry reports and profiles on companies. Query with published clips. Length: 500-9,000 words. **Pays 25-35¢/word.**

PHOTOS State availability. Captions required. Reviews negatives, transparencies, 3x5 prints, JPEG, EPS, or TIF files. Negotiates payment individually. Buys all rights.

TIPS "E-mail, fax, or mail a query outlining your experience, interests, and pay expectations. Include clippings."

⊙ WESTERN RESTAURANT NEWS

Mercury Publications, Ltd., 1313 Border St., Unit 16, Winnipeg MB R3H 0X4 Canada. (800)337-6372 ext. 213. **Fax:** (204)954-2057. **E-mail:** editorial@mercury. mb.ca; edufault@mercurypublications.ca. **Website:** www.westernrestaurantnews.com; www.mercury. mb.ca. **Contact:** Elaine Dufault, associate publisher and national accounts manager. **20% freelance written.** Bimonthly magazine covering the restaurant trade in Western Canada. Reports profiles and industry reports on associations, regional business developments, etc. *Western Restaurant News* is the authoritative voice of the food service industry in Western Canada. Offering a total package to readers, *WRN* delivers concise news articles, new product news, and coverage of the leading trade events in the West, across the country, and around the world. Estab. 1994. Circ. 14,532. Byline given. Pays 30-45 days from receipt of invoice. Offers 33% kill fee. Submit seasonal material 3 months in advance. Accepts queries by mail, fax. Accepts simultaneous submissions. Sample copy and writer's guidelines free.

NONFICTION Needs how-to, interview. Industry reports and profiles on companies. Query with published clips. "E-mail, fax, or mail a query outlining your experience, interests, and pay expectations. Include clippings." Length: 500-9,000 words. **Pays 25-35¢/word.**

PHOTOS State availability. Captions required. Reviews negatives, transparencies, 3x5 prints, JPEG, EPS, or TIFF files. Negotiates payment individually. Buys all rights.

INDUSTRIAL OPERATIONS

⊙ COMMERCE & INDUSTRY

Mercury Publications, Ltd., 1313 Border Street, Unit 16, Winnipeg MB R3H 0X4 Canada. (204)954-2085. **Fax:** (204)954-2057. **E-mail:** editorial@mercury. mb.ca. **Website:** www.commerceindustry.ca. **Contact:** Nicole Sherwood, editorial coordinator. **75% freelance written.** Bimonthly magazine covering the business and industrial sectors. Offers new product news, industry event coverage, and breaking trade

specific business stories. Industry reports and company profiles provide readers with an in-depth insight into key areas of interest in their profession. Estab. 1948. Circ. 18,876. Byline given. Pays 30-45 days from receipt of invoice. Offers 33% kill fee. Submit seasonal material 3 months in advance. Accepts queries by mail, e-mail, fax. Accepts simultaneous submissions. Responds in 2 weeks to queries. Sample copy and writer's guidelines free or by e-mail.

NONFICTION Needs how-to, interview. Industry reports and profiles on companies. Query with published clips. Length: 500-9,000 words. **Pays 25-35¢/word.**

PHOTOS State availability. Captions required. Reviews negatives, transparencies, 3x5 prints, JPEG, EPS or TIF files. Negotiates payment individually. Buys all rights.

TIPS "E-mail, fax, or mail a query outlining your experience, interests and pay expectations. Include clippings."

INDUSTRIAL WEIGH & MEASURE

WAM Publishing Company, Inc., P.O. Box 2247, Hendersonville TN 37077. (615)239-8087. **E-mail:** dave. mathieu@comcast.net. **Website:** www.weighproducts. com. **Contact:** David M. Mathieu, publisher and editor. Bimonthly magazine for users of industrial scales; covers material handling and logistics industries. Estab. 1914. Circ. 13,900. Byline given. Pays on acceptance. Offers 20% kill fee. Accepts queries by mail, e-mail, phone. Accepts simultaneous submissions. Responds in 2 weeks to queries. Sample copy available online.

NONFICTION Needs general interest, technical. **Buys 15 mss/year.** Query on technical articles; submit complete ms for general interest material. Length: 1,000-2,500 words. **Pays $175-300.**

⊙⊙⊙⊙⊙ MACHINERY & EQUIPMENT MRO

Annex Business Media, 80 Valleybrook Dr., Toronto ON M3B 2S9 Canada. (416)510-6851. **Fax:** (416)510-5134. **E-mail:** rbegg@annexweb.com. **Website:** www. mromagazine.com. **Contact:** Rehana Begg, Editor. **30% freelance written.** Bimonthly magazine looking for informative articles on issues that affect plant floor operations and maintenance. Estab. 1985. Circ. 18,000. Byline given. Pays on publication. No kill fee. Publishes ms an average of 3 months after acceptance. Editorial lead time 4 months. Submit seasonal material 4 months in advance. Accepts simultaneous submissions. Responds in 3 weeks to queries. Responds in 1 month to mss. Sample copy free. Guidelines available.

NONFICTION Needs essays, how-to, new product, technical. **Buys 6 mss/year.** Query with published clips. Length: 750-4,000 words. **Pays $200-1,400 (Canadian).**

PHOTOS State availability. Captions required. Reviews transparencies, prints. Negotiates payment individually. Buys one-time rights.

TIPS "Information can be found at our website. Call us for sample issues, ideas, etc."

MODERN MATERIALS HANDLING

Peerless Media, 111 Speen St., Suite 200, Framingham MA 01701. (508)663-1500. **E-mail:** mlevans@ehpub.com; robert.trebilcock@myfairpoint.net. **Website:** www.mmh.com. **Contact:** Michael Levans, editorial director. **40% freelance written.** Magazine published 13 times/year covering warehousing, distribution centers, and inventory. *Modern Materials Handling* is a national magazine read by managers of warehouses and distribution centers. Focuses on lively, well-written articles telling readers how they can achieve maximum facility productivity and efficiency. Covers technology, too. Estab. 1945. Circ. 81,000. Byline given. Pays on acceptance (allow 4-6 weeks for invoice processing). No kill fee. Publishes ms an average of 1 month after acceptance. Editorial lead time 3 months. Accepts queries by mail, e-mail, fax. Accepts simultaneous submissions. Sample copy and guidelines free.

NONFICTION Needs how-to, new product, technical. Special issues: State-of-the-Industry Report, Peak Performer, Salary and Wage survey, Warehouse of the Year. Doesn't want anything that doesn't deal with the topic of warehousing. No general-interest profiles or interviews. **Buys 25 mss/year.** Query with published clips. **Pays $300-650.**

PHOTOS State availability. Captions, identification of subjects required. Reviews negatives, transparencies, prints. Offers no additional payment for photos accepted with ms. Buys all rights.

TIPS "Learn a little about warehousing and distributors, and write well. We typically don't accept specific article queries, but welcome introductory letters from journalists to whom we can assign articles. But authors are welcome to request an editorial calendar and develop article queries from it."

INFORMATION SYSTEMS

JOURNAL OF INFORMATION ETHICS

McFarland & Co., Inc., Publishers, P.O. Box 611, Jefferson NC 28640. (336)246-4460. **E-mail:** hauptman@stcloudstate.edu. **90% freelance written.** Semiannual scholarly journal covering all of the information sciences. Addresses ethical issues in all of the information sciences with a deliberately interdisciplinary approach. Topics range from electronic mail monitoring to library acquisition of controversial material to archival ethics. The *Journal's* aim is to present thoughtful considerations of ethical dilemmas that arise in a rapidly evolving system of information exchange and dissemination. Estab. 1992. Byline given. Pays on publication. No kill fee. Publishes ms an average of 2 years after acceptance. Submit seasonal material 8 months in advance. Accepts queries by mail, e-mail, phone. Accepts simultaneous submissions. Sample copy for $30. Guidelines free.

NONFICTION Needs essays, reviews. **Buys 10-12 mss/year.** Send complete ms. Length: 500-3,500 words. **Pays $25-50, depending on length.**

TIPS "Familiarize yourself with the many areas subsumed under the rubric of information ethics, e.g., privacy, scholarly communication, errors, peer review, confidentiality, e-mail, etc. Present a well-rounded discussion of any fresh, current, or evolving ethical topic within the information sciences or involving real-world information collection/exchange."

SYSTEM INEWS

Penton Technology Media, 748 Whalers Way, Fort Collins CO 80525. (970)663-4700; (800)621-1544. **E-mail:** editors@iprodeveloper.com. **Website:** www.iprodeveloper.com. **40% freelance written.** Magazine, published 12 times/year, focused on programming, networking, IS management, and technology for users of IBM AS/400, iSERIES, SYSTEM i, AND IBM i platform. Estab. 1982. Circ. 30,000 (international). Byline given. Pays on publication. Offers 50% kill fee. Publishes ms an average of 3 months after acceptance. Editorial lead time 4 months. Submit seasonal material 4 months in advance. Accepts queries by e-mail. Accepts simultaneous submissions. Responds in 3 weeks to queries. Responds in 5 weeks to mss. Guidelines available online.

NONFICTION Needs technical. Query. Length: 1,500-2,500 words. **Pays $300/$500 flat fee for as-**

signed articles, depending on article quality and technical depth.

REPRINTS Send photocopy. Payment negotiable.

PHOTOS State availability. Offers no additional payment for photos accepted with ms.

COLUMNS/DEPARTMENTS Load'n'go (complete utility).

TIPS "Must have in-depth knowledge of IBM AS/400/iSERIES/SYSTEM i/IBM i computer platform."

TECHNOLOGY REVIEW

MIT, One Main St., 13th Floor, Cambridge MA 02142. (617)475-8000. **Fax:** (617)475-8042. **E-mail:** jason.pontin@technologyreview.com; david.rotman@technologyreview.com. **Website:** www.technologyreview.com. **Contact:** Jason Pontin, editor in chief; David Rotman, editor. Magazine published 10 times/year covering information technology, biotech, material science, and nanotechnology. *Technology Review* promotes the understanding of emerging technologies and their impact. Estab. 1899. Circ. 310,000. Byline given. Pays on acceptance. Accepts queries by mail, e-mail. Accepts simultaneous submissions.

NONFICTION Query with a pitch via online contact form. Length: 2,000-4,000 words. **Pays $1-3/word.**

FILLERS Short tidbits that relate laboratory prototypes on their way to market in 1-5 years. Length: 150-250 words. **Pays $1-3/word.**

INSURANCE

/ADVISOR TODAY

NAIFA, 2901 Telestar Court, Falls Church VA 22042. (703)770-8204. **E-mail:** amseka@naifa.org. **Website:** www.advisortoday.com. **Contact:** Ayo Mseka, editor in chief. **25% freelance written.** Monthly magazine covering life insurance and financial planning. "*Advisor Today* has the largest circulation among insurance and financial planning advising magazines. Founded in 1906 as *Life Association News, Advisor Today* is the official publication of the National Association of Insurance and Financial Advisors. Our mission is to provide practical information, sales ideas, resources, and business strategies to help insurance and financial advisors succeed." Estab. 1906. Circ. 110,000. Pays on acceptance or publication (by mutual agreement with editor). No kill fee. Publishes ms an average of 3 months after acceptance. Editorial lead time: 3 months. Submit seasonal material 6 months in advance. Accepts queries by mail, e-mail, fax, phone. Accepts simultaneous submissions. Sample copy free. Guidelines available online at www.advisortoday.com/about/contribute.cfm.

NONFICTION Buys 8 mss/year. "We prefer e-mail submissions in Microsoft Word format. For other formats and submission methods, please query first. For all articles and queries, contact Ayo Mseka. Web articles should cover the same subject matter covered in the magazine. The articles can be between 300-800 words and should be submitted to Ayo Mseka." Length: 2,300 words for cover articles; 1,000 words for feature articles; 650-700 words for columns and speciality articles; 300-800 words for Web articles. **Pays $800-2,000.**

JEWELRY

💲 ADORNMENT, THE MAGAZINE OF JEWELRY & RELATED ARTS

Association for the Study of Jewelry & Related Arts, 5070 Bonnie Branch Rd., Ellicott City MD 21043. **E-mail:** elyse@jewelryandrelatedarts.com. **Website:** www.jewelryandrelatedarts.com; www.asjra.net; www.jewelryconference.com. **50% freelance written.** Quarterly magazine covering jewelry, from antique to modern. "This magazine is a perk of membership in the Association for the Study of Jewelry & Related Arts. It is not sold as a stand-alone publication. It is delivered electronically." Estab. 2002. Circ. 1,000+. Byline given. Pays on publication. No kill fee. Publishes ms an average of 3 months after acceptance. Editorial lead time 3 months. Accepts queries by mail, e-mail. Responds in 1-2 weeks to queries; 1 month to mss. Sample copy free as an e-mailed PDF. Guidelines free.

NONFICTION Needs book excerpts, historical, interview, exhibition reviews—in-depth articles on jewelry subjects. "We do not want articles about retail jewelry. We write about ancient, antique, period, and unique and studio jewelers." **Buys 12-15 mss/year.** Query with published clips. Length: 1,000-3,000 words. **Pays up to $125 for assigned articles. Does not pay for unsolicited articles.**

PHOTOS "We only want photos that accompany articles. Quality must be professional. We pay $25 flat fee for them; we don't accept articles without accompanying photography. You must obtain permission for the use of photos. We won't publish without written approvals."

TIPS "Know your subject, and provide applicable credentials."

THE ENGRAVERS JOURNAL

P.O. Box 318, Brighton MI 48116. (810)229-5725. **Fax:** (810)229-8320. **E-mail:** editor@engraversjournal.com. **Website:** www.engraversjournal.com. **Contact:** Senior editor. **70% freelance written.** Monthly magazine covering the recognition and personalization industry (engraving, marking devices, awards, jewelry, and signage). "We provide practical information for the education and advancement of our readers, mainly retail business owners." Estab. 1975. Byline given. Pays on acceptance. No kill fee. Publishes ms an average of 3-9 months after acceptance. Accepts queries by mail, e-mail, fax. Accepts simultaneous submissions. Responds in 2 weeks to mss. Sample copy free. Guidelines free.

NONFICTION Needs general interest, how-to, technical. No general overviews of the industry. Length: 1,000-5,000 words. **Pays $200 and up.**

REPRINTS Send tearsheet, photocopy, or typed ms with rights for sale noted, and information about when and where the material previously appeared. Pays 50-100% of amount paid for original article.

PHOTOS Send photos. Captions, identification of subjects, model releases required. Pays variable rate.

TIPS "Articles should always be down to earth, practical, and thoroughly cover the subject with authority. We do not want the 'textbook' writing approach, vagueness, or theory—our readers look to us for sound, practical information. We use an educational slant, publishing both trade-oriented articles and general business topics of interest to a small retail-oriented readership."

JOURNALISM & WRITING

AMERICAN JOURNALISM REVIEW

University of Maryland Foundation, Knight Hall, University of Maryland, College Park MD 20742. (301)405-8805. **E-mail:** editor@ajr.org. **Website:** www.ajr.org. **Contact:** Lucy Dalglish, dean and publisher. **80% freelance written.** Bimonthly magazine covering print, broadcast, and online journalism. *American Journalism Review* covers ethical issues, trends in the industry, and coverage that falls short. Circ. 25,000. Byline given. Pays 1 month after publication. Offers 25% kill fee. Publishes ms an average of 2 months after acceptance. Editorial lead time 1 month. Accepts queries by mail, e-mail. Responds in 1 month to queries and unsolicited mss. Sample copy: $4.95 prepaid or online. Guidelines available online.

NONFICTION Needs expose. Query or send complete ms. Length: 2,000-4,000 words. **Pays $1,500-2,000.**

FILLERS Needs anecdotes, facts, short humor, short pieces. Length: 150-1,000 words. **Pays $100-250.**

TIPS "Write a short story for the front-of-the-book section. We prefer queries to completed articles. Include in a page what you'd like to write about, who you'll interview, why it's important, and why you should write it."

BOOK DEALERS WORLD

North American Bookdealers Exchange, P.O. Box 606, Cottage Grove OR 97424. (541)942-7455. **E-mail:** nabe@bookmarketingprofits.com. **Website:** www.bookmarketingprofits.com. **Contact:** Al Galasso. **50% freelance written.** Magazine covering writing, self-publishing, and marketing books by mail. Publishes 3 issues/year online. Estab. 1980. Circ. 20,000. Byline given. Pays on publication. No kill fee. Publishes ms an average of 3 months after acceptance. Accepts queries by mail, e-mail. Accepts simultaneous submissions. Responds in 1 month to queries. Sample copy available online.

NONFICTION Needs book excerpts, how-to, interview. **Buys 10 mss/year.** Send complete ms. Length: 1,000-1,500 words. **Pays $25-50.**

REPRINTS Send typed ms with rights for sale noted and information about when and where the material previously appeared. Pays 80% of amount paid for an original article.

COLUMNS/DEPARTMENTS Publisher Profile (on successful self-publishers and their marketing strategy), 250-1,000 words. **Buys 20 mss/year.** Send complete ms. **Pays $5-20.**

FILLERS Needs fillers concerning writing, publishing, or books. **Buys 6 mss/year.** Length: 100-250 words. **Pays $3-10.**

TIPS "Query first. Get a sample copy of the magazine online at website."

CANADIAN SCREENWRITER

Writers Guild of Canada, 366 Adelaide St. W., Suite 401, Toronto ON M5V 1R9 Canada. (416)979-7907. **Fax:** (416)979-9273. **E-mail:** info@wgc.ca. **Website:**

www.wgc.ca. **Contact:** Li Robbins, director of communications. **80% freelance written.** Magazine published 3 times/year covering Canadian screenwriting for television, film, and digital media. *Canadian Screenwriter* profiles Canadian screenwriters, provides industry news, and offers practical writing tips for screenwriters. Estab. 1998. Circ. 4,000. Byline given. Pays on acceptance. Offers 50% kill fee. Publishes ms an average of 1 month after acceptance. Editorial lead time 2 months. Submit seasonal material 2 months in advance. Accepts queries by e-mail. Accepts simultaneous submissions. Responds in 1 week to queries; in 1 month to mss. Sample copy free. Guidelines by e-mail.

NONFICTION Needs how-to, humor, interview. Does not want writing on foreign screenwriters; the focus is on Canadian-resident screenwriters. **Buys 12 mss/year.** Query with published clips. Length: 750-2,200 words. **Pays $1/word.**

PHOTOS State availability. Identification of subjects required. Reviews GIF/JPEG files. Negotiates payment individually. Buys one-time rights.

TIPS "Read other Canadian film and television publications."

ECONTENT MAGAZINE

Information Today, Inc., 143 Old Marlton Pike, Medford NJ 08055. **E-mail:** theresa.cramer@infotoday. com. **E-mail:** theresa.cramer@infotoday.com. **Website:** www.econtentmag.com. **Contact:** Theresa Cramer, editor. **90% freelance written.** Bi-monthly magazine covering digital content trends, strategies, etc. *EContent* is a leading authority on the businesses of digital publishing, media, and marketing, targeting executives and decision-makers in these fast-changing markets. By covering the latest tools, strategies, and thought-leaders in the digital content ecosystem, EContent magazine and EContentmag.com keep professionals ahead of the curve in order to maximize their investment in digital content strategies while building sustainable, profitable business models. Estab. 1979. Circ. 12,000. Byline given. Pays within 1 month of publication. No kill fee. Editorial lead time 3-4 months. Accepts simultaneous submissions. Responds in 3 weeks to queries; in 1 month to mss. Sample copy and writer's guidelines online.

NONFICTION Needs expose, how-to, interview, new product, opinion. No academic or straight Q&A. **Buys 48 mss/year.** Query with published clips. Submit electronically as e-mail attachment. Length: 1,000 words.

PHOTOS State availability. Captions required. Negotiates payment individually. Buys one-time rights.

COLUMNS/DEPARTMENTS Profiles (short profile of unique company, person or product), 1,200 words; New Features (breaking news of content-related topics), up to 500 words. **Buys 40 mss/year.** Query with published clips. **Pays 30-40¢/word.**

TIPS "Take a look at the website. Most of the time, an e-mail query with specific article ideas works well. A general outline of talking points is good, too. State prior experience."

◑ FREELANCE MARKET NEWS

The Writers Bureau Ltd., 8-10 Dutton St., Manchester M3 1LE England. (44)(161)819-9919. **Fax:** (44)(161)819-2842. **E-mail:** fmn@writersbureau.com. **Website:** www.freelancemarketnews.com. **15% freelance written.** Monthly newsletter covering freelance writing. For all writers, established and new, *Freelance Market News* is an excellent source of the most up-to-date information about the publishing world. It is packed with news, views and the latest advice about new publications, plus the trends and developments in established markets, in the UK and around the world. Informs readers about publications that are looking for new writers and even warn about those writers should avoid. Estab. 1968. Byline given. Pays on acceptance. No kill fee. Publishes ms an average of 3 months after acceptance. Editorial lead time 3 months. Submit seasonal material 3 months in advance. Accepts queries by mail, e-mail. Sample copy and guidelines available online.

◐ Prefers to receive a complete ms rather than a query.

NONFICTION **Buys 12 mss/year.** Length: 1,00 words. **Pays £50/1,000 words.**

COLUMNS/DEPARTMENTS New Markets (magazines which have recently been published); Fillers & Letters; Overseas Markets (obviously only English-language publications); Market Notes (established publications accepting articles, fiction, reviews, or poetry). All should be between 40 and 200 words. **Pays £40/1,000 words.**

FREELANCE WRITER'S REPORT

CNW Publishing, Inc., 45 Main St., P.O. Box A, North Stratford NH 03590-0167. (603)922-8338. **E-mail:** fwrwm@writers-editors.com. **Website:** www.writers-editors.com. **10% freelance written.** Monthly newsletter covering the business of freelance writing. *FWR* covers the marketing and business/office management aspects of running a freelance writing business. Articles must be of value to the established freelancer; nothing basic. Estab. 1982. Byline given. Pays on publication. No kill fee. Publishes ms an average of 12 months after acceptance. Editorial lead time 2 months. Submit seasonal material 2 months in advance. Accepts simultaneous submissions. Responds in 1 week to queries; 2 weeks to mss. Sample copy for 6x9 SAE with 2 first-class stamps (for back copy); $4 for current copy. Guidelines and sample copy available online.

NONFICTION Needs book excerpts. Does not want articles about the basics of freelancing. **Buys 5 mss/year.** Send complete ms by e-mail. Length: up to 900 words. **Pays 10¢/word.**

TIPS "Write in a terse, newsletter style."

MSLEXIA

Mslexia Publications Ltd., P.O. Box 656, Newcastle upon Tyne NE99 1PZ United Kingdom. (44)(191)204-8860. **E-mail:** submissions@mslexia.co.uk; postbag@mslexia.co.uk; debbie@mslexia.co.uk. **Website:** www.mslexia.co.uk. **Contact:** Debbie Taylor, editorial director. **60% freelance written.** Quarterly magazine offering advice and publishing opportunities for women writers, plus poetry and prose submissions on a different theme each issue. "*Mslexia* tells you all you need to know about exploring your creativity and getting into print. No other magazine provides *Mslexia*'s unique mix of advice and inspiration; news, reviews, interviews; competitions, events, grants; all served up with a challenging selection of new poetry and prose. *Mslexia* is read by authors and absolute beginners. A quarterly master class in the business and psychology of writing, it's the essential magazine for women who write." Estab. 1998. Circ. 9,000. Byline given. Pays on publication. Offers 50% kill fee. Publishes ms an average of 1 month after acceptance. Editorial lead time 3 months. Submit seasonal material 3 months in advance. Accepts queries by mail, e-mail, phone. Accepts simultaneous submissions. Responds in 3 months to mss. Sample copy available online. Writer's guidelines online or by e-mail.

NONFICTION Needs how-to, interview, opinion, personal experience. No general items about women or academic features. "We are only interested in features (for tertiary-educated readership) about wom-

en's writing and literature." **Buys 40 mss/year.** Query with published clips. Length: 500-2,200 words. **Pays $70-400 for assigned articles. Pays $70-300 for unsolicited articles.**

COLUMNS/DEPARTMENTS "We are open to suggestions, but would only commission 1 new column/year, probably from a UK-based writer." **Buys 12 mss/year.** Query with published clips.

FICTION See guidelines on website. "Submissions not on 1 of our current themes will be returned (if submitted with a SASE) or destroyed." **Buys 30 mss/year.** Send complete ms. Length: 50-2,200 words. **Pays £15 per 1,000 words prose plus contributor's copies.**

POETRY Needs avant-garde, free verse, haiku, traditional. Buys 40 poems/year. Submit maximum 4 poems. **Pays £25 per poem plus contributor's copies.**

TIPS "Read the magazine; subscribe if you can afford it. *Mslexia* has a particular style and relationship with its readers which is hard to assess at a quick glance. The majority of our readers live in the UK, so feature pitches should be aware of this. We never commission work without seeing a written sample first. We rarely accept unsolicited manuscripts, but prefer a short letter suggesting a feature, plus a brief bio and writing sample."

NOVEL & SHORT STORY WRITER'S MARKET

F+W Media, Inc., 10151 Carver Rd., Suite 200, Blue Ash OH 45242. (513)531-2690. **Fax:** (513)531-2686. **E-mail:** marketbookupdates@fwmedia.com. **Website:** www.writersmarket.com. **Contact:** Cris Freese, managing editor. **85% freelance written.** Annual resource book covering the fiction market. In addition to thousands of listings for places to get fiction published, *NSSWM*'s feature articles on the craft and business of fiction writing, as well as interviews with successful fiction writers, editors, and agents. Articles are unique in that they always offer an actionable take-away. In other words, readers must learn something immediately useful about the creation or marketing of fiction. Estab. 1981. Byline given. Pays on acceptance plus 45 days. Offers 25% kill fee. Accepts simultaneous submissions. Responds in 4 weeks to queries.

Accepts proposals during the summer.

NONFICTION Needs how-to, interview, personal experience. **Buys 12-15 mss/year.** Length: 1,500-2,500 words. **Pays $400-700.**

PHOTOS Send photos. Identification of subjects required. Reviews prints, GIF/JPEG files (hi-res). Offers no additional payment for photos accepted with ms.

TIPS "The best way to break into this book is to review the last few years' editions and look for aspects of the fiction industry that we haven't covered recently. Send a specific, detailed pitch stating the topic, angle, and 'take-away' of the piece, what sources you intend to use, and what qualifies you to write this article. Freelancers who have published fiction and/or have contacts in the industry have an advantage."

POETS & WRITERS MAGAZINE

90 Broad St., Suite 2100, New York NY 10004. (212)226-3586. **E-mail:** editor@pw.org. **Website:** www.pw.org/magazine. **Contact:** Kevin Larimer, editor. **95% freelance written.** Bimonthly professional trade journal for poets and fiction writers and creative nonfiction writers. Estab. 1987. Circ. 60,000. Byline given. Pays on publication. Offers 25% kill fee. Publishes ms an average of 4 months after acceptance. Submit seasonal material 4 months in advance. Accepts queries by mail, e-mail. Accepts simultaneous submissions. Responds in 2 months to mss. Sample copy: $5.95. Guidelines available online.

○ No poetry or fiction submissions.

NONFICTION Needs how-to. **Buys 35 mss/year.** Send complete ms. Length: 700-3,000 words (depending on topic).

PHOTOS State availability. Reviews color prints. Offers no additional payment for photos accepted with ms.

COLUMNS/DEPARTMENTS Literary and Publishing News, 700-1,000 words; Profiles of Emerging and Established Poets, Fiction Writers and Creative Nonfiction Writers, 2,000-3,000 words; Craft Essays and Publishing Advice, 2,000-2,500 words. Query with published clips or send complete ms. **Pays $225-500.**

TIPS "We typically assign profiles to coincide with an author's forthcoming book publication. We are not looking for the Get Rich Quick or 10 Easy Steps variety of writing and publishing advice."

QUILL & SCROLL MAGAZINE

Quill and Scroll International Honorary Society for High School Journalists, University of Iowa, School of Journalism and Mass Communication, 100 Adler Journalism Bldg., Iowa City IA 52242. (319)335-3457. **Fax:** (319)335-3989. **E-mail:** quill-scroll@uiowa.edu. **Website:** www.quillandscroll.org. **Contact:** Vanessa Shelton, executive director. **20% freelance written.** Fall and spring issues covering scholastic journalism-related topics during school year. Primary audience is high school journalism students working on and studying topics related to newspapers, yearbooks, radio, television, and online media; secondary audience is their teachers and others interested in this topic. Invites journalism students and advisers to submit mss about important lessons learned or obstacles overcome. Estab. 1926. Circ. 10,000. Byline given. Pays on acceptance and publication. No kill fee. Publishes ms an average of 4 months after acceptance. Editorial lead time 2 months. Accepts queries by mail, e-mail. Accepts simultaneous submissions. Responds in 2 weeks to queries. Guidelines available.

NONFICTION Needs essays, how-to, humor, interview, new product, opinion, personal experience, photo feature, technical, travel, types on topic. Does not want articles not pertinent to high school student journalists. Query with your submission. Length: 600-1,000 words. **Pays $100-500 for assigned articles. Pays complementary copy and $200 maximum for unsolicited articles.**

PHOTOS State availability. Reviews GIF/JPEG files. Offers no additional payment for photos accepted with ms.

QUILL MAGAZINE

Society of Professional Journalists, 3909 N. Meridian St., Indianapolis IN 46208. (317)927-8000, ext. 211. **Fax:** (317)920-4789. **E-mail:** sleadingham@spj.org. **E-mail:** quill@spj.org. **Website:** www.spj.org/quill.asp. **Contact:** Scott Leadingham, editor. **75% freelance written.** Monthly magazine covering journalism and the media industry. *Quill* is a how-to magazine written by journalists. Focuses on the industry's biggest issues while providing tips on how to become better journalists. Estab. 1912. Circ. 10,000. Byline given. Pays on acceptance. Offers 25% kill fee. Publishes ms an average of 2 months after acceptance. Editorial lead time 2-3 months. Submit seasonal material 2-3 months in advance. Accepts queries by e-mail. Accepts simultaneous submissions. Sample copy available online.

NONFICTION Needs general interest, how-to, technical. Does not want personality profiles and straight research pieces. **Buys 12 mss/year.** Query. Length: 800-2,500 words. **Pays $150-800.**

THE WRITER'S CHRONICLE

Association of Writers & Writing Programs (AWP), 4400 University Drive, George Mason University, Fairfax VA 22030-4444. (703)993-4301. **Fax:** (703)993-4302. **E-mail:** chronicle@awpwriter.org. **Website:** www.awpwriter.org. **90% freelance written.** Published 6 times during the academic year; 3 times a semester. Magazine covering the art and craft of writing. "*Writer's Chronicle* strives to: present the best essays on the craft and art of writing poetry, fiction, and nonfiction; help overcome the over-specialization of the literary arts by presenting a public forum for the appreciation, debate, and analysis of contemporary literature; present the diversity of accomplishments and points of view within contemporary literature; provide serious and committed writers and students of writing the best advice on how to manage their professional lives; provide writers who teach with new pedagogical approaches for their classrooms; provide the members and subscribers with a literary community as a compensation for a devotion to a difficult and lonely art; provide information on publishing opportunities, grants, and awards; and promote the good works of AWP, its programs, and its individual members." Estab. 1967. Circ. 35,000. Byline given. Pays on publication. No kill fee. Editorial lead time 3 months. Accepts simultaneous submissions. Responds in 2 weeks to queries. Sample copy free. Guidelines online. Reading period: February 1 through September 30.

NONFICTION Needs essays, interview, opinion. No personal essays. **Buys 15-20 mss/year.** Send complete ms. Length: 2,500-7,000 words. **Pays $18/100 words for assigned articles.**

TIPS "In general, the editors look for articles that demonstrate an excellent working knowledge of literary issues and a generosity of spirit that esteems the arguments of other writers on similar topics. When writing essays on craft, do not use your own work as an example. Keep in mind that 18,000 of our readers are students or just-emerging writers. They must become good readers before they can become good writers, so we expect essays on craft to show exemplary close readings of a variety of contemporary and older works. Essays must embody erudition, generosity, curiosity, and discernment rather than self-involvement. Writers may refer to their own travails and successes if they do so modestly, in small proportion to the other examples. We look for a generosity of spirit—a general love and command of literature as well as an expert, writerly viewpoint."

⑤⑤⑤ WRITER'S DIGEST

F+W Media, Inc., 10151 Carver Rd., Suite #200, Blue Ash OH 45242. (513)531-2690. **E-mail:** wdsubmissions@fwmedia.com. **Website:** www.writersdigest.com. **75% freelance written.** Magazine for those who want to write better, get published, and participate in the vibrant culture of writers. Readers look for specific ideas and tips that will help them succeed, whether success means getting into print, finding personal fulfillment through writing, or building and maintaining a thriving writing career and network. *Writer's Digest*, the No. 1 magazine for writers, celebrates the writing life and what it means to be a writer in today's publishing environment. Estab. 1920. Byline given. Pays on acceptance. Offers 25% kill fee. Publishes ms an average of 4 months after acceptance. Accepts simultaneous submissions. Responds in 1-4 months to queries and mss. Guidelines and editorial calendar available online (writersdigest.com/submission-guidelines).

● The magazine does not accept or read e-queries with attachments.

NONFICTION Essays; short front-of-book pieces; how-to (writing craft, business of publishing, etc.); humor; inspirational; interviews/profiles (rarely, as those are typically handled in house). Does not accept phone, snail mail, or fax queries, and queries of this nature will receive no response. Does not buy newspaper clippings or reprints of articles previously published in other mainstream media, whether in print or online. Product reviews are handled in-house. **Buys 80 mss/year.** A query should include a thorough outline that introduces your article proposal and highlights each of the points you intend to make. Your query should discuss how the article will benefit readers, why the topic is timely, and why you're the appropriate writer to discuss the topic. Please include your publishing credential related to your topic with your submission. Do not send attachments. Length: 800-2,400 words. **Pays 30-50¢/word.**

TIPS "*InkWell* is the best place for new writers to break in. We recommend you consult our editorial calendar before pitching feature-length articles. Check our writer's guidelines for more details."

WRITTEN BY

7000 W. Third St., Los Angeles CA 90048. (323)782-4574. **Fax:** (323)782-4800. **Website:** www.writtenby.com. **40% freelance written.** Magazine published 9 times/year. *Written By* is the premier magazine written by and for America's screen and TV writers. Focuses on the craft of screenwriting and covers all aspects of the entertainment industry from the perspective of the writer. Audience is screenwriters and most entertainment executives. Estab. 1987. Circ. 12,000. Byline given. Pays on acceptance. Offers 10% kill fee. Publishes ms an average of 2 months after acceptance. Editorial lead time 4 months. Submit seasonal material 4 months in advance. Accepts queries by mail, e-mail, fax, phone, online submission form. Accepts simultaneous submissions. Guidelines for #10 SASE or online contact form.

NONFICTION Needs book excerpts, essays, historical, humor, interview, opinion, personal experience, photo feature, technical. No beginner pieces on how to break into Hollywood or how to write scripts. **Buys 20 mss/year.** Query with published clips. Length: 500-3,500 words. **Pays $500-3,500 for assigned articles.**

PHOTOS State availability. Captions, identification of subjects, model releases required. Reviews transparencies. Offers no additional payment for photos accepted with ms. Buys one-time rights.

COLUMNS/DEPARTMENTS Pays $1,000 maximum.

TIPS "We are looking for more theoretical essays on screenwriting past and/or present. Also, the writer must always keep in mind that our audience is made up primarily of working writers who are inside the business; therefore all articles need to have an 'insider' feel and not be written for those who are still trying to break in to Hollywood. We prefer a hard copy of submission or e-mail."

LAW

ABA JOURNAL

American Bar Association, 321 N. Clark St., 20th Floor, Chicago IL 60654. (312)988-6018. **Fax:** (312)988-6014. **E-mail:** releases@americanbar.org. **Website:** www.abajournal.com. **Contact:** Molly McDonough. **10% freelance written.** Monthly magazine covering the trends, people, and finances of the legal profession from Wall Street to Main Street to Penn-

sylvania Avenue. The *ABA Journal* is an independent, thoughtful, and inquiring observer of the law and the legal profession. The magazine is edited for members of the American Bar Association. Circ. 380,000. Byline given. Pays on acceptance. No kill fee. Accepts queries by e-mail, fax. Accepts simultaneous submissions. Sample copy free. Guidelines available online.

NONFICTION "We don't want anything that does not have a legal theme. No poetry or fiction." **Buys 5 mss/year.** "We use freelancers with experience reporting for legal or consumer publications; most have law degrees. If you are interested in freelancing for the *Journal*, we urge you to include your résumé and published clips when you contact us with story ideas." Length: 500-3,500 words. **Pays $300-2,000 for assigned articles.**

COLUMNS/DEPARTMENTS The National Pulse/Ideas from the Front (reports on legal news and trends), 650 words; eReport (reports on legal news and trends), 500-1,500 words. "The *ABA Journal eReport* is our weekly online newsletter sent out to members." **Buys 25 mss/year.** Query with published clips. **Pays $300, regardless of story length.**

BENCH & BAR OF MINNESOTA

Minnesota State Bar Association, 600 Nicollet Mall #380, Minneapolis MN 55402. (612)333-1183; 800-882-6722. **Fax:** (612)333-4927. **E-mail:** jhaverkamp@mnbar.org. **Website:** www.mnbar.org. **Contact:** Judson Haverkamp, editor. **5% freelance written.** Magazine published 11 times/year. *Bench & Bar* seeks reportage, analysis, and commentary on changes in the law, trends and issues in the law and the legal profession, especially in Minnesota. Preference to items of practical/professional human interest to lawyers and judges. Audience is mostly Minnesota lawyers. Estab. 1931. Circ. 17,000. Byline given. Pays on acceptance. No kill fee. Publishes ms an average of 3 months after acceptance. Accepts simultaneous submissions. Responds in 1 month to queries. Guidelines for free online or by mail.

NONFICTION Does not want one-sided opinion pieces or advertorial. **Buys 2-3 mss/year.** Send query or complete ms. Length: 1,000-3,500 words. **Pays $500-1,500.**

PHOTOS State availability. Identification of subjects, model releases required. Reviews 5x7 prints. Pays $25-100 upon publication. Buys one-time rights.

CALIFORNIA LAWYER

Daily Journal Corp., 44 Montgomery St., Suite 500, San Francisco CA 94104. (415)296-2400. **Fax:** (415)296-2440. **E-mail:** cl_contributingeditor@dailyjournal.com; bo_links@dailyjournal.com. **Website:** www.callawyer.com. **Contact:** Bo Links, legal editor; Marsha Sessa, art director. **30% freelance written.** Monthly magazine of law-related articles and general-interest subjects of appeal to lawyers and judges. Primary mission is to cover the news of the world as it affects the law and lawyers, helping readers better comprehend the issues of the day and to cover changes and trends in the legal profession. Readers are all California lawyers, plus judges, legislators, and corporate executives. Although the magazine focuses on California and the West, they have subscribers in every state. *California Lawyer* is a general interest magazine for people interested in law. Estab. 1981. Circ. 140,000. Byline given. Pays on acceptance. Offers 25% kill fee. Publishes ms an average of 3 months after acceptance. Editorial lead time 3 months. Accepts queries by e-mail. Accepts simultaneous submissions. Guidelines available online.

NONFICTION Needs essays, general interest, profile. "We will consider well-researched, in-depth stories on the law, including legal trends of statewide and national significance, thought-provoking legal issues, and profiles of lawyers doing groundbreaking work. We will consider local issues if they have statewide or national implications or if you have a new unique angle to the story." **Buys 12 mss/year.** Query contributing editor: cl_contributingeditor@dailyjournal.com. Please do not send unsolicited mss. Length: 500-5,000 words. **Pays $50-2,000.**

PHOTOS Contact: Marsha Sessa, art director. State availability. Identification of subjects, model releases required. Reviews prints.

COLUMNS/DEPARTMENTS Expert Advice (specific, practical tips on an area of law or practice management), 650-750 words; Tech (lawyers and technology), up to 1,000 words; First Person (personal experience), 700 words; In House (working as corporate counsel in California), up to 1,000 words. Query appropriate editor (see website submission guidelines). **Pays $50-250.**

INSIDECOUNSEL

ALM Media, LLC, 120 Broadway, 5th Floor, New York NY 10271. (212)457-9400. **E-mail:** apaonita@alm.com. **Website:** www.insidecounsel.com. **Contact:** Anthony Paonita, editor-in-chief. **50% freelance written.** Monthly tabloid covering legal information for attorneys. *InsideCounsel* is a monthly national magazine that gives general counsel and inhouse attorneys information on legal and business issues to help them better manage corporate law departments. It routinely addresses changes and trends in law departments, litigation management, legal technology, corporate governance and inhouse careers. Law areas covered monthly include: intellectual property, international, technology, project finance, e-commerce, and litigation. All articles need to be geared toward the inhouse attorney's perspective. Estab. 1991. Circ. 45,000. Byline given. Pays on publication. No kill fee. Publishes ms an average of 3 months after acceptance. Editorial lead time 3 months. Submit seasonal material 3 months in advance. Accepts queries by mail, e-mail. Accepts simultaneous submissions. Responds in 3 weeks to queries. Sample copy for $17. Guidelines available online.

NONFICTION Buys 12-25 mss/year. Query with published clips. Length: 500-3,000 words. **Pays $500-2,000.**

PHOTOS Freelancers should state availability of photos with submission. Identification of subjects required. Reviews color transparencies, b&w prints. Offers $25-150/photo. Buys all rights.

TIPS "Our publication targets general counsel and inhouse lawyers. All articles need to speak to them, not to the general attorney population. Query with clips and a list of potential in-house sources."

⊘ NATIONAL

The Canadian Bar Association, 865 Carling Ave., Ottawa ON K1S 5S8 Canada. (613)237-2925. **Fax:** (613)237-0185. **E-mail:** beverleys@cba.org; national@cba.org. **Website:** www.nationalmagazine.ca. **Contact:** Beverley Spencer, editor in chief. **90% freelance written.** Magazine published 8 times/year covering practice trends and business developments in the law, with a focus on technology, innovation, practice management, and client relations. Estab. 1993. Circ. 37,000. Byline given. Pays on acceptance. Offers 50% kill fee. Publishes ms an average of 2 months after acceptance. Editorial lead time 2 months. Accepts queries by e-mail. Accepts simultaneous submissions. Sample copy free.

NONFICTION Buys 25 mss/year. Query with published clips. Length: 1,000-2,500 words. **Pays $1/word.**

THE NATIONAL JURIST AND PRE LAW

Cypress Magazines, 7670 Opportunity Rd #105, San Diego CA 92111. (858)300-3201; (800)296-9656. **Fax:** (858)503-7588. **E-mail:** jack@cypressmagazines.com; callahan@cypressmagazines.com. **Website:** www.nationaljurist.com. **Contact:** Jack Crittenden, editor in chief. **25% freelance written.** Bimonthly magazine covering law students and issues of interest to law students. Estab. 1991. Circ. 145,000. Pays on publication. No kill fee. Accepts queries by mail, e-mail. Accepts simultaneous submissions.

NONFICTION Needs general interest, how-to, humor, interview. **Buys 4 mss/year.** Query. Length: 750-3,000 words. **Pays $100-500.**

PHOTOS State availability. Reviews contact sheets. Negotiates payment individually.

COLUMNS/DEPARTMENTS Pays $100-500.

PARALEGAL TODAY

Conexion International Media, Inc., 6030 Marshalee Dr., Suite 455, Elkridge MD 21075-5935. (443)445-3057. **Fax:** (443)445-3257. **E-mail:** pinfanti@connexionmedia.com. **Website:** www.paralegaltoday.com. **Contact:** Patricia E. Infanti, editor in chief; Charles Buckwalter, publisher. Quarterly magazine geared toward all legal assistants/paralegals throughout the U.S. and Canada, regardless of specialty (litigation, corporate, bankruptcy, environmental law, etc.). How-to articles to help paralegals perform their jobs more effectively are most in demand, as are career and salary information, technolgoy tips, and trends pieces. Estab. 1983. Circ. 8,000. Byline given. Pays on publication. Offers kill fee ($25-50 standard rate). Editorial lead time is 10 weeks. Submit seasonal material 3 months in advance. Accepts queries by mail, e-mail, fax, online submission form. Accepts simultaneous submissions. Responds in 2 months to mss. Sample copy available online. Guidelines available online.

NONFICTION Needs interview, news (brief, hard news topics regarding paralegals), features (present information to help paralegals advance their careers). Send query letter first; if electronic, send submission as attachment. **Pays $75-300.**

PHOTOS Send photos.

TIPS "Query editor first. Features run 1,500-2,500 words with sidebars. Writers must understand our audience. There is some opportunity for investigative journalism as well as the usual features, profiles, and columns. How-to articles are especially desired. If you are a great writer who can interview effectively and really dig into the topic to grab readers' attention, we need you."

THE PENNSYLVANIA LAWYER

Pennsylvania Bar Association, 100 South St., P.O. Box 186, Harrisburg PA 17108. **E-mail:** editor@pabar.org; palawyer@editorialenterprises.com. **Website:** www.pabar.org. **Contact:** Donald C. Sarvey, editorial director. **25% freelance written. Prefers to work with published/established writers.** Bimonthly magazine published as a service to the legal profession and the members of the Pennsylvania Bar Association. Estab. 1979. Circ. 30,000. Byline given. Pays on acceptance. No kill fee. Publishes ms an average of 6 months after acceptance. Submit seasonal material 6 months in advance. Accepts queries by mail, e-mail, online submission form. Accepts simultaneous submissions. Responds in 2 months to queries and mss. Sample copy for $2. Writer's guidelines for #10 SASE or by e-mail.

NONFICTION Needs how-to, interview, law-practice management, technology. **Buys 8-10 mss/year.** Query. Length: 1,200-1,500 words. **Pays $50 for book reviews; $75-400 for assigned articles; $150 for unsolicited articles.**

PHOTOS State availability. Identification of subjects required. Reviews contact sheets. Negotiates payment individually. Buys one-time rights.

SUPER LAWYERS

Thomson Reuters, 610 Opperman Dr., Eagan MN 55123. (877)787-5290. **Website:** www.superlawyers.com. **Contact:** Erik Lundegaard, editor. **100% freelance written.** Monthly magazine covering law and politics. Publishes glossy magazines in every region of the country; all serve a legal audience and have a storytelling sensibility. Writes profiles of interesting attorneys exclusively. Estab. 1990. Byline given. Pays on acceptance. Offers 25% kill fee. Publishes ms an average of 1 month after acceptance. Editorial lead time 6 months. Submit seasonal material 6 months in advance. Accepts queries by phone, online submission form. Accepts simultaneous submissions. Sample copy free. Guidelines free.

NONFICTION Needs general interest, historical. Query. Length: 500-2,000 words. **Pays 50¢-$1.50/word.**

LUMBER

PALLET ENTERPRISE

Industrial Reporting, Inc., 10244 Timber Ridge Dr., Ashland VA 23005. (804)550-0323. **Fax:** (804)550-2181. **E-mail:** edb@ireporting.com; mbrindleypallet@gmail.com. **Website:** www.palletenterprise.com. **Contact:** Edward C. Brindley, Jr., Ph.D., publisher; Melissa Brindley, editor. **40% freelance written.** Monthly magazine covering lumber and pallet operations. The *Pallet Enterprise* is a monthly trade magazine for the sawmill, pallet, remanufacturing, and wood processing industries. Articles should offer technical, solution-oriented information. Anti-forest articles are not accepted. Articles should focus on machinery and unique ways to improve profitability/make money. Estab. 1981. Circ. 14,500. Pays on publication. Editorial lead time 2 months. Submit seasonal material 2 months in advance. Accepts queries by mail, e-mail, fax, phone. Accepts simultaneous submissions. Sample copy available online. Guidelines free.

NONFICTION Needs interview, new product, opinion, technical, industry news, environmental, forests operation/plant features. No lifestyle, humor, general news, etc. **Buys 20 mss/year.** Query with published clips. Length: 1,000-3,000 words. **Pays $200-400 for assigned articles. Pays $100-400 for unsolicited articles.**

PHOTOS State availability. Captions, identification of subjects required. Reviews 3x5 prints. Negotiates payment individually. Buys one-time rights and Web rights.

COLUMNS/DEPARTMENTS Green Watch (environmental news/opinion affecting US forests), 1,500 words. **Buys 12 mss/year.** Query with published clips. **Pays $200-400.**

TIPS "Provide unique environmental or industry-oriented articles. Many of our freelance articles are company features of sawmills, pallet manufacturers, pallet recyclers, and wood waste processors."

TIMBERWEST

TimberWest Publications, LLC, P.O. Box 610, Edmonds WA 98020. (425)778-3388. **Fax:** (425)771-3623. **E-mail:** timberwest@forestnet.com; diane@forestnet.com. **Website:** www.forestnet.com. **Contact:** Diane Mettler, managing editor. **75% freelance written.** Monthly magazine covering logging and lumber segment of the forestry industry in the Northwest. Primarily publishes profiles on loggers and their operations—with an emphasis on the machinery—in Washington, Oregon, Idaho, Montana, Northern California, and Alaska. Some timber issues are highly controversial, and although the magazine will report on the issues, this is a pro-logging publication. Does not publish articles with a negative slant on the timber industry. Estab. 1975. Circ. 10,000. Byline given. Pays on acceptance. No kill fee. Editorial lead time 2 months. Accepts queries by mail, fax. Accepts simultaneous submissions. Responds in 3 weeks to queries. Sample copy: $2. Guidelines for #10 SASE.

NONFICTION Needs historical, interview, new product. No articles that put the timber industry in a bad light, such as environmental articles against logging. **Buys 50 mss/year.** Query with published clips. Length: 1,100-1,500 words. **Pays $350.**

PHOTOS Send photos. Captions, identification of subjects required. Reviews contact sheets, transparencies, prints, GIF/JPEG files. Offers no additional payment for photos accepted with ms, but does pay $50 if shot is used on cover. Buys first rights.

FILLERS Needs facts, newsbreaks. **Buys 10 mss/year.** Length: 400-800 words. **Pays $100-250.**

TIPS "We are always interested in profiles of loggers and their operations in Alaska, Oregon, Washington, Montana, and Northern California. We also want articles pertaining to current industry topics, such as fire abatement, sustainable forests, or new technology. Read an issue to get a clear idea of the type of material *TimberWest* publishes. The audience is primarily loggers, and topics that focus on an 'evolving' timber industry versus a 'dying' industry will find a place in the magazine. When querying, a clear overview of the article will enhance acceptance."

MACHINERY & METAL

AMERICAN MACHINIST

Penton Media, 1300 E. 9th St., Cleveland OH 44114. (216)696-7000. **Fax:** (913)696-8208. **E-mail:** robert.brooks@penton.com. **Website:** www.americanmachinist.com. **Contact:** Robert Brooks, editor-in-chief. **10% freelance written.** Monthly online website covering all forms of metalworking covering all forms of metalworking. Accepts contributed features and articles. *American Machinist* is an essential online source dedicated to metalworking in the United

States. Readers are the owners and managers of metalworking shops. Publishes articles that provide the managers and owners of job shops, contract shops, and captive shops the information they need to make their operations more efficient, more productive, and more profitable. Articles are technical in nature and must be focused on technology that will help these shops to become more competitive on a global basis. Readers are skilled machinists. This is not the place for lightweight items about manufacturing. Not interested in articles on management theories. Estab. 1877. Circ. 80,000. Byline sometimes given. Offers 20% kill fee. Publishes ms an average of 1-2 months after acceptance. Editorial lead time 3-6 months. Submit seasonal material 4-6 months in advance. Accepts queries by mail, e-mail, phone. Accepts simultaneous submissions. Responds in 1-2 weeks to queries; 1 month to mss. Sample copy online.

NONFICTION Needs general interest, how-to, new product, opinion, personal experience, photo feature, technical. Query with published clips. Length: 600-2,400 words. **Pays $300-1,200.**

PHOTOS State availability. Captions, identification of subjects, model releases required. Reviews GIF/JPEG files. Negotiates payment individually. Buys all rights.

FILLERS Needs anecdotes, facts, gags, newsbreaks, short humor. **Buys 12-18 mss/year. mss/year.** Length: 50 200 words. **Pays $25 100.**

TIPS "With our exacting audience, a writer would do well to have some background working with machine tools."

CUTTING TOOL ENGINEERING

CTE Publications, Inc., 1 Northfield Plaza, Suite 240, Northfield IL 60093. (847)714-0175. **Fax:** (847)559-4444. **E-mail:** alanr@jwr.com. **Website:** www.ctemag.com. **Contact:** Alan Richter, editor. **40% freelance written.** Monthly magazine covering industrial metal cutting tools and metal cutting and grinding operations. *Cutting Tool Engineering* serves owners, managers, and engineers who work in manufacturing, specifically manufacturing that involves cutting or grinding metal or other materials. Writing should be geared toward improving manufacturing processes. Estab. 1948. Circ. 60,000. Byline given. Pays on publication. Offers 50% kill fee. Publishes ms an average of 2 months after acceptance. Editorial lead time 2 months. Accepts queries by mail, e-mail, phone. Responds in 2 months to mss. Sample copy and guidelines free.

NONFICTION Needs how-to, opinion, personal experience, profile, technical. Does not want fiction or articles that don't relate to manufacturing. **Buys 10 mss/year.** Length: 1,500-2,000 words. **Pays $750-1,100.**

PHOTOS State availability. Captions required. Reviews transparencies, prints. Negotiates payment individually. Buys all rights.

TIPS "For queries, write 2 clear paragraphs about how the proposed article will play out. Include sources that would be in the article."

EQUIPMENT JOURNAL

Pace Publishing, 5160 Explorer Dr., Unit 6, Mississauga ON L4W 4T7 Canada. (416)459-5163. **E-mail:** editor@equipmentjournal.com. **E-mail:** editor@equipmentjournal.com. **Website:** www.equipmentjournal.com. **Contact:** Nathan Medcalf. **5% freelance written.** Canada's national heavy equipment newspaper. Focuses on the construction, material handling, mining, forestry, and on-highway transportation industries. Estab. 1966. Circ. 22,000. Byline given. Pays on publication. Kill fee: $50. Publishes ms an average of 1-2 months after acceptance. Editorial lead time 2-3 months. Accepts queries by e-mail, phone. Accepts simultaneous submissions. Sample copy and guidelines free.

Looking for job stories, features, and tips.

NONFICTION Needs how-to, interview, new product, photo feature, technical. Does not want "material that falls outside of *Equipment Journal's* mandate—the Canadian equipment industry." **Buys 15 mss/year.** Send complete ms. "We prefer electronic submissions." Length: 400-900 words. **Pays 40-50¢/word.**

REPRINTS Reprint payment negotiable.

PHOTOS Contact: Nathan Medcalf, editor. State availability. Identification of subjects required. Negotiates payment individually. Buys one-time rights.

COLUMNS/DEPARTMENTS Contact: Nathan Medcalf, editor. **Buys 2 mss/year.**

TIPS "Please pitch a story, instead of asking for an assignment. We are looking for stories of construction sites."

ORNAMENTAL & MISCELLANEOUS FABRICATOR

P. O. Box 492167, Lawrenceville GA 30049. (888)516-8585. **Fax:** (888)279-7994. **E-mail:** editor@nomma.

org; todd@nomma.org. **Website:** www.nomma.org. **Contact:** Todd Daniel, editor. **20% freelance written.** "Bimonthly magazine to inform, educate, and inspire members of the ornamental and miscellaneous metalworking industry." Estab. 1959. Circ. 9,000. Byline given. Pays on publication. No kill fee. Editorial lead time 1-2 months. Accepts queries by mail, e-mail, fax. Accepts simultaneous submissions. Responds by e-mail in 1 month (include e-mail address in query). Guidelines by email.

NONFICTION Needs book excerpts, essays, general interest, historical, how-to, humor, interview, opinion, personal experience, technical. **Buys 8-12 mss/year.** Query. Length: 1,200-2,000 words. **Pays $250-400.**

REPRINTS Send tearsheet, photocopy or typed ms with rights for sale noted and information about when and where the material previously appeared. Pays 100% of amount paid for an original article.

PHOTOS Artwork and sidebars preferred. State availability. Model releases required. Reviews contact sheets, negatives, transparencies, prints.

COLUMNS/DEPARTMENTS 700-900 words. **Pays $50-100.**

TIPS "Please request and review recent issues. Contacting the editor for guidance on article topics is welcome."

SPRINGS

Spring Manufacturers Institute, 2001 Midwest Rd., Suite 106, Oak Brook IL 60523-1335. (630)495-8588. **Fax:** (630)495-8595. **E-mail:** lynne@smihq.org. **Website:** www.smihq.org. **Contact:** Lynne Carr, general manager. **10% freelance written.** Quarterly magazine covering precision mechanical spring manufacture. Articles should be aimed at spring manufacturers. Estab. 1962. Circ. 10,800. Byline given. Pays on publication. No kill fee. Publishes ms an average of 3-6 months after acceptance. Editorial lead time 4 months. Accepts simultaneous submissions. Sample copy free. Guidelines available online.

NONFICTION Needs general interest, how-to, interview, opinion, personal experience, technical. **Buys 4-6 mss/year.** Length: 2,000-10,000 words. **Pays $100-600 for assigned articles.**

PHOTOS State availability. Captions required. Reviews prints, digital photos. Offers no additional payment for photos accepted with ms. Buys one-time rights.

TIPS "In analyzing all contributions, *Springs* looks for information that will help our readers run their businesses more effectively. We are far more interested in comprehensive detail than flashy writing. In fact, we like to develop a 'partnership in expertise' with our authors; you provide the technical knowledge and we assist you with communications and presentation skills. Thus, once your article is accepted for publication, you should expect the editor to be in touch regarding the edited version of your ms. All authors receive edited copy before publication so they can verify the factual accuracy of the reworked piece."

STAMPING JOURNAL

Fabricators & Manufacturers Association (FMA), 2135 Point Blvd., Elgin IL 60123. (815)399-8700. **Fax:** (815)381-1370. **E-mail:** kateb@thefabricator.com. **Website:** www.thefabricator.com. **Contact:** Dan Davis, editor-in-chief; Kate Bachman, editor. **15% freelance written.** Bimonthly magazine covering metal stamping. Looks for how-to and educational articles—nonpromotional. Estab. 1989. Circ. 35,000. Byline given. Pays on publication. No kill fee. Editorial lead time 6 months. Accepts queries by mail, e-mail, phone. Accepts simultaneous submissions. Responds in 2 weeks to queries. Sample copy and writer's guidelines free.

NONFICTION Pays 40-80¢/word.

PHOTOS State availability. Captions, identification of subjects required. Negotiates payment individually. Rights purchased depends on photographer requirements.

TIPS "Articles should be impartial and should not describe the benefits of certain products available from certain companies. They should not be biased toward the author's or against a competitor's products or technologies. The publisher may refuse any article that does not conform to this guideline."

WELDING DESIGN & FABRICATION

Penton Media, 1300 E. 9th St., Cleveland OH 44114. (216)696-7000. **Fax:** (216)931-9524. **E-mail:** wdeditor@penton.com; robert.brooks@penton. **Website:** www.weldingdesign.com. **Contact:** Robert E. Brooks, editor. **10% freelance written.** Bimonthly magazine covering all facets of welding and running a welding business. *Welding Design & Fabrication* provides information to the owners and managers of welding shops, including business, technology and trends. We include information on engineering and technological developments that could change the business as it is currently known, and feature stories on how welders are doing business with the goal of helping our readers to be more productive, effecient, and competitive. Welding shops are very local in nature and need to be addressed as small businessmen in a field that is consolidating and becoming more challenging and more global. We do not write about business management theory as much as we write about putting into practice good management techniques that have proved to work at similar businesses. Estab. 1930. Circ. 40,000. Byline given. Pays on publication. Offers 20% kill fee. Publishes ms an average of 1-2 months after acceptance. Editorial lead time 3-6 months. Submit seasonal material 4-6 months in advance. Accepts queries by mail, e-mail, phone. Accepts simultaneous submissions. Responds in 1-2 weeks to queries. Responds in 1 month to mss. Sample copy available online.

NONFICTION Needs general interest, how-to, new product, opinion, personal experience, photo feature, technical. Query. Length: 600-2,400 words. **Pays $300-1,200.**

PHOTOS State availability. Captions, identification of subjects, model releases required. Reviews GIF/JPEG files (300 dpi). Negotiates payment individually. Buys all rights.

FILLERS Needs anecdotes, facts, gags, newsbreaks, short humor. **Buys 12-18 mss/year.** Length: 50-200 words. **Pays $25-100.**

TIPS Writers should be familiar with welding and/or metalworking and metal joining techniques. With that, calling or e-mailing me directly is the next best approach. We are interested in information that will help to make welding shops more competitive, and a writer should have a very specific idea before approaching me.

WIRE ROPE NEWS & SLING TECHNOLOGY

Wire Rope News LLC, P.O. Box 871, Clark NJ 07066. (908)486-3221. **Fax:** (732)396-4215. **E-mail:** info@wireropenews.com. **Website:** www.wireropenews.com. **Contact:** Edward Bluvias III, publisher and editorial director. **100% freelance written.** Bimonthly magazine published for manufacturers and distributors of wire rope, chain, cordage, related hardware, and sling fabricators. Content includes technical articles, news and reports describing the manufacturing and use of wire rope and related products in marine, construction, mining, aircraft and offshore drilling operations. Estab. 1979. Circ. 4,300. Byline sometimes given. Pays on acceptance. No kill fee. Publishes ms an average of 6 months after acceptance. Editorial lead time 2 months. Submit seasonal material 2 months in advance. Accepts queries by mail, fax. Accepts simultaneous submissions.

NONFICTION Needs general interest, historical, interview, photo feature, technical. **Buys 30 mss/year.** Send complete ms. Length: 2,500-5,000 words. **Pays $300-500.**

PHOTOS Send photos. Identification of subjects required. Reviews contact sheets, 5x7 prints, digital. Offers no additional payment for photos accepted with ms. Buys all rights.

TIPS We are accepting more submissions and queries by e-mail.

MAINTENANCE & SAFETY

AMERICAN WINDOW CLEANER MAGAZINE

12Twelve Publishing Corp., 750-B NW Broad St., Southern Pines NC 28387. (910)693-2644. **Fax:** (910)246-1681. **E-mail:** info@awcmag.com; karen@awcmag.com. **Website:** www.awcmag.com. **Contact:** Karen Grinter, creative director. **20% freelance written.** Bimonthly magazine on window cleaning. Produces articles to help window cleaners become more profitable, safe, professional, and feel good about what they do. Estab. 1986. Circ. 8,000. Byline given. Pays on acceptance. Offers 33% kill fee. Publishes ms an average of 4-8 months after acceptance. Editorial lead time 2 months. Submit seasonal material 3 months in advance. Accepts simultaneous submissions. Responds in 2 weeks to queries; in 1 month to mss. Sample copy free.

NONFICTION Needs how-to, humor, inspirational, interview, personal experience, photo feature. "We do not want PR-driven pieces. We want to educate—not push a particular product." **Buys 20 mss/year.** Query. Length: 500-5,000 words. **Pays $50-250.**

PHOTOS State availability. Captions required. Reviews contact sheets, transparencies, 4x6 prints. Offers $10 per photo. Buys one-time rights.

COLUMNS/DEPARTMENTS Window Cleaning Tips (tricks of the trade); 1,000-2,000 words; Humor-anecdotes-feel good-abouts (window cleaning industry); Computer High-Tech (tips on new technology), all 1,000 words. **Buys 12 mss/year.** Query. **Pays $50-100.**

TIPS *"American Window Cleaner Magazine* covers an unusual niche that gets people's curiosity. Articles that are technical in nature and emphasize practical tips or safety, and how to work more efficiently, have the best chances of being published. Articles include: window cleaning unusual buildings, landmarks; working for well-known people/celebrities; window cleaning in resorts/casinos/unusual cities; humor or satire about our industry or the public's perception of it. At some point, we make phone contact and chat to see if our interests are compatible."

PEST MANAGEMENT PROFESSIONAL

North Coast Media, 1360 E. 9th St., Suite 1070, Cleveland OH 44114. (216)706-3754. **Fax:** (216)706-3711. **E-mail:** hgooch@northcoastmedia.net. **Website:** www.mypmp.net. **Contact:** Heather Gooch, editor. Monthly magazine for professional pest management professionals and sanitarians. Estab. 1933. Circ. 20,000. Pays on publication. No kill fee. Submit seasonal material 3 months in advance. Accepts queries by mail, e-mail, phone. Accepts simultaneous submissions. Responds in 1 month to mss. Guidelines available online.

NONFICTION Needs how-to, humor, inspirational, interview, new product, personal experience, case histories, new technological breakthroughs. No general information type of articles desired. **Buys 3 mss/year.** Query. Length: 1,000-1,400 words. **Pays $150-400 minimum.**

PHOTOS Digital photos accepted; please query on specs. State availability. No additional payment for photos used with ms.

COLUMNS/DEPARTMENTS Regular columns use material oriented to this profession, 550 words.

MANAGEMENT & SUPERVISION

HUMAN RESOURCE EXECUTIVE

LRP Publications Magazine Group, P.O. Box 980, Horsham PA 19044-0980. (215)784-0910. **Fax:** (215)784-0275. **E-mail:** kfrasch@lrp.com. **E-mail:** tgarrison@lrp.com. **Website:** www.hronline.com. **Contact:** Kristen B. Frasch, managing editor; Terri Garrison, editorial assistant. **30% freelance written.** Magazine published 16 times/year serving the infor-

mation needs of chief human resource professionals/executives in companies, government agencies, and nonprofit institutions with 500 or more employees. Estab. 1987. Circ. 75,000. Byline given. Pays on acceptance. Offers kill fee. Pays 50% kill fee on assigned stories. Publishes ms an average of 2 months after acceptance. Accepts queries by mail, e-mail, fax. Accepts simultaneous submissions. Responds in 1 month to mss. Guidelines available online.

NONFICTION Needs book excerpts, interview. **Buys 16 mss/year.** Query with published clips. Length: 1,800 words. **Pays $200-1,000.**

PHOTOS State availability. Identification of subjects required. Reviews contact sheets. Offers no additional payment for photos accepted with ms. Buys first and repeat rights.

PLAYGROUND MAGAZINE

Harris Publishing, P.O. Box 595, Ashton ID 83420. (208)652-3683. **Fax:** (208)652-7856. **Website:** www.playgroundmag.com. **25% freelance written.** Magazine published quarterly covering playgrounds, play-related issues, equipment, and industry trends. *Playground Magazine* targets park and recreation management, elementary school teachers and administrators, child care facilities, and parent-group leader readership. Articles should focus on play and the playground market as a whole, including aquatic play and surfacing. Estab. 2000. Circ. 35,000. Byline given. Pays on publication. No kill fee. Publishes ms an average of 6 months after acceptance. Editorial lead time 2 months. Submit seasonal material 1 year in advance. Accepts queries by mail, e-mail. Accepts simultaneous submissions. Responds in 1 month to queries. Responds in 2 months to mss. Sample copy for $5. Guidelines for #10 SASE.

NONFICTION Needs how-to, interview, new product, opinion, personal experience, photo feature, technical, travel. *Playground Magazine* does not publish any articles that do not directly relate to play and the playground industry. **Buys 4-6 mss/year.** Query. Length: 800-1,500 words. **Pays $50-300 for assigned articles.**

PHOTOS State availability of or send photos. Captions, identification of subjects, model releases required. Reviews 35mm transparencies, GIF/JPEG files (350 dpi or better). Offers no additional payment for photos accepted with ms. Buys one-time rights.

COLUMNS/DEPARTMENTS Dream Spaces (an article that profiles a unique play area and focuses on community involvement, unique design, or human interest), 800-1,200 words. **Buys 2 mss/year.** Query. **Pays $100-300.**

TIPS "We are looking for articles that managers can use as a resource when considering playground construction, management, safety, installation, maintenance, etc. Writers should find unique angles to playground-related features such as current trends in the industry, the value of play, natural play, the need for recess, etc. We are a trade journal that offers up-to-date industry news and features that promote play and the playground industry."

MARINE & MARITIME INDUSTRIES

CURRENTS

Marine Technology Society, 1100 H St. NW, Suite LL-100, Washington DC 20005. (202)717-8705. **Fax:** (202)347-4302. **E-mail:** morganteeditorial@verizon.net. **Website:** www.mtsociety.org. **Contact:** Amy Morgante, managing editor. Bimonthly newsletter covering commercial, academic, scientific marine technology. Readers are engineers and technologists who design, develop ,and maintain the equipment and instruments used to understand and explore the oceans. The newsletter covers society news, industry news, science and technology news, and similar news. Estab. 1963. Circ. 3,200. Byline given. Pays on acceptance. No kill fee. Editorial lead time 1-2 months. Accepts queries by e-mail. Accepts simultaneous submissions. Responds in 4 weeks to queries Sample copy free.

NONFICTION Needs interview, technical. **Buys 1-6 mss/year.** Query. Length: 250-500 words. **Pays $100-500 for assigned articles.**

PROFESSIONAL MARINER

Navigator Publishing, P.O. Box 569, Portland ME 04112. (207)772-2466. **Fax:** (207)772-2879. **E-mail:** rmiller@professionalmariner.com. **Website:** www.professionalmariner.com. **Contact:** Rich Miller, editor. **75% freelance written.** Bimonthly magazine covering professional seamanship and maritime industry news. Estab. 1993. Circ. 29,000. Byline given. Pays on publication. No kill fee. Editorial lead time 3 months.

Accepts queries by mail, e-mail. Accepts simultaneous submissions.

NONFICTION Buys 15 mss/year. Query. Length: varies; short clips to long profiles/features. **Pays 25¢/word.**

PHOTOS Send photos. Captions, identification of subjects required. Reviews prints, slides. Negotiates payment individually. Buys one-time rights.

TIPS "Remember that our audience comprises maritime industry professionals. Stories must be written at a level that will benefit this group."

MEDICAL

ACP INTERNIST/ACP HOSPITALIST

American College of Physicians, 191 N. Independence Mall W., Philadelphia PA 19106-1572. (215)351-2400. **E-mail:** acpinternist@acponline.org. **E-mail:** acphospitalist@acponline.org. **Website:** www.acpinternist.org; www.acphospitalist.org. **Contact:** Jennifer Kearney-Strouse, executive editor. **40% freelance written.** Monthly magazine covering internal medicine/hospital medicine. Writes for specialists in internal medicine, not a consumer audience. Topics include clinical medicine, practice management, health information technology, and Medicare issues. Estab. 1981. Circ. 85,000 (*Internist*), 24,000 (*Hospitalist*). Byline given. Offers kill fee. Negotiable. Publishes ms an average of 2 months after acceptance. Editorial lead time 4 months. Submit seasonal material 6 months in advance. Accepts queries by e-mail. Accepts simultaneous submissions. Sample copy online. Guidelines online.

NONFICTION Needs interview. Query with published clips. Length: 700-2,000 words. **Pays $500-2,000 for assigned articles.**

PHOTOS Contact: Ryan Dubosar, senior editor. State availability. Reviews TIFF/JPEG files. Negotiates payment individually.

AHIP COVERAGE

America's Health Insurance Plans, 601 Pennsylvania Ave. NW, South Bldg., Suite 500, Washington DC 20004. (202)778-3200. **Fax:** (202)331-7487. **E-mail:** ahip@ahip.org. **Website:** www.ahip.org. **75% freelance written.** Bimonthly magazine geared toward administrators in America's health insurance companies. Articles should inform and generate interest and discussion about topics on anything from patient care to regulatory issues. Estab. 1990. Circ. 12,000. Byline given. Pays within 30 days of acceptance of article in final form. Offers 30% kill fee. Publishes ms an average of 2 months after acceptance. Editorial lead time 2 months. Submit seasonal material 4 months in advance. Accepts queries by mail, e-mail, fax. Accepts simultaneous submissions. Sample copy free.

NONFICTION Needs book excerpts, how-to, opinion. "We do not accept stories that promote products." Send complete ms. Length: 1,800-2,500 words. **Pays 65¢/word minimum.** Pays phone expenses of writers on assignment.

PHOTOS Buys all rights.

TIPS "Look for health plan success stories in your community; we like to include case studies on a variety of topics—including patient care, provider relations, regulatory issues—so that our readers can learn from their colleagues. Our readers are members of our trade association and look for advice and news. Topics relating to the quality of health plans are the ones more frequently assigned to writers, whether a feature or department. We also welcome story ideas. Just send us a letter with the details."

JEMS: JOURNAL OF EMERGENCY MEDICAL SERVICES

PennWell Corporation, 4180 La Jolla Village Dr., Suite 260, San Diego CA 92037. (800) 266-5367. **Fax:** (619) 699-6396. **E-mail:** rkelley@pennwell.com. **Website:** www.jems.com. **Contact:** Ryan Kelley, managing editor. **95% freelance written.** Monthly magazine directed to personnel who serve the pre-hospital emergency medicine industry: paramedics, EMTs, emergency physicians and nurses, administrators, EMS consultants, etc. Estab. 1980. Circ. 45,000. Byline given. Pays on publication. No kill fee. Publishes ms an average of 6 months after acceptance. Submit seasonal material 6 months in advance. Accepts queries by e-mail. Responds in 2-3 months to queries. Sample copy free by request when available. Guidelines available at www.jems.com/about/author-guidelines.

NONFICTION Needs general interest, how-to, interview, new product, personal experience, photo feature, profile, technical. Stories, poems, and personal stories. **Buys 80 mss/year.** Query Ryan Kelley with contact information, suggested title, ms document (can be an outline), a summary, a general ms classification, and photos or figures to be considered with the ms. Please also submit professional CV/resume. 1800-2400 words plus references. **Pays $100-300.**

PHOTOS State availability. Identification of subjects, model releases required. Reviews digital images. Offers $25 minimum per photo. Buys one-time rights.

COLUMNS/DEPARTMENTS Length: up to 850 words. Query with or without published clips. **Pays $50-250.**

TIPS "Please submit a one-page cover letter with your ms. Your letter should answer these questions: (1) What specifically are you going to tell *JEMS* readers about pre-hospital medical care? (2) Why do *JEMS* readers need to know this? (3) How will you make your case (i.e., literature review, original research, interviews, personal experience, observation)? Your query should explain your qualifications, as well as include previous writing samples."

MANAGED CARE

780 Township Line Rd., Yardley PA 19067. (267)685-2788. **Fax:** (267)685-2966. **E-mail:** pwehrwein@medimedia.com. **Website:** www.managedcaremag.com. **Contact:** Peter Wehrwein, editor. **75% freelance written.** Monthly magazine that delivers high-interest, full-length articles and shorter features on clinical and business aspects of the health care industry. Emphasizes practical, usable information that helps HMO medical directors and pharmacy directors cope with the options, challenges, and hazards in the rapidly changing health care industry. Estab. 1992. Circ. 60,000. Byline given. Pays on acceptance. Offers 20% kill fee. Publishes ms an average of 6 weeks after acceptance. Editorial lead time 3 months. Submit seasonal material 4 months in advance. Accepts queries by mail, e-mail, fax. Accepts simultaneous submissions. Responds in 3 weeks to queries. Responds in 2 months to mss. Sample copy free. Guidelines available online.

NONFICTION Needs book excerpts, general interest, how-to, original research and review articles that examine the relationship between health care delivery and financing. Also considered occasionally are personal experience, opinion, interview/profile, and humor pieces, but these must have a strong managed care angle and draw upon the insights of (if they are not written by) a knowledgeable managed care professional. **Buys 40 mss/year.** Query with published clips. Length: 1,000-3,000 words. **Pays 75¢/word.**

PHOTOS State availability. Reviews contact sheets, negatives, transparencies, prints. Negotiates payment individually. Buys first-time rights.

TIPS "Know our audience (health plan executives) and their needs. Study our website to see what we cover."

☾ OPTICAL PRISM

250 The East Mall, Suite 1113, Toronto ON M9B 6L3 Canada. (416)233-2487. **Fax:** (416)233-1746. **E-mail:** info@opticalprism.ca. **Website:** www.opticalprism.ca. **30% freelance written.** Magazine published 10 times/year. Covers the health, fashion, and business aspects of the optical industry in Canada. Estab. 1982. Circ. 10,000. Byline given. Pays on publication. Publishes ms an average of 2 months after acceptance. Editorial lead time 3 months. Submit seasonal material 3 months in advance. Accepts queries by mail, e-mail. Accepts simultaneous submissions. Digital copy available online.

NONFICTION Needs interview, related to optical industry. Special issues: Editorial themes and feature topics available online in media kit. Query. Length: 1,000-1,600 words. **Pays 40¢/word (Canadian).**

COLUMNS/DEPARTMENTS Insight (profiles on people in the eyewear industry—also sometimes schools and businesses), 700-1,000 words. **Buys 5 mss/year.** Query. **Pays 40¢/word.**

TIPS "Please look at our editorial themes, which are on our website, and pitch articles that are related to the themes for each issue."

PHYSICIAN MAGAZINE

Physicians News Network, 10755 Scripps Poway Parkway, Suite 615, San Diego CA 92131. (858)226-7647. **E-mail:** sheri@physiciansnetwork.com; editors@physiciansnewsnetwork.com. **Website:** www.physiciansnewsnetwork.com. **Contact:** Sheri Carr, COO/editor. **25% freelance written.** Monthly magazine covering non-technical articles of relevance to physicians. Estab. 1908. Circ. 18,000. Byline given. Pays on acceptance. Offers 10% kill fee. Publishes ms an average of 2-3 months after acceptance. Editorial lead time 2-3 months. Accepts queries by e-mail. Accepts simultaneous submissions. Responds in 4 weeks to queries. Responds in 2 months to mss. Sample copy available online.

NONFICTION Needs general interest. **Buys 12-24 mss/year.** Query with published clips. Length: 600-3,000 words. **Pays $200-600 for assigned articles.**

PHOTOS State availability.

COLUMNS/DEPARTMENTS Medical World (tips/how-to's), 800-900 words. Query with published clips. **Pays $$200-$600.**

TIPS "We want professional, well-researched articles covering policy, issues, and other concerns of physicians. No personal anecdotes or patient viewpoints."

PLASTIC SURGERY NEWS

American Society of Plastic Surgeons, 444 E. Algonquin Rd., Arlington Heights IL 60005. **Fax:** (847)981-5458. **E-mail:** mss@plasticsurgery.org. **Website:** www.plasticsurgery.org. **Contact:** Mike Stokes, managing editor. **15% freelance written.** Monthly tabloid covering plastic surgery. *Plastic Surgery News* readership is comprised primarily of plastic surgeons and those involved with the specialty (nurses, techs, industry). The magazine is distributed via subscription and to all members of the American Society of Plastic Surgeons. The magazine covers a variety of specialty-specific news and features, including trends, legislation, and clinical information. Estab. 1960. Circ. 6,000. Byline given. Pays on acceptance. Offers 25% kill fee. Publishes ms an average of 1-2 months after acceptance. Editorial lead time 1-3 months. Accepts queries by e-mail. Accepts simultaneous submissions. Responds in 2 weeks to queries. Responds in 3 months to mss. Sample copy for 10 first-class stamps. Guidelines by e-mail.

NONFICTION Needs expose, how-to, new product, technical. Does not want celebrity or entertainment based pieces. **Buys 20 mss/year.** Query with published clips. Length: 1,000-3,500 words. **Pays 20-40¢/word.**

COLUMNS/DEPARTMENTS Digital Plastic Surgeon (technology), 1,500-1,700 words.

PODIATRY MANAGEMENT

Kane Communications, Inc., 10 E. Athens Avenue, Suite 208, Ardmore PA 19003. (718)897-9700. **Fax:** (718)896-5747. **E-mail:** bblock@podiatrym.com. **Website:** www.podiatrym.com. Magazine published 9 times/year for practicing podiatrists. Aims to help the doctor of podiatric medicine to build a bigger, more successful practice, to conserve and invest his money, to keep him posted on the economic, legal, and sociological changes that affect him. Estab. 1982. Circ. 16,500. Byline given. Pays on publication. $75 kill fee. Submit seasonal material 4 months in advance. Accepts queries by e-mail. Accepts simultaneous submissions. Responds in 2 weeks to queries. Sample copy for $5 and 9x12 SAE. Guidelines for #10 SASE.

NONFICTION Buys 35 mss/year. Length: 1,500-3,000 words. **Pays $350-600.**

REPRINTS Send photocopy. Pays 33% of amount paid for an original article.

PHOTOS State availability. Pays $15 for b&w contact sheet. Buys one-time rights.

TIPS "Articles should be tailored to podiatrists, and preferably should contain quotes from podiatrists."

PRIMARY CARE OPTOMETRY NEWS

SLACK Inc., 6900 Grove Rd., Thorofare NJ 08086-9447. (856)848-1000. **Fax:** (856)848-5991. **E-mail:** editor@healio.com; optometry@healio.com. **Website:** www.healio.com/optometry. **Contact:** Michael D. De-Paolis, editor. **5% freelance written.** Monthly tabloid covering optometry. *Primary Care Optometry News* strives to be the optometric professional's definitive information source by delivering timely, accurate, authoritative and balanced reports on clinical issues, socioeconomic and legislative affairs, ophthalmic industry, and research developments, as well as updates on diagnostic and thereapeutic regimens and techniques to enhance the quality of patient care. Estab. 1996. Circ. 39,000. Byline given. Pays on publication. Offers 50% kill fee. Publishes ms an average of 2 months after acceptance. Editorial lead time 2 months. Accepts queries by mail, e-mail, fax, phone. Accepts simultaneous submissions. Responds in 2 weeks to queries. Sample copy available online. Guidelines by e-mail.

NONFICTION Needs how-to, interview, new product, opinion, technical. **Buys 20 mss/year.** Query. Length: 800-1,000 words. **Pays $350-500.**

PHOTOS State availability. Captions, model releases required. Reviews GIF/JPEG files. Offers no additional payment for photos accepted with ms. Buys all rights.

COLUMNS/DEPARTMENTS What's Your Diagnosis (case presentation), 800 words. **Buys 40 mss/year.** Query. **Pays $100-500.**

TIPS "Either e-mail or call the editor with questions or story ideas."

STRATEGIC HEALTH CARE MARKETING

Health Care Communications, 11 Heritage Ln., P.O. Box 594, Rye NY 10580. (914)967-6741; (866)641-4548. **Fax:** (914)967-3054. **E-mail:** mhumphrey@plainenglishmedia.com. **Website:** www.strategichealthcare.com. **Contact:** Matt Humphrey, publisher. **90% freelance written.** Monthly newsletter covering health care marketing and management in a wide range of settings, including hospitals, medical group practices, home health services, and managed care organizations. Emphasis is on strategies and techniques employed within the health care field and relevant applications from other service industries. Works with published/established writers only. *Strategic Health Care Marketing* is specifically seeking writers with expertise/contacts in managed care, patient satisfaction, and e-health. Estab. 1984. Byline given. Pays on publication. Offers 25% kill fee. Publishes ms an average of 2 months after acceptance. Accepts queries by mail, e-mail. Accepts simultaneous submissions. Responds in 1 month to queries. Sample copy for SAE with 9x12 envelope and 3 first-class stamps. Guidelines sent with sample copy only.

NONFICTION Needs how-to, interview, new product, technical. **Buys 50 mss/year.** Query. Length: 1,000-1,800 words. **Pays $100-500.** Sometimes pays expenses of writers on assignment with prior authorization.

PHOTOS Photos, unless necessary for subject explanation, are rarely used. State availability. Captions, model releases required. Reviews contact sheets. Offers $10-30/photo. Buys one-time rights.

TIPS "Writers with prior experience on the business beat for newspapers or newsletters will do well. We require a sophisticated, in-depth knowledge of health care and business. This is not a consumer publication—the writer with knowledge of both health care and marketing will excel. Absolutely no unsolicited mss; any received will be returned or discarded unread."

MUSIC TRADE

CLASSICAL SINGER MAGAZINE

Classical Publications, Inc., P.O. Box 1710, Draper UT 84020. (801)254-1025, ext. 14. **Fax:** (801)254-3139. **E-mail:** editorial@classicalsinger.com. **Website:** www.classicalsinger.com. **Contact:** Sara Thomas. Monthly magazine covering classical singers. Estab. 1988. Circ. 7,000. Byline given, plus bio and contact info. Pays on publication. No kill fee. Publishes ms an average of 3 months after acceptance. Editorial lead time 3 months. Submit seasonal material 3 months in advance. Accepts queries by e-mail. Accepts simultaneous submissions. Responds in 1 month to queries. Potential writers will be given password to website version of magazine and writer's guidelines online.

NONFICTION Needs book excerpts, expose, how-to, humor, interview, new product, personal experience, photo feature, religious, technical, travel, crossword puzzles on opera theme. Does not want reviews unless they are assigned. Query with published clips. Length: 500-3,000 words. **Pays 5¢/word ($50 minimum). Writers also receive 10 contributor's copies.** Pays telephone expenses of writers with assignments when Xerox copy of bill submitted.

PHOTOS Send photos. Captions required. Buys all rights.

TIPS *"Classical Singer Magazine* has a full-color glossy cover and glossy b&w and color pages inside. It ranges in size from 56 pages during the summer to 120 pages in September. Articles need to meet this mission statement: 'Information for a classical singer's career, support for a classical singer's life, and enlightenment for a classical singer's art.'"

INTERNATIONAL BLUEGRASS

International Bluegrass Music Association, 4206 Gallatin Pk., Nashville TN 37216. (615)256-3222. **Fax:** (615)256-0450. **E-mail:** info@ibma.org. **Website:** www.ibma.org. **10% freelance written.** Bimonthly newsletter of the International Bluegrass Music Association. *International Bluegrass* is the business publication for the bluegrass music industry. Interested in hard news and features concerning how to reach that potential and how to conduct business more effectively. Estab. 1985. Circ. 4,500. Byline given. Pays on publication. No kill fee. Publishes ms an average of 2 months after acceptance. Submit seasonal material 4 months in advance. Accepts queries by mail, e-mail, phone. Accepts simultaneous submissions. Responds in 1 month to queries. Sample copy for SAE with 6x9 envelope and 2 first-class stamps.

NONFICTION Needs book excerpts, essays, how-to, new product, opinion. No interview/profiles/feature stories of performers (rare exceptions) or fans. **Buys 6 mss/year.** Query. Length: 1,000-1,200 words. **Pays up to $150/article for assigned articles.**

REPRINTS Send photocopy of article and information about when and where the article previously appeared. Does not pay for reprints.

PHOTOS Send photos. Captions, identification of subjects, True required. Offers no additional payment for photos accepted with ms. Buys one-time rights.

COLUMNS/DEPARTMENTS Staff written.

TIPS "We're interested in a slant strongly toward the business end of bluegrass music. We're especially looking for material dealing with audience development and how to book bluegrass bands outside of the existing market."

THE MUSIC & SOUND RETAILER

Testa Communications, 25 Willowdale Ave., Port Washington NY 11050. (516)767-2500. **E-mail:** dferrisi@testa.com. **Website:** www.msretailer.com. **Contact:** Dan Ferrisi, editor. **10% freelance written.** Monthly magazine covering business to business publication for music instrument products. *The Music & Sound Retailer* covers the music instrument industry and is sent to all dealers of these products, including Guitar Center, Sam Ash, and all small independent stores. Estab. 1983. Circ. 11,700. Byline given. Pays on publication. Offers $100 kill fee. Editorial lead time 1 month. Submit seasonal material 2 months in advance. Accepts queries by e-mail. Accepts simultaneous submissions. Responds in 2 weeks to queries. Responds in 1 month to mss. Sample copy for #10 SASE. Guidelines free.

NONFICTION Needs how-to, new product, opinion, personal experience. Concert and CD reviews are never published; neiter are interviews with musicians. **Buys 25 mss/year.** Query with published clips. Length: 1,000-2,000 words. **Pays $300-400 for assigned and unsolicited articles.**

PHOTOS Send photos. Captions required. Reviews GIF/JPEG files. Offers no additional payment for photos accepted with ms. Buys one-time rights.

OPERA NEWS

Metropolitan Opera Guild, Inc., 70 Lincoln Center Plaza, 6th Floor, New York NY 10023. **E-mail:** info@operanews.com. **Website:** www.operanews.com. **Contact:** Kitty March. **75% freelance written.** Monthly magazine for people interested in opera—the opera professional as well as the opera audience. Estab. 1936. Circ. 105,000. Byline given. Pays on publication. No kill fee. Publishes ms an average of 4 months after acceptance. Editorial lead time 4 months. Accepts queries by e-mail. Accepts simultaneous submissions. Sample copy for $5.

NONFICTION Needs historical, interview, informational, think pieces, opera, and CD, DVD and book reviews. Does not accept works of fiction or personal remembrances. Send unsolicited mss, article pro-

posals and queries, along with several published clips. Length: 1,500-2,800 words. **Pays $450-1,200.**
PHOTOS State availability. Buys one-time rights.
COLUMNS/DEPARTMENTS Buys 24 mss/year.

OVERTONES

Handbell Musicians of America, P.O. Box 1765, Findlay OH 45839-1765. **E-mail:** jrsmith@handbellmusicians.org. **Website:** http://handbellmusicians.org/music-resources/overtones. **Contact:** J.R. Smith, publications director. **80% freelance written.** Bimonthly magazine covering English handbell ringing and conducting. *Overtones* is a 48-page magazine with extensive educational articles, photos, advertisements, and graphic work. Handbell Musicians of America is dedicated to advancing the musical art of handbell/handchime ringing through education, community, and communication. The purpose of *Overtones* is to provide a printed resource to support that mission. Offers how-to articles, inspirational stories, and interviews with well-known people and unique ensembles. Estab. 1954. Circ. 8,000. Byline given. Pays on publication. No kill fee. Publishes ms an average of 4 months after acceptance. Editorial lead time 4 months. Submit seasonal material 4 months in advance. Accepts queries by mail, e-mail. Accepts simultaneous submissions. Responds in 1 month to queries and to mss. Sample copy available by e-mail. Guidelines available online. Style guideline should follow *The Chicago Manual of Style*.

NONFICTION Needs essays, general interest, historical, how-to, inspirational, interview, religious, technical. Does not want product news or promotional material. **Buys 8-12 mss/year.** Send complete ms via e-mail, CD, DVD, or hard copy. Length: 1,200-2,000 words. **Pays $120.**

PHOTOS State availability of or send photos. Captions required. Reviews 8x10 prints, JPEG/TIFF files. Offers no additional payment for photos accepted with ms. Buys one-time rights.

COLUMNS/DEPARTMENTS Handbells in Education (topics covering the use of handbells in school setting, teaching techniques, etc.); Handbells in Worship (topics and ideas for using handbells in a church setting); Tips & Tools (variety of topics from ringing and conducting techniques to score study to maintenance); Community Connections (topics covering issues relating to the operation/administration/techniques for community groups); Music Reviews (rec-

ommendations and descriptions of music following particular themes, i.e., youth music, difficult music, seasonal, etc.). Length should be 800-1,200 words. Query. **Pays $80.**

TIPS "When writing profiles/interviews, try to determine what is especially unique or inspiring about the individual or ensemble and write from that viewpoint. Please have some expertise in handbells, education, or church music to write department articles."

PAPER

THE PAPER STOCK REPORT

McEntee Media Corp., 9815 Hazelwood Ave., Strongsville OH 44149. (440)238-6603. **Fax:** (440)238-6712. **E-mail:** ken@recycle.cc; psr@recycle.cc. **Website:** www.recycle.cc/psrpage.htm. **Contact:** Ken McEntee, editor/publisher. Bimonthly newsletter covering market trends and news in the paper recycling industry. Audience is interested in new innovative markets, applications for recovered scrap paper, as well as new laws and regulations impacting recycling. Estab. 1990. Circ. 2,000. Byline given. Pays on publication. No kill fee. Publishes ms an average of 1 month after acceptance. Editorial lead time 2 months. Submit seasonal material 2 months in advance. Accepts queries by mail, e-mail, fax, phone. Accepts simultaneous submissions. Responds in 1 month to queries. Sample copy for #10 SAE with 55¢ postage.

NONFICTION Needs book excerpts, essays, expose, general interest, historical, interview, new product, opinion, photo feature, technical, all related to paper recycling. **Buys 0-13 mss/year.** Send complete ms. Length: 250-1,000 words. **Pays $50-250 for assigned articles. Pays $25-250 for unsolicited articles.**

PHOTOS State availability. Identification of subjects required. Reviews contact sheets. Negotiates payment individually.

TIPS "Articles must be valuable to readers in terms of presenting new market opportunities or cost-saving measures."

RECYCLED PAPER NEWS

McEntee Media Corp., 9815 Hazelwood Ave., Strongsville OH 44149. (440)238-6603. **Fax:** (440)238-6712. **E-mail:** ken@recycle.cc. **Website:** www.recycle.cc. **Contact:** Ken McEntee, owner. **10% freelance written.** Monthly newsletter covering the recycling and composting industries. Interested in any news impacting the paper recycling industry, as well as other environmental issues in the paper industry, i.e., water/air pollution, chlorine-free paper, forest conservation, etc., with special emphasis on new laws and regulations. Estab. 1990. Pays on publication. No kill fee. Publishes ms an average of 2 months after acceptance. Editorial lead time 1 month. Submit seasonal material 1 month in advance. Accepts queries by mail, e-mail, fax, phone. Accepts simultaneous submissions. Responds in 2 months to queries. Sample copy for 9x12 SAE and 55¢ postage. Guidelines for #10 SASE.

NONFICTION Needs book excerpts, essays, how-to, interview, new product, opinion, personal experience, photo feature. **Buys 0-5 mss/year.** Query with published clips. **Pays $10-500.**

COLUMNS/DEPARTMENTS Query with published clips. **Pays $10-500.**

TIPS "We appreciate leads on local news regarding recycling or composting, i.e., new facilities or businesses, new laws and regulations, unique programs, situations that impact supply and demand for recyclables, etc. International developments are also of interest."

PLUMBING, HEATING, AIR CONDITIONING & REFRIGERATION

⟳ HPAC: HEATING PLUMBING AIR CONDITIONING

80 Valleybrook Dr., Toronto Ontario M3B 2S9 Canada. (416)510-5218. **Fax:** (416)510-5140. **E-mail:** smacisaac@hpacmag.com; kturner@hpacmag.com. **Website:** www.hpacmag.com. **Contact:** Sandy MacIsaac, art director; Kerry Turner, editor. **20% freelance written.** Monthly magazine. Estab. 1923. Circ. 19,500. Pays on publication. No kill fee. Publishes an average of 3 months after acceptance. Accepts queries by mail, e-mail. Accepts simultaneous submissions. Responds in 2 months to queries.

○   "We primarily want articles that show *HPAC* readers how they can increase their sales and business step-by-step based on specific examples of what others have done."

NONFICTION Needs how-to, technical. Length: 1,000-1,500 words. **Pays 50¢/word.**

REPRINTS Send tearsheet or photocopy with rights for sale noted and information about when and where the material previously appeared.

PHOTOS Prefers JPEGs or hi-res PDFs. Photos purchased with ms.

TIPS "Topics must relate directly to the day-to-day activities of *HPAC* readers in Canada. Must be detailed, with specific examples, quotes from specific people or authorities—show depth. We specifically want material from other parts of Canada besides southern Ontario. U.S. material must relate to Canadian readers' concerns."

SNIPS MAGAZINE

BNP Media, 2401 W. Big Beaver Rd., Suite 700, Troy MI 48084. (248)244-6416. **Fax:** (248)362-0317. **E-mail:** mcconnellm@bnpmedia.com. **Website:** www.snipsmag.com. **Contact:** Michael McConnell, editor. **2% freelance written.** Monthly magazine for sheet metal, heating, ventilation, air conditioning, and metal roofing contractors. Estab. 1932. No kill fee. Publishes ms an average of 3 months after acceptance. Accepts queries by mail, e-mail, fax, phone. Accepts simultaneous submissions. Call for writer's guidelines.

NONFICTION Length: under 1,000 words unless on special assignment. **Pays $200-300.**

PHOTOS Negotiable.

PRINTING

THE BIG PICTURE

ST Media Group International, 11262 Cornell Park Dr., Cincinnati OH 45242. (513)421-2050. **E-mail:** adrienne.palmer@stmediagroup.com. **Website:** www.bigpicture.net. **Contact:** Adrienne Palmer, editor-in-chief. **20% freelance written.** Magazine published 9 times/year covering wide-format digital printing. *The Big Picture* covers wide-format printing as well as digital workflow, finishing, display, capture, and other related topics. Readers include digital print providers, sign shops, commercial printers, in-house print operations, and other print providers across the country. Primarily interested in the technology and work processes behind wide-format printing, but also run trend features on segments of the industry (innovations in point-of-purchase displays, floor graphics, fine-art printing, vehicle wrapping, textile printing, etc.). Estab. 1996. Circ. 21,500 controlled. Byline given. Pays on publication. Offers 20% kill fee. Publishes ms an average of 2 months after acceptance. Editorial lead time 2 months. Accepts queries by e-mail. Accepts simultaneous submissions. Responds in 2 weeks to queries. Responds in 1 month to mss. Sample copy available online. Guidelines available.

NONFICTION Needs how-to, interview, new product, technical. Does not want broad consumer-oriented pieces that do not speak to the business and technical aspects of producing print for pay. **Buys 15-20 mss/year.** Query with published clips. Length: 1,500-2,500 words. **Pays $500-700 for assigned articles.**

PHOTOS Send photos. Reviews GIF/JPEG files hi-res. Offers no additonal payment for photos accepted with ms.

TIPS "Interest in and knowledge of the digital printing industry will position you well to break into this market. You have to be willing to drill down into the production aspects of digital printing to write for us."

IN-PLANT GRAPHICS

NAPCO Media, 1500 Spring Garden St., 12th Floor, Philadelphia PA 19130. (215)238-5321. **Fax:** (215)238-5457. **E-mail:** bobneubauer@napco.com. **Website:** www.inplantgraphics.com. **Contact:** Bob Neubauer, editor. **40% freelance written.** *In-Plant Graphics* features articles designed to help in-house printing departments increase productivity, save money, and stay competitive. *IPG* features advances in graphic arts technology and shows in-plants how to put this technology to use. Audience consists of print shop managers working for (nonprint related) corporations (i.e., hospitals, insurance companies, publishers, nonprofits), universities, and government departments. They often oversee graphic design, prepress, printing, bindery, and mailing departments. Estab. 1951. Circ. 23,100. Byline given. Pays on publication. No kill fee. Publishes ms an average of 3 months after acceptance. Editorial lead time 2 months. Submit seasonal material 3 months in advance. Accepts queries by e-mail. Accepts simultaneous submissions. Guidelines available online.

NONFICTION Needs interview, new product, technical. Special issues: See editorial calendar online. No articles on desktop publishing software or design software. No Internet publishing articles. **Buys 5 mss/year.** Query with published clips. Length: 800-1,500 words. **Pays $350-500.**

PHOTOS Photos should be at least 266 dpi. State availability. Captions, identification of subjects required. Reviews transparencies, prints. Negotiates payment individually. Buys one-time rights.

COLUMNS/DEPARTMENTS Query with published clips.

TIPS "To get published in *IPG*, writers must contact the editor with an idea in the form of a query letter that includes published writing samples. Writers who have covered the graphic arts in the past may be assigned stories for an agreed-upon fee. We don't want stories that tout only 1 vendor's products and serve as glorified commercials. All profiles must be well balanced, covering a variety of issues. If you can tell us about an in-house printing operation doing innovative things, we will be interested."

SCREEN PRINTING

ST Media Group International, 11262 Cornell Park Dr., Cincinnati OH 45242. (513)421-2050, ext. 331. **Fax:** (513)421-5144. **E-mail:** kiersten.wones@stmediagroup.com; ben.rosenfield@stmediagroup.com. **Website:** www.screenweb.com. **Contact:** Kiersten Wones, editorial assistant; Ben Rosenfield, managing editor. **30% freelance written.** Monthly magazine for the screen printing industry, including screen printers (commercial, industrial, and captive shops), suppliers and manufacturers, ad agencies, and allied profession. Estab. 1953. Circ. 17,500. Byline given. Pays on publication. No kill fee. Publishes ms an average of 3 months after acceptance. Accepts queries by mail, e-mail, fax. Accepts simultaneous submissions. Sample copy available. Guidelines for #10 SASE.

Works with a small number of new/unpublished writers each year.

NONFICTION **Buys 10-15 mss/year.** Query. Unsolicited mss not returned. Length: 2,000-3,000 words. **Pays $300-500 for major features.**

PHOTOS Cover photos negotiable; b&w or color. Published material becomes the property of the magazine.

TIPS "Be an expert in the screen-printing industry with supreme or special knowledge of a particular screen-printing process, or have special knowledge of a field or issue of particular interest to screen-printers. If the author has a working knowledge of screen printing, assignments are more readily available. General management articles are rarely used."

PROFESSIONAL PHOTOGRAPHY

NEWS PHOTOGRAPHER

National Press Photographers Association, Inc., 6677 Whitemarsh Valley Walk, Austin TX 78746-6367. **E-**

mail: magazine@nppa.org; tburton@nppa.org. **Website:** www.nppa.org. **Contact:** Tom Burton, editor. Magazine on photojournalism published 10 times/year. *News Photographer* magazine is dedicated to the advancement of still and television news photography. The magazine presents articles, interviews, profiles, history, new products, electronic imaging, and news related to the practice of photojournalism. Estab. 1946. Circ. 11,000. Byline given. Pays on acceptance. Offers 100% kill fee. Publishes ms an average of 4 months after acceptance. Editorial lead time 2 months. Submit seasonal material 2 months in advance. Accepts queries by mail, e-mail, fax, phone. Accepts simultaneous submissions. Responds in 1 month to queries. Sample copy for SAE with 9x12 envelope and 3 first-class stamps. Guidelines free.

NONFICTION Needs historical, how-to, interview, new product, opinion, personal experience, photo feature, technical. **Buys 10 mss/year.** Query. Length: 1,500 words. **Pays $300.**

PHOTOS State availability. Captions, identification of subjects required. Reviews high resolution, digital images only. Negotiates payment individually. Buys one-time rights.

COLUMNS/DEPARTMENTS Query.

THE PHOTO REVIEW

200 East Maple Avenue, Suite 200, Langhorne PA 19047. (215)891-0214. **Fax:** (215)891-9358. **E-mail:** info@photoreview.org. **Website:** www.photoreview.org. **50% freelance written.** Biannual magazine covering art photography and criticism. "*The Photo Review* publishes critical reviews of photography exhibitions and books, critical essays, and interviews. We do not publish how-to or technical articles." Estab. 1976. Circ. 2,000. Byline given. Pays on publication. No kill fee. Publishes ms an average of 9-12 months after acceptance. Editorial lead time 3 months. Submit seasonal material 6 months in advance. Accepts queries by mail. Accepts simultaneous submissions. Responds in 2 months to queries. Responds in 3 months to mss. Sample copy for $7. Email for guidelines.

NONFICTION Needs essays, historical, interview, reviews. No how-to articles. **Buys 20 mss/year.** Send complete ms. Length: 2-20 typed pages by email. **Pays $10-250.**

REPRINTS Send tearsheet, photocopy, or typed ms with rights for sale noted and information about when and where the material previously appeared. Payment varies.

PHOTOS Send photos. Captions required. Reviews electronic images. Offers no additional payment for photos accepted with ms. Buys all rights.

REAL ESTATE

💲💲 AREA DEVELOPMENT ONLINE

Halcyon Business Publications, Inc., 400 Post Ave., Westbury NY 11590. (516)338-0900, ext. 211. **Fax:** (516)338-0100. **E-mail:** gerri@areadevelopment.com. **Website:** www.areadevelopment.com. **Contact:** Geraldine Gambale, editor. **40% freelance written. Prefers to work with published/established writers.** Quarterly magazine covering corporate facility planning and site selection for industrial chief executives worldwide. Estab. 1965. Circ. 45,000. Byline given. Pays within 90 days. No kill fee. Publishes ms an average of 2 months after acceptance. Editorial lead time 2-3 months. Accepts queries by e-mail. Accepts simultaneous submissions. Responds as soon as possible to queries. Sample copy free. Guidelines available by e-mail upon request.

NONFICTION Needs historical, how-to, interview. **Buys 75 mss/year.** Query. Length: 1,200-1,500 words. **Pays 50¢/word.**

PHOTOS State availability. Captions, identification of subjects required. Reviews JPEGs of at least 300 dpi. Negotiates payment individually.

⊘💊 CANADIAN PROPERTY MANAGEMENT

Media Edge, 5255 Yonge St., Suite 1000, Toronto ON M2N 2P4 Canada. (416)512-8186. **E-mail:** barbc@mediaedge.ca. **Website:** www.reminetwork.com/canadian-property-management/home/. **Contact:** Barbara Carss, editor in chief. **10% freelance written.** Magazine published 8 times/year covering Canadian commercial, industrial, institutional (medical and educational), and residential properties. *Canadian Property Management* is a trade journal supplying building owners and property managers with Canadian industry news, case law reviews, technical updates for building operations, and events listings. Building and professional profile articles are regular features. Estab. 1985. Circ. 12,500. Byline given. Pays on publication. No kill fee. Publishes ms an average of 3 months after acceptance. Editorial lead time 2 months.

Submit seasonal material 2 months in advance. Accepts queries by mail, e-mail, phone. Accepts simultaneous submissions. Responds in 3 weeks to queries; in 2 months to mss. Sample copy: $5, subject to availability. Guidelines free.

NONFICTION Needs interview, technical. No promotional articles (i.e., marketing a product or service geared to this industry). Query with published clips. Length: 700-1,200 words. **Pays 35¢/word.**

PHOTOS State availability. Captions, identification of subjects, model releases required. Reviews transparencies, 3x5 prints, digital (at least 300 dpi). Offers no additional payment for photos accepted with ms.

TIPS "We do not accept promotional articles serving companies or their products. Freelance articles that are strong and information-based and that serve the interests and needs of property managers and building owners stand a better chance of being published. Proposals and inquiries with article ideas are appreciated the most. A good understanding of the real estate industry (management structure) is also helpful for the writer."

THE COOPERATOR

Yale Robbins, Inc., 205 Lexington Ave., 12th Floor, New York NY 10016. (212)683-5700. **Fax:** (212)545-0764. **E-mail:** editorial@cooperator.com. **Website:** www.cooperator.com. **70% freelance written.** Monthly tabloid covering real estate in the New York City metro area. *The Cooperator* covers condominium and cooperative issues in New York and beyond. It is read by condo unit owners and co-op shareholders, real estate professionals, board members and managing agents, and other service professionals. Estab. 1980. Circ. 40,000. Byline given. Pays on publication. No kill fee. Publishes ms an average of 3 months after acceptance. Submit seasonal material 3 months in advance. Accepts queries by mail, e-mail, fax. Accepts simultaneous submissions. Responds in 1 month to queries. Sample copy and writer's guidelines free.

NONFICTION Needs interview, new product, personal experience. No submissions without queries. Query with published clips. Length: 1,500-2,000 words. **Pays $325-425.**

PHOTOS State availability.

COLUMNS/DEPARTMENTS Profiles of co-op/condo-related businesses with something unique; Building Finance (investment and financing issues); Buying and Selling (market issues, etc.); Design (ar-

chitectural and interior/exterior design, lobby renovation, etc.); Building Maintenance (issues related to maintaining interior/exterior, facades, lobbies, elevators, etc.); Legal Issues Related to Co-Ops/Condos; Real Estate Trends, all 1,500 words. **Buys 100 mss/year.** Query with published clips.

TIPS "You must have experience in business, legal, or financial. Must have published clips to send in with résumè and query."

FLORIDA REALTOR MAGAZINE

Florida Association of Realtors, 7025 Augusta National Dr., Orlando FL 32822. (407)438-1400. **Fax:** (407)438-1411. **E-mail:** flrealtor@floridarealtors.org. **Website:** www.floridarealtormagazine.com. **Contact:** Doug Damerst, editor-in-chief. **70% freelance written.** Journal published 10 times/year covering the Florida real estate profession. "As the official publication of the Florida Association of Realtors, we provide helpful articles for our 125,000 members. We report new practices that lead to successful real estate careers and stay up on the trends and issues that affect business in Florida's real estate market." Estab. 1925. Circ. 114,592. Byline given. Pays on publication. No kill fee. Publishes ms an average of 2 months after acceptance. Editorial lead time 3 months. Accepts queries by mail, e-mail, fax. Sample copy available online.

NONFICTION No fiction or poetry. **Buys varying number of mss/year.** Query with published clips. Length: 800-1,500 words. **Pays $500-700.**

PHOTOS State availability of photos. Captions, identification of subjects, model releases required. Negotiates payment individually. Buys one-time print rights and Internet use rights.

COLUMNS/DEPARTMENTS Some written in-house: Law & Ethics, 900 words; Market It, 600 words; Technology & You, 800 words; ManageIt, 600 words. **Buys varying number of mss/year. Payment varies.**

TIPS "Build a solid reputation for specializing in real estate business writing in state/national publications. Read the magazine online at floridarealtors.org/magazine. Query with specific article ideas."

OFFICE BUILDINGS MAGAZINE

Yale Robbins, Inc., 205 Lexington Ave., 12th Fl., New York NY 10016. (212)683-5700. **Fax:** (212)497-0017. **E-mail:** mrosupport@mrofficespace.com. **Website:** marketing.yrpubs.com/officebuildings. **15% freelance written.** Annual magazine published in 12 separate editions covering market statistics, trends, and thinking of area professionals on the current and future state of the real estate market. Estab. 1987. Circ. 10,500. Byline sometimes given. Pays 1 month after publication. Offers kill fee. Editorial lead time 2 months. Accepts queries by mail, e-mail. Accepts simultaneous submissions. Sample copy and writer's guidelines free.

NONFICTION **Buys 15-20 mss/year.** Query with published clips. Length: 1,500-2,000 words. **Pays $600-700.**

PROPERTIES MAGAZINE

Properties Magazine, Inc., 3826 W. 158th St., Cleveland OH 44111. (216)251-2655. **Fax:** (216)251-0064. **E-mail:** mwatt@propertiesmag.com. **Website:** www. propertiesmag.com. **Contact:** Mark Watt, managing editor/art director. **25% freelance written.** Monthly magazine covering real estate, residential, commerical construction. *Properties Magazine* is published for executives in the real estate, building, banking, design, architectural, property management, tax, and law community—busy people who need the facts presented in an interesting and informative format. Estab. 1946. Circ. over 10,000. Byline given. Pays on publication. No kill fee. Publishes ms an average of 2 months after acceptance. Editorial lead time 2 months. Submit seasonal material 2 months in advance. Accepts queries by mail, fax. Accepts simultaneous submissions. Responds in 3 weeks to queries. Sample copy for $3.95.

NONFICTION Needs general interest, how-to, humor, new product. Special issues: Environmental issues (September); Security/Fire Protection (October); Tax Issues (November); Computers In Real Estate (December). **Buys 30 mss/year.** Send complete ms. Length: 500-2,000 words. **Pays 50¢/column line.**

PHOTOS Send photos. Captions required. Reviews prints. Offers no additional payment for photos accepted with ms. Negotiates payment individually. Buys one-time rights.

COLUMNS/DEPARTMENTS **Buys 25 mss/year.** Query or send complete ms. **Pays 50¢/column line.**

☺ REM

2255B Queen St. E., Suite #1178, Toronto ON M4E 1G3 Canada. (416)425-3504. **E-mail:** jim@remonline.com. **Website:** www.remonline.com. **Contact:** Jim Adair, managing editor. **35% freelance written.** Monthly Canadian trade journal covering real estate. "*REM* provides Canadian real estate agents and brokers with news and opinions they can't get anywhere

else. It is an independent publication and not affiliated with any real estate board, association, or company." Estab. 1989. Circ. 28,000. Byline given. Pays on acceptance. Offers 25% kill fee. Publishes ms an average of 2 months after acceptance. Editorial lead time 3 months. Submit seasonal material 3 months in advance. Accepts queries by mail, e-mail. Accepts simultaneous submissions. Responds in 2 weeks. Sample copy free.

NONFICTION Needs book excerpts, expose, inspirational, interview, new product, personal experience. "No articles geared to consumers about market conditions or how to choose a realtor. Must have Canadian content." **Buys 60 mss/year.** Query. Length: 500-1,500 words. **Pays $200-400.**

PHOTOS Send photos. Captions, identification of subjects required. Reviews transparencies, prints, GIF/JPEG files. Offers $25/photo. Buys one-time rights plus rights to place on REM websites.

TIPS "Stories must be of interest or practical use for Canadian realtors. Check out our website to see the types of stories we require."

ZONING PRACTICE

American Planning Association, 205 N. Michigan Ave., Suite 1200, Chicago IL 60601. (312)431-9100; (312)786-6392. **Fax:** (312)786-6700. **E-mail:** zoningpractice@planning.org. **Website:** www.planning. org/zoningpractice/. **90% freelance written.** Monthly newsletter covering land-use regulations including zoning. Publication is aimed at practicing urban planners and those involved in land-use decisions, such as zoning administrators and officials, planning commissioners, zoning boards of adjustment, land-use attorneys, developers, and others interested in this field. The material published comes from writers knowledgeable about zoning and subdivision regulations, preferably with practical experience in the field. Anything published needs to be of practical value to our audience in their everyday work. Estab. 1984. Circ. 2,000. Byline given. Pays on publication. Offers 50% kill fee. Publishes ms an average of 3 months after acceptance. Editorial lead time 6 months. Accepts queries by mail, e-mail, fax, phone. Accepts simultaneous submissions. Responds in 2 weeks to queries. Responds in 1 month to mss. Single copy: $10. Guidelines available at www.planning.org/zoningpractice/guidelines.htm.

NONFICTION Needs technical. See description. We do not need general or consumer-interest articles about zoning because this publication is aimed at practitioners. **Buys 12 mss/year.** Query. Length: 3,000-5,000 words. **Pays $300 minimum for assigned articles.**

PHOTOS State availability. Captions required. Reviews GIF/JPEG files. Negotiates payment individually. Buys all rights.

TIPS "Breaking in is easy if you know the subject matter and can write in plain English for practicing planners. We are always interested in finding new authors. We generally expect authors will earn another $200 premium for participating in an online forum called Ask the Author, in which they respond to questions from readers about their article. This requires a deep practical sense of how to make things work with regard to your topic."

RESOURCES & WASTE REDUCTION

COMPOSTING NEWS

McEntee Media Corp., 9815 Hazelwood Ave., Strongsville OH 44149. (440)238-6603. **Fax:** (440)238-6712. **E-mail:** ken@recycle.cc. **Website:** www.compostingnews.com. **Contact:** Ken McEntee, editor. **5% freelance written.** Monthly newsletter about the composting industry. *Composting News* features the latest news and vital issues of concern to the producers, marketers, and end-users of compost, mulch and other organic waste-based products. Estab. 1992. Circ. 1,000. Pays on publication. No kill fee. Publishes ms an average of 1 month after acceptance. Editorial lead time 1 month. Submit seasonal material 1 month in advance. Accepts queries by mail, e-mail, fax, phone. Accepts simultaneous submissions. Responds in 2 months to queries. Sample copy for 9x12 SAE and 55¢ postage. Guidelines for #10 SASE.

NONFICTION Needs book excerpts, essays, general interest, how-to, interview, new product, opinion, personal experience, photo feature. **Buys 0-5 mss/year.** Query with published clips. Length: 100-5,000 words. **Pays $10-500.**

COLUMNS/DEPARTMENTS Query with published clips. **Pays $10-500.**

TIPS "We appreciate leads on local news regarding composting, i.e., new facilities or business, new laws and regulations, unique programs, situations that impact supply and demand for composting. International developments are also of interest."

WATER WELL JOURNAL

National Ground Water Association, 601 Dempsey Rd., Westerville OH 43081. **Fax:** (614)898-7786. **E-mail:** tplumley@ngwa.org. **Website:** www.waterwelljournal.org. **Contact:** Thad Plumley, director of publications/editor; Mike Price, senior editor. Each month the *Water Well Journal* covers the topics of drilling, rigs and heavy equipment, pumping systems, water quality, business management, water supply, on-site waste water treatment, and diversification opportunities, including geothermal installations, environmental remediation, irrigation, dewatering, and foundation installation. It also offers updates on regulatory issues that impact the ground water industry. Circ. 24,000. Byline given. Pays on publication. Publishes ms an average of 3 months after acceptance. Editorial lead time 6 weeks. Submit seasonal material 3 months in advance. Accepts queries by mail. Accepts simultaneous submissions. Responds in 2 weeks to queries. Responds in 1 month to mss. Guidelines free.

NONFICTION Needs essays, historical, how-to, interview, new product, personal experience, photo feature, technical, business management. No company profiles or extended product releases. **Buys up to 30 mss/year.** Query with published clips. Length: 1,000-3,000 words. **Pays $150-400.**

PHOTOS State availability. Captions, identification of subjects required. Offers $50-250/photo.

TIPS "Some previous experience or knowledge in groundwater/drilling/construction industry helpful. Published clips are a must."

SELLING & MERCHANDISING

THE AMERICAN SALESMAN

National Research Bureau, 320 Valley St., Burlington IA 52601. (319)752-5415. **Fax:** (319)752-3421. **E-mail:** contact@salestrainingandtechniques.com. **E-mail:** articles@salestrainingandtechniques.com. **Website:** www.salestrainingandtechniques.com. **80% freelance written.** Monthly magazine covering sales and marketing. *The American Salesman Magazine* is designed for sales professionals. Its primary objective is to provide informative articles that develop the attitudes, skills, and personal and professional qualities of sales representatives, allowing them to use more of their potential to increase productivity and achieve goals. Byline given. Publishes ms an average of 1 month after acceptance. Editorial lead time 1 month. Submit seasonal material 2 months in advance. Accepts queries by e-mail. Accepts simultaneous submissions. Sample copy free. Guidelines by e-mail. **NONFICTION** Needs personal experience. **Buys 24 mss/year.** Send complete ms. Length: 500-1,000 words. **Pays 4¢/word.**

BALLOONS & PARTIES MAGAZINE

PartiLife Publications, LLC, 65 Sussex St., Hackensack NJ 07601. (201)441-4224. **Fax:** (201)342-8118. **E-mail:** info@balloonsandparties.com. **Website:** www.balloonsandparties.com. **Contact:** Mark Zettler, publisher. **10% freelance written.** International trade journal published bi-monthly for professional party decorators and gift delivery businesses. *BALLOONS & Parties Magazine* is published 6 times/year by PartiLife Publications, LLC, for the balloon, party, and event fields. New product data, letters, mss, and photographs should be sent as "Attention: Editor" and should include sender's full name, address, and telephone number. SASE required on all editorial submissions. All submissions considered for publication unless otherwise noted. Unsolicited materials are submitted at sender's risk and *BALLOONS & Parties*/PartiLife Publications, LLC, assumes no responsibility for unsolicited materials. Estab. 1986. Circ. 7,000. Byline given. Pays on publication. No kill fee. Publishes ms an average of 3 months after acceptance. Submit seasonal material 6 months in advance. Accepts queries by mail, e-mail, fax, phone. Accepts simultaneous submissions. Responds in 6 weeks to queries. Sample copy for SAE with 9x12 envelope.
NONFICTION Needs essays, how-to, interview, new product, personal experience, photo feature, technical. **Buys 12 mss/year.** Send complete ms. Length: 500-1,500 words. **Pays $100-300 for assigned articles. Pays $50-200 for unsolicited articles.**
REPRINTS Send typed ms with rights for sale noted and information about when and where the material previously appeared. Length: up to 2,500 words. Pays 10¢/word.
PHOTOS Send photos. Captions, identification of subjects, model releases required. Reviews 2x2 transparencies, 3x5 prints. Buys all rights.

COLUMNS/DEPARTMENTS Problem Solver (small business issues); Recipes That Cook (centerpiece ideas with detailed how-to); 400-1,000 words. Send complete ms with photos.
TIPS "Show unusual, lavish, and outstanding examples of balloon sculpture, design and decorating, and other craft projects. Offer specific how-to information. Be positive and motivational in style."

CASUAL LIVING MAGAZINE

Progresive Business Media/Today Group, 7025 Albert Pick Rd., Suite 200, Greensboro NC 27409. (336)605-1122. **Fax:** (336)605-1143. **E-mail:** wgoodson@casualliving.com. **Website:** www.casualliving.com. **Contact:** Waynette Goodson, editorial director. **10% freelance written.** Monthly magazine covering outdoor furniture and accessories, barbecue grills, spas, and more. *Casual Living* is a trade only publication for the casual furnishings and related industries, published monthly. Writes about new products, trends, and casual furniture retailers, plus industry news. Estab. 1958. Circ. 10,000. Pays on publication. Publishes ms an average of 1-2 months after acceptance. Editorial lead time 1-2 months. Submit seasonal material 2 months in advance. Accepts queries by mail, e-mail. Accepts simultaneous submissions. Responds in 2 weeks to queries. Sample copy available online.
NONFICTION Needs how-to, interview. **Buys 20 mss/year.** Query with published clips. Length: 300-1,000 words. **Pays $300-700.**
PHOTOS Contact: Alexa Boschini, editorial assistant. Identification of subjects required. Reviews GIF/JPEG files. Negotiates payment individually. Buys all rights.

CONSUMER GOODS TECHNOLOGY

Edgell Communications, 4 Middlebury Blvd., Randolph NJ 07869. (973)607-1354. **Fax:** (973)607-1395. **E-mail:** arajagopal@edgellmail.com. **Website:** www.consumergoods.edgl.com. **Contact:** Alarice Rajagopal, editor. **40% freelance written.** Monthly tabloid benchmarking business technology performance. Estab. 1987. Circ. 25,000. Byline given. Pays on publication. No kill fee. Publishes ms an average of 2 months after acceptance. Editorial lead time 3 months. Accepts queries by e-mail. Accepts simultaneous submissions. Sample copy available online. Guidelines by e-mail.

NONFICTION Needs essays, expose, interview. **Buys 60 mss/year.** Query with published clips. Length: 700-1,900 words. **Pays $600-1,200.**

PHOTOS Identification of subjects, model releases required. Negotiates payment individually. Buys all rights.

COLUMNS/DEPARTMENTS Columns 400-750 words—featured columnists. **Buys 4 mss/year.** Query with published clips. **Pays 75¢-$1/word.**

TIPS "All stories in *Consumer Goods Technology* are told through the voice of the consumer goods executive. We only quote VP-level or C-level CG executives. No vendor quotes. We're always on the lookout for freelance talent. We look in particular for writers with an in-depth understanding of the business issues faced by consumer goods firms and the technologies that are used by the industry to address those issues successfully. 'Bits and bytes' tech writing is not sought; our focus is on benchmarketing the business technology performance of CG firms, CG executives, CG vendors, and CG vendor products. Our target reader is tech-savvy, CG C-level decision maker. We write to, and about, our target reader."

DIRECT SELLING NEWS

Video Plus, 5800 Democracy Drive, Plano TX 75024. **E-mail:** tday@directsellingnews.com. **Website:** www.directsellingnews.com. **Contact:** Teresa Day, editorial director. **20% freelance written.** Monthly magazine covering direct selling/network marketing industry. Though we are a business publication, we prefer feature-style writing rather than a newsy approach. Circ. 6,000. Byline given. Pays 30 days after publication. Publishes ms an average of 1-2 months after acceptance. Editorial lead time 3 months. Submit seasonal material 3 months in advance. Accepts queries by e-mail. Accepts simultaneous submissions. Responds in 3 weeks to queries. Sample copy available online.

NONFICTION Needs general interest, how-to. Query. Length: 1,500-3,000 words. **Pays 50¢-$1/word.**

GIFTWARE NEWS

704 N. Wells St., Chicago IL 60654. (312)849-2220. **Fax:** (312)849-2174. **E-mail:** giftwarenews@talcott.com. **E-mail:** dfields@talcott.com. **Website:** www.giftwarenews.com. **Contact:** Dayna Fields, managing editor. **20% freelance written.** Monthly magazine covering gifts, collectibles, and tabletops for giftware retailers. "*Giftware News* is designed and written for those professionals involved in the retail giftware

industry. *Giftware News* serves gift stores, stationary stores, department stores, as well as other retail outlets selling giftware, stationary, party and paper, tabletop, and decorative accessories. *Giftware News* is unique in the industry with an abundance of information, a wealth of product photography, outstanding graphic design, and high-quality printing that all combine with *Giftware News*' digital products to result in a package that is unmatched by any other giftware publication." Estab. 1976. Circ. 21,000. Byline given. Pays on publication. No kill fee. Publishes ms an average of 2 months after acceptance. Submit seasonal material 6 months in advance. Accepts queries by mail, e-mail. Accepts simultaneous submissions. Responds in 2 months to mss. Sample copy: $8.

NONFICTION Needs how-to, new product. **Buys 20 mss/year.** Send complete ms. Length: 1,500-2,000 words. **Pays $400-500 for assigned articles. Pays $200-300 for unsolicited articles.**

PHOTOS Send photos. Identification of subjects required. Reviews 4x5 transparencies, 5x7 prints, electronic images. Offers no additional payment for photos accepted with ms.

COLUMNS/DEPARTMENTS Stationery, gift-baskets, collectibles, holiday, merchandise, tabletop, wedding market and display—all for the gift retailer. Length: 1,500-2,500 words. **Buys 10 mss/year.** Send complete ms. **Pays $100-250.**

TIPS "We are not looking so much for general journalists but rather experts in particular fields who can also write."

INCENTIVE

Northstar Travel Media LLC, 100 Lighting Way, Secaucus NJ 07094. (646)380-6247; (646)380-6251. **E-mail:** valonzo@ntmllc.com; apalmer@successfulmeetings.com. **Website:** www.incentivemag.com. **Contact:** Vincent Alonzo, editor in chief; Alex Palmer, managing editor. Monthly magazine covering sales promotion and employee motivation: managing and marketing through motivation. Estab. 1905. Circ. 41,000. Byline given. Pays on acceptance. No kill fee. Publishes ms an average of 3 months after acceptance. Accepts queries by mail, e-mail. Accepts simultaneous submissions. Responds in 1 month to queries; in 2 months to mss. Sample copy for SAE with 9x12 envelope.

NONFICTION Needs general interest, how-to, interview, travel, corporate case studies. **Buys 48 mss/**

year. Query with published clips. Length: 1,000-2,000 words. **Pays $250-700 for assigned articles. Does not pay for unsolicited articles.**

REPRINTS Send tearsheet and information about when and where the material previously appeared. Pays 50% of the amount paid for an original article.

PHOTOS Send photos. Identification of subjects required. Reviews contact sheets, transparencies. Offers some additional payment for photos accepted with ms.

TIPS "Read the publication, then query."

MIDWEST MEETINGS®

Hennen Publishing, 302 Sixth St. W., Suite A, Brookings SD 57006. (605)692-9559. **Fax:** (605)692-9031. **E-mail:** info@midwestmeetings.com; editor@midwestmeetings.com. **Website:** www.midwestmeetings.com. **Contact:** Randy Hennen. **20% freelance written.** Quarterly magazine covering meetings/conventions industry. "We provide information and resources to meeting/convention planners with a Midwest focus." Estab. 1996. Circ. 28,500. Byline given. Pays on acceptance. Publishes ms an average of 5 months after acceptance. Editorial lead time 3 months. Submit seasonal material 3 months in advance. Accepts queries by e-mail. Accepts simultaneous submissions. Sample copy free. Guidelines by e-mail.

NONFICTION Needs essays, general interest, historical, how-to, humor, interview, personal experience, travel. Does not want marketing pieces related to specific hotels/meeting facilities. **Buys 15-20 mss/year.** Send complete ms. Length: 500-1,000 words. **Pays 5-50¢/word.**

PHOTOS Send photos. Captions, identification of subjects and permission statements/photo releases required. Reviews JPEG/EPS/TIF files (300 dpi). Offers no additional payment for photos accepted with ms. Buys one time rights.

TIPS "If you were a meeting/event planner, what information would help you perform your job better? We like lots of quotes from industry experts, insider tips, personal experience stories, etc. If you're not sure, e-mail the editor."

NICHE

The Rosen Group, 3000 Chestnut Ave., Suite 112, Baltimore MD 21211. (410)889-3093, ext. 231. **Fax:** (410)243-7089. **E-mail:** hoped@rosengrp.com. **Website:** www.nichemagazine.com. **Contact:** Hope Daniels, editorial director. **50% freelance written.** Quarterly trade magazine for the progressive craft gallery retailer. Each issue includes retail gallery profiles, store design trends, management techniques, financial information, and merchandising strategies for small business owners, as well as articles about craft artists and craft mediums. Estab. 1988. Circ. 15,000. Byline given. Pays on publication. No kill fee. Publishes ms an average of 6-9 months after acceptance. Editorial lead time 9 months. Submit queries for seasonal material 1 year in advance. Accepts queries by e-mail. Accepts simultaneous submissions. Responds in 4-6 weeks to queries; 3 months to mss. Sample copy for $3.

NONFICTION Needs interview. **Buys 15-20 mss/year.** Query with published clips. **Pays $150-300.**

PHOTOS Send photos. Captions required. Reviews e-images only. Negotiates payment individually.

COLUMNS/DEPARTMENTS Retail Details (short items at the front of the book, general retail information); Artist Profiles (short biographies of American Craft Artists); Retail Resources (including book/video/seminar reviews and educational opportunities pertaining to retailers). Query with published clips. **Pays $25-100 per item.**

O&A MARKETING NEWS

KAL Publications, Inc., 559 S. Harbor Blvd., Suite A, Anaheim CA 92805-4525. (714)563-9300. **Fax:** (714)563-9310. **E-mail:** kathy@kalpub.com. **Website:** www.kalpub.com. **3% freelance written.** Bimonthly tabloid. *O&A Marketing News* is editorially directed to people engaged in the distribution, merchandising, installation, and servicing of gasoline, oil, TBA, quick lube, carwash, convenience store, alternative fuel, and automotive aftermarket products in the 13 Western states. Estab. 1966. Circ. 7,500. Byline sometimes given. Pays on publication. No kill fee. Publishes ms an average of 2 months after acceptance. Editorial lead time 1 month. Submit seasonal material 1 month in advance. Accepts queries by mail, e-mail, fax. Accepts simultaneous submissions. Responds in 2 months. Sample copy for SASE with 9x13 envelope and 10 first-class stamps.

NONFICTION Needs interview, photo feature, industry news. Does not want anything that doesn't pertain to the petroleum marketing industry in the 13 Western states. **Buys 35 mss/year.** Send complete ms. Length: 100-500 words. **Pays $1.25/column inch.**

PHOTOS State availability of or send photos. Captions, identification of subjects required. Reviews contact sheets, 4x6 prints, digital images. Offers $5/photo. Buys electronic rights.

COLUMNS/DEPARTMENTS Nevada News (petroleum marketing news in state of Nevada). **Buys 7 mss/year.** Send complete ms. **Pays $1.25/column inch.**

FILLERS Needs gags, short humor. **Buys 7 mss/year.** Length: 1-200 words. **Pays per column inch.**

TIPS "Seeking Western industry news pertaining to the petroleum marketing industry. It can be something simple—like a new gas station or quick lube opening. News from 'outlying' states such as Montana, Idaho, Wyoming, New Mexico, and Hawaii is always needed—but any timely, topical news-oriented stories will also be considered."

OPERATIONS & FULFILLMENT

Primedia, Inc., 761 Main Ave, Second Floor, Norwalk CT 06851. (203)358-4106. **E-mail:** dforte@accessintel.com. **Website:** www.opsandfulfillment.com. **Contact:** Daniela Forte, content manager. **25% freelance written.** Monthly magazine covering catalog/direct mail operations. *Operations & Fulfillment (O&F)* is a monthly publication that offers practical solutions for catalog online, and direct response operations management. The magazine covers such critical areas as material handling, bar coding, facility planning, transportation, call centers, warehouse management, information systems, online fulfillment and human resources. Estab. 1993. Circ. 17,600. Pays on publication. No kill fee. Publishes ms an average of 2 months after acceptance. Editorial lead time 2 months. Accepts queries by mail, e-mail, phone. Accepts simultaneous submissions. Responds in 1 week to queries. Sample copy and writer's guidelines free.

NONFICTION Needs book excerpts, how-to, interview, new product, technical. **Buys 4-6 mss/year.** Query with published clips. Length: 2,500-3,000 words. **Pays $1,000-1,800.**

PHOTOS In addition to the main article, you must include at least one sidebar of about 400 words that contains a detailed example or case study of how a direct-to-customer catalog company implements or benefits from the process you're writing about; a check list or set of practical guidelines (i.e., Twelve Ways to Ship Smarter) that describe how to implement what you suggest in the article; supporting materials such as flow charts, graphs, diagrams, illustrations and photographs (these must be clearly labeled and foot-

noted); and an author biography of no more than 75 words. Send photos. Captions, identification of subjects required.

TIPS Writers need some knowledge of the direct-to-customer industry. They should be able to deal clearly with highly technical material and provide attention to detail and painstaking research.

PRODUCE RETAILER

Vance Publishing Corp., 10901 W. 84th Ter., Suite 200, Lenexa KS 66214. (913)438-0603; (512)906-0733. **E-mail:** PamelaR@produceretailer.com; treyes@produceretailer.com. **Website:** produceretailer.com. **Contact:** Pamela Riemenschneider, editor; Tony Reyes, art director. **10% freelance written.** Monthly magazine. "*Produce Merchandising* is the only monthly journal on the market that is dedicated solely to produce merchandising information for retailers. Our purpose is to provide information about promotions, merchandising, and operations in the form of ideas and examples." Estab. 1988. Circ. 12,000. Byline given. Pays on acceptance. No kill fee. Publishes ms an average of 3 months after acceptance. Editorial lead time 3 months. Accepts queries by mail. Accepts simultaneous submissions. Responds in 2 weeks to queries. Sample copy free.

NONFICTION Needs how-to, interview, new product, photo feature, technical. **Buys 48 mss/year.** Query with published clips. Length: 1,000-1,500 words. **Pays $200-600.**

PHOTOS State availability of or send photos. Captions, identification of subjects, model releases required. Reviews color slides and 3x5 or larger prints. Offers no additional payment for photos accepted with ms. Buys all rights.

COLUMNS/DEPARTMENTS Contact: Contact editor for a specific assignment. **Buys 30 mss/year.** Query with published clips. **Pays $200-450.**

TIPS Send in clips and contact the editor with specific story ideas. Story topics are typically outlined up to a year in advance.

SMART RETAILER

Emmis Communications, P.O. Box 5000, N7528 Aanstad Rd., Iola WI 54945. (800)331-0038. **Fax:** (715)445-4053. **E-mail:** danb@jonespublishing.com. **Website:** www.smart-retailer.com. **Contact:** Dan Brownell, editor. **50% freelance written.** Magazine published 7 times/year covering independent retail, gift, and home decor. *Smart Retailer* is a trade publication for independent retailers of gifts and home accents. Estab. 1993. Circ. 32,000. Byline given. Pays 1 month after acceptance of final ms. Offers $50 kill fee. Publishes ms an average of 4-6 months after acceptance. Editorial lead time 4-6 months. Submit seasonal material 8-10 months in advance. Accepts queries by mail, e-mail, fax. Accepts simultaneous submissions. Usually responds in 4-6 weeks (only if accepted). Sample articles are available on website. Guidelines by e-mail.

NONFICTION Needs how-to, interview, new product, finance, legal, marketing, small business. No fiction, poetry, fillers, photos, artwork, or profiles of businesses, unless queried and first assigned. **Buys 20 mss/year.** Send complete ms, with résumé and published clips to: Writers Query, *Smart Retailer*. Length: 1,000-2,500 words. **Pays $275-500 for assigned articles. Pays $200-350 for unsolicited articles.** Limit agreed upon in advance.

COLUMNS/DEPARTMENTS Display & Design (store design and product display), 1,500 words; Retailer Profile (profile of retailer, assigned only), 1,800 words; Vendor Profile (profile of manufacturer, assigned only), 1,200 words; Technology (Internet, computer-related articles as applies to small retailers), 1,500 words; Marketing (marketing ideas and advice as applies to small retailers), 1,500 words; Finance (financial tips and advice as applies to small retailers), 1,500 words; Legal (legal tips and advice as applies to small retailers), 1,500 words; Employees (tips and advice on hiring, firing, and working with employees as applies to small retailers), 1,500 words. **Buys 15 mss/year.** Query with published clips or send complete ms. **Pays $250-350.**

TRAVEL GOODS SHOWCASE

Travel Goods Association, 301 North Harrison St., #412, Princeton NJ 08540. (877)842-1938. **Fax:** (877)842-1938. **E-mail:** info@travel-goods.org; cathy@travel-goods.org. **Website:** www.travel-goods. org. **Contact:** Cathy Hays. **5-10% freelance written.** Magazine published quarterly. *Travel Goods Showcase*, the largest trade magazine devoted to travel products, contains articles for retailers, dealers, manufacturers, and suppliers about luggage, business cases, personal leather goods, handbags, and accessories. Special articles report on trends in fashion, promotions, selling and marketing techniques, industry statistics, and other educational and promotional improvements and advancements. Estab. 1975. Circ. 21,000.

Byline given. Pays on acceptance. Offers $50 kill fee. Publishes ms an average of 2 months after acceptance. Editorial lead time 3 months. Submit seasonal material 2 months in advance. Accepts queries by mail, e-mail. Accepts simultaneous submissions. Responds in 2 weeks to queries; 1 month to mss. Sample copy and writer's guidelines free.

NONFICTION Needs interview, new product, technical, travel, retailer profiles with photos. No manufacturer profiles. **Buys 3 mss/year.** Query with published clips. Length: 1,200-1,600 words. **Pays $200-400.**

VM+SD

ST Media Group International, 11262 Cornell Park Dr., Cincinnati OH 45242. (513)421-2050. **Fax:** (513)421-5144. **E-mail:** carly.hagedon@stmediagroup. com; kaileigh.peyton@stmediagroup.com. **Website:** www.vmsd.com. **Contact:** Carly Hagedon, managing editor; Kaileigh Peyton, associate editor. **10% freelance written.** Monthly magazine covering retailing store design, store planning, visual merchandising, brand marketing. Estab. 1872. Circ. 20,000. Byline given. Pays on acceptance. Offers $100 kill fee. Publishes ms an average of 1-2 months after acceptance. Editorial lead time 2-3 months. Submit seasonal material 3-4 months in advance. Accepts queries by e-mail. Accepts simultaneous submissions. Sample copy free. Guidelines available online and by e-mail.

NONFICTION **Buys 2-3 mss/year.** Query with details of project, including a press release if available, high-resolution, professional photos, the date the store opened, and any other information available. Length: 500-1,000 words. **Pays $400-1,000.**

PHOTOS Send photos. Reviews GIF/JPEG files. Negotiates payment individually. Buys one-time rights.

COLUMNS/DEPARTMENTS Editorial calendar available online. **Buys 5-6 mss/year.** Query. **Pays $500-750.**

TIPS "We need to see a demonstrated understanding of our industry, its issues and major players; strong reporting and interviewing skills are also important. Merely facile writing is not enough for us."

SPORT TRADE

⊛⊛ AQUATICS INTERNATIONAL

Hanley Wood, LLC, 6222 Wilshire Blvd., Suite 600, Los Angeles CA 90048. **Fax:** (323)801-4972. **E-mail:**

jmcclain@hanleywood.com. **Website:** www.aquatic-sintl.com. **Contact:** Joanne McClain, editor-in-chief. Magazine published 10 times/year covering public swimming pools and waterparks. Devoted to the commercial and public swimming pool industries. The magazine provides detailed information on designing, building, maintaining, promoting, managing, programming, and outfitting aquatics facilities. Estab. 1989. Circ. 30,000. Byline given. Pays on publication. No kill fee. Publishes ms an average of 3 months after acceptance. Editorial lead time 3 months. Accepts simultaneous submissions. Responds in 1 month to queries. Sample copy for $10.50.

NONFICTION Needs how-to, interview, technical. **Buys 6 mss/year.** Send query letter with published clips/samples. Length: 1,500-2,500 words. **Pays $525 for assigned articles.**

COLUMNS/DEPARTMENTS Pays $250.

ARROWTRADE MAGAZINE

Arrow Trade Publishing Corp., 3479 409th Ave. NW, Braham MN 55006. (320)396-3473. **Fax:** (320)396-3206. **E-mail:** info@arrowtrademag.com. **Website:** www.arrowtrademag.com. **Contact:** Tim Dehn, editorial. **80% freelance written.** Bimonthly magazine covering the archery industry. Readers are interested in articles that help them operate their businesses better. They are primarily owners or managers of sporting goods stores and archery pro shops. Estab. 1996. Circ. 13,000. Byline given. Pays on publication. No kill fee. Publishes ms an average of 2 months after acceptance. Editorial lead time 2 months. Accepts queries by mail, e-mail, fax. Accepts simultaneous submissions. Responds in 2 weeks to queries. Responds in 2 weeks to mss. Sample copy for SAE with 9x12 envelope and 10 First-Class stamps.

NONFICTION Needs interview, new product. "Generic business articles won't work for our highly specialized audience." **Buys 24 mss/year.** Query with published clips. Length: 3,400-4,800 words. **Pays $350-550.**

PHOTOS Send photos. Captions required. Must provide digital photos on CD or DVD or sent to FTP site. Offers no additional payment for photos accepted with ms.

TIPS "Our readers are hungry for articles that help them decide what to stock and how to do a better job selling or servicing it. Articles needed typically fall into 1 of these categories: business profiles on outstanding retailers, manufacturers, or distributors; equipment articles that cover categories of gear, citing trends in the market, and detailing why products have been designed a certain way and what type of use they're best suited for; basic business articles that help dealers do a better job of promoting their business, managing their inventory, training their staff, etc. Good interviewing skills are a must, as especially in the equipment articles we like to see a minimum of 6 sources."

BOATING INDUSTRY

EPG Media, 3300 Fernbrook Lane N., Suite 200, Plymouth MN 55447. (763)383-4400. **E-mail:** jonathan.sweet@boatingindustry.com. **Website:** www.boatingindustry.com. **Contact:** Jonathan Sweet, editor-in-chief. **Less than 10% freelance written.** Bimonthly magazine covering recreational marine industry management. "We write for those in the industry—not the consumer. Our subject is the business of boating. All of our articles must be analytical and predictive, telling our readers where the industry is going, rather than where it's been." Estab. 1929. Circ. 23,000. Byline given. Pays on publication. Offers 50% kill fee. Publishes ms an average of 2 months after acceptance. Editorial lead time 2 months. Submit seasonal material 2 months in advance. Accepts queries by mail, e-mail. Accepts simultaneous submissions. Responds in 1 month to queries. Sample copy available online. Guidelines free.

NONFICTION **Buys 30 mss/year.** Query with published clips. Length: 250-2,500 words. **Pays $25-250.**

PHOTOS State availability. Captions, identification of subjects required. Reviews 2x2 transparencies, 4x6 prints. Negotiates payment individually. Buys one-time rights.

BOWLING CENTER MANAGEMENT

Luby Publishing, 122 S. Michigan Ave., Suite 1806, Chicago IL 60603. (312)341-1110. **Fax:** (312)341-1180. **E-mail:** mikem@lubypublishing.com. **Website:** www.bcmmag.com. **Contact:** Michael Mazek, editor. **50% freelance written.** Monthly magazine covering bowling centers, family entertainment. *Bowling Center Management* is the industry's leading business publication and offical trade magazien of the Bowling Proprietor's Association of America. Readers are looking for novel ways to draw more customers. Accordingly, the magazine looks for articles that effectively present such ideas. Estab. 1995. Circ. 12,000. Byline given. Pays on acceptance. Publishes ms an average of 3 months after acceptance. Editorial lead time 3 months. Submit seasonal material 6 months in advance. Accepts queries by e-mail. Accepts simultaneous submissions. Responds in 2-3 weeks to queries. Sample copy for $10.

NONFICTION Needs how-to, interview. **Buys 10-20 mss/year.** Query. Length: 750-1,500 words. **Pays $150-350.**

TIPS "Send a solid, clever query by e-mail with knowledge and interest in an industry trend."

GOLF COURSE MANAGEMENT

Golf Course Superintendents Association of America (GCSAA), 1421 Research Park Dr., Lawrence KS 66049. (785)832-4456. **Fax:** (785)832-3665. **E-mail:** shollister@gcsaa.org; mhirt@gcsaa.org; tcarson@gcsaa.org. **Website:** www.gcsaa.org. **Contact:** Scott Hollister, editor in chief; Megan Hirt, managing editor; Teresa Carson, science editor. **50% freelance written.** Monthly magazine covering the golf course superintendent. *GCM* helps the golf course superintendent become more efficient in all aspects of their job. Estab. 1924. Circ. 40,000. Byline given. Pays on acceptance. No kill fee. Publishes ms an average of 6 months after acceptance. Editorial lead time 6 months. Submit seasonal material 6 months in advance. Accepts queries by e-mail. Accepts simultaneous submissions. Responds in 3 weeks to queries; in 1 month to mss. Sample copy free. Guidelines available online.

NONFICTION Needs how-to, interview. No articles about playing golf. **Buys 40 mss/year.** Query for either feature, research, or superintendent article. Submit electronically, preferably as e-mail attachment. Send one-page synopsis or query for feature article to Scott Hollister. For research articles, submit to Teresa Carson. If you are a superintendent, contact Megan Hirt. Length: 1,500-2,500 words. **Pays $400-600.**

PHOTOS Send photos. Identification of subjects required. Offers no additional payment for photos accepted with ms. Buys all rights.

TIPS "Writers should have prior knowledge of golf course maintenance, agronomy and turfgrass science, and the overall profession of the golf course superintendent."

INTERNATIONAL BOWLING INDUSTRY

B2B Media, Inc., 12655 Ventura Blvd., Studio City CA 91604. (818)789-2695. **Fax:** (818)789-2812. **E-mail:** info@bowlingindustry.com. **Website:** www.bowl-ingindustry.com. **40% freelance written.** Online monthly magazine covering ownership and management of bowling centers (alleys) and pro shops. *IBI* publishes articles in all phases of bowling center and bowling pro shop ownership and management, among them finance, promotion, customer service, relevant technology, architecture, and capital improvement. The magazine also covers the operational areas of bowling centers and pro shops such as human resources, food and beverage, corporate and birthday parties, ancillary attractions (go-karts, gaming and the like), and retailing. Articles must have strong how-to emphasis. They must be written specifically in terms of the bowling industry, although content may be applicable more widely. Estab. 1993. Circ. 10,200. Byline given. Pays on acceptance. Offers $50 kill fee. Publishes ms an average of 3 months after acceptance. Submit seasonal material 3 months in advance. Accepts queries by mail, e-mail, fax. Accepts simultaneous submissions. Responds in 2 weeks to queries. Responds in 1 month to mss. Sample copy for #10 SASE. Guidelines free.

NONFICTION Needs how-to, interview, new product, technical. **Buys 40 mss/year.** Send complete ms. Length: 1,100-1,400 words. **Pays $250.**

PHOTOS State availability. Identification of subjects required. Reviews JPEG photos. Offers no additional payment for photos accepted with ms. Buys all rights.

TIPS "Please supply writing samples, applicable list of credits, and bio."

NSGA RETAIL FOCUS

National Sporting Goods Association, 1601 Feehanville Dr., Suite 300, Mt. Prospect IL 60056-6035. (847)296-6742. **Fax:** (847)391-9827. **E-mail:** info@nsga.org. **Website:** www.nsga.org. **Contact:** Bruce Hammond. **20% freelance written. Works with a small number of new/unpublished writers each year.** Bimonthly magazine. *NSGA Retail Focus* serves as a bimonthly trade journal for sporting goods retailers who are members of the association. Estab. 1948. Circ. 2,000. Byline given. Pays on publication. Offers kill fee. Publishes ms an average of 1 month after acceptance. Submit seasonal material 6 months in advance. Accepts queries by e-mail. Accepts simultaneous submissions. Sample copy for sae with 9x12 envelope and 5 first-class stamps.

NONFICTION Needs interview. No articles written without sporting goods retail business people in mind as the audience. In other words, no generic articles sent to several industries. **Buys 12 mss/year.** Query with published clips. **Pays $150-300.**

PHOTOS State availability. Reviews high-resolution, digital images. Payment negotiable. Buys one-time rights.

COLUMNS/DEPARTMENTS Personnel Management (succinct tips on hiring, motivating, firing, etc.); Sales Management (in-depth tips to improve sales force performance); Retail Management (detailed explanation of merchandising/inventory control); Store Design; Visual Merchandising, all 1,500 words. **Buys 12 columns/year. mss/year.** Query. **Pays $150-300.**

POOL & SPA NEWS

Hanley Wood, LLC, 6222 Wilshire Blvd., Suite 600, Los Angeles CA 90048. (323)801-4972. **Fax:** (323)801-4986. **E-mail:** jmcclain@hanleywood.com. **Website:** http://poolspanews.com. **Contact:** Joanne McClain, editor. **15% freelance written.** Semimonthly magazine covering the swimming pool and spa industry for builders, retail stores, and service firms. Estab. 1960. Circ. 16,300. Pays on publication. No kill fee. Publishes ms an average of 2 months after acceptance. Accepts queries by mail, e-mail. Accepts simultaneous submissions. Responds in 1 month to queries. Sample copy for $5 and 9x12 SAE and 11 first-class stamps.

NONFICTION Needs interview, technical. Send résumé with published clips. Length: 500-2,000 words. **Pays $150-550.**

REPRINTS Send typed ms with rights for sale noted and information about when and where the material previously appeared. Payment varies.

PHOTOS Payment varies.

COLUMNS/DEPARTMENTS Payment varies.

REFEREE

Referee Enterprises, Inc., 2017 Lathrop Ave., Racine WI 53405. (800)733-6100. **Fax:** (262)632-5460. **E-mail:** submissions@referee.com. **Website:** www.referee.com. **Contact:** Julie Sternberg, managing editor. **75% freelance written.** Monthly magazine covering sports officiating. *Referee* is a magazine for and read by sports officials of all kinds with a focus on baseball, basketball, football, softball, and soccer officiating. Estab. 1976. Circ. 40,000. Byline given. Pays on acceptance. Offers kill fee. Kill fee negotiable. Publishes ms an average of 6 months after acceptance. Editorial lead time 6 months. Accepts queries by mail, e-mail. Accepts simultaneous submissions. Responds in 2 weeks to queries; 1 month to mss. Sample copy with #10 SASE. Guidelines online.

NONFICTION Needs book excerpts, essays, historical, how-to, humor, interview, opinion, photo feature, technical. "We don't want to see articles with themes not relating to sport officiating. General sports articles, although of interest to us, will not be published." **Buys 40 mss/year.** Query with published clips. Length: 500-3,500 words. **Pays $50-400.**

PHOTOS State availability. Identification of subjects required. Reviews photos mailed on CD or DVD. Offers $35-40 per photo. Purchase of rights negotiable.

TIPS "Query first and be persistent. We may not like your idea, but that doesn't mean we won't like your next one. Professionalism pays off."

SKI AREA MANAGEMENT

Beardsley Publications, SAM, P.O. Box 644, Woodbury CT 06798. (203)263-0888. **Fax:** (203)266-0452. **E-mail:** donna@saminfo.com; jenn@saminfo.com. **Website:** www.saminfo.com. **Contact:** Donna Jacobs. **85% freelance written.** Bimonthly magazine covering everything involving the management and development of ski resorts. Report on new ideas, developments, marketing, and regulations with regard to ski and snowboard resorts. Estab. 1962. Circ. 4,500. Byline given. Pays on publication. Offers kill fee. Offers kill fee. Editorial lead time 2 months. Submit seasonal material 3 months in advance. Accepts queries by mail, e-mail. Accepts simultaneous submissions. Responds in 2 weeks to queries. Sample copy for 9x12 SAE with $3 postage or online. Guidelines for #10 SASE.

NONFICTION Needs historical, how-to, interview, new product, opinion, personal experience, technical. Does not want anything that does not specifically pertain to resort operations, management, or financing. **Buys 25-40 mss/year.** Query. Length: 500-2,500 words. **Pays $50-400.**

PHOTOS Send photos. Identification of subjects required. Reviews transparencies, prints. Offers no additional payment for photos accepted with ms. Buys one-time rights or all rights.

TIPS "Know what you are writing about. We are read by people dedicated to skiing and snowboarding and to making the resort experience the best possible for their customers. It is a trade publication read by professionals."

STONE, QUARRY & MINING

☼ CANADIAN MINING JOURNAL

BIG Mining Group, 38 Lesmill Rd., Unit 2, Toronto ON M3B 2T5 Canada. (416)510-6742. **E-mail:** editor@ canadianminingjournal.com. **Website:** www.canadianminingjournal.com. **Contact:** Marilyn Scales, interim editor. **5% freelance written.** Magazine covering mining and mineral exploration by Canadian companies. *Canadian Mining Journal* provides articles and information of practical use to those who work in the technical, administrative, and supervisory aspects of exploration, mining, and processing in the Canadian mineral exploration and mining industry. Estab. 1882. Circ. 10,000. Byline given. Pays on publication. No kill fee. Publishes ms an average of 3 months after acceptance. Submit seasonal material 3 months in advance. Accepts queries by mail, e-mail, phone. Accepts simultaneous submissions. Responds in 1 week to queries; in 1 month to mss.

NONFICTION Needs new product, personal experience, technical. **Buys 6 mss/year.** Query with published clips. Length: 500-1,400 words. **Pays $100-600.**

PHOTOS JPG with 300 dpi. State availability. Photos require caption, identification of subjects. Reviews 4x6 prints or high-resolution files. Negotiates payment individually. Buys one-time rights.

COLUMNS/DEPARTMENTS Guest editorial (opinion on controversial subject related to mining industry), 600 words. **Buys 3 mss/year.** Query with published clips.

TIPS "We need articles about mine sites that would be expensive/difficult for staff to reach. We also need to know the writer is competent to understand and describe the technology in an interesting way."

CONTEMPORARY STONE & TILE DESIGN

Business News Publishing Media, 210 Route 4 East, Suite 203, Paramus NJ 07652. (201)291-9001, ext. 8611. **Fax:** (201)291-9002. **E-mail:** jennifer@stoneworld.com. **Website:** www.stoneworld.com. **Contact:** Jennifer Richinelli, editor. Quarterly magazine covering the full range of stone and tile design and architecture—from classic and historic spaces to current projects. Estab. 1995. Circ. 21,000. Byline given. Pays on publication. No kill fee. Publishes ms an average of 3 months after acceptance. Submit seasonal material 6 months in advance. Accepts simultaneous submissions. Responds in 3 weeks to queries. Sample copy for $10.

NONFICTION Needs interview, photo feature. **Buys 8 mss/year.** Query with published clips. Length: 1,500-3,000 words. **Pays $6/column inch.**

PHOTOS State availability. Captions, identification of subjects required. Reviews transparencies, prints. Pays $10/photo accepted with ms. Buys one-time rights.

COLUMNS/DEPARTMENTS Upcoming Events (for the architecture and design community); Stone Classics (featuring historic architecture); question and answer session with a prominent architect or designer. Length: 1,500-2,000 words. **Pays $6/inch.**

TIPS "The visual aspect of the magazine is key, so architectural photography is a must for any story. Cover the entire project, but focus on the stonework or tile work and how it relates to the rest of the space. Architects are very helpful in describing their work and often provide excellent quotes. As a relatively new magazine, we are looking for freelance submissions and are open to new feature topics. This is a narrow subject, however, so it's a good idea to speak with an editor before submitting anything."

MINING PEOPLE MAGAZINE

Al Skinner, Inc., 629 Virginia St. W, P.O. Box 6247, Charleston WV 25362 Kanawha. (304)342-4129. **Fax:** (304)343-3124. **E-mail:** alskinner@ntelos.net; cpm@ ntelos.net. **Website:** www.miningpeople.org. **Contact:** Christina Karawan, managing editor; Al Skinner, editor. **50% freelance written.** Most stories are about people or historical—either narrative or biographical on all levels of coal and mining people, past and present—from mining execs down to grass roots miners. Most stories are upbeat—showing warmth of family or success from underground up! Estab. 1976. Circ. 12,300 hard copy, est. 26,000 digital. Byline given. Pays on publication. No kill fee. Publishes ms an average of 3 months after acceptance. Submit seasonal material 2 months in advance. Accepts queries by mail, e-mail, online submission form. Accepts simultaneous submissions. Responds in 3 months to mss. Sample copy for sae with 9x12 envelope and 10 first-class stamps.

NONFICTION Needs book excerpts, historical, humor, interview, personal experience, photo feature. Special issues: Calendar issue for more than 300 annual coal shows, association meetings, etc. (January); Surface Mining/Reclamation Award (July); Christmas in Coal Country (December). No poetry, fiction, or environmental attacks on the mining industry. **Buys 32 mss/year.** Query with published clips. Length: 750-2,500 words. **Pays $150-250.**

REPRINTS Send tearsheet and information about when and where the material previously appeared. Pays 50% of amount paid for an original article.

PHOTOS Send photos. Captions, identification of subjects required. Reviews contact sheets, transparencies, 5x7 prints. Buys one-time reprint rights.

COLUMNS/DEPARTMENTS Length: 300-500 words. Editorials—anything to do with current coal issues (nonpaid); Mine'ing Our Business (bull pen column—gossip—humorous anecdotes); Coal Show Coverage (freelance photojournalist coverage of any coal function across the US). **Buys 10 mss/year.** Query. **Pays $50.**

FILLERS Needs anecdotes. Length: 300 words. **Pays $35.**

TIPS "We are looking for good feature articles on coal professionals, companies—past and present, color slides (for possible cover use), and b&w photos to complement stories. Writers wanted to take photos and do journalistic coverage on coal events across the country. Slant stories more toward people and less on historical. More faces and names than old town, company store photos. Include more quotes from people who lived these moments! The following geographical areas are covered: North America and overseas."

PIT & QUARRY

Questex Media Group, 1360 E. Ninth St., Suite 1070, Cleveland OH 44114. (216)706-3711; (216)706-3747. **Fax:** (216)706-3710. **E-mail:** info@pitandquarry. com; kyanik@northcoastmedia.net. **Website:** www. pitandquarry.com. **Contact:** Kevin Yanik, managing editor. **10-20% freelance written.** Monthly magazine covering nonmetallic minerals, mining, and crushed stone. Audience has knowledge of construction-related markets, mining, minerals processing, etc. Estab. 1916. Circ. 23,000. Byline given. Pays on acceptance. No kill fee. Publishes ms an average of 2 months after acceptance. Editorial lead time 2 months. Accepts queries by e-mail. Accepts simultaneous submissions. Responds in 1 month to queries. Responds in 4 months to mss.

NONFICTION Needs how-to, interview, new product, technical. No humor or inspirational articles. **Buys 3-4 mss/year.** Query. Length: 2,000-2,500 words. **Pays $250-500 for assigned articles. Does not pay for unsolicited articles.**

PHOTOS State availability. Identification of subjects, model releases required. Offers no additional payment for photos accepted with ms. Buys one-time rights.

COLUMNS/DEPARTMENTS Brand New; Techwatch; E-business; Software Corner; Equipment Showcase. Length: 250-750 words. **Buys 5-6 mss/year.** Query. **Pays $250-300.**

TIPS "Be familiar with quarry operations (crushed stone or sand and gravel), as opposed to coal or metallic minerals mining. Know construction markets. We always need equipment-focused features on specific quarry operations."

TOY, NOVELTY & HOBBY

MODEL RETAILER

Kalmbach Publishing Co., 21027 Crossroads Circle, Waukesha WI 53187. (262)796-8776. **E-mail:** jreich@ kalmbach.com. **E-mail:** editor@modelretailer.com. **Website:** www.modelretailer.com. Elizabeth Nash, associate editor

Elizabeth Nash, associate editor; Monica Freitag, editorial associate. **Contact:** Jeff Reich, editor. **30% freelance written.** Monthly magazine. *Model Retailer* covers the business of hobby retailing, from financial and store management issues to product and industry trends. Our goal is to provide owners and managers with the tools and information they need to be successful retailers. Estab. 1987. Circ. 6,000. Byline given. Pays on acceptance. 25% kill fee. Publishes ms an average of 2 months after acceptance. Editorial lead time 3 months. Submit seasonal material 6 months in advance. Accepts queries by e-mail. Accepts simultaneous submissions. Sample copy free. Guidelines online.

NONFICTION Needs book excerpts, essays, how-to, interview, new product, nostalgic, opinion, profile, reviews. No articles that do not have a strong hobby or small retail component. **Buys 30-40 mss/year.** Query with published clips. "We welcome queries for feature articles and columns and the submission of articles sent on speculation. Queries and submissions accepted by e-mail only." Length: 800-1,600 words. **Pays $100-450.**

PHOTOS State availability. Captions, identification of subjects required. Reviews digital images. Negotiates payment individually. Buys one-time rights.

TRANSPORTATION

SCHOOL TRANSPORTATION NEWS

STN Media Co., P.O. Box 789, Redondo Beach CA 90277. (310)792-2226. **Fax:** (310)792-2231. **E-mail:** ryan@stnmedia.com; sean@stnmedia.com. **Website:** www.stnonline.com. **Contact:** Ryan Gray, editor in chief; Sean Gallagherean Gallagher, associate editor. **20% freelance written.** Monthly magazine covering school bus and pupil transportation industries in North America. Contributors to *School Transportation News* must have a basic understanding of K-12 education and automotive fleets and specifically of school buses. Articles cover such topics as manufacturing, operations, maintenance and routing software, GPS, security and legislative affairs. A familiarity with these principles is preferred. Additional industry information is available on website. New writers must perform some research of the industry or exhibit core competencies in the subject matter. Estab. 1991. Circ. 24,000. Byline given. Pays on publication. No kill fee. Editorial lead time 1-2 months. Submit seasonal material 3 months in advance. Accepts queries by e-mail. Accepts simultaneous submissions. Sample copy free. Guidelines free.

NONFICTION Needs book excerpts, general interest, historical, humor, inspirational, interview, new product, personal experience, photo feature, technical. Does not want strictly localized editorial. Wants articles that put into perspective the issues of the day. Query with published clips. Length: 600-1,200 words. **Pays $150-300.**

PHOTOS Contact: Sylvia Arroyo, managing editor. No Answer. Captions, model releases required. Reviews GIF/JPEG files. Offers $150-200/photo. Buys all rights.

COLUMNS/DEPARTMENTS Creative Special Report, Cover Story, Top Story; Book/Video Reviews (new programs/publications/training for pupil transporters), both 600 words. **Buys 40 mss/year.** Query with published clips. **Pays $150.**

TIPS "Potential freelancers should exhibit a basic proficiency in understanding school bus issues and demonstrate the ability to report on education, legislative

and business affairs, as well as a talent with feature writing. It would be helpful if the writer has previous contacts within the industry. Article pitches should be e-mailed only."

TRAVEL TRADE

CRUISE INDUSTRY NEWS

441 Lexington Ave., Suite 809, New York NY 10017. (212)986-1025. **Fax:** (212)986-1033. **E-mail:** oivind@cruiseindustrynews.com. **Website:** www.cruiseindustrynews.com. **Contact:** Oivind Mathisen, editor. **20% freelance written.** Quarterly magazine covering cruise shipping. Magazine about the business of cruise shipping for the industry, including cruise lines, shipyards, financial analysts, etc. Estab. 1991. Circ. 10,000. Byline given. Pays on acceptance or on publication. Offers 25% kill fee. Publishes ms an average of 4 months after acceptance. Editorial lead time 3 months. Accepts queries by mail. Accepts simultaneous submissions. Reponse time varies. Sample copy for $15. Guidelines for #10 SASE.

NONFICTION Needs interview, new product. No travel stories. **Buys more than 20 mss/year.** Query with published clips. Length: 500-1,500 words. **Pays $.50/word published.**

PHOTOS State availability. Pays $25-50/photo. Buys one-time rights.

LEISURE GROUP TRAVEL

Premier Tourism Marketing, 621 Plainfield Rd., Suite 406, Willowbrook IL 60527. (630)794-0696. **Fax:** (630)794-0652. **E-mail:** randy@ptmgroups.com. **E-mail:** editor@ptmgroups.com. **Website:** www.leisuregrouptravel.com. **Contact:** Randy Mink, managing editor. **35% freelance written.** Bimonthly magazine covering group travel. Covers destinations and editorial relevant to the group travel market. Estab. 1994. Circ. 15,012. Byline given. Pays on publication. No kill fee. Editorial lead time 6 months. Submit seasonal material 6 months in advance. Accepts queries by mail, e-mail. Accepts simultaneous submissions. Sample copy available online.

NONFICTION Needs travel. **Buys 75 mss/year.** Query with published clips. Length: 1,200-3,000 words. **Pays $0-1,000.**

SPECIALTY TRAVEL INDEX

Alpine Hansen, P.O. Box 458, San Anselmo CA 94979. (415)455-1643. **E-mail:** info@specialtytravel.com; aalpine@specialtytravel.com. **Website:** www.specialty-travel.com. **Contact:** Andy Alpine. **90% freelance written.** Semiannual magazine covering adventure and special interest travel. Estab. 1980. Circ. 35,000. Byline given. Pays on receipt and acceptance of all materials. No kill fee. Editorial lead time 3 month. Submit seasonal material 3 months in advance. Accepts queries by mail, e-mail. Accepts simultaneous submissions. Writer's guidelines on request.

NONFICTION Needs how-to, personal experience, photo feature, travel. **Buys 15 mss/year.** Query. Length: 1,250 words. **Pays $300 minimum.**

REPRINTS Send tearsheet. Pays 100% of amount paid for an original article.

PHOTOS State availability. Captions, identification of subjects required. Reviews EPS/TIFF files. Negotiates payment individually.

TIPS "Write about group travel and be both creative and factual. The articles should relate to both the travel agent booking the tour and the client who is traveling."

VETERINARY

ANIMAL SHELTERING

The Humane Society of the United States, P.O. Box 15276, North Hollywood CA 91615. (800)565-9226. **E-mail:** asm@humanesociety.org. **Website:** www. animalsheltering.org. **Contact:** Shevaun Brannigan, production/marketing manager; Carrie Allan, editor. **20% freelance written.** Magazine for animal care professionals and volunteers, dealing with animal welfare issues faced by animal shelters, animal control agencies, and rescue groups. Emphasis on news for the field and professional, hands-on work. Readers are shelter and animal control directors, kennel staff, field officers, humane investigators, animal control officers, animal rescuers, foster care volunteers, general volunteers, shelter veterinarians, and anyone concerned with local animal welfare issues. Estab. 1978. Circ. 6,000. Accepts simultaneous submissions. Sample copies are free; contact Shevaun Brannigan at sbrannigan@hsus.org. Guidelines available by e-mail.

NONFICTION Approximately 6-10 submissions published each year from non-staff writers; of those submissions, 50% are from writers new to the publication. **"Payment varies depending on length and complexity of piece. Longer features generally $400–600; short news pieces generally $200. We rarely take unsolicited work, so it's best to contact the editor with story ideas."**

REPRINTS "Aquires first publication rights. We also grant permission, with a credit to the magazine and writer, to readers who want to use the materials to educate their supporters, staff and volunteers. Contact asm@humanesociety.org for writers' guidelines."

PHOTOS Pays $150 for cover; $75 for inside.

TIPS "We almost always need good photos of people working with animals in an animal shelter or in the field. We do not use photos of individual dogs, cats, and other companion animals as often as we use photos of people working to protect, rescue or care for dogs, cats, and other companion animals."

VETERINARY ECONOMICS

8033 Flint St., Lenexa KS 66214. (800)255-6864. **Fax:** (913)871-3808. **E-mail:** dvmnews@advanstar.com. **Website:** veterinarybusiness.dvm360.com. **20% freelance written.** Monthly magazine covering veterinary practice management. "We address the business concerns and management needs of practicing veterinarians." Estab. 1960. Circ. 54,000. Byline given. Pays on publication. No kill fee. Publishes ms an average of 6 months after acceptance. Editorial lead time 3 months. Submit seasonal material 3 months in advance. Accepts queries by mail, e-mail. Accepts simultaneous submissions. Responds in 3 months to queries. Sample copy free. Guidelines available online.

NONFICTION Needs how-to, interview, personal experience. **Buys 24 mss/year.** Send complete ms. Length: 1,000-2,000 words. **Pays $40-350.**

PHOTOS Send photos. Captions, identification of subjects required. Reviews transparencies, prints. Offers no additional payment for photos accepted with ms. Buys one-time rights.

COLUMNS/DEPARTMENTS Practice Tips (easy, unique business tips), 250 words or fewer. Send complete ms. **Pays $40.**

TIPS "Among the topics we cover: veterinary hospital design, client relations, contractual and legal matters, investments, day-to-day management, marketing, personal finances, practice finances, personnel, collections, and taxes. We also cover news and issues within the veterinary profession; for example, articles might cover the effectiveness of Yellow Pages advertising, the growing number of women veterinarians, restrictive-covenant cases, and so on. Freelance writers are encouraged to submit proposals or outlines for articles on these topics. Most articles involve interviews with a nationwide sampling of veterinarians; we will provide the names and phone numbers if necessary. We accept only a small number of unsolicited mss each year; however, we do assign many articles to freelance writers. All material submitted by first-time contributors is read on speculation, and the review process usually takes 12-16 weeks. Our style is concise yet conversational, and all mss go through a fairly rigorous editing process. We encourage writers to provide specific examples to illustrate points made throughout their articles."

CONTESTS & AWARDS

The contests and awards listed in this section are arranged by subject. Nonfiction writers can turn immediately to nonfiction awards listed alphabetically by the name of the contest or award. The same is true for fiction writers, poets, playwrights and screenwriters, journalists, children's writers, and translators. You'll also find general book awards, fellowships offered by arts councils and foundations, and multiple category contests.

New contests and awards are announced in various writer's publications nearly every day. However, many lose their funding or fold, and sponsoring magazines go out of business just as often. **Contact names, entry fees,** and **deadlines** have been highlighted and set in bold type for your convenience.

To make sure you have all the information you need about a particular contest, always send a SASE to the contact person in the listing before entering a contest or check their website. The listings in this section are brief, and many contests have lengthy, specific rules and requirements that we could not include in our limited space. Often a specific entry form must accompany your submission.

When you receive a set of guidelines, you'll see some contests are not applicable to all writers. The writer's age, previous publication, geographic location, and length of the work are common matters of eligibility. Read the requirements to ensure you don't enter a contest for which you're not qualified.

Winning a contest or award can launch a successful writing career. Take a professional approach by doing a little extra research. Find out who the previous winner of the award was by investing in a sample copy of the magazine in which the prize-winning article, poem, or short story appeared. Attend the staged reading of an award-winning play. Your extra effort will be to your advantage in competing with writers who simply submit blindly.

PLAYWRITING & SCRIPTWRITING

10 MINUTE PLAY CONTEST & FESTIVAL

Weathervane Playhouse, 1301 Weathervane Lane, Akron OH 44313. (330)836-2626. **E-mail:** mycp@weathervaneplayhouse.com. **Website:** www.weathervaneplayhouse.com. **Contact:** Melanie YC Pepe, Artistic Director. Weathervane Community Playhouse produces high-quality live theater with volunteer artists, designers, and technicians under professional direction, provides education and training in theater arts and appreciation, and engages and entertains its audience and constituents to enrich the quality of life in Northeast Ohio. Weathervane shall be one of the foremost community-based playhouses in the country that serves a region through theater as evidenced by consistent excellence in high caliber, diverse, challenging theater productions that compel our community to attend, participate in, and discuss the ideas and human conditions that are presented on our stages. Maximum running time is 10 minutes. Less is fine. Each year there is a special prop that must be incorporated into that year's plays. See website for details. All entries must be sent electronically, as attachments. Printed plays will not be considered. Guidelines available on website. The mission of the Weathervane Playhouse 8x10 TheatreFest is to promote the art of play writing, present new works, and introduce area audiences to the short play form. The competition will provide Weathervane with recognition for quality and innovative theatre. 2017 Deadline: May 12. Submission period begins November 1. Prizes: Each of 8 finalists receive full productions of their plays during the Festival, held in mid-July. 1st Place: $350; 2nd Place: $250; 3rd Place: $150; 5 runners-up: $50 each. First round judges include individuals with experience in every area of stagecraft, including tech designers, actors, directors, stage managers, and playwrights.

A+ PLAYWRITING CONTEST FOR TEACHERS

Pioneer Drama Service, Inc., P.O. Box 4267, Englewood CO 80155. (303)779-4035. **Fax:** (303)779-4315. **E-mail:** editors@pioneerdrama.com. **E-mail:** submissions@pioneerdrama.com. **Website:** www.pioneerdrama.com. **Contact:** Lori Conary, submissions editor. Playwright must be a current or retired faculty member at an accredited K-12 public or private school

in the US or Canada. All plays submitted through this contest must have been produced within the last 2 years at the school where the playwright teaches. Rules and guidelines available online. Encourages the development of quality plays written specifically by teachers and other educators. All qualifying mss accepted for publication will be considered contest finalists. Deadline: Submissions will be accepted on an on-going basis with a June 30 cutoff each year. Prize: $500 royalty advance and a one-time $500 donation to the school theatre program where the play was first produced. Judged by editors.

APPALACHIAN FESTIVAL OF PLAYS & PLAYWRIGHTS

Barter Theatre, Box 867, c/o Barter Theatre, Abingdon VA 24212-0867. (276)619-3316. **Fax:** (276)619-3335. **E-mail:** apfestival@bartertheatre.com. **E-mail:** apfestival@bartertheatre.com. **Website:** www.bartertheatre.com. **Contact:** Nick Piper, Associate Artistic Director/Director, New Play Development. With the annual Appalachian Festival of New Plays & Playwrights, Barter Theatre wishes to celebrate new, previously unpublished/unproduced plays by playwrights from the Appalachian region. If the playwrights are not from Appalachia, the plays themselves must be about the region. Deadline: March 2. Prize: $250, a staged reading performed at Barter's Stage II theater, and some transportation compensation and housing during the time of the festival.

THE BLANK THEATRE COMPANY YOUNG PLAYWRIGHTS FESTIVAL

P.O. Box 38756, Hollywood CA 90038. (323)662-7734. **Fax:** (323)661-3903. **E-mail:** info@theblank.com. **E-mail:** submissions@youngplaywrights.com. **Website:** ypf.theblank.com. Purpose is to give young playwrights an opportunity to learn more about playwriting and to give them a chance to have their work mentored, developed, and presented by professional artists.

CALIFORNIA YOUNG PLAYWRIGHTS CONTEST

Playwrights Project, 3675 Ruffin Rd., Suite 330, San Diego CA 92123-1870. (858)384-2970. **Fax:** (858)384-2974. **E-mail:** write@playwrightsproject.org. **Website:** http://www.playwrightsproject.org/programs/contest/. **Contact:** Cecelia Kouma, Executive Director. Annual contest open to Californians under age 19. Annual contest. "Our organization and the contest is designed to nurture promising young writers. We hope to develop playwrights and audiences for live theater. We also teach playwriting." Submissions are required to be unpublished and not produced professionally. Submissions made by the author. SASE for contest rules and entry form. Scripts must be a minimum of 10 standard typewritten pages; send 2 copies. Scripts will *not* be returned. If requested, entrants receive detailed evaluation letter. Guidelines available online. Deadline: June 1. Prize: Scripts will be produced in spring at a professional theatre in San Diego. Writers submitting scripts of 10 or more pages receive a detailed script evaluation letter upon request. Judged by professionals in the theater community, a committee of 5-7; changes somewhat each year.

☺ CANADIAN AUTHORS ASSOCIATION AWARD FOR FICTION

6 West St. N., Suite 203, Orilla ON L3X 5B8 Canada. **Website:** www.canadianauthors.org. **Contact:** Anita Purcell, executive director. Award for full-length, English language literature for adults by a Canadian author. Deadline: January 15. Prize: $1,000. Judging: Each year a trustee for each award appointed by the Canadian Authors Association selects up to 3 judges. Identities of the trustee and judges are confidential.

ESSENTIAL THEATRE PLAYWRITING AWARD

The Essential Theatre, 1414 Foxhall Ln., #10, Atlanta GA 30316. (404) 212-0815. **E-mail:** pmhardy@aol.com. **Website:** www.essentialtheatre.com. **Contact:** Peter Hardy. Offered annually for unproduced, full-length plays by Georgia resident writers. No limitations as to style or subject matter. Submissions can be e-mailed in PDF or Word Documents, or sent by postal mail. See website for full guidelines. Deadline: April 23. Prize: $600 and full production.

SHUBERT FENDRICH MEMORIAL PLAYWRITING CONTEST

Pioneer Drama Service, Inc., P.O. Box 4267, Englewood CO 80155. (303)779-4035. **Fax:** (303)779-4315. **E-mail:** editors@pioneerdrama.com. **E-mail:** submissions@pioneerdrama.com. **Website:** www.pioneerdrama.com. **Contact:** Lori Conary, submissions editor. Annual competition that encourages the development of quality theatrical material for educational, community and children's theatre markets. Previously unpublished submissions only. Only considers mss with a running time between 20-90 minutes.

Open to all writers not currently published by Pioneer Drama Service. Guidelines available online. No entry fee. Cover letter, SASE for return of ms, and proof of production or staged reading must accompany all submissions. Deadline: Ongoing contest; a winner is selected by June 1 each year from all submissions received the previous year. Prize: $1,000 royalty advance in addition to publication. Judged by editors.

FILMMAKERS INTERNATIONAL SCREENWRITING AWARDS

Beverly Hills CA 90210. **E-mail:** info@filmmakers.com. **Website:** www.filmmakers.com/screenplay/. Deadlines: Early: Feb. 28; Regular: April 30; Late: May 31; Final: June 30; Extended Final: July 31. Prizes: Grand Prize: $5,000; Elite Prizes: $500 per category.

JOHN GASSNER MEMORIAL PLAYWRITING COMPETITION

New England Theatre Conference, 215 Knob Hill Dr., Hamden CT 06158. **Fax:** (203)288-5938. **E-mail:** mail@netconline.org. **E-mail:** mail@netconline.org. **Website:** www.netconline.org. Annually seeks unpublished full-length plays and scripts. Open to all. Playwrights living outside New England may participate. Submit by e-mail only. Deadline: April 15. Prize: Staged reading.

THE MARILYN HALL AWARDS FOR YOUTH THEATRE

P.O. Box 148, Beverly Hills CA 90213. **Website:** www.beverlyhillstheatreguild.com. **Contact:** Candace Coster, competition coordinator. The Marilyn Hall Awards consist of 2 monetary prizes for plays suitable for grades 6-8 (middle school) or for plays suitable for grades 9-12 (high school). The 2 prizes will be awarded on the merits of the play scripts, which includes its suitability for the intended audience. The plays should be approximately 45-75 minutes in length. There is no production connected to any of the prizes, though a staged reading is optional at the discretion of the BHTG. Unpublished submissions only. Authors must be U.S. citizens or legal residents and must sign entry form personally. Deadline: The last day of February. Submission period begins January 15. Prize: 1st Prize: $700; 2nd Prize: $300.

AURAND HARRIS MEMORIAL PLAYWRITING AWARD

The New England Theatre Conference, Inc., 215 Knob Hill Ave., Hamden CT 06518. **Fax:** (203)288-5938. **E-mail:** mail@netconline.org. **E-mail:** mail@netconline.

org. **Website:** www.netconline.org. Offered annually for an unpublished full-length play for young audiences. Guidelines available online or for SASE. Open to all. All scripts submitted by email *only*. Deadline: May 1.

HRC SHOWCASE THEATRE PLAYWRITING CONTEST

P.O. Box 940, Hudson NY 12534. (518)851-7244. **E-mail:** hrcshowcaseplaycontest@gmail.com. **Website:** www.hrc-showcasetheatre.com. **Contact:** Jesse Waldinger, chair. HRC Showcase Theatre invites submissions of full-length plays to its annual contest from new, aspiring, or established playwrights. Each submitted play should be previously unpublished, run no more than 90 minutes, require no more than 6 actors, and be suitable for presentation as a staged reading by Equity actors. No musicals or children's plays. Deadline: February 1. Prize: $500. Four runner-ups will receive $100 each.

L.A. DESIGNERS' THEATRE-COMMISSIONS

L.A. Designers' Theatre, P.O. Box 1883, Studio City CA 91614-0883. **E-mail:** ladesigners@gmail.com. **Contact:** Richard Niederberg, artistic director. "Quarterly contest to promote new work and push it through a Theatrical Production onto the conveyor belt to Filmed or Digital Origination entertainment. All submissions must be registered with the copyright office and be unpublished. Material will not be returned. Do not submit any proposal that will not fit in a #10 envelope. No rules, guidelines, fees, or entry forms. Just present an idea that can be commissioned into a full work. Proposals for as of yet uncompleted works are encouraged. Unpopular political, religious, social, or other themes are encouraged; 'street' language and nudity are acceptable. Open to any writer." Deadline: March 15, June 15, September 15, December 15. Prize: Production or publication of the work in the Los Angeles market. "We only want 'first refusal' for the Rights and a License that is clear of any legal, stated, unstated, or implied obligation to any other person or entity. You continue to *own* your work."

MCKNIGHT FELLOWSHIP IN PLAYWRITING

The Playwrights' Center, 2301 E Franklin Ave, Minneapolis MN 55406-1099. (612)332-7481. **Fax:** (612)332-6037. **E-mail:** submissions@pwcenter.org. **E-mail:** submissions@pwcenter.org. **Website:** www.pwcenter.org. **Contact:** Julia Brown, Artistic Programs Administrator. The Playwrights' Center today serves more playwrights in more ways than any other organization in the country. Applications are screened for eligibility by the Playwrights' Center and evaluated by an initial select panel of professional theater artists; finalists are then evaluated by a second panel of national theater artists. Selection is based on artistic excellence and professional achievement, and is guided by the Playwrights' Center's mission statement. The McKnight Fellowships in Playwriting recognize playwrights whose work demonstrates exceptional artistic merit and excellence in the field, and whose primary residence is in the state of Minnesota. Deadline: January 5. Prize: 2 fellowships of $25,000 each will be awarded. Additional funds of $2,500 can be used to support a play development workshop and other professional expenses.

MOONDANCE INTERNATIONAL FILM FESTIVAL

970 Ninth St., Boulder CO 80302. 303-818-5771. **E-mail:** director@moondancefilmfestival.com; moondancefestival@gmail.com. **Website:** www.moondancefilmfestival.com; www.moondancefestival.com/blog. Written works submissions: feature screenplays, short screenplays, feature & short musical screenplays, feature & short screenplays for children, 1, 2 or 3-act stageplays, mini-series for TV, television movies of the week, television pilots, libretti, musical film scripts, short stories, radio plays & short stories for children. Submission service: www.withoutabox.com/login/1240. Accepts hard-copies of submissions, as well as digital submissions. Please include your full contact info on the cover page of your entry. Check out our submission guidelines on the website. Regular deadline: May 31; late deadline: June 30, extended deadline: July 15.

☼ NATIONAL ONE-ACT PLAYWRITING COMPETITION (CANADA)

Ottawa Little Theatre, 400 King Edward Ave., Ottawa ON K1N 7M7 Canada. (613)233-8948. **Fax:** (613)233-8027. **Website:** www.ottawalittletheatre.com. **Contact:** Lynn McGuigan, executive director. Encourages literary and dramatic talent in Canada. Guidelines available online. Deadline: October 15. Prize: 1st Place: $1,000; 2nd Place: $750; 3rd Place: $500; Sybil Cooke Award for a Play Written for Children or Young People: $500. All winning plays will receive a public reading in April, and the winning playwrights will have a one-on-one meeting with a resident dramaturg. Judged by 3 adjudicators, including dramaturgs, directors who develop new work, and playwrights from across Canada.

THE PAGE INTERNATIONAL SCREENWRITING AWARDS

7510 W. Sunset Blvd., #610, Hollywood CA 90046-3408. **E-mail:** info@pageawards.com. **Website:** pageawards.com. **Contact:** Zoe Simmons, Contest Coordinator. Annual competition to discover the most talented new screenwriters from across the country and around the world. Each year, awards are presented to 31 screenwriters in 10 different genre categories: Action/Adventure, Comedy, Drama, Family Film, Historical Film, Science Fiction, Thriller/Horror, Short Film Script, TV Drama Pilot, and TV Comedy Pilot. The contest is open to all writers 18 years of age and older who have not previously earned more than $25,000 writing for film and/or television. (Please visit contest website for entry forms and a complete list of rules and regulations.) Deadlines: January 15 (early), February 15 (regular), March 15 (late), April 15 (last minute). Each year the PAGE Judges present over $50,000 in cash and prizes, including a $25,000 Grand Prize, plus Gold, Silver & Bronze Prizes in all 10 genre categories. Most importantly, the award-winning writers receive extensive publicity and industry exposure for their scripts. As a result of winning the contest, many past PAGE Award Winners now have movies and television shows in production, on the air and in theaters. Judging is done entirely by working Hollywood professionals, including industry script analysts, literary agents, managers, producers, and development executives.

SCREENPLAY FESTIVAL

15021 Ventura Blvd., #523, Sherman Oaks CA 91403. (424)248-9221. **Fax:** (866)770-2994. **E-mail:** info@screenplayfestival.com. **Website:** www.screenplay-festival.com. This festival is an opportunity to give all scriptwriters a chance to be noticed and have their work read by the power players. Entries in the feature-length competition must be more than 60 pages; entries in the short screenplay contest must be fewer than 60 pages. The Screenplay Festival was established to solve two major problems. One, it is simply too difficult for talented writers who have no "connections" to gain recognition and get their material read by legitimate agents, producers, directors and investors. Two, agents, producers, directors, and investors

complain that they cannot find any great material, but they will generally not accept "unsolicited material." This means that unless the script comes from a source that is known to them, they will not read it. Screenplay Festival was established to help eliminate this "chicken and egg" problem. By accepting all submitted screenplays and judging them based upon their quality—not their source or their standardized formatting or the quality of the brads holding them together—Screenplay Festival looks to give undiscovered screenwriters an opportunity to rise above the crowd. Deadline: September 9. Prize: $1,000 for feature film categories, $500 for television categories.

SCRIPTAPALOOZA SCREENPLAY & SHORTS COMPETITION

Endorsed by Write Brothers and Robert McKee, 310-594-5384. **E-mail:** info@scriptapalooza.com. **Website:** www.scriptapalooza.com. "From choosing our judges to creating opportunities, our top priority has always been the writer. We surround ourselves with reputable and successful companies, including many producers, literary agents, and managers who read your scripts. Our past winners have won Emmy's, been signed by agents, managers, had their scripts optioned, and even made into movies. Scriptapalooza will promote, pitch and push the semifinalists and higher for a full year." Deadline: January 6, February 1, March 10, April 17, and May 1. Prize: 1st Place: $10,000; over $50,00 in prizes for the entire competition. The top 100 scripts will be considered by over 95 production companies. Judged by over 90 producers.

SCRIPTAPALOOZA TELEVISION WRITING COMPETITION

310-594-5384. **E-mail:** info@scriptapalooza.com. **Website:** www.scriptapaloozatv.com. Bi-annual competition accepting entries in 4 categories: Reality shows, sitcoms, original pilots, and 1-hour dramas. There are more than 30 producers, agents, and managers reading the winning scripts. Two past winners won Emmys because of Scriptapalooza and 1 past entrant now writes for Comedy Central. Winners announced February 15 and August 30. For contest results, visit website. Length: Standard television format whether 1 hour, 1-half hour, or pilot. Open to any writer 18 or older. Guidelines available on website. Accepts inquiries by e-mail or phone. Deadline: October 15 and April 15. Prize: 1st Place: $500; 2nd Place:

$200; 3rd Place: $100 (in each category); production company consideration. Judged by over 25 producers. **TIPS** Pilots should be fresh, new, and easy to visualize. Spec scripts should stay current with the shows, up-to-date story lines, characters, etc.

SCRIPT PIPELINE SCREENWRITING AND TV WRITING CONTESTS

2633 Lincoln Blvd. #701, Santa Monica CA 90405. (323) 424-4243. **E-mail:** entry@scriptpipeline.com. **Website:** scriptpipeline.com. **Contact:** Matt Misetich, director of development. Script Pipeline's 14th Annual Screenwriting and 9th Annual TV Writing Contests continue a long tradition of discovering up-and-coming talent and connecting them with top producers, agencies, and managers across studio and independent markets. This process has proven enormously successful, with numerous screenwriting contest alumni worldwide finding elite representation and gaining crucial introductions to otherwise impossible-to-reach industry execs. The result thus far is over $5 million in screenplays and TV pilots sold from competition finalists and "Recommend" writers since 2003. Last season, over 5,000 scripts were entered in the Screenwriting and TV Writing contests combined, making Script Pipeline one of the leading companies reviewing spec material. Purpose: to circulate exceptional material industry-wide, support writers long-term, and launch careers. Early deadline: March 1. Regular deadline: May 1. Late Deadline: May 15. Screenwriting Contest: $25,000 in cash for the winner and $1,500 in cash to the runner-up. TV Writing Contest: $10,000 in cash for the winner and $1,000 in cash to the runner-up.

REVA SHINER COMEDY AWARD

Bloomington Playwrights Project, 107 W. 9th St., Bloomington IN 47404. **Website:** www.newplays. org. **Contact:** Susan Jones, Literary Manager. Annual award for unpublished/unproduced plays. The Bloomington Playwrights Project is a script-developing organization. Winning playwrights are expected to become part of the development process, working with the director in person or via long-distance. Check the website for more details. Deadline: October 31. Prize: $1,000, full production as a part of the Mainstage season. Judged by the literary committee of the BPP.

SHRIEKFEST HORROR/SCI-FI FILM FESTIVAL & SCREENPLAY COMPETITION

P.O. Box 950921, Lake Mary FL 32795. **E-mail:** shriekfest@aol.com. **E-mail:** shriekfest@aol.com. **Website:** www.shriekfest.com. **Contact:** Denise Gossett. "Our awards are to help screenwriters move their script up the ladder and hopefully have it made into a film. Our winners take that win and parlay it into agents, film deals, and options. No, we don't use loglines anywhere; we keep your script private." "We accept award-winning screenplays. No restrictions as long as it's in the horror/thriller or sci-fi/fantasy genres. We accept shorts and features. No specific lengths." Deadline: February 1, May 1, July 1, July 10. Prize: Trophies, product awards, usually cash. "Our awards are updated all year long as sponsors step onboard." Judged by at least 20-30 judges who are all in different aspects of the entertainment industry, such as producers, directors, writers, actors, and agents.

SKIPPING STONES YOUTH AWARDS

P.O. Box 3939, Eugene OR 97403-0939. (541)342-4956. **Fax:** (541)342-4956. **E-mail:** editor@skippingstones. org. **Website:** www.skippingstones.org. **Contact:** Arun N. Toké. Annual awards to promote creativity as well as multicultural and nature awareness in youth. Cover letter should include name, address, phone, and e-mail. Entries must be unpublished. Length: 1,000 words maximum; 30 lines maximum for poems. Open to any writer between 7 and 17 years old. Guidelines available by SASE, e-mail, or on website. Accepts inquiries by e-mail or phone. Results announced in the October-December issue of *Skipping Stones*. Winners notified by mail. For contest results, visit website. Everyone who enters receives the issue which features the award winners. Deadline: June 25. Prize: Publication in the autumn issue of *Skipping Stones*, honor certificate, subscription to magazine, plus 5 multicultural and/or nature books. Judged by editors and reviewers at *Skipping Stones* magazine.
TIPS "Be creative. Do not use stereotypes or excessive violent language or plots. Be sensitive to cultural diversity."

SOUTHERN PLAYWRIGHTS COMPETITION

Jacksonville State University, Department of English, 700 Pelham Rd. N., Jacksonville AL 36265-1602. (256)782-5412. **Fax:** (256)782-5441. **E-mail:** jmaloney@jsu.edu. **E-mail:** jmaloney@jsu.edu. **Website:** www.jsu.edu/depart/english/southpla.htm. **Contact:**

Joy Maloney. Competition for playwrights native to or a resident of Alabama, Arkansas, Florida, Georgia, Kentucky, Louisiana, Mississippi, North Carolina, South Carolina, Tennessee, Texas, Virginia, or West Virginia. Plays must deal with the Southern experience. Entries must be original, full-length plays. No musicals or adaptations will be accepted. The playwright may submit only one play. All entries must be typed, securely bound, and clearly identified. Synopsis of script must be included. No electronic entries accepted. Legal clearance of all materials not in the public domain will be the responsibility of the playwright. The Southern Playwrights Competition seeks to identify and encourage the best of Southern playwriting. Deadline: January 15. Prize: $1,000 and production of the play.

TELEVISION OUTREACH PROGRAM (TOP)

Scriptwriters Network (SWN), The Scriptwriters Network Foundation, Inc., P.O. Box 642806, Los Angeles CA 90064. **E-mail:** top@scriptwritersnetwork.org. **E-mail:** top@scriptwritersnetwork.org. **Website:** www.scriptwritersnetwork.org. **Contact:** Melessa Y. Sargent, Director. The Television Outreach Program (TOP) is a Scriptwriters Network program to support undiscovered television writing talent. The program's objective is to help writers improve their craft so that they may achieve their goals of obtaining representation, script development, mentoring and career counseling services, landing writing assignments, and/or selling their work.

THEATRE CONSPIRACY ANNUAL NEW PLAY CONTEST

Theatre Conspiracy, 10091 McGregor Blvd., Ft. Myers FL 33919. (239)936-3239. **E-mail:** info@theatreconspiracy.org. **Website:** theatreconspiracy.org. **Contact:** Bill Taylor, producing artistic director. Offered annually for full-length plays that are unproduced. Work submitted to the contest must be a full length play with 7 actors or less and have simple to moderate technical demands. Plays having up to three previous productions are welcome. No musicals. Deadline: March 30. Prize: $700 and full production. Judged by a panel of qualified theatre teachers, directors, and performers.

☻ THEATRE IN THE RAW BIENNIAL ONE-ACT PLAY WRITING CONTEST

Theatre In the Raw, 3521 Marshall St., Vancouver BC V5N 4S2 Canada. (604)708-5448. **E-mail:** theatrein-

theraw@telus.net. **Website:** www.theatreintheraw.ca. Biennial contest for an original one-act play, presented in proper stage-play format, that is unpublished and unproduced. The play (with no more than 6 characters) cannot be longer than 25 double-spaced, typed pages equal to 30 minutes. Scripts must have page numbers. Scripts are to be mailed only & will not be accepted by e-mail. Deadline: December 31. Prize: 1st Place: $200, at least 1 dramatic reading or staging of the play at a Theatre In the Raw Cafe/Venue, or as part of a mini-tour program for the One-Act Play Series Nights; 2nd Place: $100; 3rd Place: $75. Winners announced June 30.

JACKIE WHITE MEMORIAL NATIONAL CHILDREN'S PLAY WRITING CONTEST

1800 Nelwood Dr., Columbia MO 65202-1447. (573)874-5628. **E-mail:** jwmcontest@cectheatre.org. **Website:** www.cectheatre.org. **Contact:** Tom Phillips. Annual contest that encourages playwrights to write quality plays for family audiences. Previously unpublished submissions only. Submissions made by author. Play may be performed during the following season. All submissions will be read by at least 3 readers. Author will receive a written evaluation of the script. Guidelines available online. Deadline: June 1. Prize: $500 with production possible. Judging by current and past board members of CEC and by non-board members who direct plays at CEC.

WORLDFEST-HOUSTON INDEPENDENT INTERNATIONAL FILM FESTIVAL

WorldFest-Houston, 9898 Bissonnet St., Suite 650, Houston TX 77036. (713)965-9955. **Fax:** (713)965-9960. **E-mail:** entry@worldfest.org. **Website:** www.worldfest.org. mixed media art **Contact:** Entry Coordinator. WorldFest discovered Steven Spielberg, George Lucas, Ang Lee, Ridley Scott, the Coen Brothers, Francis Ford Coppola, John Lee Hancock, and David Lynch with their first awards. Screenplays must be submitted as actual printed scripts, 3-hole binders, no online reading. Competition for all genres of screenplays, plus 10 other competition categories of films and videos. Deadline: December 31; Final deadline is Jan 15. Prize: Cash, options, production deals, workshops, master classes, and seminars. Judged by a jury whose members are credentialed, experienced, award-winning writers, producers, and directors. No production assistants.

WRITE NOW

Indiana Repertory Theatre, 140 W. Washington St., Indianapolis IN 46204. 480-921-5770. **E-mail:** info@writenow.co. **Website:** www.writenow.co. The purpose of this biennial workshop is to encourage writers to create strikingly original scripts for young audiences. It provides a forum through which each playwright receives constructive criticism and the support of a development team consisting of a professional director and dramaturg. Finalists will spend approximately one week in workshop with their development team. At the end of the week, each play will be read as a part of the Write Now convening. Guidelines available online. Deadline: August 15.

YEAR END SERIES (YES) FESTIVAL OF NEW PLAYS

Theatre and Dance Program, School of the Arts, Nunn Dr., Northern Kentucky University, Highland Heights KY 41099-1007. 859.572.5648. **Fax:** (859)572-6057. **E-mail:** daniellyc1@nku.edu, or mking@nku.edu. **Website:** http://artscience.nku.edu/departments/theatre.html, https://artscience.nku.edu/content/dam/artscience/theatre/docs/16755YesFestivalFlyer.pdf. **Contact:** Michael King, co-project director; Corrie Danieley, co-project director. Receives submissions until September 30 in even-numbered years for the festivals which occur in April of odd-numbered years. Open to all writers. Flyers with submission guidelines and entry forms available on the website, or via email. Deadline: September 30. Open to submissions on May 1. Prize: $250 and an expense-paid visit (travel and housing) to Northern Kentucky University to see the play produced.

ANNA ZORNIO MEMORIAL CHILDREN'S THEATRE PLAYWRITING COMPETITION

University of New Hampshire, Department of Theatre and Dance, PCAC, 30 Academic Way, Durham NH 03824. (603)862-3038. **Fax:** (603)862-0298. **E-mail:** mike.wood@unh.edu. **Website:** http://cola.unh.edu/theatre-dance/program/anna-zornio-childrens-theatre-playwriting-award. **Contact:** Michael Wood. Offered every 4 years for unpublished well-written plays or musicals appropriate for young audiences with a maximum length of 60 minutes. May submit more than 1 play, but not more than 3. Honors the late Anna Zornio, an alumna of The University of New Hampshire, for dedication to and inspiration of playwriting for young people, K-12th grade. Deadline: March 1. Prize: $500.

ARTS COUNCILS & FELLOWSHIPS

$50,000 GIFT OF FREEDOM

A Room of Her Own Foundation, P.O. Box 778, Placitas NM 87043. **E-mail:** awards@aroho.org. **Website:** www.aroomofherownfoundation.org. **Contact:** Tracey Cravens-Gras, associate director. The publicly funded award provides very practical help—both materially and in professional guidance and moral support with mentors and advisory council—to assist women in making their creative contribution to the world. The Gift of Freedom competition will determine superior finalists from each of 3 genres: Creative nonfiction, fiction, and poetry. Open to female residents of the US. Award application cycle dates are yet to be determined. Visit website at www.aroho.org for more information about the next application window. Deadline: November 2. Prize: One genre finalist will be awarded the $50,000 Gift of Freedom grant, distributed over 2 years in support of the completion of a particular creative project. The 2 remaining genre finalists will each receive a $5,000 prize.

ALABAMA STATE COUNCIL ON THE ARTS INDIVIDUAL ARTIST FELLOWSHIP

201 Monroe St., Suite 110, Montgomery AL 36130. (334)242-4076, ext. 236. **Fax:** (334)240-3269. **E-mail:** anne.kimzey@arts.alabama.gov. **Website:** www.arts.state.al.us. **Contact:** Anne Kimzey, Literary Arts Program Manager. Must be a legal resident of Alabama who has lived in the state for 2 years prior to application. Competition receives 30+ submissions annually. Accepts inquiries by e-mail and phone. The following should be submitted: a résumé and a list of published works with reviews, if available; and a minimum of 10 pages of poetry or prose, with a maximum of 20 pages. Please label each page with title, artist's name, and date. If published, indicate where and the date of publication. Please do not submit bound material. Guidelines available in January on website. Recognizes the achievements and potential of Alabama writers. Deadline: March 1. Applications must be submitted online by eGRANT. Judged by independent peer panel. Fellowship recipients notified by mail and announced on website in June.

GEORGE BENNETT FELLOWSHIP

Phillips Exeter Academy, 20 Main Street, Exeter NH 03833. E-mail: teaching_opportunities@exeter.edu. Website: www.exeter.edu/bennettfellowship. Annual award for fellow and family to provide time and freedom from material considerations to a person seriously contemplating or pursuing a career as a writer. Applicants should have a ms in progress which they intend to complete during the fellowship period. Ms should be fiction, nonfiction, novel, short stories, or poetry. Duties: To be in residency at the Academy for the academic year; to make oneself available informally to students interested in writing. Committee favors writers who have not yet published a book with a major publisher. Deadline: November 30. A choice will be made, and all entrants notified in mid-April. Prize: Cash stipend (currently $15,260), room and board. Judged by committee of the English department.

DOBIE PAISANO WRITER'S FELLOWSHIP

The Graduate School, The University of Texas at Austin, Attn: Dobie Paisano Program, 110 Inner Campus Drive Stop G0400, Austin TX 78712-0531. (512)232-3609. Fax: (512)471-7620. E-mail: gbarton@austin.utexas.edu. Website: www.utexas.edu/ogs/Paisano. Contact: Gwen Barton. Sponsored by the Graduate School at The University of Texas at Austin and the Texas Institute of Letters, the Dobie Paisano Fellowship Program provides solitude, time, and a comfortable place for Texas writers or writers who have written significantly about Texas through fiction, nonfiction, poetry, plays, or other mediums. The Dobie Paisano Ranch is a very rural and rustic setting, and applicants should read the guidelines closely to insure their ability to reside in this secluded environment. At the time of the application, the applicant must meet one of the following requirements: (1) be a native Texan, (2) have resided in Texas at least three years at some time, or (3) have published significant work with a Texas subject. Those who meet requirement 1 or 2 do not have to meet the Texas subject matter restriction. Deadline: January 15. Applications are accepted beginning December 1 and must be post-marked no later than January 15. The Ralph A. Johnston memorial Fellowship is for a period of 4 months with a stipend of $6,250 per month. It is aimed at writers who have already demonstrated some publishing and critical success. The Jesse H. Jones Writing Fellowship is for a period of approximately 6 months with a stipend of $3,000 per month. It is aimed at, but not limited to, writers who are early in their careers.

TIPS "Three sets of each complete application must be submitted. Electronic submissions are not allowed. Guidelines and application forms are on the website (http://www.utexas.edu/ogs/Paisano/info.html) or may be requested by sending a SASE (3-ounce postage) to the above address, attention of 'Dobie Paisano Fellowship Project.'"

FELLOWSHIPS FOR CREATIVE AND PERFORMING ARTISTS AND WRITERS

American Antiquarian Society, 185 Salisbury St., Worcester MA 01609-1634. (508)755-5221. Fax: (508)754-9069. E-mail: jmoran@mwa.org; library@americanantiquarian.org. Website: www.american-antiquarian.org. Contact: James David Moran. Annual fellowship for creative and performing artists, writers, filmmakers, journalists, and other persons whose goals are to produce imaginative, non-formulaic works dealing with pre-20th century American history. Application instructions available online. Website also lists potential fellowship projects. Deadline: October 5. Prize: The stipend will be $1,350 for fellows residing on campus (rent-free) in the society's scholars' housing, located next to the main library building. The stipend will be $1,850 for fellows residing off campus. Fellows will not be paid a travel allowance. Judged by AAS staff and outside reviewers.

TIPS "Successful applicants are those whose work is for the general public rather than for academic or educational audiences."

GUGGENHEIM FELLOWSHIPS

John Simon Guggenheim Memorial Foundation, 90 Park Ave., New York NY 10016. (212)687-4470. E-mail: fellowships@gf.org. Website: www.gf.org. Often characterized as "midcareer" awards, Guggenheim Fellowships are intended for men and women who have already demonstrated exceptional capacity for productive scholarship or exceptional creative ability in the arts. Fellowships are awarded through two annual competitions: one open to citizens and permanent residents of the United States and Canada, and the other open to citizens and permanent residents of Latin America and the Caribbean. Candidates must apply to the Guggenheim Foundation in order to be considered in either of these competitions. The Foundation receives between 3,500 and 4,000 applications each year. Although no one who applies is guaranteed success in the competition, there is no prescreening: all applications are reviewed. Approximately 200 Fellowships are awarded each year. Deadline: September 15.

MARILYN HOLLINSHEAD VISITING SCHOLARS FELLOWSHIP

University of Minnesota, 113 Anderson Library, 222 21st Ave. South, Minneapolis MN 55455. **Website:** http://www.lib.umn.edu/clrc/awards-grants-and-fellowships. Marilyn Hollinshead Visiting Scholars Fund for Travel to the Kerlan Collection is available for research study. Applicants may request up to $1,500. Send a letter with the proposed purpose and plan to use specific research materials (manuscripts and art), dates, and budget (including airfare and per diem). Travel and a written report on the project must be completed and submitted in the previous year. Deadline: June 1.

HENRY HOYNS & POE/FAULKNER FELLOWSHIPS

Creative Writing Program, 219 Bryan Hall, P.O. Box 400121, University of Virginia, Charlottesville VA 22904-4121. (434)924-6675. **Fax:** (434)924-1478. **E-mail:** creativewriting@virginia.edu. **Website:** creativewriting.virginia.edu. **Contact:** Jeb Livingood, associate director. Two-year MFA program in poetry and fiction; all students receive fellowships and teaching stipends that total $18,000 in both years of study. Sample poems/prose required with application. Deadline: December 15.

MCKNIGHT ARTIST FELLOWSHIPS FOR WRITERS, LOFT AWARD(S) IN CHILDREN'S LITERATURE/CREATIVE PROSE/POETRY

The Loft Literary Center, 1011 Washington Ave. S., Suite 200, Open Book, Minneapolis MN 55415. (612)215-2575. **Fax:** (612)215-2576. **E-mail:** loft@loft.org. **Website:** www.loft.org. **Contact:** Bao Phi. "The Loft administers the McKnight Artists Fellowships for Writers. Five $25,000 awards are presented annually to accomplished Minnesota writers and spoken word artists. Four awards alternate annually between creative prose (fiction and creative nonfiction) and poetry/spoken word. The fifth award is presented in children's literature and alternates annually for writing for ages 8 and under and writing for children older than 8." The awards provide the writers the opportu-

nity to focus on their craft for the course of the fellowship year. Prize: $25,000.
TIPS "See guidelines and follow carefully and exactly."

MOONDANCER FELLOWSHIP FOR WRITING ABOUT NATURE AND THE OUTDOORS

The Writers' Colony at Dairy Hollow, 515 Spring St., Eureka Springs AR 72632. (479)253-7444. **Fax:** (479)253-9859. **E-mail:** director@writerscolony.org. **Website:** www.writerscolony.org. **Contact:** Linda Caldwell, Director. "A two-week residency for writing in any genre about any aspect of nature and the outdoors. Works may be fiction or non-fiction. Supports writing of excellence which aspires to engage the mind, body and soul in the appreciation of nature. Applications accepted until May 31." Deadline: May 31.

JENNY MCKEAN MOORE VISITING WRITER

English Department, George Washington University, Rome Hall, 801 22nd St. NW, Suite 760, Washington DC 20052. (202)994-6180. **Fax:** (202)994-7915. **E-mail:** tvmallon@gwu.edu. **Website:** https://english.columbian.gwu.edu/activities-events. **Contact:** Lisa Page, Acting Director of Creative Writing. The position is filled annually, bringing a visiting writer to The George Washington University. During each semester the Writer teaches 1 creative-writing course at the university as well as a community workshop. Seeks someone specializing in a different genre each year—fiction, poetry, creative nonfiction. Annual stipend between $50,000 and $60,000, plus reduced-rent townhouse on campus (not guaranteed). Application deadline: December 12. Annual stipend varies, depending on endowment performance; most recently, stipend was $60,000, plus reduced-rent townhouse (not guaranteed).

NICKELODEON WRITING PROGRAM

Nickelodeon, Viacom, 231 W. Olive Ave., Burbank CA 91502. (818)736-3663. **E-mail:** info.writing@nick.com. **Website:** www.nickwriting.com, www.facebook.com/nickwriting, twitter: @nickwriting. **Contact:** Karen Kirkland, Vice President. Offered annually for unpublished spec scripts. Must be 18 years or older to participate. Deadline: February 28. Prize: The Nickelodeon Writing Program offers aspiring television writers all over the globe, with diverse backgrounds and experiences, the opportunity to hone their skills while writing for our live action and animated shows. Participants will have hands-on interaction with executives writing spec scripts and pitching story ideas. The Program, developed to broaden Nickelodeon's outreach efforts, provides a salaried position for up to six months (for International writers) and up to onApplication and submission guidelines are available on our website at www.nickwriting.com. Judged by experienced script analysts and Nickelodeon executives.

NORTH CAROLINA ARTS COUNCIL REGIONAL ARTIST PROJECT GRANTS

North Carolina Arts Council, Dept. of Natural and Cultural Resources, MSC #4632, Raleigh NC 27699-4634. (919)807-6512. **Fax:** (919)807-6532. **E-mail:** david.potorti@ncdcr.gov. **Website:** www.ncarts.org. **Contact:** David Potorti, literature and theater director. See website for contact information for the consortia of local arts councils that distribute these grants. Open to any writer living in North Carolina. Deadline: Dates vary in fall/spring. Prize: $500-3,000 awarded to writers to pursue projects that further their artistic development. These grants are awarded through consortia of local arts councils. See our website for details.

NORTH CAROLINA WRITERS' FELLOWSHIPS

North Carolina Arts Council, North Carolina Arts Council, Writers' Fellowships, Department of Cultural Resources, Raleigh NC 27699-4632. (919)807-6512. **Fax:** (919)807-6532. **E-mail:** david.potorti@ncdcr.gov. **Website:** www.ncarts.org. **Contact:** David Potorti, literature and theater director. The North Carolina Arts Council offers grants to writers, spoken-word artists, playwrights, and screenwriters: fellowships (every other year). Writers must be current residents of North Carolina for at least 1 year, must remain in residence in North Carolina during the grant year, and may not pursue academic or professional degrees while receiving grant. Fellowships offered to support writers in the development and creation of their work. See website for details. Offered every even year to support writers of fiction, poetry, literary nonfiction, literary translation, and spoken word. See website for guidelines and other eligibility requirements. Deadline: November 1 of even-numbered years. Prize: $10,000 grant. Reviewed by a panel of literature professionals (writers and editors).

OREGON LITERARY FELLOWSHIPS

925 S.W. Washington, Portland OR 97205. (503)227-2583. **E-mail:** susan@literary-arts.org. **Website:** www.literary-arts.org. **Contact:** Susan Moore, Director of programs and events. Oregon Literary Fellowships are intended to help Oregon writers initiate, develop, or complete literary projects in poetry, fiction, literary nonfiction, drama, and young readers literature. Writers in the early stages of their career are encouraged to apply. The awards are merit-based. Guidelines available in February for SASE. Accepts inquiries by e-mail, phone. Oregon residents only. Recipients announced in January. Deadline: Last Friday in June. Prize: $3,000 minimum award, for approximately 8 writers and 2 publishers. Judged by out-of-state writers.

RHODE ISLAND ARTIST FELLOWSHIPS AND INDIVIDUAL PROJECT GRANTS

Rhode Island State Council on the Arts, State of Rhode Island, One Capitol Hill, 3rd Floor, Providence RI 02908. (401)222-3880. **Fax:** (401)222-3018. **E-mail:** Cristina.DiChiera@arts.ri.gov. **Website:** www.arts.ri.gov. **Contact:** Cristina DiChiera, director of individual artist programs. Annual fellowship competition is based upon panel review of poetry, fiction, and playwriting/screenwriting manuscripts. Project grants provide funds for community-based arts projects. Rhode Island artists who have lived in the state for at least 12 consecutive months may apply without a nonprofit sponsor. Applicants for all RSCA grant and award programs must be at least 18 years old and not currently enrolled in an arts-related degree program. Online application and guidelines can be found at www.arts.ri.gov/grants/guidelines/. You must be a United States citizen or Green Card holder and a current, legal resident of the State of Rhode Island. You must have established legal residence in Rhode Island for a minimum of twelve consecutive months prior to the date of application and you must be a current legal resident of the State of Rhode Island at the time that grant funds are disbursed. Rhode Island State Law (§44-30-5) defines a "resident" as someone "who is domiciled in this state" or "who is not domiciled in this state but maintains a permanent place of abode in this state and is in this state for an aggregate of more than one hundred eighty-three days of the taxable year. If an individual selected for a grant award is no longer a resident of the State of Rhode Island when funds are to be disbursed, the grant award may be withdrawn." Deadline: April 1 and October 1. Fellowship awards: $5,000 and $1,000. Grants range from $500-5,000, with an average of around $1,500. Judged by a rotating panel of artists.

WALLACE E. STEGNER FELLOWSHIPS

Creative Writing Program, Stanford University, Stanford CA 94305-2087. (650)723-0011. **Fax:** (650)723-3679. **E-mail:** stegnerfellowship@stanford.edu. **Website:** http://creativewriting.stanford.edu/about-the-fellowship. Offers 5 fellowships in poetry and 5 in fiction for promising writers who can benefit from 2 years of instruction and participation in the program. Online application preferred. "We do not require a degree for admission. No school of writing is favored over any other. Chronological age is not a consideration." Deadline: December 1. Open to submissions on September 1. Prize: Fellowships of $26,000, plus tuition of over $7,000/year.

TENNESSEE ARTS COMMISSION LITERARY FELLOWSHIP

Tennessee Arts Commission, 401 Charlotte Ave., Nashville TN 37243-0780. **Fax:** (615)741-8559. **E-mail:** lee.baird@state.tn.us. **Website:** tnartscommission.org. **Contact:** Lee Baird, director of literary programs. Awarded annually in recognition of professional Tennessee artists, i.e., individuals who have received financial compensation for their work as professional writers. Applicants must have a publication history other than vanity press. Three fellowships awarded annually to outstanding literary artists who live and work in Tennessee. Categories are in fiction, creative nonfiction, and poetry. Deadline: January 26. Prize: $5,000. Judged by an out-of-state adjudicator.

WISCONSIN INSTITUTE FOR CREATIVE WRITING FELLOWSHIP

6195B H.C. White Hall, 600 N. Park St., Madison WI 53706. **E-mail:** rfkuka@wisc.edu. **Website:** creativewriting.wisc.edu/fellowships.html. **Contact:** Sean Bishop, graduate coordinator. Fellowship provides time, space and an intellectual community for writers working on first books. Receives approximately 300 applicants a year for each genre. Judged by English Department faculty and current fellows. Candidates can have up to one published book in the genre for which they are applying. Open to any writer with either an M.F.A. or Ph.D. in creative writing. Please enclose a SASE for notification of results. Results an-nounced on website by May 1. Applicants should submit up to 10 pages of poetry or one story or excerpt of up to 30 pages and a résumé or vita directly to the program during the month of February. See instructions on website for submitting online. An applicant's name must not appear on the writing sample (which must be in ms form) but rather on a separate sheet along with address, social security number, phone number, e-mail address and title(s) of submission(s). Candidates should also supply the names and phone numbers of two references. Accepts inquiries by e-mail and phone. Deadline: Last day of February. Open to submissions on December 15. Prize: $30,000 for a 9-month appointment.

TIPS "Send your best work. Stories seem to have a small advantage over novel excerpts."

FICTION

24-HOUR SHORT STORY CONTEST

WritersWeekly.com, 5726 Cortez Rd. W., #349, Bradenton FL 34210. 305-768-0261. **Fax:** 305-768-0261. **E-mail:** writersweekly@writersweekly.com. **Website:** www.writersweekly.com/misc/contest.php. **Contact:** Angela Hoy. Popular quarterly contest in which registered entrants receive an assigned topic at start time (usually noon Central Time) and have 24 hours to write and submit a story on that topic. All submissions must be returned via e-mail. Each contest is limited to 500 people. Upon entry, entrant will receive guidelines and details on competition, including submission process. Deadline: Quarterly—see website for dates. Prize: 1st Place: $300; 2nd Place: $250; 3rd Place: $200. There are also 20 honorable mentions and 60 door prizes (randomly drawn from all participants). The top 3 winners' entries are posted on WritersWeekly.com (non-exclusive electronic rights only) and receive a Freelance Income Kit. Writers retain all rights to their work. See website for full details on prizes. Judged by Angela Hoy (publisher of WritersWeekly.com and Booklocker.com).

AEON AWARD

Albedo One/Aeon Press, Aeon Award, Albedo One, 2 Post Road, Lusk, Dublin Ireland. +353 1 8730177. **E-mail:** fraslaw@yahoo.co.uk. **Website:** www.albedo1.com. **Contact:** Frank Ludlow, event coordinator. Prestigious fiction writing competition for short stories in any speculative fiction genre, such as fantasy, science fiction, horror, or anything in-between or unclassifiable. Submit your story (which must be less than 10,000 words in length and previously unpublished) in the body of an e-mail with contact details and "Aeon Award Submission" as the subject. Deadline: November 30. Contest begins January 1. Prize: Grand Prize: €1,000; 2nd Prize: €200; and 3rd Prize: €100. The top three stories are guaranteed publication in *Albedo One*. Judged by Ian Watson, Eileen Gunn, Todd McCaffrey, and Michael Carroll.

AHWA FLASH & SHORT STORY COMPETITION

AHWA (Australian Horror Writers Association), **E-mail:** ahwacomps@australianhorror.com; ahwa@ australianhorror.com. **E-mail:** ctrost@hotmail.com. **Website:** www.australianhorror.com. **Contact:** Cameron Trost, Competitions Officer. Competition/award for short stories and flash fiction. There are 2 categories: short stories (1,001 to 8,000 words) and flash fiction (less than 1,000 words). Writers may submit to one or both categories, but entry is limited to 1 story per author per category. Send submission as an attached rtf or doc. Mail submissions only accepted as a last resort. No previously published entries will be accepted—all tales must be an original work by the author. Stories can be as violent or as bloody as the storyline dictates, but those containing gratuitous sex or violence will not be considered. Please check entries for spelling and grammar mistakes and follow standard submission guidelines (e.g., 12 point font, Ariel, Times New Roman, or Courier New, one and a half spacing between lines, with title and page number on each page). Looking for horror stories, tales that frighten, yarns that unsettle readers in their comfortable homes. All themes in this genre will be accepted, from the well-used (zombies, vampires, ghosts etc) to the highly original, so long as the story is professional and well written. Deadline: May 31. Prize: The authors of the winning Flash Fiction and Short Story entries will each receive paid publication in *Midnight Echo*, the Magazine of the AHWA and an engraved plaque. Judged by previous winners.

SHERWOOD ANDERSON FICTION AWARD

Mid-American Review, Mid-American Review, Dept. of English, Box WM, BGSU, Bowling Green OH 43403. (419)372-2725. **Fax:** (419)372-4642. **E-mail:** mar@bgsu.edu. **Website:** www.bgsu.edu/midamericanreview. **Contact:** Abigail Cloud, editor-in-chief.

Offered annually for unpublished mss (6,000 word limit). Contest is open to all writers not associated with a judge or *Mid-American Review*. Guidelines available online or for SASE. Deadline: November 1. Prize: $1,000, plus publication in the spring issue of *Mid-American Review*. Four Finalists: Notation, possible publication. Judged by editors and a well-known writer, i.e., Aimee Bender or Anthony Doerr. Judged by Charles Yu in 2017.

ARIZONA LITERARY CONTEST AND AWARDS

Arizona Authors' Association, 6939 East Chaparral Road, Paradise Valley AZ 85253-7000. (602) 554-8101. **E-mail:** AzAuthors@gmail.com. **E-mail:** AzAuthors@gmail.com. **Website:** www.azauthors.com. **Contact:** Lisa Aquilina, President. Arizona Authors' Association sponsors annual literary competition in poetry, short story, essay, unpublished novels, and published books (fiction, nonfiction, and children's literature) and Arizona Book of the Year. Cash prizes awarded ($500 Book of the Year) from Green Pieces Press and 1st, 2nd, and 3rd place in seven categories ($150, $75 and $50, respectively) from Vignetta Syndicate LLC. New category in 2017, New Drama Writing, with a grand prize of $250. All category winners are published in the *Arizona Literary Magazine*. NEW PRIZE in 2017 for Unpublished Novel category. Winner receives a standard, traditional publishing contract through IngramElliott Book Publishers. Poetry, short story, essay, and new drama writing submissions must be unpublished. Work must have been published in the current or immediate past calendar year. Considers simultaneous submissions. Entry form and guidelines available on website or upon request after submitting an SASE. Deadline: July 1. Begins accepting submissions January 1. Finalists notified by Labor Day weekend. Prizes: Grand Prize, Arizona Book of the Year Award: $500. All categories except new drama writing: 1st Prize: $150 and publication; 2nd Prize: $75 and publication; 3rd Prize: $50 and publication. New drama writing grand prize $250 and publication. Features in *Arizona Literary Magazine* can be taken instead of money and publication. 1st and 2nd prize winners in poetry, essay, and short story are nominated for the Pushcart Prize. Judged by nationwide published authors, editors, literary agents, and reviewers. Winners announced at an awards dinner and ceremony held the first Saturday in November.

BALCONES FICTION PRIZE

Austin Commmunity College, Department of Creative Writing, 1212 Rio Grande St., Austin TX 78701. (512)584-5045. **E-mail:** joconne@austincc.edu. **Website:** http://www.austincc.edu/crw/html/balcones-center.html. **Contact:** Joe O'Connell. Awarded to the best book of literary fiction published the previous year. Books of prose may be submitted by publisher or author. Send three copies. Deadline: January 31. Prize: $1,500, winner is flown to Austin for a campus reading.

THE BALTIMORE REVIEW CONTESTS

The Baltimore Review, 6514 Maplewood Rd., Baltimore MD 21212. **E-mail:** editor@baltimorereview.org. **Website:** www.baltimorereview.org. **Contact:** Barbara Westwood Diehl, senior editor. Each summer and winter issue includes a contest theme (see submissions guidelines for theme). Prizes are awarded for first, second, and third place among all categories—poetry, short stories, and creative nonfiction. All entries are considered for publication. Open to all writers. Only unpublished work will be considered. Asks only for the right to publish the work for the first time. Deadline: May 31 and November 30. Prize: 1st Place: $500; 2nd Place: $200; 3rd Place: $100. All entries are considered for publication. Provides a small compensation to all contributors. Judged by the editors of *The Baltimore Review* and a guest, final judge.

BARD FICTION PRIZE

Bard College, P.O. Box 5000, Annandale-on-Hudson NY 12504-5000. (845)758-7087. **Fax:** (845)758-7917. **E-mail:** bfp@bard.edu. **Website:** www.bard.edu/bfp. **Contact:** Irene Zedlacher. The Bard Fiction Prize is awarded to a promising, emerging writer who is an American citizen aged 39 years or younger at the time of application. Cover letter should include name, address, phone, e-mail and name of publisher where book was previously published. Entries must be previously published. Open to U.S. citizens aged 39 and below. Guidelines available by SASE, fax, phone, e-mail, or on website. Results announced by October 15. Winners notified by phone. For contest results, e-mail, or visit website. The Bard Fiction Prize is intended to encourage and support young writers of fiction to pursue their creative goals and to provide an opportunity to work in a fertile and intellectual environment. Deadline: June 15. Prize: $30,000 and appointment as writer-in-residence at Bard College for 1 semester.

Judged by a committee of 5 judges (authors associated with Bard College).

BELLEVUE LITERARY REVIEW GOLDENBERG PRIZE FOR FICTION

Bellevue Literary Review, NYU Dept of Medicine, 550 First Ave., OBV-A612, New York NY 10016. (212)263-3973. **E-mail:** info@blreview.org; stacy@blreview.org. **Website:** www.blreview.org. **Contact:** Stacy Bodziak, managing editor. The BLR prizes award outstanding writing related to themes of health, healing, illness, the mind and the body. Annual competition/award for short stories. Receives about 200-300 entries per category. Send credit card information or make checks payable to Bellevue Literary Review. Guidelines available in February. Accepts inquiries by e-mail, phone, mail. Submissions open in February. Results announced in December and made available to entrants with SASE, by e-mail, on website. Winners notified by mail, by e-mail. Entries should be unpublished. Anyone may enter contest. Length: No minimum; maximum of 5,000 words. Writers may submit own work. Deadline: July 1. Prize: $1,000 and publication in *The Bellevue Literary Review*. Honorable mention winners receive $250 and publication. BLR editors select semi-finalists to be read by an independent judge who chooses the winner. Previous judges include Nathan Englander, Jane Smiley, Francine Prose, and Andre Dubus III.

BINGHAMTON UNIVERSITY JOHN GARDNER FICTION BOOK AWARD

Creative Writing Program, Binghamton University, Binghamton University, Department of English, General Literature, and Rhetoric, Library North Room 1149, P.O. Box 6000, Binghamton NY 13902-6000. (607)777-2713. **E-mail:** cwpro@binghamton.edu. **Website:** http://binghamton.edu/english/creative-writing/. **Contact:** Maria Mazziotti Gillan, director. Contest offered annually for a novel or collection of fiction published in previous year in a press run of 500 copies or more. Each book submitted must be accompanied by an application form. Publisher may submit more than 1 book for prize consideration. Send 2 copies of each book. Guidelines available on website. Author or publisher may submit. Deadline: March 1. Prize: $1,000. Judged by a professional writer not on Binghamton University faculty.

❧ JAMES TAIT BLACK MEMORIAL PRIZES

University of Edinburgh, School of Literatures, Languages, and Cultures, 50 George Square, Edinburgh EH8 9LH Scotland. (44-13)1650-3619. **E-mail:** s.strathdee@ed.ac.uk. **Website:** http://www.ed.ac.uk/events/james-tait-black. Open to any writer. Entries must be previously published. Winners notified by phone, via publisher. Contact department of English Literature for list of winners or check website. Accepts inquiries by e-mail or phone. Eligible works must be written in English and first published or co-published in Britain in the year of the award. Works should be submitted by publishers. Deadline: December 1. Prize: Two prizes each of £10,000 are awarded: one for the best work of fiction, one for the best biography or work of that nature, published during the calendar year January 1 to December 31. Judged by professors of English Literature with the assistance of teams of postgraduate readers.

BOULEVARD SHORT FICTION CONTEST FOR EMERGING WRITERS

Boulevard Magazine, 6614 Clayton Rd., PMB #325, Richmond Heights MO 63117. (314)862-2643. **Website:** www.boulevardmagazine.org. **Contact:** Jessica Rogen, editor. Offered annually for unpublished short fiction to a writer who has not yet published a book of fiction, poetry, or creative nonfiction with a nationally distributed press. Holds first North American rights on anything not previously published. Open to any writer with no previous publication by a nationally known press. Guidelines for SASE or on website. Accepts works up to 8,000 words. Simultaneous submissions are allowed, but previously accepted or published work is ineligible. Entries will be judged by the editors of *Boulevard Magazine.* Submit online or via postal mail. Deadline: December 31. Prize: $1,500, and publication in 1 of the next year's issues.

❧ THE CAINE PRIZE FOR AFRICAN WRITING

51 Southwark St., London SE1 1RU United Kingdom. **E-mail:** info@caineprize.com. **Website:** www.caineprize.com. **Contact:** Lizzy Attree. Entries must have appeared for the first time in the 5 years prior to the closing date for submissions, which is January 31 each year. Publishers should submit 6 copies of the published original with a brief cover note (no pro forma application). "Please indicate nationality or passport held." Submissions should be made by publishers only. Only one story per author will be considered in any one year. Only fiction work is eligible. Indicative length is between 3,000 and 10,000 words. See website for more details and rules. The Caine Prize is open to writers from anywhere in Africa for work published in English. Its focus is on the short story, reflecting the contemporary development of the African story-telling tradition. Deadline: January 31. Prize: £10,000. Judges change each year.

JOHN W. CAMPBELL MEMORIAL AWARD FOR BEST SCIENCE FICTION NOVEL OF THE YEAR

English Department, University of Kansas, Lawrence KS 66045. (785)864-3380. **Fax:** (785)864-1159. **E-mail:** cmckit@ku.edu. **Website:** www.sfcenter.ku.edu/campbell.htm. **Contact:** Chris McKitterick. Honors the best science fiction novel of the year. Entries must be previously published. Open to any writer. Accepts inquiries by e-mail and fax. "Ordinarily publishers should submit work, but authors have done so when publishers would not. Send for list of jurors." Results announced in July. For contest results, send SASE. Deadline: Check website. Prize: Campbell Award trophy. Winners receive an expense-paid trip to the university to receive their award. Their names are also engraved on a permanent trophy. Judged by a jury.

❂ CANADIAN AUTHORS ASSOCIATION AWARD FOR POETRY

6 West St. N, Suite 203, Orillia ON L3V 5B8 Canada. (705)325-3926. **E-mail:** admin@canadianauthors.org. **Website:** www.canadianauthors.org. **Contact:** Anita Purcell, executive director. Offered annually for a full-length English-language book of poems for adults, by a Canadian writer. Deadline: January 31. Prize: $1,000 and a silver medal. Judging: Each year a trustee for each award appointed by the Canadian Authors Association selects up to 3 judges. Identities of the trustee and judges are confidential.

❂ CANADIAN AUTHORS ASSOCIATION EMERGING WRITER AWARD

6 West St. N., Suite 203, Orilla ON L3X 5B8 Canada. **Website:** www.canadianauthors.org. **Contact:** Anita Purcell, executive director. Annual award for a writer under 30 years of age deemed to show exceptional promise in the field of literary creation. Deadline: January 15. Prize: $500. Judging: Each year a trustee for each award appointed by the Canadian Authors

Association selects up to 3 judges. Identities of the trustee and judges are confidential.

CASCADE WRITING CONTEST & AWARDS

Oregon Christian Writers, 1075 Willow Lake Road N., Keizer Oregon 97303. **E-mail:** cascade@oregonchristianwriters.org. **E-mail:** cascade@oregonchristianwriters.org. **Website:** http://oregonchristianwriters.org/. **Contact:** Marilyn Rhoads and Julie McDonald Zander. The Cascade Awards are presented at the annual Oregon Christian Writers Summer Conference (held at the Red Lion on the River in Portland, Oregon, each August) attended by national editors, agents, and professional authors. The contest is open for both published and unpublished works in the following categories: contemporary fiction book, historical fiction book, speculative fiction book, nonfiction book, memoir book, young adult/middle grade fiction book, young adult/middle grade nonfiction book, children's chapter book and picture book (fiction and nonfiction), poetry, devotional, article, column, story, or blog post. Two additional special Cascade Awards are presented each year: the Trailblazer Award to a writer who has distinguished him/herself in the field of Christian writing; and a Writer of Promise Award for a writer who demonstrates unusual promise in the field of Christian writing. For a full list of categories, entry rules, and scoring elements, visit website. Guidelines and rules available on the website. Entry forms will be available on the first day for entry. Annual multi-genre competition to encourage both published and emerging writers in the field of Christian writing. Deadline: March 31. Submissions period begins February 14. Prize: Award certificate and pin presented at the Cascade Awards ceremony during the Oregon Christian Writers Annual Summer Conference. Finalists are listed in the conference notebook and winners are listed online. Cascade Trophies are awarded to the recipients of the Trailblazer and Writer of Promise Awards. Judged by published authors, editors, librarians, and retail book store owners and employees. Final judging by editors, agents, and published authors from the Christian publishing industry.

KAY CATTARULLA AWARD FOR BEST SHORT STORY

Texas Institute of Letters, P.O. Box 609, Round Rock TX 78680. **E-mail:** tilsecretary@yahoo.com. **Website:** www.texasinstituteofletters.org. Offered annually for work published January 1-December 31 of the previous year to recognize the best short story. The story submitted must have appeared in print for the first time to be eligible. Writers must have been born in Texas, must have lived in Texas for at least 2 consecutive years, or the subject matter of the work must be associated with Texas. See website for guidelines. See website for details and instructions on entering the competition. Deadline: January 10. Prize: $1,000.

G. S. SHARAT CHANDRA PRIZE FOR SHORT FICTION

BkMk Press, University of Missouri-Kansas City, BkMk Press, University of Missouri-Kansas City, 5100 Rockhill Rd., Kansas City MO 64110-2499. (816)235-2558. **Fax:** (816)235-2611. **E-mail:** bkmk@umkc.edu; newletters@umkc.edu. **Website:** www.umkc.edu/bkmk. **Contact:** Ben Furnish. Offered annually for the best book-length ms collection (unpublished) of short fiction in English by a living author. Translations are not eligible. Initial judging is done by a network of published writers. Final judging is done by a writer of national reputation. Guidelines for SASE, by e-mail, or on website. Short fiction collections should be approximately 125 pages minimum, 300 pages maximum, double spaced. Deadline: January 15. Prize: $1,000, plus book publication by BkMk Press.

● PEGGY CHAPMAN-ANDREWS FIRST NOVEL AWARD

P.O. Box 6910, Dorset DT6 9QB United Kingdom. **E-mail:** info@bridportprize.org.uk. **Website:** www.bridportprize.org.uk. **Contact:** Kate Wilson, Prize Administrator. Award to promote literary excellence and new writers. Enter first chapters of novel, up to 8,000 words (minimum 5,000 words) plus 300 word synopsis. Send SSAE for entry form or enter online. Deadline: May 31. Prize: 1st Place: £1,000 plus mentoring & possible publication; Runner-Up: £500. Judged by Nathan Filer with The Literary Consultancy & A.M. Heath Literary Agents.

● THE ARTHUR C. CLARKE AWARD

55 Burtt House, Fanshaw Street, London N1 6LE U.K. **E-mail:** clarkeaward@gmail.com. **Website:** www.clarkeaward.com. **Contact:** Tom Hunter, award director. Annual award presented to the best science fiction novel, published between January 1 and December 31 of the year in question, receiving its first British publication during the calendar year. Deadline: 2nd week in December. Prize: £2,016 (rising by £1 each year),

and an engraved bookend. Judged by representatives of the British Science Fiction Association, the Science Fiction Foundation, and Sci-Fi-London Film Festival.

THE DANAHY FICTION PRIZE

Tampa Review, University of Tampa, 401 W. Kennedy Blvd., Tampa FL 33606. 813-253-6266. **E-mail:** utpress@ut.edu. **Website:** www.ut.edu/TampaReview. Annual award for the best previously unpublished short fiction. Prefers mss between 500-5,000 words. Deadline: November 30. Prize: $1,000, plus publication in *Tampa Review.*

THE DEADLY QUILL SHORT STORY WRITING CONTEST

Deadly Quill Magazine, **E-mail:** lorne@deadlyquill.com. **E-mail:** contest@deadlyquill.com. **Website:** www.deadlyquill.com. **Contact:** Lorne McMIllan. "We are hoping to give an outlet for short stories that follow the tradition of The Twilight Zone, Alfred Hitchcock, and The Outer Limits." Deadline: August 31. Prizes: $250 first place; $200 second place; $150 third place. Plus, more prizes described online. Author Edward Willett, Author Lorne McMillan, Author Colin Douglas.

DEAD OF WINTER

E-mail: editors@toasted-cheese.com. **Website:** www.toasted-cheese.com. **Contact:** Stephanie Lenz, editor. The contest is a winter-themed horror fiction contest with a new topic/theme each year. Theme and word count parameters announced October 1. Entries must be unpublished. Accepts inquiries by e-mail. Cover letter should include name, address, e-mail, word count, and title. Word count parameters vary each year. Open to any writer. Deadline: December 21. Results announced January 31. Winners notified by e-mail. List of winners on website. Prize: Amazon gift certificates and publication in *Toasted Cheese.* Judged by *Toasted Cheese* editors who blind judge each contest. Each judge uses her own criteria to rate entries. **TIPS** "Stories *mustT* be based on the theme provided, stories *must* be set in winter, stories MUST fall in the horror genre, and the word count range varies each year. Any horror subgenre is welcome. Note that the judges prefer gothic, dark fantasy, erotic horror (PG-13 max), noir, psychological horror, quiet/soft horror, and suspense horror. The judges tend not to like sci-fi horror, extreme/splatter horror, Lovecraftian, etc. but, as always, the quality and creativeness of the writing come first. See previous placed Dead of Winter entries

to get an idea of what the judges enjoy reading. Please no people who don't know they're dead or overdone "monsters" (vampires, werewolves, Sasquatch, etc.). Tropes like "creepy child" or "disturbed cult leader" may be necessary to use the provided theme. Just keep your characterizations fresh and three-dimensional and you should be able to avoid the "seen it" trap. As to gore level, we'd far rather know what's going on inside a character's head than to see it on a pike. We want to be disturbed, unable to shake your story and compelled to leave on every light in the house after reading it."

WILLIAM F. DEECK MALICE DOMESTIC GRANTS FOR UNPUBLISHED WRITERS

Malice Domestic, P.O. Box 8007, Gaithersburg MD 20898-8007. **E-mail:** malicegrants@comcast.net. **Website:** www.malicedomestic.org. **Contact:** Harriette Sackler. Offered annually for unpublished work in the mystery field. Malice awards one grant to unpublished writers in the Malice Domestic genre at its annual convention in May. The competition is designed to help the next generation of Malice authors get their first work published and to foster quality Malice literature. Malice Domestic literature is loosely described as mystery stories of the Agatha Christie type, i.e., traditional mysteries. These works usually feature no excessive gore, gratuitous violence, or explicit sex. Writers who have been published previously in the mystery field, including publication of a mystery novel, short story, or dramatic work, are ineligible to apply. Members of the Malice Domestic Board of Directors and their families are ineligible to apply. Malice encourages applications from minority candidates. Guidelines online. Deadline: November 1. Prize: $2,500, plus a comprehensive registration to the following year's convention and two nights' lodging at the convention hotel.

THE JACK DYER FICTION PRIZE

Crab Orchard Review, Department of English, Mail Code 4503, Faner Hall 2380, Southern Illinois University Carbondale, 1000 Faner Drive, Carbondale IL 62901. (618)453-6833. **Fax:** (618)453-8224. **E-mail:** jtribble@siu.edu. **Website:** www.craborchardreview.siu.edu. **Contact:** Jon C. Tribble, managing editor. Annual award for unpublished short fiction. Entries should consist of 1 story up to 6,000 words maximum in length. *Crab Orchard Review* acquires first North American serial rights to all submitted work. One winner and at least 2 finalists will be chosen. Length: 6,000 words maximum. All submissions must be made through Submittable. Submissions must be unpublished original work, written in English by a U.S. citizen, permanent resident, or person who has DACA/TPS status (current students and employees at Southern Illinois University Carbondale are not eligible). See Submittable guidelines online for complete formatting instructions. The author's name should not appear on any page of the entry. Results announced by end of August. Deadline: May 17. Prize: $2,000, publication and 1-year subscription to *Crab Orchard Review*. Finalists are offered $500 and publication. Judged by editorial staff (pre-screening); winner chosen by genre editor.

TIPS "Carefully read directions for entering and follow them exactly. Send us your best work. Note that simultaneous submissions are accepted for this prize, but the winning entry must NOT be accepted elsewhere. All submissions should be made through Submittable: https://craborchardreview.submittable.com/submit."

☙ THE FAR HORIZONS AWARD FOR SHORT FICTION

The Malahat Review, University of Victoria, P.O. Box 1700, Stn CSC, Victoria BC V8W 2Y2 Canada. (250)721-8524. **Fax:** (250)472-5051. **E-mail:** malahat@uvic.ca. **E-mail:** horizons@uvic.ca. **Website:** www.malahatreview.ca. **Contact:** Patrick Grace, publicity manager. Submissions must be unpublished. No simultaneous submissions. Submit 1 piece of short fiction, 3,500 words maximum; no restrictions on subject matter or aesthetic approach. Include separate page with author's name, address, e-mail, and title; no identifying information on mss pages. E-mail submissions are accepted. Do not include SASE for results; mss will not be returned. Guidelines available on website. Winner and finalists contacted by e-mail. Open to "emerging short fiction writers from Canada, the US, and elsewhere" who have not yet published their fiction in a full-length book (48 pages or more). Deadline: May 1 of odd numbered years. Prize: $1,000 CAD, publication in fall issue of *The Malahat Review* (see separate listing in Magazines/Journals). Announced in fall on website, Facebook page, and in quarterly e-newsletter, *Malahat Lite.*

GIVAL PRESS NOVEL AWARD

Gival Press, LLC, P.O. Box 3812, Arlington VA 22203. (703)351-0079. **E-mail:** givalpress@yahoo.com. **Website:** www.givalpress.submittable.com. **Contact:** Robert L. Giron. Offered every other year for a previously original unpublished novel (not a translation). Guidelines by phone, on website, via e-mail, or by mail with SASE. Results announced late fall of same year. Winners notified by phone. Results made available to entrants with SASE, by e-mail, on website. Open to any author who writes original unpublished ms/work in English. Length: 30,000-100,000 words. Cover letter should include name, address, phone, e-mail, word count, novel title; include a short bio and short synopsis. Only the title and word count should appear on the actual ms. Writers may submit own work. Purpose is to award the best literary novel. Deadline: May 30. Prize: $3,000, plus publication of book with a standard contract and author's copies. Final judge is announced after winner is chosen. Entries read anonymously.

TIPS "Review the types of mss Gival Press has published. We stress literary works."

GIVAL PRESS SHORT STORY AWARD

Gival Press, P.O. Box 3812, Arlington VA 22203. (703)351-0079. **E-mail:** givalpress@yahoo.com. **Website:** www.givalpress.submittable.com. **Contact:** Robert L. Giron, publisher. Annual literary, short story contest. Entries must be unpublished. Open to anyone who writes original short stories, which are not a chapter of a novel, in English. Receives about 100-150 entries per category. Guidelines available online, via e-mail, or by mail. Results announced in the fall of the same year. Winners notified by phone. Results available with SASE, by e-mail, and on website. Length: 5,000-15,000 words. Include name, address, phone, e-mail, word count, title on cover letter; include short bio. Only the title and word count should be found on ms. Writers may submit their own fiction. Recognizes the best literary short story. Deadline: August 8. Prize: $1,000 and publication on website. Judged anonymously.

GLIMMER TRAIN'S FAMILY MATTERS CONTEST

Glimmer Train, P.O. Box 80430, Portland OR 97280. (503)221-0836. **Fax:** (503)221-0837. **E-mail:** eds@glimmertrain.org. **Website:** www.glimmertrain.org. **Contact:** Susan Burmeister-Brown. This contest is now held once a year, during the months of November and December. Winners are contacted on March 1. Submit online at www.glimmertrain.org. The word count for this contest generally ranges from 1,000 to 5,000 words, though up 12,000 words is fine. See complete guidelines online. Deadline: December 31. Prize: 1st Place: $2,500, publication in *Glimmer Train Stories*, and 10 copies of that issue; 2nd Place: $500 and consideration for publication; 3rd Place: $300 and consideration for publication. The editors judge.

TIPS "We are looking for stories about families of all configurations. It's fine to draw heavily on real life experiences, but the work must read like fiction and all stories accepted for publication will be presented as fiction."

GLIMMER TRAIN'S FICTION OPEN

Glimmer Train, Inc., Glimmer Train Press, Inc., P.O. Box 80430, Portland OR 97280. (503)221-0836. **Fax:** (503)221-0837. **E-mail:** eds@glimmertrain.org. **Website:** www.glimmertrain.org. **Contact:** Susan Burmeister-Brown. Submissions to this category generally range from 3,000-8,000 words, but up to 20,000 is fine. Held twice a year: March 1 - April 30 and July 1 - August 31. Submit online at www.glimmertrain.org. Winners will be called 2 months after the close of the contest. Deadline: April 30 and August 31. Prize: 1st Place: $3,000, publication in *Glimmer Train Stories*, and 10 copies of that issue; 2nd Place: $1,000 and consideration for publication; 3rd Place: $600 and consideration for publication. Judged by the editors.

TIPS This category is open to all writers and all themes. The prize was just increased in 2016.

GLIMMER TRAIN'S SHORT-STORY AWARD FOR NEW WRITERS

Glimmer Train Press, Inc., P.O. Box 80430, Portland OR 97280. (503)221-0836. **Fax:** (503)221-0837. **E-mail:** eds@glimmertrain.org. **Website:** www.glimmertrain.org. **Contact:** Susan Burmeister-Brown. Offered for any writer whose fiction hasn't appeared in a nationally distributed print publication with a circulation over 5,000. Submissions to this category generally range from 1,000–5,000 words, but up to 12,000 is fine. Held three times a year: January 1–February 29, May 1–June 30, September 1–October 31. Submit online at www.glimmertrain.org. Winners will be called 2 months after the close of the contest. Deadline: February 29, June 30, and October 31. Prize: 1st Place: $2,500, publication in *Glimmer Train Stories*, and 10

copies of that issue; 2nd Place: $500 and consideration for publication; 3rd Place: $300 and consideration for publication.

TIPS "In a recent edition of *Best American Short Stories*, of the top '100 Distinguished Short Stories,' 10 appeared in *Glimmer Train Stories*, more than any other publication in the country, including *The New Yorker*. Of those 10, 3 were those authors' first stories accepted for publication."

GLIMMER TRAIN'S VERY SHORT FICTION CONTEST

Glimmer Train Press, Inc., P.O. Box 80430, Portland OR 97280. (503)221-0836. **Fax:** (503)221-0837. **E-mail:** eds@glimmertrain.org. **Website:** www.glimmertrain.org. **Contact:** Susan Burmeister-Brown. Offered to encourage the art of the very short story. Word count: 3,000 maximum. Held twice a year: March 1–April 30 and July 1–August 31. Submit online at www.glimmertrain.org. Results announced 2 months after the close of the contest. To encourage the art of the very short story. Deadline: April 30 and August 31. Prize: 1st Place: $2,000, publication in *Glimmer Train Stories*, and 10 copies of that issue; 2nd Place: $500 and consideration for publication; 3rd Place: $300 and consideration for publication. Judged by the editors.

TIPS There is no minimum word count, though it is rare for a piece under 500 words to read as a full story.

🌀 MARJORIE GRABER-MCINNIS SHORT STORY AWARD

ACT Writers Centre, Gorman House Arts Centre, Ainslie Ave., Braddon ACT 2612 Australia. (61)(2)6262-9191. **Fax:** (61)(2)6262-9191. **E-mail:** admin@actwriters.org.au. **Website:** www.actwriters.org.au. Open theme for a short story with 1,500-3,000 words. Guidelines available on website. Open only to unpublished emerging writers residing within the ACT or region. Deadline: September 18. Submissions period begins in early September. Prize: $600 and publication. Five runners-up receive book prizes. All winners may be published in the ACT Writers Centre newsletter and on the ACT Writers Centre website.

🌀 LYNDALL HADOW/DONALD STUART SHORT STORY COMPETITION

Fellowship of Australian Writers (WA), P.O. Box 6180, Swanbourne WA 6910 Australia. (61)(8)9384-4771. **Fax:** (61)(8)9384-4854. **E-mail:** fellowshipaustralianwriterswa@gmail.com. **Website:** www.fawwa.org. Annual contest for unpublished short stories (maximum 3,000 words). Reserves the right to publish entries in a FAWWA publication or on website. Guidelines online or for SASE. Deadline: June 1. Submissions period begins April 1. Prize: 1st Place: $1,00; 2nd Place: $300; 3rd Place: $100.

HAMMETT PRIZE

International Association of Crime Writers, North American Branch, 243 Fifth Avenue, #537, New York NY 10016. **E-mail:** mfrisque@igc.org. **Website:** www.crimewritersna.org. **Contact:** Mary A. Frisque, executive director, North American Branch. Award for crime novels, story collections, nonfiction by one author. "Our reading committee seeks suggestions from publishers and they also ask the membership for recommendations." Nominations announced in January; winners announced in fall. Winners notified by e-mail or mail and recognized at awards ceremony. For contest results, send SASE or e-mail. For guidelines, send SASE or e-mail. Accepts inquiries by e-mail. Entries must be previously published. To be eligible, the book must have been published in the US or Canada during the calendar year. The author must be a US or Canadian citizen or permanent resident. Award established to honor a work of literary excellence in the field of crime writing by a US or Canadian author. Deadline: December 15. Prize: Trophy. Judged by a committee of members of the organization. The committee chooses 5 nominated books, which are then sent to 3 outside judges for a final selection. Judges are outside the crime writing field.

WILDA HEARNE FLASH FICTION CONTEST

Big Muddy: A Journal of the Mississippi River Valley, WHFF Contest, Southeast Missouri State University Press, One University Plaza, MS 2650, Cape Girardeau MO 63701. (573) 651-2044. **E-mail:** sswartwout@semo.edu. **Website:** www.semopress.com. **Contact:** Susan Swartwout, publisher. Annual competition for flash fiction, held by Southeast Missouri State University Press. Work must not be previously published. Send maximum of 500 words, double-spaced, with no identifying name on the pages, and a separate cover sheet with story title, author's name, address, and phone number. Send SASE for notification of results; all manuscripts will be recycled. Entries should be sent via postal mail. Deadline: October 1. Prize: $500 and publication in *Big Muddy: A Journal of the Mississippi River Valley*. Semi-finalists will be chosen by a team of published writers. The final manuscript will be chosen by Susan Swartwout, publisher of the Southeast Missouri State University Press.

DRUE HEINZ LITERATURE PRIZE

University of Pittsburgh Press, 7500 Thomas Blvd., Pittsburgh PA 15260. **Fax:** (412)383-2466. **E-mail:** info@upress.pitt.edu. **Website:** www.upress.pitt.edu. Offered annually to writers who have published a book-length collection of fiction or a minimum of 3 short stories or novellas in commercial magazines or literary journals of national distribution. Does not return mss. Deadline: June 30. Open to submissions on May 1. Prize: $15,000. Judged by anonymous nationally known writers such as Robert Penn Warren, Joyce Carol Oates, and Margaret Atwood.

LORIAN HEMINGWAY SHORT STORY COMPETITION

Hemingway Days Festival, P.O. Box 2011 c/o Cynthia. D. Higgs: Key West Editorial, Key West FL 33045. **E-mail:** shortstorykeywest@hushmail.com. **Website:** www.shortstorycompetition.com. **Contact:** Eva Eliot, Editorial Assistant. Offered annually for unpublished short stories up to 3,500 words. Guidelines available via mail, e-mail, or online. Accepts inquiries by e-mail, or visit website. Entries must be unpublished. Open to all writers whose work has not appeared in a nationally distributed publication with a circulation of 5,000 or more. Looking for excellence, pure and simple—no genre restrictions, no theme restrictions. We seek a writer's voice that cannot be ignored. All entrants will receive a letter from Lorian Hemingway and a list of winners, via mail or e-mail, by October 1. Results announced at the end of July during Hemingway Days festival. Winners notified by phone prior to announcement. Award to encourage literary excellence and the efforts of writers whose voices have yet to be heard. Deadline: May 15. Prizes: 1st Place: $1,500, plus publication of his or her winning story in *Cutthroat: A Journal of the Arts*; 2nd-3rd Place: $500; honorable mentions will also be awarded. Judged by a panel of writers, editors, and literary scholars selected by author Lorian Hemingway. (Lorian Hemingway is the competition's final judge.)

TONY HILLERMAN PRIZE

Wordharvest, 1063 Willow Way, Santa Fe NM 87507. (505)471-1565. **E-mail:** wordharvest@wordharvest.com. **Website:** www.wordharvest.com. **Contact:** Anne Hillerman and Jean Schaumberg, co-organizers. Awarded annually, and sponsored by St. Martin's

Press, for the best first mystery set in the Southwest. Murder or another serious crime or crimes must be at the heart of the story, with the emphasis on the solution rather than the details of the crime. Multiple entries accepted. Accepts inquiries by e-mail, phone. Entries should be unpublished; self-published work is generally accepted. Length: no less than 220 type written pages, or approximately 60,000 words. Cover letter should include name, address, phone, e-mail, list of publishing credits. Please include SASE for response. Writers may submit their own work. Entries should be mailed to St. Martin's Press: St. Martin's Minotaur/THWC Competition, St. Martin's Minotaur, 175 Fifth Ave., New York, NY 10010. Honors the contributions made by Tony Hillerman to the art and craft of the mystery. Deadline: June 1. Prize: $10,000 advance and publication by St. Martin's Press. Nominees will be selected by judges chosen by the editorial staff of St. Martin's Press, with the assistance of independent judges selected by organizers of the Tony Hillerman Writers Conference (Wordharvest), and the winner will be chosen by St. Martin's editors.

TOM HOWARD/JOHN H. REID FICTION & ESSAY CONTEST

Winning Writers, 351 Pleasant Street, PMB 222, Northampton MA 01060-3961. (866)946-9748. **Fax:** (413)280-0539. **E-mail:** adam@winningwriters.com. **Website:** www.winningwriters.com. **Contact:** Adam Cohen, President. Since 2001, Winning Writers has provided expert literary contest information to the public. Sponsors four contests. One of the "101 Best Websites for Writers" (*Writer's Digest*). Open to all writers. Submit any type of short story or essay. Both published and unpublished works are welcome. If you win a prize, requests nonexclusive rights to publish your submission online, in e-mail newsletters, in e-books, and in press releases. See website for guidelines and to submit your entry. Prefers inquiries by e-mail. Length: 6,000 words max per entry. Writers may submit own work. Winners notified by e-mail. Results made available to entrants on website. Deadline: April 30. Prizes: Two 1st prizes of $1,500 will be awarded, plus 10 honorable mentions of $100 each. Top 12 entries published online. Judged by Arthur Powers, assisted by Lauren Singer.

TIPS Read past winning entries at https://winning-writers.com/our-contests/contest-archives.

Read advice from the judge at https://winningwriters.com/resources/advice-from-arthur-powers-judge-tom-howard-fiction-essay-contest.

L. RON HUBBARD'S WRITERS OF THE FUTURE CONTEST

Author Services, Inc., P.O. Box 1630, Los Angeles CA 90078. (323)466-3310. **Fax:** (323)466-6474. **E-mail:** contests@authorservicesinc.com. **Website:** www.writersofthefuture.com. **Contact:** Joni Labaqui, contest director. Foremost competition for new and amateur writers of unpublished science fiction or fantasy short stories or novelettes. Offered to find, reward and publicize new speculative fiction writers so they may more easily attain professional writing careers. Open to writers who have not professionally published a novel or short novel, more than 2 novelettes, or more than 3 short stories. Entry stories must be unpublished. Limit 1 entry per quarter. This is an international contest. Results announced quarterly in e-newsletter. Winners notified by phone. Contest has 4 quarters. There shall be 3 cash prizes in each quarter. In addition, at the end of the year, the 4 first-place, quarterly winners will have their entries rejudged, and a grand prize winner shall be determined. Eligible entries are previously unpublished short stories or novelettes (under 17,000 words) of science fiction or fantasy. Guidelines for SASE or on website. Accepts inquiries by fax, e-mail, phone. Mss: White paper, black ink; double-spaced; typed; each page appropriately numbered with title, no author name. Include cover page with author's name, address, phone number, e-mail address (if available), as well as estimated word count and the title of the work. Online submissions are accepted. Hard copy submissions will not be returned. Deadline: December 31, March 31, June 30, September 30. Prize (awards quarterly): 1st Place: $1,000; 2nd Place: $750; and 3rd Place: $500. Annual grand prize: $5,000. Judged by David Farland (initial judge), then by a panel of 4 professional authors.

INDIANA REVIEW POETRY CONTEST

Ballantine Hall 465, Indiana University, 1020 E. Kirkwood Ave., Bloomington IN 47405-7103. **E-mail:** inreview@indiana.edu. **Website:** http://indianareview.org. **Contact:** Peter Kispert, editor. Contest for poetry in any style and on any subject. Open to any writer. Mss will not be returned. No works forthcoming elsewhere, are eligible. Simultaneous submissions accepted, but in the event of entrant withdrawal, contest fee will not be refunded. Deadline: April 1. Submission period begins February 15. Prize: $1,000, publication in the *Indiana Review* and contributor's copies. Judged by Camille Rankine.

TIPS "We look for a command of language and structure, as well as a facility with compelling and unusual subject matter. It's a good idea to obtain copies of issues featuring past winners to get a more concrete idea of what we are looking for."

INK & INSIGHTS WRITING CONTEST

Critique My Novel, 2408 W. 8th, Amarillo TX 79106. **E-mail:** contest@InkandInsights.com. **Website:** http://InkandInsights.com. **Contact:** Catherine York, contest administrator. Ink & Insights is a writing contest geared toward strengthening the skills of independent writers by focusing on feedback. Each entry is assigned four judges who specialize in the genre of the manuscript. They read, score, and comment on specific aspects of the segment. The top three mss in the Master and Nonfiction categories move on to the Agent Round and receive a guaranteed read and feedback from a panel of agents. Send the first 10,000 words of your manuscript (unpublished, self-published, or published through a vanity/independent press). Include a cover sheet that contains the following information: novel title, genre, word count of full ms, e-mail address. Do not put name on submission. See website for full details and formatting guidelines. Deadline: April 30 (regular entry), June 30 (late entry). Prize: Prizes vary depending on category. Every novel receives personal feedback from 4 judges. Judges listed on website, including the agents who will be helping choose the top winners this year.

THE IOWA SHORT FICTION AWARD & JOHN SIMMONS SHORT FICTION AWARD

Iowa Writers' Workshop, 507 N. Clinton St., 102 Dey House, Iowa City IA 52242-1000. **Website:** www.uiowapress.org. **Contact:** James McCoy, director. Annual award to give exposure to promising writers who have not yet published a book of prose. Open to any writer. Current University of Iowa students are not eligible. No application forms are necessary. Announcement of winners made early in year following competition. Winners notified by phone. No application forms are necessary. Do not send original ms. Include SASE for return of ms. Entries must be unpublished, but stories previously published in periodicals are eligible for inclusion. The ms must be a collection of short stories of at least 150 word-processed, double-spaced pages. Deadline: September 30. Submission period begins August 1. Prize: Publication by University of Iowa Press. Judged by senior Iowa Writers' Workshop members who screen mss; published fiction author of note makes final selections.

JESSE H. JONES AWARD FOR BEST WORK OF FICTION

P.O. Box 609, Round Rock TX 78680. **E-mail:** tilsecretary@yahoo.com. **Website:** http://texasinstituteofletters.org. Offered annually by Texas Institute of Letters for work published January 1-December 31 of year before award is given to recognize the writer of the best book of fiction entered in the competition. Writers must have been born in Texas, have lived in the state for at least 2 consecutive years at some time, or the subject matter of the work should be associated with the state. See website for details and information on submitting. Deadline: January 10. Prize: $6,000.

JAMES JONES FIRST NOVEL FELLOWSHIP

Wilkes University, Creative Writing Department, Wilkes University, 84 West South Street, Wilkes-Barre PA 18766. (570)408-4547. **Fax:** (570)408-3333. **E-mail:** jamesjonesfirstnovel@wilkes.edu. **Website:** www.wilkes.edu/. Offered annually for unpublished novels (must be works-in-progress). This competition is open to all U.S. citizens who have not previously published novels. Submit a 2-page (maximum) outline of the entire novel and the first 50 pages of the novel-in-progress are to be submitted. The ms must be typed and double-spaced; outline may be single-spaced. Entrants submitting via snail mail should include their name, address, telephone number, and e-mail address (if available) on the title page, but nowhere else on the manuscript. For those entrants submitting online, name, address, telephone number, and e-mail address should appear only on your cover letter. Cover letter should be dropped in the cover letter box and outline and ms should be attached as one document. The award is intended to honor the spirit of unblinking honesty, determination, and insight into modern culture exemplified by the late James Jones. Deadline: March 15. Submission period begins October 1. Prize: $10,000; 2 runners-up get $1,000 honorarium.

THE LAWRENCE FOUNDATION AWARD

Prairie Schooner, 123 Andrews Hall, University of Nebraska-Lincoln, Lincoln NE 68588-0334. (402)472-

0911. **Fax:** (402)472-9771. **E-mail:** prairieschooner@unl.edu. **Website:** www.prairieschooner.unl.edu. Offered annually for the best short story published in Prairie Schooner in the previous year. Only work published in *Prairie Schooner* in the previous year is considered. Work is nominated by editorial staff. Results announced in the Spring issue. Winners notified by mail in February or March. Prize: $1,000. Judged by editorial staff of *Prairie Schooner*.

LAWRENCE FOUNDATION PRIZE

Michigan Quarterly Review, 0576 Rackham Bldg., 915 E. Washington Street, Ann Arbor MI 48109-1070. (734)764-9265. **E-mail:** mqr@umich.edu. **Website:** www.michiganquarterlyreview.com. **Contact:** Vicki Lawrence, managing editor. This annual prize is awarded by the *Michigan Quarterly Review* editorial board to the author of the best short story published in *MQR* that year. The prize is sponsored by University of Michigan alumnus and fiction writer Leonard S. Bernstein, a trustee of the Lawrence Foundation of New York. Approximately 20 short stories are published in *MQR* each year. Guidelines available under submission guidelines on website. Prize: $1,000. Judged by editorial board.

LITERAL LATTÉ FICTION AWARD

Literal Latté, 200 E. 10th St., Suite 240, New York NY 10003. **E-mail:** litlatte@aol.com. **E-mail:** Link to submittable on www.literal-latte.com. **Website:** www.literal-latte.com. **Contact:** Edward Estlin, contributing editor. Award to provide talented writers with 3 essential tools for continued success: money, publication, and recognition. Offered annually for unpublished fiction (maximum 20,000 words). Guidelines online. Open to any writer. Deadline: January 15. Prize: 1st Place: $1,000 and publication in *Literal Latté*; 2nd Place: $300; 3rd Place: $200; also up to 7 honorable mentions. All winners published in *Literal Latté*.

LITERAL LATTE SHORT SHORTS CONTEST

Literal Latté, 200 E. 10th St., Suite 240, New York NY 10003. **E-mail:** litlatte@aol.com. **E-mail:** Link to submittable on www.literal-latte.com. **Website:** www.literal-latte.com. **Contact:** Jenine Gordon Bockman, editor. Keeping free thought free since 1994. Deadline: June 30. Prize: $500. Judged by the editors.

LITERARY FICTION CONTEST

The Writers' Workshop of Asheville, NC, Literary Fiction Contest, 387 Beaucatcher Rd., Asheville NC

28805. **E-mail:** writersw@gmail.com. **Website:** www.twwoa.org. Submit a short story or chapter of a novel of 5,000 words or less. Multiple entries are accepted. All work must be unpublished. Pages should be paper clipped, with your name, address, phone and title of work on a cover sheet. Double-space and use 12-point font. Deadline: August 30. Prize: 1st Place: Your choice of a 2 night stay at the Mountain Muse B&B in Asheville, 3 free online workshops, or 50 pages line-edited and revised by editorial staff; 2nd Place: 2 free workshops or 35 pages line-edited; 3rd Place: 1 free workshop or 25 pages line-edited; 10 Honorable Mentions. Judged by published writing instructors.

THE MARY MACKEY SHORT STORY PRIZE CATEGORY

Soul-Making Keats Literary Competition, The Webhallow House, 1544 Sweetwood Dr., Broadmoor Village CA 94015. **E-mail:** SoulKeats@mail.com. **Website:** www.soulmakingcontest.us. **Contact:** Eileen Malone. Open annually to any writer. One story/entry, up to 5,000 words. All prose works must be typed, page numbered, and double-spaced. Identify only with 3x5 card. Deadline: November 30. Prize: Cash prizes.

✪ THE MALAHAT REVIEW NOVELLA PRIZE

The Malahat Review, University of Victoria, P.O. Box 1700 STN CSC, Victoria BC V8W 2Y2 Canada. (250)721-8524. **E-mail:** malahat@uvic.ca. **E-mail:** novella@uvic.ca. **Website:** malahatreview.ca. **Contact:** Patrick Grace, publicity manager. Held in alternate (even numbered) years with the Long Poem Prize. Submit novellas between 10,000 and 20,000 words in length. Include separate page with author's name, address, e-mail, and novella title; no identifying information on mss. pages. E-mail submissions are now accepted. Do not include SASE for results; mss will not be returned. Guidelines available on website. 2010 winner was Tony Tulathimutte, 2012 winner was Naben Ruthnum, and the 2014 winner was Dora Dueck. Winner and finalists contacted by e-mail. Offered to promote unpublished novellas. Obtains first world rights. After publication rights revert to the author. Open to any writer. Deadline: February 1 (even years). Prize: $1,500 CAD and one year's subscription. Winner published in summer issue of *The Malahat Review* and announced on website, Facebook page, and in quarterly e-newsletter, *Malahat Lite*. Three recognized literary figures are assigned to judge the contest each year.

THE MAN BOOKER PRIZE

Four Colman Getty PR, 20 St Thomas Street, London SE1 9BF United Kingdom. (44)(207)697 4200. **Website:** www.themanbookerprize.com. **Contact:** Four Colman Getty PR. Books are only accepted through UK publishers. However, publication outside the UK does not disqualify a book once it is published in the UK. Open to any full-length novel (published October 1-September 30). No novellas, collections of short stories, translations, or self-published books. Open to citizens of the Commonwealth or Republic of Ireland. Deadline: July. Prize: £50,000. Judges appointed by the Booker Prize Management Committee.

MARY MCCARTHY PRIZE IN SHORT FICTION

Sarabande Books, 2234 Dundee Rd., Suite 200, Louisville KY 40205. (502)458-4028. **Fax:** (502)458-4065. **E-mail:** info@sarabandebooks.org. **Website:** www.sarabandebooks.org. **Contact:** Sarah Gorham, Editor-in-Chief. Annual competition to honor a collection of short stories, novellas, or a short novel. All mss should be between 150 and 250 pages. All finalists considered for publication. Guidelines available online. Deadline: February 15. Submission period begins January 1. Prize: $2,000 and publication (standard royalty contract).

MEMPHIS MAGAZINE FICTION CONTEST

Memphis Magazine, co-sponsored by booksellers of Laurelwood and Burke's Book Store, Fiction Contest, c/o *Memphis* magazine, P.O. Box 1738, Memphis TN 38101. (901)521-9000, ext. 451. **Fax:** (901)521-0129. **E-mail:** sadler@memphismagazine.com. **Website:** www.memphismagazine.com. **Contact:** Marilyn Sadler. Annual award for authors of short fiction living within 150 miles of Memphis. Each story should be between 2,500 and 3,500 words long. See website for guidelines and rules. Deadline: February 15. Prize: $1,000 grand prize, along with being published in the annual Cultural Issue; two honorable-mention awards of $500 each will be given if the quality of entries warrants.

DAVID NATHAN MEYERSON PRIZE FOR FICTION

Southwest Review, Southern Methodist University, P.O. Box 750374, Dallas TX 75275-0374. (214) 768-1037. **Fax:** (214) 768-1408. **E-mail:** swr@smu.edu. **Website:** www.smu.edu/southwestreview. **Contact:** Greg Brownderville, editor-in-chief. Annual award given to a writer who has not published a first book of fiction, either a novel or collection of stories. All contest entrants will receive a copy of the issue in which the winning piece appears. Submissions must be no longer than 8,000 words. Work should be printed without the author's name. Name and address should appear only on the cover letter. Submissions will not be returned. Deadline: May 1 (postmarked). Prize: $1,000 and publication in the *Southwest Review*.

TIPS "A cover letter with name, address, and other relevant information may accompany the piece which must be printed without any identifying information. Get guidelines for SASE or online."

MILKWEED NATIONAL FICTION PRIZE

1011 Washington Ave. S., Suite 300, Minneapolis MN 55415. (612)332-3192. **Fax:** (612)215-2550. **E-mail:** editor@milkweed.org. **Website:** www.milkweed.org. **Contact:** Patrick Thoman, editor and program manager. Annual award for unpublished works. Mss should be one of the following: a novel, a collection of short stories, one or more novellas, or a combination of short stories and one or more novellas. Mss should be of high literary quality and between 150-400 pages in length. Work previously published as a book in the US is not eligible, but individual stories or novellas previously published in magazines or anthologies are eligible. Guidelines available online. Deadline: Rolling submissions. Check website for details of when they're accepting mss. Prize: Publication by Milkweed Editions and a cash advance of $5,000 against royalties, agreed upon in the contractual arrangement negotiated at the time of acceptance. Judged by the editors.

MONTANA PRIZE IN FICTION

Cutbank Literary Magazine, *CutBank*, University of Montana, English Dept., LA 133, Missoula MT 59812. **E-mail:** editor.cutbank@gmail.com. **Website:** www.cutbankonline.org. **Contact:** Allison Linville, editor-in-chief. The Montana Prize in Fiction seeks to highlight work that showcases an authentic voice, a boldness of form, and a rejection of functional fixedness. Accepts online submissions only. Send a single work, no more than 35 pages. Guidelines available online. Deadline: January 15. Submissions period begins November 9. Prize: $500 and featured in the magazine. Judged by a guest judge each year.

THE HOWARD FRANK MOSHER SHORT FICTION PRIZE

Vermont College, 36 College St., Montpelier VT 05602. (802)828-8517. E-mail: hungermtn@vcfa.edu. Website: www.hungermtn.org. Contact: Samantha Kolber, managing editor. The Howard Frank Mosher Short Fiction Prize is an annual contest for short fiction. Enter one original, unpublished story under 10,000 words. Do not put name or address on the story; entries are judged blind. Accepts submissions online or via postal mail. Deadline: March 1. Prize: One first place winner receives $1,000 and publication. Two honorable mentions receive $100 each, and are considered for publication. Judged by Janet Burroway in 2016 and Caitlyn Horrocks in 2017.

NATIONAL READERS' CHOICE AWARDS

Oklahoma Romance Writers of America (OKRWA), E-mail: nrca@okrwa.com. Website: www.okrwa.com. Contact: Kathy L Wheeler. "To provide writers of romance fiction with a competition where their published novels are judged by readers." See the website for categories and descriptions. Additional award for best first book. All entries must have an original copyright date during the current contest year. Entries will be accepted from authors, editors, publishers, agents, readers, whoever wants to fill out the entry form, pay the fee, and supply the books. No limit to the number of entries, but each title may be entered only in one category. Open to any writer published by an RWA approved non-vanity/non-subsidy press. For guidelines, send e-mail or visit website. Deadline: December 1st. Prize: Plaques and finalist certificates awarded at the awards banquet hosted at the Annual National Romance Writers Convention. Judged by readers.

NATIONAL WRITERS ASSOCIATION NOVEL WRITING CONTEST

The National Writers Association, 10940 S. Parker Rd. #508, Parker CO 80134. E-mail: natlwritersassn@hotmail.com. Website: www.nationalwriters.com. Contact: Sandy Whelchel, director. Open to any genre or category. Contest begins December 1. Open to any writer. Entries must be unpublished. Length: 20,000-100,000 words. Contest forms are available on the NWA website or an attachment will be sent upon request via e-mail or with an SASE. Annual contest to help develop creative skills, to recognize and reward

outstanding ability, and to increase the opportunity for the marketing and subsequent publication of novel mss. Deadline: April 1. Prize: 1st Place: $500; 2nd Place: $250; 3rd Place: $150. Judged by editors and agents.

NATIONAL WRITERS ASSOCIATION SHORT STORY CONTEST

10940 S. Parker Rd., #508, Parker CO 80134. E-mail: natlwritersassn@hotmail.com. Website: www.nationalwriters.com. Any genre of short story manuscript may be entered. All entries must be postmarked by July 1. Contest opens April 1. Only unpublished works may be submitted. All manuscripts must be typed, double-spaced, in the English language. Maximum length is 5,000 words. Those unsure of proper manuscript format should request Research Report #35. The entry must be accompanied by an entry form (photocopies are acceptable) and return SASE if you wish the material and rating sheets returned. Submissions will be destroyed, otherwise. Receipt of entry will not be acknowledged without a return postcard. Author's name and address must appear on the first page. Entries remain the property of the author and may be submitted during the contest as long as they are not published before the final notification of winners. Final prizes will be awarded in June. The purpose of the National Writers Assn. Short Story Contest is to encourage the development of creative skills, recognize and reward outstanding ability in the area of short story writing. Prize: 1st Prize: $250; 2nd Prize: $100; 3rd Prize: $50; 4th-10th places will receive a book. 1st-3rd place winners may be asked to grant one-time rights for publication in *Authorship* magazine. Honorable Mentions receive a certificate. Judging will be based on originality, marketability, research, and reader interest. Copies of the judges evaluation sheets will be sent to entrants furnishing an SASE with their entry.

THE NELLIGAN PRIZE FOR SHORT FICTION

Colorado Review/Center for Literary Publishing, Colorado State University, 9105 Campus Delivery, Dept. of English, Colorado State University, Ft. Collins CO 80523-9105. (970)491-5449. E-mail: creview@colostate.edu. Website: http://nelliganprize.colostate.edu. Contact: Stephanie G'Schwind, editor. Annual competition/award for short stories. Receives approximately 900 stories. All entries are read blind by Colorado Review's editorial staff. Ten to fifteen entries are selected to be sent on to a final, outside judge. Stories must be unpublished and between 10 and 50 pages. "The Nelligan Prize for Short Fiction was established in memory of Liza Nelligan, a writer, editor, and friend of many in Colorado State University's English Department, where she received her master's degree in literature in 1992. By giving an award to the author of an outstanding short story each year, we hope to honor Liza Nelligan's life, her passion for writing, and her love of fiction." Deadline: March 14. Prize: $2,000 and publication of story in *Colorado Review*. Judged by a different writer each year. 2017 judge is Richard Bausch.

◐ SEAN O'FAOLAIN SHORT STORY COMPETITION

The Munster Literature Centre, Frank O'Connor House, 84 Douglas Street, Cork Ireland. +353-0214319255. **E-mail:** munsterlit@eircom.net. **Website:** www.munsterlit.ie. **Contact:** Patrick Cotter, artistic director. Entries should be unpublished. Anyone may enter contest. Length: 3,000 words max. Cover letter should include name, address, phone, e-mail, word count, novel/story title. Purpose is to reward writers of outstanding short stories. Deadline: July 31. Prize: 1st prize €2,000; 2nd prize €500. Four runners-up prizes of €100 (approx $146). All six stories to be published in *Southword Literary Journal*. First-Prize Winner offered week's residency in Anam Cara Artist's Retreat in Ireland.

FRANK O'CONNOR AWARD FOR SHORT FICTION

descant, Texas Christian University's literary journal, TCU Box 298300, Fort Worth TX 76129. **E-mail:** descant@tcu.edu. **Website:** www.descant.tcu.edu. **Contact:** Matthew Pitt, editor. Offered annually for an outstanding story accepted for publication in the current edition of the journal. Publication retains copyright but will transfer it to the author upon request. Deadline: March 31. Open to submissions September 1. Prize: $500.

ON THE PREMISES CONTEST

On The Premises, LLC, 4323 Gingham Court, Alexandria VA 22310. **E-mail:** questions@onthepremises.com. **Website:** www.onthepremises.com. **Contact:** Tarl Kudrick or Bethany Granger, co-publishers. *On the Premises* aims to promote newer and/or relatively unknown writers who can write creative, compelling stories told in effective, uncluttered, and evoca-tive prose. Each contest challenges writers to produce a great story based on a broad premise that the editors supply as part of the contest. Submissions are accepted only through web-based submissions system. Entries should be unpublished. Length: minimum 1,000 words; maximum 5,000. No name or contact info should be in ms. Writers may submit own work. Check website for details on the specific premise that writers should incorporate into their story. Results announced within 2 weeks of contest deadline. Winners notified via e-mail and with publication of *On the Premises*. Results made available to entrants on website and in publication. Deadline: Short story contests held twice a year; smaller mini-contests held four times a year; check website for exact dates. Prize: 1st Prize: $220; 2nd Prize: $160; 3rd Prize: $120; Honorable Mentions receive $60. All prize winners are published in *On the Premises* magazine in HTML and PDF format. Judged by a panel of judges with professional editing and writing experience.

TIPS "Write a compelling, creative and well-crafted short story that clearly uses the contest premise."

KENNETH PATCHEN AWARD FOR THE INNOVATIVE NOVEL

Eckhard Gerdes Publishing, 1110 Varsity Blvd., Apt. 221, DeKalb IL 60115. **E-mail:** egerdes@experimentalfiction.com. **Website:** www.experimentalfiction.com. **Contact:** Eckhard Gerdes. This award will honor the most innovative novel submitted during the previous calendar year. Kenneth Patchen is celebrated for being among the greatest innovators of American fiction, incorporating strategies of concretism, asemic writing, digression, and verbal juxtaposition into his writing long before such strategies were popularized during the height of American postmodernist experimentation in the 1970s. See guidelines and application form online at website. Deadline: All submissions must be postmarked between January 1 and July 31. Prize: $1,000 and 20 complimentary copies. Judged by novelist Dominic Ward.

THE PATERSON FICTION PRIZE

The Poetry Center at Passaic Community College, One College Blvd., Paterson NJ 07505. (973)684-6555. **Fax:** (973)523-6085. **E-mail:** mgillan@pccc.edu. **Website:** www.pccc.edu/poetry. **Contact:** Maria Mazziotti Gillan, executive director. Offered annually for a novel or collection of short fiction published the previous calendar year. For more information, visit the website or send SASE. Deadline: February 1. Prize: $1,000.

WILLIAM PEDEN PRIZE IN FICTION

The Missouri Review, 357 McReynolds Hall, Columbia MO 65211. (573)882-4474. **Fax:** (573)884-4671. **E-mail:** mutmrcontestquestion@moreview.com. **Website:** www.missourireview.com. **Contact:** Michael Nye, managing editor. Offered annually for the best story published in the past volume year of the magazine. All stories published in *The Missouri Review* are automatically considered. Guidelines online or for SASE. Prize: $1,000 and a reading/reception.

PEN/FAULKNER AWARDS FOR FICTION

PEN/Faulkner Foundation, 201 E. Capitol St. SE, Washington DC 20003. (202)898-9063. **E-mail:** awards@penfaulkner.org. **Website:** www.penfaulkner.org. **Contact:** Emma Snyder, executive director. Offered annually for best book-length work of fiction by an American citizen published in a calendar year. Deadline: October 31. Prize: $15,000 (one Winner); $5,000 (4 Finalists).

PHOEBE WINTER FICTION CONTEST

Phoebe, MSN 2D6, George Mason University, 4400 University Dr., Fairfax VA 22030. (703)993-2915. **E-mail:** phoebe@gmu.edu. **Website:** http://www.phoebejournal.com/. Offered annually for an unpublished story (25 pages maximum). Guidelines online or for SASE. First serial rights if work is accepted for publication. Purpose is to recognize new and exciting fiction. Deadline: March 19. Prize: $400 and publication in the Spring online issue. Judged by a recognized fiction writer, hired by *Phoebe* (changes each year). For 2016, the fiction judge will be Patricia Park.

TIPS Submit no more than 1 story/25 pages per entry.

EDGAR ALLAN POE AWARD

1140 Broadway, Suite 1507, New York NY 10001. (212)888-8171. **E-mail:** mwa@mysterywriters.org. **Website:** www.mysterywriters.org. Mystery Writers of America is the leading association for professional crime writers in the United States. Members of MWA include most major writers of crime fiction and nonfiction, as well as screenwriters, dramatists, editors, publishers, and other professionals in the field. Categories include: Best Novel, Best First Novel by an American Author, Best Paperback/E-Book Original, Best Fact Crime, Best Critical/Biographical, Best Short Story, Best Juvenile Mystery, Best Young Adult

Mystery, Best Television Series Episode Teleplay, and Mary Higgins Clark Award. Purpose of the award: Honor authors of distinguished works in the mystery field. Previously published submissions only. Submissions should be made by the publisher. Work must be published/produced the year of the contest. Deadline: November 30. Prize: Awards ceramic bust of "Edgar" for winner; certificates for all nominees. Judged by active status members of Mystery Writers of America (writers).

THE KATHERINE ANNE PORTER PRIZE FOR FICTION

Nimrod International Journal, The University of Tulsa, 800 S. Tucker Dr., Tulsa OK 74104. (918)631-3080. **Fax:** (918)631-3033. **E-mail:** nimrod@utulsa.edu. **Website:** www.utulsa.edu/nimrod. **Contact:** Eilis O'Neal. Submissions must be unpublished. Work must be in English or translated by original author. Author's name must not appear on ms. Include cover sheet with title, author's name, address, phone number, and e-mail address (author must have a US address by October of contest year to enter). Mark "Contest Entry" on submission envelop and cover sheet. Include SASE for results only; mss will not be returned. Guidelines available for #10 SASE or on website. 7,500-word maximum for short stories. Deadline: April 30. Prizes: 1st Place: $2,000 and publication; 2nd Place: $1,000 and publication. Judged by the *Nimrod* editors, who select the finalists, and a recognized author, who selects the winners.

PRESS 53 AWARD FOR SHORT FICTION

Press 53, 560 N. Trade St., Suite 103, Winston-Salem NC 27101. (336)770-5353. **E-mail:** kevin@press53.com. **Website:** www.press53.com. **Contact:** Kevin Morgan Watson, Publisher. Awarded to an outstanding, unpublished collection of short stories. Details and guidelines available online. Deadline: December 31. Submission period begins September 1. Finalists and winner announced no later than May 1. Publication in October. Prize: Publication of winning short story collection, $1,000 cash advance, 1/4-page color ad in *Poets & Writers* magazine, plus 10 copies of the book. Judged by Press 53 publisher Kevin Morgan Watson.

⚙ PRISM INTERNATIONAL ANNUAL SHORT FICTION CONTEST

Creative Writing Program, UBC, Buch. E462 - 1866 Main Mall, Vancouver BC V6T 1Z1 Canada.

(604)822-2514. **Fax:** (604)822-3616. **Website:** http://prismmagazine.ca/contests. **Contact:** Clara Kumagai, executive editor, promotions. Maximum word count: 6,000 words. Offered annually for unpublished work to award the best in contemporary fiction. Works of translation are eligible. Guidelines by SASE, by e-mail, or on website. Acquires first North American serial rights upon publication, and rights to publish online for promotional or archival purposes. Open to any writer except students and faculty in the Creative Writing Department at UBC, or people who have taken a creative writing course at UBC with the 2 years prior to the contest deadline. Deadline: January 31. Prize: 1st Place: $1,500; 1st Runner-up: $600; 2nd Runner-up: $400; winner is published.

○ THOMAS H. RADDALL ATLANTIC FICTION AWARD

Writers' Federation of Nova Scotia, 1113 Marginal Rd., Halifax NS B3H 4P7 Canada. (902)423-8116. **Fax:** (902)422-0881. **E-mail:** director@writers.ns.ca. **Website:** www.writers.ns.ca. **Contact:** Nate Crawford, executive director. The Thomas Head Raddall Atlantic Fiction Award is awarded for a novel or a book of short fiction by a full-time resident of Atlantic Canada. Detailed guidelines and eligibility criteria available online. Deadline: First Friday in December. Prize: Valued at $25,000 for winning title.

HAROLD U. RIBALOW PRIZE

Hadassah Magazine, Hadassah WZOA, 40 Wall Street 8th floor, New York NY 10005. (212) 451-6286. **Fax:** (212) 451-6257. **E-mail:** magtemp3@hadassah.org. **Website:** www.hadassahmagazine.org/. **Contact:** Deb Meisels, coordinator. Offered annually for English-language books of fiction (novel or short stories) on a Jewish theme published the previous year. Books should be submitted by the publisher. Administered annually by *Hadassah Magazine*. Deadline: April 7. Prize: $3,000. The official announcement of the winner will be made in the fall.

○ THE ROGERS WRITERS' TRUST FICTION PRIZE

The Writers' Trust of Canada, 460 Richmond St. W., Suite 600, Toronto ON M5V 1Y1 Canada. (416)504-8222. **Fax:** (416)504-9090. **E-mail:** info@writerstrust.com. **Website:** www.writerstrust.com. **Contact:** Amanda Hopkins. Awarded annually to the best novel or short story collection published within the previous year. Presented at the Writers' Trust Awards event held in Toronto each fall. Open to Canadian citizens and permanent residents only. Deadline: July 27. Prize: $25,000 and $2,500 to 4 finalists.

THE SATURDAY EVENING POST GREAT AMERICAN FICTION CONTEST

The Saturday Evening Post Society, 1100 Waterway Blvd., Indianapolis IN 46202. **E-mail:** fictioncontest@saturdayeveningpost.com. **Website:** www.saturdayeveningpost.com/fiction-contest. "In its nearly 3 centuries of publication, *The Saturday Evening Post* has included fiction by a who's who of American authors, including F. Scott Fitzgerald, William Faulkner, Kurt Vonnegut, Ray Bradbury, Louis L'Amour, Sinclair Lewis, Jack London, and Edgar Allan Poe. The *Post*'s fiction has not just entertained us; it has played a vital role in defining who we are as Americans. In launching this contest, we are seeking America's next great, unpublished voices." Entries must be character- or plot-driven stories in any genre of fiction that falls within the *Post*'s broad range of interest. "We are looking for stories with universal appeal touching on shared experiences and themes that will resonate with readers from diverse backgrounds and experience." Stories must be submitted by the author and previously unpublished (excluding personal websites and blogs), and 1,500-5,000 words in length. No extreme profanity or graphic sex scenes. Submit story via the online at www.saturdayeveningpost.com/fiction-contest. All submissions must be made electronically in Microsoft Word format with the author's name, address, telephone number, and e-mail address on the first page. Do not submit hard copies via the mail; physical mss will not be read. "Due to staff limitations, we will not be able to update entrants on the status of their stories. We will inform winners or runners-up within 30 days of publication. We regret we will not be able to notify non-winning entrants." Deadline: July 1. The winning story will receive $500 and publication in the magazine and online. Five runners-up will be published online and receive $100 each.

JOANNA CATHERINE SCOTT NOVEL EXCERPT PRIZE CATEGORY

Soul-Making Keats Literary Competition Category, The Webhallow House, 1544 Sweetwood Dr., Broadmoor Village CA 94015-2029. **E-mail:** soulkeats@mail.com. **Website:** www.soulmakingcontest.us. **Contact:** Eileen Malone. Open annually to any writer. Send first chapter or the first 20 pages, whichever comes first. Include a 1-page synopsis indicating category at top of page. Identify with 3x5 card only. Deadline: November 30. Prize: 1st Place: $100; 2nd Place: $50; 3rd Place: $25.

SCREAMINMAMAS MAGICAL FICTION CONTEST

1911 Cleveland St., Hollywood FL 33020. **E-mail:** screaminmamas@gmail.com. **Website:** www.screaminmamas.com/contests. **Contact:** Darlene Pistocchi, editor/managing director. This contest celebrates moms and the magical spirit of the holidays. If you had an opportunity to be anything you wanted to be, what would you be? Transport yourself! Become that character and write a short story around that character. Can be any genre. Length: 800-3,000 words. Open only to moms. Deadline: June 30. Prize: complementary subscription to magazine, plus publication.

SCREAMINMAMAS VALENTINE'S DAY CONTEST

1911 Cleveland St., Hollywood FL 33020. **E-mail:** screaminmamas@gmail.com. **Website:** www.screaminmamas.com/contests. **Contact:** Darlene Pistocchi, editor/managing director. "Looking for light romantic comedy. Can be historical or contemporary—something to lift the spirits and celebrate the gift of innocent romance that might be found in the everyday life of a busy mom." Length: 600-1,200 words. Open only to moms. Deadline: June 30. Prize: Publication, complementary print copy.

SHEEHAN YA BOOK PRIZE

Elephant Rock Books, P.O. Box 119, Ashford CT 06278. **E-mail:** elephantrockbooksya@gmail.com. **Website:** elephantrockbooks.com/ya.html. **Contact:** Jotham Burrello and Amanda Hurley. Elephant Rock is a small independent publisher. Their first YA book, *The Carnival at Bray* by Jessie Ann Foley was a Morris Award Finalist, and Printz Honor Book. Runs contest every other year. Check website for details. Guidelines are available on the website: http://www.elephantrockbooks.com./about.html#submissions. "Elephant Rock Books' teen imprint is looking for a great story to follow our critically acclaimed novel, *The Carnival at Bray*. We're after quality stories with heart, guts, and a clear voice. We're especially interested in the quirky, the hopeful, and the real. We are not particularly interested in genre fiction and prefer standalone novels, unless you've got the next *Hunger Games*. We seek writers who believe in the transfor-

mative power of a great story, so show us what you've got." Deadline: July 1. Prize: $1,000 as an advance. Judges vary year-to-year.

MARY WOLLSTONECRAFT SHELLEY PRIZE FOR IMAGINATIVE FICTION

Rosebud, ROSEBUD MAGAZINE; ROSEBUD, INC., C/O Rosebud Magazine, N3310 Asje Rd., Cambridge WI 53523. (608)423-9780. **E-mail:** jrodclark@rsbd.net. **Website:** www.rsbd.net. **Contact:** J. Roderick Clark, editor. Publishes eclectic mix of poetry, fiction and nonfiction. Genres with a literary feel okay. The Shelley Award is presented for any kind of unpublished imaginative fiction/short stories, 4,000 words or less. Entries are welcome any time. Acquires first rights. Open to any writer. Deadline: June 15 in even years. Grand Prize: $1,000. 4 runner-ups receive $100. All winners published in *Rosebud*. Judged by editor Rod Clark in 2016.

STONY BROOK SHORT FICTION PRIZE

Stony Brook Southampton, 239 Montauk Highway, Southampton NY 11968. **Website:** www.stonybrook.edu/fictionprize. "Only undergraduates enrolled full time in United States and Canadian universities and colleges for the current academic year are eligible. This prize has traditionally encouraged submissions from students with an Asian background, but we urge all students to enter." Submissions of no more than 7,500 words. All entries must be accompanied by proof of current undergraduate enrollment, such as a photocopy of a grade transcript, a class schedule or payment receipt showing your full time status. See website for full details. Deadline: March 15. Prize: $1,000.

STORYSOUTH MILLION WRITERS AWARD

E-mail: terry@storysouth.com. **Website:** www.storysouth.com. **Contact:** Terry Kennedy, editor. Annual award to honor and promote the best fiction published in online literary journals and magazines during the previous year. Anyone may nominate one story for the award. To be eligible for nomination, a story must be longer than 1,000 words. See website for details on how to nominate someone. Most literary prizes for short fiction have traditionally ignored web-published fiction. This award aims to show that world-class fiction is being published online and to promote to the larger reading and literary community. Deadline: August 15. Nominations of stories begins on March 15. Prize: Prize amounts subject to donation. Check website for details.

THEODORE STURGEON MEMORIAL AWARD FOR BEST SHORT SF OF THE YEAR

Center for the Study of SF, 1445 Jayhawk Blvd, Room 3001, University of Kansas, Lawrence KS 66045. (785)864-2518. **Fax:** (785)864-1159. **E-mail:** cssf@ku.edu. **Website:** sfcenter.ku.edu/sturgeon.htm. **Contact:** Kij Johnson, professor and associate director. Entries must be previously published. Guidelines available in December by phone, e-mail or on website. Accepts inquiries by e-mail and fax. Entrants for the Sturgeon Award are by nomination only. Results announced in July. For contest results, send SASE. Award to "honor the best science fiction short story of the year." Prize: Trophy. Winners receive expense-paid trip to the University and have their names engraved on the pernmanent trophy.

THREE CHEERS AND A TIGER

E-mail: editors@toasted-cheese.com. **Website:** tclj.toasted-cheese.com. **Contact:** Stephanie Lenz, editor. Contestants are to write a short story (following a specific theme) within 48 hours. Contests are held first weekend in Spring (mystery) and first weekend in Fall (science fiction/fantasy). Word limit announced at the start of the contest, 5 pm ET. Contest-specific information is announced 48 hours before the contest submission deadline. Results announced in April and October. Winners notified by e-mail. List of winners on website. Entries must be unpublished. Open to any writer. Accepts inquiries by e-mail. Cover letter should include name, address, e-mail, word count and title. Information should be in the body of the e-mail. It will be removed before the judging begins. Prize: Amazon gift certificates and publication. Blind-judged by *Toasted Cheese* editors. Each judge uses his or her own criteria to choose entries.

THE THURBER PRIZE FOR AMERICAN HUMOR

77 Jefferson Ave., Columbus OH 43215. **Website:** www.thurberhouse.org. Entry fee: $65 per title. Published submissions or accepted for publication in U.S. for the first time. Primarily pictorial works such as cartoon collections are not considered. Word length: no requirement. See website for application form and guidelines. Results announced in September. Winners notified in person in New York City. For contest results, visit website. This award recognizes the art of humor writing. Deadline: March 31. Prize: $5,000 for the finalist, non-cash prizes awarded to two runners-up. Judged by well-known members of the national arts community.

STEVEN TURNER AWARD FOR BEST FIRST WORK OF FICTION

6335 W. Northwest Hwy., #618, Dallas TX 75225. **Website:** www.texasinstituteofletters.org. Offered annually for work published January 1-December 31 for the best first book of fiction. Writers must have been born in Texas, have lived in the state for at least 2 consecutive years at some time, or the subject matter of the work should be associated with the state. Guidelines online. Deadline: normally first week in January; see website for specific date. Prize: $1,000.

ANNUAL VENTURA COUNTY WRITERS CLUB SHORT STORY CONTEST

Ventura County Writers Club Short Story Contest, P.O. Box 3373, Thousand Oaks CA 91362. **E-mail:** vcwc.contestchair@gmail.com. **Website:** www.venturacountywriters.com. **Contact:** Contest Chair. Annual short story contest for youth and adult writers. High school division for writers still in school. Adult division for those 18 and older. Club membership not required to enter and entries accepted worldwide as long as fees are paid, story is unpublished and in English. Enter through website. 2,500 word limit. See formatting on website. Winners get cash prizes and are published in club anthology. Deadline: November 15. Adult Prizes: 1st Place: $500; 2nd Place: $250; 3rd Place: $125. High School Prizes: 1st Place: $100; 2nd Place: $75; 3rd Place: $50.

TIPS Look at previous winning stories published in the Ventura County Star newspaper.

WAASNODE SHORT FICTION PRIZE

Passages North, Department of English, Northern Michigan University, 1401 Presque Isle Ave., Marquette MI 49855. (906)227-1203. **Fax:** (906)227-1096. **E-mail:** passages@nmu.edu. **Website:** www.passagesnorth.com. **Contact:** Jennifer Howard. Offered every 2 years to publish new voices in literary fiction (maximum 10,000 words). Guidelines for SASE or online. Submissions accepted online. Deadline: April 15. Submission period begins February 15. Prize: $1,000 and publication for winner; 2 honorable mentions are also published; all entrants receive a copy of *Passages North*. Judged by Tiphanie Yanique in 2016.

WABASH PRIZE FOR FICTION

Sycamore Review, Department of English, 500 Oval Dr., Purdue University, West Lafayette IN 47907. E-mail: sycamore@purdue.edu; sycamorefiction@purdue.edu. **Website:** www.sycamorereview.com/contest/. **Contact:** Kara Krewer, editor-in-chief. Annual contest for unpublished fiction. For each submission, send one story (limit 7,500 words). Ms pages should be numbered and should include the title of the piece. All stories must be previously unpublished. See website for more guidelines. Submit via online submissions manager. Deadline: November 15. Prize: $1,000 and publication.

THE WASHINGTON WRITERS' PUBLISHING HOUSE FICTION PRIZE

Washington Writers' Publishing House, P.O. Box 15271, Washington DC 20003. **E-mail:** wwphpress@gmail.com. **Website:** www.washingtonwriters.org. Fiction writers living within 75 miles of the Capitol are invited to submit a ms of either a novel or a collection of short stories (no more than 350 pages, double-spaced). Author's name should not appear on the manuscript. The title page of each copy should contain the title only. Provide name, address, telephone number, e-mail address, and title on a separate cover sheet accompanying the submission. A separate page for acknowledgments may be included for stories or excerpts previously published in journals and anthologies. Send electronic copies to wwphpress@gmail.com or mail paper copies and/or reading fee (check to WWPH) with SASE to: Washington Writers' Publishing House Fiction Prize, c/o Elisavietta Ritchie, P.O. Box 298, Broomes Island, MD 20615. Deadline: November 15. Submission period begins July 1. Prize: $1,000 and 50 copies of the book.

THOMAS WOLFE PRIZE AND LECTURE

North Carolina Writers' Network, Thomas Wolfe Fiction Prize, Great Smokies Writing Program, Attn: Nancy Williams, CPO #1860, UNC, Asheville NC 28805. **Website:** englishcomplit.unc.edu/wolfe. The Thomas Wolfe Fiction Prize honors internationally celebrated North Carolina novelist Thomas Wolfe. The prize is administered by Tommy Hays and the Great Smokies Writing Program at the University of North Carolina at Asheville. Competition is open to all writers, regardless of geographical location or prior publication. Submit 2 copies of an unpublished fiction ms (short story or self-contained novel excerpt) not to exceed 12 double-spaced, single-sided pages. Deadline: January 30. Submissions period begins December 1. Prize: $1,000 and potential publication in *The Thomas Wolfe Review*.

TOBIAS WOLFF AWARD FOR FICTION

Bellingham Review, Mail Stop 9053, Western Washington University, Bellingham WA 98225. (360)650-4863. **E-mail:** bellingham.review@wwu.edu. **Website:** www.bhreview.org. **Contact:** Susanne Paola Antonetta, editor-in-chief; Louis McLaughlin, managing editor. Offered annually for unpublished work. Guidelines available on website; online submissions only. Categories: novel exceprts and short stories. Entries must be unpublished. Length: 6,000 words or less per story or chapter. Open to any writer. Electronic submissions only. Enter submissions through Submittable, a link to which is available on the website. Winner announced in August and notified by e-mail. Deadline: March 15. Submissions period begins December 1. Prize: $1,000, plus publication and subscription.

WORLD FANTASY AWARDS

P.O. Box 43, Mukilteo WA 98275. **E-mail:** sfexecsec@gmail.com. **Website:** www.worldfantasy.org. **Contact:** Peter Dennis Pautz, president. Offered annually for previously published work in several categories, including life achievement, novel, novella, short story, anthology, collection, artist, special award-pro and special award-nonpro. Works are recommended by attendees of current and previous 2 years' conventions and a panel of judges. Entries must be previously published. Published submissions from previous calendar year. Word length: 10,000-40,000 for novella, 10,000 for short story. All fantasy is eligible, from supernatural horror to Tolkien-esque to sword and sorcery to the occult, and beyond. Cover letter should include name, address, phone, e-mail, word count, title, and publications where submission was previously published, submitted to the address above and the panel of judges when they appear on the website. Results announced November 1 at annual convention. For contest results, visit website. Guidelines available in December for SASE or on website. Awards to recognize excellence in fantasy literature worldwide. Deadline: June 1. Prize: Trophy. Judged by panel.

WOW! WOMEN ON WRITING QUARTERLY FLASH FICTION CONTEST

WOW! Women on Writing, P.O. Box 41104, Long Beach CA 90853. **E-mail:** contestinfo@wow-womenonwriting.com. **Website:** www.wow-womenonwriting.com/contest.php. **Contact:** Angela Mackintosh, editor. Contest offered quarterly. Entries must be 250-750 words. "We are open to all themes and genres, although we do encourage writers to take a close look at our literary agent guest judge for the season if you are serious about winning." Deadline: August 31, November 30, February 28, May 31. Prize: 1st place: $350 cash prize, $25 Amazon gift certificate, story published on WOW! Women On Writing, interview on blog; 2nd place: $250 cash prize, $25 Amazon gift certificate, story published on WOW! Women On Writing, interview on blog; 3rd place: $150 cash prize, $25 Amazon gift certificate, story published on WOW! Women On Writing, interview on blog; 7 runners up: $25 Amazon gift certificate, story published on WOW! Women on Writing, interview on blog; 10 honorable mentions: $20 gift certificate from Amazon, story title and name published on WOW!Women On Writing. Judged by a different guest every season, who is either a literary agent, acquiring editor or publisher.

WRITER'S DIGEST SHORT SHORT STORY COMPETITION

Writer's Digest, 10151 Carver Road, Suite 200, Blue Ash OH 45242. (715)445-4612; ext. 13430. **E-mail:** WritersDigestShortShortStoryCompetition@fwmedia.com. **Website:** www.writersdigest.com. **Contact:** Nicole Howard. Looking for fiction that's bold, brilliant, and brief. Send your best in 1,500 words or fewer. All entries must be original, unpublished, and not submitted elsewhere at the time of submission. *Writer's Digest* reserves one-time publication rights to the 1st-25th winning entries. Winners will be notified by Feb. 28. Early bird deadline: November 15. Final deadline: December 15. Prize: 1st Place: $3,000 and a trip to the Writer's Digest Conference; 2nd Place: $1,500; 3rd Place: $500; 4th-10th Place: $100; 11th-25th Place: $50 gift certificate for writersdigestshop.com.

ZOETROPE ALL STORY SHORT FICTION CONTEST

Zoetrope: All Story, Zoetrope: All-Story, Attn: Fiction Editor, 916 Kearny St., San Francisco CA 94133. (415)788-7500. **E-mail:** contests@all-story.com. **Website:** www.all-story.com. Annual short fiction contest.

Considers submissions of short stories and one-act plays no longer than 7,000 words. Excerpts from larger works, screenplays, treatments, and poetry will be returned unread. For details, visit the website during the summer. Deadline: October 1. Submissions period begins July 1. Prizes: 1st place: $1,000 and publication on website; 2nd place: $500; 3rd place: $250.

ZONE 3 FICTION AWARD

Zone 3, Austin Peay State University, P.O. Box 4565, Clarksville TN 37044. (931)221-7031. **Fax:** (931)221-7149. **E-mail:** wallacess@apsu.edu. **Website:** www.apsu.edu/zone3/contests. **Contact:** Susan Wallace, Managing Editor. Annual contest for unpublished fiction. Open to any fiction writer. Accepts entries online and via postal mail. Deadline: April 1. Prize: $250 and publication.

NONFICTION

ANNUAL MEMOIRS COMPETITION

The Writers' Workshop of Asheville, NC, Memoirs Contest, 387 Beaucatcher Rd., Asheville NC 28805. **E-mail:** writersw@gmail.com. **Website:** www.twwoa.org. **Contact:** Karen Ackerson. Submit a memoir of 5,000 words or less. Multiple entries are accepted. All work must be unpublished. Pages should be paper clipped, with your name, address, phone and title of work on a cover sheet. Double-space and use 12-point font. Deadline: November 30. Prize: 1st Place: A 2 night stay at the Mountain Muse B&B and 50 pages line-edited and revised by editorial staff; 2nd Place: A 2 night stay at the B&B and 50 pages line-edited; 3rd Place: 25 pages line-edited. Up to 10 Honorable Mentions. Judged by professional, published writing instructors.

ANTHEM ESSAY CONTEST

Ayn Rand Institute, P.O. Box 57044, Irvine CA 92619-7044. (949)222-6550. **Fax:** (949)222-6558. **E-mail:** essays@aynrand.org. **Website:** https://www.aynrand.org/contests. **Contact:** Anthony Loy. Offered annually to encourage analytical thinking and excellence in writing (600-1,200 word essay), and to expose students to the philosophic ideas of Ayn Rand. "For information contact your English teacher or guidance counselor or visit our website." Open to 8th, 9th and 10th graders. See website for topics. Deadline: March 29. Prize: 1st Place: $2,000; 2nd Place (5): $500; 3rd

Place (10): $200; Finalist (45): $50; Semifinalist (175): $30.

THE ASCAP DEEMS TAYLOR AWARDS

American Society of Composers, Authors & Publishers, One Lincoln Plaza, New York NY 10023. (212)621-6318. **E-mail:** jlapore@ascap.com. **Website:** www.ascap.com/music-career/support/deems-taylor-guidelines.aspx. **Contact:** Julian Lapore. The ASCAP Deems Taylor Awards program recognizes books, articles, broadcasts, and websites on the subject of music selected for their excellence. Written works must be published in the U.S. in English, during the calendar year of the awards. The subject matter may be biographical or critical, reportorial or historical—almost any form of nonfiction prose about music and/or its creators. However, instructional textbooks, how-to-guides, or works of fiction will not be accepted. Honors the memory of composer/critic/commentator Deems Taylor. Deadline: May 31. Submission period begins February 1. Prize: Several categories of cash prizes are presented to writers of award-winning books and newspaper, journal, or magazine articles (includes program notes, liner notes and on-line publications). Awards are also presented to the authors and journalists as well as to their respective publishers.

TIPS "The website will answer all questions. Please call 212-621-6318 with any additional questions."

ATLAS SHRUGGED ESSAY CONTEST

Ayn Rand Institute, P.O. Box 57044, Irvine CA 92619-7044. (949)222-6550, ext. 269. **Fax:** (949)222-6558. **E-mail:** essays@aynrand.org. **Website:** https://www.aynrand.org/contests. **Contact:** Anthony Loy. Offered annually to encourage analytical thinking and excellence in writing, and to expose students to the philosophic ideas of Ayn Rand. Open to 12th graders, college undergraduates, and graduate students. Essay length: 800-1,600 words. Essays are judged both on style and content. Guidelines and topics available on the website. The winning applicant will be judged on both style and content. Judges will look for writing that is clear, articulate and logically organized. Winning essays must demonstrate an outstanding grasp of the philosophic meaning of *Atlas Shrugged*. Essay submissions are evaluated in a fair and unbiased four-round judging process. Judges are individually selected by the Ayn Rand Institute based on a demonstrated knowledge and understanding of Ayn Rand's

works. Deadline: April 28. Prizes: 1st Place: $20,000; 2nd Place (3 awards): $2,000; 3rd Place (5 awards): $1,000; Finalists (25 awards): $100; Semifinalists (50 awards): $50.

MORTON N. COHEN AWARD

Modern Language Association of America, 85 Broad Street, suite 500, New York NY 10004-2434. (646)576-5141. **Fax:** (646)458-0030. **E-mail:** awards@mla.org. **Website:** www.mla.org. **Contact:** Coordinator of Book Prizes. Awarded in odd-numbered years for a distinguished collection of letters. At least 1 volume of the edition must have been published during the previous 2 years. Editors need not be members of the MLA. Under the terms of the award, the winning collection will be one that provides readers with a clear, accurate, and readable text; necessary background information; and succinct and eloquent introductory material and annotations. The edited collection should be in itself a work of literature. Deadline: May 1. Prize: A cash award and a certificate to be presented at the Modern Language Association's annual convention in January.

CARR P. COLLINS AWARD FOR NONFICTION

The Texas Institute of Letters, P.O. Box 609, Round Rock TX 78680. **E-mail:** tilsecretary@yahoo.com. **Website:** http://texasinstituteofletters.org/. Offered annually for work published January 1-December 31 of the previous year to recognize the best nonfiction book by a writer who was born in Texas, who has lived in the state for at least 2 consecutive years at one point, or a writer whose work has some notable connection with Texas. See website for guidelines and instructions on submitting. Deadline: January 10. Prize: $5,000.

◯ CREATIVE NONFICTION CONTEST

PRISM International, Creative Writing Program, UBC, Buch E462—1866 Main Mall, Vancouver BC V6T 1Z1 Canada. **E-mail:** promotions@prismmagazine.ca. **Website:** www.prismmagazine.ca. Maximum word count: 5,000. Offered annually for published and unpublished writers to promote and reward excellence in literary creative nonfiction. *PRISM* buys first North American serial rights upon publication. Also buys limited web rights for pieces selected for the website. Open to anyone except students and faculty of the Creative Writing Program at UBC or people who have taken a creative writing course at UBC in the 2 years prior to contest deadline. All entrants receive a 1-year subscription to *PRISM*. Entries are accepted via Submittable at http://prisminternational. submittable.com/submit or by mail. Deadline: July 15. Prize: $1,500 grand prize, $600 runner-up, and $400 second runner-up.

ANNIE DILLARD AWARD FOR CREATIVE NONFICTION

Bellingham Review, Mail Stop 9053, 516 High St., Western Washington University, Bellingham WA 98225. (360)650-4863. **E-mail:** bellingham.review@ wwu.edu. **Website:** www.bhreview.org. **Contact:** Susanne Paola Antonetta, editor-in-chief; Dayna Patterson, managing editor. Offered annually for unpublished essays on any subject and in any style. Guidelines available online. Deadline: March 15. Submission period begins December 1. Prize: $1,000, plus publication and copies. All finalists considered for publication. All entrants receive subscription. Judged by Julie Marie Wade.

TIPS "The *Bellingham Review* seeks literature of palpable quality: poems, stories, and essays so beguiling they invite us to come closer, look deeper, touch, sniff and taste their essence. We hunger for a kind of writing that nudges the limits of form or executes traditional forms exquisitely."

GORDON W. DILLON/RICHARD C. PETERSON MEMORIAL ESSAY PRIZE

American Orchid Society, Inc., American Orchid Society at Fairchild Tropical Botanic Garden, 10901 Old Cutler Rd., Coral Gables FL 33156. (305)740-2010. **Fax:** (305)740-2011. **E-mail:** theaos@aos.org. **E-mail:** rmchatton@aos.org. **Website:** www.aos.org. **Contact:** Ron McHatton. The Gordon W. Dillon\Richard C. Peterson Memorial Essay Prize is an annual writing competition. Open to amateur and professional writers. The theme is announced each May in *Orchids* magazine. All themes deal with an aspect of orchids. Acquires one-time rights. The essay must be an original, unpublished article. Submissions must be no more than 5,000 words in length. Submissions will be judged without knowledge of the identity of the author. Established to honor the memory of two former editors of the *AOS Bulletin* (now *Orchids*). Deadline: November 30. Prize: Cash prize and a certificate. Winning entry usually published in the June issue of *Orchids* magazine.

THE ILA DINA FEITELSON RESEARCH AWARD

International Literacy Association, Division of Research & Policy, P.O. Box 8139, Newark DE 19714-8139. (302)731-1600, ext. 227. **Fax:** (302)368-2449. **E-mail:** research@reading.org. **Website:** http://www.literacyworldwide.org/about-us/awards-grants. **Contact:** Wendy Logan. This is an award for an exemplary work published in English in a refereed journal that reports on an empirical study investigating aspects of literacy acquisition, such as phonemic awareness, the alphabetic principle, bilingualism, or cross-cultural studies of beginning reading. Articles may be submitted for consideration by researchers, authors, et al. Copies of the applications and guidelines can be downloaded in PDF format from the website. Deadline: January 15. Prize: $500 award and recognition at the International Literacy Association's annual conference.

THE *FOUNTAINHEAD* ESSAY CONTEST

The Ayn Rand Institute, P.O. Box 57044, Irvine CA 92619-7044. (949) 222-6550. **Fax:** (949) 222-6558. **E-mail:** essays@aynrand.org. **Website:** https://www. aynrand.org/contests. **Contact:** Anthony Loy. Competition for 11th and 12th grade students. Essays will be judged on whether the student is able to argue for and justify his or her view—not on whether the Institute agrees with the view the student expresses. Judges will look for writing that is clear, articulate and logically organized. Winning essays must demonstrate an outstanding grasp of the philosophic meaning of *The Fountainhead*. Deadline: April 26. Prizes: 1st Place: $10,000; 2nd Place: $2,000 (5 Winners); 3rd Place: $1,000 (10 Winners); Finalists: $100 (45 Winners); Semifinalists: $50 (175 Winners).

THE JOHN GUYON LITERARY NONFICTION PRIZE

Crab Orchard Review, Department of English, Faner Hall 2380 - Mail Code 4503, 1000 Faner Drive, Carbondale IL 62901. (618)453-6833. **Fax:** (618)453-8224. **E-mail:** jtribble@siu.edu. **Website:** www.craborchardreview.siu.edu. **Contact:** Jon C. Tribble, managing editor. Annual award for unpublished creative nonfiction. Not a prize for academic essays. Entries should consist of 1 creative nonfiction piece up to 6,500 words maximum in length. *Crab Orchard Review* acquires first North American serial rights to all submitted work. One winner and at least 2 finalists will be chosen. Length: 6,500 words maximum. All submissions must be made through Submittable. Submissions must be unpublished original work, written in English by a U.S. citizen, permanent resident, or person who has DACA/TPS status (current students and employees at Southern Illinois University Carbondale are not eligible). See Submittable guidelines online for complete formatting instructions. The author's name should not appear on any page of the entry. Results announced by end of August. Deadline: May 31. Submission period begins March 21. Prize: $1,250 and publication. Finalists are each offered online publication.

TIPS "Carefully read directions for entering and follow them exactly. Send us your best work. Note that simultaneous submissions are accepted for this prize, but the winning entry must NOT be accepted elsewhere. All submissions should be made through Submittable: https://craborchardreview.submittable.com/submit."

HENDRICKS AWARD

The New Netherland Institute, Cultural Education Center, Room 10D45, 222 Madison Ave., Albany NY 12230. **Fax:** (518)473-0472. **E-mail:** nyslfnn@nysed.gov. **Website:** www.newnetherlandinstitute.org. Given annually to the best book or book-length ms relating to any aspect of New Netherland and its legacy. Two categories of submissions will be considered in alternate years: (1) recently completed dissertations and unpublished book-length manuscripts, and (2) recently published books. If there is no suitable winner in the designated category in any particular year, submissions from the alternate category will be considered. In addition, submissions from previous years will be reconsidered for the Award. Entries must be based on research completed or published within three years prior to the deadline for submission. Entries may deal with any aspect of New Netherland and its legacy. Biographies of individuals whose careers illuminate aspects of the history of New Netherland and its legacy are eligible, as are manuscripts dealing with literature and the arts, provided that the methodology is historical. Deadline: March 15. Prize: $5,000 and a framed print of a painting by L.F. Tantillo. Judged by a 5-member panel of scholars.

THE HUNGER MOUNTAIN CREATIVE NONFICTION PRIZE

Vermont College, 36 College St., Montpelier VT 05602. (802)828-8517. **E-mail:** hungermtn@vcfa.edu. **Website:** www.hungermtn.org. **Contact:** Samantha Kolber, Managing Editor. Annual contest for the best writing in creative nonfiction. Submit essays under 10,000 words. Guidelines available on website. Accepts entries online or via mail. Deadline: March 1. Prize: $1,000 and publication. Two honorable mentions receive $100 each. Judged by Joni Tevis in 2017.

ILA OUTSTANDING DISSERTATION OF THE YEAR AWARD

International Literacy Association, P.O. Box 8139, Newark DE 19714-8139. (302)731-1600, ext. 227. **Fax:** (302)368-2449. **E-mail:** research@reading.org. **Website:** http://www.literacyworldwide.org/about-us/awards-grants. **Contact:** Wendy Logan, project manager. Dissertations in reading or related fields are eligible for the competition. Studies using any research approach (ethnographic, experimental, historical, survey, etc.) are encouraged. Each study is assessed in the light of this approach, the scholarly qualification of its report, and its significant contributions to knowledge within the reading field. The application process is open to those who have completed dissertations in any aspect of the field of reading or literacy of the calendar year. A routine check is made with the home university of the applicant to protect all applicants, their universities, and the International Reading Association from false claims. Studies may use any research approach (ethnographic, experimental, historical, survey, etc.). Each study will be assessed in light of its approach, its scholarship, and its significant contributions to knowledge within the reading/literacy field. Deadline: January 15.

TILIA KLEBENOV JACOBS RELIGIOUS ESSAY PRIZE CATEGORY

Soul Making Keats Literary Competition, The Webhallow House, 1544 Sweetwood Dr., Broadmoor Village CA 94015-2029. **E-mail:** SoulKeats@mail.com. **Website:** www.soulmakingcontest.us. **Contact:** Eileen Malone. Call for thoughtful writings of up to 3,000 words. "No preaching, no proselytizing." Open annually to any writer. Previously published material is accepted. Indicate category on cover page and on identifying 3x5 card. Up to 3,000 words, double-spaced. See website for more details. Deadline: November 30. Prize: 1st Place: $100; 2nd Place: $50; 3rd Place: $25.

KATHERINE SINGER KOVACS PRIZE

Modern Language Association of America, 85 Broad Street, suite 500, New York NY 10004-2434. (646)576-5141. **Fax:** (646)458-0030. **E-mail:** awards@mla.org. **Website:** www.mla.org. **Contact:** Coordinator of Book Prizes. Offered annually for an outstanding book published in English or Spanish in the field of Latin American and Spanish literatures and cultures. Competing books should be broadly interpretive works that enhance understanding of the interrelations among literature, the other arts, and society. Books must have been published in the previous year. Authors need not be members of the MLA. Must send 6 copies of book. Deadline: May 1. Prize: A cash award and a certificate to be presented at the Modern Language Association's annual convention in January.

KATHERYN KROTZER LABORDE CREATIVE NONFICTION PRIZE CATEGORY

Soul-Making Keats Literary Competition, The Webhallow House, 1544 Sweetwood Dr., Broadmoor Village CA 94015-2029. **E-mail:** SoulKeats@mail.com. **Website:** www.soulmakingcontest.us. **Contact:** Eileen Malone. Creative nonfiction is the child of fiction and journalism. Unlike fiction, the characters and events are real, not imagined. Unlike journalism, the writer is part of the story she tells, if not as a participant then as a thoughtful observer. Must be typed, page numbered, and double-spaced. Each entry up to 3,000 words. Identify only with 3x5 card. Open annually to any writer. Deadline: November 30. Prizes: First Place: $100; Second Place: $50; Third Place: $25. **TIPS** "Looking for a strong voice, a solid sense of the story, and a clear sense of one's writing style. One last note: think about the STORY you are trying to tell and don't be a slave to the truth, the whole truth, and nothing but. This is art, not sworn testimony!"

THE GILDER LEHRMAN LINCOLN PRIZE

Gettysburg College and Gilder Lehrman Institute of American History, 300 N. Washington St., Campus Box 435, Gettysburg PA 17325. (717)337-8255. **Fax:** (717)337-6596. **E-mail:** lincolnprize@gettysburg.edu. **Website:** www.gilderlehrman.org. The Gilder Lehrman Lincoln Prize, sponsored by the Gilder Lehrman Institute and Gettysburg College, is awarded annually for the finest scholarly work in English on Abraham Lincoln or the American Civil War era.

Send 6 copies of the nominated work. Deadline: November 1. Prize: $50,000.
TIPS "This contest is for adults writers only."

LITERAL LATTÉ ESSAY AWARD

Literal Latté, 200 E. 10th St., Suite 240, New York NY 10003. **E-mail:** litlatte@aol.com. **E-mail:** Go to www.literal-latte.com for link to our submittable page. **Website:** www.literal-latte.com. **Contact:** Jenine Gordon Bockman. Mind-stimulating entertainment. Free since 1994. Acquires first rights. Visit website for guidelines and tastes. Deadline: September 30. Prize: 1st Place: $1,000; 2nd Place: $300; 3rd Place: $200. Judged by the editors.

JAMES RUSSELL LOWELL PRIZE

Modern Language Association of America, 85 Broad Street, suite 500, New York NY 10004-2434. (646)576-5141. **Fax:** (646)458-0030. **E-mail:** awards@mla.org. **Website:** www.mla.org. **Contact:** Coordinator of Book Prizes. For an outstanding literary or linguistic study, a critical edition of an important work, or a critical biography. Open to studies dealing with literary theory, media, cultural history, or interdisciplinary topics. Books must be published in the previous year. Authors must be current members of the MLA. Send 6 copies of the book. Deadline: March 1. Prize: A cash award and a certificate to be presented at the Modern Language Association's annual convention in January.

RICHARD J. MARGOLIS AWARD

c/o Margolis & Bloom, LLP, 535 Boylston St., 8th Floor, Boston MA 02116. (617)267-9700, ext. 517. **Fax:** (617)267-3166. **E-mail:** hsm@margolis.com. **E-mail:** award@margolis.com. **Website:** www.margolisaward. org. **Contact:** Harry S. Margolis. Sponsored by the Blue Mountain Center, this annual award is given to a promising new journalist or essayist whose work combines warmth, humor, wisdom, and concern with social justice. Applicants should be aware that this award is for nonfiction reporting and commentary, not for creative nonfiction, fiction, or poetry. Applications should include at least 2 examples of your work (published or unpublished, 30 pages maximum) and a short biographical note including a description of your current and anticipated work. Also please indicate what you will work on while attending the Blue Mountain residency. Please send to award@margolis. com. Deadline: July 1. Prize: $5,000, plus a one month residency at the Blue Mountain Center.

HOWARD R. MARRARO PRIZE

Modern Language Association of America, 85 Broad Street, suite 500, New York NY 10004-2434. (646)576-5141. **Fax:** (646)458-0030. **E-mail:** awards@mla.org. **Website:** www.mla.org. **Contact:** Coordinator of Book Prizes. Offered in even-numbered years for an outstanding scholarly work on any phase of Italian literature or comparative literature involving Italian. Books must have been published in the previous year. Authors must be members of the MLA. Requires 4 copies of the book. Deadline: May 1. Prize: A cash award and a certificate to be presented at the Modern Language Association's annual convention in January.

KENNETH W. MILDENBERGER PRIZE

Modern Language Association of America, 85 Broad Street, suite 500, New York NY 10004-2434. (646)576-5141. **Fax:** (646)458-0030. **E-mail:** awards@mla.org. **Website:** www.mla.org. **Contact:** Coordinator of Book Prizes. Offered in odd-numbered years for a publication from the previous year in the field of language, culture, literacy, or literature with a strong application to the teaching of languages other than English. Author need not be a member of the MLA. Books must have been published in the previous 2 years. Requires 4 copies of the book. Deadline: May 1. Prize: A cash award, and a certificate, to be presented at the Modern Language Association's annual convention in January, and a year's membership in the MLA.

C. WRIGHT MILLS AWARD

The Society for the Study of Social Problems, 901 McClung Tower, University of Tennessee, Knoxville TN 37996-0490. (865)689-1531. **Fax:** (865)689-1534. **E-mail:** mkoontz3@utk.edu. **Website:** www.sssp1.org. **Contact:** Michele Smith Koontz, Administrative Officer and Meeting Manager. Offered annually for a book published the previous year that most effectively critically addresses an issue of contemporary public importance; brings to the topic a fresh, imaginative perspective; advances social scientific understanding of the topic; displays a theoretically informed view and empirical orientation; evinces quality in style of writing; and explicitly or implicitly contains implications for courses of action. Self-nominations are acceptable. Edited volumes, textbooks, fiction, and self-published works are not eligible. Deadline: December 15. Prize: $1,000 stipend.

MLA PRIZE FOR A BIBLIOGRAPHY, ARCHIVE, OR DIGITAL PROJECT

Modern Language Association of America, 85 Broad Street, Suite 500, New York NY 10004-2434. (646)576-5141. **Fax:** (646)458-0030. **E-mail:** awards@mla.org. **Website:** www.mla.org. **Contact:** Coordinator of Book Prizes. Offered in even-numbered years for an outstanding enumerative or descriptive bibliography, archive, or digital project. Open to any writer or publisher. At least 1 volume must have been published in the previous 2 years. Editors need not be members of the MLA. Criteria for determining excellence include evidence of analytical rigor, meticulous scholarship, intellectual creativity, and subject range and depth. Deadline: May 1. Prize: A cash prize and a certificate to be presented at the Modern Language Association's annual convention in January.

MLA PRIZE FOR A FIRST BOOK

Modern Language Association of America, 85 Broad Street, Suite 500, New York NY 10004-2434. (646)576-5141. **Fax:** (646)458-0030. **E-mail:** awards@mla.org. **Website:** www.mla.org. **Contact:** Coordinator of Book Prizes. Offered annually for the first book-length scholarly publication by a current member of the association. To qualify, a book must be a literary or linguistic study, a critical edition of an important work, or a critical biography. Studies dealing with literary theory, media, cultural history, and interdisciplinary topics are eligible; books that are primarily translations will not be considered. See listing for James Russell Lowe Prize—prize offered for same criteria. Deadline: March 1. Prize: A cash award and a certificate to be presented at the Modern Language Association's annual convention in January.

MLA PRIZE FOR A SCHOLARLY EDITION

Modern Language Association of America, 85 Broad Street, suite 500, New York NY 10004-2434. (646)576-5141. **Fax:** (646)458-0030. **E-mail:** awards@mla.org. **Website:** www.mla.org. Offered in odd-numbered years for an outstanding scholarly edition. Editions may be in single or multiple volumes. At least one volume must have been published in the 2 years prior to the award deadline. Editors need not be members of the MLA. To qualify for the award, an edition should be based on an examination of all available relevant textual sources; the source texts and the edited text's deviations from them should be fully described; the edition should employ editorial principles appropriate to the materials edited, and those principles should be clearly articulated in the volume; the text should be accompanied by appropriate textual and other historical contextual information; the edition should exhibit the highest standards of accuracy in the presentation of its text and apparatus; and the text and apparatus should be presented as accessibly and elegantly as possible. Deadline: May 1. Prize: A cash award and a certificate to be presented at the Modern Language Association's annual convention in January.

MLA PRIZE FOR INDEPENDENT SCHOLARS

Modern Language Association of America, 85 Broad Street, Suite 500, New York NY 10004-2434. (646)576-5141. **Fax:** (646)458-0030. **E-mail:** awards@mla.org. **Website:** www.mla.org. Offered in even-numbered years for a scholarly book in the field of English or other modern languages and literatures. Book must have been published within the 2 years prior to prize deadline. At the time of publication of the book, author must not be enrolled in a program leading to an academic degree or hold a tenured, tenure-accruing, or tenure-track position in postsecondary education. Authors need not be members of the MLA. Requires 6 copies of the book and a completed application. Deadline: May 1. Prize: A cash award, a certificate, and a year's membership in the MLA.

MONTANA PRIZE IN CREATIVE NONFICTION

CutBank Literary Magazine, *CutBank*, University of Montana, English Dept., LA 133, Missoula MT 59812. **E-mail:** editor.cutbank@gmail.com. **Website:** www.cutbankonline.org. **Contact:** Allison Linville, editor-in-chief. The Montana Prize in Creative Nonfiction seeks to highlight work that showcases an authentic voice, a boldness of form, and a rejection of functional fixedness. Accepts online submissions only. Send a single work, no more than 35 pages. Guidelines available online. Deadline: January 15. Submissions period begins November 9. Prize: $500 and featured in the magazine. Judged by a guest judge each year.

LINDA JOY MYERS MEMOIR VIGNETTE PRIZE CATEGORY

Soul-Making Keats Literary Competition, Webhallow House, 1544 Sweetwood Dr., Broadmoor Village CA 94015-2029. **E-mail:** soulkeats@mail.com. **Website:** www.soulmakingcontest.us. **Contact:** Eileen Malone. Open annually to any writer. One memoir/entry, up to 1,500 words, double spaced. Previously published

material is acceptable. Indicate category on first page. Identify only with 3x5 card. Deadline: November 30. Prize: 1st Place: $100; 2nd Place: $50; 3rd Place: $25.

NATIONAL BUSINESS BOOK AWARD

PwC and BMO Financial Group, 121 Richmond St. W., Suite 605, Toronto ON M5H 2K1 Canada. (416)868-1500. **Fax:** (416)868-1502. **Website:** www.nbbaward.com. Offered annually for books published January 1-December 31 to recognize excellence in business writing in Canada. Publishers nominate books. Deadline: December 31. Prize: $30,000 (CAN).

NATIONAL WRITERS ASSOCIATION NONFICTION CONTEST

The National Writers Association, 10940 S. Parker Rd., #508, Parker CO 80134. **E-mail:** natlwritersassn@hotmail.com. **Website:** www.nationalwriters.com. Only unpublished works may be submitted. Judging of entries will not begin until the contest ends. Nonfiction in the following areas will be accepted: articles—submission should include query letter, 1st page of manuscript, separate sheet citing 5 possible markets; essay—the complete essay and 5 possible markets on separate sheet; nonfiction book proposal including query letter, chapter by chapter outline, first chapter, bio, and market analysis. Those unsure of proper manuscript format should request Research Report #35. The purpose of the National Writers Association Nonfiction Contest is to encourage the writing of nonfiction and recognize those who excel in this field. Deadline: December 31. Prize: 1st-5th place awards. Other winners will be notified by March 31st. 1st Prize: $200 and Clearinghouse representation if winner is book proposal; 2nd Prize: $100; 3rd Prize: $50; 4th-10th places will receive a book. Honorable Mentions receive a certificate. Judging will be based on originality, marketability, research, and reader interest. Copies of the judges evaluation sheets will be sent to entrants furnishing an SASE with their entry.

NONFICTION AWARD

Saskatchewan Book Awards, Inc., P.O. Box 20025, Regina SK S4P 4J7 Canada. (306)569-1585. **E-mail:** director@bookawards.sk.ca. **Website:** www.bookawards.sk.ca. Offered annually. This award is presented to a Saskatchewan author for the best book of nonfiction, judged on the quality of writing. Deadline: November 1. Prize: $2,000 (CAD).

FRANK LAWRENCE AND HARRIET CHAPPELL OWSLEY AWARD

Southern Historical Association, Room 111 A, LeConte Hall, Athens GA 30602-1602. (706)542-8848. **Fax:** (706)542-2455. **E-mail:** sdendy@uga.edu. **Website:** thesha.org. **Contact:** Dr. John B. Boles, Editor. Awarded for a distinguished book in Southern history published in even-numbered years. The decision of the Award Committee will be announced at the annual meeting in odd-numbered years. The award carries a cash payment to be fixed by the Council, a certificate for the author(s), and a certificate for the publisher. Deadline: March 1.

THE PHI BETA KAPPA AWARD IN SCIENCE

The Phi Beta Kappa Society, 1606 New Hampshire Ave. NW, Washington DC 20009. (202)265-3808. **Fax:** (202)986-1601. **E-mail:** awards@pbk.org. **Website:** www.pbk.org/bookawards. **Contact:** Awards Coordinator. Offered annually for outstanding contributions by scientists to the literature of science. To be eligible, biographies of scientists must have a substantial critical emphasis on their scientific research. Entries must have been published in the previous calendar year. Entries must be submitted by the publisher. Entries must be preceded by a letter certifying that the book(s) conforms to all the conditions of eligibility and stating the publication date of each entry. Two copies of the book must be sent with the nomination form. Books will not be entered officially in the competition until all copies and the letter of certification have been received. Open only to original works in English and authors of US residency and publication. The intent of the award is to encourage literate and scholarly interpretations of the physical and biological sciences and mathematics; monographs and compendiums are not eligible. Deadline: January 15. Prize: $10,000.

PRESERVATION FOUNDATION CONTESTS

The Preservation Foundation, Inc, 2313 Pennington Bend, Nashville TN 37214. (615)889-2968. **E-mail:** preserve@storyhouse.org. **E-mail:** preserve@storyhouse.org. **Website:** www.storyhouse.org. **Contact:** Richard Loller, publisher. Three contests offered annually for unpublished nonfictionl: (1) Biography/Autobiography. (1,500-10,000 words)—a true story of an individual personally known to the author. Or a true story from the author's life, the whole or an episode. (2) General nonfiction (1,500-10,000 words)—any

appropriate nonfiction topic. (3) Travel nonfiction (1,500-10,000 words)—must be the true story of trip by author or someone known personally by author. Open to any previously unpublished writer. Defined as having earned no more than $750 by creative writing in any previous year. Stories must be submitted by e-mail. No paper mss can be considered. No story may be entered in more than one contest. See website for contest details. Our purpose is to "Preserve the extraordinary works of "ordinary" people. Deadline: August 31. Prize: 1st Place: $100 in each category; certificates for finalists. Judged by a jury of three judges.

❂ EVELYN RICHARDSON MEMORIAL NONFICTION AWARD

Writers' Federation of Nova Scotia, 1113 Marginal Rd., Halifax NS B3H 4P7 Canada. (902)423-8116. **Fax:** (902)422-0881. **E-mail:** director@writers.ns.ca. **Website:** www.writers.ns.ca. The Evelyn Richardson Memorial Nonfiction Award is awarded for a book of creative nonfiction by a resident of Nova Scotia. Detailed guidelines and eligibility criteria available online. Deadline: First Friday in December. Prize: Valued at $2,000 for the winning title.

ALDO AND JEANNE SCAGLIONE PRIZE FOR COMPARATIVE LITERARY STUDIES

Modern Language Association of America, 85 Broad Street, Suite 500, New York NY 10004-2434. (646)576-5141. **Fax:** (646)458-0030. **E-mail:** awards@mla.org. **Website:** www.mla.org. **Contact:** Coordinator of Book Prizes. Offered annually for outstanding scholarly work in comparative literary studies involving at least 2 literatures. Works of literary history, literary criticism, philology, and literary theory are eligible, as are works dealing with literature and other arts and disciplines, including cinema; books that are primarily translations will not be considered. Books must have been published in the past calendar year. Authors must be current members of the MLA. Requires 4 copies of the book. Deadline: May 1. Prize: A cash award and a certificate to be presented at the Modern Language Association's annual convention in January.

ALDO AND JEANNE SCAGLIONE PRIZE FOR FRENCH AND FRANCOPHONE STUDIES

Modern Language Association of America, 85 Broad Street, Suite 500, New York NY 10004-2434. (646)576-5141. **Fax:** (646)458-0030. **E-mail:** awards@mla.org. **Website:** www.mla.org. Offered annually for an outstanding scholarly work in French or francophone linguistics or literary studies. Works of literary history, literary criticism, philology, and literary theory are eligible for consideration; books that are primarily translations will not be considered. Books must have been published in the previous year. Authors must be current members of the MLA. Requires 4 copies of the book. Deadline: May 1. Prize: A cash award and a certificate to be presented at the Modern Language Association's annual convention in January.

ALDO AND JEANNE SCAGLIONE PRIZE FOR ITALIAN STUDIES

Modern Language Association of America, 85 Broad Street, Suite 500, New York NY 10004-2434. (646)576-5141. **Fax:** (646)458-0030. **E-mail:** awards@mla.org. **Website:** www.mla.org. **Contact:** Coordinator of Book Prizes. Offered in odd-number years for an outstanding scholarly work on any phase of Italian literature or culture, or comparative literature involving Italian. This shall include works that study literary or cultural theory, science, history, art, music, society, politics, cinema, and linguistics, preferably but not necessarily relating other disciplines to literature. Books must have been published in the previous year. Authors must be members of the MLA. Requires 4 copies of the book. Deadline: May 1. Prize: A cash award and a certificate to be presented at the Modern Language Association's annual convention in January.

ALDO AND JEANNE SCAGLIONE PRIZE FOR STUDIES IN GERMANIC LANGUAGES & LITERATURE

Modern Language Association of America, 85 Broad Street, Suite 500, New York NY 10004-2434. (646)576-5141. **Fax:** (646)458-0030. **E-mail:** awards@mla.org. **Website:** www.mla.org. Offered in even-numbered years for an outstanding scholarly work on the linguistics or literatures of any of the Germanic languages (Danish, Dutch, German, Norwegian, Swedish, Yiddish). Works of literary history, literary criticism, philology, and literary theory are eligible for consideration; books that are primarily translations will not be considered. Books must have been published in the previous 2 years. Authors must be members of the MLA. Requires 4 copies of the book. Deadline: May 1. Prize: A cash award, and a certificate to be presented at the Modern Language Association's annual convention in January.

ALDO AND JEANNE SCAGLIONE PUBLICATION AWARD FOR A MANUSCRIPT IN ITALIAN LITERARY STUDIES

Modern Language Association, 85 Broad Street, Suite 500, New York NY 10004-2434. (646)576-5141. **Fax:** (646)458-0030. **E-mail:** awards@mla.org. **Website:** www.mla.org. **Contact:** Coordinator of Book Prizes. Offered annually for an outstanding ms dealing with any aspect of the languages and literatures of Italy, including medieval Latin and comparative studies or intellectual history if the work's main thrust is clearly related to the humanities. Materials from ancient Rome are eligible if related to postclassical developments. Also eligible are translations of classical works of prose and poetry produced in Italy prior to 1900 in any language (e.g., neo-Latin, Greek) or in a dialect of Italian (e.g., Neapolitan, Roman, Sicilian). Eligible are book manuscripts in English or Italian that are ready for submission or already submitted to a press. Mss must be approved or ready for publication before award deadline. Authors must be current members of the MLA, residing in the United States or Canada. Requires 4 copies, plus contact and biographical information. Deadline: June 1. Prize: A cash award and a certificate to be presented at the Modern Language Association's annual convention in January.

WILLIAM SANDERS SCARBOROUGH PRIZE

Modern Language Association of America, 85 Broad Street, Suite 500, New York NY 10004-2434. (646)576-5141. **Fax:** (646)458-0030. **E-mail:** awards@mla.org. **Website:** www.mla.org. **Contact:** Coordinator of book prizes. Offered annually for an outstanding study of black American literature or culture. Books must have been published in the previous year. Authors need not be members of the MLA. Requires 4 copies of the book. Deadline: May 1. Prize: A cash award, and a certificate to be presented at the Modern Language Association's annual convention in January.

⊙ SCHOLARLY WRITING AWARD

Saskatchewan Book Awards, Inc., P.O. Box 20025, Regina SK S4P 4J7 Canada. (306)569-1585. **E-mail:** director@bookawards.sk.ca. **Website:** www.bookawards.sk.ca. **Contact:** Courtney Bates-Hardy, Executive Director. Offered annually. This award is presented to a Saskatchewan author for the best contribution to scholarship. The work must recognize or draw on specific theoretical work within a community of scholars, and participate in the creation and transmission of scholarly knowledge. Prize: $2,000 (CAD).

SCREAMINMAMAS CREATIVE NONFICTION CONTEST

1911 Cleveland St., Hollywood FL 33020. **E-mail:** screaminmamas@gmail.com. **Website:** www.screaminmamas.com/contests. **Contact:** Darlene Pistocchi, editor/managing director. "Looking for stories that revolve around the kids and/or pets. Must be true! Take an incident or scene that is embedded in your brain and share it with us. Story can be dramatic or humorous, happy or sad. Looking for the real deal." Stories should be 600-1,000 words. Open only to moms. Deadline: March 31. Prize: Publication, complementary subscription.

THE SHAUGHNESSY COHEN PRIZE FOR POLITICAL WRITING

The Writers' Trust of Canada, 460 Richmond St. W., Suite 600, Toronto ON M5V 1Y1 Canada. (416)504-8222. **Fax:** (416)504-9090. **E-mail:** info@writerstrust.com. **Website:** www.writerstrust.com. **Contact:** Amanda Hopkins. Awarded annually for a nonfiction book of outstanding literary merit that enlarges understanding of contemporary Canadian political and social issues. Presented at the Politics & the Pen event each spring in Ottawa. Open to Canadian citizens and permanent residents only. Prize: $25,000 and $2,500 to 4 finalists.

MINA P. SHAUGHNESSY PRIZE

Modern Language Association of America, 85 Broad Street, Suite 500, New York NY 10004-2434. (646)576-5141. **Fax:** (646)458-0030. **E-mail:** awards@mla.org. **Website:** www.mla.org. **Contact:** Coordinator of Book Prizes. Offered in even-numbered years for a work in the fields of language, culture, literacy, or literature with strong application to the teaching of English. Books must have been published in the previous 2 years. Authors need not be members of the MLA. Requires 4 copies of the book. Deadline: May 1. Prize: A cash prize, a certificate, to be presented at the Modern Language Association's annual convention in January, and a 1-year membership in the MLA.

CHARLES S. SYDNOR AWARD

Southern Historical Association, Rm. 111 A LeConte Hall, Athens GA 30602-1602. (706)542-8848. **Fax:** (706)542-2455. **E-mail:** sdendy@uga.edu. **Website:** sha.uga.edu/awards/syndor.htm. **Contact:** Southern Historical Association. Offered in even-numbered years for recognition of a distinguished book in Southern history published in odd-numbered years. Publishers usually submit books. Deadline: March 1.

TONY LOTHIAN PRIZE

Under the auspices of the Biographers' Club, 79 Arlington Ave., London N1 7BA United Kingdom. (44)(20)7 359 7769. **E-mail:** ariane.bankes@gmail.com. **Website:** www.biographersclub.co.uk. **Contact:** Ariane Bankes, prize administrator. Entries should consist of a synopsis and 10 pages of a sample chapter for a proposed biography, plus CV, sources and a note on the market for the book: 20 pages maximum in all, unstapled. Open to any writer who has not previously been published or commissioned or written a biography. Deadline: July 27. Prize: £2,000. Judges have included Michael Holroyd, Victoria Glendinning, Selina Hastings, Frances Spalding, Lyndall Gordon, Anne de Courcy, Nigel Hamilton, Anthony Sampson, and Mary Lovell.

WABASH PRIZE FOR NONFICTION

Sycamore Review, Department of English, 500 Oval Dr., Purdue University, West Lafayette IN 47907. **E-mail:** sycamore@purdue.edu; sycamorenf@purdue.edu. **Website:** www.sycamorereview.com/contest/. **Contact:** Kara Krewer, editor-in-chief. Annual contest for unpublished nonfiction. For each submission, send one nonfiction piece (limit 7,500 words). Ms pages should be numbered and should include the title of the piece. All stories must be previously unpublished. See website for more guidelines. Submit via online submissions manager. Deadline: April 15. Prize: $1,000 and publication.

THE HILARY WESTON WRITERS' TRUST PRIZE FOR NONFICTION

The Writers' Trust of Canada, 460 Richmond St. W., Suite 600, Toronto ON M5V 1Y1 Canada. (416)504-8222. **Fax:** (416)504-9090. **E-mail:** info@writerstrust.com. **Website:** www.writerstrust.com. **Contact:** Amanda Hopkins. Offered annually for a work of nonfiction published in the previous year. Award presented at the Writers' Trust Awards event held in Toronto each fall. Open to Canadian citizens and permanent residents only. Deadline: July 27. Prize: $60,000; $5,000 to 4 finalists.

THE ELIE WIESEL PRIZE IN ETHICS ESSAY CONTEST

The Elie Wiesel Foundation for Humanity, 555 Madison Ave., 20th Floor, New York NY 10022. **Fax:** (212)490-6006. **Website:** www.eliewieselfoundation.org. **Contact:** Leslie Meyers. This annual competition is intended to challenge undergraduate juniors and seniors in colleges and universities throughout the US to analyze ethical questions and concerns facing them in today's complex society. All students are encouraged to write thought-provoking, personal essays. Deadline: December 14. Prize: 1st Prize: $5,000; 2nd Prize: $2,500; 3rd Prize: $1,500; Honorable Mentions (2): $500. Judged by a distinguished panel of readers who evaluate all contest entries. A jury chooses the winners.

WRITING CONFERENCE WRITING CONTESTS

P.O. Box 664, Ottawa KS 66067-0664. (785)242-2947. **Fax:** (785)242-2473. **E-mail:** jbushman@writingconference.com. **E-mail:** support@studentq.com. **Website:** www.writingconference.com. **Contact:** John H. Bushman, contest director. Unpublished submissions only. Submissions made by the author or teacher. Purpose of contest: To further writing by students with awards for narration, exposition and poetry at the elementary, middle school, and high school levels. Deadline: January 8. Prize: Awards plaque and publication of winning entry in The Writers' Slate online, April issue. Judged by a panel of teachers.

YEARBOOK EXCELLENCE CONTEST

100 Adler Journalism Building, Iowa City IA 52242-2004. (319)335-3457. **Fax:** (319)335-3989. **E-mail:** quill-scroll@uiowa.edu. **Website:** www.quilland-scroll.org. **Contact:** Vanessa Shelton, executive director. High school students who are contributors to or staff members of a student yearbook at any public or private high school are invited to enter the competition. Awards will be made in each of the 18 divisions. There are two enrollment categories: Class A: more than 750 students; Class B: 749 or less. Winners will receive Quill and Scroll's National Award Gold Key and, if seniors, are eligible to apply for one of the Edward J. Nell Memorial or George and Ophelia Gallup scholarships. Open to students whose schools have Quill and Scroll charters. Previously published submissions only. Submissions made by the author or school yearbook adviser. Must be published in the 12-month span prior to contest deadline. Visit website for list of current and previous winners. Purpose is to recognize and reward student journalists for their work in yearbooks and to provide student winners an opportunity to apply for a scholarship to be used freshman year in college for students planning to major in journalism. Deadline: November 1.

ZONE 3 CREATIVE NONFICTION BOOK AWARD

Zone 3, Austin Peay State University, P.O. Box 4565, Clarksville TN 37044. (931)221-7031. **Fax:** (931)221-7149. **E-mail:** wallacess@apsu.edu. **Website:** www.apsu.edu/zone3/contests. **Contact:** Susan Wallace, Managing Editor. This competition is open to all authors writing original works in English. Looking for manuscripts that embrace creative nonfiction's potential by combining lyric exposition, researched reflection, travel dialogues, or creative criticism. Memoir, personal narrative, essay collections, and literary nonfiction are also invited. Submit one copy of ms of 150-300 pages. Accepts entries online and via postal mail. Deadline: April 1. Prize: $1,000 and publication.

WRITING FOR CHILDREN & YOUNG ADULTS

JANE ADDAMS CHILDREN'S BOOK AWARDS

Jane Addams Peace Association, 777 United Nations Plaza, 6th Floor, New York NY 10017. (212)652-8830. **E-mail:** info@janeaddamspeace.org. **Website:** www.janeaddamspeace.org. **Contact:** Heather Palmer, co-chair. The Jane Addams Children's Book Awards are given annually to the children's books published the preceding year that effectively promote the cause of peace, social justice, world community, and the equality of the sexes and all races as well as meeting conventional standards for excellence. Books eligible for this award may be fiction, poetry, or nonfiction. Books may be any length. Entries should be suitable for ages 2-12. See website for specific details on guidelines and required book themes. Deadline: December 31. Judged by a national committee of WILPF members concerned with children's books and their social values is responsible for making the changes each year.

AMERICAN ASSOCIATION OF UNIVERSITY WOMEN AWARD IN JUVENILE LITERATURE

4610 Mail Service Center, Raleigh NC 27699-4610. (919)807-7290. **E-mail:** michael.hill@ncdcr.gov. **Website:** www.ncdcr.gov. **Contact:** Michael Hill, awards coordinator. Annual award. Book must be published during the year ending June 30. Submissions made by author, author's agent or publisher. SASE for contest rules. Author must have maintained either legal residence or actual physical residence, or a combination of both, in the state of North Carolina for 3 years immediately preceding the close of the contest period. Only published work (books) eligible. Recognizes the year's best work of juvenile literature by a North Carolina resident. Deadline: July 15. Prize: Awards a cup to the winner and winner's name inscribed on a plaque displayed within the North Carolina Office of Archives and History. Judged by three-judge panel.

☙ HANS CHRISTIAN ANDERSEN AWARD

Nonnenweg 12, Postfach Basel CH-4009 Switzerland. **E-mail:** liz.page@ibby.org. **E-mail:** ibby@ibby.org. **Website:** www.ibby.org. **Contact:** Liz Page, director. The Hans Christian Andersen Award, awarded every two years by the International Board on Books for Young People (IBBY), is the highest international recognition given to an author and an illustrator of children's books. The Author's Award has been given since 1956, the Illustrator's Award since 1966. Her Majesty Queen Margrethe II of Denmark is the Patron of the Hans Christian Andersen Awards. The awards are presented at the biennial congresses of IBBY. Awarded to an author and to an illustrator, living at the time of the nomination, who by the outstanding value of their work are judged to have made a lasting contribution to literature for children and young people. The complete works of the author and of the illustrator will be taken into consideration in awarding the medal, which will be accompanied by a diploma. Candidates are nominated by National Sections of IBBY in good standing. Prize: Awards medals according to literary and artistic criteria. Judged by the Hans Christian Andersen Jury.

◐ MARILYN BAILLIE PICTURE BOOK AWARD

The Canadian Children's Book Centre, 40 Orchard View Blvd., Suite 217, Toronto ON M4R 1B9 Canada. (416)975-0010, ext. 222. **Fax:** (416)975-8970. **E-mail:** meghan@bookcentre.ca. **Website:** www.bookcentre.ca. **Contact:** Meghan Howe. The Marilyn Baillie Picture Book Award honors excellence in the illustrated picture book format. To be eligible, the book must be an original work in English, aimed at children ages 3-8, written and illustrated by Canadians and first published in Canada. Eligible genres include fiction, non-fiction and poetry. Books must be published between Jan. 1 and Dec. 31 of the previous calendar year. New editions or re-issues of previously published books are not eligible for submission. Send 5 copies of title along with a completed submission form. Deadline: mid-December annually. Prize: $20,000. **TIPS** "Please visit website for submission guidelines and eligibility criteria."

MILDRED L. BATCHELDER AWARD

50 E. Huron St., Chicago IL 60611-2795. **Website:** http://www.ala.org/alsc/awardsgrants/. The Batchelder Award is given to the most outstanding children's book originally published in a language other than English in a country other than the United States, and subsequently translated into English for publication in the US. Visit website for terms and criteria of award. The purpose of the award, a citation to an American publisher, is to encourage international exchange of quality children's books by recognizing US publishers of such books in translation. Deadline: December 31.

JOHN AND PATRICIA BEATTY AWARD

California Library Association, **E-mail:** tbronzan@sonoma.lib.ca.us. **Website:** http://www.cla-net.org/?page=113. **Contact:** Tiffany Bronzan, award chair. The California Library Association's John and Patricia Beatty Award, sponsored by Baker & Taylor, honors the author of a distinguished book for children or young adults that best promotes an awareness of California and its people. Must be a children's or young adult books published in the previous year, set in California, and highlight California's cultural heritage or future. Send title suggestiosn to the committee members. Deadline: January 31. Prize: $500 and an engraved plaque. Judged by a committee of CLA members, who select the winning title from books published in the United States during the preceding year.

◐ THE GEOFFREY BILSON AWARD FOR HISTORICAL FICTION FOR YOUNG PEOPLE

The Canadian Children's Book Centre, 40 Orchard View Blvd., Suite 217, Toronto ON M4R 1B9 Canada.

(416)975-0010, ext. 222. **Fax:** (416)975-8970. **Web-site:** www.bookcentre.ca. **Contact:** Meghan Howe. Awarded annually to reward excellence in the writing of an outstanding work of historical fiction for young readers, by a Canadian author, published in the previous calendar year. Open to Canadian citizens and residents of Canada for at least 2 years. Books must be published between January 1 and December 31 of the previous year. Books must be first foreign or first Canadian editions. Autobiographies are not eligible. Jury members will consider the following: historical setting and accuracy, strong character and plot development, well-told, original story, and stability of book for its intended age group. Send 5 copies of the title along with a completed submission form. Deadline: mid-December annually. Prize: $5,000.

THE IRMA S. AND JAMES H. BLACK AWARD

Bank Street College of Education, 610 W. 112th St., New York NY 10025-1898. (212)875-4458. **Fax:** (212)875-4558. **E-mail:** kfreda@bankstreet.edu. **Website:** http://bankstreet.edu/center-childrens-lit-erature/irma-black-award/. **Contact:** Kristin Freda. Award give to an outstanding book for young children—a book in which text and illustrations are inseparable, each enhancing and enlarging on the other to produce a singular whole. Entries must have been published during the previous calendar year. Publishers submit books. Submit only one copy of each book. Does not accept unpublished mss. Deadline: mid-December. Prize: A scroll with the recipient's name and a gold seal designed by Maurice Sendak. Judged by a committee of older children and children's literature professionals. Final judges are first-, second-, and third-grade classes at a number of cooperating schools.

☻ ANN CONNOR BRIMER BOOK AWARD

The Ann Connor Brimer Award, P.O. Box 36036, Halifax NS B3J 3S9 Canada. (902)490-2742. **Website:** www.atlanticbookawards.ca/. **Contact:** Laura Carter, Atlantic Book Awards Festival Coordinator. In 1990, the Nova Scotia Library Association established the Ann Connor Brimer Award for writers residing in Atlantic Canada who have made an outstanding contribution to writing for Atlantic Candian young people. Author must be alive and residing in Atlantic Canada at time of nomination. Book intended for youth up to the age of 15. Book in print and readily available.

Fiction or nonfiction (except textbooks). Book must have been published within the previous year. Prize: $2,000. Two shortlisted titles: $250 each.

CHILDREN'S AFRICANA BOOK AWARD

Outreach Council of the African Studies Association, c/o Rutgers University -Livingston campus, 54 Joyce Kilmer Ave., Piscataway NJ 08854. (703)549-8208; (301)585-9136. **E-mail:** africaaccess@aol.com. **E-mail:** Harriet@AfricaAccessReview.org. **Website:** www.africaaccessreview.org. **Contact:** Brenda Randolph, chairperson. The Children's Africana Book Awards are presented annually to the authors and illustrators of the best books on Africa for children and young people published or distributed in the U.S. The awards were created by the Outreach Council of the African Studies Association (ASA) to dispel stereotypes and encourage the publication and use of accurate, balanced children's materials about Africa. The awards are presented in 2 categories: Young Children and Older Readers. Entries must have been published in the calendar year previous to the award. Work submitted for awards must be suitable for children ages 4-18; a significant portion of books' content must be about Africa; must by copyrighted in the calendar year prior to award year; must be published or distributed in the US. Books should be suitable for children and young adults, ages 4-18. A significant portion of the book's content should be about Africa. Deadline: January 31 of the award year. Judged by African Studies and Children's Literature scholars. Nominated titles are read by committee members and reviewed by external African Studies scholars with specialized academic training.

CHILDREN'S BOOK GUILD AWARD FOR NONFICTION

E-mail: theguild@childrensbookguild.org. **Website:** www.childrensbookguild.org. Annual award. "One doesn't enter. One is selected. Our jury annually selects one author for the award." Honors an author or illustrator whose total work has contributed significantly to the quality of nonfiction for children. Prize: Cash and an engraved crystal paperweight. Judged by a jury of Children's Book Guild specialists, authors, and illustrators.

☻ CLA YOUNG ADULT BOOK AWARD

1150 Morrison Dr.,, Suite 400, Ottawa ON K2H 8S9 Canada. (613)232-9625. **Fax:** (613)563-9895. **E-mail:** cshea@cbvrsb.ca. **Website:** www.cla.ca. **Contact:** Carmelita Cechetto-Shea, chair. This award recognizes an author of an outstanding English language Canadian book which appeals to young adults between the ages of 13 and 18. To be eligible for consideration, the following must apply: it must be a work of fiction (novel, collection of short stories, or graphic novel), the title must be a Canadian publication in either hardcover or paperback, and the author must be a Canadian citizen or landed immigrant. The award is given annually, when merited, at the Canadian Library Association's annual conference. Deadline: December 31. Prize: $1,000.

MARGARET A. EDWARDS AWARD

50 East Huron St., Chicago IL 60611-2795. (312)280-4390 or (800)545-2433. **Fax:** (312)280-5276. **E-mail:** yalsa@ala.org. **Website:** www.ala.org/yalsa/edwards. **Contact:** Nichole O'Connor. Annual award administered by the Young Adult Library Services Association (YALSA) of the American Library Association (ALA) and sponsored by *School Library Journal* magazine. Awarded to an author whose book or books, over a period of time, have been accepted by young adults as an authentic voice that continues to illuminate their experiences and emotions, giving insight into their lives. The book or books should enable them to understand themselves, the world in which they live, and their relationship with others and with society. The book or books must be in print at the time of the nomination. Submissions must be previously published no less than 5 years prior to the first meeting of the current Margaret A. Edwards Award Committee at Midwinter Meeting. Nomination form is available on the YALSA website. Deadline: December 1. Prize: $2,000. Judged by members of the Young Adult Library Services Association.

DOROTHY CANFIELD FISHER CHILDREN'S BOOK AWARD

Midstate Library Service Center, Dorothy Canfield Fisher Book Award Committee, c/o Vermont Department of Libraries, 109 State St., Montpelier VT 05609. (802)828-6954. **E-mail:** grace.greene@state. vt.us. **Website:** www.dcfaward.org. **Contact:** Mary Linney, chair. Annual award to encourage Vermont children to become enthusiastic and discriminating readers by providing them with books of good quality by living American or Canadian authors published in the current year. E-mail for entry rules. Titles must be original work, published in the U.S., and be appropri-

ate to children in grades 4-8. The book must be copyrighted in the current year. It must be written by an American author living in the U.S. or Canada, or a Canadian author living in Canada or the U.S. Deadline: December of year book was published. Prize: Awards a scroll presented to the winning author at an award ceremony. Judged by children, grades 4-8, who vote for their favorite book.

☺ THE NORMA FLECK AWARD FOR CANADIAN CHILDREN'S NON-FICTION

The Canadian Children's Book Centre, 40 Orchard View Blvd., Suite 217, Toronto ON M4R 1B9 Canada. (416)975-0010 ext. 222. **Fax:** (416)975-8970. **E-mail:** meghan@bookcentre.ca. **Website:** www.bookcentre. ca. **Contact:** Meghan Howe. The Norma Fleck Award was established by the Fleck Family Foundation to recognize and raise the profile of exceptional nonfiction books for children. Offered annually for books published between January 1 and December 31 of the previous calendar year. Open to Canadian citizens or landed immigrants. Books must be first foreign or first Canadian editions. Nonfiction books in the following categories are eligible: culture and the arts, science, biography, history, geography, reference, sports, activities, and pastimes. Deadline: mid-December annually. Prize: $10,000. The award will go to the author unless 40% or more of the text area is composed of original illustrations, in which case the award will be divided equally between author and illustrator.

FLICKER TALE CHILDREN'S BOOK AWARD

Morton Mandan Public Library, 609 W. Main St., Mandan ND 58554. **E-mail:** laustin@cdln.info. **Website:** www.ndla.info/flickertale. **Contact:** Linda Austin. Award gives children across the state of North Dakota a chance to vote for their book of choice from a nominated list of 20: 4 in the picture book category; 4 in the intermediate category; 4 in the juvenile category (for more advanced readers); 4 in the upper grade level nonfiction category. Also promotes awareness of quality literature for children. Previously published submissions only. Submissions nominated by librarians and teachers across the state of North Dakota. Deadline: April 1. Prize: A plaque from North Dakota Library Association and banquet dinner. Judged by children in North Dakota.

THEODOR SEUSS GEISEL AWARD

Association for Library Service to Children, Division of the American Library Association, 50 E. Huron, Chicago IL 60611. (800)545-2433. **E-mail:** als-cawards@ala.org. **Website:** www.ala.org. The Theodor Seuss Geisel Award is given annually to the author(s) and illustrator(s) of the most distinguished American book for beginning readers published in English in the United States during the preceding year. The award is to recognize the author(s) and illustrator(s) who demonstrate great creativity and imagination in his/her/their literary and artistic achievements to engage children in reading. Terms and criteria for the award are listed on the website. Entry will not be returned. Deadline: December 31. Prize: Medal, given at awards ceremony during the ALA Annual Conference.

GOLDEN KITE AWARDS

Society of Children's Book Writers and Illustrators (SCBWI), SCBWI Golden Kite Awards, 8271 Beverly Blvd., Los Angeles CA 90048-4515. (323)782-1010. **Fax:** (323)782-1892. **E-mail:** bonniebader@sbcwi.org. **Website:** www.scbwi.org. Given annually to recognize excellence in children's literature in 4 categories: fiction, nonfiction, picture book text, and picture book illustration. Books submitted must be published in the previous calendar year. Both individuals and publishers may submit. Submit 4 copies of book. Submit to one category only, except in the case of picture books. Must be a current member of the SCBWI. Deadline: December 1. Prize: One Golden Kite Award Winner and one Honor Book will be chosen per category. Winners and Honorees will receive a commemorative poster also sent to publishers, bookstores, libraries, and schools; a press release; an announcement on the SCBWI website; and on SCBWI Social Networks.

⊘ AMELIA FRANCES HOWARD-GIBBON ILLUSTRATOR'S AWARD

1150 Morrison Drie, Suite 400, Ottawa ON K 2H859 Canada. (613)232-9625. **Fax:** (613)563-9895. **Website:** www.bookcentre.ca. **Contact:** Diana Cauthier. Annually awarded to an outstanding illustrator of a children's book published in Canada during the previous calendar year. The award is bestowed upon books that are suitable for children up to and including age 12. To be eligible for the award, an illustrator must be a Canadian citizen or a permanent resident of Canada, and the text of the book must be worthy of the book's illustrations. Deadline: November 30. Prize: A plaque and a check for $1,000 (CAD).

CAROL OTIS HURST CHILDREN'S BOOK PRIZE

Westfield Athenaeum, 6 Elm St., Westfield MA 01085. (413)568-7833. **Fax:** (413)568-0988. **Website:** www.westath.org. **Contact:** Pamela Weingart. The Carol Otis Hurst Children's Book Prize honors outstanding works of fiction and nonfiction, including biography and memoir, written for children and young adults through the age of eighteen that exemplify the highest standards of research, analysis, and authorship in their portrayal of the New England Experience. The prize will be presented annually to an author whose book treats the region's history as broadly conceived to encompass one or more of the following elements: political experience, social development, fine and performing artistic expression, domestic life and arts, transportation and communication, changing technology, military experience at home and abroad, schooling, business and manufacturing, workers and the labor movement, agriculture and its transformation, racial and ethnic diversity, religious life and institutions, immigration and adjustment, sports at all levels, and the evolution of popular entertainment. The public presentation of the prize will be accompanied by a reading and/or talk by the recipient at a mutually agreed upon time during the spring immediately following the publication year. Books must have been copyrighted in their original format during the calendar year, January 1 to December 31, of the year preceding the year in which the prize is awarded. Any individual, publisher, or organization may nominate a book. See website for details and guidelines. Deadline: December 31. Prize: $500.

INTERNATIONAL LITERACY ASSOCIATION CHILDREN'S AND YOUNG ADULT'S BOOK AWARDS

P.O. Box 8139, 800 Barksdale Rd., Newark DE 19714-8139. (302)731-1600, ext. 221. **E-mail:** kbaughman@reading.org. **E-mail:** committees@reading.org. **Website:** www.literacyworldwide.org. **Contact:** Kathy Baughman. The ILA Children's and Young Adults Book Awards are intended for newly published authors who show unusual promise in the children's and young adults' book field. Awards are given for fiction and nonfiction in each of three categories: primary, intermediate, and young adult. Books from all countries and published in English for the first time during the previous calendar year will be considered. See website for eligibility and criteria information. Entry should be the author's first or second book. Deadline: January 15. Prize: $1,000.

TIPS Provide believable and intriguing characters, truthful and authentic in its presentation of information and attitudes as they existed at the time and place which the story reflects.

☼ THE IODE JEAN THROOP BOOK AWARD

The Lillian H. Smith Children's Library, 239 College St., 4th St., Toronto ON M5T 1R5 Canada. (905)522-9537. **E-mail:** mcscott@torontopubliclibrary.ca; iodeontario@bellnet.ca. **Website:** www.iodeontario.ca. **Contact:** Martha Scott. Each year, the Municipal Chapter of Toronto IODE presents an award intended to encourage the publication of books for children between the ages of 6-12 years. The award-winner must be a Canadian citizen, resident in Toronto or the surrounding area, and the book must be published in Canada. Deadline: December 31. Prize: Award and cash prize of $2,000. Judged by a selected committee.

JEFFERSON CUP AWARD

P.O. Box 56312, Virginia Beach VA 23456. (757)689-0594. **Website:** www.vla.org. **Contact:** Lauri Newell, current chairperson. The Jefferson Cup honors a distinguished biography, historical fiction, or American history book for young people. The Jefferson Cup Committee's goal is to promote reading about America's past; to encourage the quality writing of United States history, biography, and historical fiction for young people; and to recognize authors in these disciplines. Deadline: January 31.

THE EZRA JACK KEATS BOOK AWARD FOR NEW WRITER AND A NEW ILLUSTRATOR

450 14th St., Brooklyn NY 11215-5702. **E-mail:** foundation@ezra-jack-keats.org. **Website:** www.ezra-jack-keats.org. Annual award to an outstanding new author and new illustrator of children's books that portray universal qualities of childhood in our multicultural world. Many past winners have gone on to distinguished careers, creating books beloved by parents, children, librarians and teachers around the world. Writers and illustrators must have had no more than 3 books previously published. Prize: $1,000 honorarium for each winner. Judged by a distinguished selection committee of early childhood education specialists, librarians, illustrators and experts in children's literature.

TIPS "Seeking books that portray the universal qualities of childhood, a strong and supportive family, and the multicultural nature of our world."

EZRA JACK KEATS/KERLAN MEMORIAL FELLOWSHIP

University of Minnesota Libraries, 113 Elmer L. Andersen Library, 222 21st Ave. S, Minneapolis MN 55455. **E-mail:** asc-clrc@umn.edu. **Website:** https://www.lib.umn.edu/clrc/awards-grants-and-fellowships. This fellowship from the Ezra Jack Keats Foundation will provide $1,500 to a talented writer and/or illustrator of children's books who wishes to use the Kerlan Collection for the furtherance of his or her artistic development. Special consideration will be given to someone who would find it difficult to finance a visit to the Kerlan Collection. The Ezra Jack Keats Fellowship recipient will receive transportation costs and a per diem allotment. See website for application deadline and for digital application materials. Winner will be notified in February. Study and written report must be completed within the calendar year. Deadline: January 30.

KENTUCKY BLUEGRASS AWARD

Website: www.kasl.us. The Kentucky Bluegrass Award is a student choice program. The KBA promotes and encourages Kentucky students in kindergarten through grade 12 to read a variety of quality literature. Each year, a KBA committee for each grade category chooses the books for the four Master Lists (K-2, 3-5, 6-8 and 9-12). All Kentucky public and private schools, as well as public libraries, are welcome to participate in the program. To nominate a book, see the website for form and details. Deadline: March 1. Judged by students who read books and choose their favorite.

CORETTA SCOTT KING BOOK AWARDS

50 E. Huron St., Chicago IL 60611-2795. (800)545-2433. **E-mail:** olos@ala.org. **Website:** www.ala.org/csk. **Contact:** Office for Diversity, Literacy and Outreach Services. The Coretta Scott King Book Awards are given annually to outstanding African American authors and illustrators of books for children and young adults that demonstrate an appreciation of African American culture and universal human values. The award commemorates the life and work of Dr. Martin Luther King, Jr., and honors his wife, Mrs. Coretta Scott King, for her courage and determination to continue the work for peace and world

brotherhood. Must be written for a youth audience in one of three categories: preschool-4th grade; 5th-8th grade; or 9th-12th grade. Book must be published in the year preceding the year the award is given, evidenced by the copyright date in the book. See website for full details, criteria, and eligibility concerns. Purpose is to encourage the artistic expression of the African American experience via literature and the graphic arts, including biographical, historical and social history treatments by African American authors and illustrators. Deadline: December 1. Judged by the Coretta Scott King Book Awards Committee.

○ THE VICKY METCALF AWARD FOR LITERATURE FOR YOUNG PEOPLE

The Writers' Trust of Canada, 460 Richmond St. W., Suite 600, Toronto ON M5V 1Y1 Canada. (416)504-8222. **E-mail:** info@writerstrust.com. **Website:** www.writerstrust.com. **Contact:** Amanda Hopkins. The Vicky Metcalf Award is presented to a Canadian writer for a body of work in children's literature at The Writers' Trust Awards event held in Toronto each fall. Open to Canadian citizens and permanent residents only. Prize: $20,000.

MILKWEED PRIZE FOR CHILDREN'S LITERATURE

Milkweed Editions, 1011 Washington Ave. S., Suite 300, Minneapolis MN 55415. (612)332-3192. **Fax:** (612)215-2550. **E-mail:** editor@milkweed.org. **Website:** www.milkweed.org. Milkweed Editions will award the Milkweed Prize for Children's Literature to the best mss for young readers that Milkweed accepts for publication during the calendar year by a writer not previously published by Milkweed. All mss for young readers submitted for publication by Milkweed are automatically entered into the competition. Seeking full-length fiction between 90-200 pages. Does not consider picture books or poetry collections for young readers. Recognizes an outstanding literary novel for readers ages 8-13 and encourage writers to turn their attention to readers in this age group. Prize: $10,000 cash prize in addition to a publishing contract negotiated at the time of acceptance. Judged by the editors of Milkweed Editions.

NATIONAL YOUNGARTS FOUNDATION

2100 Biscayne Blvd., Miami FL 33137. (305)377-1140. **Fax:** (305)377-1149. **E-mail:** info@nfaa.org; apply@youngarts.org. **Website:** www.youngarts.org. The National YoungArts Foundation (formerly known as the National Foundation for Advancement in the Arts) was established in 1981 by Lin and Ted Arison to identify and support the next generation of artists and to contribute to the cultural vitality of the nation by investing in the artistic development of talented young artists in the visual, literary, design and performing arts. Each year, there are approximately 11,000 applications submitted to YoungArts from 15-18 year old (or grades 10-12) artists, and from these, approximately 700 winners are selected who are eligible to participate in programs in Miami, New York, Los Angeles, and Washington D.C. (with Chicago and other regions in the works). YoungArts provides these emerging artists with life-changing experiences and validation by renowned mentors, access to significant scholarships, national recognition and other opportunities throughout their careers to help ensure that the nation's most outstanding emerging artists are encouraged to pursue careers in the arts. See website for details about applying. Prize: Cash awards up to $10,000.

JOHN NEWBERY MEDAL

Association for Library Service to Children, Division of the American Library Association, 50 E. Huron, Chicago IL 60611. (800)545-2433, ext. 2153. **Fax:** (312)280-5271. **E-mail:** alscawards@ala.org. **Website:** www.ala.org. The Newbery Medal is awarded annually by the American Library Association for the most distinguished contribution to American literature for children. Previously published submissions only; must be published prior to year award is given. SASE for award rules. Entries not returned. Medal awarded at Caldecott/Newbery banquet during ALA annual conference. Deadline: December 31. Judged by Newbery Award Selection Committee.

NEW VOICES AWARD

95 Madison Ave., Suite 1205, New York NY 10016. **Website:** www.leeandlow.com. Open to students. Annual award. Lee & Low Books is one of the few minority-owned publishing companies in the country and has published more than 100 first-time writers and illustrators. Winning titles include *The Blue Roses*, winner of a Patterson Prize for Books for Young People; *Janna and the Kings*, an IRA Children's Book Award Notable; and *Sixteen Years in Sixteen Seconds*, selected for the Texas Bluebonnet Award Masterlist. Submissions made by author. SASE for contest rules or visit website. Restrictions of media for illustrators:

The author must be a writer of color who is a resident of the U.S. and who has not previously published a children's picture book. For additional information, send SASE or visit Lee & Low's website. Encourages writers of color to enter the world of children's books. Deadline: September 30. Prize: $1,000 and standard publication contract (regardless of whether or not writer has an agent) along with an advance against royalties; New Voices Honor Award: $500 prize. Judged by Lee & Low editors.

THE ORIGINAL ART

128 E. 63rd St., New York NY 10065. (212)838-2560. **Fax:** (212)838-2561. **E-mail:** kim@societyillustrators.org; info@societyillustrators.org. **Website:** www.societyillustrators.org. **Contact:** Kate Feirtag, exhibition director. The Original Art is an annual exhibit created to showcase illustrations from the year's best children's books published in the US. For editors and art directors, it's an inspiration and a treasure trove of talent to draw upon. Previously published submissions only. Request "call for entries" to receive contest rules and entry forms. Works will be displayed at the Society of Illustrators Museum of American Illustration in New York City October-November annually. Deadline: July 18. Judged by 7 professional artists and editors.

HELEN KEATING OTT AWARD FOR OUTSTANDING CONTRIBUTION TO CHILDREN'S LITERATURE

CSLA, 10157 SW Barbur Blvd. #102C, Portland OR 97219. (503)244-6919. **Fax:** (503)977-3734. **E-mail:** sharperl@kent.edu. **Website:** www.cslainfo.org. **Contact:** S. Meghan Harper, awards chair. Annual award given to a person or organization that has made a significant contribution to promoting high moral and ethical values through children's literature. Recipient is honored in July during the conference. Awards certificate of recognition, the awards banquet, and one-night's stay in the hotel. A nomination for an award may be made by anyone. An application form is available online. Elements of creativity and innovation will be given high priority by the judges.

PATERSON PRIZE FOR BOOKS FOR YOUNG PEOPLE

The Poetry Center at Passaic County Community College, One College Blvd., Paterson NJ 07505. (973)684-6555. **Fax:** (973)523-6085. **E-mail:** mgillan@pccc.edu. **Website:** www.pccc.edu/poetry. **Contact:** Maria Mazziotti Gillan, executive director. Award for a book published in the previous year in each age category (Pre-K-Grade 3, Grades 4-6, Grades 7-12). Deadline: February 1. Prize: $500.

THE KATHERINE PATERSON PRIZE FOR YOUNG ADULT AND CHILDREN'S WRITING

Hunger Mountain, Vermont College of Fine Arts, 36 College St., Montpelier VT 05602. (802)828-8517. **E-mail:** hungermtn@vcfa.edu. **Website:** www.hungermtn.org. **Contact:** Samantha Kolber, Managing Editor. The annual Katherine Paterson Prize for Young Adult and Children's Writing honors the best in young adult and children's literature. Submit young adult or middle grade mss, and writing for younger children, short stories, picture books, poetry, or novel excerpts, under 10,000 words. Guidelines available on website. Deadline: March 8. Prize: $1,000 and publication for the first place winner; $100 each and publication for the three category winners. Judged by a guest judge every year. The 2016 judge is Rita Williams-Garcia, author of Newbery Honor-winning novel, *One Crazy Summer*.

PENNSYLVANIA YOUNG READERS' CHOICE AWARDS PROGRAM

Pennsylvania School Librarians Association, 134 Bisbing Road, Henryville PA 18332. **E-mail:** pyrca.psla@gmail.com. **Website:** www.psla.org. **Contact:** Alice L. Cyphers, co-coordinator. Submissions nominated by a person or group. Must be published within 5 years of the award—for example, books published in 2013 to present are eligible for the 2018-2019 award. Check the Program wiki at pyrca.wikispaces.com for submission information. View information at the Pennsylvania School Librarians' website or the Program wiki. Must be currently living in North America. The purpose of the Pennsylvania Young Reader's Choice Awards Program is to promote the reading of quality books by young people in the Commonwealth of Pennsylvania, to encourage teacher and librarian collaboration and involvement in children's literature, and to honor authors whose works have been recognized by the students of Pennsylvania. Deadline: September 15. Prize: Framed certificate to winning authors. Four awards are given, one for each of the following grade level divisions: K-3, 3-6, 6-8, YA. Judged by children of Pennsylvania (they vote).

PEN/PHYLLIS NAYLOR WORKING WRITER FELLOWSHIP

PEN America, PEN American Center, 588 Broadway, Suite 303, New York NY 10012. **E-mail:** awards@pen. org. **Website:** www.pen.org/awards. **Contact:** Arielle Anema, Literary Awards Coordinator. Offered annually to an author of children's or young-adult fiction. The Fellowship has been developed to help writers whose work is of high literary caliber but who have not yet attracted a broad readership. The Fellowship is designed to assist a writer at a crucial moment in his or her career to complete a book-length work-in-progress. Candidates have published at least one novel for children or young adults which have been received warmly by literary critics, but have not generated sufficient income to support the author. Writers must be nominated by an editor or fellow author. See website for eligibility and nomination guidelines. Deadline: Submissions open during the summer of each year. Visit PEN.org/awards for up-to-date information on deadlines. Prize: $5,000.

PLEASE TOUCH MUSEUM BOOK AWARD

Memorial Hall in Fairmount Park, 4231 Avenue of the Republic, Philadelphia PA 19131. (215)578-5153. **Fax:** (215)578-5171. **E-mail:** hboyd@pleasetouchmuseum.org. **Website:** www.pleasetouchmuseum.org. **Contact:** Heather Boyd. This prestigious award has recognized and encouraged the publication of high quality books. The award was exclusively created to recognize and encourage the writing of publications that help young children enjoy the process of learning through books, while reflecting PTM's philosophy of learning through play. The awards to to books that are imaginative, exceptionally illustrated, and help foster a child's life-long love of reading. To be eligible for consideration, a book must be distinguished in text, illustration, and ability to explore and clarify an idea for young children (ages 7 and under). Deadline: October 1. Books for each cycle must be published within previous calendar year (September-August). Judged by a panel of volunteer educators, artists, booksellers, children's authors, and librarians in conjunction with museum staff.

POCKETS FICTION-WRITING CONTEST

P.O. Box 340004, Nashville TN 37203-0004. (615)340-7333. **Fax:** (615)340-7267. **E-mail:** pockets@upperroom.org. **Website:** www.pockets.upperroom.org. **Contact:** Lynn W. Gilliam, senior editor. Designed for 6- to 12-year-olds, *Pockets* magazine offers wholesome devotional readings that teach about God's love and presence in life. The content includes fiction, scripture stories, puzzles and games, poems, recipes, colorful pictures, activities, and scripture readings. Freelance submissions of stories, poems, recipes, puzzles and games, and activities are welcome. Stories should be 750-1,000 words. Multiple submissions are permitted. Past winners are ineligible. The primary purpose of *Pockets* is to help children grow in their relationship with God and to claim the good news of the gospel of Jesus Christ by applying it to their daily lives. *Pockets* espouses respect for all human beings and for God's creation. It regards a child's faith journey as an integral part of all of life and sees prayer as undergirding that journey. Deadline: August 15. Submission period begins March 15. Prize: $500 and publication in magazine.

MICHAEL L. PRINTZ AWARD

Young Adult Library Services Association, Division of the American Library Association, 50 E. Huron, Chicago IL 60611. (800)545-2433. **Fax:** (312)280-5276. **E-mail:** yalsa@ala.org. **Website:** www.ala.org/yalsa/printz. **Contact:** Nichole O'Connor, program officer for events and conferences. The Michael L. Printz Award annually honors the best book written for teens, based entirely on its literary merit, each year. In addition, the Printz Committee names up to 4 honor books, which also represent the best writing in young adult literature. The award-winning book can be fiction, nonfiction, poetry or an anthology, and can be a work of joint authorship or editorship. The books must be published between January 1 and December 31 of the preceding year and be designated by its publisher as being either a young adult book or one published for the age range that YALSA defines as young adult, e.g. ages 12 through 18. Deadline: December 1. Judged by an award committee.

PURPLE DRAGONFLY BOOK AWARDS

Story Monsters LLC, 4696 W Tyson St, Chandler AZ 85226-2903. (480)940-8182. **Fax:** (480)940-8787. **E-mail:** Cristy@StoryMonsters.com; Linda@StoryMonsters.com. **Website:** www.DragonflyBookAwards.com. **Contact:** Cristy Bertini, contest coordinator. The Purple Dragonfly Book Awards are designed with children in mind. Awards are divided into 52 distinct subject categories, ranging from books on the environment and cooking to sports and family issues.

The Purple Dragonfly Book Awards are geared toward stories that appeal to children of all ages. The awards are open to books published in any calendar year and in any country that are available for purchase. Books entered must be printed in English. Traditionally published, partnership published and self-published books are permitted, as long as they fit the above criteria. Submit materials to: Cristy Bertini, Attn: Five Star Book Awards, 1271 Turkey St., Hardwick, MA 01082. Deadline: May 1. Prize: Grand Prize winner receives a $300 cash prize, 100 foil award seals, one hour of marketing consultation from Story Monsters LLC, as well as publicity on Dragonfly Book Awards website and inclusion in a winners' news release sent to a comprehensive list of media outlets. All first-place winners of categories will be put into a drawing for a $100 prize. In addition, each first-place winner in each category receives a certificate commemorating their accomplishment, 25 foil award seals and mention on Dragonfly Book Awards website. All winners are listed in Story Monsters Ink magazine. Judged by industry experts with specific knowledge about the categories over which they preside.

QUILL AND SCROLL WRITING, PHOTO AND MULTIMEDIA CONTEST AND BLOGGING COMPETITION

School of Journalism, Univ. of Iowa, 100 Adler Journalism Bldg., Iowa City IA 52242-2004. (319)335-3457. **Fax:** (319)335-3989. **E-mail:** quill-scroll@uiowa.edu. **E-mail:** quill-scroll@uiowa.edu. **Website:** quilland-scroll.org. **Contact:** Vanessa Shelton, contest director. Entries must have been published in a high school or profesional newspaper or website during the previous year, and must be the work of a currently enrolled high school student, when published. Open to students. Annual contest. Previously published submissions only. Submissions made by the author or school media adviser. Deadline: February 5. Prize: Winners will receive *Quill and Scroll*'s National Award Gold Key and, if seniors, are eligible to apply for one of the scholarships offered by *Quill and Scroll*. All winning entries are automatically eligible for the International Writing and Photo Sweepstakes Awards. Engraved plaque awarded to sweepstakes winners.

THE RED HOUSE CHILDREN'S BOOK AWARD

Red House Children's Book Award, 123 Frederick Road, Cheam, Sutton, Surrey SM1 2HT United Kingdom. **E-mail:** info@rhcba.co.uk. **Website:** www.redhousechildrensbookaward.co.uk. **Contact:** Sinead Kromer, national coordinator. The Red House Children's Book Award is the only national book award that is entirely voted for by children. A shortlist is drawn up from children's nominations and any child can then vote for the winner of the three categories: Books for Younger Children, Books for Younger Readers and Books for Older Readers. The book with the most votes is then crowned the winner of the Red House Children's Book Award. Deadline: December 31.

TOMÁS RIVERA MEXICAN AMERICAN CHILDREN'S BOOK AWARD

Dr. Jesse Gainer, Texas State University, 601 University Drive, San Marcos TX 78666-4613. (512)245-2357. **E-mail:** riverabookaward@txstate.edu. **Website:** www.riverabookaward.org. **Contact:** Dr. Jesse Gainer, award director. Texas State University College of Education developed the Tomas Rivera Mexican American Children's Book Award to honor authors and illustrators who create literature that depicts the Mexican American experience. The award was established in 1995 and was named in honor of Dr. Tomas Rivera, a distinguished alumnus of Texas State University. The book will be written for younger children, ages pre-K to 5th grade (awarded in even years), or older children, ages 6th grade to 12 grade (awarded in odd years). The text and illustrations will be of highest quality. The portrayal/representations of Mexican Americans will be accurate and engaging, avoid stereotypes, and reflect rich characterization. The book may be fiction or non-fiction. See website for more details and directions. Deadline: November 1.

ROCKY MOUNTAIN BOOK AWARD: ALBERTA CHILDREN'S CHOICE BOOK AWARD

Box 42, Lethbridge AB T1J 3Y3 Canada. (403)381-0855. **Website:** http://www.rmba.info. **Contact:** Michelle Dimnik, contest director. Annual contest. No entry fee. Awards: Gold medal and author tour of selected Alberta schools. Judging by students. Canadian authors and/or illustrators only. Submit entries to Richard Chase. Previously unpublished submissions only. Submissions made by author's agent or nominated by a person or group. Must be published within the 3 years prior to that year's award. Register before January 20th to take part in the Rocky Mountain Book Award. SASE for contest rules and entry forms. Purpose of contest: "Reading motivation for students, promotion of Canadian authors, illustrators and publishers."

SCBWI MAGAZINE MERIT AWARDS

4727 Wilshire Blvd., Suite 301, Los Angeles CA 90010. (323)782-1010. **Fax:** (323)782-1892. **E-mail:** grants@scbwi.org. **Website:** www.scbwi.org. **Contact:** Stephanie Gordon, award coordinator. The SCBWI is a professional organization of writers and illustrators and others interested in children's literature. Membership is open to the general public at large. All magazine work for young people by an SCBWI member—writer, artist or photographer—is eligible during the year of original publication. In the case of co-authored work, both authors must be SCBWI members. Members must submit their own work. Requirements for entrants: 4 copies each of the published work and proof of publication (may be contents page) showing the name of the magazine and the date of issue. Previously published submissions only. For rules and procedures see website. Must be a SCBWI member. Recognizes outstanding original magazine work for young people published during that year, and having been written or illustrated by members of SCBWI. Deadline: December 15 of the year of publication. Submission period begins January 1. Prize: Awards plaques and honor certificates for each of 4 categories (fiction, nonfiction, illustration and poetry). Judged by a magazine editor and two "full" SCBWI members.

SKIPPING STONES BOOK AWARDS

Skipping Stones, P.O. Box 3939, Eugene OR 97403-0939. **E-mail:** editor@SkippingStones.org. **Website:** www.skippingstones.org. **Contact:** Arun N. Toke', Exec. Editor. Open to published books, publications/magazines, educational videos, and DVDs. Annual awards. Submissions made by the author or publishers and/or producers. Send request for contest rules and entry forms or visit website. Many educational publications announce the winners of our book awards. The winning books and educational videos/DVDs are announced in the July-September issue of *Skipping Stones* and also on the website. In addition to announcements on social media pages, the reviews of winning titles are posted on website. *Skipping Stones* multicultural magazine has been published for over 28 years. Recognizes exceptional, literary and artistic contributions to juvenile/children's literature, as well as teaching resources and educational audio/video resources in the areas of multicultural awareness, nature and ecology, social issues, peace, and nonviolence. Deadline: February 28. Prize: Winners receive gold honor award seals, attractive honor certificates, and publicity via multiple outlets. Judged by a multicultural selection committee of editors, students, parents, teachers, and librarians.

SKIPPING STONES YOUTH HONOR AWARDS

P.O. Box 3939, Eugene OR 97403-0939. (541)342-4956. **E-mail:** editor@SkippingStones.org. **Website:** www.SkippingStones.org. **Contact:** Arun N. Toké, editor. Now celebrating its 29th year, *Skipping Stones* is a winner of N.A.M.E.EDPRESS, Newsstand Resources, Writer and Parent's Choice Awards. Open to students. Annual awards. Submissions made by the author. The winners are published in the October-December issue of *Skipping Stones*. Everyone who enters the contest receives the Autumn issue featuring Youth Awards. SASE for contest rules or download from website. Entries must include certificate of originality by a parent and/or teacher and a cover letter that included cultural background information on the author. Submissions can either be mailed or e-mailed. Up to ten awards are given in three categories: (1) Compositions (essays, poems, short stories, songs, travelogues, etc.): Entries should be typed (double-spaced) or neatly handwritten. Fiction or nonfiction should be limited to 1,000 words; poems to 30 lines. Non-English writings are also welcome. (2) Artwork (drawings, cartoons, paintings or photo essays with captions): Entries should have the artist's name, age and address on the back of each page. Send the originals with SASE. Black & white photos are especially welcome. Limit: 8 pieces. (3) Youth Organizations: Describe how your club or group works to: (a) preserve the nature and ecology in your area, (b) enhance the quality of life for low-income, minority or disabled or (c) improve racial or cultural harmony in your school or community. Use the same format as for compositions. Recognizes youth, 7 to 17, for their contributions to multicultural awareness, nature and ecology, social issues, peace and nonviolence. Also promotes creativity, self-esteem and writing skills and to recognize important work being done by youth organizations. Deadline: June 25. Judged by *Skipping Stones* staff.

SYDNEY TAYLOR MANUSCRIPT COMPETITION

Association of Jewish Libraries, Sydney Taylor Manuscript Award Competition, 204 Park St., Montclair NJ 07042-2903. **E-mail:** stmacajl@aol.com. **Website:** www.jewishlibraries.org/main/Awards/SydneyTaylorManuscriptAward.aspx. **Contact:** Aileen Grossberg. This competition is for unpublished writers of juvenile fiction. Material should be for readers ages 8-13. The manuscript should have universal appeal and reveal positive aspects of Jewish life that will serve to deepen the understanding of Judaism for all children. Download rules and forms from website. Must be an unpublished fiction writer or a student; also, books must range from 64-200 pages in length. "AJL assumes no responsibility for publication, but hopes this cash incentive will serve to encourage new writers of children's stories with Jewish themes for all children." To encourage new fiction of Jewish interest for readers ages 8-13. Deadline: September 30. Prize: $1,000. Judging by qualified judges from within the Association of Jewish Libraries.

SYDNEY TAYLOR BOOK AWARD

Association of Jewish Libraries, **E-mail:** chair@sydneytaylorbookaward.org. **Website:** www.sydneytaylorbookaward.org. **Contact:** Ellen Tilman, chair. The Sydney Taylor Book Award is presented annually to outstanding books for children and teens that authentically portray the Jewish experience. Deadline: November 30. Cannot guarantee that books received after November 30 will be considered. Prize: Gold medals are presented in 3 categories: younger readers, older readers, and teen readers. Honor books are awarded in silver medals, and notable books are named in each category. Winners are selected by a committee of the Association of Jewish Libraries. Each committee member must receive an individual copy of each book that is to be considered.

✪ TD CANADIAN CHILDREN'S LITERATURE AWARD

The Canadian Children's Book Centre, 40 Orchard View Blvd., Suite 217, Toronto ON M4R 1B9 Canada. (416)975-0010, ext. 222. **Fax:** (416)975-8970. **E-mail:** meghan@bookcentre.ca. **Website:** www.bookcentre.ca. **Contact:** Meghan Howe. The TD Canadian Children's Literature Award is for the most distinguished book of the year. All books, in any genre, written and illustrated by Canadians and for children ages 1-12 are eligible. Only books first published in Canada are eligible for submission. Books must be published between January 1 and December 31 of the previous calendar year. Open to Canadian citizens and/or permanent residents of Canada. Deadline: mid-December. Prizes: Two prizes of $30,000, 1 for English, 1 for French. $20,000 will be divided among the Honour Book English titles and Honour Book French titles, to a maximum of 4; $2,500 shall go to each of the publishers of the English and French grand-prize winning books for promotion and publicity.

TIPS "Please visit website for submission guidelines and eligibility criteria, as well as specific submission deadline."

VEGETARIAN ESSAY CONTEST

The Vegetarian Resource Group, P.O. Box 1463, Baltimore MD 21203. (410)366-VEGE. **Fax:** (410)366-8804. **E-mail:** vrg@vrg.org. **Website:** www.vrg.org. Write a 2-3 page essay on any aspect of vegetarianism. Entrants should base their paper on interviewing, research, and/or personal opinion. You need not be a vegetarian to enter. Three different entry categories: age 14-18; age 9-13; and age 8 and under. Prize: $50.

VFW VOICE OF DEMOCRACY

Veterans of Foreign Wars of the U.S., National Headquarters, 406 W. 34th St., Kansas City MO 64111. (816)968-1117. **E-mail:** kharmer@vfw.org. **Website:** https://www.vfw.org/VOD/. The Voice of Democracy Program is open to students in grades 9-12 (on the Nov. 1 deadline), who are enrolled in a public, private or parochial high school or home study program in the United States and its territories. Contact your local VFW Post to enter (entry must not be mailed to the VFW National Headquarters, only to a local, participating VFW Post). Purpose is to give high school students the opportunity to voice their opinions about their responsibility to our country and to convey those opinions via the broadcast media to all of America. Deadline: November 1. Prize: Winners receive awards ranging from $1,000-30,000.

LAURA INGALLS WILDER MEDAL

50 E. Huron, Chicago IL 60611. (800)545-2433. **E-mail:** alscawards@ala.org. **Website:** www.ala.org/alsc/awardsgrants/bookmedia/wildermedal. Award offered every 2 years. The Wilder Award honors an author or illustrator whose books, published in the US, have made, over a period of years, a substantial and lasting contribution to literature for children.

The candidates must be nominated by ALSC members. Medal presented at Newbery/Caldecott banquet during annual conference. Judging by Wilder Award Selection Committee.

RITA WILLIAMS YOUNG ADULT PROSE PRIZE CATEGORY

Soul-Making Keats Literary Competition, The Webhallow House, 1544 Sweetwood Drive, Broadmoor Village CA 94015-2029. **E-mail:** SoulKeats@mail.com. **Website:** www.soulmakingcontest.us. **Contact:** Eileen Malone. For writers in grades 9-12 or equivalent age. Up to 3,000 words in prose form of choice. Complete rules and guidelines available online. Deadline: November 30 (postmarked). Prize: $100 for first place; $50 for second place; $25 for third place. Judged (and sponsored) by Rita Wiliams, an Emmy-award winning investigative reporter with KTVU-TV in Oakland, California.

TIPS "This contest is for young adult writers, high school age writers; no adults writing for children."

PAUL A. WITTY OUTSTANDING LITERATURE AWARD

P.O. Box 8139, Newark DE 19714-8139. (800)336-7323. **Fax:** (302)731-1057. **Website:** www.reading.org. **Contact:** Marcie Craig Post, executive director. This award recognizes excellence in original poetry or prose written by students. Elementary and secondary students whose work is selected will receive an award. Deadline: February 2. Prize: Not less than $25 and a citation of merit.

WORK-IN-PROGRESS GRANT

Society of Children's Book Writers and Illustrators (SCBWI), 8271 Beverly Blvd., Los Angeles CA 90048. (323)782-1010. **E-mail:** grants@scbwi.org; wipgrant@scbwi.org. **Website:** www.scbwi.org. Six grants—one designated specifically for picture book text, chapter book/early readers, middle grade, young adult fiction, nonfiction, and multicultural fiction or nonfiction—to assist SCBWI members in the completion of a specific project. Open to SCBWI members only. Deadline: March 31. Open to submissions on March 1.

🐢 THE YOUNG ADULT FICTION PRIZE

Victorian Premier's Literary Awards, State Government of Victoria, The Wheeler Centre, 176 Little Lonsdale Street, Melbourne VIC 3000 Australia. (61) (3)90947800. **E-mail:** vpla@wheelercentre.com. **Website:** http://www.wheelercentre.com/projects/victori-an-premier-s-literary-awards-2016/about-the-awards. **Contact:** Project Officer. Visit website for guidelines and nomination forms. Prize: $25,000.

YOUNG READER'S CHOICE AWARD

Paxson Elementary School, 101 Evans, Missoula MT 59801. **E-mail:** hbray@missoula.lib.mt.us. **Website:** www.pnla.org. **Contact:** Honore Bray, president. The Pacific Northwest Library Association's Young Reader's Choice Award is the oldest children's choice award in the U.S. and Canada. Nominations are taken only from children, teachers, parents and librarians in the Pacific Northwest: Alaska, Alberta, British Columbia, Idaho, Montana and Washington. Nominations will not be accepted from publishers. Nominations may include fiction, nonfiction, graphic novels, anime, and manga. Nominated titles are those published 3 years prior to the award year. Deadline: February 1. Books will be judged on popularity with readers. Age appropriateness will be considered when choosing which of the three divisions a book is placed. Other considerations may include reading enjoyment; reading level; interest level; genre representation; gender representation; racial diversity; diversity of social, political, economic, or religions viewpoints; regional consideration; effectiveness of expression; and imagination. The Pacific Northwest Library Association is committed to intellectual freedom and diversity of ideas. No title will be excluded because of race, nationality, religion, gender, sexual orientation, political or social view of either the author or the material.

GENERAL

🐢 AUSTRALIAN CHRISTIAN BOOK OF THE YEAR AWARD

SparkLit, PO Box 198, Forest Hill Victoria 3131 Australia. **E-mail:** admin@sparklit.org. **E-mail:** admin@sparklit.org. **Website:** www.sparklit.org. **Contact:** The Awards Coordinator. SparkLit advances God's kingdom by empowering Christian writers and publishers. (Formerly the Society for Promoting Christian Knowledge Australia and the Australian Christian Literature Society.) The Australian Christian Book of the Year Award is given annually to an original book written by an Australian citizen normally resident in Australia. A short list is released in July. The results are announced and prizes are presented in August. The award recognizes and encourages excellence in Australian Christian writing. Deadline: March 31. Prize: $3,000 (AUD), a framed certificate and extensive promotion.

JAMIE CAT CALLAN HUMOR PRIZE

Category in the Soul-Making Keats Literary Competition, The Webhallow House, 1544 Sweetwood Dr., Broadmoor Village CA 94015-2029. **E-mail:** SoulKeats@mail.com. **Website:** www.soulmaking-contest.us. **Contact:** Eileen Malone. Any form, 2,500 words or less. One piece per entry. Previously published material is accepted. Open annually to any writer. Deadline: November 30. Prize: First Place: $100; Second Place: $50; Third Place: $25. Judged by Jamie Cat Callan.

TIPS "Make me laugh out loud."

✪ J.W. DAFOE BOOK PRIZE

J.W. Dafoe Foundation, 351 University College, University of Manitoba, Winnipeg MB R3T 2M8 Canada. **E-mail:** james.fergusson@umanitoba.ca. **Website:** www.dafoefoundation.ca. **Contact:** Dr. James Fergusson. The Dafoe Book Prize was established to honor John Dafoe, editor of the *Winnipeg Free Press* from 1900 to 1944, and is awarded each year for distinguished writing by Canadians or authors in resident in Canada that contributes to the understanding of Canada, Canadians, and/or Canada's place in the world. Books must be published January-December of previous publishing year. Co-authored books are eligible, but not edited books consisting of chapters from many different authors. Submit 4 copies of book. Deadline: December 14. Prize: $10,000. Judged by a jury of academics and lay public.

THE GLENNA LUSCHEI PRAIRIE SCHOONER AWARDS

Prairie Schooner, 123 Andrews Hall, P.O. Box 880334, Lincoln NE 68588-0334. (402)472-0911. **Fax:** (402)472-1817. **E-mail:** prairieschooner@unl.edu; psbookprize@unl.edu. **Website:** http://prairieschooner.unl.edu/. **Contact:** Kwame Dawes. Annual awards for work published in *Prairie Schooner* in the previous year. Offers one large prize and 10 smaller awards. See website for more details. Contact *Prairie Schooner* for further information. Prize: One award of $1,500 and 10 awards of $250 each.

INDEPENDENT PUBLISHER BOOK AWARDS

Jenkins Group/Independent Publisher Online, 1129 Woodmere Ave., Ste. B, Traverse City MI 49686. (231)933-0445. **Fax:** (231)933-0448. **E-mail:** jimb@bookpublishing.com. **Website:** www.independent-publisher.com. **Contact:** Jim Barnes. Honors the year's best independently published English language titles from around the world. The IPPY Awards reward those who exhibit the courage, innovation, and creativity to bring about change in the world of publishing. Independent spirit and expertise comes from publishers of all areas and budgets, and they judge books with that in mind. Entries will be accepted in over 80 categories, visit website to see details. Open to any published author. Accepts books published within the past 2 years. See website for guidelines and details. Deadline: Late February. Price of submission rises in September and December. Prize: Gold, silver and bronze medals for each category; foil seals available to all. Judged by a panel of experts representing the fields of design, writing, bookselling, library, and reviewing.

✪ INSCRIBE CONTESTS

InScribe Christian Writers' Fellowship, PO Box 99509, Edmonton AB T5B 0E1 Canada. **E-mail:** fellowscripteditor@gmail.com. **Website:** www.inscribe.org. **Contact:** Contest Director. Check Website www.inscribe.org for updated details. Contest details are included in *Fellowscipt* magazine. Deadline: Contests offered twice per year. See website for details. Prize: 1st Place: $100; 2nd Place: $50; 3rd Place: $30. InScribe reserves the right to publish winning entries in its magazine, *FellowScript*, and/or on its website Judged by a different judge for each category. All judging is blind.

DOROTHEA LANGE–PAUL TAYLOR PRIZE

Center for Documentary Studies, 1317 W. Pettigrew St., Duke University, Durham NC 27705. (919)660-3685. **Fax:** (919)681-7600. **E-mail:** caitlin.johnson@duke.edu; docstudies@duke.edu. **Website:** http://documentarystudies.duke.edu/awards/dorothea-lange-paul-taylor-prize. **Contact:** Caitlin Johnson. Award from the Center for Documentary Studies at Duke University, supporting documentary artists, working alone or in teams, who are involved in extended, on-going fieldwork projects that rely on and exploit the interplay of words and images. More information available at documentarystudies.duke.edu/awards. First announced a year after the Center for Documentary Studies' founding at Duke University, the prize was created to encourage a collaboration between documentary writers and photographers in the tradition of the acclaimed photographer Dorothea Lange and writer and social scientist Paul Taylor. Deadline: May 9. Submissions accepted starting in February. Prize: The winner receives $10,000, features in Center for Documentary Studies' print and digital publications, and inclusion in the Archive of Documentary Arts at Rubenstein Library, Duke University.

MLA PRIZE IN UNITED STATES LATINA & LATINO AND CHICANA & CHICANO LITERARY AND CULTURAL STUDIES

Modern Language Association of America, 85 Broad Street, suite 500, New York NY 10004-2434. (646)576-5141. **Fax:** (646)458-0030. **E-mail:** awards@mla.org. **Website:** www.mla.org. **Contact:** Coordinator of Book Prizes. Offered in odd-numbered years for an outstanding scholarly study in any language of United States Latina and Latino or Chicana and Chicano literature or culture. Books must have been published in the two previous years before the award. Authors must be current members of the MLA. Requires 4 copies of the book. Deadline: May 1. Prize: A cash award, and a certificate to be presented at the Modern Language Association's annual convention in January.

NACUSA YOUNG COMPOSERS' COMPETITION

Box 49256 Barrington Station, Los Angeles CA 90049. **E-mail:** nacusa@music-usa.org; membership@mail.music-usa.org; webmaster@music-usa.org. **Website:** http://music-usa.org. **Contact:** John Winsor. Applications online. Must be a paid member of NACUSA. The competition is open to all NACUSA members who are American citizens or residents, who have reached their 18th birthday but have not yet reached there 32nd birthday by the submission deadline. Encourages the composition of new American concert hall music. Deadline: December 15. Prize: All prizes come with a possible performance on a NACUSA National concert. First Prize is $400; Second Prize is $300; Third Prize is $200. Judged by a committee of experienced NACUSA composer members.

OHIOANA WALTER RUMSEY MARVIN GRANT

Ohioana Library Association, 274 E. First Ave., Suite 300, Columbus OH 43201. (614)466-3831. **Fax:** (614)728-6974. **E-mail:** ohioana@ohioana.org. **Website:** www.ohioana.org. **Contact:** David Weaver, executive director. Open to unpublished authors born in Ohio or who have lived in Ohio for a minimum of 5 years. Must be 30 years of age or younger. Guidelines for SASE or on website. Winner notified in early summer. Up to 6 pieces of prose may be submitted; maximum 60 pages, minimum 10 pages double-spaced, 12-point type. Entries must be unpublished. Award to encourage young, unpublished writers 30 years of age or younger. Competition for short stories or novels in progress. Deadline: January 31. Prize: $1,000.

DAVID RAFFELOCK AWARD FOR PUBLISHING EXCELLENCE

National Writers Association, 10940 S. Parker Rd., #508, Parker CO 80134. **E-mail:** natlwritersassn@hotmail.com. **Website:** www.nationalwriters.com. **Contact:** Sandy Whelchel. Contest is offered annually for books published the previous year. Published works only. Open to any writer. Guidelines for SASE, by e-mail, or on website. Winners will be notified by mail or phone. List of winners available for SASE or visit website. Purpose is to assist published authors in marketing their works and to reward outstanding published works. Deadline: May 15. Prize: Publicity tour, including airfare, valued at $5,000.

RAMIREZ FAMILY AWARD FOR MOST SIGNIFICANT SCHOLARLY BOOK

The Texas Institute of Letters, P.O. Box 609, Round Rock TX 78680. **E-mail:** tilsecretary@yahoo.com. **Website:** http://texasinstituteofletters.org. Offered annually for submissions published January 1-December 31 of previous year to recognize the writer of the book making the most important contribution to knowledge. Writer must have been born in Texas, have lived in the state at least 2 consecutive years at some time, or the subject matter of the book should be associated with the state. See website for guidelines. Deadline: Visit website for exact date. Prize: $2,500.

BYRON CALDWELL SMITH BOOK AWARD

The University of Kansas, Hall Center for the Humanities, 900 Sunnyside Ave., Lawrence KS 66045. (785)864-4798. **E-mail:** vbailey@ku.edu. **Website:** www.hallcenter.ku.edu. **Contact:** Victor Bailey, director. Offered in odd years. To qualify, applicants must live or be employed in Kansas and have written an outstanding book published within the previous 2 calendar years. Translations are eligible. Guidelines for SASE or online. Deadline: March 1. Prize: $1,500.

FRED WHITEHEAD AWARD FOR DESIGN OF A TRADE BOOK

Texas Institute of Letters, P.O. Box 609, Round Rock TX 78680. **E-mail:** tilsecretary@yahoo.com. **Website:** www.texasinstituteofletters.org. Offered annually for the best design for a trade book. Open to Texas residents or those who have lived in Texas for 2 consecutive years. See website for guidelines. Deadline: early January; see website for exact date. Prize: $750.

☯ THE WRITERS' TRUST ENGEL/FINDLEY AWARD

The Writers' Trust of Canada, 460 Richmond St. W., Suite 600, Toronto ON M5V 1Y1 Canada. (416)504-8222. **Fax:** (416)504-9090. **E-mail:** info@writerstrust.com. **Website:** www.writerstrust.com. **Contact:** Amanda Hopkins. The Writers' Trust Engel/Findley Award is presented annually at The Writers' Trust Awards Event, held in Toronto each fall, to a Canadian writer for a body of work in hope of continued contribution to the richness of Canadian literature. Open to Canadian citizens and permanent residents only. Prize: $25,000.

JOURNALISM

AAAS KAVLI SCIENCE JOURNALISM AWARDS

American Association for the Advancement of Science, AAAS Office of Public Programs, 1200 New York Ave. NW, Washington DC 20005. **E-mail:** sja@aaas.org. **Website:** http://sjawards.aaas.org/. **Contact:** Awards Coordinator. The AAAS Kavli Science Journalism Awards represent the pinnacle of achievement for professional journalists in the science writing field. The awards recognize outstanding reporting worldwide for a general audience and honor individuals (rather than institutions, publishers or employers) for their coverage of the sciences, engineering, and mathematics. Entries are submitted online only at http://sjawards.aaas.org. See website for guidelines and details. Deadline: August 1. Prize: $5,000 and $3,000 awards in each category; award includes trav-

el expenses to AAAS Annual Meeting for awards ceremony. Judged by committees of reporters and editors.

THE AMERICAN LEGION FOURTH ESTATE AWARD

The American Legion, The American Legion, 700 N. Pennsylvania St., Indianapolis IN 46204. (317)630-1253. **E-mail:** pr@legion.org. **Website:** www.legion.org/presscenter/fourthestate. Offered annually for journalistic works published the previous calendar year. Subject matter must deal with a topic or issue of national interest or concern. Entry must include cover letter explaining entry, and any documentation or evidence of the entry's impact on the community, state, or nation. No printed entry form. Guidelines available by SASE or online. Deadline: March 1. Prize: $2,000 stipend to defray expenses of recipient accepting the award at The American Legion National Convention in August/September. Judged by members of the Media & Communications Commission of The American Legion.

☯ ATLANTIC JOURNALISM AWARDS

46 Swanton Dr., Dartmouth NS B2W2C5 Canada. (902)478-6026. **Fax:** (902)462-1892. **E-mail:** office@ajas.ca. **Website:** ajas.ca. **Contact:** Bill Skerrett, Executive Director. Offered annually to recognize excellence and achievement by journalists in print and electronic news media in Atlantic Canada. Guidelines and online entry system available on website. Opens December 1. Entries are usually nominated by editors, news directors, etc. Freelancers are eligible to enter. The competition is open to any journalist living in Atlantic Canada whose entry was originally published or broadcast during the previous year in Atlantic Canada. Deadline: January 31. Prize: A plaque presented at an awards dinner.

INVESTIGATIVE JOURNALISM GRANT

Fund For Investigative Journalism, Fund for Investigative Journalism, 529 14th Street NW, 13th Floor, Washington DC 20045. (202)662-7564. **E-mail:** fundfij@gmail.com. **Website:** www.fij.org. **Contact:** Sandy Bergo, executive director. Offered 3 times/year for original investigative print, online, radio, and TV stories and books. Guidelines online. See website for details on applying for a grant. Deadlines: Vary. Check website. Grants of $500-10,000. (Typical grant: $5,000.)

ANSON JONES, MD, AWARDS

Texas Medical Association, 401 W. 15th St., Ste. 100, Austin TX 78701-1680. (512)370-1470. **Fax:** (512)370-1693. **E-mail:** ansonjones@texmed.org. **Website:** www.texmed.org. **Contact:** Tammy Wishard, outreach coordinator. Offered annually to Texas news media for excellence in communicating health information to the public. Open only to Texas general-interest media for work published or aired in Texas during the previous calendar year. Guidelines posted online. Deadline: January 10. $500 for winner in each category; $1,000 for Texas Health Journalist of the Year.

FRANK LUTHER MOTT-KAPPA TAU ALPHA RESEARCH AWARD IN JOURNALISM

University of Missouri School of Journalism, 76 Gannett Hall, Columbia MO 65211-1200. (573)882-7685. **E-mail:** umcjourkta@missouri.edu. **Website:** www.kappataualpha.org. **Contact:** Dr. Keith Sanders, exec. dir., Kappa Tau Alpha. Offered annually for best researched book in mass communication. Submit 6 copies; no forms required. Deadline: December 9. Prize: $1,000. Judged by a panel of university professors of journalism and mass communication and national officers of Kappa Tau Alpha.

NATIONAL MAGAZINE AWARDS

National Magazine Awards Foundation, 2300 Yonge St., Suite 1600, Toronto ON M4P 1E4 Canada. (416)939-6200. **E-mail:** staff@magazine-awards.com. **E-mail:** staff@magazine-awards.com. **Website:** www.magazine-awards.com. **Contact:** Barbara Gould. The National Magazine Awards Foundation is a bilingual, not-for-profit institution whose mission is to recognize and promote excellence in the content and creation of Canadian print and digital publications through an annual program of awards and national publicity efforts. Deadline: January 20. Cash prizes for winners. Certificates and seals for all finalists and winners. Judged by 200+ peer judges from the Canadian magazine industry.

SANOFI PASTEUR MEDAL FOR EXCELLENCE IN HEALTH RESEARCH JOURNALISM

Canadians for Health Research, P.O. Box 126, Westmount QC H3Z 2T1 Canada. (514)398-7478. **Fax:** (514)398-8361. **E-mail:** info@chrcrm.org. **Website:** www.chrcrm.org. Offered annually for work published the previous calendar year in Canadian news-

papers or magazines. Applicants must have demonstrated an interest and effort in reporting health research issues within Canada. Guidelines available on website. Deadline: April 1 (postmarked). Prize: $2,500 bursary and a medal.

SCIENCE IN SOCIETY AWARDS

National Association of Science Writers, Inc., P.O. Box 7905, Berkeley CA 94707. (510)647-9500. **E-mail:** director@nasw.org. **Website:** www.nasw.org. **Contact:** Tinsley Davis. Offered annually for investigative or interpretive reporting about the sciences and their impact on society. Categories: books, commentary and opinions, science reporting, longform science reporting, and science reporting for a local or regional market. Material may be a single article or broadcast, or a series. Works must have been first published or broadcast in North America between January 1 and December 31 of the previous year. Deadline: February 1. Prize: $2,500, and a certificate of recognition in each category.

SOVEREIGN AWARD

The Jockey Club of Canada, P.O. Box 66, Station B, Etobicoke ON M9W 5K9 Canada. (416)675-7756. **Fax:** (416)675-6378. **E-mail:** jockeyclub@bellnet.ca. **Website:** www.jockeyclubcanada.com. **Contact:** Stacie Roberts, exec. dir. The Jockey Club of Canada was founded in 1973 by E.P. Taylor to serve as the international representative of the Canadian Thoroughbred industry and to promote improvements to Thoroughbred racing and breeding, both in Canada and internationally. Submissions for these media awards must be of Canadian Thoroughbred racing or breeding content. They must have appeared in a media outlet recognized by The Jockey Club of Canada. See website for eligibility details and guidelines. Deadline: December 31.

TRANSLATION

AMERICAN-SCANDINAVIAN FOUNDATION TRANSLATION PRIZE

The American-Scandinavian Foundation, 58 Park Ave., New York NY 10016. (212)779-3587. **E-mail:** grants@amscan.org; info@amscan.org. **Website:** www.amscan.org. **Contact:** Matthew Walters, director of fellowships & grants. The annual ASF translation competition is awarded for the most outstanding translations of poetry, fiction, drama, or literary prose written by a Scandinavian author born after 1800. Accepts inquiries by e-mail, or through online application. Instructions an application available online. Entries must be unpublished. Length: No more than 50 pages for drama and fiction; no more than 25 pages for poetry. Open to any writer. Results announced in November. Winners notified by e-mail. Results available on the ASF website. Guidelines available online. Deadline: June 15. Prize: The Nadia Christensen Prize includes a $2,500 award, publication of an excerpt in *Scandinavian Review*, and a commemorative bronze medallion; The Leif and Inger Sjöberg Award, given to an individual whose literature translations have not previously been published, includes a $2,000 award, publication of an excerpt in *Scandinavian Review*, and a commemorative bronze medallion.

THE WILLIS BARNSTONE TRANSLATION PRIZE

The Evansville Review, Dept. of Creative Writing, University of Evansville, 1800 Lincoln Ave., Evansville IN 47722. (812)488-1042. **E-mail:** evansvillereview@evansville.edu. **Website:** https://www.evansville.edu/majors/creativewriting/evansvilleReview-Barnstone.cfm. The competition welcomes submissions of unpublished poetry translations from any language and time period (ancient to contemporary). The length limit for each translation is 200 lines. Deadline: December 1. Judged by Willis Barnstone.

DER-HOVANESSIAN PRIZE

New England Poetry Club, 376 School St., Watertown MA 02472. **E-mail:** contests@nepoetryclub.org. **Website:** www.nepoetryclub.org. **Contact:** Audrey Kalajin. For a translation from any language into English. Send a copy of the original. Funded by John Mahtesian. Contest open to members and nonmembers. Poems should be typed and submitted in duplicate with author's name, address, phone, and e-mail address of writer on only 1 copy. Label poems with contest name. Entries should be sent by regular mail only. Entries should be original, unpublished poems in English. No poem should be entered in more than 1 contest, nor have won a previous contest. Deadline: May 31. Prize: $200. Judges are well-known poets and sometimes winners of previous NEPC contests.

SOEURETTE DIEHL FRASER AWARD FOR BEST TRANSLATION OF A BOOK

P.O. Box 609, Round Rock TX 78680. **E-mail:** tilsecretary@yahoo.com. **Website:** http://texasinstituteoflet-

ters.org. Offered every 2 years to recognize the best translation of a literary book into English. Translator must have been born in Texas or have lived in the state for at least 2 consecutive years at some time. Check website for guidelines and instructions on submitting. Deadline: January 10. Prize: $1,000.

JOHN GLASSCO TRANSLATION PRIZE

Literary Translators' Association of Canada, 615-01 Concordia University, 1455 boul. de Maisonneuve Ouest, Montréal QC H3G 1M8 Canada. (514)848-2424, ext. 8702. **E-mail:** info@attlc-ltac.org. **Website:** http://attlc-ltac.org/john-glassco-translation-prize. **Contact:** Glassco Prize Committee. Offered annually for a translator's first book-length literary translation into French or English, published in Canada during the previous calendar year. The translator must be a Canadian citizen or permanent resident. Eligible genres include fiction, creative nonfiction, poetry, and children's books. Deadline: July 31. Prize: $1,000.

THE HAROLD MORTON LANDON TRANSLATION AWARD

Academy of American Poets, 75 Maiden Lane, Suite 901, New York NY 10038. (212)274-0343. **Fax:** (212)274-9427. **E-mail:** awards@poets.org. **Website:** www.poets.org. **Contact:** Awards Coordinator. This annual award recognizes a poetry collection translated from any language into English and published in the previous calendar year. A noted translator chooses the winning book. Deadline: February 15. Prize: $1,000.

FENIA AND YAAKOV LEVIANT MEMORIAL PRIZE IN YIDDISH STUDIES

Modern Language Association of America, 85 Broad Street, suite 500, New York NY 10004-2434. (646)576-5141. **Fax:** (646)458-0030. **E-mail:** awards@mla.org. **Website:** www.mla.org. **Contact:** Coordinator of book prizes. Offered in even-numbered years for an outstanding English translation of a Yiddish literary work or the publication of a scholarly work. Cultural studies, critical biographies, or edited works in the field of Yiddish folklore or linguistic studies are eligible to compete. See website for details on which they are accepting. Books must have been published within the past 4 years. Authors need not be members of the MLA. Requires 4 copies of the book. Deadline: May 1. Prize: A cash prize, and a certificate, to be presented at the Modern Language Association's annual convention in January.

MARSH AWARD FOR CHILDREN'S LITERATURE IN TRANSLATION

The English-Speaking Union, Dartmouth House, 37 Charles St., London En W1J 5ED United Kingdom. 020 7529 1590. **E-mail:** emma.coffey@esu.org. **Website:** www.marshcristiantrust.org; www.esu.org. **Contact:** Emma Coffey, education officer. The Marsh Award for Children's Literature in Translation, awarded biennially, was founded to celebrate the best translation of a children's book from a foreign language into English and published in the UK. It aims to spotlight the high quality and diversity of translated fiction for young readers. The Award is administered by the ESU on behalf of the Marsh Christian Trust. Submissions will be accepted from publishers for books produced for readers from 5 to 16 years of age. Guidelines and eligibility criteria available online.

PEN AWARD FOR POETRY IN TRANSLATION

PEN America, 588 Broadway, Suite 303, New York NY 10012. **E-mail:** awards@pen.org. **Website:** www.pen.org/awards. **Contact:** Arielle Anema. This award recognizes book-length translations of poetry from any language into English, published during the current calendar year. All books must have been published in the US. Translators may be of any nationality. US residency/citizenship not required. Submissions must be made publishers or literary agents. Self-published books are not eligible. Books with more than 2 translators are not eligible. Re-translations are ineligible, unless the work can be said to provide a significant revision of the original translation. Deadline: Submissions are accepted during the summer of each year. Visit PEN.org/awards for updated on deadline dates. Prize: $3,000. Judged by a single translator of poetry appointed by the PEN Translation Committee.

PEN TRANSLATION PRIZE

PEN America, 588 Broadway, Suite 303, New York NY 10012. **E-mail:** awards@pen.org. **Contact:** Arielle Anema, Literary Awards Coordinator. *PEN will only accept submissions from publishers or literary agents.* This award is offered for book-length translations from any language into English, published during the current calendar year. No technical, scientific, or bibliographic translations. Self-published books are not eligible. Although all eligible books must have been published in the United States, translators may be of any nationality; US residency or citizenship is not required. PEN will only accept submissions from publishers or literary agents. Deadline: Submissions will be accepted during the summer of each year. Visit PEN.org/awards for up-to-date information on deadlines. Prize: $3,000. Judged by three to five translators and/or writers selected by the PEN Translation Committee.

LOIS ROTH AWARD

Modern Language Association, 85 Broad Street, suite 500, New York NY 10004-2434. (646)576-5141. **Fax:** (646)458-0030. **E-mail:** awards@mla.org. **Website:** www.mla.org. Offered in odd-numbered years for an outstanding translation into English of a book-length literary work. Translators need not be members of the MLA. Translations must have been published in the previous calendar year. Requires 6 copies, plus 12-15 pages of text in the original language. Deadline: April 1. Prize: A cash award and a certificate to be presented at the Modern Language Association's annual convention in January.

ALDO AND JEANNE SCAGLIONE PRIZE FOR A TRANSLATION OF A LITERARY WORK

Modern Language Association, 85 Broad Street, suite 500, New York NY 10004-2434. (646)576-5141. **Fax:** (646)458-0030. **E-mail:** awards@mla.org. **Website:** www.mla.org. **Contact:** Coordinator of Book Prizes. Offered in even-numbered years for an outstanding translation into English of a book-length literary work. Translations must have been published in the previous calendar year. Translators need not be members of the MLA. Requires 6 copies of the book, plus 12-15 pages of text in the original language. Deadline: April 1. Prize: A cash award and a certificate to be presented at the Modern Language Association's annual convention in January.

ALDO AND JEANNE SCAGLIONE PRIZE FOR A TRANSLATION OF A SCHOLARLY STUDY OF LITERATURE

Modern Language Association of America, 85 Broad Street, Suite 500, New York NY 10004-2434. (646)576-5141. **Fax:** (646)458-0030. **E-mail:** awards@mla.org. **Website:** www.mla.org. **Contact:** Coordinator of Book Prizes. Offered in odd-numbered years for an outstanding translation into English of a book-length work of literary history, literary criticism, philology, or literary theory. Translators need not be members of the MLA. Books must have been published in the previous 2 years. Requires 4 copies of the book. Deadline: May 1. Prize: A cash award and a certificate to be presented at the Modern Language Association's annual convention in January.

ALDO AND JEANNE SCAGLIONE PRIZE FOR STUDIES IN SLAVIC LANGUAGES AND LITERATURES

Modern Language Association of America, 85 Broad Street, Suite 500, New York NY 10004-2434. (646)576-5141. **Fax:** (646)458-0030. **E-mail:** awards@mla.org. **Website:** www.mla.org. **Contact:** Coordinator of Book Prizes. Offered in odd-numbered years for an outstanding work on the linguistics or literatures of the Slavic languages. Books must have been published in the previous 2 years. Requires 4 copies of the book. Authors need not be members of the MLA. Deadline: May 1. Prize: A cash award and a certificate to be presented at the Modern Language Association's annual convention in January.

POETRY

49TH PARALLEL AWARD FOR POETRY

Western Washington University, Mail Stop 9053, Bellingham WA 98225. (360)650-4863. **E-mail:** bellingham.review@wwu.edu. **Website:** www.bhreview.org. **Contact:** Susanne Paola Antonetta, editor-in-chief; Dayna Patterson, managing editor. Annual poetry contest, supported by the *Bellingham Review*, given for a poem of any style or length. Upload entries via Submittable online. Up to 3 poems per entry. Deadline: March 15. Submissions period begins December 1. Prize: $1,000. Judged by Robert Cording.

✪ J.M. ABRAHAM POETRY PRIZE

Writers' Federation of Nova Scotia, 1113 Marginal Rd., Halifax NS B3H 4P7 Canada. (902)423-8116. **Fax:** (902)422-0881. **E-mail:** director@writers.ns.ca. **Website:** www.writers.ns.ca. The J.M. Abraham Poetry Prize is an annual award designed to honor the best book of poetry by a resident of Atlantic Canada. Formerly known as the Atlantic Poetry Prize. Detailed guidelines and eligibility criteria available online. Deadline: First Friday in December. Prize: Valued at $2,000 for the winning title.

AKRON POETRY PRIZE

The University of Akron Press, 120 E. Mill St., Suite 415, Akron OH 44308. **E-mail:** uapress@uakron.edu. **Website:** www.uakron.edu/uapress/akron-poetry-prize/. **Contact:** Mary Biddinger, editor/award director. Submissions must be unpublished. Considers simultaneous submissions (with notification of acceptance elsewhere). Submit at least 48 pages and no longer than 90 pages. See website for complete guidelines. Manuscripts will be accepted via Submittable.com between April 15 and June 15 each year. Competition receives 500+ entries. 2016 winner was Aimée Baker for *Doe*. Winner posted on website by September 30. Intimate friends, relatives, current and former students of the final judge (students in an academic, degree-conferring program or its equivalent), and current faculty, staff, students, and alumni of the University of Akron or the Northeast Ohio MFA Program (NEOMFA) are not eligible to enter the Akron Poetry Prize competition. Deadline: June 15. Open to submissions on April 15. Prize: $1,500, plus publication of a book-length ms.

THE AMERICAN POETRY REVIEW/ HONICKMAN FIRST BOOK PRIZE

320 S. Broad St., Hamilton 313, Philadelphia PA 19102. 215 717 6800. **E-mail:** escanlon@aprweb.org. **Website:** www.aprweb.org. **Contact:** Elizabeth Scanlon, editor. The prize is open to poets who have not published a book-length collection of poems with a registered ISBN. Translations are not eligible nor are works written by multiple authors. 2016 guest judge is Gabrielle Calvocoressi. Reading period: August 1-October 31. Prize: $3,000, plus publication and reading at the University of the Arts Visiting Writers Series in 2018.

THE ANHINGA PRESS-ROBERT DANA PRIZE FOR POETRY

Anhinga Press, P.O. Box 3665, Tallahassee FL 32315. **E-mail:** info@anhinga.org. **Website:** www.anhinga.org. **Contact:** Kristine Snodgrass, poetry editor. Offered annually for a book-length collection of poetry by an author writing in English. Guidelines on website. Past winners include Frank X. Gaspar, Earl S. Braggs, Julia Levine, Keith Ratzlaff, Lynn Aarti Chandhok, and Rhett Iseman Trull. Mss must be 48-80 pages, excluding front matter. Deadline: Submissions will be accepted from February 15-May 30. Prize: $2,000, a reading tour of selected Florida colleges and universities, and the winning ms will be published. Past judges include Jan Beatty, Richard Blaco, Denise Duhamel, Donald Hall, Joy Harjo, Robert Dana, Mark Jarman, and Tony Hoagland.

ART AFFAIR POETRY CONTEST

Art Affair Annual Literary Contests, Art Affair, P.O. Box 54302, Oklahoma City OK 73154. **Website:** www.shadetreecreations.com. **Contact:** Barbara Shepherd, contest chair. The annual Art Affair Poetry Contest is open to any poet. Multiple entries accepted with entry fee for each and may be mailed in the same packet. Guidelines available on website. Winners' list will be published on the Art Affair website in December. Poems must be unpublished. Submit original poems on any subject, in any style, no more than 60 lines (put line count in the upper right-hand corner of first page). Include cover page with poet's name, address, phone number, and title of poem. Do not include SASE; poems will not be returned. Deadline: October 1. Prizes: 1st Prize: $40 and certificate; 2nd Prize: $25 and certificate; and 3rd Prize: $15 and certificate. Honorable Mention certificates will be awarded at the discretion of the judges.

THE MURIEL CRAFT BAILEY MEMORIAL AWARD

4956 St. John Dr., Syracuse NY 13215. (315)488-8077. **E-mail:** poetry@comstockreview.org. **Website:** www.comstockreview.org. Annual contest for best previously unpublished poem. Deadline: July 15. Prize: 1st place: $1,000; 2nd place: $250; 3rd place: $100; honorable mentions receive 1-year subscription to *Comstock Review*. Judged by Ellen Bass in 2017.

BARROW STREET PRESS BOOK CONTEST

P.O. Box 1558, Kingston RI 02881. **Website:** www.barrowstreet.org. The Barrow Street Press Book Contest award will be given for the best previously unpublished ms of poetry in English. Submit a 50-80 page unpublished ms of original poetry in English. Please number the pages of your ms and include a table of contents and an acknowledgments page for any previously published poems. Include two title pages. The author's name, address, and telephone number should appear on the first title page only and should not appear anywhere else in the ms. The second title page should contain only the ms title. Deadline: June 30. Prize: $1,000. Judged by Denise Duhamel.

ELINOR BENEDICT POETRY PRIZE

Passages North, Northern Michigan University, 1401 Presque Isle Ave., Marquette MI 49855. **E-mail:** passages@nmu.edu. **Website:** passagesnorth.com/contests/. **Contact:** Jennifer A. Howard, Editor-in-Chief. Prize given biennially for a poem or a group of poems. Check website to see if award is currently being offered this year. Deadline: April 15. Submission period begins February 15. Prize: $1,000 and publication for winner; 2 honorable mentions are also published; all entrants receive a copy of *Passages North*.

BERMUDA TRIANGLE PRIZE

The Poet's Billow, 6135 Avon St., Portage MI 49024. **E-mail:** thepoetsbillow@gmail.com. **Website:** http://thepoetsbillow.org. **Contact:** Robert Evory. Annual award open to any writer to recognize three poems that address a theme set by the editors. Finalists with strong work will also be published. Submissions must be previously unpublished. Please submit online. Deadline: March 15. Submission period begins November 15. Prize: $50 each to three poems. The winning poems will be published and displayed in The Poet's Billow Literary Art Gallery and nominated for a Pushcart Prize. If the poet qualifies, the poem will also be submitted to The Best New Poets anthology. Judged by the editors, and, occasionally, a guest judge.

THE PATRICIA BIBBY FIRST BOOK AWARD

Patricia Bibby Award, Tebot Bach, P.O. Box 7887, Huntington Beach CA 92615-7887. **E-mail:** mifanwy@tebotbach.org; info@tebotbach.org. **Website:** www.tebotbach.org. **Contact:** Mifanwy Kaiser. Annual competition open to all poets writing in English who have not committed to publishing collections of poetry of 36 poems or more in editions of over 400 copies. Offers award and publication of a book-length poetry ms by Tebot Bach. Complete guidelines available by e-mail or on website. Deadline: November 1. Prize: $500 and book publication. Judges for each year's competition announced online.

BINGHAMTON UNIVERSITY MILT KESSLER POETRY BOOK AWARD

Binghamton University Creative Writing Program, Department of English, General Literature, and Rhetoric, Library North Room 1149, Vestal Parkway East, P.O. Box 6000, Binghamton NY 13902-6000. (607)777-2713. **Fax:** (607)777-2408. **E-mail:** cwpro@binghamton.edu. **Website:** www2.binghamton.edu/english/creative-writing/binghamton-center-for-writers. **Contact:** Maria Mazziotti Gillan, creative writing program director. Annual award for a book of poems written in English, 48 pages or more in length, selected by judges as the strongest collection of poems published in that year. Print on demand is acceptable but no self-published or vanity press work will be considered. Each book submitted must be accompanied by an application form available online. Poet or publisher may submit more than 1 book for prize consideration. Send 2 copies of each book. Deadline: March 1. Prize: $1,000.

THE BITTER OLEANDER PRESS LIBRARY OF POETRY AWARD

BOPLOPA, The Bitter Oleander Press, 4983 Tall Oaks Dr., Fayetteville NY 13066-9776. (315)637-3047. **E-mail:** info@bitteroleander.com. **Website:** www.bitteroleander.com. **Contact:** Paul B. Roth. The Bitter Oleander Press Library of Poetry Book Award replaces the 15-year long run of the Frances Locke Memorial Poetry Award. Guidelines available on website. Entrants must not be friends or employees of The Bitter Oleander Press. Deadline: June 15 (postmarked). Open to submissions on May 1. Early or late entries will be disqualified. Prize: $1,000, plus book publication of the winning ms. the following spring.

BLUE LIGHT POETRY PRIZE AND CHAPBOOK CONTEST

1563 - 45th Avenue, San Francisco CA 94122. **E-mail:** bluelightpress@aol.com. **E-mail:** bluelightpress@aol.com. **Website:** www.bluelightpress.com. **Contact:** Diane Frank, Chief Editor. The Blue Light Poetry Prize and Chapbook Contest offers a cash prize and publication by Blue Light Press (see separate listing in Book/Chapbook Publishers). Deadline: June 15. The winner will be published by Blue Light Press, with 20 copies the author's book. We have a group of poets who read manuscripts. Some years, we publish more than one winner.

TIPS "Our new anthology, *River of Earth and Sky: Poems for the Twenty-First Century,* has more than 100 poets whose work we deeply admire. It will show you the kind of poetry we love to publish."

BLUE MOUNTAIN ARTS/SPS STUDIOS POETRY CARD CONTEST

P.O. Box 1007, Boulder CO 80306. (303)449-0536. **Fax:** (303)447-0939. **E-mail:** poetrycontest@sps.com; editorial@sps.com. **Website:** www.sps.com. **Contact:** Becky Milanski. Biannual poetry card contest. All entries must be the original creation of the submitting author. Looking for original poetry that's non-rhyming, although rhyming poetry may be considered. Poems may also be considered for possible publication on greeting cards or in book anthologies. Guidelines available online. Deadline: December 31 and June 30.

Prize: 1st Place: $300; 2nd Place: $150; 3rd Place: $50. Judged by the Blue Mountain Arts editorial staff.

TIPS "We suggest that you write about real emotions and feelings and that you have some special person or occasion in mind as you write."

THE BOSTON REVIEW ANNUAL POETRY CONTEST

Poetry Contest, Boston Review, P.O. Box 425786, Cambridge MA 02142. (617)324-1360. **Fax:** (617)452-3356. **E-mail:** review@bostonreview.net. **Website:** www.bostonreview.net. Offers $1,500 and publication in *Boston Review* (see separate listing in Magazines/Journals). Any poet writing in English is eligible, unless he or she is a current student, former student, or close personal friend of the judge. Submissions must be unpublished. Submit up to 5 poems, no more than 10 pages total, via online contest entry manager. Include cover sheet with poet's name, address, and phone number; no identifying information on the poems themselves. No cover note is necessary for online submissions. No mss will be returned. Guidelines available for SASE or on website. Deadline: June 1. Winner announced in early November on website. Prize: $1,500 and publication.

BOULEVARD POETRY CONTEST FOR EMERGING POETS

PMB 325, 6614 Clayton Rd., Richmond Heights MO 63117. **E-mail:** editors@boulevardmagazine.org. **Website:** www.boulevardmagazine.org. **Contact:** Jessica Rogen, editor. Annual Emerging Poets Contest offers $1,000 and publication in *Boulevard* (see separate listing in Magazines/Journals) for the best group of 3 poems by a poet who has not yet published a book of poetry with a nationally distributed press. All entries will be considered for publication and payment at regular rates. Submissions must be unpublished. Considers simultaneous submissions. Submit 3 poems, typed; may be a sequence or unrelated. On page one of first poem type poet's name, address, phone number, and titles of the 3 poems. Deadline: June 1. Prize: $1,000 and publication.

BARBARA BRADLEY PRIZE

New England Poetry Club, 376 School St., Watertown MA 02472. **E-mail:** contests@nepoetryclub.org. **Website:** www.nepoetryclub.org. **Contact:** Audrey Kalajin. For a lyric poem under 20 lines, written by a woman. Contest open to members and nonmembers. Poems should be typed and submitted in duplicate with author's name, address, phone, and e-mail address of writer on only 1 copy. (Judges receive copies without names.) Copy only. Label poems with contest name. Entries should be sent by regular mail only. Special delivery or signature required mail will be returned by the post office. Entries should be original, unpublished poems in English. No poem should be entered in more than 1 contest, nor have won a previous contest. No entries will be returned. NEPC will not engage in correspondence regarding poems or contest decisions. Deadline: May 31. Prize: $200. Judged by well-known poets and sometimes winners of previous NEPC contests.

BRICK ROAD POETRY BOOK CONTEST

Brick Road Poetry Press, Inc., 513 Broadway, Columbus GA 31901. (706) 649-3080. **Fax:** (706) 649-3094. **E-mail:** kbadowski@brickroadpoetrypress.com. **Website:** www.brickroadpoetrypress.com. **Contact:** Ron Self and Keith Badowski, co-editors/founders. Annual competition for an original collection of 50-100 pages of poetry. Book-length poetry mss only. Simultaneous submissions accepted. Single sided, single spaced only. No more than one poem per page. Electronic submissions are accepted, see website for details. Include a cover letter with poetry publication/recognition highlights. Deadline: November 1. Submission period begins August 1. Prize: $1,000, publication in both print and e-book formats, and 25 copies of the book. May also offer publication contracts to the top finalists. Judged by Keith Badowski & Ron Self, Brick Road poetry editors.

TIPS "The best way to discover all that poetry can be and to expand the limits of your own poetry is to read expansively."

BRIGHT HILL PRESS POETRY CHAPBOOK COMPETITION

Bright Press Hill & Literary Center, 94 Church St., Treadwell NY 13846. (607)829-5055. **E-mail:** brighthillpress@stny.rr.com; wordthur@stny.rr.com. **Website:** www.brighthillpress.org. The annual Bright Hill Press Chapbook Award recognizes an outstanding collection of poetry. Guidelines available for SASE, by e-mail, or on website. Collection of original poetry, 48-64 pages, single spaced, one poem to a page (no name) with table of contents. Ms must be submitted in Times New Roman, 12 pt. type only. No illustrations, no cover suggestions. Bio and acknowledgments of poems that have been previously published should

be included in a separate document, or in comments box if submitting online. See website for more details, and information on submitting a hard copy. Deadline: December 31. Prize: A publication contract with Bright Hill Press and $1,000, publication in print format, and 30 copies of the printed book. Judged by a nationally-known poet.

TIPS "Publish your poems in literary magazines before trying to get a whole ms published. Publishing individual poems is the best way to hone your complete ms."

BRITTINGHAM PRIZE IN POETRY

University of Wisconsin Press, 1930 Monroe Street, 3rd Floor, Madison WI 5311-2059. (608)263-1110. **Fax:** (608)263-1132. **E-mail:** rwallace@wisc.edu. **E-mail:** uwiscpress@uwpress.wisc.edu. **Website:** www.wisc.edu/wisconsinpress/poetryguide.html. **Contact:** Ronald Wallace, series editor. The annual Brittingham Prize in Poetry is 1 of 2 prizes awarded by The University of Wisconsin Press (see separate listing for the Felix Pollak Prize in Poetry in this section). Beginning in 2017 the Press will publish two or three additional books annually, drawn from the contest submissions. Submissions must be unpublished as a collection, but individual poems may have been published elsewhere (publication must be acknowledged). Considers simultaneous submissions if notified of selection elsewhere. Submit 60-90 unbound ms pages, typed single-spaced (with double spaces between stanzas). Clean photocopies are acceptable. Include 1 title page with poet's name, address, and telephone number and 1 with title only. No translations. Strongly encourages electronic submissions via web page. SASE required for postal submissions. Will return results only; mss will not be returned. Guidelines available on website. The Brittingham Prize in Poetry is awarded annually to the best book-length manuscript of original poetry submitted in an open competition. The award is administered by the University of Wisconsin–Madison English Department, and the winner is chosen by a nationally recognized poet. The resulting book is published by the University of Wisconsin Press. Deadline: Submit August 15-September 15. Prize: Offers $1,000, plus publication. Judged by a distinguished poet who will remain anonymous until the winners are announced in mid-February.

BURNING BUSH POETRY PRIZE

P.O. Box 4658, Santa Rosa CA 95402. **Website:** www. bbbooks.com. Purpose of contest to reward a poet whose writing inspires others to value human life and natural world instead of values based on short-term economic advantage; speaks for community-centered values, democratic processes, especially those whose voices are seldom heard; demonstrates poetic excellence; and educates readers of the relevance of the past to the present and future. Deadline: June 1.

BOB BUSH MEMORIAL AWARD FOR FIRST BOOK OF POETRY

Texas Institute of Letters, P.O. Box 609, Round Rock TX 78680. **E-mail:** tilsecretary@yahoo.com. **Website:** www.texasinstituteofletters.org. Offered annually for best first book of poetry published in previous year. Writer must have been born in Texas, have lived in the state at least 2 consecutive years at some time, or the subject matter should be associated with the state. Deadline: See website for exact date. Prize: $1,000.

✪ CAA POETRY AWARD

Canadian Authors Association, 74 Mississaga Street E., Orillia ON L3V 1V5 Canada. **Website:** canadianauthors.org/national. Contest for full-length English-language book of poems for adults by a Canadian writer. Deadline: January.

CAROLINA WREN PRESS POETRY SERIES CONTEST

120 Morris St., Durham NC 27701. (919)560-2738. **Fax:** (919)560-2759. **E-mail:** carolinawrenpress@earthlink.net. **Website:** www.carolinawrenpress.org. **Contact:** Andrea Selch, Poetry Editor. Carolina Wren Press is a nonprofit organization whose mission is to publish quality writing, especially by writers historically neglected by mainstream publishing, and to develop diverse and vital audiences through publishing, outreach, and educational programs. Submit a copy of a 48-72 page manuscript. Manuscript should be single-spaced and paginated. Please include a table of contents. Title page should not include author information–no name, address, etc. Within the manuscript, do include a page acknowledging individual poems that have been previously published. Open only to poets who have had no more than one full-length book published. Deadline: June 15 of odd-numbered years. Prize: $1,000 and publication.

CAVE CANEM POETRY PRIZE

Cave Canem Foundation, Inc., 20 Jay St., Suite 310-A, Brooklyn NY 11201. (718)858-0000. **Website:** www. cavecanempoets.org. This 1st book award is dedicated to the discovery of exceptional mss by black poets of African descent. Deadline: March 17. 1st place: $1,000, plus publication by University of Pittsburgh Press, 15 copies of the book, and a featured reading.

JOHN CIARDI PRIZE FOR POETRY

BkMk Press, University of Missouri-Kansas City, 5101 Rockhill Rd., Kansas City MO 64110. (816)235-2558. **E-mail:** bkmk@umkc.edu. **Website:** www.newletters. org. **Contact:** Ben Furnish. Offered annually for the best book-length collection (unpublished) of poetry in English by a living author. Translations are not eligible. Guidelines for SASE, by e-mail, or on website. Poetry mss should be approximately 50-110 pages, single-spaced. Deadline: January 15. Prize: $1,000, plus book publication by BkMk Press. Judged by a network of published writers. Final judging is done by a writer of national reputation.

CIDER PRESS REVIEW BOOK AWARD

P.O. Box 33384, San Diego CA 92163. **E-mail:** editor@ciderpressreview.com. **Website:** http://ciderpressreview.com/. Annual award from *Cider Press Review*. Submissions must be unpublished as a collection, but individual poems may have been previously published elsewhere. Submit book-length ms of 48-80 pages. Submissions can be made online using the submission form on the website or by mail. If sending by mail, include 2 cover sheets—1 with title, author's name, and complete contact information; and 1 with title only, all bound with a spring clip. Does not require SASE; notification via e-mail and on the website, only. Mss cannot be returned. Online submissions must be in Word for PC or PDF format, and should not include title page with author's name. The editors strongly urge contestants to use online delivery if possible. Review the complete submission guidelines and learn more online at website. Deadline: November 30. Open to submissions on September 1. Prize: $1,500, publication, and 25 author's copies of a book length collection of poetry. Author receives a standard publishing contract. Initial print run is not less than 1,000 copies. CPR acquires first publication rights.

CLEVELAND STATE UNIVERSITY POETRY CENTER PRIZES

Cleveland State University Poetry Center, Cleveland State University Poetry Center, 2121 Euclid Avenue, Rhodes Tower, Room 1841, Cleveland OH 44115-2214. (216)687-3986. **Fax:** (216)687-6943. **E-mail:** poetrycenter@csuohio.edu. **Website:** www.csuohio.edu/poetrycenter. **Contact:** Caryl Pagel. Manuscript should contain a minimum of 48 and a maximum of 100 pages of poetry. See website for specific details and rules. Offered annually to identify, reward, and publish the best unpublished book-length poetry ms (minimum 48 pages) in 2 categories: First Book Award and Open Competition (for poets who have published at least one collection with a press run of 500). Deadline: March 31. Submissions open on January 1. Prize: First Book and Open Book Competitions awards publication and a $1,000 advance against royalties for an original manuscript of poetry in each category. Judged by Emily Kendal Frey, Siwar Masannat, Jon Woodward, Daniel Borzutzky, and Chris Kraus.

CLOCKWISE CHAPBOOK COMPETITION

Tebot Bach, Tebot Bach, Clockwise, P.O. Box 7887, Huntington Beach CA 92615. (714)968-0905. **Fax:** (714)968-4677. **E-mail:** mifanwy@tebotbach.org. **Website:** www.tebotbach.org/clockwise.html. Annual competition for a collection of poetry. Submit 24-32 pages of original poetry in English. Must be previously unpublished poetry for the full collection; individual poems may have been published. Full guidelines, including submission info, available online. Deadline: July 30. Prize: $500 and a book publication in Perfect Bound Editions. Winner announced in September with publication January. Judged by Gail Wronsky.

🌑 TOM COLLINS POETRY PRIZE

Fellowship of Australian Writers (WA), P.O. Box 6180, Swanbourne WA 6910 Australia. (61)(8)9384-4771. **Fax:** (61)(8)9384-4854. **E-mail:** fellowshipaustralianwriterswa@gmail.com. **Website:** www.fawwa.org. Annual contest for unpublished poems, maximum 60 lines. Reserves the right to publish entries in a FAWWA publication or on its website. Guidelines online or for SASE. See website for details, guidelines, and entry form. Deadline: February 5. Prize: 1st Place: $1,000; 2nd Place: $200; 43rd Place: $100 each.

THE COLORADO PRIZE FOR POETRY

Colorado Review/Center for Literary Publishing, Department of English, Colorado State University, 9105 Campus Delivery, Ft. Collins CO 80523. (970)491-5449. **E-mail:** creview@colostate.edu. **Website:** http://coloradoprize.colostate.edu. **Contact:** Stephanie G'Schwind, editor. Submission must be unpublished as a collection, but individual poems may have been published elsewhere. Submit mss of 48-100 pages of poetry on any subject, in any form, double- or single-spaced. Include 2 titles pages: 1 with ms title only, the other with ms title and poet's name, address, and phone number. Enclose SASP for notification of receipt and SASE for results; mss will not be returned. Guidelines available for SASE or by e-mail. Guidelines available for SASE or online at website. Poets can also submit online via online submission manager through website. Deadline: January 14. Prize: $2,000 and publication of a book-length ms. Judged by Susan Howe.

CONCRETE WOLF POETRY CHAPBOOK/LOUIS AWARD CONTEST

P.O. Box 445, Tillamook OR 97141. **E-mail:** concretewolfpress@gmail.com. **Website:** http://concretewolf.com. Prefers collections that have a theme, either obvious (i.e., chapbook about a divorce) or understated (i.e., all the poems mention the color blue). Likes a collection that feels more like a whole than a sampling of work. No preference as to formal or free verse. Slightly favors lyric and narrative poetry to language and concrete, but excellent examples of any style will grab their attention. Considers simultaneous submissions if notified of acceptance elsewhere. See website for details. Deadline: November 30 and March 31. Prize: Publication and author copies of a perfectly-bound collection.

THE CONNECTICUT RIVER REVIEW POETRY CONTEST

P.O. Box 270554, W. Hartford CT 06127. **E-mail:** connpoetry@comcast.net. **Website:** ctpoetry.net. Send up to 3 unpublished poems, any form, 80-line limit. Include 2 copies of each poem: 1 with complete contact informatoin and 1 with no contact information. Include a SASE. Deadline: September 30. Open to submissions on August 1. 1st Place: $400; 2nd Place: $100; 3rd Place: $50.

CPR EDITOR'S PRIZE

P.O. Box 33384, San Diego CA 92163. **E-mail:** editor@ciderpressreview.com. **Website:** http://ciderpressreview.com/bookaward. Annual award from *Cider Press Review*. Submissions must be unpublished as a collection, but individual poems may have been previously published elsewhere. Submit book-length ms of 48-80 pages of original poetry. Submissions can be made online using the submission form on the website or by mail. If sending by mail, include 2 cover sheets—1 with title, author's name, and complete contact information; and 1 with title only, all bound with a spring clip. Check website for change of address coming in the future. Include SASE for results only if no email address included; notification via email and on the website; manuscripts cannot be returned. Online submissions must be in Word for PC or PDF format, and should not include title page with author's name. The editors strongly urge contestants to use online delivery if possible. Review the complete submission guidelines and learn more online at website. Deadline: submit between April 1-June 30. Prize: $1,000, publication, and 25 author's copies of a book length collection of poetry. Author receives a standard publishing contract. Initial print run is not less than 1,000 copies. CPR acquires first publication rights. Judged by *Cider Press Review* editors.

CRAB ORCHARD SERIES IN POETRY FIRST BOOK AWARD

First Book Award, Dept. of English, Mail Code 4503, Southern Illinois University Carbondale, 1000 Faner Drive, Carbondale IL 62901. (618)453-6833. **Fax:** (618)453-8224. **E-mail:** jtribble@siu.edu. **Website:** www.craborchardreview.siu.edu. **Contact:** Jon Tribble, series editor. Annual award that selects a first book of poems for publication from an open competition of manuscripts, in English, by a U.S. citizen, permanent resident, or person who has DACA/TPS status who has neither published, who has neither published, nor committed to publish, a volume of poetry 48 pages or more in length in an edition of over 500 copies (individual poems may have been previously published; for the purposes of the Crab Orchard Series in Poetry, a ms which was in whole or in part submitted as a thesis or dissertation as a requirement for the completion of a degree is considered unpublished and is eligible). Current or former students, colleagues, and close friends of the final judge, and current and former students and employees of Southern Illinois University Carbondale and authors who have published a book with Southern Illinois University Press or have a book under contract with Southern Illinois University Press are not eligible. See website for complete formatting instructions and guidelines. Ac-

cepts submissions only through Submittable, online. Mss are recommended to be a minimum of 50 pages to a recommended maximum of 75 pages of original poetry, but no manuscript will be rejected solely because of length. Considers simultaneous submissions, but series editor must be informed immediately upon acceptance. Author's name should appear nowhere in manuscript. Do not include acknowledgments page. Deadline: July 8. Submission period begins May 15. Prize: $4,000 and publication. Judged by a published poet. Check website for current judge.

TIPS "Carefully read directions for entering and follow them exactly. Note that simultaneous submissions are accepted for this book prize, but the winning entry must NOT be accepted elsewhere. All submissions should be made through Submittable: https://craborchardseriesinpoetry.submittable.com/submit."

CRAB ORCHARD SERIES IN POETRY OPEN COMPETITION AWARDS

Department of English, Mail Code 4503, Faner Hall 2380, Southern Illinois University Carbondale, Carbondale IL 62901. (618)453-6833. **Fax:** (618)453-8224. **E-mail:** jtribble@siu.edu. **Website:** www.craborchardreview.siu.edu. **Contact:** Jon Tribble, series editor. Annual competition to award unpublished, original collections of poems written in English by United States citizens, permanent residents, or persons who have DACA/TPS status (individual poems may have been previously published; for the purposes of the Crab Orchard Series in Poetry, a ms which was in whole or in part submitted as a thesis or dissertation as a requirement for the completion of a degree is considered unpublished and is eligible). Two volumes of poems will be selected from the open competition of mss. Current or former students, colleagues, and close friends of the final judge, and current and former students and employees of Southern Illinois University Carbondale and authors who have published a book with Southern Illinois University Press or have a book under contract with Southern Illinois University Press are not eligible. See website for complete formatting instructions and guidelines. Accepts submissions only through Submittable, online. Mss are recommended to be a minimum of 50 pages to a recommended maximum of 80 pages of original poetry, but no manuscript will be rejected solely because of length. Considers simultaneous submissions, but series editor must be informed immediately upon acceptance. Deadline: November 19. Submission period begins October 1. Prize: Both winners will be awarded a publication contract with Southern Illinois University Press, a $2,500 prize, and a $1,500 as an honorarium for a reading at Southern Illinois University Carbondale. Both readings will follow the publication of the poets' collections. Judged by a published poet. Check website for current judge.

TIPS "Carefully read directions for entering and follow them exactly. Note that simultaneous submissions are accepted for this book prize, but the winning entry must NOT be accepted elsewhere. All submissions should be made through Submittable: https://craborchardseriesinpoetry.submittable.com/submit."

THE CRAZYHORSE PRIZE IN POETRY

Crazyhorse, Department of English, College of Charleston, 66 George St., Charleston SC 29424. (843)953-4470. **E-mail:** crazyhorse@cofc.edu. **Website:** http://crazyhorse.cofc.edu. **Contact:** Prize Director. The *Crazyhorse* Prize in Poetry is for a single poem. All entries will be considered for publication. Submissions must be unpublished. Submit online or by mail up to 3 original poems (no more than 10 pages). Include cover page (placed on top of ms) with poet's name, address, e-mail, and telephone number; no identifying information on mss (blind judging). Accepts multiple submissions with separate fee for each. Include SASP for notification of receipt of ms and SASE for results only; mss will not be returned. Guidelines available for SASE or on website. Deadline: January 31. Submissions period begins January 1. Prize: $2,000 and publication in *Crazyhorse*. Judged by genre judges for first round, guest judge for second round. Judges change on a yearly basis.

DANCING POETRY CONTEST

Artists Embassy International, AEI Contest Chair, Judy Cheung, 704 Brigham Ave., Santa Rosa CA 95404-5245. (707)528-0912. **E-mail:** jhcheung@comcast.net. **Website:** www.dancingpoetry.com. Any subject, any form or free verse, suitable for a general audience **Contact:** Judy Cheung, contest chair. Line Limit: 40 lines maximum each poem. No limit on number of entries. Send 2 typed, clear copies of each entry. Show name, address, telephone number, e-mail and how you heard about the contest on one copy only. Poems must be in English or include English translation. Deadline: May 15. Prizes: Three Grand Prizes will receive $100 each plus the poems will be danced and videotaped at this year's Dancing Poetry Festival; six First Prizes will receive $50 each; twelve Second Prizes will receive $25 each; and thirty Third Prizes will receive $10 each. Judged by members and associates of Artists Embassy International and the Poetic Dance Theater Company.

TIPS "We always look for something new and different including new twists to old themes, different looks at common situations, inovative concepts for dynamic, thought provoking entertainment."

JAMES DICKEY PRIZE FOR POETRY

Georgia State University, P.O. Box 3999, Atlanta GA 30302-3999. **Website:** fivepoints.gsu.edu. The James Dickey Prize for Poetry is for the best previously unpublished poem. Deadline: December 1. Open to submissions on September 1.

DREAM HORSE PRESS NATIONAL POETRY CHAPBOOK PRIZE

P.O. Box 2080, Aptos CA 95001-2080. **E-mail:** dreamhorsepress@yahoo.com. **Website:** www.dreamhorsepress.com. **Contact:** J.P. Dancing Bear, Editor/Publisher. All entries will be considered for publication. Submissions may be previously published in magazines/journals but not in books or chapbooks. Considers simultaneous submissions with notification. Submit 20-28 pages of poetry in a readable font with table of contents, acknowledgments, bio, e-mail address for results, and entry fee. Poet's name should not appear anywhere on the manuscript. Accepts multiple submissions (with separate fee for each entry). Manuscripts will be recycled after judging. Guidelines available on website. Make checks/money orders made payable to Dream Horse Press. Recent previous winners include M.R.B. Chelko, Cynthia Arrieu-King, and Ariana-Sophia Kartsonis. Deadline: June 30. Prize: $500, publication, and 25 copies of a handsomely printed chapbook. Judged is anonymous.

♻ FAR HORIZONS AWARD FOR POETRY

The Malahat Review, University of Victoria, P.O. Box 1700, Stn CSC, Victoria BC V8W 2Y2 Canada. (250)721-8524. **Fax:** (250)472-5051. **E-mail:** malahat@uvic.ca. **Website:** www.malahatreview.ca. **Contact:** Patrick Grace, publicity manager. The biennial Far Horizons Award for Poetry offers $1,000 CAD and publication in *The Malahat Review* (see separate listing in Magazines/Journals). Winner and finalists contacted by e-mail. Winner published in fall in *The Malahat Review* and announced on website, Facebook page, and in quarterly e-newsletter, *Malahat lite*. Submissions must be unpublished. No simultaneous submissions. Submit up to 3 poems per entry, each poem not to exceed 60 lines; no restrictions on subject matter or aesthetic approach. Include separate page with poet's name, address, e-mail, and poem title(s); no identifying information on mss pages. E-mail submissions are acceptable: please send to horizons@uvic.ca. Do not include SASE for results; mss will not be returned. Full guidelines available on website. Open to "emerging poets from Canada, the United States, and elsewhere" who have not yet published a full-length book (48 pages or more). Deadline: May 1 (even numbered years). Prize: $1,000.

THE JEAN FELDMAN POETRY PRIZE

Washington Writers' Publishing House, 4640 23rd Rd. N., Arlington VA 22207. **E-mail:** wwphpress@gmail.com. **Website:** www.washingtonwriters.org. **Contact:** Holly Karapetkova. Poets living within 75 miles of the Capitol are invited to submit a ms of either a novel or a collection of short stories. Ms should be 50-70 pages, single spaced. Author's name should not appear on the manuscript. The title page of each copy should contain the title only. Provide name, address, telephone number, e-mail address, and title on a separate cover sheet accompanying the submission. A separate page for acknowledgments may be included for stories or excerpts previously published in journals and anthologies. E-mail electronic copies to wwphpress@gmail.com or mail paper copies and/or reading fee (check to WWPH) with SASE to: The Jean Feldman Poetry Prize, WWPH, c/o Holly Karapetkova, 4640 23rd Rd. N., Arlington, VA 22207. Deadline: November 15. Submission period begins July 1. Prize: $1,000 and 50 copies of the book.

FIELD POETRY PRIZE

Oberlin College Press/FIELD, 50 N. Professor St., Oberlin OH 44074-1095. (440)775-8408. **Fax:** (440)775-8124. **E-mail:** oc.press@oberlin.edu. **Website:** www.oberlin.edu/ocpress/prize.htm. **Contact:** Marco Wilkinson, managing editor. Offered annually for an unpublished book-length collection of poetry (mss of 50-80 pages). Contest seeks to encourage the finest in contemporary poetry writing. Open to any writer. Deadline: May 31. Opens to submissions on May 1. Prize: $1,000 and a standard royalty contract.

THE FINISHING LINE PRESS OPEN CHAPBOOK COMPETITION

P.O. Box 1626, Georgetown KY 40324. (859)514-8966. **E-mail:** finishingbooks@aol.com. **Website:** www.finishinglinepress.com. **Contact:** Leah Maines, director. Annual competition for previously unpublished poetry chapbook.

FIRST BOOK AWARD FOR POETRY

Zone 3, Austin Peay State University, Austin Peay State University, PO Box 4565, Clarksville TN 37044. (931)221-7031. **Fax:** (931)221-7149. **E-mail:** zone3@apsu.edu. **Website:** www.apsu.edu/zone3/. **Contact:** Andrea Spofford, poetry editor; Susan Wallace, managing editor. Annual poetry award for anyone who has not published a full-length collection of poems (48 pages or more). Accepts entries via postal mail or online. Separate instructions for both, see website for guidelines and details. Deadline: May 1. Prize: $1,000 and publication.

FISH POETRY PRIZE

Fish Poetry Contest, Fish Publishing, Dunbeacon, Durrus, Bantry Co. Cork Ireland. **E-mail:** info@fishpublishing.com. **Website:** www.fishpublishing.com. **Contact:** Clem Cairns. For poems up to 300 words. Age Range: Adult. The best 10 will be published in the Fish Anthology, launched in July at the West Cork Literary Festival. Entries must not have been published before. Enter online or by post. See website for full details of competitions, and information on the Fish Editorial and Critique Services, and the Fish Online Writing Courses. Do not put your name or address or any other details on the poem, use a separate sheet. Receipt of entry will be acknowledged by e-mail. Poems will not be returned. Word count: 300 max for each poem. You may enter as many as you wish, provided there is an entry fee for each one. Full details and rules are online. Entry is deemed to be acceptance of these rules. Publishing rights of the 10 winning poems are held by Fish Publishing for one year after the publication of the Anthology. The aim of the competition is to discover and publish new writers. Deadline: March 31. Prize: $1,000. 2nd Prize: a week at Anam Cara Writers" Retreat in West Cork. Results announced May 15. Judged by Jo Shapcott in 2017.

FOLEY POETRY CONTEST

106 W. 56th St., New York NY 10019. (212)581-4640. **Fax:** (212)399-3596. **Website:** www.americamagazine.org. *America*, the national Catholic weekly by the Je-

suits of North America, sponsors the annual Foley Poetry Contest. Offers $1,000 and 2 contributor's copies for the winning poem. Winner will be announced in the mid-June issue of America and on the website. Runners-up will have their poems printed in subsequent issues of *America*. Submissions must be unpublished and may not be entered in other contests. "Submit 1 poem per person, not to exceed 30 lines of verse, in any form. Name, address, telephone number, and e-mail address (if applicable) should be appended to the bottom of the page. Poems will not be returned, and e-mailed submissions are not accepted." Guidelines available in magazine, for SASE, or on website. Competition receives more than 1,000 entries/year. Submissions must be unpublished and may not be entered in other contests. "Submit 1 poem per person, not to exceed 30 lines of verse, in any form. Name, address, telephone number, and e-mail address (if applicable) should be appended to the bottom of the page. Poems will not be returned, and e-mailed submissions are not accepted." Guidelines available in magazine, for SASE, or on website. Deadline: March 31. Open to submissions on January 1.

FOOD VERSE CONTEST

Literal Latte, 200 East 10th St., Suite 240, New York NY 10003. (212)260-5532. **E-mail:** litlatte@aol.com. **E-mail:** See link to submittable on www.literal-latte.com. **Website:** www.literal-latte.com. **Contact:** Jenine Gordon Bockman, editor. Open to any writer. Poems should have food as an ingredient. Submissions required to be unpublished. Guidelines online at website. Submit up to 2,000 words. Literal Latté acquires first rights. Annual contest to give support and exposure to great writing. Deadline: March 15. Prize: $500. Judged by the editors.

THE FOUR WAY BOOKS LEVIS PRIZE IN POETRY

Four Way Books, Box 535, Village Station, New York NY 10014. (212)334-5430. **Fax:** (212)334-5435. **E-mail:** editors@fourwaybooks.com. **Website:** www.fourwaybooks.com. **Contact:** Ryan Murphy, Assoc. Director. The Four Way Books Levis Prize in Poetry, offered biennially in even-numbered years, offers publication by Four Way Books (see separate listing in Book Publishers), honorarium, and a reading at one or more participating series In New York City. Open to any poet writing in English who has not published a book-length collection of poetry. Entry form and guidelines available on website at www.fourwaybooks.com. Deadline: March 31 (postmark or online submission). Winner announced by e-mail and on website. Prize: Publication and $1,000. Copies of winning books available through Four Way Books online and at bookstores (to the trade through University Press of New England).

GERTRUDE PRESS POETRY CHAPBOOK CONTEST

P.O. Box 28281, Portland OR 97228. **E-mail:** editor@gertrudepress.org; poetry@gertrudepress.org. **Website:** www.gertrudepress.org. Annual chapbook contest for 25-30 pages of poetry. Individual poems may have been previously published; unpublished poems are welcome. Poetry may be of any subject matter, and writers from all backgrounds are encouraged to submit. Include list of acknowledgments and cover letter indicating how poet learned of the contest. Include 1 title page with identifying information and 1 without. Guidelines available in *Gertrude* (see separate listing in Magazines/Journals), for SASE, by e-mail, or on website. Deadline: May 15. Submission period begins September 15. Prize: $200, publication and 25 complimentary copies of the chapbook.

ALLEN GINSBERG POETRY AWARDS

The Poetry Center at Passaic County Community College, One College Blvd., Paterson NJ 07505. (973)684-6555. **Fax:** (973)523-6085. **E-mail:** mgillan@pccc.edu. **Website:** www.pccc.edu/poetry. **Contact:** Maria Mazziotti Gillan, executive director. All winning poems, honorable mentions, and editor's choice poems will be published in *The Paterson Literary Review*. Winners will be asked to participate in a reading that will be held in the Paterson Historic District. Submissions must be unpublished. Submit up to 5 poems (no poem more than 2 pages long). Send 4 copies of each poem entered. Include cover sheet with poet's name, address, phone number, e-mail address and poem titles. Poet's name should not appear on poems. Include SASE for results only; poems will not be returned. Guidelines available for SASE or on website. Deadline: February 1 (postmark). Prize: 1st Prize: $1,000; 2nd Prize: $200; 3rd Prize: $100.

GIVAL PRESS POETRY AWARD

Gival Press, LLC, P.O. Box 3812, Arlington VA 22203. (703)351-0079. **E-mail:** givalpress@yahoo.com. **Website:** www.givalpress.submittable.com. **Contact:** Robert L. Giron, editor. Offered every other year for a previously unpublished poetry collection as a complete ms, which may include previously published poems; previously published poems must be acknowledged, and poet must hold rights. Guidelines for SASE, by e-mail, or online. Open to any writer, as long as the work is original, not a translation, and is written in English. The copyright remains in the author's name; certain rights fall to the publisher per the contract. Must be at least 45 typed pages of poetry, on one side only. Entrants are asked to submit their poems without any kind of identification (with the exception of the titles) and with a separate cover page with the following information: Name, address (street, city, state, and zip code), telephone number, e-mail address (if available), short bio, and a list of the poems by title. Checks drawn on American banks should be made out to Gival Press, LLC. The competition seeks to award well-written, origional poetry in English on any topic, in any style. Deadline: December 15 (postmarked). Prize: $1,000, publication, and 20 copies of the publication. The editor narrows entries to the top 10; previous winner selects top 5 and chooses the winner—all done anonymously.

PATRICIA GOEDICKE PRIZE IN POETRY

CutBank Literary Magazine, *CutBank*, University of Montana, English Dept., LA 133, Missoula MT 59812. **E-mail:** editor.cutbank@gmail.com. **Website:** www. cutbankonline.org. **Contact:** Billy Wallace, editor-in-chief. The Patricia Goedicke Prize in Poetry seeks to highlight work that showcases an authentic voice, a boldness of form, and a rejection of functional fixedness. Accepts online submissions only. Submit up to 5 poems. Guidelines available online. Deadline: January 15. Submissions period begins November 9. Prize: $500 and featured in the magazine. Judged by a guest judge each year.

GOLDEN ROSE AWARD

New England Poetry Club, 654 Green St., No. 2, Cambridge MA 02139. **E-mail:** contests@nepoetryclub. org; info@nepoetryclub.org. **Website:** www.nepoetryclub.org. **Contact:** NEPC contest coordinator. Given annually to the poet, who by their poetry and inspiration to and encouragement of other writers, has made a significant mark on American poetry. Traditionally given to a poet with some ties to New England so that a public reading may take place. Contest open to members and nonmembers. Poems should be typed and submitted in duplicate with author's name, address, phone, and e-mail address of writer on only 1 copy. (Judges receive copies without names.) Copy only. Label poems with contest name. Entries should be sent by regular mail only. Special delivery or signature required mail will be returned by the post office. Entries should be original, unpublished poems in English. No poem should be entered in more than 1 contest, nor have won a previous contest. No entries will be returned. NEPC will not engage in correspondence regarding poems or contest decisions. Deadline: May 31. Judged by well-known poets and sometimes winners of previous NEPC contests.

THE GREEN ROSE PRIZE IN POETRY

New Issues Poetry & Prose, Deptartment of English, Western Michigan University, 1903 W. Michigan Ave., Kalamazoo MI 49008-5463. **E-mail:** new-issues@ wmich.edu. **Website:** www.wmich.edu/newissues. Offered annually for unpublished poetry. The university will publish a book of poems by a poet writing in English who has published 1 or more full-length collections of poetry. *New Issues* may publish as many as 3 additional mss from this competition. Guidelines for SASE or online. *New Issues Poetry & Prose* obtains rights for first publication. Book is copyrighted in the author's name. Considers simultaneous submissions, but *New Issues* must be notified of acceptance elsewhere. Submit a ms of at least 40 pages, typed; single-spaced preferred. Clean photocopies acceptable. Do not bind; use manila folder or metal clasp. Include cover page with poet's name, address, phone number, and title of the ms. Also include brief bio, table of contents, and acknowledgments page. Submissions are also welcome through the online submission manager: www.newissuespoetryprose.submittable.com. For hardcopy manuscripts only, you may include SASP for notification of receipt of ms and SASE for results only; mss will be recycled. Guidelines available for SASE, by fax, e-mail, or on website. Winner is announced in January or February on website. The winning manuscript will be published in spring of following year. 2016 winner was Nadine Sabra Meyer (*Chrysanthemum, Chrysanthemum*). Deadline: Submit May 1-September 30. Winner is announced in January or February on website. Prize: $2,000 and publication of a book of poems.

⊙ THE GRIFFIN POETRY PRIZE

The Griffin Trust for Excellence in Poetry, 363 Parkridge Crescent, Oakville ON L6M 1A8 Canada.

(905)618-0420. **E-mail:** info@griffinpoetryprize.com. **Website:** www.griffinpoetryprize.com. **Contact:** Ruth Smith. The Griffin Poetry Prize is one of the world's most generous poetry awards. The awards go to one Canadian and one international poet for a first collection written in, or translated into, English. Submissions must come from publishers. A book of poetry must be a first-edition collection. Books should have been published in the previous calendar year. Deadline: December 31. Prize: Two $65,000 (CAD) prizes. An additional $10,000 (CAD) goes to each shortlisted poet for their participation in the Shortlist Readings. Judges are chosen annually by the Trustees of The Griffin Trust For Excellence in Poetry.

GREG GRUMMER POETRY AWARD

Phoebe, MSN 2C5, George Mason University, 4400 University Dr., Fairfax VA 22030. **E-mail:** phoebe@gmu.edu. **Website:** www.phoebejournal.com. **Contact:** Doug Luman & Janice Majewski, poetry editors. Offered annually for unpublished work. Submit up to 4 poems, no more than 10 pages total. Guidelines online. Requests first serial rights, if work is to be published, and $400 first prize. The purpose of the award is to recognize new and exciting poetry. Deadline: March 19. Prize: $400 and publication in the *Phoebe*. Judged by poet Monica Youn.

THE DONALD HALL PRIZE IN POETRY

AWP, Carty House, Mail Stop 1E3, George Mason University, Fairfax VA 22030-4444. **E-mail:** chronicle@awpwriter.org. **Website:** www.awpwriter.org. The Donald Hall Prize for Poetry offers an award of $5,500, supported by Amazon.com, and publication by the University of Pittsburgh Press. Deadline: March 3. Opens to submissions January 1.

JAMES HEARST POETRY PRIZE

North American Review, University of Northern Iowa, 1222 W. 27th St., Cedar Falls IA 50614-0516. (319)273-3026. **Fax:** (319)273-4326. **E-mail:** nar@uni.edu. **Website:** www.northamericanreview.org. Contest to find the best previously unpublished poem. Deadline: October 31. Prize: 1st place: $1,000; 2nd place: $100; 3rd place: $50. Judged by Major Jackson in 2017.

TIPS "We have noticed that long poems rarely do well—too much can go wrong in a large space. Poems that have reached the finalist stage in our competition in the past are typically 1 to 2 pages (often much shorter). Winning poems always balance interesting subject matter and consummate poetic craft. We value both free verse and formal poems."

THE HILARY THAM CAPITAL COLLECTION

The Word Works, Nancy White, c/o SUNY Adiorndack, 640 Bay Rd., Queensbury NY 12804. **E-mail:** editor@wordworksbooks.org. **Website:** www.wordworksbooks.org. **Contact:** Nancy White, editor. The Hilary Tham Capital Collection publishes only poets who volunteer for literary nonprofits. Every nominated poet is invited to submit; authors have until May 1 to send their ms via online submissions at website, or to Nancy White. Details available online. Deadline: May 1. Past judges include Denise Duhamel, Kimiko Hahn, Michael Klein, and Eduardo Corral.

THE BESS HOKIN PRIZE

Poetry, 61 W. Superior St., Chicago IL 60654. (312)787-7070. **Fax:** (312)787-6650. **E-mail:** editors@poetry-magazine.org. **Website:** www.poetrymagazine.org. Offered annually for poems published in *Poetry* during the preceding year (October-September). Upon acceptance, *Poetry* licenses exclusive worldwide first serial rights, including electronic rights, for publication, as well as non-exclusive rights to reprint, reuse, and archive the work, in any format, in perpetuity. Copyright reverts to author upon first publication. "Established in 1947 through the generosity of our late friend and guarantor, Mrs. David Hokin, and is given annually in her memory." Prize: $1,000.

FIRMAN HOUGHTON PRIZE

New England Poetry Club, 53 Regent St., Cambridge MA 02140. **E-mail:** info@nepoetryclug.org. **Website:** www.nepoetryclub.org. **Contact:** Mary Buchinger, co-president NEPC. For a lyric poem in honor of the former president of NEPC. Contest guidelines available on website. Deadline: May 31. Prize: $200. Judged by well-known poets and sometimes winners of previous NEPC contests.

ILLINOIS STATE POETRY SOCIETY ANNUAL CONTEST

Illinois State Poetry Society, 543 E. Squirrel Trail Dr., Tucson AZ 85704. **E-mail:** oasis@alharris.com. **Website:** www.illinoispoets.org. **Contact:** Alan Harris. Annual contest to encourage the crafting of excellent poetry. Guidelines and entry forms available for SASE. Deadline: September 30. Cash prizes of $50, $30, and $10. Three Honorable Mentions. Poet retains all rights. Judged by out-of-state professionals.

INDIANA REVIEW POETRY PRIZE

Indiana Review, Poetry Prize, Indiana Review, Ballantine Hall 529, 1020 E. Kirkwood Ave., Bloomington IN 47405-7103. **E-mail:** inreview@indiana.edu. **Website:** www.indianareview.org. Offered annually for unpublished work. Open to any writer. Guidelines available on website. All entries are considered for publication. Send no more than 3 poems per entry, 8 pages maximum. Each fee entitles entrant to a 1-year subscription. No longer accepts hard-copy submissions. Deadline: April 5. Submission period begins February 1. Prize: $1,000 and publication. Judged by Camille Rankine in 2016. Different judge every year.

IOWA POETRY PRIZE

University of Iowa Press, 119 West Park Rd., 100 Kuhl House, Iowa City IA 52242. (319)335-2000. **Fax:** (319)335-2055. **E-mail:** uipress@uiowa.edu. **Website:** www.uiowapress.org. Offered annually to encourage poets and their work. Submissions must be postmarked during the month of April; put name on title page only. This page will be removed before ms is judged. Open to writers of English (US citizens or not). Mss will not be returned. Previous winners are not eligible. Mss should be 50-150 pages in length. Poems included in the collection may have appeared in journals or anthologies; poems from a poet's previous collections may be included only in manuscripts of new and selected poems. Deadline: April 30. Prize: Publication under standard royalty agreement.

ALICE JAMES AWARD

Alice James Books, 114 Prescott Street, Farmington ME 04938. (207)778-7071. **Fax:** (207)778-7766. **E-mail:** ajb@alicejamesbooks.org. **Website:** www.alicejamesbooks.org. **Contact:** Alyssa Neptune, Managing Editor. For complete contest guidelines, visit website or send a SASE. Open to anyone residing in the United States. Offered annually for unpublished, full-length poetry collection. Deadline: November 1. Prize: $2,000 and publication, with an additional $1,000 honorarium for a reading at the University of Maine at Farmington.

ALICE JAMES AWARD

Alice James Books, University of Maine at Farmington, 114 Prescott St., Farmington ME 04938. (207)778-7071. **Fax:** (207)778-7766. **E-mail:** ajb@alicejamesbooks.org; info@alicejamesbooks.org. **Website:** www.alicejamesbooks.org. **Contact:** Alyssa Neptune, managing editor. Offered annually for unpublished, full-length poetry collections. Emerging and established poets are welcome. Submit 48-80 pages of poetry. Guidelines for submissions available online. Deadline: November 1. Prize: $2,000, publication, and distribution through Consortium.

RANDALL JARRELL POETRY COMPETITION

North Carolina Writers' Network, Terry L. Kennedy, MFA Writing Program, 3302 MHRA Building, UNC Greensboro, Greensboro NC 27402-6170. **E-mail:** tlkenned@uncg.edu. **Website:** www.ncwriters.org. **Contact:** Terry L. Kennedy, associate director. Offered annually for unpublished work to honor Randall Jarrell and his life at UNC Greensboro, by recognizing the best poetry submitted. The competition is open to any writer who is a legal resident of North Carolina or a member of the North Carolina Writers' Network. Submissions should be one poem only (40-line limit). Poem must be typed (single-spaced) and stapled in the left-hand corner. Author's name should not appear on the poem. Instead, include a separate cover sheet with author's name, address, e-mail address, phone number, and poem title. Poem will not be returned. Include a self-addressed stamped envelope for a list of winner and finalists. The winner and finalists will be announced in May. Deadline: March 1. Prize: $200 and publication at *storySouth* (www.storysouth.com). Judged by David Blaire in 2017.

JUNIPER PRIZE FOR POETRY

University of Massachusetts Press, East Experiment Station, 671 North Pleasant St., Amherst MA 01003. (413)545-2217. **Fax:** (413)545-1226. **E-mail:** info@umpress.umass.edu; kfisk@umpress.umass.edu. **E-mail:** poetry@umpress.umass.edu. **Website:** www.umass.edu/umpress. **Contact:** Karen Fisk, competition coordinator. The University of Massachusetts Press offers the annual Juniper Prize for Poetry, awarded in alternate years for the first and subsequent books. Considers simultaneous submissions, but if accepted for publication elsewhere, please notify immediately. Mss by more than 1 author, entries of more than 1 mss simultaneously or within the same year, and translations are not eligible. Submit paginated ms of 50-70 pages of poetry, with paginated contents page, credits page, and information on previously published books. Include 2 cover sheets: 1 with contract information, 1 without. Mss will not be returned. Guidelines available for SASE or on website. Deadline: September 30. Submissions period begins August 1. Winners announced online in April on the press website. Prize: Publication and $1,000 in addition to royalties.

BARBARA MANDIGO KELLY PEACE POETRY AWARDS

Nuclear Age Peace Foundation, PMB 121, 1187 Coast Village Rd., Suite 1, Santa Barbara CA 93108-2794. (805)965-3443. **Fax:** (805)568-0466. **E-mail:** cwarner@napf.org. **Website:** www.wagingpeace.org; www.peacecontests.org. **Contact:** Carol Warner, poetry award coordinator. The Barbara Mandigo Kelly Peace Poetry Contest was created to encourage poets to explore and illuminate positive visions of peace and the human spirit. The annual contest honors the late Barbara Kelly, a Santa Barbara poet and longtime supporter of peace issues. Awards are given in 3 categories: adult (over 18 years), youth between 12 and 18 years, and youth under 12. All submitted poems should be unpublished. Deadline: July 1 (postmarked) or e-mailed (cwarner@napf.org). Prize: Adult: $1,000; Youth (13-18): $200; Youth (12 and under): $200. Honorable Mentions may also be awarded. Judged by a committee of poets selected by the Nuclear Age Peace Foundation. The foundation reserves the right to publish and distribute the award-winning poems, including honorable mentions.

MILTON KESSLER MEMORIAL PRIZE FOR POETRY

Dept. of English, Binghamton University, Library North Room 1149, Vestal Parkway E., P.O. Box 6000, Binghamton NY 13902-6000. **Website:** www.binghamton.edu/english/creative-writing/binghamton-center-for-writers/binghamton-book-awards/kessler-poetry-awards.html. **Contact:** Maria Mazziotti Gillan, director. Annual award for best previously published book (previous year). Deadline: March 1. 1st place: $1,000.

THE JAMES LAUGHLIN AWARD

The Academy of American Poets, 584 Broadway, Suite 604, New York NY 10012. **Website:** www.poets.org. Offered since 1954, the James Laughlin Award is given to recognize and support a second book of poetry forthcoming in the next calendar year. It is named for the poet and publisher James Laughlin, who founded New Directions in 1936. The winner receives a prize of $5,000, an all-expenses-paid weeklong residency at The Betsy Hotel in Miami Beach, FL, and distribution of the winning book to approximately 1,000 Academy of American Poets members. Deadline: May 15.

LEVIS READING PRIZE

Virginia Commonwealth University, Department of English, Levis Reading Prize, VCU Department of English, 900 Park Avenue, Hibbs Hall, Room 306, P.O. Box 842005, Richmond VA 23284-2005. (804)828-1329. **Fax:** (804)828-8684. **E-mail:** bloomquistjmp@mymail.vcu.edu. **Website:** www.english.vcu.edu/mfa/levis. **Contact:** John-Michael Bloomquist. Offered annually for books of poetry published in the previous year to encourage poets early in their careers. The entry must be the writer's first or second published book of poetry. Previously published books in other genres, or previously published chapbooks or self-published material, do not count as books for this purpose. Entries may be submitted by either author or publisher, and must include three copies of the book (48 pages or more), a cover letter, and a brief biography of the author including previous publications. (Entries from vanity presses are not eligible.) The book must have been published in the previous calendar year. Entrants wishing acknowledgment of receipt must include a self-addressed stamped postcard. Deadline: February 1. Prize: $5,000 and an expense-paid trip to Richmond to present a public reading.

THE RUTH LILLY POETRY PRIZE

Poetry, 61 W. Superior St., Chicago IL 60654. (312)787-7070. **Fax:** (312)787-6650. **E-mail:** editors@poetrymagazine.org. **Website:** www.poetrymagazine.org. Awarded annually, the $100,000 Ruth Lilly Poetry Prize honors a living U.S. poet whose lifetime accomplishments warrant extraordinary recognition. Established in 1986 by Ruth Lilly, the Prize is one of the most prestigious awards given to American poets and is one of the largest literary honors for work in the English language. Deadline: No submissions or nominations considered. Prize: $100,000.

LITERAL LATTÉ POETRY AWARD

Literal Latté, 200 E. 10th St., Suite 240, New York NY 10003. **E-mail:** LitLatte@aol.com. **Website:** www.literal-latte.com. **Contact:** Jenine Gordon Bockman, editor. Offered annually to any writer for unpublished poetry (maximum 2,000 words per poem). All styles welcome. Winners published in *Literal Latté*. Acquires first rights. Deadline: Postmark by July 15. Prizes: 1st Place: $1,000; 2nd Place: $300; 3rd Place: $200. Judged by the editors.

LUMINA POETRY CONTEST

Sarah Lawrence College, Sarah Lawrence College Slonim House 1 Mead Way, Bronxville NY 10708. **Website:** www.luminajournal.com. Poetry competition held once every three years by the Sarah Lawrence College's graduate literary journal. Rotates with a fiction and nonfiction contest. Submit online. Include a 100-word bio at the bottom of cover letter. Submit up to 3 poems, 60 lines maximum per poem. Does not accept previously published material or simultaneous submissions. Deadline: October 15. Prize: 1st Place: $500 and publication; 2nd Place: $250 and publication; 3rd Place: $100 and online publication.

THE MACGUFFIN'S NATIONAL POET HUNT CONTEST

The MacGuffin, The MacGuffin, Schoolcraft College, 18600 Haggerty Rd., Livonia MI 48152. (734)462-4400, ext. 5327. **Fax:** (734)462-4679. **E-mail:** macguffin@schoolcraft.edu. **E-mail:** macguffin@schoolcraft.edu. **Website:** www.schoolcraft.edu/a-z-index/the-macguffin. **Contact:** Gordon Krupsky, managing editor. *The MacGuffin* is a national literary magazine from Schoolcraft College in Livonia, Michigan. An entry consists of three poems. Poems must not be previously published, and must be the original work of the contestant. See website for additional details. The mission of *The MacGuffin* is to encourage, support, and enhance the literary arts in the Schoolcraft College community, the region, the state, and the nation. Deadline: June 3. Submissions period begins April 1. Prize: $500. Judged by Li-Young Lee.

NAOMI LONG MADGETT POETRY AWARD

Broadside Lotus Press, Inc., 8300 East Jefferson Ave., #504, Detroit MI 48214. (313)736-5338. **E-mail:** broadsidelotus@gmail.com. **Website:** www.broadsidelotuspress.org. **Contact:** Gloria House. Offered annually to recognize an unpublished book-length poetry ms by an African American. Guidelines available online. Poems in the ms should total *approximately* 60-90 pages, exclusive of a table of contents or other optional introductory material. Poems that have been published individually in periodicals or anthologies are acceptable. Will not consider an entire collection that has been previously published. Deadline: March 1. Submission period begins January 2. Prize: $500 and publication by Lotus Press.

MAIN STREET RAG'S ANNUAL POETRY BOOK AWARD

Main Street Rag Publishing Company, P.O. Box 690100, Charlotte NC 28227-7001. (704)573-2516. **E-mail:** editor@mainstreetrag.com. **Website:** www.mainstreetrag.com. **Contact:** M. Scott Douglass, publisher/managing editor. Submit 48-84 pages of poetry, no more than 1 poem/page (individual poems may be longer than 1 page). Guidelines available on website. The purpose of this contest is to select manuscripts for publication and offer prize money to the manuscript we feel best represents our label. Deadline: January 31. Prize: 1st Place: $1,200 and 50 copies of book; runners-up are also offered publication. Judged by 1 panel that consists of *MSR* editors, associated editors and college-level instructors, and previous contest winners.

✪ THE MALAHAT REVIEW LONG POEM PRIZE

The Malahat Review, Box 1700 STN CSC, Victoria BC V8W 2Y2 Canada. **E-mail:** malahat@uvic.ca. **Website:** www.malahatreview.ca. **Contact:** Patrick Grace, publicity manager. Long Poem Prize offered in alternate years with the Novella Contest. Open to any writer. Offers 2 awards of $1,000 CAD each for a long poem or cycle (10-20 printed pages). Includes publication in *The Malahat Review* and a 1-year subscription. Open to entries from Canadian, American, and overseas authors. Obtains first world rights. Publication rights after revert to the author. Submissions must be unpublished. No simultaneous submissions. Submit a single poem or cycle of poems, 10-20 published pages (a published page equals 32 lines or less, including breaks between stanzas); no restrictions on subject matter or aesthetic approach. Include separate page with poet's name, address, e-mail, and title; no identifying information on mss pages. Do not include SASE for results; mss will not be returned. Guidelines available on website. Deadline: February 1 (odd-numbered years). Prize: Two $1,000 prizes. Winners published in the summer issue of *The Malahat Review*, announced in summer on website, Facebook page, and in quarterly e-newsletter *Malahat lite*. Judged by 3 recognized poets. Preliminary readings by editorial board.

THE MORTON MARR POETRY PRIZE

Southwest Review, Southern Methodist University, P.O. Box 750374, Dallas TX 75275-0374. (214) 768-1037. **Fax:** (214) 768-1408. **E-mail:** swr@mail.smu.

edu. **Website:** www.smu.edu/southwestreview. **Contact:** Prize coordinator. Annual award for poem(s) by a writer who has not yet published a book of poetry. Submit no more than 6 poems in a "traditional" form (e.g., sonnet, sestine, villanelle, rhymed stanzas, blank verse, et al.). Submissions will not be returned. All entrants will receive a copy of the issue in which the winning poems appear. Deadline: September 30. Prizes: $1,000 for 1st place; $500 for 2nd place; plus publication in the *Southwest Review*.

THE LENORE MARSHALL POETRY PRIZE

The Academy of American Poets, 584 Broadway, Suite 604, New York NY 10012. (212)274-0343. **Fax:** (212)274-9427. **E-mail:** awards@poets.org. **Website:** www.poets.org. Established in 1975, this $25,000 award recognizes the most outstanding book of poetry published in the United States in the previous calendar year. The prize includes distribution of the winning book hundreds of Academy of American Poets members. Deadline: May 15. Prize: $25,000.

MARSH HAWK PRESS POETRY PRIZE

Marsh Hawk Press, P.O. Box 206, East Rockaway NY 11518-0206. **E-mail:** marshhawkpress1@aol.com. **Website:** www.MarshHawkPress.org. **Contact:** Prize Director. The Marsh Hawk Press Poetry Prize offers $1,000, plus publication of a book-length ms. Additionally, The Robert Creeley Poetry Prize and The Rochelle Ratner Poetry Award, both cash prizes, go to the runners-up. Submissions must be unpublished as a collection, but individual poems may have been previously published elsewhere. Submit 48-84 pages of original poetry in any style in English, typed single-spaced, and paginated. (Longer mss will be considered if the press is queried before submission.) Contest mss may be submitted by electronic upload. See website for more information. If submitting via Post Office mail, the ms must be bound with a spring clip. Include 2 title pages: 1 with ms title, poet's name, and contact information only; 1 with ms title only (poet's name must not appear anywhere in the ms). Also include table of contents and acknowledgments page. Include SASE for results only; ms will not be returned. Guidelines available on website. Deadline: April 30. Judged by Meena Alexander in 2017.

KATHLEEN MCCLUNG SONNET PRIZE CATEGORY

Soul-Making Keats Literary Competition, The Webhallow House, 1544 Sweetwood Dr., Broadmoor Village CA 94015-2029. **E-mail:** soulkeats@mail.com. **Website:** www.soulmakingcontest.us. **Contact:** Eileen Malone. Call for Shakespearean and Petrarchan sonnets on the theme of the "beloved." Previously published material is accepted. Indicate category on cover page and on identifying 3x5 card. Open annually to any writer. Deadline: November 30. Prize:1st Place: $100; 2nd Place: $50; 3rd Place: $25.

THE KATHRYN A. MORTON PRIZE IN POETRY

Sarabande Books, Inc., 822 E. Market St., Louisville KY 40206. (502)458-4028. **E-mail:** info@sarabandebooks.org. **Website:** www.sarabandebooks.org. **Contact:** Sarah Gorham, editor-in-chief. The Kathryn A. Morton Prize in Poetry is awarded annually to a book-length ms (at least 48 pages). All finalists are considered for publication. Competition receives approximately 1,400 entries. Guidelines available online. Mss can be submitted online or via postal mail. Deadline: February 15. Submissions period begins January 1. Prize: $2,000, publication, and a standard royalty contract.

SHEILA MARGARET MOTTON PRIZE

New England Poetry Club, 2 Farrar St., Cambridge MA 02138. (617)744-6034. **E-mail:** info@nepoetryclub.org. **Website:** www.nepoetryclub.org. **Contact:** Audrey Kalajin. Awarded for a book of poems published in the last 2 years. Send 2 copies of book. Deadline: May 31. Prize: $500. Judged by well-known poets and sometimes winners of previous NEPC contests.

ERIKA MUMFORD PRIZE

New England Poetry Club, 376 School St., Watertown MA 02472. **E-mail:** contests@nepoetryclub.org. **Website:** www.nepoetryclub.org/contests.htm. **Contact:** Audrey Kalajin. Offered annually for a poem in any form about foreign culture or travel. Funded by Erika Mumford's family and friends. Contest open to members and nonmembers. Deadline: May 31. Prize: $250. Judged by well-known poets and sometimes winners of previous NEPC contests.

🟢 NATIONAL POETRY COMPETITION

The Poetry Society, 22 Betterton St., London WC2H 9BX United Kingdom. 020 7420 9880. **E-mail:** info@poetrysociety.org.uk. **Website:** www.poetrysociety.org.uk. **Contact:** Competition organizer. The Poetry Society was founded in 1909 to promote "a more general recognition and appreciation of poetry". Since then, it has grown into one of Britain's most dynamic arts organizations, representing British poetry both nationally and internationally. Today it has nearly 4000 members worldwide and publishes *The Poetry Review*. With innovative education and commissioning programs and a packed calendar of performances, readings and competitions, The Poetry Society champions poetry for all ages. Open to anyone aged 17 or over. Submissions must be unpublished (poems posted on websites are considered published). Submit original poems in English, on any subject, no more than 40 lines/poem, typed on 1 side only of A4 paper, double- or single-spaced. Each poem must be titled. No identifying information on poems. Do not staple pages. Accepts online submissions; full details available on the National Poetry Competition pages on the Poetry Society website. Entry form (required) available for A5 SAE (1 entry form covers multiple entries, may be photocopied). Include stamped SAE for notification of receipt of postal entries (confirmation of online entries will be e-mailed at time of submission); poems will not be returned. Guidelines available on website. Deadline: October 31. 1st Prize: £5,000; 2nd Prize: £2,000; 3rd Prize: £1,000; plus 7 commendations of £200 each. Winners will be published in *The Poetry Review*, and on the Poetry Society website; the top 3 winners will receive a year's free membership of The Poetry Society.

THE NATIONAL POETRY REVIEW BOOK PRIZE

The National Poetry Review, P.O. Box 2080, Aptos CA 95001-2080. **E-mail:** editor@nationalpoetryreview. com. **Website:** www.nationalpoetryreview.com; www. tnprpress.com. **Contact:** C.J. Sage, editor. Submit 45-80 pages of poetry via e-mail and PayPal (strongly preferred) or via mail. Include cover letter with bio and acknowledgments page. Include e-mail address (no SASE; mss will be recycled). Guidelines available on website. Deadline: June 30 (postmark). Prize: $1,000 plus publication and 15 copies of the book.

NATIONAL WRITERS ASSOCIATION POETRY CONTEST

The National Writers Association, 10940 S. Parker Rd. #508, Parker CO 80134. **E-mail:** natlwritersassn@hotmail.com. **Website:** www.nationalwriters.com. **Contact:** Sandy Whelchel, director. Annual contest to encourage the writing of poetry, an important form of individual expression but with a limited commercial market. Deadline: October 1. Prize: 1st Place: $100; 2nd Place: $50; 3rd Place: $25.

THE PABLO NERUDA PRIZE FOR POETRY

Nimrod International Journal, 800 S. Tucker Dr., Tulsa OK 74104. (918)631-3080. **Fax:** (918)631-3033. **E-mail:** nimrod@utulsa.edu. **Website:** www.utulsa. edu/nimrod. **Contact:** Eilis O'Neal. Annual award to discover new writers of vigor and talent. Open to US residents only. Submissions must be unpublished. Work must be in English or translated by original author. Submit 3-10 pages of poetry (1 long poem or several short poems). Poet's name must not appear on ms. Include cover sheet with poem title(s), poet's name, address, phone and fax numbers, and e-mail address (poet must have a US address by October of contest year to enter). Mark "Contest Entry" on submission envelope and cover sheet. Include SASE for results only; mss will not be returned. Guidelines available for #10 SASE or on website. Deadline: April 30. Prizes: 1st Place: $2,000 and publication; 2nd Place: $1,000 and publication. Judged by the *Nimrod* editors (finalists). A recognized author selects the winners.

THE NEW ISSUES POETRY PRIZE

New Issues Poetry & Prose, New Issues Poetry & Prose, Department of English, Western Michigan University, 1903 W. Michigan Ave., Kalamazoo MI 49008-5463. **E-mail:** new-issues@wmich.edu. **Website:** www.wmich.edu/newissues. Offered annually for publication of a first book of poems by a poet writing in English who has not previously published a full-length collection of poems in an edition of 500 or more copies. *New Issues Poetry & Prose* obtains rights for first publication. Book is copyrighted in author's name. Guidelines for SASE or online. Additional mss will be considered from those submitted to the competition for publication. Considers simultaneous submissions, but *New Issues* must be notified of acceptance elsewhere. Submit ms of at least 40 pages, typed, single-spaced preferred. Clean photocopies acceptable. Do not bind; use manila folder or metal clasp. Include cover page with poet's name, address, phone number, and title of the ms. Also include brief bio and acknowledgments page. Submissions are also welcome through the online submission manager: www.newissuespoetryprose.submittable.com. For hardcopy submissions only, you may include SASP for notification of receipt of ms and SASE for results only; no mss will be returned. Winning manuscript will be named in May and published in the next spring. Deadline: November 30. Prize: $2,000, plus publication of a book-length ms. A national judge selects the prize winner and recommends other manuscripts. The editors decide on the other books considering the judge's recommendation, but are not bound by it. 2017 judge: David Rivard.

NEW LETTERS PRIZE FOR POETRY

New Letters Awards for Writers, UMKC, University House, 5101 Rockhill Rd., Kansas City MO 64110-2499. 816-235-1168. **E-mail:** newletters@umkc.edu. **Website:** www.newletters.org. The annual New Letters Poetry Prize awards $1,500 and publication in *New Letters* (see separate listing in Magazines/Journals) to the best group of 3-6 poems. All entries will be considered for publication in *New Letters*. Submissions must be unpublished. Considers simultaneous submissions with notification upon acceptance elsewhere. Accepts multiple entries with separate fee for each. Submit up to 6 poems (need not be related). Include 2 cover sheets: 1 with poet's name, address, e-mail, phone number, prize category (poetry), and poem title(s); the second with category and poem title(s) only. No identifying information on ms pages. Accepts electronic submissions. Include SASE for notification of receipt of ms and entry number, and SASE for results only (send only 1 envelope if submitting multiple entries); mss will not be returned. Guidelines available by SASE or on website. Current students and employees of the University of Missouri-Kansas City, and current volunteer members of the *New Letters* and BkMk Press staffs, are not eligible. Deadline: May 18 (postmarked). Prize: $1,500 and publication.

NFSPS POETRY CONVENTION MADNESS CONTEST

2029 103rd Ave. NW, Coon Rapids MN 55433. **E-mail:** pwilliamstein@yahoo.com; schambersmediator@yahoo.com. **Website:** www.mnpoets.com. **Contact:** Peter Stein; Sue Chambers. Enter to win your way to the NFSPS National Poetry Convention in Chaska, MN, June 9th-13th. For more details about the event, visit www.nfspsconvention.com. Must be original work of the contestant. Deadline: January 31. Prizes: 1st Place: Hotel Lodging at Oak Ridge Convention Center for four nights, June 9th-12th. 2nd Place: Meals payed for during the course of the convention. 3rd Place: Registration to the Convention. 1st-3rd Honorable Mentions: Subscription to Poem by Post for one year.

THE NIGHTBOAT POETRY PRIZE

Nightboat Books, P.O. Box 10, Callicoon NY 12723. **E-mail:** info@nightboat.org. **Website:** www.nightboat.org. **Contact:** Stephen Motika. Annual contest for previously unpublished collection of poetry (48-90 pages). Deadline: November 15. 1st place: $1,000, plus publication and 25 copies of published book.

OHIO POETRY DAY CONTESTS

Dept. of English, Heidelberg College, 310 East Market, Tiffin OH 44883. **Website:** ohiopoetryday.blogspot.com. **Contact:** Bill Reyer, Contest Chair. Several poetry categories open to poets from Ohio and out-of-state. Prizes range $5-100. Deadline: May 31.

GUY OWEN AWARD

Southern Poetry Review, Department of Languages, Literature, and Philosophy, Armstrong Atlantic State University, 11935 Abercorn St., Savannah GA 31419-1997. (912)344-3196. **E-mail:** editor@southernpoetryreview.org. **Website:** www.southernpoetryreview.org. **Contact:** Tony Morris, associate editor. The annual Guy Owen Prize offers $1,000 and publication in *Southern Poetry Review* to the winning poem selected by a distinguished poet. All entries will be considered for publication. Submissions must be unpublished. "We consider work published online or posted there as previously published." Considers simultaneous submissions if indicated as such. Submit 3-5 poems (10 pages maximum). Include cover sheet with poet's name and contact information; no identifying information on ms pages. No e-mail or disk submissions. Include SASE for results only; mss will not be returned. Guidelines available in magazine, for SASE, by e-mail, or on website. Deadline: May 31 (postmarked). Open to submissions March 1.

PANGAEA PRIZE

The Poet's Billow, 6135 Avon St, Portage MI 49024. **E-mail:** thepoetsbillow@gmail.com. **Website:** http://thepoetsbillow.org. **Contact:** Robert Evory. Annual award open to any writer to recognize the best series of poems, ranging between two and up to seven poems in a group. Finalists with strong work will also be published. Submissions must be previously unpublished. Please submit online. Deadline: May 1. Prize: $100. The winning poem will be published and displayed in The Poet's Billow Literary Art Gallery and nominated for a Pushcart Prize. If the poet qualifies, the poem will also be submitted to The Best New Poets anthology. Judged by the editors, and, occasionally, a guest judge.

THE PATERSON POETRY PRIZE

The Poetry Center at Passaic County Community College, One College Blvd., Paterson NJ 07505. (973)684-6555. **Fax:** (973)523-6085. **E-mail:** mgillan@pccc.edu. **Website:** www.pccc.edu/poetry. **Contact:** Maria Mazziotti Gillan, executive director. The Paterson Poetry Prize offers an annual award for the strongest book of poems (48 or more pages) published in the previous year. The winner will be asked to participate in an awards ceremony and to give a reading at The Poetry Center. Minimum press run: 500 copies. Publishers may submit more than 1 title for prize consideration; 3 copies of each book must be submitted. Include SASE for results; books will not be returned (all entries will be donated to The Poetry Center Library). Guidelines and application form (required) available for SASE or on website. Deadline: February 1. Prize: $1,000.

PAVEMENT SAW PRESS CHAPBOOK AWARD

321 Empire St., Montpelier OH 43543-1301. **E-mail:** info@pavementsaw.org. **E-mail:** editor@pavement-saw.org. **Website:** www.pavementsaw.org. **Contact:** David Baratier, editor. Pavement Saw Press has been publishing steadily since the fall of 1993. Each year since 1999, they have published at least 4 full-length paperback poetry collections, with some printed in library edition hard covers, 1 chapbook, and a yearly literary journal anthology. They specialize in finding authors who have been widely published in literary journals but have not published a chapbook or full-length book. Submit up to 32 pages of poetry. Include signed cover letter with poet's name, address, phone number, e-mail, publication credits, a brief biography, and ms title. Also include 2 cover sheets: 1 with poet's contact information and ms title, 1 with the ms title only. Do not put name on mss pages except for first title page. No mss will be returned. Deadline: December 31 (postmark). Prize: Chapbook Award offers $500, publication, and 40 author copies.

JEAN PEDRICK PRIZE

New England Poetry Club, 2 Farrar St., Cambridge MA 02138. **E-mail:** contests@nepoetryclub.org. **Website:** www.nepoetryclub.org. **Contact:** Audrey Kalajin. Prize for a chapbook of poems published in the last two years. Send 2 copies of the chapbook. Deadline:

May 31. Prize: $100. Judged by well-known poets and sometimes winners of previous NEPC contests.

PEN/JOYCE OSTERWEIL AWARD FOR POETRY

PEN America, 588 Broadway, Suite 303, New York NY 10012. **E-mail:** awards@pen.org. **Website:** www.pen.org/awards. **Contact:** Arielle Anema, Literary Awards Coordinator. *Candidates may only be nominated by members of PEN.* This award recognizes the high literary character of the published work to date of a new and emerging American poet of any age, and the promise of further literary achievement. Nominated writer may not have published more than 1 book of poetry. Offered in odd-numbered years and alternates with the PEN/Voelcker Award for Poetry. Electronic letters of nomination will be requested during open submissions season. Submissions will be accepted during the summer of even-numbered year. Visit PEN.org/awards for up-to-date information on deadlines. Prize: $5,000. Judged by a panel of 3 judges selected by the PEN Awards Committee.

PENNSYLVANIA POETRY SOCIETY ANNUAL CONTESTS

5 Coachmans Court, Norwalk CT 06850. **Website:** nfsps.com/pa. **Contact:** Colleen Yarusavage. Pennsylvania Poetry Society offers several categories of poetry contests with a range of prizes from $10-100. Deadline: January 15.

PEN/VOELCKER AWARD FOR POETRY

PEN America, 588 Broadway, Suite 303, New York NY 10012. **E-mail:** awards@pen.org. **Website:** www.pen.org/awards. **Contact:** Arielle Anema, Literary Awards Coordinator. The PEN/Voelcker Award for Poetry, established by a bequest from Hunce Voelcker, this award is given to a poet whose distinguished and growing body of work to date represents a notable and accomplished presence in American literature. The poet honored by the award is one for whom the exceptional promise seen in earlier work has been fulfilled, and who continues to mature with each successive volume of poetry. The award is given in even-numbered years and carries a stipend of $5,000. Please note that submissions will only be accepted from Professional Members of PEN and that it is understood that all nominations made for the PEN/Voelcker Award supplement internal nominations made by the panel of judges. PEN Members are asked to submit a letter of nomination through an online submissions form. Deadline: Nominations from PEN Members will be accepted during the summer of each odd-numbered year. Visit PEN.org/awards for up-to-date information on deadlines. Prize: $5,000. Judged by a panel of 3 poets or other writers chosen by the PEN Literary Awards Committee.

PERUGIA PRESS PRIZE

Perugia Press, P.O. Box 60364, Florence MA 01062. **Website:** www.perugiapress.com. **Contact:** Susan Kan. Submissions must be unpublished as a collection, but individual poems may have been previously published in journals, chapbooks, and anthologies. Considers simultaneous submissions if notified of acceptance elsewhere. Follow online guidelines carefully. Electronic submissions available through website. No translations or self-published books. Multiple submissions accepted if accompanied by separate entry fee for each. Use USPS or electronic submission, not FedEx or UPS. Winner announced by April 1 by e-mail or SASE (if included with entry). The Perugia Press Prize is for a first or second poetry book by a woman. Poet must have no more than 1 previously published book of poems (chapbooks don't count). Deadline: November 15. Open to submissions on August 1. Prize: $1,000 and publication. Judged by panel of Perugia authors, booksellers, scholars, etc.

THE RICHARD PETERSON POETRY PRIZE

Crab Orchard Review, Dept. of English, Mail Code 4503, Faner Hall 2380, Southern Illinois University at Carbondale, 1000 Faner Drive, Carbondale IL 62901. (618)453-6833. **Fax:** (618)453-8224. **E-mail:** jtribble@siu.edu. **Website:** www.craborchardreview.siu. edu. **Contact:** Jon Tribble, managing editor. Annual award for unpublished poetry. Entries should consist of 1 poem up to 5 pages in length. *Crab Orchard Review* acquires first North American serial rights to all submitted work. One winner and at least 2 finalists will be chosen. Entries should consist of 1 poem up to 5 pages in length. All submissions must be made through Submittable. Submissions must be unpublished original work, written in English by a U.S. citizen, permanent resident, or person who has DACA/TPS status (current students and employees at Southern Illinois University Carbondale are not eligible). See Submittable guidelines online for complete formatting instructions. The author's name should not appear on any page of the entry. Results announced by end of August. Deadline: May 31. Submission pe-

riod begins March 21. Prize: $1,250 plus publication. Judged by the editors of *Crab Orchard Review*.

TIPS "Carefully read directions for entering and follow them exactly. Send us your best work. Note that simultaneous submissions are accepted for this prize, but the winning entry must NOT be accepted elsewhere. All submissions should be made through Submittable: https://craborchardreview.submittable.com/submit."

THE PLEIADES PRESS EDITORS PRIZE FOR POETRY

Pleiades Press, Pleiades Press, Dept of English, Martin 336, University of Central Missouri, Warrensburg MO 64093. (660)543-8106. **E-mail:** pleiades@ucmo.edu. **Website:** www.ucmo.edu/pleiades/. The annual Pleiades Press Editors Prize for Poetry is open to all American writers, regardless of previous publication. Submission must be unpublished as a collection, but individual poems may have been previously published elsewhere. Submit at least 48 pages of poetry (one copy). Include 2 cover sheets: one with ms title, poet's name, address, and phone number; the second with ms title only. Also include acknowledgments page for previously published poems. Guidelines online. Deadline: May 11. Prize: $2,000 and the winning collection will be published in paperback and nationally distributed.

THE POETRY CENTER BOOK AWARD

The Poetry Center, San Francisco State University, 1600 Holloway Ave., San Francisco CA 94132. (415)338-2227. **Fax:** (415)338-0966. **E-mail:** poetry@sfsu.edu. **Website:** www.sfsu.edu/~poetry. Offered annually for books of poetry and chapbooks, published in year of the prize. "Prize given for an extraordinary book of American poetry written in English." Please include a cover letter noting author name, book title(s), name of person issuing check, and check number. Will not consider anthologies or translations. Deadline: January 31 for books published and copywrited in the previous year. 1st place: $500 and an invitation to read in the Poetry Center Reading Series.

POETRY SOCIETY OF AMERICA AWARDS

15 Gramercy Park, New York NY 10003. **E-mail:** psa@poetrysociety.org. **Website:** www.poetrysociety.org. Offers 7 categories of poetry prizes between $250-2,500. 5 categories are open to PSA members only. Free entry for members; $15 for non-members. Submit between October 1-December 22.

POETS & PATRONS ANNUAL CHICAGOLAND POETRY CONTEST

Sponsored by Poets & Patrons of Chicago, 416 Gierz St., Downers Grove IL 60515. **E-mail:** eatonb1016@aol.com. **Website:** www.poetsandpatrons.net. **Contact:** Barbara Eaton, director. Annual contest for unpublished poetry. Guidelines available for self-addressed, stamped envelope. The purpose of the contest is to encourage the crafting of poetry. Deadline: September 1. Prize: 1st Place: $45; 2nd Place: $20; 3rd Place: $10 cash. Poet retains rights. Judged by out-of-state professionals.

POETS OUT LOUD PRIZE

Poets Out Loud, Fordham University at Lincoln Center, 113 W. 60th St., Room 924-I, New York NY 10023. (212)636-6792. **Fax:** (212)636-7153. **E-mail:** pol@fordham.edu. **Website:** www.fordham.edu/pol. Annual competition for an unpublished, full-length poetry ms (50-80 pages). Deadline: November 1. Prize: $1,000, book publication, and book launch in POL reading series.

FELIX POLLAK PRIZE IN POETRY

University of Wisconsin Press, 1930 Monroe St., 3rd Floor, Madison WI 53711. (608)263-1110. **Fax:** (608)263-1120. **E-mail:** uwiscpress@wisc.edu. **Website:** uwpress.wisc.edu. The Felix Pollak Prize in Poetry is awarded annually to the best book-length ms of original poetry submitted in an open competition. The award is administered by the University of Wisconsin–Madison English department, and the winner is chosen by a nationally recognized poet. The resulting book is published by the University of Wisconsin Press. Submissions must be unpublished as a collection, but individual poems may have been published elsewhere (publication must be acknowledged). Considers simultaneous submissions if notified of selection elsewhere. Submit 50-80 unbound ms pages, typed single-spaced (with double spaces between stanzas). Clean photocopies are acceptable. Include 1 title page with poet's name, address, and telephone number; 1 title page with title only. No translations. Complete guidelines available online. Deadline: September 15. Prize: $1,000 cash prize, plus publication.

A. POULIN, JR. POETRY PRIZE

BOA Editions, Ltd., BOA Editions, Ltd., P.O. Box 30971, Rochester NY 14603. **E-mail:** fisher@boaeditions.org. **Website:** www.boaeditions.org. The A. Poulin, Jr. Poetry Prize is awarded to honor a poet's first book, while also honoring the late founder of BOA Editions, Ltd., a not-for-profit publishing house of poetry, poetry in translation, and short fiction. Published books in other genres do not disqualify contestants from entering this contest. Send by first class or priority mail (recommended). Entrants must be a citizen or legal resident of the US. Poets who are at least 18 years of age, and who have yet to publish a full-length book collection of poetry, are eligible. Translations are not eligible. Individual poems may have been previously published in magazines, journals, anthologies, chapbooks of 32 pages or less, or self-published books of 46 pages or less, but must be submitted in ms form. Submit 48-100 pages of poetry, paginated consecutively, typed or computer-generated in 11 point font. Bind with spring clip (no paperclips). Include cover/title page with poet's name, address, telephone number, and e-mail address. Also include the table of contents, list of acknowledgments, and entry form (available for download on website). Multiple entries accepted with separate entry fee for each. No e-mail submissions. Deadline: November 30. Open to submissions on August 1. Prize: Awards $1,500 honorarium and book publication in the A. Poulin, Jr. New Poets of America Series.

PRESS 53 AWARD FOR POETRY

Press 53, 560 N. Trade St., Suite 103, Winston-Salem NC 27101. (336)770-5353. **E-mail:** kevin@press53.com. **Website:** www.press53.com. **Contact:** Kevin Morgan Watson, publisher. Awarded to an outstanding, unpublished collection of poetry. Details and guidelines available online. Deadline: July 31. Submission period begins April 1. Winner and finalists announced on by November 1. Publication in April. Prize: Publication of winning poetry collection as a Tom Lombardo Poetry Selection, $1,000 cash advance, 1/4-page color ad in Poets & Writers magazine, and 10 copies of the book. Judged by Press 53 poetry series editor Tom Lombardo.

THE PSA NATIONAL CHAPBOOK FELLOWSHIPS

Poetry Society of America, 15 Gramercy Park, New York NY 10003. (212)254-9628. **Fax:** (212)673-2352. **Website:** www.poetrysociety.org. Open to any US citizen or anyone currently living within the US who has not published a full-length poetry collection. Charges $12 entry fee. Winner receives $1,000 and welcomed as guest for a month-long artist's residency at PLAYA and invited to teach a single class at Purchase College for $1,000 under the sponsorshp of the Royal and Shirley Durst Chair in Literature. Deadline: December 22.

RATTLE POETRY PRIZE

RATTLE, 12411 Ventura Blvd., Studio City CA 91604. (818) 505-6777. **E-mail:** tim@rattle.com. **Website:** www.rattle.com. **Contact:** Timothy Green, editor. *Rattle's* mission is to promote the practice of poetry. To enter, purchase a one-year subscription to *Rattle* at the regular $20 rate. Open to writers, worldwide; poems must be written in English. No previously published works, or works accepted for publication elsewhere. No simultaneous submissions are allowed. Send up to 4 poems per entry. "More than anything, our goal is to promote a community of active poets." Deadline: July 15. Prize: One $10,000 winner and ten $200 finalists will be selected in a blind review by the editors of *Rattle* and printed in the Winter issue; one $1,000 Readers' Choice Award will then be chosen from among the finalists by subscriber and entrant vote. Judged by the editors of *Rattle.*

RHINO FOUNDERS' PRIZE

RHINO, The Poetry Forum, P.O. Box 591, Evanston IL 60204. **E-mail:** editors@rhinopoetry.org. **Website:** rhinopoetry.org. **Contact:** Editors. Send best unpublished poetry (3-5 pages). Visit website for previous winners and more information. Submit online or by mail. Include a cover letter listing your name, address, e-mail, and/or telephone number, titles of poems, how you learned about RHINO, and fee. Mss will not be returned. Deadline: October 31. Open to submissions on September 1. Prize: $500, publication, featured on website, and nominated for a Pushcart Prize. Two runners-ups will receive $50, publication, and will be featured on website. Occasionally nominates runner-up for a Pushcart Prize.

TIPS "RHINO values original voice, musicality, fresh language, and respect for the reader."

ROANOKE-CHOWAN POETRY AWARD

The North Carolina Literary & Historical Assoc., 4610 Mail Service Center, Raleigh NC 27699-4610. (919)807-7290. **Fax:** (919)733-8807. **E-mail:** michael. hill@ncdcr.gov. **Website:** litandhist.ncdcr.gov. **Contact:** Michael Hill, awards coordinator. Offers annual award for an original volume of poetry published during the 12 months ending June 30 of the year for which the award is given. Open to authors who have main-tained legal or physical residence, or a combination of both, in North Carolina for the 3 years preceding the close of the contest period. Submit 3 copies of each entry. Guidelines available for SASE or by fax or e-mail. Winner announced October 15. Deadline: July 15.

LORI RUDNITSKY FIRST BOOK PRIZE

Persea Books, P.O. Box 1388, Columbia MO 65205. **Website:** www.perseabooks.com. "This annual competition sponsors the publication of a poetry collection (at least 40 pages) by an American woman poet who has yet to publish a full-length book of poems." Deadline: October 31. Prize: $1,000, plus publication of book. In addition, the winner receives the option of an all-expenses-paid residency at the Civitella Ranieri Center, a renowned artists retreat housed in a 15th-century castle in Umbertide, Italy.

VERN RUTSALA POETRY PRIZE

P.O. Box 610, Corvallis OR 97339. (541)752-0075. **E-mail:** michael@cloudbankbooks.com. **Website:** http://www.cloudbankbooks.com/Contest.html. **Contact:** Michael Malan. For contest submissions, the writer's name, address, e-mail, and the titles of the poems pieces being submitted should be typed on a cover sheet only, not on the pages of poems. No electronic submissions. Deadline: January 2. Prize: $1,000 plus publication of full-length ms. Judged by Dennis Schmitz.

BENJAMIN SALTMAN POETRY AWARD

Red Hen Press, P.O. Box 40820, Pasadena CA 91114. (818)831-0649. **Fax:** (818)831-6659. **E-mail:** productioncoordinator@redhen.org. **Website:** www.redhen. org. Offered annually for unpublished work to publish a winning book of poetry. Open to any writer. Name on cover sheet only, 48 page minimum. Send SASE for notification. Deadline: August 31. 1st place: $3,000 and publication.

MAY SARTON AWARD

New England Poetry Club, 654 Green St., No. 2, Cambridge MA 02139. (617)744-6034. **E-mail:** contests@ nepoetryclub.org. **Website:** www.nepoetryclub.org. **Contact:** NEPC contest coordinator. "Given intermittently to a poet whose work is an inspiration to other poets. Recipients are chosen by the board." "Contest open to members and nonmembers. Poems should be typed and submitted in duplicate with author's name, address, phone, and e-mail address of writer on only 1 copy. (Judges receive copies without names.) Copy only. Label poems with contest name. Entries should be sent by regular mail only. Special delivery or signature required mail will be returned by the post office. Entries should be original, unpublished poems in English. No poem should be entered in more than 1 contest, nor have won a previous contest. No entries will be returned. NEPC will not engage in correspondence regarding poems or contest decisions." To recognize emerging poets of exceptional promise and distinguished achievement. Established to honor the memory of longtime Academy Fellow May Sarton, a poet, novelist, and teacher who during her career encouraged the work of young poets. Deadline: May 31. Prize: $250. Judges are well-known poets and sometimes winners of previous NEPC contests.

SCREAMINMAMAS MOTHER'S DAY POETRY CONTEST

1911 Cleveland St., Hollywood FL 33020. **E-mail:** screaminmamas@gmail.com. **Website:** www.screaminmamas.com/contests. **Contact:** Darlene Pistocchi, editor/managing director. "What does it mean to be a mom? There is so much to being a mom—get deep, get creative! We challenge you to explore different types of poetry: descriptive, reflective, narrative, lyric, sonnet, ballad, limerick. you can even go epic!" Open only to moms. Deadline: December 31. Prize: complementary subscription to magazine, publication.

SLAPERING HOL PRESS CHAPBOOK COMPETITION

The Hudson Valley Writers' Center, 300 Riverside Dr., Sleepy Hollow NY 10591. (914)332-5953. **Fax:** (914)332-4825. **E-mail:** info@writerscenter.org. **Website:** www.writerscenter.org. **Contact:** Margo Stever, editor. The annual competition is open to poets who have not published a book or chapbook, though individual poems may have already appeared. Manuscripts may be either a collection of poems or one long poem and should be a minimum of 16 pages and a maximum of 20 pages (not including the title page or table of contents). Purpose is to provide publishing opportunities for emerging poets. Deadline: June 15. Prize: $1,000, publication of chapbook, 20 copies of chapbook, and a reading at The Hudson Valley Writers' Center.

SLIPSTREAM ANNUAL POETRY CHAPBOOK CONTEST

Slipstream, Slipstream Poetry Contest, Dept. W-1, P.O. Box 2071, Niagara Falls NY 14301. **E-mail:** editors@slipstreampress.org. **Website:** www.slipstreampress.org. **Contact:** Dan Sicoli, co-editor. *Slipstream Magazine* is a yearly anthology of some of the best poetry you'll find today in the American small press. Send up to 40 pages of poetry: any style, format, or theme (or no theme). Send only copies of your poems, not originals. Manuscripts will no longer be returned. See website for specific details. Offered annually to help promote a poet whose work is often overlooked or ignored. Open to any writer. Deadline: December 1. Prize: $1,000, plus 50 professionally-printed copies of your book.

HELEN C. SMITH MEMORIAL AWARD FOR BEST BOOK OF POETRY

The Texas Institute of Letters, P.O. Box 609, Round Rock TX 78680. **E-mail:** tilsecretary@yahoo.com. **Website:** http://texasinstituteofletters.org/. Offered annually for the best book of poems published January 1-December 31 of previous year. Poet must have been born in Texas, have lived in the state at some time for at least 2 consecutive years, or the subject matter must be associated with the state. See website for submission details and information. Deadline: January 10. Prize: $1,200.

THE RICHARD SNYDER MEMORIAL PUBLICATION PRIZE

Ashland Poetry Press, 401 College Ave., Ashland University, Ashland OH 44805. **E-mail:** app@ashland.edu. **Website:** www.ashlandpoetrypress.com. **Contact:** Cassandra Brown, managing editor. Submissions must be unpublished in book form. Considers simultaneous submissions. Submit 50-96 pages of poetry. Competition receives 400+ entries/year. Winners will be announced in *Writer's Chronicle* and *Poets & Writers*. Copies of winning books available from Small Press Distribution and directly from the Ashland University Bookstore online. The Ashland Poetry Press publishes 2-4 books of poetry/year. Deadline: April 1. Prize: $1,000 plus book publication. Judged by Elizabeth Spires in 2016.

SOCIETY OF CLASSICAL POETS POETRY COMPETITION

The Society of Classical Poets, 11 Heather Ln., Mount Hope NY 10940. **E-mail:** submissions@classicalpoets.org. **Website:** www.classicalpoets.org. **Contact:** Evan Mantyk, president. Annual competition for a group of poems that address one or more of the following themes: beauty, Falun Dafa, great culture, or humor.

Poems must incorporate meter and rhyme. All entries are considered for publication. Submit 3-5 poems of up to 50 lines each. Deadline: December 31. Prize: $500. Judged by Evan Mantyk, the society's president.

THE SOW'S EAR CHAPBOOK COMPETITION

The Sow's Ear Review, 1748 Cave Ridge Rd., Mount Jackson VA 22842. (540)955-3955. **E-mail:** sepoetryreview@gmail.com. **Website:** www.sowsearpoetry.org. **Contact:** Sarah Kohrs, managing editor. *The Sow's Ear Poetry Review* sponsors an annual chapbook competition. Open to adults. Open to adults. Send 22-26 pages of poetry plus a title page and a table of contents, all without your name. On a separate sheet list chapbook title, your name, address, phone number, e-mail address if available, and publication credits for submitted poems, if any. No length limit on poems, but no more than one poem on a page. Simultaneous submission is allowed, but if your chapbook is accepted elsewhere, you must withdraw promptly from our competition. Poems previously published are acceptable if you hold publication rights. Send SASE or e-mail address for notification. Entries will not be returned. To submit online, visit our website. Deadline: May 1 (postmark). Prize: Offers $1,000, publication as the spring issue of the magazine, 25 author's copies, and distribution to subscribers.

THE SOW'S EAR POETRY COMPETITION

The Sow's Ear Poetry Review, 1748 Cave Ridge Road, Mount Jackson VA 22842. **E-mail:** SEPoetryReview@gmail.com. **Website:** www.sowsearpoetry.org. **Contact:** Sarah Kohrs, managing editor. Open to adults. Send unpublished poems to the address above. Please do not put your name on poems. Include a separate sheet with poem titles, name, address, phone, and e-mail address if available, or a SASE for notification of results. No length limit on poems. Simultaneous submission acceptable (checks with finalists before sending to final judge). Send poems in September or October. Deadline: November 1. Prize: $1,000, publication, and the option of publication for approximately 20 finalists.

THE EDWARD STANLEY AWARD

Prairie Schooner, 123 Andrews Hall, P.O. Box 880334, Lincoln NE 68588-0334. (402)472-0911. **Fax:** (402)472-9771. **E-mail:** prairieschooner@unl.edu. **Website:** www.prairieschooner.unl.edu. **Contact:** Editor in Chief. Offered annually for poetry published in *Prairie Schooner* in the previous year. Prize: $1,000.

STEVENS POETRY MANUSCRIPT CONTEST

NFSPS Stevens Poetry Manuscript Competition, 499 Falcon Ridge Way, Bolingbrook IL 60440. **E-mail:** stevens.nfsps@gmail.com. **Website:** www.nfsps.org. **Contact:** Wilda Morris, Chair. National Federation of State Poetry Societies (NFSPS) offers annual award of $1,000, publication of ms, and 50 author's copies for the winning poetry manuscript by a single author. Submit 48-70 pages of poetry by a single author, typewritten, or computer printed. No illustrations. No author identification in the manuscript. No more than one poem per page. May include previously published poems (acknowledgements on separate sheet). Simultaenous and multiple submissions permitted. Deadline: Fall, varies from year to year. For 2016, November 30, Submissions open November 1. Prize: $1,000, publication and 50 copies of the book.

THE RUTH STONE POETRY PRIZE

Vermont College, 36 College St., Montpelier VT 05602. (802)828-8517. **E-mail:** hungermtn@vcfa.edu. **Website:** www.hungermtn.org. **Contact:** Samantha Kolber, managing editor. The Ruth Stone Poetry Prize is an annual poetry contest. Enter up to 3 original, unpublished poems. Do not include name or address on submissions; entries are read blind. Accepts submissions online or via postal mail. Deadline: March 1. Prize: One first place winner receives $1,000 and publication on Hunger Mountain online. Two honorable mentions receive $100 and publication on Hunger Mountain online. Judged by Major Jackson in 2017.

THE ELIZABETH MATCHETT STOVER MEMORIAL AWARD

Southwest Review, Southern Methodist University, P.O. Box 750374, Dallas TX 75275-0374. (214) 768-1037. **Fax:** (214) 768-1408. **E-mail:** swr@mail.smu.edu. **Website:** www.smu.edu/southwestreview. **Contact:** Greg Brownderville, editor-in-chief. Offered annually to the best works of poetry that have appeared in the magazine in the previous year. Please note that mss are submitted for publication, not for the prizes themselves. Guidelines for SASE and online. Prize: $300. Judged by Greg Brownderville. **TIPS** "Not an open contest. Annual prize in which winners are chosen from published pieces during the preceding year."

🌑 STROKESTOWN INTERNATIONAL POETRY COMPETITION

Strokestown International Poetry Festival, Strokestown Poetry Festival Office, Strokestown, County Roscommon Ireland. (+353) 71 9633759. **E-mail:** director@strokestownpoetry.org. **Website:** www.strokestownpoetry.org. **Contact:** Martin Dyar, Director. Poem cannot exceed 70 lines. Ten short-listed poets will be invited to Strokestown for the festival. This annual competition was established to promote excellence in poetry and participation in the reading and writing of it. Acquires first publication rights. Deadline: January. Prize: 1st Place: €1,500; 2nd Place: €500; 3rd Place: €300; 3 shortlisted prizes of €100 each.

THE TAMPA REVIEW PRIZE FOR POETRY

University of Tampa, 401 W. Kennedy Blvd., Tampa FL 33606. 813-253-6266. **E-mail:** utpress@ut.edu. **Website:** www.ut.edu/tampareview. Annual award for the best previously unpublished collection of poetry (at least 48 pages, though preferably 60-100). Deadline: December 31. Prize: $2,000, plus publication.

THE TENTH GATE PRIZE

The Word Works, P. O. Box 42164, Washington D.C. 20015. **E-mail:** editor@wordworksbooks.org. **Website:** www.wordworksbooks.org. **Contact:** Leslie McGrath, Series Editor; Nancy White, Editor. Publication and $1000 cash prize awarded annually by The Word Works to a full-length ms by a poet who has already published at least 2 full-length poetry collections. Submit 48-80 pages. Include acknowledgments and past book publications in the "NOTES" section of the online submissions manager. Submit via online submissions manager: wordworksbooks.org/submissions. Founded in honor of Jane Hirshfield, The Tenth Gate Prize supports the work of mid-career poets. Deadline: July 15. Open to submissions on June 1. Prize: $1,000 and publication. Judged by the editors.

TOM HOWARD/MARGARET REID POETRY CONTEST

Winning Writers, Winning Writers, 351 Pleasant St., PMB 222, Northampton MA 01060-3961. (866)946-9748. **Fax:** (413)280-0539. **E-mail:** adam@winningwriters.com. **Website:** www.winningwriters.com. **Contact:** Adam Cohen. Winning Writers provides expert literary contest information to the public. It is one of the "101 Best Websites for Writers" (*Writer's Digest*). Offers annual awards of Tom Howard Prize, for a poem in any style or genre, and Margaret Reid Prize, for a poem that rhymes or has a traditional style. See website for guidelines and to submit your poem. Nonexclusive right to publish submissions online, in e-mail newsletters, in e-books, and in press releases. Submissions maybe published or unpublished, may have won prizes elsewhere, and may be entered in other contests. Length limit: 250 lines per poem. Deadline: September 30. Submission period begins April 15. Prizes: Two top awards of $1,500 each, with 10 Honorable Mentions of $100 each (any style). All entries that win cash prizes will be published on the Winning Writers website. Judged by Soma Mei Sheng Frazier. **TIPS** Read past winning entries and judges' remarks on website.

TOR HOUSE PRIZE FOR POETRY

Robinson Jeffers Tor House Foundation, Poetry Prize Coordinator, Tor House Foundation, Box 223240, Carmel CA 93922. (831)624-1813. **Fax:** (831)624-3696. **E-mail:** thf@torhouse.org. **Website:** www.torhouse.org. **Contact:** Eliot Ruchowitz-Roberts, Poetry Prize Coordinator. The annual Prize for Poetry is a living memorial to American poet Robinson Jeffers (1887-1962). Open to well-crafted poetry in all styles, ranging from experimental work to traditional forms, including short narrative poems. Poems must be original and unpublished. Each poem should be typed on 8 1/2" by 11" paper, and no longer than three pages. On a cover sheet only, include: name, mailing address, telephone number and email; titles of poems; bio optional. Multiple and simultaneous submissions welcome. Deadline: March 15. Prize: $1,000 honorarium for award-winning poem; $200 Honorable Mention.

KINGSLEY & KATE TUFTS POETRY AWARDS

Claremont Graduate University, Claremont Graduate University, 160 E. Tenth St., Harper East B7, Claremont CA 91711-6165. (909)621-8974. **E-mail:** tufts@cgu.edu. **Website:** www.cgu.edu/tufts. The $100,000 Kingsley Tufts Poetry Award was created to both honor the poet and provide the resources that allow artists to continue working towards the pinnacle of their craft; the Kingsley Tufts Awards goes to a book published by a mid-career poet. The $10,000 Kate Tufts Award is presented annually for a first book by a poet of genuine promise. "Any poet will tell you that the only thing more rare than meaningful recognition is a meaningful payday. For two outstanding poets each year, the Kingsley and Kate Tufts awards represent both." Deadline: July 1, for books published in the preceding year. Prize: $100,000 for the Kingsley Tufts Poetry Award and $10,000 for the Kate Tufts Discovery Award. Please see website for current judges.

☯ UTMOST CHRISTIAN POETRY CONTEST

Utmost Christian Writers Foundation, 121 Morin Maze, Edmonton Alberta T6K 1V1 Canada. (780)265-4650. **E-mail:** nnharms@telusplanet.net. **Website:** www.utmostchristianwriters.com. **Contact:** Nathan Harms, executive director. Utmost is founded on—and supported by—the dreams, interests and aspirations of individual people. Contest is only open to Christians. Poems may be rhymed or free verse, up to 60 lines, but must not have been published previously or have won any prize in any previous competition of any kind. Submit up to 5 poems. Deadline: February 28. Prizes: 1st Place: $1,000; 2nd Place: $500; 10 prizes of $100 are offered for honorable mention; $300 for best rhyming poem; and $200 for an honorable mention rhyming poem. Judged by a committee of the Directors of Utmost Christian Writers Foundation (who work under the direction of Barbara Mitchell, chief judge).

TIPS "Besides providing numerous resources for Christian writers and poets, Utmost also provides a marketplace where Christian writers and poets can sell their work. Please follow our guidelines. We receive numerous unsuitable submissions from writers. We encourage writers to submit suitable material. The best way to do this is to read the guidelines specific to your project—poetry, book reviews, articles—and then take time to look at the material we have already published in that area. The final step is to evaluate your proposed submission in comparison to the material we have used previously. If you complete these steps and strongly feel that your material is appropriate for us, we encourage you to submit it."

DANIEL VAROUJAN AWARD

New England Poetry Club, 376 School St., Watertown MA 02472. **E-mail:** contests@nepoetryclub.org. **Website:** www.nepoetryclub.org. **Contact:** Audrey Kalajin. For an unpublished poem (not a translation) worthy of Daniel Varoujan, a poet killed by the Turks in the genocide which destroyed three-fourths of the Armenian population. Previous winners may not enter again. Send entry in duplicate, one without name and address of writer. Deadline: May 31. Prize: $1,000.

Judged by well-known poets and sometimes winners of previous NEPC contests.

VASSAR MILLER PRIZE IN POETRY

University of North Texas Press, 1155 Union Circle, #311336, Denton TX 76203. (940)565-2142. **Fax:** (940)565-4590. **Website:** http://untpress.unt.edu. **Contact:** John Poch. Annual prize awarded to a collection of poetry. Submit 50-80 pages. In years when the judge is announced, it is asked that students of the judge not enter to avoid a perceived conflict. All entries should contain identifying material only on the one cover sheet. Entries are read anonymously. Deadline: Mss may be submitted between 9 A.M. on September 1 and 5 P.M. on October 31, through online submissions manager only. Prize: $1,000 and publication by University of North Texas Press. Judged by a different eminent writer selected each year. Some prefer to remain anonymous until the end of the contest.

MARICA AND JAN VILCEK PRIZE FOR POETRY

Bellevue Literary Review, New York University School of Medicine, OBV-A612, 550 First Ave., New York NY 10016. (212)263-3973. **E-mail:** info@BLReview.org. **Website:** www.BLReview.org. **Contact:** Stacy Bodziak. The annual Marica and Jan Vilcek Prize for Poetry recognizes outstanding writing related to themes of health, healing, illness, the mind, and the body. All entries will be considered for publication. No previously published poems (including Internet publication). Submit up to 3 poems (5 pages maximum). Electronic (online) submissions only; combine all poems into 1 document and use first poem as document title. See guidelines for additional submission details. Guidelines available for SASE or on website. Deadline: July 1. Prize: $1,000 for best poem and publication in *Bellevue Literary Review*. Previous judges include Mark Doty, Cornelius Eady, Naomi Shihab Nye, and Tony Hoagland.

WABASH PRIZE FOR POETRY

Sycamore Review, Department of English, 500 Oval Dr., Purdue University, West Lafayette IN 47907. **E-mail:** sycamore@purdue.edu; sycamorepoetry@purdue.edu. **Website:** www.sycamorereview.com/contest/. **Contact:** Anthony Sutton, editor-in-chief. Annual contest for unpublished poetry. For each submission, send up to 3 poems (no more than 6 total pages). Ms pages should be numbered and should include the title of each poem. See website for more guidelines.

Submit online via Submittable. Deadline: December 1. Prize: $1,000 and publication.

THE WASHINGTON PRIZE

The Word Works, Dearlove Hall, SUNY Adirondack, 640 Bay Rd., Queensbury NY 12804. **E-mail:** editor@wordworksbooks.org. **Website:** www.wordworksbooks.org. **Contact:** Rebecca Kutzer-Rice, Washington Prize administrator. In addition to its general poetry book publications, The Word Works runs four imprints: The Washington Prize, The Tenth Gate Prize, International Editions, and the Hilary Tham Capital Collection. Selections announced in late summer. Book publication planned for spring of the following year. Submit a poetry ms of 48-80 pages. Submit online with no identifying information appearing within the manuscript; or, if on paper, include 2 title pages, 1 with and 1 without author information, including an acknowledgments page, a table of contents and a brief bio. Electronic submissions are accepted at www.wordworksbooks.org/submissions. The Washington Prize allows poets from all stages of their careers to compete on a level playing field for publication and national recognition. Deadline: Submit January 15-March 15 (postmark). Prize: $1,500 and publication of a book-length ms of original poetry in English by a living US or Canadian citizen. Judged by two tiers of readers, followed by five final judges working as a panel.

WERGLE FLOMP HUMOR POETRY CONTEST

Winning Writers, 351 Pleasant St., PMB 222, Northampton MA 01060. (866)946-9748. **Fax:** (413)280-0539. **E-mail:** adam@winningwriters.com. **Website:** www.winningwriters.com. **Contact:** Adam Cohen. Winning Writers provides expert literary contest information to the public. It is one of the "101 Best Websites for Writers" (*Writer's Digest*). Submit one humor poem online. Length limit: 250 lines. The poem should be in English. Inspired gibberish is also accepted. Submissions may be previously published and may be entered in other contests. Deadline: April 1. Prize: 1st prize of $1,000; 2nd prize of $250; 10 honorable mentions of $100 each. All winners of cash prizes published on website. Judged by Jendi Reiter, assisted by Lauren Singer.
TIPS Read past winning entries and judges' remarks on website.

WHITE PINE PRESS POETRY PRIZE

White Pine Press, P.O. Box 236, Buffalo NY 14201. **E-mail:** wpine@whitepine.org. **Website:** www.whitepine.org. **Contact:** Dennis Maloney, editor. Offered annually for previously published or unpublished poets. Manuscript: 60-80 pages of original work; translations are not eligible. Poems may have appeared in magazines or limited-edition chapbooks. Open to any US citizen. Deadline: November 30 (postmarked). Prize: $1,000 and publication. Final judge is a poet of national reputation. All entries are screened by the editorial staff of White Pine Press.

STAN AND TOM WICK POETRY PRIZE

Wick Poetry Center, P.O. Box 5190, Kent OH 44240. (330)672-2067. **E-mail:** wickpoetry@kent.edu. **Website:** www.kent.edu/wick/stan-and-tom-wick-poetry-prize. **Contact:** David Hassler, director. Offered annually to a poet who has not previously published a full-length collection of poetry (a volume of 50 or more pages published in an edition of 500 or more copies). Submissions must consist of 50-70 pages of poetry, typed on one side only, with no more than one poem included on a single page. Also accepts submissions online through Submittable. See website for details and guidelines. Deadline: May 1. Submissions period begins February 1. Prize: $2,500 and publication of full-length book of poetry by Kent State University Press.

MILLER WILLIAMS POETRY PRIZE

University of Arkansas Press, McIlroy House, 105 N. McIlroy Avenue, Fayetteville AR 72701. (479)575-7258. **Fax:** (479)575-6044. **E-mail:** info@uapress.com; mbieker@uark.edu. **Website:** www.uapress.com. **Contact:** Billy Collins, judge and series editor; Mike Bieker, director. Each year, the University of Arkansas Press accepts submissions for the Miller Williams Poetry Series and from the books selected awards the Miller Williams Poetry Prize in the following summer. Mss should be between 60-90 pages. Individual poems may have been published in chapbooks, journals, and anthologies. Guidelines available online. Submit online. Deadline: September 30. Accepts submissions all year long. Prize: $5,000, publication, and featured reading at the University of Arkansas. Judged by Billy Collins, series editor.

THE J. HOWARD AND BARBARA M.J. WOOD PRIZE

Poetry, 61 W. Superior St., Chicago IL 60654. (312)787-7070. **Fax:** (312)787-6650. **E-mail:** editors@poetry-magazine.org. **Website:** www.poetrymagazine.org. Offered annually for poems published in *Poetry* during the preceding year (October-September). Upon acceptance, *Poetry* licenses exclusive worldwide first serial rights, including electronic rights, for publication, as well as non-exclusive rights to reprint, reuse, and archive the work, in any format, in perpetuity. Copyright reverts to author upon first publication. Prize: $5,000.

WORKING PEOPLE'S POETRY COMPETITION

Blue Collar Review, P.O. Box 11417, Norfolk VA 23517. **E-mail:** red-ink@earthlink.net. **Website:** www.par-tisanpress.org. Poetry should be typed as you would like to see it published, with your name and address on each page. Include cover letter with entry. Guidelines available on website. Deadline: May 15. Prize: $100, 1-year subscription to *Blue Collar Review* (see separate listing in Magazines/Journals) and 1-year posting of winning poem to website.

JAMES WRIGHT POETRY AWARD

Mid-American Review, Dept. of English, Bowling Green State University, Bowling Green OH 43403. (419)372-2725. **Fax:** (419)372-4642. **E-mail:** clouda@bgsu.edu. **Website:** www.bgsu.edu/midamericanreview. **Contact:** Abigail Cloud, poetry editor. Offered annually for unpublished poetry. Open to all writers not associated with *Mid-American Review* or judge. Guidelines available online or for SASE. Deadline: November 1. Prize: $1,000 and publication in spring issue of *Mid-American Review*. Judged by editors and a well known poet, i.e., Kathy Fagan, Bob Hicok, Michelle Boisseau. Judged by Maggie Smith in 2016.

THE YALE SERIES OF YOUNGER POETS

Yale University Press, P.O. Box 209040, New Haven CT 06520-9040. **Website:** youngerpoets.yupnet.org. The Yale Series of Younger Poets champions the most promising new American poets. The Yale Younger Poets prize is the oldest annual literary award in the United States. Open to U.S. citizens who have not published a volume of poetry; poets may have published a limited edition chapbook of 300 copies or less. Poems may have been previously published in newspapers and periodicals and used in the book ms if so

identified. No translations. Submit 48-64 pages of poetry, paginated, with each new poem starting on a new page. Accepts hard copy and electronic submissions. Deadline: November 15. Submissions period begins October 1.

ZONE 3 FIRST BOOK AWARD FOR POETRY

Zone 3, Austin Peay State University, Austin Peay State University, PO Box 4565, Clarksville TN 37044. (931)221-7031. **Fax:** (931)221-7149. **E-mail:** spofforda@aspu.edu; wallacess@apsu.edu. **Website:** www.apsu.edu/zone3/. **Contact:** Andrea Spofford, poetry editor; Susan Wallace, managing editor. Offered annually for anyone who has not published a full-length collection of poems (48 pages or more). Submit a ms of 48-80 pages. Deadline: May 1. Prize: $1,000 and publication.

MULTIPLE WRITING AREAS

● AESTHETICA ART PRIZE

Aesthetica Magazine, P.O. Box 371, York YO23 1WL United Kingdom. **E-mail:** info@aestheticamagazine.com; artprize@aestheticamagazine.com. **Website:** www.aestheticamagazine.com. The Aesthetica Art Prize is a celebration of excellence in art from across the world and offers artists the opportunity to showcase their work to wider audiences and further their involvement in the international art world. There are 4 categories: Photograpic & Digital Art, Three Dimensional Design & Sculpture, Painting & Drawing, Video Installation & Performance. See guidelines at Artwork & Photography, Fiction, and Poetry. See guidelines at www.aestheticamagazine.com. The Aesthetica Art Prize is a celebration of excellence in art from across the world and offers artists the opportunity to showcase their work to wider audiences and further their involvement in the international art world. Deadline: August 31. Prizes include: £5,000 main prize courtesy of Hiscox, £1,000 Student Prize courtesy of Hiscox, group exhibition and publication in the Aesthetica Art Prize Anthology. Entry is £15 and permits submission of 2 works in one category.

◑ ALCUIN SOCIETY BOOK DESIGN AWARDS

P.O. Box 3216, Vancouver BC V6B 3X8 Canada. (604)732-5403. **E-mail:** awards@alcuinsociety.com; info@alcuinsociety.com. **Website:** www.alcuinsociety.com. **Contact:** Leah Gordon. The Alcuin Society

Awards for Excellence in Book Design in Canada is the only national competition for book design in Canada. Winners are selected from books designed and published in Canada. Awards are presented annually at appropriate ceremonies held in each year. Winning books are exhibited nationally and internationally at the Tokyo, Frankfurt, and Leipzig Book Fairs, and are Canada's entries in the international competition in Leipzig, "Book Design from all over the World" in the following spring. Submit previously published material from the year before the award's call for entries. Submissions made by the publisher, author or designer (Canadian). Deadline: March 1. Prizes: 1st, 2nd, and 3rd in each category (at the discretion of the judges). Judged by professionals and those experienced in the field of book design.

MARIE ALEXANDER POETRY SERIES

English Department, 2801 S. University Ave., Little Rock AR 72204. **E-mail:** editor@mariealexanderseries.com. **Website:** mariealexanderseries.com. **Contact:** Nickole Brown. Annual contest for a collection of previously unpublished prose poems or flash fiction by a U.S. writer. Deadline: July 31. Open to submissions on July 1. Prize: $1,000, plus publication.

ALLIGATOR JUNIPER AWARD

Alligator Juniper/Prescott College, 220 Grove Ave., Prescott AZ 86301. (928)350-2012. **Fax:** (928)776-5102. **E-mail:** alligatorjuniper@prescott.edu. **Website:** www.prescott.edu/alligatorjuniper/national-contest/index.html. **Contact:** Skye Anicca, managing editor. Annual contest for unpublished fiction, creative nonfiction, and poetry. Open to all age levels. Each entrant receives a personal letter from staff regarding the status of their submission, as well as minor feedback on the piece. Accepts simultaneous submissions, but inform on cover letter and contact immediately, should work be selected elsewhere. Maximum length: 30 pages or 5 poems. Deadline: October 1. Prize: $1,000 plus publication in all three categories. Finalists in each genre are recognized as such, published, and paid in copies. Judged by the distinguished writers in each genre and Prescott College writing students enrolled in the Literary Journal Practicum course.

THE AMERICAN GEM LITERARY FESTIVAL

FilmMakers Magazine / Write Brothers, FilmMakers Magazine (filmmakers.com), Beverly Hills CA 90210. **E-mail:** info@filmmakers.com. **Website:** http://film-makers.com/contests/short_story/. **Contact:** Jennifer Brooks. Worldwide contest to recognize excellent short screenplays and short stories. Ms submissions must be between 3-45 pages (there is an extra fee for anything between 46-65 pages) and up to industry standards. See website for more details. Must not have been previously optioned or sold to market or to a film producer. Preferable that the ms has not yet been adapted to a screenplay. Short stories should be no more than 50 pages, double-spaced, to a maximum of 12,500 words. Must not have been previously published. Deadlines: Early: Feb 29; Regular: April 30; Late: June 30; Final: July 31. Prize: Short Script: 1st Place: $1,000. Other cash and prizes to top 5.

AMERICAN LITERARY REVIEW CONTESTS

American Literary Review, P.O. Box 311307, University of North Texas, Denton TX 76203-1307. (940)565-2755. **E-mail:** americanliteraryreview@gmail.com. **Website:** www.americanliteraryreview.com. Contest to award excellence in short fiction, creative nonfiction, and poetry. Multiple entries are acceptable, but each entry must be accompanied with a reading fee. Do not put any identifying information in the file itself; include the author's name, title(s), address, e-mail address, and phone number in the boxes provided in the online submissions manager. Short fiction: Limit 8,000 words per work. Creative nonfiction: Limit 6,500 words per work. Deadline: October 1. Submission period begins June 1. Prize: $1,000 prize for each category, along with publication in the Spring online issue of the *American Literary Review*.

ART AFFAIR SHORT STORY AND WESTERN SHORT STORY CONTESTS

Art Affair - Contest, P.O. Box 54302, Oklahoma City OK 73154. **E-mail:** artaffair@aol.com. **Website:** www.shadetreecreations.com. The annual Art Affair Writing Contests include (General) Short Story and Western Short Story categories. See separate listing for Poetry contest. Open to any writer. All short stories must be unpublished. Multiple entries accepted in both categories with separate entry fees for each. Submit original stories on any subject and timeframe for general Short Story category, and submit original western stories for Western Short Story—word limit for all entries is 5,000 words. Guidelines available on website. Put word count in the upper right-hand corner of first page; mark "Western" on western short stories. All ms must be double-spaced on 8.5x11 white paper. Type title of story on first page and headers (with page numbers) on following pages. Include cover page with writer's name, address, phone number, and manuscript title. Deadline: October 1. Prize (in both categories): 1st Place: $50; 2nd Place: $25; 3rd Place: $15.

TIPS Use proper manuscript formatting.

ARTIST TRUST FELLOWSHIP AWARD

1835 12th Ave., Seattle WA 98122. (209)467-8734, ext. 11. **Fax:** (866)218-7878. **E-mail:** info@artisttrust.org. **Website:** www.artisttrust.org. **Contact:** Miguel Guillen, program manager. Fellowships award $7,500 to practicing professional artists of exceptional talent and demonstrated ability. The Fellowship is a merit-based, not a project-based award. Recipients present a Meet the Artist Event to a community in Washington state that has little or no access to the artist and their work. Awards 14 fellowships of $7,500 and 2 residencies with $1,000 stipends at the Millay Colony. Artist Trust Fellowships are awarded in two-year cycles. Applicants must be 18 years of age or older, Washington State residents at the time of application and payment, and generative artists. Deadline: January 17. Applications available December 3. Prize: $7,500.

ARTS & LETTERS PRIZES

Arts & Letters Journal of Contemporary Culture, Campus Box 89, GC&SU, Milledgeville GA 31061. (478)445-1289. **E-mail:** al.journal@gcsu.edu. **Website:** al.gcsu.edu. **Contact:** The Editors. Offered annually for unpublished work. Deadline: March 31. Prize: $1,000 prize for each of the four major genres. Fiction, poetry, and creative nonfiction winners are published in Fall or Spring issue. The prize-winning one-act play is produced at the Georgia College campus (usually in March). Judged by the editors (initial screening); see website for final judges and further details about submitting work.

THE ATHENAEUM LITERARY AWARD

The Athenaeum of Philadelphia, 219 S. 6th St., Philadelphia PA 19106-3794. (215)925-2688. **Fax:** (215)925-3755. **E-mail:** jilly@PhilaAthenaeum.org. **Website:** http://www.philaathenaeum.org/literary.html. **Contact:** Jill LeMin Lee, Librarian. The Athenaeum Literary Award was established to recognize and encourage literary achievement among authors who are bona fide residents of Philadelphia or Pennsylvania living within a radius of 30 miles of City Hall at the time their book was written or published. Any volume of general literature is eligible; technical, scientific, and juvenile books are not included. Nominated works are reviewed on the basis of their significance and importance to the general public as well as for literary excellence. Only published works are eligible. Deadline: All nominations must be submitted prior to December 1st of the year of publication.

AUTUMN HOUSE POETRY, FICTION, AND NONFICTION PRIZES

P.O. Box 60100, Pittsburgh PA 15211. (412)381-4261. **E-mail:** info@autumnhouse.org. **E-mail:** https://autumnhousepress.submittable.com/submit. **Website:** http://autumnhouse.org. **Contact:** Christine Stroud, Editor-in-Chief. Offers annual prize and publication of book-length ms with national promotion. Submission must be unpublished as a collection, but individual poems, stories, and essays may have been previously published elsewhere. Considers simultaneous submissions. "Autumn House is a nonprofit corporation with the mission of publishing and promoting poetry and other fine literature. We have published books by Chana Bloch, Ellery Akers, Gerald Stern, Ruth L. Schwartz, Ed Ochester, Andrea Hollander, George Bilgere, Ada Limon, and many others." Submit 50-80 pages of poetry or 200-300 pages of prose (include 2 cover sheets requested). Guidelines available for SASE, by e-mail, or on website. Competition receives 1,500 entries/year. Winners announced through mailings, website, and ads in *Poets & Writers*, *American Poetry Review*, and *Writer's Chronicle* (extensive publicity for winner). Copies of winning books available from Amazon.com, Barnes & Noble, and other retailers. Deadline: June 30. Prize: The winner (in each of three categories) will receive book publication, $1,000 advance against royalties, and a $1,500 travel/publicity grant to promote his or her book. Judged by Alberto Rios (poetry), Amina Gautier (fiction), and Alison Hawthorne Deming (nonfiction).

TIPS "Include only your best work."

AWP AWARD SERIES

Association of Writers & Writing Programs, George Mason University, 4400 University Drive, MSN 1E3, Fairfax VA 22030. **E-mail:** supriya@awpwriter.org. **Website:** www.awpwriter.org. **Contact:** Supriya Bhatnagar, director of publications. AWP sponsors the Award Series, an annual competition for the publication of excellent new book-length works. The competition is open to all authors writing in English regardless of nationality or residence, and is available to published and unpublished authors alike. Guidelines on website. Entries must be unpublished. Open to any writer. Entries are not accepted via postal mail. Offered annually to foster new literary talent. Deadline: Postmarked between January 1 and February 28. Prize: AWP Prize for the Novel: $2,500 and publication by New Issues Press; Donald Hall Prize for Poetry: $5,500 and publication by the University of Pittsburgh Press; Grace Paley Prize in Short Fiction: $5,500 and publication by the University of Massachusetts Press; and AWP Prize for Creative Nonfiction: $2,500 and publication by the University of Georgia Press.

☙ THE BOARDMAN TASKER PRIZE FOR MOUNTAIN LITERATURE

The Boardman Tasker Charitable Trust, 8 Bank View Rd., Darley Abbey Derby DE22 1EJ UK. 01332 342246. **E-mail:** steve@people-matter.co.uk. **Website:** www. boardmantasker.com. **Contact:** Steve Dean. Offered annually to reward a work with a mountain theme, whether fiction, nonfiction, drama, or poetry, written in the English language (initially or in translation). Subject must be concerned with a mountain environment. Previous winners have been books on expeditions, climbing experiences, a biography of a mountaineer, novels. Guidelines available in January by e-mail or on website. Entries must be previously published. Open to any writer. Writers may obtain information, but entry is by publishers only (includes self-publishing). Awarded for a work published or distributed for the first time in the United Kingdom during the previous year. Not an anthology. The award is to honor Peter Boardman and Joe Tasker, who disappeared on Everest in 1982. Deadline: August 1. Prize: £3,000 Judged by a panel of 3 judges elected by trustees.

THE BRIAR CLIFF REVIEW FICTION, POETRY, AND CREATIVE NONFICTION COMPETITION

The Briar Cliff Review, Briar Cliff University, 3303 Rebecca St., Sioux City IA 51104-0100. **E-mail:** tricia. currans-sheehan@briarcliff.edu (editor); jeanne.emmons@briarcliff.edu (poetry). **Website:** www.bcreview.org. **Contact:** Tricia Currans-Sheehan, editor. *The Briar Cliff Review* sponsors an annual contest offering $1,000 and publication to each 1st Prize winner in fiction, poetry, and creative nonfiction. Previous year's winner and former students of editors ineligible. Winning pieces accepted for publication on the basis of first-time rights. Considers simultaneous submissions, "but notify us immediately upon acceptance elsewhere. We guarantee a considerate reading." No mss returned. Word limit for short story and creative nonfiction is 5,000. For poetry, three poems, no more than five pages total. Submit via Submittable or post. To reward good writers and showcase quality writing. Deadline: November 1. Prize: $1,000 and publication to each prize winner in fiction, poetry, and creative nonfiction. Judged by *Briar Cliff Review* editors.

☙ BRITISH CZECH AND SLOVAK ASSOCIATION WRITING COMPETITION

24 Ferndale, Tunbridge Wells Kent TN2 3NS England. **E-mail:** prize@bcsa.co.uk. **Website:** www.bcsa.co.uk/specials.html. Annual contest for original writing (entries should be 1,500-2,000 words) in English on the links between Britain and the Czech/Slovak Republics, or describing society in transition in the Republics since 1989. Entries can be fact or fiction. Topics can include history, politics, the sciences, economics, the arts, or literature. Deadline: June 30. Winners announced in November. Prize: 1st Place: £300; 2nd Place: £100.

☙ THE RBC BRONWEN WALLACE AWARD FOR EMERGING WRITERS

The Writers' Trust of Canada, 460 Richmond St. W., Suite 600, Toronto ON M5C 1P1 Canada. (416)504-8222. **Fax:** (416)504-9090. **E-mail:** info@writerstrust. com. **Website:** www.writerstrust.com. **Contact:** Amanda Hopkins. Presented annually to a Canadian writer under the age of 35 who is not yet published in book form. The award, which alternates each year between poetry and short fiction, was established in memory of Bronwen Wallace. Deadline: March 7. Prize: $10,000. Two finalists receive $2,500 each.

CHRISTIAN BOOK AWARD® PROGRAM

Evangelical Christian Publishers Association, 9633 S. 48th St., Suite 195, Phoenix AZ 85044. (480)966-3998. **Fax:** (480)966-1944. **E-mail:** info@ecpa.org. **Website:** www.ecpa.org. **Contact:** Stan Jantz, ED. The Evangelical Christian Publishers Association (ECPA) recognizes quality and encourages excellence by presenting the ECPA Christian Book Awards® (formerly known as Gold Medallion) each year. Categories include Christian Living, Biography & Memoir, Faith & Culture, Children, Young People's Literature, Devotion & Gift, Bibles, Bible Reference Works, Bible Study, Ministry Resources and New Author. All entries must be evangelical in nature and submitted through an ECPA member publisher. Books must have been published in the calendar year prior to the award. Publishing companies submitting entries must be ECPA members in good standing. See website for details. The Christian Book Awards® recognize the highest quality in Christian books and is among the oldest and most prestigious awards program in Christian publishing. Submission period runs September 1-30. Judged by ECPA members, who are experts, authors and retailers with years of experience in their field.

CLOUDBANK JOURNAL CONTEST

P.O. Box 610, Corvallis OR 97339. (541)752-0075. **E-mail:** michael@cloudbankbooks.com. **Website:** www.cloudbankbooks.com. **Contact:** Michael Malan. For contest submissions, the writer's name, address, e-mail, and the titles of the poems/flash fiction pieces being submitted should be typed on a cover sheet only, not on the pages of poems or flash fiction. Submit no more than 5 poems or flash fiction pieces (500 words or less) for the contest or for regular submissions. Deadline: April 30. Prize: $200 and publication, plus an extra copy of the issue in which the winning poem appears. Two contributors' copies will be sent to writers whose work appears in the magazine. Judged by Michael Malan and Peter Sears.

COLORADO BOOK AWARDS

Colorado Humanities & Center for the Book, 7935 E. Prentice Ave., Suite 450, Greenwood Village CO 80111. (303)894-7951. **Fax:** (303)864-9361. **E-mail:** bess@coloradohumanities.org. **Website:** www.coloradohumanities.org. **Contact:** Bess Maher. An annual program that celebrates the accomplishments of Colorado's outstanding authors, editors, illustrators, and photographers. Awards are presented in at least ten categories including anthology/collection, biography, children's, creative nonfiction, fiction, history, nonfiction, pictorial, poetry, and young adult. To be eligible for a Colorado Book Award, a primary contributor to the book must be a Colorado writer, editor, illustrator, or photographer. Current Colorado residents are eligible, as are individuals engaged in ongoing literary work in the state and authors whose personal history, identity, or literary work reflect a strong Colorado influence. Authors not currently Colorado resi-

dents who feel their work is inspired by or connected to Colorado should submit a letter with his/her entry describing the connection. Deadline: January 9.

THE CUTBANK CHAPBOOK CONTEST

CutBank Literary Magazine, *CutBank*, University of Montana, English Dept., LA 133, Missoula MT 59812. **E-mail:** editor.cutbank@gmail.com. **Website:** www.cutbankonline.org. **Contact:** Kate Barrett, editor-in-chief. This competition is open to original English language mss in the genres of poetry, fiction, and creative nonfiction. While previously published stand-alone pieces or excerpts may be included in a ms, the ms as a whole must be an unpublished work. Looking for startling, compelling, and beautiful original work. "We're looking for a fresh, powerful manuscript. Maybe it will overtake us quietly; gracefully defy genres; satisfyingly subvert our expectations; punch us in the mouth page in and page out. We're interested in both prose and poetry—and particularly work that straddles the lines between genres." Accepts online submissions only. Submit up to 25-40 pages of poetry or prose. Guidelines available online. Deadline: March 31. Submissions period begins January1. Prize: $1,000 and 25 contributor copies. Judged by a guest judge each year.

CWW ANNUAL WISCONSIN WRITERS AWARDS

Council for Wisconsin Writers, 4964 Gilkeson Rd, Waunakee WI 53597. **E-mail:** karlahuston@gmail.com. **Website:** www.wiswriters.org. **Contact:** Geoff Gilpin, president and annual awards co-chair; Karla Huston, secretary and annual awards co-chair; Sylvia Cavanaugh, annual awards co-chair; Edward Schultz, annual awards co-chair, Erik Richardson, annual awards co-chair. Offered annually for work published by Wisconsin writers during the previous calendar year. Nine awards: Major Achievement (presented in alternate years); short fiction; short nonfiction; nonfiction book; poetry book; fiction book; children's literature; Lorine Niedecker Poetry Award; Christopher Latham Sholes Award for Outstanding Service to Wisconsin Writers (presented in alternate years); Essay Award for Young Writers. Open to Wisconsin residents. Entries may be submitted via postal mail only. See website for guidelines and entry forms. Deadline: January 31. Submissions open on November 1. Prizes: First place prizes: $500. Honorable mentions: $50. List of judges available on website.

DANA AWARDS IN THE NOVEL, SHORT FICTION, AND POETRY

200 Fosseway Dr., Greensboro NC 27445. (336)644-8028. **E-mail:** danaawards@gmail.com. **Website:** www.danaawards.com. **Contact:** Mary Elizabeth Parker, chair. Three awards offered annually for unpublished work written in English. Works previously published online are not eligible. The Dana Awards are re-vamping. The Novel Award is now increased to $2,000, based on a new partnership with Blue Mary Books: Blue Mary has agreed to consider for possible publication not only the Novel Award winning manuscript, but the top 9 other Novel finalists, as well as the 30 top Novel semifinalists. The Short Fiction and Poetry Awards offer the traditional $1,000 awards each and do not offer a publishing option (currently, Blue Mary publishes only novels). See website for further updates. Categories: Novel: For the first 40 pages of a novel completed or in progress; Fiction: Short fiction (no memoirs) up to 10,000 words; Poetry: For best group of 5 poems based on excellence of all 5 (no light verse, no single poem over 100 lines). Purpose is monetary award for work that has not been previously published or received monetary award, but will accept work published simply for friends and family. Deadline: October 31 (postmarked). Prizes: $2,000 for the Novel Award; $1,000 each for the Short Fiction and Poetry awards awards.

DIAGRAM CHAPBOOK CONTEST

Department of English, University of Arizona, P.O. Box 210067, Tucson AZ 85721-0067. **E-mail:** nmp@thediagram.com; editor@thediagram.com. **Website:** www.thediagram.com/contest.html. **Contact:** Ander Monson, editor. Contest for prose or poetry manuscript between 18-44 pages. Deadline: April 28. Check website for more details. Prize: $1,000 and publication. Finalist essay also published. Judged by editors Ander Monson and Nicole Walker.

DIAGRAM/NEW MICHIGAN PRESS CHAPBOOK CONTEST

New Michigan Press, P.O. Box 210067, English, ML 424, University of Arizona, Tucson AZ 85721. **E-mail:** nmp@thediagram.com. **Website:** www.thediagram.com. **Contact:** Ander Monson, editor. The annual *DIAGRAM*/New Michigan Press Chapbook Contest offers $1,000, plus publication and author's copies, with discount on additional copies. Submit 18-44 pages of poetry, fiction, mixed-genre, or genre-bending work.

Do not send originals of anything. Include SASE. Guidelines available on website. Deadline: April 28. Prize: $1,000, plus publication. Finalist chapbooks also considered for publication.

EATON LITERARY AGENCY'S ANNUAL AWARDS PROGRAM

Eaton Literary Agency, P.O. Box 49795, Sarasota FL 34230-6795. (941)366-6589. **Fax:** (941)365-4679. **E-mail:** eatonlit@aol.com. **Website:** www.eatonliterary.com. **Contact:** Richard Lawrence, President. Offered biannually for unpublished mss. Entries must be unpublished. Open to any writer. Guidelines available for SASE, by fax, e-mail, or on website. Accepts inquiries by fax, phone, and e-mail. Results announced in April and September. Winners notified by mail. For contest results, send SASE, fax, e-mail, or visit website. Deadline: March 31 (short story); August 31 (book-length). Prize: $2,500 (book-length); $500 (short story). Judged by an independent agency in conjunction with some members of Eaton's staff.

THE VIRGINIA FAULKNER AWARD FOR EXCELLENCE IN WRITING

Prairie Schooner, 123 Andrews Hall, University of Nebraska-Lincoln, Lincoln NE 68588-0334. (402)472-0911. **Fax:** (402)472-1817. **E-mail:** PrairieSchooner@unl.edu. **Website:** www.prairieschooner.unl.edu. **Contact:** Kwame Dawes. Offered annually for work published in *Prairie Schooner* in the previous year. Categories: short stories, essays, novel excerpts, and translations. Accepts inquiries by fax and e-mail. Reads unsolicited mss between May 1 and September 1. Winning entry must have been published in *Prairie Schooner* in the year preceding the award. Results announced in the Spring issue. Winners notified by mail in February or March. Prize: $1,000. Judged by editorial board.

THE WILLIAM FAULKNER-WILLIAM WISDOM CREATIVE WRITING COMPETITION

Faulkner - Wisdom Competition, Pirate's Alley Faulkner Society, Inc., The Pirate's Alley Faulkner Society, Inc., 624 Pirate's Alley, New Orleans LA 70116-3233. (504)586-1609. **E-mail:** faulkhouse@aol.com. **Website:** www.wordsandmusic.org. general craft **Contact:** Rosemary James, award director. See guidelines posted at www.wordsandmusic.org. Deadline: May 15. Prizes: $750-7,500 depending on category. Judged by established authors, literary agents, and acquiring editors.

FISH SHORT MEMOIR PRIZE

Fish Publishing, Durrus, Bantry Co. Cork Ireland. **E-mail:** info@fishpublishing.com. **Website:** www.fishpublishing.com. Annual worldwide contest to recognize the best memoirs submitted to Fish Publishing. Submissions must not have been previously published. Enter online or via postal mail. See website for full details. Word limit: 4,000. Deadline: January 31. Prize: 1st Prize: $1,000. The 10 best memoirs will be published in the Fish Anthology, launched in July at the West Cork Literary Festival.

FREEFALL SHORT PROSE AND POETRY CONTEST

Freefall Literary Society of Calgary, 922 9th Ave. SE, Calgary AB T2G 0S4 Canada. **E-mail:** editors@freefallmagazine.ca. **Website:** www.freefallmagazine.ca. **Contact:** Ryan Stromquist, managing editor. Offered annually for unpublished work in the categories of poetry (5 poems/entry) and prose (3,000 words or less). Recognizes writers and offers publication credits in a literary magazine format. Contest rules and entry form online. Acquires first Canadian serial rights; ownership reverts to author after one-time publication. Deadline: December 31. Prize: 1st Place: $500 (CAD); 2nd Place: $250 (CAD); 3rd Place: $75; Honorable Mention: $25. All prizes include publication in the spring edition of *FreeFall Magazine*. Winners will also be invited to read at the launch of that issue, if such a launch takes place. Honorable mentions in each category will be published and may be asked to read. Travel expenses not included. Judged by current guest editor for issue (who are also published authors in Canada).

GOVERNOR GENERAL'S LITERARY AWARDS

Canada Council for the Arts, 150 Elgin St., P.O. Box 1047, Ottawa ON K1P 5V8 Canada. 1-800-263-5588, ext. 5573. **Website:** ggbooks.ca. The Canada Council for the Arts provides a wide range of grants and services to professional Canadian artists and art organizations in dance, media arts, music, theatre, writing, publishing, and the visual arts. Books must be first edition literary trade books written, translated, or illustrated by Canadian citizens or permanent residents of Canada and published in Canada or abroad in the previous year. In the case of translation, the original work must also be a Canadian-authored title. For complete eligibility criteria, deadlines, and submission procedures, please visit the website at www.canadacouncil.ca. The Governor General's Literary Awards are given annually for the best English-language and French-language work in each of 7 categories, including fiction, non-fiction, poetry, drama, children's literature (text), children's literature (illustrated books), and translation. Deadline: Depends on the book's publication date. See website for details. Prize: Each GG winner receives $25,000. Non-winning finalists receive $1,000. Publishers of the winning titles receive a $3,000 grant for promotional purposes. Evaluated by fellow authors, translators, and illustrators. For each category, a jury makes the final selection.

GREAT LAKES COLLEGES ASSOCIATION NEW WRITERS AWARD

The Great Lakes Colleges Association, 535 W. William, Suite 301, Ann Arbor MI 48103. (734)661-2350. **Fax:** (734)661-2349. **E-mail:** wegner@glca.org. **Website:** http://glca.org/program-menu/new-writers-award. **Contact:** Gregory R. Wegner, Director of Program Development. The Great Lakes Colleges Association (GLCA) is a consortium of 13 independent liberal arts colleges in Ohio, Michigan, Indiana, and Pennsylvania. Nominations should be made by the publisher and should emphasize literary excellence. A publisher can nominate only one author per year for any given category. A publisher can nominate one author in each of the three categories (poetry, fiction, creative non-fiction) in a single year if desired. Deadline: July 25. Prize: Honorarium of at least $500 for winning writers who are invited to give a reading at a member college campus. Each award winner receives invitations from several of the 13 colleges of the GLCA to visit campus. At these campus events an author will give readings, meet students and faculty, and occasionally lead discussions or classes. In addition to an honorarium for each campus visit, travel costs to colleges are paid by GLCA and its member colleges. Judged by professors of literature and writers in residence at GLCA colleges.

HACKNEY LITERARY AWARDS

4650 Old Looney Mill Rd, Birmingham AL 35243. **E-mail:** info@hackneyliteraryawards.org. **Website:** www.hackneyliteraryawards.org. **Contact:** Myra Crawford, PhD, executive director. Offered annually for unpublished novels, short stories (maximum 5,000 words), and poetry (50 line limit). Guidelines on website. Deadline: September 30 (novels), November 30 (short stories and poetry). Prize: $5,000 in annual prizes for poetry and short fiction ($2,500 national and $2,500 state level). 1st Place: $600; 2nd Place: $400; 3rd Place: $250; plus $5,000 for an unpublished novel. Competition winners will be announced on the website each March.

ERIC HOFFER AWARD

Hopewell Publications, LLC, P.O. Box 11, Titusville NJ 08560-0011. **Fax:** (609)964-1718. **E-mail:** info@hopepubs.com. **Website:** www.hofferaward.com. **Contact:** Christopher Klim, chair. Annual contest for previously published books. Recognizes excellence in independent publishing in many unique categories: Art (titles capture the experience, execution, or demonstration of the arts); Poetry (all styles); Chapbook (40 pages or less, artistic assembly); General Fiction (nongenre-specific fiction); Commercial Fiction (genre-specific fiction); Children (titles for young children); Young Adult (titles aimed at the juvenile and teen markets); Culture (titles demonstrating the human or world experience); Memoir (titles relating to personal experience); Business (titles with application to today's business environment and emerging trends); Reference (titles from traditional and emerging reference areas); Home (titles with practical applications to home or home-related issues, including family); Health (titles promoting physical, mental, and emotional well-being); Self-help (titles involving new and emerging topics in self-help); Spiritual (titles involving the mind and spirit, including relgion); Legacy Fiction and Nonfiction (titles over 2 years of age that hold particular relevance to any subject matter or form); E-book Fiction; E-book Nonfiction. Open to any writer of published work within the last 2 years, including categories for older books. This contest recognizes excellence in independent publishing in many unique categories. Also awards the Montaigne Medal for most though-provoking book, the Da Vinci Eye for best cover, and the First Horizon Award for best new authors. Results published in the US Review of Books. Deadline: January 21. Grand Prize: $2,000; honors in each category, including the Montaigne Medal (most thought-provoking), da Vinci Art (cover art), First Horizon (first book), and Best in Press (small, academic, micro, self-published).

THE JULIA WARD HOWE/BOSTON AUTHORS AWARD

The Boston Authors Club, The Boston Authors Club, 36 Sunhill Lane, Newton Center MA 02459. **E-mail:** bostonauthors@aol.com;. **Website:** www.bostonauthorsclub.org. **Contact:** Alan Lawson. This annual award honors Julia Ward Howe and her literary friends who founded the Boston Authors Club in 1900. It also honors the membership over 110 years, consisting of novelists, biographers, historians, governors, senators, philosophers, poets, playwrights, and other luminaries. There are 2 categories: trade books and books for young readers (beginning with chapter books through young adult books). Authors must live or have lived (college counts) within a hundred 100-mile radius of Boston within the last 5 years. Subsidized books, cook books and picture books are not eligible. Deadline: January 15. Prize: $1,000. Judged by the members.

INSIGHT WRITING CONTEST

Insight Magazine, 55 W. Oak Ridge Dr., Hagerstown MD 21740-7390. **Fax:** (301)393-4055. **E-mail:** insight@rhpa.org. **Website:** www.insightmagazine.org. **Contact:** Omar Miranda, editor. Annual contest for writers in the categories of student short story, general short story, and student poetry. Unpublished submissions only. General category is open to all writers; student categories must be age 22 and younger. Deadline: July 31. Prizes: Student Short and General Short Story: 1st Prize: $250; 2nd Prize: $200; 3rd Prize: $150. Student Poetry: 1st Prize: $100; 2nd Prize: $75; 3rd Prize: $50.

TIPS "Your entry must be a true, unpublished work by you, with a strong spiritual message. We appreciate the use of Bible texts."

THE IOWA REVIEW AWARD IN POETRY, FICTION, AND NONFICTION

308 EPB, University of Iowa, Iowa City IA 52242. **E-mail:** iowa-review@uiowa.edu. **Website:** www.iowareview.org. *The Iowa Review* Award in Poetry, Fiction, and Nonfiction presents $1,500 to each winner in each genre and $750 to runners-up. Winners and runners-up published in *The Iowa Review*. Submissions must be unpublished. Considers simultaneous submissions (with notification of acceptance elsewhere). Submit up to 25 pages of prose, (double-spaced) or 10 pages of poetry (1 poem or several, but no more than 1 poem per page). Submit online. Include cover

page with writer's name, address, e-mail and/or phone number, and title of each work submitted. Personal identification must not appear on ms pages. Guidelines available on website. Deadline: January 31. Submission period begins January 1. Judged by Joyelle McSweeney, Amy Gray, and Charles D'Ambrosio in 2017.

JAPAN-U.S. FRIENDSHIP COMMISSION PRIZE FOR THE TRANSLATION OF JAPANESE LITERATURE

Japanese Literary Translation Prize, Donald Keene Center of Japanese Culture, Columbia University, 507 Kent Hall 1140 Amsterdam Ave., New York NY 10027. **Website:** http://www.keenecenter.org/. **Contact:** Yoshiko Niiya, Program Coordinator. The Donald Keene Center of Japanese Culture at Columbia University annually awards Japan-U.S. Friendship Commission Prizes for the Translation of Japanese Literature. A prize is given for the best translation of a modern work or a classical work, or the prize is divided between equally distinguished translations. Translators must be citizens or permanent residents of the United States. Deadline: June 1. Prize: $6,000.

☺ THE STEPHEN LEACOCK MEMORIAL MEDAL FOR HUMOUR

149 Peter St. N., Orillia ON L3V 4Z4 Canada. (705)326-9286. **E-mail:** bettewalkerca@gmail.com. **Website:** www.leacock.ca. **Contact:** Bette Walker, award committee, Stephen Leacock Associates. The Leacock Associates awards the prestigious Leacock Medal for the best book of literary humor written by a Canadian and published in the current year. The winning author also receives a cash prize of $15,000 thanks to the generous support of the TD Financial Group. 2 runners-up are each awarded a cash prize of $1,500. Deadline: December 31. Prize: $15,000.

LEAGUE OF UTAH WRITERS CONTEST

The League of Utah Writers, The League of Utah Writers, P.O. Box 64, Lewiston UT 84320. (435)755-7609. **E-mail:** luwcontest@gmail.com; luwriters@gmail.com. **Website:** www.luwriters.org. Open to any writer, the LUW Contest provides authors an opportunity to get their work read and critiqued. Multiple categories are offered; see website for details. Entries must be the original and unpublished work of the author. Winners are announced at the Annual Writers Round-Up in September. Those not present will be notified by e-mail. Deadline: June 15. Submissions

period begins March 15. Prize: Cash prizes are awarded. Judged by professional authors and editors from outside the League.

LES FIGUES PRESS NOS BOOK CONTEST

P.O. Box 7736, Los Angeles CA 90007. (323)734-4732. **E-mail:** info@lesfigues.com. **Website:** www.lesfigues. com. **Contact:** Teresa Carmody, director. Les Figues Press creates aesthetic conversations between writers/artists and readers, especially those interested in innovative/experimental/avant-garde work. The Press intends in the most premeditated fashion to champion the trinity of Beauty, Belief, and Bawdry. Submit a 64-250 page unpublished manuscript through electronic submissions manager. Eligible submissions include: poetry, novellas, innovative novels, anti-novels, short story collections, lyric essays, hybrids, and all forms *not otherwise specified*. Guidelines available online. Deadline: September 15. Prize: $1,000, plus publication by Les Figues Press. Each entry receives LFP book.

LET'S WRITE LITERARY CONTEST

The Gulf Coast Writers Association, P.O. Box 4808, Biloxi MS 39535. **E-mail:** writerpllevin@gmail.com. **Website:** www.gcwriters.org/contest.html. **Contact:** Philip Levin. The Gulf Coast Writers Association sponsors this nationally recognized contest, which accepts unpublished poems, prose, and short stories from authors all around the US. This is an annual event which has been held for 29 years. Deadline: April 10. Prize: 1st Prize: $80; 2nd Prize: $60; 3rd Prize: $40.

THE HUGH J. LUKE AWARD

Prairie Schooner, 123 Andrews Hall, University of Nebraska-Lincoln, Lincoln NE 68588-0334. (402)472-0911. **Fax:** (402)472-1817. **E-mail:** prairieschooner@unl.edu. **Website:** www.prairieschooner.unl.edu. **Contact:** Kwame Dawes. Offered annually for work published in *Prairie Schooner* in the previous year. Results announced in the Spring issue. Winners notified by mail in February or March. Prize: $250. Judged by editorial staff of *Prairie Schooner*.

☺ MANITOBA BOOK AWARDS

Manitoba Writers' Guild, c/o Manitoba Writers' Guild, 218-100 Arthur St., Winnipeg MB R3B 1H3 Canada. (204)944-8013. **E-mail:** events@mbwriter.mb.ca. **Website:** www.manitobabookawards.com. **Contact:** Ellen MacDonald. The awards honor books written by Manitobans, published in Manitoba or about Manitoba. More than $30,000 in prizes is awarded each year to Manitoba writers. The Manitoba Book Awards celebrates literary excellence, originality and diverse talent. Some of Canada's best writers have springboarded to national and international acclaim after winning the Manitoba Book Awards. Previous winners include: Carol Shields (1993), David Bergen (1993,1996, 2009), Miriam Toews (1998, 2000), Margaret Sweatman (1991, 2001), Sandra Birdsell (1992), Jake MacDonald (2002), Allan Levine (2010), Barbara Huck (2014) and Wab Kinew (2016). The 18 awards to be presented at the 29th annual Manitoba Book Awards include Alexander Kennedy Isbister Award for Non-Fiction/Prix Alexander-Kennedy-Isbister pour les études et les essais, Beatrice Mosionier Aboriginal Writer of the Year Award /Prix Beatrice-Mosionier pour l'écrivain.e autochtone de l'année (English/Français/Indigenous Languages), Carol Shields Winnipeg Book Award/Prix littéraire Carol-Shields de la ville de Winnipeg, The Chris Johnson Award for Best Play by a Manitoba Playwright /Prix Chris-Johnson pour la meilleure pièce par un dramaturge manitobain, Eileen McTavish Sykes Award for Best First Book, John Hirsch Award for Most Promising Manitoba Writer/Prix John-Hirsch pour l'écrivain manitobain le plus prometteur, Lansdowne Prize for Poetry / Prix Lansdowne de poésie, Le Prix Littéraire Rue-Deschambault, Manuela Dias Book Design and Illustration Awards/Prix Manuela—Dias de conception graphique et d'illustration en édition—4 categories, Margaret Laurence Award for Fiction, Mary Scorer Award for Best Book by a Manitoba Publisher/ Prix Mary-Scorer pour le meilleur livre par un éditeur du Manitoba, McNally Robinson Books for Young People Awards—2 categories, McNally Robinson Book of the Year Award, and Lifetime Achievement Award—English/Français. Guidelines and submission forms available online. Open to Manitoba writers only. Publishers are encouraged to send 4 (four) copies per award of any eligible books to the Manitoba Writers' Guild on or before Dec. 1 (postmark date) for books published January 1 and October 31. The deadline for books published between November 1 and December 31, is January 15. Deadline: December 1 and January 15. Prize: Several prizes up to $5,000 (Canadian). Jurors selected by the Manitoba Writers' Guild.

THE MCGINNIS-RITCHIE MEMORIAL AWARD

Southwest Review, Southern Methodist University, P.O. Box 750374, Dallas TX 75275-0374. (214) 768-1037. Fax: (214) 768-1408. E-mail: swr@mail.smu.edu. Website: www.smu.edu/southwestreview. Contact: Greg Brownderville, editor-in-chief. The McGinnis-Ritchie Memorial Award is given annually to the best works of fiction and nonfiction that appeared in the magazine in the previous year. Mss are submitted for publication, not for the prizes themselves. Guidelines for SASE or online. Prize: $500. Judged by Greg Brownderville.

TIPS "Not an open contest. Annual prize in which winners are chosen from published pieces during the preceding year."

A MIDSUMMER TALE

E-mail: editors@toasted-cheese.com. Website: www.toasted-cheese.com. Contact: Theryn Fleming, editor. A Midsummer Tale is open to non-genre fiction and creative nonfiction. There is a different theme each year. Entries must be unpublished. Accepts inquiries by e-mail. Cover letter should include name, address, e-mail, word count, and title. Length: 1,000-5,000 words. Open to any writer. Guidelines available in April on website. Deadline: June 21. Results announced on July 31. Winners notified by e-mail. List of winners on website. Prize: Amazon gift certificates and publication in Toasted Cheese. Entries are blind-judged by at least one Toasted Cheese editor

MINNESOTA BOOK AWARDS

The Friends of the Saint Paul Public Library, 1080 Montreal Avenue, Suite 2, St. Paul MN 55116. (651)222-3242. Fax: (651)222-1988. E-mail: mnbookawards@thefriends.org; friends@thefriends.org; info@thefriends.org. Website: www.mnbookawards.org. A year-round program celebrating and honoring Minnesota's best books, culminating in an annual awards ceremony. Recognizes and honors achievement by members of Minnesota's book and book arts community. All books must be the work of a Minnesota author or primary artistic creator (current Minnesota resident who maintains a year-round residence in Minnesota). All books must be published within the calendar year prior to the Awards presentation. Deadline: Nomination should be submitted by 5:00 p.m. on the first Friday in December.

MISSISSIPPI REVIEW PRIZE

Mississippi Review, 118 College Dr., #5144, Hattiesburg MS 39406-0001. (601)266-4321. **Fax:** (601)266-5757. **E-mail:** msreview@usm.edu. **Website:** www.mississippireview.com. Annual contest starting August 1 and running until January 1. Winners and finalists will make up next spring's print issue of the national literary magazine *Mississippi Review*. Each entrant will receive a copy of the prize issue. Contest is open to all writers in English except current or former students or employees of The University of Southern Mississippi. Fiction entries should be 1,000-8,000 words, poetry entries should be 3-5 poems totaling 10 pages or less. There is no limit on the number of entries you may submit. Online submissions must be submitted through Submittable site: mississippireview.submittable.com/submit. No mss will be returned. Previously published work is ineligible. Winners will be announced in March and publication is scheduled for June of following year. Entries should have "MR Prize," author name, address, phone, e-mail and title of work on page 1. Deadline: January 1. Prize: $1,000 in fiction and poetry. Judged by Andrew Malan Milward in fiction, and Angela Ball in poetry.

MOUNTAINS & PLAINS INDEPENDENT BOOKSELLERS ASSOCIATION READING THE WEST BOOK AWARDS

Mountains & Plains Independent Booksellers Association, 3278 Big Spruce Way, Park City UT 84098. **E-mail:** Submission is via an online form, posted on the website (www.mountainsplains.org) in the fall of each year. **Website:** http://www.mountainsplains.org/reading-the-west-book-awards/. **Contact:** Laura P Burnett. Mountains & Plains Independent Booksellers Association is a professional trade organization with the primary mission of supporting independent bookseller members in a 12-state region in the West. Also welcomes as members colleagues in the book industry including authors, publishers, sales representatives, and others. The purpose of these annual awards is to honor outstanding books published in the previous calendar year which are set in the region (Arizona, Colorado, Kansas, Montana, Nebraska, Nevada, New Mexico, Oklahoma, South Dakota, Texas, Utah, and Wyoming) or that evoke the spirit of the region. The author's place of residence is immaterial for these awards. Deadline: Nomination period September 1 to December 31 for books published in the previous calendar year. Prize: All nominated titles

are listed on the website (www.mountainsplains.org). Shortlist and winning titles are recognized via a press release, e-announcement, and on the website. Winners are recognized at a Reading the West luncheon at the Fall Discovery Show and in promotional materials. Judged by 2 panels of judges, 1 for adult titles and 1 for children's titles. Other categories/panels may be convened at the Association's discretion.

NATIONAL BOOK AWARDS

The National Book Foundation, 90 Broad St., Suite 604, New York NY 10004. (212)685-0261. **E-mail:** nationalbook@nationalbook.org; agall@nationalbook.org. **Website:** www.nationalbook.org. **Contact:** Amy Gall. The National Book Foundation and the National Book Awards celebrate the best of American literature, expand its audience, and enhance the cultural value of great writing in America. The contest offers prizes in 4 categories: fiction, nonfiction, poetry, and young people's literature. Books should be published between December 1 and November 30 of the past year. Submissions must be previously published and must be entered by the publisher. General guidelines available on website. Interested publishes should phone or e-mail the Foundation. Deadline: Submit entry form, payment, and a copy of the book by July 1. Prize: $10,000 in each category. Finalists will each receive a prize of $1,000. Judged by a category specific panel of 5 judges for each category.

NATIONAL OUTDOOR BOOK AWARDS

921 S. 8th Ave., Stop 8128, Pocatello ID 83209. (208)282-3912. **E-mail:** wattron@isu.edu. **Website:** www.noba-web.org. **Contact:** Ron Watters. Nine categories: History/biography, outdoor literature, instructional texts, outdoor adventure guides, nature guides, children's books, design/artistic merit, natural history literature, and nature and the environment. Additionally, a special award, the Outdoor Classic Award, is given annually to books which, over a period of time, have proven to be exceptionally valuable works in the outdoor field. Application forms and eligibility requirements are available online. Applications for the Awards program become available in early June. Deadline: August 24. Prize: Winning books are promoted nationally and are entitled to display the National Outdoor Book Award (NOBA) medallion.

THE NEUTRINO SHORT-SHORT CONTEST

Passages North, Dept. of English, Northern Michigan University, 1401 Presque Isle Ave., Marquette MI

49855. (906)227-1203. **Fax:** (906)227-1096. **E-mail:** passages@nmu.edu. **Website:** www.passagesnorth. com. **Contact:** Jennifer Howard. Offered every 2 years to publish new voices in literary fiction, nonfiction, hybrid-essays and prose poems (maximum 1,000 words). Guidelines available for SASE or online. Deadline: April 15. Submission period begins February 15. Prize: $1,000, and publication for the winner; 2 honorable mentions also published; all entrants receive a copy of *Passages North*. Judged by Lindsay Hunter in 2016.

NEW ENGLAND BOOK AWARDS

1955 Massachusetts Ave., #2, Cambridge MA 02140. (617)547-3642. **Fax:** (617)547-3759. **E-mail:** nan@ neba.org. **Website:** http://www.newenglandbooks. org/BookAwards. **Contact:** Nan Sorenson, administrative coordinator. Annual award. Previously published submissions only. Submissions made by New England booksellers; publishers. Submit written nominations only; actual books should not be sent. Member bookstores receive materials to display winners' books. Award is given to a specific title, fiction, nonfiction, children's. The titles must be either about New England, set in New England or by an author residing in the New England. The titles must be hardcover, paperback original or reissue that was published between September 1 and August 31. Entries must be still in print and available. Deadline: June 10. Prize: Winners will receive $250 for literacy to a charity of their choice. Judged by NEIBA membership.

NEW LETTERS LITERARY AWARDS

New Letters, University of Missouri-Kansas City, 5101 Rockhill Rd., Kansas City MO 64110-2499. (816)235-1168. **Fax:** (816)235-2611. **Website:** http://www. newletters.org/writers-wanted/writing-contests. Award has 3 categories (fiction, poetry, and creative nonfiction) with 1 winner in each. Offered annually for previously unpublished work. For guidelines, send an SASE to *New Letters*, or visit http://www.newletters.org/writers-wanted/writing-contests. Deadline: May 18. Prize: 1st place: $1,500, plus publication. Judged by regional writers of prominence and experience. Final judging by someone of national repute. Previous judges include Maxine Kumin, Albert Goldbarth, Charles Simic, and Janet Burroway.

NEW MILLENNIUM AWARDS FOR FICTION, POETRY, AND NONFICTION

New Millennium Writings, 4021 Garden Dr., Knoxville TN 37918. (865)254-4880. **Website:** www.new-millenniumwritings.org. **Contact:** Alexis Williams, Editor and Publisher. No restrictions as to style, content or number of submissions. Previously published pieces acceptable if online or under 5,000 print circulation. Simultaneous and multiple submissions welcome. Each fiction or nonfiction piece is a separate entry and should total no more than 6,000 words, except for the Short-Short Fiction Award, which should total no more than 1,000 words. (Nonfiction includes essays, profiles, memoirs, interviews, creative nonfiction, travel, humor, etc.) Each poetry entry may include up to 3 poems, not to exceed 5 pages total. All 20 poetry finalists will be published. Include name, phone, address, e-mail, and category on cover page only. Apply online via submissions manager. Send SASE or IRC for list of winners or await your book. Deadline: Postmarked on or before January 31 for the Winter Awards and July 31 for the Summer Awards. Prize: $1,000 for Best Poem; $1,000 for Best Fiction; $1,000 for Best Nonfiction; $1,000 for Best Short-Short Fiction.

NEW SOUTH WRITING CONTEST

English Department, Georgia State University, P.O. Box 3970, Atlanta GA 30302-3970. **E-mail:** newsouth@gsu.edu. **Website:** newsouthjournal.com/contest. **Contact:** Stephanie Devine, editor-in-chief. Offered annually to publish the most promising work of up-and-coming writers of poetry (up to 3 poems) and fiction (9,000 word limit). Rights revert to writer upon publication. Guidelines online. Deadline: April 30. Prize: 1st Place: $1,000 in each category; 2nd Place: $250; and publication to winners. Judged by Anya Silver in poetry and Matthew Salesses in prose.
TIPS "We look for engagement with language and characters we care about."

NORTHERN CALIFORNIA BOOK AWARDS

Northern California Book Reviewers Association, c/o Poetry Flash, 1450 Fourth St. #4, Berkeley CA 94710. (510)525-5476. **E-mail:** ncbr@poetryflash.org; editor@poetryflash.org. **Website:** www.poetryflash.org. **Contact:** Joyce Jenkins, executive director. Annual Northern California Book Award for outstanding book in literature, open to books published in the current calendar year by Northern California authors.

NCBR presents annual awards to Bay Area (northern California) authors annually in fiction, nonfiction, poetry and children's literature. Previously published books only. Must be published the calendar year prior to spring awards ceremony. Submissions nominated by publishers; author or agent could also nominate published work. Send 3 copies of the book to attention: NCBR. Encourages writers and stimulates interest in books and reading. Deadline: December 28. Prize: $100 honorarium and award certificate. Judging by voting members of the Northern California Book Reviewers.

NOVA WRITES COMPETITION FOR UNPUBLISHED MANUSCRIPTS

Writers' Federation of Nova Scotia, 1113 Marginal Rd., Halifax NS B3H 4P7. (902)423-8116. **Fax:** (902)422-0881. **E-mail:** programs@writers.ns.ca. **Website:** www.writers.ns.ca. **Contact:** Robin Spittal, communications and development officer. Annual program designed to honor work by unpublished writers in all 4 Atlantic Provinces. Entry is open to writers unpublished in the category of writing they wish to enter. Prizes are presented in the fall of each year. Categories include: short form creative nonfiction, long form creative nonfiction, novel, poetry, short story, and writing for children/young adult novel. Judges return written comments when competition is concluded. Page lengths and rules vary based on categories. See website for details. Anyone resident in the Atlantic Provinces since September 1st immediately prior to the deadline date is eligible to enter. Only one entry per category is allowed. Each entry requires its own entry form and registration fee. Deadline: December 13. Prizes vary based on categories. See website for details.

OHIOANA BOOK AWARDS

Ohioana Library Association, 274 E. First Ave., Suite 300, Columbus OH 43201-3673. (614)466-3831. **Fax:** (614)728-6974. **E-mail:** ohioana@ohioana.org. **Website:** www.ohioana.org. **Contact:** David Weaver, executive director. Writers must have been born in Ohio or lived in Ohio for at least 5 years, but books about Ohio or an Ohioan need not be written by an Ohioan. Finalists announced in May and winners in July. Winners notified by mail in early summer. Offered annually to bring national attention to Ohio authors and their books, published in the last year. (Books can only be considered once.) Categories: Fiction, nonfiction, juvenile, poetry, and books about Ohio or an Ohioan. Deadline: December 31. Prize: $1,000 cash prize, certificate, and glass sculpture. Judged by a jury selected by librarians, book reviewers, writers and other knowledgeable people.

OKLAHOMA BOOK AWARDS

200 NE 18th St., Oklahoma City OK 73105. (405)521-2502. **Fax:** (405)525-7804. **E-mail:** connie.armstrong@libraries.ok.gov. **Website:** www.odl.state.ok.us/ocb. **Contact:** Connie Armstrong, executive director. This award honors Oklahoma writers and books about Oklahoma. Awards are presented to best books in fiction, nonfiction, children's, design and illustration, and poetry books about Oklahoma or books written by an author who was born, is living or has lived in Oklahoma. SASE for award rules and entry forms. Winner will be announced at banquet in Oklahoma City. The Arrell Gibson Lifetime Achievement Award is also presented each year for a body of work. Previously published submissions only. Submissions made by the author, author's agent, or entered by a person or group of people, including the publisher. Must be published during the calendar year preceding the award. Deadline: January 10. Prize: Awards a medal. Judging by a panel of 5 people for each category, generally a librarian, a working writer in the genre, booksellers, editors, etc.

OPEN SEASON AWARDS

The Malahat Review, University of Victoria, P.O. Box 1700, Stn CSC, Victoria BC V8V 2Y2 Canada. (250)721-8524. **Fax:** (250)472-5051. **E-mail:** malahat@uvic.ca. **Website:** www.malahatreview.ca. **Contact:** Patrick Grace, publicity manager. The Open Season Awards accepts entries of poetry, fiction, and creative nonfiction. Winners published in spring issue of *Malahat Review* announced in winter on website, facebook page, and in quarterly e-newsletter, *Malahat lite*. Submissions must be unpublished. No simultaneous submissions. Submit up to 3 poems of 100 lines or less; 1 piece of fiction 2,500 words maximum; or 1 piece of creative nonfiction, 2,500 words maximum. No restrictions on subject matter or aesthetic approach. Include separate page with writer's name, address, e-mail, and title(s); no identifying information on mss pages. E-mail submissions now accepted: season@uvic.ca. Do not include SASE for results; mss will not be returned. Guidelines available on website. Winners and finalists will be contacted by email. Deadline: November 1. Prize: $4,500 over three categories (poetry, fiction, creative nonfiction) and publication in *The Malahat Review* in each category.

OREGON BOOK AWARDS

925 SW Washington St., Portland OR 97205. (503)227-2583. **Fax:** (503)241-4256. **E-mail:** la@literary-arts.org. **Website:** www.literary-arts.org. **Contact:** Susan Denning, director of programs and events. The annual Oregon Book Awards celebrate Oregon authors in the areas of poetry, fiction, nonfiction, drama and young readers' literature published between August 1 and July 31 of the previous calendar year. Awards are available for every category. See website for details. Entry fee determined by initial print run; see website for details. Entries must be previously published. Oregon residents only. Accepts inquiries by phone and e-mail. Finalists announced in January. Winners announced at an awards ceremony in November. List of winners available in April. Deadline: August 26. Prize: Grant of $2,500. (Grant money could vary.) Judged by writers who are selected from outside Oregon for their expertise in a genre. Past judges include Mark Doty, Colson Whitehead and Kim Barnes.

JUDITH SIEGEL PEARSON AWARD

Judith Siegel Pearson Award, c/o Department of English, Wayne State University, Attn: Royanne Smith, 5057 Woodward Ave, Ste. 9408, Detroit MI 48202. **E-mail:** fm8146@wayne.edu. **Website:** https://wsu-writingawards.submittable.com/submit. **Contact:** Donovan Hohn. Offers an annual award for the best creative or scholarly work on a subject concerning women. The type of work accepted rotates each year: drama in 2016, poetry in 2017; nonfiction in 2018; fiction in 2019. Open to all interested writers and scholars. Only submit the appropriate genre in each year. Submit electronically on the web site listed here. Deadline: February 22. Prize: $500. Judged by members of the writing faculty of the Wayne State University English Department.

PEN CENTER USA LITERARY AWARDS

PEN Center USA, P.O. Box 6037, Beverly Hills CA 90212. (323)424-4939. **E-mail:** awards@penusa.org. **E-mail:** awards@penusa.org. **Website:** www.penusa.org. Offered for work published or produced in the previous calendar year. Open to writers living west of the Mississippi River. Award categories: fiction, poetry, research nonfiction, creative nonfiction, translation, young adult, graphic literature, drama,

screenplay, teleplay, journalism. Guidelines and submission form available on website. No anthologies or self-pubished work. Deadline: See website for details. Prize: $1,000.

PENGUIN RANDOM HOUSE CREATIVE WRITING AWARDS

One Scholarship Way, P.O. Box 297, St. Peter MN 56082. (212)782-9348. **Fax:** (212) 782-5157. **E-mail:** creativewriting@penguinrandomhouse.com. **Website:** www.penguinrandomhouse.com/creativewriting. **Contact:** Melanie Fallon Hauska, director. Offered annually for unpublished work to NYC public high school seniors. 72 awards given in literary and nonliterary categories. Four categories: poetry, fiction/drama, personal essay, and graphic novel. Applicants must be seniors (under age 21) at a New York high school. No college essays or class assignments will be accepted. Word length: 2,500 words or less. Applicants must be seniors (under age 21) at a New York high school. Results announced mid-May. Winners notified by mail and phone. For contest results, send SASE, fax, e-mail or visit website. Deadline: February 3 for all categories. Graphic Novel extended deadline: March 1st. Prize: Awards range from $500-10,000. The program usually awards just under $100,000 in scholarships.

THE PINCH LITERARY AWARDS

Literary Awards, The Pinch, Department of English, The University of Memphis, Memphis TN 38152-6176. (901)678-4591. **Website:** www.pinchjournal.com. Offered annually for unpublished short stories of 5,000 words maximum or up to three poems. Guidelines on website. Cost: $20, which is put toward one issue of *The Pinch*. Deadline: March 15. Prize: 1st place Fiction: $1,500 and publication; 1st place Poetry: $1,000 and publication. Offered annually for unpublished short stories and prose of up to 5,000 words and 1-3 poems. Deadline: March 15. Open to submissions on December 15. Prizes: $1,000 for 1st place in each category.

PNWA LITERARY CONTEST

Pacifc Northwest Writers Association, PMB 2717, 1420 NW Gilman Blvd., Suite 2, Issaquah WA 98027. (452)673-2665. **Fax:** (452)961-0768. **E-mail:** pnwa@pnwa.org. **Website:** www.pnwa.org. Annual literary contest with 12 different categories. See website for details and specific guidelines. Each entry receives 2 critiques. Winners announced at the PNWA Summer Conference, held annually in mid-July. Deadline: February 20. Prize: 1st Place: $600; 2nd Place: $300; 3rd Place: $100. Judged by an agent or editor attending the conference.

PRAIRIE SCHOONER BOOK PRIZE

Prairie Schooner and the University of Nebraska Press, Prairie Schooner Prize Series, 123 Andrews Hall, Lincoln NE 68588-0334. (402)472-0911. **E-mail:** PSBookPrize@unl.edu. **Website:** prairieschooner.unl.edu. **Contact:** Kwame Dawes, editor. Annual competition/award for poetry and short story collections. The Prairie Schooner Book Prize Series welcomes manuscripts from all living writers, including non-US citizens, writing in English. Both unpublished and published writers are welcome to submit manuscripts. Writers may enter both contests. Simultaneous submissions are accepted, but we ask that you notify us immediately if your manuscript is accepted for publication somewhere else. No past or present paid employee of Prairie Schooner or the University of Nebraska Press or current faculty or student at the University of Nebraska will be eligible for the prizes. Deadline: March 15. Prize: $3,000 and publication through the University of Nebraska Press.

THE PRESIDIO LA BAHIA AWARD

Sons of the Republic of Texas, 1717 Eighth St., Bay City TX 77414-5033. (979)245-6644. **Fax:** (979)244-3819. **E-mail:** srttexas@srttexas.org. **Website:** www.srttexas.org. **Contact:** Scott Dunbar, chairman. "Material may be submitted concerning the influence on Texas culture of our Spanish Colonial heritage in laws, customs, language, religion, architecture, art, and other related fields." Offered annually to promote suitable preservation of relics, appropriate dissemination of data, and research into Texas heritage, with particular attention to the Spanish Colonial period. Deadline: September 30. Prizes: $2,000 available annually for winning participants; 1st Place: Minimum of $1,200; 2nd and 3rd prizes at the discretion of the judges. Judged by members of the Sons of the Republic of Texas on the Presidio La Bahia Award Committee.

PRIME NUMBER MAGAZINE AWARDS

Press 53, 560 N. Trade St., Suite 103, Winston-Salem NC 27101. (336)770-5353. **Fax:** N/A. **E-mail:** kevin@press53.com. **Website:** www.press53.com. **Contact:** Kevin Morgan Watson, Publisher. Awards $1,000 in poetry and short fiction. Details and guidelines available online. Deadline: April 15. Submission period begins January 1. Finalists and winners announced by August 1. Winners published in Prime Number Magazine in October. Prize: $1,000 cash. All winners receive publication in Prime Number Magazine online. Judged by industry professionals to be named when the contest begins.

⊘ PRISM INTERNATIONAL ANNUAL SHORT FICTION, POETRY, AND CREATIVE NONFICTION CONTESTS

PRISM International, Creative Writing Program, UBC, Buch. E462, 1866 Main Mall, Vancouver BC V6T 1Z1 Canada. **E-mail:** promotions@prismmagazine.ca. **Website:** www.prismmagazine.ca. **Contact:** Claire Matthews. Offered annually for unpublished work to award the best in contemporary fiction, poetry, drama, translation, and nonfiction. Works of translation are eligible. Guidelines are available on website. Acquires first North American serial rights upon publication, and limited web rights for pieces selected for website. Open to any writer except students and faculty in the Creative Writing Department at UBC, or people who have taken a creative writing course at UBC within 2 years of the contest deadline. Entry includes subscription. Deadlines: Creative Nonfiction: July 15; Fiction: January 15; Poetry: October 15. Prize: All grand prizes are $1,500, $600 for first runner up, and $400 for second runner up. Winners are published.

PUSHCART PRIZE

Pushcart Press, P.O. Box 380, Wainscott NY 11975. (631)324-9300. **Website:** www.pushcartprize.com. **Contact:** Bill Henderson. Published every year since 1976, The Pushcart Prize - Best of the Small Presses series "is the most honored literary project in America. Hundreds of presses and thousands of writers of short stories, poetry and essays have been represented in the pages of our annual collections." Little magazine and small book press editors (print or online) may make up to six nominations from their year's publicatoins by the deadline. The nominations may be any combination of poetry, short fiction, essays or literary whatnot. Editors may nominate self-contained portions of books — for instance, a chapter from a novel. Deadline: December 1.

SUMMERFIELD G. ROBERTS AWARD

Sons of the Republic of Texas, 1717 Eighth St., Bay City TX 77414-5033. (979)245-6644. **Fax:** (979)244-3819. **E-mail:** aa-srt@son-rep-texas.net. **Website:**

www.srttexas.org. **Contact:** Edward A. Heath, Chairman. The manuscripts must be written or published during the calendar year for which the award is given. No entry may be submitted more than one time. There is no word limit on the material submitted for the award. The manuscripts may be fiction, nonfiction, poems, essays, plays, short stories, novels, or biographies. The competition is open to all writers everywhere; they need not reside in Texas nor must the publishers be in Texas. Judges each year are winners of the award in the last three years. The purpose of this award is to encourage literary effort and research about historical events and personalities during the days of the Republic of Texas,1836-1846, and to stimulate interest in this period. Deadline: January 15. Prize: $2,500.

ROYAL DRAGONFLY BOOK AWARDS

Story Monsters LLC, 4696 W. Tyson St., Chandler AZ 85226. (480)940-8182. **Fax:** (480)940-8787. **E-mail:** Cristy@StoryMonsters.com; Linda@StoryMonsters.com. **E-mail:** cristy@StoryMonsters.com. **Website:** www.DragonflyBookAwards.com. **Contact:** Cristy Bertini. Offered annually for any previously published work to honor authors for writing excellence of all types of literature—fiction and nonfiction—in 66 categories, appealing to a wide range of ages and comprehensive list of genres. Open to any title published in English. Guidelines available online. Send submissions to Cristy Bertini, Attn.: Five Star Book Awards, 1271 Turkey St., Ware, MA 01082. Deadline: October 1. Prize: Grand Prize winner receives a $300 cash prize, 100 foil award seals, one hour of marketing consultation from Story Monsters LLC, as well as publicity on Dragonfly Book Awards website and inclusion in a winners' news release sent to a comprehensive list of media outlets. All first-place winners of categories will be put into a drawing for a $100 prize. In addition, each first-place winner in each category receives a certificate commemorating their accomplishment, 25 foil award seals and mention on Dragonfly Book Awards website. All winners are listed in Story Monsters Ink magazine.

ERNEST SANDEEN PRIZE IN POETRY AND THE RICHARD SULLIVAN PRIZE IN SHORT FICTION

University of Notre Dame, Dept. of English, 356 O'Shaughnessy Hall, Notre Dame IN 46556-5639. (574)631-7526. **Fax:** (574)631-4795. **E-mail:** creative-writing@nd.edu. **Website:** http://english.nd.edu/creative-writing/publications/sandeen-sullivan-prizes. **Contact:** Director of Creative Writing. The Sandeen & Sullivan Prizes in Poetry and Short Fiction is awarded to the author who has published at least one volume of short fiction or one volume of poetry. Awarded biannually, but judged quadrennially. Though the Sandeen Prize is open to any author, with the exception of graduates of the University of Notre Dame, who has published at least one volume of short stories (Sullivan) or one collection of poetry (Sandeen), judges pay special attention to second volumes. Please include a vita and/or a biographical statement which includes your publishing history. Will also see a selection of reviews of the earlier collection. Please submit two copies of mss and inform if the mss is available on computer disk. Include an SASE for acknowledgment of receipt of your submission. If you would like your manuscript returned, please send an SASE. Manuscripts will not otherwise be returned. Submissions Period: May 1 - September 1. Prize: $1,000, a $500 award and a $500 advance against royalties from the Notre Dame Press.

SANTA FE WRITERS PROJECT LITERARY AWARDS PROGRAM

Santa Fe Writers Project, 369 Montezuma Ave., #350, Santa Fe NM 87501. **E-mail:** info@sfwp.com. **Website:** www.sfwp.com. **Contact:** Andrew Gifford. Annual contest seeking fiction and nonfiction of any genre. The Literary Awards Program was founded by a group of authors to offer recognition for excellence in writing in a time of declining support for writers and the craft of literature. Past judges have included Richard Currey, Jayne Anne Phillips, Chris Offutt, Emily St. John Mandel, and David Morrell. Deadline: July 20th. Prize: $3,300 and publication. Judged by Benjamin Percy and Mat Johnson in 2017.

☯ SASKATCHEWAN BOOK AWARDS

315-1102 Eighth Ave., Regina SK S4R 1C9 Canada. (306)569-1585. **E-mail:** director@bookawards.sk.ca. **Website:** www.bookawards.sk.ca. **Contact:** Courtney Bates-Hardy, Administrative Director. Saskatchewan Book Awards celebrates, promotes, and rewards Saskatchewan authors and publishers worthy of recognition through 14 awards, granted on an annual or semiannual basis. Awards: Fiction, Nonfiction, Poetry, Scholarly, First Book, *Prix du Livre Français*, Regina, Saskatoon, Aboriginal Peoples' Writing, Aboriginal

Peoples' Publishing, Publishing in Education, Publishing, Children's Literature/Young Adult Literature, Book of the Year. Deadline: Early November. Prize: $2,000 (CAD) for all awards except Book of the Year, which is $3,000 (CAD). Juries are made up of writing and publishing professionals from outside of Saskatchewan.

THE MONA SCHREIBER PRIZE FOR HUMOROUS FICTION & NONFICTION

3940 Laurel Canyon Blvd., #566, Studio City CA 91604. **E-mail:** brad.schreiber@att.net. **Website:** www.bradschreiber.com. **Contact:** Brad Schreiber. Established in 2000, to honor Mona Schreiber, a writer and teacher. Entry fees are the same as in 2000 and money from entries helps pay for prizes. No SASEs. Non-US entries should enclose US currency or checks written in US dollars. Include e-mail address. No previously published work. The purpose of the contest is to award the most creative humor writing, in any form, under than 750 words, in either fiction or nonfiction, including but not limited to stories, articles, essays, speeches, shopping lists, diary entries, and anything else writers dream up. Complete rules and previous winning entries On website. Deadline: December 1. Prize: 1st Place: $500; 2nd Place: $250; 3rd Place: $100. Judged by Brad Schreiber, journalist, consultant, instructor, author of among other books, the humor writing how-to *What Are You Laughing At?*
TIPS Uniqueness is suggested. Weirdness is encouraged.

☻ SHORT GRAIN CONTEST

P.O. Box 3986, Regina SK S4P 3R9 Canada. (306)791-7749. **E-mail:** grainmag@skwriter.com. **Website:** www.grainmagazine.ca/short-grain-contest. **Contact:** Jordan Morris, business administrator (inquiries only). The annual Short Grain Contest includes a category for poetry of any style up to 100 lines and fiction of any style up to 2,500 words, offering 3 prizes. Each entry must be original, unpublished, not submitted elsewhere for publication or broadcast, nor accepted elsewhere for publication or broadcast, nor entered simultaneously in any other contest or competition for which it is also eligible to win a prize. Entries must be typed on 8½x11 paper. It must be legible. No simultaneous submissions. A separate covering page must be attached to the text of your entry, and must provide the following information: Author's name, complete mailing address, telephone number, e-mail address, entry title, category name, and line count. Online submissions are accepted, see website for details. An absolutely accurate word or line count is required. No identifying information on the text pages. Entries will not be returned. Names of the winners and titles of the winning entries will be posted on the *Grain Magazine* website in August; only the winners will be notified. Deadline: April 1. Prize: $1,000, plus publication in *Grain Magazine*; 2nd Place: $750; 3rd Place: $500.

SKIPPING STONES HONOR (BOOK) AWARDS

P.O. Box 3939, Eugene OR 97403. (541)342-4956. **Fax:** (541)342-4956. **E-mail:** editor@skippingstones.org. **Website:** www.skippingstones.org. **Contact:** Arun N. Toké. *Skipping Stones* is a well respected, multicultural literary magazine now in its 29th year. For multicultural and nature books and teaching resources. Entries must be previously published. Open to published books and teaching resources that appeared in print during a 2-year period prior to the deadline date. Guidelines for SASE or e-mail and on website. Accepts inquiries by e-mail or phone. The Annual Honors list includes approximately 25 books and teaching resources in three categories. Annual award to promote multicultural and/or nature awareness through creative writings for children and teens and their educators. Seeks authentic, exceptional, child/youth friendly books that promote intercultural, international, intergenerational harmony, or understanding through creative ways. Deadline: February 29. Prize: Honor certificates; gold seals; reviews; press release/publicity. Judged by a multicultural committee of teachers, librarians, parents, students and editors.
TIPS "Books that come out of author's own research, experiences and cultural understanding seem to have an edge. We like authentic, educational, entertaining and exceptional books. There are three categories: International and Multicultural, Nature and Ecology, and Theaching Resources and educational DVDs."

THE BERNICE SLOTE AWARD

Prairie Schooner, 123 Andrews Hall, PO Box 880334, Lincoln NE 68588-0334. (402)472-0911. **Fax:** (402)472-1817. **E-mail:** PrairieSchooner@unl.edu. **Website:** www.prairieschooner.unl.edu. **Contact:** Kwame Dawes. Categories: short stories, essays and poetry. For guidelines, send SASE or visit website. Only work published in the journal during the previous year will be considered. Work is nominated by the editorial staff. Offered annually for the best work by a beginning writer published in *Prairie Schooner* in the previous year. Celebrates the best and finest writing that they have published for the year. Prize: $500. Judged by editorial staff of *Prairie Schooner*.

JEFFREY E. SMITH EDITORS' PRIZE IN FICTION, ESSAY AND POETRY

The Missouri Review, 357 McReynolds Hall, UMC, Columbia MO 65211. (573)882-4474. **Fax:** (573)884-4671. **E-mail:** contest_question@moreview.com. **Website:** www.missourireview.com. **Contact:** Editor. Offered annually for unpublished work in 3 categories: fiction, essay, and poetry. Guidelines online or for SASE. Deadline: October 15. Prize: $5,000 and publication for each category winner.

KAY SNOW WRITING CONTEST

Willamette Writers, Willamette Writers, 2108 Buck St., West Linn OR 97068. (503)305-6729. **Fax:** (503)344-6174. **E-mail:** reg@willamettewriters.com. **Website:** www.willamettewriters.org. Willamette Writers is the largest writers' organization in Oregon and one of the largest writers' organizations in the United States. It is a non-profit, tax-exempt Oregon corporation led by volunteers. Elected officials and directors administer an active program of monthly meetings, special seminars, workshops, and an annual writing conference. Continuing with established programs and starting new ones is only made possible by strong volunteer support. See website for specific details and rules. There are six different categories writers can enter: Adult Fiction, Adult Nonfiction, Poetry, Juvenile Short Story, Screenwriting, and Student Writer. The purpose of this annual writing contest, named in honor of Willamette Writer's founder, Kay Snow, is to help writers reach professional goals in writing in a broad array of categories and to encourage student writers. Deadline: April 23. Submission deadline begins January 15. Prize: One first prize of $300, one second place prize of $150, and a third place prize of $50 per winning entry in each of the six categories. Student first prize is $50, $20 for second place, $10 for third.

SOCIETY OF MIDLAND AUTHORS AWARD

Society of Midland Authors, Society of Midland Authors, P.O. Box 10419, Chicago IL 60610-0419. **E-mail:** marlenetbrill@comcast.net. **Website:** www.midlandauthors.com. **Contact:** Marlene Targ Brill, awards chair. Since 1957, the Society has presented annual awards for the best books written by Midwestern authors. The Society began in 1915. The contest is open to any title published within the year prior to the contest year. Open to adult and children's authors/poets who reside in, were born in, or have strong ties to a Midland state, which includes Illinois, Indiana, Iowa, Kansas, Michigan, Minnesota, Missouri, Nebraska, North Dakota, South Dakota, Ohio, and Wisconsin. The Society of Midland Authors (SMA) Award is presented to one title in each of six categories: adult nonfiction, adult fiction, adult biography and memoir, children's nonfiction, children's fiction, and poetry. There may be honor book winners as well. Books and entry forms must be mailed to the 3 judges in each category; for a list of judges and the entry and payment forms, visit the SMA website. Do not mail books to the society's P.O. box. The fee can be sent to the SMA P.P. box or paid via Paypal. Deadline: January 7. Prize: $500 and a plaque that is awarded at the SMA banquet in May in Chicago. Honorary winners receive a plaque.

SOUL-MAKING KEATS LITERARY COMPETITION

The Webhallow House, 1544 Sweetwood Dr., Broadmoor Village CA 94015-2029. **E-mail:** SoulKeats@mail.com. **Website:** www.soulmakingcontest.us. **Contact:** Eileen Malone, award director. Annual open contest offers cash prizes in each of 13 literary categories. Competition receives 600 entries/year. Names of winners and judges are posted on website. Winners announced in January by SASE and on website. Winners are invited to read at the Koret Auditorium, San Francisco. Event is televised. Submissions in some categories may be previously published. No names or other identifying information on mss; include 3x5 card with poet's name, address, phone, fax, e-mail, title(s) of work, and category entered. Include SASE for results only; mss will not be returned. Guidelines available on website. Deadline: November 30. Prizes: 1st Prize: $100; 2nd Prize: $50; 3rd Prize: $25.

✪ *SUBTERRAIN MAGAZINE'S* ANNUAL LUSH Triumphant Literary Awards Competition

P.O. Box 3008 MPO, Vancouver BC V6B 3X5 Canada. (604)876-8710. **Fax:** (604)879-2667. **E-mail:** subter@portal.ca. **Website:** www.subterrain.ca. Entrants may submit as many entries in as many categories as they like. Fiction: Max of 3,000 words. Poetry: A suite of 5 related poems (max of 15 pages). Creative Nonfiction (based on fact, adorned with fiction): Max of 4,000 words. All entries must be previously unpublished material and not currently under consideration in any other contest or competition. Deadline: May 15. Prize: Winners in each category will receive $1,000 cash (plus payment for publication) and publication in the Winter issue. First runner-up in each category will be published in the Spring issue of *subTerrain*.

THE TEXAS INSTITUTE OF LETTERS LITERARY AWARDS

E-mail: Betwx@aol.com. Website: www.texasinstituteofletters.org. The Texas Institute of Letters gives annual awards for books by Texas authors and writers who have produced books about Texas, including Best Books of Poetry, Fiction, and Nonfiction. Awards are also given for best Short Story, Magazine or Newspaper Article, Essay, and best Books for Children and Young Adults. Work submitted must have been published in the year stipulated, and entries may be made by authors or by their publishers. Complete guidelines and award information is available on the Texas Institute of Letters website.

⊙ TORONTO BOOK AWARDS

City of Toronto c/o Toronto Arts & Culture, Cultural Partnerships, City Hall, 9E, 100 Queen St. W., Toronto ON M5H 2N2 Canada. E-mail: shan@toronto.ca. Website: www.toronto.ca/book_awards. The Toronto Book Awards honor authors of books of literary or artistic merit that are evocative of Toronto. There are no separate categories; all books are judged together. Any fiction or nonfiction book published in English for adults and/or children that are evocative of Toronto are eligible. To be eligible, books must be published between January 1 and December 31 of previous year. Deadline: April 30. Prize: Each finalist receives $1,000 and the winning author receives $10,000 ($15,000 total in prize money available).

THE JULIA WARD HOWE AWARD

The Boston Authors Club, 33 Brayton Road, Brighton MA 02135. (617)783-1357. E-mail: alan.lawson@bc.edu. Website: www.bostonauthorsclub.org. Contact: Alan Lawson, president. Julia Ward Howe Prize offered annually in the spring for books published the previous year. Two awards are given: one for adult books of fiction, nonfiction, or poetry, and one for children's books, middle grade and young adult novels, nonfiction, or poetry. No picture books or subsidized publishers. There must be two copies of each book submitted. Authors must live within 100 miles of Boston the year their book is published. Deadline: January 15. Prize: $1,000 in each category. Several books will also be cited with no cash awards as Finalists or Highly Recommended.

THE ROBERT WATSON LITERARY PRIZE IN FICTION AND POETRY

The Robert Watson Literary Prizes, *The Greensboro Review*, MFA Writing Program, 3302 MHRA Building, Greensboro NC 27402-6170. (336)334-5459. E-mail: jlclark@uncg.edu. Website: www.greensbororeview.org. Contact: Jim Clark, editor. Offered annually for fiction (up to 25 double-spaced pages) and poetry (up to 10 pages). Entries must be unpublished. Open to any writer. Guidelines available online. Submit online: https://greensbororeview.submittable.com/submit. Deadline: September 15. Prize: $1,000 each for best short story and poem. Judged by editors of *The Greensboro Review*.

❺ WESTERN AUSTRALIAN PREMIER'S BOOK AWARDS

State Library of Western Australia, Perth Cultural Centre, 25 Francis St., Perth WA 6000 Australia. (61)(8)9427-3151. E-mail: premiersbookawards@slwa.wa.gov.au. Website: pba.slwa.wa.gov.au. Contact: Karen de San Miguel. Annual competition for Australian citizens or permanent residents of Australia, or writers whose work has Australia as its primary focus. Categories: children's books, digital narrative, fiction, nonfiction, poetry, scripts, writing for young adults, West Australian history, and Western Australian emerging writers. Submit 5 original copies of the work to be considered for the awards. All works must have been published between January 1 and December 31 of the prior year. See website for details and rules of entry. Deadline: January 31. Prize: Awards $25,000 for Premier's Prize; awards $15,000 each for the Children's Books, Digital Narrative, Fiction, and Nonfiction categories; awards $10,000 each for the Poetry, Scripts, Western Australian History, Western Australian Emerging Writers, and Writing for Young Adults; awards $5,000 for People's Choice Award.

WESTERN HERITAGE AWARDS

National Cowboy & Western Heritage Museum, 1700 NE 63rd St., Oklahoma City OK 73111-7997. (405)478-2250. Fax: (405)478-4714. Website: www.nationalcowboymuseum.org. Contact: Jessica Limestall. The

National Cowboy & Western Heritage Museum Western Heritage Awards were established to honor and encourage the legacy of those whose works in literature, music, film, and television reflect the significant stories of the American West. Accepted categories for literary entries: western novel, nonfiction book, art book, photography book, juvenile book, magazine article, or poetry book. Previously published submissions only; must be published the calendar year before the awards are presented. Requirements for entrants: The material must pertain to the development or preservation of the West, either from a historical or contemporary viewpoint. Literary entries must have been published between December 1 and November 30 of calendar year. Five copies of each published work must be furnished for judging with each entry, along with the completed entry form. Works recognized during special awards ceremonies held annually at the museum. There is an autograph party preceding the awards. Awards ceremonies are sometimes broadcast. The WHA are presented annually to encourage the accurate and artistic telling of great stories of the West through 16 categories of western literature, television, film and music; including fiction, nonfiction, children's books and poetry. See website for details and category definitions. Deadline: November 30. Prize: Awards a Wrangler bronze sculpture designed by famed western artist, John Free. Judged by a panel of judges selected each year with distinction in various fields of western art and heritage.

WESTERN WRITERS OF AMERICA

271CR 219, Encampment WY 82325. (307)329-8942. **Fax:** (307)327-5465 (call first). **E-mail:** wwa. moulton@gmail.com. **Website:** www.westernwriters.org. **Contact:** Candy Moulton, executive director. Seventeen Spur Award categories in various aspects of the American West. Send entry form with your published work. Accepts multiple submissions, each with its own entry form. The nonprofit Western Writers of America has promoted and honored the best in Western literature with the annual Spur Awards, selected by panels of judges. Awards, for material published last year, are given for works whose inspirations, image and literary excellence best represent the reality and spirit of the American West.

WESTMORELAND POETRY & SHORT STORY CONTEST

Westmoreland Arts & Heritage Festival, 252 Twin Lakes Road, Latrobe PA 15650-9415. (724)834-7474. **Fax:** (724)850-7474. **E-mail:** info@artsandheritage. com. **Website:** www.artsandheritage.com. **Contact:** Diane Shrader. Offered annually for unpublished work. Two categories: Poem and Short Story. Short story entries no longer than 4,000 words. Family-oriented festival and contest. Deadline: February 17. Prizes: Award: $200; 1st Place: $125; 2nd Place: $100; 3rd Place: $75.

WILLA LITERARY AWARD

Women Writing the West, 8547 East Arapaho Rd., #J-541, Greenwood Village CO 80112-1436. **E-mail:** Anneschroederauthor@gmail.com. **Website:** www. womenwritingthewest.org. **Contact:** Anne Schroeder. The WILLA Literary Award honors the year's best in published literature featuring women's or girls' stories set in the West. Women Writing the West (WWW), a nonprofit association of writers and other professionals writing and promoting the Women's West, underwrites and presents the nationally recognized award annually (for work published between January 1 and December 31). The award is named in honor of Pulitzer Prize winner Willa Cather, one of the country's foremost novelists. The award is given in 7 categories: historical fiction, contemporary fiction, original softcover fiction, creative nonfiction, scholarly nonfiction, poetry, and children's/young adult fiction/nonfiction. Entry forms available on the website. Deadline: November 1–February 1. Prize: $100 and a trophy. Finalist receives a plaque. Both receive digital and sticker award emblems for book covers. Notice of Winning and Finalist titles mailed to more than 4,000 booksellers, libraries, and others. Award announcement is in early August, and awards are presented to the winners and finalists at the annual WWW Fall Conference. Judged by professional librarians not affiliated with WWW.

TENNESSEE WILLIAMS/NEW ORLEANS LITERARY FESTIVAL CONTESTS

Tennessee Williams/New Orleans Literary Festival, 938 Lafayette St., Suite 514, New Orleans LA 70113. (504)581-1144. **E-mail:** info@tennesseewilliams. net. **Website:** www.tennesseewilliams.net/contests. **Contact:** Paul J. Willis. Annual contests for: Unpublished One Act, Unpublished Short Fiction, and Unpublished Poem. Plays should run no more than one hour in length. Unlimited entries per person. Production criteria include scripts requiring minimal technical support for a 100-seat theater. Cast of characters must be small. See website for additional guidelines and entry form. Fiction must not exceed 7,000 words. Poetry submissions should be 2-4 poems not exceeding 400 lines total. "Our competitions provide playwrights an opportunity to see their work fully produced before a large audience during one of the largest literary festivals in the nation, and for the festival to showcase the undiscovered talents of poetry and fiction writers." Deadline: November 1 (One Act); November 15 (Poetry); December 1 (Fiction). Prize: One Act: $1,500, staged read at the next festival, full production at the festival the following year, VIP All-Access Festival pass for two years ($1,000 value), and publication in Bayou. Poetry: $1,000, public reading at next festival, publication in Louisiana Cultural Vistas Magazine. Fiction: $1,500, public reading at next festival, publication in Louisiana Literature. Judged by an anonymous expert panel for One Act contest. Judged by special guest judges, who change every year, for fiction and poetry.

☼ THE WORD AWARDS

The Word Guild, The Word Guild, Suite # 226, 245 King George Rd, Brantford ON N3R 7N7 Canada. 800-969-9010 x 1. **E-mail:** info@thewordguild.com. **E-mail:** info@thewordguild.com. **Website:** www. thewordguild.com. **Contact:** Karen deBlieck. The Word Guild is an organization of Canadian writers and editors who are Christian, and who are committed to encouraging one another and to fostering standards of excellence in the art, craft, practice and ministry of writing. Memberships available for various experience levels. Yearly conference Write Canada (please see website for information) and features keynote speakers, continuing classes and workshops. Editors and agents on site. The Word Awards is for work published in the past year, in almost 30 categories including books, articles, essays, fiction, nonfiction, novels, short stories, songs, and poetry. Please see website for more information. Deadline: January 15. Prize $50 CAD for article and short pieces; $100 CAD for book entries. Finalists book entries are eligible for the $5,000 Grace Irwin prize. Judged by industry leaders and professionals.

WORLD'S BEST SHORT-SHORT STORY CONTEST, NARRATIVE NONFICTION CONTEST & SOUTHEAST REVIEW POETRY CONTEST

The Southeast Review, Florida State University, English Department, Tallahassee FL 32306. **E-mail:** southeastreview@gmail.com. **Website:** www.southeastreview.org. **Contact:** Erin Hoover, editor. Annual award for unpublished short-short stories (500 words or less), poetry, and narrative nonfiction (6,000 words or less). Visit website for details. Deadline: March 15. Prize: $500 per category. Winners and finalists will be published in *The Southeast Review*.

WRITER'S DIGEST ANNUAL WRITING COMPETITION

Writer's Digest, a publication of F+W Media, Inc., 10151 Carver Rd., Suite 200, Cincinnati OH 45242. (715)445-4612, ext. 13430. **E-mail:** writing-competition@fwmedia.com. **Website:** www.writersdigest. com. Writing contest with 10 categories: Inspirational Writing (spiritual/religious, maximum 2,500 words); Memoir/Personal Essay (maximum 2,000 words); Magazine Feature Article (maximum 2,000 words); Short Story (genre, maximum 4,000 words); Short Story (mainstream/literary, maximum 4,000 words); Rhyming Poetry (maximum 32 lines); Non-rhyming Poetry (maximum 32 lines); Stage Play (first 15 pages and 1-page synopsis); TV/Movie Script (first 15 pages and 1-page synopsis). Entries must be original, in English, unpublished/unproduced (except for Magazine Feature Articles), and not accepted by another publisher/producer at the time of submission. *Writer's Digest* retains one-time publication rights to the winning entries in each category. Deadline: May (early bird); June. Grand Prize: $3,000 and a trip to the Writer's Digest Conference to meet with editors and agents; 1st Place: $1,000 and $100 of Writer's Digest Books; 2nd Place: $500 and $100 of Writer's Digest Books; 3rd Place: $250 and $100 of Writer's Digest Books; 4th Place: $100 and $50 of *Writer's Digest* Books.

WRITER'S DIGEST SELF-PUBLISHED BOOK AWARDS

Writer's Digest, 10151 Carver Road, Suite #200, Blue Ash OH 45242. (715)445-4612, ext. 13430. **E-mail:** WritersDigestSelfPublishingCompetition@fwmedia. com. **Website:** www.writersdigest.com. **Contact:** Nicole Howard. Contest open to all English-language, self-published books for which the authors have paid the full cost of publication, or the cost of printing has been paid for by a grant or as part of a prize. Categories include: Mainstream/Literary Fiction, Genre Fiction, Nonfiction, Inspirational (spiritual/new age), Life Stories (biographies/autobiographies/family histories/memoirs), Children's Books, Reference Books (directories/encyclopedias/guide books), Poetry, and Middle-Grade/Young Adult Books. Judges reserve the right to re-categorize entries. Judges reserve the right to withhold prizes in any category. All winners will be notified in October. Entrants must send a printed and bound book. Entries will be evaluated on content, writing quality, and overall quality of production and appearance. No handwritten books are accepted. Books must have been published within the past 5 years from the competition deadline. Books which have previously won awards from *Writer's Digest* are not eligible. Early bird deadline: April 3. Prizes: Grand Prize: $8,000, a trip to the Writer's Digest Conference, promotion in *Writer's Digest*, 10 copies of the book will be sent to major review houses, and a guaranteed review in *Midwest Book Review*; 1st Place (9 winners): $1,000 and promotion in *Writer's Digest*; Honorable Mentions: $50 worth of Writer's Digest Books and promotion on writersdigest.com. All entrants will receive a brief commentary from one of the judges.

WRITER'S DIGEST SELF-PUBLISHED E-BOOK AWARDS

Writer's Digest, 10151 Carver Road, Suite #200, Blue Ash OH 45242. (715)445-4612, ext. 13430. **E-mail:** WritersDigestSelfPublishingCompetition@fwmedia. com. **Website:** www.writersdigest.com. **Contact:** Nicole Howard. Contest open to all English-language, self-published e-books for which the authors have paid the full cost of publication, or the cost of publication has been paid for by a grant or as part of a prize. Categories include: Mainstream/Literary Fiction, Genre Fiction, Nonfiction (includes reference books), Inspirational (spiritual/new age), Life Stories (biographies/autobiographies/family histories/memoirs), Children's Books, Poetry, and Middle-Grade/Young Adult Books. Judges reserve the right to re-categorize entries. Judges reserve the right to withhold prizes in any category. All winners will be notified by December 31. Entrants must enter online. Entrants may provide a file of the book or submit entry by the Amazon gifting process. Acceptable file types include:

.epub, .mobi, .ipa. Word processing documents will not be accepted. Entries will be evaluated on content, writing quality, and overall quality of production and appearance. Books must have been published within the past 5 years from the competition deadline. Books which have previously won awards from *Writer's Digest* are not eligible. Early bird deadline: August 6; Deadline: September 1. Prizes: Grand Prize: $5,000, promotion in *Writer's Digest*, $200 worth of Writer's Digest Books, and more; 1st Place (9 winners): $1,000 and promotion in *Writer's Digest*; Honorable Mentions: $50 worth of Writer's Digest Books and promotion on writersdigest.com. All entrants will receive a brief commentary from one of the judges.

WRITERS-EDITORS NETWORK INTERNATIONAL WRITING COMPETITION

CNW Publishing, P.O. Box A, North Stratford NH 03590-0167. **E-mail:** contestentry@writers-editors. com. **E-mail:** info@writers-editors.com. **Website:** www.writers-editors.com. **Contact:** Dana K. Cassell, executive director. Annual award to recognize publishable talent. New categories and awards for 2016: Nonfiction (unpublished or self-published; may be an article, blog post, essay/opinion piece, column, nonfiction book chapter, children's article or book chapter); fiction (unpublished or self-published; may be a short story, novel chapter, Young Adult [YA] or children's story or book chapter); poetry (unpublished or self-published; may be traditional or free verse poetry or children's verse). Guidelines available online. Open to any writer. Maximum length: 4,000 words. Accepts inquiries by e-mail, phone and mail. Entry form online. Results announced May 31. Winners notified by mail and posted on website. Results available for SASE or visit website. Deadline: March 15. Prize: 1st Place: $150 plus one year Writers-Editors membership; 2nd Place: $100; 3rd Place: $75. All winners and Honorable Mentions will receive certificates as warranted. Most Promising entry in each category will receive a free critique by a contest judge. Judged by editors, librarians, and writers.

TIPS Review full guidelines and Contest Tip Sheet at http://www.Writers-Editors.com

☼ WRITERS' GUILD OF ALBERTA AWARDS

Writers' Guild of Alberta, Percy Page Centre, 11759 Groat Rd., Edmonton AB T5M 3K6 Canada. (780)422-8174. **Fax:** (780)422-2663. **E-mail:** mail@ writersguild.ca. **Website:** writersguild.ca. **Contact:**

Executive Director. Offers the following awards: Wilfrid Eggleston Award for Nonfiction; Georges Bugnet Award for Fiction; Howard O'Hagan Award for Short Story; Stephan G. Stephansson Award for Poetry; R. Ross Annett Award for Children's Literature; Gwen Pharis Ringwood Award for Drama; Jon Whyte Memorial Essay Award; James H. Gray Award for Short Nonfiction. Eligible entries will have been published anywhere in the world between January 1 and December 31 of the current year. The authors must have been residents of Alberta for at least 12 of the 18 months prior to December 31. Unpublished mss, except in the drama and essay categories, are not eligible. Anthologies are not eligible. Works may be submitted by authors, publishers, or any interested parties. Deadline: December 31. Prize: Winning authors receive $1,500; short piece prize winners receive $700.

WRITERS' LEAGUE OF TEXAS BOOK AWARDS

Writers' League of Texas, 611 S. Congress Ave., Suite 200A-3, Austin TX 78704. (512)499-8914. **Fax:** (512)499-0441. **E-mail:** sara@writersleague.org. **E-mail:** sara@writersleague.org. **Website:** www.writersleague.org. Open to Texas authors of books published the previous year. Authors are required to show proof of Texas residency (current or past), but are not required to be members of the Writers' League of Texas. Deadline: February 28. Open to submissions October 7. Prize: $1,000 and a commemorative award.

LAMAR YORK PRIZE FOR FICTION AND NONFICTION CONTEST

The Chattahoochee Review, Georgia Perimeter College, 2101 Womack Rd., Dunwoody GA 30338-4497. (770)274-5479. **E-mail:** gpccr@gpc.edu. **Website:** thechattahoocheereview.gpc.edu. **Contact:** Anna Schachner, Editor. Offered annually for unpublished creative nonfiction and nonscholarly essays and fiction up to 5,000 words. *The Chattahoochee Review* buys first rights only for winning essay/ms for the purpose of publication in the summer issue. Entries should be submitted via Submittable. See website for details and guidelines. Deadline: January 31. Submission period begins October 1. Prize: 2 prizes of $1,000 each, plus publication. Judged by the editorial staff of *The Chattahoochee Review*.

THE YOUTH HONOR AWARDS

Skipping Stones Youth Honor Awards, Skipping Stones Magazine, Skipping Stones Magazine, P.O. Box 3939, Eugene OR 97403. (541)342-4956. **E-mail:** info@skippingstones.org. **E-mail:** editor@skippingstones.org. **Website:** www.skippingstones.org. **Contact:** Arun N. Toke, Editor and Publisher. *Skipping Stones* is an international, literary, and multicultural, children's magazine that encourages cooperation, creativity, and celebration of cultural and linguistic diversity. It explores stewardship of the ecological and social webs that nurture us. It offers a forum for communication among children from different lands and backgrounds. *Skipping Stones* expands horizons in a playful, creative way. This is a non-commercial, non-profit magazine with no advertisements. In its 28th year. Original writing and art from youth, ages 7 to 17, should be typed or neatly handwritten. The entries should be appropriate for ages 7 to 17. Prose under 1,000 words; poems under 30 lines. Word limit: 1,000. Poetry: 30 lines. Non-English and bilingual writings are welcome. To promote multicultural, international and nature awareness. Deadline: June 25. Prize: An Honor Award Certificate, a subscription to Skipping Stones and five nature and/or multicultural books. They are also invited to join the Student Review Board. Everyone who enters the contest receives the autumn issue featuring the ten winners and other noteworthy entries.

TIPS "Write from your own personal experiences. Rather than facts and figures, we prefer writings that contain critical thinking, as well as practical and constructive ideas."

PROFESSIONAL ORGANIZATIONS

AGENTS' ORGANIZATIONS

ASSOCIATION OF AUTHORS' AGENTS (AAA), 5-8 Lower John St., Golden Square, London W1F 9HA. E-mail: anthonygoff@davidhigham.co.uk. Website: www.agentsassoc.co.uk.

ASSOCIATION OF AUTHORS' REPRESENTATIVES (AAR). E-mail: info@aar-online.org. Website: www.aar-online.org.

ASSOCIATION OF TALENT AGENTS (ATA), 9255 Sunset Blvd., Suite 930, Los Angeles CA 90069. (310)274-0628. E-mail: shellie@agentassociation.com. Website: www.agentassociation.com.

WRITERS' ORGANIZATIONS

ACADEMY OF AMERICAN POETS 584 Broadway, Suite 604, New York NY 10012. E-mail: academy@poets.org. Website: www.poets.org.

AMERICAN CRIME WRITERS LEAGUE (ACWL), 17367 Hilltop Ridge Dr., Eureka MO 63205. Website: www.acwl.org.

AMERICAN INDEPENDENT WRITERS (AIW), 1001 Connecticut Ave. NW, Suite 701, Washington DC 20036. E-mail: info@aiwriters.org. Website: americanindependentwriters.org.

AMERICAN MEDICAL WRITERS ASSOCIATION (AMWA), 30 West Gude Dr., Suite 525, Rockville MD 20850-4347. E-mail: amwa@amwa.org. Website: www.amwa.org.

AMERICAN SCREENWRITERS ASSOCIATION (ASA), 269 S. Beverly Dr., Suite 2600, Beverly Hills CA 90212. (866)265-9091. E-mail: asa@goasa.com. Website: www.asascreenwriters.com.

AMERICAN TRANSLATORS ASSOCIATION (ATA), 225 Reinekers Ln., Suite 590, Alexandria VA 22314. (703)683-6100. E-mail: ata@atanet.org. Website: www.atanet.org.

EDUCATION WRITERS ASSOCIATION (EWA), 2122 P St., NW Suite 201, Washington DC 20037. E-mail: ewa@ewa.org. Website: ewa.org.

HORROR WRITERS ASSOCIATION (HWA), 244 5th Ave., Suite 2767, New York NY 10001. E-mail: hwa@horror.org. Website: www.horror.org.

THE INTERNATIONAL WOMEN'S WRITING GUILD (IWWG), P.O. Box 810, Gracie Station, New York NY 10028. Website: www.iwwg.com.

MYSTERY WRITERS OF AMERICA (MWA), 1140 Broadway, Suite 1507, New York NY 10001. (212)888-8171. E-mail: mwa@mysterywriters.org. Website: www.mysterywriters.org.

NATIONAL ASSOCIATION OF SCIENCE WRITERS (NASW), P.O. Box 7905, Berkeley, CA 94707. (510)647-9500. E-mail: lfriedmann@nasw.org. Website: www.nasw.org.

NATIONAL ASSOCIATION OF WOMEN WRITERS (NAWW), 24165 IH-10 W., Suite 217-637, San Antonio TX 78257. Phone/Fax: (866)821-5829. Website: www.naww.org.

ORGANIZATION OF BLACK SCREENWRITERS (OBS). 1999 W. Adams Blvd., Mezzanine, Los Angeles CA 90018. Website: www.obswriter.com.

OUTDOOR WRITERS ASSOCIATION OF AMERICA (OWAA), 121 Hickory St., Suite 1, Missoula MT 59801. E-mail: krhoades@owaa.org. Website: www.owaa.org.

POETRY SOCIETY OF AMERICA (PSA), 15 Gramercy Park, New York NY 10003. Website: www.poetrysociety.org.

POETS & WRITERS, 90 Broad St., Suite 2100, New York NY 10004. (212)226-3586. Fax: (212)226-3963. Website: www.pw.org.

ROMANCE WRITERS OF AMERICA (RWA), 114615 Benfer Rd., Houston TX 77069. (832)717-5200. Fax: (832)717-5201. E-mail: info@rwanational.org. Website: www.rwanational.org.

SCIENCE FICTION AND FANTASY WRITERS OF AMERICA (SFWA), P.O. Box 877, Chestertown MD 21620. E-mail: execdir@sfwa.org. Website: www.sfwa.org.

SOCIETY OF AMERICAN BUSINESS EDITORS & WRITERS (SABEW), University of Missouri, School of Journalism, 30 Neff Annex, Columbia MO 65211. (602) 496-7862. E-mail: sabew@sabew.org. Website: www.sabew.org.

SOCIETY OF AMERICAN TRAVEL WRITERS (SATW), 7044 S. 13 St., Oak Creek WI 53154. E-mail: satw@satw.org. Website: www.satw.org.

SOCIETY OF CHILDREN'S BOOK WRITERS & ILLUSTRATORS (SCBWI), 8271 Beverly Blvd., Los Angeles CA 90048. E-mail: scbwi@scbwi.org. Website: www.scbwi.org.

WESTERN WRITERS OF AMERICA (WWA). E-mail: spiritfire@kc.rr.com. Website: www.westernwriters.org.

INDUSTRY ORGANIZATIONS

AMERICAN BOOKSELLERS ASSOCIATION (ABA), 200 White Plains Rd., Suite 600, Tarrytown NY 10591. (914)591-2665. E-mail:

info@bookweb.org. Website: www.bookweb.org.

AMERICAN SOCIETY OF JOURNALISTS & AUTHORS (ASJA), 1501 Broadway, Suite 302, New York NY 10036. (212)997-0947. E-mail: director@asja.org. Website: www.asja.org.

ASSOCIATION FOR WOMEN IN COMMUNICATIONS (AWC), 3337 Duke St., Alexandria VA 22314. (703)370-7436. E-mail: info@womcom.org. Website: www.womcom.org.

ASSOCIATION OF AMERICAN PUBLISHERS (AAP), 71 5th Ave., 2nd Floor, New York NY 10003. Website: www.publishers.org.

THE ASSOCIATION OF WRITERS & WRITING PROGRAMS (AWP), Mail Stop 1E3, George Mason University, Fairfax VA 22030. Website: www.awpwriter.org.

THE AUTHORS GUILD, INC., 31 E. 32nd St., 7th Floor, New York NY 10016. E-mail: staff@authorsguild.org. Website: authorsguild.org.

CANADIAN AUTHORS ASSOCIATION (CAA), P.O. Box 581, Stn. Main Orilla ON L3V 6K5 Canada. Website: www.canauthors.org.

CHRISTIAN BOOKSELLERS ASSOCIATION (CBA), P.O. Box 62000, Colorado Springs CO 80962. Website: www.cbaonline.org.

THE DRAMATISTS GUILD OF AMERICA, 1501 Broadway, Suite 701, New York NY 10036. Website: www.dramatistsguild.com.

NATIONAL LEAGUE OF AMERICAN PEN WOMEN (NLAPW), 1300 17th St. NW, Washington DC 20036-1973. Website: www.americanpenwomen.org.

NATIONAL WRITERS ASSOCIATION (NWA), 10940 S. Parker Rd., #508, Parker CO 80134. Website: www.nationalwriters.com

NATIONAL WRITERS UNION (NWU), 256 West 38th St., Suite 703, New York, NY 10018. E-mail: nwu@nwu.org. Website: www.nwu.org.

PEN AMERICAN CENTER, 588 Broadway, Suite 303, New York NY 10012-3225. E-mail: pen@pen.org. Website: www.pen.org.

THE PLAYWRIGHTS GUILD OF CANADA (PGC), 215 Spadina Ave., Suite #210, Toronto ON M5T 2C7 Canada. E-mail: info@playwrightsguild.ca. Website: www.playwrightsguild.com.

VOLUNTEER LAWYERS FOR THE ARTS (VLA), One E. 53rd St., 6th Floor, New York NY 10022. (212)319-2787. Website: www.vlany.org.

WOMEN IN FILM (WIF), 6100 Wilshire Blvd., Suite 710, Los Angeles CA 90048. E-mail: info@wif.org. Website: www.wif.org.

WOMEN'S NATIONAL BOOK ASSOCIATION (WNBA), P.O. Box 237, FDR Station, New York NY 10150. E-mail: publicity@bookbuzz.com. Website: www.wnba-books.org.

WRITERS GUILD OF ALBERTA (WGA), 11759 Groat Rd., Edmonton AB T5M 3K6 Canada. E-mail: mail@writersguild.ab.ca. Website: writersguild.ab.ca.

WRITERS GUILD OF AMERICA-EAST (WGA), 555 W. 57th St., Suite 1230, New York NY 10019. E-mail: info@wgaeast.org. Website: www.wgaeast.org.

WRITERS GUILD OF AMERICA-WEST (WGA), 7000 W. Third St., Los Angeles CA 90048. Website: www.wga.org.

WRITERS UNION OF CANADA (TWUC), 90 Richmond St. E., Suite 200, Toronto ON M5C 1P1 Canada. E-mail: info@writersunion.ca. Website: www.writersunion.ca.

GLOSSARY

#10 ENVELOPE. A standard, business-size envelope.

ADVANCE. A sum of money a publisher pays a writer prior to the publication of a book. It is usually paid in installments, such as one-half on signing contract; one-half on delivery of complete and satisfactory manuscript.

AGENT. A liaison between a writer and editor or publisher. An agent shops a manuscript around, receiving a commission when the manuscript is accepted. Agents usually take a 10-15% fee from the advance and royalties.

ARC. Advance reader copy.

ASSIGNMENT. Editor asks a writer to produce a specific article for an agreed-upon fee.

AUCTION. Publishers sometimes bid for the acquisition of a book manuscript that has excellent sales prospects. The bids are for the amount of the author's advance, advertising and promotional expenses, royalty percentage, etc. Auctions are conducted by agents.

AVANT-GARDE. Writing that is innovative in form, style, or subject.

BACKLIST. A publisher's list of its books that were not published during the current season, but that are still in print.

BIMONTHLY. Every two months.

BIO. A sentence or brief paragraph about the writer; can include education and work experience.

BIWEEKLY. Every two weeks.

BLOG. Short for weblog. Used by writers to build platform by posting regular commentary, observations, poems, tips, etc.

BLURB. The copy on paperback book covers or hard cover book dust jackets, either promoting the book and the author or featuring testimonials from book reviewers or well-known people in the book's field. Also called flap copy or jacket copy.

BOILERPLATE. A standardized contract.

BOUND GALLEYS. Prepublication edition of book, usually photocopies of final galley proofs; also known as "bound proofs."

BYLINE. Name of the author appearing with the published piece.

CATEGORY FICTION. A term used to include all types of fiction.

CHAPBOOK. A small booklet usually paperback of poetry, ballads, or tales.

CIRCULATION. The number of subscribers to a magazine.

CLIPS. Samples, usually from newspapers or magazines, of a writer's published work.

COFFEE-TABLE BOOK. A heavily illustrated oversize book.

COMMERCIAL NOVELS. Novels designed to appeal to a broad audience. These are often broken down into categories such as western, mystery and romance. See also genre.

CONTRIBUTOR'S COPIES. Copies of the issues of magazines sent to the author in which the author's work appears.

CO-PUBLISHING. Arrangement where author and publisher share publications costs and profits of a book. Also known as cooperative publishing.

COPYEDITING. Editing a manuscript for grammar, punctuation, printing style, and factual accuracy.

COPYRIGHT. A means to protect an author's work.

COVER LETTER. A brief letter that accompanies the manuscript being sent to an agent or editor.

CREATIVE NONFICTION. Nonfictional writing that uses an innovative approach to the subject and creative language.

CRITIQUING SERVICE. An editing service in which writers pay a fee for comments on the salability or other qualities of their manuscript. Fees vary, as do the quality of the critiques.

CV. Curriculum vita. A brief listing of qualifications and career accomplishments.

ELECTRONIC RIGHTS. Secondary or subsidiary rights dealing with electronic/multimedia formats (i.e., the Internet, CD-ROMs, electronic magazines).

ELECTRONIC SUBMISSION. A submission made by modem or on computer disk.

EROTICA. Fiction that is sexually oriented.

EVALUATION FEES. Fees an agent may charge to evaluate material. The extent and quality of this evaluation varies, but comments usually concern salability of the manuscript.

FAIR USE. A provision of the copyright law that says short passages from copyrighted material may be used without infringing on the owner's rights.

FEATURE. An article giving the reader information of human interest rather than news.

FILLER. A short item used by an editor to "fill" out a newspaper column or magazine page. It could be a joke, an anecdote, etc.

FILM RIGHTS. Rights sold or optioned by the agent/author to a person in the film industry, enabling the book to be made into a movie.

FOREIGN RIGHTS. Translation or reprint rights to be sold abroad.

FRONTLIST. A publisher's list of books that are new to the current season.

GALLEYS. First typeset version of manuscript that has not yet been divided into pages.

GENRE. Refers either to a general classification of writing, such as the novel or the poem, or to the categories within those classifications, such as the problem novel or the sonnet.

GHOSTWRITER. Writer who puts into literary form an article, speech, story, or book based on another person's ideas or knowledge.

GRAPHIC NOVEL. A story in graphic form, long comic strip, or heavily illustrated story; of 40 pages or more.

HI-LO. A type of fiction that offers a high level of interest for readers at a low reading level.

HIGH CONCEPT. A story idea easily expressed in a quick, one-line description.

HONORARIUM. Token payment.

HOOK. Aspect of the work that sets it apart from others and draws in the reader/viewer.

HOW-TO. Books and magazine articles offering a combination of information and advice in describing how something can be accomplished.

IMPRINT. Name applied to a publisher's specific line of books.

JOINT CONTRACT. A legal agreement between a publisher and two or more authors, establishing provisions for the division of royalties the book generates.

KILL FEE. Fee for a complete article that was assigned and then cancelled.

LEAD TIME. The time between the acquisition of a manuscript by an editor and its actual publication.

LITERARY FICTION. The general category of serious, non-formulaic, intelligent fiction.

MAINSTREAM FICTION. Fiction that transcends popular novel categories such as mystery, romance and science fiction.

MARKETING FEE. Fee charged by some agents to cover marketing expenses. It may be used to cover postage, telephone calls, faxes, photocopying or any other expense incurred in marketing a manuscript.

MASS MARKET. Non-specialized books of wide appeal directed toward a large audience.

MEMOIR. A narrative recounting a writer's (or fictional narrator's) personal or family history; specifics may be altered, though essentially considered nonfiction.

MIDDLE GRADE OR MID-GRADE. The general classification of books written for readers approximately ages 9-11. Also called middle readers.

MIDLIST. Those titles on a publisher's list that are not expected to be big sellers, but are expected to have limited/modest sales.

MODEL RELEASE. A paper signed by the subject of a photograph giving the photographer permission to use the photograph.

MULTIPLE CONTRACT. Book contract with an agreement for a future book(s).

MULTIPLE SUBMISSIONS. Sending more than one book or article idea to a publisher at the same time.

NARRATIVE NONFICTION. A narrative presentation of actual events.

NET ROYALTY. A royalty payment based on the amount of money a book publisher receives on the sale of a book after booksellers' discounts, special sales discounts and returns.

NOVELLA. A short novel, or a long short story; approximately 7,000 to 15,000 words.

ON SPEC. An editor expresses an interest in a proposed article idea and agrees to consider the finished piece for publication "on speculation." The editor is under no obligation to buy the finished manuscript.

ONE-TIME RIGHTS. Rights allowing a manuscript to be published one time. The work can be sold again by the writer without violating the contract.

OPTION CLAUSE. A contract clause giving a publisher the right to publish an author's next book.

PAYMENT ON ACCEPTANCE. The editor sends you a check for your article, story or poem as soon as he decides to publish it.

PAYMENT ON PUBLICATION. The editor doesn't send you a check for your material until it is published.

PEN NAME. The use of a name other than your legal name on articles, stories or books. Also called a pseudonym.

PHOTO FEATURE. Feature in which the emphasis is on the photographs rather than on accompanying written material.

PICTURE BOOK. A type of book aimed at preschoolers to 8-year-olds that tells a story using a combination of text and artwork, or artwork only.

PLATFORM. A writer's speaking experience, interview skills, website and other abilities which help form a following of potential buyers for that author's book.

POD. Print on demand.

PROOFREADING. Close reading and correction of a manuscript's typographical errors.

PROPOSAL. A summary of a proposed book submitted to a publisher, particularly used for nonfiction manuscripts. A proposal often contains an individualized cover letter, one-page overview of the book, marketing information, competitive books, author information, chapter-by-chapter outline, and two to three sample chapters.

QUERY. A letter that sells an idea to an editor or agent. Usually a query is brief (no more than one page) and uses attention-getting prose.

REMAINDERS. Copies of a book that are slow to sell and can be purchased from the publisher at a reduced price.

REPORTING TIME. The time it takes for an

editor to report to the author on his/her query or manuscript.

REPRINT RIGHTS. The rights to republish a book after its initial printing.

ROYALTIES, STANDARD HARDCOVER BOOK. 10 percent of the retail price on the first 5,000 copies sold; 12 percent on the next 5,000; 15 percent thereafter.

ROYALTIES, STANDARD MASS PAPERBACK BOOK. 4-8 percent of the retail price on the first 150,000 copies sold.

ROYALTIES, STANDARD TRADE PAPERBACK BOOK. No less than 6 percent of list price on the first 20,000 copies; 7½ percent thereafter.

SASE. Self-addressed, stamped envelope; should be included with all correspondence.

SELF-PUBLISHING. In this arrangement the author pays for manufacturing, production and marketing of his book and keeps all income derived from the book sales.

SEMIMONTHLY. Twice per month.

SEMIWEEKLY. Twice per week.

SERIAL. Published periodically, such as a newspaper or magazine.

SERIAL FICTION. Fiction published in a magazine in installments, often broken off at a suspenseful spot.

SERIAL RIGHTS. The right for a newspaper or magazine to publish sections of a manuscript.

SHORT-SHORT. A complete short story of 1,500 words.

SIDEBAR. A feature presented as a companion to a straight news report (or main magazine article) giving sidelights on human-interest aspects or sometimes elucidating just one aspect of the story.

SIMULTANEOUS SUBMISSIONS. Sending the same article, story or poem to several publishers at the same time. Some publishers refuse to consider such submissions.

SLANT. The approach or style of a story or article that will appeal to readers of a specific magazine.

SLICE-OF-LIFE VIGNETTE. A short fiction piece intended to realistically depict an interesting moment of everyday living.

SLUSH PILE. The stack of unsolicited or misdirected manuscripts received by an editor or book publisher.

SOCIAL NETWORKS. Websites that connect users: sometimes generally, other times around specific interests. Four popular ones at the moment are Facebook, Twitter, Instagram and LinkedIn.

SUBAGENT. An agent handling certain subsidiary rights, usually working in conjuction with the agent who handled the book rights. The percentage paid the book agent is increased to pay the subagent.

SUBSIDIARY RIGHTS. All rights other than book publishing rights included in a book publishing contract, such as paperback rights, book club rights and movie rights. Part of an agent's job is to negotiate those rights and advise you on which to sell and which to keep.

SUBSIDY PUBLISHER. A book publisher who charges the author for the cost to typeset and print his book, the jacket, etc., as opposed to a royalty publisher who pays the author.

SYNOPSIS. A brief summary of a story, novel or play. As part of a book proposal, it is a comprehensive summary condensed in a page or page and a half, single-spaced.

TABLOID. Newspaper format publication on about half the size of the regular newspaper page.

TEARSHEET. Page from a magazine or newspaper containing your printed story, article, poem or ad.

TOC. Table of Contents.

TRADE BOOK. Either a hardcover or softcover book; subject matter frequently concerns a special interest for a general audience; sold mainly in bookstores.

TRADE PAPERBACK. A soft-bound volume published and designed for the general public; available mainly in bookstores.

TRANSLATION RIGHTS. Sold to a foreign agent or foreign publisher.

UNSOLICITED MANUSCRIPT. A story, article, poem or book that an editor did not specifically ask to see.

YA. Young adult books.

BOOK PUBLISHERS SUBJECT INDEX

//

FICTION

ADVENTURE

Abbeville Press
Archaia
Atheneum Books for Young Readers
Berkley/NAL
Bloomsbury Children's Books
Bold Strokes Books, Inc.
Cedar Fort, Inc.
Children's Brains are Yummy (CBAY) Books
Clarion Books
Covenant Communications, Inc.
Curiosity Quills
Dial Books for Young Readers
Divertir
Dutton Adult Trade
Father's Press
Frances Lincoln Children's Books
Glencannon Press, The
Goosebottom Books
Grey Gecko Press
HarperCollins
Holiday House, Inc.
Hopewell Publications
Houghton Mifflin Harcourt Books for Children
JourneyForth
Kaeden Books
Kane/Miller Book Publishers
Kitchen Publishing Co., LLC, Denis
Knox Robinson Publishing
Lantana Publishing
Leapfrog Press

Little, Brown Books for Young Readers
Manor House Publishing, Inc.
Martin Sisters Publishing, LLC
Marvel Comics
McBooks Press
McElderry Books, Margaret K.
Melange Books, LLC
Milkweed for Young Readers
Mondial
Nelson, Tommy
New Libri Press
North Atlantic Books
Orca Book Publishers
PageSpring Publishing
Pants On Fire Press
Paradise Cay Publications
Pauline Books & Media
Philomel Books
Pinata Books
Plexus Publishing, Inc.
Putnam's Sons Hardcover, GP
Rebelight Publishing, Inc.
Ring of Fire Publishing LLC
Saguaro Books, LLC
Salvo Press
Severn House Publishers
Shipwreckt Books Publishing Company LLC
Splashing Cow Books
Stoneslide Books
Sunbury Press, Inc.
Sweet Cherry Publishing
Tantor Media
Tor Books

Tumblehome Learning
WaterBrook Multnomah Publishing Group
Zumaya Publications, LLC

COMIC BOOKS
Fantagraphics Books, Inc.
Guernica Editions
Immedium
Insomniac Press
Marvel Comics
NBM Publishing
Papercutz
Shipwreckt Books Publishing Company LLC
Soft Skull Press Inc.
Splashing Cow Books
Stone Bridge Press
Sweet Cherry Publishing

CONFESSION
Ballantine Bantam Dell
Crystal Spirit Publishing, Inc.
Martin Sisters Publishing, LLC
Soft Skull Press Inc.
Sunbury Press, Inc.

CONTEMPORARY
Arte Publico Press
Bookouture
Bottom Dog Press, Inc.
Canterbury House Publishing, Ltd.
Cave Hollow Press
Cedar Fort, Inc.
Crystal Spirit Publishing, Inc.
Curiosity Quills
Divertir
Filbert Publishing
Folded Word
Gival Press
Grey Gecko Press
Guernica Editions
Hopewell Publications
Knox Robinson Publishing
Little, Brown and Co. Adult Trade Books
Melange Books, LLC
NBM Publishing
PageSpring Publishing
Pauline Books & Media
Persea Books
Rebelight Publishing, Inc.
Ring of Fire Publishing LLC
Ripple Grove Press
Riverhead Books
Saint Martin's Press, LLC
Sakura Publishing & Technologies
Scribe Publications
Soft Skull Press Inc.

Splashing Cow Books
Stone Bridge Press
Stoneslide Books
Sunbury Press, Inc.
Sweet Cherry Publishing
Tantor Media
Tightrope Books
Titan Press
Vintage Anchor Publishing
Zumaya Publications, LLC

EROTICA
Bold Strokes Books, Inc.
Bookouture
Changeling Press LLC
Crescent Moon Publishing
Crystal Spirit Publishing, Inc.
Curiosity Quills
Grove/Atlantic, Inc.
Kitchen Publishing Co., LLC, Denis
Loose Id
Melange Books, LLC
Mondial
NBM Publishing
Soft Skull Press Inc.
Stone Bridge Press
Tantor Media
World Weaver Press

ETHNIC
Arsenal Pulp Press
Arte Publico Press
Atheneum Books for Young Readers
Ballantine Bantam Dell
Bancroft Press
Bookouture
Bottom Dog Press, Inc.
Carolina Wren Press
Changeling Press LLC
Coteau Books
Crystal Spirit Publishing, Inc.
Fernwood Publishing, Ltd.
Gertrude Press
Goosebottom Books
Grey Gecko Press
Guernica Editions
Houghton Mifflin Harcourt Books for Children
Insomniac Press
Interlink Publishing Group, Inc.
Kensington Publishing Corp.
Lantana Publishing
Leapfrog Press
Mage Publishers, Inc.
Mondial
New Directions

Nortia Press
Philomel Books
Red Hen Press
Sakura Publishing & Technologies
Shipwreckt Books Publishing Company LLC
Soho Press, Inc.
Splashing Cow Books
Sunbury Press, Inc.
Texas Tech University Press
Tightrope Books
University of New Mexico Press
Zumaya Publications, LLC

EXPERIMENTAL

Anvil Press
Atheneum Books for Young Readers
BlazeVOX Books
Carolina Wren Press
Coach House Books
Crescent Moon Publishing
Gertrude Press
Guernica Editions
Hopewell Publications
Insomniac Press
Kelsey Street Press
Lantana Publishing
Leapfrog Press
Livingston Press
Manor House Publishing, Inc.
Milkweed Editions
New Directions
New Libri Press
Nightscape Press
Paycock Press
Pedlar Press
Red Hen Press
Ring of Fire Publishing LLC
Shipwreckt Books Publishing Company LLC
Small Beer Press
Soft Skull Press Inc.
Stoneslide Books
Subito Press
Sunbury Press, Inc.
Tantor Media
Tightrope Books

FANTASY

Ace Science Fiction and Fantasy
AMG Publishers
Archaia
Atheneum Books for Young Readers
Ballantine Bantam Dell
Bloomsbury Children's Books
Bold Strokes Books, Inc.
Bookouture

Brucedale Press, The
Cedar Fort, Inc.
Changeling Press LLC
Children's Brains are Yummy (CBAY) Books
Coteau Books
Curiosity Quills
DAW Books, Inc.
Del Rey Books
Dial Books for Young Readers
Divertir
Edge Science Fiction and Fantasy Publishing
Frances Lincoln Children's Books
Goosebottom Books
Greenwillow Books
Grey Gecko Press
Hadley Rille Books
HarperCollins
Harper Voyager
Hopewell Publications
Kaeden Books
Kane/Miller Book Publishers
Knox Robinson Publishing
Lantana Publishing
Little, Brown Books for Young Readers
Martin Sisters Publishing, LLC
Marvel Comics
McElderry Books, Margaret K.
Medallion Press
Melange Books, LLC
Milkweed for Young Readers
Moody Publishers
New Libri Press
Nightscape Press
PageSpring Publishing
Pants On Fire Press
Papercutz
Philomel Books
Puffin Books
Rebelight Publishing, Inc.
Ring of Fire Publishing LLC
Saguaro Books, LLC
Saint Martin's Press, LLC
Severn House Publishers
Shipwreckt Books Publishing Company LLC
Simon & Schuster Books for Young Readers
Splashing Cow Books
Stoneslide Books
Sunbury Press, Inc.
Sweet Cherry Publishing
Tantor Media
Tor Books
Twilight Times Books
World Weaver Press
Zumaya Publications, LLC

FEMINIST

Arsenal Pulp Press
Ballantine Bantam Dell
Bancroft Press
Brucedale Press, The
Carolina Wren Press
Cleis Press
Coteau Books
Crescent Moon Publishing
Crystal Spirit Publishing, Inc.
Fernwood Publishing, Ltd.
Gertrude Press
Gival Press
Goosebottom Books
Grey Gecko Press
Guernica Editions
Leapfrog Press
Little, Brown Books for Young Readers
Mage Publishers, Inc.
PageSpring Publishing
Pedlar Press
Red Hen Press
Tantor Media
Tightrope Books
Véhicule Press
Zumaya Publications, LLC

GAY

Bold Strokes Books, Inc.
Bookouture
Bottom Dog Press, Inc.
Changeling Press LLC
Crystal Spirit Publishing, Inc.
Curiosity Quills
Fernwood Publishing, Ltd.
Gertrude Press
Gival Press
Goosebottom Books
Grey Gecko Press
Guernica Editions
Hopewell Publications
Leapfrog Press
Lethe Press
Melange Books, LLC
Orca Book Publishers
Pedlar Press
Soft Skull Press Inc.
Tantor Media
Tightrope Books
University of Wisconsin Press
Zumaya Publications, LLC

GOTHIC

Atheneum Books for Young Readers
Black Lyon Publishing

Bold Strokes Books, Inc.
Curiosity Quills
Divertir
HarperCollins
Manor House Publishing, Inc.
Melange Books, LLC
Ring of Fire Publishing LLC
Stoneslide Books
Sunbury Press, Inc.
Sweet Cherry Publishing
Tantor Media
Zumaya Publications, LLC

HI-LO

Curiosity Quills
JourneyForth
Orca Book Publishers
PageSpring Publishing
University of Wisconsin Press

HISTORICAL

Academy Chicago Publishers
Atheneum Books for Young Readers
Avon Romance
Ballantine Bantam Dell
Bancroft Press
Beil, Publisher, Inc., Frederic C.
Berkley/NAL
Bethany House Publishers
Black Lyon Publishing
Bloomsbury Children's Books
Bold Strokes Books, Inc.
Bookouture
Bottom Dog Press, Inc.
Brucedale Press, The
Calkins Creek
Canterbury House Publishing, Ltd.
Cedar Fort, Inc.
Changeling Press LLC
Clarion Books
Constable & Robinson, Ltd.
Coteau Books
Covenant Communications, Inc.
Cross-Cultural Communications
Curiosity Quills
Divertir
Dutton Adult Trade
Father's Press
Fernwood Publishing, Ltd.
Folded Word
Frances Lincoln Children's Books
Gival Press
Glencannon Press, The
Goosebottom Books
Grey Gecko Press

HarperCollins
Holiday House, Inc.
Hopewell Publications
Houghton Mifflin Harcourt Books for Children
Inverted-A
JourneyForth
Kaeden Books
Kane/Miller Book Publishers
Kensington Publishing Corp.
Kitchen Publishing Co., LLC, Denis
Knox Robinson Publishing
Leapfrog Press
Little, Brown Books for Young Readers
Mage Publishers, Inc.
Manor House Publishing, Inc.
Martin Sisters Publishing, LLC
McDonald & Woodward Publishing Co., The
McElderry Books, Margaret K.
Medallion Press
Melange Books, LLC
Merriam Press
Milkweed for Young Readers
Mondial
Moody Publishers
New Directions
New Libri Press
Nortia Press
PageSpring Publishing
Pants On Fire Press
Peace Hill Press
Pelican Publishing Company
Philomel Books
Pocol Press
Rebelight Publishing, Inc.
Red Hen Press
Revell
Saguaro Books, LLC
Saint Martin's Press, LLC
Scribe Publications
Severn House Publishers
Shipwreckt Books Publishing Company LLC
Simon & Schuster Books for Young Readers
Soho Press, Inc.
Splashing Cow Books
Stoneslide Books
Sunbury Press, Inc.
Tantor Media
Tor Books
Torrey House Press, LLC
Touchwood Editions
Twilight Times Books
University of Arkansas Press, The
WaterBrook Multnomah Publishing Group
Zumaya Publications, LLC

HORROR

Archaia
Atheneum Books for Young Readers
Bold Strokes Books, Inc.
Changeling Press LLC
Curiosity Quills
Divertir
Edge Science Fiction and Fantasy Publishing
Goosebottom Books
Grey Gecko Press
Grove/Atlantic, Inc.
Kelsey Street Press
Kensington Publishing Corp.
Kitchen Publishing Co., LLC, Denis
Knox Robinson Publishing
Manor House Publishing, Inc.
Marvel Comics
Medallion Press
New Libri Press
Nightscape Press
Pocol Press
Rebelight Publishing, Inc.
Ring of Fire Publishing LLC
Saint Martin's Press, LLC
Sakura Publishing & Technologies
Severn House Publishers
Sunbury Press, Inc.
Sweet Cherry Publishing
Tantor Media
Zumaya Publications, LLC

HUMOR

Atheneum Books for Young Readers
Ballantine Bantam Dell
Bancroft Press
Bloomsbury Children's Books
Brucedale Press, The
Cartwheel Books
Cedar Fort, Inc.
Clarion Books
Coteau Books
Crystal Spirit Publishing, Inc.
Curiosity Quills
Divertir
Folded Word
Frances Lincoln Children's Books
Gertrude Press
Goosebottom Books
Greenwillow Books
Grey Gecko Press
Holiday House, Inc.
Hopewell Publications
Houghton Mifflin Harcourt Books for Children
Insomniac Press
Kaeden Books

Kitchen Publishing Co., LLC, Denis
Little, Brown Books for Young Readers
Manor House Publishing, Inc.
Martin Sisters Publishing, LLC
Marvel Comics
Milkweed for Young Readers
NBM Publishing
New Directions
PageSpring Publishing
Pants On Fire Press
Papercutz
Rebelight Publishing, Inc.
Ripple Grove Press
Scribe Publications
Shipwreckt Books Publishing Company LLC
Simon & Schuster Books for Young Readers
Soho Press, Inc.
Splashing Cow Books
Stoneslide Books
Sunbury Press, Inc.
Sweet Cherry Publishing
Tantor Media
Tor Books
Twilight Times Books
Zumaya Publications, LLC

JUVENILE

Barefoot Books
BelleBooks
Bloomsbury Children's Books
Brucedale Press, The
Candlewick Press
Cartwheel Books
Cedar Fort, Inc.
Changeling Press LLC
Children's Brains are Yummy (CBAY) Books
Coteau Books
Craigmore Creations
Creston Books
Crystal Spirit Publishing, Inc.
Curiosity Quills
Dial Books for Young Readers
Dutton Children's Books
Familius
Farrar, Straus & Giroux
Father's Press
Forward Movement
Frances Lincoln Children's Books
Goosebottom Books
Grey Gecko Press
Grosset & Dunlap Publishers
Hachai Publishing
Hendrick-Long Publishing Co., Inc.
Hopewell Publications
Houghton Mifflin Harcourt Books for Children

JourneyForth
Just Us Books, Inc.
Kane/Miller Book Publishers
Leapfrog Press
Levine Books, Arthur A.
Mandala Publishing
Manor House Publishing, Inc.
Martin Sisters Publishing, LLC
Nelson, Tommy
Orca Book Publishers
PageSpring Publishing
Pants On Fire Press
Papercutz
Pauline Books & Media
Peace Hill Press
Peachtree Children's Books
Pelican Publishing Company
Philomel Books
Pinata Books
Rebelight Publishing, Inc.
Ring of Fire Publishing LLC
Ripple Grove Press
Saguaro Books, LLC
Salina Bookshelf
Scholastic Press
Simon & Schuster Books for Young Readers
Splashing Cow Books
Sunbury Press, Inc.
Sweet Cherry Publishing
Tafelberg Publishers
Tantor Media
Tradewind Books
Tumblehome Learning
Twilight Times Books
Tyndale House Publishers, Inc.
Worthy Kids/Ideals Books
Zumaya Publications, LLC

LESBIAN

Bold Strokes Books, Inc.
Bookouture
Curiosity Quills
Fernwood Publishing, Ltd.
Gertrude Press
Gival Press
Grey Gecko Press
Guernica Editions
Leapfrog Press
Lethe Press
Melange Books, LLC
Orca Book Publishers
Pedlar Press
Soft Skull Press Inc.
Tantor Media
Tightrope Books

University of Wisconsin Press
Zumaya Publications, LLC

LITERARY

Algonquin Books of Chapel Hill
Anvil Press
Arcade Publishing
Arch Street Press
Arsenal Pulp Press
Arte Publico Press
Avon Romance
Ballantine Bantam Dell
Bancroft Press
Beil, Publisher, Inc., Frederic C.
Bellevue Literary Press
Berkley/NAL
BkMk Press
Black Lawrence Press
BOA Editions, Ltd.
Bold Strokes Books, Inc.
Bottom Dog Press, Inc.
Brucedale Press, The
Canterbury House Publishing, Ltd.
Carnegie Mellon University Press
Carolina Wren Press
Cave Hollow Press
Cedar Fort, Inc.
Changeling Press LLC
Cleis Press
Coach House Books
Coteau Books
Crescent Moon Publishing
Crystal Spirit Publishing, Inc.
Curiosity Quills
Dufour Editions
Dundurn Press, Ltd.
Dutton Adult Trade
Father's Press
Fence Books
Fernwood Publishing, Ltd.
Folded Word
Gertrude Press
Gival Press
Godine, Publisher, David R.
Goosebottom Books
Goose Lane Editions
Greenwillow Books
Grey Gecko Press
Grove/Atlantic, Inc.
Guernica Editions
Hampton Roads Publishing Co., Inc.
HarperCollins
Holiday House, Inc.
Hopewell Publications
Houghton Mifflin Harcourt Books for Children

Insomniac Press
Kitchen Publishing Co., LLC, Denis
Knox Robinson Publishing
Leapfrog Press
Little, Brown and Co. Adult Trade Books
Livingston Press
Mage Publishers, Inc.
Manor House Publishing, Inc.
Martin Sisters Publishing, LLC
Medallion Press
Michigan State University Press
Mondial
NBM Publishing
New Directions
NeWest Publishers Ltd.
New Issues Poetry & Prose
New Libri Press
North Atlantic Books
Nortia Press
Oolichan Books
Orca Book Publishers
PageSpring Publishing
Paul Dry Books
Paycock Press
Pedlar Press
Persea Books
Philomel Books
Pocol Press
Press 53
Putnam's Sons Hardcover, GP
Red Hen Press
Ring of Fire Publishing LLC
Ripple Grove Press
River City Publishing
Riverhead Books
Ronsdale Press
Saint Martin's Press, LLC
Salvo Press
Sarabande Books, Inc.
Scribe Publications
Scribner
Seven Stories Press
Shipwreckt Books Publishing Company LLC
Small Beer Press
Soft Skull Press Inc.
Soho Press, Inc.
Splashing Cow Books
Stone Bridge Press
Stoneslide Books
Subito Press
Talese, Nan A.
Tantor Media
Thistledown Press Ltd.
Tightrope Books
Titan Press

Torrey House Press, LLC
Twilight Times Books
University of Alaska Press
University of Michigan Press
University of New Mexico Press
University of Tampa Press
Véhicule Press
Viking
Vintage Anchor Publishing
WaterBrook Multnomah Publishing Group
Zumaya Publications, LLC

MAINSTREAM
Arte Publico Press
Bold Strokes Books, Inc.
Bookouture
Canterbury House Publishing, Ltd.
Cave Hollow Press
Cedar Fort, Inc.
Crystal Spirit Publishing, Inc.
Curiosity Quills
Divertir
Filbert Publishing
Gertrude Press
Glencannon Press, The
Goosebottom Books
Grey Gecko Press
Hopewell Publications
Kensington Publishing Corp.
Knox Robinson Publishing
Leapfrog Press
Little, Brown and Co. Adult Trade Books
Martin Sisters Publishing, LLC
Medallion Press
Melange Books, LLC
New Libri Press
PageSpring Publishing
Rebelight Publishing, Inc.
Ring of Fire Publishing LLC
Ripple Grove Press
Riverhead Books
Soft Skull Press Inc.
Splashing Cow Books
Stoneslide Books
Sunbury Press, Inc.
Sweet Cherry Publishing
Tantor Media
Titan Press
Touchwood Editions
Twilight Times Books
Vintage Anchor Publishing

MILITARY
Cedar Fort, Inc.
Changeling Press LLC

Glencannon Press, The
Grey Gecko Press
Martin Sisters Publishing, LLC
McBooks Press
Merriam Press
New Libri Press
Nortia Press
Saguaro Books, LLC
Scribe Publications
Sunbury Press, Inc.
Tantor Media
Twilight Times Books
Zumaya Publications, LLC

MULTICULTURAL
Arsenal Pulp Press
Ballantine Bantam Dell
Bloomsbury Children's Books
Cedar Fort, Inc.
Changeling Press LLC
Chronicle Books for Children
Coteau Books
Creston Books
Cross-Cultural Communications
Crystal Spirit Publishing, Inc.
Curiosity Quills
Fernwood Publishing, Ltd.
Frances Lincoln Children's Books
Gertrude Press
Gival Press
Glencannon Press, The
Godine, Publisher, David R.
Goosebottom Books
Grey Gecko Press
Guernica Editions
Kane/Miller Book Publishers
Kelsey Street Press
Kensington Publishing Corp.
Lantana Publishing
Leapfrog Press
Melange Books, LLC
Mondial
North Atlantic Books
Oneworld Publications
Orca Book Publishers
PageSpring Publishing
Piano Press
Rebelight Publishing, Inc.
Ripple Grove Press
Saguaro Books, LLC
Sakura Publishing & Technologies
Shipwreckt Books Publishing Company LLC
Soft Skull Press Inc.
Splashing Cow Books
Sunbury Press, Inc.

Tantor Media
Texas Tech University Press
ThunderStone Books
Tightrope Books
Tradewind Books
University of New Mexico Press
Zumaya Publications, LLC

MULTIMEDIA
Coteau Books
Curiosity Quills
Piano Press
Tantor Media

MYSTERY
Academy Chicago Publishers
Archaia
Atheneum Books for Young Readers
Avon Romance
Ballantine Bantam Dell
Bancroft Press
Berkley/NAL
Bloomsbury Children's Books
Bold Strokes Books, Inc.
Bookouture
Brucedale Press, The
Canterbury House Publishing, Ltd.
Cartwheel Books
Cave Hollow Press
Cedar Fort, Inc.
Changeling Press LLC
Children's Brains are Yummy (CBAY) Books
Clarion Books
Constable & Robinson, Ltd.
Coteau Books
Covenant Communications, Inc.
Curiosity Quills
Divertir
Dundurn Press, Ltd.
Dunne Books, Thomas
Dutton Adult Trade
Father's Press
Filbert Publishing
Glencannon Press, The
Goosebottom Books
Greenwillow Books
Grey Gecko Press
Harlequin Intrigue
HarperCollins
Hopewell Publications
Houghton Mifflin Harcourt Books for Children
Insomniac Press
JourneyForth
Kaeden Books
Kane/Miller Book Publishers

Kelsey Street Press
Kensington Publishing Corp.
Kitchen Publishing Co., LLC, Denis
Little, Brown Books for Young Readers
Manor House Publishing, Inc.
Martin Sisters Publishing, LLC
McElderry Books, Margaret K.
Medallion Press
Melange Books, LLC
Mondial
Moody Publishers
Nelson, Tommy
New Libri Press
North Atlantic Books

Oceanview Publishing
Orca Book Publishers
PageSpring Publishing
Plexus Publishing, Inc.
Pocket Books
Pocol Press
Poisoned Pencil, The
Poisoned Pen Press
Rebelight Publishing, Inc.
Ring of Fire Publishing LLC
Saguaro Books, LLC
Saint Martin's Press, LLC
Salvo Press
Scribe Publications
Scribner
Severn House Publishers
Shipwreckt Books Publishing Company LLC
Simon & Schuster Books for Young Readers
Soho Press, Inc.
Splashing Cow Books
Stoneslide Books
Strategic Media Books
Sunbury Press, Inc.
Tantor Media
Tor Books
Touchwood Editions
Twilight Times Books
University of Wisconsin Press
Viking
WaterBrook Multnomah Publishing Group
Zumaya Publications, LLC

OCCULT
Divertir
Grey Gecko Press
Kensington Publishing Corp.
Kitchen Publishing Co., LLC, Denis
Lethe Press
Manor House Publishing, Inc.
Ring of Fire Publishing LLC

Playlab Press

POETRY
Bloomsbury Children's Books
Blue Light Press
BOA Editions, Ltd.
Bronze Man Books
Brucedale Press, The
Carnegie Mellon University Press
Carolina Wren Press
Coach House Books
Coteau Books
Cross-Cultural Communications
Fence Books
Folded Word
Gival Press
Godine, Publisher, David R.
Guernica Editions
Insomniac Press
Kelsey Street Press
Leapfrog Press
Manor House Publishing, Inc.
Merriam Press
Mondial
New Directions
New Issues Poetry & Prose
Paycock Press
Pedlar Press
Red Hen Press
Scribe Publications
Shipwreckt Books Publishing Company LLC
Tightrope Books
University of Tampa Press

POETRY IN TRANSLATION
Blue Light Press
BOA Editions, Ltd.
Carnegie Mellon University Press
Cross-Cultural Communications
Folded Word
Gival Press
Godine, Publisher, David R.
Guernica Editions
Martin Sisters Publishing, LLC
New Directions
Red Hen Press
Tightrope Books

REGIONAL
Bancroft Press
Canterbury House Publishing, Ltd.
Cedar Fort, Inc.
Coteau Books
Covenant Communications, Inc.
Down the Shore Publishing
Father's Press

echnologies

LLC

PICTURE BOOKS

Bloomsbury Children's Books
Bronze Man Books
Candlewick Press
Cartwheel Books
Craigmore Creations
Creston Books
Dial Books for Young Readers
Familius
Farrar, Straus & Giroux
Flashlight Press
Frances Lincoln Children's Books
Goosebottom Books
Greenwillow Books
HarperCollins Children's Books/HarperCollins
    Publishers
Houghton Mifflin Harcourt Books for Children
Immedium
Inverted-A
Kane/Miller Book Publishers
Lantana Publishing
Levine Books, Arthur A.
McElderry Books, Margaret K.
Nelson, Tommy
Orca Book Publishers
Pauline Books & Media
Peace Hill Press
Peachtree Children's Books
Philomel Books
Piano Press
Pinata Books
Puffin Books
Ripple Grove Press
Scholastic Press
Scribe Publications
Simon & Schuster Books for Young Readers
Splashing Cow Books
Sweet Cherry Publishing
ThunderStone Books
Tor Books
Tradewind Books
Woodbine House

PLAYS
Brucedale Press, The
Coteau Books
Guernica Editions
Hopewell Publications

Fernwood Publishing, Ltd.
Folded Word
Grey Gecko Press
Manor House Publishing, Inc.
Martin Sisters Publishing, LLC
New Directions
North Atlantic Books
PageSpring Publishing
Philomel Books
Pineapple Press, Inc.
River City Publishing
Shipwreckt Books Publishing Company LLC
Sunbury Press, Inc.
ThunderStone Books
Touchwood Editions
Twilight Times Books
University of Arkansas Press, The
University of Michigan Press
University of New Mexico Press
University of Wisconsin Press
Véhicule Press

RELIGIOUS

Cedar Fort, Inc.
Covenant Communications, Inc.
Crystal Spirit Publishing, Inc.
Eerdmans Publishing Co., William B.
Father's Press
Kregel Publications
Mandala Publishing
Martin Sisters Publishing, LLC
Messianic Jewish Publishers
Moody Publishers
Nelson, Tommy
Pacific Press Publishing Association
Pauline Books & Media
Revell
Sunbury Press, Inc.
Tantor Media
Texas Tech University Press
WaterBrook Multnomah Publishing Group
Whitaker House

ROMANCE

Avon Romance
Ballantine Bantam Dell
Berkley/NAL
Black Lyon Publishing
Black Velvet Seductions Publishing
Bold Strokes Books, Inc.
Bookouture
Brucedale Press, The
Canterbury House Publishing, Ltd.
Cedar Fort, Inc.
Changeling Press LLC

Covenant Communications, Inc.
Crystal Spirit Publishing, Inc.
Curiosity Quills
Divertir
Filbert Publishing
Grey Gecko Press
Harlequin Blaze
Harlequin Desire
Harlequin Intrigue
Harlequin Superromance
Kensington Publishing Corp.
Knox Robinson Publishing
Loose Id
Manor House Publishing, Inc.
Martin Sisters Publishing, LLC
Medallion Press
Melange Books, LLC
Mondial
PageSpring Publishing
Pants On Fire Press
Pauline Books & Media
Pocket Books
Rebelight Publishing, Inc.
Ring of Fire Publishing LLC
Severn House Publishers
Sunbury Press, Inc.
Tafelberg Publishers
Tantor Media
Tyndale House Publishers, Inc.
WaterBrook Multnomah Publishing Group
World Weaver Press
Zumaya Publications, LLC

SCIENCE FICTION

Ace Science Fiction and Fantasy
Archaia
Atheneum Books for Young Readers
Avon Romance
Bancroft Press
Bloomsbury Children's Books
Bold Strokes Books, Inc.
Bookouture
Cedar Fort, Inc.
Changeling Press LLC
Children's Brains are Yummy (CBAY) Books
Curiosity Quills
DAW Books, Inc.
Del Rey Books
Divertir
Edge Science Fiction and Fantasy Publishing
Goosebottom Books
Grey Gecko Press
Grove/Atlantic, Inc.
Hadley Rille Books
HarperCollins

Harper Voyager
Kitchen Publishing Co., LLC, Denis
Knox Robinson Publishing
Leapfrog Press
Lethe Press
Little, Brown Books for Young Readers
Martin Sisters Publishing, LLC
Marvel Comics
Medallion Press
Melange Books, LLC
Moody Publishers
New Libri Press
Nightscape Press
North Atlantic Books
PageSpring Publishing
Pants On Fire Press
Puffin Books
Rebelight Publishing, Inc.
Ring of Fire Publishing LLC
Saguaro Books, LLC
Saint Martin's Press, LLC
Salvo Press
Shipwreckt Books Publishing Company LLC
Simon & Schuster Books for Young Readers
Splashing Cow Books
Stoneslide Books
Sunbury Press, Inc.
Sweet Cherry Publishing
Tantor Media
Tor Books
Twilight Times Books
WaterBrook Multnomah Publishing Group
World Weaver Press
Zumaya Publications, LLC

SHORT STORY COLLECTIONS
Anvil Press
Arcade Publishing
Arsenal Pulp Press
Ballantine Bantam Dell
BkMk Press
Black Lawrence Press
BlazeVOX Books
Blue Light Press
BOA Editions, Ltd.
Bottom Dog Press, Inc.
Brucedale Press, The
Carnegie Mellon University Press
Carolina Wren Press
Children's Brains are Yummy (CBAY) Books
Coteau Books
Crescent Moon Publishing
Crystal Spirit Publishing, Inc.
Dufour Editions
Dutton Adult Trade

Folded Word
Gertrude Press
Goose Lane Editions
Graywolf Press
Grey Gecko Press
Grove/Atlantic, Inc.
Guernica Editions
Hadley Rille Books
Hopewell Publications
Kaeden Books
Leapfrog Press
Mage Publishers, Inc.
Manor House Publishing, Inc.
Martin Sisters Publishing, LLC
Milkweed Editions
Mondial
New Directions
Nightscape Press
Paul Dry Books
Paycock Press
Pedlar Press
Persea Books
Philomel Books
Pocol Press
Press 53
Red Hen Press
Red Tuque Books
Ring of Fire Publishing LLC
River City Publishing
Ronsdale Press
Sarabande Books, Inc.
Scribe Publications
Severn House Publishers
Small Beer Press
Soft Skull Press Inc.
Splashing Cow Books
Stoneslide Books
Sunbury Press, Inc.
Tantor Media
Thistledown Press Ltd.
Tightrope Books
Titan Press
University of North Texas Press
University of Wisconsin Press
Vintage Anchor Publishing
Zumaya Publications, LLC

SPIRITUAL
Ballantine Bantam Dell
Berkley/NAL
Cedar Fort, Inc.
Changeling Press LLC
Coteau Books
Covenant Communications, Inc.
Crystal Spirit Publishing, Inc.

Hampton Roads Publishing Co., Inc.
Hopewell Publications
Mandala Publishing
Martin Sisters Publishing, LLC
North Atlantic Books
Pauline Books & Media
Pocol Press
Splashing Cow Books
Sunbury Press, Inc.
Tantor Media
Unity House
WaterBrook Multnomah Publishing Group
Zumaya Publications, LLC

SPORTS

Atheneum Books for Young Readers
Bloomsbury Children's Books
Cedar Fort, Inc.
Coteau Books
Frances Lincoln Children's Books
Grey Gecko Press
JourneyForth
Kaeden Books
Martin Sisters Publishing, LLC
Orca Book Publishers
PageSpring Publishing
Pocol Press
Rebelight Publishing, Inc.
Saguaro Books, LLC
Splashing Cow Books
Sunbury Press, Inc.
Tantor Media

SUSPENSE

Atheneum Books for Young Readers
Ballantine Bantam Dell
Berkley/NAL
Bloomsbury Children's Books
Bold Strokes Books, Inc.
Bookouture
Canterbury House Publishing, Ltd.
Cedar Fort, Inc.
Changeling Press LLC
Children's Brains are Yummy (CBAY) Books
Clarion Books
Covenant Communications, Inc.
Curiosity Quills
Divertir
Dunne Books, Thomas
Dutton Adult Trade
Father's Press
Filbert Publishing
Goosebottom Books
Grey Gecko Press
Grove/Atlantic, Inc.

Harlequin Intrigue
HarperCollins
Hopewell Publications
Houghton Mifflin Harcourt Books for Children
Insomniac Press
Kaeden Books
Kensington Publishing Corp.
Little, Brown Books for Young Readers
Martin Sisters Publishing, LLC
Medallion Press
Melange Books, LLC
New Directions
Nightscape Press
Oceanview Publishing
PageSpring Publishing
Pants On Fire Press
Pocket Books
Putnam's Sons Hardcover, GP
Rebelight Publishing, Inc.
Revell
Ring of Fire Publishing LLC
Saguaro Books, LLC
Saint Martin's Press, LLC
Salvo Press
Scribe Publications
Scribner
Severn House Publishers
Shipwreckt Books Publishing Company LLC
Splashing Cow Books
Stoneslide Books
Strategic Media Books
Sunbury Press, Inc.
Tantor Media
Tor Books
Twilight Times Books
Viking
WaterBrook Multnomah Publishing Group
Zumaya Publications, LLC

TRANSLATION

Arcade Publishing
Ballantine Bantam Dell
Bancroft Press
Black Lawrence Press
Crescent Moon Publishing
Cross-Cultural Communications
Dufour Editions
Gival Press
Godine, Publisher, David R.
Guernica Editions
Inverted-A
Milkweed Editions
Mondial
NBM Publishing
New Directions

New Libri Press
Papercutz
Paul Dry Books
Persea Books
Philomel Books
Scribe Publications
Stone Bridge Press
Subito Press
University of New Mexico Press
Véhicule Press

WAR

Cedar Fort, Inc.
Changeling Press LLC
Glencannon Press, The
Grey Gecko Press
Inverted-A
Martin Sisters Publishing, LLC
McBooks Press
Merriam Press
New Libri Press
Nortia Press
Saguaro Books, LLC
Scribe Publications
Twilight Times Books
Zumaya Publications, LLC

WESTERN

Atheneum Books for Young Readers
Berkley/NAL
Bold Strokes Books, Inc.
Bookouture
Cedar Fort, Inc.
Changeling Press LLC
Father's Press
Glencannon Press, The
Grey Gecko Press
Grove/Atlantic, Inc.
HarperCollins
JourneyForth
Kensington Publishing Corp.
Martin Sisters Publishing, LLC
Melange Books, LLC
New Libri Press
Philomel Books
Pocket Books
Pocol Press
Ring of Fire Publishing LLC
Saguaro Books, LLC
Saint Martin's Press, LLC
Splashing Cow Books
Sunbury Press, Inc.
Tantor Media
Texas Tech University Press
Zumaya Publications, LLC

YOUNG ADULT

Abrams, Harry N., Inc.
AMG Publishers
Avon Romance
Bancroft Press
BelleBooks
Berkley/NAL
Bethany House Publishers
Bloomsbury Children's Books
Bold Strokes Books, Inc.
Brucedale Press, The
Candlewick Press
Cedar Fort, Inc.
Changeling Press LLC
Charlesbridge Publishing
Children's Brains are Yummy (CBAY) Books
Chronicle Books for Children
Craigmore Creations
Creston Books
Crystal Spirit Publishing, Inc.
Curiosity Quills
Dial Books for Young Readers
Divertir
Dundurn Press, Ltd.
Dutton Children's Books
Edge Science Fiction and Fantasy Publishing
Familius
Farrar, Straus & Giroux
Father's Press
Fernwood Publishing, Ltd.
Frances Lincoln Children's Books
Glencannon Press, The
Godine, Publisher, David R.
Goosebottom Books
Grey Gecko Press
HarperCollins Children's Books/HarperCollins
    Publishers
Hendrick-Long Publishing Co., Inc.
Hopewell Publications
Houghton Mifflin Harcourt Books for Children
Inverted-A
JourneyForth
Kregel Publications
Leapfrog Press
Levine Books, Arthur A.
Manor House Publishing, Inc.
Martin Sisters Publishing, LLC
Marvel Comics
McElderry Books, Margaret K.
Medallion Press
Melange Books, LLC
Milkweed Editions
Moody Publishers
NBM Publishing

New Libri Press
Nightscape Press
Orca Book Publishers
PageSpring Publishing
Pants On Fire Press
Papercutz
Paul Dry Books
Pauline Books & Media
Peace Hill Press
Peachtree Children's Books
Persea Books
Philomel Books
Pinata Books
Poisoned Pencil, The
Puffin Books
Rebelight Publishing, Inc.
Ring of Fire Publishing LLC
Saguaro Books, LLC
Scribe Publications
Shipwreckt Books Publishing Company LLC
Simon & Schuster Books for Young Readers
Sunbury Press, Inc.
Sweet Cherry Publishing
Tantor Media
Tightrope Books
Tor Books
Tu Books
Twilight Times Books
Zumaya Publications, LLC

NONFICTION

AGRICULTURE
ASM Press
Ball Publishing
Cedar Fort, Inc.
Chelsea Green Publishing Co.
Cornell University Press
Dover Publications, Inc.
Fernwood Publishing, Ltd.
Hancock House Publishers
High Plains Press
Hobar Publications
Indiana Historical Society Press
Krieger Publishing Co.
Lyons Press, The
Milkweed Editions
New Libri Press
New Society Publishers
North Atlantic Books
Paul Dry Books
Reference Service Press
Shipwreckt Books Publishing Company LLC
Stipes Publishing LLC
Sun Books / Sun Publishing

Sunbury Press, Inc.
Tantor Media
University of Iowa Press
Windward Publishing

ALTERNATIVE LIFESTYLES
BlueBridge
Bottom Dog Press, Inc.
Chelsea Green Publishing Co.
Crystal Spirit Publishing, Inc.
Findhorn Press
Hay House, Inc.
New Society Publishers
New World Library
Red Moon Press
Reed Publishers, Robert D.
Seal Press
Shipwreckt Books Publishing Company LLC
Sun Books / Sun Publishing
Tantor Media
Tightrope Books

AMERICANA
AMG Publishers
Atheneum Books for Young Readers
BlueBridge
Burford Books
Cedar Fort, Inc.
Clarion Books
Crescent Moon Publishing
Dover Publications, Inc.
Down the Shore Publishing
Familius
Filter Press, LLC
Glenbridge Publishing, Ltd.
Godine, Publisher, David R.
Golden West Books
Heritage Books, Inc.
Heyday Books
High Plains Press
History Publishing Company, LLC.
Holiday House, Inc.
Iconografix/Enthusiast Books
Inverted-A
Kane/Miller Book Publishers
Kensington Publishing Corp.
Lehigh University Press
Lyons Press, The
Martin Sisters Publishing, LLC
Merriam Press
Minnesota Historical Society Press
Motorbooks
Ohio University Press
Pelican Publishing Company
Santa Monica Press

Seal Press
Shipwreckt Books Publishing Company LLC
Strategic Media Books
Sun Books / Sun Publishing
Sunbury Press, Inc.
Tantor Media
University of Akron Press
University of Alaska Press
University of Arizona Press
University of Illinois Press
University of New Mexico Press
University of North Carolina Press, The
University of North Texas Press
University of Pennsylvania Press
University of Tennessee Press, The
University Press of Kansas
University Press of Mississippi
Vanderbilt University Press
Voyageur Press
Yale University Press

ANIMALS

ABDO Publishing Co.
Alpine Publications
ASM Press
Atheneum Books for Young Readers
Ballantine Bantam Dell
Balzer & Bray
BlueBridge
Burford Books
Capall Bann Publishing
Cartwheel Books
Cedar Fort, Inc.
Charlesbridge Publishing
Chronicle Books for Children
Craigmore Creations
Dawn Publications
Dover Publications, Inc.
Dutton Children's Books
Encante Press, LLC
Epicenter Press, Inc.
Father's Press
Findhorn Press
Formac Publishing Co. Ltd.
Frances Lincoln Books
Frances Lincoln Children's Books
Hancock House Publishers
Heinemann Educational Publishers
Heritage House Publishing Co., Ltd.
Hobar Publications
Houghton Mifflin Harcourt Books for Children
JourneyForth
Kaeden Books
Kensington Publishing Corp.
Krieger Publishing Co.

Little, Brown Books for Young Readers
Lyons Press, The
McDonald & Woodward Publishing Co., The
Milkweed Editions
Mountain Press Publishing Co.
Newsage Press
New Society Publishers
New World Library
Peachtree Children's Books
Putnam's Sons Hardcover, GP
Rio Nuevo Publishers
Sasquatch Books
Shipwreckt Books Publishing Company LLC
Sterling Publishing Co., Inc.
Storey Publishing
Sunbury Press, Inc.
Tantor Media
Trafalgar Square Books
University of Alaska Press
University of Illinois Press
Whitecap Books, Ltd.
Willow Creek Press
Windward Publishing

ANTHROPOLOGY

Algora Publishing
BlueBridge
Cedar Fort, Inc.
Craigmore Creations
Fernwood Publishing, Ltd.
Heritage House Publishing Co., Ltd.
North Atlantic Books
Ohio University Press
Paragon House Publishers
Strawberries Press
Sunbury Press, Inc.
Tantor Media
University of Akron Press
University of New Mexico Press
University of Wisconsin Press

ARCHEOLOGY

Algora Publishing
BlueBridge
Cedar Fort, Inc.
Craigmore Creations
North Atlantic Books
Southern Illinois University Press
Strawberries Press
Sunbury Press, Inc.
University of Akron Press
University of New Mexico Press
University of Tennessee Press, The
University Press of Kansas

ARCHITECTURE

BlueBridge
Bronze Man Books
Fairleigh Dickinson University Press
Grey Gecko Press
McDonald & Woodward Publishing Co., The
North Atlantic Books
PPI (Professional Publications, Inc.)
Strawberries Press
Sunbury Press, Inc.
University of Arkansas Press, The
University of Calgary Press
University of New Mexico Press
University of Tennessee Press, The

ART

Abbeville Press
Arch Street Press
BlueBridge
Bronze Man Books
Chronicle Books
Fairleigh Dickinson University Press
Godine, Publisher, David R.
Grey Gecko Press
Heritage House Publishing Co., Ltd.
IMPACT Books
Medallion Press
Milkweed Editions
North Atlantic Books
North Light Books
Palettes & Quills
Paraclete Press
Red Moon Press
Rotovision
Santa Monica Press
Strawberries Press
Sunbury Press, Inc.
Tightrope Books
University of Calgary Press
University of New Mexico Press
University of North Texas Press

ASTROLOGY

Capall Bann Publishing
Hay House, Inc.
North Atlantic Books
Sun Books / Sun Publishing
Sunbury Press, Inc.
Tantor Media

BEAUTY

Chronicle Books
Familius
New Society Publishers

BUSINESS

Addicus Books, Inc.
Amacom Books
Ankerwycke
Arch Street Press
Cedar Fort, Inc.
Chelsea Green Publishing Co.
Craftsman Book Co.
Crystal Spirit Publishing, Inc.
Entrepreneur Press
Heritage House Publishing Co., Ltd.
History Publishing Company, LLC.
Information Today, Inc.
International Wealth Success
InterVarsity Press
Maven House Press
New Forums Press
New Libri Press
New Society Publishers
New World Library
North Atlantic Books
Oneworld Publications
Passkey Publications
Printing Industries of America
Reed Publishers, Robert D.
Stone Bridge Press
Sunbury Press, Inc.
Tantor Media
Ten Speed Press
Wiley & Sons, Inc., John

CAREER GUIDANCE

Amacom Books
American Counseling Association
Entrepreneur Press
Facts On File, Inc.
Frances Lincoln Books
Frances Lincoln Children's Books
New World Library
Reed Publishers, Robert D.
Search Institute Press
Sun Books / Sun Publishing
Sunbury Press, Inc.
Ten Speed Press

CHILD GUIDANCE

Amacom Books
Ballantine Bantam Dell
Beacon Press
Berkley/NAL
Bethany House Publishers
Broadway Books
Cedar Fort, Inc.
Clarkson Potter
Encounter Books

Familius
FamilyLife Publishing
Free Spirit Publishing, Inc.
Great Potential Press
Gryphon House, Inc.
Harvard Common Press, The
Harvest House Publishers
Health Communications, Inc.
InterVarsity Press
Kensington Publishing Corp.
 Inc.
Martin Sisters Publishing, LLC
McGraw-Hill Professional Business
Moody Publishers
NavPress
New Hope Publishers
New Horizon Press
New Libri Press
New Society Publishers
New World Library
North Atlantic Books
Pacific Press Publishing Association
Pauline Books & Media
Peachtree Children's Books
Putnam's Sons Hardcover, GP
Reed Publishers, Robert D.
Revell
Seal Press
Search Institute Press
Sentient Publications
Sourcebooks, Inc.
Square One Publishers, Inc.
Sunbury Press, Inc.
Tantor Media
Tyndale House Publishers, Inc.
Viking
WaterBrook Multnomah Publishing Group
Western Psychological Services
Workman Publishing Co.
Yogi Impressions Books Pvt. Ltd.

CINEMA

BearManor Media
Fairleigh Dickinson University Press
Jain Publishing Co.
Santa Monica Press
Stone Bridge Press
University of Calgary Press
World Weaver Press

COMMUNICATIONS

Amacom Books
Arch Street Press
Cedar Fort, Inc.
Duquesne University Press

Fairleigh Dickinson University Press
Fernwood Publishing, Ltd.
Filbert Publishing
New Society Publishers
Printing Industries of America
Reed Publishers, Robert D.
Sunbury Press, Inc.
Tantor Media
University of Calgary Press
Wiley & Sons, Inc., John

COMMUNITY

Arch Street Press
Ballantine Bantam Dell
Berrett-Koehler Publishers, Inc.
BlueBridge
Chelsea Green Publishing Co.
Fernwood Publishing, Ltd.
Findhorn Press
Heritage House Publishing Co., Ltd.
Judson Press
Minnesota Historical Society Press
New Society Publishers
North Atlantic Books
Reed Publishers, Robert D.
Search Institute Press
Second Story Press

COMPUTERS

New Libri Press
Sunbury Press, Inc.
Wiley & Sons, Inc., John

CONTEMPORARY CULTURE

Arch Street Press
BlueBridge
Bottom Dog Press, Inc.
Broadway Books
Clarity Press, Inc.
Da Capo Press
Divertir
Facts On File, Inc.
Fairleigh Dickinson University Press
Fernwood Publishing, Ltd.
Graywolf Press
Grey Gecko Press
Hendrickson Publishers, Inc.
Heritage House Publishing Co., Ltd.
History Publishing Company, LLC.
IMPACT Books
InterVarsity Press
JourneyForth
Kensington Publishing Corp.
Martin Sisters Publishing, LLC
Methuen Publishing Ltd.

Milkweed Editions
Minnesota Historical Society Press
New Society Publishers
New World Library
North Atlantic Books
Paul Dry Books
Persea Books
Putnam's Sons Hardcover, GP
Red Moon Press
Reed Publishers, Robert D.
Sakura Publishing & Technologies
Santa Monica Press
Seal Press
Second Story Press
Sentient Publications
Soft Skull Press Inc.
Strategic Media Books
Sunbury Press, Inc.
Talese, Nan A.
Tantor Media
Tightrope Books
University of Iowa Press
Vivisphere Publishing

COOKING
Andrews McMeel Universal
Balzer & Bray
Blair, Publisher, John F.
Burford Books
Cedar Fort, Inc.
Chelsea Green Publishing Co.
Chronicle Books
Familius
Fox Chapel Publishing
Frances Lincoln Books
Frances Lincoln Children's Books
Grey Gecko Press
Hay House, Inc.
Martin Sisters Publishing, LLC
Minnesota Historical Society Press
New Libri Press
New Society Publishers
North Atlantic Books
Saint Johann Press
Shambhala Publications, Inc.
Square One Publishers, Inc.
Tantor Media
Ten Speed Press
Touchwood Editions
University of North Texas Press
Voyageur Press

COUNSELING
Familius
Free Spirit Publishing, Inc.

New World Library
Reed Publishers, Robert D.
Search Institute Press
Sunbury Press, Inc.

CRAFTS
Capall Bann Publishing
Cedar Fort, Inc.
Chronicle Books
Divertir
Fox Chapel Publishing
Interweave Press
Linden Publishing, Inc.
Palettes & Quills
Saint Johann Press
Shambhala Publications, Inc.
STC Craft
Stone Bridge Press
Sunbury Press, Inc.
Ten Speed Press

CREATIVE NONFICTION
Algora Publishing
Appalachian Mountain Club Books
Arch Street Press
Arsenal Pulp Press
Ballantine Bantam Dell
Berkley/NAL
Blair, Publisher, John F.
BlueBridge
Capall Bann Publishing
Cedar Fort, Inc.
Charlesbridge Publishing
Coffee House Press
Coteau Books
Craigmore Creations
Crossroad Publishing Company, The
Crystal Spirit Publishing, Inc.
Da Capo Press
Dream of Things
Father's Press
Fernwood Publishing, Ltd.
Filbert Publishing
Folded Word
Formac Publishing Co. Ltd.
Fox Chapel Publishing
Gival Press
Godine, Publisher, David R.
Goosebottom Books
Grey Gecko Press
Grove/Atlantic, Inc.
Guernica Editions
Hendrickson Publishers, Inc.
Heritage House Publishing Co., Ltd.
History Publishing Company, LLC.

IMPACT Books
Jonathan David Publishers, Inc.
JourneyForth
Kaeden Books
Langmarc Publishing
Martin Sisters Publishing, LLC
Milkweed Editions
Minnesota Historical Society Press
MSI Press
New Horizon Press
New Libri Press
Palettes & Quills
Palgrave Macmillan
Peachtree Children's Books
Pedlar Press
Red Rock Press
Rotovision
Sakura Publishing & Technologies
Santa Monica Press
Seal Press
Second Story Press
Sentient Publications
Shipwreckt Books Publishing Company LLC
Soft Skull Press Inc.
Soho Press, Inc.
Stone Bridge Press
Strawberries Press
Sunbury Press, Inc.
Tantor Media
ThunderStone Books
Tightrope Books
Titan Press
Torrey House Press, LLC
Touchwood Editions
Travelers' Tales
Twilight Times Books
University of Akron Press
University of Iowa Press
University of North Texas Press
Zumaya Publications, LLC

DANCE
Algora Publishing
Balzer & Bray
BearManor Media
Fairleigh Dickinson University Press
University of Wisconsin Press

ECONOMICS
Addicus Books, Inc.
Amacom Books
Arch Street Press
BlueBridge
Cedar Fort, Inc.
Chelsea Green Publishing Co.

Clarity Press, Inc.
Crystal Spirit Publishing, Inc.
Fairleigh Dickinson University Press
Fernwood Publishing, Ltd.
History Publishing Company, LLC.
InterVarsity Press
Maven House Press
New Libri Press
New Society Publishers
North Atlantic Books
Oneworld Publications
Paragon House Publishers
Passkey Publications
Printing Industries of America
Sunbury Press, Inc.
Tantor Media
Wiley & Sons, Inc., John

EDUCATION
Abingdon Press
Algora Publishing
Amacom Books
American Catholic Press
American Counseling Association
AMG Publishers
APA Books
Arch Street Press
ASA, Aviation Supplies & Academics
ASM Press
Association for Supervision and Curriculum Development
Baker Academic
Ballantine Bantam Dell
Beacon Press
Between the Lines
Bloomsbury Continuum
Bull Publishing Co.
Capstone Professional
Carnegie Mellon University Press
Carson-Dellosa Publishing Co., Inc.
Cato Institute
Cedar Fort, Inc.
College Board, The
Colourpoint Books
Corwin Press, Inc.
Encounter Books
Enete Enterprises
Facts On File, Inc.
FamilyLife Publishing
Fernwood Publishing, Ltd.
Finney Company, Inc.
Fordham University Press
Free Spirit Publishing, Inc.
Future Horizons
Gival Press

Great Potential Press
Group Publishing, Inc.
Grove/Atlantic, Inc.
Gryphon House, Inc.
Hay House, Inc.
Hein & Co., Inc., William S.
Heinemann Educational Publishers
Hendrickson Publishers, Inc.
Hobar Publications
Human Kinetics Publishers, Inc.
Incentive Publications, Inc.
Information Today, Inc.
Jossey-Bass
Krieger Publishing Co.
LRP Publications, Inc.
Mandala Publishing
Martin Sisters Publishing, LLC
McGraw-Hill Professional Business
Medical Group Management Association
MSI Press
New Forums Press
New Hope Publishers
New Society Publishers
Nova Press
Ohio State University Press
Palgrave Macmillan
Peace Hill Press
Peachtree Children's Books
Peterson's
Pfeiffer
Presses de l'Universite de Montreal
Printing Industries of America
Prometheus Books
Prufrock Press, Inc.
Puffin Books
Red Moon Press
Reed Publishers, Robert D.
Reference Service Press
Salina Bookshelf
Santa Monica Press
Scribner
Search Institute Press
Sentient Publications
Stenhouse Publishers
Strawberries Press
Sunbury Press, Inc.
SuperCollege
Tantor Media
Teachers College Press
Texas Western Press
ThunderStone Books
UMI (Urban Ministries, Inc.)
University of Alaska Press
Vanderbilt University Press
Van Schaik Publishers

Velazquez Press
Walch Publishing
Wiley & Sons, Inc., John
Yale University Press

ELECTRONICS
New Libri Press
North Atlantic Books
Sunbury Press, Inc.

ENTERTAINMENT
BearManor Media
Hendrickson Publishers, Inc.
Palettes & Quills
Reed Publishers, Robert D.
Sakura Publishing & Technologies
Santa Monica Press
Search Institute Press
Soft Skull Press Inc.
Sunbury Press, Inc.
Tantor Media
Titan Press

ENVIRONMENT
Algora Publishing
Appalachian Mountain Club Books
Arch Street Press
Balzer & Bray
BlueBridge
Bucknell University Press
Chelsea Green Publishing Co.
Clarity Press, Inc.
Craigmore Creations
Encante Press, LLC
Fernwood Publishing, Ltd.
Frances Lincoln Books
Frances Lincoln Children's Books
Grey Gecko Press
Heritage House Publishing Co., Ltd.
High Plains Press
Jain Publishing Co.
JourneyForth
McDonald & Woodward Publishing Co., The
Milkweed Editions
New Libri Press
New Society Publishers
New World Library
North Atlantic Books
Red Moon Press
Reed Publishers, Robert D.
Ruka Press
Scribe Publications
Seaworthy Publications, Inc.
Second Story Press
Sentient Publications
Shipwreckt Books Publishing Company LLC

Strategic Media Books
Strawberries Press
Sun Books / Sun Publishing
Texas Tech University Press
Torrey House Press, LLC
University of Akron Press
University of Calgary Press
University of Iowa Press
University of Wisconsin Press
University Press of Kansas
Voyageur Press

ETHNIC
Arsenal Pulp Press
Arte Publico Press
Barricade Books, Inc.
Beacon Press
BlueBridge
Bucknell University Press
Carolina Wren Press
Clarity Press, Inc.
Cornell University Press
Coteau Books
Crossroad Publishing Company, The
Crystal Spirit Publishing, Inc.
Encounter Books
Epicenter Press, Inc.
Fairleigh Dickinson University Press
Fernwood Publishing, Ltd.
Filter Press, LLC
Guernica Editions
Hachai Publishing
Hancock House Publishers
Heinemann Educational Publishers
Heritage Books, Inc.
Heritage House Publishing Co., Ltd.
Heyday Books
Hill Books, Lawrence
Holy Cross Orthodox Press
Houghton Mifflin Harcourt Books for Children
Indiana Historical Society Press
InterVarsity Press
Jonathan David Publishers, Inc.
Little, Brown Books for Young Readers
Mage Publishers, Inc.
Minnesota Historical Society Press
Mitchell Lane Publishers, Inc.
Mondial
Naturegraph Publishers, Inc.
NeWest Publishers Ltd.
New York University Press
Nortia Press
Palgrave Macmillan
Peachtree Children's Books
Pelican Publishing Company

Pinata Books
Red Hen Press
Red Moon Press
Reed Publishers, Robert D.
Reference Service Press
Rutgers University Press
Sakura Publishing & Technologies
Salem Press, Inc.
Salina Bookshelf
Scribner
Seal Press
Shipwreckt Books Publishing Company LLC
Soho Press, Inc.
Stanford University Press
Sterling Publishing Co., Inc.
Strategic Media Books
Strawberries Press
Sunbury Press, Inc.
Temple University Press
Texas Tech University Press
Tightrope Books
University of Alaska Press
University of Arizona Press
University of Nevada Press
University of New Mexico Press
University of North Texas Press
University of Texas Press
University of Washington Press
University Press of Mississippi
Vanderbilt University Press
YMAA Publication Center

FASHION
New Society Publishers
Quite Specific Media Group, Ltd.

FILM
Fairleigh Dickinson University Press
Hendrickson Publishers, Inc.
Jain Publishing Co.
Sakura Publishing & Technologies
Santa Monica Press
Stone Bridge Press
University of Calgary Press
University of Wisconsin Press

FINANCE
Algora Publishing
Amacom Books
Arch Street Press
Familius
International Wealth Success
New Society Publishers
North Atlantic Books
Passkey Publications
Wiley & Sons, Inc., John

FOODS

Burford Books
Cedar Fort, Inc.
Chelsea Green Publishing Co.
Conari Press
Familius
Grey Gecko Press
Hay House, Inc.
New Society Publishers
North Atlantic Books
Saint Johann Press
Shipwreckt Books Publishing Company LLC
Tantor Media
University of Arkansas Press, The
University of Wisconsin Press

GAMES

Andrews McMeel Universal
Sakura Publishing & Technologies
Search Institute Press
Tantor Media

GARDENING

Ball Publishing
BlueBridge
Capall Bann Publishing
Cedar Fort, Inc.
Chelsea Green Publishing Co.
Crescent Moon Publishing
Godine, Publisher, David R.
Hobar Publications
Martin Sisters Publishing, LLC
Milkweed Editions
Nelson, Inc., Thomas
New Libri Press
New Society Publishers
North Atlantic Books
Peachtree Children's Books
Rio Nuevo Publishers
Sasquatch Books
Sentient Publications
Shipwreckt Books Publishing Company LLC
Sterling Publishing Co., Inc.
Storey Publishing
University of New Mexico Press
University of North Carolina Press, The
Whitecap Books, Ltd.
Willow Creek Press
Windward Publishing
Workman Publishing Co.

GAY

American Counseling Association
Bold Strokes Books, Inc.
Carolina Wren Press

Fairleigh Dickinson University Press
Fernwood Publishing, Ltd.
Gival Press

Milkweed Editions
North Atlantic Books
Orca Book Publishers
Pedlar Press
Reed Publishers, Robert D.
Seal Press
Second Story Press
Shipwreckt Books Publishing Company LLC
Tantor Media
Tightrope Books
University of Wisconsin Press

GOVERNMENT

Algora Publishing
Amacom Books
Arch Street Press
Chelsea Green Publishing Co.
Clarity Press, Inc.
Divertir
Encante Press, LLC
Fairleigh Dickinson University Press
Fernwood Publishing, Ltd.
History Publishing Company, LLC.
Milkweed Editions
Nortia Press
Ohio University Press
Paragon House Publishers
Shipwreckt Books Publishing Company LLC
Strategic Media Books
Sunbury Press, Inc.
Tantor Media
University of North Texas Press
University Press of Kansas

HEALTH

Addicus Books, Inc.
Arch Street Press
Cedar Fort, Inc.
Chelsea Green Publishing Co.
Conari Press
Constable & Robinson, Ltd.
Enete Enterprises
Familius
Fernwood Publishing, Ltd.
Findhorn Press
Hay House, Inc.
Health Communications, Inc.
Health Professions Press
Idyll Arbor, Inc.
Medallion Press
Medical Group Management Association

MSI Press
New Society Publishers
North Atlantic Books
Piccadilly Books, Ltd.
Reed Publishers, Robert D.
Seal Press
Second Story Press
Shipwreckt Books Publishing Company LLC
Square One Publishers, Inc.
Sunbury Press, Inc.
Tantor Media
Wiley & Sons, Inc., John

HISTORY

ABDO Publishing Co.
Academy Chicago Publishers
Algora Publishing
Allan Publishing, Ltd., Ian
AMG Publishers
Arcade Publishing
Arcadia Publishing
Arch Street Press
Arsenal Pulp Press
ASM Press
Atheneum Books for Young Readers
Ballantine Bantam Dell
Ball Publishers, Jonathan
Balzer & Bray
Barricade Books, Inc.
Basic Books
Beil, Publisher, Inc., Frederic C.
Berkley/NAL
Between the Lines
Black Dome Press Corp.
Blair, Publisher, John F.
Bloomsbury Continuum
BlueBridge
Broadway Books
Brucedale Press, The
Bucknell University Press
Burford Books
Calkins Creek
Carnegie Mellon University Press
Cartwheel Books
Catholic University of America Press
Cedar Fort, Inc.
Chand & Company Ltd., S.
Charlesbridge Publishing
Clarion Books
Clarity Press, Inc.
Constable & Robinson, Ltd.
Cornell University Press
Coteau Books
Covenant Communications, Inc.
CQ Press

Da Capo Press
Divertir
Dover Publications, Inc.
Down the Shore Publishing
Dufour Editions
Dundurn Press, Ltd.
Dunne Books, Thomas
Dutton Children's Books
Eerdmans Publishing Co., William B.
Encounter Books
Enslow Publishers, Inc.
Epicenter Press, Inc.
Facts On File, Inc.
Fairleigh Dickinson University Press
Father's Press
Fernwood Publishing, Ltd.
Filter Press, LLC
Flyleaf Press
Fordham University Press
Foreign Policy Association
Formac Publishing Co. Ltd.
Frances Lincoln Books
Frances Lincoln Children's Books
Glenbridge Publishing, Ltd.
Glencannon Press, The
Godine, Publisher, David R.
Golden West Books
Goosebottom Books
Goose Lane Editions
Grey Gecko Press
Guernica Editions
Hancock House Publishers
Heinemann Educational Publishers
Hellgate Press
Hendrick-Long Publishing Co., Inc.
Hendrickson Publishers, Inc.
Heritage Books, Inc.
Heritage House Publishing Co., Ltd.
Heyday Books
High Plains Press
Hill and Wang
Hill Books, Lawrence
History Publishing Company, LLC.
Holiday House, Inc.
Houghton Mifflin Harcourt Books for Children
Ibex Publishers
Iconografix/Enthusiast Books
ILR Press
Indiana Historical Society Press
InterVarsity Press
Irish Academic Press
Iron Gate Publishing
Jewish Lights Publishing
Johns Hopkins University Press, The
Johnson Books

JourneyForth
Kane/Miller Book Publishers
Kensington Publishing Corp.
Kent State University Press
Knox Robinson Publishing
Kregel Publications
Krieger Publishing Co.
Lehigh University Press
Linden Publishing, Inc.
Little, Brown Books for Young Readers
Lyons Press, The
Mage Publishers, Inc.
Manor House Publishing, Inc.
Martin Sisters Publishing, LLC
McBooks Press
McClelland & Stewart, Ltd.
McDonald & Woodward Publishing Co., The
McElderry Books, Margaret K.
McFarland & Co., Inc., Publishers
Merriam Press
Methuen Publishing Ltd.
Milkweed Editions
Minnesota Historical Society Press
Missouri Historical Society Press
Mondial
Montana Historical Society Press
Motorbooks
Mountain Press Publishing Co.
NeWest Publishers Ltd.
New Forums Press
North Carolina Office of Archives and History

North Point Press
Ohio State University Press
Ohio University Press
Oolichan Books
Owen Publishers, Peter
Owen, Richard C., Publishers, Inc.
Palgrave Macmillan
Paragon House Publishers
Paul Dry Books
Peace Hill Press
Peachtree Children's Books
Pelican Publishing Company
Presses de l'Universite de Montreal
Prometheus Books
P & R Publishing Co.
Puffin Books
Quite Specific Media Group, Ltd.
Red Moon Press
Reed Publishers, Robert D.
Reference Service Press
Rio Nuevo Publishers
Ronsdale Press
Rutgers University Press

Saint Johann Press
Sakura Publishing & Technologies
Salem Press, Inc.
Santa Monica Press
Sasquatch Books
Scribe Publications
Scribner
Second Story Press
Sentient Publications
Shipwreckt Books Publishing Company LLC
Simon & Schuster Books for Young Readers
Sourcebooks, Inc.
Southern Illinois University Press
Stanford University Press
Strategic Media Books
Sun Books / Sun Publishing
Sunbury Press, Inc.
Talese, Nan A.
Tantor Media
Teachers College Press
Temple University Press
Texas Tech University Press
Texas Western Press
Touchwood Editions
University of Akron Press
University of Alabama Press, The
University of Alaska Press
University of Alberta Press, The
University of Arkansas Press, The
University of Calgary Press
University of California Press
University of Georgia Press
University of Illinois Press
University of Iowa Press
University of Maine Press
University of Nevada Press
University of New Mexico Press
University of North Carolina Press, The
University of North Texas Press
University of Pennsylvania Press
University of South Carolina Press
University of Tennessee Press, The
University of Texas Press
University of Washington Press
University of Wisconsin Press
University Press of Kentucky
Utah State University Press
Vanderbilt University Press
Véhicule Press
Verso
Viking
Voyageur Press
Walch Publishing
Whitecap Books, Ltd.
William Morrow

Wisconsin Historical Society Press
Yale University Press
YMAA Publication Center

HOBBIES

Allan Publishing, Ltd., Ian
Burford Books
Cedar Fort, Inc.
C&T Publishing
Divertir
Dover Publications, Inc.
Familius
Flyleaf Press
Iconografix/Enthusiast Books
IMPACT Books
Interweave Press
Kensington Publishing Corp.
Linden Publishing, Inc.
Little, Brown Books for Young Readers
Motorbooks
New Libri Press
Red Moon Press
Saint Johann Press
Sakura Publishing & Technologies
Shipwreckt Books Publishing Company LLC
Square One Publishers, Inc.
Sterling Publishing Co., Inc.
Strawberries Press
Sunbury Press, Inc.
Voyageur Press

HORTICULTURE

ASM Press
Cedar Fort, Inc.
Hancock House Publishers
High Plains Press
New Society Publishers
North Atlantic Books
Shipwreckt Books Publishing Company LLC
Tantor Media

HOUSE AND HOME

Cedar Fort, Inc.
Chronicle Books
Martin Sisters Publishing, LLC
New Libri Press
New Society Publishers
Shipwreckt Books Publishing Company LLC
Stone Bridge Press
Sunbury Press, Inc.

HUMANITIES

ABC-CLIO/Greenwood
Arch Street Press
Beil, Publisher, Inc., Frederic C.
BlueBridge

Bottom Dog Press, Inc.
Duquesne University Press
Fernwood Publishing, Ltd.
Heinemann Educational Publishers
Hendrickson Publishers, Inc.
Heritage House Publishing Co., Ltd.
Ibex Publishers
Jain Publishing Co.
Johns Hopkins University Press, The
Knox Robinson Publishing
Martin Sisters Publishing, LLC
Milkweed Editions
MSI Press
New Society Publishers
Nortia Press
Red Moon Press
Reed Publishers, Robert D.
Sakura Publishing & Technologies
Santa Monica Press
Stanford University Press
Sunbury Press, Inc.
University of Akron Press
University of Arkansas Press, The
University of Calgary Press
University of Iowa Press
University of New Mexico Press
University of North Texas Press

LABOR

Arch Street Press
Clarity Press, Inc.
Fernwood Publishing, Ltd.
Martin Sisters Publishing, LLC
New Society Publishers
Second Story Press
University of Akron Press

LANGUAGE

Algora Publishing
Arch Street Press
Godine, Publisher, David R.
Hendrickson Publishers, Inc.
Ibex Publishers
Luna Bisonte Prods
Martin Sisters Publishing, LLC
Milkweed Editions
Ohio University Press
Red Moon Press
Reed Publishers, Robert D.
Santa Monica Press
Southern Illinois University Press
Stone Bridge Press
Sunbury Press, Inc.
ThunderStone Books
Tightrope Books

White Pine Press

LAW

Addicus Books, Inc.
Arch Street Press
Bucknell University Press
Clarity Press, Inc.
Fairleigh Dickinson University Press
Fernwood Publishing, Ltd.
Godine, Publisher, David R.
Hein & Co., Inc., William S.
Martin Sisters Publishing, LLC
Tantor Media
Texas Tech University Press
University of Akron Press

LESBIAN

American Counseling Association
Bold Strokes Books, Inc.
Carolina Wren Press
Fairleigh Dickinson University Press
Fernwood Publishing, Ltd.
Gival Press
North Atlantic Books
Orca Book Publishers
Reed Publishers, Robert D.
Seal Press
Second Story Press
Shipwreckt Books Publishing Company LLC
Tantor Media
Tightrope Books
University of Wisconsin Press

LITERARY CRITICISM

ABC-CLIO/Greenwood
Arch Street Press
BenBella Books
BlueBridge
Bucknell University Press
Carnegie Mellon University Press
Duquesne University Press
Facts On File, Inc.
Fairleigh Dickinson University Press
Godine, Publisher, David R.
Guernica Editions
Irish Academic Press
Johns Hopkins University Press, The
Kent State University Press
Mondial
Ohio State University Press
Palettes & Quills
Paul Dry Books
Peachtree Children's Books
Pedlar Press
Persea Books
Playlab Press

Quite Specific Media Group, Ltd.
Red Moon Press
Ronsdale Press
Stanford University Press
Tantor Media
Texas Tech University Press
Tightrope Books
Titan Press
Twilight Times Books
University of Akron Press
University of Alabama Press, The
University of Arkansas Press, The
University of Calgary Press
University of Iowa Press
University of New Mexico Press
University of Pennsylvania Press
University of Tennessee Press, The
University of Texas Press
University Press of Mississippi

LITERATURE

Algora Publishing
Arch Street Press
Backwaters Press, The
Beil, Publisher, Inc., Frederic C.
Blair, Publisher, John F.
Blue Light Press
Bronze Man Books
Carolina Wren Press
Folded Word
Gival Press
Godine, Publisher, David R.
Guernica Editions
Hendrickson Publishers, Inc.
Ibex Publishers
Luna Bisonte Prods
Martin Sisters Publishing, LLC
Milkweed Editions
New Forums Press
Ohio University Press
Owen Publishers, Peter
Palettes & Quills
Pedlar Press
Persea Books
Plan B Press
Red Moon Press
Reed Publishers, Robert D.
Ronsdale Press
Rose Alley Press
Sakura Publishing & Technologies
Salmon Poetry
Santa Monica Press
Second Story Press
Shearsman Books, LTD
Soft Skull Press Inc.

Stone Bridge Press
Sunbury Press, Inc.
Texas Tech University Press
Thistledown Press Ltd.
ThunderStone Books
Tightrope Books
Travelers' Tales
University of Calgary Press
University of New Mexico Press
White Pine Press

MARINE SUBJECTS
Glencannon Press, The
Grey Gecko Press
Heritage House Publishing Co., Ltd.
McBooks Press
Orca Book Publishers
Salmon Poetry
Seaworthy Publications, Inc.
Strawberries Press
Tantor Media

MEDICINE
Chelsea Green Publishing Co.
Constable & Robinson, Ltd.
Eastland Press
Familius
Idyll Arbor, Inc.
North Atlantic Books
Piccadilly Books, Ltd.
Shipwreckt Books Publishing Company LLC

MEMOIRS
Arcade Publishing
Arch Street Press
Ballantine Bantam Dell
BearManor Media
Beil, Publisher, Inc., Frederic C.
Blair, Publisher, John F.
Bold Strokes Books, Inc.
Bottom Dog Press, Inc.
Broadway Books
Brucedale Press, The
Canterbury House Publishing, Ltd.
Carnegie Mellon University Press
Clarkson Potter
Coffee House Press
Coteau Books
Cross-Cultural Communications
Crystal Spirit Publishing, Inc.
Da Capo Press
Dream of Things
Encounter Books
Enete Enterprises
Familius

Gival Press
Grove/Atlantic, Inc.
Guernica Editions
Hellgate Press
Heritage Books, Inc.
High Plains Press
Kensington Publishing Corp.
Loyola Press
Martin Sisters Publishing, LLC
Merriam Press
Minnesota Historical Society Press
Mondial
MSI Press
North Atlantic Books
Owen Publishers, Peter
Paul Dry Books
Persea Books
Red Hen Press
Red Moon Press
Reed Publishers, Robert D.
Sakura Publishing & Technologies
Santa Monica Press
Scribe Publications
Seal Press
Second Story Press
Shearsman Books, LTD
Shipwreckt Books Publishing Company LLC
Soho Press, Inc.
Stone Bridge Press
Strategic Media Books
Sunbury Press, Inc.
Tafelberg Publishers
Tantor Media
Tightrope Books
Touchwood Editions
Travelers' Tales
Twilight Times Books
University of Calgary Press
University of New Mexico Press
University of Wisconsin Press
Véhicule Press
Zumaya Publications, LLC

MILITARY
Algora Publishing
AMG Publishers
Burford Books
Cedar Fort, Inc.
Clarity Press, Inc.
Constable & Robinson, Ltd.
Grey Gecko Press
Hellgate Press
Heritage Books, Inc.
History Publishing Company, LLC.
Merriam Press

New Forums Press
Nortia Press
Ohio University Press
Paragon House Publishers
Reed Publishers, Robert D.
Saint Johann Press
Sakura Publishing & Technologies
Shipwreckt Books Publishing Company LLC
Southern Illinois University Press
Strategic Media Books
Sunbury Press, Inc.
Tantor Media
Twilight Times Books
University of Calgary Press
University of North Texas Press
University of Tennessee Press, The
University Press of Kansas

MONEY

Algora Publishing
Martin Sisters Publishing, LLC
New Society Publishers
North Atlantic Books
Passkey Publications
Reed Publishers, Robert D.
Sunbury Press, Inc.
Tantor Media

MULTICULTURAL

American Counseling Association
APA Books
Arch Street Press
Arsenal Pulp Press
Balzer & Bray
BlueBridge
Broadway Books
Bucknell University Press
Carolina Wren Press
Charlesbridge Publishing
Chronicle Books for Children
Clarity Press, Inc.
Craigmore Creations
Cross-Cultural Communications
Crystal Spirit Publishing, Inc.
Encounter Books
Facts On File, Inc.
Fairleigh Dickinson University Press
Fernwood Publishing, Ltd.
Formac Publishing Co. Ltd.
Frances Lincoln Books
Frances Lincoln Children's Books
Gival Press
Goosebottom Books
Great Potential Press
Guernica Editions

Heritage House Publishing Co., Ltd.
Hill Books, Lawrence
Immedium
Insomniac Press
InterVarsity Press
Jain Publishing Co.
Jonathan David Publishers, Inc.
Judson Press
Kaya Press
Kensington Publishing Corp.
Milkweed Editions
Minnesota Historical Society Press
Missouri Historical Society Press
Mitchell Lane Publishers, Inc.
Mondial
Naturegraph Publishers, Inc.
New Hope Publishers
Newsage Press
North Atlantic Books
Ohio State University Press
Orca Book Publishers
Palgrave Macmillan
Parallax Press
Paul Dry Books
Peachtree Children's Books
Pelican Publishing Company
Red Moon Press
Reed Publishers, Robert D.
Rutgers University Press
Seal Press
Second Story Press
Shipwreckt Books Publishing Company LLC
Strategic Media Books
Tantor Media
ThunderStone Books
Tightrope Books
University of Akron Press
University of Iowa Press
University of New Mexico Press
University of North Carolina Press, The
University of North Texas Press
University of Washington Press
Vanderbilt University Press
Volcano Press, Inc.
White Pine Press
Yogi Impressions Books Pvt. Ltd.

MUSIC

Algora Publishing
Arch Street Press
Balzer & Bray
Fairleigh Dickinson University Press
JourneyForth
Minnesota Historical Society Press
Palettes & Quills

Piano Press
Red Moon Press
Sakura Publishing & Technologies
Santa Monica Press
Sunbury Press, Inc.
Tantor Media
University of North Texas Press
University of Tennessee Press, The
Voyageur Press

NATURE

Algora Publishing
Appalachian Mountain Club Books
Arch Street Press
Balzer & Bray
BlueBridge
Cedar Fort, Inc.
Craigmore Creations
Encante Press, LLC
Findhorn Press
Folded Word
Frances Lincoln Books
Frances Lincoln Children's Books
Grey Gecko Press
High Plains Press
JourneyForth
McDonald & Woodward Publishing Co., The
Menasha Ridge Press
Milkweed Editions
New Libri Press
New Society Publishers
New World Library
North Atlantic Books
Ohio University Press
Red Moon Press
Reed Publishers, Robert D.
Ruka Press
Shipwreckt Books Publishing Company LLC
Stone Bridge Press
Strategic Media Books
Strawberries Press
Sunbury Press, Inc.
Torrey House Press, LLC
Twilight Times Books
University of Iowa Press
University of New Mexico Press
University of North Texas Press
University Press of Kansas
Voyageur Press

NEW AGE

Berkley/NAL
Berrett-Koehler Publishers, Inc.
Broadway Books
Capall Bann Publishing

Chronicle Books
Findhorn Press
Hampton Roads Publishing Co., Inc.
Hay House, Inc.
Idyll Arbor, Inc.
Llewellyn Publications
Naturegraph Publishers, Inc.
New World Library
North Atlantic Books
Ozark Mountain Publishing, LLC
Paragon House Publishers
Prometheus Books
Red Moon Press
Red Wheel/Weiser
Reed Publishers, Robert D.
Sterling Publishing Co., Inc.
Sun Books / Sun Publishing
Sunbury Press, Inc.
Tantor Media
Twilight Times Books
Zumaya Publications, LLC

NUTRITION

Amacom Books
Facts On File, Inc.
Familius
Hay House, Inc.
Martin Sisters Publishing, LLC
New Society Publishers
North Atlantic Books
Piccadilly Books, Ltd.
Reed Publishers, Robert D.
Saint Johann Press
Shipwreckt Books Publishing Company LLC
Square One Publishers, Inc.

PARENTING

AMG Publishers
Bronze Man Books
Conari Press
Familius
Health Communications, Inc.
Judson Press
Martin Sisters Publishing, LLC
MSI Press
New Libri Press
New Society Publishers
New World Library
Paragon House Publishers
Reed Publishers, Robert D.
Santa Monica Press
Seal Press
Search Institute Press
Shambhala Publications, Inc.

PHILOSOPHY

Algora Publishing
Arch Street Press
Beacon Press
Bloomsbury Continuum
BlueBridge
Broadview Press, Inc.
Bucknell University Press
Capall Bann Publishing
Catholic University of America Press
Cornell University Press
Crescent Moon Publishing
Dover Publications, Inc.
Duquesne University Press
Eerdmans Publishing Co., William B.
Encounter Books
Fairleigh Dickinson University Press
Fernwood Publishing, Ltd.
Fordham University Press
Glenbridge Publishing, Ltd.
Grove/Atlantic, Inc.
Guernica Editions
Hay House, Inc.
Hohm Press
InterVarsity Press
Jain Publishing Co.
Jewish Lights Publishing
Kensington Publishing Corp.
Mandala Publishing
McClelland & Stewart, Ltd.
Melbourne University Publishing, Ltd.
Mondial
MSI Press
New Society Publishers
North Atlantic Books
Open Court Publishing Co.
Ozark Mountain Publishing, LLC
Pacific Press Publishing Association
Palgrave Macmillan
Paragon House Publishers
Paul Dry Books
Philosophy Documentation Center
Presses de l'Universite de Montreal
Prometheus Books
Red Moon Press
Reed Publishers, Robert D.
Rose Alley Press
Saint Augustine's Press
Saint PAULS
Sakura Publishing & Technologies
Salem Press, Inc.
Scribner
Sentient Publications
Stanford University Press
Stone Bridge Press
Swedenborg Foundation
Talese, Nan A.
Tantor Media
Teachers College Press
University of Illinois Press
University of North Carolina Press, The
Vanderbilt University Press
Verso
Viking
Wisdom Publications
Yale University Press
YMAA Publication Center

PHOTOGRAPHY

Allworth Press
Amherst Media, Inc.
Atheneum Books for Young Readers
Black Dome Press Corp.
Brucedale Press, The
Clarion Books
Clarkson Potter
Constable & Robinson, Ltd.
Dover Publications, Inc.
Focal Press
Godine, Publisher, David R.
Grey Gecko Press
Mandala Publishing
McClelland & Stewart, Ltd.
Minnesota Historical Society Press
Motorbooks
Palettes & Quills
Phaidon Press
Red Moon Press
Santa Monica Press
Sentient Publications
Strawberries Press
Temple University Press
University of New Mexico Press
University of North Carolina Press, The
University of North Texas Press
University of Washington Press

POLITICS

Algora Publishing
BlueBridge
Chelsea Green Publishing Co.
Clarity Press, Inc.
Constable & Robinson, Ltd.
Divertir
Encante Press, LLC
Facts On File, Inc.
Fernwood Publishing, Ltd.
Guernica Editions
Heritage House Publishing Co., Ltd.
History Publishing Company, LLC.

Inverted-A
Milkweed Editions
Minnesota Historical Society Press
New Society Publishers
North Atlantic Books
Ohio University Press
Paragon House Publishers
Seal Press
Second Story Press
Shipwreckt Books Publishing Company LLC
Strategic Media Books
University of Akron Press
University of Alabama Press, The
University of Calgary Press
University of North Texas Press
University Press of Kansas

POP CULTURE
Chronicle Books
Guernica Editions
Heritage House Publishing Co., Ltd.
Minnesota Historical Society Press
Red Moon Press
Sakura Publishing & Technologies
Santa Monica Press
Seal Press
Soft Skull Press Inc.
Stone Bridge Press
University of Iowa Press
University of New Mexico Press
World Weaver Press

PSYCHIC
Capall Bann Publishing
Hay House, Inc.
Idyll Arbor, Inc.
North Atlantic Books
Sunbury Press, Inc.

PSYCHOLOGY
Algora Publishing
American Counseling Association
APA Books
Atheneum Books for Young Readers
Baker Academic
Barricade Books, Inc.
Basic Books
Berkley/NAL
BlueBridge
Broadway Books
Bucknell University Press
Clarkson Potter
Constable & Robinson, Ltd.
Duquesne University Press
Eerdmans Publishing Co., William B.
Emis, Inc.

Encounter Books
Fairleigh Dickinson University Press
Findhorn Press
Great Potential Press
Grove/Atlantic, Inc.
Guernica Editions
Hay House, Inc.
Health Communications, Inc.
Health Professions Press
Heinemann Educational Publishers
Human Kinetics Publishers, Inc.
Idyll Arbor, Inc.
InterVarsity Press
Jain Publishing Co.
Jossey-Bass
Kensington Publishing Corp.
Llewellyn Publications
Martin Sisters Publishing, LLC
McClelland & Stewart, Ltd.
Methuen Publishing Ltd.
Mondial
MSI Press
New Harbinger Publications
New Horizon Press
New York University Press
North Atlantic Books
Paragon House Publishers
Pfeiffer
Presses de l'Universite de Montreal
Prometheus Books
Red Moon Press
Reed Publishers, Robert D.
Safer Society Press
Sakura Publishing & Technologies
Salem Press, Inc.
Scribe Publications
Scribner
Sentient Publications
Sourcebooks, Inc.
Square One Publishers, Inc.
Stanford University Press
Tantor Media
University of Akron Press
Wiley & Sons, Inc., John
Wisdom Publications
Yale University Press

PUBLIC AFFAIRS
BlueBridge
Divertir
Heritage House Publishing Co., Ltd.
North Atlantic Books
Nortia Press
Search Institute Press
Sunbury Press, Inc.

University of Calgary Press

REAL ESTATE
International Wealth Success
Passkey Publications

RECREATION
Abrams, Harry N., Inc.
Appalachian Mountain Club Books
Atheneum Books for Young Readers
Ballantine Bantam Dell
Burford Books
Career Press, Inc., The
Cartwheel Books
Cedar Fort, Inc.
Enslow Publishers, Inc.
Epicenter Press, Inc.
Heyday Books
Human Kinetics Publishers, Inc.
Idyll Arbor, Inc.
Johnson Books
Kensington Publishing Corp.
Little, Brown Books for Young Readers
Lyons Press, The
McClelland & Stewart, Ltd.
McFarland & Co., Inc., Publishers
Menasha Ridge Press
Mountaineers Books, The
New Libri Press
Owen, Richard C., Publishers, Inc.
Paradise Cay Publications
Peachtree Children's Books
Red Moon Press
Sasquatch Books
Shipwreckt Books Publishing Company LLC
Sterling Publishing Co., Inc.
Stipes Publishing LLC
Touchwood Editions
Triumph Books
Venture Publishing, Inc.
Whitecap Books, Ltd.
Wilderness Press
Willow Creek Press
Windward Publishing

REGIONAL
Appalachian Mountain Club Books
Arte Publico Press
Avalon Travel Publishing
Bancroft Press
Black Dome Press Corp.
Blair, Publisher, John F.
Canterbury House Publishing, Ltd.
Cedar Fort, Inc.
Cornell University Press
Coteau Books

Craigmore Creations
Down the Shore Publishing
Dundurn Press, Ltd.
Eerdmans Publishing Co., William B.
Epicenter Press, Inc.
Fairleigh Dickinson University Press
Fernwood Publishing, Ltd.
Filter Press, LLC
Fordham University Press
Formac Publishing Co. Ltd.
Goose Lane Editions
Guernica Editions
Hancock House Publishers
Heinemann Educational Publishers
Hendrick-Long Publishing Co., Inc.
Heritage Books, Inc.
Heritage House Publishing Co., Ltd.
Heyday Books
High Plains Press
Johns Hopkins University Press, The
Johnson Books
Kensington Publishing Corp.
Kent State University Press
Linden Publishing, Inc.
Martin Sisters Publishing, LLC
Minnesota Historical Society Press
Missouri Historical Society Press
Montana Historical Society Press
Mountaineers Books, The
Mountain Press Publishing Co.
New Forums Press
New Society Publishers
New York University Press
North Carolina Office of Archives and History
Ohio State University Press
Ohio University Press
Oregon State University Press
Palgrave Macmillan
Peachtree Children's Books
Pelican Publishing Company
Pineapple Press, Inc.
Quill Driver Books
Rio Nuevo Publishers
Ronsdale Press
Rutgers University Press
Sakura Publishing & Technologies
Santa Monica Press
Sasquatch Books
Seaworthy Publications, Inc.
Shipwreckt Books Publishing Company LLC
Smith, Publisher, Gibbs
Southern Illinois University Press
Strategic Media Books
Sun Books / Sun Publishing
Sunbury Press, Inc.

Temple University Press
Texas Tech University Press
Texas Western Press
ThunderStone Books
Touchwood Editions
University of Akron Press
University of Alaska Press
University of Alberta Press, The
University of Arizona Press
University of Arkansas Press, The
University of Calgary Press
University of Georgia Press
University of Illinois Press
University of Iowa Press
University of Maine Press
University of Nevada Press
University of New Mexico Press
University of North Carolina Press, The
University of North Texas Press
University of South Carolina Press
University of Tennessee Press, The
University of Texas Press
University of Washington Press
University Press of Kansas
University Press of Kentucky
University Press of Mississippi
Utah State University Press
Véhicule Press
Voyageur Press
Whitecap Books, Ltd.

RELIGION

Abingdon Press
ACTA Publications
Algora Publishing
American Catholic Press
American Counseling Association
AMG Publishers
Atheneum Books for Young Readers
Baker Academic
Ballantine Bantam Dell
Beacon Press
Bloomsbury Continuum
BlueBridge
Broadview Press, Inc.
Capall Bann Publishing
Catholic University of America Press
Cedar Fort, Inc.
Chalice Press
Covenant Communications, Inc.
Crescent Moon Publishing
Crossroad Publishing Company, The
Crystal Spirit Publishing, Inc.
Darton, Longman & Todd
Dover Publications, Inc.

Duquesne University Press
Eerdmans Publishing Co., William B.
Encounter Books
Facts On File, Inc.
Fairleigh Dickinson University Press
FamilyLife Publishing
Father's Press
Fordham University Press
Fortress Press
Forward Movement
Frances Lincoln Books
Frances Lincoln Children's Books
Group Publishing, Inc.
Hachai Publishing
Harvest House Publishers
Heinemann Educational Publishers
Hendrickson Publishers, Inc.
Hohm Press
Holy Cross Orthodox Press
Insomniac Press
InterVarsity Press
Jain Publishing Co.
Jewish Lights Publishing
Johns Hopkins University Press, The
Jonathan David Publishers, Inc.
Jossey-Bass
JourneyForth
Judaica Press
Judson Press
Kar-Ben Publishing
Knox Robinson Publishing
Kregel Publications
Liguori Publications
Loyola Press
Mandala Publishing
McClelland & Stewart, Ltd.
Messianic Jewish Publishers
Moody Publishers
MSI Press
Nelson, Inc., Thomas
Nelson, Tommy
New Hope Publishers
New World Library
New York University Press
North Atlantic Books
Nortia Press
Pacific Press Publishing Association
Palgrave Macmillan
Paraclete Press
Paragon House Publishers
Parallax Press
Paul Dry Books
Pauline Books & Media
Paulist Press
Pelican Publishing Company

Pfeiffer
Pilgrim Press, The
Prometheus Books
P & R Publishing Co.
Putnam's Sons Hardcover, GP
Reference Service Press
Revell
Rio Nuevo Publishers
Rutgers University Press
Saint Augustine's Press
Saint Johann Press
Saint Mary's Press
Saint PAULS
Sakura Publishing & Technologies
Scarecrow Press, Inc.
Scribner
Skinner House Books
Square One Publishers, Inc.
Stanford University Press
Sunbury Press, Inc.
Swedenborg Foundation
Tantor Media
Tyndale House Publishers, Inc.
UMI (Urban Ministries, Inc.)
Unity House
University of Alabama Press, The
University of New Mexico Press
University of North Carolina Press, The
University of South Carolina Press
University of Tennessee Press, The
WaterBrook Multnomah Publishing Group
Wesleyan Publishing House
Westminster John Knox Press
Whitaker House
Wisdom Publications
Yale University Press
Yogi Impressions Books Pvt. Ltd.

SCIENCE

ABDO Publishing Co.
Algora Publishing
Amacom Books
American Chemical Society
American Water Works Association
APA Books
ASM Press
Atheneum Books for Young Readers
Balzer & Bray
BenBella Books
BlueBridge
Carnegie Mellon University Press
Cartwheel Books
Charlesbridge Publishing
Chelsea Green Publishing Co.
Chemical Publishing Co., Inc.

Chronicle Books for Children
Constable & Robinson, Ltd.
Craigmore Creations
CSLI Publications
Dover Publications, Inc.
Dutton Children's Books
Encante Press, LLC
Encounter Books
Enslow Publishers, Inc.
Fordham University Press
Grosset & Dunlap Publishers
Grove/Atlantic, Inc.
Heinemann Educational Publishers
Hobar Publications
Holiday House, Inc.
Houghton Mifflin Harcourt Books for Children
Idyll Arbor, Inc.
Information Today, Inc.
International Press
InterVarsity Press
Johns Hopkins University Press, The
Johnson Books
Kaeden Books
Krieger Publishing Co.
Lehigh University Press
Little, Brown Books for Young Readers
McClelland & Stewart, Ltd.
McDonald & Woodward Publishing Co., The
Melbourne University Publishing, Ltd.
Mountain Press Publishing Co.
Naturegraph Publishers, Inc.
New Libri Press
New Society Publishers
North Atlantic Books
No Starch Press, Inc.
Oregon State University Press
Owen, Richard C., Publishers, Inc.
Peachtree Children's Books
PPI (Professional Publications, Inc.)
Putnam's Sons Hardcover, GP
Reference Service Press
Ruka Press
Salem Press, Inc.
Salina Bookshelf
Scribner
Sentient Publications
Sourcebooks, Inc.
Stanford University Press
Sterling Publishing Co., Inc.
Stipes Publishing LLC
Strawberries Press
Sunbury Press, Inc.
Tantor Media
Texas Western Press
ThunderStone Books

Tumblehome Learning
University of Alaska Press
University of Maine Press
University of New Mexico Press
University of Texas Press
Walch Publishing
Wiley & Sons, Inc., John
Windward Publishing
Yale University Press

SEX

Arsenal Pulp Press
Ballantine Bantam Dell
Broadway Books
Crystal Spirit Publishing, Inc.
FamilyLife Publishing
Fernwood Publishing, Ltd.
Kensington Publishing Corp.
Manor House Publishing, Inc.
Mondial
New Libri Press
Sakura Publishing & Technologies
Seal Press
Stone Bridge Press
Sunbury Press, Inc.
Tantor Media

SOCIAL SCIENCES

ABC-CLIO/Greenwood
American Counseling Association
APA Books
Arch Street Press
Balzer & Bray
Between the Lines
BlueBridge
Bottom Dog Press, Inc.
Cedar Fort, Inc.
Da Capo Press
Duquesne University Press
Fernwood Publishing, Ltd.
Goosebottom Books
Grove/Atlantic, Inc.
Guernica Editions
Heinemann Educational Publishers
Hendrickson Publishers, Inc.
History Publishing Company, LLC.
InterVarsity Press
Jain Publishing Co.
Kaeden Books
Manor House Publishing, Inc.
Melbourne University Publishing, Ltd.
New Society Publishers
North Atlantic Books
Nortia Press
Paragon House Publishers

Peachtree Children's Books
Reed Publishers, Robert D.
Santa Monica Press
Search Institute Press
Sentient Publications
Stanford University Press
Tantor Media
Texas Western Press
University of Calgary Press
University of New Mexico Press
University of North Texas Press
University of Washington Press
Van Schaik Publishers

SOCIOLOGY

Algora Publishing
APA Books
Arch Street Press
Arsenal Pulp Press
Atheneum Books for Young Readers
Barricade Books, Inc.
Basic Books
Between the Lines
Bloomsbury Continuum
BlueBridge
Bucknell University Press
Carnegie Mellon University Press
Cato Institute
Cornell University Press
Eerdmans Publishing Co., William B.
Encounter Books
Enslow Publishers, Inc.
Fairleigh Dickinson University Press
Fernwood Publishing, Ltd.
Fordham University Press
Glenbridge Publishing, Ltd.
Hay House, Inc.
History Publishing Company, LLC.
ILR Press
InterVarsity Press
Mage Publishers, Inc.
Manor House Publishing, Inc.
Martin Sisters Publishing, LLC
McClelland & Stewart, Ltd.
McFarland & Co., Inc., Publishers
Mondial
New Forums Press
New York University Press
North Atlantic Books
Nortia Press
Ohio State University Press
Ohio University Press
Palgrave Macmillan
Presses de l'Universite de Montreal
Reed Publishers, Robert D.

Reference Service Press
Rutgers University Press
Salem Press, Inc.
Second Story Press
Sentient Publications
Stanford University Press
Talese, Nan A.
Tantor Media
Teachers College Press
Temple University Press
University of Illinois Press
University of Pennsylvania Press
Véhicule Press
Venture Publishing, Inc.
Verso
Yale University Press

SOFTWARE

American Water Works Association
Craftsman Book Co.
Microsoft Press
New Libri Press
Nova Press
Philosophy Documentation Center
SAS Publishing

SPIRITUALITY

ACTA Publications
American Catholic Press
American Counseling Association
AMG Publishers
Arch Street Press
Ballantine Bantam Dell
Berrett-Koehler Publishers, Inc.
BlueBridge
Bottom Dog Press, Inc.
Broadway Books
Capall Bann Publishing
Cedar Fort, Inc.
Conari Press
Covenant Communications, Inc.
Crossroad Publishing Company, The
Crystal Spirit Publishing, Inc.
Darton, Longman & Todd
FamilyLife Publishing
Filbert Publishing
Findhorn Press
Hampton Roads Publishing Co., Inc.
Hay House, Inc.
Hendrickson Publishers, Inc.
Ibex Publishers
Idyll Arbor, Inc.
InterVarsity Press
Jain Publishing Co.
Jewish Lights Publishing

JourneyForth
Judson Press
Liguori Publications
Loyola Press
Mandala Publishing
Manor House Publishing, Inc.
Martin Sisters Publishing, LLC
Moody Publishers
MSI Press
Nelson, Inc., Thomas
New Society Publishers
New World Library
North Atlantic Books
Ozark Mountain Publishing, LLC
Pacific Press Publishing Association
Palgrave Macmillan
Paragon House Publishers
Parallax Press
Pauline Books & Media
P & R Publishing Co.
Red Moon Press
Red Wheel/Weiser
Reed Publishers, Robert D.
Rio Nuevo Publishers
Saint Johann Press
Saint PAULS
Sentient Publications
Shipwreckt Books Publishing Company LLC
Square One Publishers, Inc.
Stone Bridge Press
Sunbury Press, Inc.
Swedenborg Foundation
Tantor Media
Travelers' Tales
UMI (Urban Ministries, Inc.)
WaterBrook Multnomah Publishing Group
Westminster John Knox Press
Wisdom Publications
YMAA Publication Center
Yogi Impressions Books Pvt. Ltd.
Zumaya Publications, LLC

SPORTS

ABDO Publishing Co.
Allan Publishing, Ltd., Ian
Atheneum Books for Young Readers
Ball Publishers, Jonathan
Balzer & Bray
Bancroft Press
Broadway Books
Burford Books
Cartwheel Books
Coaches Choice
Coteau Books
Da Capo Press

Dover Publications, Inc.
Dunne Books, Thomas
Enslow Publishers, Inc.
Facts On File, Inc.
Grove/Atlantic, Inc.
Heinemann Educational Publishers
Houghton Mifflin Harcourt Books for Children
Human Kinetics Publishers, Inc.
Indiana Historical Society Press
Jonathan David Publishers, Inc.
JourneyForth
Kane/Miller Book Publishers
Kensington Publishing Corp.
Little, Brown Books for Young Readers
Lyons Press, The
McClelland & Stewart, Ltd.
McGraw-Hill Professional Business
Menasha Ridge Press
Methuen Publishing Ltd.
Missouri Historical Society Press
Mountaineers Books, The
North Atlantic Books
Orca Book Publishers
Owen, Richard C., Publishers, Inc.
Paradise Cay Publications
Peachtree Children's Books
Pelican Publishing Company
Putnam's Sons Hardcover, GP
Saint Johann Press
Saint Martin's Press, LLC
Santa Monica Press
Sasquatch Books
Scarecrow Press, Inc.
Seaworthy Publications, Inc.
Shipwreckt Books Publishing Company LLC
Sourcebooks, Inc.
Square One Publishers, Inc.
Sterling Publishing Co., Inc.
Strawberries Press
Sunbury Press, Inc.
Tantor Media
Texas Tech University Press
Triumph Books
University of Illinois Press
Voyageur Press
Willow Creek Press
Windward Publishing
Workman Publishing Co.
YMAA Publication Center

STAGE
BearManor Media
Inverted-A
Santa Monica Press
Southern Illinois University Press

TRANSLATION
Algora Publishing
Arch Street Press
Arte Publico Press
Carnegie Mellon University Press
Clarkson Potter
Cornell University Press
Da Capo Press
Dover Publications, Inc.
Dufour Editions
Eerdmans Publishing Co., William B.
Fernwood Publishing, Ltd.
Fordham University Press
Gival Press
Great Potential Press
Grove/Atlantic, Inc.
Guernica Editions
Hippopotamus Press
Ibex Publishers
Inverted-A
Italica Press
Mage Publishers, Inc.
McClelland & Stewart, Ltd.
Milkweed Editions
Mondial
Motorbooks
Mountaineers Books, The
New Libri Press
Owen Publishers, Peter
Palgrave Macmillan
Paul Dry Books
Persea Books
Presses de l'Universite de Montreal
P & R Publishing Co.
Quite Specific Media Group, Ltd.
Red Moon Press
Shearsman Books, LTD
ThunderStone Books
University of Alaska Press
University of California Press
University of Illinois Press
University of New Mexico Press
University of North Carolina Press, The
University of Texas Press
White Pine Press

TRANSPORTATION
Glencannon Press, The
Strawberries Press
Sunbury Press, Inc.

TRAVEL
Academy Chicago Publishers
Allan Publishing, Ltd., Ian
Arcade Publishing

Arsenal Pulp Press
Atheneum Books for Young Readers
Avalon Travel Publishing
Ballantine Bantam Dell
Ball Publishers, Jonathan
Bergli Books
Blair, Publisher, John F.
BlueBridge
Broadway Books
Burford Books
Constable & Robinson, Ltd.
Coteau Books
Crescent Moon Publishing
Cyclotour Guide Books
Da Capo Press
Dover Publications, Inc.
Encante Press, LLC
Enete Enterprises
Fodor's Travel Publications, Inc.
Folded Word
Formac Publishing Co. Ltd.
Glencannon Press, The
Great Potential Press
Grey Gecko Press
Heyday Books
Johnson Books
Kensington Publishing Corp.
Lonely Planet Publications
McClelland & Stewart, Ltd.
McDonald & Woodward Publishing Co., The
Menasha Ridge Press
Montana Historical Society Press
Mountaineers Books, The
MSI Press
New Libri Press
North Atlantic Books
North Point Press
Owen Publishers, Peter
Paradise Cay Publications
Peachtree Children's Books
Persea Books
Putnam's Sons Hardcover, GP
Red Moon Press
Reed Publishers, Robert D.
Rio Nuevo Publishers
Sakura Publishing & Technologies
Santa Monica Press
Sasquatch Books
Seal Press
Seaworthy Publications, Inc.
Sentient Publications
Square One Publishers, Inc.
Stone Bridge Press
Sunbury Press, Inc.
Travelers' Tales

University of Iowa Press
University of New Mexico Press
University of Wisconsin Press
Whitecap Books, Ltd.
Willow Creek Press
Workman Publishing Co.

TRUE CRIME

Ballantine Bantam Dell
Barricade Books, Inc.
Berkley/NAL
Kensington Publishing Corp.
Kent State University Press
Linden Publishing, Inc.
Reed Publishers, Robert D.
Sakura Publishing & Technologies
University of Iowa Press
University of New Mexico Press

WAR

Algora Publishing
AMG Publishers
Cedar Fort, Inc.
Constable & Robinson, Ltd.
Glencannon Press, The
Grey Gecko Press
Hellgate Press
Heritage House Publishing Co., Ltd.
History Publishing Company, LLC.
Merriam Press
New Forums Press
Nortia Press
Shipwreckt Books Publishing Company LLC
Southern Illinois University Press
Strategic Media Books
Sunbury Press, Inc.
University of North Texas Press
University of Tennessee Press, The
University Press of Kansas

WOMENS ISSUES

Algora Publishing
American Counseling Association
AMG Publishers
BlueBridge
Bottom Dog Press, Inc.
Carolina Wren Press
Cedar Fort, Inc.
Conari Press
Crystal Spirit Publishing, Inc.
Fairleigh Dickinson University Press
Fernwood Publishing, Ltd.
Gival Press
Hay House, Inc.
Hellgate Press
Heritage House Publishing Co., Ltd.

Judson Press
Martin Sisters Publishing, LLC
MSI Press
New World Library
North Atlantic Books
Nortia Press
Puffin Books
Reed Publishers, Robert D.
Seal Press
Second Story Press
Shipwreckt Books Publishing Company LLC
Stone Bridge Press
Tantor Media
Tightrope Books
Travelers' Tales
University of New Mexico Press
University of North Texas Press

WOMENS STUDIES
Algora Publishing
American Counseling Association
Arch Street Press
BlueBridge
Conari Press
Crystal Spirit Publishing, Inc.
Facts On File, Inc.
Fairleigh Dickinson University Press
Fernwood Publishing, Ltd.
Gival Press
Goosebottom Books
Martin Sisters Publishing, LLC
North Atlantic Books
Puffin Books
Reed Publishers, Robert D.
Seal Press
Second Story Press
Southern Illinois University Press
Tantor Media
Tightrope Books
Twilight Times Books
University of Calgary Press
University of Iowa Press
University of New Mexico Press
University of North Texas Press

WORLD AFFAIRS
Arch Street Press
Beacon Press

BlueBridge
Clarity Press, Inc.
Da Capo Press
Divertir
Fairleigh Dickinson University Press
Fernwood Publishing, Ltd.
Hellgate Press
History Publishing Company, LLC.
Milkweed Editions
North Atlantic Books
Paragon House Publishers
Reed Publishers, Robert D.
Sakura Publishing & Technologies
Shipwreckt Books Publishing Company LLC
Strategic Media Books
Sunbury Press, Inc.
Tantor Media
Travelers' Tales

YOUNG ADULT
AMG Publishers
Bold Strokes Books, Inc.
Cedar Fort, Inc.
Craigmore Creations
Crystal Spirit Publishing, Inc.
Facts On File, Inc.
Familius
Fernwood Publishing, Ltd.
Frances Lincoln Children's Books
Godine, Publisher, David R.
Goosebottom Books
Health Communications, Inc.
JourneyForth
Kane/Miller Book Publishers
Orca Book Publishers
Pauline Books & Media
Persea Books
Second Story Press
Shipwreckt Books Publishing Company LLC
Strawberries Press
Sunbury Press, Inc.
Tantor Media
Thistledown Press Ltd.
Tu Books
Twilight Times Books

GENERAL INDEX

$50,000 Gift of Freedom 715
10 Minute Play Contest & Festival 709
24-Hour Short Story Contest 719
49th Parallel Award for Poetry 768
417 Magazine 553

A
A+ Playwriting Center for Teachers 709
A-R Editions, Inc. 203
A.T. Journeys 587
A&U 434
AAAS Kavli Science Journalism Awards 764
AARP Bulletin 569
AARP The Magazine 569
ABA Journal 675
Abbeville Family 191
Abbeville Press 191
ABC-CLIO/Greenwood 191
ABDO Publishing Co. 191
Abel Literary Agency, Dominick 135
Abilities 438
Abingdon Press 191
Abraham Poetry Prize, J.M. 768
Abrams Books for Young Readers 192
Abrams 192
Academy Chicago Publishers 192
Ace Science Fiction and Fantasy 192
ACP Internist 683
Acres U.S.A. 649
ACTA Publications 192
Acuta Journal, The 639
Ad Astra 572
Adams Literary 135
Adbusters 435
Addams Children's Book Awards, Jane 749

Addicus Books, Inc. 193
Adirondack Life 555
Adornment, The Magazine of Jewelry & Related Arts
    669
Adventure Cyclist 581
Advisor Today 669
Advisor's Edge 655
Advocate, The 450
Aeon Award 719
AeroSafety World Magazine 615
Aesthetica Art Prize 795
AFP Exchange 655
African American Golfer's Digest 585
African Pilot 423
African-American Career World 428
Ag Journal 649
Ag Weekly 649
Agni 486
AHIP Coverage 683
Ahsahta Press 193
AHWA Flash & Short Story Competition 720
Air and Space 423
Air Force Times 531
Airbrush Action Magazine 609
Airforce 531
AKC Gazette 413
Akron Life 557
Akron Poetry Prize 768
Alabama Heritage 539
Alabama Living 539
Alabama State Council on Arts Artist Fellowship 715
Aladdin 193
Alaska 540
Alaska Business Monthly 424
Alaska Quarterly Review 480
Albedo One 481

albemarle 561
Alberta Venture 425
Alberta Views 541
Alcuin Society Book Design Awards 795
Alexander Poetry Series, Marie 796
Algonquin Books of Chapel Hill 194
Algonquin Young Readers 194
Algora Publishing 194
Aliterate 487
Alive Now 562
All You 599
Allan Publishing, Ltd., Ian 194
Allegory 487
Allen & Unwin 194
Alligator Juniper Award 796
Allure 599
Allworth Press 195
Almanac for Farmers & City Folk, The 451
Alpine Publications 195
Alternatives Journal 533
AMACOM Books 195
Amadeus Press 196
Ambassador Magazine 442
Amberjack Publishing 196
America's Civil War 461
American Agriculturist 650
American Angler 589
American Archaeology 573
American Association of University Women Award in
    Juvenile Literature 750
American Baby 429
American Book Review 621
American Catholic Press 196
American Chemical Society 196
American Cinematographer 645
American City & County 658
American Correctional Association 197
American Counseling Association 197
American Craft 464
American Digger 464
American Educator 464
American Federation of Astrologers 197
American Fitness 457
American Fruit Grower 650
American Gardener, The 472
American Gem Literary Festival, The 796
American Heritage 460
American History 460
American Hunter 590
American Journalism Review 670
American Legacy 460
American Legion Fourth Estate Award, The 764
American Legion Magazine, The 451
American Literary Review Contests 796
American Machinist 678
American Motorcyclist 422
American Poetry Review 488
American Poetry Review/Henickman First Book Prize
    768
American Quarter Horse Journal 413

American Quilter's Society 197
American Rifleman 587
American Salesman, The 694
American Scholar 452
American Short Fiction 488
American Snowmobiler 594
American Songwriter 594
American Spectator 537
American Theatre 646
American Turf Monthly 588
American Water Works Association 198
American Window Cleaner Magazine 681
American Wine Society Journal 446
American-Scandinavian Foundation Translation Prize
    765
AMG Publishers 198
Amherst Media, Inc. 198
Amster Literary Enterprises, Betsy 135
Amulet Books 199
Analog Science Fiction & Fact 575
Ancient Paths 488
Andersen Award, Hans Christian 750
Andersen Press
Anderson Fiction Award, Sherwood 720
Andrews McMeel Universal 199
Angus Journal 650
Anhinga Press 199
Anhinga Press-Robert Dana Prize for Poetry, The 768
Animal Sheltering 706
Ankerwycke 199
Ann Arbor Observer 550
Annick Press, Ltd. 200
Annual Memoirs Competition 739
Anthem Essay Contest 739
Antigonish Review, The 489
Antioch Review 490
Antique Trader 465
Antiqueweek 609
Anvil Press 200
APA Books 200
Apex Magazine 575
Apogee Photo Magazine 536
Aponte Literary Agency 136
Appalachian Festival of Plays & Playwrights 709
Appalachian Mountain Club Books 200
Appaloosa Journal 413
Appraisers Standard 609
Aquatics International 699
Aquila 479
Arbordale Publishing 201
Arc Poetry Magazine 490
Arcade Publishing 202
Arcadia Publishing 202
Arch Street Press 202
Archaeology 573
Archaia 202
Area Development Online 691
Arizona Foothills 540
Arizona Highways 540
Arizona Literary Contest & Book Awards 720

Arizona Wildlife Views 591
Arrow Publications, LLC 203
Arrowtrade Magazine 700
Arsenal Pulp Press 203
Art Affair Poetry Contest 769
Art Affair Short Story and Western Short Story
    Contests 796
Art Materials Retailer 610
Art Times 491
Arte Publico Press 204
Arthritis Today 438
Artilleryman, The 461
Artist Trust Fellowship Award 797
Artist's Magazine, The 416
Artlink 416
Arts & Activities 636
Arts & Letters Journal of Contemporary Culture 491
Arts & Letters Prizes 797
ASA, Aviation Supplies & Academics 204
Asahi Publishing 204
ASCAP Deems Taylor Awards 740
ASCE Press 204
ASCP Skin Deep 616
Ashland Poetry Press 205
Asimov's Science Fiction 576
ASM Press 205
Association for Supervision and Curriculum Develop-
    ment 205
Astragal Press 205
Astronomy 573
ATA Magazine, The 636
Athenaeum Literary Award, The 797
Atheneum Books for Young Readers 206
Atlanta Home Improvement 473
Atlanta Homes and Lifestyles 473
Atlanta Parent 430
Atlanta Tribune 545
Atlantic Business Magazine 425
Atlantic Journalism Awards 764
Atlantic Monthly 452
Atlantic Salmon Journal, The 591
Atlas Shrugged Essay Contest 740
Australian Christian Book of the Year Award 761
Auto Restorer 612
Autograph Magazine 465
Automated Builder 632
AutoWeek 432
Autumn House Poetry, Fiction, and Nonfiction Prizes
    797
Avalon Travel Publishing 206
Aviation History 423
Aviation International News 615
Avon Romance 206
AWP Award Series 797
Axelrod Agency, The 136
AZURE (Architecture, Design, Interiors, Curiosity)
    416

B

Backbeat Books 206

Backpacker Magazine 587
Backroads 595
Backwaters Press, The 206
Backwoods Home Magazine 578
Bacon Busters 591
Baen Books 207
Bailey Memorial Award, The Muriel Craft 769
Bailiwick Press 207
Baillie Picture Book Award, Marilyn 750
Baker Academic 207
Baker Books 208
Balcones Fiction Prize 721
Ball Publishers, Jonathan 208
Ball Publishing 208
Ballantine Books 208
BALLOONS & Parties Magazine 695
Baltimore Review Contests, The 721
Baltimore Review, The 491
Balzer & Bray 208
Bancroft Press 209
Bantam Books 209
Bar & Beverage Business Magazine 619
Barbour Publishing, Inc. 209
Bard Fiction Prize 721
Barefoot Books 209
Barnstone Translation Prize, Willis 766
Barone Literary Agency 136
Barrelhouse 492
Barricade Books, Inc. 210
Barrons Translation Prize, Willis 766
Barrow Street Press Book Contest 769
BARTENDER * Magazine 665
Baseball America 581
Baseline 536
Basic Books 210
Bassmaster 592
Batchelder Award, Mildred L. 750
Baylor University Press 210
Beacon Hill Press of Kansas City 211
Beacon Press 211
Beadwork 465
Bear Star Press 211
BearManor Media 211
Beatdom 492
Beatty Award, John and Patricia 750
Beauty Store Business 616
Bee Culture 651
Behrman House Inc. 212
Beil, Publisher, Inc., Frederic C. 212
BelleBooks 212
Bellevue Literary Press 212
Bellevue Literary Review Goldenberg Prize for Fiction
    721
BenBella Books 213
Bench & Bar of Minnesota 675
Benedict Poetry Prize, Elinor 769
Bennett Fellowship, George 716
Bent Agency, The 136
Bentley Publishers 213
Bergli Books 213

Berkley 213
Bermuda Triangle Prize 769
Berrett-Koehler Publishers, Inc. 213
Bess Press 214
Bethany House Publishers 214
Better Homes and Gardens 474
Between the Lines 214
Beyond Words Publishing, Inc. 215
Bibby First Book Award, The Patricia 769
Big Picture, The 689
Big Pulp 492
Bijur Literary Agency, Vicky 137
Bilingual Review Press 215
Bilson Award for Historical Fiction for Young People,
    The Geoffrey 750
Binghamton Univ John Gardner Fiction Book Award
    721
Binghamton University Milt Kessler Poetry Book
    Award 769
Birch Book Press 215
Bird Watcher's Digest 534
Birds & Blooms 474
Birmingham Parent 430
Bitter Oleander Press Library of Poetry Award, The
    770
BkMk Press 216
Black Award, The Irma S. and James H. 751
Black Dome Press Corp. 216
Black Lawrence Press 216
Black Literary Agency, David 137
Black Lyon Publishing 216
Black Memorial Prizes, James Tait 722
Black Ocean 216
Black Rose Writing 216
Black Velvet Seductions Publishing 217
Blair, Publisher, John F. 217
Blank Theatre Company Young Playwrights Festival,
    The 709
BlazeVOX 218
Blind Eye Books 218
Bloomberg Businessweek 426
Bloomberg Press 218
Bloomsbury Children's Books 219
Bloomsbury Continuum 219
Blue Light Poetry Prize and Chapbook Contest 770
Blue Light Press 219
Blue Mountain Arts/SPS Studios Poetry Card Contest
    770
Blue Mountain Press 220
Blue River Press 220
BlueBridge 219
BNA Books 220
BOA Editions, Ltd. 220
Boardman Tasker Prize for Mountain Literature, The
    798
Boating Industry 700
Bold Strokes Books, Inc. 221
Bomb Magazine 493
Bon Appetit 447
Book Cents Literary Agency, LLC 138

Book Dealers World 670
Book Group, The 139
BookEnds Literary Agency 138
Bookfish Books 221
Bookouture 221
Books for All Times 222
Boston Review 435
Boston Review Annual Poetry Contest, The 770
Bottom Dog Press, Inc. 222
Boulevard 493
Boulevard Poetry Contest for Emerging Poets 770
Boulevard Short Fiction Contest for Emerging Writers
    722
Bowling Center Management 700
Boyds Mills Press 222
Boys' Life 479
Bradford Literary Agency 139
Bradley Prize, Barbara 770
Brahman Journal, The 651
Brand Packaging 606
Brandt & Hochman Literary Agents, Inc. 140
Brattle Agency, The 140
Braun Associates, Inc., Barbara 140
Braziller, George 222
Bread for God's Children 562
Brealey Publishing, Nicholas 222
Brewers Publications 223
Briar Cliff Review Fiction, Poetry, and Creative Non-
    fiction Competition, The 798
Brick 494
Brick Books 223
Brick Road Poetry Book Contest 771
Brick Road Poetry Press, Inc. 223
Bright Hill Press Poetry Chapbook Competition 771
Brimer Book Award, Ann Connor 751
British Czech and Slovak Assoc Writing Competition
    798
British Heritage Travel 461
Brittingham Prize in Poetry 771
Broadview Press, Inc. 224
Broadway Books 224
Bronwen Wallace Memorial Award, The RBC 798
Bronze Man Books 225
Brown Literary Agency, Inc., Andrea 142
Brown, Ltd., Curtis 141
Browne & Miller Literary Associates, LLC 141
Brucedale Press, The 225
Bucknell University Press 225
Bugle 592
Bull Publishing Co. 226
Burford Books 226
Burning Bush Poetry Prize 772
Burnside Review 494
Bush Memorial Award for First Book of Poetry, Bob
    772
Business Fleet 613
Business NH Magazine 426
Business Travel Executive 624
Buster Books 226
Bykofsky Associates, Inc., Sheree 142

C

C&T Publishing 226
CAA Poetry Award 772
Cadet Quest Magazine 480
Caine Prize for African Writing, The 722
California Lawyer 676
California Young Playwrights Contest 709
Calkins Creek 227
Calyx Books 227
Cameron & Associates, Kimberley 143
Campbell Memorial Award for Best Science Fiction
    Novel of the Year, John W. 722
Canadian Authors Association Award for Poetry 722
Canadian Authors Association Award for Poetry 722
Canadian Authors Association Award for Fiction 710
Canadian Authors Association Emerging Writer
    Award 722
Canadian Consulting Engineer 642
Canadian Mining Journal 703
Canadian Property Management 691
Canadian Screenwriter 670
Canadian Woodworking and Home Improvement
    466
Candlewick Press 227
Cannell Literary Agency, Cynthia 143
Canterbury House Publishing, Ltd. 227
Capall Bann Publishing 228
Cape Cod LIFE 550
Capilano Review, The 494
Capital Talent Agency 143
Capstone Press 228
Capstone Professional 228
Car and Driver 422
Career Press, Inc., The 228
Careers & the disABLED 439
Carnegie Mellon University Press 228
Carolina Wren Press 229
Carolina Wren Press Poetry Series Contest 772
Carolrhoda Books, Inc. 229
Carson-Dellosa Publishing Co., Inc. 229
Cartwheel Books 229
Carvainis Agency, Inc., Maria 143
Cascade Writing Contest & Awards 723
Casual Living 695
Cat Callan Humor Prize, Jamie 762
Catholic University of America Press 230
Cato Institute 230
Cattarulla Award for Best Short Story, Kay 723
Cattleman, The 651
Cave Canem Poetry Prize 772
Cave Hollow Press 230
CBA Retailers+Resources 625
Cedar Fort, Inc. 230
Celtic Life International 443
Centerstream Publishing 231
Chalberg & Sussman 144
Chalice Press 231
Chand & Company Ltd., S. 231
Chandra Prize for Short Fiction, G. S. Sharat 723
Changeling Press LLC 231

Chapman-Andrews First Novel Award, Peggy 723
Charles Press, Publishers 232
Charlesbridge Publishing 232
Charlotte Magazine 556
Chelsea Green Publishing Co. 233
Chemical Publishing Co., Inc. 233
Chesapeake Bay Magazine 582
Chesapeake Family Life 431
Chicago Parent 431
Chicago Review Press 234
Chicken Soup for the Soul 495
Child's Play (International) Ltd. 234
Children's Africana Book Award 751
Children's Book Guild Award for Nonfiction 751
Children's Brains are Yummy (CBAY) Books 234
Christian Book Awards 798
Christian Communicator 628
Christian Focus Publications 235
Christian Living in the Mature Years 569
Christian Science Monitor, The 453
Chronicle Books 235
Chronicle Books for Children 235
Church Publishing, Inc. 236
Ciardi Prize for Poetry, John 772
Cider Press Review Book Award 772
Cincinnati Magazine 557
Cincinnati Review, The 495
City Lights Books 236
CLA Young Adult Book Award 751
Clarion Books 236
Clarity Press, Inc. 236
Clark Associates, WM 144
Clarke Award, The Arthur C. 723
Clarkson Potter 237
Classic Toy Trains 466
Classical Singer Magazine 686
Cleis Press 237
Cleveland State University Poetry Center 237
Cleveland State University Poetry Center Prizes 773
Clockwise Chapbook Competition 773
Cloudbank Journal Contest 799
Coach House Books 238
Coaches Choice 238
Coffe House Press 238
Cohen Award, Morton N. 740
College Board, The 238
College Press Publishing Co. 239
Collin, Literary Agent, Frances 145
Collins Award For Nonfiction, Carr P. 740
Collins Poetry Prize, Tom 773
Colorado Book Awards 799
Colorado Prize for Poetry, The 773
Colorado Review 495
Colourpoint Books 239
Commerce & Industry 667
Common Ground 436
Commonweal 537
Composites Manufacturing 643
Composting News 694
Computer World 640

Conari Press 239
Concordia Publishing House 239
Concrete Producer, The 633
Concrete Wolf Poetry Chapbook Contest 773
Condè Nast Traveler 596
Confrontation 496
Congdon Associates Inc., Don 145
Connecticut River Review Poetry Contest, The 773
Connectionist 643
Constable & Robinson, Ltd. 239
Consumer Goods Technology 695
Contract Management 625
Contracting Profits 625
Contrary 496
Cooking Light 447
Contemporary Stone & Tile Design 703
Convenience Distribution 661
Cooperator, The 692
Copper Canyon Press 240
Copper Nickel 497
Cornell University Press 240
Corvisiero Literary Agency 146
Corwin Press, Inc. 240
Cosmetics 617
Cosmopolitan 599
Coteau Books 240
Cotton Grower Magazine 652
Country Living 475
County 658
Covenant Communications, Inc. 241
CPR Editor's Prize 773
CQ Press 241
Crab Orchard Review 497
Crab Orchard Series in Poetry First Book Award 774
Crab Orchard Series in Poetry Open Competition
    Awards 774
Crabtree Publishing Company 241
Craftsman Book Co. 242
Craigmore Creations 242
Crazyhorse 498
Crazyhorse Prize in Poetry, The 775
Creative Company 242
Creative Media Agency, Inc. 146
Creative Nonfiction 498
Creative Nonfiction Contest 740
Credit Today 656
Credit Union Management 656
Crescent Moon Publishing 242
Creston Books 243
Cross-Cultural Communications 243
Crossroad Publishing Company, The 243
Crossway 243
Crown Business 244
Crown Publishing Group 244
Crucible 499
Cruise Industry News 705
Crystal Spirit Publishing, Inc. 244
CSLI Publications 244
Curiosity Quills Press 244
Curious Fox 245

Current Nursing in Geriatric Care 663
Currents 683
Curtis Associates, Richard 147
Curve Magazine 450
CutBank Chapbook Contest, The 799
Cutting Tool Engineering 679
CWW Annual Wisconsin Writers Awards 799
Cycle California! Magazine 581
Cycle Publications, Inc. 245
Cyclotour Guide Books 245

D

Da Capo Press 245
Dafoe Book Prize, J.W. 762
Dail Literary Agency, Inc., Laura 147
Dana Awards in the Novel, Short Fiction, and Poetry
    800
Danahy Fiction Prize, The 724
Dance International 441
DanceTeacher 646
Dancing Poetry Contest 775
Darhansoff & Verrill Literary Agents 148
Dark Horse Comics 246
Dark, The 499
Darton, Longman & Todd 246
DAW Books, Inc. 246
Dawn Publications 246
Dawson Associates, Liza 148
Dawson Books, Kathy 247
Dayspa 617
Dead of Winter 724
Deadly Quill Short Story Writing Contest, The 724
DECA Direct 606
december 499
Deeck Malice Domestic Grants for Unpublished Writ-
    ers, William F. 724
DeFiore and Co. 149
Del Rey Books 247
Delacorte Press 247
Delaware Beach Life 542
Delbourgo Associates, Inc., Joelle 149
Der-Hovanessian Prize 766
Diabetes Health 439
Diabetes Self-Management 440
DIAGRAM Chapbook Contest 800
Dial Books for Young Readers 247
Dial Press 248
Dialogue 440
Dickey Prize for Poetry, James 775
Dig Into History 480
Digital Manga 248
Digital Output 640
Digger 657
Dijkstra Literary Agency, Sandra 150
Dillard Award for Creative Nonfiction, Annie 741
Dillon/Richard C. Peterson Memorial Essay Prize,
    Gordon W. 741
Direct Selling News 696
Divertir Publishing 248
DK Publishing 248

Dobie Paisano Writer's Fellowship 716
Donadio & Olson, Inc. 150
Doubleday Canada 248
Dover Publications, Inc. 248
Down the Shore Publishing 249
Draft 447
Dragon Moon Press 249
Dramatics Magazine 646
Dream Horse Press National Poetry Chapbook Prize 775
Dream of Things 249
Ducts 500
Dufour Editions 249
Dundurn Press, Ltd. 250
Dunedin Academic Press, Ltd. 250
Dunham Literary, Inc. 150
Dunne Books, Thomas 250
Dunow, Carlson, & Lerner Agency 151
Duquesne University Press 250
Dutton Adult Trade 250
Dutton Children's Books 250
Dyer Fiction Prize, The Jack 724
Dynamite Entertainment 251
Dystel & Goderich Literary Management 151
Dzanc Books 251

E

Early American Life 475
Eastland Press 251
Eaton Literary Agency's Annual Awards Program 800
Ebony 453
Ecco Press, The 252
EContent Magazine 671
Eden Street Literary 152
Edge Science Fiction and Fantasy Publishing 252
EDGE YK 542
Editions Du Noroit 252
Edupress, Inc. 252
Edwards Award, Margaret A. 752
Eerdmans Publishing Co., William B. 252
Einstein Literary Management 152
Ekus Group, LLC, The Lisa 153
el Restaurante 665
Electrical Apparatus 641
Electrical Business 642
Elle 599
Ellenberg Literary Agency, Ethan 153
Elliott Wave International Publications 426
Ellipsis 500
Elm Books 253
Emis, Inc. 253
emmy 647
Empire Literary 153
Encante Press, LLC 253
Encounter Books 253
Enete Enterprises 253
Engravers Journal, The 670
Enslow Publishers, Inc. 254
Entangled Teen 254
Entertainment Weekly 441

Entrepreneur Press 254
Enterprise Minnesota 643
Epicenter Press, Inc. 254
Equipment Journal 679
Erosion Control 644
Escapees 596
ESPACE 417
ESPN The Magazine 585
Esquire 530
Essence 599
Essential Theatre Playwriting Award 710
Eth Literary Representation, Felicia 154
Evangelical Missions Quarterly 563
Evans Inc., Mary 154
Evansville Living 548
Event 500
Every Day With Rachel Ray 448
Executive Golfer 586
Eyewear Publishing 255

F

F+W 258, 466
Fabrics + Furnishings International 623
Faces 481
Facts On File, Inc. 255
Fairbank Literary Representation 154
Fairleigh Dickinson University Press 255
Faith Today 563
Familius 256
Family Circle 453
Family Handyman 475
Family Motor Coaching 597
Family Tree Magazine 467
Familyfun 431
FamilyLife Publishing 256
Fantagraphics Books, Inc. 256
Far Horizons Award for Poetry 775
Far Horizons Award for Short Fiction, The 725
Farcountry Press 257
Farm & Ranch Living 571
Farrar, Straus & Giroux 257
Farrar, Straus & Giroux for Young Readers 257
Fast Company 436
Fat Fox Books 257
Fate Magazine 420
Father's Press 253
Faulkner Award for Excellence in Writing, The Virginia 800
FCA Magazine 564
Federal Credit Union 656
Feed Lot Magazine 652
Feitelson Research Award, The ILA Dina 741
Feiwel and Friends 258
Feldman Literary, Leigh 155
Feldman Poetry Prize, The Jean 776
Fellowships for Creative and Performing Artists and Writers 716
Fence Books 258
Fenderbender 613
Fendrich Memorial Playwriting Contest, Shubert 710

Ferguson Publishing Co. 258
Fernwood Publishing, Ltd. 259
Fibre Focus 467
Fickling Books, David 259
Fiddlehead, The 501
Field & Stream 593
FIELD 502
FIELD Poetry Prize 776
Fifteen 501 556
FILBERT PUBLISHING 259
Filling Station 502
FilmMakers International Screenwriting Awards 710
Filter Press, LLC 260
Finch Literary Agency, Diana 155
Findhorn Press 260
Fine Woodworking 467
FinePrint Literary Management 156
Finescale Modeler 468
Finishing Line Press Open Chapbook Competition 776
Finney Company, Inc. 260
Fire Chief 659
Firehouse 659
FireRescue 660
First Book Award for Poetry 776
First for Women 600
First Line, The 502
First Second 260
Fish Poetry Prize 776
Fish Short Memoir Prize 801
Fisher Children's Book Award, Dorothy Canfield 752
Fitzhenry & Whiteside Ltd. 260
Five Points 503
Flagpole Magazine 546
Flashlight Press 261
Flannery Literary 156
Flaunt 436
Fleck Award for Canadian Children's Nonfiction, The Norma 752
Fleet Solutions 613
Fletcher & Company 156
Flicker Tale Children's Book Award 752
Flight Journal 424
Florida Grower 652
Florida Realtor 692
Fluent Magazine 544
Flying Adventures 424
Flying Eye Books 261
Flyleaf Press 261
Focal Press 261
Fodor's Travel Publications, Inc. 261
Folded Word 262
Foley Poetry Contest 776
Folio Literary Management, LLC 157
Food & Wine 448
Food Network Magazine 448
Food Verse Contest 777
Footwear Plus 632
Forbes 426
Fordham University Press 262

Foreign Policy Association 263
Forensic Teacher Magazine, The 636
Foreword Reviews 621
Form 417
Formac Publishing Co. Ltd. 263
Format Magazine 606
Fortress Press 263
Fortune 426
Forward Movement 263
Foster Publishing, Inc., Walter 263
Fountainhead, The Essay Contest 741
Four Way Books 263
Four Way Books Intro Prize in Poetry, The 777
Fox Chapel Publishing 264
Frances Lincoln Books 264
Frances Lincoln Children's Books 264
Franciscan Media Press 264
Franklin Watts 265
Fraser Award For Best Translation of a Book, Soeurette Diehl 766
Fredericks Literary Agency, Inc., Jeanne 158
Free Spirit Publishing, Inc. 265
Freedson's Publishing Network, Grace 158
FreeFall Magazine 503
FreeFall Short Prose and Poetry Contest 801
Freelance Market News 671
Freelance Writer's Report 671
Freeman: Ideas on Liberty, The 537
Fresh Cut 662
Friedman Literary Agency, Rebecca 159
Friedrich Agency, The 159
Friend Magazine, The 481
Fruit Growers News 653
Ft.Myers Magazine 543
Fulcrum Publishing 265
Full Circle Literary, LLC 159
Fun for Kidz 481
Funny Times 478
Fur-Fish-Game 593
Future Horizons 266
FutureCycle Press 266

G

G Agency, LLC, The 159
Game Informer 449
Games World of Puzzles 449
Gassner Memorial Playwriting Competition, John 710
Gateway 461
Gay & Lesbian Review, The 450
Geisel Award, Theodor Seuss 752
Gelfman Schneider Literary Agents, Inc. 160
Georgia Magazine 546
Georgia Review, The 504
German Life 443
Gertrude 451
Gertrude Press 266
Gertrude Press Poetry Chapbook Contest 777
Gettysburg Review, The 504
Ghosh Literary 160

Gibbs Smith 266
Giftware News 696
Ginsberg Poetry Awards, Allen 777
Girls' Life 482
Gival Press 267
Gival Press Novel Award 725
Gival Press Poetry Award 777
Gival Press Short Story Award 725
Glamour 600
Glass Literary Management 160
Glassco Translation Prize, John 766
Glenbridge Publishing, Ltd. 267
Glencannon Press, The 267
Glenna Luschei Prairie Schooner Awards, The 762
Glimmer Train Stories 504
Glimmer Train's Family Matters Contest 725
Glimmer Train's Fiction Open 726
Glimmer Train's Short-Story Award for New Writers 726
Glimmer Train's Very Short Fiction Contest 726
Global Lion Intellectual Property Management 161
Globe 441
Godine, Publisher, David R. 267
Goedicke Prize in Poetry, Patricia 778
Goldblatt Literary LLC, Barry 161
Golden Books for Young Readers Group 268
Golden Kite Awards 753
Golden Rose Award 778
Golden West Books 268
Goldin Literary Agency, Inc., Frances 161
Golf Course Management 701
Golf Digest 586
Golf Magazine 437
Golf Tips 586
Good Fruit Grower 653
Good Housekeeping 475
Good Magazine 437
Good Old Boat 582
Goodman Literary Agency, Irene 162
Goose Lane Editions 268
Goosebottom Books 268
Gourmet Traveller Wine 448
Governor General's Literary Awards 801
GQ 531
Graber-McInnis Short Story Award, Marjorie 726
Grad Literary Agency, Inc., Doug 162
Gradpsych 539
Grain 505
Grain Journal 653
Grasslimb 505
Graywolf Press 269
Great Lakes Colleges Association New Writers Award 801
Great Potential Press 269
Green Rose Prize in Poetry, The 778
Green Teacher 534
Greenburger Associates, Inc., Sanford J. 163
Greenhaven Press 269
Greenhouse Literary Agency, The 163
Greenwillow Books 269

Grey Gecko Press 269
Griffin Poetry Prize, The 778
Grosset & Dunlap Publishers 270
Groundwood Books 270
Group Magazine 628
Group Publishing, Inc. 270
Grove/Atlantic, Inc. 271
Growertalks 657
Grummer Poetry Award, Greg 779
Gryphon House, Inc. 271
Guernica Editions 271
Guggenheim Fellowships 716
Guitar Player 532
Gulf Coast: A Journal of Literature and Fine Arts 506
Gulf Publishing Company 272
Gun Digest Books 272
Guyon Literary Nonfiction Prize, The John 741

H
Hachai Publishing 272
Hackney Literary Awards 801
Hadassah Magazine 444
Hadley Rille Books 273
Hadow/Donald Stuart Short Story Competition, Lyndall 726
Hall Awards for Youth Theatre, The Marilyn 710
Hall Prize in Poetry, Donald 779
Hammett Prize 727
Hampton Roads Publishing Co., Inc. 273
Hancock House Publishers 273
Handwoven 468
Hanser Publications 274
Hard Hat News 633
Harlequin Blaze 274
Harlequin Desire 274
Harlequin Intrigue 275
Harlequin Superromance 275
Harmony Ink Press 275
Harper Perennial 276
Harper Voyager 276
HarperBusiness 275
HarperCollins 276
HarperCollins Canada, Ltd. 276
HarperCollins Children's Books/HarperCollins Publishers 276
Harris Literary Agency, Inc., The Joy 164
Harris Memorial Playwriting Award, Aurand 710
Hartman Publishing, Inc. 277
Harvard Common Press, The 277
Harvest House Publishers 277
Hawkins & Associates, Inc., John 164
Hay House, Inc. 277
Health 457
Health Communications, Inc. 278
Health Professions Press 278
Hearne Flash Fiction Contest, Wilda 727
Hearst Poetry Prize, James 779
Heartland Boating 583
Hein & Co., Inc., William S. 278
Heinz Literature Prize, Drue 727

Hellgate Press 278
Hemingway Short Story Competition, Lorian 727
Hendrick-Long Publishing Co., Inc. 278
Hendricks Award 742
Hendrickson Publishers, Inc. 279
Henshaw Group, Richard 164
Heritage Books, Inc. 279
Heritage House Publishing Co., Ltd. 279
Heyday Books 280
HGTV Magazine 476
High Country News 535
High Plains Press 280
Hilary Tham Capital Collection, The 779
Hill and Wang 280
Hill Books, Lawrence 280
Hill Country Sun 560
Hillerman Prize, Tony 727
Hilton Head Monthly 559
Hippocrene Books, Inc. 281
Hippopotamus Press 281
Hispanic Career World 428
Hispanic Outlook in Higher Education 637
History Magazine 462
History Publishing Company, LLC. 281
Hitchcock's Mystery Magazine, Alfred 533
Hobar Publications 281
Hobby Farms 571
Hoffer Award, Eric 802
Hohm Press 282
Hokin Prize, The Bess 779
Holiday House, Inc. 282
Hollins Critic 506
Hollinshead Visiting Scholars Fellowship, Marilyn 717
Holloway Literary 165
Holt, Henry 282
Holy Cross Orthodox Press 282
Home Business Magazine 434
Home Energy Magazine 634
Home Furnishings Retailer 663
Honolulu Magazine 546
Hoof Beats 589
Hoot 507
Hope for Women 600
Hopewell Publications 283
Horizon Edition Magazine 479
Horse Canada 414
Horse Illustrated 414
Horticulture 476
Hospitality Technology 665
Hotelier 666
Houghton Mifflin Harcourt Books for Children 283
Houghton Mifflin Harcourt Co. 283
Houghton Prize, Firman 779
House Beautiful 476
House of Anansi Press 283
Houseboat Magazine 583
HOW 610
HOW Books 284
Howard-Gibbon Illustrator's Award, Amelia Frances 753
Howard/John H. Reid Fiction & Essay Contest, Tom 728
Howe/Boston Authors Award, The Julia Ward 802
Hoyns & Poe/Faulkner Fellowships, Henry 717
HPAC: Heating Plumbing Air Conditioning 689
HRC Showcase Theatre Playwriting Contest 711
HSG Agency 165
Hubbard's Writers of the Future Contest, L. Ron 728
Hubbub 507
Hudson Valley Parent 431
Human Kinetics Publishers, Inc. 284
Human Resource Executive 682
Hunger Mountain 507
Hunger Mountain Creative Nonfiction Prize, The 742
Hurst Children's Book Prize, Carol Otis 753
Hyde Park Living 557

I

Ibex Publishers 284
Iconoclast 508
Iconografix/Enthusiast Books 284
Idaho Review, The 509
IDW Publishing 284
Idyll Arbor, Inc. 285
ILA Outstanding Dissertation of the Year Award 742
Ilium Press 285
Illinois Entertainer 547
Illinois State Poetry Society Annual Contest 779
Illumen 509
ILR Press 285
Image 509
Image Comics 285
Imbrifex Books 286
Immedium 286
IMPACT Books 286
IMPACT Magazine 457
Impact Publishers, Inc. 287
Impressions 632
In New York 555
In Touch Weekly 441
In-Plant Graphics 690
Incentive 696
Incentive Publications, Inc. 287
Independent Publisher Book Awards 762
Indiana Historical Society Press 287
Indiana Review 510
Indiana Review Poetry Contest 728
Indiana Review Poetry Prize 780
Industrial Weigh & Measure 667
Information Today, Inc. 287
Infoworld 536
Ink & Insights Writing Contest 729
InScribe Contests 762
Insidecouncel 676
Insight Writing Contest 802
Insomniac Press 288
Inspired Senior Living 570
InStyle 601
Intents 626

Interior Construction 634
Interlink Publishing Group, Inc. 288
Intermission 558
International Bluegrass 687
International Bowling Industry 701
International Examiner 444
International Foundation of Employee Benefit Plans 288
International Literacy Association Children's and Young Adult's Book Awards 753
International Living 597
International Marine 289
International Press 289
International Society for Technology in Education (ISTE) 289
International Wealth Success 289
InterVarsity Press 290
Interweave Crochet 468
Interweave Knits 469
Interweave Press 290
Inventors Digest 574
Inverted-A 290
Investigative Journalism Grant 764
IODE Jean Throop Book Award, The 754
Iowa Poetry Prize 780
Iowa Review Award in Poetry, Fiction, and Nonfiction, The 802
Iowa Review, The 510
Iowa Short Fiction Award & John Simmons Short Fiction Award, The 729
Iowan, The 548
Irish Academic Press 291
Iron Gate Publishing 291
Italian America 444
Italica Press 291

J

Jack and Jill 482
Jacobs Religious Essay Prize Category, Tilia Klebenov 742
Jain Publishing Co. 291
James Award, Alice 780
James Books, Alice 292
Japan-U.S. Friendship Commission Prize for the Translation of Japanese Literature 803
Jarrell Poetry Competition, Randall 780
Jefferson Cup Award 754
JEMS 684
Jewish Lights Publishing 292
Johns Hopkins University Press, The 292
Johnson Books 292
Jones Award for Best Work of Fiction, Jesse H. 729
Jones First Novel Fellowship, James 729
Jones, MD, Awards, Anson 765
Jossey-Bass 293
Journal Of Adventist Education, The 629
Journal of Information Ethics 668
JourneyForth 293
Judaica Press 293
Judson Press 293

Juniper Prize For Poetry 780
Just Labs 414
Just Us Books, Inc. 294

K

Kaeden Books 294
Kaleidoscope 440
Kalmbach Publishing Co. 294
Kane/Miller Book Publishers 295
Kansas! 549
Kar-Ben Publishing 295
Kashrus Magazine 448
Kasma Magazine 511
Kaya Press 296
KC Magazine 553
Keats New Writer and New Illustrator Awards, The Ezra Jack 754
Keats/Kerlan Memorial Fellowship, Ezra Jack 754
Kelly Peace Poetry Awards, Barbara Mandigo 781
Kelsey Street Press 296
Kensington Publishing Corp. 296
Kent State University Press 296
Kentucky Bluegrass Award 754
Kentucky Living 549
Kentucky Monthly 549
Kenyon Review, The 511
Kessler Memorial Prize for Poetry, Milton 781
Keys for Kids Devotional 564
Khabar 445
Kids Can Press 297
King Book Awards, Coretta Scott 754
Kiplinger's Personal Finance 434
Kirkbride Bible Co., Inc. 297
Kitchen and Bath Design News 623
Kitchen Publishing Co., LLC, Denis 297
Kitplanes 469
Klinger, Inc., Harvey 165
Knight Agency, The 166
Knopf 297
KNOWAtlanta Magazine 546
Knox Robinson Publishing 298
Konner Literary Agency, Linda 167
Kovacs Prize, Katherine Singer 743
Krause Publications 298
Kregel Publications 298
Krichevsky Literary Agency, Inc., Stuart 167
Krieger Publishing Co. 299
KT Literary 167
Kung Fu Tai Chi 594

L

L.A. Designers' Theatre-Commissions 711
Laborde Creative Nonfiction Prize Category, Katheryn Krotzer 743
Ladies' Home Journal 601
Lady Churchill's Rosebud Wristlet 512
Lake Country Journal 551
Lake Superior Magazine 552
Lakeland Boating 583

Land, The 653
Landon Translation Award, The Harold Morton 766
Lane Report, The 426
Lange, Dorothea–Paul Taylor Prize 762
Langmarc Publishing 299
Lantana Publishing 299
Lapidary Journal Jewelry Artist 470
Lapwing Publications 299
Laughlin Award, James 781
Law Enforcement Technology 660
Lawrence Foundation Award, The 729
Lawrence Foundation Prize 730
Leadership Journal 629
Leading Edge 576
League of Utah Writers Contest 803
Leapfrog Press 300
Lee & Low Books 300
Lehigh University Press 301
Lehrman Lincoln Prize, The Gilder 743
Leisure Group Travel 705
Leonard Books, Hal 301
Les Figues Press 301
Les Figues Press NOS Book Contest 803
Leshne Agency, The 168
Lethe Press 301
Let's Write Literary Contest 803
Leviant Memorial Prize in Yiddish Studies, Fenia and
    Yaakov 766
Levine Books, Arthur A. 301
Levine Greenberg Rostan Literary Agency, Inc. 169
Levis Reading Prize 781
Levy Creative Management 169
LexisNexis Canada, Inc. 301
Life Cycle Books 302
Light and Life Magazine 564
Lighthouse Digest 462
Liguori Publications 302
Lilith Magazine 445
Lillenas Publishing Co. 302
Lilly Poetry Prize, The Ruth 781
Linden Publishing, Inc. 302
Line 512
LION 418
Listen & Live Audio 302
Literal Latté Essay Award 743
Literal Latté Fiction Award 730
Literal Latté Poetry Award 781
Literal Latté Short Shorts Contest 730
Literary Fiction Contest 730
Little Pickle Press 303
Little Simon 303
Little Tiger Press 303
Little, Brown and Co. Adult Trade Books 303
Little, Brown Books for Young Readers 303
LIVE 565
Livingston Press 304
Llewellyn Publications 304
Log Home Living 476
Lonely Planet Publications 304
Long Island Woman 601

Lookout, The 566
Loose Id 304
Lord Literistic, Inc., Sterling 169
Lost Treasure, Inc. 470
Lowell Prize, James Russell 743
Lowenstein Associates Inc. 170
Loyola Press 304
LRP Publications, Inc. 305
LSU Press 305
Luke Award, The Hugh J. 803
LUMINA Poetry Contest 782
Luna Bisonte Prods 305
Lutheran Digest, The 566
Lyons Press, The 305

M

Maass Literary Agency, Donald 171
Maccoby Literary Agency, Gina 171
MacGuffin National Poet Hunt Contest, The 782
Machinery & Equipment MRO 667
Mackey Short Story Prize Category, The Mary 730
Madgett Poetry Award, Naomi Long 782
Magazine of Fantasy & Science Fiction, The 577
Mage Publishers, Inc. 305
Magenta Publishing for the Arts 305
Magination Press 306
Main Street Rag's Poetry Book Award 782
Maine Organic Farmer & Gardener 654
Mainebiz 626
Make-up Artist Magazine 647
Malahat Review Long Poem Prize, The 782
Malahat Review Novella Prize, The 730
Malahat Review, The 513
Man Booker Prize, The 731
Managed Care 684
Mandala Publishing 306
Manitoba Book Awards 803
Mann Agency, Carol 172
Mānoa: A Pacific Journal of International Writing 513
Manor House Publishing, Inc. 306
Mansion Street Literary Management 172
Manus & Associates Literary Agency, Inc. 172
Marcil Literary Agency, LLC, The Denise 173
Margolis Award, Richard J. 743
Marine Corps Times 532
Mariner Books 307
Marlena Agency 173
Marr Poetry Prize, The Morton 782
Marraro Prize, Howard R. 744
Marsh Award for Children's Literature in Translation
    767
Marsh Hawk Press Poetry Prize 783
Marshall Agency, The Evan 173
Marshall Poetry Prize, Lenore 783
Martin Sisters Publishing Company, Inc. 307
Marvel Comics 307
Massage Magazine 617
Master Books 307
Mature Living 570
Maven House Press 308

Maverick Duck Press 308
Maverick Musicals and Plays 308
Maxim 531
MC Press 310
McBooks Press 308
McBride Literary Agency, Margret 174
McCarthy Prize in Short Fiction, Mary 731
McClelland & Stewart, Ltd. 309
McClung Sonnet Prize Category, Kathleen 783
McCormick Literary 174
McDonald & Woodward Publishing Co., The 309
McElderry Books, Margaret K. 309
McFarland & Co., Inc., Publishers 309
McGinnis-Ritchie Memorial Award, The 804
McGraw-Hill Professional Business 310
McIntosh & Otis, Inc. 174
McKnight Fellowship in Playwriting 711
McKnight Artist Fellowships for Writers, Loft
    Award(s) in Children's Literature/Creative Prose/
    Poetry 717
McSweeney's Poetry Series 310
Medallion Press 310
Media for Living, Valley Living Magazine 432
Media Inc. 606
Medical Group Management Association 311
Medical Physics Publishing 311
Melange Books, LLC 311
Melbourne University Publishing, Ltd. 311
Memphis Downtowner Magazine 560
Memphis Magazine Fiction Contest 731
Men's Health 531
Menasha Ridge Press 311
Mendel Media Group, LLC 175
Merriam Press 312
MESSAGE Magazine 566
Messianic Jewish Publishers 312
Metal Powder Industries Federation 312
Metal Roofing 634
Metcalf Award for Literature for Young People, The
    Vicky 755
Methuen Publishing Ltd. 313
Metro Magazine (Australia) 441
MetroKids 432
Meyerson Prize for Fiction, David Nathan 731
MFRTech EJournal 644
MHQ: The Quarterly Journal of Military History 462
Miami University Press 313
Michigan History 551
Michigan Hospitality Review 620
Michigan State University Press 313
Microsoft Press 313
Midwest Home 477
Midwest Living 544
Midwest Meetings® 697
MidWest Outdoors 593
Mildenberger Prize, Kenneth W. 744
Military History 463
Military Officer 532
Military Vehicles 470
Milkweed Editions 313

Milkweed for Young Readers 314
Milkweed National Fiction Prize 731
Milkweed Prize for Children's Literature 755
Millbrook Press, The 314
Mills Award, C. Wright 744
Milwaukee Magazine 561
Miniature Donkey Talk 404
Mining People Magazine 703
Minnesota Book Awards 804
Minnesota Historical Society Press 314
Minority Engineer 644
Mississippi Review Prize 805
Missouri Historical Society Press 315
Missouri Life 553
Missouri Review, The 513
Mitchell Lane Publishers, Inc. 315
MLA Prize for a Bibliography, Archive, or Digital
    Project 744
MLA Prize for a First Book 744
MLA Prize for a Scholarly Edition 744
MLA Prize for Independent Scholars 745
MLA Prize in United States Latina & Latino and Chi-
    cana & Chicano Literary and Cultural Studies 763
Model Retailer 704
Modern Haiku 514
Modern Materials Handling 668
Moment 445
Monday Magazine 542
Mondial 315
Money 427
Monsoon Books 316
Montana Historical Society Press 316
Montana Prize in Creative Nonfiction 745
Montana Prize in Fiction 731
Moody Publishers 316
Moondance International Film Festival 711
Moondancer Fellowship for Writing About Nature
    and the Outdoors, The 717
Moore Visiting Writer, Jenny McKean 717
MORE 601
Morpheus Tales 577
Morton Prize in Poetry, The Kathryn A. 783
Mosher Short Fiction Prize, The Howard Frank 732
Mother Earth News 571
Mother Jones 437
Motor Trend 422
Motorbooks 317
MotorHome 598
Mott-Kappa Tau Alpha Research Award in Journalism,
    Frank Luther 765
Motton Prize, Sheila Margaret 783
Mountain Living 477
Mountain Press Publishing Co. 317
Mountaineers Books 317
Mountains & Plains Independent Booksellers Associa-
    tion Reading the West Book Awards 805
MovieMaker Magazine 442
Moving Parts Press 317
Mpls. St. Paul Magazine 552
MSI Press 318

Mslexia 672
Mumford Prize, Erika 783
Mushing Magazine 594
Music & Sound Retailer 687
Music Connection 532
Musky Hunter Magazine 594
Mussio Ventures Publishing Ltd. 318
Muzzle Blasts 587
Myers Memoir Vignette Prize Category, Linda Joy 745
Mythic Delirium 578

N

Na'amat Woman 602
NACUSA Young Composers' Competition 763
Naggar Literary Agency, Inc., Jean V. 176
Nailpro 618
Nails 618
Narrative Magazine 514
Nation, The 537
National 676
National Black MBA Magazine 427
National Book Awards 805
National Business Book Award 745
National Communications Magazine 470
National Geographic 453
National Geographic Children's Books 318
National Geographic Kids 483
National Jurist and Pre Law, The 677
National Magazine Awards 765
National One-Act Playwriting Competition (Canada) 711
National Outdoor Book Awards 805
National Parks Magazine 535
National Poetry Competition 783
National Poetry Review Book Prize 784
National Readers' Choice Awards 732
National Review 538
National Writers Association Nonfiction Contest 745
National Writers Association Novel Writing Contest 732
National Writers Association Poetry Contest 784
National Writers Association Short Story Contest 732
National YoungArts Foundation 755
Native Peoples Magazine 446
Nature 535
Nature Friend Magazine 483
Naturegraph Publishers, Inc. 318
Naval Institute Press 319
NavPress 319
NBM Publishing 319
Nelligan Prize for Short Fiction, The 732
Nelson Literary Agency 176
Nelson, Inc., Thomas 319
Nelson, Tommy 319
Neruda Prize for Poetry, The Pablo 784
Netcomposites 634
Network Journal, The 427
Neutrino Short-Short Contest, The 805
Nevada Magazine 553

New Directions 319
New England Book Awards 806
New England Review 515
New Forums Press 320
New Harbinger Publications 320
New Hope Publishers 321
New Horizon Press 321
New Issues Poetry & Prose 321
New Issues Poetry Prize, The 784
New Jersey Monthly 554
New Leaf Literary & Media, Inc. 176
New Letters 515
New Letters Literary Awards 806
New Letters Prize for Poetry 785
New Libri Press 321
New Mexico Magazine 554
New Millennium Awards for Fiction, Poetry, and Nonfiction 806
New Mobility 418
New Moon Girls 484
New Ohio Review 516
New Quarterly, The 516
New Rivers Press 322
New Society Publishers 322
New South Writing Contest 806
New Voices Award 755
New World Library 322
New York University Press 323
New Yorker, The 454
Newbery Medal, John 755
NeWest Publishers Ltd. 320
Newman Literary, Dana 147
News Photographer 690
Newsage Press 322
Nextstepu Magazine 428
NFSPS Poetry Convention Madness Contest 785
NICHE 697
Nickelodeon Writing Program 717
Nightboat Books 323
Nightboat Poetry Prize 785
Nightscape Press 323
Ninety-Six Press 323
Ninth Letter 517
No Starch Press, Inc. 325
Nolo 323
Nomad Press 324
Nonfiction Award 745
North Atlantic Books 324
North Carolina Arts Council Regional Artist Project Grants 718
North Carolina Office of Archives and History 324
North Carolina Writers' Fellowships 718
North Light Books 324
Northern California Book Awards 806
NorthSouth Books 325
Northwest Quarterly Magazine 547
Nortia Press 325
Norton & Company, Inc., W.W. 325
Nosy Crow Publishing 326
Notre Dame Magazine 429

Notre Dame Review 517
Nova Press 326
Nova Writes Competition for Unpublished Manuscripts 807
Novel & Short Story Writer's Market 672
NSGA Retail Focus 701
Nursebooks.org 326
Nurseweek 663
Nursing 664

O

O, The Oprah Magazine 602
O'Connor Award for Short Fiction, Frank 733
O'Dwyer's PR Report 607
O'Faolain Short Story Competition, Sean 733
O&A Marketing News 697
Oak Knoll Press 326
Ober Associates, Harold 177
Oberlin College Press 327
Oceanview Publishing 327
Office Buildings Magazine 692
Ohio Poetry Day Contests 785
Ohio State University Press 327
Ohio University Press 327
Ohioana Book Awards 807
Ohioana Walter Rumsey Marvin Grant 763
Oklahoma Book Awards 807
Oldie Magazine, The 437
Omnidawn Publishing 328
On Course 484
On Spec 578
On The Mark Press 328
On The Premises Contest 733
One 567
One Story 517
Oneworld Publications 328
Onion World 654
OnStage Publishing 328
Oolichan Books 328
Open Court Publishing Co. 329
Open Season Awards 807
Opera News 687
Operations & Fulfillment 698
Optical Prism 685
Orange Coast 541
Orbis 518
Orca Book Publishers 329
Orchard Books (US) 329
Oregon Book Awards 808
Oregon Coast 558
Oregon Literary Fellowships 718
Oregon State University Press 330
Oreilly Media 330
Original Art, The 756
Ornamental & Miscellaneous Fabricator 679
Ott Award for Outstanding Contribution to Children's Literature, Helen Keating 756
Our Sunday Visitor, Inc. 330
Overdrive 613
Overtime 518

Overtones 688
Owen Award, Guy 785
Owen Publishers, Peter 331
Owen, Richard C., Publishers, Inc. 330
Owsley Award, Frank Lawrence And Harriet Chappell 746
Oxford University Press 331
Oxford University Press: Southern Africa 331
Ozark Mountain Publishing, Inc. 331

P

P & R Publishing Co. 331
Pacific Coast Business Times 428
Pacific Press Publishing Association 332
PAGE International Screenwriting Awards, The 712
PageSpring Publishing 332
Painted Bride Quarterly 518
Pajama Press 333
Paladin Press 333
Palettes & Quills 334
Palgrave Macmillan 334
Pallet Enterprise 678
Pangaea Prize 785
PANK 518
Pantheon Books 335
Pants On Fire Press 335
Paper Stock Report, The 688
Papercutz 335
Paraclete Press 335
Paradise Cay Publications 335
Paragon House Publishers 336
Paralegal Today 677
Parallax Press 336
Parents 433
Parnassus: Poetry in Review 519
Passkey Publications 336
Pastel Journal 611
Patchen Award for the Innovative Novel, Kenneth 733
Paterson Fiction Prize, The 733
Paterson Poetry Prize, The 786
Paterson Prize for Books for Young People 756
Paterson Prize for Young Adult and Children's Writing, The Katherine 756
Paul Dry Books 336
Pauline Books & Media 337
Paulist Press 337
Pavement Saw Press Chapbook Award 786
Paycock Press 338
Peachtree Children's Books 338
Peachtree Publishers, Ltd. 338
Pearson Award, Judith Siegel 808
Peden Prize in Fiction, William 734
Pedestal Magazine, The 519
Pedlar Press 338
Pedrick Prize, Jean 786
Pelican Publishing Company 339
PEN Award for Poetry in Translation 767
PEN Center USA Literary Awards 808
PEN Translation Prize 767

PEN/Faulkner Awards for Fiction 734
PEN/Joyce Osterweil Award for Poetry 786
PEN/Phyllis Naylor Working Writer Fellowship 757
PEN/Voelcker Award for Poetry 786
Penguin Canada, Ltd. 339
Penguin Group USA 339
Penguin Random House Creative Writing Awards 808
Penguin Random House, LLC 339
Pennsylvania Heritage 559
Pennsylvania Lawyer 677
Pennsylvania Poetry Society Annual Contests 786
Pennsylvania Young Readers' Choice Awards Program 756
People 454
People StyleWatch 438
Perkins Agency, L. 177
Permanent Press, The 339
Persea Books 340
Perugia Press 340
Perugia Press Prize 787
Pest Management Professional 682
Peter Pauper Press, Inc. 340
Petersen's Bowhunting 580
Peterson Poetry Prize, The Richard 787
Peterson's 340
Pfeiffer 341
Pflaum Publishing Group 341
Phaidon Press 341
Phi Beta Kappa Award in Science, The 746
Philomel Books 341
Philosophy Documentation Center 341
Phoebe Winter Fiction Contest 734
Photo Review, The 691
Physician 685
Piano Press 342
Piatkus Books 342
Picador USA 342
Piccadilly Books, Ltd. 342
Pilgrim Press, The 342
Piñata Books 343
Pinch Literary Awards, The 808
Pineapple Press, Inc. 343
Pit & Quarry 704
Pizza Today 666
Plan B Press 343
Planet 520
Planning 660
Plastic Surgery News 685
Playground Magazine 682
Playlab Press 344
Please Touch Museum Book Award 757
Pleiades 520
Pleiades Press Editors Prize for Poetry 787
Plexus Publishing, Inc. 344
Ploughshares 521
PNWA Literary Contest 808
POB Magazine 635
Pocket Books 344
Pockets Fiction-Writing Contest 757

Pocol Press 344
Podiatry Management 685
Poe Award, Edgar Allan 734
Poetry 521
Poetry Center Book Award 787
Poetry Ireland Review 521
Poetry Society of America Awards 787
Poets & Patrons Annual Chicagoland Poetry Contest 788
Poets & Writers Magazine 673
Poets Out Loud Prize 788
Point 567
Poisoned Pen Press 345
POISONED PENCIL, THE 344
Police and Security News 661
Polis Books 345
Pollak Prize in Poetry, Felix 788
Pontoon & Deck Boat 584
Pool & Spa News 702
Popular Mechanics 471
Popular Science 574
Popular Woodworking Books 345
Popular Woodworking Magazine 471
Porter Prize for Fiction, The Katherine Anne 734
Poulin, Jr. Poetry Prize, A. 788
PPI (Professional Publications, Inc.) 346
Prairie Journal, The 522
Prairie Messenger 567
Prairie Schooner Book Prize 809
Precast Inc. 635
Presa Press 346
Preservation Foundation Contests 746
Presidio La Bahia Award, The 809
Press 53 346
Press 53 Award for Poetry 788
Press 53 Award for Short Fiction 734
Press Here 347
Presses de l'Universite de Montreal 347
Prestwick House, Inc. 347
Prevention 458
Price Stern Sloan, Inc. 347
Priest, The 630
Primary Care Optometry News 686
Prime Number Magazine Awards 809
Princeton Architectural Press 347
Princeton Book Co. 348
Princeton University Press 348
Print 611
Printing Industries of America 348
Printz Award, Michael L. 757
Prism International 522
Prism International Annual Short Fiction Contest 734
PRISM International Annual Short Fiction, Poetry, and Creative Nonfiction Contests 809
Produce Business 654
Produce News, The 662
Produce Retailer 698
Professional Artist 611
Professional Mariner 683

Professional Pilot 616
Progressive Populist 538
Prometheus Books 348
PROMO 607
Properties 693
Prospect Agency 178
Prufrock Press, Inc. 349
PSA National Chapbook Fellowships 788
PTO Today 637
Public Power 642
Puffin Books 349
Pulse 619
Purdue University Press 349
Purple Dragonfly Book Awards 757
Purpose 568
Pushcart Prize 809
Putnam's Sons Hardcover, GP 350
Putnam's, G.P., Sons, Penguin Young Readers Group 350

Q

Qualified Remodeler 623
Quantum Fairy Tales 578
Que 350
Quill 673
Quill & Scroll Magazine 673
Quill and Scroll Writing, Photo and Multimedia Contest, and Blogging Competition 758
Quill Driver Books 350
Quite Specific Media Group, Ltd. 350

R

Raddall Atlantic Fiction Award, Thomas H. 735
Raffelock Award for Publishing Excellence, David 763
Rag, The 523
Ragged Sky Press 350
Railway Track and Structures 645
Raleigh Review Literary & Arts Magazine 523
Ramirez Family Award for Most Significant Scholarly Book 763
Random House Children's Books 351
Random House Children's Publishers UK 351
Random House Publishing Group 351
Rattapallax Press 351
RATTLE 524
RATTLE Poetry Prize 789
Razorbill 351
Reader's Digest 454
Real Simple 602
Rebelight Publishing, Inc. 352
Recycled Paper News 688
Red Deer Press 352
Red Hen Press 352
Red House Children's Book Award, The 758
Red Moon Press 353
Red Rock Press 353
Red Sage Publishing, Inc. 353
Red Tuque Books, Inc. 353
Red Wheel/Weiser 354

Redbook Magazine 602
Redleaf Lane 353
Reed Publishers, Robert D. 354
Referee 702
Reference Service Press 354
Regal Hoffman & Associates, LLC 178
REM 693
Remodeling 624
Retail Info Systems News 626
Reunions Magazine 455
Revell 354
RHINO Founders' Prize 789
Rhode Island Artist Fellowships and Individual Project Grants 718
Ribalow Prize, Harold U. 735
Richardson Memorial Nonfiction Award, Evelyn 746
Ring of Fire Publishing LLC 355
Rio Nuevo Publishers 355
Ripple Grove Press 355
Rittenberg Literary Agency, Inc., Ann 179
River City Publishing 355
Rivera Mexican American Children's Book Award, Tomás 758
Riverhead Books 356
Roanoke-Chowan Poetry Award 789
Roaring Brook Press 356
Robbins Literary Agency, B.J. 179
Roberts Award, Summerfield G. 809
Rocky Mountain Book Award: Alberta Children's Choice Book Award 758
Rocky Mountain Books 356
Rodale Books 356
Rogers Writers' Trust Fiction Prize, The 735
Rolling Stone 533
Ronsdale Press 356
Room 524
Rose Alley Press 357
Rosen Publishing 357
Rosenkranz Literary Agency, Rita 179
Ross Literary Agency, Andy 180
Ross Yoon Agency 157
Roth Award, Lois 767
Rotovision 357
Rowman & Littlefield Publishing Group 357
Royal Dragonfly Book Awards 810
RTJ's Creative Catechist 630
RTOHQ: The Magazine 627
Rudnitsky First Book Prize, Lori 789
Ruka Press 358
Rutgers University Press 358
Rutsala Poetry Prize, Vern 789
RVBusiness 614
Ryan Publishing Enterprises, Regina 181

S

Saddleback Educational Publishing 358
Sadler Children's Literary 181
SAE International 358
Safer Society Press 359
Sagalyn Agency / ICM Partners, The 182

Saguaro Books, LLC 359
Sailing Breezes 584
Saint Martin's Press, LLC 359
Saint Mary's Press 359
Saint PAULS 359
Sakura Publishing & Technologies 360
Salem Press, Inc. 360
Salina Bookshelf 360
Salmon Poetry 361
Saltman Poetry Award, Benjamin 789
Salvo Press 361
Sandeen Prize in Poetry and the Richard Sullivan
    Prize in Short Fiction, Ernest 810
Sanders & Associates, Victoria 182
Sanofi Pasteur Medal for Excellence in Health Re-
    search Journalism 765
Santa Fe Writers Project Literary Awards Program
    810
Santa Monica Press 361
Santé Magazine 620
Sarabande Books, Inc. 361
Sarton Award, May 789
SAS Publishing 362
Saskatchewan Book Awards 810
Sasquatch Books 362
Saturday Evening Post Great American Fiction Con-
    test, The 735
Saturnalia Books 363
Scaglione Prize for a Translation of a Literary Work,
    Aldo and Jeanne 767
Scaglione Prize for a Translation of a Scholarly Study
    of Literature, Aldo and Jeanne 767
Scaglione Prize for Comparative Literary Studies,
    Aldo and Jeanne 746
Scaglione Prize for French and Francophone Studies,
    Aldo and Jeanne 746
Scaglione Prize for Italian Studies, Aldo and Jeanne
    747
Scaglione Prize for Studies in Germanic Languages &
    Literature, Aldo and Jeanne 747
Scaglione Prize for Studies in Slavic Languages and
    Literatures, Aldo and Jeanne 768
Scaglione Publication Award for a Manuscript in Ital-
    ian Literary Studies, Aldo and Jeanne 747
Scarborough Prize, William Sanders 747
Scarecrow Press, Inc. 363
SCBWI Magazine Merit Awards 759
Schiffer Publishing, Ltd. 363
Schocken Books 364
Scholarly Writing Award 747
Scholastic Press 364
School Nurse News 664
School Transportation News 705
SchoolArts Magazine 638
Schreiber Prize for Humorous Fiction & Nonfiction,
    The Mona 811
Schulman Literary Agency LLC, Susan 182
Schwartz & Wade Books 364
Science in Society Awards 765
Scifaikuest 579

Scott Novel Excerpt Prize Category, Joanna Catherine
    735
Scouting 419
ScreaminMamas Creative Nonfiction Contest 748
ScreaminMamas Magical Fiction Contest 736
ScreaminMamas Mother's Day Poetry Contest 790
ScreaminMamas Valentine's Day Contest 736
Screen Education 648
Screen Printing 690
Screenplay Festival 712
Scribe Publications 364
Scribner 365
Script Pipeline Screenwriting and TV Writing Con-
    tests 713
Scriptapalooza Screenplay & SHORTS Competition
    712
Scriptapalooza Television Writing Competition 712
Seal Press 365
Search Institute Press 365
Seaworthy Publications, Inc. 365
Second Story Press 366
Secret Place, The 568
Security Dealer & Integrator 627
Seedling Continental Press 366
Self 603
Self-Counsel Press 366
Sentient Publications 366
Sequestrum 524
Serendipity Literary Agency 183
Servicing Management 657
Seven Stories Press 366
Seventeen Magazine 595
Severn House Publishers 367
Sewanee Review, The 525
Shambhala Publications, Inc. 367
Shape 458
Shaughnessy Cohen Prize for Political Writing, The
    748
Shaughnessy Prize, Mina P. 748
Shearsman Books, LTD 367
Sheehan YA Book Prize 736
Sheep! Magazine 654
Shelley Prize for Imaginative Fiction, Mary Woll-
    stonecraft 736
Shenandoah 525
Sherman Associates, Inc., Wendy 183
SHINE brightly 484
Shiner Comedy Award, Reva 713
Shipwreckt Books Publishing Company LLC 367
Short Grain Contest 811
Shriekfest Horror/SciFi Film Festival & Screenplay
    Competition 713
Sibling Rivalry Press 368
Sign Builder Illustrated 607
Silman-James Press 368
Silver Dolphin Books 368
Silver Lake Publishing 369
Silverfish Review Press 368
Simon & Schuster 369
Simon & Schuster Books for Young Readers 369

Simply Read Books 369
Ski Area Management 702
Skin Inc. 619
Skinner House Books 369
Skipping Stones Book Awards 759
Skipping Stones Youth Awards 713
Skipping Stones Youth Honor Awards 759
Skurnick Books, Lizzie 370
Sky Pony Press 370
Slapering Hol Press Chapbook Competition 790
Sleeping Bear Press 370
Slipstream Annual Poetry Chapbook Contest 790
Slote Award, The Bernice 811
Small Beer Press 370
Smallholder Magazine 655
Smart Business 627
Smart Retailer 698
Smith And Kraus Publishers, Inc. 370
Smith Book Award, Byron Caldwell 763
Smith Memorial Award for Best Book of Poetry,
    Helen C. 790
Smith, Publisher, Gibbs 371
Smithsonian Magazine 455
Snips Magazine 689
Snow Writing Contest, Kay 812
Snyder Memorial Publication Prize, The Richard 790
Socal Meetings + Events 608
Society of Classical Poets Poetry Competition 790
Society of Midland Authors Award 812
Soft Skull Press Inc. 371
Soho Press, Inc. 371
Soul-Making Keats Literary Competition 812
Sound & Video Contractor 640
Sourcebooks Casablanca 372
Sourcebooks Fire 372
Sourcebooks Landmark 372
Sourcebooks, Inc. 371
Southern Illinois University Press 373
Southern Living 544
Southern Playwrights Competition 713
Southern Theatre 648
Sovereign Award 765
Sow's Ear Chapbook Competition 791
Sow's Ear Poetry Competition, The 791
Space and Time 579
Sparkle 485
Specialty Travel Index 705
Spencer Hill Press 373
Spencerhill Associates 183
Spinner Books 373
Spitzer Literary Agency, Inc., Philip G. 184
Splashing Cow Books 373
Sports Illustrated 585
Springs 680
SQL Server 641
Square One Publishers, Inc. 373
St. Augustine's Press 374
Stained Glass 622
Stamats Meetings Media 627
Stamping Journal 680

Standard Publishing 374
Stanford University Press 374
Stanley Award, The Edward 791
Star Bright Books 374
Star*Line 525
Stardate 575
STC Craft 374
Steel Toe Books 374
Stegner Fellowships, Wallace E. 719
Stenhouse Publishers 375
Sterling Publishing Co., Inc. 375
Stewart Living, Martha 477
Stimola Literary Studio 184
Stipes Publishing LLC 375
Stone Arch Books 376
Stone Bridge Press 376
Stone Poetry Prize, The Ruth 791
Stone Soup 486
Stoneslide Books 376
Stonesong 184
Stony Brook Short Fiction Prize 736
Storey Publishing 376
Storie 526
storySouth Million Writers Award 736
Stover Memorial Award, The Elizabeth Matchett 791
Strand Magazine, The 526
Strange Horizons 580
Strategic Health Care Marketing 686
Strategic Media Books 377
Straus Agency, Inc., Robin 185
Strawberries Press 377
Stringer Literary Agency, LLC, The 185
Strokestown International Poetry Competition 792
Sturgeon Memorial Award for Best Short SF of the
    Year, Theodore 737
Stylus Publishing, LLC 378
Subito Press 378
subTerrain 526
subTERRAIN Magazine's Annual Literary Awards
    Competition: The Lush Triumphant 812
Subtropics 527
Sun Books / Sun Publishing 378
Sunbury Press, Inc. 378
Sunrise River Press 379
Sunset Magazine 544
Sunstone Press 379
Super Lawyers 677
SuperCollege 379
Supervision Magazine 628
Swan Scythe Press 379
Swedenborg Foundation 379
Sweeney Agency, LLC, Emma 186
Sweet Cherry Publishing 380
Sydnor Award, Charles S. 748
Syracuse University Press 380
System iNews 668

T

Tafelberg Publishers 380
Talese, Nan A. 380

Tampa Review Prize for Poetry 792
Tantor Media 381
Taste of Home 449
Taylor Book Award, Sydney 760
TD Canadian Children's Literature Award 760
Teachers & Writers Magazine 638
Teachers College Press 381
Teachers of Vision 638
Teaching Theatre 639
Teaching Tolerance 639
Tebot Bach 381
Tech Directions 645
Technology Review 669
Teen Vogue 595
Tegen Books, Katherine 381
Television Outreach Program (TOP) 714
Temple University Press 382
Ten Speed Press 382
Tennessee Arts Commission Literary Fellowship 719
Tenth Gate Prize, The 792
Texas Architect 611
Texas Gardener 477
Texas Institute of Letters Literary Awards, The 813
Texas Meetings + Events 608
Texas Parks & Wildlife 560
Texas Tech University Press 382
Texas Western Press 382
Textile World 632
Theatre Conspiracy Annual New Play Contest 714
Theatre In the Raw Biennial One-Act Play Writing
    Contest 714
THEMA 527
This Old House 478
Thistledown Press Ltd. 383
Thompson Literary Agency 186
Thomson Reuters 383
Three Cheers and a Tiger 737
Threepenny Review, The 528
ThunderStone Books 383
Thurber Prize for American Humor, The 737
Tia Chucha Press 384
Tightrope Books 384
Tilbury House Publishers 384
TimberWest 678
TIME 456
Tin House 528
Tin House Books 384
Tire News 614
Titan Press 385
Toastmaster magazine 419
Today's Catholic Teacher 631
Today's Parent 433
Tom Howard/Margaret Reid Poetry Contest 792
Tony Lothian Prize 748
Top Cow Productions, Inc. 385
Tor Books 385
Tor House Prize for Poetry 792
Toronto Book Awards 813
Torrey House Press, LLC 385
Touchwood Editions 385

Tower Publishing 386
Tradewind Books 386
Traditional Home 478
Trafalgar Square Books 386
Trains 463
Travel + Leisure 598
Travel Goods Showcase 699
Travelers' Tales 386
Tree Care Industry Magazine 658
Triada U.S. Literary Agency, Inc. 186
Triangle Square 387
Trinity Foundation, The 387
Tristan Publishing 387
Triumph Books 387
Truman State University Press 387
Tu Books 387
Tufts Poetry Awards 792
Tumblehome Learning 388
Turner Award for Best First Work of Fiction, Steven
    737
Turnstone Press 388
TV Guide 442
Twilight Times Books 389
Two Dollar Radio 389
Two Sylvias Press 389
Tyndale House Publishers, Inc. 389

U

U.S. Catholic 568
U.S. News & World Report 538
UMI (Urban Ministries, Inc.) 390
Unbridled Books 390
Underground Construction 636
Union Literary 187
Unity House 390
University of Akron Press 390
University of Alabama Press, The 391
University of Alaska Press 391
University of Alberta Press, The 391
University of Arizona Press 392
University of Arkansas Press, The 392
University of Calgary Press 392
University of California Press 392
University of Chicago Press, The 392
University of Georgia Press 393
University of Illinois Press 393
University of Iowa Press 393
University of Maine Press 393
University of Michigan Press 394
University of Nevada Press 394
University of New Mexico Press 394
University of North Carolina Press, The 394
University of North Texas Press 395
University of Oklahoma Press 395
University of Ottawa Press 395
University of Pennsylvania Press 396
University of Pittsburgh Press 396
University of South Carolina 396
University of Tampa Press 396
University of Tennessee Press, The 397

University of Texas Press 397
University of Washington Press 397
University of Wisconsin Press 397
University Press of Kansas 398
University Press of Kentucky 398
University Press of Mississippi 398
Unter Agency, The 187
Upscale Magazine 446
US Glass, Metal & Glazing 623
Us Weekly 442
USA Hockey 588
Usborne Publishing 398
USDF Connection 415
Utah State University Press 399
Utmost Christian Poetry Contest 793
Utne Reader 438

V

Van Schaik Publishers 399
Vanderbilt University Press 399
Vanity Fair 438
Varoujan Award, Daniel 793
Vassar Miller Prize in Poetry 793
Vegetable Growers News, The 655
Vegetarian Essay Contest 760
Vehicule Press 399
Velazquez Press 399
Ventura County Writers Club Short Story Contest 737
Venture Publishing, Inc. 400
Venues Today 649
Verso 400
Vertigo 400
Veterinary Economics 706
VFW Magazine 420
VFW Voice of Democracy 760
Vibrant Life 458
Victorian Homes 470
Video Librarian 622
Vietnam 463
Viking 400
Viking Children's Books 400
Vilcek Prize for Poetry, Marica and Jan 793
Villard Books 400
Vineyard & Winery Management 621
Vintage Anchor Publishing 401
Vivisphere Publishing 401
Viz Media LLC 401
VM+SD 699
Voyageur Press 401

W

Waasnode Short Fiction Prize 737
Wabash Prize for Fiction 738
Wabash Prize for Nonfiction 748
Wabash Prize for Poetry 793
Wake Forest University Press 401
Walch Publishing 402
Wales Literary Agency, Inc. 188
Walls & Ceilings 624

Ward Howe Award, The Julia 813
Washington State University Press 402
Washington Writers' Publishing House 402
Washington Writers' Publishing House Fiction Prize, The 738
Water Well Journal 694
WaterBrook Multnomah Publishing Group 403
Watercolor Artist 612
Watson Literary Prizes in Fiction and Poetry, The Robert 813
Wave Books 403
Waveland Press, Inc. 403
Waywiser Press 403
Webber Associates Literary Management, CK 144
WebMD the Magazine 459
Weight Watchers 459
Welding Design & Fabrication 680
Wells Arms Literary 188
Wergle Flomp Humor Poetry Contest 794
Wernick & Pratt Agency 188
Wesleyan Publishing House 403
Wesleyan University Press 403
West Suburban Living 548
Westchester Magazine 555
Westerly 529
Western & Eastern Treasures 472
Western Australian Premier's Book Awards 813
Western Canada Highway News 614
Western Grocer Magazine 662
Western Heritage Awards 813
Western Hotelier Magazine 666
Western Journey 599
Western Psychological Services 404
Western Restaurant News 667
Western Writers of America 814
Westminster John Knox Press 404
Westmoreland Poetry & Short Story Contest 814
Weston Writers' Trust Prize for Nonfiction, The Hilary 748
Where 543
Whitaker House 404
White Mane Kids 405
White Memorial National Children's Playwriting Contest, Jackie 714
White Pine Press 405
White Pine Press Poetry Prize 794
Whitecap Books, Ltd. 404
Whitehead, Fred, Award for Design of a Trade Book 764
Whitman, Albert & Company 405
Wick Poetry Prize, Stan and Tom 794
Wiesel Prize in Ethics Essay Contest, The Elie 749
Wild Rose Press 406
Wild West 463
Wilder Medal, Laura Ingalls 760
Wilderness Press 406
Wiley & Sons, Inc., John 406
WILLA Literary Award 814
William Morrow 406
Williams Young Adult Prose Prize Category, Rita 761

Williams/New Orleans Literary Festival Contests, Tennessee 814
Williams Poetry Prize, Miller 794
Willow Creek Press 406
Windward Publishing 407
Wine Enthusiast Magazine 449
Wines & Vines 621
Wire Rope News & Sling Technology 681
Wired 536
Wisconsin Historical Society Press 407
Wisconsin Institute for Creative Writing Fellowship 719
Wisdom Publications 407
Wiseman Books, Paula 407
Witches and Pagans 421
Witty Outstanding Literature Award, Paul A. 761
Wolfe Prize and Lecture, Thomas 738
Wolff Award for Fiction, Tobias 738
Woman Engineer 645
Woman's Day 603
Woman's World 603
Women's Health 604
Wood Prize, The J. Howard and Barbara M.J. 795
Woodbine House 408
Worcester Magazine 550
Word Awards, The 815
Wordsong 408
Work-In-Progress Grant 761
Workers Write! 529
Workforce Diversity For Engineering & IT Professionals 429
Working Mother 433
Working People's Poetry Competition 795
Workman Publishing Co. 408
World Book, Inc. 408
World Fantasy Awards 738
World Policy Journal 538
World Weaver Press 408
World's Best Short Short Story Contest, Narrative Nonfiction Contest, & Southeast Review Poetry Contest 815
Worldfest-Houston Independent International Film Festival 714
Worthy Kids/Ideals Books 409
WOW! Women on Writing Quarterly Flash Fiction Contest 739
Wright Poetry Award, James 795
Write Bloody Publishing 409
Write Now 715
Writer's Chronicle, The 674
Writer's Digest 674
Writer's Digest Books 409
Writer's Digest Annual Writing Competition 815
Writer's Digest Self-Published Book Awards 815
Writer's Digest Self-Published e-Book Awards 816
Writer's Digest Short Short Story Competition 739
Writers-Editors Network International Writing Competition 816
Writers' Guild of Alberta Awards 816
Writers' League of Texas Book Awards 817
Writers' Trust Engel/Findley Award, The 764
Writing Conference Writing Contests 749
Written By 675
Wyoming Living 558
Wyoming Rural Electric News 562

Y

Yachting 584
Yachting Monthly 585
Yale Review, The 529
Yale Series of Younger Poets, The 795
Yale University Press 410
Yankee 545
Year End Series (YES) Festival of New Plays 715
Yearbook Excellence Contest 749
Yellow Shoe Fiction Series 410
Yes! Magazine 456
YMAA Publication Center 410
Yoga Journal 459
Yogi Impressions Books Pvt. Ltd. 410
York Prize for Fiction and Nonfiction Contest, Lamar 817
Young Adult Fiction Prize, The 761
Young Reader's Choice Award 761
Young Rider 415
Youth Honor Award Program, The 817
Youth Today 661
YouthWorker Journal 631

Z

Zebra Books 410
Zest Books 410
Zink 604
Zoetrope Short Story Contest 739
Zoetrope: All-Story 530
Zone 3 Creative Nonfiction Book Award 749
Zone 3 Fiction Award 739
Zone 3 First Book Award for Poetry 795
Zoning Practice 693
Zornio Memorial Children's Theatre Playwriting Competition, Anna 715
Zumaya Publications, LLC 411
ZYZZYVA 530